D1330459

CLONTARF

DUBLIN

DUBLIN BAY

Clontarf

Clontarf

Colm Lennon

Irish Historic Towns Atlas
Dublin suburbs No. 1

Series editors: Colm Lennon and Jacinta Prunty
Cartographic editor: Sarah Gearty
Editorial assistant: Angela Byrne

IRISH HISTORIC TOWNS ATLAS
Editors: Raymond Gillespie, H.B. Clarke, Jacinta Prunty, Michael Potterton
Consultant editors: Anngret Simms, J.H. Andrews
Cartographic editor: Sarah Gearty
Editorial assistants: Jennifer Moore, Frank Cullen

Acadamh Ríoga na hÉireann
Royal Irish Academy

Clontarf

First published 2018 by the Royal Irish Academy
in association with Dublin City Council

Maps prepared in association with Ordnance Survey Ireland

Irish Historic Towns Atlas
Royal Irish Academy
19 Dawson Street
Dublin 2

www.ria.ie
www.ihta.ie

Text © 2018 Colm Lennon

Copyright © The Royal Irish Academy

ISBN 978-1-908997-72-2

British Library Cataloguing-in-Publication Data. A catalogue record is available from the British Library.

Thanks are due to the institutions mentioned in the captions and in the list of maps (pp 81–2) and illustrations (p. 129) for permission to reproduce material in their custody.

Maps 1, 3–6, 30 and photography for plate 1 © Ordnance Survey Ireland/Government of Ireland, copyright permit no. MP 003917.

Figures 1–9 drawn by Sarah Gearty and Frank Cullen

Design: Fidelma Slattery
Printed in Italy by Printer Trento

5 4 3 2 1

Front endpaper: Dublin from railway bridge at Hollybrook, *c.* 1850, by Edward Radclyffe (National Library of Ireland)
Back endpaper: Traffic map, 1925 (*Dublin civic survey*)
Previous pages: Sheds of Clontarf, 1785, by John Laporte (British Library)

DIGITAL VERSION: the Topographical information section and further study maps are downloadable and available for research via www.ihta.ie. Go to 'Additional Resources' and use the code 'clontarf01' (available 2018).

Contents

Acknowledgements   vi

Preface   vii

Introduction   1

The topographical development of Clontarf   7

Topographical information   33

Appendix   73

Maps   79

Further notes   127

List of illustrations   129

Selected bibliography and key to abbreviations   130

General abbreviations   135

Acknowledgements

In the course of their work on this atlas and the research that preceded it, the author and editors have been greatly assisted by many people in libraries, archives and other institutions, and in the locality of Clontarf. Anne Rosenbusch contributed to the project under the auspices of the Irish Historic Towns Atlas research team. The staff in the library of the Royal Irish Academy have been unfailingly helpful, including Siobhán Fitzpatrick, Sophie Evans, Amy Hughes, Bernadette Cunningham and Dave McKeon, as have colleagues throughout the institution, particularly Peter Harbison. Ruth Hegarty and the team in the publications office provided valuable advice and asistance. Special thanks are due to Elizabeth Mullins in University College Dublin, School of History, Jane Nolan, University College Dublin Library, Paul Ferguson and Paul Mulligan of the Glucksman Map Library, Trinity College, Dublin, Mary Broderick of the National Library of Ireland, Sean McDermott, Dublin City Council, Mary Clark of Dublin City Library and Archive and the staffs of the Valuation Office, Dublin and the National Archives of Ireland. Arnold Horner very kindly advised on the selection of maps and Andrew Bonar Law generously supplied images. The project has been supported from the outset by Dublin City Council and thanks are due to Charles Duggan, Heritage Officer, for facilitating this collaboration.

Colm Lennon would like to acknowledge the supportiveness and friendship of his colleagues in the Department of History in Maynooth University. Maighréad Ní Mhurchadha kindly agreed to the use of an unpublished paper on Clontarf. Thanks are also due to Máire Ní Chearbhaill, Robin Kavanagh, Nick Maxwell and Séamas Ó Maitiú. He has drawn on the local knowledge and expertise of many in Clontarf: Claire Gogarty, whose work on the building of the suburb has been invaluable, Douglas Appleyard, who generously shared information on Clontarf and Hollybrook, Bernardine Ruddy, Joan Ussher Sharkey, Kay and Joe Lonergan, Brian Wray, David Evans, Colette Gill, Madeleine Bradley, Fintan O'Meara, Dennis McIntyre, Ian Murphy and Fiona and Kevin Williams, as well as members of the Clontarf Historical Society and Raheny Heritage Society. He acknowledges with love the support of his wife, Margaret, daughters, Róisín, Deirdre, Caoimhe, son-in-law Niall, and grandsons, Cian and Eoin.

Preface

Since 1986 the Irish Historic Towns Atlas, as part of an international project, has published atlases of representative types of Irish towns. The aim has been to explore the morphological development of towns as a reflection of their underlying social, economic, cultural and political structures. In most cases each town has fitted neatly into one atlas, but for the larger towns and cities it has proved necessary to concentrate on urban cores. While this has many practical advantages it means that suburbs have received less attention than they deserve. As well as having their own identity and personality, suburbs contribute to the multi-centred nature of the nineteenth-century city. This tension between local identity and the forces of urbanisation will serve to show the dynamic interdependence of suburb and metropolis. Organised along Irish Historic Towns Atlas lines, this series of suburban atlases allows us to capture a different aspect of the urban experience and to engage in comparative study of suburban life. Complementary to the main atlas series, it deserves as much attention as the more extended coverage of urban cores and should promote an exciting and expansive approach to the Irish urban past.

Raymond Gillespie, H.B. Clarke, Jacinta Prunty, Michael Potterton, September 2017

Overleaf: Beached boats at Clontarf,
looking north, 19th cent., by O.M. Latham

Introduction

The success of the Irish Historic Towns Atlas (IHTA) project over the past forty years is attested to by its ongoing series of town atlases (twenty-eight of which have appeared to date), and its many ancillary publications. The atlas has also, through its fascicles and annual conferences, encouraged the comparative study of towns within Ireland, Britain and across the continent of Europe, in harmony with the recommendations of the International Commission for the History of the Towns. Many experts in cartography, historical geography, archaeology and urban history in Ireland have served both on the editorial board and as advisers or authors of individual fascicles in the towns atlas series. The enterprise to date has resulted in the compilation of huge resources of information for the interpretation of topographical history and has helped to conceptualise the study of comparative urban development over a *longue durée*.

While the capital city of Ireland has been accorded special treatment, in that its atlas has been divided into separate parts, the same organising principles as govern those of other towns have characterised the fascicles of Dublin that have been published to date. Thus, the three parts of *Dublin* provide long views of urban growth and contain the same core elements of maps and texts as the other town atlases. The first part of *Dublin* traces the topographical history down to 1610, the second to 1756 and the third to 1847, while the fourth will eventually bring it down to the twentieth century. Although comparatively vast in its physical extent, for the purposes of the atlas, Dublin city incorporates only the area bounded by the circular roads and the two canals, the Royal to the north and the Grand to the south. As is evident from the principal map in *Dublin, part III*, based on the Ordnance Survey of 1847, the built-up area of the city was already expanding into districts outside these perimeters.

Although extramural quarters were a feature of the immediate neighbourhood of Dublin from the late middle ages, it was in the nineteenth century that the phenomenon of suburbanisation resulted from the settlement of large populations in the urban hinterland took hold. The migration, which was driven by political, social and economic factors, impinged on what had been outlying villages on the urban periphery. Communities of older inhabitants and newcomers together were faced with forming new topographical and municipal identities. The most complete form of suburban integration in the Dublin region was through the constitution of townships, self-governing enclaves that had devolved powers of local taxation and administration. In all, nine of these suburban townships evolved in the Victorian period – Rathmines and Rathgar, Pembroke, Blackrock, Kingstown, Dalkey, Killiney, Kilmainham, Drumcondra and Clontarf. The last-mentioned trio were absorbed within the municipal boundaries of Dublin in 1900, while the rest, by then urban district councils, were abolished in 1930. Districts within the present-day Dublin City Council boundary are the first to be dealt with in this series of suburban atlases.

Even in those Dublin suburbs that did not evolve into townships in the nineteenth century, there were issues of local topographical, cultural and social identification. Municipal boundaries, forms of transportation and the lure of the seaside to excursionists, for example, were among the factors that affected relations between the metropolis and traditional village centres. Bray, Co. Wicklow, already the subject of a town atlas by K.M. Davies (no. 9 in the IHTA series), provides a valuable case study of a suburban town in which development was thus shaped through the symbiosis of city and locality.

In this new series, a number of townships and suburbs within the area that comprised the county of Dublin (now administered by Dublin City Council, as well as the local authorities of Fingal, South County, and Dún Laoghaire and Rathdown) will be the subject of atlases, organised along IHTA lines. As well as establishing the distinctive topographical identity of the individual village or suburb, each unit of the series will explore the relationship between city and district in so far as this has

shaped the pattern of settlement through the ages. In respect of the former aim, the roots of suburban communities will be examined by showing the evolution over time of modern-day topographical features, including streets and roads, waterways, religious sites and substantial houses. This process necessarily entails the delineation of localities, which could be cross-cut by several sets of boundaries, including those of manor, parish, townland and estate ownership, and in some cases will allow for natural combinations of smaller settlements to be defined as areas for study. As to the elucidation of aspects of the history of the city through suburban studies, the series will analyse the dynamics of residential areas aspiring to preserve their ambience in the face of the expansion of metropolitan borders, maritime and public utilities, and recreational facilities in the neighbourhood of Dublin. In thus considering the balance of interests of traditional village centres and estate cores on the one hand and the municipality and port of Dublin on the other, the suburbs series should complement parts I–IV of the IHTA of Dublin city.

In this regard, the proven composition and methodology of the atlas in terms of a combination of maps and texts are carried over into the suburbs series. As with the main town series, there are maps common to all of the atlases presented in large format followed by facsimile reproductions, as the cartographical heritage allows. This section is completed by the provision of base maps to encourage further study. The textual element is introduced by an extended essay interpreting the maps and evidence for settlement history from the first emergence of a recognisable village or suburb down to the late twentieth century. The essay also contains text maps and other illustrations as appropriate. As with the atlases of towns, there is a gazetteer section entitled, Topographical information, collating data down to about 1970 under the standard twenty-two headings of the IHTA, in so far as this is feasible and relevant to each place, with standardised references and abbreviations. The selected bibliography lists important works devoted to a township or suburb for the period, especially those of topographical relevance, and is not necessarily confined to works cited in the footnotes. Other sources mentioned in the footnotes are not separately tabulated, except where their titles have been abbreviated in a way that requires explanation. Abbreviations of more general application for the whole series are listed after the bibliography at the end of the volume.

The atlas expresses the belief that, within the context of the comparative analysis of the topography of European towns, a suburban series makes a valuable contribution to studying the changes associated with modern urban expansion and the interdependency of city and suburbs. As such, it should be useful not only to students and teachers of history, geography, archaeology and architecture, but also to planners, conservationists and local government officers, and thus directly or indirectly to all residents and visitors in the township or suburban areas concerned.

Colm Lennon, Jacinta Prunty, September 2017

Overleaf: View of Dublin from Clontarf,
looking south-east, 1796–8, by William Ashford

The topographical development of Clontarf

People have been attracted to Clontarf through the ages not just because of its proximity to Dublin, but also because of the natural features of the terrain and coastline. It is located in the low-lying floodplain of the Rivers Liffey and Tolka on the north side of Dublin Bay, between the latter river to the west and the escarpment of the Sutton/Howth peninsula to the east. Clontarf has a carboniferous limestone base covered with a fertile soil in its inland areas,[1] which facilitated the reclamation of lands suitable for successful arable and pastoral farming well before the late middle ages. At least until the late seventeenth century, part of the landscape was fairly thickly wooded with an outgrowth of the woods at Santry and Coolock.[2] Along the coastal stretch from the Tolka estuary to Sutton there was a tract of tidal mudflats and slobland, overflowed by the tide, much of which was not finally reclaimed until the twentieth century. The tidal channels were suitable for fishing, as well as the farming of shellfish, including oysters. Off the shore, the waters of the bay were affected by estuarine deposits that clogged the passages of the Liffey, preventing navigation to the city by all but the smallest of boats. Two maritime features assisted Clontarf in exploiting the difficulties of Dublin port and in becoming a thriving fishing and trading post: the small sliver of land off the western end of the shoreline, which came to be called Clontarf Island, provided shelter for shipping, and a comparatively deep anchorage known as Clontarf Pool allowed larger vessels to put in on its lee side.[3]

A small number of archaeological finds point to some settlement at Clontarf in prehistoric times.[4] At least two burial mounds, one to the west of the district near the old railway station and the other to the east at Conquer Hill, were noted by Charles Mount as possibly indicating Bronze Age activity. In the early medieval period, Clontarf came under the sway of a ruler from one of the branches of the kingdom of Brega, as well as the bishop of Finglas, the nearest early Christian ecclesiastical dignitary. A tradition persists that a monastery was founded at Clontarf by St Comgall in the mid-sixth century, but no near-contemporary documentary or physical evidence of such a foundation survives. Any settlement in the district would have been on the road from Dublin to Howth, and thus vulnerable to early Viking raids on the east coast. The only definite evidence of settlement in the hinterland is the presence of a weir at Clontarf (*corad Chluana Tarb*), mentioned in a chronicle of 1014 referring to the death of Brian Boru's grandson, Toirrdelbach, during the eponymous battle. It has been suggested that this was located where a late medieval bridge was built at Ballybough over the River Tolka.[5] While much of the fighting in the battle of that year may have been along the elevated ridge between the Liffey and the Tolka, placename as well as annalistic evidence points to its having had its climax along the north strand, as the stretch of shoreline between the city and Clontarf was called (and from which the modern thoroughfare from the city derives its name). Tidal phenomena and shoreline events, which are described so vividly in the narratives of the battle, suggest very strongly that at least some of the action took place to the north-east of the Tolka in the area known today as Clontarf.[6]

By the later twelfth century there was a settlement established at Clontarf, as indicated in the grant by Henry II of a 'vill near Dublin called Clumtorp' (later rendered as Clenmthorp) to the Knights Templar about 1172.[7] Perhaps the most intriguing sign of the possible interplay between Scandinavian and Irish there before the arrival of the Anglo-Normans is the dual form of the placename: the Irish language form of Cluain Tarbh is rendered Clenmthorp, a Norse-sounding version, in the grant of the 1170s to the Knights Templar. As well as acquiring rights to the vill, their grant entitled them to full ecclesiastical jurisdiction over the parish of Clontarf. Under the auspices of the Templars a manor of just under 400 acres was developed and farmed at Clontarf. At its heart, a manorial residence and church, situated about 150 m apart, stood at the north end of a village street that led southwards to the sea. According to an inquisition of 1308, the bulk of the manorial territory was under the plough, while the balance consisted of pasture, meadow and woodland. Half of the fields were given over to the cultivation of wheat, oats, barley and legumes. There was a mill in the vicinity for the processing of cereals. The Templars had herds of cows and pigs and flocks of sheep in the meadows and pastures, as well as plough-horses and oxen, and produce of the manorial economy included cheese, bacon and wool, as well as grain. A coastal village grew around the small port of Clontarf (Fig. 1).[8]

The order of the Knights Templar was formally dissolved in 1312 and its possessions were granted to its rival order, the Hospital of St John of Jerusalem, which took over the manor and parish of Clontarf in the same year.[9] The Hospitallers continued to foster farming on the manor, renting farms to members of the gentry, and they extended hospitality in their house at Clontarf through a system of pensions.[10] Communications between Clontarf and the neighbouring city were improved with the construction of a stone bridge over the Tolka in 1313 by John le Decer, a former mayor of Dublin.[11] Contact by sea was also facilitated during the fourteenth and fifteenth centuries, owing to the development of Clontarf harbour.[12] Fishing and trading activity expanded through the port of Clontarf from the late fourteenth century, as evidenced by royal licences for exporting wheat and other goods.[13] Merchants from Clontarf engaged in trade with Chester and other ports in England and Wales in the fifteenth and early sixteenth centuries.[14]

The formal dissolution of Clontarf and the other Hospitaller houses under Henry VIII took place on 22 November 1540. The surrendering prior, John Rawson, was granted an annual pension of 500 marks and the title of Viscount Clontarf for life.[15] The estate and rectory, including the hall with two towers, as well as 383½ acres, the island and pool of Clontarf,[16] and Prior's Wood near Coolock were granted to Matthew King and his wife, Elizabeth, niece of John Rawson.[17] Among the head tenants on the manor were members of leading Pale families, such as Patrick White, who was related to the neighbouring landlord family of St Lawrence,

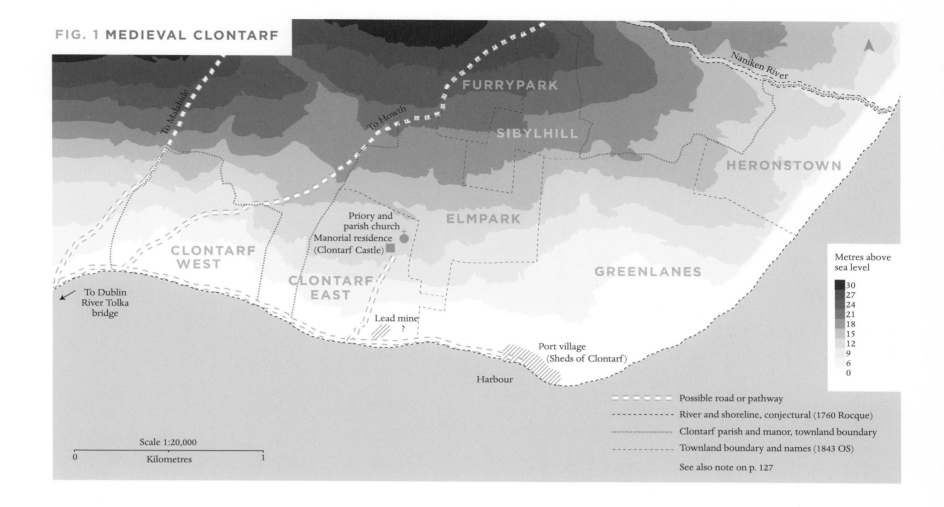

FIG. 1 MEDIEVAL CLONTARF

FURRYPARK

Naniken River

SIBYLHILL

To Malahide

To Howth

HERONSTOWN

Priory and
parish church
Manorial residence
(Clontarf Castle)

ELMPARK

CLONTARF
WEST

CLONTARF
EAST

GREENLANES

To Dublin
River Tolka
bridge

Lead mine
?

Metres above
sea level

30
27
24
21
18
15
12
9
6
0

Port village
(Sheds of Clontarf)

Harbour

Scale 1:20,000

0   Kilometres   1

– – – – –   Possible road or pathway

– – – – –   River and shoreline, conjectural (1760 Rocque)

· · · · ·   Clontarf parish and manor, townland boundary

– – – – –   Townland boundary and names (1843 OS)

See also note on p. 127

and the Bathes of Drumcondra. Rich agrarian and maritime resources made Clontarf the subject of competition between gentry families from the later Tudor period.[18] The manor produced a large grain harvest annually, and a windmill operated there by the seventeenth century. Local fishermen zealously guarded their rights to the fisheries and the port of Clontarf benefited from the trade of the local merchant fleet with Britain and the Continent, exporting agricultural produce and importing wine, among other commodities. Rights to the foreshore of Clontarf became more contentious in the early modern period as the mineral resources began to be exploited. The extraction of lead from the mine discovered on the coast near the village did not begin until the eighteenth century, but stone from an adjacent quarry was used in an elaborate operation for the repair of the cathedral of Christ Church in the city in the 1560s.[19]

In the late 1590s George King, grandson of the original grantee, Matthew, became embroiled in a bitter feud over the ownership of Clontarf with a powerful official, Sir Geoffrey Fenton. In August 1600 Fenton was granted 'the manor, preceptory, lordship and town of Clontarf', including 'the prior's wood', as well as the rectory with its tithe income, full rights to the shoreline and entitlement to fish in Carlingford Bay, all at a rent of £20 per annum.[20] The Fentons allied in marriage with the richest of the recently-arrived English

planters, Richard Boyle, earl of Cork, who in 1614 purchased the manor of Clontarf. Boyle was for some years the absentee landlord of Clontarf and eventually, in part exchange for leases of the manor of Dungarvan, he transferred the manor and parsonage of Clontarf back to George King.[21] King's rigorous exploitation of the fisheries and anchorage rights along the northern shore of Dublin Bay and his fish-processing operation at the Sheds at Clontarf Head brought him into conflict with the nearby municipality. The city authorities retaliated by granting a lease of Clontarf Island and Furlong (just off the coast at Clontarf Head) to the civic recorder to test the extent of the city's franchises. They also developed and promoted an alternative herring fishery at Ringsend, across the bay, in the 1620s. To judge by the emergence of a fishing centre at Clontarf, called Herringtowne, by the end of seventeenth century, the attempt to undermine the fisheries there was not a success (Map 11).[22]

When the rebellion of 1641 broke out, George King joined the uprising of the Catholic gentry of the Pale.[23] In retaliation for the looting of an English ship, Sir Charles Coote, governor of Dublin, burnt the town and the castle of Clontarf on 15 December 1641. Many buildings were destroyed and the King family was outlawed.[24] Eventually the confiscated estate of 590 acres, including the Hollybrooks and the Island, was granted to a prominent supporter of Oliver Cromwell, John Blackwell, who

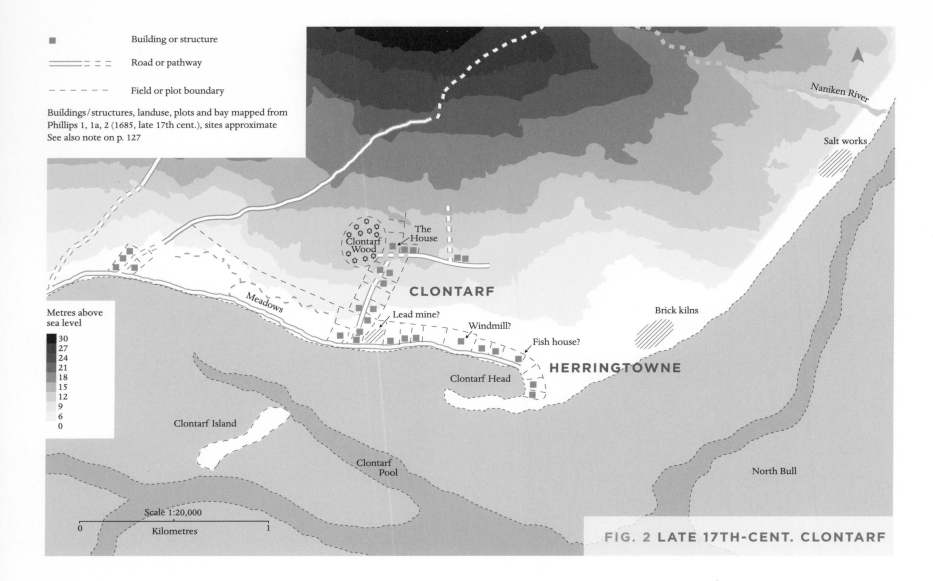

Naniken River

Salt works

The
House

Clontarf
Wood

CLONTARF

Meadows

Lead mine?

Windmill?

Brick kilns

Fish house?

HERRINGTOWNE

Clontarf Head

Metres above
sea level

30
27
24
21
18
15
12
9
6
0

Clontarf Island

Clontarf
Pool

North Bull

Scale 1:20,000

0   Kilometres   1

FIG. 2 LATE 17TH-CENT. CLONTARF

sold it on to Captain John Vernon, quartermaster of the Cromwellian army, in 1656.[25] When the Civil Survey was conducted in the mid-1650s, it was found that, of the 560 acres surveyed, 448 were arable, 100 were pasture and twelve meadow. Among the buildings listed were a castle and a slated stone house, a stone bawn or enclosure and a dove house. Nearby in the village were several thatched cottages, a windmill and a decayed church. Clontarf Island was included as part of the manorial possessions, as well as a fishery belonging to the lord of the manor.[26] After the Restoration, Captain John Vernon's cousin, Colonel Edward Vernon, assumed ownership of the manor and township of Clontarf, 'with Hollybrook and the island of Clontarf', on 26 October 1660.[27] His title was contested by the heirs of George King of Clontarf and by his cousin, Captain John Vernon, and the latter's son, also John. The intra-Vernon dispute was not settled until about 1730, when the main Clontarf estate was taken over by a Captain John Vernon, grand-nephew of Colonel Edward. An unbroken period of Vernon lordship of Clontarf ensued, which lasted into the twentieth century.[28]

The early modern manor of Clontarf was bounded by the sea to the south, the road from Dublin to Baldoyle to the west and north, and the Naniken River to the east (Fig. 2). A poll tax carried out for Ireland in 1660 found that there were seventy-nine taxpayers in Clontarf, of whom forty-five were English, and Protestant, and thirty-four were Irish.[29] The refurbishment of the castle and estate, begun by John Vernon, the Cromwellian grantee, continued after the Restoration. The Vernons also oversaw the construction of a new church on the site of the old one, which had been described as 'decayed' in the Civil Survey. A royal grant of 1675 gave the new landlord a manorial court, power to lay out a private deer park of 300 acres, and the right to hold two fairs annually.[30] Among the topographical features displayed on the earliest maps of the district was Clontarf Island, shown first on the Down Survey map. The island was designated a quarantine for plague victims in 1666.[31] Sir Bernard de Gomme's map of Dublin harbour of 1673 shows some details of the Clontarf coastline (Map 7).[32] Thomas Phillips's more detailed maps of the 1680s indicate the manor-house or castle at the core of the estate, from which a road ran south to the coast, lined by a number of houses. To the west of the castle was an oval-shaped area of woodland named Clantarff Wood. To the east were depicted for the first time the herring sheds (Maps 8–10).[33]

The small settlement named Herringtowne was shown on a contemporary map by Greenville Collins (Map 11). Also indicated by Phillips, to the east of the 'fish house', were brick kilns and salt works (Maps 8–9).[34]

Significant topographical changes in the coastal shape of Clontarf were prefigured in the maps of the marine surveyors before and after 1700. The depth of water in Clontarf Pool and some of the other anchorages in the inner bay was decreasing noticeably. As part of the project to counteract the silting up of the central channel of Dublin port, a Ballast Board was established in 1707 to initiate engineering and reclamation works in the Liffey estuary. Plans to address specific problems of navigation in the northern bay, including one by Captain Perry in 1721 for a marine canal between Fairview and Sutton, did not materialise (Map 13).[35] Meanwhile, Dublin municipality proposed an elaborate scheme of reclamation of the north strand, involving the allocation of 134 lots for building and development, in 1717. This plan envisaged the canalising of the Tolka estuary between two blocks of reclaimed land, the northernmost of which would impinge directly on the Clontarf shoreline as far as the avenue leading to the castle (Map 12).[36] The development may have been still-born, as least in respect of its northern half, but the municipal council pushed ahead with its claims over the coastal waters of Clontarf by granting the oyster beds at Crab Lough and the Furlong to a city alderman as lessee for a term of years.[37] John Vernon, who had objected vociferously to quarrying for stone and sand on the shore of the manor, responded by banning the entry of the corporation's party for riding the franchises from the shore at Clontarf in 1731, and followed up by having his oration of remonstration published.[38]

By the time that John Rocque surveyed the district for his Dublin county map of 1760, the Vernons were firmly ensconced as owners of Clontarf Castle and estate (Map 14). Rocque depicts the 590-acre manor, along the southern perimeter of which runs a dotted line demarcating the city's franchises, as containing a mixture of pasture and arable fields, as well as landscaped gardens. At the core of the estate was the village, with the Vernon mansion and gardens as its hub. Abutting the wall north of the castle grounds was the church enclosed in its small churchyard. Along the avenue leading to the castle there are about a dozen 'well-built houses', as a slightly later directory termed it, mostly with gardens.[39] Also prominent is the Southwell family residence opposite the castle, called Yew Park or Elm View, nestling in the northern angle of the later Castle Avenue/Seafield Road West junction. Among the other large houses shown are the Royal Charter School (built in 1748), Furrypark, Sibyl Hill and Verville. Also prominently displayed is the cluster of small buildings called the Sheds at the fishing port of Clontarf. Among the coastal features delineated by Rocque are Clontarf Island, Clontarf Pool and the oyster beds. The North Bull is depicted as a sandbank overswept by the water and divided from the mainland by a narrow creek called the Raheny Lake. High-tide water is shown as covering the entire expanse up to the strand (called the North Strand as far as Dollymount).[40]

The proprietors of the more than twenty mansions in Clontarf in the late eighteenth century, each with estates of several acres, evidently sought rural seats in close proximity to the metropolis.[41] These members of the parliament and judiciary, as well as bankers and merchants, looked to the Vernon family, who presided over the district from their base at Clontarf Castle, for the preservation of its rural character. Vernon patronage extended not only to the cultural life of this polite society, but also to the leasing of land for the construction of the 'beautiful seats' of gentle families (Map 15), the control of industrial projects such as the mining of lead and the refining of salt on the coast, and supervision of the grand jury system in the district.[42] The growth of the coastal community at the Sheds appears to have occurred through the subleasing of small plots to fishing families, who built cottages near the premises of the revenue officers (Figs 3, 4).[43] Contemporary illustrations

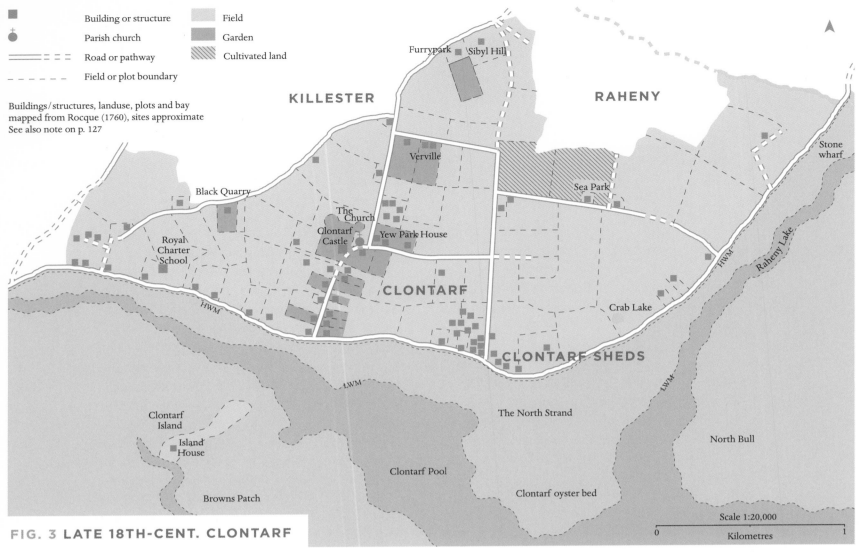

KILLESTER

RAHENY

Furrypark Sibyl Hill

Stone
wharf

Verville

Black Quarry

Sea Park

HWM

Royal
Charter
School

The
Church
Clontarf
Castle   Yew Park House

Raheny Lake

CLONTARF

Crab Lake

HWM

CLONTARF SHEDS

LWM

LWM

Clontarf
Island

The North Strand

North Bull

Island
House

Clontarf Pool

Clontarf oyster bed

Browns Patch

Scale 1:20,000

0   1
Kilometres

FIG. 3 LATE 18TH-CENT. CLONTARF

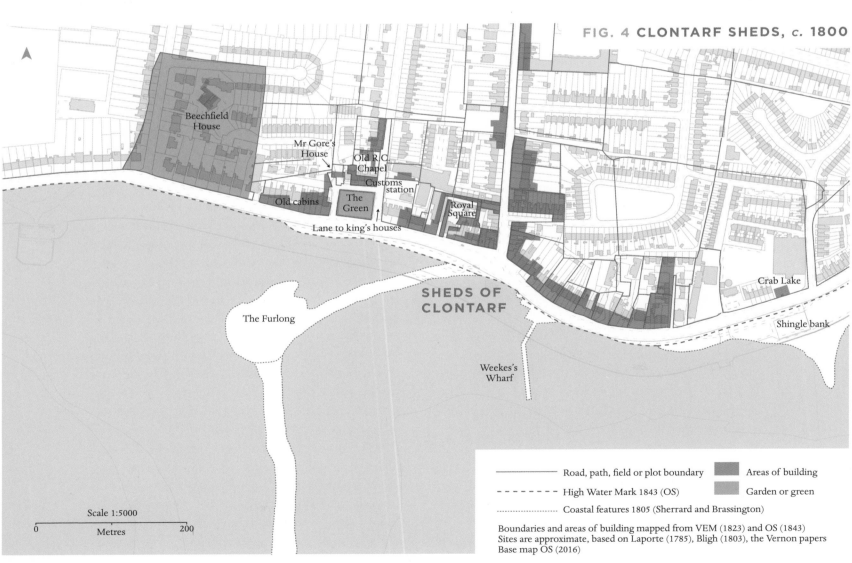

FIG. 4 CLONTARF SHEDS, *c.* 1800

Beechfield
House

Mr Gore's
House

Old R.C.
Chapel
Customs
station

Old cabins

The
Green

Royal
Square

Lane to king's houses

Crab Lake

SHEDS OF
CLONTARF

The Furlong

Shingle bank

Weekes's
Wharf

Scale 1:5000

0   200
Metres

of the Sheds show these single-storey structures. John Laporte's painting of the Sheds in 1785 (p. 51) depicts a wharf that had been constructed by a local philanthropist, Christmas Weekes (along with a reservoir and pumping system for supplying ships with water),[44] and four-wheeled bathing machines, indicating the rise of sea-bathing as a popular activity in the north inner bay. Unlike in the case of Bray, Co. Wicklow, however, where the lure of the seaside promoted rapid urban growth, there was little encouragement forthcoming from the landlords of Clontarf for the early tourist trade. On the seaward side, the equation of the Furlong with the coastal protrusion at the Sheds shown in earlier maps is clearly depicted in Sherrard and Brassington's map of 1805 (Map 17).[45]

Despite the efforts of the Vernons and other Clontarf proprietors such as the Guinnesses of St Anne's estate to keep the outside world at bay, the nineteenth century witnessed the inexorable growth of municipal and leisure influences in the district. These came about in large part owing to the construction of the Great North Wall, or Bull Wall, in 1819. Marine surveyors, including Captain William Bligh in 1803, had proffered a number of proposed locations (Map 16) but the eventual point of departure for the project under Ballast Board control was Crab Lake House, just west of Seafield Road East in the Dollymount district. In conjunction with this in 1820, the civic corporation set about acquiring the rights of the Vernons to the North Bull, three years later letting the fishery there to one William Campbell. The building of the wooden bridge, across Crab Lake water (first shown on Map 19), and the stone causeway extending 2.7 km from the shore was completed in 1824 under the supervision of Francis Giles. Besides greatly aiding the eradication of the sand-bar at the entry to the Liffey estuary,[46] the structure altered the ecology off Clontarf through the promotion of accelerated growth of the small sandy island on the North Bull. Extending north-eastwards from the wall towards Sutton Creek, the Bull Island in 1843 is shown as being 2.56 km in length, and it eventually attained almost 5 km, with the sweep of

Dollymount Strand on its seaward side. The island became an attraction for visitors and day-trippers drawn by sea-bathing and other forms of aquatic and sporting activity such as sailing, rowing, shooting and golf (Fig. 5).[47]

While new opportunities for leisure tourism may have opened up in Clontarf from the early nineteenth century, the attrition of local fisheries and natural resources precluded any significant industrial development. Within twenty years of the construction of the Bull Wall, the Sheds had decayed as a fishing village, as is confirmed in D'Alton's statement in 1838 that 'the Sheds of Clontarf have long since vanished with the good days of the fishermen'.[48] At their most productive, the fisheries off Clontarf were highly lucrative for landlords and fishers alike, producing shell-fish such as mussels, oysters, cockles and lobsters, and fish species such as herring, mackerel and turbot. The shrinkage of the stocks of herrings and oysters in the inner bay may have made the issue of ownership of fishing grounds academic, as was symbolised by the award of a shilling to George Vernon in 1814 in acknowledgement of his right of fishery on the strand near the North Lotts.[49] The substandard cottages and cabins of 200 fishing families were cleared to make way for the new Roman Catholic church of St John the Baptist in the 1830s,[50] the maritime community being rehoused by J.E.V. Vernon in cottages to the north of the church. The landward natural resources of the district – stone, salt, clay for brick-making and lead – may likewise have been almost exhausted by the Victorian period. The last-named commodity had been mined fairly intensively for half a century from the 1750s, but by 1818 conditions for the extraction of lead had deteriorated owing to the constant flooding of the mineshaft on the shore (Map 18).[51]

The Vernon family, under the headship of John Vernon from 1833, attempted to uphold the autonomy of the old manorial area, standing out against many innovative developments, including incipient suburbanisation. A survey of the manor of Clontarf

FIG. 5 DEVELOPMENT OF NORTH BULL ISLAND

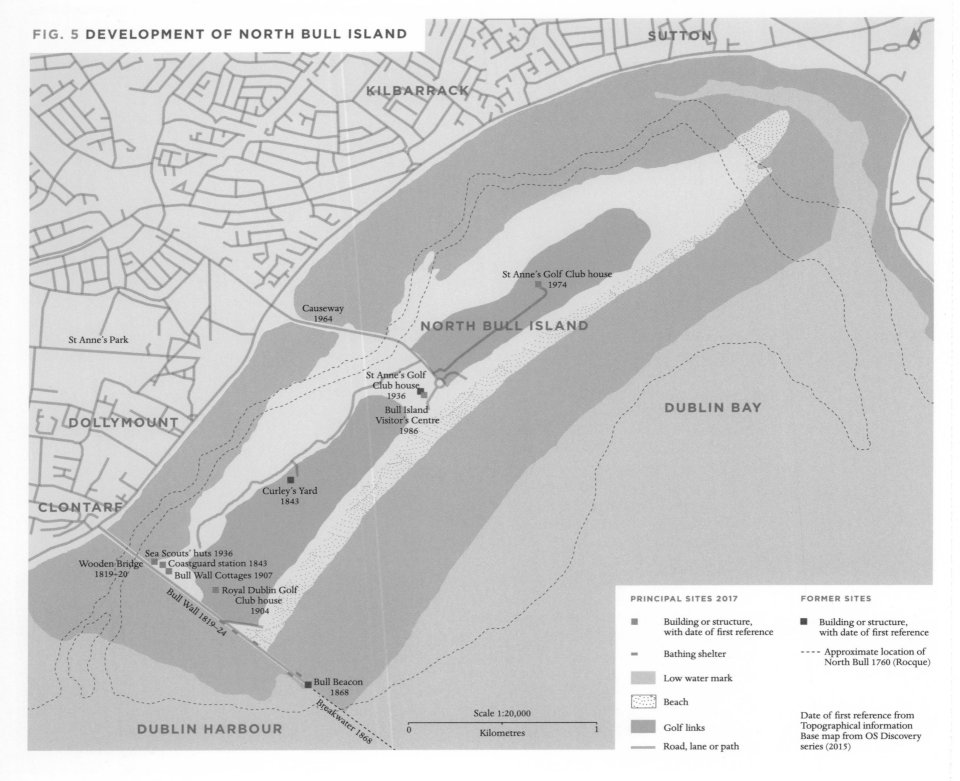

SUTTON

KILBARRACK

St Anne's Golf Club house
1974

Causeway
1964

NORTH BULL ISLAND

St Anne's Park

DUBLIN BAY

St Anne's Golf
Club house
1936

Bull Island
Visitor's Centre
1986

DOLLYMOUNT

Curley's Yard
1843

CLONTARF

Sea Scouts' huts 1936
Wooden Bridge   Coastguard station 1843
1819-20   Bull Wall Cottages 1907
Royal Dublin Golf
Club house
1904

Bull Wall 1819-24

PRINCIPAL SITES 2017

▪ Building or structure,
with date of first reference

– Bathing shelter

Low water mark

Beach

Golf links

Road, lane or path

FORMER SITES

▪ Building or structure,
with date of first reference

---- Approximate location of
North Bull 1760 (Rocque)

Date of first reference from
Topographical information
Base map from OS Discovery
series (2015)

Bull Beacon
1868

Breakwater 1868

DUBLIN HARBOUR

Scale 1:20,000

0   Kilometres   1

---

and its principal inhabitants in 1823 reflected the traditional rights of the manorial lords (Map 20). Symbolically, when in the mid-1830s the Vernons embarked upon a major refurbishment of their ancient house, the 'new' mansion was designed to hark back to a manorial and baronial past.[52] As listed in Lewis's *Topographical dictionary* and as displayed on the earliest Ordnance Survey map (Map 21), there were almost forty large mansions set in their own grounds dispersed throughout the district. The few clusters of habitation shown on the latter are on lower Castle Avenue, along the T-junction of Vernon Avenue and the coast road, and fronting the sea to the east of the Bull Wall. Under the patronage of the Vernons and other philanthropic families, new institutions were established, including an Anglican parochial school and a Catholic one in the old chapel on the west side

of Vernon Avenue. The site for the new Roman Catholic church was donated by John Vernon, and he later provided another on Seafield Road for a new Church of Ireland parish church to replace the old one on Castle Avenue. With a population of 3,314 in 1837 according to Lewis, Clontarf was a substantial community, though *Thom's directory* lists only about 150 premises in 1839.[53] Prominent among the residents listed were members of the legal, medical and clerical professions, with several merchants and a small number of people involved in trade, including provisioning and hospitality.

Overall, there was little development in the early 1840s to prefigure Clontarf's later growth as a suburb, since landed and leisure interests appeared to hold sway. Indeed, the middle decades of the century witnessed an opposing trend through the consolidation of a great landed estate under new nobility, in concert with two long-established land-lords. Centred on St Anne's mansion in the eastern lands of Clontarf, the estate of Benjamin Lee Guinness and his son, Arthur, Lord Ardilaun, took shape through propitious leases from John Vernon and the earl of Howth, who was the proprietor of Raheny and Killester. Through the acquisition of existing estate houses and lodges with attached lands, the Guinness family had built up a 500-acre estate in Clontarf and Raheny by the 1880s, thus precluding any suburban development over a vast tract. Instead, St Anne's estate was laid out in beautifully landscaped gardens and tree-lined walks, focused on St Anne's mansion built by 1837 by Benjamin Lee Guinness and incorporating part of Thornhill, an older house on the site. Satellite estate houses, including Bedford Lodge, Baymount Castle and Sibyl Hill, as well as other cottages and lodges at Raheny, were absorbed by the Guinnesses. Lord Ardilaun sponsored the building of a new Anglican parish church at Raheny and he constructed a tunnel for pedestrians along a right of way from north to south underneath his splendid new avenue from St Anne's mansion to Sibyl Hill. He also negotiated possession of most of North Bull Island through leases from Vernon and Howth, selectively conserving walking, bathing and sporting rights.[54]

The earliest modern suburbs began to form around village hubs in the county area of Dublin by the 1830s and, notwithstanding the protectiveness of its landowners, Clontarf by its very proximity to the city alone would prove to be attractive to migrant urban-dwellers (Fig. 6).[55] It did not provide the industrial opportunities of other contiguous communities such as Kilmainham or Irishtown/Ringsend. It had, however, beautiful coastal views within the inner bay, unlike the seaside locations of Blackrock, Dalkey and Kingstown, which were farther from the centre. Moreover, the popularity of Bray as a residential town from the early nineteenth century demonstrated that leisure resorts were not incompatible with suburban living, especially with a metropolitan connection by rail.

Lack of infrastructure for building development in Clontarf, in areas such as sewerage and drainage, lighting and paving, may have been a factor of size as well as of landlord indifference, but shortness of commuting journeys by public transport or by foot would prove to be a strong countervailing incentive to settlement for urban workers, as was also the case in Drumcondra. Besides, the reform of local government in the county, evident in the successful adoption of independent township status by Rathmines, opened out possibilities for similar arrangements for Clontarf. Local communities outside the canal peripheries of Dublin provided a rich variety of more healthful, spacious and autarkic milieux for thousands of urbanites, whether fleeing insalubrious conditions or perceived municipal disfranchisement within the city.

By the late 1850s, barriers to suburban growth in the Clontarf district were being clearly identified by building interests there and unfavourable comparisons drawn with the progress of south-side suburbs. Environmental handicaps of access through the dockland and industrial area of East Wall and North Strand, and along a malodorous slobland at Fairview between Annesley Bridge and the new railway embankment, were difficult to surmount. More amenable to remediation was the problem of unsightly, ruinous and unsafe cottages and bathing cabins, which lined the coastal sweep out towards Dollymount on land owned by the Vernon and St Lawrence landlords. The comparative slowness of these landlords, particularly the Vernons, to demolish the 'tottering structures' seemed to critics to bespeak a less than encouraging attitude to the development of new residences. Also symptomatic were the neglect of sewerage facilities and property boundaries, excessive tolls and charges for the transportation of building materials, and the failure to construct proper docking facilities for boats. Above all, potential property developers complained of comparatively short leases, typically of 150 years, and excessive ground rents of 4s. 6d. per foot of frontage on sites offered by the Vernon estate. Restrictive conditions on speculative building, including insistence on architectural embellishments such as bow windows, caused the price of housing to become prohibitively expensive. Vernon countered by saying that he was making available at a reasonable cost sites upon which detached or terraced houses costing £400 or £500 could be built in a style that fittingly replaced the offending cabins.[56]

New mansions such as Castilla, Sunnyside and Blackheath House were built by owner-occupiers from the late 1850s on sites leased from John Vernon and set back from the coast in verdant terrain known as Green Lanes. By contrast, speculative developers were responsible for constructing terraces from as early as the 1840s, mostly along the seafront and some comprising just two semi-detached houses (Map 2). These included Gresham Villas built by Thomas Gresham, the hotelier, and Warrenpoint, developed by Isaac Warren, steward of the Vernon estate. By the 1860s such commercial enterprises were spreading along the main arteries of Castle Avenue and Vernon Avenue, as well as the coast road. Walpole Terrace and Rossborough Terrace were erected on Castle and Vernon Avenues, respectively, but it was along Strand Road and Street, which later became Clontarf Road, that most of the investment in new property took place in the middle decades of the century. From Vernon Parade to the west to Seabank Terrace to the east, at least a dozen terraces of four to twelve houses and villas, ranging in value from £300–£400 to £1,000, were completed by businessmen and builders on plots leased from the Vernon estate. Among the most active developers were George Tickell, a furniture magnate, William Graham, a timber merchant, Frederick Thorpe and Patrick Cullen, builders, and Francis Byrne and Frederick Bowles, gentlemen. Architects who had worked on suburban building projects elsewhere in Dublin were called upon to design new premises in Clontarf, as in the case of John J. Lyons who collaborated with Tickell on the eleven houses of Victoria Terrace in the 1860s (Map 22).[57]

The comparatively sluggish development of Clontarf as a suburb notwithstanding, a campaign to constitute the district a township was successful by the end of the decade. Already seven suburbs on the south side of Dublin, beginning with Kingstown in 1834, had availed themselves of this status to run their local administration autonomously. The townships gave the ruling commissioners the right to raise taxation locally in return for which they funded the provision of services, including sewerage, lighting, paving and water supplies. Driven in the main by successful property owners and professionals, the townships asserted their independence of the jurisdiction of the reformed Dublin municipality within the canals and attracted large numbers of settlers to set up their residences within their franchises. Before 1869 Clontarf fell under the authority of the Co. Dublin grand jury through the barony of Coolock, but funding and services under this system, including the maintenance of a proper sea wall to prevent flooding, had proved to be extremely inadequate. What caused a complacent landowning elite to contemplate a new form of local government was the threat posed in 1865 by a private enterprise scheme for the dumping of Dublin city sewage on the shore at Clontarf and the flooding of low-lying land there. Protests by Vernon and Benjamin Guinness to Dublin Corporation were successful, but the evident vulnerability of the district to exploitation by outside interests fuelled the campaign for a township. Despite the opposition of leading landlords, including Vernon and George Tickell, to the details of the bill, Clontarf was in 1869 established as a township containing 1,300 acres, the area of Ballybough and Fairview between Annesley Bridge and the railway bridge at Clontarf being incorporated therein to provide critical mass (Map 23).[58]

The twelve commissioners of Clontarf township, of whom John Vernon was constituted chairman for life, represented major property-owning and business interests, including building development. Besides Vernon, Sir Arthur Guinness (later Lord Ardilaun), George Tickell, Francis Byrne and William Graham, other prominent commissioners who served terms were Archibald Tisdall of Sunnyside, Graham Lemon of Yew Park (a confectionery magnate), Graham Black of Blackheath and William Prescott of Lucerne (owner of a major laundry and dye-works). A rate for the township was struck annually to cover charges for basic services, including sanitation, water and lighting, as well as poor law relief and public health, amounting to 4s. 6d. at its peak but averaging about 3s. 5d. for every pound of rateable valuation.[59] Within a year of its establishment, the township entered into a contract with the Alliance Gas Company for gas-lamps along the roads and avenues of Clontarf. By the early 1870s Clontarf had been connected up to Dublin Corporation's Vartry water supply. Responsibility for roads in the expanding district now passed from the county grand jury to the commissioners. Paving and flagging of the pavements of Clontarf got under way in the late 1880s and were eventually completed in the 1890s. A key feature of the built environment over which the commissioners now had control was the sea-wall along the strand road. Costly repairs to its span were constantly required after erosion and flooding due to storms, as in 1877 when the sum of £465 was expended.[60]

Despite an increase in the total rateable valuation of the district between 1869 and 1900, the township struggled to meet the annual costs of maintenance, let alone the improvement of local infrastructure. The financial burden on ratepayers compounded the grievances of those in the Ballybough area who complained bitterly about the acute problem of the outfall from the city sewerage system at the mouth of the Tolka, which created a cesspool at Fairview. They objected, moreover, to the insouciant attitude (as they saw it) of the landowning cabal among the commissioners of Clontarf, where the effects of the nuisance were mitigated somewhat by the action of the tides in the bay. Vernon and the substantial property owners had objected to Dublin city's proposal in the 1860s and 1870s for a main drainage system, fearing the possibility of seepage along the coastline.[61] When a serious proposal for the annexation of Clontarf and other townships to Dublin municipality was made in 1879, it received the backing of a significant number of ratepayers. John Vernon, who was simultaneously contesting the compulsory purchase by Dublin Port and Docks Board of 900 acres off the Clontarf shoreline, stood out against the plan, however, despite Clontarf township's being 'practically a bankrupt concern'.[62] The issue of a major scheme of waste disposal proved to be intractable under local governance and its solution played a large part in the eventual absorption of the township within the municipality of Dublin in 1900, after which Clontarf and Fairview were connected to the main drainage system at the expense of the ratepayers of the enlarged city.[63]

Although transportation was not within the direct remit of the township administration, the commissioners were generally supportive of private operators of services to and from the Clontarf district. The original proposal for the running of the Dublin to Drogheda railway through Clontarf in the 1830s had been opposed by the Vernons and other landowners, the trains eventually being routed along an embankment and bridges skirting the west of the district from 1844 (Map 1). The opening of a railway station on the line at Clontarf was premature, since it closed in the mid-1850s owing to insufficient passenger traffic. Meanwhile an omnibus link to central Dublin was successful, the frequent services being used to attract buyers of houses in the new terraces along the coastal route. The coming of horse-drawn trams to Clontarf in 1873 was encouraged by the township: not only did the tramway company pay an annual way-leave fee for passage through the district, but also it co-operated in local road-widening and anti-flooding schemes. A new electrified service of the Dublin United Tramways Company commenced in 1897 with the erection of pillars for the overhead wiring being accompanied by the installation of electric lamp standards. By 1900 when, despite some objections, the Clontarf tramway was extended from Dollymount along the coast to Howth, the service was carrying the largest passenger loads of any city route (Map 4). And a ratepayers' movement for a rail halt was successful when the new Clontarf

FIG. 6 SUBURBAN DEVELOPMENT, 1843–1907

c. 1843

c. 1843–68

c. 1868–90

c. 1890–1907

Base map redrawn from OS (1907)
See also note on p. 127

Scale 1: 8000

0   Metres   500

station opened at Howth Road in 1898. It had been argued that, since the township's population of 6,000 increased to 10,000 in the summer, the trams were unable to cope with the traffic.[64]

While omnibus, tramway and rail services gave a boost to holiday-making and day-tripping on the major bank holidays of the year, tourism and leisure pursuits were carefully controlled by the township commissioners in later Victorian Clontarf. Visitors were catered for by 1900 by a number of hotels and taverns, including the Dollymount and Fingal House hotels and Mooney's public house, confectioners' shops and a restaurant named Keely's.[65] Longer-stay visitors could avail themselves of summer lettings along the strand road in one of the many cottages and villas that were built between the 1870s and 1900. Bathing conditions gave rise to health concerns owing to sewage and industrial effluent, especially in the vicinity of Clontarf Island. In 1881 the Clontarf Baths and Assembly Rooms, located just off the coast between Castle and Vernon Avenues, were established. Within a few years, the baths were attracting over 25,000 swimmers during the five-month season.[66] North Bull Island provided a beautiful and circumscribed environment for pleasure seekers. Sports such as horse-racing, athletics and riflery, and aquatic pursuits such as boating and sailing were common on and around the island. Lord Ardilaun of St Anne's estate became the owner of the island, buying the eastern part from Edward Vernon in 1902 and stipulating the right of the public to walk the land and bathe from the Wall and foreshore. Many sporting clubs and associations came into being in Clontarf in the Victorian period, including the Royal Dublin Golf Club, the Yacht and Boat Club, the Cricket and Rugby Football Club and the Lawn Tennis Club, all of which had established their own premises with landlord patronage by the early twentieth century.[67]

Under the Boundaries Act of 1900, Clontarf was formally absorbed under the aegis of Dublin Corporation, bringing the era of township government to an end. Yet as recently as 1893–4 a town hall had been constructed on the seafront as a symbol of local self-confidence.[68] Substantial suburban growth seemed to be under way by the late 1890s: after a faltering start during the 1860s, when the number of residents actually declined, there was an increase of 60% in the population of the township area from 1885 to 1901.[69] Several new roads were opened up in western Clontarf in the decades at the turn of the century, including Hollybrook Road, St Lawrence Road (Map 23) and Haddon Road, while on the older thoroughfares to the east, as well as along the shore, spaces between individual houses and terraces were gradually filled in. Elsewhere, the buildings and grounds of large residences and villas continued to dominate along avenues such as Mount Prospect and Seafield. In the Conquer Hill district, behind the Dublin United Tramways garage, the company built rows of small cottages for tramway workers, including Tramway Cottages or Tram Terrace, while after 1900 some local authority housing was erected in the same location.[70]

For a perspective on the suburban character of Clontarf in 1901, the census records of that year for the major new avenues may be adduced. While Hollybrook and St Lawrence Roads evolved over at least two decades of piecemeal growth (the latter with leases from the earl of Howth as proprietor of the land), Haddon Road was built more quickly, perhaps because of the initiative of the main builder, John Kennedy. All were constructed as blocks of individual terraces of up to six houses, with leases normally specifying uniformity of alignment and other features. St Lawrence Road, for example, emerged as an ensemble of red-bricked houses, though with variations of porches, bay windows and iron decoration. That road comprised at least twelve separately numbered terraces, as well as individual units, built in the 1880s and 1890s, but by 1897 all of the housing was consecutively numbered (Fig. 7). More than two-thirds of the heads of household enumerated on the three roads were from outside the Dublin metropolitan area, almost half hailing from the Irish provinces and a quarter from overseas, mostly Britain. There was an average of one domestic servant per household

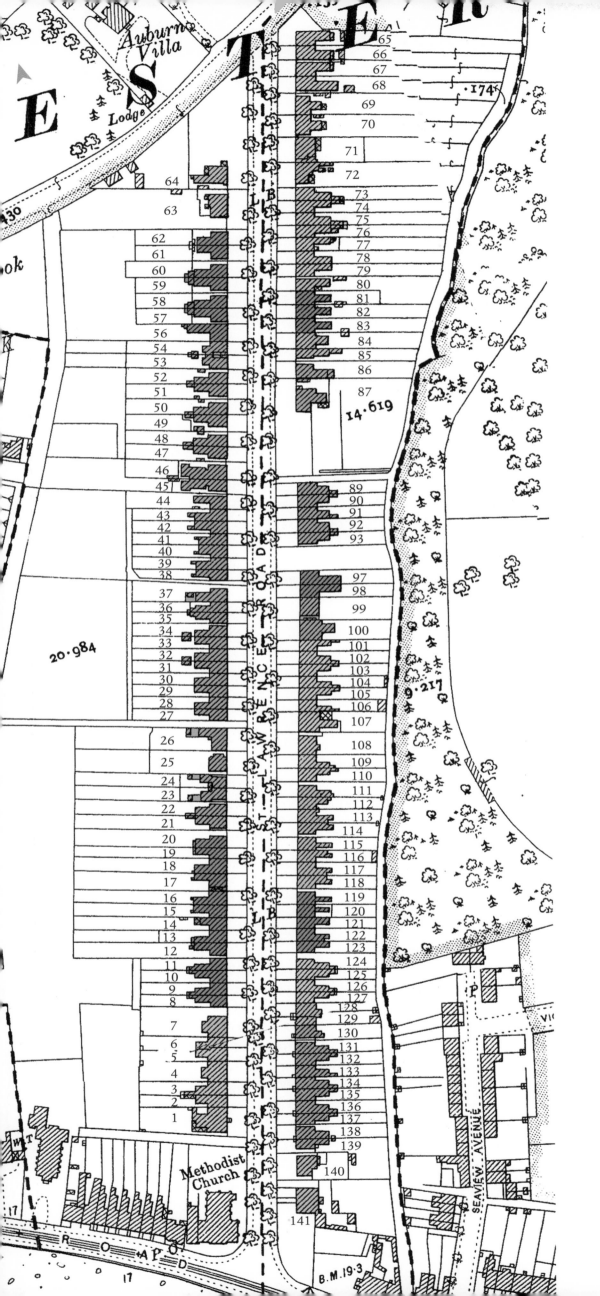

FIG. 7 DEVELOPMENT OF ST LAWRENCE ROAD

DATE OF BUILDING

- To 1883
- 1884–90
- 1891–6
- 1897–1907

NAMED HOUSES

3	Tally House
18	Castle House
23	Brooklyn
37	Hollyfort House
43	Lyndhurst
53	San Remo
54	Mentone
56	Ballyneety House
63	Bal Ivor
64	Girniegoe
65	Wilford
67	Elmina
68	Valetta
69	Croft's House
70	Ballynacurry House
71	Glenmaurice House
72	Woodville
80	Ellesmere
82	Masnabulle
84	Dungooley
85	Fernville
86	Avoneal
99	Woodside
102	The Gables
107	St Lawrence House
108	Madeley
118	Cullrathin
128	Ardilaun
129	Lincluden
130	Seaforth
133	Rostrevor
138	Belvoir
139	Trasna
140	Hollywood
141	Annadale

TERRACES

1–6	Hope Terrace
56–62	Nora Villas
65–70	St Aloysius Terrace
73–9	Pulteney Terrace
80–83	Ellesmere
97–8	St George's Terrace
101–07	Laird Terrace
108–10	Madeley Terrace
111–18	St Patrick's Terrace
119–23	Zetland Terrace
124–7	The Mall

Base map OS (1907)
Sources for date of buildings:
Thom, Gogarty, Val. 3, OS,
Electoral rolls

Scale 1: 2000

0   Metres   100

in 1901 and, of those in employment outside the home, just over 40% were engaged in skilled man- ufacturing and clerical occupations, 20% were professionals or higher civil servants and about 25% were of the employer or managerial class. About one-sixth of household heads were living on pensions or private sources of income.[71]

The denominational composition of the newly settled population in the west of Clontarf reflected the overall pattern of religious affiliation in the suburb at large. Just over 40% of the inhabitants were Roman Catholic (including the vast majority of domestic servants), 32% were members of the Church of Ireland, about 13% were Presbyterians and 9% were Methodists.[72] The expanding reli- gious communities also effected changes in parish development and church building in the district. The new Anglican church of St John the Baptist, which had opened on a site donated by John Vernon on Seafield Road in 1866, was extended to accommodate 130 additional worshippers in 1899.[73] Similarly, St John the Baptist Roman Catholic church was extended and enhanced before the end of the century.[74] A new church for the Presbyterian congregation was opened for services in 1890 on a site at the south-east junction of Howth Road and the coast road. The Methodist community at Clontarf, which had had a chapel since 1868, also acquired a new church on the seafront at the bottom of St Lawrence Road in 1906 to accommo- date nearly 500 people.[75]

Clontarf's incorporation within the municipality of Dublin in 1900 marked the end of centuries of local independence as first manor and then town- ship. Opponents of the move, including Lord Ardilaun, had argued strenuously that the locale was not an urban one,[76] but rather a 'seaside place', apart from Dublin, and they also feared the cost of increased taxation if city rates were applied. By contrast, protagonists of corporation rule, resi- dent mainly in Fairview, put forward a strong case for the extension of the city's boundaries, pointing to the general neglect of their area under the administration of the township and to the

specific issue of drainage. In the dismantling of the township, the western parts of Fairview and Ballybough were decoupled from the Clontarf section to the east of the railway embankment and two separate municipal wards – Clontarf West (mainly for Fairview and Ballybough) and Clontarf East – were established (Map 5).[77] The corporation of Dublin, under the aegis of which the district now fell, had the metropoli- tan resources to undertake major infrastructural projects that were too costly for local funding. But although the municipality made a substantial contribution to the shaping of twentieth-century Clontarf, the decades after 1900 witnessed a con- stant struggle to balance the interests of the local village community and the environmental and economic concerns of the greater Dublin area.

Large engineering projects were undertaken by Dublin Corporation for the general health and salubriousness of the district in the first decade of the new century. First among these was the long-delayed reclamation of the Fairview slobland, which was of obvious benefit not just to residents in the immediate locality but also to those who valued a more picturesque approach to Clontarf.[78] Fifty-eight acres of the foreshore acquired from the Dublin Port and Docks Board from Annesley Bridge to the railway embankment were infilled with city refuse and the new Fairview Park was ready for landscaping by the end of 1910.[79] More complex were the corporation schemes for bring- ing Clontarf within the main drainage and electric lighting systems of the greater city, work on which began in earnest in 1905. The drainage works involved huge excavations from the city centre to Clontarf and then the main sewer was laid outside the sea wall along the front as far as St Anne's. A system of connecting drains and pumping util- ities was also incorporated. By the end of 1911 most of the work of connecting the suburb up with the city sewerage system was finished. Contemporaneously, the laying down of mains for the installation of electric lighting of the roads in the neighbourhood was undertaken and the work was mostly complete by 1911.[80]

FIG. 8 VALUATION OF BUILDINGS IN VERNON AVENUE AREA, c. 1900

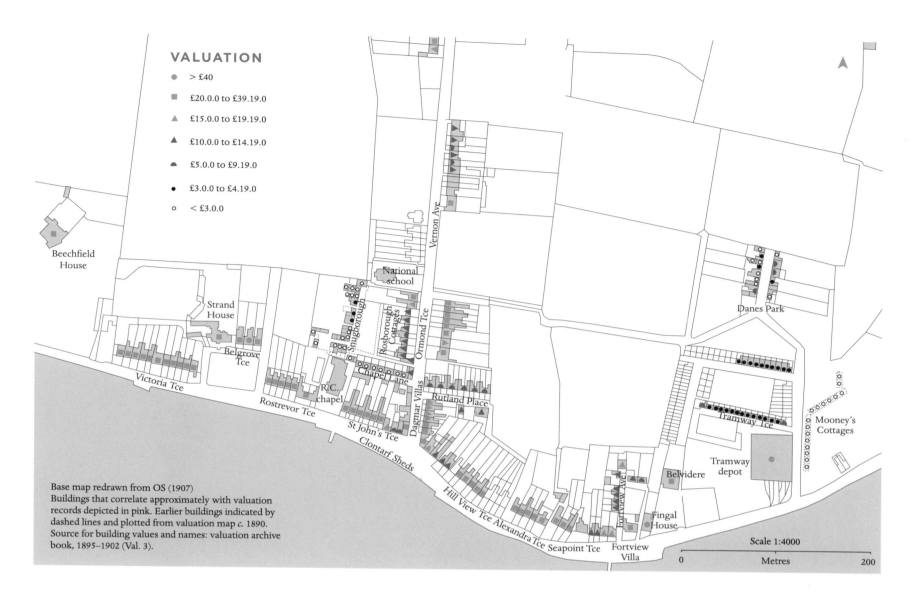

VALUATION

- ● > £40
- ■ £20.0.0 to £39.19.0
- ▲ £15.0.0 to £19.19.0
- ▲ £10.0.0 to £14.19.0
- ◗ £5.0.0 to £9.19.0
- ● £3.0.0 to £4.19.0
- ○ < £3.0.0

Base map redrawn from OS (1907)
Buildings that correlate approximately with valuation
records depicted in pink. Earlier buildings indicated by
dashed lines and plotted from valuation map c. 1890.
Source for building values and names: valuation archive
book, 1895–1902 (Val. 3).

Scale 1:4000

0   Metres   200

While substantial expenditure was being devoted to reclamation, drainage and lighting schemes, the overall direction of suburban development was less certain in the first quarter of the twentieth century, responsibility falling between the municipality and its agencies on the one hand, and local landed and commercial interests on the other. Despite the corporation's acquisition of the right to a 150-foot strip along 3 km of the seafront from the Vernon estate in 1921, for example, the scheme for making a promenade through refuse dumping was deferred in the 1920s, mainly owing to objections of residents to noxious odours and dirt. Moreover, complaints by local associations about the poor state of the foreshore and the lack of amenities for visitors to Bull Island were complicated by ownership being divided between St Anne's estate and the Port and Docks Board.[81] More fundamentally, however, the residential character of Clontarf was at issue, with its hundreds of acres of land available for settlement being considered in the context of planning for Dublin's growth and the alleviation of its housing crisis. A small amount of local authority accommodation had been provided in Clontarf in the

vicinity of the tramway depot by 1913 (Fig. 8) and additional proposals of the housing inquiry in that year included the building of more corporation housing in the district, at a density of twenty cottages per acre, with other plantations in large garden settings for rural homesteaders.[82] In the context of a major civic survey, a prize-winning plan for the future of Dublin by Patrick Abercrombie in 1914 incorporated many proposals for the development of Clontarf, including some privately-built housing for working class people, a reclaimed parkway to the north of the Tolka estuary stretching to the Bull Wall, and a new village centre at the Vernon Avenue/Seafield Road East intersection from which would radiate a series of concentric roadways (Map 24).[83]

Local building work was set aside during the period of World War One and national revolution from 1914 to 1922. There was strong enlistment in the district in the military services for the war. Clontarf was directly affected by the take-over of Bull Island for the drilling of troops and was also touched by the targeting of the railway line by rebel bases in neighbouring Marino during the Easter 1916 rising.

When building resumed in the 1920s, all of the housing constructed was by private development, though with at times considerable support from Dublin Corporation. Much of it was piecemeal in the form of the infilling of spaces by local developers who built terraces or estates of up to a dozen houses on existing roads such as Vernon Avenue and Hollybrook Road or on newer thoroughfares such as Victoria Road and Seaview Avenue. Increasing foresight in the planning of suburban development was evident in municipal provision for future expansion of the drainage scheme in granting individual permissions for connections and in the road-widening scheme for Howth Road, north-east of Castle Avenue, for example. Speculative building was encouraged, especially in the more rural area to the east of Vernon Avenue, by the corporation's taking on the full cost of building new roadways from 1924. The Vernon estate began to take a more active part in promoting development, with a view to controlling the type of building and construction in the district. In 1925 the estate advertised free building sites in certain parts of Clontarf, ground rent only being payable, to encourage construction, particularly of bungalows, with the help of government housing grants. Among the building enterprises attracted were some public utility societies, which facilitated reasonably priced housing through state grants to builders and which were funded by private investors who were motivated by philanthropy as well as by the prospect of modest profits.[84]

A trend towards owner occupation rather than rental of new housing became more marked in general from the mid-1920s and this was facilitated in Clontarf in a number of ways. As elsewhere, Clontarf house-buyers, who were mainly middle class, were able to avail themselves of preferential loans from Dublin Corporation under the Small Dwellings Acquisitions Act. A formal arrangement between the corporation and the Vernon estate, which came into being in 1928, entailed the Vernons leasing dozens of building plots along the proposed connecting road between Castle Avenue and Vernon Avenue (called Kincora Road), as well as Belgrove Road, to the civic authority.

The corporation then negotiated with individual private builders and public utility societies for the construction of new houses, many of them reasonably priced bungalows built to the satisfaction of the city and estate architects. These dwellings yielded both ground rents and rates to the city. This system of 'assisted private enterprise' in building projects was familiar in other suburbs, which were otherwise dominated by public housing, including the newly-built Marino and Drimnagh. Meanwhile, private development continued in Clontarf during the 1930s, when most of the building of Oulton Road, Seafield Road East, Mount Prospect Avenue and Dollymount Avenue was completed on lands of the Vernon estate. In addition the Blackheath estate was built and the main thoroughfare taken in charge, in conjunction with which the widening of Castle Avenue was undertaken by Dublin Corporation on land ceded by the new landowner.[85]

The shape of the modern suburb of Clontarf was emerging clearly by the mid-twentieth century (Fig. 9). The construction of low-density bungalows with large gardens and semi-detached houses or villas on reasonably priced sites made for a distinctive residential style on the newly opened or extended roads in central and eastern Clontarf in the 1940s and 1950s, including Dollymount Grove, Dollymount Park, Mount Prospect Grove and Vernon Drive. Furthermore, the development of housing estates and later blocks of apartments on the grounds of large mansions such as Castilla, Oakley and Sea Park (some of which were demolished) swallowed up much of the farmland in the former Green Lanes of north-central Clontarf. The pattern of demographic growth in the new suburb was reflected in the establishing of two chapels-of-ease for the Roman Catholic parish of St John the Baptist – first in 1925 that of St Anthony in the converted former town hall to the west and then in 1956 in the newly-built St Gabriel's Church in Dollymount to the east.[86] The founding or expanding of educational, health and welfare institutions, such as Belgrove and Greenlanes primary schools, the secondary schools of Holy Faith convent, St Paul's and Mountjoy and Marine (later Mount

Temple Comprehensive School), the orthopaedic hospital and the Central Remedial Clinic, also contributed much to social capital in the locality.

The attractiveness of the growing suburb for new residents was enhanced by environmental improvements under Dublin Corporation management. After a slow start, real progress on the construction of the seafront promenade began to be made from the later 1930s onwards. The sea-wall, built by 1934, ran from the railway embankment to the Bull Wall and infilling of the space between it and the road was carried on by Dutch dredgers with sand and gravel from the seabed and by dumpers depositing city refuse. Gradually, a frontage of 2,650 m was reclaimed and by the mid-1950s the promenade was ready for planting with trees, shrubs and flowers and for the erection of shelters at intervals along its length. The problem of flooding was thereby alleviated, but by no means finally solved.[87] A scheme for a marine lake and pleasure-ground to the east of the Bull Wall, popularly dubbed the Blue Lagoon, and closely associated with the promenade project, came to little, but a new causeway to Bull Island from the seafront was built by the mid-1960s. While improving access to the island for visitors and vehicles, the new amenity raised concerns about conservation of birds and other wildlife, protection of which falls today to Dublin City Council as owners of most of the island.[88] To complement its guardianship of Bull Island, the corporation also took on a conservatory and developmental role in respect of St Anne's estate, which it purchased from the Guinness family in the 1930s for £62,000. Although St Anne's mansion was destroyed by fire in 1943, the bulk of the estate has been preserved as a public park, apart from some housing along the Raheny fringe.[89]

As well as benefiting from the seaside and parkland ambience, residents of the Clontarf district had the advantage of continuing easy access to the centre of Dublin city through efficient public transport. The closure of the Dublin United Tramways Company's service from Nelson's Pillar to Dollymount in 1939 and of the Clontarf and Hill of Howth Tramway Company's service from Dollymount to Howth village in 1941 had brought to an end a transport system that had helped to transform it into a successful suburb (Map 25). With the ending of the tramway system, however, bus services, which were already in strong competition for passengers, took over both seafront and inland routes and the original tram depot at Conquer Hill became Clontarf bus garage. A major improvement in the roadway infrastructure along the shore came with the opening in 1948 of the thoroughfare between Mount Prospect Avenue and Watermill Road (Raheny) and of its extension towards Sutton that became known as James Larkin Road. Meanwhile, the Clontarf railway station near the Howth Road bridge continued to function on the Great Northern Railway service until its closure in 1956. Two years earlier, the station had gained national prominence as the terminus of the Belfast to Dublin rail service in the aftermath of the sweeping away of the Tolka railway bridge by flood waters. A local rail service was not restored until 1 September 1997 when Clontarf Road station was opened on the Dublin Area Rapid Transit line just south of the railway bridge.[90]

By the later 1960s, when the population of the ward of Clontarf East had trebled to 34,000 in the thirty years from 1936, the character of modern Clontarf was well established and the road network more or less complete. Within the bounds of railway line, promenade, island and parkland, the district had the coherence of a garden suburb. The architecture was a harmonious ensemble of mostly terraced red brick houses and villa-style bungalows, shaped by the maritime location, while the older residential roadways blended with new suburban housing. Development at the heart of the neighbourhood was sealed by the building of the Kincora estate of three- and four-bedroomed houses on the demesne lands of the castle, which were sold in 1955 by the Oulton family, successors to the Vernons as proprietors. During the last three decades of the twentieth century the existing features of the built environment accommodated, without too much incongruity, the erection of

FIG. 9 SUBURBAN DEVELOPMENT, 1907–2016

c. 1907

c. 1907–36

c. 1936–71

c. 1971–2016

Base map OS (2016)
See also note on p. 127

Scale 1: 8000

0   Metres   500

over two dozen developments of townhouses and apartment blocks, mostly between houses on thoroughfares such as Castle Avenue, Vernon Avenue, St Lawrence Road, Kincora Road and Clontarf Road, or on the sites of demolished large mansions. As to names, while many have been ascribed the appellation 'court', the former sylvan rusticity of the district has been conjured up in Redcourt Oaks, Mount Prospect Lawns, Seafield Downs and Vernon Heath (Maps 26–8).[91]

Although Lord Ardilaun's description of Clontarf in 1900 as 'a seaside place' (as opposed to a quarter in a proposed enlarged Dublin) flew in the face of its rapid suburbanisation in the late Victorian period, he encapsulated therein the essence of its *rus in urbe* quality that he and his fellow landlords had fought to preserve. Of all of the districts in closest proximity to the perimeter formed by the canals, however, Clontarf (with the possible exception of Drumcondra) was the one whose aloofness from full civic engagement was most seriously challenged. Its very closeness to the city centre, its penuriousness as a local authority and its relative failure in the business of tourism made it all the more dependent on municipal support. Dublin Corporation eschewed the extension to its new borough of Clontarf of its public housing projects, as in nearby Marino for example, but was nevertheless extremely influential in realising its vision for the settlement there of hundreds of families of modest income as owners of attractive houses and gardens. This was engineered through a variety of schemes, including grants to individuals and societies as builders, subsidised loans to buyers and mediation between developers and the principal landlord, the Vernon family. The patronage role of landowners such as the Vernons, Guinnesses and Tickells in the later nineteenth century, evident in their donations to local religious, charitable and recreational groups and associations, was filled in the twentieth by Dublin Corporation, most notably in its development and protection of green spaces for sporting and leisure activities. While the influx of thousands of newcomers to the district, many of them from non-urban backgrounds, may have rendered difficult the formation of local identity,

it is ironic that the former village characteristics of Clontarf, which were engulfed in a tide of rapid urbanisation, have come to the fore in the last two decades. This tendency is physically evident in the corporation's promotion of the junction of lower Vernon Avenue with the seafront as a locale of modern urban design, including new street lighting and paving, which chimes with local business and cultural interests.[92] It is also perceptible in the emergence of a community spirit combining a sense of an older heritage with its self-conscious assertion of the rights of locality in the face of metropolitan forces.[93] The erection of a series of fine graphic panels commemorating the battle of Clontarf along the seafront in 2014, drawing on local knowledge, professional expertise and public funding, exemplifies very well this sense of communal pride and practical association.

Notes

[1] Murphy and Potterton, p. 34.
[2] Dunton, p. 366.
[3] Murphy and Potterton, p. 37.
[4] Charles Mount, 'The collection of early and middle Bronze Age material culture in south-east Ireland', in *RIA Proc.*, ci C (2001), p. 14. See also J.D. Bateson, 'Roman material from Ireland: a re-consideration', in *RIA Proc.*, lxxiii C (1973), p. 13.
[5] M.V. Ronan (ed.), 'Royal visitation of Dublin, 1615', in *Archivium Hibernicum*, viii (1941), p. 35; Patricia Fagan and Anngret Simms, 'Villages in County Dublin: their origins and inheritance', in Aalen and Whelan, p. 86. See also Murphy and Potterton, p. 215; *Cog. Gaedhel*, p. 193.
[6] *Cog. Gaedhel*, p. 193; Máire Ní Mhaonaigh, *Brian Boru: Ireland's greatest king?* (Stroud, 2007), pp 65, 76–7, 99; John Ryan, 'The battle of Clontarf', in *RSAI Jn.*, lxviii (1938), pp 32–7; Darren McGettigan, *The battle of Clontarf, Good Friday 1014* (Dublin, 2013), pp 93–4; Seán Duffy, *Brian Boru and the battle of Clontarf* (Dublin, 2013), pp 203, 214–15.
[7] *Cal. doc. Ire., 1171–1251*, pp 13, 225; *Cal. doc. Ire., 1252–84*, p. 368; *Cal. doc. Ire., 1285–92*, p. 329; Mary Valante, 'Dublin's economic relations with hinterland and periphery in the later Viking age', in Seán Duffy (ed.), *Medieval Dublin I: proceedings of the Friends of Medieval Dublin symposium 1999* (Dublin, 2000), pp 69–83.
[8] Mac Niocaill, 1967, pp 188, 214–15; Philomena Connolly and Geoffrey Martin (eds), *The Dublin guild merchant roll, c. 1190–1265* (Dublin, 1992), pp 8, 29, 80, 104.
[9] Wood, pp 350–60; Falkiner, pp 275–317.
[10] Charles McNeill, 'The Hospitallers at Kilmainham and their guests', in *RSAI Jn.*, liv (1924), pp 15–30; *Reg. Kilmainham*, pp 9, 11, 26, 32, 44, 73, 84, 85, 93, 125.
[11] Book of Howth, p. 130.
[12] A.E.J. Went, 'Fisheries of the River Liffey. Notes on the corporation fishery up to the dissolution of the monasteries', in *RSAI Jn.*, lxxxiii (1953), pp 166–8.
[13] C.V. Smith, *Dalkey: society and economy in a small medieval town* (Dublin, 1996), pp 45–50; *Rot. pat. Hib.*, pp 105, 209, 212, 213.
[14] W.R. Childs, 'Irish merchants and seamen in late medieval England', in *IHS*, xxxii (2000), p. 24; A.J. Fletcher, 'The earliest extant recension of the Dublin Chronicle: an edition, with commentary',

in John Bradley, A.J. Fletcher and Anngret Simms (eds), *Dublin in the medieval world: studies in honour of Howard B. Clarke* (Dublin, 2009), p. 400; *Cal. exch. inq.*, pp 15–16, 22.

[15] *Cal. exch. inq.*, pp 110–11; *L.P. Hen. VIII*, xvi, p. 13; M.A. Lyons, 'John Rawson, Viscount Clontarff (1470?–1547?)', in *ODNB*.

[16] *Extents Ir. mon. possessions*, p. 89.

[17] *Cal. exch. inq.*, pp 90–91.

[18] 'Acts of the privy council in Ireland, 1556–1571', ed. J.T. Gilbert, in *Historical Manuscripts Commission, fifteenth report*, appendix, part III (London, 1897), pp 13, 90, 91; *Cal. exch. inq.*, pp 148, 167; F.E. Ball, *Howth and its owners* (Dublin, 1917), p. 54.

[19] *Proctor's accounts*, pp 50–80; Warburton *et al.*, ii, p. 1251.

[20] *Cal. S.P. Ire., 1599–1600*, pp 214, 278, 375–6; *Cal. S.P. Ire., 1600–01*, p. 58; *Cal. S.P. Ire., 1601–03*, p. 495; *Cal. pat. rolls Ire., 1576–1603*, pp 544–5, 570.

[21] Grosart, i, pp 57, 166, 181–2; Grosart, ii, p. 6.

[22] De Courcy, pp 157, 169; *Ancient records*, iii, pp 132, 139–40, 146–7, 177–8, 198, 238–9.

[23] Depositions, 809, ff 214r–215r, 273r, 276r–276v; 810, f. 244r; 821, f. 231r.

[24] *Calendar of the manuscripts of the marquess of Ormonde, preserved at Kilkenny Castle* (new series, 8 vols, London, 1902–20), ii, p. 46; John Temple, *The Irish rebellion* (Dublin, 1713), pp 151–2; Gilbert, i, pp 41–4; R.S., *A collection of some of the murthers and massacres committed on the Irish in Ireland since 23rd of October 1641* (London, 1662), pp 8–9; Depositions, 809, f. 276r.

[25] *Cal. S.P. Ire., 1660–62*, pp 76, 433; *Cal. S.P. Ire., 1669–70*, p. 447; G.E. Aylmer, 'Blackwell, John (1624–1701)', in *ODNB*; 'Case of John Vernon' *c.* 1680, Archbishop Marsh's Library, Dublin, MS Z I 1 13; D'Alton, p. 46; *Cal. S.P. dom., 1689–1702*, p. 201.

[26] *CS*, vii, p. 176.

[27] *Cal. S.P. Ire., 1660–62*, pp 60, 71, 366.

[28] 'Case of John Vernon' *c.* 1680; 'Case of Mary Vernon', *c.* 1715, Archbishop Marsh's Library, Dublin, MS Z I 1 13; *Reports of cases upon appeals and writs of error in the high court of parliament, 1701–1779*, ed. Josiah Browne (London, 1781), iv, pp 383–96.

[29] *Census, 1659*, pp 382–92; *Ninth report of the Royal Commission on Historical Manuscripts, part II: appendix and index* (London, 1884), p. 130; *Hearth money roll*, p. 394.

[30] *Cal. S.P. Ire., 1675–6*, p. 155.

[31] Murphy and Potterton, p. 429; *Ancient records*, iv, p. 379.

[32] De Gomme.

[33] Phillips 1.

[34] Collins, p. 100; WSC maps.

[35] John Perry, *The description of a method humbly proposed for the making of a better depth coming over the barr of Dublin; as also for the making of a bason within the harbour* (Dublin, 1721), pp 1–12.

[36] Bolton; McCullough, p. 50.

[37] *Ancient records*, vii, pp 439–40.

[38] *Speech of Captain John Vernon opposing the lord mayor on the riding of the franchises of Dublin at their attempting to enter his mannor of Clontarf, 6 August 1731* (Dublin, 1731).

[39] *Post chaise companion*, p. 308.

[40] Rocque.

[41] Gogarty, pp 19–61, 78.

[42] For the charter school, see Ruddy, 2004.

[43] Ní Mhurchadha, p. 34.

[44] For an account of Weekes's wharf and water system, see *Post chaise companion*, pp 308–9.

[45] See, for example, Mary Davies, '*That favourite resort*': the story of *Bray, County Wicklow* (Bray, 2007), pp 84–9.

[46] Flood; De Courcy, p. 53.

[47] See D.T. Flood, 'Historical evidence for the growth of North Bull Island', in D.W. Jeffrey *et al.* (eds), *North Bull Island, Dublin Bay: a modern coastal natural history* (Dublin, 1977), pp 9–12; J.S. Jackson, 'The future of the island', in Jeffrey *et al.*, *North Bull Island*, pp 114–24.

[48] D'Alton, p. 52.

[49] A.E.J. Went, 'Historical notes on the oyster fisheries of Ireland', in *RIA Proc.*, lxii C (1961–3), pp 199, 216.

[50] D'Alton, p. 52.

[51] Warburton *et al.*, ii, p. 1250; Knowles, pp 12–13.

[52] Hardy; *IPJ* 12.9.1840.

[53] Lewis, i, pp 376–7; Thom.

[54] Gogarty, pp 51–5, 62–101; Sharkey, pp 63–5.

[55] For a discussion of modern suburban development in Dublin, see Ó Maitiú, pp 19–46; Daly, pp 118–22, 152–202. For a conceptualisation à propos of medieval Dublin, see H.B. Clarke, *The four parts of the city: high life and low life in the suburbs of medieval Dublin* (Dublin, 2003).

[56] *Ir. Builder* 1.7.1859, 15.4.1861, 15.5.1861, 1.7.1861, 1.8.1861, 15.8.1861, 1.9.1861, 15.9.1861, 1.5.1862, 1.8.1862; Daly, pp 165–8.

[57] Thom, 1862–1901; Gogarty, pp 91–2, 96–7, 100, 101, 104, 131–60, 167–78.

[58] Daly, pp 165–8, 251; Ó Maitiú, pp 43–4; *Report of royal commission appointed to enquire into the boundaries and municipal areas of certain cities and towns in Ireland*, pt 1, HC 1881 (2725) xxx, pp 9–10.

[59] *FJ* 1.1.1869, 5.1.1869, 21.4.1869, 8.5.1869, 26.6.1869, 31.7.1872.

[60] Ibid. 28.3.1870, 12.11.1870, 23.10.1877, 18.6.1886, 27.3.1889, 23.3.1893.

[61] Ibid. 9.8.1870, 28.2.1871.

[62] Ibid. 1.4.1879, 12.2.1886, 4.9.1889; Ó Maitiú, p. 119.

[63] *FJ* 9.8.1870, 27.3.1891, 18.5.1893, 18.12.1893, 7.8.1897, 13.11.1899, 9.1.1900, 22.1.1900.

[64] Ibid. 20.3.1875, 12.9.1894, 24.8.1895, 16.12.1896, 1.4.1898, 11.1.1899; *Ir. Times* 10.8.1895; J.M.C. Kilroy, 'Transport', in V.J. McBrierty (ed.), *The Howth peninsula: its history, lore and legend* (Dublin, 1981), pp 94–7; Murphy, pp 5–6, 8–9.

[65] *FJ* 10.4.1882; *Ir. Times* 12.3.1879; Thom, 1900; Gogarty, pp 86–7, 120, 149, 155.

[66] *Ir. Times* 6.1.1881, 5.2.1884; Ruddy, 2009.

[67] Sharkey, pp 63–5; *Ir. Times* 14.7.1875, 18.8.1925; 'Club history', Clontarf Rugby Club website, available at www.clontarfrugby.com/about-2/club-history/ (last accessed 10 Sept. 2016); Gogarty, pp 82–3.

[68] *Ir. Times* 25.1.1893, 22.12.1893, 1.3.1894.

[69] Ó Maitiú, p. 66; Daly, pp 147–9, 165–8.

[70] Gogarty, pp 155, 162–3,164–6, 172.

[71] Census returns, 1901.

[72] Ibid.; see also Daly, pp 147–9.

[73] McIntyre, pp 56–8; DIA; *Ir. Times* 11.3.1899.

[74] *FJ* 30.6.1842; McIntyre, p. 45; Donnelly, pt 14, pp 33–7.

[75] Clontarf and Scots Presbyterian Church website, available at http://www.clontarfchurch.ie (last accessed 10 Sept. 2016); DIA; Levistone Cooney, p. 158; *Ir. Times* 17.5.1890, 8.10.1906.

[76] *Ir. Times* 4.7.1900.

[77] Ibid. 3.7.1900.

[78] Ibid. 31.7.1902, 1.8.1902, 21.7.1904.

[79] Ibid. 31.7.1902, 1.8.1902, 21.7.1904, 6.9.1904, 15.6.1905, 27.11.1906, 12.8.1910, 8.10.1910.

[80] Ibid. 20.1.1900, 22.1.1904, 8.11.1904, 15.7.1905, 24.11.1905, 13.2.1906, 15.2.1906, 1.8.1906, 4.9.1906, 25.9.1906, 1.11.1911.

[81] Ibid. 1.5.1900, 21.2.1901, 24.12.1904, 24.2.1905, 16.3.1905, 2.11.1906, 23.3.1909, 9.9.1909, 22.6.1910.

[82] McManus, pp 36, 38.

[83] *Dublin civic survey*; Abercrombie *et al.*

[84] Lennon, 2014, pp 216–20; McManus, pp 282–6, 294–5, 355.

[85] McManus, pp 286–95.

[86] Gogarty, pp 186–214; *Ir. Times* 11.8.1925, 5.6.1926; *Souvenir brochure*.

[87] *Ir. Times* 7.11.1905, 14.8.1937, 4.11.1944, 6.6.1945, 10.12.1952, 30.12.1952, 19.8.1953, 2.11.1956, 23.3.1959.

[88] Ibid. 8.1.1931, 25.1.1956, 11.7.1963, 30.3.1967; Jackson, 'The future of the island', pp 116–24.

[89] Sharkey, pp 79–97; Knowles, pp 22–31; Kilroy, 'Transport', pp 94–7; Murphy, pp 5–6, 89; *Ir. Times* 1.9.1997.

[90] Knowles, pp 22–31; Kilroy, 'Transport', pp 94–7; Murphy, pp 5–6, 8–9; *Ir. Times* 1.9.1997.

[91] Gogarty, pp 214–16.

[92] *Ir. Times* 28.7.2000.

[93] See, for example, ibid. 14.10.2011, 15.10.2011, 18.10.2011.

Overleaf: Royal Charter School, Clontarf Road, looking east, 1794, by William Ashford

Topographical
information

From medieval times onwards references to the changing topography of Clontarf can be found in a wide range of documentary sources including maps. The following section, included across the suburbs series, draws from many of these sources, collecting information on topographical features that originated before *c.* 1970 and collating them under twenty-two standardised headings. The gazetteer format enables individual sites to be followed through over time, by theme, giving reference information in each case. The methodology upon which the gazetteer is constructed is introduced below with further notes on p. 128. These principles follow the pattern of the main Irish Historic Towns Atlas series, allowing links to be made between the city of Dublin and its suburbs.

The area covered by the Topographical information includes the former manor and parish of Clontarf, which was bounded by the sea in the south extending from Marino Crescent in the west to the Naniken River in the east as far as the junction of Howth Road and Sybil Hill Road in the north. The extent includes St Lawrence Road in the barony of Killester South, which was not part of the manor or parish of Clontarf.

Sections **1–9** give information on the suburb as a whole including various placename forms, legal status and population figures. Section **10** tabulates streets by their present-day name in alphabetical order. Sections **11–22** are concerned with functions of the suburb, such as religion, manufacturing and education, with a select list of residences provided at the end. Entries in these sections are laid out chronologically by categories: for example, mills are listed before brick kilns, because the oldest mill pre-dates the oldest brick kiln.

Sites are located, where possible, according to their orientation to the nearest street and by grid reference (these relate to the eastings and northings shown on Map 3, pp 91–4). Abbreviated sources referred to are explained in the bibliography and general abbreviations on pp 130–39.

1. NAME

Early spellings

Cluain Tarbh *c.* 1100 (*Cog. Gaedhel*, 176).
Clumtorp *c.* 1172, 1199 (*Cal. doc. Ire., 1171–1251*, 13).
Cluntarf 1186 (*Chartul. St Mary's*, i, 173).
Clumtorf 1227 (*Cal. doc. Ire., 1171–1251*, 225).
Clenmthorp 1286–7 (*Cal. doc. Ire., 1285–92*, 329).
Clontarff 1377 (*Rot. pat. Hib.*, 105).
Clantarf 1395 (*Rot. pat. Hib.*, 152).
Clontaff 1540 (*L.P. Henry VIII*, xvi, 13).
Clontarfe 1577 (*Christ Church deeds*, 120), 1654–6 (*CS*, vii, 176).
Clanturf alias Clantafe 1660 (*Cal. S.P. Ire., 1660–62*, 71).
Clantarfe 1685 (Petty).
Clantarff late 17th cent. (Phillips 2b).
Clantaff 1699 (Dunton, 371).
Clandaf 1728 (Brooking).
Clontarf 1760 (Rocque) to present.

Current spellings

Cluain Tarbh
Clontarf

Derivation

Cluain tarbh, meadow of bulls (MacGiolla Phádraig, 127–8).

2. LEGAL STATUS

Vill *c.* 1172 (*Cal. doc. Ire., 1171–1251*, 13).
Manor 1308 (Mac Niocaill, 1967, 188).
Manor of Clontarf, with courts leet and baron, and right to hold 2 fairs annually 1675 (*Cal. S.P. dom., 1675–6*, 155).
Township 1869 (32 & 33 Vict., c. 85).
Urban District Council 1899 under Local Government (Ireland) Act 1898 (61 & 62 Vict., c. 37).
Dublin municipal ward 1900 (63 & 64 Vict., c. 264).

3. PARLIAMENTARY STATUS

Part of County Dublin constituency until 1885 (Lewis, i, 522; D'Alton, 14, 24; Walker, 272–3).
Part of North County Dublin constituency 1885–1918 (Walker, 348).
Parliamentary constituency of Dublin Clontarf 1918–22 (Walker, 388).
Part of Dublin North constituency 1923–37 (Electoral Act, 1923, 12).
Part of Dublin North-East constituency 1937–77 (Electoral Act, 1935, 5).
Parliamentary constituency of Dublin Clontarf 1977–81 (Electoral Act, 1974, 7).
Part of Dublin North-Central constituency 1977–2012 (Electoral Act, 1980, 17).

4. PROPRIETORIAL STATUS

Vill of Clontarf granted to Knights Templar in *c.* 1172 (*Cal. doc. Ire., 1171–1251*, 13).
Clontarf granted to Richard de Burgh, earl of Ulster in 1310 (*Cal. fine rolls, 1307–19*, 76).
Clontarf granted to Knights Hospitaller of St John of Jerusalem in 1312 (Wood, 358, 365).
Clontarf granted to Matthew King by the crown in 1539 (*Cal. exch. inq.*, 90–91; Archdall, ii, 126).
Clontarf granted to Geoffrey Fenton by the crown in 1600 (*Cal. pat. rolls Ire., 1576–1603*, 544–5, 570).
Clontarf purchased by Richard Boyle, earl of Cork in 1614 (Grosart, i, 57).
George King resumed ownership of Clontarf in 1620 (Grosart, ii, 280).
Clontarf granted to John Blackwell in 1649 (*Cal. S.P. Ire., 1660–62*, 76, 433).
Clontarf purchased by John Vernon in 1656 (*Cal. S.P. Ire., 1660–62*, 76, 433).
Clontarf granted to Edward Vernon in 1660 (*Cal. S.P. Ire., 1660–62*, 60, 71, 366).

5. MUNICIPAL BOUNDARY

Extent of manor, preceptory and lordship of Clontarf 1600 (*Cal. pat. rolls Ire., 1576–1603*, 570).
Dublin municipal boundary with Clontarf as recorded in the riding of the franchises 1603 (*Ancient records*, i, 197–8).
Parish boundary defined in 1836 (OSN); mapped in 1843 (OS).
Township boundary defined in 1869 (32 & 33 Vict., c. 85). Mapped in 1890 (Thom map).
Municipal boundary defined in 1900 (63 & 64 Vict., c. 264). Mapped in 1907 (OS).

6. ADMINISTRATIVE LOCATION

Dyflinnarskíri (Dublinshire) *c.* 1000 (Bradley, 43–4).
County: Dublin, shired in 1210 (D'Alton, 12).
Barony: Coolock 1215 (D'Alton, 27–8).
Civil parish: Clontarf 1654–6 (*CS*, vii, 176); Killester 1843 (OS).
Townlands: Clontarf, Clontarf East, Clontarf Sheds, Clontarf West, Elm Park, Greenlanes, Heronstown, Killester South 1836 (OSN). Mapped in 1843 (OS).
Poor law union: Dublin North, formed in 1839 (Workhouse).
Poor law electoral division: Clontarf 1839 (Workhouse).
District electoral division: Clontarf 1898 (61 & 62 Vict., c. 37). Clontarf East, Clontarf West 1900 (63 & 64 Vict., c. 264). Clontarf 2013 (*Local electoral area rept*, 45).

7. ADMINISTRATIVE DIVISIONS

Wards: Clontarf East, Clontarf West 1900 (63 & 64 Vict., c. 264). Mapped in 1907 (OS).

8. POPULATION

1660 — 79[1]	1891 — 2,938[11]	1971 — 32,537
1821 — 2,687[2]	1901 — 6,930[12]	1979 — 29,206
1831 — 3,323[3]	1911 — 8,967	1981 — 28,247
1837 — 3,314[4]	1926 — 13,507	1986 — 26,978
1841 — 2,664[5]	1936 — 12,582	1991 — 26,290
1851 — 2,682[6]	1946 — 15,309	1996 — 26,119
1861 — 2,470[7]	1951 — 22,244	2002 — 26,642
1871 — 2,396[8]	1956 — 38,718	2006 — 26,568
1881 — 2,894[9]	1961 — 39,505	2011 — 26,639
1885 — 4,210[10]	1966 — 34,000	2016 — 27,905

(Source: *Census*, unless otherwise stated.)

NOTES

[1] *Census, 1659*, 382–92.
[2] *Census*, 1831.
[3] 1,309 in town.
[4] Lewis, i, 376.
[5] Parish.
[6] Parish.
[7] Parish; 2,868 in Electoral District of Clontarf.
[8] Parish; 3,442 in township.
[9] Parish; 4,210 township.
[10] Township (Ó Maitiú, 66).
[11] Parish; 5,238 in township.
[12] In 1901–2016 inclusive, *Census* figures for Clontarf East and West wards have been totalled, excluding part of Fairview where possible.

9. HOUSING

	Number of houses			
	Inhabited	Uninhabited	Building	Total
1540				20[1]
1664				31[2]
1821	481	53	0	534
1831	493	28	1	522
1841	362	37	1	400
1851	407	38	4	449
1861	413	51	1	465
1871	435	51	3	489
1881	478	50	15	543
1891	507	36	0	543
1901	720	71	6	797
1911	815	59	2	876

	1st-class	2nd-class	3rd-class	4th-class	Unoccupied	Total[3]
1841	90	170	69	34	37	400
1851	115	342	20	63	55	595
1861	108	228	40	1	8	425

Classes as defined in 1861 Census:
4th: predominantly mud cabins with 1 room and window only.
3rd: better, with 2–4 rooms and windows.
2nd: good, with 5–9 rooms and windows.
1st: all houses of a better description than classes 2–4.

(Source: *Census*, unless otherwise stated.)

NOTES

[1] *Extents Ir. mon. possessions*, 89.
[2] Hearth money roll, 394.
[3] All figures refer to Clontarf parish.

CLONTARF CASTLE, 1805, BY THOMAS SNAGG

10. STREETS

Alfie Byrne Road/
Bóthar Ailf
Uí Bhroin

(Clontarf Rd [west] S., 717947, 736005).
Alfie Byrne Road, laid out on reclaimed
land (see **18** Utilities: land reclamation)
by 1970; 2016 (OS). Alfie Byrne Road/
Bóthar Ailf Uí Bhroin 2017 (nameplate;
Logainm).

Back Lane

Location unknown, possibly same as
Byrne's Hill or Lane [north] (*q.v.*). Back
Lane 1850 (Val. 2). For other Back Lanes,
see Belgrove Road [south], Churchgate
Avenue, Conquer Hill Road, Danespark.

Back Strand Road

See Seafield Road West.

Baymount Park/
Páirc Chnocán
an Chuain

(Clontarf Rd [east] N., 721378, 736746).
Baymount Park 1971, 2016 (OS).
Baymount Park/Páirc Árd an Chuain
2017 (nameplate). Baymount Park/Páirc
Chnocán an Chuain 2017 (Logainm).

Beechfield Lane

(Clontarf Rd [mid] N., 719635, 736268).
Unnamed 1843–1907 (OS). Beechfield
Lane 1914 (Vernon papers). Unnamed
1936–71 (OS); 2017. See also Tudor's or
Tutor's Avenue.

Belgrove Road/
Bóthar Belgrove
[north]

(Clontarf Rd [mid] N., 719935, 736072).
Belgrove Road, extended in 1928
(*Ir. Times* 5.4.1928). Belgrove Road
1936–2016 (OS). Belgrove Road/Bóthar
Sarchoille 2017 (nameplate). Belgrove
Road/Bóthar Belgrove 2017 (Logainm).

Belgrove Road/
Bóthar Belgrove
[south]

(Clontarf Rd [mid] N., 719916, 735925).
Unnamed 1843 (OS). Back Lane 1850
(Val. 2). Lane 1855 (Val. 3). Unnamed
1907 (OS). Rutland Avenue, renamed
Belgrove Road in 1927 (McManus,
286). Extended to N. in 1928 (*Ir. Times*
5.4.1928). Belgrove Road 1936–2016
(OS). Belgrove Road/Bóthar Belgrove
2017 (Logainm).

Black Quarry Lane

See Strandville Avenue East.

Black Quarry Road

See Howth Road [south].

Blackbush Lane

See Mount Prospect Avenue [east].

Blackheath Avenue/
Ascaill an
Fhraoigh Dhuibh

(Vernon Ave [north] W., 719937, 736701).
Development approved in 1936; laid out
in *c.* 1936–55 (Gogarty, 208). Blackheath

Avenue 1958 (*Thom*). Blackheath Drive 1970–71; Blackheath Avenue 2016 (OS). Blackheath Avenue/Ascaill an Fhraoigh Dhuibh 2017 (nameplate; Logainm).

Blackheath Drive/ Céide an Fhraoigh Dhuibh (Vernon Ave [north] W., 719839, 736708). Development approved in 1936; laid out in *c.* 1936–55 (Gogarty, 208). Blackheath Drive 1939 (McManus, 293), 1949 (*Thom*), 1970–71, 2016 (OS). Blackheath Drive/Céide an Fhraoigh Dhuibh 2017 (Logainm). For another Blackheath Drive, see previous entry.

Blackheath Gardens/ Gairdíní an Fhraoigh Dhuibh (Castle Ave [north] E., 719582, 736578). Development approved in 1936; laid out in *c.* 1936–55 (Gogarty, 208). Blackheath Gardens 1939 (*Thom*), 1970–71, 2016 (OS). Blackheath Gardens/Gairdíní an Fhraoigh Dhuibh 2017 (nameplate; Logainm).

Blackheath Grove/ Garrán an Fhraoigh Dhuibh (Vernon Ave [north] W., 719738, 736711). Development approved in 1936; laid out in *c.* 1936–55 (Gogarty, 208). Blackheath Grove 1949 (*Thom*), 1970–71; N. end built over by 2016 (OS). Blackheath Grove/Garrán an Fhraoigh Dhuibh 2017 (nameplate; Logainm).

Blackheath Park/ Páirc an Fhraoigh Dhuibh (Vernon Ave [north] W., 719829, 736633). Development approved in 1936; laid out in *c.* 1936–55 (Gogarty, 208). Blackheath Park 1939 (*Thom*), 1970, 2016 (OS). Blackheath Park/Páirc an Fhraoigh Dhuibh 2017 (nameplate; Logainm).

Brewery Lane Vernon Ave, site unknown. Brewery Lane 1893 (*FJ* 5.5.1893). Brewery Lane, implied in Brewery Lane Field (see **14** Primary production) 1895 (Vernon papers).

Brian Boroimhe or Brian Boru Avenue/Ascaill Bhriain Bhórú (Vernon Ave [south] E., 720371, 735903). Brian Boroimhe Avenue 1907 (Vernon papers). Brian Boru Avenue 1907 (OS), 1911 (Census returns), 1936–2016 (OS). Brian Boru Avenue/Ascaill Bhriain Bhórú 2017 (nameplate; Logainm).

Brian Boru Street/ Sráid Bhriain Bhórú (Vernon Ave [south] E., 720387, 735950). Brian Boru Street 1907 (OS), 1911 (Census returns), 1936–2016 (OS). Brian Boru Street/Sráid Brian Bóirme 2017 (nameplate). Brian Boru Street/Sráid Bhriain Bhórú 2017 (Logainm).

Brighton Avenue/ Ascaill Brighton (Howth Rd [south] W., 718094, 736621). Brighton Avenue 1907–2016 (OS). Brighton Avenue/Ascal Brighton 2017 (nameplate). Brighton Avenue/Ascaill Brighton 2017 (Logainm).

Byrne's Cottages See Byrne's Hill or Lane [south].

Byrne's Hill or Lane [north] (Clontarf Rd [east] N., 721039, 736368). Back Lane 1864 (Val. 3). Byrne's Lane 1868–1935 (OS). Byrne's Lane and Byrne's Hill 1948 (*Ir. Times* 18.12.1948). Demolished by 1952 (Lynch, 104). See also **22** Residence: Byrne's Cottages.

Byrne's Hill or Lane [south] (Clontarf Rd [east] N., 721157, 736317). Byrne's Cottages 1864 (Val. 3). Byrne's Lane 1868–1935 (OS). Byrne's Lane and Byrne's Hill 1948 (*Ir. Times* 18.12.1948). Demolished by 1952 (Lynch, 104). See also **22** Residence: Byrne's Cottages.

Cabra Parade See Seaview Avenue North [south].

Castilla Park/Páirc Castilla (Vernon Ave [north] W., 719993, 736536). Castilla Park, laid out on site of former Castilla (see **22** Residence) in 1958 (Gogarty, 101); 1969 (*Thom*), 1970, 2016 (OS). Castilla Park/Páirc Chastilla 2017 (nameplate). Castilla Park/Páirc Castilla 2017 (Logainm).

Castle Avenue/ Ascaill an Chaisleáin [north] (719471, 736504). Unnamed 1685 (Phillips 1), 1730 (Price), 1760 (Rocque). Green Lane 1816 (Taylor). Unnamed 1821 (Duncan), 1823 (VEM), 1843 (OS). Castle Avenue 1848 (*FJ* 23.2.1848), 1862 (*Thom*). Unnamed 1868; Castle Avenue 1907–35 (OS). To be widened 1936 (McManus, 293). Castle Avenue 1970–71, 2016 (OS). Castle Avenue/Ascaill an Chaisleáin 2017 (nameplate; Logainm).

Castle Avenue/ Ascaill an Chaisleáin [south] (719225, 736134). Unnamed 1685 (Phillips 1), 1717 (Bolton), 1730 (Price). Street of Clontarf 1740 (*FDJ* 13.5.1740). Unnamed 1760 (Rocque), 1803 (Bligh), 1805 (Snagg). Town of Clontarf 1805 (Sherrard and Brassington). Unnamed 1816 (Taylor), 1821 (Duncan). 'Street of the town of Clontarf' 1822 (Gogarty, 130). Unnamed 1823 (VEM), 1843 (OS). Castle Avenue 1848 (*FJ* 23.2.1848), 1862 (*Thom*), 1868–2016 (OS). Castle Avenue/Ascaill an Chaisleáin 2017 (nameplate; Logainm).

Castle Grove/Garrán an Chaisleáin

(Howth Rd [north] S., 719369, 736926). Castle Grove 1949 (*Thom*), 1971, 2016 (OS). Castle Grove/Garrán an Chaisleáin 2017 (nameplate; Logainm).

Castle Road/Bóthar an Chaisleáin

(Castle Ave [south] E., 719439, 736225). Castle Road 1949 (*Thom*), 1970–71, 2016 (OS). Castle Road/Bóthar an Chaisleáin 2017 (nameplate; Logainm).

Castle View/Radharc an Chaisleáin

(Castle Ave [north] E., 719522, 736368). Unnamed 1935, 1970–71; Castle View 2016 (OS). Castle View/Radharc an Chaisleáin 2017 (nameplate; Logainm).

Castlewood Road

See Haddon Road.

Causeway Road/Bóthar an Tóchair

(Clontarf Rd [east] S., 722738, 737366). Under construction 1963 (*Ir. Times* 20.2.1963). Completed in 1964 (Lynch, 90). Causeway in use by pedestrians 1969 (*Ir. Times* 31.3.1969). Depicted 1971; Causeway Road 2016 (OS). Causeway Road/Bóthar an Tóchair 2017 (Logainm).

Cecil Avenue/Ascaill Shicil

(Howth Rd [south] W., 718059, 736662). Cecil Avenue 1907–2016 (OS). Cecil Avenue/Ascaill Cecil 2017 (nameplate). Cecil Avenue/Ascaill Shicil 2017 (Logainm).

Chapel House Square

Location unknown. Chapel House Square, many houses roofless and in ruins 1861 (*Ir. Builder* 1.7.1861). Chapel House Square 1863 (*Ir. Times* 15.9.1863).

Chapel Lane

See Churchgate Avenue.

Chapel Yard

Clontarf Rd [mid], site unknown. Chapel Yard 1806 (Vernon papers).

Charlemont Road/Bóthar Charlemont [north]

(Howth Rd [south] W., 718060, 736618). Unnamed 1874 (Thom map). Charlemont Road 1900 (Val. 3), 1907–2016 (OS). Charlemont Road/Bóthar Charlemont 2017 (nameplate; Logainm).

Charlemont Road/Bóthar Charlemont [south]

(Howth Rd [south] W., 718060, 736618). Unnamed 1843 (OS). Charlemont Road 1900 (Val. 3), 1907–2016 (OS). Charlemont Road/Bóthar Charlemont 2017 (nameplate; Logainm).

Charter Row

See Marino Avenue.

Church Lane

Location unknown. Church Lane 1908 (Vernon papers).

Churchgate Avenue/Ascaill Gheata an Teampaill

(Vernon Ave [south] W., 720039, 735923). Unnamed 1843 (OS). Back Lane 1855 (Val. 3). Unnamed 1868 (OS). Chapel Lane 1884 (Vernon papers). Unnamed 1907 (OS). Chapel Lane 1911 (Census returns). Rutland Lane 1936; Churchgate Avenue 1970 (OS), 1972 (*Ir. Times* 14.6.1972), 2016 (OS). Churchgate Avenue/Ascal Gheata an Teampaill 2017 (nameplate). Churchgate Avenue/Ascaill Gheata an Teampaill 2017 (Logainm).

Clontarf Park/Páirc Chluain Tarbh

(Vernon Ave [south] E., 720201, 735894). Rutland Place 1816 (Taylor), 1823 (VEM). Victoria Place 1843 (OS). Rutland Place 1850 (Val. 2), 1855 (Val. 3), 1868, 1907 (OS). Rutland Place and Lane 1911 (Census returns). Rutland Place 1936 (OS). Clontarf Park 1958 (*Thom*); extended to E., partly over Queen's Park and Corinthians Football Grounds (see **21** Entertainment, memorials and societies) by 1970; 2016 (OS). Clontarf Park/Páirc Chluain Tarbh 2017 (nameplate; Logainm).

Clontarf Road/Bóthar Chluain Tarbh [east]

(721091, 736131). Unnamed 1730 (Price), 1760 (Rocque). Strand Road 1816 (Longfield 4). Unnamed 1816 (Taylor), 1821 (Duncan). Strand Road 1823 (VEM). Unnamed 1843–68; Clontarf Road 1907–2016 (OS). Clontarf Road/Bóthar Cluain Tairbh 2017 (nameplate). Clontarf Road/Bóthar Chluain Tarbh 2017 (Logainm).

Clontarf Road/Bóthar Chluain Tarbh [mid]

(720261, 735734). 'The road below the Shades of Clontarf' 1718 (*Ancient records*, vii, 66–7). Unnamed 1760 (Rocque). Sheds of Clontarf 1805 (Sherrard and Brassington). Unnamed 1816 (Taylor), 1821 (Duncan). Sheds of Clontarf 1836 (OSN). Clontarf Sheds 1843 (OS), 1850 (Val. 2). Clontarf Road 1907–2016 (OS). Clontarf Road/Bóthar Cluain Tairbh 2017 (nameplate). Clontarf Road/Bóthar Chluain Tarbh 2017 (Logainm).

Clontarf Road/Bóthar Chluain Tarbh [west]

(719170, 735954). Unnamed 1685 (Phillips 1). The Strand 1717 (Bolton). Unnamed 1730 (Price), 1760 (Rocque). Strand Road, bounding Lord Howth's land 1791 (Vernon papers). Unnamed

1816 (Taylor). Strand Road 1822 (Gogarty, 130). To Clontarf and Howth 1843 (OS). Clontarf Strand 1850 (*Thom*). Strand Street 1850 (Val. 2). Clontarf Road 1853 (McFarland, 7). Clontarf Strand 1855 (Val. 3). Unnamed 1868 (OS). Strand Road 1888 (Vernon papers), 1904 (*Thom*). Clontarf Road 1907 (OS). Strand Road 1909 (Electoral rolls). Sea Road 1911 (Census returns). Strand Road 1914 (Electoral rolls). Clontarf Road 1936–2016 (OS). Clontarf Road/ Bóthar Cluain Tairbh 2017 (nameplate). Clontarf Road/Bóthar Chluain Tarbh 2017 (Logainm).

Clontarf Sheds	See Clontarf Road [mid]; **14** Primary production: Sheds of Clontarf; **22** Residence: The Sheds.
Clontarf Strand	See Clontarf Road [west].
Conquer Hill Avenue/Ascaill Chnoc an Bhua	(Vernon Ave [south] E., 720426, 735888). Tramway Cottages 1901 (Census returns). Tram Terrace 1906 (*Ir. Times* 14.4.1906), 1907 (OS), 1910 (*Ir. Times* 6.10.1910). Tramway Cottages 1911 (Census returns). Tram Terrace 1936

(OS). Conquer Hill Avenue 1958 (*Thom*), 1970, 2016 (OS). Conquer Hill Avenue/ Ascal an Choinigéir 2017 (nameplate). Conquer Hill Avenue/Ascaill Chnoc an Bhua 2017 (Logainm).

Conquer Hill Road/ Bóthar Chnoc an Bhua	(Clontarf Rd [mid] N., 720486, 735892). Unnamed 1843 (OS). Back Lane 1850 (Val. 2). Mooney's Row 1881; Mooney's Lane 1894, 1900 (*FJ* 18.11.1881, 9.5.1894, 11.6.1900). 'New road, formerly Mooney's Lane' 1901 (Gogarty, 155). Mooney's Lane 1904 (*Ir. Times* 15.10.1904), 1905 (McManus, 116–17). Conquer Hill Road 1907 (OS), 1911 (Census returns). Mooney's Lane 1914 (Prunty, 281). Conquer Hill Road 1936–2016 (OS). Conquer Hill Road/ Bóthar an Choinigéir 2017 (nameplate). Conquer Hill Road/Bóthar Chnoc an Bhua 2017 (Logainm).
Copeland Avenue/ Ascaill Chóplainn	(Howth Rd [south] N., 718138, 736701). Laid out in 1933 (Gogarty, 206). Copeland Avenue 1935–2016 (OS). Copeland Avenue/Ascal Cóplainn 2017 (nameplate). Copeland Avenue/Ascaill Chóplainn 2017 (Logainm).

SHEDS OF CLONTARF, 1785, BY FRANCIS WHEATLEY

Copeland Grove/Garrán Chóplainn (Howth Rd [south] N., 718247, 736723). Copeland Grove 1950 (*Ir. Press* 19.8.1950), 1970, 2016 (OS). Copeland Grove/Garrán Cóplainn 2017 (nameplate). Copeland Grove/Garrán Chóplainn 2017 (Logainm).

Crescent Place/Plás an Chorráin (Howth Rd [south] N., 717975, 736545), partly on site of former lane (*q.v.*). Stable Lane 1872 (Val. 3). Crescent Place 1889–2016 (OS). Crescent Place/Plás an Corráin (nameplate). Crescent Place/Plás an Chorráin 2017 (Logainm).

Crescent, The See Marino Crescent.

Danespark or Dean's Park (Vernon Ave [south] E., 720447, 736044). Back Lane 1850 (Val. 2). Unnamed 1868 (OS). Danespark 1873 (*Ir. Times* 2.8.1873). Dean's Park 1893, 1896 (Vernon papers). Danespark 1901 (Census returns). Unnamed 1907 (OS). Danespark 1911 (Census returns), 1936 (OS). Built over in *c.* 1948 (*Ir. Times* 13.3.1948).

Dollymount Avenue/Ascaill Chnocán Doirinne (Clontarf Rd [east] W., 721123, 736623). Laid out in 1933 (McManus, 292). Dollymount Avenue 1935–2016 (OS). Dollymount Avenue/Ascaill Chnocán Doirinne 2017 (nameplate; Logainm). For another Dollymount Avenue, see Mount Prospect Avenue [east] and [west].

Dollymount Grove/Garrán Chnocán Doirinne (Vernon Ave [north] E., 720769, 736519). Dollymount Grove 1958 (*Thom*), 1970, 2016 (OS). Dollymount Grove/Garrán Baile na gCorr (nameplate). Dollymount Grove/Garrán Chnocán Doirinne 2017 (Logainm).

Dollymount Park/Páirc Chnocán Doirinne (Clontarf Rd [east] W., 720940, 736384). Dollymount Park 1949 (*Thom*), 1970, 2016 (OS). Dollymount Park/Páirc Chnocán Doirinne 2017 (nameplate; Logainm).

Dollymount Rise/Ard Chnocán Doirinne (Clontarf Rd [east] W., 721133, 736463). Dollymount Rise, laid out on site of former Kincora House (see **22** Residence) by 1970 (OS); 1981 (*Thom*), 2016 (OS). Dollymount Rise/Ard Chnocán Doirinne 2017 (nameplate; Logainm).

Doyles Lane/Lána Uí Dhúill (Clontarf Rd [east] N., 721294, 736409). Unnamed 1760 (Rocque), 1843–1907; Doyle's Lane 1935; unnamed 1970; Doyles Lane 2016 (OS). Doyle's Lane/Lána Doyle 2017 (nameplate). Doyles Lane/Lána Uí Dhúill 2017 (Logainm).

Dunluce Road/Bóthar Dhún Libhse (Howth Rd [north] S., 719799, 737208). Unnamed 1935 (OS). Dunluce Road 1939 (*Thom*), 1971, 2016 (OS). Dunluce Road/Bóthar Dhún Libhse 2017 (nameplate; Logainm).

Dunseverick Road/Bóthar Dhún Sobharice (Howth Rd [north] S., 719430, 737022). Newly built houses 1947; Dunseverick Road 1948 (*Ir. Times* 21.11.1947, 12.4.1948), 1971, 2016 (OS). Dunseverick Road/Bóthar Dhúnsobharice 2017 (nameplate). Dunseverick Road/Bóthar Dhún Sobharice 2017 (Logainm).

Dye House or Dyehouse Lane See Strandville Avenue East.

Fairville See Vernon Avenue [west].

Fingal Avenue (Clontarf Rd [mid] N., 720324, 735780). Fingal Avenue 1863 (*Thom*), 1868–1936; unnamed 1970; closed by 2016 (OS).

Fortview Avenue or Terrace/Ascaill Radharc an Dúin (Clontarf Rd [mid] N., 720303, 735789). Fortview Avenue 1850 (Val. 2), 1855 (Val. 3), 1861 (*Ir. Builder* 1.7.1861). Fort View Avenue 1868; Fortview Avenue 1907, 1936 (OS). Fortview Terrace 1950 (*Ir. Times* 7.7.1950). Fortview Avenue 1969 (*Thom*), 1970, 2016 (OS). Fortview Avenue/Ascal Radharc an Dúna 2017 (nameplate). Fortview Avenue/Ascaill Radharc an Dúin 2017 (Logainm).

Furry Park Road/Bóthar Pháirc an Aitinn (Howth Rd [north] S., 719807, 737312). Laid out during development of Furry Park estate (see **22** Residence) from 1936 (Gogarty, 208). Furry Park Road 1971, 2016 (OS). Furry Park Road/Bóthar Pháirc an Aitinn 2017 (nameplate; Logainm).

Green Lane, Green Lanes or Greenlanes See Castle Avenue [north], Mount Prospect Avenue [west], Vernon Avenue [north], Vernon Avenue [west].

Haddon Park/Páirc Ui Aidín (Clontarf Rd [west] N., 718890, 736163). Haddon Park 1911 (Census returns), 1929 (*Thom*), 1936–2016 (OS). Haddon Park/Páirc Uí hAidín 2017 (nameplate).

Haddon Park/Páirc Ui Aidín 2017 (Logainm).

Haddon Road/Bóthar Uí Aidín (Clontarf Rd [west] N., 719057, 736080). New road 1894 (Gogarty, 172), 1895 (Vernon papers). Castlewood Road 1895; Haddon Road 1899 (Val. 3), 1907–2016 (OS). Haddon Road/Bóthar Ó hAidín 2017 (nameplate). Haddon Road/Bóthar Uí Aidín 2017 (Logainm).

Hollybrook Avenue See Hollybrook Park.

Hollybrook Grove/ Garrán Shruthán an Chuilinn (Clontarf Rd [west] N., 718349, 736463). Hollybrook Grove 1958 (*Thom*), 1971, 2016 (OS). Hollybrook Grove/Garrán Cuileannsruth 2017 (nameplate). Hollybrook Grove/Garrán Shruthán an Chuilinn 2017 (Logainm).

Hollybrook Mews (Clontarf Rd [west] N., 718588, 736578). Lane; gate, N. end 1812 (Longfield 3). Unnamed 1843–1971; Hollybrook Mews 2016 (OS).

Hollybrook Park/ Páirc Shruthán an Chuilinn (Howth Rd [south] S., 718628, 736618). Hollybrook Avenue; gate, W. end 1812 (Longfield 3). Unnamed 1843 (OS). Hollybrook Park 1864 (Val. 3). Unnamed 1868 (OS). Hollybrook Park 1883 (*Thom*), 1889, 1907 (OS), 1929 (*Thom*). Unnamed 1935–6; Hollybrook Park 1971, 2016 (OS). Hollybrook Park/Páirc Shruthán an Chuilinn 2017 (Logainm).

Hollybrook Road/ Bóthar Shruthán an Chuilinn (Clontarf Rd [west] N., 718605, 736425). Hollybrook Road 1900 (Val. 3), 1907–2016 (OS). Hollybrook Road/Bóthar Chuileann tSruth 2017 (nameplate). Hollybrook Road/Bóthar Shruthán an Chuilinn 2017 (Logainm).

Howth Road/Bóthar Bhinn Éadair [north] (719096, 736907). The Road to Beldole 1730 (Price). Unnamed 1760 (Rocque). Killester Road 1789 (*Commons votes*, 1789, 269). Road from Dublin to Raheny 1812 (Longfield 3). Unnamed 1816 (Taylor), 1821 (Duncan). Road to Raheny and Howth 1843 (OS). Howth Road 1864–7 (Val. 3). To Howth 1868; Howth Road 1889–2016 (OS). Howth Road/Bóthar Bhinn Éadair 2017 (nameplate; Logainm).

Howth Road/Bóthar Bhinn Éadair [south] (718214, 736558). Unnamed 1685 (Phillips 1), 1730 (Price), 1760 (Rocque).

Black Quarry Road 1789 (*Commons votes*, 1789, 269). Road 1803 (Bligh). Unnamed 1816 (Taylor), 1821 (Duncan), 1843 (OS). Howth Road 1864–7 (Val. 3). Unnamed 1868; Howth Road 1889–2016 (OS). Howth Road/Bóthar Bhinn Éadair 2017 (nameplate; Logainm).

James Larkin Road/ Bóthar Shéamais Uí Lorcáin (Clontarf Rd [east] E., 721730, 736910). James Larkin Road, extension of Clontarf Road [east] (*q.v.*) to E., opened in 1948 (Gogarty, 189). James Larkin Road/Bóthar Séamas Ó Lorcáin 1949 (datestone). James Larkin Road 1970, 2016 (OS). James Larkin Road/Bóthar Shéamais Uí Lorcáin 2017 (Logainm).

Killester Road Clontarf Rd [west] N., site unknown, possibly same as St Lawrence Road (*q.v.*). Killester Road 1872, 1873 (Val. 3). For another Killester Road, see Howth Road [north].

Kincora Avenue/ Ascaill Cheann Cora (Clontarf Rd [west] N., 719024, 736323). Laid out, on former grounds of Clontarf Castle (see **22** Residence) in 1955–9 (Gogarty, 212). Kincora Avenue 1958 (*Thom*), 1971, 2016 (OS). Kincora Avenue/Ascaill Cheann Córa 2017 (nameplate). Kincora Avenue/Ascaill Cheann Cora 2017 (Logainm).

Kincora Drive/Céide Cheann Cora (Castle Ave [north] W., 720893, 736078). Laid out, on former grounds of Clontarf Castle (see **22** Residence) in 1955–9 (Gogarty, 212). Kincora Drive 1963 (*Ir. Times* 8.5.1963), 1970–71, 2016 (OS). Kincora Drive/Céide Cheann Córa 2017 (nameplate). Kincora Drive/Céide Cheann Cora 2017 (Logainm).

Kincora Grove/ Garrán Cheann Cora (Castle Ave [north] W., 719284, 736666). Laid out, on former grounds of Clontarf Castle (see **22** Residence) in 1955–9 (Gogarty, 212). Kincora Grove 1961 (*Ir. Times* 5.10.1961), 1970–71, 2016 (OS). Kincora Grove/Garrán Cheann Cora 2017 (nameplate; Logainm).

Kincora Park/Páirc Cheann Cora (Clontarf Rd [mid] N., 719732, 736108). Kincora Park 1949 (*Thom*), 1970, 2016 (OS). Kincora Park/Páirc Ceann Coradh 2017 (nameplate). Kincora Park/Páirc Cheann Cora 2017 (Logainm).

LANE FROM SEAFIELD ROAD WEST TO OULTON ROAD, *c.* 1910

Kincora Road/Bóthar Cheann Cora
(Clontarf Rd [mid] N., 719777, 736226). Planned and leased in 1927 (McManus, 287–8). New road 1927 (Vernon papers). Opened in 1928 (*Ir. Times* 24.4.1928). Kincora Road 1936–2016 (OS). Kincora Road/Bóthar Cheann Cora 2017 (nameplate; Logainm).

Lane (1)
Clontarf Rd [mid], site unknown. A lane to the kinges houses (see **13** Administration: customs station) 1806 (Vernon papers). For another Lane, see Belgrove Rd [south], Hollybrook Mews.

Lane (2)
(Howth Rd [south] N., 717889, 736520). Lane 1823 (VEM). Unnamed 1843 (OS). Built over during laying out of Crescent Place by 1889 (*q.v.*). For another Lane, see Belgrove Rd [south], Hollybrook Mews.

Lane (3)
Vernon Ave, site unknown. A lane adjoining Vernon Avenue 1860–62
(Vernon papers). For another Lane, see Belgrove Rd [south], Hollybrook Mews.

Laneway
(Clontarf Rd [west] N., 719002, 736054). Unnamed 1868 (OS). A laneway 1895 (Vernon papers). Unnamed 1907–1970 (OS).

Lawrence Grove/Garráin Labhrais
(Howth Rd [south] S., 718757, 736583). Lawrence Grove 1971, 2016 (OS). Lawrence Grove/Garráin Labhrais 2017 (nameplate; Logainm).

Long Lane
Location unknown. Long Lane 1903–4 (Vernon papers).

Malahide Road/Bóthar Mhullach Íde
(Clontarf Rd [west] N., 717919, 736650). Unnamed 1685 (Phillips 1), 1760 (Rocque). Road 1803 (Bligh). Unnamed 1816 (Taylor), 1821 (Duncan). To Coolock 1823 (VEM). To Malahide 1843 (OS). Malahide Road 1852 (Vernon papers), 1864 (Val. 3). To Malahide

MARINO CRESCENT, 1812, BY B. KING

1868; Malahide Road 1889–2016 (OS). Malahide Road/Bóthar Mhullach Íde 2017 (nameplate; Logainm).

Marino Crescent/ Corrán Marino
(Howth Rd [south] W., 717941, 736458). Laid out in 1792 (Cosgrave, 93). Crescent 1803 (Bligh). The Crescent 1812 (King). Crescent 1816 (Taylor), 1821 (Duncan), 1823 (VEM). The Crescent 1836 (OSN). Crescent 1843 (OS). Marino Crescent 1850 (*Thom*). The Crescent 1850 (Val. 2). Marino Crescent 1864–7 (Val. 3), 1868–2016 (OS). The Crescent/An Corrán 2017 (nameplate). Marino Crescent/ Corrán Marino 2017 (Logainm).

Marino or Merino Avenue/Ascaill Marino
(Howth Rd [south] W., 718013, 736702). Charter Row 1816 (Taylor). Unnamed 1821 (Duncan). Merino Avenue 1823 (VEM). Marino Avenue 1843–2016 (OS). Marino Avenue/Ascaill Mhuirne 2017 (nameplate). Marino Avenue/Ascaill Marino 2017 (Logainm).

Moat Lane/Lána an Mhóta
(Vernon Ave [south] E., 720188, 736002). Unnamed 1843–1970; Moat Lane, extended to E. by 2016 (OS). Moat Lane/Lána an Mhóta 2017 (Logainm).

Mooney's Lane or Row
See Conquer Hill Road.

Moore or Moore's Place
Clontarf Rd, site unknown. Moore's Place 1875 (*Thom*), 1876; Moore Place 1879 (*FJ* 23.11.1876, 14.4.1879). Moore's Place 1881 (*Thom*).

Mount Prospect Avenue/Ascaill Chnocán an Radhairc [east]
(Vernon Ave [north] E., 721300, 736941). Dollymount Avenue 1747 (Gogarty, 163). Road from Howth to Dublin 1816 (Longfield 4). Unnamed 1816 (Taylor), 1821 (Duncan), 1823 (VEM). Blackbush Lane 1843–68 (OS), 1894 (Vernon papers). Mount Prospect Avenue 1907 (OS), 1908 (*Thom*); partly widened in 1928 (*Ir. Times* 5.4.1928); 1935–2016 (OS). Mount Prospect Avenue/Ascaill

Árd na Teamhrach 2017 (nameplate). Mount Prospect Avenue/Ascaill Chnocán an Radhairc 2017 (Logainm).

Mount Prospect Avenue/Ascaill Chnocán an Radhairc [west] (Vernon Ave [north] E., 720511 736679). Dollymount Avenue 1747 (Gogarty, 163). Unnamed 1760 (Rocque), 1816 (Taylor), 1821 (Duncan). Green Lane 1843 (OS). Green Lanes 1849 (*Thom*), 1868 (OS), 1903 (*Thom*). Mount Prospect Avenue 1907 (OS), 1908 (*Thom*); partly widened in 1928 (*Ir. Times* 5.4.1928); 1935–2016 (OS). Mount Prospect Avenue/Ascaill Árd na Teamhrach 2017 (nameplate). Mount Prospect Avenue/Ascaill Chnocán an Radhairc 2017 (Logainm).

Mount Prospect Drive/Céide Chnocán an Radhairc (Vernon Ave [north] E., 720655, 736893). Mount Prospect Drive 1949 (*Thom*), 1971, 2016 (OS). Mount Prospect Drive/Céide Ard na Teamhrach 2017 (nameplate). Mount Prospect Drive/Céide Chnocán an Radhairc 2017 (Logainm).

Mount Prospect Grove/Garrán Chnocán an Radhairc (Vernon Ave [north] E., 720289, 736733). Mount Prospect Grove 1949 (*Thom*), 1970, 2016 (OS). Mount Prospect Grove/Garrán Árd na Teamhrach 2017 (nameplate). Mount Prospect Grove/Garrán Chnocán an Radhairc 2017 (Logainm).

Mount Prospect Park/Páirc Chnocán an Radhairc (Vernon Ave [north] E., 720508, 736821). Mountprospect Park 1935 (OS). Mount Prospect Park 1939 (*Thom*), 1971, 2016 (OS). Mount Prospect Park/Páirc Chnocán an Radhairc 2017 (nameplate; Logainm).

Oakley Estate or Park/Páirc Oakley (Vernon Ave [north] W., 720030,736714). Oakley Estate, laid out on site of former Oakley (see **22** Residence) by 1960 (*Ir. Times* 30.11.1960). Oakley Park 1970, 2016 (OS). Oakley Park/Páirc Oakley 2017 (nameplate; Logainm). See also **22** Residence: Oakley Park.

Oulton Road/Bóthar Oulton (Clontarf Rd [west] N., 719628, 736096). Opened in 1932 (McManus, 292). Oulton Road 1932 (*Ir. Times* 21.9.1932), 1936–2016 (OS). Oulton Road/Bóthar Oulton 2017 (nameplate; Logainm).

Queen Victoria Street See Victoria Road.

Royal Square (Clontarf Rd [mid] N., 720015, 735904). Royal Square 1823 (VEM), 1834 (Vernon papers). Demolished, partly built over by R.C. church in 1836 (see **11** Religion: St John the Baptist Catholic Church).

Rutland Avenue See Belgrove Road [south].

Rutland Lane See Churchgate Avenue, Clontarf Park.

Rutland Place See Clontarf Park.

St Gabriel's Road/Bóthar Naomh Gaibréal (Clontarf Rd [east] W., 720855, 736435). Laid out in 1956 (Gogarty, 213). St Gabriel's Road 1964 (*Ir. Independent* 9.1.1964), 1970, 2016 (OS). St Gabriel's Road/Bóthar Naomh Gaibréal 2017 (nameplate; Logainm).

St Joseph or Joseph's Square/Cearnóg Iósaif (Vernon Ave [south] W., 719996, 735992). Laid out shortly after 1837 (Gogarty, 137). Unnamed 1868 (OS). St Joseph's Square (formerly Snugboro) 1900 (Vernon papers). Unnamed 1907 (OS). St Joseph's Square 1909 (Vernon papers), 1929 (*Thom*). St Joseph Square 1936; St Joseph's Square 1970 (OS), 1989 (*Ir. Times* 20.9.1989), 2016 (OS). St Josephs Square/Cearnóg Shan Seosaimh 2017 (nameplate). Saint Joseph's Square/Cearnóg Iósaif 2017 (Logainm). See also **22** Residence: Snugboro.

St Laurence, St Lawrence or St Lawrences Road/Bóthar San Labhrás (Clontarf Rd [west] N., 718830, 736458). S. portion laid out by 1868 (OS). Begun in 1871 (Gogarty, 165). St Laurence Road 1873 (*Ir. Times* 9.12.1873). St Lawrence Road 1873–6 (Val. 3). St Lawrences Road 1890 (OS). St Lawrence Road 1892 (*Thom*), 1907–2016 (OS). St Lawrence Road/Bóthar Shan Labhráis 2017 (nameplate). St Lawrence Road/Bóthar San Labhrás 2017 (Logainm).

Sea Road See Clontarf Road [west].

Sea View Avenue See Seafield Road East.

Seafield Avenue North See Seaview Avenue North.

Seafield or Sea Field Avenue/Ascaill Ghort na Mara (Vernon Ave [north] E., 720394, 736535). Laid out in 1933 (Gogarty, 206). Seafield Avenue 1935–2016 (OS). Seafield Avenue/Ascaill Ghort na Mara 2017 (nameplate; Logainm). For other

Seafield Avenues, see Seafield Road East, Seafield Road West.

Seafield Road or Seafield Road East/ Bóthar Ghort na Mara Thoir
(Vernon Ave [south] E., 720589, 736334). Sea View Avenue 1816 (Taylor), 1821 (Duncan). Sea Field Avenue 1823 (VEM). Seafield Avenue 1834 (Vernon papers). 'A road or avenue leading from Clontarf Castle to the shore in very good repair' 1836 (OSN). Seafield Avenue 1843–68 (OS), 1886 (*FJ* 3.5.1886), 1896 (Vernon papers). Seafield Road 1901 (*Thom*), 1907; Seafield Road East 1935–2016 (OS). Seafield Road East/Bóthar Ghort na Mara Thoir 2017 (nameplate; Logainm).

Seafield Road or Seafield Road West/ Bóthar Ghort na Mara Thiar
(Vernon Ave [south] W., 719777, 736386). Unnamed 1685 (Phillips 1), 1760 (Rocque), 1816 (Taylor). Back Strand Road *c.* 1819 (Vernon papers). Unnamed 1821 (Duncan), 1823 (VEM). Seafield Avenue 1841 (*FJ* 21.8.1841), 1843 (OS). Seafield Road 1901 (*Thom*), 1907 (OS), 1924 (Vernon papers). Seafield Road West 1935–2016 (OS). Seafield Road West/Bóthar Ghort na Mara Thiar 2017 (nameplate; Logainm).

Seapark Drive/Céide Pháirc na Mara
(Clontarf Rd [east] N., 720727, 736185). Seapark Drive 1949 (*Thom*), 1970, 2016 (OS). Seapark Drive/Céide Pháirc na Mara 2017 (nameplate; Logainm).

Seapark Road/ Bóthar Pháirc na Mara
(Clontarf Rd [mid] N., 720601, 736508). Land granted for road 'to be called Seapark Road' in 1933 (Gogarty, 205). Seapark Road 1935–2016 (OS). Seapark Road/Bóthar Pháirc na Mara 2017 (nameplate; Logainm).

Seaview Avenue or Seaview Avenue North/Ascaill Radharc na Mara Thuaidh [north]
(Clontarf Rd [west] N., 718862, 736139). Seaview Avenue 1850 (*Thom*), 1868–1907 (OS), 1918 (Vernon papers). Seaview Avenue North 1936; Seafield Avenue North 1970; Seaview Avenue North 2016 (OS). Seaview Avenue North/ Ascal Radharc na Mara Thuaidh 2017 (nameplate). Seaview Avenue North/ Ascaill Radharc na Mara Thuaidh 2017 (Logainm).

Seaview Avenue or Seaview Avenue North/Ascaill Radharc na Mara Thuaidh [south]
(Clontarf Rd [west] N., 718841, 736084). Seaview Avenue 1850 (*Thom*), 1868–90 (OS). Cabra Parade 1898 (Thom map). Seaview Avenue 1907 (OS). Cabra Parade 1910; Seaview Avenue 1918 (Vernon papers). Seaview Avenue North 1936; Seafield Avenue North 1970; Seaview Avenue North 2016 (OS). Seaview Avenue North/Ascaill Radharc na Mara Thuaidh 2017 (nameplate). Seaview Avenue North/Ascaill Radharc na Mara Thuaidh 2017 (Logainm).

Sheds of Clontarf
See Clontarf Road [mid].

Stable Lane
See Crescent Place.

Stiles Road, The/ Bóthar na Strapaí
(Clontarf Rd [west] N., 719041, 736605). Styles Road laid out, partly on site of former Northbank and Rosemount Cottage (see **22** Residence), by 1939 (OS). The Stiles Road 1945 (Vernon papers), 1949 (*Thom*), 1971, 2016 (OS). The Stiles Road/Bóthar na Strapaí 2017 (nameplate; Logainm).

Stiles, The or Stiles Court, The/Cúirt Stiles
(Castle Ave [north] W., 719309, 736721). The Stiles 1935; unnamed 1970–71 (OS). Stiles Court 1993 (*Ir. Times* 14.10.1993). The Stiles Court 2016 (OS). Stiles Court/ Cúirt na Strapaí 2017 (nameplate). Stiles Court/Cúirt Stiles 2017 (Logainm).

Strand Road or Street
See Clontarf Road [east], Clontarf Road [west].

Strand, The
See Clontarf Road [west].

Strandville Avenue or Strandville Avenue East/Ascaill Bhaile na Trá Thoir
(Clontarf Rd [west] N., 718410, 736445). Black Quarry Lane 1789 (*Commons votes*, 1789, 269). Dye H. Lane 1816 (Taylor). Unnamed 1821 (Duncan). Dye House Lane 1823 (VEM). Strandville Avenue, known as Strandville Villa 1841 (*FJ* 3.7.1841). Unnamed 1843 (OS). Dyehouse Lane 1846 (*FJ* 1.9.1846). Strandville Avenue 1850 (*Thom*), 1868–1907 (OS), 1909 (Electoral rolls). Strandville Avenue East 1935–2016 (OS). Strandville Avenue East/Ascaill Bhailtín na Trá Thoir 2017 (nameplate). Strandville Avenue East/Ascaill Bhaile na Trá Thoir 2017 (Logainm).

Strandville Villa
See previous entry.

Street of Clontarf
See Castle Avenue [south].

Styles Road
See Stiles Road, The.

Sybil Hill Road/
Bóthar Chnoc Shibéal

(Howth Rd [north] S., 720160, 737119). Sybil Hill Road 1968 (*Ir. Times* 14.11.1968), 1971, 2016 (OS). Sybil Hill Road/Bóthar Chnoc Shibéal 2017 (nameplate; Logainm).

Tram Terrace

See Conquer Hill Avenue.

Tramway Cottages

See Conquer Hill Avenue.

Tudor's or Tutor's
Avenue

Vernon Ave [south] W., site unknown, possibly same as Beechfield Lane (*q.v.*). Tutor's Avenue 1904; Tudor's Avenue 1908 (*Thom*).

Vernon Avenue/
Ascaill Vernon
[north]

(720115, 736473). Unnamed 1760 (Rocque). Green Lane 1816 (Taylor). Unnamed 1821 (Duncan), 1823 (VEM). Vernon Avenue, 'a bye-road leading from Clontarf parochial school through the Sheds of Clontarf and to the shore in good repair' 1836 (OSN); 1842 (*FJ* 9.12.1842). Unnamed 1843 (OS). Green Lanes 1849 (*Thom*). Vernon Avenue 1850 (Val. 2). Green Lanes 1852 (*Thom*), 1868 (OS). Greenlanes 1903 (*Thom*). Vernon Avenue 1907–2016 (OS). Vernon Avenue/Ascal Vernon 2017 (nameplate). Vernon Avenue/Ascaill Vernon 2017 (Logainm).

Vernon Avenue/
Ascaill Vernon
[south]

(7200088, 736030). Unnamed 1760 (Rocque), 1816 (Taylor), 1821 (Duncan), 1823 (VEM). Vernon Avenue, 'a bye-road leading from Clontarf parochial school through the Sheds of Clontarf and to the shore in good repair' 1836 (OSN); 1843–2016 (OS). Vernon Avenue/Ascal Vernon 2017 (nameplate). Vernon Avenue/Ascaill Vernon 2017 (Logainm).

Vernon Avenue/
Ascaill Vernon [west]

(719890, 737022). Unnamed 1760 (Rocque). Fairville 1816 (Taylor). Unnamed 1821 (Duncan). Green Lane 1823 (VEM). 'A bye road in good repair passing to the south of Furry Park House and Sibyl Hill House' 1836 (OSN). Unnamed 1843 (OS). Green Lanes 1849, 1861 (*Thom*). Unnamed 1868 (OS). Greenlanes 1903 (*Thom*). Verville Road 1903–4 (Vernon papers). Unnamed 1907, 1935; Vernon Avenue 1971, 2016 (OS). Vernon Avenue/Ascal Vernon 2017 (nameplate). Vernon Avenue/Ascaill Vernon 2017 (Logainm).

Vernon Drive/
Céide Vernon

(Vernon Ave [west] N., 720077, 737090). Vernon Drive 1958 (*Thom*), 1971, 2016 (OS). Vernon Drive/Céide Vernon 2017 (nameplate; Logainm).

Vernon Gardens/
Gairdíní Vernon

(Vernon Ave [south] E., 720205, 736049). Vernon Gardens, laid out in 1924 (Gogarty, 200); 1929 (*Thom*), 1936–2016 (OS). Vernon Gardens/Gairdíní Vernon 2017 (nameplate; Logainm).

Vernon Grove/
Garrán Vernon

(Vernon Ave [south] E., 720320, 736048). Laid out in 1924 (Gogarty, 200). Vernon Grove 1929 (*Thom*), 1936–2016 (OS). Vernon Grove/Garrán Vernon 2017 (nameplate; Logainm).

Vernon Park/Páirc
Vernon

(Vernon Ave [north] E., 720251, 736538). Vernon Park 1939–2016 (OS). Vernon Park/Páirc Bhearnon 2017 (nameplate). Vernon Park/Páirc Vernon 2017 (Logainm).

Verville Road

See Vernon Avenue [west].

Victoria Place

See Clontarf Park.

Victoria Road/
Bóthar Victoria

(Castle Ave [south] W., 719080, 736199). Unnamed 1843 (OS). Victoria Road 1903 (*Thom*); widened and extended to W., partly on site of former Frankfort House (see **22** Residence), by 1907 (OS). Queen Victoria Street 1918 (Vernon papers). Victoria Road 1936–2016 (OS). Victoria Road/Bóthar Victoria 2017 (nameplate; Logainm).

Victoria Terrace/
Ardán Victoria

(Clontarf Rd [mid] N., 719813, 735956). Unnamed 1843–1970; Victoria Terrace 2016 (OS). Victoria Terrace 2017 (nameplate). Victoria Terrace/Ardán Victoria 2017 (Logainm).

Victoria Villas/
Bailtíní Victoria

(Howth Rd [south] W., 718000, 736615). Victoria Villas 1904 (*Thom*), 1907–2016 (OS). Victoria Villas/Bailtíní Buaidhe 2017 (nameplate). Victoria Villas/Bailtíní Victoria 2017 (Logainm).

11. RELIGION

Early Christian monastery of Clontarf, location unknown. Reputedly founded by St Comgall in mid-6th cent. (D'Alton, 37). See also next entry.

Clontarf preceptory (Knights Templar), Castle Ave W., site unknown, possibly on site of previous entry. Founded in *c.* 1172 (Falkiner, 306). Preceptory of Clontarf 1185 (Wood, 331). Transferred to Knights Hospitaller in 1311 (Falkiner, 306). Clontarf priory 1348 (*Reg. Kilmainham*, 125). Dissolved in 1540; hall, 2 towers, kitchen, other houses 1541 (*Extents Ir. mon. possessions*, 89). Church and parsonage granted to Matthew King in 1542 (*Cal. exch. inq.*, 91). See also **14** Primary production: rabbit warrens.

St John's Church (C. of I.), Castle Ave [north] W. (719414, 736507). Parish church, appropriated to Matthew King 1542 (Archdall, 126). Rebuilt in 1609 (McIntyre, 56). Church decayed 1654–6 (*CS*, vii, 176). Rebuilt in late 17th or early 18th cent. (Aalen and Whelan, 161). The church 1760 (Rocque). Church 1816 (Taylor), 1821 (Duncan), 1823 (VEM). St John's Church 1836 (OSN). Church 1843 (OS). Parish church 1845 (Val. 1). Clontarf church 1855 (Brett). Parish church moved to new site in 1866 (see next entry). Church (in ruins) 1868–2016 (OS). See also **20** Education: Greenlanes School; **21** Entertainment, memorials and societies: parochial hall.

Cemetery: grave yard 1843–1907; cemetery 1970–71, 2016 (OS).
Church yard: 1806 (Vernon papers).

St John the Baptist's Church (C. of I.), Seafield Rd West S. (719638, 736382). Built to replace former church (see previous entry), foundation stone laid in 1864 (Gogarty, 102); completed in 1866 (*Ir. Times* 15.5.1866). Church 1868 (OS). Extended in 1899 (*Ir. Times* 11.3.1899). St John the Baptist's Ch. 1907 (OS). Clontarf Episcopal Church 1914 (Vernon papers). St John the Baptist's Church 1935; church (C. of I.) 1970–71; St John the Baptist's Church 2016 (OS). See also **21** Entertainment, memorials and societies: tennis ground; **22** Residence: The Old Rectory.

R.C. chapel, Vernon Ave [south] W. (719903, 735944). Chapel 1805 (Sherrard and Brassington), 1816 (Taylor), 1821 (Duncan), 1823 (VEM). Old R.C. chapel 1836 (OSN). In use as school 1837 (see **20** Education). Old R.C. chapel (in ruins) 1843 (OS). Plot, formerly Roman Catholic chapel and yard 1845 (Val. 1).

St John the Baptist Catholic Church, Clontarf Rd [mid] N. (719995, 735921), partly on site of former Royal Square (see **10** Streets) and former Snugboro (see **22** Residence). Chapel, proposed in 1834 (Vernon papers). New chapel at Clontarf Sheds 1836 (OSN). Completed in 1838 (Donnelly, 27–32). Dedicated in 1842 (*FJ* 30.6.1842). R.C. chapel 1843 (OS). Roman Catholic chaple and yard 1845 (Val. 1). R.C. chapel, yard 1855 (Val. 3). R.C. chapel 1868 (OS). Addition to apse in 1893 (Gogarty, 72). Extended in 1895 (Donnelly, 33–7). R.C. church 1907 (OS). 2 porches added in 1910–11 (Gogarty, 72). Catholic church 1936; church (Catholic) 1970, 2016 (OS). Saint John the Baptist Catholic Church 2017. See also **22** Residence: presbytery.

St Anthony's Catholic Church, Clontarf Rd [west] N., in former Town Hall (see **13** Administration). Established in 1925 (*Ir. Times* 11.8.1925). St Anthony's Cath. Ch 1936 (OS). Damaged by fire in 1971 (*Ir. Independent* 4.1.1971). Church (Catholic) 1971 (OS). Converted to community centre (see **21** Entertainment, memorials and societies: St Anthony's Hall), church moved to new site in 1975 (see next entry).

St Anthony's Catholic Church, St Lawrence Rd W. (718675, 736263). Built to replace former church (see previous entry) in 1975 (*Ir. Press* 24.11.1975). Church (Catholic) 2016 (OS). Saint Anthony's Catholic Church 2017.

Saint Gabriel's Catholic Church, St Gabriel's Rd E. (720923, 736432). Built in 1956 (*Souvenir brochure*). Church (Catholic) 1970, 2016 (OS). Saint Gabriel's Catholic Church 2017. See also **21** Entertainment, memorials and societies: community centre.

Nunnery (Dominican), Vernon Ave [north] E. (720150, 736713). Moved from N. Brunswick Street in 1808 (Genevieve, 240–41). Nunnery 1816 (Taylor), 1821 (Duncan). Unnamed 1823 (VEM). Former nunnery, residents removed to Cabra in *c.* 1825 (Lewis, i, 376). Converted to private residence by 1836 (see **22** Residence: Vernon House).

Carmelite monastery, location unknown. Monastery of Discalced Carmelites 1836 (OSN). Carmelite monastery, chapel 1837 (Lewis, i, 376).

Loreto Sisters convent, Dollymount Ave N., in former Baymount Castle (see **22** Residence). Loreto Sisters convent, established in 1842 (Ruddy, 2006, 174). Converted to school in 1847 (see **20** Education: St Mary's Abbey of Loreto Catholic Girls' Boarding School).

Daughters of Charity convent, Mount Prospect Ave [west] E., in former Mount Prospect (see **22** Residence). St Vincent de Paul female orphanage, established in 1873 (Gogarty, 39–40). Daughters of Charity orphanage 1901 (Census returns). Mount Prospect 1907 (OS). Mount Prospect orphanage 1918 (Vernon papers). Building altered and extended in 1919; house granted to Daughters of Charity in 1934 (Gogarty, 40). Mount Prospect Convent, chapel 1935 (OS). In use as convent only from *c.* 1960s (Gogarty, 40). Convent 1970, 2016 (OS). Daughters of Charity convent 2017.

Holy Faith convent, Clontarf Rd [mid] N., in former constabulary barracks (see **13** Administration). Convent, Sisters of the Holy Faith 1890 (Val. 3). Convent 1905 (Vernon papers), 1907–70 (OS). Holy Faith convent 2017. See also **20** Education: Holy Faith schools.

Clontarf Methodist Church, St Lawrence Rd W. (718725, 736159). Built in 1867 (Levistone Cooney, 158). Opened in 1868 (Gogarty, 103). Extended in 1881 (Levistone Cooney, 158). Methodist church 1890 (OS). Methodist chapel 1895–1902 (Val. 3). Demolished, rebuilt in 1906 (*Ir. Times* 8.10.1906). Methodist church 1907, 1935; church (Methodist) 1970,

2016 (OS). Clontarf Methodist Church 2017. See also **20** Education: Sunday school.

Clontarf and Scots Presbyterian Church, Clontarf Rd [west] N. (718024, 736368). Foundation stone laid in 1889 (Gogarty, 113). Built in 1890 (*Ir. Times* 18.4.1890). Presbyterian church 1898 (Thom map), 1907 (OS). Vestry added in 1931–2 (Gogarty, 114). Church (Presbyterian) 1970, 2016 (OS). Clontarf and Scots Presbyterian Church 2017. See also **20** Education: Howth Road Mixed National School; **22** Residence: manse.

Manresa Retreat House, Dollymount Ave N., in former Baymount Preparatory School (see **20** Education). House of Studies, Manresa House (Society of Jesus) established in 1948 (Ruddy, 2006, 179). Manresa Retreat House 1970, 2016 (OS).

Vincentian Provincial Office, Sybil Hill Rd E., in former Sibyl Hill (see **22** Residence). House occupied by Vincentian Fathers Congregation in 1950 (local information). College 1971 (OS). Vincentian Provincial Office 2017. See also **20** Education: St Paul's College.

12. DEFENCE

Castle, Castle Ave [south] W. (719344, 736451). Manor house of Knights Templar from 13th cent., implied in manorial extent of Clontarf, including outbuildings 1308 (Mac Niocaill, 1967, 188, 214–15). 'A hall, two towers' 1540 (*Extents Ir. mon. possessions*, 89). Burnt down in 1641 (Gilbert, i, 41–4). Castle, adjoining slated stone house, stone bawn, dove-house, orchard 1656 (*CS*, vii, 176). Building with 11 hearths 1664 (Hearth money roll, 394). The House late 17th cent. (Phillips 1a). Unnamed 1730 (Price), 1760 (Rocque). Clontarf Castle 1772 (Beranger). 'A fine edifice, with noble rooms, and a very pleasant garden and demesne' 1787 (*Dublin guide*, 110). Clontarf Castle 1803 (Bligh), 1805 (Snagg). Castle 1816 (Taylor). Clontarf Castle 1817 (Turner). Castle 1821 (Duncan). Clontarf Demesne, lawn, ruins, stable yard 1823 (VEM). Mansion house called Clontarf Castle 1828 (Vernon papers). Castle of Clontarf 1834 (Hardy, 274). Demolished, rebuilt as private residence in 1836–7 (see **22** Residence: Clontarf Castle).

CLONTARF AND SCOTS PRESBYTERIAN CHURCH, *c.* 1910

13. ADMINISTRATION

Customs station, Clontarf Rd [mid], site unknown. Customs station 1698; King's house 1758 (Ní Mhurchadha, 18, 50). Kinges houses 1806 (Vernon papers).

Customs officers' watch house, location unknown. 1717; decommissioned in 1722 (Ní Mhurchadha, 20, 24).

Two mile stone, Howth Rd [south] W. (717980, 736391). 1823 (VEM).

Post offices:

    Location unknown. 1824 (Vernon papers).

    Clontarf Rd [mid] N. (719816, 735915). 1843 (OS).

    Vernon Ave [south] E. (720114, 736151). 1876–1899 (Val. 3).

    Vernon Ave, site unknown, possibly same as previous entry. 1897 (Vernon papers).

    Clontarf Rd [east] N. (721179, 736229). 1907 (OS).

    Clontarf Rd [mid] N. (720064, 735862). 1907 (OS).

    Clontarf Rd [west] N., in former Anna Villa (see 22 Residence). 1907 (OS).

    Clontarf Rd [east] N. (721239, 736315). 1936 (OS).

    Clontarf Rd [west] N. (718666, 736172). 1970, 2016 (OS).

Coastguard station, North Bull Island (see 14 Primary production), S. end (721324, 735820). Coastguard station 1843; coast guard station, flagstaff 1868 (OS). Coast Guard station house 1876–95 (Val. 3). Coastguard station 1907 (OS). Destroyed in 1921; surrendered in 1928 (Board of Works cal., 12772/21, 17669/27).

Coastguard station, Clontarf Rd [mid] N. (720297, 735826). 1849 (*Thom*), 1851 (Val. 3).

Police station, Clontarf Rd [mid] N. (719835, 735908). 1843 (OS). Moved to new premises in 1846 (see next entry).

Constabulary barracks, Clontarf Rd [mid] N. (719962, 735899). Moved from former premises (see previous entry) to private residence purchased by Royal Irish Constabulary in 1846 (Gogarty, 115). Constabulary 1850 (Val. 2). Police barrack 1862 (*Ir. Builder* 1.5.1862). Police barrack 1864–7 (Val. 3). Constabulary B. 1868 (OS). Constabulary barracks for auction 1889 (*FJ* 19.11.1889). Converted to Holy Faith convent (see 11 Religion) and Holy Faith convent school for girls in 1890 (see 20 Education).

Dublin County Constabulary headquarters, location unknown. 1869 (*FJ* 26.6.1869).

CLONTARF CASTLE, 1772, BY GABRIEL BERANGER

Dublin Metropolitan Police station, Clontarf Rd [mid] N. (720251, 735765). Police barrack 1891 (Val. 3). RIC barracks 1894 (*Thom*). Constabulary barracks 1896 (Val. 3). Royal Irish Constabulary barracks, taken over by Dublin Metropolitan Police in 1902–3 (*Public works rept 71*, 35). Police station 1903 (*Thom*), 1907 (OS). DMP station 1908 (*Thom*). Unnamed 1936–1970 (OS). Private residence 2017.

Garda Síochána station, Strandville Ave East E. (718456, 736289). Designed in 1907–9 (Gogarty, 187). Police barracks, constabulary huts 1909 (Electoral rolls). Metropolitan police barracks 1911 (Census returns). G.S. station 1935–6; Garda Síochána station 1971, 2016 (OS), 2017. See also **21** Entertainment, memorials and societies: ball alley.

Clontarf police barracks, Seaview Ave, location unknown. 1918 (Vernon papers).

Letter box, Clontarf Rd [west] N. (718919, 736017). 1868, 1890 (OS).

Pillar letter box, Clontarf Rd [east] N. (721255, 736311). 1868 (OS).

Letter box, St Lawrence Rd W. (718889, 736691). Pillar letter box 1889; letter box 1907 (OS).

Town Hall, Clontarf Rd [west] N. (718649, 736217). Foundation stone laid in 1893; opened in 1894 (*FJ* 22.12.1893, 25.4.1894). Town Hall 1898 (Thom map). In use as police court 1902–3 (*Public works rept 71*, 35). Town Hall 1907 (OS), 1909 (Electoral rolls). In use as cinema 1920s (Gogarty, 119). Converted to St Anthony's Catholic Church in 1925 (see **11** Religion).

Lifeguard hut, North Bull Island (see **21** Entertainment, memorials and societies), S. end (721884, 735421). 1971 (OS).

Lifeguard hut, North Bull Island (see **21** Entertainment, memorials and societies), S. end (722115, 735665). 1971 (OS).

14. PRIMARY PRODUCTION

Tomar's wood, location unknown. Caill Tomair 1000 (*Ann. Inisf.*, 174), 1014 (*Cog. Gaedhel*, 190).

Clantarff Wood, Castle Ave [south] W. (719770, 736506). Late 17th cent. (Phillips 1a). See also next entries.

Clontarf Wood, location unknown, possibly same as previous entry. 1699 (Dunton, 366).

Woods of Clontarf, location unknown, possibly same as previous entries. 1780 (*Saunders Newsletter* 5.5.1780).

Weir of Clontarf (corad Chluana Tarb), location unknown. 1014 (*Cog. Gaedhel*, 192–3).

Weir, Strandville Ave East E. (718462, 736520). 1889–1936 (OS).

Rabbit warrens, locations unknown, associated with Clontarf preceptory (see **11** Religion). Rabbit warrens of Clontarf priory 1348 (*Reg. Kilmainham*, 125).

Farm, location unknown. Busshells Ferme 1540 (*Extents Ir. mon. possessions*, 89).

Farm, location unknown. Whiteferme 1540 (*Extents Ir. mon. possessions*, 89).

Farm yard, Vernon Ave [west] S. (719886, 737006). 1823 (VEM).

Lead mine, location unknown, possibly same as next entry. 'Vein of lead at Clontarf' 1563 (*Cal. S.P. Ire.*, 1509–73, 225).

Lead mine, Clontarf Rd [mid] S. (719386, 735893). Opened in 1768 (Warburton *et al.*, ii, 1251). Lead mine 1816 (Taylor). Mineshaft flooded, mining deteriorated by 1818 (Warburton *et al.*, ii, 1250). Mine house 1823 (VEM). 'Hole made in search of lead' 1843–68; depicted 1907, 1936 (OS). Last remaining shaft incorporated into base of shelter (see **18** Utilities) during building of promenade (see **21** Entertainment, memorials and societies) in *c.* 1956 (Arch. Survey, DU019-033). See also next and previous entries.

Mine, location unknown, possibly same as previous entry. Mine of lead, copper ore and other minerals 1809 (Vernon papers).

Lead mine, Clontarf Rd [east] N., near Crab Lake (see below), site unknown. 'At Crab Lake there was once a lead mine' 1819 (Vernon papers).

Lead mine, Howth Rd [south] S. (719097, 736840). 'Pump and site of old lead mine' 1843–68 (OS). See also **18** Utilities: pump.

Quarry, location unknown, possibly same as next entry. 1565 (*Proctor's accounts*, 50).

Quarry, Clontarf Rd [west] N. (719300, 735971). Quarry 1715 (*Ancient records*, vii, 7), 1717 (Bolton). Old quarry 1823 (VEM). Quarry 1843 (OS). See also previous entry.

Black Quarry, Howth Rd [south] W. (718451, 736762). Black Quarry 1760 (Rocque), 1816 (Taylor). Black Quarrys 1821 (Duncan). Black Quarries 1823 (VEM), 1824 (Vernon papers). Black Quarry 1843 (OS). See also next entry.

Stone quarries, near Mount Temple (see **22** Residence), possibly same as previous entry. 1824 (Vernon papers).

The Furlong, Clontarf Rd [mid] S. (719726, 735618). 'The furlong of Clontarf' 1603; leased to the recorder of Dublin in 1621; lease renewed in 1624 (*Ancient records*, i, 197–8; iii, 132, 146–7). Forlongs 1717 (Bolton). The Furlong 1803 (Bligh), 1805 (Sherrard and Brassington), 1816 (Taylor). Unnamed 1819 (Giles). The Furlong 1821 (Duncan), 1823 (VEM). The Furlong, gravel bank 1836 (OSN). The Furlong 1843–68 (OS).

Sheds of Clontarf, Clontarf Rd [mid] N. (720095, 735841). 'Making fish' at Clontarf 1630 (*Ancient records*, iii, 146–7). Salting of herrings at Clontarf 1644 (Depositions, 809, f. 243). Fish House 1685 (Phillips 1). The Shades of Clontarf 1718 (*Ancient records*, vii, 66–7). 'Shed or house of landing commonly called the Shed of Clontarf and known by the name of the Sign of the ship' 1719 (Ní Mhurchadha, 7). Herring Shelds 1730 (Price). Sheds of Clontarf 1760 (Rocque). Shades of Clontarff 1767 (De Courcy, 81). Sheds of Clontarf, 'so called from several sheds or pent-houses, being originally erected there for persons employed in preserving fish, of which great quantities were formerly cured' 1786 (*Post chaise companion*, 308). The Sheds, used for curing of herring and preparation of oysters until *c.* 1800 (Gogarty, 15, 73). Sheds of Clontarf, 'long since vanished' 1838 (D'Alton, 52). See also below, The Green; **10** Streets: Clontarf Road [mid]; **22** Residence: The Sheds.

Cockle fishery, location unknown. Place of salted herrings and cockle gathering 1641 (Depositions, 809, f. 243).

North Bull fishery, location unknown. Salmon pool 1693 (Collins), 1730 (*Ancient records*, vii, 515). North Bull fishery 1823 (De Courcy, 158).

Fishery of Clontarf, Dublin Bay (721836, 735432). 1800 (Vernon papers).

Bull park, location unknown. 1659 (*Ancient records*, iv, 169).

Hollybrook Park, Howth Rd [south] S. (718671, 736656). Meadow or pasture commonly called Hollybrooks 1678 (Vernon papers). 'Land called the two thirds of Hollibrook' 1735; lands of Hollybrooke 1800 (Vernon papers). Hollybrook Park 1812 (Longfield 3), 1816 (Taylor); 'formerly a park' 1836 (OSN).

North Bull Island, Dublin Bay (722294, 736384). The North Bull late 17th cent. (Phillips 2a). North Bull 1760 (Rocque), 1800 (Vernon papers), 1816 (Longfield 4). Sand Island or Green Island 1819 (Giles). North Bull Bank 1836 (OSN). North Bull 1843 (OS). North Bull Island, in pasture 1845 (Val. 1). North Bull 1850 (Val. 2), 1868 (OS). North Bull Island, purchased by Lord Ardilaun in 1902 (Sharkey, 63–5). North Bull 1907 (OS). North Bull Island, designated as bird sanctuary in 1931 (see **21** Entertainment, memorials and societies). See also **13** Administration: coastguard station; **18** Utilities: Bull Wall.

Great Meadow, 'manor of Clontarf' (see **2** Legal status). 1752 (Vernon papers).

Greenlanes, Mount Prospect Ave [west] S. (720569, 736435). Depicted as area under cultivation 1760 (Rocque). Green Lanes of Clontarf 1836 (OSN). Greenlanes 1843 (OS). See also below, The Green.

Mary Field, Clontarf Rd [east] N., site unknown. 1792 (Longfield 1).

Slip Field, Clontarf Rd [east] N., site unknown. 1792 (Longfield 1).

The Green, Clontarf Rd [mid] N. (719882, 735923). The Green 1805 (Sherrard and Brassington). Green of the Sheds 1806 (Vernon papers). The Green 1823 (VEM). Unnamed 1843 (OS). The Green, commonage formerly occupied by fishermen of The Sheds (see above, Sheds of Clontarf), enclosed in c. 1836; 1845 (Val. 1). Unnamed 1868–1907 (OS). In use as tennis ground by 1970 (see **21** Entertainment, memorials and societies).

Far Field, Mount Prospect Ave [east] E. (721393, 737308). 1816 (Longfield 4). Built over by glasshouses by 1907 (OS).

Lodge Field, Mount Prospect Ave [east] E. (721294, 737029). 1816 (Longfield 4).

Battery Field, Malahide Rd E. (718127, 736806). 1823 (VEM).

Garden, Castle Ave [south] E. (719283, 736203). 1823 (VEM).

Dempseys Furry Park, 'manor of Clontarf' (see **2** Legal status). 1836 (Vernon papers).

Lynches Park, 'manor of Clontarf' (see **2** Legal status). 1836 (Vernon papers).

Slashers Park, 'manor of Clontarf' (see **2** Legal status). 1836 (Vernon papers).

Town meadow, 'manor of Clontarf' (see **2** Legal status). 1836 (Vernon papers).

Silver Acre, Howth Rd [south] S. (719115, 736900). Silver Acre 1843, 1868; unnamed 1907 (OS).

Heron's Field, location unknown. 1861 (Vernon papers).

The Mine Field, location unknown. 1882 (Vernon papers).

Heronstown Field, Mount Prospect Ave [east] S., site unknown. 1894 (Vernon papers).

Brewery Lane Field, Vernon Ave, site unknown. 1895 (Vernon papers).

Moat Field, Vernon Ave, site unknown. 1895 (Vernon papers).

School House Field, Vernon Ave, site unknown. 1895 (Vernon papers).

Milestone Fields, Sybil Hill, site unknown. 1898 (Vernon papers).

Church Fields, Castle Ave E., site unknown. 1902 (Vernon papers).

Middle Field, Crab Lake, site unknown. 1910 (Vernon papers).

Castilla Green, location unknown. 1917 (Vernon papers).

Church Field, location unknown. 1917 (Vernon papers).

Reilly's Field, location unknown. 1917 (Vernon papers).

Seafield, Clontarf estate, location unknown. 1917 (Vernon papers).

The Styles paddock, Clontarf Rd [west] N., site unknown. The Styles paddock, formerly grazing land 1937 (Gogarty, 209).

Oyster beds, Crab Lough, Dublin Harbour. (720556, 735647). Crablake oyster-beds 1718 (*Ancient records*, vii, 67). Clontarf oyster bed 1760 (Rocque). Oyster beds of Clontarf 1786, 1793 (Vernon papers). Clontarf oyster beds 1816 (Taylor). Crablake oyster-beds 1819 (Giles). Oyster bed 1823 (VEM). Oyster beds 1843–68 (OS). Oyster bank, not fished 1869 (Val. 3). See also next entry.

Oyster beds, location unknown, possibly same as previous entry, associated with Strand House (see **22** Residence: Summerville House). Oyster beds leased to Margaret Dugan 1917–22 (Gogarty, 111).

Crab Lake, Clontarf Rd [east] N. (720770, 736073). Unnamed 1760 (Rocque). Cold Harbour Water 1816 (Taylor). Crab Lake 1819 (Vernon papers). Water 1823 (VEM). Crab Lake, 'small lake containing 1.75 roods' 1836 (OSN). Crab Lake 1843–1907; Crab Lake, marsh 1936 (OS). Built over in *c.* 1982 (local information).

Melon pits, Clontarf Rd [mid] N., site unknown. 1778 (*Saunders Newsletter* 8.4.1778).

Nursery, Clontarf Rd, site unknown, possibly on site of later nurseries (see next entry). 1820 (*FJ* 27.1.1820).

Watson's Nurseries, Clontarf Rd [west] N. (718291, 736350). Opened in 1880 (Ruddy, 2014, 21). Nursery, well (covered) 1890; Clontarf Nurseries, glasshouses depicted 1907 (OS). Watson's Nurseries 1909 (*Thom*). Closed by 1920 (Ruddy, 2014, 27). See also previous entry; **22** Residence: Hollybrook Cottage, Simla Lodge.

Piggery, Strandville Ave East E. (718458, 736443). 1823 (VEM).

Piggery, Clontarf East, site unknown. Frances Milford 1845 (Val. 1). See also **16** Trades and services: laundry; **17** Transport: boat house.

Piggery, Clontarf West, site unknown. Patrick Carrule 1845 (Val. 1).

Piggery, Seafield Rd West N., site unknown, associated with Greenlanes School (see **20** Education). 1845 (Val. 1). See also **16** Trades and services: store.

Pond, Clontarf Rd [mid] N. (719459, 735969). 1823 (VEM).

Pond, Vernon Ave [north] W. (720115, 736840). Pond 1843; unnamed 1868 (OS).

Pond, Seafield Rd East N. (721112, 736179). Pond 1843; unnamed 1907 (OS).

15. MANUFACTURING

Mill of Clontarf, location unknown. *c.* 1313 (Book of Howth, 130).

Windmill, Clontarf Strand, site unknown. 1654–6 (*CS*, vii, 176), 1655 (DS).

Brick kilns, Clontarf Rd [east] N. (720798, 736005). Brick mills 1685; brick kills 1685 (Phillips 1, 2). Brick kilns 1730 (Price). See also next entry.

Millpond, Clontarf Rd [east] N. (720798, 736005), associated with brick kilns (see previous entry). Late 17th cent. (Phillips 2b).

Saltworks, Clontarf Rd [east] S. (721624, 736876). Salt works 1685 (Phillips 2). Salt house 1711 (*Dublin Intelligence* 20.3.1711). Salt pipes laid on the Strand for salt works 1733 (Brown, iv, 130).

Cotton manufactory, Clontarf Rd [west] N., near Royal Charter School (see **20** Education), site unknown. Cotton manufactory, established by Baron Hamilton 1786 (*Post chaise companion*, 308).

Smithy, Clontarf Rd [west] N. (718643, 736194). 1868 (OS).

Engineering works, Seapark Rd W. (720553, 736262). Engineering works 1970; demolished, built over by 2016 (OS).

16. TRADES AND SERVICES

Fairs. Fairs to be held on 10 and 11 April, 5 and 6 October, granted to Edward Vernon 1675 (*Cal. S.P. Ire., 1675–6*, 155). April fair 1729 (*FDJ* 12.3.1729).

City Arms Inn, between Ballybough Bridge and Howth Rd, site unknown. 1709 (*Flying Post* 9.2.1709).

Ship Inn, junction Malahide Rd/Clontarf Rd [west], site unknown. 1717 (Bolton). See also next entry.

Ship Inn, near Clontarf harbour, site unknown, possibly same as previous entry. 1719 (RD 24/540/14656).

Inn of Clontarf, location unknown, possibly same as next entry. 1729 (RD 61/331/41520).

Inn, Castle Ave, site unknown. 1740 (*FDJ* 13.5.1740). See also previous entry.

Guy, Earl of Warwick Inn, Clontarf Rd [mid] N., site unknown. 1748 (RD 138/496/94070). See also next entry.

Vernon Inn, Clontarf Rd [mid] N., site unknown, possibly same as previous entry. 1758 (RD 215/347/142005).

Star and Garter, Clontarf Rd [mid] N., site unknown. 1764 (Gogarty, 73).

Coaching inn, Howth Rd [south] S. (718625, 736692). Coaching inn, coach yard, farrier's yard, livery stables 1809 (Gogarty, 84–5). Unnamed 1843; public house 1868; unnamed 1889–1971 (OS). Harry Byrne's pub 2017.

Dollymount House Hotel, Clontarf Rd [east] N. (721203, 736274). Tavern 1782 (Lynch, 104). Byrne's inn 1839 (*Thom*). Byrne's hotel and restaurant 1886 (*FJ* 30.8.1886). Dollymount Hotel 1906 (*Ir. Times* 2.11.1906). Doyle's hotel 1909 (*Thom*). Dollymount Hotel 1936 (OS). Dollymount House, formerly Dollymount Inn, closed in 2006; demolished in 2013 (Gogarty, 86). See also **17** Transport: landing stage.

Bram Stoker Hotel, Clontarf Rd [mid] N. (720329, 735772). Fingal House, built in 1897; Fingal Hotel and restaurant, sold in 1899 (*Ir. Times* 17.4.1897, 7.1.1899). Fingal House 1916 (Vernon papers). Sold in 1970 (*Ir. Times* 27.11.1970). Hotel 2016 (OS). Bram Stoker Hotel 2017.

Hotel, Hollybrook Park S., on site of former Hollybrook House (see **22** Residence). Hotel 1971 (OS). Demolished in 2003 (Lynch, 151).

Hotel, Howth Rd [south] S., on site of former Silveracre (see **22** Residence). Hotel 1971; De La Salle Provincialate 2016 (OS).

Clontarf Castle Hotel, Castle Ave [south] W., in former Clontarf Castle (see **22** Residence). Opened in 1973 (*Sunday Times* 1.7.2007). Refurbished and extended in 1995 (*Ir. Times* 26.4.1995). Clontarf Castle Hotel 2016 (OS).

Laundry, Clontarf East, site unknown. Frances Milford 1845 (Val. 1). See also **14** Primary production: piggery; **17** Transport: boat house.

Store, Seafield Rd West N., site unknown, associated with Greenlanes School (see **20** Education). 1845 (Val. 1). See also **14** Primary production: piggery.

The Sheds public house, Clontarf Rd [mid] N. (720096, 735844). Livery stable and public house, opened by 1847 (Gogarty, 149). Public house 1868; The Sheds P.H. 1907, 1936; unnamed 1970, 2016 (OS). Connolly's The Sheds 2017.

The Yacht public house, Clontarf Rd [west] N., in former St Edmund's (see **22** Residence). St Edmunds public house 1868; St Edmunds 1890 (OS), 1898 (Thom map). Unnamed 1907 (OS). St Edmund's, partly converted to Mrs McCoy's girls' school by 1911 (see **20** Education). St Edmund's 1936 (OS). Rebuilt as The Yacht public house by *c.* 1950 (Gogarty, 143). The Yacht 2017.

Stone depot, Clontarf Rd [west] N. (717851, 736380). 1889 (OS). Replaced by electricity station by 1907 (see **18** Utilities).

Stone depot, Clontarf Rd [west] S. (718838, 736040). 1890 (OS).

Commercial Buildings, Clontarf Rd [west] N. (718593, 736202). 1909 (Electoral rolls), 1911 (Census returns).

Printing works, Malahide Rd E. (718002, 736754). 1970 (OS).

17. TRANSPORT

Weekes's Wharf, Clontarf Rd [mid] S. (719784, 735866). Depicted 1785 (Laporte). Built by Christmas Weekes by 1786 (*Post chaise companion*, 308–9). 'A commodious wharf' 1787 (*Dublin guide*, 112). Weeks Wharf 1803 (Bligh). Weekes's Wharf 1805 (Sherrard and Brassington). Pier 1821 (Duncan). See also next entry; **18** Utilities: aqueduct, reservoir.

Wharf quay, location unknown, possibly same as previous entry. Wharf quay, enclosed with iron railing and stone base 1836 (Vernon papers).

Cold Harbour, Clontarf Rd [east] S. (721026, 736014). Cold Harbour 1803 (Bligh). Cold Harb. 1821 (Duncan). Cold Harbour 1843–68; walls demolished by 1907 (OS).

Bull Bridge, Crablake Water, Clontarf Rd [east] to Bull Wall (see **18** Utilities). (721098, 735959). Built in 1819–20 (De Courcy, 52). Unnamed 1821 (Duncan). Bridge 1831 (*FJ* 12.8.1831). Wooden Bridge 1843–68; unnamed 1907; Bull Bridge 1936, 1970, 2016 (OS).

Naniken Bridge, Naniken River, Clontarf Rd [east] E. end. (721986, 737227). Naniken Bridge 1843–68; Naniken Bridge 1907, 1936; unnamed 2016 (OS).

Coach house, Clontarf Rd [mid], site unknown. Granted to Edward Piers in 1836 (Gogarty, 80).

WINDMILL, 1655, FROM DOWN SURVEY MAP BY WILLIAM WRIGHT

DUBLIN AND DROGHEDA RAILWAY VIADUCT, 1853,
BY EDWARD McFARLAND

Railway bridge, Clontarf Rd [west]. (718100, 736315). Double-arched skew bridge, built for Great Northern Railway (Ireland) (see below: railway line) in 1842–3 (Gamble, ii, 291). Unnamed 1843 (OS). Dublin and Drogheda railway viaduct 1853 (McFarland, 7). Unnamed 1868–2016 (OS). Railway bridge 2017.

Railway bridge, Howth Rd [north]. (718472, 736655). Metal bridge built for Great Northern Railway (Ireland) (see below: railway line) in 1842–3 (Gamble, ii, 291). Unnamed 1843–2016 (OS). Railway bridge 2017.

Railway bridge, Tolka River. (717460, 735742). Unnamed 1843; Great Northern Railway (Ireland) 1907 (OS). Swept away by floods in 1954; replaced by new bridge in 1956 (*Ir. Times* 9.2.1956). Unnamed 2016 (OS). Railway bridge 2017.

Railway bridge, Tolka River. (717697, 735953). Unnamed 1843, 1868; Great Northern Railway (Ireland) 1907 (OS). Demolished during land reclamation for laying out of Fairview Park in early 20th cent. (see **18** Utilities: land reclamation; **21** Entertainment, memorials and societies: Fairview Park).

Railway line. Great Northern Railway (Ireland), Dublin–Drogheda, double line, opened in 1844 (Gamble, ii, 292–3). Railway to Drogheda 1843 (OS). Dublin and Drogheda Railway 1850 (Val. 2), 1868 (OS), 1874 (Thom map). Great Northern Railway 1890 (OS), 1898 (Thom map). Great Northern Railway (Ireland) 1907; Great Northern Railway (Ireland) to Belfast 1936 (OS). Iarnród Éireann, Dublin–Belfast line; Dublin Area Rapid Transit commuter rail, Greystones–Howth 2017. See also **18** Utilities: electric telegraph.

Clontarf Railway Station, Clontarf Rd [west] N., site unknown, near Kingscourt House and baths (see **21** Entertainment, memorial and societies). Completed by 1844 (Ó Maitiú, 43). Hourly service 1845 (*FJ* 19.6.1845). Closed in 1855 (Ó Maitiú, 43).

Clontarf Railway Station, Howth Rd [south] W. (718522, 736671). Opened in 1898 (Ruddy, 2008, 188). Clontarf station 1907, 1935–6 (OS). Closed in 1956 (*Ir. Times* 4.9.1956). Private residence 2017.

Boat house, Clontarf East, site unknown. Frances Milford 1845 (Val. 1). See also **14** Primary production: piggery; **16** Trades and services: laundry.

Horse-drawn tram. Dublin United Tramway Co. line to Dollymount opened in 1873 (Murphy, 3). Replaced by electrified tram in 1897 (see next entry).

Electric tram, Dublin United Tramway Co., O'Connell St, Dublin, to junction Belview Terrace/Clontarf Rd [east]. Dollymount tram electrified, replaced former horse-drawn tram (see previous entry) in 1897 (Gogarty, 159, 106). Clontarf and Hill of Howth Tramroad Co., Dollymount–Howth tramline opened in 1900; line taken over by Dublin United Tramway Co. in 1907 (Murphy, 6). Tramway 1907, 1935 (OS). Clontarf–Howth tramline replaced by bus service in 1939 (Gogarty, 189). Dollymount–Howth tramline closed in 1941 (Lennon, 2014, 232).

Tram shed, Clontarf Rd [mid] N. (720458, 735845). Tramway garage, built by Dublin United Tramway Co. in 1874 (Gogarty, 106). Tramway depôt 1895 (Val. 3). Horse tram sheds, stables converted to power station, car shed, repair shops in 1897 (Corcoran, 57). Tram shed 1907, 1936 (OS). Converted to bus depot by 1970 (see next entry).

Dublin Bus Depot, Clontarf Rd [mid] N., in former tram shed (see previous entry). Bus depot 1970, 2016 (OS). Dublin Bus Depot 2017.

Tram shelter, Clontarf Rd [east] S. (721329, 736379). Tram shelter *c.* 1890 (Val. 3). Depicted 1939, 1970 (OS). Demolished, rebuilt in 2016 (local information).

Wooden boat-slip, Clontarf Rd [west] S., opposite Haddon Rd, site unknown. Partly washed away in 1903 (*Ir. Times* 7.3.1903).

Landing stage, Clontarf Rd [east] S. (721228, 736245), associated with Dollymount House Hotel (see **16** Trades and services). Landing stage 1907, 1936; demolished by 1970 (OS).

Landing stage, Clontarf Rd [mid] S. (719992, 735854). Landing stage 1907; demolished by 1970 (OS).

Landing stage, Clontarf Rd [mid] S. (720288, 735685). Landing stage 1907; demolished by 1970 (OS).

Landing stage, Clontarf Rd [east] S. (721399, 736475). Landing stage 1935, 1970; partly demolished by 2016 (OS).

Landing stage, Clontarf Rd [mid] S. (720290, 735728), associated with Clontarf Yacht and Boat Club (see **21** Entertainment, memorials and societies). Landing stage 1936; landing stage, pillar, slipway 1970 (OS). Slipway 2017.

Car park, Clontarf Rd [west] N. (718783, 736119). Car park 1970, 2016 (OS); 2017.

Car park, Clontarf Rd [west] S. (718630, 736152). Car park, laid out on reclaimed ground (see **18** Utilities: land reclamation) by 1970; car park 2016 (OS); 2017.

Car park, Blackheath Ave N. (719847, 736793). 1970–71; built over by 2016 (OS).

Cycle lane, Alfie Byrne Rd, E. side. (718187, 736031). 1970, 2016 (OS); 2017.

18. UTILITIES

Sea wall, Clontarf Rd S., Clontarf Rd [mid] to Clontarf Rd [west]. Wall damaged in 1774 (*Hibernian Journal* 28.9.1774). Rampier wall proposed in 1789 (*Commons votes, 1789*, 269). Sea wall, repaired by Board of Works in 1837 (*Public works rept 5*, 32). Wall damaged by storm in 1844 (*Glasgow Herald* 14.10.1844). Repaired in 1877 (*FJ* 23.10.1877). Sections of wall depicted 1907 (OS). Replaced by new wall in 1923 (see next entry).

Sea wall, Clontarf Rd S., railway bridge (see **17** Transport) to Bull Wall (see below). Proposed, to replace former wall (see previous entry), as outer edge of promenade (see **21** Entertainment, memorials and societies) in 1921 (*Ir. Times* 26.7.1921). Rights to foreshore strip 150 feet wide, 2 miles long acquired by Dublin Corporation, infilling commenced in 1921 (Lennon, 2014, 221). Building in progress 1923 (*Ir. Times* 9.8.1923). Foundation of outer sea wall begun in 1932; completed in 1934 (Gogarty, 183). Partly complete 1936 (OS). Completed in 1937 (*Ir. Times* 14.8.1937).

Break water, Clontarf Rd [mid] S., site unknown. Several ranges of piles of timber 1787 (*Dublin guide*, 112).

Bull Wall, Bull Bridge (see **17** Transport) to North Bull Island (see **14** Primary production), S. end (721504, 735648). Enclosure of part of North Bull proposed in 1819 (Vernon papers). Building begun in 1819 (De Courcy, 53). New wall or breakwater 1821 (Duncan). New wall 1823 (VEM). Completed in *c.* 1824 (Flood, 152). New wall or breakwater (called the Bull Wall) 1843; Bull Wall 1868–2016 (OS). See also **21** Entertainment, memorials and societies: bathing shelters.

Beating buoy: 1843 (OS).

Breakwater: depicted, poles, tower 1868; breakwater 1907, 1936 (OS); 2017.

Bull Beacon: Bull Beacon 1868; unnamed 1907 (OS).

Buoy: 1843 (OS).

Latrines: latrines 1936 (OS); toilet 2017.

Shelter: 1936, 2016 (OS).

Aqueduct, Clontarf Rd [mid], site unknown, associated with Weekes's Wharf (see **17** Transport). Depicted 1785 (Laporte). Built by Christmas Weekes to supply ships with water by 1786 (*Post chaise companion*, 308–9). Aqueduct 1787 (*Dublin guide*, 111).

Reservoir, Clontarf Rd [mid], site unknown, associated with Weekes's Wharf (see **17** Transport). Depicted 1785 (Laporte). Built by Christmas Weekes to supply ships with water by 1786 (*Post chaise companion*, 308–9). Reservoir 1787 (*Dublin guide*, 111).

Reservoir, Clontarf Rd [east] W. (721717, 736927). Reservoir 1843; bath 1868; unnamed 1907, 1936 (OS). Stone basin, overgrown 2017.

Pumps, 2, Clontarf Rd [mid], sites unknown. 1787 (*Dublin guide*, 111).

Pump, location unknown, possibly same as next entry. Pump, hole 1804 (Longfield 2).

Pump, Howth Rd [south] S. (719097, 736840). 'Pump and site of old lead mine' 1843–68 (OS). See also **14** Primary production: lead mine.

BULL BRIDGE AND BULL WALL, c. 1910

Hollybrook Well, Hollybrook Park S. (718577, 736486). Spring well 1812 (Longfield 3). Hollybrook Well 1836 (OSN), 1843–68 (OS), 1898 (Thom map). Built over by 1907 (OS).

St Dennis Well, The Stiles Rd E. (719191, 736707). St Denis Well 1836 (OSN). St Dennis Well 1843 (OS).

Brian Boroimhe's Well, Castle Ave [south] E. (719237, 736142). Brian Boru's Well, covered over by memorial plaque 1850 (*Ir. Builder* 15.8.1884). Brian Boroimhe's Well 1868, 1907; Brian Boroimhe's Well (covered) 1936; Brian Boroimhe's Well 1970, 2016 (OS). Brian Boroihm's Well 2017 (plaque).

St Philip's Well, The Stiles Rd E. (719139, 736779). St Philip's Well 1868; St Philip's Well (site of) 1907; St Philip's Well 1935; built over by 1970–71 (OS).

Curley's Yard, North Bull Island, S. end (722317, 736400), associated with Royal Dublin Golf Club (see **21** Entertainment, memorials and societies). Unnamed 1843; unnamed, well 1907; Curley's Yard 1936; unnamed 1970 (OS). Greenkeepers' depot 2017.

Mounds:

Mount Prospect Ave [east] S. (720938, 736507). Depicted 1843; mound 1868; depicted 1907, 1935 (OS). 'Mound site' excavated in 2003 (*Excavations, 2003*, 113).

Vernon Ave [south] E. (720225, 736112). Depicted 1843; mound 1868 (OS). 'Two sepulchral mounds near Clontarf village' 1888 (Wakeman 2).

Vernon Ave [south] E. (720359, 735979). Depicted 1843; mound 1868 (OS). 'Two sepulchral mounds near Clontarf village' 1888 (Wakeman 2).

Blackheath Park N. (719908, 736660). 1868 (OS).

Near Marino Crescent, site unknown. *c.* 1874–87 (Wakeman 1).

Near Conquer Hill, site unknown, possibly same as mound at Mount Prospect Ave [east] S. (see above). Sepulchral mound 1888 (Wakeman 3).

Electric telegraph, along Great Northern Railway (Ireland) line (see **17** Transport: railway line). Electric telegraph 1868 (OS). British and Irish Magnetic Telegraph Company 1869; Rt. Hon. Her Majesty's Postmaster General 1871 (Val. 3).

Telegraph, location unknown, possibly same as previous entry. Electric and International Telegraph Company 1869; Rt. Hon. Her Majesty's Postmaster General 1871 (Val. 3).

North Bull Lighthouse, Bull Wall (see above), E. end (723205, 734325). Beacon 1868; North Bull Lighthouse (revolving white) 1907 (OS). North Bull Lighthouse 2017.

Street lighting. Gas lighting installed by 1870 (*FJ* 28.3.1870). Gas mains and pipes, Alliance and Dublin Consumers Gas Company 1876 (Val. 3). Standards for electric lighting erected by 1898 (*FJ* 7.9.1898). Mains electricity installed for street lighting by 1911 (*Ir. Times* 1.11.1911).

Two Sepulchral Mounds close to Clontarf village,
a little inland from the street, to the westward
From a sketch made by me in 1888
W. F. Wakeman.

MOUNDS, VERNON AVENUE, 1888, BY WILLIAM WAKEMAN

Fountains:
    Howth Rd [south] S. (718544, 736657). 1889 (OS).
    Seaview Ave North [south] W. (718854, 736134). 1890 (OS).
    Strandville Ave East E. (718459, 736243). 1890 (OS).
    Danespark E. (720453, 736046). 1936 (OS).
    North Bull Island (see **21** Entertainment, memorials and societies), S. end (721342, 735782). 1936, 1971 (OS).
    North Bull Island (see **21** Entertainment, memorials and societies), S. end. (721766, 735446). 1971 (OS).
    North Bull Island (see **21** Entertainment, memorials and societies), S. end. (721832, 735389). 1971 (OS).
    North Bull Island (see **21** Entertainment, memorials and societies), S. end. (722067, 735623). 1971 (OS).
    North Bull Island (see **21** Entertainment, memorials and societies), S. end. (722085, 735643). 1971 (OS).
Street paving. Flagging of pavements completed by 1893 (*FJ* 23.3.1893).
Telephone lines. Telephone poles erected 1899–1908 (Vernon papers).
Land reclamation, Clontarf Rd [west] S. (717701, 736197). Fairview sloblands purchased by Dublin Corporation from Dublin Port and Docks Board for laying out as Fairview Park (see **21** Entertainment, memorials and societies) in 1904 (*Ir. Times* 2.8.1904). See also **17** Transport: railway bridge.

Land reclamation, Clontarf Rd [west] S. (718087, 736110). Sloblands reclaimed in 1960s (local information). See also **10** Streets: Alfie Byrne Road; **20** Education: children's traffic school; **21** Entertainment, memorials and societies: sports ground.
Land reclamation, Clontarf Rd S., railway bridge (see **17** Transport) to Bull Wall (see above). Land reclaimed during laying out of promenade (see **21** Entertainment, memorials and societies) and sea wall (see above) in 1921–56 (*Ir. Times* 26.7.1921, 2.11.1956). See also **17** Transport: car park.
Sewage works. Main drainage for district begun, sewer laid outside sea wall (see above), from Dublin city centre to St Anne's (see **22** Residence) in 1905; completed by 1911 (*Ir. Times* 15.7.1905, 24.11.1905, 1.11.1911).
Pumping station, Clontarf Rd [west] S. (718046, 736316). Clontarf sewage pumping station (Dublin Corporation), air chambers (2), sewage sumps 1935–6; pumping station 1970, 2016 (OS). Dublin City wastewater services 2017.
Electricity station, Clontarf Rd [west] N., on site of former stone depot (see **16** Trades and services). Electricity sub-station 1907; electricity station 1970, 2016 (OS); 2017.
Electricity station, Clontarf Rd [west] S. (718042, 736312). Electricity station 1970, 2016 (OS); 2017.

Electricity station, Sybil Hill Rd E. (720197, 736980). Electricity station 1971, 2016 (OS); 2017.

Gasometer, Clontarf Rd [east] W. (721670, 736875). 1907 (OS).

Telephone exchange, Castle Ave [south] S. (719404, 736267). Built in 1926 (Gogarty, 118). Telephone exchange 1928 (Board of Works cal., 23687/28), 1935–2016 (OS). Eir offices 2017.

Shelter, Clontarf Rd [mid] S., on site of former lead mine (see **14** Primary production). Depicted 1970, 2016 (OS). Shelter 2017.

Shelter, Clontarf Rd [mid] S. (720259, 735696). Shelter 1970, 2016 (OS); 2017.

Toilets, Clontarf Rd [mid] S. (720061, 735807). 1970 (OS). Built over by pumphouse in 2007 (De Paor).

19. HEALTH

Pest houses, 2, Clontarf Island (see **21** Entertainment, memorials and societies), sites unknown. Clontarf Island designated quarantine for plague victims in 1666 (Murphy and Potterton, 429). 2 pest houses 1682 (*Ancient records*, iv, 379).

Dispensary, Castle Ave [south] W. (719221, 736163). Dispensary 1863 (Val. 3), 1907; demolished, built over by private residence by 1936 (OS).

Dispensary, Clontarf Park S. (720154, 735887). 1936 (OS).

Dispensary, Sybil Hill Rd E. (720179, 736976). Dispensary 1971; health centre 2016 (OS). Vernon Avenue Health Centre 2017.

Orthopaedic hospital, Blackheath Park N., in former Blackheath (see **22** Residence). Orthopaedic hospital, opened in 1941 (*Ir. Times* 27.3.1941). Hospital 1970–71 (OS). Patients transferred to new premises, building in use as offices by 2013 (Gogarty, 104). Hospital 2016 (OS). Incorporated Orthopaedic Hospital of Ireland 2017.

Nurses' home: designed in 1949–54 (Gogarty, 195).

Central Remedial Clinic, Vernon Ave [west] S. (719694, 736935). Opened in 1968 (*Ir. Times* 6.12.1968). Central Remedial Clinic 1971, 2016 (OS).

Irish Wheelchair Association National Headquarters, Blackheath Ave N. (719781, 736835). Opened in 1968 (*Ir. Times* 21.5.1968). Irish Wheelchair Association 2016 (OS).

First aid hut, North Bull Island (see **21** Entertainment, memorials and societies), S. end (722062, 735622). 1971 (OS).

20. EDUCATION

Royal Charter School, Clontarf Rd [west] N. (718340, 736290). Foundation stone laid in 1748 (*Pue's Occurrences* 16.4.1748). Royal Charter School 1760 (Rocque). Charter school 1782 (Vernon papers). Royal Charter School 1794 (Ashford), 1795 (Jukes). Charter school 1803 (Bligh). Royal Charter School 1816 (Taylor). Charter school 1821 (Duncan). Royal Charter School, cistern, pond, pump, steps, yard 1823 (VEM). School 1825 (*Ir. educ. rept 1*, 105). Closed in 1831 (Ruddy, 2004, 76). Converted to Kingscourt House and baths in 1834 (see **21** Entertainment, memorials and societies).

Infirmary: erected in 1794 (Ruddy, 2004, 71); 'hospital at Clontarf school' 1825 (*Ir. educ. rept 1*, 283).

Seminary, Castle Ave [south] E. (719200, 736040). 1823 (VEM).

St Mary's Abbey of Loreto Catholic Girls' Boarding School, Dollymount Ave N., in former Baymount Castle (see **22** Residence). School, John Keily *c.* 1834 (Ruddy, 2006, 173). Baymount House and Boarding School 1836 (OSN). Building reverted to private residence in 1838–47; St Mary's Abbey of Loreto Catholic Girls' Boarding School, opened in 1847; burnt in 1854; rebuilt, reopened in 1855; closed in 1862 (Ruddy, 2006, 173–6). See also **11** Religion: Loreto Sisters convent.

Greenlanes School, Seafield Rd West N., in former Cottage (see **22** Residence), associated with St John's Church (C. of I.) (see **11** Religion). Church of Ireland parochial school, donated by J.E.V. Vernon in 1835 (Lewis, i, 377). Parochial school 1836 (OSN). School house 1843 (OS). School house (boys), school house (girls), school house (infants) 1845 (Val. 1). Parochial schoolhouse 1850 (Val. 2), 1855 (Val. 3). Parochial school 1868 (OS). Granted for use as parochial hall in 1880 (Gogarty, 110). School 1907; Greenlanes School 1935 (OS). Moved to new premises in 1952 (see next entry). Demolished in *c.* 2000 (Gogarty, 198). See also **14** Primary production: piggery; **16** Trades and services: store.

Greenlanes National School, Seafield Ave E. (720498, 736551). School house built, pupils moved from former premises (see previous entry) in 1952 (*Ir. Times* 13.9.1952). School 1970; school, sports ground 2016 (OS). Greenlanes National School 2017.

School, Vernon Ave [south] W., in former R.C. chapel (see **11** Religion). School, 100 boys and girls 1837 (Lewis, i, 377).

School room, Greenlanes, site unknown. School room, John Vernon Esq. 1845 (Val. 1).

Catholic national school, Vernon Ave [south] W. (720044, 736032). Clontarf National Schools 1847 (McIntyre, 45), 1868 (OS). Extended in 1903 (Gogarty, 121). School 1907, 1936 (OS). Pupils transferred to new premises, Seafield Rd West S., in 1940 (see next entry).

National school, Seafield Rd West S., in former Belgrove (see **22** Residence). Scoil Eoin Baiste, national school for boys and girls, pupils transferred from Vernon Ave [south] W. (see previous entry), in 1940 (datestone). Male pupils transferred to new premises in 1960s; female pupils transferred to new premises in 1969 (see below, Belgrove Senior Boys' School, Belgrove Girls' Schools). Unnamed 1970–71 (OS). Converted to GAA clubhouse in 1998 (local information).

Belgrove Senior Boys' School, Seafield Rd West S. (719969, 736344). Belgrove Boys' School, built to replace former premises (see previous entry) in 1960s (Gogarty, 42). School 1970 (OS). Extended in 2012 (Gogarty, 42). Saint John the Baptist National School 2016 (OS). St John the Baptist Senior Boys' School, Belgrove Senior Boys' School 2017.

Belgrove Girls' Schools, Seafield Rd West S. (719843, 736344). Girls' school, built to replace former premises (see above, national school) in 1969 (Gogarty, 42). School 1970–71;

extensively remodelled by 2016 (OS). Belgrove Girls' Schools 2017.

Miss Mathew's boarding and day school, Annesbrook Terrace (see **22** Residence), site unknown. 1881 (*Thom*).

Holy Faith convent school for girls, Clontarf Rd [mid] N., in former constabulary barracks (see **13** Administration), associated with Holy Faith convent (see **11** Religion). Opened in 1890; school room for boys to be established 1893 (Val. 3). Replaced by new school in 1953 (see below, Holy Faith secondary school).

Holy Faith secondary school, Clontarf Rd [mid] N., in former presbytery (see **22** Residence), associated with Holy Faith convent (see **11** Religion). School 1936 (OS). Replaced by new building in 1953 (see next entry).

Holy Faith secondary school, Clontarf Rd [mid] N., on site of former presbytery (see **22** Residence). Built to replace former schools (see previous entries) in 1953 (*Ir. Times* 3.10.1953). School 1970, 2016 (OS). Holy Faith secondary school 2017. See also **21** Entertainment, memorials and societies: tennis ground.

Howth Road Mixed National School, Clontarf Rd [west] N. (718062, 736357), associated with Clontarf and Scots Presbyterian Church (see **11** Religion). Howth Road National Schools, built in 1890 (datestone). Extended in 1894 (Gogarty, 114). School 1898 (Thom map), 1907 (OS). Boys' and girls' schools amalgamated in 1950 (Gogarty, 114). School 1970 (OS). Amalgamated with infants' school in 1971 (Gogarty, 114). School 2016 (OS). Howth Road Mixed National School 2017.

Sunday school, St Lawrence Rd W., in Clontarf Methodist Church (see **11** Religion). 1895–1902 (Val. 3).

Misses Brown ladies' school, St Lawrence Rd W. (718775, 736336). 1897 (*Thom*), 1901 (Census returns).

Baymount Preparatory School, Dollymount Ave N., in former Baymount Castle (see **22** Residence). Baymount Preparatory School, opened in 1904 (Ruddy, 2006, 177). Baymount Castle 1907; Baymount 1935 (OS). School closed in 1946; in use as kindergarten 1946–8 (Ruddy, 2006, 177–8). Buildings sold to Jesuits, converted to Manresa Retreat House in 1948 (see **11** Religion).
Lodges, 2: 1907, 1935 (OS).

Hibernian Marine School, Seafield Rd East N. (720797, 736413). Moved from former premises on Sir John Rogerson's Quay, opened in 1904 (Gogarty, 123). Hibernian Marine School, 60 boarding and day pupils 1904 (De Courcy, 192). Hibernian Marine School 1907, 1935 (OS). Amalgamated with Mountjoy School (see below, Mount Temple Comprehensive School) in 1968; demolished in *c.* 1974 (De Courcy, 192).

Mrs McCoy's girls' school, Strandville Ave East, site unknown. 1909 (*Thom*). Moved to new premises by 1911 (see next entry).

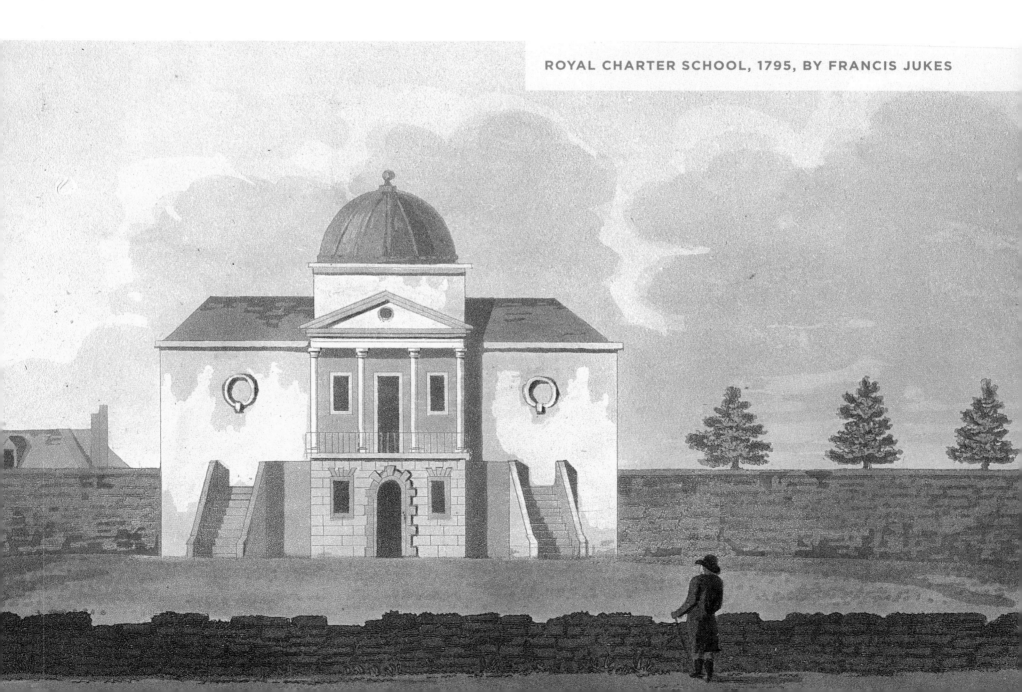

ROYAL CHARTER SCHOOL, 1795, BY FRANCIS JUKES

Mrs McCoy's girls' school, Clontarf Rd [west] N., in part of St Edmund's public house (see **16** Trades and services). Moved from former premises (see previous entry) by 1911 (Census returns).

Belgrove Preparatory School, Belgrove Rd [north] W. (719909, 736044). Belgrove School 1936 (OS). Belgrove Preparatory School 1939 (*Ir. Times* 6.9.1939).

Kostka College, Seafield Rd East S., in former Rosetta (see **22** Residence). Kostka College, opened in 1943 (*Ir. Independent* 31.7.1943). College 1970 (OS). Closed in 1980 (local information). Demolished, built over by apartments by 2013 (Gogarty, 50).

Mount Temple Comprehensive School, Malahide Rd E., in former Mount Temple (see **22** Residence). School moved from former premises on Mountjoy Square in 1949; amalgamated with Hibernian Marine School (see above) to form Mountjoy and Marine School in 1968; amalgamated with Bertrand and Russell School, Mount Temple Comprehensive established in 1970 (Ruddy, 2008, 191–2). Mountjoy School 1971; Mount Temple Comprehensive School, gym, 2 hockey pitches, sports ground 2016 (OS). See also **21** Entertainment, memorials and societies: basketball grounds.

St Paul's College, Sybil Hill Rd E. (720244, 737353). St Paul's Boys' Secondary School opened, pupils moved from former premises (see **22** Residence: Sibyl Hill) in 1950 (Gogarty, 28). College, tennis grounds 1971; college 2016 (OS). St Paul's College 2017. See also **11** Religion: Vincentian Provincial Office.

St Brigid's National School, Howth Rd [north] S. (720080, 737599). School 1971, 2016 (OS). St Brigid's National School 2017.

Children's traffic school, Clontarf Rd [west] S. (718058, 736195). Traffic school, laid out on reclaimed ground (see **18** Utilities: land reclamation) by 1970 (OS). Children's traffic school, established in 1971 (*Ir. Times* 11.6.1976). Closed in *c.* 2005 (*Evening Herald* 8.6.2009).

21. ENTERTAINMENT, MEMORIALS AND SOCIETIES

Clontarf Island bathing, Dublin Harbour. (718281, 735189). Island of Clontarf 1621, 1624 (*Ancient records*, iii, 132, 146–7). Island 1655 (DS). Clantarfe Eyle 1673 (de Gomme). Island of Clontarf 1678 (Vernon papers). Clantarf Island 1685 (Phillips 1, 2). Clontarff Island 1717 (Bolton). Clandaf Isle 1730 (Price). Clontarf Island, Island House 1760 (Rocque). Island of Clontarf 1800 (Vernon papers). Clontarf Island 1803 (Bligh), 1816 (Taylor), 1821 (Duncan), 1843 (OS). Clontarf Island, locally known as Bathing Island in 19th cent. (De Courcy, 80). Clontarf Island overflowed, house swept away by storm in 1844 (*Glasgow Herald* 14.10.1844). Island of Clontarf, granted to William Collins for use as bathing place and pleasure ground 1868 (Vernon papers). Clontarf Island, bathing pond 1868 (OS). Bathing place

1875 (*Ir. Times* 29.10.1875). Old Clontarf Island 1878; Island of Clontarf overflowed by high tide 1908 (Williams, 165, 168). See also **19** Health: pest houses.

Bathing place, Clontarf Rd [mid] S., Sheds of Clontarf, site unknown. 1836 (OSN).

Bathing cabins, location unknown. 'Very convenient little edifices, in the form of small houses' 1787 (*Dublin guide*, 111).

Bathing platform, Fortview Ave, site unknown. 1861 (*Ir. Builder* 1.7.1861).

Bathing boxes, Clontarf Rd [mid] S. (718997, 735962). 1868, 1890 (OS).

Bathing box, Clontarf Rd [west] S. (718883, 736016). 1890 (OS).

Bathing shelter, Bull Wall N. (see **18** Utilities). (722104, 735181). Designed by Herbert Simms in 1934 (Archiseek). Bathing shelter 1936, 1971 (OS); 2017.

Bathing shelter, Bull Wall N. (see **18** Utilities). (722319, 735014). Designed by Herbert Simms in 1934 (Archiseek). Bathing shelter 1936 (OS); 2017.

Bathing shelter, Bull Wall S. (see **18** Utilities). (722225, 735077). Designed by Herbert Simms in 1934 (Archiseek). Bathing shelter 1936, 1971 (OS). Ladies Bathing Shelter, Mens Bathing Shelter 2017 (mural inscription).

Gents Bathing Shelter, Bull Wall S. (see **18** Utilities). (721989, 735262). Designed by Herbert Simms in 1934 (Archiseek). Bathing shelter 1936, 1971 (OS). Gents Bathing Shelter 2017 (mural inscription).

Ladies Bathing Shelter, Bull Wall S. (see **18** Utilities). (721848, 735372). Designed by Herbert Simms in 1934 (Archiseek). Bathing shelter 1936, 1971 (OS). Ladies Bathing Shelter 2017 (mural inscription).

Ball court, Clontarf Rd [mid] N. (720010, 735888). 1823 (VEM).

Ball alley, Strandville Ave East E. (718455, 736317), associated with Garda Síochána station (see **13** Administration). Ball alley 1935–2016 (OS); 2017.

Kingscourt House and baths, Clontarf Rd [west] N., in former Royal Charter School (see **20** Education). Kingscourt Baths, established in 1834 (Gogarty, 70). Kingscourt House and baths, 'hot, cold and plunge baths' 1836 (OSN). Hot and cold sea-water baths 1837 (Lewis, i, 376). Royal Kingscourt Baths 1842 (*Dublin almanac*). Kingscourt House, baths 1843 (OS). Kingscourt House and baths 1845 (Val. 1). Kingscourt House and baths, 'hot, cold, shower and plunge baths' 1850 (Val. 2). Kingscourt Baths, renovated in 1863 (*FJ* 4.4.1863). Kings Court House, baths, offices 1864 (Val. 3). Kingscourt House, baths 1868 (OS). House converted to private residence by 1874 (see **22** Residence: Kingscourt House). Baths 1890 (OS), 1898 (Thom map).

Clontarf Baths, Clontarf Rd [west] S. (719457, 735861). Clontarf Baths and Assembly Rooms proposed in 1879–80 (Gogarty, 108). Built in 1881 (Ruddy, 2009, 30). Clontarf Baths 1904 (Vernon papers), 1907–70 (OS). Closed in 1990s (Gogarty, 109). Clontarf baths 2016 (OS). In development as seawater baths with cafe and restaurant 2017 (*Ir. Times* 31.7.2017).See also below, bandstand; Clontarf Swimming Club.

Marino Crescent Pleasure Grounds, Clontarf Rd [west] N. (717940, 736413). Unnamed 1843 (OS). The Creasent on pleasure ground 1845 (Val. 1). Pleasure grounds 1866; Marino Crescent Pleasure Grounds 1915 (Vernon papers).

Clontarf Cricket and Football (rugby) Club, Vernon Ave, site unknown. Established by 1875 (Gogarty, 121). Moved to new premises after 1875 (see next entry).

Clontarf Cricket and Football (rugby) Club, Clontarf Rd [mid] N., in Clontarf Yacht and Boat Club (see below). Moved from former premises (see previous entry) after 1875 (Gogarty, 121). Moved to new premises by 1889 (see next entry).

Clontarf Cricket and Football (rugby) Club, Howth Rd [south] E. (718077, 736421). Clontarf Cricket Club, moved from former premises (see previous entry) by 1889; field for use by Clontarf Cricket Club 1893 (Vernon papers). Moved to new premises in 1896 (see next entry).

Clontarf Rugby Club, Cricket and Football Clubs, Castle Ave [north] W. (719444, 736760). Opened, moved from former premises (see previous entry) in 1896 (Gogarty, 121). Field leased for use as cricket ground by Clontarf Cricket Club 1896; lease renewed in 1901 (Vernon papers). Clontarf Cricket and Football Ground 1935; sport ground, stand 1970–71; sports ground 2016 (OS). Clontarf Rugby Club, Cricket and Football Clubs 2017.

Club house: wooden pavilion with tin roof to be erected 1896 (Vernon papers); unnamed 1907; club house 1935; Clontarf Cricket Club, extended by 1970–71, 2016 (OS).

Pavilion: built in 1908 (Gogarty, 121).

Clontarf Yacht and Boat Club, Clontarf Rd [mid] N., in former Belvidere and former Fingal Cottage (see 22 Residence). Clontarf Yacht and Boat Club premises 1875 (Gogarty, 82). Clontarf Boat Club 1895 (Val. 3). Belvidere 1907 (OS). Belvidere, Clontarf Boat Club and assembly rooms 1915 (Gogarty, 83). Clontarf Yacht and Boat Club 1936; yacht club 1970, 2016 (OS). Clontarf Yacht and Boat Club 2017. See also above, Clontarf Cricket and Football (rugby) Club; 17 Transport: landing stage.

Boat shed: built after 1968 (Gogarty, 83).

Parochial hall, Seafield Rd West N. (719997, 736413), associated with St John's Church (C. of I.) (see 11 Religion). Built in 1879 (Ir. Builder 1.1.1879). Parochial hall 1895 (Vernon papers). Unnamed 1907; hall, extended by 1970 (OS). Demolished, moved to new premises in 1990s (Gogarty, 110).

Hall, Castle Grove N. (719501, 736974). Hall 1971, 2016 (OS). Headquarters, 92nd Dublin Clontarf St Anthony's Scout Group 2017.

St Anthony's Hall, Clontarf Rd [west] N., in former St Anthony's Catholic Church (see 11 Religion). Community centre 1975 (Gogarty, 119). Hall 2016 (OS). St Anthony's Hall 2017.

Clontarf Swimming Club, Clontarf Rd [west] S., in Clontarf Baths (see above). Founded in 1884 (Ruddy, 2009, 32).

Clontarf Lawn Tennis Club, St Lawrence Rd W. (718803, 736544). Founded in 1887 (Gogarty, 112). Moved to new premises by 1891 (see next entry).

Clontarf Lawn Tennis Club, Oulton Rd W. (719525, 736102). Moved from former premises (see previous entry) by 1891 (Val. 3). Clontarf Tennis Ground 1936; unnamed 1970 (OS). Pavilion burnt down in 1982; rebuilt by 1984; new clubhouse opened in 2007 (CLTC). Clontarf Lawn Tennis Club 2016 (OS).

Pavilion: 1936–2016 (OS).

Lido Tennis Ground, The Stiles Court N. (719316, 736795). Unnamed 1907; Lido Tennis Ground 1935; sports ground 1970–71; sports ground, stand 2016 (OS).

Pavilion: 1935; demolished by 1971 (OS).

Tennis courts, Seafield Rd West S. (719637, 736343), associated with St John the Baptist's Church (C. of I.) (see 11 Religion). Beechfield Lawn Tennis Club 1914 (Vernon papers). Tennis ground 1935, 1970–71; tennis courts 2016 (OS); 2017.

Pavilion: wooden pavilion to be erected 1914 (Vernon papers); pavilion 1935, 1970–71 (OS).

Arcadian Lawn Tennis Ground, Kincora Rd S. (719420, 736187). Arcadian Lawn Tennis Ground 1936; built over by 1971 (OS).

Tudor Tennis Ground, Castle Ave [south] E. (719313, 736024). Tudor Tennis Ground 1936; tennis grounds 1970; sports ground 2016 (OS).

Pavilion: 1936; demolished, replaced by new pavilion by 1970 (see next entry).

Pavilion: built to replace former pavilion (see previous entry) by 1970; pavilion 2016 (OS).

Tennis ground, Clontarf Rd [mid] N., on former Green (see 14 Primary production), associated with Holy Faith secondary school (see 20 Education). Tennis ground 1970 (OS). Holy Faith school tennis courts 2013 (Gogarty, 146). Tennis ground 2016 (OS); 2017.

Royal Dublin Golf Club, North Bull Island (see below), S. end (721711, 735557). Dublin Golf Club 1889 (Lynch, 87, 89). Royal Dublin Golf Club, club house 1891 (Val. 3). Lease of portion of North Bull to Royal Dublin Golf Club 1892; sale of lands at North Bull to Royal Dublin Golf Club 1903 (Vernon papers). Golf links 1907; Royal Dublin Golf Links, flag staff, 2 shelters 1936; Royal Dublin Golf Links, car park, 3 shelters 1971; Royal Dublin Golf Club, golf links 2016 (OS). See also 18 Utilities: Curley's Yard.

Club house: built in 1904 (RDGC, 26); club house 1907, 1936 (OS); burnt down in 1943; new club house built in 1953 (RDGC, 30, 51); club house 1971 (OS).

Clontarf Golf Club and Bowling Club, Malahide Rd E. (718643, 737119). Clontarf Club, opened in 1912 (Ir. Times 27.5.1912). Clontarf Golf Course 1971; Clontarf Golf Club and Bowling Club 2016 (OS).

St Anne's Golf Club, North Bull Island (see below), N. end (723936, 737710). Founded in 1921 (Sharkey, 69). St Anne's Golf Links, shelter 1936; St Anne's Golf Links 1971 (OS). New clubhouse opened in 1974; new course inaugurated in 1989 (Ir. Times 14.8.1974, 2.9.1989). St Anne's Golf Club 2017.

Club house: St Anne's Golf Club House 1936; club house 1971 (OS); built over by Bull Island Visitor's Centre in 1986 (Lynch, 101).

Fairview Park, Clontarf Rd [west] S. (717543, 736066). Fairview sloblands (see **18** Utilities: land reclamation) purchased by Dublin Corporation from Dublin Port and Docks Board for laying out as public park 1904; park in use for recreation and concerts 1910; formal design for layout of park 1915; new roadway (for cyclists and pedestrians) laid out in 1926 (*Ir. Times* 2.8.1904, 7.6.1910, 8.11.1915, 11.3.1926). Fairview Park, nursery 1936; Fairview Park, extended to E. of railway line (see **17** Transport), basketball ground, pavilion, playground 1970 (OS). Fairview Park 2017. See also **17** Transport: railway bridge.

North Bull Island, Dublin Bay (722294, 736384). Island, formerly in pasture (see **14** Primary production: North Bull Island) designated as bird sanctuary 1931 (Wild Birds Protection Act, 1930, 16). North Bull Island 1936 (OS). Island, excluding lands of Royal Dublin Golf Club (see above), purchased by Dublin Corporation in 1954 (Dáil deb., 315, no. 9, 28.6.1979). North Bull Island 1971, 2016 (OS). North Bull Island/Oileán an Bhulla Thuaidh 2017 (nameplate). See also above, St Anne's Golf Club; below, Sea Scouts' huts; **13** Administration: lifeguard huts; **18** Utilities: Curley's Yard, fountains; **19** Health: first aid hut.

Brian Boru Park, Brian Boru St S. (720428, 735922). Brian Boru Park 1936; built over by 1970 (OS).

Bandstand, Clontarf Rd [west] S. (719387, 735894), associated with Clontarf Baths (see above). Depicted 1907–2016 (OS). Bandstand 2017.

Promenade, Clontarf Rd S., railway bridge (see **17** Transport) to Bull Wall (see **18** Utilities) (719571, 735932). 150-foot wide promenade proposed with sea wall on reclaimed land (see **18** Utilities) in 1921; completed in 1956 (*Ir. Times* 26.7.1921, 2.11.1956). Unnamed 1970–71 (OS). Promenade 2017. See also **14** Primary production: lead mine; **17** Transport: car park; **18** Utilities: sea wall.

Tudor Park, Oulton Rd E. (719838, 736106). Tudor Park, club ground of Eason's football team 1930 (*Ir. Times* 26.4.1930). Moved to new premises in 1958 (see next entry).

Belgrove Football Club, Mount Prospect Ave [west] N. (720377, 736864). Sports ground, pavilion 1935 (OS). Belgrove Football Club, established in 1947 (*Ir. Times* 6.2.1954). Belgrove Football Club, moved from former premises in St Anne's Park in 1958; Eason's football team moved from former premises (see previous entry) in 1958 (Lynch, 126). Sports ground, pavilion 1971 (OS). Pavilion burnt down in 1975 (Lynch, 126). Grounds built over by 2016 (OS).

Bronol Club Ground, Mount Prospect Ave [west] N. (720500, 736924). Bronol Club Ground, pavilion 1935; built over by 1970 (OS).

CLONTARF ISLAND, 1878, BY ALEXANDER WILLIAMS

B. & I. Football Ground, Kincora Rd S. (720315, 736173). B. & I. Football Ground, pavilion 1936 (OS).

Brian Boru Football Ground, Kincora Rd S. (720463, 736134). 1936 (OS).

Corinthians Football Ground, Clontarf Rd [mid] N. (720199, 735923). Corinthians Football Ground 1936 (OS). Built over by Clontarf Park extension by 1970 (see **10** Streets).

Queen's Park Football Ground, Clontarf Rd [mid] N. (720290, 735920). Queen's Park Football Ground 1936 (OS). Built over by Clontarf Park extension by 1970 (see **10** Streets).

Basketball grounds, Strandville Ave East W. (718361 736352), associated with Mount Temple Comprehensive School (see **20** Education). Mountjoy School sports ground, pavilion 1935–6; basketball grounds, partly built over by 1971 (OS).

Basketball ground, Blackheath Park N. (719835, 736797). 1970–71 (OS).

Scoil Uí Chonaill GAA Club, Clontarf Rd [west] N. (719438, 736097). O Connell School Sports Ground 1936 (OS). O'Connell's Schools GAA Club 1950 (*O'Connell's Schools*). Sports ground 1970, 2016 (OS). Scoil Uí Chonaill GAA Club 2017.

Sea Scouts' huts, 2, North Bull Island (see above), S. end (721307, 735827; 721366, 735815). 1936 (OS).

James Larkin Memorial, James Larkin Rd E. (721620, 736769). James Larkin Road/Bóthar Séamas Ó Lorcáin 1949 (datestone). James Larkin Memorial 1970 (OS); 2017.

Star of the Sea (Realt na Mara) statue, Bull Wall, E. end (722354, 734985). Star of the Sea (Realt na Mara) statue, erected at cost of £17,000 in 1972 (*Ir. Times* 25.9.1972). Star of the Sea memorial 2017.

Community centre, St Gabriel's Rd E., associated with Saint Gabriel's Catholic Church (see **11** Religion). (720946, 736524). Built in 1960s (Gogarty, 213). Community centre, car park 1970; extended by 2016 (OS).

Sports ground, Clontarf Rd [west] S. (718138, 736110). All-weather surface, running track, 2 sand pits, laid out on reclaimed ground (see **18** Utilities: land reclamation) by 1970; sports ground 2016 (OS).

Sports ground, Clontarf Rd [west] N. (719386, 736082). Sports ground, pavilion, tennis grounds 1970; sports ground 2016 (OS).

Playground, Blackheath Park N. (719706, 736715). 1970–71 (OS).

Swimming pool, Sybil Hill Rd E. (720177, 737613). Swimming pool 1971 (OS). Closed in 2006 (*Ir. Independent* 27.7.2006).

ROYAL DUBLIN GOLF CLUB HOUSE, NORTH BULL ISLAND, *c.* 1910

22. RESIDENCE

(See also appendix on pp 73–5)

Single and paired houses

Furrypark, Howth Rd [north] E. (719784, 737408). Built by 1731 (Gogarty, 23). Furry Park 1760 (Rocque); garden 1823 (VEM). Furry Park House 1836 (OSN). Furry Park 1843 (OS). Unnamed 1845 (Val. 1). Furry Park 1868; Furrypark 1907; Furrypark, fountain 1935; unnamed 1971 (OS). Refurbished in c. 1985 (Ir. Times 30.3.1985). Divided into apartments in 1990s (Gogarty, 26).

    Gate lodge: unnamed 1843 (OS); gate lodge 1850 (Val. 2); lodge 1868–1935 (OS).

    Tea cottage: 1843–68; demolished by 1907 (OS).

Sibyl Hill, Sybil Hill Rd E. (720267, 737508). Built in 1730s (Gogarty, 28). Unnamed 1760 (Rocque). Extended in 1808 (Gogarty, 28). Sable Hill 1816 (Taylor). Sybil Hill 1821 (Duncan). Sybil Hill, garden 1823 (VEM). Sibyl Hill 1836 (OSN). Sybil Hill 1837 (Lewis, i, 376). Sibyl Hill House 1843 (OS). Sibyl Hill 1850 (Val. 2). Sibyl Hill House 1868; Sibyl Hill 1907, 1935 (OS). Temporarily converted to school before building of St Paul's College in 1950 (see 20 Education). House occupied by Vincentian Fathers Congregation in 1950 (see 11 Religion: Vincentian Provincial Office).

    Gate lodges: 2 gate lodges 1843 (OS), 1850 (Val. 2); lodge 1868; 2 lodges 1907, 1935 (OS).

Oakley, Vernon Ave [north] W. (720049, 736761). Cottage Park, built by 1740 (Gogarty, 76). Cottage Park 1816 (Taylor), 1821 (Duncan), 1823 (VEM). Cottage Park House 1836 (OSN). Cottage Park 1843 (OS), 1845 (Val. 1). Oakley 1868–1935 (OS). Demolished, built over by Oakley Park by 1960 (see below; 10 Streets).

Ivy Lodge, Castle Ave [south] W. (719240, 736237). Built in mid-18th cent. (Gogarty, 132). Unnamed 1843 (OS). The Bungalow 1865 (Val. 3). Unnamed 1868–71 (OS). Ivy Lodge 2013 (Gogarty, 132). Unnamed 2016 (OS).

Verville, Vernon Ave [west] S. (719837, 736996). Built by 1758 (Gogarty, 33). Unnamed 1760 (Rocque). Verville 1816 (Taylor), 1821 (Duncan), 1823 (VEM). Verville House 1836 (OSN). Verville 1843 (OS). Converted to asylum in 1859 (see below).

    Lodge: 1868; unnamed 1907 (OS).

    Summer house: turret 1823 (VEM); summer house 1843 (OS).

Sea Park, Mount Prospect Ave [west] N. (720620, 736733). Unnamed 1760 (Rocque); laundry 1823 (VEM). Seapark 1833 (Ruddy, 2006, 174). Dollymount House 1836 (Gogarty, 37). Sea Park House 1836 (OSN). Dollymount 1837 (Lewis, i, 376). Sea Park 1843–1935 (OS). Sold in 1964 (Ir. Times 10.7.1964). Demolished, built over by Seapark Apartments in 1967 (see below).

    Lodge: unnamed 1843; lodge 1868; unnamed 1907, 1935 (OS); demolished, built over by 2013 (Gogarty, 38).

Yew Park House, Castle Ave [north] E. (719495, 736490). Unnamed 1760 (Rocque). 'The fine seat and beautiful gardens of Lady Southwell' 1786 (Post chaise companion, 308). Unnamed 1816 (Taylor), 1821 (Duncan). Yew View 1823 (Gogarty, 30). Elmview, seat 1823 (VEM). Elm View 1836 (OSN), 1843 (OS). Elm Park 1855 (Gogarty, 30). Yew Park 1864 (FJ 16.7.1864), 1868 (OS). Elm View, otherwise Yew Park 1876; Elm Park 1884 (Vernon papers). Yew Park 1907 (OS). Elm View, otherwise Yew Park 1908 (Vernon papers). Yew View 1910 (Thom). Yew Park House 1935; demolished by 1970–71 (OS); built over by Seafield Court apartments by 2013 (Gogarty, 32).

    Lodge: 1843, 1868; demolished by 1907 (OS).

    Lodge: 1868, 1907 (OS); 1908 (Vernon papers); extended by 1935 (OS); Elm View gatehouse 2014 (Gogarty, 30–31).

Bay View, Mount Prospect Ave [west] N. (720424, 736719). 'A new house' 1762 (Gogarty, 56). Bayview 1786 (Post chaise companion, 309). Bay View 1816 (Taylor). Bayview 1821 (Duncan), 1823 (VEM). Bay View House 1836 (OSN). Bay View 1843–1907 (OS). Demolished by 1954 (Gogarty, 57).

Baymount Castle, Dollymount Ave N. (721232, 736734). Granby Hill 1763; Baymount House 1800 (Ruddy, 2006, 172–73). Baymount 1803 (Bligh), 1821 (Duncan). Bay Mount 1823 (VEM). In use as boarding school (see 20 Education: St Mary's Abbey of Loreto Catholic Girls' Boarding School) c. 1834–8 (Ruddy, 2006, 172–3). Baymount House, residence of J. Keily 1837 (Lewis, i, 376). Rebuilt in 1838 (Gogarty, 59). Baymount, reverted to private residence in 1838 (Ruddy, 2006, 173–4). Bought by Loreto Sisters, converted to convent in 1842 (see 11 Religion: Loreto Sisters convent). Baymount Castle 1843 (OS), 1845 (Val. 1). Converted to school in 1847 (see 20 Education: St Mary's Abbey of Loreto Catholic Girls' Boarding School). Reconverted to private residence in 1862 (Ruddy, 2006, 176–7). Baymount Castle 1866 (Vernon papers), 1868 (OS), 1886 (FJ 16.11.1886). Baymount Castle, 'land ... formerly called Granby Hill' 1898 (Vernon papers). Converted to Baymount Preparatory School in 1904 (see 20 Education).

    Gate lodges: gate lodge 1843 (OS); 2 gate lodges 1850 (Val. 2); 2 lodges 1868 (OS).

Ormond Villa, Vernon Ave [south] E. (720108, 735971). Built in c. 1773–1816 (Gogarty, 139). Unnamed 1843 (OS). Ormond House 1851 (FJ 17.3.1851). Unnamed 1907 (OS). Ormond Hall 1912; Ormond Villa 1914 (Vernon papers). Façade extant 2013 (Gogarty, 139).

Crab Lake, Clontarf Rd [mid] N. (720447, 735789). Crablaugh 1776 (Vernon papers). Crablake 1803 (Bligh), 1816 (Vernon papers). Crablake House 1816 (Taylor), 1821 (Duncan). Crab Lake 1823 (VEM), 1837 (Lewis, i, 376), 1850 (Thom).

Simla Lodge, Strandville Ave East E. (718432, 736397), associated with Watson's Nurseries (see 14 Primary production). Simla Lodge, built in 1776 (Gogarty, 77); 1868–1936; unnamed 1971, 2016 (OS). Simla Lodge 2017 (nameplate).

Wood Ville, Howth Rd [north] E. (719331, 736976). Built by 1791 (Gogarty, 78). Unnamed 1823 (VEM). Woodville House 1836 (OSN). Wood Ville 1843; Wood Vale 1868 (OS). Woodville 1894 (Vernon papers). Wood Ville 1907, 1935; demolished by 1971 (OS).

Lodge: unnamed 1843; lodge 1868, 1907; demolished by 1971 (OS).

Mount Temple, Malahide Rd E. (718297, 736915). Built before 1799 (Ruddy, 2008, 184). Mount Temple 1816 (Taylor). Mt Temple 1821 (Duncan). Mount Temple 1823 (VEM). Mount Temple, repair of damage 1824; house and demesne of Mount Temple 1828 (Vernon papers). Mount Temple House 1836 (OSN). Mount Temple 1843–1907; Mount Temple, tennis ground 1935–6 (OS). Converted to school in 1949 (see **20** Education: Mount Temple Comprehensive School).

Gate lodge: gate lodge 1843–68; 2 lodges 1907; lodge 1935–6; unnamed 1971, 2016 (OS); gate lodge 2017.

Beechfield House, Oulton Rd E. (719693, 736062). Depicted, Dobbs 1803 (Bligh). Beachfield 1816 (Taylor). Beachfield, erroneously sited at Vernon Ave [south] W. 1821 (Duncan). Unnamed 1823 (VEM). Peachfield House 1836 (OSN). Beachfield 1837 (Lewis, i, 376). Beachfield House 1843 (OS). Divided into 2 dwellings by 1861 (see also below, Tudor House). Beachfield House 1868, 1907 (OS). Beechfield House 1918 (Gogarty, 45), 1936; unnamed 1970 (OS). Beechfield House, converted to apartments after 1995 (Gogarty, 45).

Lodge: gate lodge 1843; lodge 1868, 1907; demolished by 1970 (OS).

Blackbush, Clontarf Rd [east] N., site unknown. 1803 (Bligh).

Cabin, Clontarf Rd [east] N., site unknown. 1803 (Bligh).

Cabin, Clontarf Rd [east] N., site unknown. 1803 (Bligh).

Dolly Mount, Clontarf Rd [east] N., site unknown. 1803 (Bligh).

Gore's House, Victoria Terrace N. (719860, 735961). Gore's 1803 (Bligh).

Welch's House, Clontarf Rd [east] N., site unknown. Welch's 1803 (Bligh).

Hollybrook House, Hollybrook Park S. (718591, 736620). Built by 1812 (Gogarty, 84). Holly Brook 1821 (Duncan). Unnamed 1823 (VEM). Hollybrook House 1836 (OSN), 1843; Hollybrook House, churning machine 1889; Hollybrook House 1907, 1935–6 (OS). Demolished, built over by hotel by 1971 (see **16** Trades and services).

Thornhill, Mount Prospect Ave [east] N. (721684, 737201). Built on Blackbush lands leased from Vernons in 1814 (Sharkey, 13). Demesne of Thorn Hill, house depicted 1816 (Longfield 4). Thorn Hill 1821 (Duncan); haggard, lawn, yard 1823 (VEM). Modern 2-storey slated house 1836 (OSN). Thornhill 1837 (Lewis, i, 376). Demolished, partly built over by St Anne's in *c.* 1836–7 (see below).

Bedford Lodge, Mount Prospect Ave [east] N. (721416, 736919). Bedford Lodge 1816 (Longfield 4), 1821 (Duncan), 1823 (VEM), 1836 (OSN), 1843–1971 (OS). Parks Headquarters of Dublin Corporation *c.* 1975–95; private residence 2013 (Gogarty, 62). Bedford Lodge 2017 (nameplate).

Merchamp, Vernon Ave [south] E. (720173, 736413). Merchamp 1816 (Taylor). Mercamp 1821 (Duncan), 1823 (VEM). Merchamp 1837 (Lewis, i, 376). Merchamp Lodge 1843 (OS). House converted to 2 detached dwellings (see also below, Rosetta) in 1862 (Gogarty, 49). Merchamp Lodge 1866–7 (Val. 3). Merchamp 1868–1935 (OS). Divided into

apartments by 1935 (Gogarty, 49). Demolished by 1970 (OS). Built over by apartments by 2013 (Gogarty, 50).

Gate lodge: gate lodge 1843; lodge 1868–1935; demolished by 1970 (OS).

Moss Grove, Seafield Rd East S. (719958, 736371). Moss Grove 1816 (Taylor), 1821 (Duncan). Unnamed 1843; demolished by 1907 (OS).

Prospect Cottage, Mount Prospect Ave [west] N. (720872, 736629). 1816 (Taylor).

Seaview, Clontarf Rd [west] N. (718910, 736061). Sea View 1820 (Vernon papers), 1821 (Duncan), 1843 (OS). Seaview 1852 (*Thom*). Unnamed 1868 (OS). Seaview 1870 (*Thom*), 1888 (Vernon papers). Ontario 1890 (OS), 1895 (Vernon papers), 1897 (*Thom*). Unnamed 1907 (OS). Seaview 1908 (*Thom*). Extant 2013 (Gogarty, 66).

Silveracre, Howth Rd [south] S. (719053, 736809). Silver Acre 1821 (Duncan). Silverfield House 1843–1907; Silveracre 1935 (OS). Replaced by hotel by 1971 (see **16** Trades and services).

Annsbrook, Clontarf Rd [west] N. (718302, 736309). Unnamed 1823 (VEM). Ann's Brook House 1836 (OSN). Annsbrook 1843 (OS). Demolished, built over by Annesbook Terrace by 1852 (see below).

Auburn, Seafield Rd East S. (720548, 736328). Cottage 1823 (VEM). Unnamed 1843; Seafield Cottage 1868, 1907 (OS), 1909 (Electoral rolls). Auburn 1935; unnamed 1970 (OS). Rebuilt by 2017.

Belgrove, Seafield Rd West S. (719910, 736353). Unnamed 1823 (VEM). Belgrove House 1836 (OSN). Bellgrove House 1843–1907; Belgrove 1935 (OS). Purchased by R.C. church, converted to national school in 1940 (see **20** Education).

Lodge: 1868–1935; unnamed 1970–71 (OS); extant 2013 (Gogarty, 42); Belgrove Lodge 2017 (nameplate).

Boroimhe Lodge, Clontarf Rd [east] N. (720965, 736069). Unnamed 1823 (VEM). Barohme (Boroimhe/Borumha) Lodge 1836 (OSN). Boroimhe Lodge 1843 (OS). Borohme Lodge 1850 (*Thom*). Boroimhe Lodge, summer house 1868 (OS). Boroimhe 1891; 'formerly Bird's Nest' 1898 (*FJ* 13.8.1891, 30.11.1898). Permission granted to convert to restaurant, Mrs Kenny 1898 (*Ir. Builder* 1.12.1898). In use as house for destitute children 1899 (Val. 3). Boroimhe Lodge 1907 (OS). Vacant 1915 (Gogarty, 68). Boroimhe Lodge 1936 (OS). Extant 1947; demolished by 2013 (Gogarty, 68).

Cottage, Howth Rd [north] E. (719151, 736918). Cottage 1823 (VEM). Depicted as ruins 1843 (OS).

Cottage, Mount Prospect Ave [west] N. (719988, 736414). Cottage 1823 (VEM). Unnamed 1843, 1907 (OS).

Cottage, Seafield Rd East N. (720547, 736355). Cottage 1823 (VEM). Unnamed 1843, 1907 (OS).

Cottage, Seafield Rd West N. (719988, 736414). Cottage 1823 (VEM). Converted to Greenlanes School in 1835 (see **20** Education).

Danesfield, Seafield Rd East N. (721120, 736254). Unnamed 1823 (VEM). Danes Field 1836 (OSN). Danesfield 1837 (Lewis, i, 376). Danesfield House 1843 (OS). Danesfield 1850 (*Thom*). Danesfield House 1868 (OS). Danesfield 1887 (Vernon papers). Danesfield House 1907; Danesfield 1936;

demolished by 1970 (OS). Built over by Danes Court apartments by 2013 (Gogarty, 47).

Lodge: unnamed 1843; lodge 1868, 1907; demolished by 1970 (OS).

Eagleville, Strandville Ave East E. (718429, 736442). Strandville 1823 (VEM), 1836 (OSN), 1837 (Lewis, i, 376). Strand Ville 1843 (OS). Strandville House 1845 (Val. 1). Eagle Ville 1868–1936; Eagleville 1971; demolished by 2016 (OS).

Grace Ville, Blackheath Park N. (719528, 736645). Grace Ville 1823 (VEM), 1843–68 (OS). Demolished, built over by Blackheath in 1872 (see below).

Hollybrook Park, Hollybrook Park S. (718654, 736648). Hollybrook Park 1823 (VEM). 'Several scattered houses in what was formerly a park' 1836 (OSN). Hollybrook Park 1843; Hollybrook Park, cesspool 1889; Hollybrook Park 1907, 1935–6 (OS).

Lodge: 1889; unnamed 1907 (OS).

Marino Lodge, Marino Crescent N. (718046, 736500). Unnamed 1823 (VEM). Marino Lodge 1843; demolished by 1907 (OS).

Moira Lodge, Clontarf Rd [west] N. (718900, 736066). Built by 1823 (Gogarty, 64). Moira Lodge 1837 (Lewis, i, 377). Unnamed 1843; Moira Lodge 1868, 1890 (OS), 1898 (Thom map). Unnamed 1907 (OS). Moira Lodge 1914 (Vernon papers), 1947 (Gogarty, 64). Moira Lodge 2017 (nameplate).

Mount Prospect, Mount Prospect Ave [west] E. (720912, 736625). Prospect 1823 (VEM). Mount Prospect House 1836 (OSN). Prospect 1837 (Lewis, i, 376). Mount Prospect 1843–68 (OS). House converted to St Vincent de Paul female orphanage in 1873 (see 11 Religion: Daughters of Charity convent).

Old Ivy House, Howth Rd [south] W. (718035, 736490). Old Ivy House 1823 (VEM). Unnamed 1843 (OS).

Prospect Terrace, Clontarf Rd [west] N. (718823, 736083). Unnamed 1823 (VEM). Prospect 1843 (OS), 1854 (Thom), 1866–7 (Val. 3). Unnamed 1868 (OS). Prospect Terrace 1888 (Vernon papers), 1890; unnamed, redeveloped by 1907 (OS).

Seafield House, Seafield Rd East S. (720975, 736143). Sea Field, garden 1823 (VEM). Seafield House 1836 (OSN). Seafield 1843–1907; Seafield House 1936; unnamed 1970 (OS). Ruinous in 1970s; demolished, built over by Seafield Downs estate by 2013 (Gogarty, 48).

Gate lodge: gate lodge 1843; lodge 1868; demolished by 1907 (OS).

Strandville, Hollybrook Rd W. (718561, 736317). Unnamed 1823 (VEM). Strandville House 1836 (OSN), 1843; Strand Ville 1868, 1890 (OS), 1898 (Thom map). Strandvilla 1907; Strandville 1935–6; unnamed, divided into 2 dwellings by 1971 (OS).

Balmoral Lodge, Castle Ave [south] W. (719230, 736211). Built in c. 1825 (Gogarty, 131). Unnamed 1843 (OS). Belmount Lodge 1863 (Val. 3). Balmoral Lodge 1868; unnamed 1907 (OS). Balmoral Lodge 1909 (Electoral rolls). Unnamed 1970 (OS). Balmoral Lodge 2013 (Gogarty, 131).

Baymount, Clontarf Rd [west] N. (719267, 735994). Baymount House 1836 (OSN). Unnamed 1843 (OS). Baymount 1861

(Thom), 1864–7 (Val. 3), 1868–1970 (OS). Demolished, built over by Danesfort apartments by 1988 (Gogarty, 88).

Fortview Villa, Clontarf Rd [mid] N. (720312, 735767). Built by 1836 (Gogarty, 67). Fort View 1843 (OS). Fortview 1852; Fortview Ville 1853 (Thom). Fort View Villa 1868 (OS). Fortview Villa 1875; Fortview 1894; Fortview Villa 1903 (Thom). Vacant 1915 (Gogarty, 67). Fortview Villa 1920 (Thom). Unnamed 1970 (OS). Extensively refurbished in c. 1993 (Gogarty, 67).

Lake View, Clontarf Rd [east] N. (721248, 736330). Lake View 1836 (Vernon papers). Lakeview Cottage 1843–68; Lake View 1907, 1935; demolished, built over by 1970 (OS).

Vernon House, Vernon Ave [north] E., in former nunnery (see 11 Religion). Convent House 1836 (OSN), 1843 (OS), 1845 (Val. 1), 1868, 1907 (OS). Old Convent House 1916; Convent House 1928 (Vernon papers). Vernon House 1935 (OS). House collapsed in 1960s; built over by Duncan Court apartments by 2013 (Gogarty, 36).

Gate lodge: gate lodge 1843; lodge 1868; unnamed 1907 (OS); gate lodge 1916 (Vernon papers).

Clontarf Castle, Castle Ave [south] W., on site of former castle (see 12 Defence). Built in 1836–7 (Gogarty, 21). 'A large, handsome mansion in the castle style, not quite finished' 1836 (OSN). Restored by 1840 (IPJ 12.9.1840). Clontarf Castle 1843 (OS). Dwelling, dwelling tower 1845 (Val. 1). Clontarf Castle 1868–1971 (OS). Sold, converted to hotel in 1973 (see 16 Trades and services: Clontarf Castle Hotel). See also 10 Streets: Kincora Avenue, Kincora Drive, Kincora Grove.

Castle gardens: let 1918 (Vernon papers).

Lodge: gate lodge 1843; lodge 1868–1935; unnamed 1970–71 (OS).

St Anne's, Mount Prospect Ave [east] N. Built, partly on site of former Thornhill (see above), in c. 1836–7 (Sharkey, 9–14). St Ann's House 1836 (OSN). St Ann's 1843; St Ann's, fountain, grotto, summer house, tool house 1868 (OS). Rebuilt in 1873–81 (Gogarty, 52). St Ann's, tower 1907; St Anne's, fountain, sun dial, tank (covered), tower, well 1935 (OS). Destroyed by fire in 1943 (Ir. Times 4.1.1944; Sharkey, 14). Ruins demolished in 1968 (Gogarty, 55).

Gate lodges: gate lodge 1843 (OS); 3 gate lodges 1850 (Val. 2); 3 lodges 1868–1935 (OS).

Wooden bridge: 1843 (OS).

Merville, Fortview Ave, site unknown. 1837 (Lewis, i, 376), 1854 (Thom).

Alverno, Castle Ave [south] W. (719144, 736008). Unnamed 1843; Tivoli House 1864–7 (Val. 3), 1868, 1907; Alverno 1936; unnamed 1970 (OS). Demolished, built over by Alverno Apartments in 1984–6 (Ir. Times 10.2.1984, 23.5.1984, 21.2.1986).

Auburn House, Seafield Rd East S. (720546, 736303). Unnamed 1843; Auburn Lodge 1868, 1907; Auburn House 1935; unnamed 1970; demolished by 2016 (OS).

Belvidere, Clontarf Rd [mid] N. (720351, 735822). Belvidere 1843 (OS). Belvedere 1850 (Thom). Belvidere 1855 (Val. 3), 1868 (OS). Converted to Clontarf Yacht and Boat Club premises in 1875 (see 21 Entertainment, memorials and societies).

CLONTARF CASTLE, AFTER RESTORATION, 1840

Danes Fort, Castle Ave [south] E. (719212, 735988). Unnamed 1843 (OS). Danesfort 1864–7 (Val. 3). Danes Fort 1868–1936 (OS). Sold in 1959 (Gogarty, 88). Demolished by 1970 (OS). Built over by Danesfort apartments in 1988 (Gogarty, 88).

Fingal Cottage, Clontarf Rd [mid] N. (720336, 735814). Unnamed 1843 (OS). Fingal Cottage 1855, 1873 (Val. 3). Converted to Clontarf Yacht and Boat Club premises in 1875 (see **21** Entertainment, memorials and societies).

Hollybrook, Howth Rd [south] S. (718690, 736692). Unnamed 1843; Hollybrook 1868–1936 (OS).

Moat Cottage, Brian Boru St N. (720433, 736026). Unnamed 1843; Moat Cottage 1868; unnamed 1907 (OS).

St Edmund's, Clontarf Rd [west] N. (718793, 736099). Unnamed 1843 (OS). St Edmund's, residence of Graham Lemon 1861 (*Ir. Builder* 1.7.1861). Converted to public house by 1868 (see **16** Trades and services: The Yacht).

St James's, Hollybrook Park N. (718650, 736670). Unnamed 1843–89 (OS). St James's 1897 (*Thom*), 1907, 1935–6; unnamed 1971; Saint James's 2016 (OS).

Seapoint House, Clontarf Rd [mid] N. (720501, 735816). Unnamed 1843 (OS). Seapoint Lodge 1849 (Gogarty, 98). Sea Point House 1868 (OS). Seapoint House 1898; 'premises formerly known as Seapoint House' 1904 (Vernon papers). Demolished by 1907 (OS).

Seabank Cottage, Mount Prospect Ave [west] N. (720880, 736637). Unnamed 1843, 1907; Seabank Cottage 1935; demolished by 1970 (OS).

Springvale, Clontarf Rd [west] N. (718581, 736211). Unnamed 1843; Spring Vale 1868, 1890 (OS), 1898 (Thom map). Springvale 1900 (Vernon papers).

Strandville Cottage, Clontarf Rd [west] N. (718590, 736229). Unnamed 1843; Strandville Cottage 1890 (OS); 'in very bad repair' 1905 (Vernon papers). Demolished by 1907 (OS).

Strandville House, Strandville Ave East E. (718430, 736366). Unnamed 1843; Strandville House 1868, 1890 (OS), 1898 (Thom map), 1905 (Vernon papers). Unnamed 1907 (OS). Strandville House 1909 (Electoral rolls). Demolished by 1971 (OS).

Willow Brook, Strandville Ave East E. (718464, 736350). Willow Brook 1843 (Ruddy, 2014, 20–21), 1890–1936; unnamed 1971; demolished by 2016 (OS).

Wood Park, Vernon Ave [north] E. (720181, 736912). Wood Park 1843–68 (OS). Woodpark 1870 (*FJ* 30.4.1870). Wood Park 1907, 1935; unnamed 1971 (OS). Demolished, built over by Vernon Heath estate by 2013 (Gogarty, 75).

Woodside, Vernon Ave [south] W. (720089, 736286). Unnamed 1843; Woodside 1868 (OS). Incorporated into Woodside Terrace in 1872 (see below).

Iverna House, Clontarf Rd [east] W. (721372, 736595). Built in *c.* 1843; Eagle Lodge *c.* 1870 (Gogarty, 93–4). Iverna House 1935; unnamed 1970 (OS). Iverna House 2013 (Gogarty, 94).

Mount Vernon, Clontarf Rd [east] W. (721416, 736555). Built in *c.* 1843 (Gogarty, 93–4). Mount Vernon 1850 (*Thom*), 1868–1935; unnamed 1970 (OS). Mount Vernon 2013 (Gogarty, 93–4).

Ardnardeen, Castle Ave [south] E. (719245, 736101). Ardnardeen Villa, built in *c.* 1846 (Gogarty, 95). Ardnardeen 1868 (OS), 1897 (*Thom*). Unnamed 1907 (OS). Demolished, site vacant by 2013 (Gogarty, 95). New house built in 2017.

Fortview House, Clontarf Rd [mid] N. (720259, 735764). Fortview House 1850, 1852 (*Thom*). Fortview 1855 (Val. 3). Unnamed 1868 (OS). Fortview House 1875, 1920 (*Thom*).

Gresham Villas, Clontarf Rd [east] N. (721295, 736392). Gresham's Buildings 1850, 1897 (*Thom*). Unnamed 1907 (OS). Gresham Buildings 1909 (Electoral rolls). Gresham Villas 1911 (Census returns), 1935 (OS). Gresham Buildings or Villas, in use as offices 2013 (Gogarty, 92). Gresham House 2017.

Kincora House, Clontarf Rd [east] N. (721143, 736447). Built by 1854 (Gogarty, 98). Kinkora 1854 (*FJ* 5.10.1854), 1868, 1907; Kincora House 1935 (OS). Demolished, built over by Dollymount Rise by 1970 (see **10** Streets).

Everton, Castle Ave [south] E. (719249, 736110). Built by 1855 (Gogarty, 133). Everton 1868 (OS), 1897 (*Thom*). Unnamed 1907, 1970 (OS). Demolished by 2013 (Gogarty, 133). New house built in 2017.

Moyville, Castle Ave [south] E. (719261, 736185). Built by 1857 (Gogarty, 99). Moyville 1868 (OS), 1893 (Vernon papers), 1897 (*Thom*). Unnamed 1907 (OS). Moyville 1909 (Electoral rolls). Unnamed 1970 (OS). Moyville 2013 (Gogarty, 99).

Sunnyside, Vernon Ave [north] W. (719993, 736653). Built in 1858 (Gogarty, 100). Sunnyside 1868–1970 (OS). Demolished, built over by Blackheath Court in 1986 (*Ir. Times* 7.2.1986).

Castilla, Vernon Ave [north] W. (720003, 736529). Built by 1859 (Gogarty, 101). Castilla 1868, 1907; Castilla, fountain 1935 (OS). Demolished, built over by Castilla Park in 1958 (see **10** Streets).

Lodge: 1868–1935 (OS).

Tudor House, Oulton Rd E., in part of Beechfield House (see above). Beechfield Lodge 1861 (Gogarty, 43–4), 1868 (OS). Tudor Lodge or Tudor House 1899 (Gogarty, 45). Tudor House 1903 (Vernon papers), 1907, 1936; unnamed 1970 (OS). Tudor House, converted to apartments after 1995 (Gogarty, 45).

Gate lodge: 1903 (Vernon papers).

Rosetta, Seafield Rd East S. (720186, 736355). Built, in half of former Merchamp (see above) in 1862 (Gogarty, 49). Rosetta 1868–1935 (OS). Converted to Kostka College in 1943 (see **20** Education).

Frankfort House, Castle Ave [south] W. (719206, 736181). Frankfort House 1863 (Val. 3), 1868 (OS), 1897 (*Thom*). Demolished, laid over by widening of Victoria Rd by 1907 (see **10** Streets).

Glaslynn, Hollybrook Park S. (718555, 736642). Glaslinn 1863 (*FJ* 10.7.1863). Glaslinn, aquarium, 4 foot bridges, fountain 1889–90; Glaslynn, 2 foot bridges 1907 (OS). Glasslynn 1909 (Electoral rolls). Glaslynn, foot bridge, fountain 1935–6; unnamed 1971; Glasslyn 2016 (OS). Glaslynn 2017 (nameplate).

Lodge: lodge 1889–1936; unnamed 1971; replaced by Glaslyn Apartments in 2001 (*Ir. Times* 14.9.2001).

Cozy Lodge, Seaview Ave North [south] W. (718857, 736145). Cozy Lodge 1864 (Val. 3). Unnamed 1868 (OS). Cosy Lodge 1888 (Vernon papers). Cozy Lodge 1897 (*Thom*).

Hollybrook Cottage, Hollybrook Mews W. (718551, 736527), associated with Watson's Nurseries (see **14** Primary production). Hollybrook Cottage 1864 (Val. 3), 1868, 1890 (OS); accommodation for nurserymen in late 19th cent. (Ruddy, 2014, 24); 1907, 1935–6; unnamed 1971; demolished, built over by 2016 (OS).

Strandville House, Clontarf Rd [west] N. (718623, 736221). Strandville House 1864 (Val. 3), 1890; unnamed 1907 (OS).

Strandville Lodge, Clontarf Rd [west] N. (718518, 736239). Strandville Lodge 1864 (Val. 3), 1868, 1890 (OS), 1897 (*Thom*). Unnamed 1907 (OS). Strandville Lodge 1909 (Electoral rolls).

Elmview Lodge, Marino Ave N. (717979, 736738). Elmview Lodge 1864–7 (Val. 3), 1868; rebuilt, St David's by 1889 (OS). Elmview Lodge 1898 (Thom map). Unnamed 1907 (OS).

Hollybrook Lodge, Howth Rd [south] S. (718253, 736560). Hollybrook Lodge 1865 (Val. 3), 1890 (OS), 1897 (*Thom*). Unnamed 1907 (OS). Hollybrook Lodge 1909 (Electoral rolls).

Arthurlic Cottage, Clontarf Rd [mid] N. (718889, 736072). 1865–7 (Val. 3).

Alti Villa, Fortview Ave W. (720290, 735819). Alti Villa 1868; unnamed 1907 (OS).

Anna Cottage, Clontarf Rd [west] N. (718670, 736171). 1868 (OS).

Blandford Lodge, Clontarf Rd [west] N. (718516, 736235). Blandford Lodge 1868, 1890 (OS), 1898 (Thom map). Unnamed 1907 (OS).

Brookside Cottage, Clontarf Rd [west] N. (718484, 736249). Brookside Cottage 1868, 1890 (OS), 1898 (Thom map). Unnamed 1907 (OS). Brookside Cottage 1909 (Electoral rolls).

Manor House, Castle Ave [south] E. (719268, 736277). Manor House 1868 (OS), 1897 (*Thom*). Demolished, built over by 1907 (OS).

Northbank House, Seaview Ave North [north] N. (718886, 736262). Northbank House 1868, 1890 (OS). Northbank Cottage 1907 (Vernon papers). Unnamed 1907 (OS). Northbank 1915 (Vernon papers). Demolished, laid over by The Stiles Road by 1939 (see **10** Streets).

Palmyra, Vernon Ave [south] E. (720106, 735948). 1868 (OS), 1897 (*Thom*).

Rosemount Cottage, Seaview Ave North [north] N. (718896, 736260). Rosemount Cottage 1868 (OS). Rosemount 1888 (Vernon papers). Rosemount Cottage 1890 (OS), 1898 (Thom map). Unnamed 1907 (OS). Rosemount 1915 (Vernon papers). Demolished, laid over by The Stiles Road by 1939 (see **10** Streets).

Seaview House, Seaview Ave North [south] E. (718870, 736130). Seaview House 1868, 1890; unnamed, divided into 2 dwellings by 1907 (OS).

Summerville House, Clontarf Rd [mid] N. (719870, 735961). Unnamed 1868 (OS). Strand House 1887 (Vernon papers), 1897 (*Thom*). Unnamed 1907 (OS). Summerville 1909 (Electoral rolls). Somerville, rebuilding 1916 (Vernon papers). Strand House 1922 (Gogarty, 111). Summerville House 1936 (OS). Sold in 1965 (Gogarty, 111). Unnamed 1970 (OS). Demolished, built over by Summerville estate in 1992 (Gogarty, 111). See also **14** Primary production: oyster beds.

White Hill, Clontarf Rd [west] N. (718706, 736151). 1868 (OS).

Blackheath, Blackheath Park N., on site of former Grace Ville (see above). Built in 1872; extended in 1879–80 (Gogarty, 104). Black Heath, otherwise Graceville 1884 (Vernon papers). Blackheath 1891 (*FJ* 9.9.1891), 1907, 1935 (OS). Converted to hospital in 1941 (see **19** Health: orthopaedic hospital).
Lodge: 1907, 1935; demolished, built over by 1970–71 (OS).

Kingscourt House, Clontarf Rd [west] N., in former Kingscourt House and baths (see **21** Entertainment, memorials and societies). Converted to private residence by 1874 (Ruddy, 2009, 28). King's Court House, in use as depôt for holding crown witnesses 1883–8 (Ruddy, 2014, 23). Kingscourt House 1890, 1907 (OS). Known as 'Informers' Home' early 20th cent. (Knowles, 8). Building extant 1912 (Ruddy, 2004, 77).

The Old Rectory, Seafield Rd West S. (719695, 736365), associated with St John the Baptist's Church (C. of I.) (see **11** Religion). Glebe House, built in 1877 (*Ir. Builder* 15.8.1877); 1887 (Vernon papers). Rectory 1907, 1935; unnamed 1970–71 (OS). Private residence 2013 (Gogarty, 107). The Old Rectory 2017 (nameplate).

St George's Terrace, Howth Rd [south] S. (718227, 736536). Built in 1877 (Gogarty, 161). George's Terrace 1890 (OS), 1898 (Thom map). Unnamed 1907 (OS). St George's Terrace 1908–15 (Electoral rolls).

Ellesmere, St Lawrence Rd E. (718904, 736642). Ellesmere 1889 (OS). Extended to terrace of four houses by 1893 (see below, Ellesmere).

Glenmaurice House, St Lawrence Rd E. (718924, 736714). Glenmaurice, flagstaff 1889 (OS). Glenmaurice House 1897 (*Thom*). Unnamed 1907 (OS). Glenmaurice House 1908 (*Thom*). Private residence 2017.

Manse, Haddon Rd E. (719067, 736007), associated with Clontarf and Scots Presbyterian Church (see **11** Religion). Built in 1889 (Gogarty, 114). Manse 1895 (Vernon papers), 1907, 1936 (OS). Sold in 1967 (Gogarty, 114). Demolished, built over by Haddon Court apartments by 2013 (Gogarty, 114).

Marino House, Malahide Rd E. (717881, 736518). Marino House 1889, 1907–36; unnamed 1970 (OS). Kavanagh's Marino House pub 2017.

Samuelville, Malahide Rd E. (717984, 736744). Samuelville 1889; unnamed 1907 (OS).

Wood Ville, St Lawrence Rd E. (718918, 736702). Wood Ville, flagstaff 1889 (OS). Woodville 1897 (*Thom*). Unnamed 1907 (OS). Woodville 1908 (*Thom*). Wood Ville 2017 (nameplate).

Anna Villa, Clontarf Rd [west] N. (718700, 736155). Anna Villa 1890 (OS), 1897 (*Thom*). Converted to post office by 1907 (see **13** Administration).

Annadale, St Lawrence Rd E. (718772, 736153). Annadale 1890 (OS), 1897 (*Thom*). Unnamed 1907 (OS). Annadale 1908 (*Thom*).

Ardilaun, St Lawrence Rd E. (718800, 736256). Ardilaun 1890 (OS). Ardilaun Villas 1897 (*Thom*). Unnamed 1907 (OS). Ardilaun 1908 (*Thom*).

Elsinore, Howth Rd [south] S. (718214, 736526). Elsinore 1890 (OS), 1898 (Thom map). Unnamed 1907 (OS). Elsinore 1909 (Electoral rolls), 2017 (nameplate).

Floraville, Howth Rd [south] N. (718066, 736478). Flora Ville 1890 (OS), 1897 (*Thom*). Flora Villa 1898 (Thom map). Unnamed 1907 (OS). Floraville 1909 (Electoral rolls).

Frankville, Howth Rd [south] N. (718060, 736476). Frank Ville 1890 (OS), 1897 (*Thom*). Unnamed 1907 (OS). Frankville 1909 (Electoral rolls).

Hollywood, St Lawrence Rd E. (718777, 736173). Hollywood 1890, 1897 (*Thom*). Unnamed 1907 (OS). Hollywood 1909 (Electoral rolls).

Lincluden, St Lawrence Rd E. (718794, 736250). Lincluden 1890 (OS), 1897 (*Thom*). Unnamed 1907 (OS). Lincluden 1909 (Electoral rolls).

Lonsdale House, St Lawrence Rd W. (718753, 736260). Lonsdale House 1890 (OS), 1898 (Thom map). Unnamed 1907 (OS).

Seaview Cottage, Howth Rd [south] N. (718163, 736550). Seaview Cottage 1890 (OS), 1897 (*Thom*). Unnamed 1907 (OS). Seaview Cottage 1909 (Electoral rolls).

Whitehall Cottages, Clontarf Rd [west] N. (718652, 736178). Whitehall Cottages 1890 (OS), 1898 (Thom map). 1 of 2 houses demolished by 1907 (OS).

Willmount, Howth Rd [south] S. (718207, 736523). Wilmont 1890; unnamed 1907 (OS). Willmount 1909 (Electoral rolls).

Tristram Villas, St Lawrence Rd W. (718871, 736696). Tristram Villas 1894 (*Thom*); 'newly-erected' 1895 (*Ir. Times* 19.10.1895); 1904 (*Thom*).

Lucerne, Castle Ave [south] E. (719343, 736266). Built in 1896 (Gogarty, 118). Lucerne 1907, 1935; unnamed 1970–71 (OS). Divided into apartments by 2013 (Gogarty, 118).

Waverley, Howth Rd [south] S. (718161, 736486). Built in 1896 (Gogarty, 177). Waverley 1903 (Vernon papers), 1909 (Electoral rolls), 2017 (nameplate).

Woodstock, Howth Rd [south] S. (718156, 736480). Built in 1896 (Gogarty, 177). Woodstock 1903 (Vernon papers), 1909 (Electoral rolls).

Bleak House, Marino Ave N. (718041, 736693). 1898 (Thom map).

Altona House, Howth Rd [south] W. (718188, 736505). Altona 1897 (*Thom*), 1901 (*Ir. Times* 11.12.1901). Unnamed 1907 (OS). Altona House 1909 (Electoral rolls).

Castlewood House, Haddon Rd W., formerly part of Castlewood Terrace (see below). Castlewood House 1897 (*Thom*), 1903 (Vernon papers). Unnamed 1907 (OS). Castlewood House 1909 (Electoral rolls), 2017 (nameplate).

Nora Brook, Howth Rd [south] S. (719004, 736788). Nora Brook 1897 (*Thom*), 1907, 1935; unnamed 1971 (OS). Demolished in 2016 (local information). In residential development 2017.

Glenavon, Howth Rd [south] W. (718133, 736527). Glenavon, for sale 1902 (*Ir. Times* 17.1.1902). Unnamed 1907 (OS). Glenavon 1909 (Electoral rolls), 2017 (nameplate).

Glenbower, Howth Rd [south] W. (718125, 736455). Glenbower, for sale 1902 (*Ir. Times* 17.1.1902). Unnamed 1907 (OS). Glenbower 1909 (Electoral rolls), 2017 (nameplate).

Glendalough, Howth Rd [south] W. (718139, 736530). Glendalough, for sale 1902 (*Ir. Times* 17.1.1902). Unnamed 1907 (OS). Glendalough 1909 (Electoral rolls), 2017 (nameplate).

Redcourt, Seafield Rd East N. (720869, 736333). Redcourt 1904 (Gogarty, 122), 1907–70 (OS). Demolished, laid over by Redcourt Oaks by 2004 (*Ir. Times* 3.6.2004).

Fingal, Clontarf Rd [mid] N. (720330, 735771). Unnamed 1907; Fingal 1936 (OS).

Lauraville, Howth Rd [south] S. (719168, 736951). Lauraville 1907, 1935 (OS).

St Helen's, Haddon Rd E. (719067, 736033). St Helen's 1907, 1936 (OS), 2017 (nameplate).

Holly Lodge, Howth Rd [south] W. (718156, 736555). Holly Lodge 1909 (Electoral rolls), 1920 (*Ir. Times* 17.8.1920).

Ferndale, Howth Rd [north] S. (719221, 736992). Ferndale 1935 (OS), 2017 (gatepost inscription).

Redpark, Howth Rd [south] S. (719188, 736965). Red Park 1935 (OS). Redpark 2017 (nameplate).

Dumyat, Lawrence Grove E. (718808, 736707). 1935–6 (OS).

Sunville, Copeland Ave S. (718199, 736576). 1935–6 (OS).

Presbytery, Clontarf Rd [mid] N. (719997, 735945), associated with St John the Baptist Catholic Church (see **11** Religion). Presbytery 1936 (OS). Built over by Holy Faith secondary school in 1953 (see **20** Education).

Caragh, Castle Ave [south] S. (719307, 736272). 1970–71 (OS), 2017 (nameplate).

The Lodge, Castle Ave [south] S. (719316, 736258). 1970–71 (OS).

Almshouses and private asylums

Widows' asylum, Belgrove Rd [south] W. (719906, 735997). Alms house for widows 1836 (OSN). Almshouse for 12 widows 1837 (Lewis, i, 376). Widow's asylum 1843, 1868 (OS). Widows' alms house 1894 (*Thom*). Demolished by 1907 (OS).

Alms house, Belgrove Rd [south] W., site unknown. Revd Dr Reed 1845 (Val. 1).

Alms house and widows asylum, Belgrove Rd [south] W., site unknown. Revd Dr Reed 1845 (Val. 1).

House for poor widows, Belgrove Rd [south] W., site unknown. Revd Dr Reed 1845 (Val. 1).

Asylum, Vernon Ave [west] S., in former Verville (see above). Private asylum for ladies, established in 1859 (Gogarty, 33–4). Verville 1868, 1907 (OS), 1911 (Vernon papers). Asylum 1911 (Census returns). Verville Retreat (private mental hospital) 1935; hospital 1971, 2016 (OS).

Rows and terraces

The Sheds, Clontarf Rd [mid] N. (720099, 735841). Sheds of Clontarf 1785 (Laporte). The Sheds of Clontarfe 1785 (Wheatley). 'Old cabins now standing at the Sheds' 1806 (Vernon papers). Sheds of Hoath and Clontarf 1812 (King). Clontarf Sheds 1850 (Val. 2). The Sheds 1857 (Vernon papers). Clontarf Sheds 1868 (OS), 1901 (*Thom*). The Sheds 1911 (Census returns). See also **10** Streets: Clontarf Road [mid]; **14** Primary production: Sheds of Clontarf.

Snugboro, St Joseph's Sq. (719996, 735992). 200 families removed from former dwellings for building of new church (see **11** Religion: St John the Baptist Catholic Church) in *c.* 1837 (Gogarty, 137; Lynch, 48). Snugborough 1855 (Val. 3). 'Rookeries termed Snugboro' 1861 (*Ir. Builder* 1.7.1861). Snugborough 1863 (*Thom*); 20 cottages 1889; Snugboro 1899 (*FJ* 16.11.1889, 12.5.1899); 'in a very ruinous state', to be improved 1905 (Vernon papers). See also **10** Streets: St Joseph's Square.

St John's Terrace, Clontarf Rd [mid] N. (720027, 735886). Built in 1843 (Gogarty, 167). St John's Terrace 1846 (*FJ* 8.5.1846), 1850 (Val. 2), 1868–1936 (OS).

Vernon Terrace, Vernon Ave [south] E. (720112, 736161). Unnamed 1843; Crampton Villa 1868; Vernon Terrace 1907, 1936; unnamed 1970; partially demolished by 2016 (OS).

Hillview Terrace, Clontarf Rd [mid] N. (720141, 735804). Built in 1846 (Gogarty, 150). Hillview Terrace 1856 (*FJ* 31.1.1856). Hill View Terrace 1868 (OS). Hillview Terrace 1894 (*FJ* 10.9.1894). Unnamed 1907 (OS). Hillview Terrace 1911 (Census returns). Extant 2013 (Gogarty, 151).

Warrenpoint, Haddon Rd W. (718973, 736048). Built in 1847 (Gogarty, 96). Warrenpoint 1852 (*Thom*), 1868–1936 (OS).
   Lodge: gate lodge 1864 (Val. 3); lodge 1890–1936 (OS); private residence 2017.

Rutland Terrace, Clontarf Rd [mid] N. (720169, 735792). Rutland Terrace 1850 (Val. 2), 1861 (*Ir. Builder* 1.7.1861), 1868 (OS).

Seaview Terrace, Clontarf Rd [west] N. (718871, 736080). Seaview Terrace 1850 (*Thom*), 1864 (Val. 3). Unnamed 1868 (OS). Seaview Terrace 1888 (Vernon papers), 1890 (OS), 1903 (*Thom*). Unnamed 1907 (OS). Seaview Terrace 1909 (Electoral rolls).

Vernon Parade, Clontarf Rd [west] N. (718216, 736317). Vernon Parade 1850 (Val. 2), 1868, 1890 (OS), 1898 (Thom map). Unnamed 1907 (OS). Vernon Parade 1908 (*Thom*).

Ormond Terrace, Vernon Ave [south] E. (720110, 735966). Ormond Terrace 1851 (Gogarty, 138), 1857 (*FJ* 21.3.1857). Ormonde Terrace 1861 (*Thom*). Ormond Terrace 1868 (OS), 1901 (Census returns).

Annesbrook Terrace, Clontarf Rd [west] N., on site of former Annsbrook (see above). Annsbrook 1852 (*Thom*). Anns Brook 1868 (OS). Annesbrook 1870 (*Thom*). Anns Brook, pedestal 1890; Anns Brook 1907 (OS). Annesbook Terrace 1911 (Census returns). Demolished by 1971 (OS).

Rossborough Terrace, Vernon Ave [south] W. (720065, 735972). Rossborough Terrace 1852; Rosborough Cottages 1861 (*Thom*), 1868 (Val. 3), 1897 (*Thom*). Rossborough Terrace 1903 (*Thom*), 1911 (Census returns).

Walpole Terrace, Castle Ave [south] W. (719238, 736241). Built in 1859 (Gogarty, 132). Walpole Terrace 1861 (*Thom*), 1868–1935 (OS), 2017 (nameplate).

Rostrevor Terrace, Clontarf Rd [mid] N. (719937, 735908). Built in 1861 (Gogarty, 147). Rostrevor Terrace 1868 (OS), 1889 (Vernon papers). Unnamed 1907 (OS). Rostrevor Terrace 1911 (Census returns).

Alexandra Terrace, Clontarf Rd [mid] N. (720194, 735781). Built by 1863 (Gogarty, 152). Alexandra Terrace 1864 (*Thom*), 1868 (OS), 1897 (Vernon papers). Unnamed 1907 (OS). Two of 5 houses demolished, built over by Vernon Court apartments by 2013 (Gogarty, 152).

Byrne's Cottages, Clontarf Rd [east] N. (721094 736353). Byrne's Cottages 1863 (*Thom*), 1864 (Val. 3); 6 small cottages 1871; 20 cottages 1949 (*Thom*). Demolished by 1952 (Lynch, 104). See also **10** Streets: Byrne's Hill or Lane.

Seabank Terrace, Clontarf Rd [east] W. (721526, 736696). Seabank Terrace 1863 (*Thom*), 1868, 1907 (OS), 1908 (*Thom*). Sea Bank Terrace 1911 (Census returns). Seabank Terrace 1936 (OS).

Casino Terrace, Malahide Rd E. (717918, 736585). Casino Terrace 1864 (Val. 3), 1868–1907 (OS), 1909 (Electoral rolls). Casino 2017 (nameplate).

Fingal Terrace, Howth Rd [south] N. (718045, 736479). Fingal Terrace 1864 (Val. 3). Fingall Terrace 1868, 1890; unnamed 1907 (OS). Fingal Terrace 1909 (Electoral rolls).

Marino Cottages, Malahide Rd E. (717903, 736566). Marino Cottages 1864 (Val. 3), 1868; Marino Terrace 1889, 1907 (OS). Marino Cottages 2017 (nameplate).

Winston Ville, Malahide Rd E. (717952, 736673). Winstonville 1864 (Val. 3). Winston Ville 1868; Wiston Ville 1889 (OS), 1898 (Thom map). Unnamed 1907 (OS). Winston Villas 1909 (Electoral rolls). Winston Ville 2016 (OS). Winstonville House, Winston Ville 2017 (nameplate).

Hollybrook Terrace, Howth Rd [south] E. (718247, 736551). Hollybrook Terrace 1865 (Val. 3), 1868, 1890; unnamed 1907 (OS). Hollybrook Terrace 1909 (Electoral rolls). Unnamed 1935–2016 (OS). Private residence 2017.

Seapoint Terrace, Clontarf Rd [mid] N. (720242, 735768). Built by 1865 (Gogarty, 153). Sea Point Terrace 1868; unnamed 1907 (OS). Seapoint Terrace 1908, 1929 (*Thom*).

Victoria Terrace, Clontarf Rd [mid] N. (719824, 735931). Victoria Terrace 1865 (*Thom*), 1868 (OS). Victoria Place 1870 (*Thom*). Victoria Terrace 1884 (Vernon papers), 1907, 1936; unnamed 1970 (OS). Refurbished in 1990 (*Ir. Times* 25.10.1990). Victoria Terrace 2016 (OS), 2017 (nameplate).

Mooney's Cottages, Conquer Hill Rd E. (720501, 735869). Unnamed 1868 (OS). Poor housing conditions 1894 (*FJ* 9.5.1894). Mooney's Lane Cottages 1894 (Vernon papers). Mooney's Cottages 1898 (*Thom*), 1901 (Census returns). Mooney's Lane housing scheme, 47 new houses planned 1903 (*Ir. Times* 25.3.1903). New houses built in 1904 (DIA). Mooney's Cottages 1905 (*Ir. Builder* 11.3.1905). Unnamed 1907 (OS). Mooney's Cottages 1911 (Census returns).

SEAFRONT HOUSES, EARLY 20TH CENT.

Clontarf. Dublin

Telleden Cottages, Clontarf Rd [east] W. (721387, 736556). Telleden 1868 (OS). Tellenden 1897 (*Thom*). Unnamed 1907 (OS). Telleden Cottages 1911 (Census returns).

Woodside Terrace, Vernon Ave [south] W., incorporating former Woodside (see above). Woodside Terrace, formed of 2 existing houses in 1872 (Gogarty, 105). Woodside 1879, 1897 (Vernon papers). Unnamed 1907 (OS). Woodside 1911 (Census returns). Extant 2013 (Gogarty, 105). Private residence 2017.

Charlemont Terrace, Malahide Rd E. (717940, 736639). Charlemont Terrace 1875 (Val. 3), 1889, 1907 (OS), 1909 (Electoral rolls), 2017 (nameplate).

St Anne's Villas, Clontarf Rd [east] W. (721383, 736510). Built in 1880–83 (Gogarty, 174). St Anne's Villas 1907 (OS). St Anne's Terrace 1911 (Census returns). St Anne's Villas 1935 (OS).

Aloysius Terrace, St Lawrence Rd E. (718932, 736748). Built by 1883 (Gogarty, 165–6). Aloysius Terrace 1889 (OS), 1898 (*Thom* map).

Esplanade Villas, Clontarf Rd [east] W. (721394, 736529). Esplanade Villas 1883, 1897 (*Thom*). Unnamed 1907; Esplanade Villas 1935 (OS).

Hope Terrace, St Lawrence Rd W. (718744, 736233). Built by 1883 (Gogarty, 165–6). Hope Terrace 1890 (OS), 1898 (*Thom* map). Unnamed 1907 (OS). Hope Terrace 1909 (Electoral rolls), 2017 (nameplate).

Laird Terrace, St Lawrence Rd E. (718849, 736434). Built by 1883 (Gogarty, 165–6). Laird Terrace 1890 (OS), 1898 (*Thom* map), 2017 (nameplate).

Madeley Terrace, St Lawrence Rd E. (718838, 736390). Built by 1883 (Gogarty, 165–6). Madeley Terrace 1890 (OS), 1898 (*Thom* map).

Pulteney Terrace, St Lawrence Rd E. (718909, 736663). Built by 1883 (Gogarty, 165–6). Pulteney Terrace 1889 (OS), 1898 (*Thom* map), 2017 (nameplate).

The Mall, St Lawrence Rd E. (718804, 736273). Built by 1883 (Gogarty, 165–6). The Mall 1890 (OS).

St Patrick's Terrace, St Lawrence Rd E. (718826, 736348). Built in 1887 (Gogarty, 166). St Patrick's Terrace 1890 (OS), 1898 (*Thom* map).

Alpha Cottages, Malahide Rd E. (717896, 736552). 1889, 1907 (OS), 1909 (Electoral rolls).

Como Terrace, Howth Rd [south] S. (718190, 736509). Como Terrace 1890 (OS), 1898 (*Thom* map). Unnamed 1907 (OS). Como Terrace 1909 (Electoral rolls).

Rialto Terrace, Howth Rd [south] S. (718169, 736493). Rialto Terrace 1890 (OS). Rialto 1897 (*Thom*). Rialto Terrace 1898 (*Thom* map).

Victoria Terrace, St Lawrence Rd E. (718813, 736303). 1890 (OS).

Whitehall Terrace, Clontarf Rd [west] N. (718677, 736169). 1890 (OS), 1904 (*Thom*).

Seafield Terrace, Seafield Rd West S. (719559, 736407). Built in *c.* 1890–98 (Gogarty, 175). Seafield Terrace 1907, 1935 (OS).

Zetland Terrace, St Lawrence Rd E. (718813, 736300). 5 houses, built in 1891 (Gogarty, 166). Zetland Terrace 1892 (*Thom*), 1908–15 (Electoral rolls).

Dagmar Villas, Vernon Ave [south] E. (720093, 735879). Dagmar Villas 1892 (Vernon papers), 1908 (*Thom*), 1910 (Gogarty, 138). Daemar Villas 1911 (Census returns). Dagmar Villas 1924 (*Ir. Times* 24.1.1924).

Ellesmere, St Lawrence Rd E. (718906, 736640). Ellesmere, 4 houses, incorporating former Ellesmere (see above) 1893 (Val. 3); 1894 (*Thom*). Unnamed 1907 (OS). Ellesmere 1908 (*Thom*).

Belview Terrace, Clontarf Rd [east] N. (721319, 736431). Built by 1894 (Gogarty, 158). Belview Terrace 1907 (OS). Bellview Terrace 1909 (Electoral rolls). Belview Terrace 1935 (OS).

St George's Terrace, St Lawrence Rd E. (718864, 736482). 1896 (*Thom*), 1908–15 (Electoral rolls).

Albert Terrace, Clontarf Rd [east] N. (721182, 736244). New row of 5 houses 1897 (*Thom*). Albert Terrace 1907, 1936 (OS).

Castlewood Terrace, Haddon Rd W. (719030, 736045). Castlewood Terrace 1899 (*Thom*). Unnamed 1907 (OS). Castlewood Terrace 1908 (*Thom*), 1914 (Electoral rolls). See also above, Castlewood House.

Beechfield Terrace, Vernon Ave [south] W. (72007, 736072). Building commenced in 1901 (Gogarty, 136). Beechfield Terrace 1907 (OS). Beachfield Terrace 1910 (Vernon papers). Beechfield Terrace 1936 (OS).

Conquer Hill Terrace, Clontarf Rd [east] N. (720869, 736008). Conquer Hill, 12 houses 1901 (Census returns). Unnamed 1907 (OS). Conquer Hill 1908 (*Thom*). Conquer Hill Terrace 1909 (Electoral rolls). Conquer Hill 1911 (Census returns). Conquer Hill Terrace 1949 (*Thom*).

Conquer Terrace, Clontarf Rd [east] N., site unknown, near Crab Lake (see **14** Primary production). 1903 (*Thom*), 1911 (Census returns), 1929 (*Thom*).

Pretoria Villas, Clontarf Rd [east] N. (720752, 735947). 1903 (*Thom*), 1907, 1936 (OS).

Ardilaun Villas, Clontarf Rd [east] N. (721344, 736460). 1907, 1935 (OS).

Bull Wall Cottages, Bull Wall N. (see **18** Utilities) (721345, 735806). Unnamed 1907; Bull Wall Cottages 1936–2016 (OS).

Redhall Terrace, Vernon Ave [south] E. (720110, 735994). Unnamed 1907 (OS). Redhall Terrace 1910 (Vernon papers), 1911 (Census returns), 1915 (Gogarty, 140).

Stiles Cottages, The Stiles Court S. (719242, 736738). Unnamed 1907; Stiles Cottages 1935; unnamed 1970–71; extended by 2016 (OS).

Housing estates and flat complexes

Furry Park estate, Howth Rd [north] S. (719817, 737341). Development of 150 houses approved in 1936 (Gogarty, 208). See also **10** Streets: Furry Park Road.

Vernon Park, Vernon Ave [north] E. (720263, 736627). 62 houses laid out in 1936 (Gogarty, 191). Vernon Park 1939 (*Thom*), 1970, 2016 (OS).

Oakley Park, Vernon Ave [north] W., on site of former Oakley (see above). Oakley Estate 1960 (*Ir. Times* 30.11.1960). Oakley Park 1970, 2016 (OS). See also **10** Streets: Oakley Park.

Seapark Apartments, Mount Prospect Ave [west] N., on site of former Sea Park (see above). Built in 1967 (Gogarty, 38). Flats, 2 car parks 1970; Seapark, 2 car parks 2016 (OS).

Appendix

Clontarf: houses and terraces, listed by road or street

1897

The residences listed here are those named in 1897 (*Thom*), when consecutive numbering of the houses began to be adopted. This demonstrates the range of named houses and terraces in Clontarf immediately prior to a period of construction and expansion. It also represents a mid-point between the publication of the 1890 and 1907 OS maps.

Castle Ave: Ardnardeen, Baymount, Belgrove, Blackheath, Castle Terrace, Clontarf Castle, Danesfort, Everton, Frankfort House, Hughenden, Manor House, Moyville, Sandon, The Rectory, Tivoli House.

Clontarf Rd: Adelaide Terrace, Albert Terrace, Alexandra Terrace, Annesbrook, Ardilaun Villas, Belgrove Villas, Belview Terrace, Cabra Villas, Gresham's Buildings, Hillview Terrace, Kingscourt House, Mountain View, Rostrevor Terrace, St Anne's Villas, St John's Terrace, Seabank Terrace, Seapoint Terrace, Seatonville, Seaview Terrace, The Manse, Vernon Parade, Victoria Terrace, Walpole Terrace, Warrenpoint.

Clontarf Sheds: Grace Dieu, Vernon House.

Conquer Hill Rd: Mooney's Cottages.

Dollymount: Baymount Castle, Baymount Cottage, Bedford Lodge, Belvidere House, Boroihme Lodge, Danesfield, Esplanade Villas, Kinkora, Lakeview, Mount Vernon, Mount Vernon Cottages, Seafield, Tellenden.

Fortview: Bedford Lodge, Fortview House, Fortview Villa, Leinster Lodge, South View, Virginia Lodge.

Greenlanes: Bayview House, Castilla, Oakley, Seapark, Verville, Woodpark.

Haddon Rd: Auburn, Castlewood House, St Raphael's.

Hollybrook Park: Ashbrook, Auburn Villa, Glaslinn, Glenvar, Greenmount, Hollybrook, Hollybrook Cottage, Hollybrook Park, Hollybrook Park House, Nora Brook, St James's, Silver Acre.

Howth Rd: Altona, Como Terrace, Fingal Terrace, Flora Ville, Frankville, George's Terrace, Hollybrook, Hollybrook Lodge, Hollybrook Terrace, Mount Temple, Rialto, Seaview Cottage.

Malahide Rd: Marino Terrace.

Mount Prospect Ave: St Anne's.

St Lawrence Rd: Annadale, Ardilaun, Avoneal, Bal Ivor, Belvoir, Brooklyn, Castle House, Croft's House, Cullrathin, Dungooley, Elmina, Garrynacurry House, Girniegoe, Glenmaurice House, Hollywood, Leinster Lodge, Lincluden, Madeley, Mentone, St Lawrence House, San Remo, Seaforth, South View, Trasna, Valetta, Virginia Lodge, Wilford, Woodside, Woodville.

Seafield Ave: Auburn Lodge, Rosetta, Seafield Cottage.

Seaview: Moira Lodge, Ontario.

Seaview Ave: Blandford Lodge, Cabra Parade, Cozy Lodge, North Bank Cottage, Rosemount, Seaview House.

Strandville: Anna Villa, Beachfield House, Beachfield Lodge, Blandford Lodge, Brookside, St Edmund's, Springvale, Strand House, Strandvilla, Strandville Cottage, Strandville Lodge.

Strandville Ave: Eagle Ville, Simla Lodge, Strandville House, Willowbrook.

Vernon Ave: Convent House, Dagmar Villas, Eleanor Terrace, Merchamp, Ormond Hall, Ormond Villa, Palmyra, Rossborough Cottages, Rutland House, Sunnyside, The Cottage, Woodside (*Thom*).

1909

Castle Ave: Balmoral Lodge, Clontarf Castle, Mount Oriel, Moyville, Walpole Terrace.

Charlemont Rd: Cecilia Terrace.

Clontarf Rd: Anna Villa, Annesbrook, Baymount, Bedford Lodge, Beechfield, Belview Terrace, Boroimhe Lodge, Brookside Cottage, Cabra Villas, Danesfort, Fingal House, Gresham Buildings, Hillview Terrace, Mount Vernon, Pretoria Villas, Rostrevor Terrace, St Anne's, St Anne's Villas, St Edmond's, St Ellen's Villas, St John's Terrace, Seabank Terrace, Seapoint Terrace, Seaview Terrace, Strandville Lodge, Summerville, Tudor House, Unavarra, Victoria Terrace, Victoria Villas.

Conquer Hill: Clareville, Conquer Hill Terrace.

Dollymount: Albert Terrace, Bellview Terrace.

Haddon Rd: Castlewood House, Glenomra, St Helen's, Warrenpoint.

Hollybrook Park: Glencoe, Hollybrook House, St Dymphna's, Tullyallan.

Hollybrook Rd: Ellerslie, Glasslynn, Hollybrook Cottage.

Howth Rd: Altona House, Ashbrook, Auburn Villa, Avora, Belvidere, Belview, Clandeboye, Como Terrace, Dalriada, Elsinore, Fingal Terrace, Floraville, Frankville, Freame Mount, Glenarm, Glenavon, Glenbeight, Glenbower, Glenbrook, Glendalough, Glenvale, Glenvar, Glenwood, Greenmount, Greenore, Hazeldene, Holly Lodge, Hollybrook, Hollybrook Lodge, Hollybrook Terrace, Howth Castle, Iona, Killester Park, Lyndale, Mentana, Mount Temple, Norabrook, Railway Cottage, Rialto House, Riga House, St Denis, St

George's Terrace, St Joseph's, St Michael's, Seaview Cottage, The Villa, Waverley, Williamville, Willmount, Woodfield, Woodstock.

Malahide Rd: Alpha Cottages, Casino Terrace, Charlemont Terrace, Failta, Glenmore, Marino Demesne, Marino House, Winston Villas.

St Lawrence Rd: Ballyneely House, Crofton House, Girnigoe, Glencaura, Hollywood, Hope Terrace, Lincluden, St George's Terrace, The Ranche, Trasna, Wilford, Zetland Terrace.

Seafield Rd: Redcourt.

Seafield Rd East: Holmdale, Kentdene, Seafield Cottage.

Strandville Ave East: Eagleville, Simla Lodge, Strandville House, Strandville Lodge, Willow Brook.

Vernon Ave: Beachfield Terrace, Dagmar Villas, Merchamp, Rutland House, Woodside Villa (Electoral rolls).

Overleaf: Dublin from railway bridge at Hollybrook,
c. 1850, by Edward Radclyffe

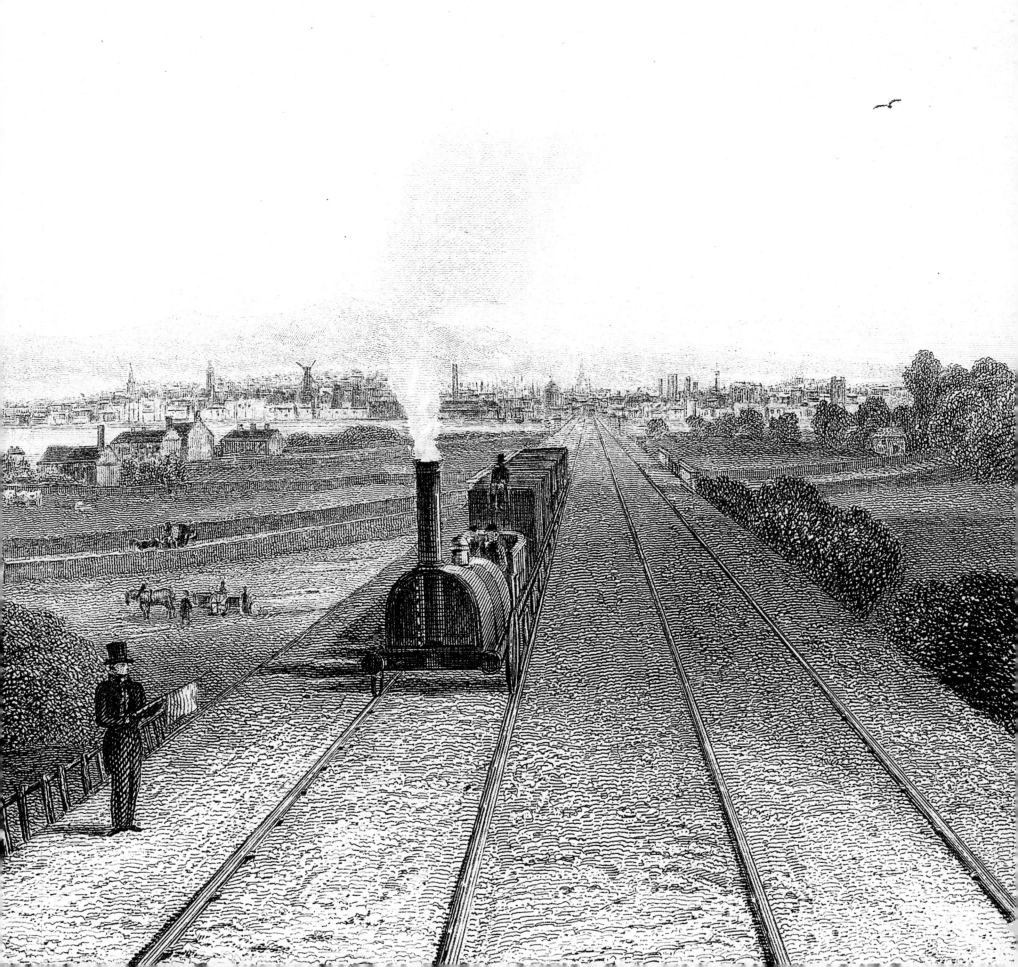

Maps

Changes to the topography of Clontarf are vividly recorded in maps and views. Some of these early views have been used alongside period reconstructions and thematic maps to illustrate the text. The following section, included across the suburbs series, is dedicated to the cartographic record. Maps and plates are presented in a style based on that of the main Irish Historic Towns Atlas series, allowing links to be made between the city of Dublin and its suburbs.

The section begins with the presentation of core maps that follow the guidelines for the European Historic Towns Atlas and allow comparative study. Map 1 shows the suburb in its mid-nineteenth-century setting at 1:50,000 and has been prepared from the first edition of the one-inch to the mile (1:63,360) Ordnance Survey map of Dublin (1860). Map 2, considered the principal map for each atlas, is a large-scale representation of the suburb in the nineteenth century. For this series, this is a reproduction of the original twenty-five inch (1:2500) Ordnance Survey parish map for Co. Dublin (1863–70) at the reduced scale of 1:5000 with an extract at 1:2500 also included. The third core map (Map 3) is a modern Ordnance Survey town plan at 1:5000, which includes contours (3 m intervals) and grid co-ordinates (100 m intervals, Irish Transverse Mercator). Maps 4 and 5, also at 1:5000, depict the urban area in the early to mid-twentieth century and have been compiled using the twenty-five inch (1:2500) Ordnance Survey plans (1906–9) and subsequent revision of 1935–8. Map 6 is an extract from Ordnance Survey Ireland's most recent edition of the Discovery series (1:50,000). Finally, a modern air photograph is included as plate 1 at 1:5000.

Following these are reproductions of historic maps (facsimiles) in chronological order from the seventeenth century onwards. Some of these, such as maps by Thomas Phillips (1685), John Rocque (1760) and the Ordnance Survey (from 1843) cover the city as a whole and comparative extracts may be expected across the Dublin suburbs atlases.

Unlike the town series, which is loose leaf with some folded pages, large maps are spread over multiple pages with an index on p. 80. Pages have perforated edges to allow users to disassemble their atlas, to join and compare the maps, should they so wish. Captions are kept to a minimum, with full details being given on the introductory list on pp 81–2.

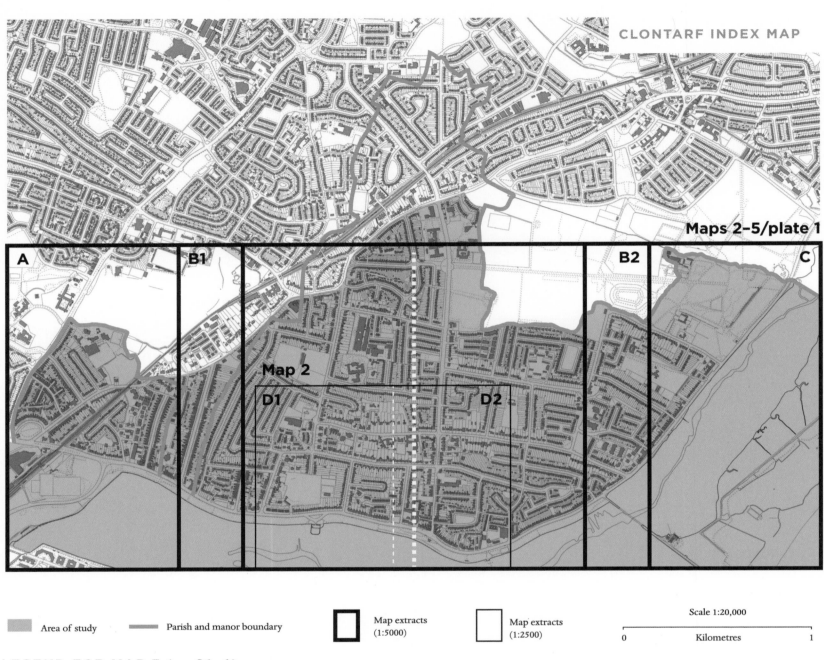

Maps 2–5/plate 1

A B1 B2 C

Map 2

D1 D2

Area of study	Parish and manor boundary	Map extracts (1:5000)

Map extracts (1:2500)

Scale 1:20,000

0 Kilometres 1

LEGEND FOR MAP 3 (pp 91–4)

· · · · · · · · · Townland boundary

━ ━ ━ ━ County boundary

━ ━ ━ ━ ━ Barony boundary

━ ━ ━ ━ Urban district

━ ━ ━ ━ Parish boundary

+ 29.7 Spot height in metres

⌒ 6 Contours in metres

═ ═ ═ ═ ═ ═ ═ Unfenced road or footpath

─ ─ ─ ─ ─ ─ ─ Verge

G S Sta	Garda Síochána (police) station
P O	Post Office
F B	Footbridge
Chy	Chimney
Fn	Fountain
Sch	School
HWM	High Water Mark
LWM	Low Water Mark
ES	Electricity Station
CR	Centre Road / River
UND	Undefined
CYMS	Catholic Young Men's Society
LB	Letter Box
TK	Tank
UDC	Urban District Council

Maps

Map 1   **Dublin city and suburbs, 1860**   83
Ordnance Survey of Ireland, scale 1:50,000
Reproduced courtesy of the National Library of Ireland.
© Ordnance Survey Ireland/Government of Ireland.

Map 2   **Parish of Clontarf, 1868**   84
Ordnance Survey of Ireland, scale 1:5000 (A–C), 1:2500 (D)
Reproduced courtesy of the National Library of Ireland.

Map 3   **Clontarf, 2016**   91
Ordnance Survey Ireland, scale 1:5000
© Ordnance Survey Ireland/Government of Ireland.

Map 4   **Clontarf, 1907**   95
Ordnance Survey of Ireland, scale 1:5000
© Ordnance Survey Ireland/Government of Ireland.

Map 5   **Clontarf, 1935–6**   99
Ordnance Survey of Ireland, scale 1:5000
© Ordnance Survey Ireland/Government of Ireland.

Plate 1   **Aerial view of Clontarf, 2013**   103
Ordnance Survey Ireland, Scale 1:5000
© Ordnance Survey Ireland/Government of Ireland.

Map 6   **Dublin city and suburbs, 2015**   107
Ordnance Survey Ireland, Discovery series, scale 1:50,000
© Ordnance Survey Ireland/Government of Ireland.

Map 7   **Clontarf, 1673, De Gomme**   108
'The city and suburbs of Dublin, from Kilmainham to Rings-End', 1673,
by Bernard de Gomme, extract. Reproduced courtesy of the National Maritime
Museum, Greenwich, P/49 (11).

Map 8   **Clontarf, 1685, Phillips (2)**   108
'Bay and harbour of Dublin', 1685, by Thomas Phillips, extract.
Reproduced courtesy of the British Library, Maps K Top 53 3 2.

Map 9   **Clontarf, 1685, Phillips (1)**   109
'An exact survey of the citty of Dublin and part of the harbour', 1685,
by Thomas Phillips, extract. Reproduced courtesy of the British Library,
Maps K Top 53 8.

Map 10   **Clontarf, late 17th cent., Phillips (1a)**   109
Modified copy of 'An exact survey of the citty of Dublin and
part of the harbour', by Thomas Phillips (Map 9), late 17th cent., extract.
Reproduced courtesy of the Royal Irish Academy, RR MC 3/7.

Map 11   **Clontarf, 1693, Collins**   110
Map of Dublin Bay, from *Great Britain's coasting-pilot*
(London, 1693), extract. Reproduced courtesy of Andrew Bonar Law.

Map 12   **Clontarf, 1717, Bolton**   110
'A map of the strand of the north side of the channel of the river Anna Liffe',
1717, by Thomas Bolton, extract. Reproduced courtesy of Dublin City Library
and Archive.

Map 13   **Clontarf, 1730, Price**   110
'A correct chart of the city and harbour of Dublin', 1730,
by Charles Price, extract. Reproduced courtesy of Andrew Bonar Law.

Map 14   **Clontarf, 1760, Rocque**   111
An actual survey of the county of Dublin, by John Rocque (Dublin, 1760;
reprinted London, 1802), extract. Reproduced courtesy of the Royal Irish Academy,
RR/MC/6/12.

Map 15 **Hollybrook Park, 1812, Longfield (3)** 111
'A map of a holding at Hollybrook Park near Clontarf', 1812,
by John Longfield. Reproduced courtesy of the National Library of Ireland,
21/F/51 (115).

Map 16 **Clontarf, 1803, Bligh** 112
'Survey of the bay of Dublin', 1803, by William Bligh, extract.
Reproduced courtesy of Andrew Bonar Law.

Map 17 **Clontarf, 1805, Sherrard and Brassington** 112
'A map of the boundaries of the county of the city of Dublin
on the north east side thereof', 1805, by Sherrard and Brassington, extract.
Reproduced courtesy of Adam's Auctioneers.

Map 18 **Clontarf, 1816, Taylor** 113
Taylor's map of the environs of Dublin, by John Taylor, scale two inches to one
mile (Dublin, 1816), extract. Reproduced courtesy of the Royal Irish Academy,
RR/31/2/B/1.

Map 19 **Clontarf, 1821, Duncan** 113
Map of the county of Dublin, by William Duncan (Dublin, 1821), extract.
Reproduced courtesy of Andrew Bonar Law.

Map 20 **Manor of Clontarf, 1823, VEM** 114
'Survey of the manor of Clontarf in the barony of Coolock and County of
Dublin. The estate of George Vernon Esquire', 1823, by Sherrard, Brassington
and Greene, scale ten perches to an inch. University College Dublin, School of
History, private collection. With transcribed and printed reference table.

Map 21 **Clontarf, 1843, OS** 116
Ordnance Survey six-inch map of Co. Dublin, 1843, sheets 18 and 19, extract,
reproduced to scale (1:10,560).

Map 22 **Clontarf, 1869–75, OS** 117
Ordnance Survey six-inch map of Co. Dublin, 1869–75, sheets 18 and 19,
extract, reproduced to scale (1:10,560).

Map 23 **Township of Clontarf, 1898, Thom map** 118
'Map of the city of Dublin and its environs', 1898, from *Thom's Irish almanac and
official directory*, extract. Reproduced courtesy of University College Dublin Digital Library.

Map 24 **New Town Plan, 1914, Abercrombie** 119
'City of Dublin New Town Plan, no. 4, zoning plan', 1914, from Patrick
Abercrombie *et al. Dublin of the future: the new town plan* (Dublin, 1922), extract.
Reproduced courtesy of the Royal Irish Academy.

Map 25 **Traffic, 1925, Dublin civic survey** 120
Traffic map from *The Dublin civic survey report* (Liverpool, 1925), extract.
Reproduced courtesy of Arnold Horner.

Map 26 **Clontarf, 1931, OS** 121
Ordnance Survey, Dublin and environs, scale 1:20,000, 1931, extract.
Reproduced courtesy of Trinity College Dublin (Map Library).

Map 27 **Clontarf, 1948, OS** 121
Ordnance Survey, Dublin, popular edition, scale 1:25,000, 1948, extract.
Reproduced courtesy of Trinity College Dublin (Map Library).

Map 28 **Clontarf, 1969, OS** 121
Ordnance Survey, Dublin City North, 8th popular edition,
scale 1:18,000, 1969, extract. © Ordnance Survey Ireland/Government of Ireland.

Map 29 **Further study, 1907** 122
Clontarf base map, redrawn from Ordnance Survey, 1907. Scale 1:10,000.

Map 30 **Further study, 2016** 123
Clontarf base map, Ordnance Survey Ireland, 2016. Scale 1:10,000.
© Ordnance Survey Ireland/Government of Ireland.

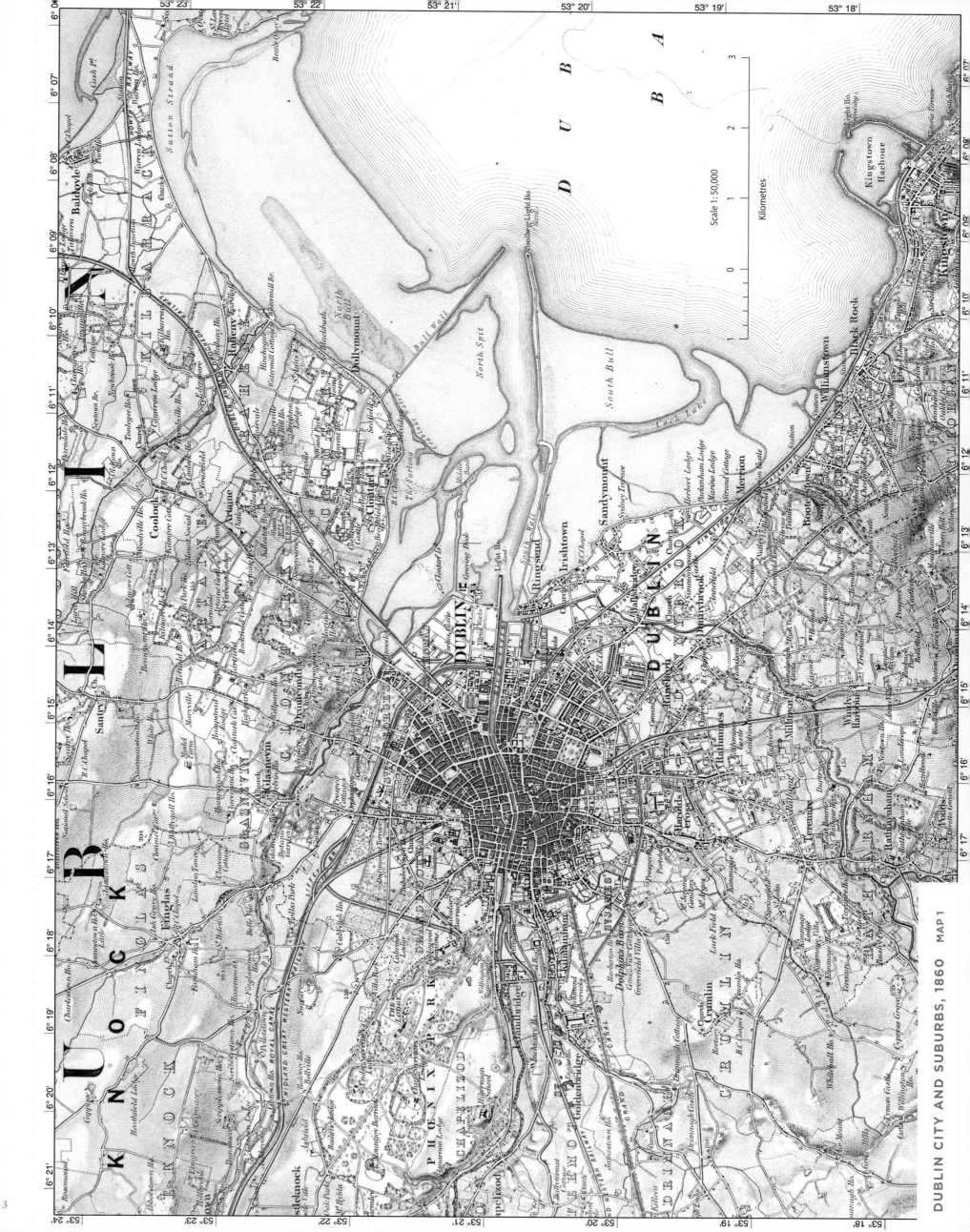

DUBLIN CITY AND SUBURBS, 1860   MAP 1

Clontarf Castle

2

35

36

Yew Park

Grave
Yard
Church
(in Ruins.)

5

Lodge

45

Church

ARE EAST

46

Lodge.....D^d

10

78

Walpole Terrace

9

47

Manor Ho.

8

48

35

34

77

Balmoral Lodge

36

Frankfort Ho.

Moville

23

Brian Boroimhe's Well

79

Clontarf

33

27

80

81

84

Everton

Beachfield Lodge

24

Ardnardeen

Bea

25

28

31

32

82

83

85

Ho.

29

26

Baymount

Lodge

Danes Fort

30

21

Hole made in search of Lead

Hole made in search of Lead

Victori

Scale 1: 2500

25   0   100   200

Metres

Castilla

31

39

37

38

40

41

48

G R

50

Parochial School

42

Lodge

49

43

44

Lod

Lodge

Merchamp
52

Rosetta

62

55

Bellgrove House

53

Woodside

56

57

60

61²

110

59¹

Sum². Ho.

Crampton Villa

111²

61

109

93

95

Ruin.

108

Mound

112

field House

116

Moat Cott

92

96

Clontarf Nat¹. Schools

107

113

Mound

89

97

Widows Asylum

100

101

106

114

Ormond Ter.
Palmyra

118

129

87

88

98

R.C. Chapel

102

99

Avenue

103

104

115

Rutland Place

119

122

a Terrace

Rostrevor Ter.

Constabulary B

Sᵗ John's Terrace

P.H

120

Clontarf Sheds

Att Villa

Bel

Hill View Ter.

Rutland Ter.

Alexandra Ter.

Sea Point

CLONTURK Pʰ

To Malahide

Lodge

Mount Temple

3a

4

5

6

7

8

10

G.P.O 2 Miles

11

12

Elmview Lodge

Marino Avenue

15

Winston Ville

14 19

20

17

9

C L O N T A R F W E S T

18

13

36

21 L

24

23

Casino Terrace

22

Marino Cottages

25

26

27

28

Fingall Terrace

Hollybrook Terrace

33

Hollybrook Lodge

35

34

37

Marino Crescent

29

30

32

DUBLIN AND DROGHEDA RAILWAY

Electric Telegraph

To Howth

37

48

46

Hollybrook Park

49

50

5¹ᵃ

51

Hollybrook Ho.

Hollybrook Cottage

Hollybrook Well

44

45

43

52

53

54

Eagle Ville

Strandville Avenue

56

55

Simla Lodge

40

42

Strandville Ho.

42a.

Vernon Parade

38

39

Halls Brook

Kingscourt Ho.

57

Strand Ville

31

59

Baths

60

Brookside Cottage

Spring Val.

RAILWAY

Telegraph

C L O

Northbank Ho.

Rosemount Cottage

12

15

Seaview Ho.

Warrenpoint

Scale 1 : 5000

100   50   0   100   200   300

Metres

PARISH OF CLONTARF, 1868   MAP 2 (A)

PARISH OF CLONTARF, 1868   MAP 2 (B1)

PARISH OF CLONTARF, 1868   MAP 2 (B2)

St. Anns

Blackbush Lane

HER Lane STOWN

Lodge

Lodge

Bedford Lodge

Lodge

Baymount Castle

Seabank Terrace

Mount Prospect

Bath

Lodge

Mount Vernon

Telleden

Mound

Kinkora

NORTH B
(Clontarf Parish)

Byrnes Lane

Lakeview Cottage

Dollymount

Danesfield Ho.

Lodge

Seafield

Lodge

Cold Harbour

Covered at Extraordinary High Tides

Wooden Bridge

Stone
(Marked 1000 ft)

Covered at Extraordinary High Tides

Coast Guard Station

Covered at Extraordinary High Tides

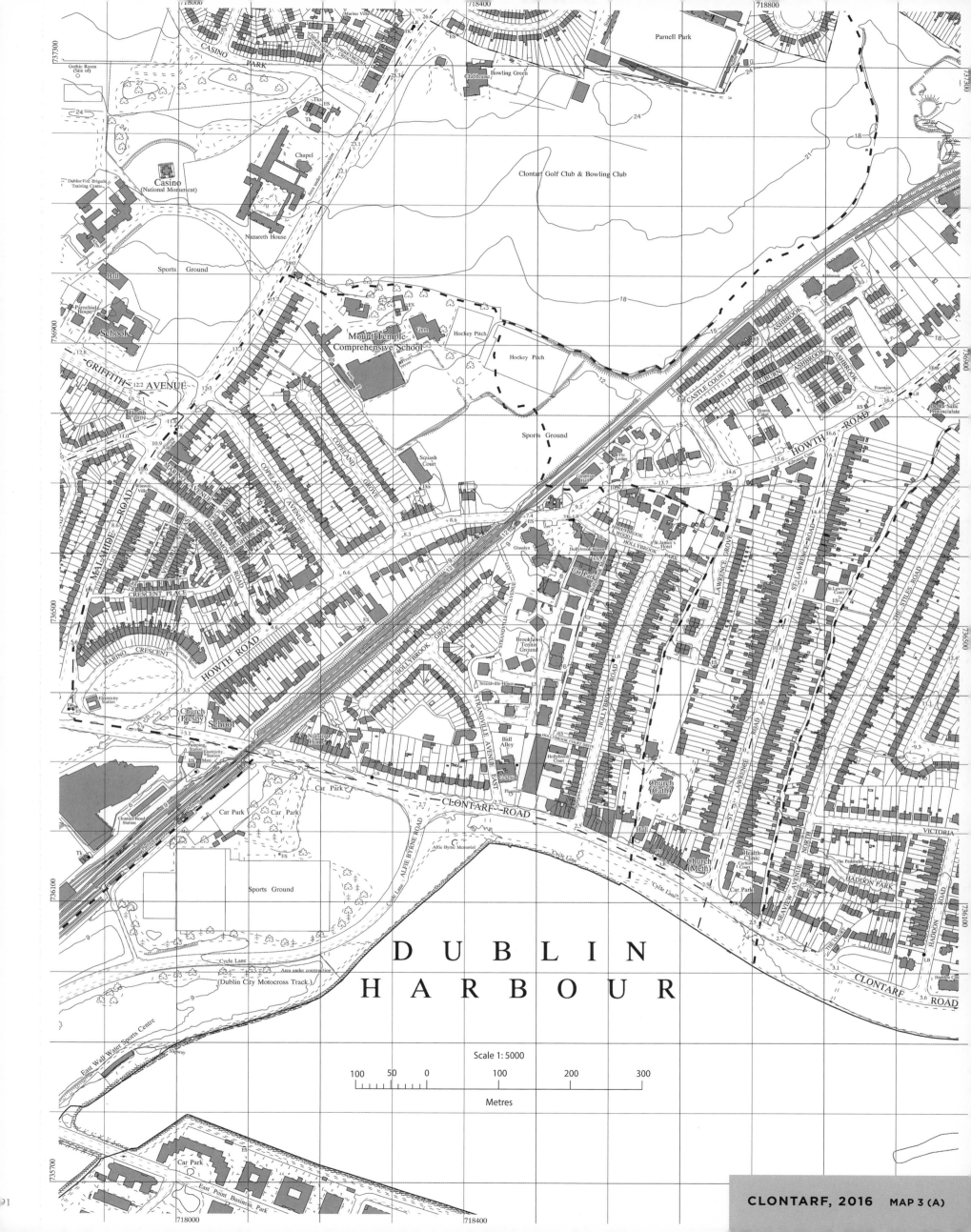

DUBLIN

HARBOUR

Scale 1: 5000

100 50 0 100 200 300

Metres

DUBLIN

HARBOUR

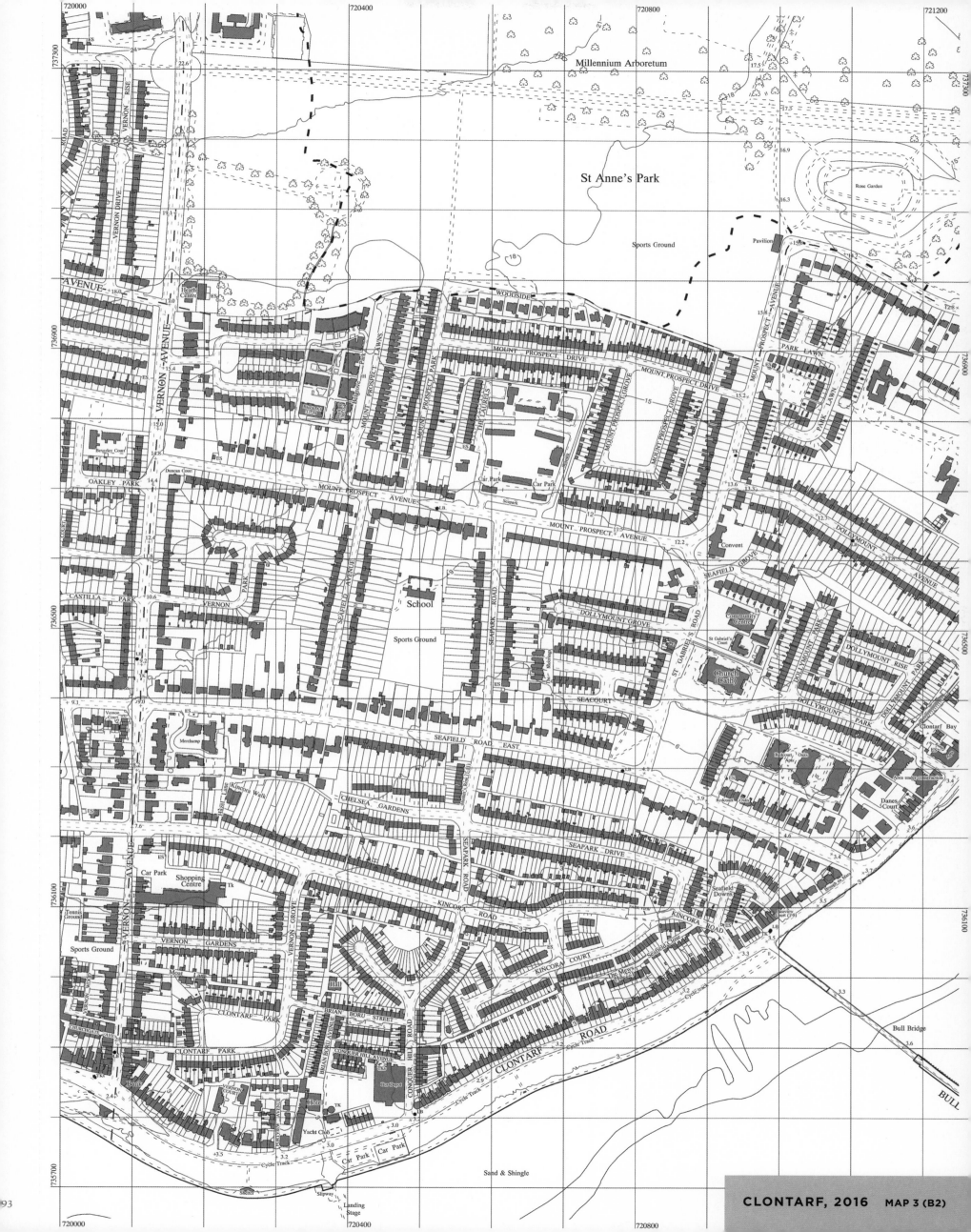

CLONTARF, 2016 MAP 3 (B2)

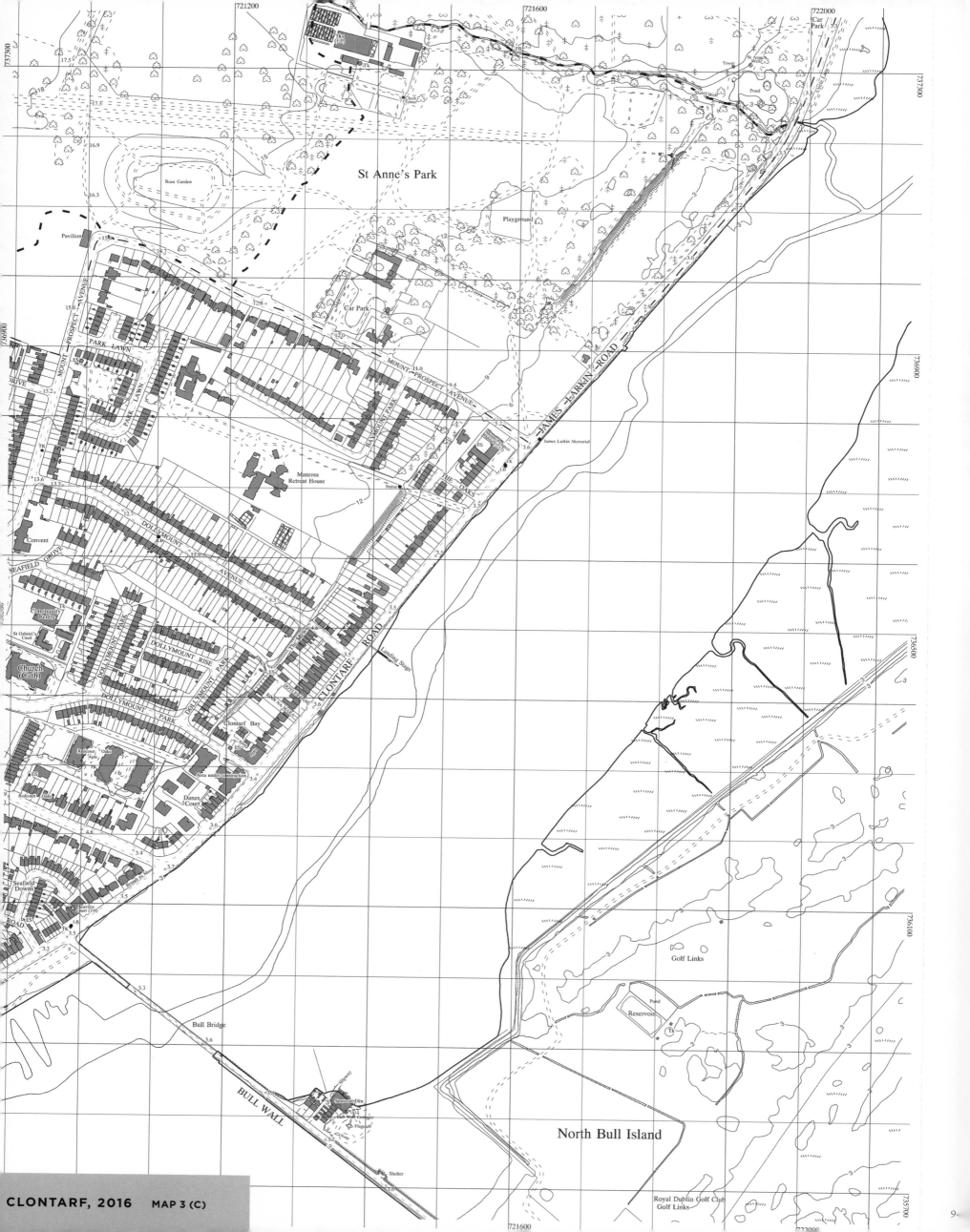

St Anne's Park

Rose Garden

Pavilion

Playground

Car Park

MOUNT PROSPECT AVENUE
PARK LAWN
PARK LAWN
RAYMOUNT PARK
MOUNT PROSPECT AVENUE

JAMES LARKIN ROAD
James Larkin Memorial

Manresa
Retreat House

THE OAKS

Convent

SEAFIELD GROVE

DOLLYMOUNT AVENUE

DOLLYMOUNT PARK

Community
Centre

St Gabriel's
Court

Church
(Cath)

DOLLYMOUNT RISE

DOLLYMOUNT PARK

CLONTARF ROAD

Landing Stage

Clontarf Bay

Redcourt
Apts

Area under construction

Danes
Court

Seafield
Downs

Seaview Court (130)

ROAD

Bull Bridge

Golf Links

Pond
Reservoir

BULL WALL

Seascourt Den

Shelter

North Bull Island

Royal Dublin Golf Club
Golf Links

CLONTARF, 1907   MAP 4 (A)

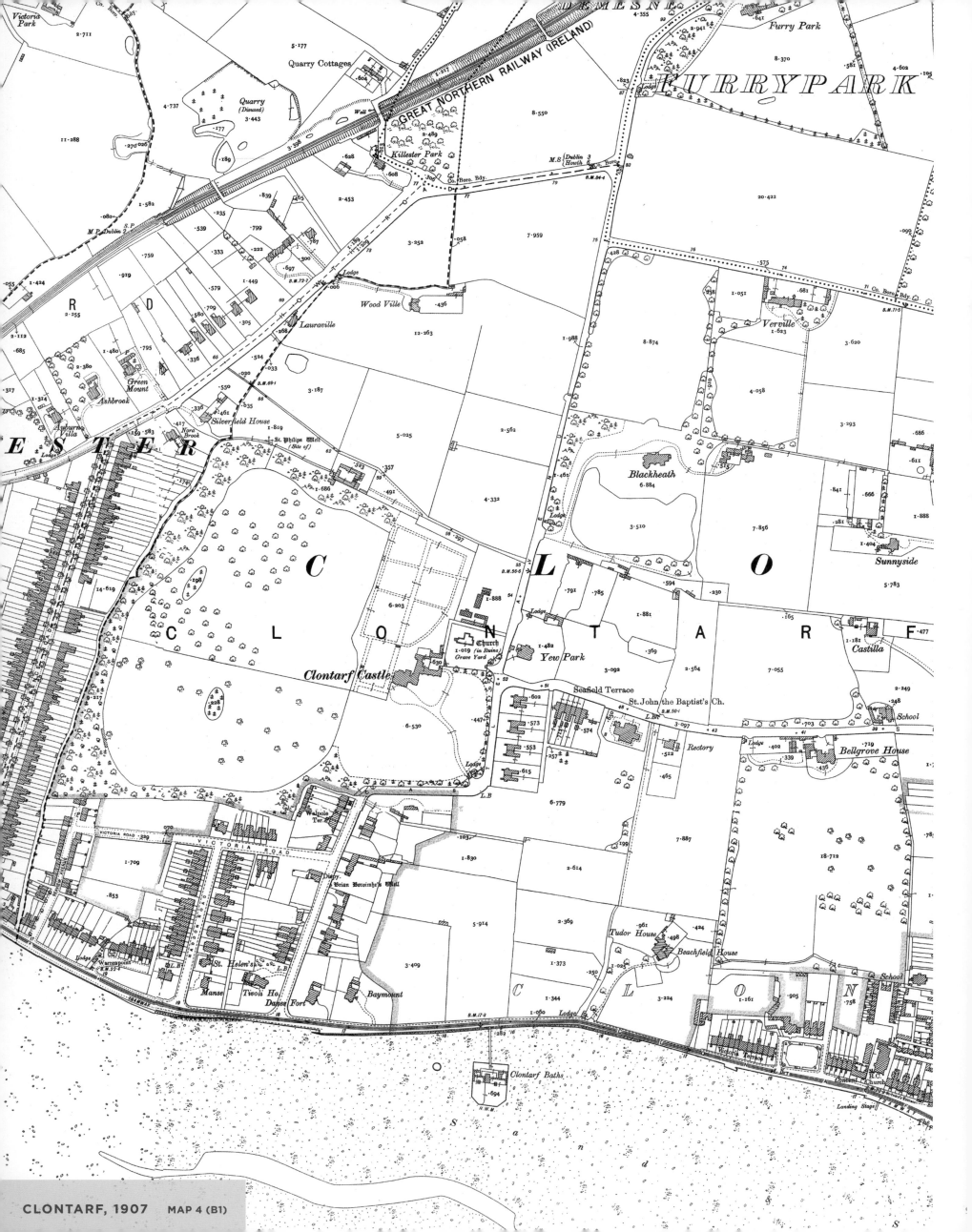

CLONTARF, 1907   MAP 4 (B1)

MAP 4 (B2)   CLONTARF, 1907

CLONTARF, 1907   MAP 4 (C)

CLONTARF, 1935-6   MAP 5 (A)

CLONTARF, 1935-6   MAP 5 (B1)

CLONTARF, 1935-6   MAP 5 (B2)

CLONTARF, 1935-6   MAP 5 (C)

CLONTARF, 1673, DE GOMME   MAP 7

CLONTARF, 1685, PHILLIPS (2)   MAP 8

CLONTARF, 1685, PHILLIPS (1) MAP 9

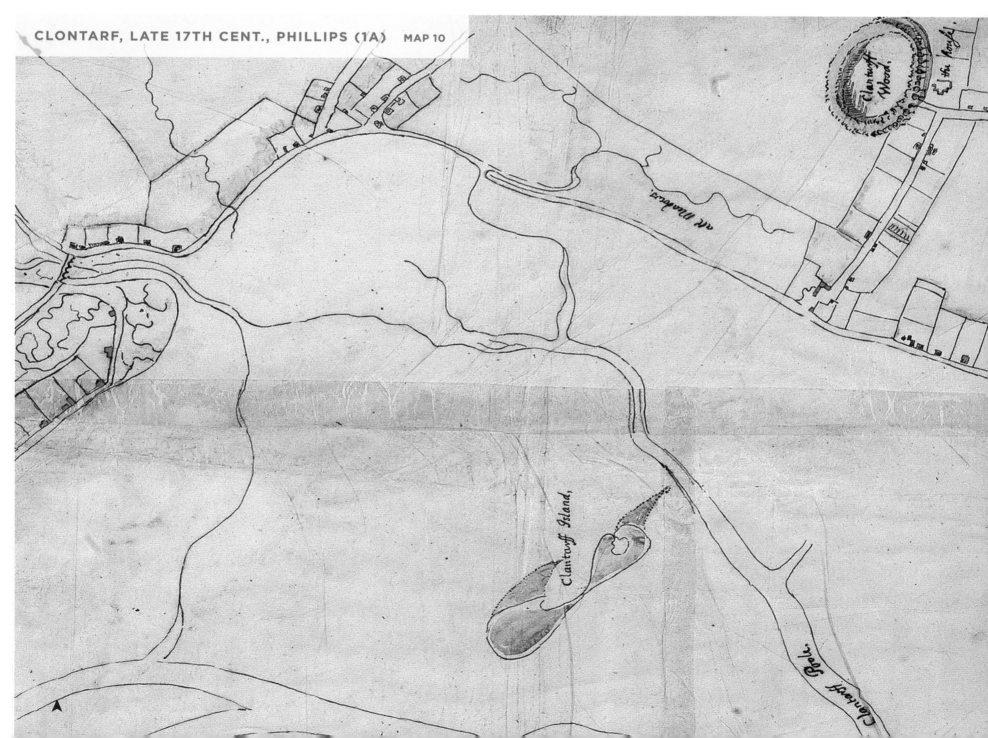

CLONTARF, LATE 17TH CENT., PHILLIPS (1A) MAP 10

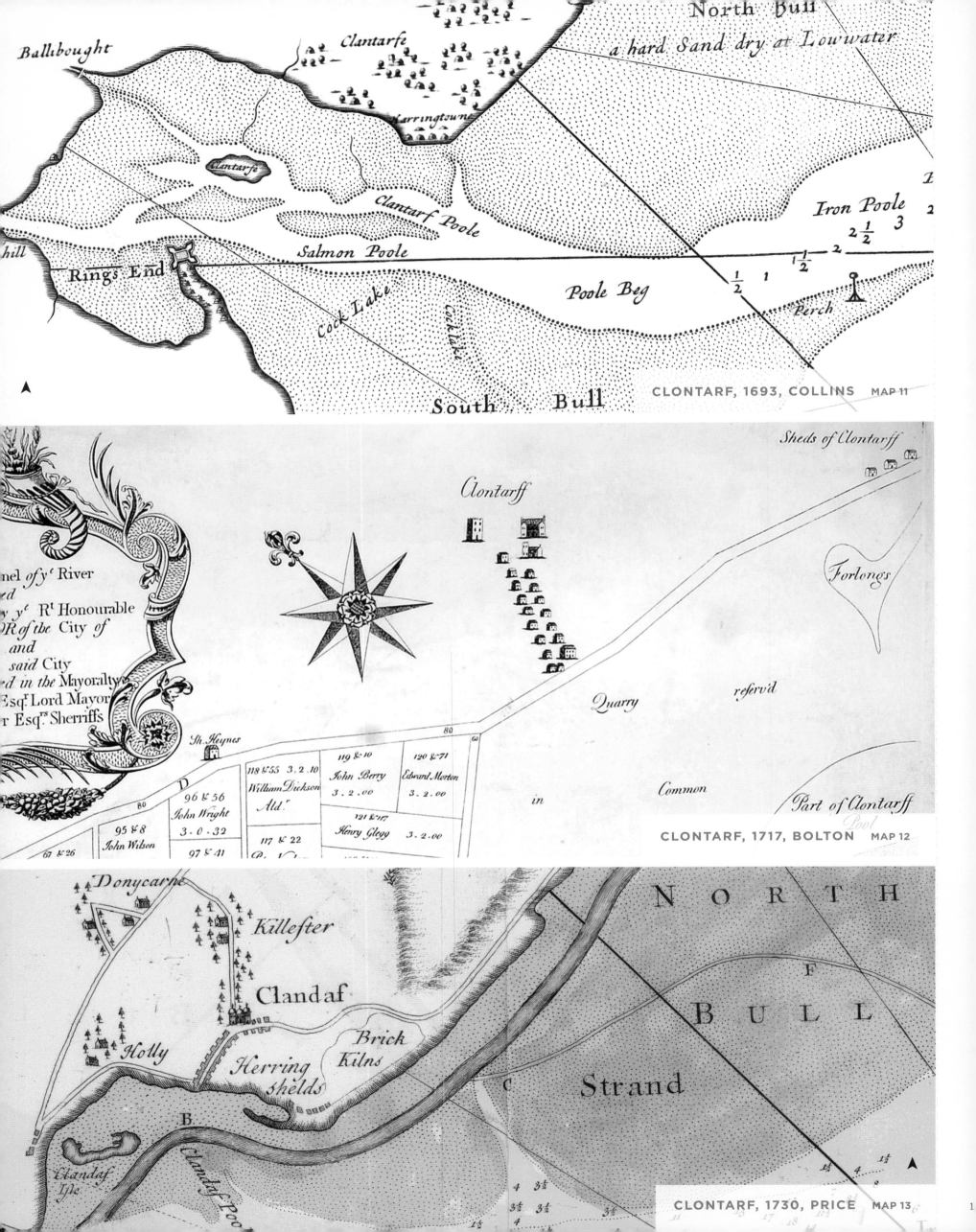

Map 11 (top):

Ballibought

Clantarfe

North Bull

a hard Sand dry at Lowwater

Clantarfe

Harringtowne

Clantarf Poole

Iron Poole

2 1/2   3

Salmon Poole

2 1/2

2

hill

Rings End

1/2   1   1 1/2

Cock Lake

Cocklake

Poole Beg

Perch

South Bull

CLONTARF, 1693, COLLINS   MAP 11

Map 12 (middle):

Sheds of Clontarff

Clontarff

...nel of yᵉ River
...ed
...y yᵉ Rᵗ Honourable
...OR of the City of
...and
...said City
...d in the Mayoralty
...Esqʳ Lord Mayor
...r Esqʳˢ Sherriffs

Forlongs

Quarry   reserv'd

80

Common

in

Part of Clontarff

Pool

Sh. Heynes

D

118 & 55   3.2.10   119 & 10   120 & 71

William Dickson   John Berry   Edward Morton

96 & 56   Aldᵗ   3.2.00   3.2.00

80   John Wright

3.0.32

95 & 8   117 & 22   121 & 117

67 & 26   John Wilson   97 & 41   Henry Glegg   3.2.00

CLONTARF, 1717, BOLTON   MAP 12

Map 13 (bottom):

Donycarne

Killester

NORTH

F

Clandaf

BULL

Holly

Brick Kilns

Herring shelds

Strand

B

Clandaf Isle

1 1/4   4   1 1/4   8

Clandaf Pool

4   3 1/4

3 1/4   3 1/4

1 1/4

CLONTARF, 1730, PRICE   MAP 13

NORTH BU

NORTH STRAND

THE ST. A. North

CLONTARF POOL

Ballybough River

Clontarf Island

Island House

BROWNS PATCH

THE HA RB OUR

Packet & Moorings

THE PILES

Wagge Green

The Church Road

North Strand Road

North Strand

Ballybough

Road from Dublin to Raheny

YARD

0 - 2 - 5½
Garden   Lawn

Mr A Keffes holding

Gate   wall

Hollybrook Avenue

wall and Paling

Mr Plunkets

holding

Gate

Lane

wall and paling

field
a r p
2 . 1 . 25

Caseys holding

wall

Passage

Spring
well

wall

Mr Plunkets field

House Offices Garden & Lawn   a r p   0 - 2 - 5½

Field ——

Total exclusive of Road   } 2 . 1 . 25
or Avenue ————

2 " 3 " 30½

100 ft to an Inch

South

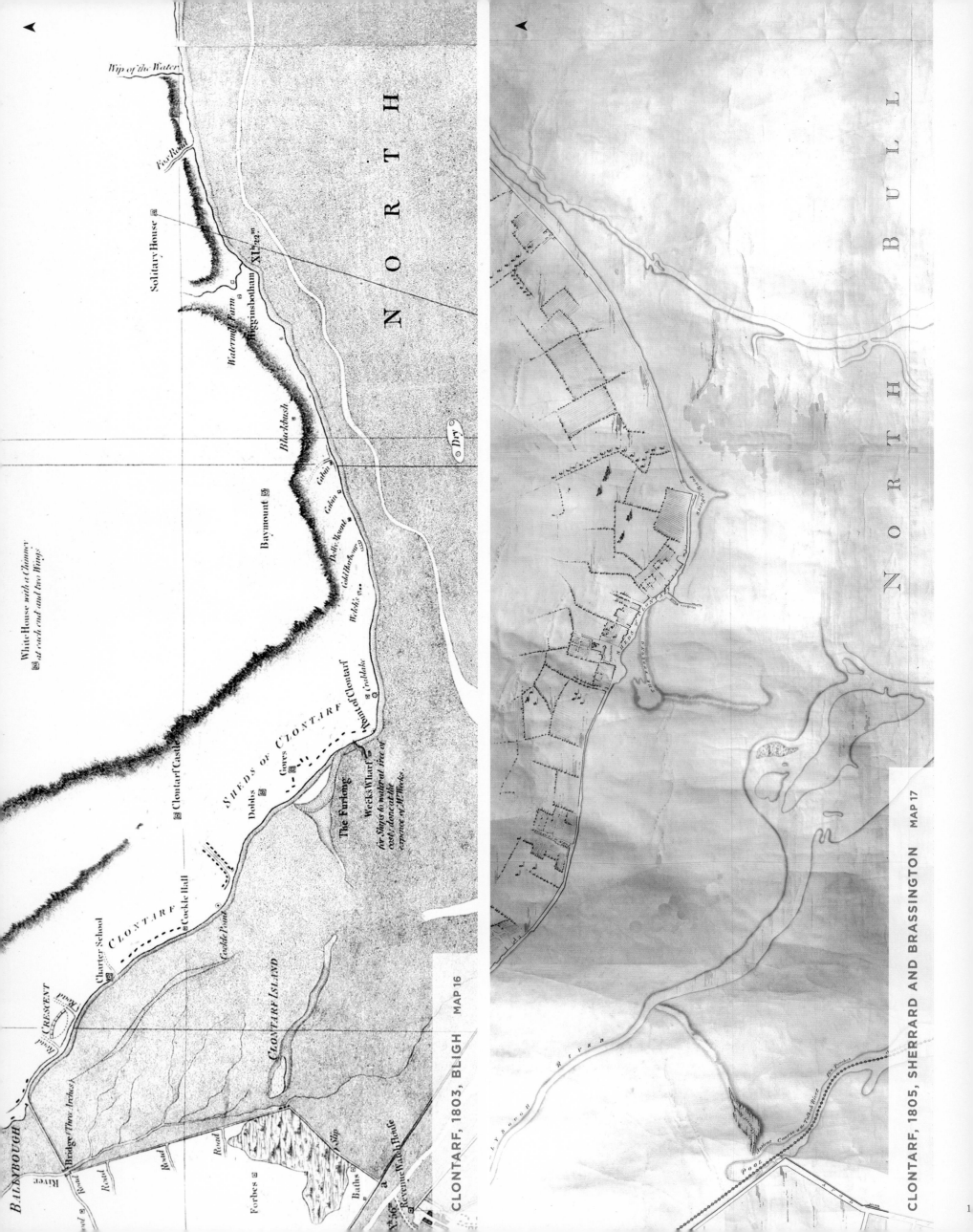

CLONTARF, 1803, BLIGH   MAP 16

CLONTARF, 1805, SHERRARD AND BRASSINGTON   MAP 17

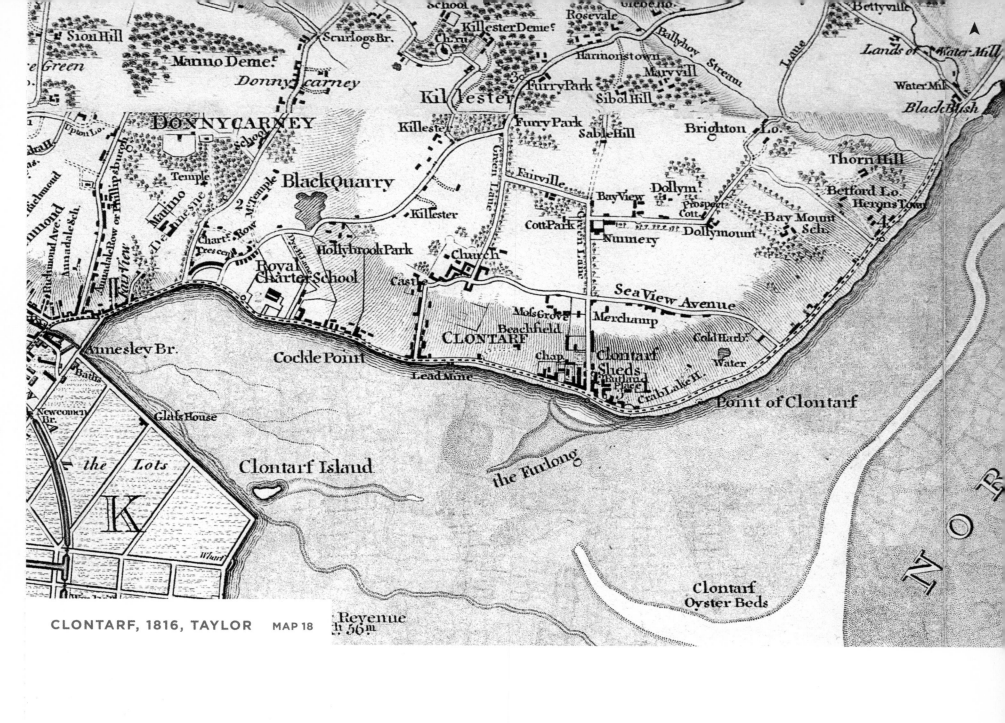

CLONTARF, 1816, TAYLOR   MAP 18

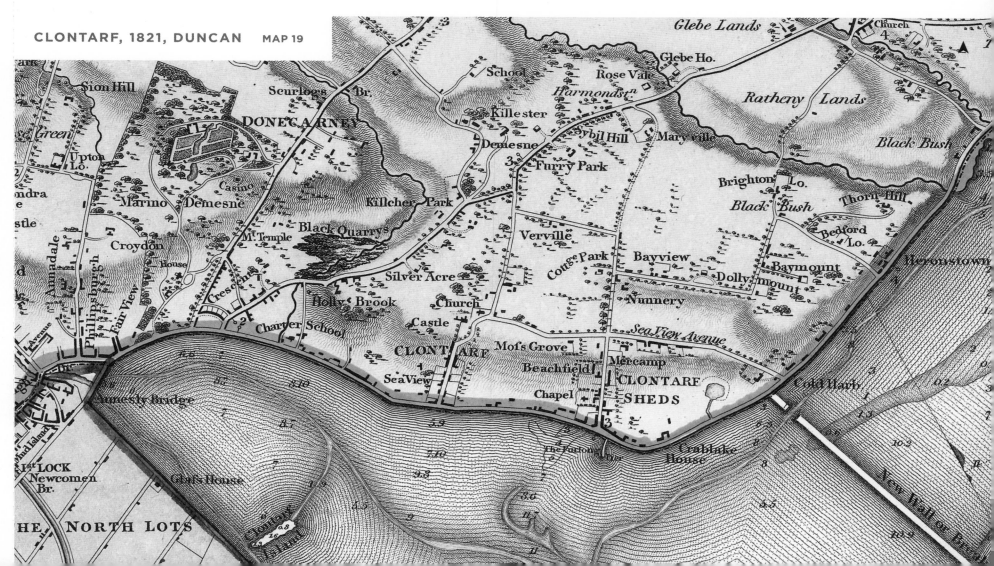

CLONTARF, 1821, DUNCAN   MAP 19

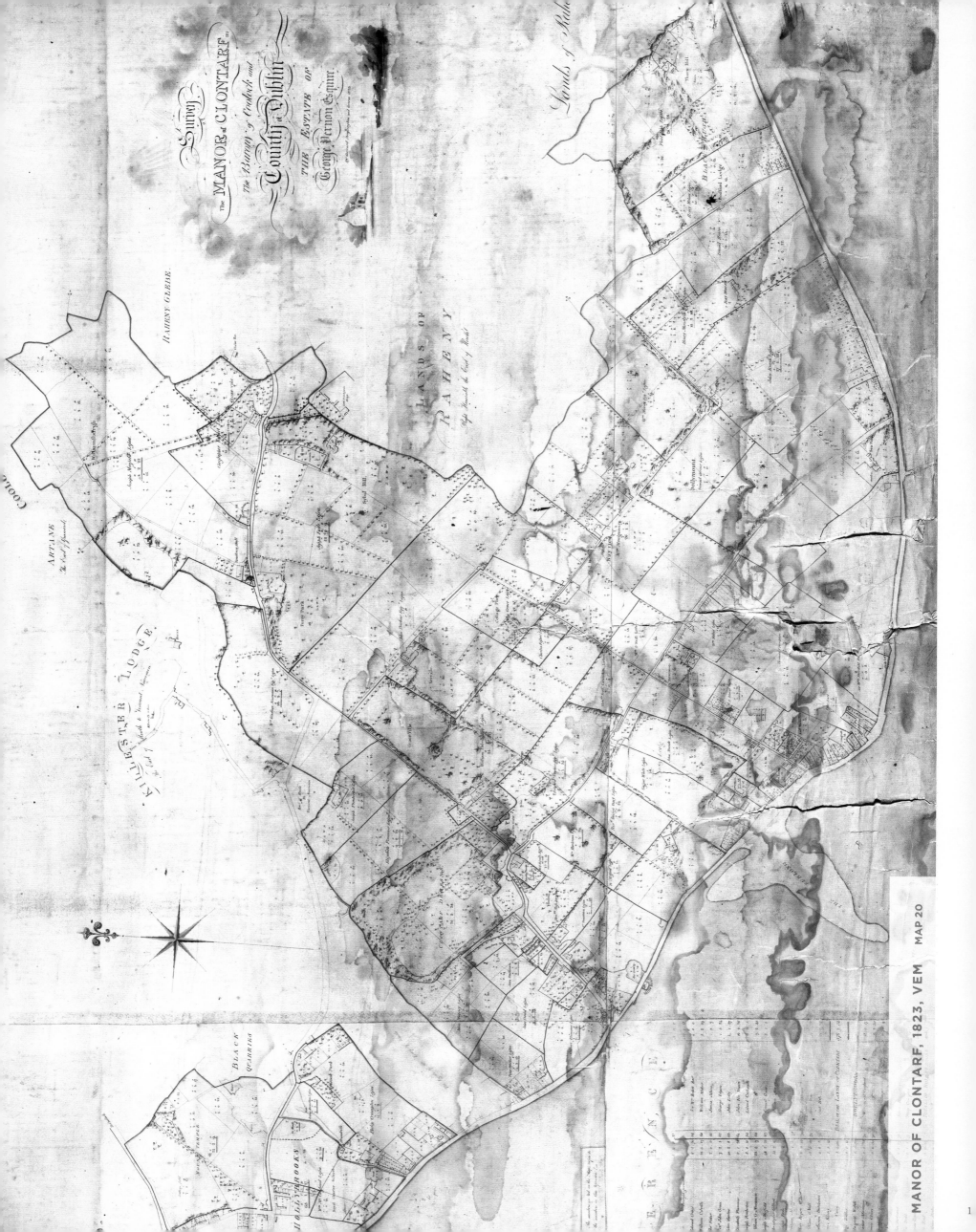

REFERENCE TO SURVEY OF THE MANOR OF CLONTARF, 1823

No.	Lessee	A.	R.	P.
	Lands of Clontarf			
1.	Clontarf Demesne	20	3	8
2.	Church Yard	0	2	36
3.	John Mooney	8	0	10
4.	Peter Walker	4	3	15
5.	John Dodd	4	3	39
6.	do. (at will)	0	1	24
7.	John Sullivan	2	1	6
8.	Miss Blundell	0	0	16
9.	Hon. Miss Smythe	1	2	20
10.	Claim'd by G. Plummer	0	0	35
11.	Gilbert Plummer	7	2	12
12.	do.	7	1	15
13.	Mine House and Yard	0	0	11
14.	John Templeton	2	1	10
15.	Hon. Miss Smythe	3	3	18
16.	Timothy Dunn	0	3	32
17.	W. Colville (at will)	1	2	6
18.	William Harkness	4	3	29
19.	B. Mitford	1	2	14
20.	T. Bunbury	7	0	18
21.	Rev. George Vesey	5	2	22
22.	Gasper White	8	0	36
23.	John Marsden	7	2	27
24.	Chapel Yard & Cabin	0	0	30
25.	Commissioners of Customs	0	0	9
26.	The Green	0	2	36
27.	Wm. O'Neill	0	3	26
28.	Edward Kane	7	1	2
29.	Hon. F. Cavendish	4	0	3
	Carried forward	**116**	**0**	**35**
30.	Edward Croker	11	1	35
31.	William Colville	25	3	27
32.	Chas. Fisher	2	0	0
33.	Revd. John Grace	7	2	3
34.	John Barlow	40	2	8
35.	Elizabeth Plummer	11	1	28
36.	Joseph Pemberton	8	0	10
37.	William G. Newcomen	16	3	7
38.	Joseph Merfield	48	2	22
39.	Christopher Gilbert	15	2	16
40.	Joseph Fade	42	0	9
41.	William Montgomery	26	1	3
42.	Mary Rogers Widow	0	3	16
43.	William O'Neill	3	3	10
44.	Catherine Hutcheson	4	0	3
45.	Henry Kinsey	1	3	15
46.	—Carey	1	3	25
47.	Peter Walker	0	3	13
48.	Margaret Walsh	0	0	22
49.	Connor Manning	0	0	28
50.	James Cleere	0	0	35
51.	K. Fonge	0	1	5
52.	J. Langstaff	0	1	25
53.	John Bertrand	0	0	27
54.	John Dodd	0	1	1
55.	Thomas Conolly	0	1	22
56.	Peter Earl	3	0	31
57.	Anthony Weeks	1	2	23
58.	Thomas Crampton	11	2	14
	Carried forward	**410**	**1**	**0**
59.	Sir Wm. Burdell Bart.	4	0	5
60.	William Maher	3	2	29
61.	James Malone	1	3	7
62.	George Ingham	1	3	24
63.	John Kelly	14	1	37
64.	John King Irwin	12	2	26
65.	Leland Crosthwaite	6	3	5
66.	do.	7	2	35
67.	Samuel Garner	8	1	0
68.	William Muray	1	2	34
69.	John Keogh	27	1	15
70.	Henry Meredyth	12	2	16
71.	Daniel Hearn	13	1	14
72.	Henry Wilme	10	0	38
73.	Paul Hale	28	3	28
	Total of the Lands of Clontarf	**576**	**2**	**33**
	Hollybrooks			
74.	William McCausland	18	0	17
75.	do.	9	2	30
76.	Mount Temple	22	2	9
77.	In Hands	0	3	17
78.	Baron Hamilton	2	2	25
79.	Philip Crampton	14	2	9
	Total of Hollybrooks	**68**	**1**	**27**
	General total	**645**	**0**	**20**

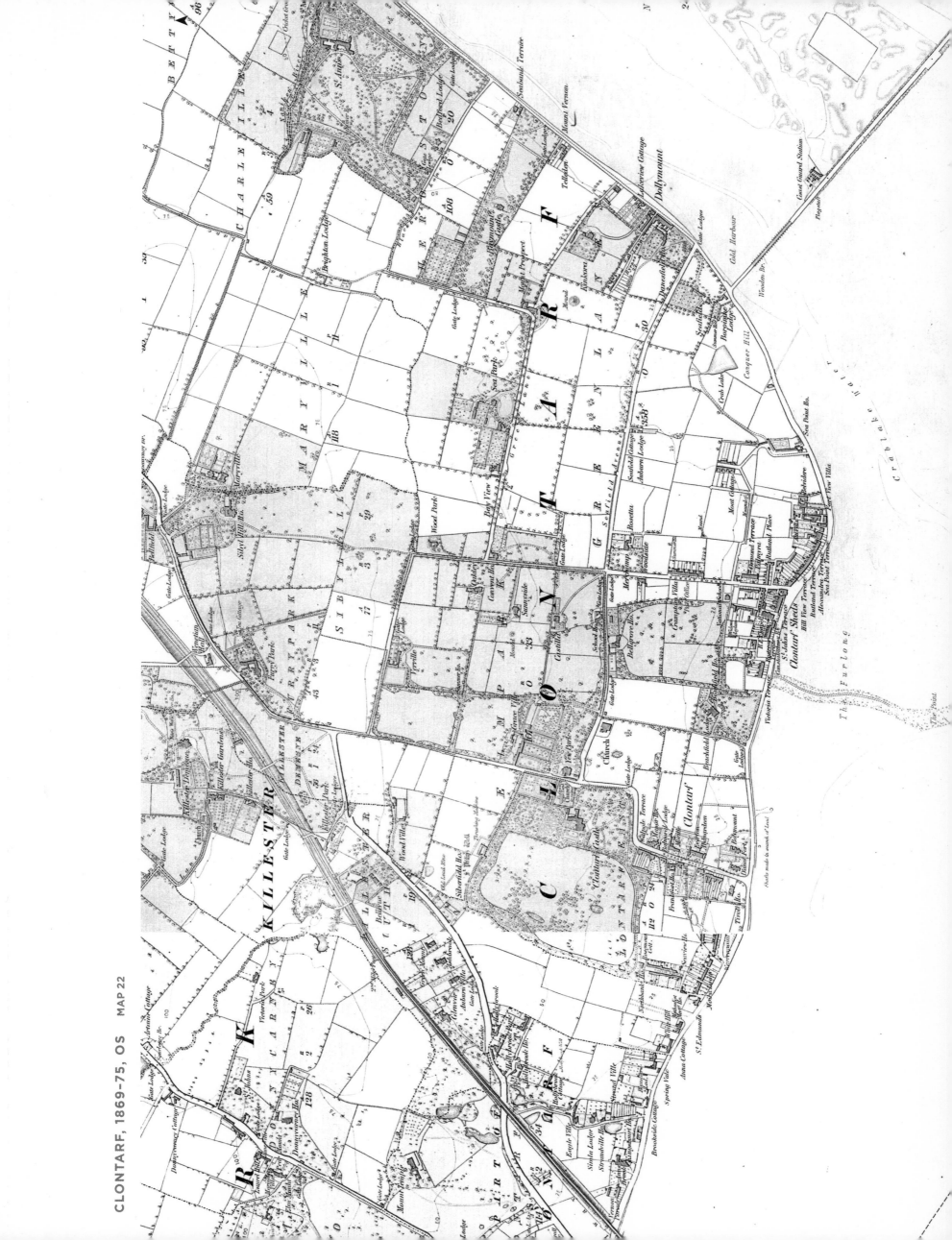

TOWNSHIP OF CLONTARF, 1898, THOM MAP   MAP 23

PLAN

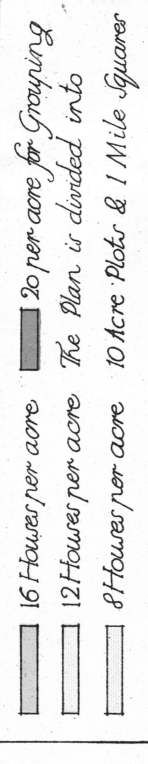

16 Houses per acre	20 per acre for Grouping
12 Houses per acre	The Plan is divided into
8 Houses per acre	10 Acre Plots & 1 Mile Squares

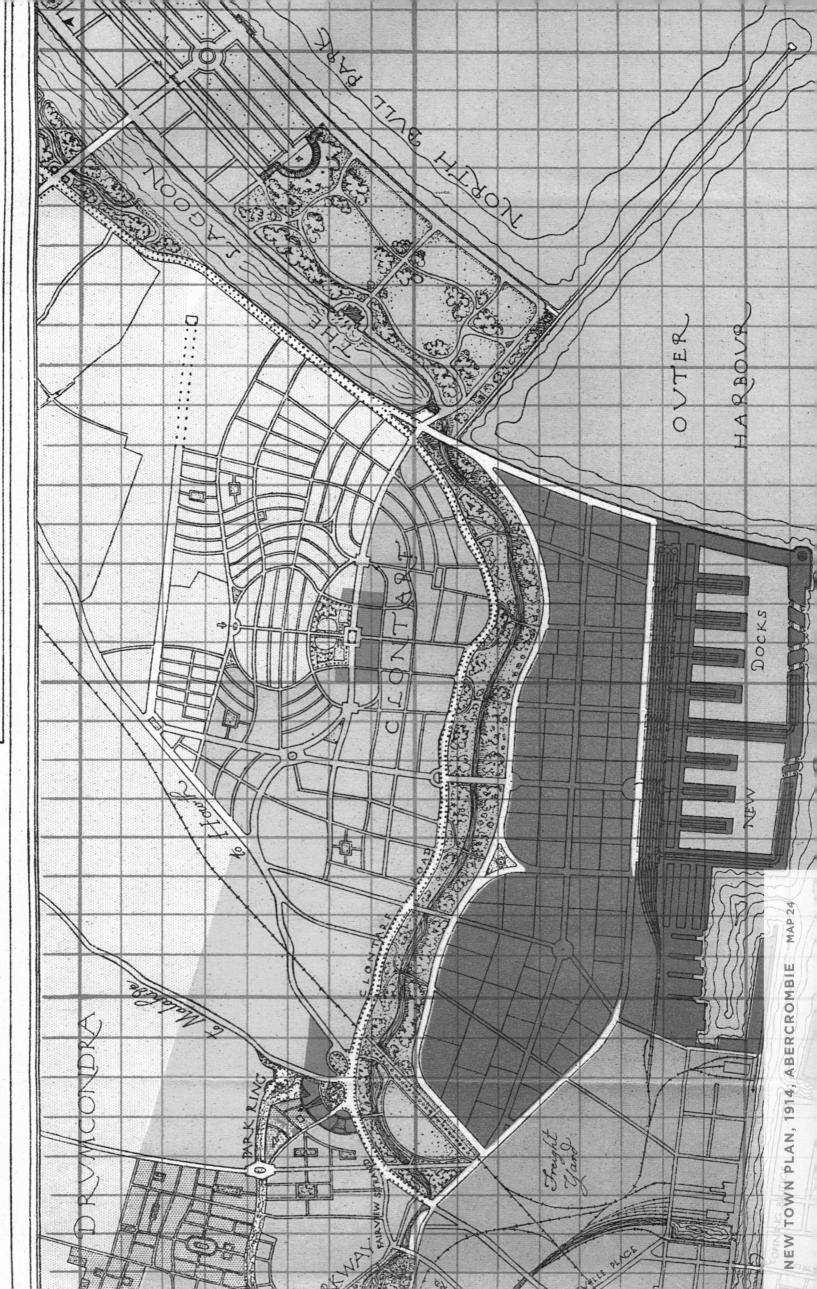

LAGOON

THE

NORTH BULL PARK

OUTER

HARBOUR

CLONTARF

DOCKS

NEW

CLONTARF ROAD

PARK KING

to Howth

to Malahide

PARKWAY FAIRVIEW STRAND

DRUMCONDRA

Freight Yard

NEW TOWN PLAN, 1914, ABERCROMBIE   MAP 24

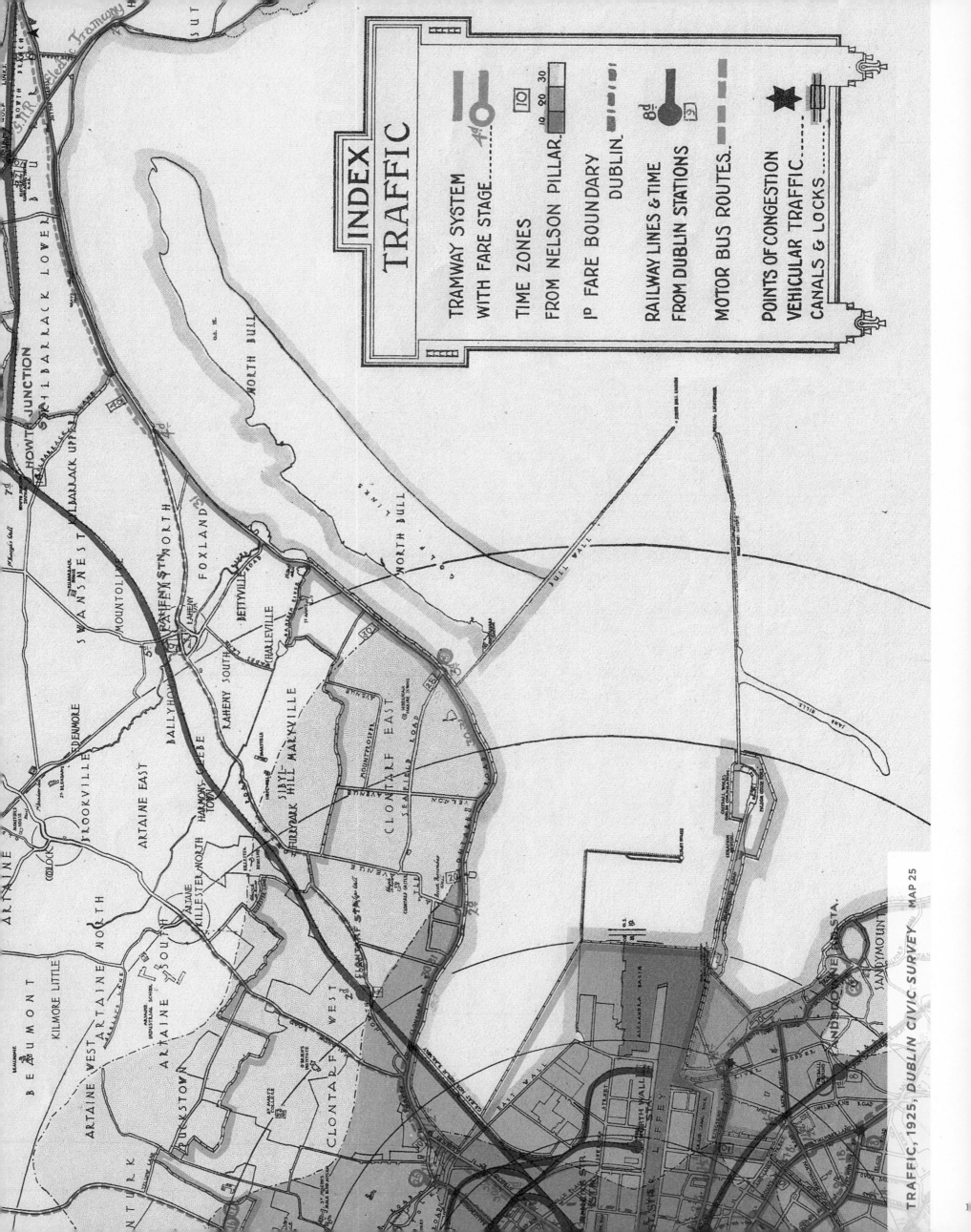

INDEX

TRAFFIC

TRAMWAY SYSTEM
WITH FARE STAGE 4ᵈ

TIME ZONES

FROM NELSON PILLAR.

1ᴾ FARE BOUNDARY
DUBLIN.

RAILWAY LINES & TIME
FROM DUBLIN STATIONS 8ᵈ

MOTOR BUS ROUTES.

POINTS OF CONGESTION
VEHICULAR TRAFFIC.......
CANALS & LOCKS ....

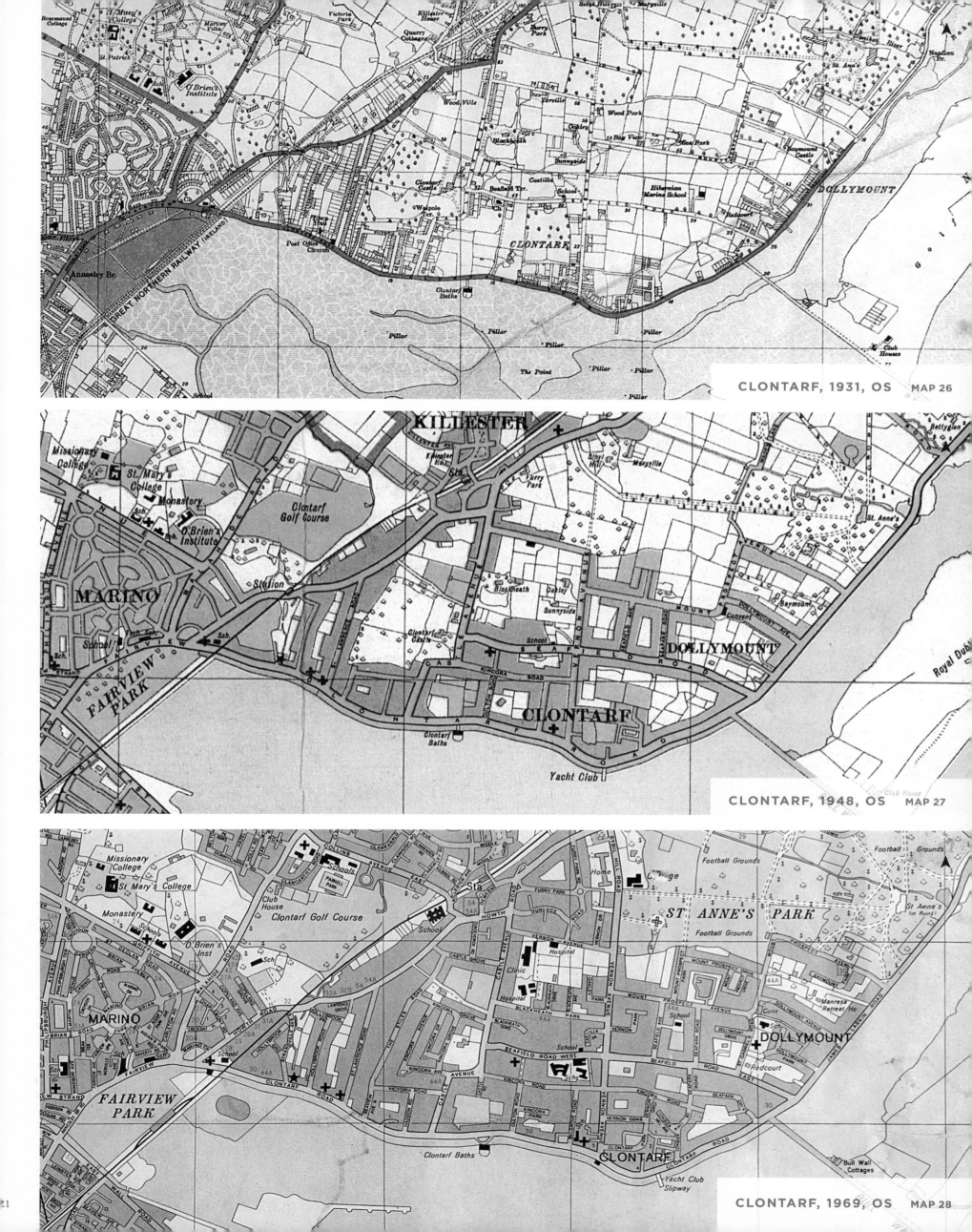

CLONTARF, 1931, OS   MAP 26

CLONTARF, 1948, OS   MAP 27

CLONTARF, 1969, OS   MAP 28

Scale 1:10,000

Metres

200   100   0   200   400

FURTHER STUDY, 1907   MAP 29

Scale 1 : 10,000

Metres

400

200

100

0

100

200

Previous pages: View of Clontarf, looking east, late 18th cent.

Further notes

Period reconstructions and thematic maps
Figs 1–9, pp 7–29

For the suburbs series, five reconstructions aim to show the development of the chosen area of study from its origins down to the present day (for Clontarf, Figs 1–3, 6 and 9). Two further maps focus on a selected street or area but may be utilised in a broadly comparative way between suburbs — one tracing the development of a chosen street and another plotting the valuation of buildings in *c*. 1900 (for Clontarf, Figs 7 and 8 respectively). Additional maps are included to highlight topographical features or themes specific to the suburb in question. For Clontarf, these focus on the area known as the Sheds (Fig. 4) and Bull Island (Fig. 5).

Figs 1–3 show key topographical features in Clontarf from the medieval period to the late eighteenth century at a scale of 1:20,000. Sites, taken from the Topographical information section and select historic maps, are depicted with standard symbols and lines that do not reflect actual dimensions. Where there is a doubt about location, a question mark (for sites) or dashed lines (for roads or boundaries) are used.

Figs 1 and 2 use a base of modern contours at 3 m intervals. In Fig. 1, modern placenames are included in grey. Contemporary placenames are depicted in black.

In Figs 2 and 3, the shore and bay features have been plotted from the contemporary maps of Thomas Phillips (1685) and John Rocque (1760). The low water line, indicated by a deeper shade of blue, has been estimated using those same sources. In Fig. 1, topographical detail for the bay is limited to a conjectural, generalised shoreline, based on the eighteenth-century depiction by Rocque.

Figs 6 and 9 show the approximate extent of the built-up area at different stages during the nineteenth and twentieth centuries at a scale of 1:8000, using key Ordnance Survey maps from 1843 to 1907 and 1907 to 2016. Streets, roads, lanes, rail/tram lines and buildings with their associated plots are shaded according to their main phase of development. Where properties include extensive garden or parkland, shading has been generalised and limited to the main building and immediate area. The map does not necessarily indicate the age of individual buildings depicted on the 1907 or 2016 base maps, which may have been redeveloped or demolished since their initial construction.

Topographical information
pp 33–72

Primary source material is listed to approximately 1970. Features originating after this date are listed only in exceptional cases.

The list of early spellings in section **1** seeks to give a representative selection of placename forms. It is confined to the earliest and latest examples noted of the variants deemed to be the most significant. Where necessary the earliest noted attestation of the commonest spelling in each of these categories is also given.

Street names are listed in alphabetical order in section **10**. The first entry for each street gives its present-day name according to the most authoritative source, with versions in Irish taken from the Placename Database of Ireland (Logainm), where available. This is followed in the right-hand column by the nearest main thoroughfare in brackets, and the street's first identifiable appearance, named or unnamed, in a map or other record and the various names subsequently applied to it in chronological order of occurrence.

Entries under each heading in sections **11–22** are arranged in chronological order by categories: for example, mills are listed before brick kilns, because the oldest mill pre-dates the oldest brick kiln. In general, dates of initiation and cessation are specified as such. Where these are unknown, the first and last recorded dates are given, and references of intermediate date are omitted except where corroborative evidence appears necessary. In source-citations, a pair of years joined by a hyphen includes all intervening years for which that source is available: thus 1843–1907 (OS) means all Ordnance Survey maps from 1843 to 1907 inclusive.

The section on residence (**22**) is not intended to embrace more than a small fraction of the dwelling houses in the suburb. The main criteria for inclusion are (1) contribution to the townscape, past or present; (2) significance in defining critical stages in the history of urban or suburban housing; (3) abundance of documentation, especially for houses representative of a large class of dwellings. Biographical associations are not in themselves a ground for inclusion. Only residences that can be located to at least a street location, or that are named in two or more primary sources, have been included. Supplementary information is provided in the appendix (pp 73–5), which lists houses and terraces named in selected sources.

Sites are located, where possible, according to their orientation to the nearest street and by grid reference (these relate to the eastings and northings shown on Map 3, pp 91–4). 'Site unknown' is stated for features that cannot be precisely placed along a street, with 'location unknown' being used in cases where no locational evidence has been found. Grid references are given in Irish Transverse Mercator co-ordinates. They indicate the approximate centre of the feature in question.

Abbreviated source-references are explained in the bibliography and general abbreviations on pp 130–39.

List of illustrations

Maps and plates listed on pp 81–2

ii–iii, 51   Sheds of Clontarf, Weekes's Wharf, Clontarf Road, 1785, by John Laporte. Reproduced courtesy of the British Library, Maps K Top 53 21 c.

viii–ix   Beached boats at Clontarf, looking north, 19th cent., by O.M. Latham. Reproduced courtesy of the National Gallery of Ireland, 2497.

4–5   View of Dublin from Clontarf, looking south-east, 1796–8, by William Ashford. Reproduced courtesy of the National Gallery of Ireland, 4137.

30–31   Royal Charter School, Clontarf Road, looking east, 1794, by William Ashford. Reproduced courtesy of the National Gallery of Ireland, 577.

36   Clontarf Castle, Castle Avenue, 1805, by Thomas Snagg. Reproduced courtesy of Whyte's.

39   Sheds of Clontarf, Clontarf Road, 1785, by Francis Wheatley. Reproduced courtesy of the British Library, Maps K Top 53 25.

42   Lane from Seafield Road West and continuing to Oulton Road, c. 1910. Reproduced courtesy of the National Library of Ireland, ET A375.

43   Marino Crescent, 1812, by B. King. Reproduced courtesy of the National Library of Ireland, PD 1983 TX 95.

48   Clontarf and Scots Presbyterian Church, Clontarf Road, c. 1910. Reproduced courtesy of the National Library of Ireland, Eas 1667.

49   Clontarf Castle, 1772, by Gabriel Beranger. Reproduced courtesy of the National Library of Ireland, PD 1958 TX 71.

53   Windmill, Clontarf Strand, 1655, from Down Survey map by William Wright. Reproduced courtesy of the Royal Irish Academy.

54   Dublin and Drogheda railway viaduct, 1853, by Edward McFarland. Reproduced courtesy of the National Library of Ireland, PD 1986 TX, p. 7.

56   Bull Bridge and Bull Wall, c. 1910. Reproduced courtesy of the National Library of Ireland, Eas 1752.

57   Mounds, Vernon Avenue, 1888, by William Wakeman. Reproduced courtesy of the Royal Irish Academy, 12 T 12 (13).

59   Royal Charter School, Clontarf Road, 1795, by Francis Jukes. Reproduced courtesy of the British Library, Maps K Top 53 2 f.

62   Clontarf Island, 1878, by Alexander Williams (*Irish Naturalist*, xvii (1908), facing p. 165). Reproduced courtesy of the Royal Irish Academy.

63   Royal Dublin Golf Club house, North Bull Island, c. 1910. Reproduced courtesy of the National Library of Ireland, Eas 1669.

67   Clontarf Castle, after restoration, 1840 (*Irish Penny Journal* 12.9.1840). Reproduced courtesy of the National Library of Ireland.

71   Seafront houses, Vernon Avenue, early 20th cent. Irish Historical Picture Company.

76–7   Dublin from railway bridge at Hollybrook, c. 1850, by Edward Radclyffe. Reproduced courtesy of the National Library of Ireland, ET A375.

124–5   View of Clontarf, looking east, late 18th cent. Reproduced courtesy of the National Library of Ireland, ET B404.

Selected bibliography and key to abbreviations

(Other abbreviations are explained in the general list for the series on pp 135–9)

Archdall	Archdall, Mervyn. *Monasticon Hibernicum*. Dublin, 1786. Ashford, William. 'A view of Dublin from Clontarf', 1796–8. Oil on canvas. NGI, 4137.
Ashford	Ashford, William. 'The Royal Charter School, Clontarf, County Dublin', 1794. Oil on canvas. NGI, 577.
Beranger	Beranger, Gabriel. 'Clontarf Castle', 1772. Watercolour. NLI, PD 1958 TX 71.
Bligh	Bligh, William. 'Survey of the bay of Dublin', 1803. Map library, TCD. (Map 16).
Board of Works cal.	Board of Works calendar of papers in National Archives, 1848–1935. Available at http://www.opw.ie/en/media/board-of-works-calendar-of-papers-in-national-archives-1848-1935.pdf (last accessed 7 July 2017). Cited by National Archives file number.
Bolton	'A map of the strand of the north side of the channel of the river Anna Liffe as it was granted and set out in Easter assembly 1717 by the right honourable Thomas Bolton Esqr.', 1717. BL, Add. MS 29,881. (Map 12).
Book of Howth	Brewer, J.S. and Bullen, William (eds). 'The book of Howth'. In *Cal. Carew MSS*, v (London, 1871), pp 1–259. Bowles, John. *A new and correct map of the bay and harbour of Dublin*. London, 1728.
Bradley	Bradley, John. 'Some reflections on the problem of Scandinavian settlement in the hinterland of Dublin during the ninth century'. In John Bradley, A.J. Fletcher and Anngret Simms (eds), *Dublin in the medieval world: studies in honour of Howard B. Clarke*. Dublin, 2009, pp 39–62.
Brett	Brett, John. 'Clontarf church, Co. Dublin', 1855. Photocopy of catalogue entry. Irish Art Research Centre (TRIARC) Crookshank-Glin Collection.
Brown	Brown, J. (ed.). *Reports of cases upon appeals and writs of error in the High Court of Parliament, 1701–1779*. 7 vols. London, 1779–83.
Chartul. St Mary's	*Chartularies of St Mary's Abbey, Dublin ... and annals of Ireland, 1162–1370*. Ed. J.T. Gilbert. 2 vols. London, 1884–6.

CLTC	Clontarf Lawn Tennis Club website. Available at clontarfltc.com (last accessed 1 May 2016).
Cog. Gaedhel	*Cogadh Gaedhel re Gallaibh: the War of the Gaedhil with the Gaill* ... Ed. J.H. Todd. London, 1867.
Collins	Collins, Greenville. *Great Britain's coasting-pilot being a new and exact survey of the sea-coast of England* ... London, 1693. (Map 11).
Commons votes, 1789	*Votes of the house of commons in the parliament of Ireland* ... 1789. Dublin, 1789.
Corcoran	Corcoran, Michael. *Through streets broad and narrow: a history of Dublin trams*. Hersham, 2008.
Cosgrave	Cosgrave, Dillon. *North Dublin: city and environs*. Dublin, 1909; 2nd ed. Dublin, 2005.
Dáil deb.	Dáil Éireann debates, 1919–. Available at http://oireachtasdebates.oireachtas.ie (last accessed 6 July 2017).
De Courcy	De Courcy, J.W. *The Liffey in Dublin*. Dublin, 1996.
De Paor	De Paor architects website. Available at http://www.depaor.com/projects/clontarf-road.php (last accessed 27 Oct. 2016).
Depositions	Depositions etc. relating to the years 1641–53. TCD, MSS 809–41.
DS	Down Survey. Wright, William. 'The barony of Coolock in the county of Dublin', 1655, scale 160 perches to an inch. Available at http://downsurvey.tcd.ie (last accessed 3 July 2017).
Dublin Intelligence	*Dublin Intelligence*. Dublin, 1690–93. *The Dublin Intelligence*, later *The Dublin Intelligence or Oxman-Town News-Letter containing a variety of foreign and domestick news*. Dublin, 1702–32.
Dunton	Dunton, John. *The Dublin scuffle*. Dublin, 1699.
Evening Herald	*Evening Herald*. Dublin, 1891–.
Falkiner	Falkiner, C.L. 'The hospital of St John of Jerusalem in Ireland'. In *RIA Proc.*, xxvi C (1906–7), pp 275–317.
FDJ	*Faulkner's Dublin Journal*. Dublin, 1725–1825.
FJ	*Freeman's Journal*. Dublin, 1763–1924.
Flood	Flood, D.T. 'The birth of the Bull Island'. In *DHR*, xxviii (1975), pp 142–53.
Flying Post	*The Flying Post: or, the Postmaster*. Dublin, 1699–1712.
Gamble	Gamble, Noel. 'The Dublin and Drogheda railway: part 1 & 2'. In *Journal of the Irish Railway Record Society*, xi (1974), pp 224–34, 283–93.
Genevieve	Genevieve, Mary. 'Mrs Bellew's family in Channel Row'. In *DHR*, xxii (1968), pp 230–41.
Gilbert	Gilbert, J.T. (ed.). *A contemporary history of affairs in Ireland, from A.D. 1641 to 1652* ... . 3 vols. Dublin, 1879.
Giles	Giles, Francis. 'Map of the North Bull', 1819. Dublin Port and Docks Board.
Glasgow Herald	*Glasgow Herald*. Glasgow, 1783–.
Gogarty	Gogarty, Claire. *From village to suburb: the building of Clontarf since 1760*. Dublin, 2013.
Grosart	Grosart, A.B. *The Lismore papers: autobiographical notes, remembrances and diaries of Sir Richard Boyle, first and 'great' earl of Cork*. 5 vols, London, 1886.
Hardy	Hardy, P. Dixon. 'A day's ramble on the north side of the city'. In *Dublin Penny Journal*, ii (1834), pp 273–5.
Hearth money roll	'Hearth money roll for County Dublin, continued, 1664'. In *Journal of the County Kildare Archaeological Society*, xi (1930–33), pp 386–466.

Hibernian Journal	*Hibernian Journal.* Dublin, 1771–1822.
IPJ	*The Irish Penny Journal.* Dublin, 1840–41.
Ir. educ. rept 1	*First report of the commissioners of inquiry into education in Ireland*, appendix 134. HC 1825 (400), xii.
Ir. Independent	*Irish Independent.* Dublin, 1905–.
Ir. Press	*Irish Press.* Dublin, 1931–95.
Ir. Times	*The Irish Times.* Dublin, 1859–.
Jukes	Jukes, Francis. 'Royal Charter School', 1795. Aquatint and etching with hand colouring. BL, Maps K Top 53 2 f.
King	King, B. 'The Crescent near Clontarf and Lord Charlemont's house from the N. wall', 1812. Pencil drawing. NLI, PD 1983 TX 95.
Knowles	Knowles, F.W.R. *Old Clontarf.* Dublin, [*c.* 1970].
Laporte	Laporte, John. 'Dublin Bay, from Clontarf', 1785. Etching with hand colouring. BL, Maps K Top 53 21 c.
	Latham, O.M. 'Beached boats at Clontarf, Dublin', 19th cent. Graphite on watercolour paper. NGI, 2497.
Lennon, 2014	Lennon, Colm. *That field of glory: the story of Clontarf, from battleground to garden suburb.* Dublin, 2014.
Levistone Cooney	Levistone Cooney, D.A. 'The Methodist chapels in Dublin'. In *DHR*, lvii (2004), pp 152–63.
Local electoral area rept	*Local electoral area boundary committee report.* Dublin, 2013. Available at www.boundarycommittee.ie (last accessed 10 Sept. 2016).
Longfield 1–4	Longfield Map Collection. (1) Brownrigg, John. 'A survey of a piece of ground called the Slip Field near Clontarf in the Barony of Coolock and County of Dublin let by A. Savage Esq. to John Ash', 1792, scale ten perches to an inch. NLI, MS 21/F/51 (81); (2) Brownrigg & Co. 'A map of part of the lands of Clontarf in the Barony of Coolock and Co. Dublin. Let by W. Pemberton Esq. to Thos. Butler Esq.', 1804, scale 40 feet to an inch. NLI, MS 21/F/51 (101); (3) Longfield, John. 'A map of a holding at Hollybrook Park near Clontarf in the County of Dublin let by – to Armstrong Esq.', 1812, scale 100 feet to an inch. NLI, MS 21/F/51 (115) (Map 15); (4) Longfield, John. 'A survey of the demesne of Thorn Hill in the Parish of Clontarf and Co. of Dublin, belonging to Mrs Bull, by J.L', 1816, scale 10 perches to an inch. NLI, MS 21/F/51 (141).
L.P. Henry VIII	*Letters and papers, foreign and domestic, of the reign of Henry VIII, 1509–13* [etc.]. 21 vols in 36. London, 1862–1932.
Lynch	Lynch, Val. *No thoroughfare on the tram road: history of Clontarf and its environs.* Dublin, 2007.
Mac Niocaill, 1967	Mac Niocaill, Gearóid (ed.). 'Documents relating to the suppression of the Templars in Ireland'. In *Analecta Hibernica*, xxiv (1967), pp 183–226.
MacGiolla Phádraig	MacGiolla Phádraig, Brian. 'The Irish form of "Clontarf"'. In *DHR*, xi (1950), pp 127–8.
McFarland	McFarland, Edward. 'A drive from Dublin to Howth returning by Clontarf in 1853'. Watercolour. NLI, PD 1986 TX.
McIntyre	McIntyre, Dennis. *The meadow of the bull: a history of Clontarf.* Dublin, 1987.
	McNally, Kieran. *The island imagined by the sea: a history of Bull Island.* Dublin, 2014.

Murphy	Murphy, F.J. 'Dublin trams 1872–1959'. In *DHR*, 33 (1979), pp 2–9.
Ní Mhurchadha	Ní Mhurchadha, Maighréad. 'Clontarf'. Unpublished paper, [2003].
O'Connell's Schools	*O'Connell's Schools commemorative booklet*. Dublin, 2000.
ODNB	*Oxford dictionary of national biography*. Ed. H.C.G. Matthew and B.H. Harrison. 61 vols. Oxford, 2004. Also available at www.oxforddnb.com (last accessed 3 Aug. 2016).
OS	Ordnance Survey. Maps of parish of Clontarf: scale 1:2500, surveyed in 1868 (Map 2); scale 1:1056, surveyed in 1889–90 (printed in 1889–90). Maps of Co. Dublin: scale 1:10,560, sheets 18, 19, surveyed in 1837 (engraved in 1837), corrected to 1843 (Map 21), revised in 1869–75 (Map 22); scale 1:2500, sheets xix. 1, 2, 4, 5, 8 surveyed in 1837, revised in 1907 (published in 1910) (Map 4); revised in 1935–6 (printed in 1938) (Map 5); scale 1:1000, sheets 3198. 3, 4, 5, 8, 9, 10, 13, 14, 15, 18, 19, 20, sheets 3199. 1, 2, 6, 7, 11,12, 16, 17, surveyed in 1970–71; scale 1:5000, surveyed in 2016 (Map 3).
OSN	Ordnance Survey name books, Dublin city and county, 1836. NAI, OS 144. Typescript copy, DCLA.
Phillips 1, 1a	(1) Phillips, Thomas. 'An exact survey of the citty of Dublin and part of the harbour', 1685. BL, Maps K Top 53 8. (Map 9). Later copies RIA, MC 3/5, 10, 11, 13, 15. (1a) Modified copy of (1), [late 17th cent.]. RIA, RR MC 3/7. (Map 10). Another version, RIA, RR MC 3/12.
Phillips 2, 2a, 2b	(2) Phillips, Thomas. 'The bay and harbour of Dublin', 1685. BL, Maps K Top 53 3 2. (Map 8). (2a) Modified copy of (2), [late 17th cent.]. RIA, RR MC 3/9. (2b) Modified copy of (2), [late 17th cent.]. RIA, RR MC 3/6.
Post chaise companion	*The post chaise companion: or traveller's directory through Ireland*. Dublin, 1786.
Price	Price, Charles. 'A correct chart of the city and harbour of Dublin', 1730. Map library, TCD. (Map 12).
Proctor's accounts	*The proctor's accounts of Peter Lewis 1564–1565*. Ed. Raymond Gillespie. Dublin, 1996.
Public works rept 5	*Fifth annual report of the commissioners of public works in Ireland*. HC 1837 (483), xxxiii, p. 32.
Public works rept 71	*Seventy-first annual report of the commissioners of public works in Ireland*. HC 1903 [Cd. 1748], xviii, p. 289.
Pue's Occurrences	*Impartial occurrences foreign and domestick*, later *Pue's Occurrences*. Dublin, 1703–88.
	Radclyffe, Edward. 'Dublin from railway bridge at Hollybrook', *c.* 1850. NLI, ET A365.
RDGC	*The Royal Dublin Golf Club, 1885–1985*. Dublin, 1985.
Reg. Kilmainham	*Registrum de Kilmainham: register of chapter acts of the hospital of Saint John of Jerusalem in Ireland, 1326–39, under the grand prior, Sir Roger Outlawe … *. Ed. Charles McNeill. IMC. Dublin, n.d. [1932].
Ruddy, 2004	Ruddy, Bernardine. 'The Royal Charter School, Clontarf'. In *DHR*, lvii (2004), pp 64–80.
Ruddy, 2006	Ruddy, Bernardine. 'Baymount Castle, Clontarf'. In *DHR*, lxix (2006), pp 171–81.
Ruddy, 2008	Ruddy, Bernardine. 'Mount Temple, Clontarf'. In *DHR*, lxi (2008), pp 183–93.

Ruddy, 2009	Ruddy, Bernardine. 'Clontarf baths and assembly rooms'. In *DHR*, lxii (2009), pp 27–35.
Ruddy, 2014	Ruddy, Bernardine. 'William Watson's Clontarf nursery, 1880–1920'. In *DHR*, lxvii (2014), pp 19–28.
Saunders Newsletter	*Saunders Newsletter*. Dublin, 1746–1879.
Sharkey	Sharkey, Joan Ussher. *St Anne's: the story of a Guinness estate*. Dublin, 2002.
Sherrard and Brassington	Sherrard and Brassington. 'A map of the boundaries of the county of the city of Dublin on the north east side thereof', 1805. Private collection. (Map 17).
Snagg	Snagg, Thomas. 'View of Clontarf Castle', 1805. Private collection.
Souvenir brochure	*Souvenir brochure of official opening of Church of St Gabriel, Clontarf, Dublin*. Dublin, 1956.
Sunday Times	*Sunday Times*. Irish ed., Dublin, 1993–.
Val. 1, 2, 3	Records of the General Valuation Office relating to Clontarf. (1) Valuation Office field and house books, 1845, NAI, 5.0870–71. (2) Printed tenement valuation, Union of North Dublin, 1850. (3) Manuscript revision books and related maps (1:1056), Clontarf, 1855–1902. Valuation Office, Dublin.
VEM	Vernon estate map. Sherrard, Brassington and Greene. 'Survey of the manor of Clontarf in the barony of Coolock and County of Dublin. The estate of George Vernon Esquire', 1823, scale ten perches to an inch. Vernon papers, University College Dublin, School of History, private collection, S6/15. Used by permission. (Map 20).
Vernon papers	Vernon papers, [1728–1916], University College Dublin, School of History. Private collection, S6/15. Used by permission.
Wakeman 1	Wakeman, W.F. 'Mound near the Crescent, Clontarf', *c.* 1874–87. NLI, PD 1992 TX (2).
Wakeman 2	Wakeman, W.F. 'Two sepulchral mounds close to Clontarf village, a little inland from the street, to the west ward', 1888. Watercolour. RIA 12 T 12 (13).
Wakeman 3	Wakeman, W.F. 'Sepulchral mound at Conquer Hill between Clontarf and Howth', 1888. Watercolour. RIA 12 T 12 (14).
Wheatley	Wheatley, Francis. 'The Sheds of Clontarfe', 1785. BL, Maps K Top 53 25.
Wild Birds Protection Act	Wild Birds Protection Acts, 1930–76. Available at www.irishstatutebook.ie (last accessed 5 July 2017). Cited by act number.
Williams	Williams, Alexander. 'Bird life in Dublin Bay. The passing of Clontarf Island'. In *Irish Naturalist*, xvii (1908), pp 165–70.
Wood	Wood, Herbert. 'The Templars in Ireland'. In *RIA Proc.*, xxvi C (1906–7), pp 327–77.
Workhouse	The workhouse: the story of an institution website. Available at: www.workhouses.org.uk (last accessed 6 June 2017).
WSC maps	Wide Street Commission maps. DCLA, C1/S1/130, 131.

General abbreviations

AAI	*Art and Architecture of Ireland*. Ed. Andrew Carpenter and others. 5 vols. Dublin, New Haven, London, 2014.
Aalen and Whelan	Aalen, F.H.A. and Whelan, Kevin (eds). *Dublin city and county: from prehistory to present: studies in honour of J.H. Andrews*. Dublin, 1992.
Abercrombie *et al.*	Abercrombie, Patrick, *et al. Dublin of the future: the new town plan*. Dublin, 1922.
AFM	*Annála ríoghachta Éireann: Annals of the kingdom of Ireland by the Four Masters, from the earliest period to the year 1616*. Ed. John O'Donovan. 7 vols. Dublin, 1851.
ALC	*The Annals of Loch Cé: a chronicle of Irish affairs from A.D. 1014 to A.D. 1590*. Ed. W.M. Hennessy. 2 vols. London, 1871.
Ancient records	*Calendar of ancient records of Dublin in the possession of the municipal corporation*. Ed. J.T. Gilbert and R.M. Gilbert. 19 vols. Dublin, 1889–1944.
Ann. Clon.	*The Annals of Clonmacnoise, being annals of Ireland from the earliest period to A.D. 1408, translated into English, A.D. 1627, by Conell Mageoghagan*. Ed. Denis Murphy. Dublin, 1896.
Ann. Conn.	*Annála Connacht: the Annals of Connacht (A.D. 1224–1544)*. Ed. A.M. Freeman. Dublin, 1944.
Ann. Inisf.	*The Annals of Inisfallen (MS Rawlinson B 503)*. Ed. Seán Mac Airt. Dublin, 1951.
Ann. Tig.	The Annals of Tigernach. Ed. Whitley Stokes. Facsimile reprint from *Revue Celtique*, xvi–xviii (1895–7). 2 vols. Lampeter, 1993.
Arch. Survey	Archaeological Survey of Ireland. National Monuments Service. Available at www.archaeology.ie (last accessed 6 June 2017).
Archiseek	Archiseek website. Available at www.archiseek.com (last accessed 6 June 2017).
AU 1, 2	(1) *Annála Uladh, Annals of Ulster … : a chronicle of Irish affairs, 431 to 1541*. Ed. W.M. Hennessy and Bartholomew MacCarthy. 4 vols. 2nd ed. Dublin, 1998; (2) *The Annals of Ulster (to A.D. 1131), pt 1, Text and translation*. Ed. Seán Mac Airt and Gearóid Mac Niocaill. Dublin, 1983.

BL	British Library, London.
Bodl.	Bodleian Library, Oxford.
Bonar Law and Bonar Law	Bonar Law, Andrew and Bonar Law, Charlotte. *A contribution towards a catalogue of the printed maps of Dublin city and county.* 2 vols. Dublin, 2005.
Boundary com. rept	*Municipal boundaries commission (Ireland)*, pt III, *Report and evidence.* HC 1881 [C.3089], 1.
Brooking	Brooking, Charles. *A map of the city and suburbs of Dublin. And also the archbishop and earl of Meaths liberties with the bounds of each parish, drawn from an actual survey.* With inset *A prospect of the city of Dublin from the north.* Dublin, 1728.
Cal. Carew MSS	*Calendar of the Carew manuscripts preserved in the archiepiscopal library at Lambeth, 1515–74* [etc.]. 6 vols. London, 1867–73.
Cal. chart. rolls	*Calendar of the charter rolls, 1226–57* [etc]. 6 vols. London, 1903–27.
Cal. doc. Ire.	*Calendar of documents relating to Ireland, 1171–1251* [etc.]. 5 vols. London, 1875–86.
Cal. exch. inq.	*Calendar of exchequer inquisitions, 1455–1699* [etc.]. Dublin, 1991–.
Cal. fine rolls	*Calendar of the fine rolls, 1271–1307* [etc.]. 22 vols. London, 1911–62.
Cal. justic. rolls Ire.	*Calendar of the justiciary rolls or proceedings in the court of the justiciar of Ireland, 1295–1303* [etc.]. 3 vols. Dublin, 1905–56.
Cal. papal letters	*Calendar of entries in the papal registers relating to Great Britain and Ireland: papal letters, 1198–1304* [etc.]. London and Dublin, 1893–.
Cal. pat. rolls	*Calendar of the patent rolls, 1216–25* [etc]. London, 1901–.
Cal. pat. rolls Ire.	*Calendar of the patent and close rolls of chancery in Ireland.* 3 vols. Dublin, 1861–3.
Cal. pat. rolls Ire., Jas I	*Irish patent rolls of James I: facsimile of the Irish record commissioners' calendar prepared prior to 1830.* IMC, Dublin, 1966.
Cal. S.P. dom.	*Calendar of state papers, domestic series, 1547–1580* [etc.]. London 1856–.
Cal. S.P. Ire.	*Calendar of the state papers relating to Ireland, 1509–73* [etc.]. 24 vols. London, 1860–1910.
Cal. treas. bks	*Calendar of treasury books.* 32 vols. London, 1904–62.
Census, 1659	*A census of Ireland circa 1659.* Ed. Séamus Pender. IMC, Dublin, 1939; reprinted, 2002.
Census, 1821 [etc.]	Printed census reports (for full references see W.E. Vaughan and A.J. Fitzpatrick, *Irish historical statistics 1821–1971* (Dublin, 1978), pp 355–61).
Census returns, 1901 [etc.]	Unpublished census returns, NAI.
Chartae	*Chartae, privilegia et immunitates, being transcripts of charters and privileges to cities, towns, abbeys, and other bodies corporate … .* Dublin, 1829–30.
Christ Church deeds	'Calendar to Christ Church deeds'. In *PRI repts D.K. 20–24.* Dublin, 1888–92. Index in *PRI rept D.K. 27*, pp 3–101. Reprinted, with additional material and new index, as *Christ Church deeds*, ed. M.J. McEnery and Raymond Refaussé. Dublin, 2001 (cited by deed number).
Chron. Scot.	*Chronicum Scotorum: a chronicle of Irish affairs … to A.D. 1135, with a supplement … from 1141 to 1150.* Ed. W.M. Hennessy. London, 1866.

Clarke	Clarke, H.B. *Dublin, part I, to 1610* (*IHTA*, no. 11). Dublin, 2002.
C. of I.	Church of Ireland.
Commons' jn. Ire.	*Journals of the house of commons of the kingdom of Ireland.* Printed in four series (for full lists see H.D. Gribbon, 'Journals of the Irish house of commons', *An Leabharlann: the Irish Library*, 2nd ser., ii (1985), pp 52–5).
CS	*The civil survey, A.D. 1654–6.* Ed. R.C. Simington. 10 vols. IMC, Dublin, 1931–61.
D'Alton	D'Alton, John. *The history of the county of Dublin.* Dublin, 1838. Reprinted Cork, 1976.
Daly	Daly, Mary. *Dublin: the deposed capital: a social and economic history, 1860–1914.* Cork, 1984.
DCLA	Dublin City Library and Archive. Pearse Street, Dublin.
De Gomme	[De Gomme, Bernard]. 'The city and suburbs of Dublin, from Kilmainham to Rings-End wherein the rivers, streets, lanes, allys, churches, gates & c. are exactly described, 1673'. Scale 1760 yards to one English mile. National Maritime Museum, Greenwich, P/49 (11).
DHR	*Dublin Historical Record.* Dublin, 1938–.
DIA	Dictionary of Irish Architects online. Available at www.dia.ie (last accessed 14 May 2016).
DIB	*Dictionary of Irish Biography: from the earliest times to the year 2002.* Ed. James McGuire and James Quinn. 9 vols. Cambridge, 2009. Available at dib.cambridge.org (last accessed 25 July 2016).
Donnelly	Donnelly, Nicholas. *A short history of some Dublin parishes.* 17 parts, Dublin, [*c.* 1905–16]; reprinted Blackrock, 1983.
Dublin almanac	*The Dublin almanac and general advertiser of Ireland.* Dublin, 1834–50.
Dublin civic survey	*The Dublin civic survey report.* Liverpool, 1925.
Dublin guide	Lewis, Richard. *The Dublin guide: or a description of the city of Dublin* … Dublin, 1787.
Duncan	Duncan, William. *Map of the county of Dublin*, 8 sheets. Dublin, 1821.
Education repts	*Reports from the commissioners of the board of education in Ireland.* HC 1813 (47), v.
Electoral Act	The Electoral Acts, 1923–1980. Available at www. irishstatutebook.ie (last accessed 24 Oct. 2016). Cited by act number.
Electoral rolls, 1908 [etc.]	Borough of the City of Dublin Register of Local Government Voters, 1908–15. Clontarf West Ward. Available at http:// databases.dublincity.ie/advanced.php (last accessed 5 July 2017).
Endowed schools rept	*Report of the commissioners for enquiring into the endowed schools in Ireland.* HC 1857–8 [2336], xxii, pt iv; 1881 [2831], xxxv, pt i.
Excavations	*Excavations 1969: summary accounts of archaeological excavations in Ireland* [etc.]. Dublin and Bray, 1969–76, 1985–. Available at www.excavations.ie (last accessed 17 Nov. 2016).
Extents Ir. mon. possessions	*Extents of Irish monastic possessions, 1540–41, from manuscripts in the Public Record Office, London.* Ed. N.B. White. IMC, Dublin, 1943.
Fairs and markets rept	*Report of the commissioners appointed to inquire into the state of the fairs and markets in Ireland.* HC 1852–3 [1674], xli.
Fiants	'Calendar of fiants of Henry VIII … Elizabeth'. In *PRI repts D.K.* 7–22. Dublin, 1875–90. Reprinted as *The Irish fiants of the Tudor sovereigns* … . 4 vols. Dublin, 1994.

Goodbody	Goodbody, Rob. *Dublin, part III, 1756 to 1847 (IHTA, no. 26).* Dublin, 2014.
Gwynn and Hadcock	Gwynn, Aubrey and Hadcock, R.N. *Medieval religious houses: Ireland.* London, 1970.
HC	House of commons sessional paper.
IAA	Irish Architectural Archive, Dublin.
IHS	*Irish Historical Studies.* Dublin, 1938–.
IHTA	*Irish Historic Towns Atlas.* Ed. J.H. Andrews, Anngret Simms, H.B. Clarke, Raymond Gillespie and Jacinta Prunty. Dublin, 1986–.
IMC	Irish Manuscripts Commission.
Ir. Builder	*The Irish Builder and Engineer.* Dublin, 1867–. Formerly *The Dublin Builder.* Dublin, 1859–66.
Lennon	Lennon, Colm. *Dublin, part II, 1610 to 1756 (IHTA, no. 19).* Dublin, 2008.
Lewis	Lewis, Samuel. *A topographical dictionary of Ireland.* 2 vols with atlas. London, 1837.
Logainm	Logainm. Bunachar logainmneacha na hÉireann — Placenames database of Ireland. Available at www.logainm.ie (last accessed 9 June 2017).
Lucas	Lucas, Richard. *A general directory of the kingdom of Ireland … .* Dublin, 1788.
Mac Niocaill	Mac Niocaill, Gearóid. *Na buirgéisí, xii–xv aois.* 2 vols. Dublin, 1964.
McCullough	McCullough, Niall. *Dublin, an urban history: the plan of the city.* Dublin, 2007.
McManus	McManus, Ruth. *Dublin, 1910–1940: shaping the city and suburbs.* Dublin, 2002.
Mun. boundary repts	*Municipal corporation boundaries (Ireland) reports and plans.* HC 1837 (301), xxix.
Mun. corp. Ire. rept	*Municipal corporations (Ireland), appendices to the first report of the commissioners.* HC 1835, xxvii, xxviii; 1836, xxiv.
Murphy and Potterton	Murphy, Margaret and Potterton, Michael. *The Dublin region in the middle ages: settlement, land-use and economy.* Dublin, 2010.
NAI	National Archives of Ireland, Dublin. Formerly Public Record Office of Ireland.
NGI	National Gallery of Ireland, Dublin.
NHI	*A new history of Ireland.* Ed. T.W. Moody, F.X. Martin, F.J. Byrne, and others. 9 vols. Oxford, 1976–2005.
NIAH intro./survey	National inventory of architectural heritage. *An introduction to the architectural heritage of County Meath* [etc.]. Dublin, 2002–. Survey available at www.buildingsofireland.com (last accessed 9 June 2017).
NLI	National Library of Ireland, Dublin.
Ó Maitiú	Ó Maitiú, Séamus. *Dublin's suburban towns, 1834–1930.* Dublin, 2003.
OSM	Ordnance Survey memoirs, RIA.
Parl. boundary repts	*Parliamentary representation: boundary reports, Ireland.* HC 1831–2 (519), xliii.
Parl. gaz.	*The parliamentary gazetteer of Ireland.* 3 vols. London, 1846.
Petty	Petty, William. *Hiberniae delineatio quoad hactenus licuit perfectissima … .* [London], 1685.

Pigot	*Pigot's national commercial directory of Ireland.* Dublin, 1824.
Pratt	Pratt, Henry. *A map of the kingdom of Ireland newly corrected and improved … with plans of the citys and fortified towns … .* London, [1708]. Reprinted Dublin, [1732].
Primary educ. returns	*Royal commission of inquiry, primary education (Ireland), vi, Educational census. Returns showing the number of children actually present in each primary school on 25th June 1868 … .* HC 1870 [C.6.v], xxviii, pt V.
PRI rept D.K. 1 [etc.]	*First [etc.] report of the deputy keeper of the public records in Ireland.* Dublin, 1869–1936.
PRONI	Public Record Office of Northern Ireland, Belfast.
Prunty	Prunty, Jacinta. *Maps and map-making in local history.* Dublin, 2004.
Publ. instr. rept 1	*First report of the commissioners on public instruction, Ireland.* HC 1835 [45, 46], xxxiii.
Publ. instr. rept 2	*Second report of the commissioners on public instruction, Ireland.* HC 1835 [47], xxxiv.
RC	Roman Catholic.
RCB	Representative Church Body Library, Dublin.
RD	Registry of Deeds, Dublin, memorials of deeds.
RIA / *RIA Proc.*	Royal Irish Academy, Dublin (*Proceedings of*), Dublin, 1836–.
Rocque	Rocque, John. *An actual survey of the county of Dublin, 1760.* 4 sheets. Dublin, 1760; reprinted London, 1802.
Rot. pat. Hib.	*Rotulorum patentium et clausorum cancellariae Hiberniae calendarium.* i, pt 1, *Hen. II–Hen. VII.* Ed. Edward Tresham. Dublin, 1828.
RSAI Jn.	*Journal of the Royal Society of Antiquaries of Ireland.* Dublin, 1850–.
Slater	*Slater's national commercial directory of Ireland.* Manchester, 1846, etc.
Stat. Ire.	*The statutes at large passed in the parliaments held in Ireland … .* 22 vols. Dublin, 1786–1801.
Taylor	Taylor, John. *Taylor's map of the environs of Dublin.* Dublin, 1816. Scale 2 inches to one mile.
Taylor and Skinner	Taylor, George and Skinner, Andrew. *Maps of the roads of Ireland, surveyed in 1777.* London and Dublin, 1778.
TCD	Trinity College, Dublin.
Thom	*Thom's Irish almanac and official directory.* Dublin, 1844, etc.
Thom map	'Map of the city of Dublin and its environs, constructed for Thom's almanac and official directory'. In *Thom*, 1871, etc. UCD School of Geography, Planning and Environmental Policy. Available at http://digital.ucd.ie/view/ucdlib:33009 (last accessed 6 June 2017).
Thomas	Thomas, Avril. *The walled towns of Ireland.* 2 vols. Dublin, 1992.
TNA: PRO	The National Archives: Public Record Office, Kew.
UJA	*Ulster Journal of Archaeology.* Belfast, 1853–.
Urb. Arch. Survey	Urban Archaeology Survey, National Monuments Service, Department of the Environment, Heritage and Local Government.
Walker	Walker, B.M. (ed.). *Parliamentary election results in Ireland, 1801–1922.* Dublin, 1978.
Warburton *et al.*	Warburton, John, Whitelaw, James and Walsh, Robert. *History of the city of Dublin.* 2 vols. London, 1818.
Watson	Watson, John, and others. *The gentleman and citizen's almanack.* Dublin, 1729–1844.

The Irish Historic Towns Atlas (IHTA) project was established in 1981 with the aim of recording the historical geography of a selection of Irish towns, both large and small. To date, twenty-eight towns atlases have been published. In addition, the project has produced a number of ancillary publications, including pocket maps, guides to urban mapping and a set of proceedings of its annual seminar on 'Maps and texts'. The Dublin suburbs series, of which this volume is part, now complements the main towns atlas series.

The Irish Historic Towns Atlas project has played a major role in promoting Irish urban studies within a European scholarly milieu, through its active participation in the International Commission for the History of Towns. The Irish series is part of a larger project to facilitate the comparative study of towns in Europe based on a unified system of cartographical principles. Over 500 towns atlases have been published under the European project.

www.ihta.ie

Early Medieval China

Early Medieval China

❖

A SOURCEBOOK

Edited by

Wendy Swartz, Robert Ford Campany, Yang Lu,
and Jessey J. C. Choo

COLUMBIA UNIVERSITY PRESS

NEW YORK

The volume editors and Columbia University Press wish to express their appreciation for the grant provided by the New Perspectives on Chinese Culture and Society program of the American Council of Learned Societies and the Chiang Ching-kuo Foundation toward the cost of publishing this book.

Columbia University Press
Publishers Since 1893
New York   Chichester, West Sussex
cup.columbia.edu

Library of Congress Cataloging-in-Publication Data
Early medieval China : a sourcebook / edited by Wendy Swartz, Robert Ford Campany, Yang Lu, and Jessey J. C. Choo.
pages   cm.
Includes bibliographical references and index.
ISBN 978-0-231-15986-9 (cloth : alk. paper)
ISBN 978-0-231-15987-6 (pbk. : alk. paper)
ISBN 978-0-231-53100-9 (e-book)
1. China—Civilization—221 B.C.–960 A.D.   2. China—Intellectual life—221 B.C.–960 A.D.   3. Chinese literature—220–589—History and criticism.   I. Swartz, Wendy, 1972– author, editor of compilation.   II. Campany, Robert Ford, 1959– author, editor of compilation   III. Lu, Yang, 1965– author, editor of compilation.   IV. Choo, Jessey Jiun-Chyi, 1973– author, editor of compilation.
DS747.42E37 2013
931'.04—dc23
2012048486

Columbia University Press books are printed on permanent and durable acid-free paper.
This book is printed on paper with recycled content.
Printed in the United States of America

COVER DESIGN: SHAINA ANDREWS

COVER IMAGE:

OFFERING PROCESSION OF THE EMPRESS AS DONOR WITH HER COURT, CHINESE, FROM LONGMEN, BINYANG CENTRAL CAVE, HENAN PROVINCE, CA. 522 C.E. NORTHERN WEI DYNASTY.

THE NELSON-ATKINS MUSEUM OF ART, KANSAS CITY, MISSOURI

c 10 9 8 7 6 5 4 3 2 1
p 10 9 8 7 6 5 4 3 2

CONTENTS

Chronological Contents   xi
Acknowledgments   xv
A Note on the Translations   xvii
Abbreviations   xix

Introduction   1

PART I
The North and the South
Jessey J. C. Choo
11

1. Return to the North?
The Debate on Moving the Capital Back to Luoyang
Jessey J. C. Choo
17

2. The Disputation at Pengcheng:
Accounts from the *Wei shu* and the *Song shu*
Albert E. Dien
32

3. Between Imitation and Mockery:
The Southern Treatments of Northern Cultures
Jessey J. C. Choo
60

4. Literary Imagination of the North and South
Ping Wang
77

PART II
Governing Mechanisms and Social Reality
Yang Lu
89

5. Managing Locality in Early Medieval China:
Evidence from Changsha
Yang Lu
95

6. Classical Scholarship in the Shu Region: The Case of Qiao Zhou
J. Michael Farmer
108

7. Ranking Men and Assessing Talent:
Xiahou Xuan's Response to an Inquiry by Sima Yi
Timothy M. Davis
125

8. On Land and Wealth: Liu Zishang's "Petition on Closing Off Mountains
and Lakes" and Yang Xi's "Discussion on
Abolishing Old Regulations Regarding Mountains and Marshes"
Charles Holcombe
147

9. Crime and Punishment:
The Case of Liu Hui in the *Wei shu*
Jen-der Lee
156

10. Marriage and Social Status:
Shen Yue's "Impeaching Wang Yuan"
David R. Knechtges
166

11. Religion and Society on the Silk Road:
The Inscriptional Evidence from Turfan
Huaiyu Chen
176

PART III
Cultural Capital
Wendy Swartz
195

12. The Art of Discourse:
Xi Kang's "Sound Is Without Sadness or Joy"
Robert Ashmore
201

13. Poetry on the Mysterious:
The Writings of Sun Chuo
Paul W. Kroll
230

14. The Art of Poetry Writing:
Liu Xiaochuo's "Becoming the Number-One
Person for the Number-One Position"
Ping Wang
245

15. Six Poems from a Liang Dynasty Princely Court
Xiaofei Tian
256

16. Pei Ziye's "Discourse on Insect Carving"
Jack W. Chen
267

17. Classifying the Literary Tradition:
Zhi Yu's "Discourse on Literary Compositions
Divided by Genre"
Wendy Swartz
274

18. Zhong Rong's Preface to *Grades of the Poets*
Stephen Owen
287

19. Book Collecting and Cataloging in the Age of
Manuscript Culture: Xiao Yi's *Master of the
Golden Tower* and Ruan Xiaoxu's Preface to *Seven Records*
Xiaofei Tian
307

PART IV
Imaging Self and Other
Wendy Swartz
325

20. Biographies of Recluses:
Huangfu Mi's *Accounts of High-Minded Men*
Alan Berkowitz
333

21. Classifications of People and Conduct:
Liu Shao's *Treatise on Personality* and Liu Yiqing's
Recent Anecdotes from the Talk of the Ages
Jack W. Chen
350

22. The Literary Community at the Court of
the Liang Crown Prince
Ping Wang
370

23. Self-Narration:
Tao Yuanming's "Biography of the Master of Five Willows"
and Yuan Can's "Biography of the Master of Wonderful Virtue"
Wendy Swartz
382

24. On Political and Personal Fate:
Three Selections from Jiang Yan's Prose and Verse
Paul W. Kroll
388

25. The Shadow Image in the Cave:
Discourse on Icons
Eugene Wang
405

PART V
Everyday Life
Jessey J. C. Choo and Albert E. Dien
429

26. Dietary Habits: Shu Xi's "Rhapsody on Pasta"
David R. Knechtges
447

27. The Epitaph of a Third-Century Wet Nurse, Xu Yi
Jen-der Lee
458

28. Festival and Ritual Calendar:
Selections from *Record of the Year and Seasons of Jing-Chu*
Ian Chapman
468

29. Custom and Society:
The Family Instructions of Mr. Yan
Albert E. Dien
494

30. Adoption and Motherhood:
"The Petition Submitted by Lady [née] Yu"
Jessey J. C. Choo
511

31. Estate Culture in Early Medieval China:
The Case of Shi Chong
David R. Knechtges
530

PART VI
Relations with the Unseen World
Robert Ford Campany
539

32. Biographies of Eight Autocremators
and Huijiao's "Critical Evaluation"
James A. Benn
543

33. Divine Instructions for an Official
Stephen R. Bokenkamp
561

34. Tales of Strange Events
Robert Ford Campany
576

35. Texts for Stabilizing Tombs
Timothy M. Davis
592

36. Reciting Scriptures to Move the Spirits
Clarke Hudson
613

37. Confucian Views of the Supernatural
Keith N. Knapp
640

38. Encounters in Mountains
Gil Raz
652

List of Contributors   683
Index   689

CHRONOLOGICAL CONTENTS

Ca. 180s–ca. 230s   5. Managing Locality in Early Medieval China: Evidence from Changsha   95

Third century onward   37. Confucian Views of the Supernatural   640

Early–mid-third century   21. Classifications of People and Conduct: Liu Shao's *Treatise on Personality*   350

239–244   7. Ranking Men and Assessing Talent: Xiahou Xuan's Response to an Inquiry by Sima Yi   125

Mid-third century   20. Biographies of Recluses: Huangfu Mi's *Accounts of High-Minded Men*   333

12. The Art of Discourse: Xi Kang's "Sound Is Without Sadness or Joy"   201

6. Classical Scholarship in the Shu Region: The Case of Qiao Zhou   108

252 onward   35. Texts for Stabilizing Tombs   592

291   26. Dietary Habits: Shu Xi's "Rhapsody on Pasta"   447

296   31. Estate Culture in Early Medieval China: The Case of Shi Chong   530

299   27. The Epitaph of a Third-Century Wet Nurse, Xu Yi   458

Ca. 300   17. Classifying the Literary Tradition: Zhi Yu's
                                    "Discourse on Literary Compositions Divided
                                    by Genre"   274

Early fourth–late tenth century   3. Between Imitation and Mockery:
                                    The Southern Treatments of Northern
                                    Cultures   60

From 317   38. Encounters in Mountains   652

330   30. Adoption and Motherhood: "The Petition
                                    Submitted by Lady [née] Yu"   511

Ca. 345–ca. 360   13. Poetry on the Mysterious: The Writings of
                                    Sun Chuo   230

362   1. Return to the North? The Debate on Moving
                                    the Capital Back to Luoyang   17

364–370   33. Divine Instructions for an Official   561

Ca. 400   36. Reciting Scriptures to Move the Spirits   613

Ca. 412–429   25. The Shadow Image in the Cave: Discourse
                                    on Icons   405

Ca. 415–427   23. Self-Narration: Tao Yuanming's "Biography
                                    of the Master of Five Willows"   382

Ca. 430   21. Classifications of People and Conduct: Liu
                                    Yiqing's *Recent Anecdotes from the Talk of the
                                    Ages*   350

Ca. 440   34. Tales of Strange Events   576

451   2. The Disputation at Pengcheng: Accounts
                                    from the *Wei shu* and the *Song shu*   32

Ca. 460s   8. On Land and Wealth: Liu Zishang's
                                    "Petition on Closing Off Mountains and Lakes"
                                    and Yang Xi's "Discussion on Abolishing
                                    Old Regulations Regarding Mountains and
                                    Marshes"   147

Mid-fifth century   23. Self-Narration: Yuan Can's "Biography of
                                    the Master of Wonderful Virtue"   382

                                    24. On Political and Personal Fate: Three
                                    Selections from Jiang Yan's Prose and
                                    Verse   388

Ca. 480s   4. Literary Imagination of the North and
                                    South   77

490   10. Marriage and Social Status: Shen Yue's
                                    "Impeaching Wang Yuan"   166

Late fifth–early sixth century   16. Pei Ziye's "Discourse on Insect
                                    Carving"   267

Early sixth century   32. Biographies of Eight Autocremators and
                                    Huijiao's "Critical Evaluation"   543

Ca. 505–510   14. The Art of Poetry Writing: Liu Xiaochuo's
                               "Becoming the Number-One Person for the
                               "Number-One Position" 245

513–518   18. Zhong Rong's Preface to *Grades of the
                               Poets* 287

517–519   22. The Literary Community at the Court of
                               the Liang Crown Prince 370

523   19. Book Collecting and Cataloging in the Age
                               of Manuscript Culture: Ruan Xiaoxu's Preface
                               to *Seven Records* 307

523–530   15. Six Poems from a Liang Dynasty Princely
                               Court 256

Mid-sixth century   19. Book Collecting and Cataloging in the Age
                               of Manuscript Culture: Xiao Yi's *Master of the
                               Golden Tower* 307

554   9. Crime and Punishment: The Case of Liu
                               Hui in the *Wei shu* 156

556   11. Religion and Society on the Silk Road:
                               The Inscriptional Evidence from Turfan 176

Completed by 565   28. Festival and Ritual Calendar: Selections
                               from *Record of the Year and Seasons of
                               Jing-Chu* 468

Completed ca. 590s   29. Custom and Society: *The Family Instruc-
                               tions of Mr. Yan* 494

ACKNOWLEDGMENTS

For a project many years in the making, we have many people to thank who helped along the way. We are grateful to the following scholars who offered feedback and encouragement during the early phase of the project: Cheng Yu-yu, Benjamin Elman, Paul Goldin, Martin Kern, Li Fengmao, Liu Yuan-ju, Willard Peterson, Andrew Plaks, Michael Puett, Stephen Teiser, and, especially, Xiaofei Tian. We also thank the Department of East Asian Studies at Princeton University for hosting a planning meeting in 2006 and the Department of East Asian Languages and Cultures at Columbia University for hosting a conference in 2007 during which the first draft of the volume was produced. The Princeton meeting was funded by the East Asian Studies Program, Council of the Humanities, Princeton Institute for International and Regional Studies (PIIRS), and the Shelby Cullom Davis Center for Historical Studies. The two rapporteurs for the Princeton meeting, Ian Chapman and Alexei Ditter, and the two rapporteurs for the Columbia conference, Linda Feng and Nina Duthie, provided the contributors with meticulous and helpful notes from the proceedings of the meetings. Gregory Patterson deftly managed the logistics for the conference and helped ensure its success.

Several scholars from China generously spent their time to discuss certain issues in parts 1 and 2 of this volume; their admirable erudition has enriched those sections: Hou Xudong, Hu Baoguo, Luo Xin, and Meng Yanhong.

We would like to acknowledge the two anonymous readers, who took great care in reading the manuscript and offered insightful comments that have helped improve the volume in substantial ways.

The administrative staff of the History Department at the University of Missouri–Kansas City provided crucial support as the editors prepared the final manuscript. At Columbia University Press, we thank editor Jennifer Crewe, whose reputation for excellent judgment is justified in every way, and manuscript editor Irene Pavitt, whose expertise in handling large-scale projects was valuable in every instance. We especially appreciate Margaret B. Yamashita's careful editorial work in a volume of this length and complexity. We also thank Asya Graf, whose professionalism, efficiency, and good cheer made the publication process more enjoyable.

This project was made possible by a generous conference grant and publication subsidy from the American Council of Learned Societies and the Chiang Ching-kuo Foundation. We also thank the Rutgers University Research Council for providing a grant that subsidized the final preparation of this manuscript.

A NOTE ON THE TRANSLATIONS

This volume uses the *pinyin* system for romanizing Chinese throughout, silently emending other systems in quoted secondary works as necessary. Chinese names are rendered in their Chinese order, with the surname first and the personal name last. Dates given after personal names are those of birth and death. Reign dates given after the temple name of rulers are indicated by "r." When the exact dates of a person are unknown, the approximate period of activity is indicated by "fl." Although the editors of this volume have standardized the translation of certain common terms, such as "league" (*li* 里) and "byname" (*zi* 字), we have kept the different translations of some terms, such as the still debated *jiu* 酒 (wine or ale).

For the translation of official titles, we have followed, when possible, Charles O. Hucker, *A Dictionary of Official Titles in Imperial China* (Stanford, Calif.: Stanford University Press, 1985). All citations of dynastic histories are from the standard Zhonghua shuju editions, published between 1959 and 1977. The titles of all dynastic histories have been abbreviated, except *Sui shu*, which shares the same initials (*SS*) as another often cited history, *Song shu*. When referring to the Classics, the editors have left the choice to each scholar of using *pinyin* or an English translation—for example, *Shangshu* 尚書 (or *Shujing* 書經) or *Classic of Documents*; *Shijing* 詩經 or *Classic of Poetry* (or *Odes*); *Liji* 禮記 or *Record of Rites*; and *Lunyu* 論語 or *Analects*.

ABBREVIATIONS

BQS   *Bei Qi shu* 北齊書 by Li Baiyao 李百藥 (565–648). Beijing: Zhonghua shuju, 1972.

BS   *Bei shi* 北史 by Li Yanshou 李延壽 (fl. ca. 629). Beijing: Zhonghua shuju, 1974.

CLEAR   *Chinese Literature: Essays, Articles, Reviews.*

CS   *Chen shu* 陳書 by Yao Silian 姚思廉 (557–637). Beijing: Zhonghua shuju, 1972.

CSJC   *Congshu jicheng chubian* 叢書集成初編. Beijing: Zhonghua shuju, 1985.

DZ   *Daozang* 道藏. Works in the Ming-era Daoist canon (*Zhengtong daozang*) are cited by the number assigned to them in Kristofer M. Schipper and Franciscus Verellen, eds., *The Taoist Canon: A Historical Companion to the Daozang* (Chicago: University of Chicago Press, 2004), followed by fascicle and page numbers (a indicates recto, b verso) and sometimes line number.

HBXD   *Han Wei Liuchao biji xiaoshuo daguan* 漢魏六朝筆記小說大觀. Edited by Wang Genlin 王根林 et al. Shanghai: Shanghai guji, 1999.

HHS   *Hou Han shu* 後漢書 by Fan Ye 范曄 (398–445). Beijing: Zhonghua shuju, 1965.

HJAS   *Harvard Journal of Asiatic Studies.*

HS   *Han shu* 漢書 by Ban Gu 班固 (32–92). Beijing: Zhonghua shuju, 1962.

JS   *Jin shu* 晉書 by Fang Xuanling 房玄齡 (579–648) et al. Beijing: Zhonghua shuju, 1974.

JTS   *Jiu Tang shu* 舊唐書 by Liu Xu 劉昫 (887–946). Beijing: Zhonghua shuju, 1975.

LBXJ   *Lidai biji xiaoshuo jicheng* 歷代筆記小說集成. Shijiazhuang: Hebei jiaoyu chubanshe, 1994.

LS   *Liang shu* 梁書 by Yao Silian 姚思廉 (557–637). Beijing: Zhonghua shuju, 1973.

LX   *Gu xiaoshuo gouchen* 古小說鉤沈 by Lu Xun 魯迅. Beijing: Renmin wenxue chubanshe, 1954.

NQS   *Nan Qi shu* 南齊書 by Xiao Zixian 蕭子顯 (489–537). Beijing: Zhonghua shuju, 1972.

NS   *Nan shi* 南史 by Li Yanshou 李延壽 (ca. 629). Beijing: Zhonghua shuju, 1975.

QW   *Quan Shanggu Sandai Qin Han Sanguo Liuchao wen* 全上古三代秦漢三國六朝文. Compiled by Yan Kejun 嚴可均 (1762–1843). Beijing: Zhonghua shuju, 1958.

SBBY   *Sibu beiyao* 四部備要. Shanghai: Zhonghua shuju, 1927–1935.

SBCK   *Sibu congkan* 四部叢刊. Shanghai: Commercial Press, 1920–1922.

SGZ   *Sanguo zhi* 三國志 by Chen Shou 陳壽 (233–297). Beijing: Zhonghua shuju, 1957.

SJ   *Shi ji* 史記 by Sima Qian 司馬遷 (ca. 145–86 B.C.E.). Beijing: Zhonghua shuju, 1959.

SKQS   *Siku quanshu* 四庫全書. *Yingyin Wenyuange Siku quanshu* 景印文淵閣四庫全書. Taibei: Taiwan Shangwu yinshuguan, 1983–1986.

SS   *Song shu* 宋書 by Shen Yue 沈約 (441–513). Beijing: Zhonghua shuju, 1974.

SSJZ   *Shisan jing zhushu* 十三經註疏. Taibei: Yiwen yinshuguan, 1965.

SSJZZ   *Shisan jing zhushu zhengliben* 十三經注疏整理本. Beijing: Peking University Press, 2000.

T   *Taishō shinshū daizōkyō* 大正新脩大藏經. Edited by Takakusu Junjirō 高楠順次郎 and Watanabe Kaigyoku 渡邊海旭. Tokyo: Taishō issaikyō kankōkai, 1924–1932. Texts are cited by the number assigned to them in this edition, followed by the volume number, page number, and, in some cases, register (a, b, or c) and line number.

TP   *T'oung Pao* 通報.

TPGJ   *Taiping guangji* 太平廣記. Compiled by Li Fang 李昉 (925–996). Beijing: Zhonghua shuju, 1961.

TPYL   *Taiping yulan* 太平御覽. Compiled by Li Fang 李昉 (925–996). *SBCK* vols. 1–7. Taibei: Shangwu yinshuguan, 1975.

WS   *Wei shu* 魏書 by Wei Shou 魏收 (505–572). Beijing: Zhonghua shuju, 1974.

XS   *Xian Qin Han Wei Jin Nanbeichao shi* 先秦漢魏晉南北朝詩. Compiled by Lu Qinli 逯欽立. Beijing: Zhonghua shuju, 1983.

ZGXZ   *Zhongguo gudai xiaoshuo zongmu* 中國古代小說總目. Compiled by Shi Changyu 石昌渝. Taiyuan: Shanxi jiaoyu, 2004.

ZS   *Zhou shu* 周書 by Linghu Defen 令狐德棻 (583–666) et al. Beijing: Zhonghua shuju, 1971.

ZZJC   *Zhuzi jicheng* 諸子集成. Beijing: Zhonghua shuju, 1954.

ZZTJ   *Zizhi tongjian* 資治通鑒 by Sima Guang 司馬光 (1019–1086) et al. Beijing: Zhonghua shuju, 1956.

Early Medieval China

Introduction

The Six Dynasties period is also variously referred to in modern Western scholarship as Early Medieval China, the Northern and Southern Dynasties, and the Period of Division or Disunion. It was the longest period of political fragmentation in China's imperial history and appears to have had a definite beginning and ending. It began when Cao Pi, the head of the powerful Cao family, deposed the last emperor of the Eastern Han and founded the Wei dynasty in 220 C.E. It ended when Yang Jian, the founder of the Sui dynasty, reunified China under his rule in 589. During this span of political fragmentation, there was a brief period of unity. The Western Jin dynasty managed to hold China together for several decades, from the destruction of the Wu kingdom in 280 to the sack of Luoyang in 311, even though the dynasty itself endured a civil war fought among members of the ruling house from 291 to 306. In turn, the sack of Luoyang by the Xiongnu leaders Liu Cong and Liu Yao marked the beginning of the nomadic invasions from northern China and a succession of alien regimes. During this time, with the support of émigré elites in southern China, Sima Rui established a new dynasty in the name of Jin. From this time on, the large region south of the Yangtze River was ruled by a string of dynasties founded by Han Chinese elites. Despite a number of ambitious campaigns launched by various Northern and Southern regimes, this geographical and political division persisted until the Sui dynasty, arguably the last Northern dynasty, conquered Chen, the last Southern dynasty, in 589 and thus once again brought China together under one sovereignty.

This narrative, with its emphasis on the rise and fall of political entities, obscures profound and complex continuities, as well as changes in the society. China in 300 was vastly different from China in 600. However one parses it, politically or geographically, China in 300 more or less continued Han dynasty traditions and practices. In contrast, China in 600 was not a re-creation of Han uniformity but a new order forged through many drastic and thorough transformations that took place in the intervening centuries, an order that had its own ideological foundation, ethnic makeup, and economic infrastructure.

The changes in northern China were abrupt and drastic, the most apparent being the changes in ethnic makeup and relationships. Just before the fourth century, massive numbers of people termed "barbarians" by the Han people began migrating into the traditional Chinese heartland. Traditional historiography specifically names and discusses the so-called Five Barbarians (wu hu 五胡)—Xiongnu, Xianbei, Jie, Di, and Qiang—who conquered the North and established, either simultaneously or consecutively, their own political regimes. But the picture of ethnic diversity in the North was in fact much more complicated. Other non-Han ethnic peoples, such as the Sogdians, Turks, and Koreans, also played significant roles in shaping the culture and politics. The manifestations of the tension between the non-Han and the Han peoples also varied across places and times, displayed either violently in political upheavals or more peacefully in ritual debates at court. The degree of tension between the two should not, however, be exaggerated, as the rivalries and confrontations among the non-Han ethnic groups were often even more intense and violent.

The conquest of northern China by non-Han ethnic groups was not simply the result of the persistent confrontations between steppe nomads and sedentary peoples or the collapse of the once mighty Han Empire, as traditional historiography often asserts. Instead, it was part of a much larger and lengthy process that connected the Eurasian steppe and China, a process that brought peoples, ideas, and cultures into contact with those of China, which were shaped and reshaped by those interactions. The interests of the non-Han ethnic groups in controlling the Chinese heartland were as much a matter of shrewd investment as of raw ambition. For example, the Qiang people had a significant presence in northwestern China, where they served in the Han frontier army during the last decades of the dynasty. Then, after the collapse of orderly rule, they fought mostly for control of the territories they had already inhabited for several generations.

Similarly, any linear representation of cultural assimilation and the sinicizing process in the North is problematic. The non-Han ethnic "invaders" had a more sophisticated understanding of China than traditional historians gave them credit for, and in some cases, they had a better grasp of Chinese cultural traditions than did those who invaded the same areas decades later. The early leaders of the Five Barbarians clearly were familiar with, if not fully in command of, the subtleties of the codes of conduct, symbols of power, and forces of ideology—in short, Han statecraft. They readily utilized and manipulated these elements to their own advantage, as well as mixing them with elements from their own cultures to achieve effective rule. Liu Yuan, the Xiongnu leader who established the first non-Han regime in the North, rallied his people with the rhetoric of restoring the Xiongnu Empire and gained support from the native Chinese by emphasizing his familial tie with the Han imperial house. In this early stage, although the ruling elites of these non-Han ethnic groups were not hostile to Chinese culture, they did not necessarily embrace it. Any overt push toward sinicization tended to cause resentment, resistance, and even armed confrontation, and it continued to have such effects well into the second half of the Northern Dynasties.

Throughout the history of early medieval China, warfare was common. Since the North was more frequently at war, one might assume that it was consumed by violence and chaos. But the Northern society often enjoyed periods of remarkable stability and economic growth as well, especially during the rule of stronger regimes. The population displacement, the breakdown of infrastructure, and the decline of locally entrenched powers offered newly arrived non-Han conquerors rare opportunities to build their sociopolitical control by possessing and allocating human and material resources. For the first time in the history of imperial China, a government could directly control and redistribute previously cultivated land on a scale that revolutionized the methods of taxation and fundamentally altered the economy. As they were incorporated in the new political order, the rural communities maintained roughly the same structure they had at the end of the Han. This structural stability thus made them the best channels through which to propagate the political ideologies, social conduct, and religious practices fostered by the Northern regimes.

The changes in the South matched those of the North in scale and complexity. While all Southern Dynasties were founded by ethnically Han elites, their social and political foundations were not consistently the same. One widely accepted view among scholars is as follows: the Southern Dynasties were politically weak and militarily incompetent; the Southern rulers often succumbed to the dominance of the great clans and had little ability to impose effective government; and the Southern courts were superior in culture and economy only when compared with their Northern neighbors. This view is rather simplistic, however. The rulers of the Southern Dynasties were often just as politically ambitious and creative as their non-Han counterparts in the North. They were equally adept at manipulating existing cultural and political elements to shape their political identity and assert imperial authority. Although the Southern courts did not achieve any lasting victories in reclaiming the Chinese heartland, they were able to fend off the numerous military offensives launched by Northern regimes. The length of the political division between the North and the South was therefore more a testament to these rulers' considerable political resolve and organizational skills than to their failures in these areas.

Modern scholars, especially those in Japan and the West, have often labeled the Six Dynasties as an age of aristocratic rule. Many Marxist historians in China, in contrast, have called the Six Dynasties a period of "feudalism." Although neither of these anachronistic characterizations captures the idiosyncratic nature of the period, they do call attention to the dominant influence of kinship-based groups in social and political life. These groups, whether they were the Great Clans of Shandong or leading nomadic tribes, constantly challenged the model of imperial authority developed in the Han dynasty. Compared with other periods in the history of imperial China, in the Six Dynasties the social and political status of an individual depended more on the social recognition of his family and reputation than on the office he held. That is, the channels for social mobility and access to political power were less often open to those who were not members of these exclusive groups. These kinship-based groups, however, were generally conscious of their privileged position in society, and in turn, their efforts to sustain that position sustained the society. Because their longevity ensured the survival of many cultural and political traditions, we find it difficult to support the claim that these kinship-based groups always placed private interests ahead of imperial authority or the public good. The hereditary status enjoyed by members of these kinship-based groups may indeed have been aristocratic, but there were different kinds of aristocracy during this period. For example, even the Great Clans of Shandong had varied interactions with the imperial authorities and the society at large, and each of them managed these interactions differently depending on their own relative geographical and political dominance. Having sketched, in the briefest terms possible, the overall shape of this period's history, we turn next to the organization and rationale of this volume.

Academic readers will immediately notice that this volume is organized thematically, with the texts arranged to suggest new ways of thinking about the period. The six parts offer a categorization that focuses less on modern disciplinary boundaries and more on the issues and discursive spheres that animated the early medieval period. We feel that a thematic organization better captures both the cross-fertilization of various fields and the complex realities of the period. By transcending modern disciplinary boundaries (or, even when most of the entries in the parts are texts that might fall under the purview of a single discipline, by choosing and introducing them thematically), we sought to avoid the academic arbitrariness in labeling texts from early medieval China as historical, literary, or religious. Most of the texts that survived from this period were produced by writers who saw themselves first and foremost as literati and who shared the goal of connecting their writings with the grand cultural and political traditions they inherited. By reading these texts outside a particular disciplinary boundary, they may be seen through a different set of lenses and appreciated for their rich texture. For example, Sun Chuo's memorial to the Eastern Jin throne concerning whether to move the capital from Jiankang back to Luoyang was written in parallel prose and is at once a calculated political work, a masterly piece of rhetoric, and a dazzling display of literary art. In another case, stories of paranormal events both featured what we today think of as "religious" topics and were understood by their authors and readers as a subbranch of history.

This volume is organized around six themes:

- Part I. The North and the South
- Part II. Governing Mechanisms and Social Reality
- Part III. Cultural Capital
- Part IV. Imaging Self and Other
- Part V. Everyday Life
- Part VI. Relations with the Unseen World

We decided on these six themes because they best capture some of the major dynamic developments of the period. We also are using them to address specific scholarly agendas of our own:

- To highlight areas of scholarship that have seen remarkable advancement in recent years (such as parts IV and VI)
- To bring attention to areas that could and should be further developed (such as parts III and V) by adapting prevalent and useful cultural theories (i.e., Pierre Bourdieu's "cultural capital" and Michel de Certeau's "everyday life")
- To provide the cultural and historical contexts for the period that will lay the foundation for future research projects (such as parts I and II)

Texts that are included in one part could certainly be used to highlight the theme of another part. This interconnection of themes is due to both the richness of the sources themselves and the sophistication of scholarly interpretations that cut across genres and disciplines. For example, Shen Yue's "Impeaching Wang Yuan" in part II, "Governing Mechanisms and Social Reality," could easily be placed in part V, "Everyday Life," where it would illuminate the self-definition of social class and the economic interests of the gentry elite in the Southern Dynasties. Likewise, excerpts from the *Outer Chapters* of *The Master Who Embraces Simplicity* included in part I, "The North and the South," would contribute much to the topics of self-reference and autobiography featured in part IV, "Imaging Self and Other." The thematic categories proposed in this volume are thus intended to highlight, rather than limit, the complexities of the early medieval period.

During the early medieval period, various group identities were continually redefined through challenges and adaptations. The physical and social landscapes faced by the people of this era changed more rapidly than in any recent generations. Large-scale conquests and resettlements led to frequent restructurings of the relationship between the land and the people. Also during this period, many new political forms and ideologies were formed. All regimes, whether in the North or the South, attempted to augment their political authority by refashioning existing political models or even inventing new ones in the name of emulating the past. On a smaller scale, the gentry class, in particular, used its social advantage and cultural capital to make gains in the political sphere, sharing power with the ruler, especially in the Eastern Jin dynasty. Cultural enterprises became both a vehicle for individual expression and the articulation of a unique personality, as well as a means to gain sociopolitical privileges. Negotiations between traditional and newly imported religions led the people of that time to consider anew their ontological understanding of their own existence and the mundane and supernatural world around them. The boundaries among the various religious teachings often blurred: religious teachings (e.g., canon, vocabulary, ideas, and practices) were shaped by the interactions with one another, and scholars today are (prudently) far less certain about the origins of certain notions. Material culture also became much more complex and rich in this period. Everyday objects and activities became the subject matter of intellectual elites' writings. New forms of urban planning, architecture, apparel, food, and furnishings appeared, leading to, as well as reinforced by, emerging lifestyles and social behaviors. As with the changes and improvements to the physical environment, new tactics that allowed people to negotiate the rapidly shifting everyday realities also became much more discernible.

The entries in each of the six parts in this volume illustrate in an interdisciplinary way the part's main theme and open with a critical narrative providing the historical and conceptual background for that particular subject. In most cases, the contributing scholars, each with a particular expertise, selected a text or a set of excerpts that he or she deemed best to demonstrate a given subject. Part I, "The North and the South," explores the ways in which, as imagined cultural spheres, the ideas of the North and the South were constructed and reflected on in contemporary sources. Although the conceptualization of the "North" and the "South" has a long history, today these two terms most commonly refer to the cultural and political divisions created when the seminomadic tribesmen who had long settled within the Chinese borders forced the Western Jin court to flee from the Chinese heartland—that is, the Yellow River basin. Subsequently, some remnants of the Chinese ruling elite set up the Eastern Jin dynasty south of the Yangzi River. Its establishment left a North that was ruled by a number of short-lived non- or semi-Chinese regimes and a South ruled by a sequence of Chinese dynasties, with the Yangzi River serving as the natural border between the two. For more than two hundred years, no Northern regime was able to conquer the South, and no Southern regime could reclaim much of the lost land in the North; each developed a unique blend of cultures, ethnicities, and social and political institutions that responded to domestic necessities and foreign challenges. The entries in part I suggest that the shifting boundary between the two depended as much on political-military realities as on the discursive and geographical spheres in which the speakers were situated. Warfare and massive deracination exposed an unprecedented number of people to languages, customs, topographies, and climates different from their own. The repeated displacement of social and cultural institutions also introduced new complications and challenged established boundaries, real or imaginary. The process of differentiating between the North and the South and assigning them attributes was also one of self-realization for the residents of the respective locales. Common identities were solidified when one party encountered "the other," either literally or figuratively. Recent studies of literature, especially poetry, have demonstrated how cultural imagination often superseded actual experience in complex and ambivalent representations of the other, be it the North or the South. The landmark memorials by Huan Wen and Sun Chuo that circulated in the Eastern Jin court concerning the prospect of returning to Luoyang are prime examples of conflicted longings: returning to native lands that had been laid waste by wars or staying safely in a strange new place that was becoming home. Aside from being a bibliophile of all things "Daoist," Ge Hong also made some of the most astute observations on the adaptation, transformation, and vulgarization of Northern culture in the South. Li Xiaobo and Zhang Chang, emissaries of the warring Northern Wei and Liu Song states, respectively, engaged in a dazzling verbal duel outside the besieged city, Pengcheng, playing on themes of cultural and political differences. The entries in part I therefore focus not only on the differences between the North and the South but also on the processes that produced and shaped them and the political mechanisms that underlay them.

The early medieval period witnessed dramatic reorganizations of the social and political order and the impact of new ideologies on those structural changes. The Han imperial model, which still overshadowed its variant political successors through its institutional legacy and its presence in the public imagination, was repeatedly challenged by both domestic and foreign interventions and improvisations. The entries in part II, "Governing Mechanisms and Social Reality," address these changes on multiple levels. The focus is on the processes through which ideologies, both cultural and political, were constructed, accepted, and reevaluated, as well as on their social and economic implications. Part II reexamines some well-known developments, such as the Nine Ranks system (the basis for official selection and employment), the economic policies adopted by the Southern state(s) to advance the interests of its ruling members, and the contesting views on marriage that defined the status of the social elite.

It also deals with matters that have not yet received adequate scholarly attention in the West, such as the reorganization of local administration and the state patronage of religion in border regions. The bamboo slips excavated from Changsha and the commemorative Buddhist stele of Gaochang are prime examples. The former reveals both the changes and the continuities of the Han dynasty and the Wu kingdom in their respective systems for managing local populations, while the latter highlights the power of religious patronage in shaping the identity of a multiethnic state. In the past, the study of elite ideologies of this period has often overemphasized "mysterious learning" (*xuanxue*) or "pure talk" (*qingtan*), which explored the ontological nature of social and political values among the intellectual elite. Part II offers a long-overdue survey of the presence of the classical tradition in scholarly, particularly classicist (often termed "Confucian"), commentaries in various intellectual enterprises of the period, including historiography, lexicography, and cosmography. The entries here suggest that classicism played a role even in the formation of both Buddhist and Daoist scholastic traditions, including their canons. Rather than treat this period as one in which classical learning was in decline—as has been the recent scholarly norm—part II approaches it as a time in which the skills developed through classical learning were being applied to broader areas of the production and organization of knowledge.

In part III, "Cultural Capital," the concept of knowledge, competence, and accomplishments that were accumulated and transmitted within the literati class provides a useful framework for examining literature and the arts. The notion of cultural capital enables us to pose complex questions about the production, organization, and evaluation of "culture" in one of the most intellectually creative periods in Chinese history. What were the cultural issues and phenomena associated with the conception of *wen* (defined as "refined literature"), and how could cultural competence and intellectual stock be converted into sociopolitical gain? The entries in part III examine the major building blocks of cultural capital for early medieval literati: the arts of discourse and poetry writing (which defined the intellectual elite), literary theory and criticism (which accounted for literary production), and treatises on collection and classification (which took stock of accumulated cultural wealth). The rhetorical art of argument is illustrated by Xi Kang's major essay "Sound Is Without Sadness or Joy," which also constitutes an important document on early medieval music theory. The selections of poems by influential writers of the period, such as Sun Chuo, Xiao Gang, and Liu Xiaochuo, demonstrate the increasingly complex art of poetic composition. These examples also underscore the increasing importance of poetry as an indicator of cultural literacy and social legitimacy. As cultural capital accumulated, efforts to manage, categorize, and rank the components of the literary heritage multiplied as well. Anthology making (Zhi Yu's "Discourse on Literary Compositions Divided by Genre") and literary criticism (Pei Ziye's "Discourse on Insect Carving" and Zhong Rong's *Grades of the*

Poets) aimed to organize the literary tradition and set standards in the face of a proliferation of texts. As texts multiplied and were disseminated in the book culture of the latter part of the early medieval period, scholars attempted to collect the books of the realm (Xiao Yi's private collection contained eighty thousand scrolls, not counting the imperial library collection that was later added to his own) and to catalog the books of the realm (Ruan Xiaoxu's *Seven Records*). Two early documents on book collection and cataloging, Ruan Xiaoxu's preface to his bibliographic catalog and an excerpt from Xiao Yi's *Master of the Golden Tower*, moreover reveal how the literati conceived of their libraries and their organization.

Part IV, "Imaging Self and Other," examines the practices of fashioning the past, oneself, and others (including a transcendent, radical "other," the Buddha). It includes translations of biographies of recluses (excerpts from Huangfu Mi's *Accounts of High-Minded Men*), a hugely important category for understanding early medieval social and political values, as well as excerpts from Liu Shao's *Treatise on Personality* (a major political work that became the foundation for official selection during this period) and the fifth-century collection of stories about the gentry class, *Recent Anecdotes from the Talk of the Ages*, both of which highlight the major issues of the day: selfhood, identity, character appraisal, and the classification of human types and conduct. Poems by Xiao Tong and his courtiers illustrate literary group identity, and the texts on self-narration (Tao Yuanming and Jiang Yan) foreground issues of self-representation. How to narrate oneself or others was a crucial question for Chinese historiography, inasmuch as the history of China is arguably recounted through the lives of individuals rather than institutions. The entries in part IV thus challenge the prevailing view that the early medieval period witnessed the rise of individualism and the awareness of selfhood. Although there is no doubt that Han social values and behavioral norms were seriously (and sometimes comically) challenged in the Wei and Jin dynasties, it is equally certain that people living before this era had experienced self-awareness as unique individuals. Accordingly, part IV offers another set of vantage points from which to view the complex social changes of the era: an expansion of typological models, the development of an elaborate classification of behavior and of a sophisticated vocabulary for character appraisal, and experimentation with literary forms of self-representation. Rather than suggesting the rise of self-awareness (another recently prevalent scholarly trope concerning our period), these early medieval developments point to the rise of a more sophisticated articulation of notions of selfhood and personality.

One of the new areas of research that this volume incorporates is the study of material culture and everyday life in early medieval China. Both transmitted and recently excavated sources offer insight into how people during this period lived each day and articulated the meaning of life through acts such as consumption, production, and possession. Part V, "Everyday Life," deals with the material condition of everyday surroundings, on the one hand, and the newly invented or repackaged concepts that helped regulate, reshape, and/or give new interpretations to everyday experiences, on the other. The texts translated and discussed here include ritual and festival calendars (around which people's lives were organized), dietary habits, domestic relationships, child custody and litigations, and the estate culture of the landed gentry.

Finally, whereas the study of the religions of the early medieval period has boomed in the past twenty years, much of recent scholarship has tended to focus on one of the major traditions—predominantly Buddhism and Daoism—in isolation from other religious currents. But people often participated in more than one of these traditions; the "great traditions" model left other aspects of religion out of the picture; and many elements of China's religions were formed in conversation with (or in explicit opposition to) elements of others. Therefore, rather than being organized according to the great traditions or "isms," part VI, "Relations with the Unseen World," focuses on a single unifying theme: relations between human beings and the denizens of the unseen world of spirits, gods, and buddhas. The selections in this part are from previously untranslated scriptures, biographies, narratives of anomalies, treatises, and documents placed in tombs. Although Western-language studies and translations of religious texts of this period have multiplied dramatically in recent years, we still lack translations of many important works and also genres of texts (such as sacred biographies and other short narratives, inscriptions, and tomb documents) usually ignored in favor of the major scriptures and treatises. Part VI builds on the momentum of recent scholarship by introducing a few of the many texts that have not yet been adequately studied.

PART I

The North and the South

"North" and "South" are used in this book as multivalent, relational terms, designating not only a geographic difference but also two sets of cultural and political attributes distinctive to each region. Throughout the history of early and medieval China, no fixed boundaries separated the two, but the North almost always refers to the Yellow River basin, the heart of the cultural and political realm. The South was commonly defined vis-à-vis the North, the perceived center of the Chinese world. Accordingly, the South denoted the area beyond the southernmost reach of the center's direct control. Even though the South referred to a series of political entities—among them the powerful states of Wu 吳, Yue 越, and Chu 楚, which more or less occupied the lower reaches of the Yangzi River—it remained the archetypal "other," whose landscapes, languages, people, and customs were alien and exotic compared with those of the center. In both the cultural imagination and political reality, the transformative teaching (*jiaohua* 教化) flowed in only one direction, from north to south.

After the Yongjia disorder 永嘉之亂 in 311 C.E. and the removal of the court to Jiankang 建康 in 318 C.E.—a series of events in which the Jin royal house was driven out of Luoyang by advancing Xiongnu forces and was forced to cede its territories in and around the Yellow River basin—the North was no longer the center. Two zones that were different but equal emerged from this cultural and political landscape: the "barbarian"-occupied North and the

"Chinese"-dominated South. Neither could conquer the other by force or culture. Therefore, as some scholars have observed, it was during the Northern and Southern Dynasties when the imagination of the North versus that of the South first took shape.[1] The documents translated in part I attest to the shifting cultural interactions between, and perceptions of, the North and the South from the third to the sixth century. These documents illustrate the ways in which the differences between the two were constructed and the preoccupation with forms and standards. Most of these documents were written by Southerners. This is not the preference of the contributors to part I but a result of the unevenness of the surviving sources. This unevenness, in turn, may suggest that the Southerners (including the Northerners who immigrated to the South in the aftermath of the Yongjia disorder) were more obsessed with constructing a cultural identity for themselves along the lines of the North and the South. Although the process by which the images of the North and the South were construed is much too complicated to represent linearly, a chronological examination of these source materials nevertheless yields many clues to the changes as well as continuations.

In chapter 4, Ping Wang points out that since the time of poet Qu Yuan 屈原 (ca. 340–ca. 277 B.C.E.), the South was regarded in literary imagination as a place for the exiled and dispossessed, even though the Southern elites, especially those from the Wu area, actively participated in the culture and governance of the center during the next four hundred years. The South was construed as a region where the civilizing influence of the center encountered lush wilderness and sensual abandonment. At once subversive and seductive, the South was where rites and propriety came undone. The fall of the Han dynasty in 220 C.E. and the splitting of the empire into three competing kingdoms, each occupying an established cultural locus with a long history—Wei 魏 on the Central Plain, Wu 吳 at the Yangzi delta, and Shu 蜀 in Sichuan—did not affect the perceived cultural supremacy of the North. In fact, the subsequent Wei-Jin dominance over the other two states might be seen as reaffirming the cultural and political centrality of the North. Ge Hong 葛洪 (283–343) observed and commented on this in his collection of essays entitled with his sobriquet, *The Master Who Embraces Simplicity* (*Baopuzi* 抱朴子). Himself a Southerner whose family had served the Han, Wu, and the conquering Jin regimes, Ge Hong was keenly aware of the deep sense of cultural inferiority felt by his peers. In the excerpts that I translated in chapter 3 from the *Outer Chapters* (*Waipian* 外篇), he insists that the Wu area had long upheld the classical tradition and saw no shortage of able and virtuous men steeped in Confucian learning. Ge Hong felt as though he was living in an age of decline in governance and moral cultivation. To follow blindly the latest fashions and social practices at the court in Luoyang, as his fellow Southerners had done, was to deny their own cultural heritage, which itself was rooted in Zhou orthodoxy. Ge Hong was describing and complaining about a universally revered North that was the cultural, geographical, and political center of both the realm and its trendsetting elite, even though its customs and practices deviated from what the classics prescribed. Ge Hong resented the Northerners' contempt for the Southerners, feeling that he and his countrymen were being treated with only slightly more respect than illiterate barbarians. The North that Ge Hong railed against soon lost its cultural sovereignty as the members of the Jin court fled across the Yangzi River to settle at the old capital of the Wu state. The Northern elites, no longer in possession of the Central Plain, lost geographical support for their claim of cultural superiority. The trendsetters now became the guests of the perceived trend followers.

Several new constructs of the North and the South resulted from the Jin court's removal to the area south of the Yangzi River. Most immediately noticeable were the cultural and political divides between the non-Chinese regimes in the North and the Chinese regime in the South and that between the émigré Northern elites and the locals in the Southern courts. To the Northerners who took refuge in the South, like Wang Dao 王導 (276–339) and his fellow courtiers partying at the "New Stop" (Xinting 新停) discussed by Ping Wang in chapter 4, the image of the South as the land of the exiled and dispossessed continued, though it did not last long. The changes came as part of the political consolidation of various factions within the Jin court in exile. Hoping to regroup and reclaim lost patrimony, the émigré elites partly sided with the Jin royal house, which was much reduced in stature and prestige, and partly tried to replace it. The alliance formed in the face of foreign threats was therefore an unhappy marriage undertaken out of necessity. Moreover, the Northerners had to depend for support on their gracious hosts, whom they continued to hold in contempt. The conflicts of interest were frequent and intense. The energy and resources invested in securing the South led to the construction of a North that was lost and, in turn, reinforced the need to further invest in a South culturally and politically dominated by Northerners.

The memorials that Huan Wen 桓溫 (312–373) and Sun Chuo 孫綽 (314–371) submitted to Eastern Jin Emperor Ai 哀帝 (r. 361–365) regarding the relocation of the court to the newly recovered Luoyang were products of this contention. To the second and third generations of Northerners who were born and raised in the South, the North was as foreign to them as the South had been to their forefathers. It had been plundered by the "barbarians" and laid waste by wars. Its desolate landscape was haunted by the ghosts from the neglected ancestral tombs. Once the source of the advanced Han civilization, the North occupied by non-Han people was now the bastardized "other," whose classical traditions had become hopelessly compromised. The descendants of the émigré elites thus considered themselves the sole heirs of the Han. But even as Huan Wen and Sun Chuo were conjuring up an image of a ruined North, they also were reaffirming its symbolic importance as the original cultural and political center. This was where the rightful ruler of All Under Heaven must rule. But a sovereign's legitimacy also was based on his virtue. Huan Wen, arguing for the court's return, insisted on the emperor's filial duties to the imperial mausoleums in the suburb of Luoyang. Sun Chuo countered this argument, claiming that a truly virtuous sovereign would place the well-being of his people before that of his ancestors. Besides, there now were numerous ancestral graves in the South that needed maintenance as well. The double bind in which the Northerners' descendants in the South found themselves meant regarding the old North as lost, the new North as usurped, and the South as a home that needed defending.

The relationship between the newly aligned North and the South was highly competitive. At stake were the cultural and political legitimacy and the survival of individual regimes. This contentious relationship is illustrated in the accounts of the disputation between the envoys of the Northern Wei 北魏 and the Liu Song 劉宋 states outside the besieged city of Pengcheng 彭城 in 451 C.E., translated in chapter 2 by Albert E. Dien. Driven by the desire to unify China, the Northern Wei emperor, Tuoba Dao 拓拔燾 (r. 424–451), launched a full-scale assault on the territories northwest of the Yangzi River held by the Liu Song regime, with the intent to conquer the Southern state once and for all. The Liu Song emperor, Liu Yilong 劉義隆 (r. 424–453), retaliated. Pengcheng—a city that should have been easy for the Northern Wei army to overcome—held out, and the battle outside the city gate became one of discourse and posturing. Li Xiaobo 李孝伯 (d. 459) and Zhang Chang 張暢 (408–457), representing the Northern Wei and Liu Song, respectively, dueled in words and manners. Both insisted on the political legitimacy of their respective states. Both tried to outshine the other in speech, argumentation, and deportment in their attempts at psychological intimidation. Ultimately, this battle of force and diplomacy ended in a draw. The verbal assaults continued as the court historians of the respective states took to their brushes to recount the disputation. In Dien's carefully correlated passages from the *History of the Wei* (*Wei shu* 魏書) and the *History of the Song* (*Song shu* 宋書), both Li Xiaobo and Zhang Chang were celebrated at each other's expense. The North and the South here were cultural and political equals: each had strengths and weaknesses, and neither could overpower the other. Verbal assault as a comparative sport became wholly expected and thoroughly entertaining, as seen in the story that I translated in chapter 3 about Lu Sidao 盧思道 (535–586). The mission of the Northern Qi's 北齊 envoy to the Southern Chen 南陳 reportedly culminated in mutual disparagement. At the state banquet, the Southerners ridiculed the Northern diet and, by extension, the Northerners' perceived barbarism. In return, the Northerners ridiculed the Southern expression of familial affection. This story in the Northern Song 北宋 compilation *Extensive Records of the Taiping Era* (*Taiping guangji* 太平廣記, completed in 978) was, at best, historically inaccurate. Lu Sidao did visit the Southern Chen court, but as the envoy of the Sui 隋 and not the Northern Qi. Even so, this story, as a source produced after Sui, a Northern regime that had finally reunified the realm, is interesting because it shows us that the famous literati from the North were perceived as winning the cultural war.

The tipping of balance toward the North's imagined cultural superiority was not just the result of its political-military victory over the South. The victory also was rooted in at least two contemporaneous developments. The first was the continuing clash between the descendants of the Northern émigrés and their hosts. The former prided themselves on being the heirs of the orthodox classical tradition and stereotypically viewed the latter as uncultured. In response, the Southerners drew on a self-pride that would have made Ge Hong proud. Ping Wang examines one Southerner's resentment of the émigrés' arrogance, packaged in a self-effacing eloquence, in the accusatory letter from Zhang Chong 張充 (449–514) to Wang Jian 王儉 (452–489). The attack was provoked when Wang, an illustrious member of a prestigious Northern family, withheld a promotion that the Southern Qi 南齊 emperor granted to Zhang's father, claiming his Southern family's lack of civility. Zhang Chong openly rejected the cultural standards that Wang Jian represented and on which he insisted using to measure others. Zhang Chong retaliated by bringing up the Southern tradition of reclusion and evoking the useless against the useful, the unlearned against the cultivated, the simple against the refined, and the austere against the decadent. His letter is nothing less than a rejection of the artificial culture that Wang, a Northerner, had brought to the South. Even though it was a culture that originated in the North, it was inauthentic. Zhang's view of the South's high culture is surprisingly similar to how the occupants of the North came to view the South.

The excerpts that I translated in chapter 3 from the *Family Instructions of Mr. Yan (Yanshi jiaxun* 顏氏家訓) by Yan Zhitui 顏之推 (531–591) show a new common cultural standard and transregional elite emerging. In the midst of the rapid rise and fall of numerous Chinese and non-Chinese dynasties was a group of literary technocrats known for their erudition in Confucian classics and skill in rescript writing. Even though not all of them came from prestigious elite families or sold their services to the highest bidder, many of them had illustrious careers in the court of their employers. Yan Zhitui was one such person. A Southerner from an émigré family, he defected to the Northern Qi in the chaos at the end of the Southern Liang and the Eastern and Western Wei. Yan spent most of his life in the North. In *Family Instructions*, he notes the many cultural similarities and differences between the North and the South without placing his own family in either camp. To him, each side had its own shortcomings and backwardness, so the way for his children to survive was to maintain cultural respectability in both the North and the South. How he prepared and educated his children thus is crucial to our understanding of this new transregional high culture that was slowly taking shape in the final years before the great reunification.

After all the setbacks and transformations, disarrays and realignments, mastery of the Confucian classics remained at the core of all cultural refinements and lent legitimacy to any ambition to dominate the culture or politics of the realm. This was not the Han Confucian scholarship that was situated at and emanated from the cultural, geographical, and political center of the Middle Kingdom, but a new Confucian scholarship that itself was the center and had the power to transport those who mastered it to the cultural and political heart of an empire, wherever it might be. The North and the South that this self-proclaimed "man who had thrice lost his nation" (*san wei wangguo zhiren* 三為亡國之人)[2] captured in the instructions he left for his children were ending. By now, neither the North nor the South was the same as it had been described at the beginning of part I, and neither remained much longer as Yan Zhitui described them. Although there would always be a North and a South even in the unified empire of the future, they would never be the same as the North and the South in early medieval China.

Jessey J. C. Choo

NOTES

1.   Xiaofei Tian, *Beacon Fire and Shooting Star: The Literary Culture of the Liang (502–557)* (Cambridge, Mass.: Harvard University Asia Center, 2007), 311.

2.   Yan Zhitui 顏之推, "Rhapsody on a View of My Life" (*Guan wosheng fu* 觀我生賦), quoted in full in his official biography in *BQS* 45.618–26.

1. Return to the North?

The Debate on Moving the Capital Back to Luoyang

JESSEY J. C. CHOO

A proposal that circulated in the court of the Eastern Jin Emperor Ai 東晉哀帝 (r. 361–365) sought to reestablish the recently recovered Luoyang as the capital of the state and to repopulate it with those who had fled to the South. The year was 362 C.E., and by this time, the Jin court had been "temporarily" held in Jiankang 建康 for nearly five decades. The author of this proposal was Huan Wen 桓溫 (312–373), an ambitious statesman and the military commander who had reconquered the city.[1] Filled with references to the filial piety of the emperor and, in fact, of every man, the proposal asked a serious moral question: How could ancestral tombs be abandoned to the whim of invaders? While most of the courtiers vehemently opposed the proposal in private, they could not oppose Huan Wen in public until Sun Chuo 孫綽 (314–371) came to their aid.[2] This was one of the rare occasions in which Sun Chuo, a politically savvy literatus, inserted himself into court politics. His judiciously reasoned and eloquently phrased memorial against Huan Wen's proposal did not merely win the debate; it also became his crowning achievement as a statesman. Both Huan Wen's and his memorials are translated here in their entirety.

Since the first decade of the fourth century, Luoyang, once the cultural and political center of the Jin dynasty, had been repeatedly sacked and occupied by non-Han ethic groups. The sixteen-year-long civil war fought among various factions of the royal family, known as the Rebellion of the Eight Imperial

Princes (*bawang zhi luan* 八王之亂),[3] did not end until 306. The conflicts had exhausted resources, caused widespread suffering and great loss of lives, and left the dynasty vulnerable to external threats. One such threat was from Liu Yuan 劉淵 (d. 310), who, along with the Xiongnu tribesmen he led, was slowly but steadily chipping away at the dynasty's territory in the northeast and testing the strength of the Jin army at various strategic locations. Declaring himself the heir to the Han throne, Liu Yuan founded the state of Han Zhao 漢趙 and established its capital in Pingyang 平陽 in 308.[4] The ranks of the Han Zhao army were filled with highly skilled fighters drawn from many seminomadic tribes, chief among which was the Xianbei 鮮卑. Almost immediately after the dynasty was created, Han Zhao sent forces to attack Jin strongholds in the Yellow River basin, which included Luoyang. While the city was able to fend off its attackers this time, it became increasingly isolated as nearby fortresses were taken one after another by Liu Yuan's marauding troops.

Within the city, however, the Jin court, under the lackluster leadership of Emperor Huai 懷帝 (r. 306–312), remained deeply fractious.[5] The internecine conflict between the emperor and his treasonous kinsman Sima Yue 司馬越, the Prince of Donghai 東海王, came to a head in the fifth year (311) of the Yongjia era. The second Han Zhao emperor, Liu Cong 劉聰 (d. 318),[6] the son of Liu Yuan, pounced on this opportunity in a series of events that later men, including Huan Wen and Sun Chuo, referred to as the Yongjia disorder (*yongjia zhi luan* 永嘉之亂). First, the Han Zhao army annihilated Sima Yue's troops, a hundred thousand strong and the best of the Jin military, in the confusion following the prince's untimely death (of natural causes). The Han Zhao army then sacked Luoyang, in the process wiping out the remaining Jin forces and capturing Emperor Huai. The emperor was taken to Pingyang and executed, but not before being thoroughly humiliated in public.[7] The Yongjia disorder clearly was a devastating blow to the dynasty, although some remnants of the Jin court managed to regroup in Chang'an and rally behind Emperor Min 愍帝 (r. 313–317), Emperor Huai's hapless nephew. Despite having few men and inadequate supplies to defend themselves, they were able to hang on for four years, thanks only to the struggles for dominance between the Han Zhao and other tribal forces. In 316, Emperor Min finally surrendered both the city and himself to the menacing Han Zhao army, thereby yielding all the Jin territory north of the Huai River.[8] Although Chang'an was where the Jin court made its last stand in what would soon be referred to as "the North," it was Luoyang that came to symbolize the loss that was seared into the Jin people's collective memory for years to come.

The Jin dynasty survived through Sima Rui 司馬睿, the Prince of Langye 琅邪王, who established a new court in Jiankang and reigned as Emperor Zhongzong 中宗 (r. 318–322).[9] His new regime was one of compromises from the beginning. For political legitimacy, it needed the support of the elite who had fled the carnage in the North, but it also depended on the hospitality and assistance of the local great clans of the South in order to govern. Satisfying the Northern émigrés' hunger for land while protecting the local elite's entrenched interests was a difficult balancing act for Emperor Zhongzong and his successors. Within the émigré elites, those arriving early jealously guarded their positions in the South against those arriving later.[10] Their conflicts of interest created an instability that weakened imperial authority and hampered its efforts to recover the North.

The safety of the exiled court in the South relied on both the military prowess of gifted commanders and the natural barrier provided by the Yangzi River. But the prestige and influence of these military commanders, which grew with each battle won in defending the South or in reclaiming lost Northern territory, made the court increasingly suspicious of their power and motives. Consequently, it was unwilling to support any enterprise that might be in a position to recover the North.[11] The reclamation of territory, however, remained popular and served as a source of political legitimacy. As they gained popular support with their military victories, the commanders, feeling no particular loyalty to the fickle court, frequently considered founding their own dynasties.[12] Huan Wen was one such man.

Huan Wen, the son of the Governor of Xuancheng (Xuancheng *taishou* 宣城 太守) and Princess Nankang 南康公主, the daughter of Emperor Ming 明帝 (r. 322–325), was a master strategist. When the Cheng Han 成漢 kingdom founded by the Di 氐 people in Sichuan fell into discord in 346, Huan Wen volunteered to lead an expedition to reconquer the land. The court was initially pessimistic about his chances for success: Sichuan was remote; the roads leading to it were dangerous; and his army was relatively small compared with that of the Cheng Han. Defying expectations, however, Huan Wen captured both Chengdu, the capital city of Cheng Han, and its ruler, Li Shi 李勢 (d. 361). Moreover, he proved his aptitude for governance by quickly restoring order after the war. He retained and promoted local talents to attend to daily operations and won the support of the defeated people.[13] The campaign in Sichuan earned Huan Wen both great acclaim and the court's distrust. Therefore, in 350, when various Northern regimes began to fight with one another for dominance, the court bypassed Huan Wen and sent Yin Hao 殷浩 (303–356) with an expedition to the North to exploit the unrest. Unfortunately, Yin Hao turned out to be more of an expert on "conversation on the mysterious [Dao]" (*xuanyan* 玄言) than on military affairs.[14] In addition to suffering a series of defeats, Yin Hao also managed to lose many capable commanders to defections, the most notable of whom was Yao Xiang 姚襄 (331–357), who quickly gained control of a sizable territory between the Yellow and the Huai Rivers.[15] These outcomes left the court with no choice but to replace Yin Hao with Huan Wen in 354. With victory after victory, the new commander in chief quickly reaffirmed his perceived ability and popularity.

Huan Wen routed the army of the Former Qin 前秦, another state founded by the Di people, and laid siege to its capital, Chang'an. When he arrived in the vicinity of the city, the inhabitants turned out in great numbers to welcome him and to express their delight in seeing the return of the Jin army.[16] But Huan Wen chose not to press on and instead soon withdrew his troops and returned to the South. His reasons for doing so remain unclear. Modern historians disagree on the cause of his retreat. Both Chen Yinke 陳寅恪 and Wang Zhongluo 王仲犖 suggest that a shortage of supplies was to blame. Chen Yinke, in particular, cites the example of Huan's retreat to support his argument that the South was unable to conquer the North in part because of the difficulties in transporting the provisions necessary to sustain a northern campaign.[17] Tian Yuqing 田餘慶 offers a much more cynical reading of the situation. He acknowledges that Huan Wen indeed encountered difficulties in securing adequate supplies for his troops because the defenders of the city had burned nearby farms before his arrival but also indicates that there were other reasons. For example, rumors had begun to circulate at court that Huan Wen might have designs on the throne. To Huan Wen, by the time of his withdrawal, the campaign had more than fulfilled its intended purposes: it had not only enhanced his prestige but also had fortified his position vis-à-vis his opponents. Consequently, there was little benefit in continuing the siege and risking the political capital he had accumulated.[18] His withdrawal thus ended a campaign commonly regarded as greatly successful, and for many people, it established Huan Wen as a hero.

In 356, when Yao Xiang attempted to seize Luoyang from his base in the Huai River basin, Huan Wen launched his second full-scale campaign and again achieved a resounding victory. He defeated Yao Xiang, recovered Luoyang, repaired the Jin's imperial mausoleums, and was set to attack the Former Yan 前燕 (founded by the Murong 慕容 clan of Xianbei in 337) as well as the Former Qin. Yet, as with the last campaign, he soon turned back to the South, leaving behind only a few troops to defend the strongholds in the area. By 358, most of what he had reclaimed had fallen once again to the Former Yan, and by 362 Luoyang was facing another invasion. It was at this moment of renewed urgency that Huan Wen submitted his memorial to persuade the emperor to move the court back to Luoyang and repopulate the city with those who had been displaced during the Yongjia disorder. He wrote in his memorial that there had been an opportunity to reclaim the North ever since the recovery of Sichuan but that the bickering at court had created an environment adverse to capitalizing on it. He urged the emperor, in his great wisdom and even greater sense of filial piety, to firmly support the enterprise. Huan Wen also pointed out that by right and duty, the Son of Heaven must rule from the center and not from the southern corner of the realm. In order for the emperor to assume his proper role and bring peace to All Under Heaven, he must occupy his proper place at the heart of the Central Plain. He must not allow those who had fled to the South to give up hope of returning or permit those who had been stranded in the North to suffer any longer under barbarian rule. By moving the court back to Luoyang and encouraging the émigrés to return, Huan Wen argued that the emperor could attend to the imperial mausoleums, rebuild the North, solidify territorial gains, and become known in history as the monarch who restored the dynasty to its former glory. Finally, Huan Wen entreated the emperor to accept his offer to secure the North in anticipation of the royal return and also to rule against those at court who gave precedence to their own interests and safety.

Sun Chuo's biographer treated his objection to Huan Wen's proposal as a pivotal episode in Sun's life, one in which Sun showed his mettle. He claimed that most courtiers, fearful of Huan Wen, did not dare reveal their reservations. Only Sun Chuo was brave enough to memorialize the throne and provide the opposition with both persuasive arguments and a voice. Sun Chuo pointed out that the loss of the North was in large part because the Central Plain lacked natural barriers to aid its defense against barbarian raiders. It was a problem that Huan Wen, no matter how brilliant a military strategist, could not resolve. Sun Chuo argued for conservatism, that it would be better to give up what could not be defended and to secure what had already been made safe. Besides, Sun Chuo reasoned, it would be neither practical nor sensible to send the Northern refugees back from where they came, since after years of warfare, their farms in the North had been devastated and they already had settled in the South. Any attempt to move the court, he maintained, would be reckless and disruptive, sacrificing safety and risking starvation merely in order to reoccupy a capital that could not be defended. Sun Chuo proposed instead a ten-year plan to be implemented in several stages. First, the court should dispatch an experienced military commander to Luoyang who would fortify the defense of the imperial mausoleums and pacify the areas surrounding the capital. After completing this first step and securing viable supply lines, this commander should then clear the fields and restore agricultural production. Finally, while these two stages were being carried out, the court in the South should build up its financial and military strength. Given that the emperor and Huan Wen were still in their prime, there was no pressing need for immediate relocation. Sun Chuo mused that the day for the court to return to the North would surely arrive during their lifetimes.

In their memorials, both Huan Wen and Sun Chuo appealed to the emperor's filial devotion, stressing the importance of protecting the imperial mausoleums from invaders. Both also built their arguments on poignant images of Luoyang now in ruins and the North desolated. While to both men the North was a ghost-filled landscape, Huan Wen expressed confidence in his ability to exorcise it, whereas Sun Chuo viewed this confidence with great trepidation. When the emperor accepted Sun Chuo's idea and turned down Huan Wen's, it appeared that the image of a North forever lost had won the day.

The ensuing events, however, proved that Huan Wen's proposal was not as reckless as Sun Chuo made it out to be, nor was Sun Chuo's proposal lacking tactical shrewdness. As Huan Wen predicted, the military commander stationed in Luoyang, Chen You 陳祐,[19] was unable to hold the city long enough to implement even the first stage of Sun Chuo's plan. With the court scarcely invested in Luoyang's defense, the Former Yan easily took possession of it in 365. In response to the loss of Luoyang, Huan Wen launched his third and final northern campaign in 369. This time he suffered a spectacular defeat when his deputy, Yuan Zhen 袁真,[20] failed to secure the supply lines over the waterway before their provisions ran out. Destroyed along with Huan Wen's fifty thousand troops was the last real chance for the Eastern Jin to recover Luoyang and the North.

FURTHER READING

For a general introduction to major armed conflicts between the North and South, in English, see David Graff, *Medieval Chinese Warfare, 300–900* (London: Routledge, 2002). Tang Zhangru 唐長孺 provides a detailed analysis of various nomadic forces in the North at the end of the Western Jin in *Wei Jin Nanbeichao shi lunchong* 魏晉南北朝史論叢 (Shijiazhuang: Hebei jiaoyu chubanshe, 2000). Several discussions of the three northern campaigns led by Huan Wen are available in Chinese, including Chen Yinke 陳寅恪, *Wei Jin Nanbeichao shi jiangyan lu* 魏晉南北朝史講演錄 (1987; repr., Hefei: Huanshan shushe, 2000); Tian Yuqing 田餘慶, *Dong Jin menfa zhengzhi* 東晉門閥政治 (1989; repr., Beijing: Beijing daxue chubanshe, 2005); and Wang Zhongluo 王仲犖, *Wei Jin Nanbeichao shi* 魏晉南北朝史 (Shanghai: Shanghai renmin chubanshe, 2003). Hu Baoguo 胡寶國 discusses in detail the formations of different identities and conflicts of interests within the émigré elite in "Liang Jin shiqi de 'nanren' yü 'beiren'" 兩晉時期的'南人'與'北人,' *Wenshi* 文史 73 (2005): 49–58, and "Wandu beiren yü Dong-Jin zhongqi de lishi bianhua" 晚渡北人與東晉中期的歷史變化, *Beida shixue* 北大史學 14 (2009): 94–111. Interested readers can also find an informative discussion of Sun Chuo's life and work in Paul W. Kroll, chapter 13 of this volume.

HUAN WEN 桓溫

Memorial

In the first year of the Longhe reign [362 C.E.], invaders [i.e., the Former Yan] threatened Henan, and Governor [*Taishou* 太守] Dai Shi 戴施[21] fled. The General

Commanding the Troops [*Guanjun jianjun* 冠軍將軍], Chen You 陳祐, asked urgently for reinforcements. [Huan] Wen ordered the Governor of Jinling 竟陵, Deng Xia 鄧遐,[22] to lead three thousand men to help [Chen] You and sought to move the capital back to Luoyang. He presented a memorial to the throne:

Bashu 巴蜀[23] already has been pacified and the offending barbarians destroyed. The opportune time has arrived, and the signs of peace and prosperity have become clear. Yet, circumstances have turned against [us], and the imperial strategies have repeatedly been disrupted, allowing the two rebels [i.e., the Former Qin and the Former Yan states] to rise again. The realm has fallen apart; the area between the Yellow and Luo Rivers is now desolated; and the imperial mausoleums are threatened. Thus, [people] far and near are anguished and distressed; their heartaches surpass those of the past. [I] lie prostrate on the ground [before the throne]. Your Majesty is endowed with the grace of Qian Kun 乾坤 and Nature 自然 and possess the profound virtue [that was the character of the] sage-ruler Fu Xi. [Your Majesty] was a phoenix [i.e., a prince] resting in the fief and is now a dragon [i.e., the emperor] soaring to the ends of the imperial reach. Despite their being unpredictable, no aspect of current affairs escapes [your] sublime perception. As for the prevarications of men, [Your Majesty] thoroughly understands them. Therefore, the Nine Provinces [*jiuyu* 九域; i.e., China proper] pay allegiance to you, and people of distant lands stand on tiptoe awaiting the arrival of your rule. Your care [for the people] reaches the clouds and folds into its embrace all within the four borders. Now the moment is at hand for the imperial court to devise a long-term plan and to begin extensive operations to recover the old capital [i.e., Luoyang] and bring order to Hua Xia [i.e., China proper]. [This mission] will allow the gentle breeze and warm sunshine to extend to even the remotest areas and will send the frosty might and wintry gale to sweep away [the enemies] without exception. How could such [a mission] not receive the blessing of the spirits and unite [the will of] Heaven and men? The Yangzi and Yellow Rivers are far apart; even the horses [that travel with the speed of] wind find this is so. Even as those devoted to the righteous causes have faced repeated defeats, the loyal warriors press on without any regrets. Moreover, when the Big Dipper returns [to the center of the sky], every star looks to it [for direction]; when its upstream changes course, the Gu Creek downstream follows. The survivors of the Jin will rejoice at having the imperial power [return to the area]; the knaves and miscreants will know that the day of their destruction is near. We will ride on the longing for peace and strike with the force of thunder. The two subversives will end their lives of their own accord without our sending troops to annihilate them. Those who are adaptable prefer going with the flow, and those who are enlightened excel at responding to opportunities. [Because we are as] steady as stone, we can achieve our mission. The tide is turning. If [we] the *peng* bird[24] does not spread its wings [to take advantage of the favorable wind], we will forever root ourselves in the southern corner and abandon the divine provinces [*shenzhou* 神州; i.e., China proper]. Even children who are merely five *chi* 尺 tall will cover their mouths and sigh [at this].

What the sage-king of old initiated and those of great virtue attended to was the delineation of the Nine Provinces [*jiuzhou* 九州; i.e., China proper] and the creation of the Nine Fiefdoms [*jiufu* 九服].[25] [They] gave precedence to the center and subordinated [to it] the various principalities [*zhuxia* 諸夏]. [They did this] because [like] the stylus of a sundial, [the sovereign] casts shadow from the center, thus evenly distributing frost or dew [i.e., imperial displeasure or favor] throughout the realm and bringing the courtiers of ten thousand nations and the four seas to pay tribute to the imperial court. Ever since the powerful barbarians unleashed violence, China proper [*Zhonghua* 中華] has fallen into chaos; [the people] have become desperate and dispossessed; and [the imperial court] has temporarily relocated to the region of Yang 揚 and Yue 越. A worm lies waiting for its opportunity to transform itself into a dragon; a dragon conceals itself anticipating its moment to ride on the winds and clouds. [These humble postures] are preferable in adversity, but they are not natural positions. Since the widespread loss and chaos [i.e., the Yongjia disorder] some fifty years ago, the elders have passed away, and their descendants [came when they] were still young [and] have ceased to converse in their native dialects. The [new] practices have become customs. [They] have given up the hope [of returning to the North] and found happiness and contentment in this haven; though they may reminisce [about their native land] with regret, they no longer lament [its loss]. Your humble servant is mediocre and weak, and my talent is insufficient to complete the duty. But since I assumed this hallowed office that is charged with this great task, I will wear out my muscles and bones, deplete my strength to lead, remove thistles and thorns, and expel the ravenous and cruel beasts. I request that all those who have migrated to the area south of the Yangzi River since the Yongjia disorder be resettled to the north in order to populate the region south of the Yellow River. They should resume their old industries, return to their homes and lands, devote themselves to farming and weaving, and take advantage of the three seasons [of agriculture]. [Once the people] are guided with righteousness and united with propriety, both civil and martial [values] will be manifested. Those who are faithful and obedient will flourish; the wells and cities will be repaired; and law and order will be maintained. After this, Your Majesty can magnify the brightness of the sun, moon, and stars; adorn the banners with feathers; dress in full imperial regalia; and lead the court to cross the river. Who, then, in this world will not feel ecstatic?

When the public sentiment is tamed by peace, it is difficult to initiate any plan; when an extraordinary measure [is proposed], many people will doubt [that it will be successful]. I humbly request that Your Majesty deliberate with your subtle acumen and make an unconventional decision to give me the responsibility to bring about the restoration and entrust me with the work to complete the mission. If this mission is fulfilled and the deed accomplished, then Your Majesty's glory will exceed that of any previous sovereigns [and be comparable to that of] the Zhou King Xuan 周宣王 [r. 828–782 B.C.E.] in achieving restoration.[26] If this mission does not succeed, then it will be my fault. Even if I were to pick up my undershirt and enter a cauldron,[27] I would find [any punishment] as sweet as water chestnuts.

The throne decreed: "More than fifty years have passed [since the time of] the loss and chaos. The barbarians have indulged in violence and continue in their evil ways. Speaking longingly and looking to the [north]west, our heart is overfilled with regrets. We know you want to lead the three armies to wash away the filth, clean up the central territory, and recover the old capital. If you do not devote your life to the country, how could you propose such a mission?! Regarding the ways in which various situations ought to be handled, we leave them to your competent judgment. However, the area between the Yellow and Luo Rivers is wasteland; thus, there will be much to manage. We now give to you the burden of taking the initiative." Thereupon, the court reappointed [Huan Wen] to oversee the three provinces of Bing 并, Si 司, and Ji 冀 [i.e., the northwestern frontier]. Moreover, because Jiao 交 and Guang 廣 Provinces [in the southeast] were too remote, [Huan Wen] was relieved of his duties as the Commander in Chief [*Dudu* 都督] [of the forces in the southeastern frontier]. [Huan Wen] submitted a petition to refuse [the new appointment]. The court [countered it by] also appointing him to the posts of Palace Attendant [*Shizhong* 侍中], Grand Defender in Chief [*Da sima* 大司馬], and Commander in Chief of All Internal and External Military Expeditions [*Dudu zhongwai zhujunshi* 都督中外諸軍事] and bestowed on him the Golden Axes [*huangyue* 黃鉞][28] [for use in the battlefield].

[*JS* 98.2572–74]

Sun Chuo 孫綽

Memorial

At this time [362 C.E.], the Grand Defender in Chief [*Dasima* 大司馬], Huan Wen, longed to bring order to the central states. Because the [area] south of the Yellow River had only recently been pacified, he sought to move the capital city to Luoyang. The court was afraid of [Huan] Wen and dared not disagree. The land in the North was desolate, and the people were suspicious and fearful [of the move]. Even though everyone knew that the plan must not go ahead, no one dared to be the first to object. [Sun] Chuo presented the throne with a memorial that stated:

I lie prostrated and read the memorial of the Great General of the Western Campaign [*Zhengxi dajiangjun* 征西大將軍], [Huan] Wen. He proposes to personally lead the three armed forces, quell the two invaders [*erkou* 二寇],[29] purify the Yellow and Wei Rivers, and cleanse the ancient capital. Then [he would] unfurl the divine banner [with the speed of] lightning, ferry the courtiers across the Yangzi River, relocate the imperial residence to the central land [*zhongtu* 中土], and right the [position of the] Yuheng 玉衡 star[30] at the northern celestial pole [*tianji* 天極]. Such a grand plan has not been proposed for many generations and, [if achieved,] would indeed be the greatest event in a thousand years.

But what your servant [i.e., Sun Chuo] has in his mind is apprehension. In my humble opinion, no ruler has achieved meritorious deeds by leading the righteous to suppress violence and to assuage [the people] without geographical advantages and popular support. Emperors Huai 懷帝 and Min 愍帝 were not competent, and both were captives in the capital of Qin [i.e., Pingyang 平陽, the capital city of the Han Zhao kingdom (319–329)], thereby allowing barbarian armies to invade repeatedly. The divine provinces lost their precepts and became filled with chaos because [their rulers] had strayed from the Way. The heartland of the [ancient] Xia kingdom [*Zhong Xia* 中夏; i.e., China proper] immediately fell into ruin, and turmoil was everywhere. In the hundreds of counties and thousands of cities, not a single well was left intact; why is this? The land could not be defended, and for this reason, [the people] fled. The blessing of Heaven [*tianzuo* 天祚] was not revoked, and Emperor Zhongzong soared as a dragon.[31] It was not only because his steadfastness had earned him the assistance from Heaven and the people but also because the Yangzi River of ten thousand *li* had formed a natural barrier; thus the state could be defended. The *Classic of Changes* states that "kings and princes build on tough terrain in order to defend their states. The timely knowledge of tough terrain is important indeed!"[32] The effectiveness [of such a defensive strategy] has already been demonstrated. Those who offer grand speeches for victory want to take the route that leads us away from a defensible position; yet [our] verifiable strengths and estimable capabilities leave us no choice but to preserve this small area in order to secure our existence. It has been some sixty years since the loss and chaos; the population was so decimated that not even one in a hundred was left. The hills in the area between the Yellow and Luo 洛 Rivers were laid waste, and all the provinces were made barren. Wells were boarded up and woods were warped, the crisscross footpaths that divided the fields vanished, and the livelihood of countless [people] could not again be supported. People fled to the area south of the Yangzi River and have lived here for several generations. The survivors are [now] the mature children and grown grand-children [of the original immigrants]; the dead are in graves that line up one next to the other. While the longing for the northern wind[33] affects their plain hearts, the sorrow they currently are experiencing is more pressing still. If the capital were to be relocated and the carts headed back, then the five imperial mausoleums [in Jiankang] would be left behind in a faraway region. If we were once again displaced to a distant land [i.e., the North], then the security of these imperial mausoleums [in the South] could not be guaranteed. Would not filial thoughts then gnaw at Your [Majesty's] divine heart?

[Huan] Wen's action sincerely aims to broadly survey the causes and effects and make long-term plans on behalf of the state. Had there been no urgent threat to the imperial mausoleums [in Luoyang], he would not have initiated this proposal and alone carried out the hardest assignment under Heaven. Currently, he is so dedicated as to forget to eat, and he glows with loyalty and indignation that anyone who is attentive could sense. However, the myriad people are shaken and frightened, and among them, many perceive fear and danger; how could they not think that the [chance of] revisiting old happiness is remote and the sorrow of heading toward death is near? Why is this so? After having put down roots in the area south of the Yangzi River for several decades, to uproot [the popu-lace] now would be to suddenly drive them to barren land, dragging them ten thousand *li* to pass through dangerous terrain and sail across the deep, and [causing] them to leave their [ancestral] graves and give up their livelihoods. The rich do not have [in store] three years' worth of food; the poor do not have enough rice for one meal. They neither can sell their land or houses again nor have the means to procure boats and carts. [They should not be made to] leave behind a country where they feel safe and happy and to adjust to a place that has been ravaged. [They should not be made to] depart from a place where safety is certain and to head into danger [like the precarious situation of] stacked eggs. [If they were to be made to resettle in the North], they would fall during the journey or drift away or drown in rivers, and only a few among many would reach their destination. People are the foundation of the country. To eradicate the invaders is to care for the people. To have the people die in order to anni-hilate those invaders—is this the right way to achieve peace? It is better that those who are benevolent have pity [on the people] and that the state carefully evaluate [the strategy]. Since time immemorial, the capital cities of emperors and kings have not remained in the same location. When thriving, the capital city is located at the center [of the realm] and swells to a large size; when languishing, it perseveres, awaiting for opportunity. The [imperial] virtue must not be surpassed, and each household must have three years' worth of provisions; only then can [the court] begin to

strategize about the affairs [that would bring about] great peace. Now neither the Heaven's timing nor men's action is in place. If we were to unify
the world at once, wouldn't it be difficult to proceed?

My foolish plan is, first, to send someone both renowned and capable
to Luoyang, to erect two fortresses to protect the imperial mausoleums,
pacify Liang 梁 and Xu 許 Provinces, and cleanse the [area] south of the
[Yellow] River. Then after the waterway has been opened for transporting
[provisions], [he] could devote his energy to opening the wasteland, widening the fields, and growing grain, so that he may slowly build up the
funds for relocation. Therefore, when the invaders [i.e., the non-Han ethnic groups] see signs of their decline, they will flee far away. If they remain seditious and refuse to change and, moreover, prefer to go to their
deaths, the various armies of the North and the South shall ride like the
wind and arrive like thunder, like extending one's hand to soothe an itch
or a pain and swiftly responding to one's needs from head to toe. The
imperial mausoleums would then be secured, and the heartland of the
[ancient] Xia kingdom would be walled off. In the meantime, may Your
Majesty wear the ceremonial robes of the noblest purple [i.e., preside over
the court], extend virtuous governance, personally practice the extreme
thriftiness of the Han Emperor Wen 漢文帝 [r. 180–157 B.C.E.], refrain
from granting small favors, save on expenditures for entertainment,
scrutinize the courtiers, exercise the armored armies, and put priority on
nourishing the soldiers and vanquishing the invaders. If such practices
could be kept up for ten years without ceasing, then the poor would increase in wealth and cowards would be filled with courage, and as people
learn about [Your Majesty's] heavenly virtue, they would approach death
as if coming home. To make this the policy is to keep open all options; for
what reason shall the established principle behind hundreds of victories
be cast off and All Under Heaven be gambled away in one throw? Your
Majesty has many springs and autumns ahead, and [Huan] Wen could
still carry out his grand plan. The emperor and ministers together diligently nurture this virtuous enterprise, and when caution brings great
fortune,[34] would this not be happiness?

Today as [Huan] Wen chants [his] grand proposition, Your Majesty and
the court all agree with him. Your servant is insignificant and alone presents his humble observations. Never before has [the climate at court]
been so difficult for a person to express his opinions. Why does an incon-
sequential person such as myself insist on being heard by the [Son of]
Heaven? I simply believe that this should be a court that has no taboo
subjects, [so] sentiments that are expressed by fools, or schemes put forward by collectors of firewood, could be judged by the great sage [i.e., the
emperor] on their merits. Thus I am casting away my concern [about the
consequence] and brave the chance of giving offense in presenting [my

proposal]. If Your Majesty would condescend and give me your attention, and [if Huan] Wen would consider [my proposal] just for a moment, it would be to fulfill the wish of billions of people by yielding to only one person. If I thus commit a grave offense and [arouse] your desire to have me killed in public, as long as my utmost sincerity could reach above, even if I must accept the death sentence, although I may be under the [Yellow] Springs and the Earth, my corpse would stay uncorrupted forever.

Huan Wen read Chuo's memorial and was not pleased. He said [to his staff]: "Send a message to Xingong 興公:[35] Why not look to your [own] "Rhapsody on Fulfilling My Original Resolve" [*Suichu fu* 遂初賦][36] before poking your nose into state affairs under discussion by others?!"

[*JS* 56.1544–47]

NOTES

1. *JS* 98.2568–80 contains a biography of Huan Wen 桓溫, an influential personage who dominated the Jin court for five reigns. Many anecdotes about him are scattered across the texts from this time.

2. For a biography of Sun Chuo 孫綽, see *JS* 56.1544–47. For additional information on his life and works, see Paul W. Kroll, chapter 13 of this volume.

3. The eight princes were the Prince of Runan (Sima Liang 司馬亮), Prince of Chu 楚王 (Sima Wei 司馬瑋), Prince of Zhao 趙王 (Sima Lun 司馬倫), Prince of Qi 齊王 (Sima Jiong 司馬冏), Prince of Hejian 河間王 (Sima Yong 司馬顒), Prince of Chengdu 成都王 (Sima Yin 司馬穎), Prince of Changsha 長沙王 (Sima Yi 司馬乂), and Prince of Donghai 東海王 (Sima Yue 司馬越). Their biographies are collected in *JS* 59.1589–1630. For a brief account of the event in English, see David A. Graff, *Medieval Chinese Warfare, 300–900* (London: Routledge, 2002), 44–47.

4. For an account of the career of Liu Yuan 劉淵, see *JS* 101.2645–52. He gave the state he founded the name Han 漢 because he claimed to be descended from the royal house of the Han dynasty. In 319, his successors changed the name to Zhao 趙, as it then held the territory that belonged to the Zhao kingdom during the Warring States period. Later historians thus often refer to the state as Han Zhao 漢趙.

5. For a chronicle of the reign of Emperor Huai 懷帝, see *JS* 5.115–25.

6. For an account of the career of Liu Cong 劉聰, see *JS* 102.2657–77.

7. The emperor was ordered to serve wine as if he were a servant at a state banquet. See *JS* 5.125.

8. For a chronicle of the reign of Emperor Min, see *JS* 5.125–37.

9. For a chronicle of the reign of Emperor Zhongzong 中宗, see *JS* 6.143–58.

10. Hu Baoguo 胡寶國, "Wandu beiren yu Dong Jin zhongqi de lishi bianhua" 晚渡北人與東晉中期的歷史變化, *Beida shixue* 北大史學 14 (2009): 94–111.

11. Zu Di 祖逖 (266–321), Tao Kan 陶侃 (259–334), and Yu Liang 庾亮 (289–340) are three examples. According to *JS* 62.1693–97, Zu Di recovered a large area south of the Yellow

River but received insufficient support from the court, which was plagued by intrigue. He died regretting the missed opportunities. In the end, all that he had recovered was lost to the state of Later Zhao 後趙 (319–351). According to *JS* 66.1768–79, Tao Kan suppressed various rebellions in the South, retook Xiangyang from the Later Zhao, and was poised to send troops northward in 332. The court and, later, the author of the *Jin shu*, doubted his loyalty. Although Yu Liang, according to *JS* 73.1915–24, was in a position to attack the Later Zhao when its first ruler died, he was held back by the court. Like Zu Di, he died disappointed.

12. Wang Dun 王敦 (266–324) and Su Jun 蘇峻 (d. 328) are good examples. For their biographies, see *JS* 98.2553–67 and 100.2628–31.

13. *JS* 68.2569.

14. For the official biography of Yin Hao 殷浩, see *JS* 77.2042–47.

15. Yao Xiang 姚襄 was a much-loved leader of the Qiang 羌 people and an extremely gifted warrior. Even Fu Jian 苻堅, the emperor of Former Qin 前秦 (r. 357–385) and the one who defeated and killed him in battle, greatly admired him. For the biography of Yao Xiang, see *JS* 116.2962–64.

16. *JS* 68.2571.

17. Chen Yinke 陳寅恪, "Nanbei duili xingshi fenxi" 南北對立形勢分析, in *Wei Jin Nanbeichao shi jiangyan lu* 魏晉南北朝史講演錄 (1987; repr., Hefei: Huanshan shushe, 2000), 226–39; Wang Zhongluo 王仲犖, *Wei Jin Nanbeichao shi* 魏晉南北朝史 (Shanghai: Shanghai renmin chubanshe, 2003), 312.

18. Tian Yuqing 田餘慶, *Dong Jin menfa zhengzhi* 東晉門閥政治 (1989; repr., Beijing: Beijing daxue chubanshe, 2005), 182.

19. Although Chen You does not have a biography in the *Jin shu*, what took place during his tenure as the commander stationed in Luoyang is briefly recounted in the biography of his deputy, Shen Jin 沈勁 (d. 365), as chronicled in *JS* 89.2317–18.

20. There is no official biography of Yuan Zhen.

21. There is no official biography of Dai Shi.

22. There is no official biography of Deng Xia.

23. Here Ba Shu refers to the kingdom of Cheng Han 成漢, founded in 304 C.E. by the Di 氐 people in Sichuan. Huan Wen led a military campaign against this kingdom in 346 and captured the capital city and its ruler, Li Shi 李勢 (r. 343–347). See *JS* 98.2562 and 121.3047–48.

24. Peng is a fabled bird of enormous size and great wingspan that is mentioned in the section "Xiaoyao you" in *Zhuangzi* 1. For an English translation, see Burton Watson, trans., *Chuang Tzu* (New York: Columbia University Press, 1996), 23.

25. The Nine Fiefdoms are surveyed in the "Border Duties" (*Zhigangshi* 職方氏) section under the Summer Ministry (*Xiaguan* 夏官) in the *Zhouli* 周禮. See *Zhouli zhushu* 周禮注疏; and *SSJZZ* 33.1030.

26. King Xuan of Zhou is known for restoring the Western Zhou dynasty through his efforts to drive the barbarian invaders out of Zhou territories. See *Shi ji* 史記 4.144–45; and *Guoyu* 國語 1.15–26.

27. This was one of the capital punishments, in which the criminal was placed in a cauldron of boiling water and cooked alive. See *HS*, "Treatise on Law and Punishment" (*Xingfazhi* 刑法志), 23.1096.

28. They were displayed when the Son of Heaven was present on the battlefield. With them, Huan Wen was now the representative of the emperor and could exercise the prerogatives of the Son of Heaven at war.

29. The two invaders refer to Former Qin and Former Yan.

30. Yuheng, also known as Lianzhen 廉貞, is one of the seven stars forming the Big Dipper.

31. Zhongzong was the temple name of Sima Rui 司馬睿. He was the Prince of Langye 琅邪王 and served Emperor Min as his chief minister and the commander of the armies. He regrouped the Jin forces after the Yongjia disorder and established a court in exile south of the Yangtze. After Emperor Min died in captivity, Sima Rui ascended the throne and was recognized as the first emperor (*yuandi* 元帝) of the Eastern Jin. For his biography, see *JS* 6.143–58.

32. *Classic of Changes* (*Yijing* 易經), hexagram 29 (*Kan* 坎); *Zhouyi Zhengyi* 周易正義; *SSJZZ* 3.154.

33. The northern wind alludes to the famous couplet "The Turkish horse cleaves to the northern wind / the Yue bird nests on the southern branches" from the Nineteen Old Poems no. 1.

34. *Classic of Changes*, hexagram 2 (*Kun* 坤); *Zhouyi Zhengyi* 1.31.

35. Xinggong is the courtesy name of Sun Chuo.

36. The rhapsody that cemented Sun Chuo's fame as a virtuous recluse is no longer extant. *Recent Anecdotes from the Talk of the Ages* (*Shishuo xinyu* 世說新語) states that he built a house in the mountain and planted a pine tree in front of it, claiming that he had had enough of the worldly pursuits. See Yu Jiaxi 余嘉錫, ed. and comm., *Shishuo xinyu jianshu* 世說新語箋疏 (Shanghai: Shanghai guji chubanshe, 1993), 84.72–73. Huan Wen's snide comment points out that contrary to his claim, Sun Chuo did not turn down the court appointments that his famed rhapsody earned him. See *JS* 56.1544.

2. The Disputation at Pengcheng

Accounts from the *Wei shu* and the *Song shu*

ALBERT E. DIEN

This disputation took place on January 14, 451, outside the city wall of Pengcheng 彭城. The Northern Wei Emperor Shizu 世祖, Tuoba Dao 拓拔燾 (r. 424–452), personally led an army to lay siege to the city during his southward campaign against the state of Song. (Song is usually called the Liu Song 劉宋, after the surname of its imperial family, to distinguish it from the later, more famous Song dynasty.) Tuoba Dao sent Li Xiaobo 李孝伯 (d. 459),[1] one of his ministers, to discuss terms with the Seneschal (*Zhangshi* 長史) of the city, Zhang Chang 張暢 (408–457),[2] but their disputation did not lead to an agreement. After failing to take the city by direct assault, Tuoba Dao moved on with his main force on January 18 to continue his southward campaign.

HISTORICAL BACKGROUND

The Jin 晉 dynasty lost control of northern China in 317 when numerous non-Chinese tribesmen established a series of short-lived regimes, termed the Sixteen States (*shiliuguo* 十六國), and the area descended into a period of turbulence and hardship. One of these groups, the Tuoba 拓拔, a part of the Xianbei 鮮卑 confederation that had moved south out of the steppe lands, was able to

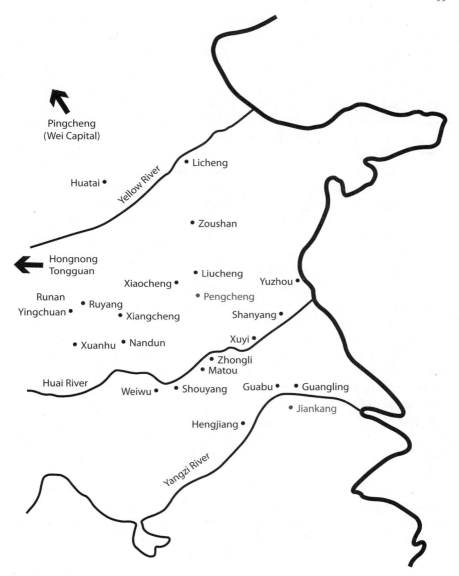

Map of the campaign of 450/451.

defeat its rivals and bring all of northern China under its control. Their state, the Northern Wei (Bei Wei 北魏) established in 386, remained in power until 535, when it was split in two by rival factions.

When it abandoned the North in 317, the Jin state moved its capital to Jiankang 建康, modern Nanjing 南京, and managed to survive until 420 when one of its generals, Liu Yu 劉裕, took the throne and established the Liu Song state, which lasted until 479. At the time in question, the throne was occupied by Emperor Taizu 太祖, Liu Yilong 劉義隆 (r. 424–453).

The core of the Northern Wei was the Yellow River and the territory to its north, while that of the Liu Song was the Yangzi River and the land to its south. The area that each sought to control was that of the Huai River basin. To a large extent, the Liu Song held sway over much of the northern bank of the Huai, but that territory seems to have been a buffer zone. During this period, warfare was not one of defined lines of defense but one of defenders holed up in walled cities capable of sending out troops at opportune times while the attacking marauding armies ranged throughout the land, keeping a wary eye on the security of their supply lines and routes of possible retreat. Siege craft became highly developed. We find mention of towers built to look down on the besieged city and from which to be able to let loose barrages of arrows while sappers were at work undermining the walls. Defenders poured hot melted oils down on the attackers and sorties to throw them off balance. Exaggeration was the order of the day, with bodies described as being piled as high as the walls; in any case, it must have been a bloody business. At one point, the Northern Wei emperor, threatening to throw his troops into the fray no matter what the cost, said that losses incurred by the various minority groups that made up his army would only mean fewer rebels in their home territories in future years.

The campaign of 450/451, during which the disputation examined here took place, was only one in a long series between the Northern and Southern states, for each was determined to bring all of China under its control. This was not just a matter of border realignment. Rather, this phase of the struggle began with what seems to have been a trial run. The Northern Wei emperor led a purported force of 100,000 south in the second month of 450. The border garrisons of Liu Song were told to hold their ground if the attack was small and to fall back to Shouyang 壽陽, on the south bank of the Huai River, if it was large. Although the cities of Nandun 南頓 and Yingchuan 穎川 were abandoned, reinforcements were sent to make a stand at Xuanhu 懸瓠, the administrative center of Runan Commandery 汝南, which was quickly put under siege. Failing to breach the walls after forty-two days, the Northern Wei forces abandoned their attempt, and in the fourth month, their armies returned north.

The emperor of the Liu Song was determined to retaliate, despite the advice of his own military advisers. In the seventh month, the state made preparations for war and appealed to all levels of the population to contribute. From the highest nobility down to the wealthy commoners, all were to contribute to the treasury, and the northeastern regions mobilized their manpower to supplement the standing army. But voluntary donations proved inadequate, and considerably larger contributions were mandated. The forces along the Huai River were to assemble at Xuyi 盱眙, and those at the Yangzi River were to gather at Guangling 廣陵. In the face of this threat, the Northern Wei emperor refused to be overly concerned, saying that the horses would be in better condition in the autumn and that there was plenty of time to gear up.

The Song armies moved north, and the first contact was at Huatai 滑臺, the administrative center of the Northern Wei's Yan region 兗州, north of the Yellow River. In response, in the ninth month, the Northern Wei gathered an army purportedly of a million men. The Song general, Wang Xuanmo 王玄謨 (388–468), in the face of such a threat, pulled back.[3] The Northern Wei attempted to use the river vessels, which had been captured when Wang retreated, to block a Song fleet of a hundred boats that had been sent upriver as an advance force. But the Song fleet broke free and sailed down river to Licheng 歷城, where an outpost was established.

The Northern Wei army, led by the emperor himself, had crossed the Yellow River on September 27 to carry the battle to the Liu Song. The forces were divided into five prongs to force the enemy to divide its strength. Since the attacking armies generally lived off the land, it also made better sense to take different routes. The main force, under the emperor, headed for Zoushan 鄒山. The commandery governor, Cui Yeli 崔耶利,[4] was captured, and for some reason, a stele, erected by the Qin Emperor Shihuang 秦始皇 (259–210 B.C.E.), was pulled down. Meanwhile, on the right flank, the Northern Wei army was making rapid progress on its way to the key point of Shouyang, on the Huai River. When Xuanhu and Xiangcheng 襄城 fell, the Liu Song state, fearing that Shouyang would be next, recalled the army it had sent north, which had seized Hongnong 弘農 on the Yellow River and was about to attack the Tongguan Pass 潼關. This ended the Liu Song's attempt to carry the battle to the North. The battle between these two armies took place at Weiwu, close to Shouyang. The Liu Song army, which met the enemy in the open rather than taking advantage of the city walls, was destroyed. Other cities farther downriver, Matou 馬頭 and Zhongli 鐘離, were also taken and Shouyang was isolated.

Meanwhile, the army led by the Northern Wei emperor reached Xiaocheng 蕭城, only some ten *li* from Pengcheng. The defenders of the city held a council of war to decide what to do. An adequate force was stationed there to defend the city, but there was a potential shortage of supplies. Both the choices proposed involved abandoning Pengcheng. The first choice was to move the army to Licheng, where there were adequate stores but which was some distance north. The other was to make a run for the coast, to reach Yuzhou 鬱洲, and from there to set sail to the Yangzi and hence to the capital at Jiankang. These were risky strategies, and the argument by Zhang Chang to remain and defend the city carried the day. On the *renzi* 壬子 day of the eleventh month—January 14, 451—the Northern Wei army arrived at Pengcheng, which is where the disputation between Li Xiaobo and Zhang Chang, the topic of this chapter, took place.

The Northern Wei emperor did not stay there long. When he could not take the city by direct assault, he led the main force southward on January 18 to make good his threat to water his horses at the Yangzi River. Some detachments were sent toward Guangling; others, toward Shanyang 山陽 and Hengjiang 横江. These armies ranged throughout the countryside with a scorched-earth policy, destroying as they went. On January 21, the main Northern Wei army reached the Huai River; the Liu Song now attempted to group its forces at Xuyi. The difficulty facing the Northern Wei was that there was not enough forage available south of the Huai River, and men and animals began to suffer from hunger. Attacks on Xuyi to gain the supplies stored there failed, so, leaving some men to continue the siege, the army moved farther south. On February 1, it reached Guabu 瓜步 on the Yangzi and began preparing rafts to cross the river. By now Jiankang was in a panic. Some inhabitants were fleeing; all men who could be commandeered were called to arms; poisoned wine was set out as booby traps; and large rewards were declared for the head of the Northern Wei emperor. To protect himself, Tuoba Dao drank only water brought by camel from the North.

The Northern Wei did not dare to move further against Jiankang while Xuyi remained a threat to their rear. Tuoba Dao requested that the defenders of Xuyi provide him with some wine, as he had at Pengcheng. Instead, a jug of urine was sent out of the city. Furious, the emperor had a bed of nails prepared for the governor of Xuyi and intensified his efforts to bring down the city. Despite all efforts, the city held out for a month. By that time, an epidemic was raging in the Northern Wei army. There were rumors that a naval force from Jiankang would be sailing up the Huai River to bring aid to Xuyi, and Pengcheng, still holding out, imperiled the return route. Finally Tuoba Dao decided to end the stalemate and to return to the North. On April 19, he burned all the siege weapons and began his retreat, reaching his own capital at Pingcheng 平城, modern Datong 大同, on April 26. He left behind a ravaged area with a terrible loss of life, including half his own army. Hostilities between the North and the South continued sporadically for another century or more; only in 589 was the country finally brought under a unified rule.

HISTORIOGRAPHY

In China, the past is a series of concrete events and overt acts, and history is a register of them. It is expected that the history be exact and dispassionate without the projection of the personality of the registrar. Because a verbatim reproduction of previous records seemed a natural and reasonable method to produce an impersonal record of events, historical writing became not an original composition but a compilation of choice selections from earlier works. It is made up of exact transcriptions because compilations of documents were not expected to be paraphrased. On the surface, the compilation is a primitive type, a synthesis of the simplest kind. It is sometimes described as a scissors-and-paste approach, the dissection and arrangement of fragments in chronological sequence. But this is misleading, for the process is much more complex. While the historian in China remained the archivist who manipulated and edited texts but rarely wrote his own versions—he collected the facts, discreetly filtered them, and presented those of greater moment to speak for themselves—his standing as a historian was judged on how well he manipulated and calibrated the texts.

One could establish a hierarchy of reliability with a careful examination of the various types of dialogue. Anecdotes, stock phrases, and direct speech of various sorts all lead one to suspect that the historian is not basing his work on completely reliable materials. But while the classical Greek historian Thucydides made no pretense that his speeches were anything but what was called for in the specific occasion, the Chinese historian recorded the direct speech in his text as verbatim. Sometimes it is clear from the context and formality of the style that a written document has been made into someone's speech and so has some reliability, but often records of conversations must have been inventions of the historian or of some secondhand source.

In treating the classical historians, Erich Auerbach, in *Mimesis: The Representation of Reality in Western Literature*, argues that the grand style of historiography requires grandiloquent speeches, which, as a rule, are fictitious. Their function is the graphic dramatization of a given occurrence or, at times, the presentation of great political or moral ideas; in either case, they are intended as rhetorical bravura pieces. That is, they are presented as set pieces, deriving from the tradition of the rhetoricians, who were accustomed to composing speeches as they might have been delivered by someone at some specific time. In Thucydides, one can discern three sorts of these speeches: first, what he composed on the basis of hindsight for a speech known to have been given; second, speeches that were appropriate for the speaker and may well have been given but for which there was no evidence; and third, those based on the reports of others. But the question is why Thucydides, who was concerned with accuracy, used such speeches for which he made no claim for objective reporting. He obviously felt that only by using such material could he show the emotions and motives of the men, which were as important as their deeds. It probably never occurred to him that anyone would read his versions of the speeches as exact and verbatim transcripts of the originals.

In the Chinese case, we also find the use of speech in a form that reminds us of Auerbach's description of the graphic dramatization. In addition to the ethical and rhetorical preoccupations, the real point of an event recorded in the histories is its use as a basis for an effective exchange of words. Lu Jia 陸賈 (ca. 240–170 B.C.E.), a famous scholar of the early Han, argued with Liu Bang 劉邦 (r. 202–195 B.C.E.), the founder of the dynasty, that the empire could not be ruled from horseback and that if one were to hold on to the state, learning was necessary. How tame that exchange would have been if the historian had simply said that Lu taught Liu the value of ancient writings. But if the dialogues were frequently fictitious, what happened to the standards of truth held by the historians? Was it that, as in the West, there was an acceptance of these speeches simply as a convention and that we have here a parallel between the two cultures? This may have been so with the first standard history, the *Records of the Historian (Shi ji* 史記) by Sima Qian 司馬遷 (ca. 145–ca. 86 B.C.E.), but as Chinese historiography became more structured and as the individuality of the historian became more constricted, it may well be that such speeches came to be invented less and less and that the historians in China were forced to seek other means of accomplishing their needs, such as less reliable written sources, and this may be the case for the text of the disputation at Pengcheng.

It is not often that one has the opportunity to compare the same incident in such detail in two of the standard histories. Apparently, a transcript, no doubt highly edited, had been prepared at the time of the meeting between Li Xiaobo and Zhang Chang and then circulated. The *History of the Song (Song shu* 宋書), compiled by Shen Yue 沈約 (441–513), was completed in 464, while the *History of the Wei (Wei shu* 魏書) by Wei Shou 魏收 (506–572) was presented to the throne in 554. Both histories included their version of the event, playing off the same transcript but making changes that would make their version more acceptable to their regional loyalties. Although the *History of the Wei* was the later of the two, it would not appear that Wei Shou had the last word on some topics.

In the following, the texts recording the disputation in the two sources, the *History of the Wei* and the *History of the Song*, are divided into parallel segments. For the most part, the texts remain largely the same and thus true to a source text, even to the point of including material reflecting badly on the reporting side. Where there are differences between the two texts, they seem to indicate how the versions were manipulated to the advantage of the particular party. Note also the careful use of terminology to underline the claims to legitimacy by each side.

FURTHER READING

For studies of warfare in medieval China, that by Frank A. Kierman Jr. and John K. Fairbank, eds., *Chinese Ways in Warfare* (Cambridge, Mass.: Harvard University Press, 1974), has long been the standard, but a more recent publication by David Andrew Graff, *Medieval Chinese Warfare, 300–900* (London: Routledge, 2002), adds a great deal more material. Three detailed studies by Benjamin E. Wallacker, "Studies in Medieval Chinese Siegecraft: The Siege of Chien-k'ang, A.D. 548–549," *Journal of Asian History* 5, no. 1 (1971): 35–54; "Studies in Medieval Chinese Siegecraft: The Siege of Ying-ch'uan, A.D. 548–549," *Journal of Asian Studies* 30, no. 3 (1971): 611–22; and "Studies in Medieval

Chinese Siegecraft: The Siege of Yu-pi, A.D. 546," *Journal of Asian Studies* 28, no. 4 (1969): 789–802, have much to offer.

The various essays in W. G. Beasley and E. G. Pulleyblank, *Historians of China and Japan* (Oxford: Oxford University Press, 1961); and Donald D. Leslie, Colin Mackerras, and Wang Gungwu, eds., *Essays on the Sources for Chinese History* (Canberra: Australian National University Press, 1973), explore the subject of Chinese historiography in some detail. On the question of direct speech, there is an extensive discussion in Hans Bielenstein, "The Restoration of the Han Dynasty," *Bulletin of the Museum of Far Eastern Art* 26 (1954): 21–40. More generally, on the reliability of the Chinese sources, given the historiographic methodology involved, see the issues raised by Clyde B. Sargent, "Subsidized History: Pan Ku and the Historical Records of the Former Han Dynasty," *Far Eastern Quarterly* 3 (1944): 119–43; and Homer H. Dubs, "The Reliability of Chinese Histories," *Far Eastern Quarterly* 6 (1946): 23–43.

THE CAST

The protagonists

NORTHERN WEI	LIU SONG
Li Xiaobo	Zhang Chang

The titles by which the individuals are identified by the two sides

NORTHERN WEI	THE INDIVIDUAL	LIU SONG
Shizu; His Majesty	Tuoba Dao, emperor of the Northern Wei (r. 424–451)	Wei ruler; Dao
	Liu Yilong, emperor of the Song (r. 424–453)	Taizu
Pacifying the North General	Liu Jun, son of the Song Emperor Liu Yilong, and future emperor (r. 454–464)	Shizu
Defender in Chief	Liu Yigong, brother of the Song Emperor Liu Yilong	Defender in Chief

Toward the end of the [Taiping] Zhenjun [reign] [440–451], the [imperial] chariots [i.e., the emperor] [opened a] southern campaign and led [the armies] out to Pengcheng 彭城. The son of Liu Yilong 劉義隆,[5] Jun 駿,[6] the Pacifying the North General [*Anbei jiangjun* 安北將軍], Regional Inspector [*Cishi* 刺史] of Xuzhou 徐州, and Prince of Wuling 武陵王, sent his general Ma Wengong 馬文恭

[died soon after 454][7] to lead more than ten thousand horse and foot [soldiers] to go to Xiaocheng 蕭城. [Our] advance army attacked and defeated them; Wengong fled, but we captured a company leader, Kuai Ying 蒯應.[8] When Yilong heard that the grand army was proceeding south, he then sent his younger brother, the Defender in Chief [*Taiwei* 太尉] and Prince of Jiangxia 江夏王, Yigong 義恭,[9] to lead a host to go to Pengcheng.

When [Northern Wei Emperor] Shizu 世祖,[10] reached Pengcheng, he ascended Yafu Mound 亞父冢[11] in order to look down into the city and had Kuai Ying escorted to the Small Market Gate [*xiaoshimen* 小市門] to make known Shizu's pronouncement and to ask after the health of Yigong and the others; he was also charged to describe in his own words the defeat at Xiaocheng. Yigong and the others asked Ying, "Did the Wei emperor himself come or not?" Ying said, "He personally came." They then asked, "Where is he now?" Ying said, "He is southwest of the city." They also asked, "How many horse and foot [soldiers] does he have?" Ying said, "The main army has more than 400,000." Jun then sent someone to present two vessels of wine and a hundred stalks of sugarcane and to request camels.

[*WS* 53.1168–72]

When Shizu[12] garrisoned Pengcheng, [Zhang] Chang 張暢 served as the Seneschal of the Pacifying the North General [*Anbei zhangshi* 安北長史] and the Governor of Pei Commandery [*Peijun taishou* 沛郡太守]. In 450 the "braided caitiff"[13] Tuoba Dao 托跋燾 invaded the South. The Defender in Chief and Prince of Jiangxia, Yigong, took full command of the various armies and went out to garrison Peng[cheng] on the Si 泗.[14] At that time Dao personally led the large host and had already arrived at Xiaocheng [i.e., Xiao District], a bit more than ten *li* from Pengcheng.[15] Although the military strength at Pengcheng was substantial, the military supplies were inadequate. Yigong wanted to abandon Pengcheng and return south, and the discussion lasted a whole day without [their] reaching a decision. At that time the forces at Licheng 歷城 were undersized, but the foodstuffs were ample.[16] The Adjutant of the Central Troops [*Zhongbing canjun* 中兵參軍] of the Pacifying the North General, Shen Qingzhi 沈慶之 [386–465],[17] advocated that the vehicle encampment be made to form an "enclosed box" [*hanxiang* 函箱] array[18] and that the elite troops form outer wings, to carry the two princes with their wives and women[19] straightaway and hurry to Licheng, and to allocate troops to stay with Protector General [*Hujun* 護軍] Xiao Sihua 蕭思話 [400–455][20] to defend [Pengcheng]. He Xun 何勖 [dates unknown],[21] the Seneschal of the Defender in Chief [*Taiwei zhangshi* 太尉長史], did not agree but wanted to roll up the mat [i.e., for one and all] to flee to Yuzhou 鬱洲 and return to the capital by sea. Yigong had already decided to withdraw, but he had yet to choose between the two arguments, so he assembled the whole staff to discuss it. They all were agitated but had no other counsel to offer.[22] Chang said, "If reaching Licheng or Yuzhou is reasonable, how could this lowly official dare not offer enthusiastic support? At present inside the city, there is an insufficiency of food, and the common folk all want to leave, but because the gates are barred with such strictness, none can depart, though they want to. Once there is movement afoot [and the gates open], everyone will scatter, and so how could we reach our goal? At present, although the military stores are in short supply, they are not yet exhausted. When one estimates that they are about to be used up, then at that point there are a number of fitting [responses]; why would one toss aside a stratagem that is perfectly safe and seek a path that holds such peril and dangers? If this plan [of retreating] must be used, this lowly official requests that his neck's blood wet the duke's horse's hooves." When Shizu heard Chang's advice, he said to Gongyi, "Since Uncle[23] is in charge of the troops, I do not dare to intervene in whether we stay or leave. I, Daomin 道民,[24] shamefully am the city head.[25] I have damaged our dominance and invited in brigandage. My sense of shame is deep indeed! If we were to abandon the garrison and flee, in truth I could not show my face again at the court; I would hope to survive or perish together with this city. One cannot differ with Seneschal Zhang's words." Since Chang's words were firm and Shizu, moreover, approved of his advice, Yigong then ceased [considering leaving Pengcheng].

At the time, [Emperor] Taizu 太祖[26] had sent Supernumerary Gentleman Cavalier Attendant 員外散騎侍郎 Xu Yuan 徐爰 [394–475][27] by post horse to go to Pengcheng to estimate how far the rice and grain would stretch. When he left, the city dispatched horsemen to accompany him. When Dao 燾[28] learned of this, he sent several hundred cavalry to pursue them, but Yuan had already crossed the Huai [River] and managed to escape. At first when Yuan left and those inside the city heard that the caitiff were pursuing him, they worried that Yuan had been captured, that the measurements of the rice had fallen to the caitiff, and that they would know that food was in short supply in the city. Yigong was anxious and fearful beyond measure and again wanted to flee. But the day that Yuan escaped [that pursuit], the great caitiff host arrived at Pengcheng.

When Dao first arrived, he ascended the Yafu Mound south of the city and, at the Ximatai 戲馬臺, erected a felt tent. Previously, before Dao had arrived, [Emperor] Shizu had sent his general Ma Wengong to Xiaocheng. His force had been defeated by the caitiff; Wengong managed to escape, but his company commander Kuai Ying was seized. He was brought to the Small Market Gate [to deliver a message] and said, "The Wei ruler extends his greetings to the Pacifying the North [General]. He has come from afar and is exhausted. If you have sugarcane and wine, could you part with some?" At that point the Company Commander Defending the City [*Fangcheng duizhu* 防城隊主], Liang Fanian 梁法念 [dates unknown],[29] replied, "Please tell me what you have heard." Ying then described the defeat at Xiaocheng. [Fanian] then asked Ying, "Has the ruler of the caitiff come himself?" [Ying] replied, "He has come." [Fanian] said,

"Where is he now?" Ying raised his hand and pointed to the southwest. Again [Fanian] asked, "How many horse and men?" He replied, "More than 400,000." Fanian reported Dao's words to [Emperor] Shizu, and [Emperor] Shizu dispatched someone to reply, "We know traveling is very taxing; we now present you with two vessels of wine and a hundred stalks of sugarcane. We hear that you have camels; perhaps you could send one."[30]

[SS 59.1599–1605]

I

The next day at dawn, Shizu again ascended the Yafu Mound and dispatched [Li] Xiaobo 李孝伯 to the Small Market [Gate]; Jun also dispatched his seneschal Zhang Chang to face Xiaobo. Xiaobo from a distance asked Chang's surname, and Chang replied, "My surname is Zhang." Xiaobo then said, "Is this Seneschal Zhang?" Chang said, "Sir, how do you come to know me?" Xiaobo said, "Since I have some familiarity with this land, how would I not know you?" (WS)

Zhang Chang looked at them from atop the wall, and the caitiff envoy asked, "Isn't that Seneschal Zhang?" Chang said, "How do you, Sir, come to know [me]?" The caitiff envoy replied, "Sir, your reputation is widely known, enough to allow me to know it." (SS)

II

Chang asked Xiaobo, "What then, Sir, is your surname, and what office do you hold?" Xiaobo said, "I am only a fellow in the ranks, why bother asking? Still it is [high] enough, Sir, that we may be matched." (WS)

Chang then asked the caitiff envoy's surname, and he replied, "I am a Xianbei and have no surname. More than this I am not permitted to say." Chang then asked, "What position do you, Sir, hold?" [The caitiff envoy] replied, "The Xianbei official ranks are different [from yours] and cannot be briefly explained; still it is adequate to match yours, Sir." (SS)

III

Xiaobo said, "His Majesty has a pronouncement [that says], 'The Defender in Chief and Pacifying the North [General] might come out of the gates for a short time. We would meet with them. We furthermore are not going to attack Pengcheng; why do you weary the officers and men that the walls be well prepared?' He now dispatches as gifts these camels as well as a sable robe and some other things." Chang said, "The term 'pronouncement' can be promulgated only in your own state; how can it be called that here?" Xiaobo said, "Your lordships the Defender in Chief and Pacifying the North [General], are they not subjects?" Chang replied, "They are." Xiaobo then said, "Our court grandly encompasses myriad states, and in all the territory within these shores, there are none who dare not serve as vassal; granted that he is the lord of neighboring states, how would we not call it a pronouncement to the vassals of neighboring states?" (WS)

At dawn the next day, Dao again went up the Ximatai and again sent an envoy [i.e., Li Xiaobo] to the Small Market Gate to say, "The ruler of the Wei extends his greetings to the Pacifying the North [General]. The Pacifying the North [General] might come out the gate for a short time. We would meet with the Pacifying the North [General]. We furthermore are not going to attack this city; why does the Pacifying the North [General] weary the officers and men on the wall? Moreover, mules, donkeys, and camels are products of the Northern state; I now give them to you, and also some other things." Moreover, [the envoy] told the Small Market Gate company commander, "Since there are provisions, you, Sir, could move the south gate to receive them?" Dao sent a camel, mule, horse, sable robe, and some drink and foodstuffs. But when they arrived at the south gate, the gate had been locked, and the requested key had not yet been produced. (SS)

IV

Xiaobo further asked Chang, "What was the point of hurriedly shutting the gates and breaching the bridge?" Chang said, "Because the Wei emperor's military ramparts had not yet been erected and his officers and men were exhausted, and among our 100,000 elite troops, everyone's thoughts were on [fighting] even to death; therefore the two princes, fearing that we too easily would shamefully overwhelm [the enemy], had the [gates of the] city shut; that is all. We await your resting the foot and horse [i.e., troops], and then together we shall engage on the battlefield; on a set day we shall divert ourselves."[31] (WS)

The caitiff envoy went on to ask, "What was the point of hurriedly shutting the gates and breaching the bridge?" Chang replied, "Because the Wei ruler's military ramparts had not yet been erected and his officers and men were exhausted, and among our 100,000 elite troops everyone's thoughts were on [fighting] even to death; therefore the two princes, fearing that we too easily would shamefully overwhelm [the enemy], had the [gates of the] city shut; that is all. We await your resting the foot and horse [i.e., troops], and then together we shall engage on the battlefield; on a set day we shall divert ourselves." (SS)

V

Xiaobo said, "Issuing orders to proceed or to stop are the ordinary affairs of commanding officers, and moreover they ought to have a plan in making decisions. Of what use is there in destroying a bridge and closing the gates? And further, why exaggerate that in this city in such difficult straits, there are a hundred thousand [troops]? Moreover, we have one million excellent horses that we could brag about on this point." (*WS*)

The caitiff envoy said, "A leader ought to have a plan in making decisions. Of what use is there in destroying a bridge and closing the gates? And further, why exaggerate that there are 100,000 [troops]? Moreover, we have more than enough excellent fleet-footed horses; even if cavalrymen as numerous as the clouds were brought together from the four directions, we could stand them off." (*SS*)

VI

Chang said, "Princes and nobles establish the alignments of the troops; how is it just a matter of commands? For if I were to brag to you, Sir, I would have said a million, so in saying a hundred thousand, it is really only the two princes' entourage that they ordinarily maintain. Within the walls here are the people, gentle and common, craftsmen, and soldiers of several regions, that I have not yet mentioned. We basically fight using men; we do not fight using an adequacy of horses. Moreover, the northern lands of Ji 冀 [32] is where horses are bred; why, Sir, would you use fleet-footed [horses] to brag about?" Xiaobo said, "The placement of troops by kings and nobles is truly as you say, and opening and shutting [gates] is common, but what is this shutting down? And what is the sense in dismantling bridges? Defense of this city is what your side is well versed in; open-field battle is what we excel at. Our reliance on horses is like you, Sir, relying on walls." (*WS*)

Chang said, "Nobles and princes establish the alignments of the troops; how is it just a matter of commands? For if I were to brag to you, Sir, I would have said a million, so saying a hundred thousand, it is really only the two princes' entourage that they ordinarily maintain. Within the walls here are the people, gentle and common of several regions, and two units of soldiers, that I have not yet mentioned. We basically fight with wisdom; we do not fight using horses' hooves. Moreover, the northern lands of Ji is where horses are bred; why, Sir, do you use fleet-footed [horses] to brag about?" The caitiff envoy said, "Not so. In defending walled cities, you, Sir, excel, but in open-field battle we excel. Our reliance on horses is like you, Sir, relying on walls." (*SS*)

VII

Within the city there was a certain Bei Si 貝思 [dates unknown],[33] who had once gone to the [Northern Wei] capital. Yigong dispatched him to take a look, and Si recognized that it was Xiaobo. Si then came forward and asked Xiaobo, "Minister Li is [perhaps] weary from his journey." Xiaobo said, "This matter ought to be common knowledge." Si replied, "Because it is common knowledge, I offer my commiseration." Xiaobo said, "I thank you, Sir, for your thoughtfulness." (WS)

Within the city there was a certain Bei Si, who had once been in the Northern state. Yigong dispatched him to take a look, and Si recognized that it was the caitiff minister Li Xiaobo. Si then asked, "Minister Li is [perhaps] weary from his journey." Xiangbo said, "This matter ought to be common knowledge." Si replied, "Because it is common knowledge, I offer my commiseration." Xiaobo said, "I thank you, Sir, for your thoughtfulness." (SS)

VIII

The gates were then opened, and Chang, alone and without staff, emerged to receive the presents. Xiaobo said, "The emperor has ordered that the sable robe be given to the Defender in Chief and that the camel[s], mule[s], and horse[s] be given to the Pacifying the North [General], while the grape wine and various food stuffs are advanced to be equally shared." (WS)

The gates were then opened, and Chang, alone and without staff, emerged to meet Xiaobo and to receive the presents of foodstuffs. The caitiff envoy said, "The sable robe is to be given to the Defender in Chief, and the camel[s] and mule[s] are to be given to the Pacifying the North [General], while the grape wine and various viands are to be shared by the uncle and nephew." (SS)

IX

Dao, moreover, asked for wine and sweet oranges [ganju 甘橘]. (SS)

X

Chang said, "The two princes, respectively, say to the Wei emperor that they know he desires to favor them with an audience and that they have always wanted to meet face to face, but they have received a command from their court to humbly remain in their frontier posts, and vassals are to have no cross-border contacts; therefore there is no allowance for private meetings." (*WS*)

Chang passed on a comment by [Emperor] Shizu: "We extend our greetings to the Wei ruler. We know you desire a meeting, and we have long looked forward to meet you face to face, but we have received a command from the court to humbly remain in our frontier post, and vassals are to have no cross-border contacts; our regret is not quickly dissipated." (*SS*)

XI

[Chang continued,] "Furthermore, preparing for the defense of city is customary for garrisons at the frontier. We are happy to be employed in it; therefore, though fatigued, we have no resentment. The Defender in Chief and the Garrison Army [General] have received the things sent over; as for the Wei ruler's purpose, we know that he again must have sweet oranges. Now we deliver them as before. The Defender in Chief realizes that the northern lands are a cold region and leather riding breeches are necessary. We now give them to the Wei ruler. Conch shell tumblers [*luobei* 螺杯] and variegated dumplings [*zazong* 雜粽] are prized in the South, and the Garrison Army [General] now has them sent over." This message had not yet been sent when Dao again dispatched an envoy to order Xiaobo to transmit another message, which went, "The Wei ruler has a proclamation to tell the Defender in Chief and the Pacifying the North [General] that soon some cavalry will arrive and there will be chariots behind [them]. Now we sit in a formal manner with nothing to do; if there is a gaming device, could we borrow it?" Chang said, "A gaming device, of course, can be requested."

[Chang continued,] "But in talking to the two princes, these are not humble phrases. Furthermore, the term 'a proclamation' really is proper for distribution in your state; how can it be termed so here?" Xiaobo said, "What is the difference between 'proclaim' or 'speak,' or between 'we' and 'I'?" Chang said, "One can talk about how terms used in communication came about. When one speaks, then, there are degrees [of status] of honored and debased. What you heretofore termed a 'proclamation' is not what I dare hear." Xiaobo then said, "His lordship the Defender in Chief and the Pacifying the North [General], are they not subjects?" Chang replied, "They are." Xiaobo said, "As the ruler of a neighboring state, how would he not [use the] term 'proclamations' in reference to the subjects of neighboring states?" Chang said, "This term 'ruler' cannot yet be heard in the Central State [*Zhonghua* 中華]; how much more, then, given the eminence of these princes, would you yet speak of 'the ruler of a neighboring state'?"[34] (*SS*)

XII

Yigong presented a pair of leather breeches, and Jun proffered two vessels of wine and a hundred stalks of sugarcane. (WS)

XIII

Xiaobo said, "There is another pronouncement: 'The Defender in Chief and the Pacifying the North [General] have long been cut off from news from the south and surely are very concerned and anxious. If you desire to dispatch a letter, we can provide protection to deliver it; if you require horsemen, we can also provide the horses to deliver it.'" Chang said, "In this area there are many roads; messengers day and night come and go; on this account, we would not further trouble the Wei emperor." Xiaobo said, "We also know there are water routes, but apparently they have been cut off by the White Bandits." Chang said, "You, Sirs, dress in white, and so are called the White Bandits." Xiaobo laughed and said, "The present-day White Bandits apparently differ from the Yellow Turbans and Red Eyebrows."[35] Chang said, "The Yellow Turbans and Red Eyebrows have not been south of the Yangzi." Xiaobo said, "Although they have not been south of the Yangzi, they have not been distant from the Xu 徐 area."[36] (WS)

Xiaobo said, "The Wei ruler says to the Defender in Chief and the Garrison Army [General], 'You are both young and separated from news from the south and so are surely very concerned and anxious. If you desire to dispatch a letter, we can provide protection to deliver it. If you require horsemen, we can also provide the horses to deliver it.'" Chang said, "In this area there are many roads; messengers day and night come and go; on this account, we would not further trouble the Wei ruler." Xiaobo said, "We also know there are water routes, but apparently they have been cut off by the White Bandits." Chang said, "You, Sirs, dress in white, and so are called the White Bandits." Xiaobo laughed and said, "The present-day White Bandits apparently differ from the Yellow Turbans and Red Eyebrows." Chang said, "The Yellow Turbans and Red Eyebrows have not been south of the Yangzi." Xiaobo said, "Although they have not been south of the Yangzi, they have not been far from the Qing 青 and Xu 徐 areas."[37] Chang said, "At present, at Qing and Xu there truly are bandits, but they are not White Bandits." (SS)

XIV

Xiaobo said, "Previously I inquired after the Pacifying the North [General]; why has there been no report for so long?" Chang said, "The two princes value their privacy, and to inform them of the inquiry is difficult." Xiaobo said, "The Duke of Zhou grasped his hair [while washing it] and spit out his food [while eating].[38] Why is it that the two princes alone value their privacy?" Chang said, "Grasping one's hair and spitting out food was not said in reference to men of a neighboring state." Xiaobo said, "My native state is still near; when a neighboring state is near, one ought to be fully respectful. Furthermore, when guests arrive, there are the [appropriate] formalities, [and] the host ought to meet with the [appropriate] formalities." Chang said, "Yesterday when we saw the guests arrive at the gate, they had not yet displayed the [appropriate] formalities." Xiaobo said, "It was not that the guests arrived without [appropriate] formalities; it was that the host was flustered and that there were no due measures for attending to the guests." (*WS*)

The caitiff envoys said, "Previously we [asked to] borrow the gaming device; why has [it] not come out?" Chang said, "The two princes value their privacy, and to inform them of the request is difficult." Xiaobo said, "The Duke of Zhou grasped his hair [while washing it] and spit out his food [while eating]. Why is it that the two princes alone value their privacy?" Chang said, "Grasping hair and spitting out food originally was granted only to [those of] the Central State [*Zhongguo* 中國]." Xiaobo said, "[Meeting] a guest has rules of propriety; the host then selects [the appropriate ones]."[39] Chang said, "Yesterday when we saw the guests arriving at the gate, they had not yet displayed the [appropriate] formalities." (*SS*)

XV

After a short time, they sent out the gaming device and thereupon presented it. (*SS*)

XVI

Xiaobo further said, "There is an imperial pronouncement: 'Cheng Tianzuo 程天祚 [d. 466][40] is a mere ordinary person, and we certainly know that he is not one of the select few of south of the Yangzi. Recently at Ruyang, having received nine wounds, he fell into the Yin River, and we had him pulled out. In general when people's flesh and blood have been separated, they then think to draw together. We hear that that his younger brother is here; why has he not been dispatched to come out briefly? He could then return. Why would we detain one person?'" Chang said, "We know that you desire that Cheng Tianzuo and his younger brother rejoin, and we already have insisted that he be dispatched, but he has strongly refused to go." Xiaobo said, "How could it be that a son or a younger brother gain news of their father or elder brother and yet not be willing to see him; this is even worse than wild animals. How could the customs of your honorable land have come to this?" (WS)

Dao again sent someone to say, "The Wei ruler extends his greetings to the Pacifying the North [General]. Cheng Tianzuo is a mere ordinary person, and we certainly know that he is not one of the admirable ones of the Song court. Recently at Ruyang, having received nine wounds, he fell into the Yin River, and we with our [own] hands pulled him out. In general when people's flesh and blood have been separated, they then think to draw together. We have already spoken of it. But his younger brother firmly declines to come. You should now order him to come so that they may see each other." Cheng Tianfu 程天福 said to the envoy, "My elder brother received the command of Ruyang and was unable to carry it to death. We each are in a different state; why this bother to see each other?" (SS)

XVII

Shizu also dispatched felt rugs to be given one each to Yigong and Jun, as well as nine sorts of salts and barbarian-made fermented black bean sauce [huchi 胡豉]. Xiaobo said, "There has been a later imperial pronouncement: Each of these various salts has an appropriate use. The white is edible salt; His Majesty consumes it himself. The black salt cures bloating of the stomach and intestines; grind up six ounces [zhu 銖] and take it with wine; the 'barbarian' salt cures eye pain; the Rong 戎 [tribes on the western frontier] salt cures all sorts of sores; the remaining four, red salt, the variegated color salt, the odoriferous salt, and the horse-tooth salt are not edible." (WS)

Dao also sent a felt rug each, nine sorts of salts, and a barbarian-made fermented bean sauce. [The messenger said,] "Each of these various salts has an appropriate use. The white salt the Wei ruler himself consumes. The black salt cures bloating of the stomach and intestines; finely scrape off six ounces [zhu 銖] and take it with wine; the 'barbarian' salt cures eye pain; the rou 柔 salt[41] is not to be eaten; it cures horses' backbone sores; the remaining four, red salt, the variegated color salt, the odoriferous salt, and the horse-tooth salt, are not edible. The barbarian-made fermented bean sauce is what [people] in the central [regions] eat. The yellow-sweet [huanggan 黃甘] [i.e., oranges] fortunately are abundant in your country, can you spare some?" (SS)

XVIII

"Why do the Defender in Chief and Pacifying the North [General] not dispatch people to come into our presence? Although the feelings of one to another cannot be plumbed, still they would see our size, know our age, and see what sort of a person we are.'" Chang said, "The Wei emperor has long been described by those coming and going [between our states]. Minister Li himself acts according to orders received and so is not troubled that [these feelings] between us are not plumbed. Therefore [we] do not respond." (WS)

[Dao's messenger] further said, "The Wei ruler extends his greetings to the Defender in Chief and Pacifying the North [General]. Why do not they dispatch people to come into our presence? Although the feelings of one to another cannot be plumbed, still they would see our size, know our age, and see what sort of a person we are. If the various attendants are not able to be dispatched, it is also possible to send junior staff members to come."

Chang further made known [his superior's] intention and replied, "The appearance, ability, and strength of the Wei ruler have long been described by those coming and going [between our states]. Minister Li himself acts according to orders received and so is not troubled that [these feelings] between us are not plumbed. Therefore we do not respond." (SS)

XIX

Yigong presented ten wax candles, and Jun presented a piece of brocade. (WS)

[Dao's messenger] further said, "The Wei ruler is pained that in previously [offering to] present a horse, he did not at all express his intent. If the Pacifying the North [General] requires a large horse, we ought then to send it. If he requires a Sichuan horse, we also have an excellent one." Chang said, "The Pacifying the North [General] does not lack fine steeds; the gift was your idea and not what we sought."

Yigong bestowed[42] ten large candles. Shizu also sent a piece of brocade[43] and said, "[We] know you need more yellow sweet [oranges]. We really are not stingy, but we cannot send enough for your whole army. What we previously sent to the Wei ruler ought not yet to have been exhausted. Therefore we will not hand over anymore." Dao again requested sugarcane and pomegranates. Chang said, "Pomegranates are produced at Yexia 鄴下,[44] so you should not be lacking them." (SS)

XX

Xiaobo said, "You, Sir, are a gentleman of the southern land. Why do you wear straw sandals? When you, Sir, wear these, what do the officers and men say?" Chang said, "Referring to me a gentleman is very embarrassing. But it is because

I am a nonmilitary [person]; when one receives orders to command troops, leisure clothing is not permitted during military deployment." (WS)

Xiaobo then said, "You, Sir, belong to the high elite[45] of the southern land. Why do you wear straw sandals? When you, Sir, wear these, what do the officers and men say?" Chang said, "Referring to me as 'high elite' is very embarrassing. But it is because I am a nonmilitary [person]; when one receives orders to command troops, leisure clothing is not permitted during military deployment." (SS)

XXI

Xiaobo further said, "Seneschal, I am a man of the central regions and have long dwelled in the Northern state, cut off from the Hua customs. We are but steps apart, and yet we cannot fully express ourselves.[46] I am surrounded by Northerners who listen to my words; you, Seneschal, should comprehend my meaning."[47] (SS)

XXII

Xiaobo said, "The Prince of Yongchang 永昌王,[48] who has recently been garrisoned at Chang'an, now has led eighty thousand crack cavalry advancing straight into the area south of the Huai [River]; Shouchun 壽春 has likewise closed its gates to defend itself and does not dare to engage us. Previously we sent the head of Liu Kangzu 劉康祖 [d. 450],[49] whom you have seen. Wang Xuanmo,[50] as is well known, is of ordinary talent. What is the point of employing such persons so that it results in flight and defeat? Since then, we have advanced more than seven hundred li beyond the border, and your leader has not been able once to put up any resistance. At the Zou Mountain 鄒山 defiles on which you relied, our advance force for the first time has engaged. Cui Xieli subsequently entered a cave, and our officers and men dragged him out upside down. His Majesty spared his life, so today he is with us here. Furthermore, how could you make light of [the situation] and dispatch Ma Wengong to go to Xiao District [= Xiaocheng] to have him observe the situation and then retreat? Your people are very angry and resentful; they say that in peaceful times, [you] took their taxes and silk but that when dire difficulties arose, [you] were unable to give them succor."
    Chang said, "We know that [the Prince of] Yongchang has already crossed into [the area] south of the Huai [River]. In recently arrived dispatches, there has been no news of Kangzu being defeated. Wang Xuanmo is a subordinate commander of the South; we do not say he has talent, but because he is a Northerner, he therefore became a guide for the vanguard. The main army had not yet arrived, and as the river was frozen over, Xuanmo came to the conclusion

that he ought to retreat. This was not yet a miscalculation, but because he was returning at night, it caused the cavalry mounts to panic. Our Xuanhu 懸瓠 is a small town, and Chen Xian 陳憲 [dates unknown] was a junior officer. The Wei emperor emptied his state to attack and besiege and, for weeks, could not take it.[51] Hu Shengzhi 胡盛之 [dates unknown] was a subaltern junior officer who did not lead even three squads; as soon as he crossed the Ge River 翮水, the lords and subjects of the Wei state fled and scattered, barely managing to escape.[52] The troops of Huatai 滑臺 do not have much to be ashamed of. Although the small outpost at Zou Mountain has some strategic importance, the people along the river are, for the most part, recent adherents. They had just begun to appreciate the effect of a good administration, but because the banditry had not yet been brought to a halt, [the court] sent Cui Xieli to calm [the situation]; that is all. Now that it has fallen, of what loss is it to the state? The Wei emperor personally led an army of a hundred thousand and has brought under control a certain Cui Xieli; is that worth mentioning? When we recently heard that the people of Xiao District had all taken to the mountain defiles, we merely sent Ma Wengong with ten companies to respond to them. Wengong first sent out three companies and even made your main encampment leave. Ji Xuanjing 稽玄敬 arrived with a hundred boats at Liucheng 留城, and the Wei army fled in defeat. [For us] to scorn an enemy to this extent: is it not pitiful?[53]

The populace of these kingly realms separately dwells along the banks of the river. When the two states engage in warfare, they ought to bring both comfort and nourishment [to those people], but after the Wei armies crossed the border, events have transpired beyond what one would have imagined. If the officials did not fail the people, of what have the people to complain? We know that you have come seven hundred *li* into our territory without encountering resistance. This, first of all, is the Defender in Chief's marvelous planning and, second, is a part of the sagely strategy [of the Prince] of Wuling 武陵. Although I have no foreknowledge of the critical affairs of army and state, since the use of arms has its critical point, I would not be inclined to talk with you about it." (*WS*)

Xiaobo further said, "The [Prince of] Yongchang, who recently has been garrisoned at Chang'an, now has led eighty thousand crack cavalry advancing straight into the area south of the Huai [River]; Shouchun has long closed its gates to defend itself and does not dare to engage us. Previously we sent the head of Liu Kangzu, whom you have seen. Wang Xuanmo, as is well known, is of ordinary talent. What is the point of the Southern state's employing such persons so that it comes to flight and defeat? Since we have advanced more than seven hundred *li* beyond the border, your leader has not been able once to put up any resistance. At the Zou Mountain defiles on which you, Sirs, relied, our advance force for the first time has engaged. Cui Xieli subsequently went hiding in a cave, and our officers and men there dragged him out upside down. The Wei ruler granted him his life, so today he is with us here. Further, how could you make light of the situation and dispatch Ma Wengong to go to Xiao District to have him observe the situation and then retreat and yield? Your people are very angry and resentful; they say that in peaceful times, [you] took their taxes and silk but when dire difficulties arose, [you] were unable to give them succor."

Chang said, "We know that [the Prince of] Yongchang has already crossed into [the area] south of the Huai. In recently arrived dispatches, there has been no news that Kangzu was defeated by him. Wang Xuanmo is a subordinate commander of the South; we do not say he has talent, but because he is a Northerner, he therefore became a guide for the vanguard. The main army had not yet arrived, and as the river was frozen over, Xuanmo came to the conclusion that he ought to retreat. This was not a failing on his part, but because he was returning at night, it caused the cavalry mounts to fall into some disorder. Our Xuanhu is a small town, and Chen Xian was a junior officer. The Wei ruler emptied his state and, for weeks, could not occupy it. Hu Shengzhi was a subaltern junior officer who does not lead even one squad; as soon as he first crossed the Rong River 融水, the lords and subjects of the Wei state fled and scattered, barely managing to escape. The troops of Huatai do not have much to be ashamed of. Although the small outpost at Zou Mountain has some strategic importance, the people along the river are, for the most part, recent adherents. They had just begun to appreciate the effect of the sagelike administration, but as the banditry had not yet been brought to a halt, [the court] sent Cui Xieli to calm [the situation]; that is all. Now that it has fallen into the caitiff's hands, of what loss is it to the state? The Wei ruler personally led an army of a hundred thousand; is bringing under control a certain Cui Xieli worth speaking about? When we recently heard that when the people of Xiao District[54] had all taken to the mountain defiles, we merely sent Ma Wengong with ten companies to show [our concern]. Wengong says he first sent out three companies and made your main encampment leave.[55] Ji Xuanjing arrived with a hundred cavalrymen at Liucheng, and the Wei army fled in defeat. [For us] to have such contempt for an enemy, is it not pitiful?

The people of these kingly realms live separately along the banks of the river. When the two states engage in warfare, they ought bring both comfort and nourishment [to those people], but after the Wei armies crossed the border, they have recklessly behaved in a destructive and cruel manner; events have transpired beyond what one would have imagined, stemming from your being without the Way. If the officials did not disappoint the people, why should the people be resentful? We know that you have come seven hundred *li* into our territory without encountering any resistance. This, first of all, is the Defender in Chief's marvelous planning and, second, is a part of the sagely strategy of the garrison army [general]. I have no foreknowledge of the critical affairs of administering the state, but since troop deployments have stratagems, even if I had heard, I would not be at liberty to talk to you about it." (*SS*)

XXIII

Xiaobo said, "You, Sir, rely on this baseless prattle and respond with equivocation. This is what is meant by 'When words are evasive, I know that [the mind] is at its wit's end.'"[56] (WS)

XXIV

"Moreover, His Majesty does not take upon himself to besiege this city but will personally lead his army straight to Guabu 瓜步. If the southward campaign is successful, there will be no need to attack and lay siege to the city; and if the southward campaign is not victorious, then Pengcheng is not what he wants. We now ought to [go] south with the intention of watering our horses in the Jiang and the lake."[57] Chang said, "Whether you leave or stay, suit yourself. If the Wei emperor subsequently is able to water his horses at the Yangzi, then it is not to accord with the Way of Heaven."[58] Xiaobo said, "From north to south, there really is only the influence of man; as for watering the horses at the Yangzi, how does it involve only the Way of Heaven?" (WS)

Xiaobo said, "The Wei ruler does not take upon himself to besiege this city but will personally lead his army straight to Guabu. If the southward campaign is successful, there will be no need to attack and lay siege to Pengcheng; and if it is not successful, Pengcheng is not what [he] requires. We now ought to [go] south, to water [our horses] in the Jiang and the lake to alleviate their thirst." Chang said, "Whether you leave or stay, suit yourself. If the caitiff horses subsequently are able to drink at the Yangzi, then it is not the Way of Heaven. We should each return and report back [to our superiors]; in time, this will become clearer." (SS)

XXV

Chang then turned to return, and Xiaobo said after him, "You, Seneschal, are very much loved and respected by me, and we are but a step apart; I regret that we cannot hold hands." (SS)

XXVI

When Chang was about to return to the city, he said to Xiaobo, "The date for the destruction of Ji[59] certainly has been set, and we will see each other soon. If

you, Sir, are able to come to the Song court, today would be the start of our coming to know each other." (WS)

Chang turned to him and said, "Please take care. The date for the destruction
of Ji certainly has been set, and we will see each other soon. If you, Sir, were
able to turn to the Song court, today would be the start of our coming to know
each other." Xiaobo said, "We may await this in the uncertain future." (SS)

XXVII

Xiaobo said, "Now I ought first to go to Jianye 建業[60] to await you, Sir. I fear that
when you, Sir, with the two princes are facing shackles and pleading your
crimes, you will not have time to see me." (WS)

XXVIII

Dao again dispatched [someone] to go to the two princes to borrow a lute, a
pipa, a zither, a flute, and a set of weiqi pieces. Yigong in reply said, "Having
accepted the responsibility of conducting a military campaign, I do not [have
the means to] make an offer of musical instruments. When we have a banquet
here, the administration has the garrison staff order up dancing girls and have
a hundred strings; they are a treasure of Jiangnan, and I now extend them to
you." Shizu said, "Holding a post on [one of] the Four Mountains,[61] I had not
earlier thought [to bring such material]; besides, musicians are readily available. Furthermore, having observed the various parting gifts given by princes
who have visited, there is this pipa that I now give to you. I also offer this weiqi
set." (SS)

XXIX

In manner, Xiaobo was relaxed and refined, and his responses came very
smoothly. Chang and his associates sighed deeply. Shizu was very pleased
and advanced his enfeoffment to the Duke of Xuancheng [Xuancheng gong
宣城公]. (WS)

In his speech and disputation Xiaobo was a treasure of the North. Chang responded easily and was articulate; his pronunciation was precise and elegant;
and his manner was splendid. Xiaobo and his attendants all looked at one another and sighed. (SS)

NOTES

1. For biographies of Li Xiaobo 李孝伯 (d. 459), a distinguished literatus at the Northern Wei court, see *WS* 53.1167–72; and *BS* 33.1220–22.

2. For biographies of Zhang Chang 張暢 (408–457), the other protagonist in this exchange, see *SS* 46.1398–1400 and 59.1598–1606; and *NS* 32.828–32.

3. For biographies of Wang Xuanmou 王玄謨 (388–468), see *SS* 76.1973–76; and *NS* 16.464. He faced execution because he was accused of failing to meet the enemy, but in a dream he was told to recite the *Guanyin Sutra* (*Gaowang Guanshiyin jing* 高王觀世音經) a thousand times, which he did, and to which he credited his escape from punishment. He went on to have a distinguished career and died at the age of eighty.

4. Cui Yeli 崔耶利 was the head of the frontier guard post at Zou Mountain, as well as Grand Protector of the commanderies of Lu 魯 and Yangping 陽平. He was overwhelmed by the large Northern Wei army and, according to the Southern sources, died in battle. See *SS* 95.2350. In the record of the debate in the *Wei shu*, his name is given as Cui Xieli 崔邪利.

5. Liu Yilong 劉義隆 was the reigning Song Emperor Wen 文, temple name Taizu 太祖 (r. 424–453).

6. Liu Jun 劉駿 was the third son of Liu Yilong, posthumous name Xiaowu 孝武 and temple name Shizu 世祖 (r. 454–464). He was named General Pacifying the North and Regional Inspector of Xuzhou, garrisoning Pengcheng in 448. He was eighteen years old at that time.

7. Ma Wengong 馬文恭 (died soon after 454) has a very brief notice in *SS* 45.1378.

8. Kuai Ying 蒯應 is mentioned in the histories only in reference to these events.

9. For biographies of Liu Yigong 劉義恭 (413–465), see *SS* 61.1640; and *NS* 13.370. He did not conduct himself well in this crisis and subsequently was demoted. See *SS* 61.1644.

10. Shizu 世祖 here refers to Tuoba Dao 拓跋燾 (r. 424–452), the Northern Wei emperor, not to be confused with Liu Jun, a future emperor of the Song, whose temple name also was Shizu 世祖.

11. *SS* 59.1600 says that he erected his felt tent—that is, his headquarters—on the Play Horse Tower (*ximatai* 戲馬臺), which was atop the mound. In his commentary to *ZZTJ* 125.3955, Hu Sanxing 胡三省 says that the structure was south of Pengcheng.

12. Shizu is the temple name of Liu Jun, who came to the throne after the events recounted here took place. But the practice in dynastic histories is to refer to an emperor by his posthumous or temple name even before he took the throne. In the *Wei shu*, he is referred to as the Pacifying the North General, his post at the time. He should not be confused with Tuoba Dao, who had the same temple name.

13. "Braided caitiff," the term used in Southern texts for the Xianbei conquerors of the North, referred to their practice of wearing their hair in a braid.

14. The Si is the name of the river flowing by Pengcheng.

15. *SS* 46.1397 has the enemy several tens of *li* from Pengcheng.

16. It would seem to be foolhardy to make a trek of such a distance northward toward the enemy state, but the hundred boats that had earlier made it downriver to Licheng may

have carried ample supplies for what was intended as a Song campaign into Wei territory. Being located on the Huai River, it may also have been a part of the plan to use the boats, if necessary, for an escape by water. Another possibility is that Licheng is a mistake for Liucheng, a shorter distance north of Pengcheng and also associated with a hundred boats. See note 53.

17. For biographies of Shen Qingzhi 沈慶之 (386–465), see *SS* 77.1996; and *NS* 37.953. He had a distinguished military career but was forced to commit suicide in 465 during the reign of a mad emperor.

18. It is not clear what form this formation took. The name occurs only a few times in the histories of this period. *WS* 4.2810 mentions it as one of three military formations, the other two being "fish scale" and "four door."

19. For *yuan* 媛 (beauties), *ZZTJ* 125.3954 has *nü* 女.

20. For biographies of Xiao Sihua 蕭思話 (400–455), see *SS* 78.2011–18; and *NS* 18.494. His biography says only that he assisted in the defense of Pengcheng.

21. He Xun 何勖 (dates unknown) has no biographies in the standard histories.

22. These discussions could become quite heated. Once when the emperor asked a couple of civil officials to question some military advice put forward by Shen Qingzhi, Shen said that when planting, one asked a farmer for advice; when weaving, one asked a weaver, so why, he wondered, did the emperor in this case turn to "white-faced scholars"? See *SS* 77.1999.

23. He says "Uncle" (*a-fu* 阿父) because Liu Yigong was a stepbrother of Wendi, Shizu's father.

24. Daomin 道民 was Shizu's childhood name; to use it in this way is a sign of humility.

25. Hu Sanxing explains that since Liu Jun, the future Shizu, was at this time the Regional Inspector of Xuzhou, his administrative center was at Pengcheng. See *ZZTJ* 125.3954–55.

26. Emperor Taizu was Liu Yilong 劉義隆 (r. 424–453), Liu Jun's father.

27. For biographies of Xu Yuan 徐爰 (394–475), see *SS* 94.2306; and *NS* 77.1917.

28. Dao is Tuoba Dao, the emperor of the Northern Wei and the leader of this campaign.

29. Liang Fanian 梁法念 (dates unknown) makes his only entry here in the standard histories.

30. A shorter version of the same text is included in *SS* 46.1397–99.

31. The use of *xi* 戲 (to play, to divert) to allude to battle occurs in *Zuozhuan*, Duke Xi 28; and James Legge, *The Ch'un ts'ew with the Tso chuen* (Hong Kong: Lane, Crawford, preface dated 1872), 209, where Legge translates the sentence, "Let me have a game with your men."

32. Ji was a term for northern China based on a traditional division of China into nine regions.

33. Bei Si 貝思 (dates unknown) has no biographies in the standard histories.

34. This paragraph appears in *WS* 3.

35. The Yellow Turbans and Red Eyebrows refer to the rebel movements at the end of the Western Han and Eastern Han, respectively.

36. Xu was the northeastern region of the Song state.

37. Qing and Xu are in the northeastern part of the Song state.

38. The Duke of Zhou said that when anyone of merit called on him, he would stop washing his hair or eating a meal even three times lest the visitors be turned away. See *Records of the Historian* (*Shi ji* 史記 33.1518).

39. *Zuozhuan*, Duke Yin 11; Legge, *Ch'un ts'ew with the Tso chuen*, 32.

40. Cheng Tianzuo 程天祚 (d. 466) was an able military figure who managed to escape from Northern Wei detention when the troops began their retreat, and he went on to a distinguished career. He has a short biographical notice in *SS* 74.1923.

41. *Rou* 柔 (soft) may refer to the Ruoruo or Ruanruan, the name of a northern people, especially as it is said to cure a horse's ailment.

42. *Xiang* 餉, rather than xian 獻, implies a gift from a superior.

43. Similarly, the use of *zhi* 致, and not *xian*, signifies an exchange between, at best, equals.

44. Yexia 鄴下, the modern Anyang 安陽, had been a capital of Northern states and here, by extension, may refer to the Northern state in general.

45. *Gaoliang* 膏粱 (literally, "rich food") refers to the highest level of the official elite. See A. Dien, "Elite Lineages and the T'o-pa Accommodation: A Study of the Edict of 495," *Journal of the Economic and Social History of the Orient* 19, no. 1 (1975): 67.

46. Here *wu* 武 has the meaning of *ji* 迹 (footsteps).

47. It is difficult to make out what Xiaobo wanted to say to Chang that he did not want others to hear. This particular exchange is not reported in other sources.

48. Tuoba Ren 仁 was the nephew of Tuoba Dao, the reigning Northern Wei emperor. He was executed in 453 for attempting rebellion. See *WS* 5.112 and 17.415. According to *SS* 50.1447 and 95.2350, his Xianbei name was Kurenzhen 庫仁真, which has been suggested to be a transcription of the Turco-Mongolian *qoyinčin-qoninčin* (sheep herdsman). See Peter Boodberg, "The Language of the T'o-Pa Wei," *Harvard Journal of Asiatic Studies* 1 (1936): 167–85.

49. According to the biography of Liu Kangzu 劉康祖 (d. 450) in *SS* 50.1446–48, he put up a brave but vain struggle, meeting the eighty thousand strong Northern Wei army with only eight thousand of his own men.

50. On Wang Xuanmou, see note 3.

51. An account of the successful defense of Xuanhu for forty-two days led by Chen Xian 陳憲 is found in *SS* 95.2345. Chen was promoted because of his efforts and shared the ten thousand bolts of cloth awarded him with the defenders of the city.

52. The bravery of Hu Shengzhi 胡盛之 (dates unknown) is cited in *SS* 50.1447–48. The name of the river, also pronounced He, is given as Yong 融 in *SS* 59.1604. An editorial note in *WS* 53.1190 states that both are probably in error.

53. Ji Xuanjing 嵇玄敬 has no biographies in the standard histories. *SS* 95.2350 says that he was sent as a lookout by Yigong, and in the *Song shu* version of this debate (59.1604), it says that he arrived with one hundred cavalrymen. Liucheng was either on or close to a large lake, the Weishan 微山. It may be that the boats rather than the cavalrymen is correct.

54. Xiang 相 is an error for 縣 (district).

55. The difference of one word, 彼 and 後, leads to different punctuation; I follow *Wei shu*.

56. *Mengzi* 孟子, *SSJZ* 3A.9b; James Legge, *The Works of Mencius* (Hong Kong: Hong Kong University Press, 1960, preface dated 1861), 191.

57. *Jiang Hu* 江湖 has a number of meanings and connotations. Here the reference may be to the Yangzi and to Dongting 洞庭 Lake.

58. According to *ZZTJ* 125.3957, what Zhang Chang had in mind was a current children's ditty, which says that if the Wei horses drank at the Yangzi, the Wei emperor would die. Such children's ditties were believed to have predictive value. The Wei emperor was referred to by his child name, Foli 佛狸, ancient Chinese pronunciation pjuət-lji, a transcription of Turkish *buri* (wolf).

59. Ji may refer either to the capital of the Northern Wei at Jizhou or to Ji as the ancient northern region.

60. Jianye 建業, an earlier name for Jiankang, at modern Nanjing, was the capital of the Song.

61. Traditionally, there were four sacred mountains, one in each direction. According to the *Classic of Documents* (*Shangshu* 尚書), during the king's inspection tours, the feudal lords would pay court to the king at the mountain in their region. See *Classic of Documents*, *SSJZ* 80.6a; James Legge, *The Shoo King* (Hong Kong: Hong Kong University Press, 1960, preface dated 1865), 531.

3. Between Imitation and Mockery

The Southern Treatments of Northern Cultures

JESSEY J. C. CHOO

Separating oneself from others is a basic mechanism in crafting one's identity. Cultural differences, especially those between what was perceived as the center and the periphery, have been constantly reassessed throughout China's long history. The period beginning with the founding of the Jin dynasty in 265 C.E. and ending with the unification of China by the Sui dynasty in 589 was marked by profound changes. For much of this time, China was politically divided. Gone with political uniformity was the dominance of Confucian classicism as the source of principles that informed cultural practices and social customs. Frequent exposure to political upheavals and rapid shifts in demography and geography made medieval Chinese intellectuals more perceptive of changes and adaptations in languages and social customs and also to their impacts on culture and society. The excerpts I have translated in this chapter are from *The Master Who Embraces Simplicity* (*Baopuzi* 抱朴子, completed in 317) by Ge Hong 葛洪 (284–363?), *Family Instructions of Mr. Yan* (*Yanshi jiaxun* 顏氏家訓, completed ca. 590s) by Yan Zhitui 顏之推 (531–after 591), and the "Tale of Lu Sidao" (*Lu Sidao* 盧思道) in *Extensive Records of the Taiping Era* (*Taiping Guangji* 太平廣記, completed in 978).[1] All provide keen observations of the cultural differences between the people of the North and those of the South. These observations are both detailed and valuable, due in no small part to the extensive travels of the authors beyond their native land. Both Ge and Yan lived for extended periods of time among those whom they observed. What also makes their accounts interesting is that they were written at different but equally pivotal moments in the early medieval period, and together they reveal the anxiety about and the resistance to cultural changes over time. Their attention to language and ritual proprieties (particularly the rules pertaining to mourning), which constitute the core of cultural, ethnic, and class identity, gives us a rare window into the formation and expansion of a new type of elite, whose membership transcended the political and geographical confines of the age. Because this elite served in various regimes in both the North and the South, they became the movers and shakers of a shared high culture that derived its authority from its ability to represent Confucianism in ways relevant to contemporary politics and practices bridging the universal and the particular.

Ge Hong, self-styled as the Master Who Embraces Simplicity, is a familiar figure to students of Daoism. He has long been considered central to the development of the Daoist religion in the early medieval period. Western scholars, however, have paid little attention to his overall erudition and have often overlooked the fact that many of his works were on other subjects. For someone who wrote so much, a great amount of which has survived, his life story remains largely a mystery. Like the immortals whose biographies he transcribed, he remains only a faint trace of his true form hidden away from mundane eyes. Historians both past and present do not have much information about Ge Hong except what he himself imparted in the work he named after his sobriquet.

Ge Hong came from a prominent Southern family, many of whose members mastered classical learning and served in the Han and Later Wu governments. He was born in 284, not long after Western Jin conquered the Wu state and unified China for the first time since the demise of the Han dynasty. Although the unification did not last long, it became the backdrop against which Ge Hong's early life should be interpreted. After the unification, Ge Hong's father, Ti 悌, served the Jin regime as the Governor of Shaoling (Shaoling *taishou* 邵陵 太守). When he was twelve, Ge Hong's formal education ended when his father died. In his autobiography, the last of the *Outer Chapters*, Ge Hong claims to have taught himself Confucian learning by reading, copying, and reciting borrowed books. By his own admission, his self-learning was far from consistent, but he remained a voracious reader throughout his life. In his late teens, Ge Hong studied with Zheng Yin 鄭隱 (dates unknown), whom he credits for providing him with a more well-rounded, if still idiosyncratic, education. Zheng Yin was a disciple of Ge Xuan 葛玄, Ge Hong's grand-uncle, who was famous for his knowledge of the occult. Zheng Yin also was an expert on the Classics, especially the *Record of Rites* (*Liji* 禮記) and the *Classic of Documents* (*Shujing* 書經). He began to concentrate on Daoist teachings and practices only in his later years. Ge Hong's own intellectual development later followed a similar trajectory. Zheng Yin once commented on the strengths and weaknesses of Ge Hong's learning. He thought that Ge Hong had only breadth and no depth in knowledge and focused too much on "worldly" accomplishments: the five Classics, three Histories, philosophies of the hundred schools, and skills in writing poetry and essays.[2] The excerpts from the *Outer Chapters* translated here fall into this "worldly" category. Although Ge Hong later moved his focus to the "other-worldly," his interest in a broad range of subjects remained his principal strength. Under Zheng Yin's tutelage, Ge Hong acquired the needed discipline to digest and consolidate his wide knowledge, and he learned a number of skills that would be useful to him later in life. In addition, during this time he transformed himself from a sickly youth into a proficient martial artist, claiming that he could seize bare-handed a blade wielded by an enemy.[3] But Ge Hong was then still a young man in his twenties and wanted to carry on the family tradition of becoming an official. Thus when Zheng Yin left for Mount Huo 霍山 in search of seclusion from the chaos of the world, Ge Hong joined the military.

Ge Hong was in the force that put down the rebellion of Shi Bing 石冰 in 304. He subsequently went on to Luoyang in hopes of procuring rare books and perhaps of receiving further recognition or even an official position. What he found was a capital city half ruined by years of warfare among members of the fractious royal family. Ge Hong thus decided to move to the more peaceful South and became an Adjutant (*Canjunshi* 參軍事) in the retinue of his friend Ji Han 嵇含,[4] who had recently been appointed as the Regional Inspector of Guangzhou (Guangzhou *cishi* 廣州刺史). But Ji was killed on the way to the South, and Ge Hong was stuck there for several years. It was at this time that he became a disciple and son-in-law of Bao Jing 鮑靚 (b. ca. 260), the Governor of Nanhai (Nanhai *taishou* 南海太守), and learned from him skills in divination and medicine. This apparently was a pivotal point in Ge Hong's life, for after this he turned his intellectual energy and literary output away from the materials that he had begun to circulate in 317 as the *Outer Chapters*. Ge Hong was then thirty-five years old. He now received the recognition he had sought earlier from the Jin government: he was awarded a pension of two hundred households in Jurong 句容 by Sima Rui 司馬睿, later the Eastern Jin Emperor Yuan (r. 317–321), and then a series of honorary posts, but he soon gave up most of these in order to concentrate on his personal cultivation.

The excerpts from chapters 15, 25, and 26 of the *Outer Chapters* contain Ge Hong's observations and criticisms of what his contemporaries from the Wu area perceived as the superior culture and courtly fashion in Luoyang. In all these passages, he displays not only his erudition in the classics and histories but also a strong sense of "Southern pride." In the excerpt from "Examination and Promotion," he laments the decline of Confucian learning in the South after the unification and blames it on the policy that the Western Jin court implemented to pacify the conquered people. This policy exempted tribute scholars (*gongshi* 貢士) from areas that had previously been part of the Wu state from examination and directly appointed them to posts in local governments.[5] In other words, this was a policy from which Ge Hong never benefited, partly because of his father's untimely demise. In any case, he interprets the preferential treatment given to the Southerners as nothing more than a veiled contempt for the conquered as mere barbarians. Those of his contemporaries who obtained offices in this way, he complains, had no interest in true learning but instead were preoccupied with imitating the latest courtly fashion and competing with one another in frivolous pursuits.

What Ge Hong meant by courtly fashion is revealed in the excerpts from the chapters "Sickened by Absurdities" and "Ridiculing the Confused." One trend that Ge Hong regarded as absurd was the promiscuous sexual conduct that his fellow Southerners claimed was common among members of the nobility and elites at the capital. He points out that such conduct resulted from a perverse understanding that the North was the source of etiquette and ritual propriety. This may have been true in the age of the Duke of Zhou and Confucius, but not anymore. In any case, such practices were not appropriate in a "well-governed realm." There was more to Ge Hong's complaint, however. He suggests that his lack of rank and office—another sign of the court's ineptitude in governance— made it impossible for him to halt the spread of the immoral practices from the North that his contemporaries so eagerly embraced. His indignation, he claims, had earned him the reputation of being unconventional and outmoded. But this was a reputation that Ge Hong treasured as one of his defining character-istics, and he mentions it often in his work.[6]

In the excerpts from "Ridiculing the Confused," Ge Hong further illustrates his fellow Southerners' hunger for capital fashions. They imitated not only the clothes and manners of the elites at Luoyang but also their stylized wailing and drunken partying at funerals. The total disregard of the Southern tradition rooted in classical teachings angered Ge Hong. But in arguing against such wholesale adaptation of contemporary Northern practices, he uses the same reasoning that motivated it in the first place: since the classical age, Northern culture had been continually revered as the universal tradition. Consequently, in his criticism, Ge Hong inadvertently confirms the North's perceived superiority. But this would change after the Jin court reconstituted itself in Jiankang in the heart of the for-mer Wu state, after losing the North to non-Chinese tribes. The capital of the state was now firmly based in the South, and the resulting cultural practices and social customs became a mixture of both Northern and Southern. Whether Ge Hong's contemporaries continued to propagate the courtly fashions is beyond the scope of this chapter. But when Yan Zhitui, another Southerner, records his ob-servations of the cultural differences between North and South, he shows an objectivity and apparent fairness that Ge Hong and his contemporaries did not.

Ge Hong and Yan Zhitui had a number of personal experiences that were similar. Much like Ge Hong, Yan Zhitui came from a family steeped in Confu-cian learning. His ancestors had migrated with the Jin court to the South and had served in successive Han-Chinese regimes. When he was only in his early teens, Yan Zhitui also lost his father and was raised by his elder brother, Zhiyi

之儀.⁷ In contrast to Ge Hong's seriousness and self-possession, Yan Zhitui was a wild youth, much criticized for his love of drink and disregard of etiquette. Although he later became a courtier known for his ability, discretion, and propriety, his frequent drunkenness remained a weakness. Both Ge Hong and Yan Zhitui lived in an age of chaos, and both witnessed much warfare. Unlike Ge Hong, however, Yan Zhitui seemed to have sought worldly honors throughout his life, despite his repeated claims to have done otherwise. A close examination of his autobiographical rhapsody "A View of My Life" (*Guan wosheng fu* 觀我生賦)⁸ and his *Family Instructions* reveals an individual anxious to know how his political career would be viewed. Yan Zhitui served in the courts of the Southern Liang, Northern Qi, Northern Zhou, and, finally, Sui. Despite being three times a government official of the conquered dynasty, he usually served by choice, especially for the Northern Qi. His personal life no doubt suffered because of the vicissitudes of his time, but his political career did not appear to have been much affected. During the reign of the Northern Qi Emperor Wenxuan 北齊文宣帝 (r. 529–559), Yan Zhitui rose rapidly in rank and, after serving at the chancellery in various capacities, was put in charge of drafting key government documents. Yan Zhitui's frequent drunkenness remained a problem. But his supervisor was instructed to overlook it. Yan Zhitui continued to thrive as a great literary technocrat whose political instincts and savvy helped him survive court intrigues. But because he represented himself as a technocrat, he lacked Ge Hong's ambition to remedy social ills. Yan's commentaries on cultural practices and social customs in his *Family Instructions* were less passionate. Instead, he was more concerned about how his descendants could achieve and maintain cultural respectability in a multicultural environment. Thus even though he described and compared the practices and customs of the North and the South, he did so with the desire to define through seemingly unbiased evaluations a transregional high culture that he and those like him shared. In this way, his *Family Instructions* anticipated the culture embraced by the members of the great clans and revered by the people in the unified Sui and Tang dynasties.

The excerpts from Yan Zhitui's *Family Instructions* translated here deal with mourning customs and language. Yan Zhitui, like Ge Hong, was concerned about the appropriate styles of wailing in funerals, although Yan was more circumspect. He first cites the instructions for wailing found in the Classics and their commentaries and then describes the differences between wailing in the North and the South. Leaving readers to decide for themselves which is superior, his comments are both pedagogically and politically ingenious. Yan Zhitui, like Ge Hong, also felt that language, particularly pronunciation and speech, was crucial to a gentleman's respectability. Whereas Ge Hong was merciless in his attacks on his fellow Southerners who mimicked Northern speech, calling them pathetic and laughable, Yan Zhitui was more reserved. He described how most elite speakers of Northern and Southern dialects, each in their own ways, muddled the pronunciation. Despite his apparent fair-mindedness, what he wanted to emphasize was the superb education in phonology that he passed on to his children. Whether living in the South or the North, the Yans managed to maintain their "perfect" accent. Considering that phonology was fundamental to poetic composition and essential to the display of refinement, Yan Zhitui could hardly have been more boastful of his own family tradition.

Lu Sidao (盧思道, 535–586),[9] the protagonist of the last excerpt from *Extensive Records of the Taiping Era*, was Yan Zhitui's colleague in three successive governments. They both earned their literary reputation serving at the chancellery of the Northern Qi Emperor Wenxuan. After the Northern Zhou's conquest of Northern Qi, they went on together to serve at the Northern Zhou court. Finally, when the Northern Zhou was replaced, they became members of the Sui officialdom. Although usually employed in the same capacity as Yan Zhitui (if not in the same office at the same time), Lu Sidao was never a technocrat. He was a poet, and in personality and fortune, the two men could not have been more different. Lu Sidao was known for his flamboyance; he was brash and had a general disregard for responsibility. He would be appointed to a noteworthy office; then dismissed for misconduct, such as insubordination or misappropriation of funds; and finally appointed to another noteworthy office because of his irrepressible poetic talent. This pattern was repeated several times throughout Lu Sidao's political career. He even once escaped death on the chopping block by a remarkable demonstration of his compositional skills. Yan Zhitui did not have much to say about Lu Sidao, only briefly stating in the *Family Instructions* that he disliked Lu's kind of elegance.[10] The excerpt here is a celebration of Lu Sidao's literary prowess in a poetry competition featuring him, as an emissary of the Northern Qi, and the courtiers of the Southern Chen. National pride was at stake, and both sides tried their utmost to humiliate their opponents. Needless to say, the outcome of the contest was predictable. There are reasons to believe that this story is apocryphal. Lu Sidao did indeed serve as an emissary to the Chen court, but he represented the Sui rather than the Northern Qi state. If the contest did indeed take place, it would have been no more than three years before the Southern Chen's demise, when the Chen emperor showed very little concern about the survival of his state and was on friendly terms with his Sui counterpart. Regardless of its authenticity, what makes the contest interesting is that both sides had formed stereotypical images of the other, neither of which was flattering. In their efforts to portray the other as coarse and barbaric, we can see that the Southerners clearly did not find Northern cuisine civilized. Had Ge Hong been at the party, he surely would have been amused.

FURTHER READING

For details on how the Western Jin court treated the Wu people and on how the Eastern Jin court treated those Northerners who arrived later than most, see

Zhou Yiliang 周一良, *Wei Jin Nanbeichao shi zhaji* 魏晉南北朝史札記 (Beijing: Zhonghua shuju, 1985), 72–75, 190–92. Hu Baoguo 胡寶國 analyzes the changing label of "Northerners" and "Southerners" in "Liang-Jin shiqi the 'nanren' yu 'beiren'" 兩晉時期的'南人' 與 '北人', *Wenshi* 73 (2005): 49–58, and the ill treatments received by and the political disadvantages of these latecomers in "Wangdu beiren yu Dong Jin zhongqi de lishi bianhua" 晚渡北人與東晉中期的歷史變化, *Beida shixue* 北大史學 14 (2009): 94–111. Although Ge Hong's life and contributions to the developments of medieval Daoism have been the focus of numerous studies, his classical learning and critiques of contemporary politics and society have mostly escaped scholarly attention in the West. The most thorough examination of his life and achievements in areas other than Daoism is Jay Sailey, *The Master Who Embraces Simplicity: A Study of the Philosopher Ko Hung, A.D. 283–343* (San Francisco: Chinese Materials Center, 1978), in which twenty-one of the fifty *Outer Chapters* are translated. Matthew Wells's article, "Self as Historical Artifact: Ge Hong and Early Chinese Autobiography," *Early Medieval China* 9 (2004): 71–103, deals with the historicity of Ge Hong's self-portrayal in the last of the *Outer Chapters*. For Ge Hong's life and the *Outer Chapters* in particular, see Wu Feng 武鋒, *Ge Hong Baopuzi waipian yanjiu* 葛洪《抱朴子外篇》研究 (Beijing: Guangming ribao chubanshe, 2010). For specific studies of topics such as languages and dialects, see Chen Yinke 陳寅恪, "Dong Jin Nanchao zhi Wu yu" 東晉南朝之吳語, originally published in 1936 and now collected and reprinted in *Jinmingguan conggao erbian* 今明館叢稿二編 (Beijing: Sanlian shuju, 2001), 304–9; and Richard B. Mather, "A Note on the Dialects of Luoyang and Nanking During the Six Dynasties," in *Wen-lin: Studies in the Chinese Humanities*, ed. Tse-tung Chow (Madison: University of Wisconsin Press, 1976), 247–56. For a complete English translation of *Yanshi jiaxun*, see Teng Ssu-Yü, *Family Instruction for the Yen Clan: An Annotated Translation with Introduction* (Leiden: Brill, 1968). *Yanshi jiaxun* has been the basis for many works comparing the North and the South. For an example in Chinese, see Gu Xiangming 顧向明 and Wang Dajian 王大建, "Yanshi jiaxun zhong Nanbeichao shizu fengsu wenhua xianxiang tanxi" 《顏氏家訓》中南北朝士族風俗文化現象探析, *Zhengzhou daxue xuebao (zhexue shehui kexueban)* 鄭州大學學報 (哲學社會科學版) 4 (2006). Of the numerous modern studies of the social practices and customs of the North and South in the Six Dynasties period, the most recognizable examples are Zhang Chengzong 張承宗 and Wei Xiangdong 魏向東, *Zhongguo fengsu tongshi: Wei Jin Nanbeichao juan* 中國風俗通史——魏晉南北朝卷 (Shanghai: Shanghai wenyi chubanshe, 2001); and Zhu Daiwei 朱大渭, Liu Chi 劉馳, Liang Mancang 梁滿倉, and Cheng Yong 陳勇, *Wei Jin Nanbeichao shehui shenghuoshi* 魏晉南北朝社會生活史 (Beijing: Zhongguo shehui kexue chubanshe, 1998). The most comprehensive treatment in English of the customs and material culture of this period is Albert E. Dien, *Six Dynasties Civilization* (New Haven, Conn.: Yale University Press, 2007).

GE HONG 葛洪

The Master Who Embraces Simplicity
(*Baopuzi* 抱樸子)

THE OUTER CHAPTERS: "EXAMINATION AND PROMOTION"
(*SHENJU* 審舉) (EXCERPT)

The Master Who Embraces Simplicity says: "Now All Under Heaven is united, and all within the Nine Borders [*jiugai* 九垓][11] are one in customs. The imperial institutions and policies should therefore be the same as if they were one. Even when measuring insignificant objects, one cannot apply different standards; how can there be a difference when evaluating the character of personages? The area south of the Yangzi River [*Jiangbiao* 江表] may be remote and hidden away near the coast. It nevertheless has been transformed by the Way and has followed the teachings of the *Rites* for more than one thousand years. Although in the past it was briefly separated [politically from the rest of the realm], [the separation lasted] no more than one hundred years,[12] [during which] Ru 儒 learning was not neglected or cast aside. Only [because] it was a smaller area compared with the Central Provinces [*Zhongzhou* 中州], the number of [its] personages could not match that [of the Central Provinces]. Those who excelled in virtue, conduct, talent, and learning, [such as] Ziyou 子游 [505–443][13] and Zhongren 仲任 [27–97],[14] were not inferior to [those of] the Upper States [*shangguo* 上國].[15]

"Back then when the land of Wu first became a part [of the realm], its tribute scholars [*gongshi* 貢士] were exempted from examination in order to appease [the local hostility]. Now there has been great peace for nearly forty years,[16] [and] if [the court] continues to exempt [the Wu tribute scholars] from examination, it will result in Ru learning in the southeast being weaker than in the past. This is to see [the Wu tribute scholars] the same as those who wear their clothes with a left lapel [*zuoren* 左衽][17] and not to distinguish them [from the barbarians]. Besides, a nobleman cares for the people by treating them according to the [proper] rites [*li* 禮]. How much more so when [one] is a parent [who brings them] ease and happiness?[18] There are laws that bring calamities to and decrees that harm [the moral] transformations of [the people]; this is what I would call [this policy]. Nowadays, those tribute scholars who are exempt from examination are all into apparel and fast steeds; with these they compete for an empty reputation. Who would still open a book and read the writing [in it]? Hence the saying, 'It is enough to defeat [a man] by overwhelming him with comfort.'"[19]

[Yang Mingzhao 楊明照, ed. and comm.,
Baopuzi waipian jiaojian 抱朴子外篇校箋
(Beijing: Zhonghua shuju, 1991), 1:411–14]

"SICKENED BY ABSURDITIES" (*JIMIU* 疾謬) (EXCERPT)

The degree to which the ancients learned to stop debauchery and prevent prof-
ligacy at the first sign may be considered extreme. Those who cultivate [this
prohibition] are noblemen, and those who resist it are sinners. Whenever the
prohibition was loosened, some men would go through a hole in the wall to
[meet their lovers] at Shanggong 上宫; when the net allowed any gaps, some
women [would] go to Sangzhong 桑中 to elope [with their lovers].[20] Given free
rein, [their passion] would grow more fiery than the blazing flame of Yunmeng
雲夢.[21] When the dammed water of ten thousand depths is released, how can it
be swept away by brooms or stopped by a pinch of soil? And yet by now, the
people are accustomed to such [behaviors], and all say, "This is how the nobility
and elites conduct themselves at the capital and in the Upper States."

I always refute it with "The Central States themselves were where the rituals
and etiquettes were created. Could this be the rituals and etiquette? These [be-
haviors] have become prevalent at a time of degradation and chaos. These are not
the traditional customs of a well-governed realm. Even Lao Dan 老聃 [i.e., Laozi],
the purest and humblest [of men], did not dare to look at what he desired, in
order to prevent the disruption of his mind.[22] If Liuxia Hui 柳下惠, the most
immaculate and exemplary [of men], was made to frequent unwholesome banquets, sensuality could not help but emerge from within him, and desire [would
then] become visible on his face.[23] Besides, [the number of] those who are less
affected by sensuality are no more than one in ten thousand, and those who can
suppress sensuality are still more difficult to find. When exposed to such tempta-
tions, how can [one] hold out for long?"

How can a man of humble [rank]—despite knowing that these practices are
not worthy of introduction and lacking both title and power—correct [them]?[24]
He often feels indignant about [the situation]. He thus earns the resentment of
those people and comes to be viewed [by them] as a rustic and unsophisticated
man who cannot follow what is appropriate to these times. I expect myself to
trust only my own [judgment]. How could I be at peace when I do what I thought
I should not and follow what others thought I should! This is not the only thing
I find lamentable. I have always [felt] this. [These practices] have gone on for so
long that I do not know what to do about them. Those who are stained by these
wicked practices are going with the flow that will lead to a common ruin[25]—
why would they listen to advice that grates on their ears and turn back from
their long trail to the East?[26]

[*Baopuzi waipian jiaojian* 1:625–28]

"RIDICULING THE CONFUSED" (*JIHUO* 譏惑) (EXCERPT)

Since the loss of and chaos [in the North],[27] fashions keep changing. [The styles
of] caps, shoes, gowns, and garments and the tailoring of sleeves and cuffs vary

from day to day, month to month, and do not remain constant. Suddenly [they are] long, [and then] suddenly [they are] short. At one time [they are] broad, [and] at another [they are] narrow. Quickly [they are] raised, [and then] quickly [they are] lowered. [The people sometimes prefer] coarse, or [they sometimes prefer] fine. The [styles of] apparel are as changeable as are [the wearers] earnestly copying [the fashion trends]. Those who are interested in such things imitate [the fashions] from dawn to dusk. Thus there is a saying: "[When] the capital urbanites prize thick eyebrows, all those who live in far corners [paint their eyebrows to cover] half their foreheads."[28]

I am just an ordinary person. I am not good at following popular practices. I cannot keep up with the changes in fashion; thus [my apparel] remains the same. I would not throw out [my clothes] if they have not yet worn out. Although people point and laugh at me, I ignore them. It is not because I want to go against the norm but because I sense no urgency. While many customs of the Upper States are superior to those in the area south of the Yangzi River, some still should be criticized. When a gentleman carries out the rites, he should not seek to follow popular practices. It is said that [even after] a man leaves his own country to move to another, he does not cease to observe the practices of his native land. For people who reside in the land of their forefathers, what reason do they have to abandon their traditions and force others to learn their ways?

The excellent calligraphers of Wu 吳 include Huang Xiang 皇象,[29] Liu Zuan 劉纂,[30] Cen Boran 岑伯然, and Zhu Jiping 朱季平[31]—they all were the finest of their generation. Similarly, the Central Provinces [*Zhongzhou* 中州] had Zhong Yuanchang 鍾元常 [151–230],[32] Hu Kongming 胡孔明 [161–250],[33] Zhang Zhi 張芝 [d. ca. 192],[34] and Suo Jing 索靖 [209–303][35]—each of them was the greatest of his state. All [of them] adhered to the traditional scripts and were proficient in the Zhou [1045–256 B.C.E.] practices. Thus I say [that] it is unnecessary to abandon the methods that one has known and to dedicate oneself to learn the calligraphy of the Central States [*Zhongguo* 中國]. How much more true [when] one changes one's pronunciation to mimic Northern speech. One cannot mimic it well. Mimicking is [in itself] pathetic and laughable. Of all the [acts] "to master the gait of [the people of] Handan 邯鄲 and be ridiculed for the crawl,"[36] so to speak, this one [i.e., to mimic Northern pronunciation] is relatively harmless.

Some people mourn the dead by imitating the wailing [practiced] in the Central States. [Their imitation] lacks any feeling of affection. Zhong Yi 鍾儀 [d. 582 B.C.E.?][37] and Zhuang Xi 莊舄 [dates unknown][38] of old did not forget their native chants. The ancients thought [that how they behaved] was appropriate. Confucius said: "One [wails] for a lost parent in the same way as an infant [wails] for his mother. That kind of wailing does not have a typical sound!"[39] It is better for the grief to be excessive and the rites insufficient.[40] Where is the beauty or ugliness in wailing to relieve one's sorrow? To regulate and adorn how it sounds is not what one does when "grief stricken."[41]

I have also heard that while observing the great mourning, the elites could sometimes become ill and take stone powder [*shisan* 石散].[42] They have several meals a day to enhance the effects of the drug and drink wine to preserve their lives. When their illness becomes critical, they cannot endure any wind or cold. Screens, curtains, cushions, and mattresses are laid out for their comfort. Thus every vulgar man who has wealth and power ceases to assume the position of a mourner [at a funeral] and spends all his time in a separate room, where he sits on a high bed layered with coverlets, feasts on delicious foods, and drinks a liberal amount [of wine]. Some even drink with close friends, filling one another's cup as it becomes empty, to the point of drunkenness. They say: "This is the practice of the capital Luoyang." What a pity![43]

[*Baopuzi waipian jiaojian* 2, 26.11–20]

YAN ZHITUI 顏之推

Family Instructions of Mr. Yan (*Yanshi jiaxun* 顏氏家訓)

"CUSTOMS AND MANNERS" (*FENGCAO* 風操) (EXCERPT)

The "Xianzhuan" 閒傳 chapter of the *Record of Rites*[44] states: "The wailing for those who wear the mourning clothes of *zhanshuai* 斬縗[45] sends forth the sound and does not turn. The wailing for those who wear the mourning clothes of *qishuai* 齊縗[46] sends forth the sound tentatively and then calls it back. The wailing for those who wear the mourning clothes of *dagong* 大功[47] makes the sound quiver three times. For those who wear the mourning clothes of *xiaogong* 小功[48] or *sima* 緦麻,[49] showing a sad face is enough. One expresses sadness through modulations of the voice."[50] The *Classic of Filial Piety* [*Xiaojing* 孝經] states, "Wail, but do not prolong the voice."[51] These all suggest that the sounds of wailing have varying degrees of lightness and gravity, simplicity and ostentation. The *Rites* labels the wailing with the word *hao* 號; thus wailing could also contain verses [*ci* 辭]. In the area south of the Yangzi River, mourners often wail with words of sorrow. In the area east of the [Taihang 太行] Mountains [covering roughly the North, excluding the area around Chang'an], the chief mourners [wail] to beseech the Blue Heaven [*cangtian* 蒼天]. Those whose mourning obligations do not exceed one year [*qigong* 期功] need only speak of their deep sorrow. In other words, they wail with words rather than without [them].

When [people] in the South suffer a significant loss [i.e., any loss that requires wearing the *zhanshuai* mourning garb], they end their friendship with any acquaintance who lives in the same town but fails to come to offer condolences within three days. After the end of the mourning, even if they meet [the person], they avoid him, resenting him for not feeling sorry for them. Those who are [prevented from expressing their condolences in person] for some reason or because of the distance can send a letter [of sympathy]. If they do not send a letter, they will be treated in the same fashion. The custom of the North is not like this. In the area south of the Yangzi River, a person who goes to offer condolences does not hold hands with those with whom he is not acquainted, other than with the chief mourner. If one is acquainted only with a wearer of the lighter mourning garb and not with the chief mourner, then he does not need to go to the place of funeral but should leave a calling card and visit his house on another day.

> [Wang Liqi 王利器, ed. and comm.,
> *Yanshi jiaxun jijie* 顏氏家訓集解
> (Beijing: Zhonghua shuju, 1993), 95–98]

"ON PRONUNCIATION AND SPEECH"
(*YINCI* 音辭) (EXCERPT)

People of the Nine Provinces [*jiuzhou* 九州][52] speak in different dialects. This has been the norm since the beginning of mankind. [. . .] The land and waters of the South are mild and gentle; [thus] the sound [of Southern speech] is bright and crisp. The shortcoming is its shallowness. Its expressions are mostly vulgar. The mountains and rivers in the North are solemn and deep; [thus] the sound [of Northern speech] is baritone and rotund, taking after the simplicity and ruggedness [of the landscape]. The expressions contain many ancient terms. However, Southern [speech] is finer when spoken by nobles and gentlemen; Northern [speech] is better when spoken by villagers and peasants. One could distinguish in a few words a Southern gentleman from a commoner, even if they exchanged clothes. One would have difficulty differentiating between a Northern courtier and a countryman even after listening [to them] all day from behind a wall. Moreover, Southern speech has been influenced by [the dialects of] Wu 吳 and Yue 越; Northern speech has [the languages of] barbarians 夷 and captives 虜 mixed into it. Both have deep flaws that cannot be discussed in detail here. [. . .] Since I arrived at Ye 鄴, I find only Cui Ziyue 崔子約 [d. 560?] and his nephew Cui Zhan 崔瞻 [d. 580],[53] Li Zuren 李祖仁 and his younger brother, Li Wei 李蔚,[54] to be knowledgeable in speech and slightly more accurate [in pronunciation]. *Resolving Doubts About Sounds and Rhymes* [*Yinyun jueyi* 音韻決疑], composed by Li Jijie 李季節 [lived during Northern Qi], contains many mistakes.[55] *The Classification of Rhymes* [*Qieyun* 切韻], devised by Yang Xiuzhi 陽休之, is perfunctory.[56] The [pronunciation of the] children of my house, since their childhood, has been watched and corrected. I take any mispronunciation of a character as my own fault. When determining what an object should be called, I dare not utter its name without first consulting books and records—this you know well.

> [*Yanshi jiaxun jijie*, 529–45]

The Tale of Lu Sidao (*Lu sidao* 盧思道) (excerpt)

Lu Sidao 盧思道 of the Northern Qi went as an emissary to the Chen 陳 state. The Chen ruler ordered the elite members of his court to prepare wine and food and had a feast with Sidao, in which they linked verses and composed poetry. The person who went first took the opportunity to ridicule the Northerner by saying: "Elm trees thrive with the desire to feed men 榆生欲飽漢 / Grass grows tall so as to fatten donkeys" 草長正肥驢. The people in the North ate elm seeds and there was no donkey in the land of Wu, thus this couplet. Sidao wielded the brush and quickly continued: "Sharing the rice steamer but not the rice 共甑分炊米 / Using the same frying pan [and yet] each cooks his or her [own] fish" 同鐺各煮魚. The people in the South had no fond feelings [for family members]; they cooked together yet ate separately, thus Sidao wrote this couplet. The Wu people [i.e., Southerners] were ashamed of it.

[*TPGJ* 247.1915]

NOTES

1. The story was first recorded by Yang Songjie 陽松玠, a contemporary and perhaps even a colleague of Lu Sidao 盧思道 (535–586), in *Marsh of Discourse* (*Tansou* 談藪). The complete work is no longer extant. Huang Dahong 黃大宏 recently published an annotated edition of a reconstructed version based on what he gleaned from various premodern sources, including the *Extensive Records of the Taiping Era* (*Taiping guangji* 太平廣記). See Huang Dahong, *Badai tansou jiaojian* 八代談藪校箋 (Beijing: Zhonghua shuju, 2010).

2. Wang Ming 王明, ed., *Baopuzi neipian jiaoshi* 抱朴子內篇校釋 (Beijing: Zhonghua shuju, 1985), 19.332.

3. Yang Mingzhao 楊明照, ed. and comm., *Baopuzi waipian jiaojian* 抱朴子外篇校箋 (Beijing: Zhonghua shuju, 1991), 50.708–9.

4. For the official biography of Ji Han 嵇含 (264–306), courtesy name Jundao 君道, see *JS* 89.2301–3.

5. Tribute scholars were local talents presented to the imperial court by the feudal states. The *Record of Rites* states that "feudal vassals at the annual presentation give scholars [*shi*] as tribute to the Son of Heaven." They were then to be evaluated in the areas of archery, music, physics, and propriety. See *Liji zhushu* 禮記註疏, *SSJZZ* 62.1015. Yan Buke 閻步克 convincingly argues that the Jin court offered the great clans of the Wu state different kinds of preferential treatment, including the exemption from examination before the initial appointment to the bureaucracy, in *Chaju zhidu bianqian shigao* 察舉制度變遷史稿 (Shenyang: Liaoning daxue chubanshe, 1997), 182–83.

6. This is evident in at least one of the excerpts here and the last *Outer Chapter* (i.e., his autobiography).

7. For the official biography of Yan Zhiyi 顏之儀 (523–591), see *BS* 83.2796–97; and *ZS* 40.719–21.

8. It is quoted in full in his official biography, in *BQS* 45.618–26.

9. For the official biography of Lu Sidao, see *Sui shu* 57.1397–1403.

10. Wang Liqi 王利器, ed. and comm., *Yanshi jiaxun jijie* 顏氏家訓集解 (Beijing: Zhonghua shuju, 1993), 9.296.

11. The Nine Borders (*jiugai* 九垓) is a general term for China proper.

12. What Ge Hong refers to as a "brief separation" was the rule of the Wu kingdom that lasted from 222 to 280.

13. Ziyou 子游 was the courtesy name of Yan Yan 言偃 (505–443 B.C.E.). A disciple of Confucius, he was renowned for his literary talent. According to Sima Qian, he was also the only known disciple of Confucius who came from the area south of the Yangzi River. See *Records of the Historian* (*Shi ji* 史記) 67.2201.

14. Zhongren 仲任 was the courtesy name of the Eastern Han scholar Wang Chong 王充 (27–97). His biography states that he was a native of Kuaiji 會稽, an ancient city located south of the Yangzi River. See *Hou Han shu* 49.1629.

15. The Tang classicist Kong Yinda 孔穎達 (574–648) suggested in his annotations to *Zuozhuan* that the Central Provinces were also referred to as the Upper States (*shangguo* 上國) because they were upstream of the rivers that ran through the Wu and Chu states. See *Chunqiu Zuozhuan zhengyi* 春秋左傳正義, *SSJZZ* 53.907. Here, Ge Hong appears to use the Central Provinces as a synonym for China proper north of the Yangzi River.

16. The Jin state conquered Wu in 280 C.E. It is reasonable to assume that Ge Hong wrote this particular passage after the removal of the Jin court to Jiankang in 316. While modern scholars have generally accepted Ge's claim that he completed *Master Who Embraces Simplicity* in 317, various statements, including this one, in the *Outer Chapters* put it in doubt.

17. *Lunyu zhushu* 論語註疏, *SSJZZ* 14.218–19. Confucius considered those who wore their clothes with a left lapel to be barbarians.

18. The parent here refers to the emperor, who, as the ruler, should treat his people as his children. See *Classic of Poetry* (*Shijing* 詩經) 251.

19. For an alternative translation, see Jay Sailey, *The Master Who Embraces Simplicity: A Study of the Philosopher Ko Hung, A.D. 283–343* (San Francisco: Chinese Material Center, 1978), 99–101.

20. *Classic of Poetry* 48. The relevant lines are "She is expecting me in Sangzhong 期我乎桑中 / she is meeting with me in Shanggong 要我乎上宮 / and she will accompany me to Qishang" 送我乎淇之上矣.

21. The "Tribute of Yu" states that Yunmeng was a swamp located in the area south of the Yangzi River. See *Shangshu zhengyi* 尚書正義, *SSJZZ* 6.178.

22. *Laozi* 3.

23. Liuxia Hui 柳下惠 was the posthumous honorific of Zhan Huo 展獲. He served as Chief Judge (*Shishi* 士師) in the Lu court of Duke Xi 魯僖公 (r. 659–627 B.C.E.) and Duke Wen 魯文公 (r. 626–609 B.C.E.). See *Chunqiu Zuozhuan zhengyi* 春秋左傳正義, *SSJZZ*, Duke Wen 2, 18.303. Even Confucius and Mengzi praised his fairness, honesty, and

integrity. See *Lunyu zhushu* 論語注疏 18.166; and *Mengzi zhushu* 孟子注疏, *SSJZZ* 3b.118–19. Here Ge Hong is referring to an incident in which Hui remained unmoved by seduction. See *Classic of Poetry* 200.

24. The man of humble rank may be Ge Hong himself.

25. *Classic of Poetry* 195: "Like that stream flowing from a spring 如彼泉流 / all will sink together in a common ruin" 無淪胥以敗.

26. In *Hanfeizi* 韓非子, *juan* 35. Ge Hong is suggesting that those who have adopted wicked practices are as mad as the madman who went east. This is actually a story told by Huizi 惠子 (390–317 B.C.E.). "A madman goes east. The one who chases him also goes east. By going east they are the same. The reason for which they go east is different. Thus the saying—those who have done the same thing should not be unexamined [i.e., treated in the same way]." For an alternative translation, see Sailey, *Master Who Embraces Simplicity*, 146–47.

27. The loss and chaos here are most likely a reference to the conquest of the Wu state in 280 by the Western Jin rather than the Yongjia disorder 永嘉之亂 (310–312).

28. *Dongguan Hanji* 東觀漢記, *The Biography of Ma Liao* 馬廖傳, *juan* 7. Ma Liao was a son of Ma Yuan 馬援 (14 B.C.E.–49 C.E.), a famous general of the Eastern Han. He petitioned the court to reform social customs, particularly fashion trends. He stated:

Those in the capital favored tall coiffures,	城中好高髻
those of the four corners then wore their hair one *chi* tall;	四方高一尺
those in the capital favored thick eyebrows,	城中好廣眉
those of the four corners then painted theirs to cover half the forehead;	四方且半額
those in the capital favored wide sleeves,	城中好大袖
those of the four corners used up much cloth [in copying the style].	四方全匹帛

29. Huang Xiang 皇象 (dates unknown), a talented calligrapher, is noted in *SGZ* 63.1245–46). None of his work survives.

30. It is unclear whether this Liu Zuan 劉纂 was the person with the same name mentioned in *Sanguo zhi*. While Ge Hong maintained that Liu Zuan was a celebrated calligrapher like Huang Xiang, the few passages in which this name is mentioned neither support nor refute his claim. See *SGZ* 50.1198, 56.1312, 60.1385, and 64.1446.

31. Cen Boran 岑伯然 and Zhu Jiping 朱季平 are unknown outside this text.

32. Yuanchang 元常 was the courtesy name of the renowned Three Kingdoms calligrapher Zhong Yao 鍾繇 (151–230). For his biography, see *SGZ* 13.391–99.

33. Kongming 孔明 was the courtesy name of another renowned Three Kingdoms calligrapher Hu Zhao 胡昭 (161–250). For his biography, see *SGZ* 11.361–66.

34. Zhang Zhi 張芝 (d. ca. 192) was a celebrated calligrapher of the Eastern Han dynasty known for his exquisite cursive script. He was briefly mentioned in his father's biography in *Hou Han shu* 65.2144. Although he greatly influenced calligraphers of subsequent generations, the first comprehensive evaluation of his works known to us did not appear until the High Tang, when the critic Zhang Huaiguan 張懷瓘 (fl. 710s) discussed

them at length in glowing terms and praised them as divine (*shenpin* 神品) in *Appraising Calligraphy* (*Shu duan* 書斷).

35. Suo Jing 索靖 (209–303) was a grandson of Zhang Zhi's sister. Deeply influenced by Zhang's style, Suo also specialized in cursive script. He served as Secretarial Court Gentleman (*Shangshu lang* 尚書郎) in the court of the Han Emperor Wu (r. 141–87 B.C.E.). For his biography, see *JS* 60.1648–60.

36. This refers to the story of a man from Shouling 壽陵 who attempted to imitate the gait of the urbanites in the Zhao 趙 capital. He failed. Since he could no longer recall how he used to walk, he ended up crawling back to his native land. See *Zhuangzi* 17, "Qiushui."

37. Zhong Yi 鍾儀 (d. 582 B.C.E.?) was a musician in the Chu 楚 court who was captured by the Jin army and became a prisoner of war. See *Chunqiu Zuozhuan zhengyi* 26.835–36. When Duke Jing of Jin 晉景公 (r. 599–582 B.C.E.) inspected the army, he met and had Zhong Yi play music for him. Zhong Yi played him the Chu music. *Zuozhuan* 26.847–49 reports that Duke Jing praised Zhong for "not forgetting his origins" (*buwangben* 不忘本).

38. Zhuang Xi 莊舄 was a man from Yue 越 who served in the Chu court. When the Chu king asked him if he missed his native land, Zhuang replied that whenever he became homesick, he spoke the Yue dialect. The Chu king then sent someone to spy on Zhuang and found that he spoke only the Yue dialect at home. See *SJ* 70.2301.

39. In the *Record of Rites*, it was Zengzi 曾子 (505–432 B.C.E.), a respected disciple of Confucius, rather than Confucius himself, who made this comment. See *Liji zhushu* 42. 1410–11.

40. This statement was made by Zilu 子路 (542–480 B.C.E.), a disciple of Confucius. See *Liji zhushu* 7.250.

41. Here Ge Hong complains about the stylized dirges that became popular at this time. It appears that people were competing with one another in singing laments.

42. The stone powder 石散 is likely the "five-mineral powder" 五石散. It was a restorative drug made of fluorine, quartz, red bole clay, stalactite, and sulfur, and it allegedly cured many illnesses and aided in the cultivation of life. Here Ge Hong appears to share the belief that it could save lives. Because the drug caused fever, many ate cold food and took cold baths to counterbalance it; hence the drug was also called "cold-food powder." Its consumption was widely popular among the elites during the medieval period. Information about the drug and its use can be found in Li Ling 李零, *Zhongguo fangshu xukao* 中國方術續考 (Beijing: Dongfang chubanshe, 2001), 341–49.

43. For an alternative translation, see Sailey, *Master Who Embraces Simplicity*, 156–60.

44. *Yanshi jiaxun jijie* 2.95–98. See also Teng Ssu-Yü, *Family Instruction for the Yen Clan: An Annotated Translation with Introduction* (Leiden: Brill, 1968), 34–35.

45. *Zhanshuai* 斬縗 is the heaviest mourning wear of the five degrees of relations (*wufu* 五服) specified in the *Record of Rites*. It is made from the roughest sackcloth with no trimmings. It was to be worn for three years (usually twenty-five or twenty-seven months) by a son or an unmarried daughter for his or her father, by a father for his eldest son, by a married woman for her parents-in-law, and by a wife or concubine for her husband. See *Yili zhushu* 儀禮註疏 29.639–50.

46. *Qishuai* is the second heaviest mourning wear of the five degrees of relations. It is made from the roughest sackcloth with trimmings. The duration of the mourning period depended on the degree of relation between the mourner and the dead. See *Yili zhushu* 30.651–73 and 31.674–91.

47. *Dagong* is the middle mourning wear of the five degrees of relations. It is made from finer sackcloth with trimmings. The duration of the mourning period depended on the degree of relation between the mourner and the dead. See *Yili zhushu* 31.691–97 and 32.698–709.

48. *Xiaogong* is the second lightest mourning wear of the five degrees of relations. It is made from sackcloth of finer quality with trimmings. The length of the observation is five months. See *Yili zhushu* 32.709–15 and 33.716–22.

49. *Sima* is the lightest mourning wear of the five degrees of relations. It is made from the finest sackcloth with decorated trimmings. The length of observation is three months. See *Yili zhushu* 33.722–33.

50. *Liji zhushu* 37.1807.

51. *Xiaojing zhushu* 孝經註疏, *SSJZZ* 9.67.

52. Teng, *Family Instruction for the Yen Clan*, 187–90. Nine Provinces is a general term for China proper. There are different opinions about which provinces are included in the nine.

53. Cui Zhan 崔瞻 (d. 580) was a prominent statesman and literatus of the Northern Qi. In addition to his literary talent, he was known for his handsome appearance and cultural refinement. For his official biographies, see *BQS* 23.336–37; and *BS* 24.875–76. Cui Ziyue 崔子約 was actually two years younger than his nephew Zhan. True to the reputation of his family, Ziyue, too, was known for his handsome appearance. He was Court Gentleman for Evaluations (*Kaogonglang* 考功郎) when he died sometime between 559 and 560. For his official biography, see *BS* 24.879.

54. Li Zuren 李祖仁 and Li Wei 李蔚 were sons of Li Xie 李諧. Father and sons all were prominent statesmen. See *BS* 43.1604–6.

55. Jijie was the courtesy name of Li Gai 李概 (dates unknown). His scholarship was famous, and his disregard for proper dress codes was infamous. He was a close friend of Cui Zhan, the contemporary model of refinement. See *BS* 21.1211–12. His *Resolving Doubts About Sounds and Rhymes* (*Yinyun jueyi* 音韻決疑) has not survived.

56. Yang Xiuzhi 陽休之 (d. 582) was an illustrious statesman whose official career extended from the last years of the Northern Wei through the Northern Qi to the early days of the Sui. His contemporaries revered his scholarship and considered him a literary master (*wenjiang* 文匠). For his biographies, see *BQS* 42.560–64; and *BS* 47.1724–28. His *Classification of Rhymes* is no longer extant.

4. Literary Imagination of the North and South

PING WANG

The literary history of the Southern Dynasties starts with a poem lamenting the loss of homeland. In this poem, the famous "Rhapsody on Climbing the Tower" (*Denglou fu* 登樓賦), Wang Can 王粲 (177–217) describes the peerless beauty of the southern land of Jing-Chu 荊楚, where he may have lived for more than a decade but which he declines to call home. He recalls the dislocated men of the South and the North alike who tenaciously cling to their wish to return home. Wang Can believes this is a desire innate not only in human beings but also in birds and beasts. Failing to find consolation in the South, the poet ends his lament noting his insomnia.[1] Wang Can's homesickness is shared by a group of Northern scholars at the turn of the third century C.E. who, after the fall of Luoyang and then Chang'an, which was caused by Dong Zhuo's insurrection, fled south to seek employment with Liu Biao 劉表 (142–208), the Governor of Jingzhou 荊州. Finding themselves at the mercy of a martial despot, some of these writers likely felt that they were in the wrong place to display and use their talents. Mi Heng 彌衡 (ca. 173–198), a man from Shandong, which was also Wang Can's hometown, wrote a rhapsody describing the sorrowful fate of a beautiful parrot that has been captured and confined to a cage. The analogy between the bird's loss of its home grove and Mi Heng's own feeling of alienation makes it clear that this piece, like Wang Can's rhapsody, is about a Northerner's frustration over the "loss of home grove."[2] Fortunately, most of these writers—though not including Mi Heng, who was executed in 198—were able to return north to join Cao Cao's court around 208, and Wang Can became the brightest of the Jian'an writers who "spent a fair amount of time feasting and drinking and going on entertaining little excursions through beautiful gardens and parks."[3] They also produced literary pieces that testify to their experiences until the good days were cut short by a pandemic in 217 that killed four of the seven masters.[4]

Exactly one century later, in 317, after the Jin regime lost its capital, Luoyang 洛陽, and the surrounding central plains to the Xiongnu, dozens of aristocratic families, following the Jin prince Sima Rui 司馬睿, abandoned their homes and moved south of the Yellow River (modern Henan and Shandong Provinces) to settle in the lower reaches of the Yangzi. The scale of this disaster is comparable to the Norman Conquest of England in 1066. The precarious regime that Sima Rui established under the protection of the Langye Wang family had to appease the resisting indigenous Wu gentry class as well as acculturate the newcomers to the new geographical and cultural environment. The gap between the newly settled and the native power groups, however, was as wide as the Yangzi River that originally separated them. Finding themselves at odds with the people and land, the Northerners could not bring themselves to appreciate what their new home had to offer. Like Wang Can, who was unaffected by the beautiful scenery of Jing-Chu, the aristocrats from Luoyang wept only when seeing the grandeur of the Yangzi River. The fifth-century collection *Recent Anecdotes from the Talk of the Ages* (*Shishuo xinyu* 世說新語) records just such an incident:

> Whenever the day was fair, those who had crossed the Yangzi River would gather on the grass at Xinting to drink and feast. On one occasion, Zhou Yi 周顗 [269–322], who was part of the group, sighed and remarked, "The scene is not unlike the old days in the North; it's just that naturally there's a difference between these mountains and rivers and those." All those present looked at one another and wept. It was only Chancellor Wang Dao 王導 [276–339], who, looking very grave, replied with deep emotion, "We should all unite our strength around the royal house and recover the sacred provinces. To what end do we sit here facing one another like so many 'captives of Chu'?"[5]

The name of the place where the Northerners held their gathering was Xinting 新亭, a post station and a popular spot for excursions. The name is also a pun on "new stop." That is, to the Northerners, the place that they now called home was just a temporary stop. For the Han Chinese for more than a millennium, comparing their home on the Central Plain with the South was an experience too new to arouse familiar sentiments. The South was all that the North was not. Wang Dao's comment about Jiangdong 江東 (literally, "east of the

Yangzi," another reference to the lower reaches of the Yangzi, especially the Wu area) as a "cramped place" is one of many examples of how the new settlers viewed the South.[6] The geography of the Yangzi River area is mountainous and lacks the Central Plain's vast expanses of land.[7] In literature and culture, the South carries a taint of exile from the time of the first known Chinese poet, Qu Yuan 屈原 (ca. 340–ca. 277 B.C.E.), a Southerner whose magnum opus, "Encountering Sorrow," is about exile and dislocation. When Jia Yi 賈誼 (200–168 B.C.E.), a prodigy from Luoyang, found himself banished to the damp and low wet country of Chu, he could not help but reach out to his predecessor by drowning a piece of writing in the river where Qu Yuan supposedly committed suicide. Qu Yuan's and Jia Yi's personae and writings, as well as the emotions connected with exile, were acknowledged by the Han historian Sima Qian 司馬遷 (ca. 145–ca. 86 B.C.E.), who himself encountered great sorrow. In history and literature, the South represents a place of banishment and sojourn, loss and nostalgia, illusion and disillusion. It was situated on the margins of Han culture. To Han Chinese, it was the other. Both the allure and the revulsion of the South are seen in the ambivalent representation of the Southern girls depicted in the *Classic of Poetry* (*Shijing* 詩經) 9, "Han guang" 漢廣, who are at the same time subversive forces of the orthodox culture and sublime creatures of elusive charm.[8] The descriptive label *yin* 淫, so often applied to Southern culture, religious practices, and arts, meant an erosion of and encroachment on rites and propriety, or what is firmly prescribed and should be upheld and adhered to closely, which may be designated as *ze* 則.

This prejudice against the South was by no means warranted. Historically, Southern elites, especially those from the Wu area, were known as upholders of Zhou 周 orthodox rites. Prince Ji Zha 季札 (576–484 B.C.E.) of Wu 吳, for example, was highly praised and honored for declining to succeed his father. Indeed, by the end of the Eastern Han, Southerners were a considerable presence at the imperial court.[9] The courts of Sun Quan 孫權 (182–252) and Liu Biao, who controlled the Yangzi River region, attracted not only the Southern local elites but also talented men from the North. The long and mutual infiltration and influence between the proponents of Southern culture and their Northern counterparts left such indelible marks of cultural prestige on the elites of both sides of the Yangzi that any attempt to claim superiority of any kind led to fierce combat, albeit sometimes in the civilized form of writing. In his article "Sweet-Peel Orange or Southern Gold," David R. Knechtges elegantly shows us the most notable cultural clashes between the North and the South as reflected in the writings of Lu Ji 陸機 and Pan Yue 潘岳.[10] Another, lesser-known yet eloquent accusation was made in the disguise of a self-defense by the Southerner Zhang Chong 張充 (449–514) against the Qi 齊 (479–501) court magnate Wang Jian 王儉 (452–489), a member of one of the most prestigious Northern aristocratic families. An upholder of ritual and propriety at the Qi court, Wang Jian denied a promotion granted to Zhang Chong's father because of the latter's family origin and several uncivilized sons, Zhang Chong being one of them. To defend his own and his family's reputation, Zhang Chong addresses a letter to Wang Jian in which he mocks the self-conceited Northerner and challenges his self-granted cultural superiority. Throughout the text, the writer sarcastically contrasts his own lowliness with Wang Jian's excellence. These insincere words of praise can be read only as an attack. Also using self-derision, Zhang Chong reminds Wang Jian of the most basic virtue of humility. The opening line of his letter puts Zhang Chong himself and Wang Jian into two camps whose boundaries are both geographical and political: Wu versus Langye—that is, South versus North—and an unemployed man versus a court attendant. Zhang Chong then discusses at length the various ways of "activity and inactivity" and roads to "ascent and descent" at court. By theorizing a person's "nature"—what leads one to seek quietude—he affirms his own integrity and virtue. Evoking moral exemplars who remain outside court, he places them above the court officials. Zhang Chong's own tenure at court gives him credibility to ridicule the hypocrisy of the prestigious group or court bureaucracy, of which Wang Jian is a devoted member and guardian. That is, both Zhang's access to and rejection of the cultural world represented by Wang Jian implicitly upsets the hierarchy of the two men.

The ideal and idyllic portrayal of a reclusive lifestyle made famous by Tao Qian 陶潛 (365–427) effectively excludes Wang Jian from the new aesthetic world of Southern birth and creation. This admiration for and adventure in the natural world as personal realization and philosophical revelation had been in fashion since the fall of the Han. When the leading Northern families poured into the South, those with the means were able to make a claim on the less crowded southeastern coastal region, where the beauty of its mountains and rivers are best seen in the lines by Gu Kaizhi 顧愷之 (ca. 345–406): "Thousands of cliffs rise in a contest of beauty; myriad streams run in rapid race. Plants and trees luxuriantly grow, like multicolored nimbuses ascending."[11] The Lanting 蘭亭 gathering planned by the aesthete Wang Xizhi 王羲之 (321–361 or 303–361) and the attachment to Eastern Mountain in Guiji of the charismatic prime minister Xie An 謝安 (320–385) reinforced the grandeur of nature and the lifestyle it produced. The dynamic and static effects of the scene described by Zhang Chong, ostensibly displaying pride in his taste, is well balanced. The first few lines bring to life the movement of the tidal bore and rock slides, contrasted with the picture of various kinds of plants growing in perfect harmony. Such wonders induce worthy men to shun society, yet Zhang Chong finds himself misunderstood by others and laments the absence of "the one who knows the tone" to share his joy. This is, of course, a hidden accusation of Wang Jian of lacking cultural depth and taste. What follows in the letter focuses on Wang Jian's merits and virtue. While lavishly praising Wang Jian, Zhang Chong nonetheless succeeds in underrating himself. The sarcasm of the letter's two portraits allows Zhang Chong to question both Wang Jian as a person and the value system that he defends. The efficacy of the letter is evidenced by a double reward: fame and gain. Not only was Zhang Chong promoted in office, but his letter was deemed worthy of being quoted in full in the official histories. Even though Wang Jian, the intended recipient of the letter, was infuriated by it, the audience for the Southerner's self-defense seemed to approve of it.

FURTHER READING

Xiaofei Tian, "The Cultural Construction of the North and South," in *Beacon Fire and Shooting Star: The Literary Culture of the Liang (502–557)* (Cambridge, Mass.: Harvard University Asia Center, 2007), 310–66. For a discussion of the clashes between Northern court officials and the Southern elite toward the end of the third century, see David R. Knechtges, "Sweet-Peel Orange or Southern Gold? Regional Identity in Western Jin Literature," in *Studies in Early Medieval Chinese Literature and Cultural History: In Honor of Richard B. Mather and Donald Holzman*, ed. Paul W. Kroll and David R. Knechtges (Boulder, Colo.: T'ang Studies Society, 2003), 27–79. For discussions of Six Dynasties practices and discourse on reclusion, see Alan Berkowitz, *Patterns of Disengagement: The Practice and Portrayal of Reclusion in Medieval China* (Stanford, Calif.: Stanford University Press, 2000); Wang Yongping 王永平, *Zhonggu shiren qianyi yu wenhua jiaoliu* 中古士人遷移與文化交流 (Beijing: Shehui kexue wenxian chubanshe, 2005); and Yao Dazhong 姚大中, *Nanfang de fengqi* 南方的奮起 (Taibei: Sanmin, 1981).

A man from Wu hereby writes to the lord's attendant from Langye:

I

Recently, the distance between us is long.	頃日路
Continuous rain blocks the light of the sun.	愁霖韜晦
The alternation between chill and heat has been uneven.	涼暑未平
I hope you are keeping up in nourishment.	想無虧攝
When I am fortunate to take a break from fishing,	充幸以魚釣之閑
or have leisure time after harvesting with the sickle,	鎌採之暇
I amuse myself with scrolls,	時復以卷軸自娛
And roam through histories.	逍遙前史
Spanning the myriad ages,	從橫萬古

paths leading to action and nonaction vary.　　　　動默之路多端

Over the countless centuries,　　　　　　　　　　紛綸百年

the ways leading to promotion and demotion
　　are not one.　　　　　　　　　　　　　　　昇降之途不一

Therefore, that circular vessels move and square
　　ones remain motionless　　　　　　　　　故以圓行方止

is only a matter of difference in nature.　　　　　器之異也

Metal is solid and water is liquid;　　　　　　　　金剛水柔

This is a distinction in nature.　　　　　　　　　性之別也

Those who are good at curbing their natures　　　善御性者

do not go against the quality of metal or water.　　不違金水之質

Those who are good at making vessels　　　　　善為器者

do not change the utility of circle and square.　　不易方圓之用

Thereupon,　　　　　　　　　　　　　　　所以

there is the loftiness of Beihai who hung up his
　　hairpin and sash;[12]　　　　　　　　　北海掛簪帶之高

There is also the nobleness of Henan who turned
　　down the imperial offer.[13]　　　　　　　河南降璽書之貴

I, throughout my life, have lacked company,　　　充生平少偶

Nor have I troubled myself with gain or fame.　　不以利欲干懷

For the thirty-six years of my life　　　　　　　三十六年

I have been able to hold myself detached,
　　dwelling in poverty.　　　　　　　　　差得以棲貧自澹

With an unwavering determination,　　　　　　介然之志

I dwell alone on a precipitous frosty cliff.　　　峭聳霜崖

With steadfast resolve,　　　　　　　　　　確乎之情

I traverse the peaks near the ocean.　　　　　峯橫海岸

Once I wore streaming tassels at Heavenly
　　Emolument Gallery;[14]　　　　　　　影纓天閣

Now I have cast off the glory of "palace
　　and temple."　　　　　　　　　　　既謝廊廟之華

In the past, I wore an embellished sash at
　　Cloud Terrace;[15]　　　　　　　　綴組雲臺

Yet in the end I was put to shame by those
　　prestigious members at court.　　　終慚衣冠之秀

II

Some people cast their tracks along the riverbank;　　所以擯跡江皋

some feigned madness along the edge of the
　　field ridge.　　　　　　　　　　陽狂隴畔者

This is, indeed, due to their having a proud spirit and
    being unconventional and obstinate;　　　　　　　實由氣岸疏凝

the direction of their disposition is toward
    uprightness and aloofness.　　　　　　　　　　情塗狷隔

In solitude, they practice their principles;　　　　獨師懷抱

they do not receive approval from ordinary persons.　不見許於俗人

They alone appear outstanding on the divine cliff;　　孤秀神崖

for they had often been hindered and hampered in
    the world.　　　　　　　　　　　　　　　　每遭回於在世

Therefore, Huan Tan, with his direct remonstration,　故君山直上

became straitened in his prime years.[16]　　　　　蹙壓於當年

Zhu Bo, despite his lofty deeds,　　　　　　　　叔陽夐舉

Was frustrated for eternity.[17]　　　　　　　　　堪秉乎千載

This is also why I have long dwelled with fish and birds.　充所以長羣魚鳥

Fully shaded in the pine-covered cove,　　　　　　畢影松阿

a field of three or four hectares,　　　　　　　　半頃之田

is enough to pay off the taxes.[18]　　　　　　　　足以輸稅

A house of an acre,　　　　　　　　　　　　　五畝之宅

is surrounded by mulberry and hemp.[19]　　　　　樹以桑麻

I whistle and chant among the rivers and gullies.　　嘯歌於川澤之間

Above Mian Lake, I mull over writings from the past;　諷味於澠池之上

I let my boat float on the lake where the "Fisherman"
    roamed.　　　　　　　　　　　　　　　　　泛濫於漁父之遊

I recline and rest beneath the "Divine Residence";[20]　偃息於卜居之下

This is simply the way things are;　　　　　　　　如此而已

What else can I ask for?　　　　　　　　　　　充何謝焉

As for:　　　　　　　　　　　　　　　　　　若

a projecting crag that blocks the sun　　　　　　夫驚巖罩日

and roaring waves that beat against the sky;　　　壯海逢天

protruding rocks collapse into the deep chasm;　　竦石崩尋

sundered defiles fall for thousands of feet.　　　　分危落仞

Cinnamon and thoroughwort bright and supple　　桂蘭綺靡

intermingle in the nooks of the mountain.　　　　叢雜於山幽

Pine and cypress solemn and stately　　　　　　松柏森陰

grow together at the bends of the gulley.　　　　相繚於澗曲

Seeing these, Yuanqing does not return;[21]　　　　元卿於是乎不歸

For this reason, Boxiu, frequently goes thither.[22]　伯休亦以茲長往

At other times I go fishing by the river,　　　　　若延飛竿釣渚

cleanse my feet in the Cang River.　　　　　　　濯足滄洲

Alone I let myself go among the mists;　　　　　獨浪煙霞

I rest at ease under the wind and moon.　　　　　高臥風月

Casually and slowly, I play the zither and drink wine.　悠悠琴酒

Yet my cave is far, and who could come and join me?   岫遠誰來

Brilliant conversations, elegant as they are,   灼灼文談

have no purpose but to exhaust my mind.   空罷方寸

Unaware, I have come long and far over a   不覺鬱然千里
    thousand leagues;

my road is blocked by rivers and streams.   路阻江川

Every time when the west wind rises,   每至西風

How could I not look back?   何嘗不眷

Tentatively, in my sickness,   聊因疾隙

I put a few thoughts in mind;   略舉諸襟

with such humble words,   持此片言

I plead for lofty hearing.   輕枉高聽

III

As for you, Sir,   丈人

barely in your forties,   歲路未強

having excelled in learning, you serve the court.   學優而仕

Your principle is to assist the myriads;   道佐蒼生

your preeminence traverses beyond the ocean.   功橫海望

At court, you show sincerity comparable to   入朝則協
    that of Changqian;   長倩之誠

When away from the court, in giving your opinions,   出議則抗
    you bear integrity like that of Zhongzi.   仲子之節

Indeed, you claim the sublime virtue in this age;   可謂盛德維時

you are the lonely pine tree, singularly outstanding.   孤松獨秀者也

[To you], the "simple treading" [of reclusion] is not   素履未詳
    yet acquainted,

this journey [into reclusion] will be a dark   斯旅尚眇
    and dim mystery.

The scholar from Maoling harbored longing upon   茂陵之彥,
    seeing the canopied carriage;   望冠蓋而長懷

the commoner of Ba Mound heaved a long sigh   霸山之氓, 佇衣
    waiting for the curtained cart.   車而聳歎

What a shame!   得無惜乎

If you were to don swan attire, yoke a chariot,   若鴻裝撰御

let the crane cart hover in the sky,   鶴駕軒空

then the cliffs wouldn't be too bleak,   則岸不辭枯

mountains would be covered in moist.   山被其潤

Rare birds and unusual feathered creatures would   奇禽異羽,
    wait on the cliffs;   或嚴際而逢迎

a hint of mist and a strand of smoke emerge above
    the grove, lingering and accumulating. 弱霧輕煙，
[Then] 乍林端而葐蒀
The Eastern Capital is not to be marveled at; 東都不足奇
The Southern Mountain has no deemed value. 南山豈為貴

IV

I, Chong, am a commoner from west of Mount Kun, 充昆西之百姓
an ordinary man from south of Mount Tai. 岱表之一民
I raise silkworms, and thereby I have clothes; 蠶而衣
I plow and so I have food. 耕且食
I am not capable of 不能
serving lords and marquises, 事王侯
seeking like-minded friends, 覓知己
visiting contemporaries, 造時人
flaunting my eloquence. 騁遊說
Instead, I have tumbled about among butchers 蓬轉於屠博之間
    and gamblers;
The pleasure of that has been great indeed! 其歡甚矣
You, Sir, in your early years served at Receiving 丈人早遇承華
    Splendor.[23]
Then you were commissioned with ritual matters. 中逢崇禮
Relying on the Superior One's concern, 肆上之眷
your reputation has been known from early on. 望溢於早辰
Words from a rustic like me 鄉下之言
are surely erroneous and reckless. 謬延於造次
If the entire world regards Chong as insane, 然舉世皆謂
 充為狂

how could I argue with them? 充亦何能與諸
 君道之哉

Hereby, 是以
I divulge what I have seen and heard; 披聞見
I pour out my innermost thoughts. 掃心胸
I make known my life experience; 述平生
I expound on "speech or reticence." 論語默
The only person with whom I can communicate in 所以通夢交魂
    dreams or through journeying souls,
To whom I can present my deepest thoughts? 推衿送抱者
It is only you, my honorable sir, no one else. 其惟丈人而已
The mountain road is far and long; 關山夐阻

After I finish my letter, I have no one to
  entrust it to.
If I happen to see a woodcutter,
I will ask him to deliver the letter.

書罷莫因

儻遇樵者
妄塵執事

[LS 21.328]

NOTES

1. For an annotated translation of "Denglou fu" 登樓賦, see Xiao Tong, comp., *Wen xuan, or Selections of Refined Literature*, vol. 2, *Rhapsodies on Sacrifices, Hunting, Travel, Sightseeing, Palaces and Halls, Rivers and Seas*, trans. David R. Knechtges (Princeton, N.J.: Princeton University Press, 1987), 236–42.

2. For an annotated translation of "Yingwu fu" 鸚鵡賦, see Xiao Tong, comp., *Wen xuan, or Selections of Refined Literature*, vol. 3, *Rhapsodies on Natural Phenomena, Birds and Animals, Aspirations and Feelings, Sorrowful Laments, Literature, Music, and Passions*, trans. David R. Knechtges (Princeton, N.J.: Princeton University Press, 1996), 49–57.

3. Robert Joe Cutter, "Cao Zhi's (192–232) Symposium Poems," *CLEAR* 6 (1984): 3.

4. For some of their pieces, see *Wen xuan* 文選 (Shanghai: Shanghai guji, 1986), 42.1896–97.

5. Yu Jiaxi 余嘉錫, *Shishuo xinyu jianshu* 世說新語箋疏 (Taibei: Huazheng shuju, 1984), 92. The translation is based on Liu I-ch'ing [Liu Yiqing], comp., *Shih-shuo Hsin-yü: A New Account of the Tales of the World*, 2nd ed., trans. Richard B. Mather (Ann Arbor: Center for Chinese Studies, University of Michigan, 2002), 47, with some modifications.

6. Liu I-ch'ing, comp., *New Account*, 156.

7. For discussions of the controversy over the demarcation between the North and the South and working definitions of the South, see Yao Dazhong 姚大中, *Nanfang de fengqi* 南方的奮起 (Taibei: Sanmin, 1981), 187; Hu A'xiang 胡阿祥, *Wei Jin bentu wenxue dili yanjiu* 魏晉本土文學地理研究 (Nanjing: Nanjing daxue chubanshe, 2001), 131–32; and Xiao Bing 蕭兵, *Chu wenhua yu meixue* 楚文化與美學 (Taibei: Wenjin chubanshe, 2000), 35.

8. I am referring to the songs in the "Ernan" 二南 and "Chen feng" 陳風, especially *Classic of Poetry (Shi jing* 詩經) 9, 22, 136, 137.

9. Wang Yongping 王永平, *Zhonggu shiren qianyi yu wenhua jiaoliu* 中古士人遷移與文化交流 (Beijing: Shehui kexue wenxian chubanshe, 2005), 12–27.

10. David R. Knechtges, "Sweet-Peel Orange or Southern Gold? Regional Identity in Western Jin Literature," in *Studies in Early Medieval Chinese Literature and Cultural History: In Honor of Richard B. Mather and Donald Holzman*, ed. Paul W. Kroll and David R. Knechtges (Boulder, Colo.: T'ang Studies Society, 2003), 27–79.

11. *JS* 62.2404; *Shishuo xinyu jianshu* 143 (2/88); Shih-hsiang Ch'en, trans., *Biography of Ku K'ai-chih*, Chinese Dynastic Histories Translations, no. 2 (Berkeley: University of California Press, 1961), 13. See also Liu I-ch'ing, comp., *New Account*, 74.

12. Beihai 北海 is referring to the Later Han recluse Pang Meng 龐盟 (dates unknown), who was a native of Beihai (Changle County 昌樂 of Shandong). See *HHS* 83.2759–60; and Alan Berkowitz, *Patterns of Disengagement: The Practice and Portrayal of Reclusion in Medieval China* (Stanford, Calif.: Stanford University Press, 2000), 164n.67, 89n.98, 166n.82, 183.

13. The identification of Henan 河南 is not certain. One possibility is that Henan refers to the Two Elders from Yewang 野王二老, who appear in *HHS* 83.2758. They turned down the offer of office from Emperor Guangwu 光武帝 (r. 25–57) after they had given the emperor their counsel.

14. Heavenly Emolument Gallery refers to the Former Han imperial library. See *HS* 87B.3584. Zhang Chong served as Drafter for the Heir Apparent (*Taizi sheren* 太子舍人). See *LS* 21.328.

15. Cloud Terrace is the Eastern Han terrace where Emperor Guangwu used to hold his court meetings. See *HHS* 6.250 and 36.1236. Here it refers to the Qi court where Zhang Chong once served as Court Gentleman of the Imperial Secretariat (*Shangshu dian zhonglang* 尚書殿中郎). See *LS* 21.328.

16. For information about Huan Tan 桓談 (dates unknown), see *HHS* 28A.950–61.

17. Shuyang 叔陽 is Zhu Bo's 朱勃 (Western Han) style name. See *HHS* 24.850.

18. This line is a verbatim reference to Jiang Yan 江淹 (444–505), "A Discussion on Reclusion with Friends" (*Yu youren lunyin shu* 與友人論隱書). See *QW* 38.3171a–b.

19. This line alludes to *Mencius*. See *Mengzi zhushu* 孟子註疏, *SSJZ* 1A.12a.

20. "Fisherman" and "Divine Residence" are titles of pieces from *Lyrics of Chu* (*Chuci* 楚辭).

21. Yuanqing 元卿 is the style name of Jiang Xu 蔣詡 (69–17 B.C.E.), a recluse from Duling 杜陵. See *Sanfu juelu* 三輔決錄, *CSJC*, 1st ser., 15.

22. Boxiu 伯修 refers to Han Kang 韓康 (dates unknown). See *HHS* 83.2770; and Berkowitz, *Patterns of Disengagement*, 117.

23. Receiving Splendor refers to the crown prince's palace.

PART II

Governing Mechanisms and Social Reality

The Six Dynasties period was born in cataclysm. Although the turmoil did not necessarily rip apart the social and political structure established in the Qin 秦 (221–206 B.C.E.) and Han 漢 (206 B.C.E.–220 C.E.) dynasties, it affected the pace and direction of subsequent developments. Changes often appeared rapidly and unexpectedly, with some having only transient effects and others leaving a lasting and often idiosyncratic imprint. New political and institutional mechanisms often borrowed from diverse cultural and intellectual traditions. The documents translated in part II showcase the unsettling and inventive nature of the period, as they describe a wide range of phenomena: the Wu 吳 (229–280) kingdom's elaborate system of population control, the eclectic use by Qiao Zhou 譙周 (ca. 200–270) of the Confucian Classics and prophecies in revamping political discourse, the ambivalence of the Northern Wei 北魏 (286–557) regarding the application of criminal law to the nobility, and the eloquent defense of endogamous marriage by Shen Yue 沈約 (441–513).

The Six Dynasties also is often characterized as a time when the imperial authority was in steady decline, threatened by the rise of the great clans and military strongmen. These two groups differed from each other in their social background and public images, and they often competed with each other. Having originated as local magnates, the great clans distinguished themselves by social reputation, public service, and cultural achievement. Their ascendancy to national prominence also made them the caretakers of culture and the arbiters of political and social matters. In addition, their unique position gave them tremendous leverage to acquire economic and political privileges, which they used to solidify their status in the realm for many generations, thereby placing their own survival over that of the regimes they served. In fact, their pedigrees and nearly hereditary control of government posts have led modern scholars to label them as aristocrats. In contrast, the backgrounds of the military men were more diverse culturally, ethnically, and socially, a diversity that they used in various combinations to gain power. They achieved their status through their service to private or state powers or by successful conquests.

The pattern of power during this time was extremely complicated. Studies show that imperial authority did not always retreat in the face of challenges and that the relationship between one's official position and one's social identity remained close. Members of the great clans had to secure their status through their continuous participation in governance and their monopoly of prestigious bureaucratic offices. As Mark Lewis observed, "Office holding, and the hierarchy of offices, had become more and more a matter of status and a demonstration of social rank, and less and less a marker of actual power."[1] The regimes in both the North and the South were inclined toward centralization, and they all made various reforms in the areas of governance, laws, finance, and rituals in order to strengthen the state's claim of authority and control over human and material resources. Their successes at centralization did not, however, necessarily undermine the great clans or the military establishment.

One of these reforms pertained to the selection of officials to serve in the government. During the Han dynasty, the relationship between the imperial center and its periphery was built on the mechanism of local recommendations. Through this system, the periphery became directly involved in the production and reproduction of the central bureaucracy. But this mechanism fell apart in the waning days of the dynasty as it pressed subsequent regimes, such as the Wei 魏 kingdom (220–265), to pursue an alternative method of recruitment. The resulting institutions, the Nine Ranks system (*jiupin* 九品) and the Office of Rectifiers (i.e., the "impartial and just" judges [*zhongzheng* 中正]), altered the balance between center and periphery in the selection process. The process of staffing the central bureaucracy became more centralized and, as Tang Zhangru 唐長孺 points out, effectively undermined local representation.[2] Meanwhile, the great clans that were already established in the central bureaucracy increasingly monopolized these institutions and further dominated the political establishment. Those who did not belong to the great clans had only limited access to the prestigious official posts and thus became marginalized. In short, the new institutions strengthened the political control of those at the capital of the empire.

These changes, nonetheless, had their critics. Liu Yi 劉毅, a courtier active during the Wei and the Western Jin, called the Office of the Rectifiers the "of-

fice of the wicked" (*jianfu* 姦府). He considered the office to be the root of political malfeasance, as the Rectifiers and the great clans usually had close ties.
Accordingly, Liu called for a return to the Han dynasty's practice of local recommendation.[3] Xiahou Xuan 夏侯玄 (209–254), whose proposals concerning this
issue are introduced in chapter 7 by Timothy M. Davis, took a more subtle approach. He contended that because the Rectifiers were in a position to assess
the candidates' character, the Imperial Secretariat should have the authority to
judge their abilities and make the appropriate appointments. The issues here
were not only the practice of governance but also the criteria for evaluation.
Who was worthy of the office: the virtuous or the talented? Xiahou Xuan, a
leading advocate of "mysterious (or dark) learning" (*xuanxue* 玄學), took the
philosophical position that the "name" (*ming* 名) must match the "substance"
(*shi* 實). He saw an intrinsic connection between virtue and talent, that one's
virtue by reputation should be manifested as talent in reality. Thus Xiahou Xuan's
proposal to have the Rectifiers judge the virtue and the Imperial Secretariat
choose the talent was an attempt to balance the "public opinion" of a candidate
and the government's administrative mandate.[4]

"Mysterious learning" was not the only intellectual current influencing political discourse and practice. Confucian classicism, with its emphasis on the
exegesis of the Classics, continued to play a significant role in shaping political
and social views. As J. Michael Farmer shows in chapter 6, the writings of Qiao
Zhou provide important examples. His scholarship, which combined prophecy,
historiography, and Confucian exegesis, shows that the Han dynasty's culture
had deep roots in the South. He presented his subtle criticism of contemporary
politics in the form of a commentary to the *Spring and Autumn Annals* (*Chunqiu jueyu* 春秋決獄). His famous disciple, Chen Shou 陳壽 (233–297), inherited
and further developed this particular line of scholarship in the *Chronicle of the
Three Kingdoms* (*Sanguo zhi* 三國志). Qiao Zhou's and Chen Shou's efforts exemplify the continuation of the Han's scholarly tradition and its relevance to
the post-Han world.

The so-called aristocracy in the Six Dynasties period was not a homoge-
neous group whose members shared a uniform political vision, cultural inclination, social network, and lifestyle. Instead, they differed in their geographical
and social origins, the sources of their power, their marriage patterns, and
their relationships with the dynasts. The ethnically Chinese Cui 崔 and Li 李
clans from Hebei 河北 in the sixth century may have had more in common
with the ethnically Xianbei 鮮卑 elite than with the émigré Wang 王 and Xie
謝 clans at the Southern courts. Even within this loosely defined group, though,
there was a clear distinction between the elite clans and those of humbler origins, and between those from the North and the South. The fortunes of these
clans also continually rose and fell. Until the end of the Eastern Jin, for example, the émigré clans enjoyed a significantly higher status than that of the clans
whose roots were in the South. This situation changed, however, in the Liu

Song 劉宋 dynasty (420–479), when professional military officers and men of humble lineage surged in influence and the scions of the Southern clans began to produce their own cultural spokesmen. The Shen 沈 clan of Wuxing 吳興, which originally were local potentates in the Jiangnan 江南 region, became a dominant family under the Qi (479–502) and the Liang (502–557) regimes. The discussion by Shen Yue 沈約 (441–513) of the impeachment of Wang Yuan 王源, which is translated and discussed in chapter 10 by David R. Knechtges, is a telling case of the unrelenting efforts of such new elites to demarcate the boundary between the commoners and the gentry. This insistence on maintaining social hierarchy coincided with an increase in social mobility.

Beginning with the demise of the Eastern Han, the new regimes competed with powerful private estates and landholders for control of the population and the land, a process that Charles Holcombe discusses in chapter 8 in his introduction to "Petition for Closing Off Mountains and Lakes" (*Shangyan shanhu zhi jin* 上言山湖之禁) by Liu Zishang 劉子尚. But the documents from the Eastern Han and the Wu kingdom that were discovered in Dongpailou 東牌樓 and Zoumalou 走馬樓 remind us how little historians knew about the state's ability to control the local population and revenues during a time of political instability.

Penal law is another area in which the Six Dynasties witnessed major changes, which I examine in chapter 5. The new regimes realized that they had to consolidate and strengthen their position by designing and implementing stricter legal codes. Legalist ideas once again became valued, even though legalism as a political philosophy did not necessarily hold sway in daily governance. The wooden and bamboo documents from Zoumalou illustrate both continuities and changes in legal practices as China moved from the Han into the Three Kingdoms period. These legal case documents give us insight into the judicial process and the application of laws in more peripheral areas such as Changsha 長沙. At a higher social level, new conceptions of law were developed as well. Jen-der Lee's discussion of Liu Hui 劉輝 and the case of domestic violence against his wife, Princess Lanling 蘭陵, in the Northern Wei illustrates the different moral standards in the North after its invasion by nomadic peoples. In this age of disunity, there was little shared sense of familial ethics, especially among members of the upper class. Indeed, when those in the ruling elite perceived that their interests conflicted with Confucian ethics, they often worked to undermine them. At this time, the law had not yet fully acknowledged the principle of the husband's superiority over his wife.

In addition to these more traditional mechanisms, religion reemerged as a device that the state could use to represent and repackage its political image. In regard to organization and effectiveness, the multifaceted nature of religious ideas and practices in the Six Dynasties period gave the state flexible means of maintaining political order, building political authority, and delineating the identity of the ruling elite. Foreign religions not only supplied an attractive alternative to native traditions, but were crucial to the construction of ethnic identities. The patronage and protection that government officials of Gaochang 高昌, a small kingdom along the Silk Road, offered to Buddhist monasteries suggested that they were indicative of both religious faith and political theater. As Huaiyu Chen demonstrates in chapter 11, religious patronage had become one of the political rituals of the period.

Yang Lu

NOTES

1. Mark Edward Lewis, *China Between Empires: The Northern and Southern Dynasties* (Cambridge, Mass.: Belknap Press of Harvard University Press, 2009), 43.

2. Tang Zhangru 唐長孺, "Jiupin zhongzheng zhi shi shi" 九品中正制試釋, in *Wei Jin Nan-beichao shi luncong* 魏晉南北朝史論叢 (1955), in *Tang Zhangru wenji* 唐長孺文集 (Beijing: Zhonghua shuju, 2011), 1:81–121.

3. Liu Yi's petition is preserved in *JS* 45.1273–77.

4. For a valuable discussion of Xiahou Xuan's view of this issue, see Jing Shuhui 景蜀慧, "Cai xing tong yi li he yu Xianhou Xuan xuanju 'fenxu' zhiyi'" 才性同異離合與夏侯玄 '選舉分敘'之議, *Zhongshan daxue xuebao* 中山大學學報 (Shehui kexue ban 社會科學版) 43, no. 3 (2003): 64–70.

5. Managing Locality in Early Medieval China

Evidence from Changsha

YANG LU

Modern scholars agree that the richest and most reliable information about how the government of early imperial China operated at various levels comes from excavated documents written on bamboo and wooden slips. Spectacular finds in Juyan 居延, Zhangjiashan 張家山, and Yinwan 尹灣 shed much light on the scope and structure of the local Qin and Han administrations. Until two accidental discoveries in Changsha 長沙, however, historians knew very little about the local administration and society during the transitional period between the Eastern Han 東漢 (25–220) and the Three Kingdoms 三國 (220–280), during which political upheavals destroyed the existing order and made managing the local population a daunting task for the new regime.

DISCOVERIES

In July 1996, a large cache of bamboo baskets filled with bamboo and wooden slips was found in a well located near a street named Zoumalou 走馬樓 in the city of Changsha in Hunan 湖南 Province. The most recent estimate places the quantity at more than 140,000 strips. Although a few of the strips are documents composed as early as the twenty-fifth year of the Jian'an reign of the Eastern Han (220 C.E.), the majority are dated in the Jiahe era (232–238) of the Wu 吳 kingdom. Most are administrative records of Lingxiang District 臨湘縣, the seat of Changsha Commandery 長沙郡 while the area was under the occupation of the Wu kingdom.[1] After this discovery, archaeologists salvaged, from wells nearby, at least three more deposits of bamboo and wooden slips dating back to both the Western and Eastern Han. One such cache, found in 2004 near Dongpailou 東牌樓 Street, consists of 206 strips, for a total of 208 documents,[2] all of which are dated to the reign of the Eastern Han Emperor Ling 靈帝 (r. 168–189).[3] The reason that these documents were deposited in wells is not known. But given the precedence of using wells as trash dumps, both the Zoumalou and Dongpailou caches were most likely abandoned files.[4]

Despite the small quantity, the Dongpailou documents yield valuable information about the communication and judicial practices in the waning years of the Eastern Han. Unlike the Zoumalou documents, which were written on both bamboo and wooden strips, the Dongpailou documents were written only on wooden tablets and strips. These documents consist mostly of official and private correspondence delivered by the postal relay station (youting 郵亭) in Lingxiang District. The other documents are item descriptions (shimu 事目), household registries (huji 戶籍), name cards (mingci 名刺), contracts (juanshu 券書), certificates (qianpai 簽牌, literally "signboards"), miscellaneous inventories (zazhang 雜賬), calligraphic exercises in various scripts (xizijian 習字簡), and other, unidentifiable fragments. The writers of these documents were most likely low-level clerks serving in the local government.[5]

The Zoumalou documents offer a comprehensive picture of how the people in this strategic Middle Yangtze region lived. Among the slips are a great number of personal and governmental contracts, administrative reports, judicial records, household registries, and inventory records. The documents are written on five different materials: long wooden strips, shorter wooden strips, bamboo strips, wooden tablets, and signboards. So far, about 12,000 slips have been published, in four volumes. One volume is a transcription of 2,141 wooden strips called bie 莂; they are taxation records of the clerical and farming households (limin tianjia 吏民田家) in the fourth and fifth years (234 and 235 C.E.) of the Jiahe era. The other three volumes are transcriptions of more than 28,500 bamboo strips concerning taxation, registries, contracts, and other topics. The bie are among the most unusual and interesting finds. These are documents written on multiple wooden strips, each roughly 1.5 inches wide and 19 inches long.[6] They most likely are tax records containing detailed household information. Each bie document has two identical halves, one for the local tax collectors and the other for the district government's registries.[7]

MANAGING LOCAL SOCIETY IN THE
MIDDLE YANGZI REGION

Changsha had been one of the commanderies under the jurisdiction of Jing-zhou 荊州 region since the Eastern Han. The region had a mixed population of both ethnic Han migrants and aboriginal tribes and was contested by various forces following the dynasty's demise. Both the Liu Bei 劉備 and Sun Quan 孫權 regimes considered this area a launching pad for their dominance of the entire middle Yangzi region and a buffer zone for the protection of their political center. In 215, the Wu kingdom finally outmaneuvered its rival and took control of the region,[8] which remained part of the Wu territory until the Western Jin unified the South in 280. The Zoumalou documents thus reflect the continuity and change in Changsha's local administration during this socially and politically tumultuous period.

Changsha Commandery was sparsely populated, and its inhabitants engaged in hunting, gathering, and some agriculture. It was the Wu government that introduced large-scale land cultivation in order to fill the state's coffers and bring the population (especially the aboriginals known as Wuling Man 武陵蠻) under control. The Zoumalou documents indicate that the commandery had a great quantity of arable land, whose productivity rivaled that of the Central Plain.[9] They also reveal a strong military presence, as the military commissioners often were directly involved in collecting taxes.[10] Nevertheless, it is unclear who, the government or individual farmers, actually owned the land. The term appearing most frequently in the Zoumalou documents referring to cultivated land, *diantian* 佃田, is also the one most debated by scholars. Some argue that it refers to the "leased land" and that the farmers were government tenants. Others maintain that the term simply means "to cultivate," as it also was commonly used in Qin, Han, and other early medieval texts.[11]

As portrayed in the Zoumalou documents, the Wu government had a sophisticated system of managing both land and taxation. It carefully categorized different types of land for different tax rates. In addition to land taxes and head taxes (*kou qian* 口錢 and *suan qian* 算錢), which were standard in the Han dynasty, the Wu government also imposed a household tax (*zi suan* 訾算) and other special taxes. Currency was in wide circulation in the area and appears to have been used by the local people to pay their taxes, along with payments in cloth and other items. This suggests more commercial activities than scholars previously estimated.[12]

The Zoumalou documents also provide detailed information about the organization of the local government, the functions of different local agencies, the salaries of the different ranks of government officials, the tax and labor obligations of various social classes, and the management of storehouses. The basic settlement units for the local populace appear to have been the hill (*qiu* 丘) and the village (*li* 里), both under the supervision of the district (*xian* 縣), although the connection between *qiu* and *li* remains unclear at this point.[13] In turn, the district was overseen by the region (*zhou* 州). During peaceful times, commandery inspectors (*duyou* 督郵) served as the midlevel managers who reported to the regional governor (*zhoutaishou* 州太守) what they had learned from the clerks whom they dispatched to monitor justice and taxation. Because the Changsha area was considered a frontier commandery (*bianjun* 邊郡), the garrison forces stationed in the region also were involved in local management. For example, the Zoumalou documents tell us that garrison commanders would sometimes send in personnel to inspect the supplies for the military campaigns against the aboriginal Wuling tribes.

Despite the region's intermittent turmoil, the census reports and household registries are fairly detailed. The Wu government often categorized households based on professions, recording information such as the age and gender of each family member and the name and number of the household's slaves. The records of artisan households list the masters and apprentices.[14] These census reports were often compiled into a volume identified by the date and the name of the locale surveyed, followed by the statistics. These documents also reveal an important aspect of local administration: the existence of an enormous number of clerical households and the Wu government's exploitation of them.[15] As shown in the texts translated here and corroborated by accounts in the official histories, if one man served as a government clerk, then the rest of the adult males in his household also had to serve as government clerks. For example, in a case described in an directive issued in 258 c.e., the father and elder brothers served in the capital (*ducheng* 都城), and the other male members of the household were clerks in various regional governments.[16] This was a continuation of a practice that began in the Han dynasty. As two of the texts in this chapter show, the position of clerk came to be a hereditary profession that was passed from one generation to the next. The members of military and artisanal households also held hereditary, specialized positions.

EVIDENCE OF JUDICIAL PRACTICE

In addition to taxes and household registration, justice was essential to local governance. Modern scholars have little information about the Wu justice system and its relationship to the Han system. This is one area for which the Dongpailou and Zoumalou documents offer valuable insights. Although neither cache contains texts of legal codes like those discovered in Zhangjiashan, they do provide examples of legal cases describing local proceedings. Two such documents are translated here. The one from Dongpailou reports a legal case from the sixth year of the Guanghe era (183 c.e.), involving two villagers who sued each other, which reveals much about the laws pertaining to inheritance and the procedures of settlement outside the court. The other example is a report from Zoumalou on the investigation of a case of embezzlement during the Jiahe era. A local storage manager named Xu Di 許迪 misappropriated, for his own personal use, a huge quantity of rice from the government proceeds from the salt monopoly. When the rice was found to be missing from storage, Xu Di made a secret attempt to return what he took. But he was caught and, after repeated interrogation, confessed. The investigation involved authorities from all three levels of local government, from the regional governor, to the local inspectors, down to the district clerks.[17] These cases, although they took place decades apart and were very different, were handled by clerks reporting to the local inspector. These cases also show the continuation of the Han's local judicial and surveillance system based on local inspectors.

FURTHER READING

For a transcription of the Dongpailou and Zoumalou documents published so far, as well as information about the materials, see Changsha shi wenwu kaogu yanjiusuo 長沙市文物考古研究所 and Zhongguo wenwu chubanshe 中國文物出版社, eds., *Changsha Dongpailou Dong Han jiandu* 長沙東牌樓東漢簡牘 (Beijing: Wenwu chubanshe, 2006); Zoumalou Wujian zhengli zu 走馬樓吳簡整理組, ed., *Changsha Zoumalou Sanguo Wujian Jiahe limin tianjia bie* 長沙走馬樓三國吳簡・嘉禾吏民田家莂 (Beijing: Wenwu chubanshe, 1999); and Zoumalou jiandu zhengli zu, ed., *Changsha Zoumalou Sanguo Wujian・zhujian* 長沙走馬樓三國吳簡・竹簡, 3 vols. (Beijing: Wenwu chubanshe, 2003–2008).

EXCERPTS FROM EASTERN HAN DOCUMENTS FROM DONGPAILOU, CHANGSHA

Report on a Settlement over Disputed Land

I

On the day of *wuwu* 戊午 [i.e., the tenth day] in the month of *jiyou* 己酉 [i.e., the ninth month] of the sixth year of the Guanghe era [183 C.E.], the Inspector [*Jian* 監] of Linxiang, Li Yong 李永, and the Supervisor for Cases of Theft and Robbery [*Li du dao zei* 例督盜賊], Yin He 殷何, prostrate themselves, braving the death sentence to report the following:

II

The dispatch [*xi* 檄] of the Central Office of the Local Inspector [*Zhongbu duyou* 中部督郵] states:

A [commoner] male adult Li Jian 李建 filed a suit against male adults Jing Zhang 精張 and Jing Xi 精昔. He claimed that his mother Jing Zheng 精娃 acquired a piece of field [in which one could sow seeds weighing] 13 *dan*[18] three years ago, which generated a taxable income of no more than 102 small *dan* of grain stalks. The funeral for his maternal grandfather [Jing] Zong 宗 took place,

III

at the closing of which [Jing] Zhang and Xi forcibly seized [a portion of the field in which one could sow seeds weighing] 8 *dan*. When confronted, Zhang and Xi refused to return the land. The commoner [i.e., Li Jian] filed [for an injunction] himself, and his statement was certified. Why did Zhang [and Xi] seize [Li] Jian's land? When the application for an injunction arrived at the Office of the Inspector [*Jian bu* 監部], the clerks on duty detained Zhang and Xi, verified

IV

the location of the land [in question], and forwarded the clear-cut evidence to the appropriate authority for judgment according to the law. [Yin] He prostrated himself, braving the death sentence, [to report that] upon receiving the application for an injunction, [I] took the carriage way to the office at the post station of Chouzhong 仇重亭 to interrogate Zhang and Xi and called Jian's father [Li] Sheng 升 to give his testimony. All of them said:

V

Sheng is a native of Luo 羅. Zhang and Xi are natives of this county. Earlier, Sheng took as his wife [Jing] Zheng [i.e., the mother of Li Jian, the plaintiff] the daughter of [Jing] Zong, who was the full-blooded elder brother of [Jing] Zhang. She gave birth to a daughter named Ti 替, Ti's younger brother named Jian 建, Jian's younger brother named Yan 顏, and Yan's younger sister named Tiao 條.[19] [Jing] Xi was a younger brother of Zhang. Zong became ill and

VI

then died, and his corpse was laid out in the hall. Then Zheng also died. Zong had no son but left some property: a field of eight *dan*. Ti and Jian were still young then. Zhang, Sheng, and Xi provided for the funeral, upon whose completion Sheng returned to Luo, and Zhang and Xi personally cultivated and lived off Zong's

VII

field. I first confirmed that Zhang was the younger brother of Zong and that Jian was the male heir of Zheng; each had his own allotted land [*koufentian* 口分田]. Of the aforementioned land, [a portion the size of] two *dan* should be given to Zhang, and the remaining six *dan* to Jian. For what Zhang and Xi harvested this year

VIII

from Jian's six *dan*, the tax payment should be equally divided among Zhang, Jian, and Xi. Since they already have settled the dispute by themselves, there is no further need for investigation and mediation. [I] have exhausted my ability to verify [the claims]; if there are any new developments after the case is closed, [I] will continue my investigation and send another report. [Yin] He trembled in

IX

fear and prostrated himself, braving the death sentence to report [this].

X

The inspector of Linxiang, Li Yong, verified that the report submitted by the supervisor for cases of theft and robbery, Yin He, matches the written settlement of the land in dispute between the adult males Li Jian and Jing Zhang.

Submitted to

XI

the office

The twenty-sixth day of the ninth month, approved.[20]

[*Changsha Dongpailou Dong Han jiandu*, no. 5, 73–74]

Report from the Local Administration

The Acting Magistrate of Linxiang 臨湘守令, Chen Su 臣蕭?, respectfully reports: The region of Jinnan 荆南 is frequently under the assault of local bandits. As a result, the local residents have ceased paying their legally required tributes and taxes and are hoping that they will receive an act of grace to be exempted from their annual taxes. Because of the years with no [tax] payments, the granaries are empty of rice, and warehouses are empty of cash and cloth. But the village clerks who are responsible for collecting the taxes are still making an effort [to collect the taxes]. Therefore, if there is an act of grace, a [tax] exemption should not be included. In addition, garrisons stationed in Zhaoling 昭陵 and Liandao 連道[21] encountered unexpected disturbances. Consequently, the clerks on duty returned to their homes and are not willing to respond to our calls. Moreover, they stored their crossbows and abandoned their arrows. [This situation deeply concerns me.][22]

[*Changsha Dongpailou Dong Han jiandu*, no. 12, 77–78]

ADMINISTRATIVE DOCUMENTS OF THE KINGDOM OF WU FROM ZOUMALOU, CHANGSHA

Household Register

Yin Lian 殷連, Promoter of Agriculture [*Quannongyuan* 勸農掾] in Dongxiang township 東鄉, following the instruction [sent by his superior], compiled a register listing the names and ages of the male adults of the clerical households in the township. [Here is the result of the investigation]: Within the boundary of the township, there are three clerical households, among which two male members, a father and a son, both with crippled feet,[23] fled to another place. Other members of these households volunteered to carry out their duties. The ages of all the members have been truthfully recorded and verified. There should be nothing amiss. In the future, if another official discovers any fraudulent claims, Lian will accept responsibility and receive a penalty. On the fourth year of the Jiahe era, the twenty-sixth day of the eighth month, [Yin Lian] split the register and kept part of it as a record.

[*Changsha Zoumalou Sanguo Wujian Jiahe limin tianjia bie*, 32]

Qu Guang 區光, Promoter of Agriculture in Guangcheng township 廣成鄉, following the instruction [sent by his superior], compiled a register listing the names and ages of the male adults of the clerical households in the township.

[Here is the result of the investigation]: Within the boundary of the township, there are seven clerical households, and the total number of male members [fathers, sons, etc.] of these households is twenty-three. Among them, four have a physical deformity such as crippled feet or deafness; one has died of illness; four others have either run away or have followed their household masters to serve in clerical offices; twelve are minors; one is farming on exempted land; and one has already begun to serve as a county clerk. I have verified their names and ages. There should be nothing amiss. In the future, if another official discovers any fraudulent claims, Guang will accept responsibility and receive a penalty. In the fourth year of the Jiahe era, on the twenty-sixth day of the eighth month, [Qu Guang] split the register and kept part of it as a record.

> [*Changsha Zoumalou Sanguo Wujian Jiahe limin tianjia bie*, 32]

In the jurisdiction of Wuchang 吳昌 County, the number of artisans is fourteen; the number of their family members is thirty-seven; [and] the total number of people [in this category] is fifty-one.

> [*Changsha Zoumalou Sanguo Wujian, zhujian*, vol. 1, 1017]

In the jurisdiction of Liuyang 劉陽 County, the number of artisans is twelve; the number of their family members is twenty-nine; [and] the total number of people [in this category] is forty-one.

> [*Changsha Zoumalou Sanguo Wujian, zhujian*, vol. 1, 1033]

Taxation Record

Huang Zheng 黃政, a male from Shangsu Village, farms nine *ting* 町 of land, totaling twenty-five *mou*,[24] seventeen of which are land with a two-year fixed tax rate. Among them, thirteen *mou* are considered "drought" land [*hantian* 旱田] so no tax in cloth is required; the tax assessed for eight *mou* of reclaimed land [*yulitian* 餘力田] is three *hu* and two *dou* of rice; [and] the tax assessed for the five *mou* of fixed-rate land is six *hu* of rice. The total grain tax is nine *hu* and two *dou*. In addition, each *mou* is taxed at two *chi* of cloth. The tax of nine *hu* and two *dou* of rice was collected by granary clerks Zhang Man 張曼 and Zhou Dong 周棟 on the tenth day of the eleventh month of the fifth year of [the Jiahe reign]. The total cloth tax is two *zhang* and six *chi*. This tax, which was converted into one *hu* and seven *dou* of rice, was collected by warehouse clerk Pan Lü 潘慮 on the ninth day [or the tenth day] of the first month of the sixth year of the [Jiahe era].[25] The "drought" land was not charged a cash tax. The mature land was charged 80 cash for each *mou*. The total cash tax of 1,030 cash was collected by warehouse clerk Fan Shen 潘慎 on the twentieth day of the first month of the sixth year of the [Jiahe reign]. On the twentieth day of the second month of the sixth year of the Jiahe era, Zhang Ti 張惕, a clerk from the Department of Farming Households [*Tianhu cao* 田戶曹], verified this.

> [*Changsha Zoumalou Sanguo Wujian Jiahe limin tianjia bie*, no. 5.92, 176]

Judicial Record

I

Recording Administrator [*Lushiyuan* 錄事掾] Pan Wan 潘琬 prostrates himself fearfully and reports: In the fourth year of the [Jiahe era], the seventh day, [and the] eleventh month, after receiving an order from the commandery inspector to investigate Clerk Xu Di 許迪, Wan, along with Verification Clerk [*Heshili* 核事吏] Zhao Tan 趙譚,

II

Population-Control Administrator [*Budianyuan* 部典掾] Zhen Ruo 烝若, and Scribal Clerk [*Zhuzheshi* 主者史] Li Zhu 李珠 thoroughly interrogated Xu Di. Here is his confession: Xu Di sold salt from the official warehouse in the amount of 426 *hu*, 1 *dou*, 9 *sheng*, 8 *he*, and 4 *shao*.

III

In exchange, Di received rice in the amount of 2,561 *hu*, 6 *dou*, and 9 *sheng*. Di transferred 2,449 *hu* and 1 *sheng* to granary clerks Deng Long 鄧隆 and Gu Rong 穀榮. Di

IV

took possession of the remaining 112 *hu*, 6 *dou*, and 8 *sheng* of rice with the intention of consuming it later. This plot was discovered by granary clerk Liao 廖, who was on duty. Therefore, Di secretly returned to the local granary the amount of rice he had taken, which was collected by granary clerk Huang Ying 黃瑛.

V

[Realizing that once] the accounting records were presented to the commandery defender [supervising military provisions], Di would be charged with serious crimes, he repeatedly claimed that he had not taken the rice. After repeated interrogation, Di finally confessed that he had stolen the rice. Throughout his detention and interrogation,

VI

we never used the five methods of torture [to seek his confession]. Based on [the evidence], Di admitted to the crime. So we did not convict him wrongly. I beg the county office to report this crime again to the higher authority. I attach here the explanation and respectfully send the report. Wan again fearfully

VII

prostrates himself.

VIII

Approved. On the twenty-ninth day, the day of Wuxu 戊戌, second month.

[*Changsha Zoumalou Sanguo Wujian Jiahe limin tianjia bie*, 34]

NOTES

1. For the initial reports on the discovery, see Changsha shi wenwu gongzuodui 長沙市文物工作隊 and Changsha shi wenwu kaogu yanjiusuo 長沙市文物考古研究所, eds., "Changsha Zoumalou J22 fajue jianbao" 長沙走馬樓 J22 發掘簡報, *Wenwu* 5 (1999): 4–25; and "Changsha Zoumalou ershier hao jing fajue baogao" 長沙走馬樓二十二號井發掘報告, in *Changsha Zoumalou Sanguo Wujian limin tianjia bie* 長沙走馬樓三國吳簡· 吏民田家莂, ed. Zoumalou jiandu zhenglizu 走馬樓簡牘整理組 (Beijing: Wenwu chubanshe, 1999), 1:30–35. For an overview of the study of the Zoumalou documents, see Wang Su 王素, "Changsha Zoumalou Sanguo Wujian yanjiu de huigu yu zhanwang" 長沙走馬樓三國吳簡研究的回顧與展望, in *Wujian yanjiu* 吳簡研究, no. 1 (Beijing: Chongwen shuju, 2003), 1–39.

2. For the initial report on the discovery, see Changsha shi wenwu kaogu yanjiusuo 長沙市文物考古研究所, ed., "Changsha Dongpailou qi hao gujing (J7) fajue jianbao" 長沙東牌樓 7號古井 (J7) 發掘簡報, *Wenwu* 12 (2005): 13. Of the 206 wooden strips with scripts, 2 strips belong to one document, and 3 strips have two different documents on each side, so the total number of documents adds up to 208. For details, see Wang Su 王素, "Changsha Dongpailou Dong-Han jiandu gaishu" 長沙東牌樓東漢簡牘概述, in *Changsha Dongpailou Dong-Han jiandu* 長沙東牌樓東漢簡牘 (Beijing: Wenwu chubanshe, 2006), 73.

3. For the dates of the Dongpailou documents, see Wang Su, "Changsha Dongpailou Dong-Han jiandu gaishu," 69–70.

4. In 2002, a large quantity of bamboo slips were found in a well in Liye 里耶, west of Hunan Province, most of which are administrative documents of the Qin dynasty. See Pian Yujian 駢宇騫 and Duan Shu'an 段書安, *Ershi shiji chutu jianbo zongshu* 二十世紀出

土簡帛綜述 (Beijing: Wenwu chubanshe, 2006), 478–79. Scholars generally agree that these Qin strips were abandoned governmental archives. See Hsing I-tien 邢義田, "Cong chutu ziliao kan Qin Han juluo xingtai he xiangli xingzheng" 從出土資料看秦漢聚落形態和鄉里行政, in *Zhongguo shi xinlun: Jiceng shehui fence* 中國史新論: 基層社會分冊, ed. Huang Kuan-chong 黃寬重 (Taibei: Academia Sinica, 2009), 60–61.

5. Wang Su, "Changsha Dongpailou Dong-Han jiandu gaishu," 73–74.

6. Song Shaohua 宋少華, "Changsha Sanguo Wujian baohu zhengli yu yanjiu de xin jinzhan" 長沙三國吳簡保護整理與研究的新進展, in *Changsha Sanguo Wujian ji bainian lai jianbo faxian yu yanjiu guoji xueshu yantaohui lunwenji* 長沙三國吳簡暨百年來簡帛發現與研究國際學術研討會論文集, ed. Changsha shi wenwu kaogu yanjiusuo (Beijing: Zhonghua shuju, 2005), 9–10.

7. For a general discussion of the *bie* of clerical and farming households in the fourth and fifth years of the Jiahe reign, see Hu Pingsheng 胡平生, "Jiahe si nian limin tianjia bie yanjiu" 嘉禾四年吏民田家莂研究, in *Changsha Sanguo Wujian ji bainian lai jianbo faxian yu yanjiu guoji xueshu yantaohui lunwenji*, 34–50.

8. For a study of the aboriginal population of the Changsha region during the Three Kingdoms period, see Wei Bin 魏斌, "Wujian shixing: Zaoqi Changsha bianhu yu zuqun wenti" 吳簡釋姓: 早期長沙編戶與族群問題, *Wei Jin Nanbeichao Sui Tang shi ziliao* 魏晉南北朝隋唐史資料 24 (2008): 23–45.

9. Gao Min 高敏, "Cong *Jiahe limin tianjiabie* kan Changsha jun yidai de minqing fengsu yu shehui jingji zhuangkuang" 從《嘉禾吏民田家莂》看長沙郡一帶的民情風俗與社會經濟狀況, in *Changsha Zoumalou jiandu yanjiu* 長沙走馬樓簡牘研究 (Guilin: Guangxi shifan daxue chubanshe, 2008), 41–43.

10. For an informative account on this issue, see He Dezhang 何德章, *Zhongguo jingji tongshi* 中國經濟通史 (Changsha: Hunan renmin chubanshe, 2002), 3:302–6.

11. Hou Xudong 侯旭東, "Zoumalou zhujian de xianmi yu tianmu jilu" 走馬樓竹簡的限米與田畝記錄, *Wujian yanjiu* 2 (2006): 164. I concur with his observation and would like to add that the term appearing in Qin and Han texts that is closer to the later meaning of "lease" is perhaps *dai* 貸.

12. Gao Min, "Cong Changsha Zoumalou Sanguo Wujian kan Sun Quan shiqi de shangpin jingji zhuangkuang" 從長沙走馬樓三國吳簡看孫權時期的商品經濟狀況, in *Changsha Zoumalou jiandu yanjiu*, 117–30.

13. The difference between *qiu* and *li* as they are used in the Zoumalou documents has been the center of many academic discussions. For more information about these opinions, see Hou Xudong 侯旭東, "Changsha Zoumalou Wu jian 'li' 'qiu' guanxi zai yanjiu" 長沙走馬樓吳簡'里''丘'關係再研究, *Wei Jin Nanbeichao Sui Tang ziliao* 23 (2006): 4–26.

14. For a study of the artisan household, see Han Shufeng 韓樹峰, "Changsha Zoumalou Sanguo Wujian suojian shizuo kao" 長沙走馬樓三國吳簡所見師佐考, *Wujian yanjiu* 1 (2004): 167–89.

15. Since the publication of the Zoumalou documents, scholars have been focusing on the issue of the clerical household and have offered different opinions about it. For a concise discussion of the development of the clerical household in the Wu kingdom, see Gao Min, "Cong *Jiahe limin tianjiabie* zhong de 'zhu li' zhuangkuang kan liyi zhi de

xingcheng yu yanbian" 從《嘉禾吏民田家莂》中的'諸吏'狀況看吏役制的形成與演變, in *Changsha Zoumalou jiandu yanjiu*, 44–53. On the issue of labor services of clerical households under the Sun regime, see Meng Yanhong 孟彥弘, "Wujian suojian de 'zidi' yu Sun Wu de lihu zhi—jian lun Wei Jin de yi hu wei yi zhi zhi" 吳簡所見的'子弟'與孫吳的吏戶制—兼論魏晉的以戶爲役之制, *Wei Jin Nan Bei chao Sui Tang shi ziliao* 23 (2008): 1–22.

16. *SGZ* 5.1105.

17. For a study of this document, see Wang Su 王素, "Changsha Zoumalou Sanguo Sun Wu jiandu san wenshu xintan" 長沙走馬樓三國孫吳簡牘三文書新探, *Wenwu* 9 (1999): 43–50.

18. The character used for measurement here is *dan* 石. It means that the land can be sown with up to a weight of thirteen *dan* of seeds.

19. In short, the plaintiff was a maternal nephew of the defendants.

20. For the translation of this document, I consulted Ye Yuying 葉玉英, "Dong Han jiandu *He cong shu* suo jian Dong-Han ruogan zhidu tansuo" 東漢簡牘《和從書》所見東漢若干制度探索, *Journal of Xiamen University (Art & Sciences)* 6 (2009): 100–105, 112.

21. Both Zhaoling and Liandao are counties under the jurisdiction of Changsha Commendary. See Wang Su 王素, "Changsha Dongpailou Dong-Han jiandu xuanshi" 長沙東牌樓東漢簡牘選釋, *Wenwu* 12 (2005): 71.

22. The slips containing this document that survived do not have a date.

23. The characters for "crippled feet" are *xing zhong* 刑踵. On other occasions, they are called as *zhong zu* 踵足. This physical deformity is mentioned frequently in the Zoumalou documents, and some scholars suggest that it may have resulted from self-inflicted injury in order to avoid working. But this suggestion is not persuasive because the Zoumalou records also show that young children are often listed as having this deformity. A more plausible explanation is that this was simply a way to describe a deformity, whether it was self-inflicted or the result of natural causes.

24. "Farms nine *ting* of land" is the translation of 佃田九町.

25. The original strip has both the ninth day and the tenth day in this line; thus one of them must be an error made by the scribe.

6. Classical Scholarship in the Shu Region

The Case of Qiao Zhou

J. MICHAEL FARMER

S hu 蜀, a geographic and administrative designation for the region occupying much of present-day Sichuan Province and the surrounding areas, was for a long time part of early Chinese polity, but in many ways it maintained its own distinctive intellectual and cultural traditions. Early bronze inscriptions indicate the participation of a state called "Shu" in the Zhou 周 conquest of Yin 殷 in the twelfth century B.C.E., and Shu remained an established part of the Zhou feudal state until its defeat by Qin 秦 in 316 B.C.E. Under Qin rule, Shu was accorded the administrative status of a commandery, a designation that continued to be used throughout the Han 漢. Following the collapse of the Han dynasty in 220 C.E., Shu and its major city of Chengdu 成都 became the capital of, under Liu Bei 劉備 (161–223), the independent state of Han 漢 (better known by its informal name of Shu or Shu-Han 蜀漢).[1] Shu was brought back into the fold in 264 and became a constituent part of the newly established Jin 晉 dynasty in 265.

Throughout the five hundred–year period spanning roughly 200 B.C.E. to 300 C.E., several unique intellectual traditions emerged from Shu. During the Western Han period, several men of Shu gained a reputation at the Han court for their ability to compose rhapsodies (*fu* 賦), poetic works that employed exhaustive descriptions of things, often to impart a moral message. The literary talents of Sima Xiangru 司馬相如 (179–117 B.C.E.), Wang Bao 王褒 (d. ca. 61

B.C.E.), and Yang Xiong 揚雄 (53 B.C.E.–23 C.E.) came to exemplify the region's intellectual activity during the Western Han. In the middle of the Han period, a new current of thought sprang from Shu. Zhuang Zun 莊遵 (also known as Yan Junping 嚴君平), a reclusive scholar from Chengdu, compiled commentaries to and taught the texts of the early Daoist tradition, the *Laozi* 老子 and the *Zhuangzi* 莊子. Zhuang's commentaries were eclectic, combining early Daoist mysticism with Confucian ethics and pragmatism. His main disciple, Yang Xiong, stopped writing rhapsodies and followed Zhuang Zun down the path of syncretic scholarship. Yang Xiong's main contribution to the intellectual world of mid–Han Shu was his opus *The Supreme Mystery* (*Taixuan* 太玄), a work based on the hexagrams of the *Classic of Changes* (*Yijing* 易經). This work attempted to articulate a cosmic order by combining elements from both the Daoist and the Confucian traditions. Later, scholars of the third century C.E. promoted *The Supreme Mystery* and established a new wave of thought in north China known as "mysterious learning" (*xuanxue* 玄學).

During the Eastern Han, another intellectual tradition gained popularity in Shu and beyond. Mantic artists (*fangshi* 方士) of the region practiced various methods of divination and prophecy, often linking matters of the natural world to those of the political. One outgrowth of this tradition of the mantic arts in Shu was the establishment of Daoism as an organized, communal religion in the second century C.E. Zhang Ling 張陵, a mantic artist from north of Chengdu, received a visit from the deified Daoist sage Laozi, who issued a code of communal governance and commanded Zhang Ling to establish a community of believers who would survive the coming apocalypse and become the "seed people" of a new age of peace and harmony. The activities of another branch of the Shu mantic arts tradition headed by members of the Yang 楊 clan of Guanghan 廣漢 Commandery came to typify the scholarly world of Shu during the Eastern Han and Three Kingdoms periods. Key among the practices of the Yang lineage was prophecy by means of celestial observation (astrology) and prophetic wordplay. These prophecies were generally related to immediate political matters, and leaders at both the imperial court and local government offices regularly consulted with the mantic artists, though owing to the obviously dangerous nature of offering advice on matters of state, many of them refused to become involved with politics and instead lived in reclusion.

Qiao Zhou 譙周 (ca. 200–270), the author of the documents translated in this chapter, was the final heir to the mantic traditions of the Yang family and the originator of a new critical approach to the Confucian canon and history. Qiao Zhou was born in the eastern part of present-day Sichuan Province around 200 C.E. The traditional biography of Qiao Zhou reports that his father, a noted scholar of the canon and history, died while Qiao Zhou was still young, and as a result, he grew up in relative poverty. Nonetheless, Qiao Zhou dedicated himself to learning and sought training from two highly regarded scholars of Shu: Du Qiong 杜瓊 and Qin Mi 秦密. From Du Qiong, himself a member of the

Yang family's intellectual lineage, Qiao Zhou learned the methods of celestial observation and prophecy based on decoding cryptic speech, both of which were hallmarks of the long-standing Shu intellectual tradition. With Qin Mi, Qiao Zhou studied canonical texts and history and expanded on his teacher's critical view of the past. In 223, Qiao Zhou was appointed to a post at the newly established Shu-Han imperial academy in Chengdu. For the next three decades he served as an educator at the academy and later as an unofficial tutor to the heir apparent of the state of Shu-Han. In 257/258, he became involved in court debates over military policy and, as a result, was promoted to high office. Six years later, when the invading armies of Wei approached the capital, Qiao Zhou advised his ruler to surrender and spare the lives of the imperial family and the citizens of Shu-Han. The emperor heeded his advice, and much bloodshed was averted. In the winter of 270, Qiao Zhou died at his home.

Sadly, most of Qiao Zhou's writings have been lost, and only a handful of fragments remain from what once were lengthy works. Consequently, the documents translated here lack the cohesion of integral works, but they are sufficient to illustrate the breadth of Qiao Zhou's scholarship and, by extension, the range of intellectual activity in early medieval Shu.

The first group of documents, collected under the heading "Prophecies," contains three selections from Qiao Zhou's prophetic works. One addresses the impending fall of Qiao's state of Shu-Han, in which Qiao employs the method of decoding a form of cryptic and prophetic speech known as "inconsistent words" to predict the fall of the state. The method of "inconsistent words" entails identifying unintended double meanings in common sayings. These double meanings were thought to be one way in which Heaven's will was communicated to man. The second prophecy predicts the death of King Wen of Jin, Sima Zhao 司馬昭 (265 C.E.). This prophecy was based on celestial observation and wordplay. In the final prophecy presented here, Qiao Zhou correctly foretells the end of his lineage, although the manner in which this prophecy was determined remains a mystery.

The second selection, "Discourse on Enemy States" (*Chouguo lun* 仇國論), is a literary account of a debate held at the Shu-Han court in the year 257 or 258 between Qiao Zhou and a high-ranking official named Chen Zhi 陳祇 (d. 258). In it, the two officials debate the merits and weaknesses of a proposal to mount an offensive military campaign in the north against the rival state of Wei. Qiao Zhou, as the allegorical interlocutor Mr. Falling-Down Fool, opposes such a campaign, whereas Chen Zhi, represented as Mr. Lofty-Worthy Minister, argues in favor of it. Both parties use appeals to historical precedence to make their cases. The essay itself was written in the literary form of "hypothetical discourse" (*shelun* 設論), with Chen Zhi's questions presented in straightforward prose and Qiao Zhou's replies offered in elegant rhymed verse. Qiao Zhou's biography notes that he was not skilled in public speaking or debate, and so this polished account of the debate may well be more what Qiao Zhou wished he had said than an actual transcript of the historical debate itself. It is useful to compare Qiao's argument with the "Memorial on Deploying the Army" (*Chushi biao* 出師表) by the former chancellor of Shu-Han, Zhuge Liang 諸葛亮, which had been submitted to the throne in 227, thirty years earlier.[2]

The third group of documents, under the heading "Exegesis on Ritual," comes from a collection of critical commentaries on the Confucian canon. The largest work, *Discourse on Truths and Falsehoods in the Five Canonical Texts* (*Wujing ranfou lun* 五經然否論), appears to have been a collection of essays addressing topics contained in the five Confucian Classics. Only Qiao's comments on various aspects of ritual have survived, with many collected in the Tang dynasty's institutional compendium *Comprehensive History of Institutions* (*Tongdian* 通典).[3] In these passages, Qiao Zhou takes issue with the finer points of detail regarding several important ritual practices. In the first selection, he addresses the problem of the chronological age of King Cheng of Zhou 周成王 when he was "capped," the traditional rite of passage from childhood to adulthood. Qiao bases his explanation on the reading of one canonical text against another, indicative of his critical approach to both the canon and history. The second selection discusses the proper age of marriage for young men and women at various levels of society. Again, Qiao argues both for and against individual passages from the canon. The third selection presents the canonical views on mourning attire, reflecting the opinion of the leading commentator of the late Han, Zheng Xuan 鄭玄, as well as Qiao Zhou's own views on the topic. The final selection is a long discussion of the protocol for paying condolences after the death of an individual. Although today's readers may find the details presented in this selection as odd, the proper performance of these rituals was of great concern to people in early medieval China. Indeed, given the rather vague and often contradictory accounts found in the canonical texts, the views of exegetes like Zheng Xuan and Qiao Zhou were viewed as necessary for understanding proper conduct under diverse circumstances.

Qiao Zhou's best-known work is *Investigations of Ancient History* (*Gushi kao* 古史考). This history has long been considered one of the earliest commentaries on the *Records of the Historian* (*Shi ji* 史記) by Sima Qian 司馬遷 (ca. 145–ca. 86 B.C.E.), but a careful analysis of the surviving text (about one hundred passages) suggests that the *Investigations of Ancient History* was intended as a much larger critique of efforts to chronicle China's ancient past. In the work, Qiao Zhou "corrected" errors of nomenclature, chronology, and interpretation in not only Sima Qian's history but also in several other early Chinese histories. The basis for Qiao's "corrections" was typically the historical texts from the Confucian canon, in particular, the *Classic of Documents* (*Shangshu* 尚書) and *Zuo Tradition on the Spring and Autumn Annals* (*Zuozhuan* 左傳). But in the spirit of honest criticism, Qiao also took issue with some of the facts and interpretations of the canonical histories. In this sense, he seems to have been concerned with presenting an accurate picture of the past and did not slavishly follow the opinions of his sources or brutally criticize the earlier histories just for the sake of argument. Qiao's *Investigations of Ancient History* has been deemed the earliest work of Chinese historical criticism and was widely cited by scholars through the Tang dynasty. The selections translated are a collection of comments regarding legendary culture bearers and their influence on Chinese culture, brief stories of famous worthies, and a direct assessment of Sima Qian himself.

FURTHER READING

For a general overview of the intellectual traditions of early Shu, see Jia Shunxian 賈順先 and Dai Dalu 戴大祿, eds., *Sichuan sixiang jia* 四川思想家 (Chengdu: Ba-Shu chubanshe, 1987); and Michael Nylan, "Afterword: The Legacies of the Chengdu Plain," in *Ancient Sichuan: Treasures from a Lost Civilization*, ed. Robert Bagley (Seattle: Seattle Art Museum, 2001). For more detailed studies of the intellectual activity during the Western Han, see Aat Vervoorn, "Zhuang Zun: A Daoist Philosopher of the Late First Century B.C.," *Monumenta Serica* 38 (1988/1989): 69–94; and Michael Nylan and Nathan Sivin, "The First Neo-Confucian: An Introduction to Yang Hsiung's '*Canon of Supreme Mystery*' (*T'ai hsuan ching*, c. 4 B.C.)," in *Chinese Ideas About Nature and Society: Studies in Honour of Derk Bodde*, ed. Charles Le Blanc and Susan Blader (Hong Kong: Hong Kong University Press, 1987). The intellectual traditions of Shu during the Eastern Han are treated in Cheng Yuanmin 程元敏, "Dong Han Shu Yang Hou jingwei xue zongchuan" 東漢蜀楊厚經緯學宗傳, *Guoli bianyiguan guankan* 國立編譯館館刊 17, no. 1 (1988): 31–48, and 17, no. 2 (1988): 19–39; and Yoshikawa Tadao 吉川忠夫, "Shuku ni okeru shin'i no gaku no dentō" 蜀における讖緯の學の傳統, in *Shin'i shisō no sōgōteki kenkyū* 讖緯思想の綜合的研究, ed. Yasui Kōzan 安居香山 (Tokyo: Kokusho kankōkai, 1984). These studies of the intellectual activity in Shu can be contrasted with the following works, which discuss the intellectual traditions in northern China during the late Han and Three Kingdoms periods: Étienne Balazs, "Political Philosophy and Social Crisis at the End of the Han Dynasty," and "Nihilistic Revolt or Mystical Escapism: Currents of Thought in China During the Third Century," both in *Chinese Civilization and Bureaucracy: Variations on a Theme*, trans. H. M. Wright (New Haven, Conn.: Yale University Press, 1964). For an introduction to *xuanxue* (mysterious learning), see Yu Yingshi, "Individualism and the Neo-Taoist Movement in Wei-Chin China," in *Individualism and Holism: Studies in Confucian and Taoist Values*, ed. Donald J. Munro (Ann Arbor: Center for Chinese Studies, University of Michigan, 1985). See also the three-volume study of the famous *xuanxue* scholar Wang Bi 王弼: Rudolph G. Wagner, *The Craft of a Chinese Commentator: Wang Bi on the Laozi* (Albany: State University of New York Press, 2000); *Language, Ontology, and Political Philosophy in China: Wang Bi's Scholarly*

Exploration of the Dark (Xuanxue) (Albany: State University of New York Press, 2003); and *A Chinese Reading of the Daodejing: Wang Bi's Commentary on the Laozi with Critical Text and Translation* (Albany: State University of New York Press, 2003). For an overview of the mantic and prophetic traditions of early medieval China, see Wolfram Eberhard, "The Political Function of Astronomy and Astronomers in Han China," in *Chinese Thought and Institutions*, ed. John K. Fairbank (Chicago: University of Chicago Press, 1957); Kenneth J. DeWoskin, trans., *Doctors, Diviners, and Magicians of Ancient China: Biographies of Fang-shih* (New York: Columbia University Press, 1983); C. Y. Hsu, "The Activities and Influences of Fang-shih," *Asian Culture* 19, no. 2 (1991): 59–86; and Lu Zongli, *Power of the Words: Chen Prophecy in Chinese Politics, A.D. 265–618* (Bern: Peter Lang, 2003). For studies of exegesis of canonical and historical texts in early and medieval China, see John Henderson, *Scripture, Canon, and Commentary: A Comparison of Confucian and Western Exegesis* (Princeton, N.J.: Princeton University Press, 1991); Daniel K. Gardner, "Confucian Commentary and Chinese Intellectual History," *Journal of Asian Studies* 57, no. 2 (1998): 397–422; and Lu Yaodong 逯耀東, *Wei Jin shixue de sixiang yu shehui jichu* 魏晉史學的思想與社會基礎 (Taibei: Dongda tushu, 2000). For a detailed study of Qiao Zhou's life and intellectual activity, see J. Michael Farmer, *The Talent of Shu: Qiao Zhou and the Intellectual World of Early Medieval Sichuan* (Albany: State University of New York Press, 2007). Complete translations of Qiao Zhou's extant writings can be found in J. Michael Farmer, "The World of the Mind in Early Medieval Sichuan" (Ph.D. diss., University of Wisconsin–Madison, 2001). Additional, brief studies of Qiao Zhou can be found in Long Xianzhao 龍顯昭, "Qiao Zhou" 譙周, in *Sichuan sixiang jia* 四川思想家, ed. Jia Shunxian 賈順先 and Dai Dalu 戴大祿 (Chengdu: Ba-Shu chubanshe, 1987); and Yang Puwei 洋卜為, "Kouwen Qiao Zhou" 叩問譙周, *Sanguo zhi shuyuan yuankan* 三國志書院院刊 (2000): 47.

Prophecies

1. REGARDING THE FALL OF SHU

The [*Zuo*] *Tradition on the Spring and Autumn* [*Zuozhuan* 左傳] says that Duke Mu 穆 of Jin 晉 named the crown prince Chou 仇 [Enemy] and his younger brother Chengshi 成師 [Becoming a General]. Shi Fu 師服 said, "These are indeed peculiar names you have given your sons! A good spouse is called a principal wife [*fei* 妃], [and] a complaining spouse is called an enemy [*chou* 仇]. Now you name the crown prince Chou and his younger brother Chengshi. This is the beginning of disorder, and I fear that [the younger brother] will replace [the crown prince]!" Afterward, it turned out just as [Shi] Fu had said.⁴

Emperor Ling 靈 of Han 漢 named his two sons "Marquis Shi" 史侯 and "Marquis Dong" 董侯. [Both] were established as emperors, and both were dispensed with and made marquises, similar to what Shi Fu had said.[5]

The taboo name of the former sovereign [Liu Bei 劉備] taboo name was Bei 備, meaning "complete." The taboo name of the later sovereign [Liu Shan] is Shan 禪, meaning "to give away." It is like saying that the Lius have already completed [their rule] and are [ready] to give it to others. The significance of this is really like the naming of the sons of Duke Mu and Emperor Ling.

[SGZ 42.1022; JS 28.834; SS 31.899]

2. REGARDING THE DEATH OF SIMA ZHAO 司馬昭 (265 C.E.)

In the summer of the second year of the Xianxi 咸熙 period [265], Wen Li 文立[6] [d. 280] of Ba 巴 Commandery returned to Shu from Luoyang and called on [Qiao] Zhou. While [Qiao] Zhou was speaking, he wrote on a tablet. [When Qiao showed] it to [Wen] Li, it said,

"*Dianwu* unexpectedly in *yueyou* will die" [典午忽兮, 月酉沒兮].

Dianwu refers to Sima. *Yueyou* refers to the eighth month. In the eighth month, King Wen will pass away.[7]

[SGZ 42.1032]

3. REGARDING THE END OF QIAO ZHOU'S LINEAGE

When Qiao Zhou was nearing death [270 C.E.], he instructed his sons, saying, "One of my descendants will have blonde hair and black teeth. My lineage will end with him." When Qiao Zhou's grandson Zong 縱 was born, his hair was blonde and his teeth were black. At the end of the Jin, Inspector Mao Qu 毛璩 placed Qiao Zong in command of seven hundred men from Baitu 白徒 and sent them from the Fu 涪 River to punish Huan Xuan 桓玄. The men from the west were not pleased about marching such a distance, so they forced Qiao Zong to be their leader and attacked Baxi 巴西, slaughtering [the people of] Yi 益 Province and killing Mao Qu. [Qiao Zong] proclaimed himself the King of Chengdu. In Yixi 義熙 9 [414 C.E.], Zhu Lingshi 朱齡石[8] attacked and pacified the area. [Qiao Zong] died as [Qiao] Zhou had said [he would].[9]

[*Yuanhe junguo zhi* 33.849; *Sanguo zhi jijie* 42.23b–24a]

DISCOURSE ON ENEMY STATES

At this time, troops were sent out many times. The people were weighed down with distress. Qiao Zhou and the prefect of the masters of writing, Chen Zhi 陳祗,[10] discoursed on the merits and demerits [of these campaigns]. Returning to his home, he wrote this, calling it "Discourse on Enemy States." It reads:

The Vestigial State [Shu] is small, while the Newly Founded State [Wei] is large. They fought for [control of] the world and became enemies. The Vestigial State had one Mr. Lofty-Worthy Minister [Chen Zhi] who asked Mr. Falling-Down Fool [Qiao Zhou], saying,

> Now the affairs of state are unstable. From top to bottom, minds are troubled. In the past, the weak were able to overcome the strong. By what art was this accomplished?

Mr. Falling-Down Fool replied,

I have heard of this.	吾聞之
When a state is large and has no worries, it frequently becomes very indolent.	處大無患者恆多慢
When a state is small and has worries, it frequently ponders ways to make things good.	處小有憂者恆思善
Great indolence results in chaos.	多慢則生亂
Pondering ways to make things good results in order	思善則生治
This is a constant principle.	理之常也
For this reason, King Wen [of Zhou 周] nourished the people and, by means of a few, took many.	故周文養民，以少取多
Gou Jian [of Yue 越] had sympathy for the masses and, by means of the weak, killed the strong.	勾踐卹眾，以弱斃彊
This is the art.	此其術也

Mr. Lofty-Worthy Minister said,

> Previously, Xiang [Yu] 項羽 was strong, and Han [Liu Bang 劉邦] was weak. They fought each other without a day of rest. As a result, Xiang Yu and Han agreed on Honggou 鴻溝 as a boundary, both wishing to return and give rest to their people. Zhang Liang 張良 thought that when the people's minds were stable, it would be difficult to move them. Subsequently, [Liu Bang's] troops pursued [Xiang] Yu and, in the end, killed Mr. Xiang. Why is it that we must follow the affairs of King Wen? The Newly Founded State has trouble and sickness. Because of this fissure, I [want to] attack their frontier, hoping to add to their troubles and destroy them.

Mr. Falling-Down Fool replied,

In the times of Yin and Zhou,	當殷周之際
kings and lords were honored for generations;	王侯世尊
relationships between sovereigns and subject were long secure;	君臣久固

and the people were accustomed to these.　民習所專

Deep roots are difficult to pull up.　深根者難拔

For this reason, the secure are difficult　據固者難遷
　　to move.

At that time, how could the Han founder　當此之時,
　　grasp the sword, whip the horse, and take　雖漢祖安能杖劍
　　the country?　鞭馬而取天下乎

After Qin dismissed the feudal lords,　當秦罷侯置守之後

the people were exhausted under corvée,　民疲秦役

and the subcelestial realm collapsed　天下土崩
　　[like a mud wall].

Each year there was a change in sovereigns;　或歲改主

each month a change in dukes.　或月易公

[The people] were surprised like birds　鳥驚獸駭
　　and startled like beasts,

not knowing where to turn.　莫知所從

Then, the powerful began to contend　於是豪彊並爭

like tigers splitting and wolves dividing　虎裂狼分
　　[the land].

Those who were quick [to act] gained much.　疾博者獲多

Those who were tardy were swallowed up.　遲後者見吞

Now, both we and the Newly Founded State　今我與肇建
　　have passed our states to the next generation.　皆傳國易世矣

These are not like the chaotic times at the　既非秦末鼎沸之時
　　end of the Qin.

These [times] are similar to the conditions　實有六國
　　during the time of the Six States, when　並據之勢
　　each held separate influence.

This is why we can act as a King Wen　故可為文王

but not as the Han founder.　難為漢祖

When the people are exhausted by corvée,　夫民疲勞則騷擾
　　vexations will arise.　之兆生

When those on top are indolent and those　上慢下暴則
　　on bottom are agitated, the country is　瓦解之形起
　　bound to collapse.

There is a saying that goes, "It is better to　諺曰: 射幸數跌,
　　aim carefully and then shoot, than to　不如審發
　　shoot and miss frequently."

Therefore, the wise man does not shift　是故智者不為
　　his objective for small profit　小利移目

or change his path for the illusory.　不為意似改步

When the time is right, then he acts.　時可而後動

When the many [factors] are in accord, then he reaches out.	數合而後舉
Therefore, the troops [commanded by] Tang 湯 and Wu 武[11] did not need to attack twice to overcome.	故湯武之師不再戰而克
Certainly, this is because they valued the people's labors and moved at the right time.	誠重民勞而度時審也
If you follow the extreme and constantly march troops,	如遂極武黷征
the country will collapse [like a mud wall].	土崩勢生
If you are unfortunate and encounter difficulty,	不幸遇難
even though you are a wise man, you cannot plan for this.	雖有智者將不能謀之矣
As for extraordinary strategies, coming and going in the spaceless, bursting through and cutting off the routes, passing the valleys and overcoming the mountains, and crossing Mengjin[12] without means of boat and oar, I am but a fool and certainly inadequate [to discuss] this.	若乃奇變縱橫, 出入無間, 衝波截轍 超谷越山, 不由舟楫而 濟盟津者, 我愚子也 實所不及

Later, [Qiao Zhou] was transferred to be imperial household grandee, second only to the nine ministers in rank. Even though he was not involved in governmental affairs, [Qiao] Zhou was highly esteemed because of his scholarly actions. He was often consulted on important matters, and he at once relied on the Classics to respond. Later, young scholars often asked him difficult questions.

[*SGZ* 42.1029–30]

Exegesis on Ritual

1. REGARDING THE CAPPING OF KING CHENG

The old text of the *Classic of Documents* [*Shangshu* 尚][13] says that when King Wu 武王 died, King Cheng 成王 was only thirteen *sui*. King Wu died in the *gengchen* 庚辰 year. In the *renwu* 壬午 year, the Duke of Zhou 周公 went to reside in the east, and in the *guiwei* 癸未 year, he returned.[14] "The Duke's Capping"[15] records that the Duke of Zhou capped King Cheng and ordered the scribes to write words of blessing.[16] This was to remove the mourning cap. Before the Duke of Zhou returned, King Cheng was capped with the leather-trimmed cap.[17] When he opened the metal-bound coffer, he was sixteen. When King Cheng was fifteen, the Duke of Zhou capped him and then departed.

[*Tongdian* 56.1571]

2. REGARDING THE PROPER AGE OF MARRIAGE[18]

The state cannot continue long without an heir. For that reason, the [sons of the] Son of Heaven, and the feudal lords are capped at age fifteen. They also take a wife at age fifteen. In order to take a wife, they must be capped. In following the way of husband and wife, the king teaches them the root. One cannot follow the way of children and govern them [according to the] rites. At age fifteen, they are mature children and next are adults. It is desirable that a ruler of men soon have posterity. For that reason, the *Classic of Documents* says that King Cheng was capped at age fifteen. This is written in the "Metal-Bound Coffer" [*Jinteng* 金縢].[19] The "Matchmaker" chapter of the *Rites of Zhou* [*Zhouli* 周禮] says, "Today, males take a wife at age thirty, and females are taken in marriage at age twenty."[20] The "Regulations of the Household" [*Jialing* 家令] says, "Females receive the hairpin at age fifteen."[21] This is what is known as an engagement.[22] For this reason, males from age twenty to thirty and females from age fifteen to twenty all marry or are given in marriage. Before this [age] is too soon. After this [age] is too late. Most people are married or marry. Some consider it [a matter of] worth and beauty. Others consider it [a matter of] physiognomy. How can this be [a matter] only of age? If [the age] must be reduced by ten years, then they are husband and wife. This topples [the notion of] worth, beauty, and physiognomy. If this is a [matter only of] age, then what use are the rites? However, [if] a man takes a wife at age thirty and a woman is given in marriage at age twenty, to speak of limits [on the ages] of marriage is impossible. Moreover, it exceeds these. For that reason, at age thirty, Shun was not married. The *Classic of Documents* calls this "an unmarried man."[23] The *Record of Rites* [*Liji* 禮記] says, "Girls who are not given in marriage by age twenty, who elope during midspring should not be forbidden to elope." One who elopes is not in accordance [with the rites]. A matchmaker should arrange to give them in marriage.[24]

[*Guliang zhuan*, Wen 12]

3. REGARDING MOURNING ATTIRE[25]

The regulations on wearing trimmed sackcloth for three years in "Mourning Attire" [*Sangfu* 喪服][26] say, "[Mourn for] an adoptive mother as if she were your own mother."[27] When the father is still alive, this regulation is not observed in mourning for an adoptive mother. The new text ["Mourning Attire"] argues that if adopted by an honored concubine when the father is still alive, [the adopted son] will wear trimmed sackcloth for one year. If adopted by a lesser con-

cubine when the father is still alive, [the adopted son] will observe the Greater
Mourning for nine months. [Commenting on] the old text ["Mourning Attire"],
Mister Zheng [Xuan] says,

> This is based on the son of a concubine of a grandee or officer who has
> been appointed by the father to be [adopted as] son to mother. The son of
> a concubine of a grandee who has been appointed [to be adopted] by the
> father observes the Greater Mourning for his mother. The son of a concu-
> bine of an officer who has been appointed [to be adopted] mourns for the
> one year for his mother. A grandee reduces mourning by one level. An
> officer without rank does not accordingly reduce.[28] When the father dies,
> all [mourning periods] are extended.[29]

According to the *Record of Rites*, "When the father is still alive, the son of a
grandee by a concubine observes the Greater Mourning for his mother."[30] This
does not distinguish between [the rank of] honored or lesser [concubines]. If
one is not [descended] from a principal wife, then if a grandee reduces mourning by one level, the sons of his concubine will likewise reduce one level. As the
concubine of a grandee, though honored, she is not of one body with her ruler
(husband). How can [mourning for her] not be reduced? On all of these distinctions, the new text [version] does not compare with the old text [version].

[*Tongdian* 94.2556]

4. REGARDING THE PROPER MANNER
OF PAYING CONDOLENCES

When the ruler of a state mourns for a high minister or grandee, he wears a
leather cap and starched sackcloth while in his residence. When he goes out on
other business, he does likewise. When he pays his condolences, he wears
starched sackcloth and a cloth hat with a band around it. After three months,
he returns to [the clothing worn for] felicitous matters. When he pays his condolences to a king, he wears a hat with a band around it and imitation sackcloth. This he wears when he is going to be at the funeral rites, but when he
goes out on other matters, he does not [wear it]. When a duke or grandee pays
his condolences to the concubines [of the deceased], he [observes the mourning]
as if he were paying the condolences of a ruler to a high minister or grandee of
another state. He wears a leather cap and starched sackcloth, but no band
around his cap. When a ruler sends an envoy to pay condolences, the presiding
mourner meets him outside the apartment door. In receiving the envoy, he
does not wail but enters first by the right of the door and stands facing north.
The envoy enters, ascending the west stairs, facing east. The presiding mourner
proceeds to the center of the hall. The envoy presents the ruler's message. The
presiding mourner wails, bows three times, stamping after completing [each
bow]. When the envoy departs, the presiding mourner escorts him outside the
door, taking his leave with a bow. When a ruler sends an envoy with burial

clothes, the envoy takes the collar in his right hand and the belt in his left and delivers his message. He then enters the chamber, lays the clothing by the corpse, then departs. The rest is the same as for a visit of condolence. After the Dressing Ritual, the clothing is not placed by the corpse but is placed on the mat east of the corpse. The presiding mourner goes out to see off [the envoy]. He bows to his guest and to all those in attendance. He takes his place at the bottom of the steps, facing east wailing and stamping. He then returns to the chamber. When a grandee pays his condolences, he wears starched sackcloth. To wear muslin cloth and come for funerary matters is called *xi* 錫.[31] When an officer pays his condolences, he wears imitation sackcloth. This is to wear starched sackcloth as the upper garment and a plain lower garment in imitation of what is worn on felicitous occasions. Their caps are all in accordance with their sackcloth. When they return to their homes, they still wear a cap with a band around it while in their residences. When they go out on other business, they remove the band. After three months, there is the burial. They then wear the clothes for felicitous occasions. Five generations of brothers dress in the same way for one another. When a grandee pays his condolences to his subject, the procedure is different. The presiding mourner does not welcome him outside the door. The ruler enters and takes a place below the hall, facing west. The presiding mourner faces north. The other mourners face south.

[*Tongdian*, 83.2256]

EXEGESIS ON ANCIENT HISTORY

1. REGARDING ANCIENT CULTURE BEARERS

At the beginning of antiquity, people licked dewdrops and ate grass and fruits. They lived in caves in the wilds and lived in the mountains. Thus, they ate birds and beasts, wore their feathers and skins, drank [their] blood, and ate fur. Those who lived near water ate fish, turtles, snails, and clams. Because they did not yet have fire, the stench of rotten [food] caused much harm to their digestive tracts. At that time, a sagacious man ruled by the virtue of fire. He created the fire bow and made fire. He taught the people how to cook food. He cast metal to make knives. The common people rejoiced greatly. He was called the Fire Driller. Following him were the three surnames, down to the time when Fuxi organized marriage according to the hairpin and leather [cap] and made the rites. He invented the lesser and greater lutes and made the music.

[Zhang Zongyuan, "Recompilation of Qiao Zhou's *Gushi kao*," 1.11b;
Zhang Zongyuan 章宗源, "Qiao Zhou *Gushi kao*" 譙周古史考,
in *Pingjinguan congshu* 平津觀叢書 (*Baibu congshu* edition)
(Taibei: Yiwen yinshu guan, 1968)]

The Yellow Thearch invented the cart. Heavy loads could be pulled great distances. Later, in the time of the Shaohao 少昊, they were pulled by oxen. In the time of Yu 禹, Xi Zhong 奚仲 [introduced] the pulling by horses.

> [*Xu Hanshu zhi*, 29.3642n.3; Zhang Zongyuan,
> "Recompilation of Qiao Zhou's *Gushi kao*," 1.3b]

Shun 舜 invented the earthenware coffin. Tang 湯 invented the wooden coffin.

> [*TPYL* 551.3b; Zhang Zongyuan,
> "Recompilation of Qiao Zhou's *Gushi kao*," 1.12b]

Yu 禹 made an earthen chamber to surround the coffin.

> [*HHS* 39.1316n.5; Zhang Zongyuan,
> "Recompilation of Qiao Zhou's *Gushi kao*," 1.4b]

The Duke of Zhou invented the feathered coffin ornaments.[32]

> [*TPYL* 552.5a; Zhang Zongyuan,
> "Recompilation of Qiao Zhou's *Gushi kao*," 1.12b]

2. REGARDING FAMOUS WORTHIES

Bo Yi 伯夷 and Shu Qi 叔齊 were two sons of Gu Zhu 孤竹 at the end of the Yin dynasty. They lived in seclusion on Mount Shouyang 首陽山, picking and eating ferns. A woman from the wilds said to them, "Because of your principles, you do not eat the grain of Zhou. These are also Zhou's plants." Because of this, they starved to death.[33]

> [*Wenxuan* 54.2348; Zhang Zongyuan,
> "Recompilation of Qiao Zhou's *Gushi kao*," 1.9a]

Xu You 許由 was a man from the time of Yao 堯. He lived in seclusion on Mount Ji 箕山, peaceful and without desires. Because of this, Yao entreated him. [Xu You] completely rejected [the offer]. Therefore, people of the time praised his lack of desire. They revered him greatly, saying, "Yao wanted to yield the subcelestial realm to Xu You. Xu You was humiliated when he heard this, then washed his ears." Others said, "There was also a Nest Father [Chao fu 巢父][34] whose intent was the same as Xu You." Others said, "During the Xia, those who lived in nests were called Nest Fathers." This [matter] cannot be known. All the records speak much of Xu You but little of Nest Father.

> [*Wenxuan* 55.2386; Zhang Zongyuan,
> "Recompilation of Qiao Zhou's *Gushi kao*," 1.9a]

When Gongsun Shu 公孫述 seized power in Shu, a man of Shu named Ren Yong 任永 claimed to be blind. When Gongsun Shu fell, Yong washed his eyes, and approaching a mirror, [his eyes] of their own accord flashed. He said, "When the times are clear, then the eyes are bright."[35]

[*Wenxuan* 46.2060; Zhang Zongyuan,
"Recompilation of Qiao Zhou's *Gushi kao*," 1.9a]

3. REGARDING THE GRAND SCRIBE, SIMA QIAN

Seeing this discourse by the Grand Scribe, he certainly had a great love for the strange![36]

[*Shiji suoyin*, 74.2346n.8; Zhang Zongyuan,
"Recompilation of Qiao Zhou's *Gushi kao*," 1.7b]

NOTES

1. In order to more clearly distinguish between the geographic region of Shu and the third-century state founded by Liu Bei, I use the more general term "Shu" to refer to the region and the later term "Shu-Han" to refer to the state. For a detailed discussion of nomenclature, see J. Michael Farmer, "What's in a Name? On the Appellative 'Shu' in Early Medieval Chinese Historiography," *Journal of the American Oriental Society* 121, no. 2 (2001): 44–59.

2. The memorial by Zhuge Liang 諸葛亮 is preserved in his biography in the *Records of the Three States*, *SGZ* 35.919–20. For an English translation, see Robert Joe Cutter, trans., "On Deploying the Army," in *Classical Chinese Literature: An Anthology of Translations*, ed. John Minford and Joseph S. M. Lau (New York: Columbia University Press, 2000), 593–96.

3. Fragments of the *Discourse on Truth and Falsehoods in the Five Canonical Texts* by Qiao Zhou 譙周 were collected by two important Qing scholars: Wang Mo 王莫 and Ma Guo-han 馬國翰.

4. *Zuozhuan, Shisanjing zhushu* (*SSZ*) ed. (Beijing: Zhonghua shuju, 1981), Duke Huan 2.

5. *HHS* 10B.449–50.

6. Wen Li was one of Qiao Zhou's disciples.

7. Sima Zhao, King Wen of Jin, did in fact die in the eighth month of 265. See *JS* 3.44. The first half of this prophecy is based on two types of word play. *Dian* 典 (code) is synonymous with *si* 司 (code). *Wu* 午 is one of the twelve celestial stems, and its corresponding animal is the horse (*ma* 馬). Hence, the combination of these two terms form "Sima." Subsequently, the term *dianwu* came to refer to the Sima family and their Jin dynasty. The second half of the prophecy is astronomical; that is, when the moon (*yue* 月) enters the astral sector of *you* 酉, it is the eighth month.

8. Zhu Lingshi 朱齡石 was the inspector of Yi Province, the highest-ranking officer in the region.

9. The *JS* biography of Qiao Zong 譙縱 offers a fuller account of the rebellion. Additional references to Qiao Zong and his uprising are scattered throughout the early dynastic histories. For the most detailed account, see *JS* 100.2636–39.

10. Chen Zhi 陳祗 (d. 258) was a child prodigy who rose rapidly at the Shu court. Greatly trusted and loved by the emperor, at the time of the debate he and the eunuch Huang Hao 黃皓 were the two most powerful individuals at court. See *SGZ* 39.987–989.

11. Cheng Tang 成湯 was the founding ruler of Yin. King Wu was the son of King Wen and the founding ruler of the Zhou.

12. Mengjin was a ford located on the Yellow River and the site of the battle in which King Wu of Zhou defeated King Zhou of Yin and established the Zhou dynasty.

13. The old text, the *Classic of Documents* (*Shangshu* 尚書), refers to the edition of this text supposedly found in the walls of Confucius's ancestral home in Qufu by Kong Anguo 孔安國 (d. ca. 100 B.C.E.). This version of the *Documents* was considered orthodox until 175 C.E., when the new text edition was granted that distinction.

14. *Renwu* and *guiwei* are successive years in the *jiazi* sixty-year cycle.

15. There is no such section in the current *Etiquette and Rituals* (*Yili* 儀禮), though the text does mention the capping of a ducal heir.

16. There is no mention of the Duke of Zhou capping King Cheng in the *Rites*. The words of blessing were presumably those ordered by the Duke of Zhou upon King Cheng's illness. See *Records of the Historian* (*Sh iji* 史記), 33.1510.

17. This cap was dark in color and trimmed with leather, and was worn by kings while in the field or on hunting expeditions. The bestowal of this cap on King Cheng at this time would have indicated an end to the mourning period. See *Zhouli zhushu* 周禮註疏, *SSZ* 21.782.

18. This fragment appears under the title *Discourse on Truths and Falsehoods in the Five Canonical Texts* (*Wujing ranfou lun* 五經然否論). In it, Qiao Zhou appears to be commenting on a passage in the *Guliang* commentary on the *Spring and Autumn Annals*, which reads, "A son should be capped at age twenty. Once capped, [the marriage] can be arranged. At thirty, a husband takes his wife. A girl should be engaged at age fifteen. At twenty she is given in marriage." See *Guliang zhuan* 穀梁傳, *SSZ*, Duke Wen 12.

19. This information is not found in the *Classic of Documents*.

20. *Zhouli zhushu, SSZ* 14.733.

21. "Regulations of the Household" (*Jialing* 家令) is a chapter of the *Record of Rites* (*Liji* 禮記). A general discussion of the events associated with various ages of both males and females is provided in this chapter. The text in the *Record of Rites* differs only slightly from Qiao Zhou's quotation. See *Liji zhengyi* 禮記正義, *SSZ* 28.243.

22. The details of the engagement ritual are found in *Yili zhushu* 儀禮註疏, *SSZ* 6.26–27. Qiao Zhou appears to be referring to the time between the receipt of the hairpin and the marriage as the engagement.

23. *Classic of Documents* (*Shangshu zhengyi* 尚書正義), *SSZ* 2.11.

24. It is unclear which text Qiao Zhou is referring to, as this passage is not in the surviving editions of the three ritual texts.

25. This fragment appears under the title "Collected Illustrations" (*Jitu* 集圖) and was likely a part of Qiao Zhou's larger collection of writings on ritual, *Discourse on Truths and Falsehoods in the Five Canonical Texts*.

26. "Mourning Attire" (*Sangfu* 喪服) was a chapter title in *Etiquette and Rituals*.

27. *Yili zhushu* 30.159. For the proper mourning of a mother while the father is still alive, see 30.160.

28. That is, the period of mourning to be observed is reduced.

29. *Yili zhushu* 30.159.

30. This passage is not in the *Etiquette and Rituals.*

31. Taking its name from the *xi* 錫, the starched sackcloth garment worn. See *Yili zhushu* 34.180.

32. On different types of early coffins and their ornamentation, see *Liji zhengyi* 6.47–48.

33. Qiao Zhou's account differs from the standard story in Sima Qian's *Records of the Historian* by adding the comments of the "woman from the wilds." For the traditional account; see 61.2123.

34. "Nest Father" refers to another famous early recluse who was said to have lived in a nest like a bird.

35. A lengthier version of this story appears in the *Records of the States South of Mount Hua* (*Huayang guo zhi* 華陽國志,10B.582), a fourth-century local history of the Sichuan region, compiled by Chang Qu 常璩. This account notes that his son drowned in a well in front of him and that his wife committed adultery in his presence, but he gave no indication of seeing these events. After his sight was restored, his wife committed suicide.

36. Yang Xiong 揚雄 made a similar appraisal of Sima Qian. In his *Model Sayings* (*Fayan* 法言), Yang Xiong wrote, "Zhongni [Confucius] loved much—he loved righteousness. Zichang [Sima Qian] loved much—he loved the strange" (18.507).

7. Ranking Men and Assessing Talent

Xiahou Xuan's Response to an Inquiry by Sima Yi

TIMOTHY M. DAVIS

As the administrative apparatus of expanding states became increasingly bureaucratic and centralized during the Eastern Zhou 東周 (770–256 B.C.E), the need to accurately assess the talent of retainers and other courtiers emerged as a key concern for the rulers of these domains. Following the unification of the Chinese realm under the Qin 秦 (221–207 B.C.E) and the Han 漢 (202 B.C.E.–220 C.E.) dynasties, the necessity of developing criteria to determine the strengths of potential candidates for government office became all the more pressing. A number of procedures were established to meet these needs.

During the Han dynasty, the most prestigious way to enter the state bureaucracy was through imperial summons. The Son of Heaven personally interviewed those called to court, and if the candidate satisfied His Highness's expectations, he was assigned to a suitable post.[1] Another avenue of special nomination was the *ren* 任 (appointment) privilege. This practice allowed high-ranking officials who had served in an official capacity for at least three years to nominate a close family member, such as a brother or a son, to serve in the bureaucracy.[2] Beyond this, each year provincial officials were allowed to recommend a certain number of admirable individuals for service in the central administration. Most candidates were recommended on the basis of moral integrity, although some were advanced because they consistently offered candid remonstration, and others were nominated for their mastery of a particular discipline, such as military strategy or legal precedent.[3] During the Jin 晉 dynasty (265–420), promising young men were occasionally singled out by commandery or provincial officials as "Pure, Pristine, and of Uncommon Conduct" (qingbai yixing 清白異行) and recommended for public service. Others were described as hailing from "Cold and Plain" (hansu 寒素) households.[4] The term hansu refers to an elite local family that, in recent generations, had not produced an officeholder in the imperial bureaucracy. A person deemed worthy of this designation was thought to be undefiled by worldly ways, uncorrupted by excessive luxury or ease, and disinclined to exaggerate personal accomplishment—and thus well suited to public service.

Besides the appointments granted on this ad hoc basis, more consistent practices of recruitment were also established. Beginning in the middle of the Western Han (202 B.C.E.–6 C.E.), all commanderies and kingdoms were required to annually submit the names of two men deemed "Filial and Incorrupt" (xiaolian 孝廉) to the central administration as candidates for official appointment. This practice provided around 200 potential officials each year.[5] Laws were subsequently revised so that one appointee was selected for every 200,000 people. In regions with a small population, candidates were recommended less frequently. But even in the least populous areas, one candidate was recommended every three years. These revisions increased the number of candidates to between 250 and 300 a year.[6] Even more prestigious than the designation "Filial and Incorrupt" were those nominated as "Cultivated Talents" (xiucai 秀才 or maocai 茂才). The Three Dukes (San gong 三公), the Chamberlain for Attendants (Guangluxun 光祿勳), and the Regional Inspectors (Cishi 刺史) of the various provinces each nominated one candidate a year for this honor. The candidate designated a "Cultivated Talent" could immediately receive an appointment as the head of a local administrative unit, such as a district, without undergoing the usual trial appointment as a palace guard.[7] High officials were also authorized to appoint subordinate staff as they saw fit, and a significant number of low-level officials entered the bureaucracy this way.

The Imperial Academy (Taixue 太學) was another institution established to provide a pool of educated potential officials. Each year, a few promising students were chosen by examination to fill low-level posts in both the central and the local governments. In addition, Erudites (boshi 博士) of the academy were occasionally transferred to other offices within the bureaucracy.[8] Finally, in times of economic need, low-ranking positions were put up for sale. For example, during the Western Han, Emperor Wu 武帝 (r. 141–87 B.C.E) used the revenues obtained from the sale of offices to help finance the large-scale military campaigns required to carry out his vision of imperial expansion. The sale of offices was even more common during the Eastern Han (25–220) when mounting fiscal problems compelled emperors not only to authorize the sale of minor offices with increasing regularity, but also to require those promoted to high office to pay a substantial fee before taking up their new post.[9]

As this description demonstrates, the avenues for entering government service during the early imperial era were fairly limited. In fact, the majority of those who filled positions in the central administration gained their initial bureaucratic experience in the provinces as locally appointed bureaucrats who were subsequently recommended for higher offices.

Eastern Han territory was divided into thirteen provinces, each overseen by a regional inspector.[10] The provinces were subdivided into commanderies (*jun* 郡) and kingdoms (*guo* 國), headed by a grand administrator (*taishou* 太守) or a chancellor (*chengxiang* 丞相), respectively. The commanderies and kingdoms were further partitioned into districts (*xiang* 鄉), presided over by a prefect (*ling* 令) or chief (*zhang* 長). The central court appointed the heads of these regional administrative units, but the clerks and staff members were recruited locally. This arrangement naturally favored members of prominent local families, primarily because imperial officials were assigned to their provincial posts on a temporary basis, so when they had to find staff for their offices, they had no other recourse but to rely on recommendations by prominent local families. This relationship helped reduce tensions between the local and central organs of power by giving regional magnates an opportunity to participate in the governance of their immediate communities and by affording them the prospect of entering the central administration through the recommendation system. Despite such efforts to satisfy the various parties involved, the favoritism shown to some elite lineages provoked statements of dissatisfaction from all levels of elite society, even including some Eastern Han emperors.[11]

The following edict, issued by Emperor Zhang 章帝 (r. 75–88) in 76, conveys the most direct expression of disappointment: "The regional inspectors, grand administrators, and chancellors of today cannot distinguish truth from falsehood. [Those they designate] 'Cultivated Talents' and 'Filial and Incorrupt,' even if they lived to be a hundred years old would still fail to stand out, and yet we are obligated to commission them to govern affairs. This is truly unspeakable!"[12]

Decades later, the situation had apparently not improved. In 132, Emperor Shun 順帝 (r. 125–144), concerned that appointees were not measuring up to their laudatory letters of recommendation, ordered those candidates recommended as "Filial and Incorrupt" to sit for an examination to test their knowledge of the Classics.[13] This edict was enforced for a half dozen years under the supervision of the Director of the Imperial Secretariat (*Shangshu ling* 尚書令), Zuo Xiong 左雄 (d. 138). But after Zuo's death, the practice of administering regular exams declined once again.[14] Despite efforts to evaluate candidates on the basis of moral character and real administrative ability, many recognized that the current recommendation process needed further reform.

In addition to the frustrations expressed by these emperors, some members of the official class took to publicly voicing their dissatisfaction with the short-comings of the recommendation process, the corruption at court, and the usur-pation of authority by eunuch staff members. As a result, "pure criticism" (*qingyi* 清議) emerged as an alternative means of promulgating evaluations of individual character. The early pure critics were associated with the Imperial Academy. They passed judgment on individuals in the form of short, memorable phrases. Depending on the tenor of the critique, either the subject's reputation could suf-fer serious damage, or his fame might be significantly enhanced. As a practice initiated by members of the literati class, pure criticism strengthened the litera-ti's claims to social and political authority.[15] Further challenges and revisions to the recommendation system ensued as Han authority declined.

When Han rule collapsed at the beginning of the third century C.E., several contenders for military, political, and cultural authority surfaced. Following a series of stunning military victories, Cao Cao 曹操 (155–220) emerged as the de facto leader in northern China. To establish firm rule over the expanding terri-tory under his control, Cao Cao had to enlarge his bureaucratic apparatus. Den-nis Grafflin has identified several of the critical constituencies that Cao Cao needed to satisfy in order to realize this essential development. First, he had to purge the remaining Han loyalists from his bureaucratic ranks; second, he had to provide opportunities for ambitious local leaders to advance by means of ser-vice to the Wei; and, finally, he had to assimilate the following three groups into his new regime: his early supporters, those remaining Han officials who were willing to serve in his administration, and fresh talent.[16] Without accomplish-ing this, his government could not long endure.

To meet these needs, Cao Cao advocated a pragmatic approach to evaluating and employing talent. He expressed his guiding principles in a series of edicts issued between 210 and 217.[17] These documents emphasized appointment to office based on individual talent and practical skill rather than on strict adher-ence to a code of ethical propriety. After Cao Cao's death in 220, his successor, Cao Pi 曹丕 (187–226, Wei Emperor Wen 魏文帝, r. 220–226), recognized that the Cao family could never hope to maintain authority without the support of powerful aristocratic families. Consequently, when staffing his imperial ad-ministration at the capital and filling positions in the bureaucratic leadership in the provinces, Cao Pi was compelled to consider first those men who had re-ceived high local ranks in their home districts.[18] To handle these recruitment needs, the court instituted the Nine Ranks system (*jiupin zhi* 九品制). The im-perial secretary, Chen Qun 陳羣 (d. 236), was charged with standardizing the procedures by which it opperated.[19]

In this system, rectifiers or "Impartial and Just" judges (*zhongzheng* 中正) were assigned to each commandery and kingdom in order to rank all potential candidates for office within their particular jurisdiction on a nine-point scale, with one being the highest and nine the lowest.[20] The Ministry of Personnel

(*Libu* 吏部), operating under the direction of the Imperial Secretariat, then took into account these "local ranks" (*xiangpin* 鄉品) when assigning a candidate to an official post in the imperial bureaucracy. Besides the local ranks, each post in the bureaucracy carried an "official rank" (*guanpin* 官品). In general, one's local rank was considered four ranks below the official rank. For example, a local rank of three could result in an appointment to a position in the central administration with an official rank of seven.[21] The rectifiers themselves were selected from powerful local families. Although the rankings were reassessed every three years, the candidates for bureaucratic office were almost exclusively drawn from the aristocracy. Moreover, the small number of rectifiers made an adequate investigation of each candidate impossible, forcing them to rely on local evaluations. This meant that locally prominent aristocratic families with land, wealth, education, and reputation not only became the authorities behind the recommendation system but also monopolized the candidacies for office that this system produced. The aristocracy thus used the Nine Ranks system to perpetuate its own interests: once members of a particular family had been assigned high rank, it became easier for them to maintain their political influence and social status.

This system continued to operate after imperial power was transferred from the Cao to the Sima family. The usurping regent Sima Yi 司馬懿 (179–251) was, after all, able to maintain his hold on power only with the support of powerful aristocratic families. (Sima Yi's rise to power is discussed in greater detail later.) He thus could not afford to alienate these influential clans by tampering too much with the Nine Ranks system, although he does seem to have initiated the appointment of a grand rectifier (*da zhongzheng* 大中正) to supervise the recommendation process at the provincial level.[22] Through this innovation, Sima Yi could more easily control who was deemed eligible for official appointment and thereby gradually staff the bureaucracy with his supporters. Such abuses of the Nine Ranks system, and the dangers of factional politics in general, contributed to the decision by some gentlemen to seek fulfillment in scholarly endeavors and social activity outside government service. Nonetheless, the general utility of the system in subordinating powerful regional elites, while still providing them with meaningful ways of wielding authority, made the Nine Ranks system a more or less viable institution throughout the early medieval period (220–589). Even so, a major change occurred during the Sui (581–618) and Tang (618–907) dynasties when the means of selecting talent for government office shifted from reliance on the rectifiers' rankings to performance in the developing civil service examination system.

The documents translated in this chapter consist of three items:

- A lengthy "opinion" (*yi* 議) written by Xiahou Xuan 夏侯玄 (209–254) in response to the request by the Grand Mentor (*Taifu* 太傅), Sima Yi, that he comment on "current affairs" (*shishi* 時事)

- A brief letter conveying Sima Yi's response to Xiahou Xuan's opinion
- A second letter providing Xiahou Xuan's reply to Sima Yi's letter[23]

Each of the three sections of Xiahou Xuan's initial opinion addresses an area of concern related to the administration of the state: (1) Thoughts on Assessing Talent and Employing Able Officials, (2) A Proposal to Streamline the Bureaucracy, and (3) A Proposal to Enforce Sumptuary Regulations.[24] This exchange, which is recorded in Xiahou Xuan's biography from *The Chronicle of the Three Kingdoms* (*Sanguo zhi* 三國志),[25] is an important primary source on the bureaucratic institutions and processes used to maintain order and authority in the early medieval period.

These three documents must have been written sometime between Sima Yi's appointment as Grand Mentor in 239 and Xiahou Xuan's participation in the 244 campaign against Shu Han 蜀漢 (this campaign is discussed in greater detail later). According to the account in *The Chronicle of the Three Kingdoms*, Sima Yi was serving as Grand Mentor at the time he sought Xiahou Xuan's counsel. Xiahou Xuan's opinions are immediately followed by a passage relating both his appointment as general of the Western Expedition and the campaign itself.[26] Therefore, Lu Kanru's 陸侃如 suggestion, that Xiahou Xuan composed his opinion in 240 C.E., is certainly possible.[27] Some additional historical background will help clarify the significance of this particular exchange.

Just before his death in 239 C.E. at the relatively early age of thirty-five, the second Wei emperor, Cao Rui 曹叡 (205–239, Emperor Ming 明帝, r. 226–239), having no sons of his own, declared a distant relative, Cao Fang 曹芳 (232–274, Emperor Fei 廢帝, r. 240–254), his adopted heir and successor.[28] Because Cao Fang was a mere boy of seven *sui* when he ascended the throne, the dying emperor expressed his desire for a capable regent to assist the child sovereign who would succeed him. Initially the emperor had decided that Cao Yu 曹宇, a son of Cao Cao, would serve as regent.[29] But then His Highness was swayed by the carefully contrived reasoning of his confidential ministers Liu Fang 劉放 (d. 250) and Sun Zi 孫資 (d. 251), who feared that such a development would threaten their own positions at court. These two men successfully persuaded the rapidly declining emperor to change his mind and instead appoint the Militant General (*Wuwei jiangjun* 武衛將軍), Cao Shuang 曹爽 (d. 249), and the Defender in Chief (*Taiwei* 太尉), Sima Yi, to act together as co-regents.[30] This decision was secured when Cao Yu firmly indicated his intention to yield the regency to others.[31]

As the emperor drew near death, he placed Cao Shuang in several key positions, including General in Chief (*Dajiangjun* 大將軍), Commander in Chief of All Military Affairs Within and Without the Capital (*Dudu zhongwai zhujunshi* 都督中外諸軍事), and Overseer of the Secretariat (*Lu shangshu shi* 錄尚書事). Sima Yi was also personally informed by the emperor of his own new weighty responsibilities. Soon after Cao Fang's enthronement in January 239, Sima Yi was promoted to serve with Cao Shuang as joint commanders in chief and joint overseers of the secretariat. Moreover, both he and Cao Shuang were made Palace Attendants (*Shizhong* 侍中).[32] Not long after these developments, Cao Shuang asked the new emperor to shift Sima Yi to the post of General in Chief,[33] but on March 13, 239, Sima Yi was instead elevated to the position of Grand Mentor (*Taifu* 太傅). Concern for his personal safety was the ostensible reason cited for this promotion; deliberations at court yielded the observation that "in all previous cases, Grand Ministers of War had died in office."[34] Other motives, however, were likely behind the reappointment. *The Chronicle of the Three Kingdoms* informs us that the attempt to appoint Sima Yi to the office of General in Chief was actually instigated by Cao Shuang and his supporters to ensure that as the sole Overseer of the Secretariat, he would have access to all the memorials sent to the imperial throne before Sima Yi could review them.[35]

Owing to close ties to the Wei royal house, the Xiahou family quickly became involved in the rivalry between the Cao and Sima families. Xiahou Xuan's granduncle, Xiahou Yuan 夏侯淵 (d. 219), was an early ally of Cao Cao and was married to Cao's sister.[36] Xiahou Yuan also fought beside Cao Cao at Guandu 官渡 in 200 C.E. when they annihilated the forces of their rival Yuan Shao 袁紹 (d. 202). Following this momentous victory, Xiahou Yuan experienced a string of military successes that included the forced surrender of the Daoist theocrat Zhang Lu 張魯 in 215. In fact, some of Xiahou Yuan's later victories were fought alongside Cao Shuang's father, Cao Zhen 曹真 (d. 231).[37] Xiahou Yuan's series of triumphant campaigns eventually came to an end in 219 when he was defeated by the forces of Liu Bei 劉備 (161–223) near Mount Dingjun 定軍山 in eastern Hanzhong Commandery 漢中郡. Xiahou Yuan's nephew, Xiahou Shang 夏侯尚 (d. 225), also married into the Cao family. He served on Cao Cao's staff and was a close companion of Cao Pi. When Cao Cao died in 220, Xiahou Shang was among those who accompanied the king's body back to Ye 業 for burial. He continued to serve the Wei regime in positions of civil and military responsibility.[38]

Xiahou Xuan, the son of Xiahou Shang, quickly established a fine reputation of his own. Not long after undergoing the capping ceremony,[39] he was appointed to the positions of Cavalier Attendant (*Sanqi* 散騎) and Gentleman Attendant at the Palace Gate (*Huangmen shilang* 黃門侍郎). His contemporaries admired him not only for his noble birth, dignified manner, and keen intellect but also for his ability to remain calm in distressing circumstances and for his conversational prowess.[40] Xiahou Xuan limited his circle of intimates to only a few individuals. Several anecdotes note his reluctance to mix with men he considered beneath him in refinement or ability. For example, when just twenty years old, Xiahou Xuan was invited to an audience with Emperor Ming, who had him seated next to Mao Zeng 毛曾, the empress's younger brother. Mao Zeng was delighted with the seating arrangement, but Xiahou Xuan's displeasure was revealed in his countenance. The emperor was offended and demoted him to Supervisor of the Palace Guard (*Yulin jian* 羽林監).[41]

Xiahou Xuan's career improved when his cousin Cao Shuang was installed as co-regent. These kinship ties, together with Xuan's remarkable natural abilities, led to his promotion as Cavalier Attendant-in-Ordinary (*Sanqi changshi* 散騎常侍) and Capital Protector (*Zhonghujun* 中護軍).[42] A few years later, Xiahou Xuan and other supporters convinced Cao Shuang that a successful military campaign would help bolster his claims to authority. Another motive for the proposed offensive was to help counter the respect and admiration that Sima Yi's splendid military career had earned for him. Plans were drawn up for a campaign to be led by Cao Shuang against the armies of the enemy state Shu-Han 蜀漢. In 244, Xiahou Xuan was promoted to general of the Western Expedition (*Zhengxi jiangjun* 征西將軍). Shortly thereafter, he set out with Cao Shuang and his troops by way of the Luo valley 駱谷 to punish Shu-Han in Hanzhong 漢中. Encountering difficult terrain and faced with tenacious opposition, the campaign was quickly aborted, and Cao Shuang and his generals returned to the capital, having suffered heavy losses.[43]

Cao Shuang was better equipped for his role as an arbiter of culture and a patron of lively intellectual repartee. Under his leadership, the Zhengshi era (240–249) became known as the golden age of pure conversation (*qingtan* 清談). It was during this time that the talents of Wang Bi 王弼 (226–249), He Yan 何晏 (190–249), and others were matched in displays of elocutionary prowess. With his prestige on the rise, Cao Shuang felt confident enough to seize sole control of the court in 247. In response, Sima Yi withdrew from active participation in government. Feigning illness, he lured Cao Shuang into a false sense of security while secretly devising plans for a countercoup.

On February 5, 249, Sima Yi moved against Cao Shuang and his supporting faction as they journeyed to pay their respects at the Cao family tombs. Sima Yi took control of the capital troops and accused Cao Shuang of planning usurpation. Sima Yi's skillful manipulation of the organs of military and civil authority resulted in the execution of Cao Shuang and many of his proponents and family members. A short time later, on February 18, having accomplished his purge, Sima Yi had himself appointed Chancellor (*Chengxiang* 丞相) and proceeded to fill the highest government posts with his backers. Because of his close association with the Cao family, Xiahou Xuan was reassigned to the less significant post of Chamberlain for Dependencies (*Da honglu* 大鴻臚) and was later transferred to Chamberlain for Ceremonials (*Taichang* 太常). Sima Yi passed away in 251, but not before placing military and civil authority under the control of his son Sima Shi 司馬師 (208–255), who was appointed General in Chief.

Sima Shi's authority, however, did not go unchallenged, as a number of Wei loyalists attempted to restore the Cao family to a position of power. One such attempt, initiated by the Director of the Imperial Secretariat (*Zhongshu ling* 中書令), Li Feng 李豐 (d. 254), is particularly relevant to our discussion. Li Feng, like

Xiahou Xuan, was linked to the Cao family by marriage; his son Li Tao 李韜 (d. 254) was married to the Wei Emperor Ming's daughter, the princess of Qi 齊. Yet, despite these close ties to the Cao clan, Li Feng was greatly admired by Sima Shi, who regarded him favorably and held him in close confidence. Notwithstanding such agreeable treatment, Li Feng remained inwardly loyal to the Wei. Furthermore, he felt impelled to demonstrate his commitment to the House of Wei in dramatic fashion. Li Feng recognized that both Xiahou Xuan and the empress's father, Zhang Qi 張緝 (d. 254), had been shut out of meaningful government service because of their close association with the Cao-Wei royal house.[44] Hoping to harness their unfulfilled ambitions, Li Feng approached both men and confided in them that he wished to force Sima Shi from power and have Xiahou Xuan serve as regent. Since Zhang Qi hailed from the same native locale as Li Feng, Pingyi Commandery 馮翊 in Yong Province 雍州, he was all the more inclined to lend his support.[45] In the end, both Xiahou Xuan and Zhang Qi pledged to support Li Feng's risky proposal.

Li Feng subsequently devised a scheme involving the support of palace troops. According to this plan, Li and his allies would take advantage of a ceremonial occasion when one of the palace women was to be promoted to the status of Honorable Lady (*Guiren* 貴人).[46] At the height of the ceremony, Li and his operatives would lead officials and palace troops in revolt, with the goal of executing Sima Shi. He would then be replaced by Xiahou Xuan, who would serve as the new General in Chief and imperial regent.[47]

Sima Shi caught wind of the plot before it could be carried out and summoned Li Feng to his presence. Li Feng, unaware that Sima Shi had discovered his plan, went to the audience, where he was questioned explicitly concerning the matter. One source claims that on this occasion, Li Feng defiantly stated, "You and your father have harbored an insidious plot, and want to overthrow the dynasty. It is a pity my strength is not sufficient to seize and exterminate you."[48] Sima Shi, incensed at Li Feng's brazen manner, commanded a subordinate to strike him with the hilt of his sword. The blow was of such force that Li Feng died on the spot.[49] Shortly after this confrontation, Xiahou Xuan, Zhang Qi, and others were implicated in the affair. Xiahou Xuan was convicted of "high treason and acting without morals" (*dani wudao* 大逆無道) and sentenced to public execution in the Eastern Market. He remained the epitome of self-composure to the end: on the day of his death, we are told, his "facial complexion remained unaltered and his bearing and movements were natural and easy."[50]

Governing during this volatile period required the deft use of political institutions to skillfully discern loyal talent, properly employ capable men, and effectively manipulate the symbols of authority to maintain a delicate balance between aristocratic influence, on the one hand, and the civil and military authority of the central administration, on the other. Capable men who chose to offer their service to the court, whether they did so enthusiastically or reluctantly, also subjected themselves to substantial risk. The following documents thus should be read in light of this uncertain era of intertwining kinship and power relations.

FURTHER READING

For relevant historical background on the Wei–Jin transition, see Achilles Fang, trans., *The Chronicle of the Three Kingdoms (220–265)*, 2 vols. (1952; repr., Cambridge, Mass.: Harvard University Press, 1965); Donald Holzman, *Poetry and Politics: The Life and Works of Juan Chi, A.D. 210–263* (Cambridge: Cambridge University Press, 1976); Rafe de Crespigny, "Three Kingdoms and Western Jin: A History of China in the Third Century A.D.," *East Asian History*, no. 1 (1991): 1–36, and no. 2 (1991): 143–64; Anthony B. Fairbank, "Ssu-ma I (179–251): Wei Statesman and Chin Founder: An Historiographical Inquiry" (Ph.D. diss., University of Washington, 1994); Charles Holcombe, *In the Shadow of the Han* (Honolulu: University of Hawai'i Press, 1994); and Howard Goodman, *Ts'ao P'i Transcendent: Political Culture and Dynasty-Founding in China at the End of the Han* (London: RoutledgeCurzon, 1998). For studies of the recruitment system of the late Han, see Rafe de Crespigny, "The Recruitment System of the Imperial Bureaucracy of Later Han," *Chung Chi Journal* 6, no. 1 (1966): 67–78, and "Recruitment Revisited: The Commissioned Civil Service of the Later Han," *Early Medieval China* 13–14, part 2 (2008): 1–47; and Hans Bielenstein, *The Bureaucracy of Han Times* (Cambridge: Cambridge University Press, 1980), 132–42, 199–203. Useful studies on the processes and institutions for assessing talent and ranking men in early medieval China include the seminal study by Miyazaki Ichisada, *Kyūhin kanjinhō no kenkyū* (Kyoto: Tōyōshi kenkyūkai, 1956). And in Western languages, see Donald Holzman, "Les débuts du système médiéval de choix et de classement des fonctionnaires: Les Neuf Catégories et l'Impartial et Juste," in *Mélanges publiés par l'Institut des haute études chinoises* (Paris: Presses universitaires de France, 1957), 1:387–414; and Dennis Grafflin, "Reinventing China: Pseudobureaucracy in the Early Southern Dynasties," in *State and Society in Early Medieval China*, ed. Albert E. Dien (Stanford, Calif.: Stanford University Press, 1990), 139–70. Dien's introduction to this collection of essays also contains a useful overview of important issues (see esp. 10–15). Holcombe has a succinct account of how the literati class used the Nine Ranks system to elevate its social status during the Late Han and early medieval period in "The Institutional Machinery of Literati Ascendance," in *In the Shadow of the Han*, 73–84. Mark Edward Lewis summarizes relevant trends in early medieval social, cultural, and political history in "The Rise of the Great Families," in *China Between Empires: The Northern and Southern Dynasties* (Cambridge, Mass.: Belknap Press of Harvard University Press, 2009), 28–53. Two additional influential studies of medieval Chinese social structures are David

Johnson, *The Medieval Chinese Oligarchy* (Boulder, Colo.: Westview Press, 1977); and Patricia Buckley Ebrey, *The Aristocratic Families of Early Imperial China: A Case Study of the Po-Ling Ts'ui Family* (Cambridge: Cambridge University Press, 1978). Finally, Fang translated several additional primary sources on assessing talent and ranking men during this period from *Zizhi tongjian* 資治通鑒 (*Chronicle of the Three Kingdoms*), 1:533–41.

Xiahou Xuan 夏侯玄

Response to Grand Mentor Sima Yi's Request That He Comment on "Current Affairs"

The Grand Mentor [*Taifu* 太傅], Prince Xuan of the Sima clan 司馬宣王,[51] asked about current affairs [*shishi* 時事]. [Xiahou] Xuan 夏侯玄 [209–254] submitted the following opinion:

THOUGHTS ON ASSESSING TALENT
AND EMPLOYING ABLE OFFICIALS

Managing talent and employing men is the prerogative of the state. Therefore, the act of "weighing in the balance" [*quanheng* 銓衡] is wholly reserved for the Imperial Secretariat—and constitutes the high official's responsibility to assign allotments [of administrative duty] [*fen,* 分].[52] Filial conduct is realized in the village lanes. Therefore, [distinguishing between] the excellent and the inferior [candidate] is the responsibility of local officials—and constitutes the lower official's privilege to determine ranks [*xu* 敘].[53] Now, if you desire [to provide] pure instruction and [promote] judicious selection, [the key lies in] clarifying these duties and privileges—above all, do not let [superiors and subordinates] interfere with each other.[54]

Why is this?

If high officials bypass their assigned duty [to make appointments], I fear that departure from fundamentals will follow and that the swift path to meddling with power will be opened. If local officials overstep their privilege to determine rank, I fear the penetration of outside [influence] on the [bestowal of] Celestial Ranks and the [unacceptable] proliferation of portals to crucial authority.[55] If those below have access to the [process of bestowing] Celestial Ranks—this will be [tantamount to] commoners interfering in the prerogatives [of the state]. When there are multiple portals to crucial authority—this is the origin of confusion and disorder.

Indeed, several years have past since [the system using] rectifiers [*zhongzheng* 中正] to rank local administrative talent [was established], yet there is still confusion and disarray. I have yet to hear of any standardized arrangement. How is this not due to the [authority] to distribute allotted responsibility and the privilege to determine rank being at odds? [High and low officials] have each abandoned the basis from which essentials are derived. If you command rectifiers alone to examine conduct and group [candidates for office] into classes, such grouping into classes ought to be implemented equitably, and only then should [a candidate] be assigned an official post [by the Secretariat].

Why is this?

If a person's filial conduct is notably displayed within the family gates, how could he not be loyal and respectful in office? If a person's humaneness [ren 仁] and capacity to imagine himself in another's place [shu 恕] are praised across the nine-clan relations [jiuzu 九族], how could he not successfully engage in governance? If a person's fair judgment [yiduan 義斷] is carried out in the townships and villages, how could he not be suited to serving [in positions of central] responsibility? These three categories [of men] are selected by the rectifiers.[56] Even if [those chosen] are not assigned offices and titles, their [fitness for] appointment to office bears acknowledgment.[57]

[If we accept that] with conduct [xing 行], there is that which is significant and that which is minor, and that with comparisons [bi 比], there is the higher and the lower, then the class [liu 流] [of men] responsible [for governing] likewise becomes brilliantly clear and distinguishable. Why allow the rectifiers to disrupt the mechanisms for "weighing in the balance" from below[58] and grasp crucial authority entrusted to those above—[leading] superiors and subordinates to encroach on one another's [prerogatives], thereby producing confusion and error? Moreover, the Imperial Secretariat oversees those below by examining merits and collating deficiencies. [In addition,] the associates of the various [lower] offices each have a chief official who investigates them morning and night—nothing is as thoroughly scrutinized as this. [In contrast,] if critiques at the village level are taken as the [sole] consideration for passing judgment, causing the higher officials [responsible for] weighing and ranking [potential candidates] to forfeit their positions, the multitude will race about in a panic; and although one desires mores and customs to be pure and tranquil, would this even be possible?

The Celestial Dais is remote and distant, cut off from the thoughts of the multitude.[59] Those who are able to access it [first] effect change in their immediate proximity.[60] Who does not dress up and adorn [himself] to acquire what he seeks?[61] If there is such a path to [obtaining] that which he seeks, then [there will be those who] dress up [the achievements of] their own household [to obtain recognition]; shortly thereafter this will not be as good as self-promotion in the district and villages; and, again, shortly thereafter even this will not be as good as seeking self-promotions at the provincial and territorial [level]. If [you allow] this path to open, you will suffer the afflictions of [falsely] adorned truth and a departure from fundamentals. Even if you subject [such deceivers] to severe reprimand at the hands of the rectifiers [in the form of low local ranks] and reprove them with reforming punishments, this will not be effective. How can [such an approach] compare with causing each [official] to be guided by [the dictates of] his assigned duties?

Each chief official considers the abilities and deficiencies of his subordinates and makes recommendations to the Imperial Secretariat. The Imperial Secretariat then, in accordance with the rankings by ability and deficiency made [previously] by the chief officials, and after consulting the classifications of virtuous conduct made by the local officials, forms its own classifications, thereby avoiding partiality or favoritism. In that case, the rectifiers need only examine the traces [ji 迹] of [the candidate's] conduct to discern his hierarchical position and settle the judgment on his type and category, thereby avoiding [excessively] elevated or debased [rankings]. The Imperial Secretariat considers all of this [input] together, and if [a candidate] it has appointed turns out to have defects or faults, the responsibility naturally will lie with the [recommending] officials. The rankings provided by the chief officials and the classification formed by the rectifiers are then compared [by the Imperial Secretariat, which,] in accordance with the rankings and statistics, employs [the candidate]. If [those employed] do not measure up, the burden of responsibility will lie outside [the secretariat].[62] Accordingly, mutual consultation among these internal and external authorities [results in] successes and failures having their places [of accountability] and brings about the mutual rectification of formal procedures. [Considering this system of checks and balances,] who could [falsely] adorn [a candidate]? [When the process operates like] this, then the hearts of the people will be settled and affairs orderly, customs and mores tranquil, and administrative talent properly assessed.

A PROPOSAL TO STREAMLINE THE BUREAUCRACY

[Xiahou Xuan] was also of the following opinion:

In ancient times, when offices were established, their purpose was to bring relief and nourishment to the congregation of living things and to coordinate the activities of the people. Therefore, [the former kings] created for them lords and elders to watch over and shepherd them. Of chief importance to effectively watching over and shepherding the people is "uniformity" [yi 一] and "specialization" [zhuan 專]. If there is uniformity, then official responsibilities are fixed, and superiors and subordinates are at peace; if there is specialization, then the tasks of office are orderly, and affairs are no longer vexing. Moreover, if affairs are simplified and tasks orderly, both superiors and subordinates will be at peace and there will be none who are unruly. The former kings established myriad states, and although the details can no longer be investigated, they distinguished borders and drew boundaries, each maintaining their lands and territories; it was not a system of redundancies that haltered and fettered them.

Moving on to investigate the privileges associated with the five noble ranks of the Yin [ca. 1570–ca. 1045 B.C.E.] and Zhou [ca. 1045–256 B.C.E.] eras,[63] we find there were distinctions only between lesser and greater or noble and base. There were no lords [*jun* 君], officials [*guan* 官], ministers [*chen* 臣], or people [*min* 民], with dual strands [of special interest] hampering and obstructing one another. Now, if the coordination of officials is not uniform, then the tasks of office will not be well tended. If the tasks of office are not well tended, how can affairs be simplified? If affairs are not simplified, how can the people attain tranquillity? If the people are not tranquil, then depravity and malice will arise together, and treacherous falsehoods will flourish and mature. The former kings comprehended this and hence made specialists of officials and made uniform the tasks that they coordinated.

Beginning in the age of Qin, the way of the sages was not followed; offices were managed according to self-interest, and subordinates were treated with treachery. Fearing that the ministers and officers would not tend to their duties, they established overseeing pastors [*jianmu* 監牧] to correct them. Then fearing that the overseeing pastors would accommodate the crooked [*rongqu* 容曲], they established official inspectors [*sicha* 司察] to restrain them. Ministers and pastors harassed each other; overseers and inspectors managed each other; the people harbored rebellious hearts; and superiors and subordinates [engaged in] completely separate activities.

The Han inherited these tendencies, and not one [of its rulers] was able to set things right or [effect] reforms. The house of Wei emerged, and even though the model precedents of the five noble ranks were difficult to restore immediately, by not relaxing for a single day, they were able to generally establish the ceremonies and standards used to make rules and regulations uniform.

Currently, senior clerks preside over [lesser] clerks and the people; an additional stratum [above them] are the grand administrators of [the various] commanderies; and another [bureaucratic] layer above them are the regional inspectors. If we consider [the tasks] that commandery [officials] manage, they are largely the same as [those currently handled by] regional officials—there is no need for such redundancy. It is appropriate to do away with the grand administrators of [the various] commanderies and employ only the regional inspectors. If the position of regional inspector is maintained, then supervision will not be discarded, and the myriad commandery clerks can return home to personally engage in agricultural enterprises, thereby reducing troublesome waste and abundantly increasing wealth and the cultivation of grain. This is the first point.

All the talented men of the larger townships are fit to serve as grand administrators of [the various] commanderies. However, litigation concerning right and wrong always produces differences of opinion. If there is smooth compliance, then there is peace; if a person values [only] his own [opinion], then there is conflict. Now, [the key to] harmonizing the fine [flavors] of a stew lies in [successfully] combining the different [ingredients]. What is beneficial to both superiors and subordinates is the ability to come together. Smooth compliance results in peace; this is [similar to] a single harmony played together on large and small zithers. If you cleanse [the bureaucracy] and get rid of [this superfluous office], then management will be pared down, and affairs will be simplified. This is the second point.

Then there are those officials administering commandery affairs; their task is to oversee the various townships, but they nourish and protect [the interests of their own] clique and kin [and those from the] districts and settlements of their home regions. If they are unable to satisfy deficiencies, they will rely on their honorable [status] to extort wealth, and the people will be brought to hardship and distress. Calamity is born of this. If all of these [unjust officials] were brought to comply [with propriety], then the source of disorder would be blocked automatically. This is the third point.

Currently we are heirs to [a period of] decline;[64] the people have been devastated; the worthy and talented are rare; those [capable of] bearing responsibility for affairs are few; and the good officials of the commandery and district frequently do not amount to more than a single individual. The commanderies accept the most accomplished [men] from the districts, and those remaining are dispersed in lower positions. Moreover, when clerks come up for selection, [it is believed that] posts in the commandery should be filled first. The result is that those officials closest to the people are exclusively obtained from the lowest strata and that those officiating over the people's fate are often the most obstinate and base. Now if we consider [all these factors] together and appoint to clerkships more officials chosen for purity and goodness, then a great transformation will flow forth, and the people—and, indeed, all creatures—will find tranquillity. This is the fourth point.

The regulations stipulate that [the heads of] districts of ten thousand households be named grand administrators of commanderies, that those [overseeing] more than five thousand [households] be called metropolitan commandants, and that those [overseeing] fewer than a thousand households [be called] prefects or chiefs, as in the past. Beginning from the chiefs on up, [you should] examine the criteria [ke 課] for promotion and shift [them] to employment [elsewhere in the bureaucracy]: transfers based on ability should result in higher office and an increase in [the number of households] over which they preside. This is the privilege of ordering [society] by advancing the talented and raising the meritorious. Once the main warp threads of the system are fixed, then managing talent will be orderly, and regulating merit [will be] completely clear. This is the fifth point.

If you eliminate the position of grand administrator for [each] commandery, then [knowledge of] district [affairs] can straightaway reach [you]; matters will not be concealed or kept from you; and [talented] officials will not remain stagnant. Although [a restoration of] the customs of the Three Eras may not yet be possible, a transformation to simplicity and uniformity can perhaps be brought about.[65] In any case, the reduction of expenditures for the people lies in this.

A PROPOSAL TO ENFORCE SUMPTUARY REGULATIONS

[Xiahou Xuan] was also of the following opinion:[66]

The alternating application of ornament [*wen* 文] and substance [*zhi* 質] is like the cyclical emergence of the four seasons. The king embodies heaven and conforms to the inner pattern of things. He must accordingly descend in order to thoroughly comprehend [all that is relevant to governing his state].[67] If [the trend of] the times is toward a fullness of substance, then provide ornament through ritual. If the [trend of the] times is toward extravagance, then rescue it with substance. Now we have inherited the vestiges of the hundred kings, and the Qin and Han have preserved their lingering influence. As the customs of the time approach [excessive] ornament, it is suitable to significantly alter them in order to change the people's desires. In the current system of ranks—everyone—from dukes and the arrayed marquises on down and from the position of General in Chief on up—is clothed in damask brocades, patterned mesh, delicate silks, and gold and silver filigree. Below them, multicolored vestments are pervasive among the more humble classes. Although each of the higher and lower grades exhibits distinctiveness, the regulations [current among] court ministers set them on par with the "Most Revered," and the colors [heavenly] black and [earthly] yellow have penetrated to even the lower [classes].[68]

Now, it is not possible to ensure that the markets refrain from selling decorative and lovely hues, that merchants refrain from trafficking in goods that are difficult to acquire [*nande zhi huo* 難得之貨], and that craftsmen refrain from producing carved objects. For this reason, it is proper to align [your conduct], in general, with the fundamentals [of the former kings]; [you should] "weigh and measure" the appropriate [blend] of ornament and substance according to ancient laws and adopt their core standards to make your rituals and rules. Chariots, carriages, clothing, and banners should all accord with the substantial and unadorned. Forbid the latest customs, [which encourage] ostentatious activity; and cause those families involved in managing court affairs (and other households with status) to do without such adornments as brocade damask, dual-colored clothing, and exquisitely crafted things. From high to low [ornament should be used] only to the point that distinctions from the simple and plain reveal that there are grades and classes—and nothing more. Do not allow [people] to exceed perceivable distinctions of one or two [grades]. If a person [is worthy] of a special dispensation based on merit or virtue, this is a special favor of His Highness's grace, and all [such cases must be] reported to the authorities, after which [the recipient] can wear or use [the distinguishing items granted to him].

The superior's transformation of his subordinates is like the wind bending the grass; if instruction concerning the simple and plain emanates from the court, then those with minds set to draw near extravagance will naturally fade away below.[69]

PRINCE XUAN

Letter in Reply

Prince Xuan responded with a letter saying:

[Your ideas regarding] the evaluation of officials and the selection of talent, paring down superfluous offices and reforming dress regulations are all most excellent. As for the [claim that the] rites are mainly carried out in the townships and villages and regarding the court's role in investigating affairs, this is largely as you have presented them, but the inherited practices among [these entities] cannot be changed suddenly.

During the Qin, there were no regional inspectors, only commandery governors and senior clerks. Although the house of Han had regional inspectors, they implemented only six regulatory responsibilities and nothing more. Therefore the regional inspectors were called "Those Conveyed by Carriage" [chuanche 傳車], and their subordinate officials were referred to as attendants [congshi 從事]. None of the posts they occupied was permanent, and their clerks did not become [imperial] ministers. Later they were transferred to [serve as] official administrators and nothing more.

Long ago, Jia Yi 賈誼 [ca. 200–168 B.C.E.] also lamented the problems with the system of dress regulations, and the Han Emperor Wen 文帝 [r. 180–157 B.C.E.] himself wore coarse silk, and still they remained unable to cause either high or low officials to accord with his wishes.[70] I fear that these three matters will have to await a worthy man of ability before they can be carried out.

XIAHOU XUAN

Response to Prince Xuan's Letter

[Xiahou] Xuan again wrote a letter that said:

Although Emperor Wen of the Han wore coarse silk, he was unable to correct laws and standards. [This was because] both internally and externally, [there were those who] usurped [the privileges associated with particular] forms of dress. [In addition,] favored ministers received unlimited special dispensations.[71] If extrapolating from this, we make further observations, [the emperor's behavior] seems to indicate that this was an attempt to establish his own reputation [for frugality], without intending to honestly regulate the system.

Currently, dukes and marquises command the age and serve as state counselors. By tracing [precedence] back to high antiquity, you can bring about ultimate order; by constraining the branches, you can rectify the trunk.[72] If restraint is solidified at the top, then [moral] transformation will proceed among the masses. Now it is time for proper change. If you maintain diligence of heart, then the day a command is given, the response of those below will be just like an echo following a voice. Still, you display modesty by saying, "I await one with ability." This is like Yi [Yin] or the [Duke of] Zhou refusing to correct the standards of Yin 殷 or the [House of] Ji 姬. Your humble servant is baffled by this.

[*SGZ* 9.295–98]

NOTES

1. Hans Bielenstein, *The Bureaucracy of Han Times* (Cambridge: Cambridge University Press, 1980), 132; Rafe de Crespigny, "Recruitment Revisited: The Commissioned Civil Service of the Later Han," *Early Medieval China* 13–14, part 2 (2008): 29.

2. Rafe de Crespigny, "The Recruitment System of the Imperial Bureaucracy of Later Han," *Chung Chi Journal* 6, no. 1 (1966): 68, and "Recruitment Revisited," 19–20; Bielenstein, *Bureaucracy of Han Times*, 62. This privilege was reserved for officials holding positions ranked at 2,000 *shi* and above.

3. De Crespigny, "Recruitment Revisited," 24–28.

4. For example, see the biographies of Ji Dan 紀瞻 and Fan Qiao 范喬 in, respectively, *JS* 68.1819 and 94.2433. Fan was also designated "Pure, Pristine, and of Uncommon Conduct."

5. De Crespigny, "Recruitment System," 69, and "Recruitment Revisited," 15; Bielenstein, *Bureaucracy in Han Times*, 134–35.

6. De Crespigny, "Recruitment System," 69, and "Recruitment Revisited," 15; Bielenstein, *Bureaucracy in Han Times*, 134–35.

7. De Crespigny, "Recruitment System," 71, and "Recruitment Revisited," 20–21.

8. De Crespigny, "Recruitment Revisited," 34–39.

9. De Crespigny, "Recruitment System," 68, and "Recruitment Revisited," 41–44.

10. There were thirteen regions (*zhou* 州) under Chinese control in 140 C.E. See Hans Bielenstein, "Wang Mang, the Restoration of the Han Dynasty, and Later Han," in *The Cambridge History of China*, vol. 1, *The Ch'in and Han Empires, 221 B.C.–A.D. 220*, ed. Denis Twitchett and Michael Loewe (Cambridge: Cambridge University Press, 1986), 252–53, map 12.

11. For the relevant edicts written, respectively, by Emperor Ming 明帝 (r. 57–75), Emperor Zhang, and Emperor He 和帝 (r. 88–106), see *HHS* 2.98, 3.133, and 4.176.

12. *HHS* 3.133. One of the most contemptuous statements against inflated recommendations is the essay "Recommendations of Substance" (*Shigong* 實貢), composed by Wang Fu 王符 (ca. 90–165), translated in Margaret Pearson, *Wang Fu and the Comments of a Recluse* (Tempe: Center for Asian Studies, Arizona State University, 1989), 124–28.

13. *HHS* 6.261.

14. De Crespigny, "Recruitment System," 70; Donald Holzman, "Les débuts du système médiéval de choix et de classement des fonctionnaires: Les Neuf Catégories et l'Imparial

et Juste," in *Mélanges publiés par l'Institut des haute études chinoises* (Paris: Presses universitaires de France, 1957), 1:390.

15. Charles Holcombe, *In the Shadow of the Han* (Honolulu: University of Hawai'i Press, 1994), 73–84.

16. Dennis Grafflin, "Reinventing China: Pseudobureaucracy in the Early Southern Dynasties," in *State and Society in Early Medieval China*, ed. Albert E. Dien (Stanford, Calif.: Stanford University Press, 1990), 147.

17. For a translation and discussion of these edicts, see Paul W. Kroll, "Portraits of Ts'ao Ts'ao: Literary Studies on the Man and the Myth" (Ph.D. diss., University of Michigan, 1976), 17–24.

18. Holzman, "Les débuts du système médiéval," 392–93; Grafflin, "Reinventing China," 147–48.

19. *SGZ* 22.635. Shen Yue 沈約 (441–513) attributes the invention of the Nine Ranks system to Cao Cao as an expedient practice implemented "in the midst of the army, on the spur of the moment" (*SS* 94.2301; Grafflin, "Reinventing China," 147).

20. Holcombe, *In the Shadow of the Han*, 79. Whereas Charles Hucker translates *zhongzheng* 中正 as "Rectifier," Holzman prefers "L'Impartial et Juste" and Holcombe, "Arbiter." See Charles O. Hucker, *A Dictionary of Official Titles in Imperial China* (Stanford, Calif.: Stanford University Press, 1985), 189; and Holzman, "Les débuts du système médiéval," 387.

21. Assignment to a particular rank was far from formulaic; complex social, political, and cultural factors influenced how local and official ranks were determined. See Grafflin, "Reinventing China," 145–69; and Holcombe, *In the Shadow of the Han*, 73–84.

22. A portion of Sima Yi's opinion proposing the establishment of Grand Rectifiers is preserved in *TPYL* 265.9b. See also the discussion of this document in Holzman, "Les débuts du système médiéval," 397–98.

23. Very little of Xiahou Xuan's literary corpus has survived. Besides the lengthy opinion and brief letter addressed to Sima Yi, we have a few fragmentary texts, including some lines from a "Rhapsody on the Imperial Heir" (*Huang yin fu* 皇胤賦); part of an essay on corporal punishment, "Rouxing lun" 肉刑論; and an excerpt from a discourse on music, "Bian yue lun" 辨樂論. The only other complete text by Xiahou Xuan to survive the vicissitudes of time is his essay on the Warring States general Yue Yi: "Yue Yi lun" 樂毅論. The last work fared better than the rest because copies of the text, written in the calligraphic hand of Wang Xizhi 王羲之 (ca. 303–ca. 361), were preserved in later collections as an exemplary model of Wang's regular script (*kaishu* 楷書). For the texts of Xiahou Xuan's extant literary works, see *Quan San guo wen* 21.1265b–1168a.

24. These divisions, and the headings provided for them, are absent in the original document.

25. *SGZ* 9.295–98.

26. *SGZ* 9.298.

27. Lu Kanru 陸侃如, *Zhonggu wenxue xinian* 中古文學繫念 (Beijing: Renmin wenxue chubanshe, 1985), 535.

28. The true family history of Cao Fang, also known as the prince of Qi 齊王, was kept secret from the court. Sun Sheng's 孫盛 (ca. 302–373) *Wei shi Chunqiu* 魏氏春秋 relates that

"some claim that [Cao Fang] was the son of [Cao] Kai 曹楷, Prince of Rencheng 任城王" (*SGZ* 4.117n.1). If true, that would make him Cao Rui's first cousin once removed.

29. Cao Yu's mother was Lady Huan. Cao Yu married a daughter of Zhang Lu, head of the Celestial Masters community based in the Hanzhong valley of Shu-Han. The Wei Emperor Ming greatly admired and respected him. On January 16, 239, when the emperor's health was failing, he appointed Cao Yu as General in Chief, in anticipation that he would serve as regent. Six days later, on January 22, 239, after Cao Yu indicated he would not accept the position, the emperor retracted the appointment and personally informed Sima Yi that he had been chosen to serve as joint regent with Cao Shuang. Emperor Ming passed away that same day. See *SGZ* 3.113–14.

30. The Militant General was one of three generals who shared command of the imperial guard at the capital. The Defender in Chief was one of the Three Dukes (*San gong* 三公), the most eminent advisers to the emperor. See Hucker, *Dictionary of Official Titles*, 574, 485.

31. *SGZ* 20.582.

32. Palace attendant was a title reserved for the emperor's closest advisers.

33. *SGZ* 9.282.

34. *JS* 1.13.

35. *SGZ* 9.282. The Grand Mentor was one of the Three Dukes. See Hucker, *Dictionary of Official Titles*, 477.

36. For a brief biography of Xiahou Yuan, see *SGZ* 9.270–72.

37. Cao Zhen provided Cao Cao with crucial military support in the early days of the Wei and was appointed General in Chief on February 3, 227. Cao Zhen was also well respected by Cao Pi (Wei Emperor Wen) and was among the four generals who received his final testamentary edict to serve as joint regents for Cao Rui (Emperor Ming). Sima Yi was also counted among the four. For a brief biography of Cao Zhen, see *SGZ* 9.280–82.

38. For a brief biography of Xiahou Shang, see *SGZ* 9.293–94.

39. This rite marked a young man's entry into adulthood.

40. Liu Yiqing 劉義慶, *Shishuo xinyu* 世說新語 (Shanghai: Shanghai guji chubanshe, 1993), 8/8, 14/4.

41. *Shishuo xinyu* 5/7 and 14/3; *JS* 9.295.

42. The Capital Protector "commanded one of two military forces garrisoned around the capital" (Hucker, *Dictionary of Official Titles*, 190).

43. *JS* 1.15; *ZZTJ* 74.2358; Achilles Fang, trans., *The Chronicle of the Three Kingdoms (220–265)*, 2 vols. (Cambridge, Mass.: Harvard University Press, 1965), 1:672–81.

44. Zhang Qi's daughter was made empress sometime during the second month of the fourth year of the Jiaping era (252). She was deposed, following her father's conviction on charges of treason, during the third month of 254. See *SGZ* 4.125 and 4.128.

45. The commandery seat was located about seventy-five miles northeast of modern Xi'an in Shaanxi Province.

46. In the hierarchy of palace women, "Honorable Lady" is one rank beneath that of empress.

47. *SGZ* 9.300n.2; Fang, *Chronicle of the Three Kingdoms*, 2.174n.7.

48. *SGZ* 9.300n.3, translated in Fang, *Chronicle of the Three Kingdoms*, 2.172n.6.3.

49. *SGZ* 9.299.

50. *SGZ* 9.299. Compare *Shishuo xinyu* 5/6.

51. Prince Xuan is Sima Yi 司馬懿 (179–251). When the principality of Jin 晉國 was established in 258, Sima Yi was given the posthumous title Prince Xuan 宣王. Later, when Sima Yan 司馬炎 (236–290, Jin Emperor Wu 武帝, r. 266–290) accepted the abdication of the last Wei 魏 ruler in 266 c.e., Sima Yi's posthumous title was elevated to August Sovereign Xuan 宣皇帝. See *JS* 1.20; and Anthony Bruce Fairbank, "Ssu-ma I (179–251): Wei Statesman and Chin Founder, An Historiographical Inquiry" (Ph.D. diss., University of Washington, 1994), 354. Sima Yi was appointed Grand Mentor on March 13, 239. See *JS* 1.13.

52. The Imperial Secretariat (*Shangshu* 尚書) is referred to synecdochically throughout the text as the Dais and Pavilion (*taige* 臺閣). The "allotments of administrative duty" (*fen* 分) are those associated with official appointment in the imperial bureaucracy.

53. Local ranks were determined by the rectifiers, who were part of the Ministry of Education (*Situ fu* 司徒府), but the authority to appoint a candidate to office in the central administration, and the assignment of official rank that accompanied such a posting, was reserved for the Ministry of Personnel (*Libu* 吏部), under the supervision of the Imperial Secretariat.

54. In other words, Xiahou Xuan is advocating that the regional and central authorities maintain a separation of powers, each operating within its own jurisdiction.

55. The term "Celestial Ranks" (*tianjue* 天爵) refers to the official ranks (*guanpin* 官品) issued by the Imperial Secretariat. The proliferation of multiple portals to authority refers to the development of political factions at court.

56. The three categories are those just mentioned: the humane, the one capable of using himself to gauge the feelings of others, and the one capable of rendering sound judgment.

57. In other words, local officials determine fitness for office, but imperial officials should be the ones making actual appointments to positions in the central administration.

58. That is, local recommenders from the districts and commanderies should not suggest appointing a candidate to any official post in the central administration.

59. The "Celestial Dais" (*tiantai* 天臺) refers to the imperial court.

60. That is, those able to attain appointment in the central administration must first establish a reputation in their native locale.

61. In other words, who does not embellish his accomplishments and credentials to seek promotion?

62. In other words, the responsibility rests with those providing the initial local rank.

63. The "five noble ranks" (*wudeng* 五等) refer to the five feudal ranks of duke (*gong* 公), marquis (*hou* 侯), earl (*bo* 伯), viscount (*zi* 子), and baron (*nan* 男).

64. The decline is manifest in the collapse of the Han dynasty and the subsequent political disunion.

65. The "Three Eras" are the Xia, Shang, and Zhou.

66. One reason for this concern about sumptuary regulations (i.e., the rules dictating the types of outward display authorized for an individual of a given rank) was that Emperor Ming and others at his court were fond of ostentatious exhibition and excess. Such practices were apparent even among the masses.

67. In other words, the emperor must descend from his exalted position at the pinnacle of the state to learn about the activities of his ministers and officials, and to ascertain the needs of the people.

68. The "Most Revered" (*zhizun* 至尊) is the emperor.

69. Compare *Analects* 12/19.

70. *HS* 48.2242–43. This statement refers to Jia Yi's "Memorial to the Throne Setting Out the Affairs of Government" (*Shang shu chen zhengshi* 上疏陳政事).

71. That is, exemptions from the requirements of sumptuary regulations.

72. In other words, by suppressing outward breaches of etiquette, one can correct the problem at its core.

8. On Land and Wealth

Liu Zishang's "Petition on Closing Off Mountains and Lakes"
and Yang Xi's "Discussion on Abolishing Old Regulations
Regarding Mountains and Marshes"

CHARLES HOLCOMBE

As the early medieval Chinese economy gradually becomes better understood, the picture that is emerging is of a China that was surprisingly
commercialized and prosperous, as well as culturally vibrant and richly cosmo-
politan. The contrast with conditions in early medieval Europe is particularly
striking and, indeed, calls into question the very assumption that China even
had a "medieval" period, at least as defined according to the standard European
sequence of historical stages. It is true that Chinese commerce did suffer an
abrupt contraction in the fourth century, somewhat parallel to the one that afflicted western Europe, but it was largely confined to northern China and was
relatively brief in duration.[1] The long-term trend during these centuries, especially in southern China, was toward greater commercial prosperity. Whereas
western Europe withdrew into a relatively self-sufficient and isolated agrarian
feudal manorial economy, China enjoyed booming economic growth and increased international contacts.[2] The "manors" (first called *shu* 墅, and later
zhuangyuan 莊園) that did begin to appear in this era were involved in a process
of commercialization that made them significantly unlike the feudal manors of
medieval Europe.[3] This commercialization—combined with the relatively vigorous survival of centralized bureaucratic imperial government and the lack of
any enduring military aristocracy in China—is why the European medieval
feudal model may be somewhat inappropriate for China.

It is, however, also true that beginning in the Han dynasty (202 B.C.E.–220 C.E.) there had been growing economic polarization in China, associated with the emergence of large landed estates. As a result, many small farmers were reduced to the status of servants, tenant farmers, refugees, or bandits.[4] As Cui Shi 崔寔 (b. ca. 110 C.E.) complained in the late Han dynasty, "Then fathers and sons lower their heads to serve wealthy people as servants . . . [and] if the harvest is slightly un-prosperous, they become vagrants in the valleys."[5] This appearance of whole new categories of personal dependents, un-taxable by the state, is often cited as evidence of "feudalism" in China.[6]

The end of the Han dynasty in 220 was followed by a period of division, which reached a peak with the virtually complete collapse of centralized imperial government in northern China in the early fourth century, due to catastrophic civil wars. Meanwhile, the Southern dynasties were continuing the trend established in the Han dynasty toward the private accumulation of land by wealthy families, with only modest attempts at government regulation to limit excessive polarization.[7] For example, the "occupation of fields and levying of fields" (zhantian ketian 占田課田) regulations that were first promulgated in 280 and that served as an (increasingly neglected) standard for much of the Southern dynasties, fixed both the maximum amount of farmland that ordinary adult males were supposedly allowed to possess, as well as a smaller minimum amount that they were obliged to farm for tax purposes, with variances for gender and age and extra allowances for official rank.[8] Despite such regulations, the overall trend was toward privatization. The reply to a proposal in 273 to prohibit the sale of property by commoners, for example, was that whatever may have been the case in antiquity, since the establishment of the empire it had been the practice that "royal law cannot regulate people's private [affairs]."[9] By 512, privatization had progressed to the point that one Southern dynasty gentleman even felt entitled to refuse to sell his villa to an emperor. The angry emperor was finally able to compel him to surrender the land only in exchange for its market value.[10]

The large private estates that became characteristic of the Southern dynasties from the fourth through the sixth century were not medieval European-style self-sufficient feudal manors but were operated, to some extent at least, for profit, sometimes by wage labor, as part of a widespread general process of commercial development.[11] This was especially true for the estates of the upwardly mobile commoners (shuzu hanmen 庶族寒門), who, by the fifth century, were rapidly undercutting the more leisured (and therefore presumably less ambitiously driven) established Great Families (shizu 士族).[12] Even members of the established Great Families sometimes applied themselves industriously to developing their holdings, however, as in the case of the villa operated by one renowned poet in early-fifth-century Zhejiang, which was designed so that "the farm paths crisscross, the embankments intersect, [and] the guided channels draw the flow, circulating evenly through the irrigation ditches."[13] Among the crops being grown commercially in Lingnan (modern Guangdong, Guangxi, and northern Vietnam) in the late Southern dynasties were oranges and tangerines, lichees, coconuts, sugarcane, and aloe wood.[14] In fact, it has been pointed out that even in the North, the use of monetary prices to indicate the value of agricultural products in a sixth-century agricultural text, the *Essential Skills of the Common People* (*Qimin yaoshu* 齊民要術), is evidence of some degree of commercialization.[15]

We have, regrettably, only scattered anecdotal evidence with which to measure the extent of Southern dynasty commercial development. There was, for example, the fifth-century "saying" that if "a Guangzhou [i.e., Canton, a city especially important to maritime trade] Regional Inspector [*Cishi* 刺史] passes through the city gate only once, he will obtain 30 million [cash]."[16] One early-sixth-century prince was alleged to have accumulated more than 3 billion in cash in storehouses at his residence.[17] In 548, when the Southern capital was besieged by rebels, the defenders are reported to have gathered 50 billion in cash and silk from various agencies in the city.[18] Not only is it impossible to know whether any of these figures are anything more than wild flights of fancy, but we also should acknowledge that the Chinese number *yi* 億, which is translated here using its smaller and generally older value of 100,000, can be somewhat vague and was in the mid-sixth century just then in the process of being semistandardized at the larger value of 100 million.[19] But the mere fact that the sixth-century Chinese needed a number for 100 million may be in itself suggestive. Clearly, people at the time were thinking occasionally in terms of staggeringly large figures. Another clue, suggestive of Southern dynasty prosperity, is the likelihood that the Southern capital, Jiankang 建康 (modern Nanjing), was the largest city in the world in the early sixth century, with a population of perhaps 1.4 million.[20] One historian has even daringly suggested that military conquest and reunification from the north under the Sui and early Tang dynasties (after 589) may have actually caused a temporary setback to the commercial development of southern China.[21]

Although the monetization of the economy and commercial development surely did enable a fortunate few to enjoy luxurious lifestyles in the late Southern dynasties, it is also true that independent taxpaying small farmers were simultaneously being squeezed by the resulting inflation and often were reduced to dependence.[22] One sixth-century author lamented that "the majority of the people" had been reduced to private retainers (*buqu* 部曲) and that "the land was deserted and the towns scattered."[23] An early-sixth-century official allegedly boasted openly that wherever he was posted, he extracted so much from the place that the waters, mountains, fields, and even "the common people in the villages are exhausted."[24] An emperor otherwise known for his tolerance of elite abuses nonetheless complained in an edict of 541 that "powerful families and wealthy households often take possession of public fields and rent them out at high rates to poor people."[25] When the Southern capital was besieged in 548, the rebel leader (himself no ordinary peasant) could appeal for support by writing that "in recent years, favorites have held power, and stripped the common people to satisfy their lusts."[26] However effective this appeal may, or may not, have been, after a lengthy siege the city did eventually fall, and the Southern dynasties never fully recovered from this devastating rebellion.

It was in this context of the Southern dynasties' commercial development and simultaneous economic polarization, in the years before the great rebellion of 548 to 552, that the private enclosure of mountains and fens (*shan ze* 山澤) became an issue. Much earlier, during the preimperial Warring States era (403–221 B.C.E.), governments may have imposed state monopolies on mountains and marshes for the purpose of compelling their subjects to engage in agriculture, rather than be tempted to live a more carefree life gathering minerals and firewood, and hunting and fishing in the wild. "Monopolize the mountains and fens; then the people who hate farming, are negligent and lazy, and have multiple wants, will have no place to go to eat. If they have no place to go to eat, then they must farm," recommended the ancient Legalist classic, the *Book of Lord Shang* (*Shang jun shu* 商君書).[27]

Under the empire (after 221 B.C.E.), however, this policy appears to have lapsed. While the enclosure of mountains and fens remained an exclusive imperial prerogative, unenclosed mountains, forests, rivers, and marshes apparently came to be regarded as public resources available to everyone.[28] With the intense competition for land that accompanied the development of the Southern dynasties, and the large-scale influx of refugees from the North in the fourth century, good farmland became a scarce commodity, and wealthy families began (illegally) occupying mountains and fens as well.[29] Somewhat similar to the (also controversial) much later English enclosure movement, such private occupation may have contributed to overall economic development and benefited individual families while simultaneously also ending public access and causing real hardship for some people. As Wang Huzhi 王胡之 (d. 371) had already noted in the fourth century, "If a common person throws a fishing line or drops a fish trap, they always seize his fishing gear, and it is not released until he hands over ten rolls [of fabric, as a penalty]."[30] In 413 it was reported that "mountains, lakes, rivers, and marshes are all monopolized by the strong, and the common people are always charged a fee for gathering firewood and fishing."[31]

Southern dynasty governments repeatedly issued stern injunctions prohibiting the private enclosure of mountains and fens, beginning in 336 and then again in 413, 440, 453, and 463. The effectiveness of these bans must have been limited, however, and eventually the government was forced to recognize the fait accompli and, for the first time, formally legalize the private

possession of mountains and fens.[32] It is this pivotal moment that is described in the text translated here. This passage illustrates both the process of
vigorous private commercial development that, from roughly the sixth century until early modern times, drove both China to become the world's leading economy and some of the trade-offs involved in that process. As Mark Elvin explains in his pioneering environmental history of China, *The Retreat of
the Elephants*, the large-scale development of China's land resources over a
period of several thousand years unleashed a massive human transformation
of the natural landscape, which in recent centuries has left China without
much remaining wilderness.[33]

FURTHER READING

For detailed studies of the Southern dynasty economy, see Liu Shufen, "Jiankang and the Commercial Empire of the Southern Dynasties: Change and Continuity in Medieval Chinese Economic History," in *Culture and Power in the
Reconstitution of the Chinese Realm, 200–600*, ed. Scott Pearce, Audrey Spiro,
and Patricia Ebrey (Cambridge, Mass.: Harvard University Press, 2001), 35–52;
Liu Shufen 劉淑芬, "San zhi liu shiji Zhe-dong diqu de jingji fazhan" 三至六世
紀浙東地區的經濟發展, in *Liuchao de chengshi yu shehui* 六朝的城市與社會, by
Liu Shufen (1987; repr., Taibei: Taiwan xuesheng shuju, 1992), 195–253; and
Kawakatsu Yoshio 川勝義雄, "Kahei keizai no shinten to Kō Kei no ran" 貨幣經
濟の進展と侯景の乱, in *Rikuchō kizokusei shakai no kenkyū* 六朝貴族制社會の
研究 (1962; repr., Tokyo: Iwanami shoten, 1982), 349–405. A standard survey of
the economies of both the Northern and Southern dynasties is Tao Xisheng 陶
希聖 and Wu Xianqing 武仙卿, *Nanbeichao jingji shi* 南北朝經濟史 (1937; repr.,
Taibei: Shihuo chubanshe, 1979). For landholding in both the Northern and
Southern dynasties, see Gao Min 高敏, *Qin-Han Wei-Jin Nanbeichao tudi zhidu
yanjiu* 秦漢魏晉南北朝土地制度研究 (Kaifeng: Zhongzhou guji chubanshe,
1986). For a general overview by a distinguished senior historian, see Tang
Zhangru 唐長孺, *Wei Jin Nanbeichao Sui Tang shi san lun: Zhongguo fengjian
shehui de xingcheng he qianqi de bianhua* 魏晉南北朝隋唐史三論: 中國封建社會的
形成和前期的變化 (Wuhan: Wuhan daxue chubanshe, 1993). A good recent
summary of the period is Zhang Chengzong 張承宗, Tian Zebin 田澤濱, and
He Rongchang 何榮昌, eds., *Liuchao shi* 六朝史 (Zhenjiang: Jiangsu guji chubanshe, 1991). For a sweeping survey of ecological considerations in Chinese
history, see Mark Elvin, *The Retreat of the Elephants: An Environmental History
of China* (New Haven, Conn.: Yale University Press, 2004).

Biography of Yang Xi (*Yangxi zhuan* 羊希傳)

LIU ZISHANG 劉子尚, "PETITION ON CLOSING OFF
MOUNTAINS AND LAKES" (*SHANGYAN SHANHU ZHI JIN*
上言山湖之禁), AND YANG XI 羊希, REPLY:
"DISCUSSION ON ABOLISHING OLD REGULATIONS
REGARDING MOUNTAINS AND MARSHES"
(*KANGE SHANZE JIUKE YI* 刊革山澤舊科議)

At the beginning of the Daming reign period [457–465] [Yang Xi (dates un-known)][34] was Left Assistant Director of the Department of State Affairs [*Shangshu zuo cheng* 尚書左丞]. At the time, the Regional Inspector of Yangzhou [Yangzhou *cishi* 揚州刺史], the Prince of Xiyang, [Liu] Zishang [西陽王子尚, ca. 451–465],[35] petitioned:

> Although there are long-standing rules forbidding [encroachment on] mountains and lakes, the popular custom is [for the people] to follow each other's [example] in neglecting and not respecting them. They clear the mountains by burning and dam the waters, preserving them for their [own] family's benefit. Recently, this neglect has grown worse daily. The wealthy and strong take over mountains and occupy them; the poor and weak have no place to rely on for grass or wood for fuel. [The situation] for lands for fishing and gathering is also like this. This is truly a profound corruption that injures governance, which ought to be eliminated by the government and, with some adjustments to the old articles, an enduring system reissued.

There was an official who consulted the Renchen 壬辰 Edict [of 336, which stated]:

> The occupation of mountains and the guarding of marshes are assessed according to the law for robbery. All those who steal more than ten feet will be publicly executed.[36]

[Yang] Xi [, however,] held:

> The Renchen regulations are harsh in their prohibitions. Since they are hard to comply with in managing business, they have rightly been re-laxed with the times. Moreover, the occupation of mountains and the blocking of waters have spread and multiplied, mutually continuing as before, becoming prior possessions. If we were to suddenly do away with them in one morning, it could easily result in sorrow and resentment. Today we will attend to abolishing [the old rules] and establishing [new] regulations in five articles. Whichever mountains and marshes have pre-viously been regularly cleared by burning and planted with tended bam-boo, timber, and miscellaneous fruits in renewable groves, as well as ponds, lakes, rivers, and seas with fishing weirs and places with loach and

swordfish that are regularly improved and maintained, will be permitted to not be evicted. Officials of the first and second rank will be allowed to occupy three *qing* 頃 [about thirty-six acres] of mountains; of the third and fourth rank, two *qing* fifty *mu* 畝 [about thirty acres]; of the fifth and sixth rank, two [*qing*, about twenty-four acres]; of the seventh and eighth rank, one *qing* fifty *mu* [about eighteen acres]; of the ninth rank and commoners, one *qing* [about twelve acres]. All, according to the fixed standards, will be noted in the property registers. If they had previously already occupied a mountain, they cannot occupy more. If their prior occupation was insufficient, they may occupy enough [more] to comply with the limits. If it is old property that was not previously noted, it uniformly cannot be prohibited. [But] if there is a [new] offender, anything more than a foot of water or land will be counted together with stolen goods and assessed according to the regular law for robbery. [As for the preexisting regulations,] repeal the Renchen rules from the second year of the Xiankang reign period [i.e., 336].

[The court] complied with this [recommendation].

[*SS* 54.1536–37]

NOTES

1. Jiang Fuya 蔣福亞, "Wei Jin Nanbeichao shiqi de shangpin jingji he chuantong shichang" 魏晉南北朝時期的商品經濟和傳統市場, *Zhongguo jingji shi yanjiu* 中國經濟史研究, no. 3 (2001): 108–19.

2. Miyazaki Ichisada 宮崎市定 draws the economic contrast between Carolingian Europe and Tang China in *Dai-Tō teikoku: Chūgoku no chūsei* 大唐帝国: 中国の中世, in *Miyazaki Ichisada zenshū* 宮崎市定全集 (1968; repr., Tokyo: Iwanami shoten, 1993), 8:256–57.

3. Li Qing 李卿 and Yang Jiping 楊際平, "Han, Wei, Jin, Nanbeichao de jiazu, zongzu, yu suowei de 'zhuangyuan-zhi' guanxi bianxi" 漢魏晉南北朝的家族、宗族與所謂的 '莊園制' 關係辨析, *Zhongguo shehui jingji shi yanjiu* 中國社會經濟史研究, no. 4 (2003): 21–26; Miyazaki, *Dai-Tō teikoku*, 256; Wu Tingyu 烏廷玉, "Tang-chao 'zhuangyuan' shuo de chansheng, fazhan, ji qi zai Zhongguo de liuchuan he yingxiang" 唐朝'莊園'說的產生發展及其在中國的流傳和影響, *Shixue jikan* 史學集刊, no. 3 (2000): 75–81; Zhao Gang 趙岡 and Chen Zhongyi 陳鍾毅, *Zhongguo tudi zhidu shi* 中國土地制度史 (Taibei: Lianjing chuban, 1982), 19.

4. Luo Tonghua 羅彤華, *Handai de liumin wenti* 漢代的流民問題 (Taibei: Taiwan xuesheng shuju, 1989), 71–80. For polarization, see also Luo Tonghua, "Zheng li linbu shilun: Handai renkou yilailü yu pinfu chaju zhi yanjiu" 鄭里廩簿試論: 漢代人口依賴率與貧富差距之研究, *Xin shi xue* 新史學 3, no. 1 (1992): 36–40.

5. Cui Shi 崔寔, "Zheng lun" 政論, in "Quan Hou Han wen," *QW* 46.726.

6. He Ziquan 何茲全, "Han Wei zhi ji renshen yifu guanxi xiang lishu guanxi de zhuanhua" 漢魏之際人身依附關係向隸屬關係的轉化, *Hebei xuekan* 河北學刊 6 (2003): 146–50;

Tang Zhangru 唐長孺, "Clients and Bound Retainers in the Six Dynasties Period," in *State and Society in Early Medieval China*, ed. Albert E. Dien (Stanford, Calif.: Stanford University Press, 1990), 111–38.

7. Tao Xisheng 陶希聖 and Wu Xianqing 武仙卿, *Nanbeichao jingji shi* 南北朝經濟史 (1937; repr., Taibei: Shihuo chubanshe, 1979), 31–32; Li Hu 黎虎, "Xi Jin zhantianzhi de lishi yuanyuan" 西晉占田制的歷史淵源, in *Wei Jin Nanbeichao shilun* 魏晉南北朝史論 (1985; repr., Beijing: Xueyuan chubanshe, 1999), 222, 224, 230, 240–41.

8. Zhang Chengzong 張承宗, Tian Zebin 田澤濱, and He Rongchang 何榮昌, eds., *Liuchao shi* 六朝史 (Zhenjiang: Jiangsu guji chubanshe, 1991), 115–16.

9. *JS* 46.1310–11.

10. *LS* 7.159. See also Zhang Chengzong et al., *Liuchao shi*, 124.

11. Liu Shufen 劉淑芬, "San zhi liu shiji Zhe-dong diqu de jingji fazhan" 三至六世紀浙東地區的經濟發展, in *Liuchao de chengshi yu shehui* 六朝的城市與社會 (1987; repr., Taibei: Taiwan xuesheng shuju, 1992), 225; Wan Shengnan 萬繩楠, *Wei Jin Nanbeichao shi lungao* 魏晉南北朝史論稿 (Hefei: Anhui jiaoyu chubanshe, 1983), 215–18; Kawamoto Yoshiaki 川本芳昭, *Chūka no hōkai to kakudai: Gi-Shin Nanbokuchō* 中華の崩壊と擴大: 魏晉南北朝 (Tokyo: Kōdansha, 2005), 147.

12. Zhang Chengzong et al., *Liuchao shi*, 171–78; Gao Min 高敏, *Qin-Han Wei-Jin Nanbeichao tudi zhidu yanjiu* 秦漢魏晉南北朝土地制度研究 (Kaifeng: Zhongzhou guji chubanshe, 1986), 210–19.

13. *SS* 67.1754, 1760.

14. Lü Chunsheng 呂春盛, *Chen-chao de zhengzhi jiegou yu zuqun wenti* 陳朝的政治結構與族群問題 (Taibei: Daoxiang chubanshe, 2001), 54.

15. Cao Xiaoli 操曉理, "Shiliuguo Beichao de qianbi wenti" 十六國北朝的錢幣問題, *Zhongguo jingji shi yanjiu* 中國經濟史研究, no. 1 (2004): 123.

16. *NQS* 32.578.

17. *NS* 51.1278.

18. *ZZTJ*, 162.5002.

19. Liu Xueyao 劉學銚, *Wu-hu shi lun* 五胡史論 (Taibei: Nantian shuju, 2001), 404. For *yi*, see Zhongwen da cidian bianzuan weiyuanhui, ed., *Zhongwen da cidian* 中文大辭典, 中文大辭典編纂委員會, 1st rev. ed. (Taibei: Zhonghua xueshuyuan, 1980), 1:1219, entry 1177.

20. Liu Shufen, "Jiankang and the Commercial Empire of the Southern Dynasties: Change and Continuity in Medieval Chinese Economic History," in *Culture and Power in the Reconstitution of the Chinese Realm, 200–600*, ed. Scott Pearce, Audrey Spiro, and Patricia Ebrey (Cambridge, Mass.: Harvard University Press, 2001), 35, 254n.2.

21. Kawakatsu Yoshio 川勝義雄, *Chūgoku no rekishi 3: Gi-Shin Nanbokuchō* 中国の歴史 3: 魏晉南北朝 (Tokyo: Kōdansha, 1981), 267–68; "La décadence de l'aristocratie chinoise sous les Dynasties du Sud," *Acta Asiatica* 21 (1971): 38; and "Kahei keizai no shinten to Kō Kei no ran" 貨幣經濟の進展と侯景の乱, in *Rikuchō kizokusei shakai no kenkyū* 六朝貴族制社會の研究 (1962; repr., Tokyo: Iwanami shoten, 1982), 369.

22. Zhang Chengzong 張承宗 and Wei Xiangdong 魏向東, *Zhongguo fengsu tongshi: Wei Jin Nanbeichao juan* 中國風俗通史: 魏晉南北朝卷 (Shanghai: Shanghai wenyi chubanshe,

2001), 438; Takahashi Tetsu 高橋徹, "Rikuchō-ki Kōnan no shō-nōmin" 六朝期江南の小農民, *Shichō* 史潮 107 (1969): 82; Kawakatsu Yoshio, "Kahei keizai," 371, 386; Kawamoto Yoshiaki, *Chūka no hōkai to kakudai*, 148–49.

23. He Zhiyuan 何之元 (ca. 503–593), "Liang Dian" 梁典, in Li Fang 李昉 (925–996), *Wenyuan yinghua* 文苑英華 (Taibei: Huawen shuju, 1965), 754.4731.

24. *LS* 28.422.

25. *LS* 3.86.

26. *Zizhi tongjian* 161.4991.

27. *Shang jun shu, zhuyi* 商君書注譯, annot. Gao Heng 高亨 (ca. third century B.C.E.) (Beijing: Zhonghua shuju, 1974), 23; Mark Elvin, *The Retreat of the Elephants: An Environmental History of China* (New Haven, Conn.: Yale University Press, 2004), 104.

28. Tang Zhangru 唐長孺, *San zhi liu shiji Jiangnan da tudi suoyouzhi de fazhan* 三至六世紀江南大土地所有制的發展 (1957; repr., Taibei: Baishu chubanshe, n.d.), 64–65, and *Wei Jin Nanbeichao Sui Tang shi san lun: Zhongguo fengjian shehui de xingcheng he qianqi de bianhua* 魏晉南北朝隋唐史三論:中國封建社會的形成和前期的變化 (Wuhan: Wuhan daxue chubanshe, 1993), 112.

29. Tao Xisheng and Wu Xianqing, *Nanbeichao jingji shi*, 34.

30. Wang Huzhi 王胡之, "Wang Huzhi yu Yu Anxi jian" 王胡之與庾安西箋, in "Quan Jin wen," *QW* 20.1572.

31. *SS* 2.29.

32. Tang Zhangru, *San zhi liu shiji*, 65, 67; Wang Zhongluo 王仲犖, *Wei Jin Nanbeichao shi* 魏晉南北朝史 (Shanghai: Shanghai renmin chubanshe, 1980), 422–23.

33. Elvin, *Retreat of the Elephants*, 84–85.

34. Yang Xi was a talented official from a relatively humble Shandong family. While serving as Regional Inspector of Guangzhou 廣州刺史, he was killed by rebels sometime after 467. The text translated here comes from his biography.

35. It is unlikely that this petition was really personally composed by the young prince. It was, instead, surely drafted in his name by court attendants. The prince, Liu Zishang, was the second son of the Song Emperor Xiaowu (r. 453–464). After the "Dethroned Emperor" Feidi was overthrown in 465, this prince was also put to death at the tender age of fifteen. For his biography, which may paint an exaggerated picture of his character deficiencies, see *SS* 80.2058–59.

36. The passage translated here appears to be the only surviving mention of this law.

9. Crime and Punishment

The Case of Liu Hui in the *Wei shu*

JEN-DER LEE

The ruling authorities generally try to systematize the ethics of marriage and family, believing that they often help stabilize society.[1] In western Europe in the Middle Ages, biblical teaching on marriage and family was interpreted and taught by the twelfth-century canonists, not only to direct people toward a more sacred life, but also to increase the church's secular influence. Through the ecclesiastical courts, the church established its authority to regulate the laity's marriage customs and to provide spiritual justification for its marital ethics.[2] In contrast, in China, the Confucian Classics provided the ethics of marriage and family, and the state, instead of a religious organization, undertook the task of enforcing them.

Since the late nineteenth century, traditional Chinese society has been perceived as Confucian, and the state, with a legal mechanism at its disposal, was often seen as a willing participant in the "inevitable" development of Confucianization. However, like the Catholic Church before monastic reform, the state (or, better, states) in early medieval China was not yet powerful enough to enforce its will. During the disunion between the third and the sixth centuries, no single state could rule all of China. Moreover, ethnic diversities, struggles for political survival, and differences in social structure all contributed to discrepancies in ethical values, both between states and within a single government. The issue, then, was not whether the ruling authorities intended to Confucianize society through the codification of classical ethics but, first, what aspects of marital and familial ethics would be made law; second, how these laws would be enacted; and, third, who the ruling authorities would be.

To understand the complicated interactions among the three issues in the codification of classical ethics, we must scrutinize statutes and cases and also analyze the rationale and arguments behind them. What I discuss and translate in this chapter is a case recorded in the "Monograph on Law" (*Xingfa zhi* 刑罰志) in the *Wei shu* 魏書, the history of the Northern Wei (386–534), a dynasty founded by the Tuoba 拓跋 clan of the nomadic Xianbei 鮮卑 people. This disastrous case involved Grand Princess Lanling 蘭陵, the daughter of Emperor Xiaowen 孝文 (r. 471–499), who was famous for his sinification movement, and her husband, Liu Hui 劉輝, the grandson of a surrendered imperial clansman from the Southern Liu-Song 劉宋 dynasty (420–479). The couple's marriage was marred by Liu Hui's extramarital affairs and ended with the princess's miscarriage and death. The legal debates surrounding the case are recorded in the "Monograph on Law," and the vicissitudes of their marriage are described in Liu Hui's biography in the *Wei shu*. The case concerned sex crimes, marital violence, concealment, and family members' collective responsibilities, all of which were important aspects of the more general problem of codifying classical ethics. In arguing the case, court officials cited statutes and precedents from earlier periods, exemplifying how the Northern Wei both continued and deviated from the legal practices of their predecessors in the Han and subsequent dynasties.

According to Liu Hui's biography in the *Wei shu*, the princess is said to have been very jealous and once even killed a maid whom Hui had impregnated. When that did not calm her fury, the princess aborted and mutilated the unborn child, stuffed the maid with straw, and showed her naked to Hui. Appalled and angered by the princess's behavior, Hui decided to ignore her. The situation was reported to Empress Dowager Ling 靈太后 (r. 516–528), the princess's sister-in-law and the reigning regent of the Northern Wei government at that time. After an investigation, Hui was divested of his noble title and was divorced. One year later, however, the princess asked to be reunited with him. At first, the empress dowager was reluctant to grant her request, for fear that the princess had not changed her behavior, but after repeated pleas, she eventually agreed. It is said that the empress dowager not only escorted the princess out of the imperial palace personally, but also asked her to exercise more discretion in the future.[3]

Sometime between 519 and 520, when the princess was pregnant, Hui committed adultery with both Rongfei 容妃, the sister of the commoner Zhang Zhishou 張智壽, and Hui-meng 慧猛, the sister of Chen Qinghe 陳慶和.[4] According to Liu Hui's biography, the princess changed her tactics and kept her temper under control. But after being provoked by her female relatives, she started fighting with Hui again. Hui thereupon pushed her out of bed, beat her, and stamped on her, causing a miscarriage. He then fled. A reward was offered for Liu Hui's arrest, and the ones already caught were to be punished. Both measures were opposed by Cui Zuan 崔纂, then the Director of the Three Dukes (*San gong lang zhong* 三公郎中) in the Department of State Affairs (*Shang shu sheng* 尚書省), and his colleagues. Cui Zuan's argument consists of four major points, including the judgments for the three parties involved and his contention over the division of bureaucratic power.

Cui Zuan's first point addresses the verdict for Liu Hui. Although the "Monograph on Law" does not explain why the arrest warrant treats Liu Hui as a traitor, Cui Zuan's argument provides some hints. Since the Han dynasty, a person who killed an imperial family member had been considered a traitor.[5] That the imperial authority applied this reasoning to charge Liu Hui with treason suggests that it considered the aborted child mainly the princess's flesh and thus a member of the imperial family. This finding, however, contradicts the idea of a patriarchal family described in the *Etiquette and Rituals* (*Yili* 儀禮), according to which one's principal parental relation is with one's father, not one's mother. Thus when Cui Zuan cites the "law of assault" (*doulü* 鬥律) to propose a sentence of hard labor for Hui's killing his own child, he actually is arguing for recognition of the patriarchal family described in the Confucian Classics.

Cui Zuan's second point concerns the two adulterous women. He uses an earlier statute to contend that Liu Hui, as the principal criminal, should be arrested and judged before the women, as his accessories, are put on trial. Besides, he points out, because Rongfei's and Huimeng's only crime was adultery, they should not have been sentenced to slavery. Although Cui Zuan did not refer to any law code regarding the penalty for adultery, his colleague You Zhao 游肇, Right Vice Director (*You pu yi* 右僕射) in the Department of State Affairs, came to his support and also called for the women to be sentenced to hard labor.

Cui Zuan's third point focuses on the innocence of the two brothers and the unfair application of collective responsibilities to their sentence. What Cui Zuan is referring to here are the two most important items in the codification of Confucian ethics: the permitted concealment by family members and the collective responsibility of the family as a whole. Both practices were based on the scope of the patriarchal family, which is defined by the *Etiquette and Rituals* as a system called "the five degrees of mourning" (*wu fu* 五服). The statute on concealment was codified in the mid-first century B.C.E. during the Han dynasty, which allowed *jiqin* 期親, family members with a one-year mourning obligation, such as siblings, to conceal one another's criminal behavior. The case of treason that prompted debates on women's collective responsibility took place near the end of the Cao-Wei 曹魏 rule (220–265) and finally led to the modification of the relevant laws in the beginning of the Western Jin 晉 (265–316). Cui Zuan's reference to them indicates that the once nomadic Xianbei continued the law of their Han predecessors and illustrates Cui's own efforts to integrate Confucian family ethics in legal decisions.

The fourth aspect of Cui Zuan's argument pertains to the division of duties and power in government. He protests the participation of the Department of Chancellery (*Men xia sheng* 門下省) in legal cases and states that it was not the department's responsibility to decide on a verdict. Whose responsibility was it, then? Cui Zuan does not explicitly say. But there is good reason to believe that the Department of State Affairs should have been the office in charge, especially when all the disagreements came from officials of that department. Yuan Xiuyi 元修義, Imperial Secretary (*Shang-shu* 尚書) in the Department of State Affairs, supported Cui Zuan's argument regarding the brothers' innocence and cited the *Spring and Autumn Annals* (*Chunqiu* 春秋) to prove the ending of connections between a married woman and her birth family. You Zhao, the Right Vice Director mentioned earlier, also agreed with Cui Zuan's objections, asking the court to put the appropriate office in charge and retry the case.

All these arguments and proposals, however, were not appreciated by the imperial authority—that is, Empress Dowager Ling, who ruled on behalf of her teenage son. Consequently, the imperial decree following these discussions not only confirmed the earlier verdicts, but also punished Cui Zuan and his colleagues.

Grand Princess Lanling died from the miscarriage after the punishment was meted out. The *Wei shu* states that the empress dowager was so sad that she not only attended the funeral, sobbing, but also accompanied the funeral procession for several miles out of the capital. Later she told one of her officials that she could not help but weep because the princess tolerated Liu Hui and never spoke up, even though he repeatedly insulted her. According to the *Wei shu*, she stated, "There was no such [woman] in the past, nor is there any such [woman] today. That is why I feel so sorry." Although Liu Hui was later captured, he was pardoned by an amnesty granted immediately before his execution. He regained his noble and official titles in 522 but died, presumably a natural death, the following year.[6]

The "Monograph on Law" covers the legal development over the 150 years of the Northern Wei, and fully one-sixth of it is devoted to this case. At the end of the nineteenth century, an essay on legal thought by the reformist judge Shen Jiaben 沈家本 (1840–1913) even used this case as an example.[7] Indeed, the substantial and lasting interest in Liu Hui's case testifies to its significance and gives us valuable insights into the relationship of state, family, and ethics in early medieval China. Moreover, inspired by today's historiography, we can see in this story a rare opportunity to exercise our newly acquired sensitivity to the issues of class, ethnicity, and gender. In this case, the match was a marriage between a nomadic princess and the offspring of a surrendered ethnic Han. The debate was between the imperial regent, a nomadic woman ruler who wanted to avenge her sister-in-law, and her legal bureaucrats, who had either a Han ethnic origin or a Confucian educational background. The story concerns both members of the imperial family and commoners, and the debates were mainly about the verdicts for commoners.

The case of Liu Hui therefore serves as an instructive example and a point of departure for us to examine the three issues in the codification of Confucian ethics. The first issue—the inculcation of marital and familial ethics into the law, Cui Zuan's citation of the "law of assault," his reference to concealment by family members, and his insistence on the brothers' innocence—illustrates the idea of a patriarchal family in accordance with the *wu fu* mourning system. The key point is, first, that a woman's family identity shifts after her marriage and, second, that her status is inferior to that of her husband in her husband's family.

In regard to the second issue, the implementation of these ethical standards, imperial decrees were most often cited to prove progress in the codification of Confucian ethics. For instance, early in the Western Jin, it was decreed that the five degrees of mourning be employed as a principle for legal decisions. That is, the justices would be permitted to impose several levels of penalties to show and ensure the family's hierarchy should its members become involved in legal cases. Nonetheless, the serious debates and final decisions concerning Liu Hui's story, some two hundred years after the Western Jin decree, suggest that codifying classical values was difficult. The application of patriarchal ideals in rendering verdicts varied among cases in different regimes owing to many different factors—court politics, pleas from powerful aristocrats, influences arising from a nomadic cultural background, as well as the individual characteristics of different rulers—all of which in turn relate to the third issue, the makeup of the ruling authority. The road to Confucianization could be bumpy, and it was not favored unconditionally by the imperial court when it ran counter to the imperial interest. In Liu Hui's case, that interest comprised class, gender, and ethnicity.

FURTHER READING

For a detailed analysis of Liu Hui's case and its significance in the codification of Confucian ethics in medieval China, see Jen-der Lee, "The Death of a Princess: Codifying Classical Family Ethics in Early Medieval China," in *Presence and Presentation: Women in the Chinese Literati Tradition*, ed. Sherry Mou (New York: St. Martin's Press, 1999), 1–37. For women rulers of medieval China and their influence on the revision of laws, see Kang Le 康樂, *Cong Xijiao dao Nanjiao* 從西郊到南郊 (Taibei: Daohe Press, 1995), part 2, "Empress Dowager Wenming" 文明太后, 111–64. See also Jo-shui Chen, "Empress Wu and Proto-Feminist Sentiments in Tang China," in *Imperial Rulership and Cultural Change in Traditional China*, ed. Frederick Brandauer and Chu-chieh Huang (Seattle: University of Washington Press, 1995), 77–116. For a classic work on Confucian influence on Chinese law, see Ch'ü T'ung-tsu, *Law and Society in Traditional China* (The Hague: Mouton, 1965). For pre-Confucian society and its legal practices in Han times, see Jack Dull, "Marriage and Divorce in Han China: A Glimpse at 'Pre-Confucian' Society," in *Chinese Family Law and Social Change in Historical and Comparative Perspective*, ed. David C. Buxbaum (Seattle: University of Washington Press, 1978), 23–74. For a more general discussion of legal practices in medieval China, see Chen Yinke 陳寅恪, "Sui Tang zhidu yuanyuan lüelungao" 隋唐制度淵源略論稿, in *Chen Yinke xiansheng lunwen ji* 陳寅恪先生論文集 (1944; repr., Taibei: Jiusi chubanshe, 1977).

❖

The Case of Liu Hui

In the Shengui era [518–519], Grand Princess Lanling's husband, Commandant Escort [*Fu ma du wei* 駙馬都尉] Liu Hui, committed adultery with Zhang Zhishou's sister Rongfei and Chen Qinghe's sister Huimeng, both commoners of Heyin 河陰 County, and beat the pregnant princess, which caused her miscarriage. Hui feared being punished and fled. The Department of Chancellery issued the [following] verdict: "Everyone [involved in the adultery] is sentenced to death, and Zhishou and Qinghe are banished to the borderland, since they knew of the situation but did not [try to] prevent it." The imperial decree stated, "The proposal is approved except that Rongfei and Huimeng are exempted from the death penalty. They shall be punished by having their head shaved and by being beaten, followed by becoming palace slaves."

Cui Zuan, Director of the Three Dukes in the Department of State Affairs, dissented, saying, "I humbly read the imperial decree, which rewards the one who arrests Liu Hui: if he is a worker, he will be promoted two degrees in the office; if he is a commoner, he will receive one degree into the nobility; if he is from a special-service household, he will be exempted from his service; and if he is a slave, he will be set free. Even though Liu Hui has not committed treason, the reward [for catching him] is equal to those offered for catching the traitor Liu Xuanming 劉宣明.[8] Moreover, the Department of Chancellery proposes, 'Rongfei and Huimeng committed adultery with Hui; they confused him and made him angry at the princess, thus causing him to beat her and to harm her fetus. Although there is no corresponding regulation in the law, their crime deserves a severe penalty, and therefore they should be sentenced to death. The families of Zhishou and the others will be banished to Dunhuang 敦煌 to serve in the military.' The imperial benevolence is extensive and [thus] will not carry out the verdict immediately. But even though it has pardoned their lives, I personally think it still is not right. The law is what the High Emperor relied on to rule All Under Heaven; it should not be strengthened or weakened because of favor or anger, and it should not be affected and altered by affinity or distance. According to the 'law of assault': 'Grandparents and parents who, out of anger, kill their grandchildren or children with a weapon will be sentenced to five years' labor, a person who kills by beating will be sentenced to four years' labor. If a person kills intentionally out of love or hatred, the punishment will be one degree more severe.' Even though the princess married down and has more prestige than an ordinary spouse, she is still a man's wife. [Consequently,] one cannot consider her fetus to not be her husband's child. In addition, according to the old statute issued by the previous court in the fourth year of the Yongping era [511], 'All penalties concerning banishment and death should wait for the principal criminal to be given the verdict before the accessories [to the crime] are judged.' To investigate the branch, one must start from the root. The sentence should be postponed while Hui is still in hiding; in no way should one put aside the principal criminal while punishing the accessories. Banishment and death are different punishments, and now may not be the time to decide [between them]. Officials of the Department of Chancellery belong to the imperial palace, and their job is to report cases and memorials. In the past, when Bing Ji was the prime minister, he did not bother with street fights but investigated the panting of oxen. Was this not for the sake of division of government?[9] What Rongfei and others did was adultery. If they had been caught in the dirty beds, their [crime] would have been obvious, and they should have been sentenced according to the relevant laws. Why, [then,] were they judged as if they had offended the palace and [thus] were sentenced to slavery? According to Zhishou's testimony, his sister is married to the Manager of Requisitioned Labor Administration [Si shi cao canjun 司士曹參軍], Luo Xiangui 羅顯貴, and has produced two daughters with her husband; therefore, she is the mother of another family. The Record of Rites [Liji 禮記] states that a woman does not marry two husbands, just as a person does not have two heavens. If she behaves badly in private, the blame will fall on her husband; the fault is not her brother's. In the past, during the Wei Jin dynasties when collective execution among the five lineages was still being used, a pregnant mother could still be put to death [for a crime committed by a member of her birth family] after her child was born. To contest [this sentence], He Zeng 何曾 argued, 'An unmarried woman should be responsible for charges against her parents, whereas a married woman should be punished for [crimes committed by] her husband's family.' This has been the irrevocable and right order and the common principle in the past and the present. The law allows a person to conceal a family member if the latter commits an ordinary crime, much less the shameful act of adultery. How can one ask a brother to testify [against his sister for her adultery]? Here the punishments [according to the verdicts] exceed the criminals' wrongdoings, and human relations [according to the verdicts] go against legal precedents. According to the law, there is no collective responsibility for adultery. [The court] should not increase the brothers' punishment because of its anger with Hui. To execute a man in the market is to abandon him along with the people, whereas to ennoble a man in the court is to honor him along with the people. Both actions should show [that the court] has no secrets under heaven and is not deceiving people's ears and eyes. How can one carry out within the Four Seas a verdict that is not in accordance with the correct laws? Once the laws and norms have been lost, even the speediest horse cannot get them back! Since the imperial decree has been issued, it should be followed, but those decisions that are not legal should be reconsidered."

Yuan Xiuyi, the imperial secretary of the Department of State Affairs, stated, "In the past, when Ai Jiang 哀姜 violated the rites in the kingdom of Lu 魯, [her brother,] the Duke of Qi 齊, took her back and executed her, and thus was criticized in the *Spring and Autumn Annals* [*Chunqiu* 春秋].[10] Also, when Xia Ji 夏姬 committed adultery in the kingdom of Chen 陳, people blamed only [her son] Zhengshu 徵舒, but not her parents.[11] [Both cases] show that a woman['s status] is established outside [her family] and that any crime she commits while violating the rites does not concern her birth family. How can the brothers be responsible for the sins of their married sisters?" You Zhao, the Right Vice Director of the Department of State Affairs, submitted a memorial to the throne that says, "Your humble and unworthy subjects participate in this important office and have the duty to provide good suggestions and to remove the bad ones. The Department of Chancellery is responsible for delivering orders and documents in and out [of the palace] and is an excellent [source of] general regulations. There are offices for handling the cases of wicked people violating the law. It is not the business [of the Department of Chancellery] to investigate felonies and to pass judgment. The adulterous behaviors of Rongfei and others should be punished only by hard labor. The law does not say that they should be executed.[12] Indeed, according to the legal codes and precedents, it is too severe to find a brother responsible for his married sister. Moreover, although Hui did run away, he does not deserve the death penalty; it also is excessive to issue a reward to catch him that equals the one to catch a traitor. A verdict that does not follow the law should be reconsidered. I beg [the court] to put the appropriate office in charge and to retry every aspect of the case."

The imperial decree states, "Hui broke the laws and violated the norms, and his crime cannot be pardoned. The substantial reward is offered to ensure his arrest. Rongfei and Huimeng committed adultery with Hui; they indulged their passions and confused Hui, which caused the princess's tragedy. If [they are] not executed, how can [the court] punish and purge [others in the future]? Although the brothers should not be responsible for their married sisters' crimes, Zhishou and Qinghe knew of their sisters' adultery but did not prevent it from happening; they tempted Liu Hui and collaborated in the shameful infidelity. They corrupted customs and defiled mores and [so] should be punished more severely. That is why the Department of Chancellery, instead of a regular office, was asked to try the case. How can it be considered an ordinary case and follow the usual procedures? Moreover, there have been imperial jurisdictions since ancient times: How can all cases belong to the legal bureaucracy? The Department of State Affairs should work on the basics and serve as the [imperial] spokesman. Not learning how deeply it violates the norms and not knowing how much it violates the customs, [the Department of State Affairs] has deviated from the correct way and arbitrarily executed the law. It has utterly betrayed our trust and therefore seriously deserves punishment. [Accordingly,] Cui Zuan shall be removed from his office, and the other court officials from the Department of State Affairs shall be deprived of their salary for a season."[13]

[WS 111.2886–88]

NOTES

1.   Part of this introduction draws material from Jen-der Lee, "The Death of a Princess: Codifying Classical Family Ethics in Early Medieval China," in *Presence and Presentation: Women in the Chinese Literati Tradition*, ed. Sherry Mou (New York: St. Martin's Press, 1999), 1–37.

2.   For canon law on Christian marriage, see Charles Donahue Jr., "The Canon Law on the Formation of Marriage and Social Practice in the Later Middle Ages," *Journal of Family History* 18 (1983): 144–58. For the Catholic Church's assumption of power through the institution of marriage, see Georges Duby, *The Knight, the Lady and the Priest: The Making of Modern Marriage in Medieval France*, trans. Barbara Bray (New York: Pantheon Books, 1983), 282–84.

3.   *WS* 59.1311–12.

4.   The sources disagree over precisely when the crime was committed. Liu Hui's biography in the *Wei shu* states that he committed adultery early in the Zhengguang era (520–524), but the "Monograph on Law" in the *Wei shu's* records that this took place in the Shengui era (518–519). See *WS* 59.1312 and 111.2886.

5.   Wang Chien-wen 王健文, "Xi- Han lüling yu guojia zhengdangxing: yi lüling zhongde budao wei zhongxin" 西漢律令與國家正當性—以律令中的"不道"為中心, *Xin shi xue* 新史學 3, no. 3 (1992): 1–36.

6.   *WS* 59.1312.

7.   Shen Jiaben 沈家本, *Jiyi wencun* 寄簃文存 (Taibei: Commercial Press, 1976), *juan* 4, "Learning to Make a Verdict" (*Xue duan* 學斷).

8.   For this earlier treason case, see *WS* 9.229 and 58.1292.

9.   Bing Ji 邴吉 was the prime minister of the Han Emperor Xuan (r. 73–49) who inquired about the oxen's panting and not about street fights because he believed that the prime minister was responsible for watching the climate that affected agriculture and people's welfare and that the police should be responsible for street fights. For his story, see *HS* 74.3147.

10. Ai Jiang was married to Duke Zhuang 莊公 of the Lu kingdom, committed adultery with Zhuang's brother, and participated in the succession struggles after Zhuang died. Her elder brother, Duke Huan 桓公 of the Qi kingdom, took her back, executed her, and returned her body to the successor of the Lu in 659 B.C.E. See the record of this event in *Zuozhuan zhushu* 左傳注疏, *SSJZ* 29.197–98.

11. After her husband died, Xia Ji committed adultery with two court officials and the Duke of Chen. Her son, Xia Zhengshu, was so angry that he killed the duke. The two court officials consequently feared for their lives and asked the kingdom of Chu for asylum, thus giving the ambitious King Zhuang of the Chu a chance to kill Zhengshu and eliminate the kingdom of Chen, in 599 B.C.E. See the record of this event in *Zuozhuan zhushu* 22.380–82.

12. There are no records showing the specific penalty for fornication and adultery in the Northern Wei dynasty. But the Tang Code, issued with annotations in 653, lists one and a half years for fornication and two years of hard labor for adultery. See Wallace Johnson, *The T'ang Code*, 2 vols. (1979; repr., Princeton, N.J.: Princeton University Press, 1997).

13. For reading *yishi* 一時 to mean a season of three months in the Northern Wei's salary system, see Zhou Yiliang 周一良, "Banlu yu shangren" 班祿與商人, in *Wei Jin Nanbeichao shi zhaji* 魏晉南北朝史札記 (Beijing: Zhonghua shuju, 1985), 397–99.

10. Marriage and Social Status

Shen Yue's "Impeaching Wang Yuan"

DAVID R. KNECHTGES

In the period from 490 to 494, while serving at the Southern Qi court, Shen Yue 沈約 (441–513) presented to the emperor a number of petitions requesting the impeachment of officials for improper conduct.[1] The only complete impeachment petition that has survived is "Impeaching Wang Yuan" (*Zou tan Wang Yuan* 奏彈王源), which is preserved in the *Wen xuan*.[2] When he wrote this impeachment petition, Shen Yue concurrently held the positions of Gentleman Attendant at the Yellow Gate (*Jishi huangmen* 給事黃門), Palace Aide to the Censor in Chief (*Yushi zhongcheng* 御史中丞), and "Impartial and Just" (*Zhongzheng* 中正) from his native commandery of Wuxing 吳興 (modern Wuxing, Zhejiang). The *Wen xuan* commentator Li Shan 李善 (d. 689) cites the now lost *Annals of the Southern Qi* (*Qi chunqiu* 齊春秋) by Shen Yue's contemporary Wu Jun 吳均 (469–520), which says that Shen Yue served as Palace Aide (to the Censor in Chief) in Yongming 8 (490).[3] Thus his petition to impeach Wang Yuan is usually dated to this year.[4]

In his petition, Shen Yue calls for the impeachment of Wang Yuan 王源, who is from the Wang family of Donghai 東海. His great-grandfather was Wang Ya 王雅 (334–400), who was the great-grandson of the famous scholar Wang Su 王肅 (196–256). During the Eastern Jin, Wang Ya held high positions under Emperor Xiaowu 孝武 (r. 373–396).[5] Shen Yue wishes Wang Yuan to be impeached on the grounds that he has arranged to marry his daughter to the son of Man Zhangzhi 滿璋之, a local wealthy official of questionable pedigree.

Shen Yue's petition to impeach Wang Yuan is an important source for both the history of marriage and the study of social classes in the Six Dynasties period. This impeachment case is interesting also for what it tells us about the impeachment process itself. Shen Yue begins his petition by citing ancient precedents that justify endogamy. Although he admits that no universal standard applies to all situations, he insists that marriage should be between families of the same social status. According to Shen, members of the *shi* 士 (gentry) clans have ignored this rule since Song times: "Family relationships are muddled and confused, and no regard is given to whether someone is menial or common." During the Liu-Song period, there is evidence of widespread intermarriage between gentry and commoner families. Indeed, so many members of the gentry class violated the endogamy rule that in 461 Emperor Xiaowu 孝武 (r. 454–464) issued a decree ordering that all gentry who married commoners be assigned to military service. Consequently, "many gentry evaded service and fled." Some of them even hid in lakes and mountains and became bandits.[6]

Shen attributes this violation of the social code to one motive: financial gain. "They trade and sell [the reputations] of their grandfathers and great-grandfathers and consider it a means of commerce." Yan Zhitui 顏之推 complains about the same practice in his *Yanshi jiaxun* 顏氏家訓: "In recent times in marrying off a daughter or taking a wife, people sell a daughter to acquire a dowry and purchase a wife in exchange for silk. They measure [the status of] fathers and grandfathers, calculating it to millimeters and centimeters, with one party demanding much and the other offering little, no different from in the marketplace."[7]

Shen Yue also is offended by the false pedigree that the Man family had given to the matchmaker. Shen's first statement about his investigation is somewhat ambiguous: "[I] could not distinguish gentry from commoner" (*shi shu mo bian* 士庶莫辨). David Johnson interprets this to mean that not all of Man Zhangzhi's ancestors were from a *shi* background.[8] Richard Mather renders the phrase to say that the Man family made "no distinction between gentry and commoner."[9] It is not certain what this means. It is possible that *shi shu mo bian* simply means there was not enough information to determine whether the Man family was gentry or commoner. But Shen was adamant on one point. He was certain that Man Zhangzhi and his son were not descendants of the famous Mans of the Western Jin. Shen Yue was evidently quite concerned about the accuracy of family registers. In 507 he presented a petition to Emperor Wu recommending that the old Jin and Song registers be consulted to verify the gentry pedigrees that various officials were now claiming for themselves.[10] In the petition Shen states that "during the two periods of the Song and Qi, gentry and commoner could not be distinguished" (*shi shu bu fen* 士庶不分).[11] Perhaps the case of Wang Yuan was an example of an indeterminate pedigree.

The Qing-dynasty scholar Zhang Yun'ao 張雲璈 (1747–1829) argues that Shen Yue wrongly accused Wang Yuan. He observes that the 490 edict forbade marriage between gentry and the commoner classes of merchants and artisans, but it did not forbid marriage between upper gentry and lower gentry (*hansu* 寒素). Zhang also notes that both Man Zhangzhi and his son held respectable posts serving the Qi house, and there should not have been any impediment to a marriage to a member of Wang Yuan's family.[12] Perhaps Shen Yue was more concerned about Man Zhangzhi's putative fabrication of his family pedigree than about the violation of the endogamy code, which, even according to Shen Yue, was not strictly observed from Liu-Song times on.

Finally, what may have most outraged Shen Yue was Wang Yuan's mercenary treatment of marriage. Not only did he obtain a large bridal present of 50,000 cash (or 50,000 strings of cash if one follows the interpretation of the *Wen xuan chao* commentary), but he also used part of it to purchase a concubine. As Shen Yue puts it, he converted these funds "into something to fill his bed and sleeping mat." In Shen's view, Wang Yuan's behavior was not only mercenary but lustful.

FURTHER READING

For studies of Shen Yue, see Suzuki Torao 鈴木虎雄, "Shin Kyūbun nenpo" 沈休文年譜, in *Kano kyōju kanreki kinen Shinagaku ronsō* 狩野教授還曆記念支那學論叢 (Tokyo: Kōbundō shobō, 1928), 567–617, Chinese trans. by Ma Daoyuan 馬導源, *Shen Yue nianpu* 沈約年譜 (Shanghai: Shangwu yinshuguan, 1935). See also Yoshikawa Tadao 吉川忠雄, "Shin Yaku no denki to sono seikatsu" 沈約の傳記とその生活, *Tōkai daigaku kiyō, bungakubu* 11 (1968): 30–45; Richard Mather, *The Poet Shen Yüeh (441–513): The Reticent Marquis* (Princeton, N.J.: Princeton University Press, 1988); Lin Jiali 林家驪, *Shen Yue yanjiu* 沈約研究 (Hangzhou: Hangzhou daxue chubanshe, 1999); and Luo Guowei 羅國威. "Shen Yue Ren Fang nianpu" 沈約任昉年譜, *Xueshu jilin* 12 (1997): 226–89, repr. in *Liuchao zuojia nianpu jiyao* 六朝作家年譜輯要, ed. Liu Yuejin 劉躍進 and Fan Ziye 范子燁 (Ha'erbin: Heilongjian jiaoyu chubanshe, 1999), 383–447. Finally, see Kishiro Mayako 稀代麻也子, *Sōsho no naka no Shin Yaku ikiru to iu koto* 『宋書』のなか沈約生きるということ (Tokyo: Kyūko shoin, 2004). On Shen Yue's impeachment of Wang Yuan, see David Johnson, *The Medieval Chinese Oligarchy* (Boulder, Colo.: Westview Press, 1977); Nakamori Kenji 中森健二, "Shin Yaku no 'Sodan Ō Gen' ni tsuite" 沈約の《奏彈王源》について, *Gakurin* 7 (1986): 43–52; Richard B. Mather, "Intermarriage as a Gauge of Family Status in the Southern Dynasties," in *State and Society in Early Medieval China*, ed. Albert E. Dien (Stanford, Calif.: Stanford University Press, 1990), 211–28; and Cheng

Zhangcan 程章粲, "Shen Yue 'Zou tan Wang Yuan' yu Nanchao shifeng kao bian" 沈約《奏彈王源》與南朝士風考辨, *Chuantong wenhua yu xiandaihua* 18 (1995–1996): 19–25, repr. in Cheng Zhangcan 程章粲, *Shizu yu Liuchao wenxue* 世族與六朝文學 (Ha'erbin: Heilongjiang jiaoyu chubanshe, 1998), 179–93. On marriage in early medieval China, see Jen-der Lee, "Women and Marriage in China During the Period of Disunion" (Ph.D. diss., University of Washington, 1992); Gu Xiangming 顧向明, "Zhonggu shiqi de shishu hunyin ji 'mai hun' xisu" 中古時期的士庶婚姻及'賣婚'習俗, *Minsu yanjiu* 3 (2002): 104–11; and Li Jinhe 李金河, *Wei Jin Sui Tang hunyin xingtai yanjiu* 魏晉隋唐婚姻形態研究 (Ji-nan: Qi Lu shushe, 2005).

SHEN YUE 沈約

Impeaching Wang Yuan (*Zou tan Wang Yuan* 奏彈王源)

Gentleman Attendant at the Yellow Gate, concurrently Palace Aide to the Censor in Chief, and Impartial and Just from Wuxing, Shen Yue, kneeling and touching his head on the ground states the following:

I have heard: "Qi was too large to make a proper match [for the heir designate of Zheng];[13] this is recorded in the pronouncements of the past. [Juan Buyi] refused Huo Guang and would not marry his daughter,[14] and his acclaim was handed down in records of feats of yore. As for establishing harmonious accord between two families[15] and distinguishing the proper relationship between well-matched mates, whether high or low, debased or lofty, truly a single standard does not apply. But a person truly should base himself on family status and not distort the proper order [of relationships], thus ensuring that Qin and Jin are equals[16] and that the rivers Jing and Wei do not mix with each other.[17]

Ever since the Song lost control of the realm, the rites and moral teaching have declined. Now the clans that dress in gowns and caps increasingly ignore rules of precedence. Family relationships are muddled and confused, and no regard is given to whether someone is menial or common. They trade and sell the [reputations of] their grandfathers and great-grandfathers and consider it a means of commerce. Bright eyed and thick skinned, they do not have the slightest sense of shame or fear.

As for the heirs of a family of consummate virtue—their generations of accomplishment are something to be cherished. Even the Luan and Xi families are not too far removed from their former glory.[18] Upon reaching adulthood, a man takes a wife. The families from which they purloin lucre are none other than lackeys and minions.[19] After having her headcloth tied and departing for her husband's home,[20] the holder of the dustpan and broom loses her proper place.[21] Upon hearing of this, men of strong principle are sad at heart, and hoary elders sigh over it.

Since the current dynasty has governed the realm, it has greatly changed the canons and laws. Although we have removed the old and promulgated the new,[22] this custom has not been eliminated. The reason that Your Majesty sits at court with a screen at his back and speaks out is because he wishes to purge vile customs. I truly am a fainthearted sort and have erroneously been given charge of the imperial laws. Even though I have the resolve to bury my chariot wheels[23] and I do not submit to powerful and influential men, yet tiny creatures like foxes and rats do harm to the great Way.[24]

It has been rumored that Wang Yuan of Donghai married a daughter to the Man family of Fuyang [in modern Zhejing]. Although Yuan's moral character is mean and base,[25] in fact he is a scion from an illustrious line. His great-grandfather Wang Ya rose to the position of the eighth order.[26] His grandfather Wang Shaoqing served in the palace's curtained chambers.[27] His father Wang Xuan rose to serve the imperial heir, and he also occupied the status of "pure and eminent."[28] Wang Yuan frequently has received an appointment as guard in various bureaus and has been ranked with the highest nobility. Yet on the pretext of marriage to establish bonds of friendship with another family—it was only to seek profit. In bringing stain and disgrace upon his class, no offense could be more severe than this.

Wang Yuan physically is in a distant place,[29] and I have now apprehended the matchmaker, Liu Sizhi, and bade him come to the censorate to be interrogated. Sizhi has set forth the lineage of Man Zhangzhi of Wu Commandery. He said: "Zhangzhi is from an old family of Gaoping, a descendant of Man Chong and Man Fen.[30] In terms of assets, the family is comfortable and well off, and I was entrusted to find a bride for their son Luan. Having been informed by Wang Yuan that he was utterly destitute, I immediately searched the genealogical and service record of Man Zhangzhi. Upon seeing that Zhangzhi had served as Attendant Gentleman in a principality and that Luan also had served as Chief Bureau Clerk for Wang Ci in Wu Commandery,[31] Yuan and his son consulted together and decided to conclude a marriage. Zhangzhi tendered 50,000 cash as a betrothal present. Yuan had previously lost his wife, and he also took the remainder of the present to take a concubine." What the matchmaker testified to tallies exactly with what I had learned through rumor.

I privately looked into Zhangzhi's family background and could not distinguish gentry from commoner. Man Fen died in the Western Court,[32] and his descendants were exterminated.[33] No heir of Wuqiu is known in the Eastern Jin.[34] That this is a false claim is self-evident. That the Wang and Man families would form bonds of marriage is truly shocking! How different this is from the friendly relations between the Pan and Yang families.[35] Furthermore, he purchased a concubine and took a secondary wife, using the betrothal gift as an asset. The funds he received to marry off his daughter he converted into some-

thing to fill his bed and sleeping mat. Such debased passions and excessive behavior he engaged in without compunction. To correct his evil and rectify his
deviance truly must be determined on the basis of this impeachment document. Wang Yuan is the guilty party.

Your servant solemnly offers the following opinion: Nan Commandery aide
Wang Yuan,[36] shamelessly relying on his forebears' status, was able to join the
ranks of the ribboned and capped. He is like other people in appearance, but
he differs from them in his heart. He treated the rite of seeking marriage in the
same way as bearing cloth to trade for silk.[37] Furthermore, he is not of our kind.
The proverbs of the former wise sages say: Sweet-smelling and foul-smelling
herbs are not mixed together.[38] I have learned this from the canons of old. How
could a descendant from a high ministerial family give his daughter in marriage to a man who was in charge of a storehouse? Why should a Zi from Song
and a bream from the Yellow River share the same grave as a ghost who is a
mere menial or lackey?[39] If one from exalted status descends to humble status,
even though he acts for himself, he demeans his ancestors and disgraces his
kin. This is a very serious matter. If this practice is not eradicated, it will spread
out from its source, besmirching the family line and blackening the household,
until it covers every house. We should deal with him according to the clearly
stipulated written statutes and banish him from his class so that his clan,
which has already been disgraced, will feel eternal shame about what happened
in the past and so that those who are about to contract marriage alliances will
alter their ill intent in the future.

Your servant and other officials have consulted and deliberated, and based
on the matters before us, we request that Yuan be dismissed from the office
that he now occupies and that he be banned from office for the rest of his life.
An order should immediately be issued restricting him to quarters but overseeing affairs as before.[40] Based on Yuan's official rank, the impeachment
should be written on yellow paper, but your servant has used white paper to
inform you.[41] Your servant Yue, with sincere trepidation, with sincere fear,
states his case.

[*Wen xuan* 40.1812–16]

NOTES

1.   There are six extant impeachment petitions. See Chen Qingyun 陳慶元, ed. and comm.,
     Shen Yue ji jiao jian 沈約集校箋 (Hangzhou: Zhejiang guji chubanshe, 1995), 3.99–105.
     Shen is also thought to have written a humorous parody of an impeachment petition
     called "The Tall Bamboo Impeaches the Banana" (*Xiu zhu tan ganjiao wen* 修竹彈甘蕉文).
     See *Shen Yue ji jiao jian* 3.106.
2.   *Wen xuan* 40.1812–16. For translations, see David Johnson, *The Medieval Chinese
     Oligarchy* (Boulder, Colo.: Westview Press, 1977), 9–10 (partial); Richard B. Mather,

"Intermarriage as a Gauge of Family Status in the Southern Dynasties," in *State and Society in Early Medieval China*, ed. Albert E. Dien (Stanford, Calif.: Stanford University Press, 1990), 221–27 (partial); and Obi Kōichi 小尾郊一, *Monzen* 文選, *Zenshasku kanbun taikei* 全釋漢文大系 30 (Tokyo: Shusisha, 1976), 438–52.

3. *Wen xuan* 41.1812.

4. Yao Zhenli 姚振黎, *Shen Yue jiqi xueshu yanjiu* 沈約及其學術研究 (Taibei: Wen shi zhe chubanshe, 1989), 37; Liu Yuejin 劉躍進, *Yongming wenxue yanjiu* 永明文學研究 (Taibei: Wenjin chubanshe, 1991), 244–45; Chen Qingyuan 陳慶元, *Shen Yue ji jiao jian*, 559; Cao Daoheng 曹道衡 and Liu Yuejin 劉躍進, *Nanbeichao wenxue biannian shi* 南北朝文學編年史 (Beijing: Renmin wenxue chubanshe, 2000), 281–82.

5. For the biography of Wang Ya, see *JS* 83.2179–81.

6. *ZZTJ* 129.4058–59; Xu Song 許嵩 (eighth century), *Jiankang shilu* 建康實錄, punc. and coll. Zhang Chenshi 張忱石 (Beijing: Zhonghua shuju, 1986), 13.483.

7. Wang Liqi 王利器, ed. and comm., *Yanshi jiaxun jijie* 顏氏家訓集解 (Beijing: Zhonghua shuju, 1993), 5.53.

8. Johnson, *Medieval Chinese Oligarchy*, 11.

9. Mather, "Intermarriage as a Gauge of Family Status," 225.

10. Liu Yuejin, *Yongming wenxue yanjiu*, 290–91.

11. "Quan Liang wen," 27.8a.

12. Zhang Yun'ao 張雲璈, *Xuanxue jiaoyan* 選學膠言 (1822; repr., Taibei: Guangwen shuju, 1966), 17.12b–14a.

13. The Marquis of Qi 齊 wished to marry his daughter Wenjiang 文姜 to the heir designate Hu 忽 of Zheng 鄭. Hu declined. When someone asked the reason for this, Hu replied, "Each person has a proper match. Qi is large, and she is not my proper match." See *Zuozhuan*, Duke Huan 6. The heir designate Hu was the future Duke Zhao 昭 of Zheng (r. 696–695 B.C.E.).

14. When Juan Buyi 雋不疑 was serving as governor of the capital, the grand general Huo Guang 霍光 wished to marry his daughter to him. Buyi adamantly refused and was unwilling to make a match with him. See *HS* 71.3038.

15. *Liji zhushu* 禮記注疏, in *SSJZ* 61.999b: "The marriage rite is intended to join the affection between families of different surnames. Above, it is for the purpose of serving the ancestral temple, and below, it is for the purpose of continuing the family line."

16. *Zuozhuan*, Duke Xi 23: "The Earl of Qin presented [Chong'er] with five daughters among whom was Huaiying 懷嬴 [the wife of Duke Huai of Jin]. She held the wash basin and poured the water for him to wash. When he was finished, he flicked the water off his hands [rather than wiping them with a towel; this was a breach of etiquette]. Angered by this, Huaiying said, 'Qin and Jin are equals, why do you demean me?'"

17. In the conventional formulation, the waters of the Jing River were clear, while those of the Wei River were considered cloudy.

18. The Luan and Xi were prominent families of the Jin state that had been reduced to low status. See *Zuozhuan*, Duke Zhao 3.

19. Shen Yue borrows a phrase from the "Defense Against Ridicule" (*Jie chao* 解嘲) by Yang Xiong 揚雄 (53 B.C.E.–18 C.E.): "Sima Xiangru purloined lucre from Master Zhuo." See

Wen xuan 45.2012. Sima Xiangru eloped with the daughter of the wealthy Shu merchant Zhuo Wangsun 卓王孫. Later, Zhuo gave the couple a handsome dowry. See *Records of the Historian (Shi ji* 史記) 117.3000–3001.

20. *Classic of Poetry (Shijing* 詩經) 156:

The mother ties her headcloth,	親結其縭
Nine and ten are the rules of proper conduct.	九十其儀

Before a bride leaves for her husband's house, her mother ties her headcloth to signify the attachment to her new family.

21. The holder of the dustpan and broom is the bride. Shen Yue says here that she marries beneath her station.

22. *Zuozhuan*, Duke Zhao 17: "In the winter there was a comet in Dachen, [its tail] extending west to the Celestial Han. Shenxu said, 'The comet is a means by which to remove the old and promulgate the new.'"

23. *HHS* 56.1817: "In the first year of Han'an [142], Emperor Shun selected eight emissaries to tour the country and inspect customs. All the envoys were famous elder scholars, except for Zhang Gang 張綱. All the elders received high positions, and Zhang, being the youngest, received the lowest-ranking post. The elders all immediately went to their assigned posts, but Gang buried his chariot wheels at the capital residence in Luoyang. He said, 'With dholes and wolves blocking the road, how can one inquire about foxes?'" He then presented a petition to have the corrupt but powerful official Liang Ji impeached.

24. *Yanzi chunqiu* 晏子春秋 7.7a–8a: Duke Jing asked Yanzi, "Is there a constant among the worries about governing a state?" Yanzi replied, "Slanderers and flatterers hiding at the ruler's side are like rats in the altar of the soil that cannot be smoked out [because one might burn down the altar in doing so]."

25. According to the *Wen xuan chao* 文選鈔, a Tang commentary preserved in the *Wen xuan jizhu*, Wang Yuan was of short stature, and so he was "mean and base." See *Tang chao Wen xuan jizhu huicun* 2:414.

26. Wang Ya 王雅 (334–400) held high positions under Emperor Xiaowu 孝武 (r. 373–396) of the Eastern Jin. For his biography, see *JS* 83.2179–81. In the idealized official rank system of the *Zhou li*, there were nine orders. The eighth order included the Three Excellencies (*San gong* 三公), which were the highest ministerial ranks.

27. Wang Shaoqing 王少卿 was Wang Ya's third son, who served as a princely attendant.

28. Nothing else is known about Wang Xuan 王璿.

29. Wang Yuan was serving in Nan Commandery at the time.

30. Man Chong 滿寵 (d. 242) was a military commander under the Wei. Under Cao Cao, he waged battles against Yuan Shao and Sun Quan. When Cao Pi took the throne, Man Chong led a defeat against Wu in Jiangling. Man Fen 滿奮 (d. 304) was a grandson of Man Chong. He rose from his position as Director of the Ministry of Personnel to Regional Inspector of Jizhou. He was commissioned to present the seals and ribbons of office to Sima Lun 司馬倫 (d. 301) after he briefly was installed on the imperial throne. See *ZZTJ* 84.2651. In 304, he joined several other officials in a plot against Shangguan

Si 上官巳, who had put the heir designate Sima Tan 司馬覃 under their protection in Luoyang. He was killed when the plot was exposed. See *JS* 61.1663 and 82.2143. Gao-ping 高平 was a kingdom established by the Western Jin in 265. Its administrative center was Changyi 昌邑 (south of modern Juye 巨野, Shandong).

31. Wang Ci 王慈 (441–491) had his ancestral home in Linyi, Langye. He was a son of Wang Sengqian 王僧虔 (426–485). For his biography, see *NQS* 46.802–4.

32. The Western Court refers to Luoyang, which was the capital of the Western Jin.

33. Li Shan cites the *Annals of Jin* (*Jin ji* 晉紀) by Gan Bao 干寶, which says that Miao Yuan 苗願 killed Metropolitan Commandant Man Fen. See *Wen xuan* 41.1815. Miao Yuan was a subordinate of Shangguan Si 上官巳, the satrap who had taken control of Luoyang in 303. Presumably, he ordered Miao Yuan to put Man Fen to death.

34. Wuqiu 武秋 is Man Fen's courtesy name.

35. Pan Yue 潘岳 (247–300) was married to the daughter of Yang Zhao 楊肇 (d. 275). The Pan and Yang families came from the area of Xingyang (modern Xingyang, Henan) and apparently had close relationships for several generations. Thus in his "Dirge for Yang Zhongwu," Pan Yue says: "The friendly relations between the Pan and Yang families, / Are long lasting and time honored" (*Wen xuan* 56.2446). Yang Zhongwu is Yang Sui 楊綏 (270–299), his wife's nephew.

36. Nan Commandery is located southeast of modern Jiangling, Hubei.

37. *Classic of Poetry* 58:

A merry fellow of the folk,	氓之蚩蚩
You brought cloth to trade for silk.	抱布貿絲
You did not come to trade for silk,	匪來貿絲
You came to seek me in marriage.	來即我謀

38. *Kongzi jiayu* 孔子家語, *SBCK* 8.1b: "Sweet-smelling and foul-smelling herbs are not stored in the same vessel."

39. *Classic of Poetry* 138:

Why when eating fish,	豈其食魚
Must there be bream from the Yellow River?	必河之魴
Why in taking a wife,	豈其取妻
Must there be a Jiang from Qi?	必齊之姜
Why in eating fish,	豈其食魚
Must there be a Zi from Song?	必宋之子

40. Here Shen Yue uses a series of formulaic phrases that frequently are found in impeachment petitions. The first is *jinzhi* 禁止, which literally means "to restrict" or "to confine." According to the "Monograph on the Bureaucracy," when a person was impeached for an offense, the Chamberlain for Attendants (*Guanglu xun* 光祿勳) was obliged to "confine the person [to his quarters]. *Jinzhi* means that the person cannot enter the palace offices. This is because the Chamberlain for Attendants is in charge of the palace gates" (*SS* 39.1229). What seems to be implied here is that until the case reached its final disposition, the charged person was put under house arrest and was prevented from

consorting with close associates. The second phrase, *shi shi ru gu* 視事如故, has received various interpretations. I have followed the explanation by Lu Shanjing 陸善經: "He is prohibited and not allowed to take up his ranked order at court, but he oversees official matters as usual" (*Tang chao Wen xuan jizhu huicun* 2:430).

41.   The *Wen xuan chao* explains that based on his "high rank," Wang Yuan's case would normally be reported on yellow paper. However, because of his crime, Shen Yue does not use paper appropriate to his rank but reports it on plain white paper. See *Tang chao Wen xuan jizhu huicun* 2:431.

11. Religion and Society on the Silk Road

The Inscriptional Evidence from Turfan

HUAIYU CHEN

From the first century B.C.E., when Emperor Wu of the Han dynasty stretched his power to the northwestern corner of his empire, to the eleventh century, when the Tangut empire occupied the area, the Silk Road functioned as a major venue for the exchange of goods, faith, and material culture between central China and Central Asia, India, and Iran. Persian and Sogdian merchants were the most active traders between China and the western regions, traveling from Luoyang and Chang'an to Antioch and Byzantine via India and Bactria. The eastern part of the Silk Road, Chinese Turkestan—nowadays known as the Xinjiang Uygur Autonomous Region—was an extraordinary hub embracing civilizations from all directions, which is explicitly illustrated in numerous manuscripts, inscriptions, and other cultural relics uncovered from this region. Despite the rise and fall of many small kingdoms through the ages, some cities survived as centers and sustained their multiethnic, multilingual, and multireligious environments. Turfan is one of those great cities on the Silk Road.

Turfan is the modern Uygur name for an oasis city located in the eastern part of the present-day Xinjiang Uygur Autonomous Region in the People's Republic of China, though in the historical materials, it appears under different names in different languages. Turfan offers a great opportunity for examining multiculturalism in early medieval China. Although the majority of the city's population today is Muslim, in the medieval period it was a center for Buddhism and, later in the eleventh and twelfth centuries, for Central Asian Manichaeism and Nestorianism. Many caves with enormous statues and magnificent wall paintings illustrate the flourishing of Buddhism in Turfan in ancient times. The city's political and military significance on the Silk Road can be traced to the Han dynasty (202 B.C.E.–197 C.E.). At that time, it was called Jushi 車師 and was a crucial garrison site for the Han in support of its military campaign against the Xiongnu. Since Han power protected trade between the Han and Central Asia, Turfan also rapidly became a trade center. Later, in the early medieval period, Turfan was known as Gaochang 高昌, which became the name of an independent kingdom from the fifth to the seventh century until it surrendered to the Tang empire in 640. After the Tang took over the region, it absorbed Turfan into its political and institutional administration and renamed it Xizhou 西州,[1] although in local sources, Gaochang remained a popular name for the area. In 755, with the breakout of the An Lushan rebellion, the Tang began having difficulty maintaining control of its peripheral regions, including Gaochang. The rise of the Tibetan empire from the south and that of the Uygur empire from the north undermined the Tang's political authority in its northwestern region, as these two empires continually blocked the Tang's economic and military support of Gaochang. During the eighth and ninth centuries, the Tibetan, Uygur, and Tang powers variously occupied Gaochang. In 840, the Uygurs in the Gaochang area established their own political regime, marking the rise of the Gaochang Uygur kingdom. It lasted for several hundred years before eventually falling to the Mongol empire under Genghis Khan in the thirteenth century. During the Yuan dynasty, like other regions in Chinese Turkestan, Turfan gradually absorbed Islamic culture, and Muslims from different family and cultural backgrounds occupied the area. The Ming government, which followed, never extended its authority to the Turfan area, and only a few Chinese travelers visited the area and left accounts of their travel. Later, during the Qing dynasty, Emperor Qianlong launched a campaign reclaiming political authority of Turfan, and since then, Turfan has remained a part of the Chinese regime.

What makes Turfan important to early medieval Chinese history? Turfan, or Gaochang, developed its own kingdom and culture when the Chinese empire fell apart between the Han and Tang dynasties. When the great Buddhist pilgrim Xuanzang passed through the Gaochang kingdom, he received great respect and financial support from the king, a devout Buddhist. Like another oasis kingdom in the southern part of Chinese Turkestan, Khotan, Gaochang was an important Buddhist kingdom during the medieval period that supplied assistance to Central Asian monks and Chinese pilgrims. How did Gaochang become a Buddhist center? Buddhism arrived in central China around the first century B.C.E. Surprisingly, however, there is no explicit evidence of Buddhism in the Gaochang area earlier than the third century. Without clearly dated manuscripts, inscriptions, and other visual materials, it is uncertain how Buddhism could have bypassed the Gaochang area. But by the fourth century, and especially the fifth century, texts and inscriptions reveal Gaochang as a center of Buddhism.

When Buddhism came to China during the Han dynasty, it was not yet flourishing in Turfan. Buddhism grew in this area mainly through the efforts of the exiled government of the Northern Liang, especially under the reign of Juqu Anzhou 且渠安周. But it did not flourish until the sixth century, when the Qu family came to power in this small kingdom. Ironically, Buddhism arrived in Turfan from the west across the Pamir plateau but was promoted by the Northern Liang regime from the east, via the Hexi corridor 河西走廊. The Northern Liang was founded by Juqu Mengxun 且渠蒙遜 in 397, and later, in 439, it fell under the Northern Wei. Mengxun's brother Anzhou and a group of loyalists fled to Gaochang and established an independent kingdom that lasted from 443 to 460. During the fifth century, the people living in the Gaochang area believed in and made offerings to their local deities. After 460, Gaochang was under the control of several powerful clans, such as the Kan 闞, Zhang 張, Ma 馬, and Qu 麴. Only the Qu family, however, managed to sustain its regime for more than a century, from 502 to 640, which allowed it to develop its own political institutions and religious culture. Under the Qu regime, Buddhism greatly expanded its influence, and Gaochang became its center on the northern route linking the Hexi corridor and Central Asia.

In the sixth century, Buddhism became powerful and popular among both the elite class and the common people. Many manuscripts of Buddhist scripture uncovered from this region are from the sixth and seventh centuries, in addition to inventory lists from the sixth century containing Buddhist elements. One of the earliest lists dates from 543 and belonged to a man named Zhang Hong, living in Astana, and his two wives. Of interest is the colophon at the end of the list, which states that a nun, Guoyuan 果願, sincerely invoked the Five-Path God and that a layperson, Xiaozi 孝姿, observed the five precepts and practiced the ten kindnesses. From this period until the fall of the Qu kingdom in 640, Buddhism had a central role in the political, economic, and social life of the Gaochang area. More than 165 monasteries and several thousand monks and nuns were living in Gaochang during this time, and many monasteries and monks owned lands and gardens. The large monastic population thus forced the government to establish an institution for registering monks and nuns and collecting taxes from them. As landowners, these monks and nuns supported themselves primarily by farming their own lands, which was very different from the monasteries in central China, where the monks and nuns hired local laborers to farm the monasteries' lands.

Several hundred Buddhist manuscripts from the Qu reign have been uncovered. Most of them are Mahayana scriptures popular in central China, including the *Pranjña-parāmitā* texts, the *Lotus Sutra*, and the *Mahāparinirvana Sutra*. Many scriptures are from the versions translated by Kumārajīva 鳩摩羅什 and Dharmaṣena 曇無懺. So it seems that the major resources for Buddhism in the Gaochang area were the translation centers in Liangzhou 涼州 (modern Wuwei) and Chang'an 長安. Although there was a large Buddhist population and it occupied a key position on the Silk Road, Gaochang did not become an important translation center. Given that Buddhism was growing primarily under the rule of the Juqu family, naturally the Juqu family brought many Buddhist scriptures from their homeland of Liangzhou. Kumārajīva stayed in Liangzhou from 386 to 401 and was an active translator. Although the majority of Buddhist manuscripts found in Turfan originated in Liangzhou and Chang'an, a few came from the Southern dynasties, particularly in the Liu-Song and Liang periods. Two manuscripts of the *Lotus Sutra* dated 477 contain colophons indicating that they were offered by Xiao Daocheng 蕭道成, an influential general in the Liu-Song dynasty. The Buddhist scriptures thus appear to have been brought to Gaochang as political gifts from the Southern dynasties.

Buddhist manuscripts are not the only evidence of Buddhism in Gaochang; Buddhist caves and steles in Gaochang can even tell us more about the religion there. Many of the wall paintings preserved in these caves reflect the local practice of Buddhism. In Toyuq, a cave of the Gaochang period called Dingguku 丁穀窟 has wall paintings depicting meditation and the practice of contemplation that can be linked to the manuscripts found in this area, particularly the Mahayana sutras on meditation. A number of copies of such Pure Land texts as the *Amitābha Sutra* and the *Sutra for Visualizing the Buddha of Infinite Life* have also been found in Gaochang, which might indicate the popularity of the Pure Land practice. According to the stele erected by Juqu Anzhou, the Maitreya Buddha was especially popular locally. It is noteworthy that the monks in Gaochang were not vegetarians, as a monastic account sheet found in an Astana tomb (72 TAM 151: 102–3) shows that the monastery bought and stored some meat for the local monks' daily consumption.[2] In sum, the practice of Buddhist monks and nuns, as well as laypeople, in Gaochang was diverse and rich.

Besides the manuscripts and wall paintings, two steles are essential to our understanding of Buddhism in early medieval Gaochang. The first is the stele commissioned by Juqu Anzhou for his virtue in promoting Buddhism, whose text was translated into English in 2004.[3] The second is the stele commissioned by Qu Binzhi (or Qu Bin) 麴斌芝 for establishing a monastery and making offerings. In the following, I offer short introductions to both steles and an English translation of the stele inscription by Qu Binzhi.

The Stele for the Virtue of Establishing a Buddhist Temple by the Great Liang King Juqu Anzhou was discovered by the German art historian Albert Grünwedel during his expedition in the Turfan area in 1902/1903. According to Grünwedel, the stele was uncovered in a temple ruin in the royal area located in the northern section of Kora Khocho 哈喇和卓 (Gaochang), which indicates that it belonged to a royal temple. The stone was originally preserved in the Museum für Völkerkunde Berlin but was later destroyed by bombing during World War II. However, the stele was known to Chinese scholars as early as the Qing, when an official, Duan Fang 端方, visited Berlin in 1905 and brought back a rubbing. In Germany in 1907, Otto Franke first published his study of the stele inscription. Indeed, the stele has attracted the attention of numerous scholars for its significance in understanding the political, economic, and religious context of Turfan in the fifth century.

The stele is about 4.5 feet in height and about 1.2 feet in width. There are a total of twenty-two lines, with forty-seven characters in each line, of which about a thousand characters have survived. The minor damage to the upper part destroyed about a hundred characters. The inscription clearly contains two sections: fourteen lines of prose and a seven-line eulogy. The top line indicates that the inscription was composed by the Vice Director of the Palace Secretariat 中書郎中, Xiahou Can 夏侯粲, and the last line tells that the inscription was commissioned in the third year of the Chengping 承平 period (445), under the supervision of a Buddhist dharma master, Fakai 法鎧, and the Director of Construction Services 典作禦史, Suo Ning 索寧.[4] It is uncertain whether Fakai was the abbot of the newly established temple. But since his name appears along with that of the local director of Construction Services, it suggests that the Buddhist community and the political authority worked together on the construction of this temple.

This stele is crucial to our understanding of the political and religious context of fifth-century Turfan. After the Northern Liang was defeated by the Northern Wei in 439, the king, Juqu Mujian 且渠牧建, fled westward along the Hexi corridor. In 442, Mujian and his refugees relocated to the Turfan region, where he died two years later. His brother Wuhui 無諱 came to power and established the Chengping reign period (443–460). Then, two years after Wuhui's death, Anzhou became king. The stele apparently was erected in the second year after Anzhou took power in Gaochang. Following his family heritage, Anzhou was a devout Buddhist, and a number of manuscripts have colophons indicating that Anzhou had produced the manuscripts as offerings, including *Chishijing* 持世經, *Foshuo pusazang jing* 佛說菩薩藏經, *Shizhu piposha lun* 十住毗婆沙論, and *Huayan jing* 華嚴經. The first three texts were translated by Kumārajīva, and the last was translated by Buddhabadra. In the meantime, because of the dire circumstances the regime experienced in its last several years, it apparently sought Buddhist protection. The regime faced the threat of not only the Northern Wei but also famine. A local monk, Fajin 法進, even imitated the Buddha's action in the Jataka tales by offering his own flesh to feed hungry refugees. Anzhou's engagement with Buddhism is also made explicit in this stele.

The inscription of this stele falls into roughly four sections. The first praises Buddhist teachings and the Buddha. The second is dedicated to a Buddhist master who helped the king promote Buddhism to protect the regime. In particular, this master instructed him about the Maitreya Buddha, the One Vehicle, and the Ten Stages. The third section talks about Anzhou's practicing Buddhism and politics as a dharma king. Despite his political exigencies, Anzhou nonetheless engaged in Buddhist practice, founded a Buddhist temple, commissioned Buddhist statues, and ordered the court historian to record these events. The last section is a eulogy dedicating the Buddhist temple.

The Stele for Establishing a Temple by the Ningshuo General Qu Binzhi is important, too, to our understanding of the political and religious history of Turfan in early medieval China. It was discovered by local peasants in Astana, in the Turfan region, in May 1911 but was soon lost because of the turbulence accompanying the regime's transition. Many leading scholars of the early twentieth century, including Luo Zhenyu 羅振玉, Wang Guowei 王國維, and Naito Konan 內藤湖南, wrote essays on the stele. Huang Wenbi 黃文弼 produced the most comprehensive transcription, and later, Ikeda On 池田溫 wrote another study of its transcription and its political and religious context. According to Ikeda, the recto side of the stele has thirty-one lines, each containing 41 characters. There seem to have been more than 1,100 characters in total, but only 1,086 have survived. The verso side contains thirty-one lines, each with 38 characters. Of the total of 1,178 characters, only 1,016 characters have survived.

This stele was first commissioned by Qu Binzhi in the first year of the Jianchang 建昌 period (556) when he donated his land to the local Buddhist community and established a Buddhist temple there. The stele was erected to commemorate this event. Later, in the fifteenth year of the Jianchang period (575), after his son Qu Liang had renovated the temple, he commissioned another inscription on the verso side of the stele, honoring his father's lifetime achievements. In my discussion of the different sides of the stele, I refer to both Qu Binzhi's inscription and Qu Liang's inscription.

According to Qu Binzhi's inscription, Qu Binzhi donated his land to establish a Buddhist temple in 555 in order to celebrate the peace treaty signed between the Gaochang kingdom and the Turkic kingdom. Although Qu Binzhi was a general while fighting against the Turks, he soon became the Gaochang's representative in the negotiations. In 555, the war ended, and both sides celebrated the political marriage between Qu Baomao 麴寶茂, the king of the Gaochang kingdom, and the princess of Tuobo Khan 陀缽可汗 of the Turks. Both Qu Baomao and Qu Binzhi were grandsons of Qu Jian 麴堅. Qu Binzhi was the Magistrate of Xinxing County 新興縣令 in 555. He donated land in the western part of this county (modern Shengjinkou 勝金口) and established a temple there, which perhaps is the Ningrong temple 寧戎寺 in other textual sources, such as the Buddhist manuscripts found in this area. According to Qu Binzhi's inscription, numerous officials, including the king of the Gaochang kingdom, Qu Baomao, attended the dedication ceremony. Many of the high-ranking officials were from the Qu family, and some of the local Buddhist monastic leaders also were present. As noted, Qu Binzhi's son Qu Liang commissioned another inscription on the back, praising the life of his father, who had dedicated himself to his government and the Buddhist community. In the inscription, Qu Binzhi's title is given as Grand Secretariat Director 绾曹郎中, the highest civil official in the Gaochang government.

Because of the dearth of materials, we do not know the extent to which Buddhism was practiced at the local level in early medieval China, but the steles from Turfan offer us a vivid image of the interaction between Buddhism and local political power. First, the local rulers had a political interest in supporting Buddhism for protection against outside military threats. Second was the hope that Buddhism would bring peace and prosperity to local citizens during a time of famine. Third, the big families, especially the royal family, had the most important role in providing lands and constructing Buddhist temples. Fourth, the stele inscription reveals that Gaochang's political system had been influenced in numerous ways by both the Turkic empire in the north and the Chinese empire in the east.

FURTHER READING

For an introduction to the local history of Turfan region in early medieval period, see Zhang Guangda 張廣達 and Rong Xinjiang 榮新江, "A Concise History of the Turfan Oasis and Its Exploration," *Asia Major*, 3rd ser., 11, part 2, 1998 (1999): 13–36. For a short history of Buddhism in Turfan in the fifth and sixth centuries, see Valerie Hansen, "The Path of Buddhism into China: The View from Turfan," *Asia Major*, 3rd ser., 11, part 2, 1998 (1999): 37–66; and Yao Chongxin 姚崇新, "Bei Liang wangzu yu Gaochang fojiao" 北涼王族與高昌佛教, *Xinjiang shifan daxue xuebao* 新疆師範大學學報, no. 1 (1996): 68–77. For the archaeological investigation of steles in the Turfan area, see Albert Grünwedel, *Bericht über archäologische Arbeiten in Idikuschari und Umgebung im Winter 1902/03*, Abhandlungen der Kgl. Bayerischen Akademie der Wissenschaften I, Klasse l, 24, vol. 1 (Munich: Verlag der Bayerischen Akademie der Wissenschaften, 1905). For early transcriptions of the stele inscriptions, see Otto Franke, *Eine chinesische Tempel-inschrift aus Idikušari bei Turfan* (Berlin, 1907). For modern transcriptions and studies of these stele inscriptions and their historical significance, see Ikeda On 池田溫, "Kōshō sanbi ryakkō" 高昌三碑略考, in *Mikami Tsuguo hakushi kiju kinen ronbunshū: rekishihen* 三上次男博士喜寿記念論文集 (Tokyo: Heibonsha, 1985), 102–20; Jiang Wenguang 蔣文光, "Guben Bei Liang Juqu Anzhou zaofosi bei yanjiu" 孤本北涼且渠安周造佛寺碑研究, *Xinjiang wenwu*, no. 2 (1989): 55–74; and Rong Xinjiang, "Juqu Anzhou bei yu Gaochang da Liang zhengquan" 且渠安周碑與高昌大涼政權, *Yanjing xuebao*, n.s., 5 (1998): 65–92, and "Juqu Anzhou's Inscription and the Daliang Kingdom in

Turfan," in *Turfan Revisited: The First Century of Research into the Art and Cultures of the Silk Road*, ed. D. Durkin-Meisterernst et al. (Berlin: Dietrich Reimer Verlag, 2004), 268–75.

The Stele of Qu Binzhi

CONVENTIONS

[X] the number of X's indicates the number of missing characters; in instances where the number is uncertain, X is followed by a question mark

[X, word(s)] reconstructed missing character(s)

[#] the number within brackets indicates the number of blank spaces preceding an official title; in instances where the number is uncertain, X is followed by the number sign

[He] added the subject

Each numbered passage represents one vertical line on the stele

[RECTO] RECORD OF DONATIONS FOR TEMPLE CONSTRUCTION, BY QU BINZHI, MAGISTRATE OF XINXING COUNTY IN GAOCHANG [*GAOCHANG XINXING LING QU BINZHI ZAOSI SHIRU JI* 高昌新興令麴斌芝造寺施入記]

1. On the twenty-third day of the twelfth month in the *yihai* year 乙亥歲, the first year of the Jianchang 建昌 period [556], the white-robe disciple,[5] the Assault-Resisting General [*Zhechong jiangjun* 折衝將軍], the Magistrate of Xinxing County [Xinxing *ling* 新興令] Qu Binzhi kowtows [XXXXXXXX] all within the territory

2. [XX] assembled monks. Evoke the Majesty Bright King [*Mingwang dianxia* 明王殿下] and speak: civil and military officials and their attendants, and [X] Tathāgatha invokes [XXX] directions. The sound of Sanskrit reverberated,[6] and the [Buddhist] principle reached as high as ten thousand grades. [X, Therefore] for the spirit embracers in the three realms, their innate nature often enjoyed [X]

3. taking refuge; for consciousness embracers in the six realms,[7] their fruits were purified by themselves and gave [merits] back to them. The transformation of benevolence harmonized [X, in] the great thousand world, and the river of generosity moistened the [X, dust] realm. The custom of Mara gradually [X]; and the wind of taming and controlling[8] strongly rose. Five stages of the impure world[9] became the fossil;[10]

4. [X] hell[11] was radically transformed to be the enlightenment place.[12] Then his chariot rested in the Twin Trees,[13] and his light was hidden in Vulture

Peak.[14] Those people who humbly cherished their honest faith constructed temples and drew images, carving cliffs and accumulating mud, melting metal and chopping wood. The touching place struggled for rising; with the method, it succeeded [X].

5. On the images in various temples like a star network and monastic buildings diffused like clouds. The begging gentlemen who were afraid of demons [X] the crows resided and relied on. Worship and confession dispersed sins, and concentration and diligence led to receiving fruits, which was called the magnificent enterprise for controlling life[15] and the wonderful method for expanding the way.[16] Binzhi properly

6. [X] spiritual deities. In his early adulthood he was punished with disaster. His two parents passed away, leaving him without support and [X]. He often miserably sighed at night and felt the sigh of the wind tree;[17] and he considered establishing the afterlife merits for repaying the kindness that he received [from his parents]. He seriously dispensed the living supplies, [X] absorbing [X]

7. thought. To the west of the Xinxing County seat, [he] constructed and erected one Buddhist temple, covering the lack of [X]. There was a rough initiative, and gardens and fields were all offered, which have not been signed and recorded. I was concerned that the superficial years easily passed and the [personal] body and life were difficult to preserve. I hope to preserve [X]. I wrote

8. a plain letter that lists the purposes of donation, which shall be passed on for eternity. The temple is endowed with forty *mu* of fields and wetlands, which reach the path in the east and lean on the valley in the south. Next, the northern wetland of the temple shares the borders in the north with the lone tower of Pan Shouzhi 潘守智 and the vegetable garden of Zhou Yaozhen 周耀真.

9. [It] shares the [X, border] in the east with the vegetable gardens of the Zhen family 鎮家 and Master Zide. The gardens and fields of the temple are all irrigated by the sprinkled water. Next, the pond-fields of the temple reach the fields of the temple of the Zhang clan in the north, the ditch in the east, and [X] in the west. Next, the pond

10. in the wetland of Qincheng 秦城 reaches [the land of] Yi Zhongxuan 已忠玄 and receives from the [XX] channel of the Zhen family. The channel reaches the path of Luozhong 螺中道 in the south, the wetland of Qincheng in the west, the pond of Gouju 茍居 [and] the fields of [X] Zhongguo 忠郭 in the north. Next, the superior [X] three *fen* 三分 on the flatland

11. reaches the path in the north and the pond of the Bu family 卜家 in the west. Next, the [X] *fen* in the pond of Three Pavilions 三亭 reaches the channel in the north, the fields of Hou Gansui 侯干歲 in the west, the pond of Cao Wu'an 曹武安 in the south, and the pond-field on the flatland in the east. Next, [the land in the pond

12. of [X] family was one *fen* 一分. Next, an area of the residential district in the city reaches [X] in the west, the temple of the Sun clan in the north, the city wall in the east, and the house of Xin Zhongyou 辛眾祐 in the south.[18] All the items just listed were used for donation and permanently serve as supplies for the feast. I wish that the

13. sound of bells always rang. The dharma performance was always fresh. The worthy and the bright inherited from one to another, and the achievements and enterprises were not in decline. [I] hope to return this merit, praying to His Majesty the Brilliant King for displaying yin and yang in order to match the flourishing and regulating four seasons[19] in order to equal the outstanding. Everlasting brilliance contended with

14. the eastern clock, and benevolent longevity was second to Southern Mountain. The ultimate virtue elevated with the days and the mysterious [X] afar from the ages. The Jade Branches and the State Leaves, as well as civil and military officials and their attendants, all held faith and embraced loyalty and exhausted their honesty and integrity. They all obeyed the order for the interest of the public and reported and administrated affairs on time.

15. Various regions were joyful and desirous, and the barbarian tribes converted to our customs. I also wish the spirits of King Zhaowu 照武王 and the five kings after him had crossed the river of desires and reached the bank of liberation, wonderfully traveling around the Pure Land and often meeting with the Buddha. I also wish Father's and Mother's

16. deceased spirits and the past spirits of family members all passed over the three realms, and traveled spiritually [through] the [X] realm, facing the holy and enjoying the sound, and obtained the fruits of enlightenment. I and my family members, all sentient beings, universally received this celebration and permanently secured future prosperity. Later, if there are

17. nonfilial descendants, from blood relatives and affines, who rely on power, [X] peculate monastic property, and the temple abbot does not serve well, [causing] unjustifiable expenses, making the one thousand–year merits break immediately, and causing the feast food and monastic supplies to be discontinued by one

18. person. The punishment for this transgression, as the scripture clearly states, of using [XX] has a fine of twenty *jin* of gold, with ten *jin* of gold going to the donor and ten *jin* of gold going to the temple. After having paid what he was fined, he must [still] donate as usual. [XX] the Buddhist assembly, floating compassion

19. the Holy Lord, raining kindness on worthy officials and good attendants and deigning to sign one [X]. It is ordered to receive the resonance at once and pass this evidence to later generations. How is the greatness of the blessing rewards not great? The disciple, Qu Binzhi, joining palms [Vandana], respectfully says:

20. Gaochang Great Monk, [1] Upper Seat, [1] Middle Seat, [1] [XX = Xiazuo, Lower Seat], [1] Vinaya Mastering Learning Feast Host Yuantai Archivist,[20] [1] Karmadāna, [1] Expanding Way Mastering Learning Feast Host, [1] Dharma Master Karmadāna

21. Arbiter [1] Dhyana Master, [1] Arbiter [1] Dharma Master, [2] Arbiter Dhyana Master, [1] Dharma Master, [1] Dhyana Master, [1] Dharma Master, [1] Dhyana Master [12]

22. Commissioned with Extraordinary Powers, Cavalry General, Commander Unequaled in Honor, Commander in Chief of All Military Affairs in Gua Prefecture [modern Yulin, Gansu Province, near Dunhuang],[21] Director of the Chancellery, Prefect of Guan Prefecture, and Dynasty-Founding Commandery Duke in Xiping, [X] Xiying 希瑩 [X] Duodie wuhai[22]

23. Ilig-bäg[23] King of Gaochang Qu Baomao, [4] Right Guard General, Tog-bäg Khan,[24] Tudun-bäg,[25] and Magistrate of Gaochang Qu Qiangu [11]

24. [2] General Commanding the Troops in charge of State Farms in Ningrong County Qu Shaohui, [1] Raising-Awesome General and Prefect of Hengjie in Charge of the Guards Qu, [1] Broadening-Awesome General and Grand Secretariat Director Qu,

25. [2] Administrator [Zhangshi 長史] and Building-Forces General in charge of Ministry of Military Appointments [Qu], [1] Administrator and Tiger-Awesome General in charge of Ministry of Provisions Qu, [1] Administrator and Awesome-Afar General in charge of Ministry of Personnel Qu, [1] Running-River General

26. [2] Qu, [1] Administrator and Awesome-Afar General in charge of Ministry of [Granaries] Ma, [1] Administrator and Awesome-Afar General in charge of Ministry of Sacrifices Yin, [1] Administrator and Pacifying-Desert General in charge of Ministry of Receptions Fan, [1]

27. [2] Administrator He 和, [1] Assistant Administrator [Sima 司馬] of Ministry of Revenue Zhang, [1] [X] Awesome General and Assistant Administrator of Ministry of Personnel Gao, [1] Assistant Administrator of Ministry of Receptions Gao, [1] Assistant Administrator of Ministry of Granaries Yan, [1] Assistant Administrator of Ministry of Military Appointments Gao, [2]

28. [2] Assistant Administrator of Ministry of Sacrifices Qu, [1] Assistant Administrator of Ministry of Provisions [X], [1] Examiner of Chancellery [Menxia jiaolang 門下校郎] Jiao, [1] Examiner of Chancellery Gong, [1] Secretarial Receptionist [Tongshi sheren 通事舍人] Zhang, [1] Secretarial Receptionist [X], [1] [X?]

29. [2] [Xin]xing Monk Upper Seat, [1] Middle Seat, [1] Lower Seat, [1] Archivist, [1] Dharma Master, [1] Dhyana Master, [1] Dharma Master, [1] Dhyana Master, [1] Karmadāna, [1] Xinxing [XX] [1] [X?]

30. [2] [X?] Office Manager of Bureau of Military Appointments, [2] Office Manager of Bureau of Farms Wei, [1] Adjutant of Bureau of Receptionists Dai, [1]

Adjutant of Bureau of Receptionists Qi, [1] Adjutant of Bureau of Farms [X], [1] Department [X?]

31. [2] [X?] Unrestricting and Prestige General, [1] [X] General Yin, Tiger's Teeth General Wei, [1] Children and brother General Lü, [1] Archivist of Bureau of Farms Feng, [1] Bureau of Military Appointment [X?]

[VERSO] EULOGY FOR FOUNDING A TEMPLE,
BY GAOCHANG GRAND SECRETARIAT DIRECTOR
QU BIN 高昌綰曹郎中麴斌造寺銘

1. [#?] The Pacifying the North General and Grand Secretariat [Director Qu Bin XX] Temple Eulogy

2. [#?] Ah! The dharma body was wonderful and boundless, and [XXXXX]; the ultimate rhythm was mysterious, which was the root of assembly conversation. [XX] mutually achieved, the true image was illuminated in such a way that [XX] became manifested. [XXX]

3. [X, XINXIANG] *LING*, TIGER AWESOME QU ZHEN[26] became more explicit. Its function could cultivate [X, XXXX] myriad beings. Alas, rivers and oceans! Why do [they] not follow it? However, sentient beings are dizzy and blinded [and] for a long time sleep in the subjected night. [They] exit and enter the three residences, and [XX]

4. [#?] the realm of six paths.[27] Sunk [XX], crossed [XXX]. For this the Buddha[28] bequeathed the compassion of the dharma mother and equally distributed the love of [his] nephew. His trace descended from the heavenly palace, and his body was born in the imperial mansion, illustrating [XXX].

5. [#?] [He] struggled to complete the great enlightenment and expand the Four Noble Truths [XXXX, X] the Six Perfections of Wisdom[29] in the spiritual house. He raised the enlightenment grades[30] for glorifying the age, and expanded the perfections of wisdom[31] for enlightening laypeople. It was high upon high, and its height was immeasurable. It was deep [and beyond deep] and

6. [X, ADMINISTRATOR], PACIFYING WAVES Qu Xuan Its depth was unfathomable. Having realized that the matter had [X, XX] pure realm.[32] Both the heavens and beings[33] were sad with respect, and their condolence stimulated the mountains and rivers. Therefore all living beings watched the two trees[34] and sighed. The fellows embracing ether [XX]

7. [#?] tree and the eyes of the Chu kingdom. Thus carving [XXX, X] the form of his previous life, decorated with red and green[35] colors, representing his image as he was still alive. There is a way-reaching gentleman Pacifying the North General and Grand Secretariat Director Qu

8. [#?] Bin, who was the uncle of [XXX] from the Jincheng Commandery 金城郡 of He Region 河州 [modern Lanzhou, Gansu Province]. He planted the jade root in the Ji River[36] and pulled up the jade stem from the heavenly branch.

From an early age, he showed the manner of a beautiful jade; while grow-ing up [XXX] the trace.

9. [X, GRAND SECRETARIAT] DIRECTOR QU BIN His heavenly genius was elegantly growing and his heroic strategy [XX. XX] like a sacrificial vessel for the ancestral shrine [*hulian* 瑚璉], and he held his weapon re-sponsibly. At the age of nineteen, he was promoted to Awesome-Afar Gen-eral 威遠將軍 and the Magistrate of Hengjie County 橫截令. His virtue passed on like a breeze, and his [power to] transform advanced god-like. [X] and beating

10. [#?] were not practiced, and his governance was fair and litigations ended. [XXXX], though not enough to be praised. Even the teaching of Wu Yin could not be equal to his. Later he was transferred to the [posts of] Resist-ing-Assault General and the Magistrate of Xinxing County. He exhorted [X] and boosted three kinds of

11. [#?] agriculture. [The cultivation of] mulberry and hemp[37] was orderly and prosperous, and the granary [XXX]. [He] governed [his people] with virtue and unified them with rites; [under his governance] people understood honor and shame, and righteousness and modesty flourished. Later the Turks became strong and powerful, and their might shook the Shuofang 朔方 area [modern Ningxia and eastern Gansu]. [They] enhanced [their] troops

12. [#?] and trained [their] soldiers, invading our northern border. [XXXX] military appointment, receiving the strategy of achieving triumph. The hawk flew out of confinement; and the tiger marched into enemy territory. The military forces confronted each other; in accordance with the situa-tion, we withdrew. The ruler [XXX]

13. [XX] DIRECTOR QU REN counted the time; [he] profoundly understood [XXXX. X] safety and had danger in mind, making decisions in accor-dance with the situation. Thus he was willing to develop a friendship [with the Turks] and permanently preserve our state borders. For [Qu Bin's] talent for professional responses, nobody could equal, therefore [the ruler] dispatched

14. [#?] him to the court of the Turks. From afar [XX; XX] discussed the situa-tional judgments and showed them [both] disasters and blessings. The [Turkic] ruler admired his heroic manner. The [Turkic] soldiers and people feared his powerful strategy. Then they agreed to an alliance and con-tracted a marriage [between the two ruling houses]. [XX]

15. [#?] and returned. Since then, the border [XXX. XX] without concerns. Spears and spikes were wrapped up, bows and arrows were stored, all of which was due to the efforts of this gentleman. For his accomplishments, he was granted a higher rank of nobility and was promoted to be the Force-Shaking General and the Administrator of the Ministry of Personnel [*Minbu zhangshi* 民部長史].

16. [#?] [He was] the column base [XXX, X] the brackets of the vessel of the state. [He] wrapped solidness and softness in the lapel of his intelligence and embraced the civil and military [talents] in his arms. His reputation was not superficial; it was actually earned. [He] [XX][38] loved

17. [#?] and esteemed the mysterious tradition[39] and floated his spirit [XX. XXX] illusion, and [his] insights reached emptiness and existence.[40] Even though he personally administered day-to-day affairs, his will remained in tranquil meditation. His body was confined in a secular web, yet his mind traveled beyond [mundane] things. [He] preferred [X] deep [X],

18. [X Bo]hai LADY GAO'S IMAGE animated and communicated with the principle. His younger brother [Administrator and Pacifying Waves] General in charge of the affairs of civil officials [Qu] Xuan.[41] [Qu Xuan's] charm was elegant and extraordinary, and he was endowed with situational judgment and innovative intelligence. He not only followed the wise but also revered the spirits. [Compared with him], Bing Yuan 邴原 [ca. second–third century] of the Han dynasty was not

19. [#?] worth glorifying;[42] Pan Ni 潘尼 [ca. 250–311] of the Jin dynasty,[43] [XXXX]. While listening to the trials, he had a forgiving mind and was willing to sympathize with the prisoners. Those who were sentenced to be spanked and beaten did not forget his kindness, and those who were sentenced to have their feet amputated still were moved by his thoughtfulness. His body was luminous, relaxed, yet solemn;

20. [#?] his appearance was superior, pure, and beyond reach.[44] Thus he can [XXXX], respectfully practiced Buddhist affairs. Therefore in the west of the city where he governed, there was an illustrious place; he exhaustively donated precious property and built such a numinous temple. Since he decided [X, XX]

21. [#?] constructed house. The silver plate[45] crossed the Milky Way [XXXXX] leaped. The golden bell[46] resounded like the amazing music of the fragrant mountain. Rooms and corridors went round and round; their arrangement followed the Jetavana; meditation rooms linked window by window, [they were] concealed like Tuṣita.

22. [#?] [X] LADY SHI'S IMAGE The orchid tree embraced smoke and hundred flowers [XX, XXX] blossomed. All day they competed for radiance. Green water rippled, sending an elegant sound. A blue wind touched trees, emitting a dense air. Indeed, it was the divine residence for the holy one, and a wondrous location for resting the mind.

23. [#?] Achievements [XX, XXX] entrusted. His [Qu Bin's] heir Tiger-Awesome General and the Magistrate of Xinxing County [Qu] Liang longed to continue his father's achievement and felt he must shoulder [his father's] responsibilities.[47] He climbed [X] mountain to

24. [#?] mourn and admire, longing for [his] parents and grieving for the [X, XXX] days. He sighed that the great virtue [of his parents] could not be

reached.[48] He erected the monumental stele to publicize [their] virtue and hoped for ten thousand years [their] brilliance would be passed on. Its eulogy is as follows:

25. [#?] [X] LADY MENG'S IMAGE The spiritual enlightenment is vast and grand, neither existence nor nonexistence. [XXXX], either reality or delusion. Its form does not have a fixed shape. The going and coming are effortless. Speaking with unusual rhythm, stretching and [X] with time. Pitying the bird in the net, and [X]

26. [#?] the fish in the wok. From the heavenly hall [he] descended [his] trace and into the imperial palace [XX. XX] resonated and pointed out the mysterious path. His virtue covered the great thousand worlds and enticed with three chariots. Once he accomplished his tasks, he withdrew. [His] moving transformation returned to myriad beings; [XX]

27. [#?] became aware of [their] residence. Refined gold and polished jade, [XXXX]. Relying on such blessings, it could permanently witness the eternal life. Ah, Gentleman Qu, his heroic manner reached beyond the Milky Way. He entered the imperial court and was dispatched to the barbarian [X]. [His] benevolence and righteousness

28. [#?] THE WIFE OF THE YOUNGER BROTHER LADY XIN'S IMAGE were cherished, and property and silk were devalued; his kindness was the same as spring [X] and [XX] autumn clouds. He sympathized with the poor and cared about the widowed; he praised the wise and rewarded charity. He respected and taught the right time for agriculture, which led to the plentiful harvest of five grains. In addition to his military strategy, his civil administration was brilliant.

29. [#?] His chariot was parallel to that of the five officials,[49] and his wheel tracks could equal those of the ten assistants.[50] Emptiness [XXX], and truthfulness and falseness both understood. [He] divided [X] and gave up sleep and always stayed fully dressed until dawn. Why [did he stay up] until dawn? He looked up and investigated the mysterious tradition. He poured out treasure and exhausted money, respectfully [X]

30. [#?] holy image. Its skillfulness exhausted all crafts in the world, and its beauty was second only to the work of nature. [XXX] ground, and flying [XX] sky. In the garden elegant water flowed, and in the forest fragrant wind blew. Most beautiful and most good, [it was] eulogized endlessly. Ventured to erect [XX],

31. [#?] carving this hidden merit. Dancing without [X. XXXX]. [3] In the ninth month of the *yiwei* year, the fifteenth year of the Yanchang era [575],[51] [1] after ten days the inscription was completed.

[Ikeda On 池田温, "Kōshō sanbi ryakkō" 高昌三碑略考, in *Mikami Tsuguo hakushi kiju kinen ronbunshū: rekishihen* 三上次男博士喜壽記念論文集:歷史編 (Tokyo: Heibonsha, 1985), 110–13]

NOTES

1. Zhang Guangda 張廣達 and Rong Xinjiang 榮新江, "A Concise History of the Turfan Oasis and Its Exploration," *Asia Major*, 3rd ser., 11, part 2, 1998 (1999): 13–36.

2. Tang Zhangru 唐長儒 et al., *Tulufan chutu wenshu* 吐魯番出土文書 (Beijing: Wenwu chubanshe, 1983), 4:193.

3. Rong Xinjiang, "Juqu Anzhou's Inscription and the Daliang Kingdom in Turfan," in *Turfan Revisited: The First Century of Research into the Art and Cultures of the Silk Road*, ed. D. Durkin-Meisterernst et al. (Berlin: Reimer, 2004), 268–75.

4. Some scholars have suggested that the temple was actually completed in 449.

5. Lay Buddhists wore white robes in the early medieval period. In contrast, Buddhist monastic members wore black robes.

6. In a Buddhist context, "the sound of Sanskrit reverberated" usually is a metaphor for reciting Buddhist scriptures.

7. *Liuqu* 六趣 is the six realms for sentient beings: hells, hungry ghosts, animals, human beings, *asuras*, and *devas*.

8. Taming and controlling indicate the teaching of the Buddha. The Buddha was said to be able to tame and control sentient beings who suffered in the six realms for their bad karma.

9. Here these five stages of the impure world (*wuzhuo* 五濁) refer to the five kaṣāya periods of impurity: the *kalpa* in decay; the deterioration of view; the passions and delusions of desire, anger, stupidity, pride, and doubt; the increase in human misery and the decrease in happiness; and the gradual diminishment of human life to ten years.

10. Literally, this sentence reads as the five stages of the impure world becoming rock, which actually means the impure world becoming the past, a fossil.

11. *Nili* 泥犁 (Skt. *niraya*).

12. *Daochang* 道場 (Skt. *bodhimaṇḍa*).

13. *Shuanglin* 雙林 refers to the *śāla* trees under which the Buddha entered nirvana.

14. *Jiufeng* 鷲峰, which refers to Gṛdhrakūṭa, near Rājagṛha. These sentences describe the virtue of the Buddha and his departure from this world.

15. Here it means achieving longevity.

16. Besides helping to lengthen life, the practice could advance Buddhist teaching.

17. The allusion to the wind tree indicates the death of his parents.

18. The Chinese name Zhongyou 衆祐 (literally, "protecting the assembly") refers to one of the Buddha's ten titles.

19. *Sixu* 四序, the order of the four seasons.

20. *Dianlu* 典錄 usually appears in Chinese sources as *dianpu* 典簿.

21. Guazhou 瓜州, which usually appears with Shazhou 沙州 (modern Dunhuang).

22. Duofudie wuhai 多浮跌無亥. These five characters, along with the missing characters as well as *xiying*, must be the transliteration of the official Turkic title, but unfortunately I cannot identify the original transcription and its meaning.

23. Xilifa 希利發 was a Turkic title for a king. See Omeljan Pritsak, "Von den Karluk zu den Karachaniden," *Zeitschrift der Deutschen Morgenländischen Gesellschaft* 101 (1950): 270–300. Alessio Bombaci, however, suggests that it is from the Turkic title Eltäbär, in "On

the Ancient Turkic Title Eltäbär," in *Proceedings of the Ninth Meeting of the Permanent International Altaistic Conference*, Naples, Italy, 1970, 1–66.

24. Duobohan 多波旱. This may be a different transliteration of Tuobahan 拓跋汗, a Turkic title. For the study of Tog-bäg, see An-King Lim, "On the Etymology of T'o-Pa," *Central Asiatic Journal* 44, no. 1 (2000): 30–44.

25. Toutunfa 鍮屯發. In Chinese sources, it often appears as Tutunfa 吐屯發, a Turkic title.

26. The title and name heading this line—as well as those heading lines 6, 9, 13, 18, 22, 25, and 28—most likely represent a type of caption that accompanied images that are no longer visible.

27. *Liudao* 六道, which is the same as *liuqu*. See note 7.

28. Nengren 能仁 (literally, "mighty in loving kindness") is one of the Buddha's ten titles.

29. The Six Perfections of Wisdom refer to the six *pāramitās*: *dāna* (charity or donation), *śīla* (observing the precepts), *kṣānti* (patience), *vīrya* (progress), *dhyāna* (meditation and contemplation), and *prajñā* (wisdom).

30. *Daopin* 道品 refers to the thirty-seven conditions leading to enlightenment: the four states of memory (*smṛtyupasthāna*), the four proper lines of exertion (*samyakprahāṇa*), the four steps toward supernatural power (*ṛddhipāda*), the five spiritual faculties (*pañca indriyāṇi*), their five powers (*pañca balāni*), the seven degrees of enlightenment (*sapta bodhyaṅga*), and the eightfold noble path (*aṣṭa-mārga*).

31. *Bore* 波若, usually *bore* 般若, Skt. *prājñā*.

32. Although three characters are missing here, this sentence apparently is delivering the message that the Buddha has died or has entered his final nirvana.

33. The "heavens and beings" refer to the two beings in the six realms.

34. The Buddha achieved his final nirvana under two *śāla* trees, which indicate his departure from this world.

35. *Danqing* 丹青, red and green, refers to traditional Chinese painting.

36. Jishui 姬水.

37. Literally, *sang* 桑 and *ma* 麻 (mulberry and hemp) refer to traditional Chinese agriculture.

38. I suspect that an adverb defining "loved and esteemed" is missing here.

39. *Xuanzong* 玄宗 (mysterious tradition) refers to Buddhism.

40. *Kongyou* 空有 (emptiness and being) refers to Buddhist ontology.

41. Xuan 暄. Qu Xuan was Qu Binzhi's younger brother.

42. Bing Yuan, who lived in the late Han dynasty, was glorified as a typical Confucian scholar who observed the Confucian rites and institutions. In 208, the powerful general Cao Cao lost his beloved son Cao Chong, and Bing Yuan's daughter had just passed away. Cao Cao asked to bury his son with Bing Yuan's daughter, but Bing Yuan turned down his request because he thought that it would violate Confucian rites.

43. Pan Ni was a distinguished writer in the Western Jin dynasty and devoted himself to learning and writing. He was killed during the Xiongnu invasion near Luoyang.

44. This rhetoric is used to suggest the inaccessible and unparalleled nature of his physical body.

45. The "silver plate" is the moon.

46. The bell is an important ritual instrument in a Buddhist monastery.

47. This allusion is from the *Zuo Commentary* to the *Spring and Autumn Annals* 左傳.

48. This allusion is from the *Classic of Poetry* (*Shijing* 詩經).

49. This allusion to the five wise officials may indicate, in different texts, a different set of five people. In the *Analects*, according to He Yan's commentary, it refers to those who helped the sage-king Shun: Yu 禹, Ji 稷, Xie 契, Gao Yao 皋陶, and Bo Yi 伯益. In the *Classic of Documents* (*Shangshu* 尚書), the five officials are those who helped the Zhou King Wen: Guo Shu 虢叔, Hong Yao 閎夭, San Yi Sheng 散宜生, Tai Dian 泰顚, and Nangong Kuo 南宮括. In *Lü's Spring and Autumn Annals* (*Lüshi chunqiu* 呂氏春秋), the five are those who helped the Zhou King Wuwang: Zhou Gong Dan 周公旦, Shao Gong Shi 召公奭, Tai Wang Gong 太公望, Bi Gong Gao 畢公高, and Su Gong Fensheng 蘇公忿生.

50. In the *Classic of Documents*, the ten servants who helped the Zhou King Wu are Zhou Gong Dan 周公旦, Shao Gong Shi 召公奭, Tai Gong Wang 太公望, Bi Gong Gao 畢公高, Rong Gong 榮公, Tai Dian 泰顚, Hong Yao 閎夭, San Yi Sheng 散宜生, Nangong Shi 南宮適, and wife of King Wen 文母公.

51. The *yiwei* year 乙未 here refers to 575, the fifteenth year of the Yanchang era.

PART III

Cultural Capital

The Six Dynasties period witnessed important transformations in the conception of cultural supremacy. Cultural phenomena were closely associated with the notion of *wen*, which often and specifically referred to "refined literature" or "elegant writings" in this period.[1] The educated class developed a variety of ways to participate in their cultural heritage, such as philosophical conversation, the creation of new literary genres, literary criticism, and the making of anthologies. Part III is concerned with the production, organization, and evaluation of cultural accomplishments in the Six Dynasties. The steady accumulation and transmission of a certain cultural wealth through the subscription to a set of shared texts and methods as well as goals of study identified the membership of the literati elite and ensured its privileges. Cultural capital—defined as competence in interpreting cultural codes and products, a competence that is accumulated and transmitted within a family or, more broadly, a social class—provides a useful framework in which to discuss developments in the fields of literature and cultural arts.[2] This knowledge or intellectual stock, moreover, could be converted into economic or political gain, as the texts discussed in this part suggest.

Oral argument and poetry writing defined, to a spectacular extent, the literati culture of early medieval China. "Pure conversation" (*qingtan* 清談), a scholarly and social activity popular among the gentry elite, involved debates on metaphysics, epistemology, and behavior, as well as on reconciliations between the "Three Mysterious Works" (*san xuan* 三玄: the *Classic of Changes* [*Yijing* 易經], the *Classic of the Way and Virtue* [*Daodejing* 道德經, or *Laozi* 老子], and the *Zhuangzi* 莊子) and the Classics. From a certain vantage point, pure conversation can be viewed as an intellectual game and competitive performance with its own rules, criteria, and accoutrements (including the distinctive sambar-tail chowry, a whisk-like accoutrement held by the debaters), many episodes of which are recorded in the fifth-century collection of anecdotes *Recent Anecdotes from the Talk of the Ages* (*Shishuo xinyu* 世說新語).[3] At stake, however, were the social reputation and, in some cases, the political career of the conversationalists. Men occupying the highest political office during the Jin dynasty took conversation seriously. Indeed, Charles Holcombe argues that an "understanding of the universal pattern of the Dao was the key to successful government, and . . . [w]ithin the medieval literati worldview the literati proclivity for abstruse metaphysical discussion was not viewed as a distraction from administrative duty, but the best qualification for it."[4] Pure conversation developed from the art of discourse (*lun* 論) associated with the masters of rhetoric from the Zhengshi period (240–248), such as Xi Kang (223–262), whose famous work "Sound Is Without Sadness or Joy" is translated and discussed here by Robert Ashmore.

This essay is a textual representation of a staged dialogue between a "host" (*zhuren* 主人), who maintains the position named by the title, and a "guest" (*ke* 客), who challenges that position. The host refutes a series of interpretations of classical examples of sounds containing emotions raised by the guest and argues in several instances for what would be described today as an "arbitrariness of signs": tones and sounds are "inconstant," and the "same things often bear different designations" among different regions and customs. Therefore, sounds may move their auditors differently. Moreover, the effect of sounds should not be confused with their inherent property; that is, sounds may cause the release of a given emotion, but they cannot be said to possess that emotion.

During the Six Dynasties, poetry writing became increasingly a sure marker of cultural literacy and social legitimacy. As Ping Wang observes in her discussion of the rise of the arriviste Liu Xiaochuo 劉孝綽 (481–539) to a very high position in the court of the Liang Emperor Wu, the art of poetry writing became an "important site of competition for cultural prestige." Literary competence (e.g., the ability to draft edicts and proclamations on behalf of rulers and to write poetry in court functions) had always been useful for a literatus's political career, but during the late Six Dynasties, literary achievements became an especially important means for advancement into a prominent political station. As Xiaofei Tian points out, family lineage, which had dominated for centuries as the main path to high political office, was "no longer the only standard for judging a man." Instead, "possession of *wen*" defined a new cultural elite, and cultural competence became the "family business" for hitherto lesser social groups or ambitious clans.[5]

The family of Liu Xiaochuo belonged precisely to this new cultural elite. Within merely a few generations, the Liu clan of Pengcheng rose in prominence, and their literary accomplishments played no small role in their rise, as Ping Wang explains here.[6] Poetry writing became a favorite occupation for those seeking social or political advancement, as it did for men already established in high places. The six poems written by the prince of Jin'an, Xiao Gang, and his principal courtiers, translated by Xiaofei Tian, illustrate this literary competence at work. These poems commemorate an offering made by Xiao Gang at the Temple of the Exalted Emperor of the Han, Liu Bang. This symbolic act taps into the political capital of the founding emperor of the great Han dynasty, appropriated here through cultural means (i.e., poetry writing) and thereby, as Tian contends, affirms the political legitimacy of the new Liang dynasty.

The practice of allusion and quotation became an increasingly integral part of the art of poetry writing. In the poetic tradition that developed during the Six Dynasties, when writing became deeply embedded in the already established vocabularies of responses to the outer world, the goal of the poet was not only to learn the repertoire of responsiveness but also to build on it. Writing well, like reading well, meant demonstrating both a command of the literary tradition and cultural codes, and the ability to appropriate them. Allusion and quotation enable a writer to display knowledge and appreciation of the past in complex and economical ways; that is, they can amplify a poem of limited characters by drawing in extratextual associations and tapping into larger systems of signification. In a good example, Liu Xiaochuo couches his message to Ren Fang, whose patronage he sought, in poetic allusions. Literary competence is equally required to decipher the codes within which the message is inscribed, as can be seen in Ren Fang's response. Another example, the poetry of Sun Chuo, brings to the foreground a specific type of quotation that became prevalent during the Wei and Jin dynasties. References to the "Three Mysterious Works" in the written discourse and pure conversation discussed earlier extended to poetic composition as well. As Paul W. Kroll points out, the *xuanyan shi* (verse on the mysterious) by Sun Chuo, among many others, delved into metaphysical, epistemological, and semiotic issues by drawing extensively from the "Three Mysterious Works."

As the cultural capital of the literati accumulated, the question of how to manage this wealth guided various endeavors in the field of literature. One important means of ordering cultural capital was anthology making, which became increasingly commonplace over the Six Dynasties, culminating in the influential compilation *Selections of Refined Literature* (*Wen xuan* 文選), supervised by the crown prince of Liang, Xiao Tong. The earliest-known anthology of diverse genres dates to the late third and early fourth centuries, the *Anthology of*

Literary Compositions Divided by Genre (*Wenzhang liubie ji* 文章流別集), by Zhi Yu 摯虞 (d. 311), which was a model for Xiao Tong's anthology. In my discussion of the discourse that was part of the *Anthology*, I frame Zhi Yu's work as a response to a growing situation in the literary field: a proliferation of genres and forms as well as works by individual writers. The easier availability of paper enabled the increasingly widespread circulation of manuscripts and their duplication, hence a greater likelihood of preserving and transmitting texts.

The proliferation of both genres and examples also created more confusion among genres. Zhi Yu's "Discourse" tackles this issue, as the extant passages reveal that he not only scrupulously defines each genre and discusses exemplary works but also singles out cases of confusing one genre for another (e.g., Yang Xiong's "Laud for Zhao Chongguo" resembles more an elegantia than a laud). The classification of various literary genres into a system likely developed from the interest in the late Han and early Wei in classifying and evaluating people. This interest is well represented by many anecdotes in the *Recent Anecdotes from the Talk of the Ages* illustrating the sort of character appraisal and categorization of human behavior that was the milieu of Zhi Yu's work. Zhi Yu's efforts at organizing the diverse genres and elevating models led the authors of the "Treatise on Bibliography" (*Jing ji zhi* 經籍志) of the *History of the Sui* (*Sui shu* 隋書) to describe his work as follows: "Zhi Yu, who pitied the readers who labored in exhaustion [due to the sheer volume of available works], therefore selected only the peacocks and kingfishers and mowed and cut out the overgrown weeds."[7]

Other extant examples of literary criticism from the period show a similar concern for taking stock of literary developments, evaluating examples, and rectifying standards. For example, "Discourse on Insect Carving" (*Diaocong lun* 雕蟲論) by Pei Ziye 裴子野 (469–530), translated and analyzed here by Jack W. Chen, surveys the historical development of poetry from the *Classic of Poetry* (*Shijing* 詩經) to his own time. There is a strong sense of exigency in Pei Ziye's conservative poetics: what he perceives as "depraved and ornate" literature was a sure sign of a chaotic age. For Pei Ziye, the moral and ethical purpose found in canonical poetry had degenerated into an ornate formalism that was applied to little other than "grasses and trees" and "wind and clouds."

With the flourishing of literary production as manifested by a proliferation of both genres and examples, literary criticism also rose to new heights. A contemporary of Pei Ziye, Zhong Rong 鍾嶸 (ca. 468–518), wrote the earliest major work of poetic criticism, *Grades of the Poets* (*Shipin* 詩品), whose system is built by the triple tasks of determination of filiation (for the fuller entries), assessment of poetic style, and assignment of rank. As Stephen Owen observes in his introduction to Zhong Rong's preface to the *Grades of the Poets*, Zhong Rong's work of evaluation and judgment was in part a response to the "craze for poetry" that had culminated by his time, which produced an excess of bad examples ("commonplace sounds and impure norms of genre"). Equally of concern to Zhong Rong was that there were too many opinions and judgments, hence "no standard to rely on." Zhong Rong thus set out to "write" down the oral judgments of Liu Hui 劉繪 (458–502), who possessed "exceptional taste." The systematic organization of poets and their poetic output in the *Grades of the Poets* reads like a definitive expression of literary competence. Owen also looks at the question of who was the actual arbiter of taste, Zhong Rong or Liu Hui.

The accumulation of cultural capital also assumed physical form in book collections. The first known writing on book collecting is by the Liang Prince of Xiaodong, Xiao Yi, as discussed here by Xiaofei Tian. Born into privilege, Xiao Yi began amassing what became one of the largest private book collections in the late Six Dynasties at the tender age of six, when he received a set of Confucian Classics from his father, the Liang Emperor Wu. The relevant chapter from Xiao Yi's *Master of the Golden Tower* (*Jinlouzi* 金樓子) is invaluable to our understanding of not only book culture but also the circulation of texts in the early medieval Chinese manuscript culture. This chapter offers illuminating details about the various modes of book acquisition (hand copying, purchase), as well as which manuscript editions were most prized owing to the paper and ink used. The widespread proliferation and dissemination of texts in the late Six Dynasties formed the context in which Ruan Xiaoxu 阮孝緒 (479–536), a private scholar, sought to produce a comprehensive catalog of books in the realm. "One hopes that all the hidden records and lost titles of the world have been included in this catalog," he writes in the preface to his *Seven Records* (*Qi lu* 七錄), the second work translated and discussed by Tian. In his preface, Ruan evaluates the organization of previous catalogs (e.g., those by Liu Xiang and Wang Jian) and explains how he builds on the older systems. The preface is a rich document that details the ways in which knowledge could be classified and organized in early medieval China and, by extension, reflects an impressive effort to order the cultural capital of the realm.

Wendy Swartz

NOTES

1.   On the notion of *wen* in the Six Dynasties, specifically in the *Wen xuan*, see David R. Knechtges, introduction to Xiao Tong, comp., *Wen xuan, or Selections of Refined Literature*, vol. 1, *Rhapsodies on Metropolises and Capitals*, trans. David R. Knechtges (Princeton, N.J.: Princeton University Press, 1982), 17–21, 52.

2.   My discussion of "cultural capital" is informed by Pierre Bourdieu, *Distinction: A Social Critique of the Judgement of Taste*, trans. Richard Nice (Cambridge, Mass.: Harvard University Press, 1984); and Pierre Bourdieu, *The Field of Cultural Production*, trans. Randal Johnson (New York: Columbia University Press, 1993).

3.   Jack W. Chen, chapter 21 of this volume.

4.   Charles Holcombe, *In the Shadow of the Han: Literati Thought and Society at the Beginning of the Southern Dynasties* (Honolulu: University of Hawai'i Press, 1994), 133.

5.   Xiaofei Tian, *Beacon Fire and Shooting Star: The Literary Culture of the Liang (502–557)* (Cambridge, Mass.: Harvard University Asia Center, 2007), 9, 47.

6.   It is noteworthy that even families that for centuries had belonged to the top echelon of society sought to foreground their excellence in the literary field rather than in politics. For example, Wang Yun of the illustrious Langye Wang clan proudly tells his sons that unlike other clans that have passed on literary talent for merely a few generations, the Wang clan has excelled in literary achievements for seven continuous generations, with each member producing his own collected works. Tian discusses the example of Wang Yun in *Beacon Fire and Shooting Star*, 48–49.

7.   *Sui shu* 35.1089.

12. The Art of Discourse

Xi Kang's "Sound Is Without Sadness or Joy"

Retracing the origins of a word or phrase in everyday speech sometimes provides a surprising reminder of the distances separating our familiar mental world from the mental worlds of past ages. The English word "undermine," for example, is an abstract, though quite ordinary, expression—describing the effect, say, of contradictory evidence on an argument, of embarrassing revelations on someone's social standing, and so on—yet when we reflect on the word's origins, we remind ourselves with a slight shock that it began as a concrete word, a word whose currency implied a community of speakers for whom the technologies and tactics of a now long-vanished mode of siege warfare were a commonplace point of reference. Similarly, reflecting on the evolution of the familiar Chinese expression *tan he rong yi* 談何容易 can provide an indication of the distance between some of our commonplace notions about speech and action and those of premodern China.

In its modern usage, the phrase *tan he rong yi* is generally construed as if it meant "the things you talk about—do you suppose they are really so easy?" In effect, the phrase works something like the English idiom "talk is cheap." Like that English phrase, the modern Chinese expression *tan he rong yi* hinges on an assumed opposition between mere talk and real action. When we look at the classical sources from which the phrase *tan he rong yi* derives, however, we discover that its original sense was quite different. In its proper classical construal it means "conversation—do you think that's an easy thing?" Rather than assuming a distinction between (easy) speech and (difficult) action, the phrase emphasizes precisely that conversation *is* a kind of action and one, moreover, that may be fraught with difficulty.

The following quotation, from a letter written in the 470s or so by Wang Sengqian 王僧虔 (426–485) to his sons, reveals much about a particular medieval Chinese mode of "conversation," its difficulties, and the cultural and social stakes involved:

> Dongfang Shuo had the saying, "How can 'conversation' be considered easy?" [*tan he rong yi*].[1] On viewing the various *xuan* texts, my ambitions ran rampant, and my innards were tugged: while focusing on a single book, I'd memorize several dozen commentators, one by one. From youth straight through to old age, my hands have never been without a book, and still I dare not speak lightly of these things. You've unrolled your *Laozi* as far as about five feet from the beginning of the scroll and don't yet know what Wang Bi has said or what He Yan's argument is, where Ma Rong and Zheng Xuan differ, or what the *Exegetical Principles* elucidate.[2] Yet you are already grandly swishing your yak-tail whisks and referring to yourselves as Masters of Conversation. This is the most reckless course of action one could imagine. What if Magistrate Yuan were to command you to speak of the *Changes*, or Secretary Xie to incite you to speak of the *Zhuangzi*, or Mr. Zhang from Wuxing to sound you out in a discussion of the *Laozi*? Do you really suppose that at that point you would be able to backtrack and say, "I never read them"? Conversation is thus like archery: when the earlier shooter has hit a target, the later ones must be able to hit it as well; if they can't, then they will lose the wager.
>
> Besides, there are the discourses and commentaries of the hundred schools, the "eight categories" of Jingzhou, and those discourses on "Endowment versus Nature," the "Four Fundamentals," and "Sound Is Without Sadness or Joy"—all these things are common fodder for masters of speaking, just like the furnishings and provisions one must prepare in advance of the arrival of guests. And you have not so much as heard of or glanced over these things. Do you suppose that anyone would presume to receive an illustrious guest without first making sure that all was in order in the kitchen?[3]

The "conversation" discussed here is the specific and formalized mode of philosophical and exegetical disputation often termed "pure conversation" (*qing tan* 清談) or "conversation about the Mysterious" (*xuan tan* 玄談). The central range of topics for conversations of this type would be difficult points of interpretation raised by the "Three Mysterious Works" (*san xuan* 三玄)—the *Classic of Changes* (*Yijing* 易經), the *Laozi* 老子, and the *Zhuangzi* 莊子—and particularly the paradoxes involved in accommodating the implications of those works with the authority of the Five Classics. Wang Sengqian describes how he has devoted his entire life to becoming versed in the lore on which the conversationalist must draw but that he dares not, even in old age, claim to be an adept in the form.

What comes through most clearly here is Wang Sengqian's concern, ultimately a practical one, about the possible consequences of his sons' rash behavior in setting themselves up as conversationalists without adequate training. As the letter makes clear, conversation is a form of social exchange through which prestige and reputation may be either gained or lost; the topics may seem abstruse, but the stakes are quite real. Wang himself was particularly aware of such issues because he was descended from one of the most prominent families of the old Jin aristocracy, the Langye Wangs, but his family's real power and prestige were on the wane. Later in this letter, Wang Sengqian goes on at some length about the uncertainty whether his sons will be able to obtain official posts through ancestral privilege as a way of bringing home to them the importance of making sound career choices. This letter, then, is fundamentally about household management—"economics" in its primordial sense. Unconvinced as he seems that venturing out into elite society as conversationalists is the right choice for his sons, "pure conversation" is clearly, in Wang Sengqian's view, a viable career for the right sort of person with the proper training. The comparison at the end of the preceding passage, linking the scholarly preparation of the aspiring conversationalist to the laying in of provisions by a judicious head of household, vividly reminds us that the preparations involved in training a conversationalist were in a very real sense a form of cultural capital, whose successful management could lead to fortune.[4]

What, then, were the "provisions" that the aspiring conversationalist would need to lay in? Wang Sengqian's survey divides the necessary items into a few discrete categories. First, it was necessary to digest the full range of earlier interpretations of the "Three Mysterious Works" themselves. Second, one also had to know a broader range of scholarly and philosophical lore, including the ancient philosophical schools and their commentaries. The "eight categories of Jingzhou" is perhaps the layer of preparation that subsequent history has rendered most obscure: this term refers to the texts and the tradition of scholarship that emerged in the southwestern city of Jingzhou during the transition from the late Eastern Han to the Wei. In the endgame of the civil strife that ended the Eastern Han, Liu Biao 劉表 (d. 208) assembled probably the single most important center of scholarly activity, in the form of both scholars and books, at Jingzhou, in hopes of eventually parlaying this geographical and cultural position into the rulership of a new dynasty. The project, of course, failed, but the legacy of Jingzhou scholarship, in the transmission of texts and in former Jingzhou scholars, played a key role in forming the particular analytical vocabulary of Wei dynasty philosophical discourse.

A final layer in the formation of the successful conversationalist as outlined by Wang Sengqian comprises the recognized "classics" of the conversational genre itself: a roster of difficult or paradoxical theses that might be sustained or refuted in debate, especially because they had been discussed in canonical essays by the Wei dynasty figures who were regarded as the founders of this genre of conversation. The Jin and the later tradition of "pure conversation" came to look back to the Wei as its golden age and referred to the recollected conversations of the masters of that age (and the texts embodying their conversational style) as the "tone of the Zhengshi reign" (240–248) (*Zhengshi zhi yin* 正始之音). Along with "Sound Is Without Sadness or Joy"—the topic given its definitive treatment by Xi Kang (223–262) in the essay translated in this chapter—Wang mentions the topics "Discourse on the Endowments Versus Nature" (*Cai xing lun* 才性論) and "The Four Fundamentals [of Human Capacities]" (*Si ben lun* 四本論), those subjects in the analysis of human character and ability most closely associated with Xi Kang's near contemporary and bitter (indeed, in the end, deadly) enemy, Zhong Hui 鍾會 (224–263). Other standards of the conversational repertoire included questions such as the validity of techniques for prolonging one's life span (also treated by Xi Kang in the essay "On Nourishing Life" [*Yang sheng lun* 養生論]) and the question of the adequacy or inadequacy of language, as explored in discourses on both sides of the thesis "words exhaust (or do not exhaust) meaning" (*yan jin* [*bu jin*] *yi* 言盡 [不盡] 意).

If we compare the various commentaries to the "Three Mysterious Works" with the fixed patterns for openings and defenses studied by students of chess, then classic discourses like these are perhaps analogous to the actual games of grandmasters, studied and picked apart by students of the game to gain a sense of how that repertoire of basic patterns might play out in an actual exchange. Such classics of the discourse genre could help the aspiring conversationalist by both illustrating general strategies and giving guidance on handling those very same theses, which appear to have been commonly recycled in later conversational practice, as we see in the following anecdote about the Langye Wang clan's most illustrious ancestor, Wang Dao 王導 (276–339): "Of old it was said that after Prime Minister Wang crossed to the south,[5] he spoke of only three theses: 'sound is without sadness or joy,' 'nourishing life,' and 'words exhaust meaning.' But his treatment of them was supple and full of novel insights, entering into every imaginable connection."[6]

Wang Dao, then, is an adept economist: like the host whose kitchen staff is able to present a plentiful supply of delicacies starting from simple ingredients and a limited budget, he successfully carries off the role of conversationalist while limiting himself to only a few familiar theses of the genre. Such anecdotes remind us of the ways in which it makes sense to think of Xi Kang's "Sound Is Without Sorrow or Joy" as not simply an essay laying out a particular philosophical position but, in a real sense, a form of cultural capital.

Xi Kang's essay itself is not, of course, an actual example of the art of conversation, but it does, like many other written works in the genre of the discourse (*lun* 論), adopt the form of dramatic dialogue, in which a "host"—referred to here as the "host of the Eastern Wilds" (*dongye zhuren* 東野主人)—maintains the thesis that gives the discourse its name, against a series of "refutations" (*nan* 難) put forward by a "guest"—here called the "guest from Qin" (*Qin ke* 秦客). Other discourses are written directly in the person of the author, often followed by series of "refutations" and "replies" in the form of actual letter exchanges with other writers. Moreover, even in instances of actual face-to-face conversations such as those documented in the *Recent Anecdotes from the Talk of the Ages* (*Shishuo xinyu* 世說新語) and other sources, it was conventional for the two main participants to adopt the roles of "host" and "guest" and for the exchange to unfold around some central thesis that the "host" maintained against the refutations of the "guest." When the participants had exhausted one thesis and wanted to go on to another, they could even reverse roles, like chess players switching black and white between games. Thus written "discourse" and oral "conversation" share a sort of chicken-and-egg relation that makes it impossible to determine which plays the leading role.

Xi Kang's discourse also reflects the various layers of textual and exegetical expertise that came to characterize the genre of "pure conversation." The thesis "Sound Is Without Sorrow or Joy" would have sounded deliberately paradoxical to its first medieval readers, for precisely the reason laid out by the "guest" in the opening salvo of the exchange. There would seem to be ample classical documentation, in both the "Record of Music" (*Yueji* 樂記) chapter of the *Record of Rites* (*Liji* 禮記) and the "Great Preface" (*Da xu* 大序) of the Mao-school commentary on the *Classic of Poetry* (*Shijing* 詩經), that "sound" did indeed have joy and sadness (see section 1A). The task of the "host," then, is not simply to lay out a novel thesis about the relation between sound and emotions but to show how his understanding coheres with the authority of these classical dicta. Thus his task is both philosophical, in laying out his understanding of the relations between emotions and sounds, and exegetical, in the sense that his account ultimately is an explanation of how we ought to understand the classical authorities invoked at the outset by the "guest" so as to eliminate the apparent contradiction.

The main classical authorities referred to in Xi Kang's discourse are the *Record of Rites* and the Mao-school "Great Preface," along with episodes from the *Classic of Documents* (*Shangshu* 尚書) describing the institution of music by sage-kings of the past and, in particular, the *Analects*, a text invoked for both its descriptions of Confucius's responses to music and (by the "host" in particular) its embodiment of an authoritative conversational voice. In the texts that may have appeared in Wang Sengqian's catalog of "pure conversation" discourse, there are occasional echoes of the *Classic of Changes* and the *Laozi*, but the primary source here is the *Zhuangzi*, especially the long discussion of various kinds of sound that appears in that book's second chapter, the "Discourse on Thinking of Things as Being on the Same Level" (*Qiwu lun* 齊物論). The technical concepts that Xi Kang invokes are borrowed from the vocabulary of Wei discussions of epistemology and the judgment of human nature and capacities that we associate with such writers as Liu Shao 劉劭 (d. ca. 239) and Xu Gan 徐 幹. Xi Kang's indebtedness to the Wei fashion for the sort of epistemological analysis of the relations between "name" and "actuality" that we see, for example, in Xu Gan is particularly evident.

The "host of the Eastern wilds" is committed from the very outset to arguing that when the *Record of Rites* says "the tone of the state nearing dissolution is sad and longing," it does not really mean what the words might seem to mean; that is, there is not an actual "tone" that is "sad." It is not surprising, then, that his arguments do not adhere strictly or consistently to the *Record of Rites'* terminology for sound and music. They do, however, assume a familiarity with that terminology. To paraphrase, the *Record of Rites* assumes a three-tiered hierarchy of types of sound, in which each higher level subsumes those beneath it:

1. *sheng* 聲 (sound): This is the most basic level and includes animal cries, the human voice apart from its conscious patterning, or any undifferentiated sound.

2. *yin* 音 (tone): This is sound plus patterning, human song or speech, as well as the whole gamut of musical sounds. Animals have *sheng* but not *yin*. Although the "host" does not consistently observe a distinction between *sheng* and *yin*, his arguments often rely on associations specific to one or the other.

3. *yue* 樂 (music): In the classical sense, this term is given in the *Record of Rites* (and, for example, in Xunzi's "Yue lun"). It does not describe ordinary human music (which remains at the level of "tone") but designates "music in the sense that the sages intended when instituting it." *Yue* in this narrow classical sense and *yue* in its more ordinary sense do share one feature not possessed by the English word "music": they both include dance as well as instrumental and vocal music.

Several notable tendencies in discussions of "music" in the "classical" sense are shared, for example, by both Xunzi's and Xi Kang's essays on music:

1. "Music" turns out not to be primarily a matter of sound per se. To the extent that it is associated with actual sounds, these are sounds of the very distant past.

2. Discussion of this ancient sagely "music" tends to elide the distinction between the sense of *yue* 樂 as "music" and *le* 樂 as "joy," the implicit argument being that at root, "music" is simply the sages' provision for channel-

ing and preserving human joy. This strand of argument is shared by Xi Kang's discourse with both Xunzi and the "Discourse on Music" written by Xi Kang's own contemporary Ruan Ji 阮籍 (210–263).

3. Understanding of "music" in this sense is deemed, in the *Record of Rites*, to be the exclusive prerogative of the "cultivated person" (*junzi* 君子) and beyond the capacities of ordinary people. Anecdotal traditions in this vein describe sometimes preternatural feats of understanding via listening to music, or simply to voices or mere sounds. As we will see, such examples provide much of the basis for the refutations the "guest" presents against the thesis maintained by the "host."

"Conversation—do you think that's an easy thing?" Notes can go only so far in conveying a sense of the density and virtuosity of intertextual play in Xi Kang's essay. To better follow how the arguments unfold, it may be desirable first to read and become familiar with—at a minimum—the "Great Preface" and the "Record of Music," the *Zhuangzi*'s "Discourse on Thinking of Things as Being on the Same Level," along with the "Discourses on Music" by Xunzi and Ruan Ji. Xi Kang himself was a master zither player, who became equally renowned for the virtuosity of his argumentation. By bringing to mind as much as we can of the historical and textual setting of his discourse, we may at least indirectly come to appreciate this classic example of the "tone of the Zhengshi era."[7]

FURTHER READING

As noted in the introduction, the single best way to understand Xi Kang's discourse is to read and become familiar with the main reference texts he cites, particularly the "Record of Music" chapter of the *Record of Rites*, the Mao-school "Great Preface" to the *Classic of Poetry*, and *Zhuangzi* 2, "Qiwu lun." For complete annotated translations of all of Xi Kang's works in the "*lun*" form, see Robert Henricks, *Philosophy and Argumentation in Third-Century China: The Essays of Hsi K'ang* (Princeton, N.J.: Princeton University Press, 1983). For an introduction to some of the main traditional texts and legends surrounding the nature and powers of music, see Kenneth DeWoskin, *A Song for One or Two: Music and the Concept of Art in Early China* (Ann Arbor: University of Michigan Press, 1982). Donald Holzman's *La vie et la pensée de Hi K'ang (223–262 ap. J.-C.)* (Leiden: Brill, 1957) is a survey of Xi Kang's life and works and their historical setting. Robert Hans van Gulik's *Hsi K'ang and His Poetical Essay on the Lute* (Tokyo: Sophia University Press, 1941) provides a translation and discussion of another renowned work of Xi Kang's on a musical topic. The discussion of the Wei thinker Xu Gan in John Makeham's *Name and Actuality in Early Chinese Thought* (Albany: State University of New York Press, 1994) gives a useful context for some of the terms and concepts drawn on in Xi Kang's essay and others in this vein. The best short introduction to the distinctive trends in Wei and Jin thought is Tang Yongtong 湯用彤, *Wei Jin xuanxue lungao* 魏晉玄學論稿 (Beijing: Zhonghua shuju, 1962). Finally, He Qimin 何啓民, *Wei Jin sixiang yu tanfeng* 魏晉思想與談風 (Taibei: Zhongguo xueshu zhuzuo jiangzhu weiyuan-hui, 1967), is a richly documented study relating developments in philosophical discourse and the formal art of "conversation" during this period.

XI KANG

Sound Is Without Sadness or Joy

1A. There was a guest from Qin who posed a question of the host of the East Wilds, saying, "We have it from discourses of the past that 'the tone of the well-governed age is peaceful and joyous; the tone of the state nearing dissolution is sad and longing.'[8] Order and discord are matters of government, yet tones and sounds resonate with them; thus inward states of sadness and longing are manifested through instruments of stone and metal; the indices of peace and joy take shape in sounds of pipes and strings. Moreover, Confucius heard the *shao* music and recognized the attainments of Shun;[9] Ji Zha listened to the strings and knew the manners of the many states[10]—these are established facts from the historical record, accepted without question by the worthies of the past. And now you alone hold that 'sound is without sadness or joy'—where is your justification? If you have some fine instruction for me, then I would like to hear your account of this."

1B.i. The host replied to him, saying, "This teaching is long been ne-glected, with no one to rescue it from obscurity; thus a succession of ages have been caused to be indiscriminate with regard to names and actualities. Today, led on by your gracious incitement, I will speak of some small portion of this topic.[11] Now, heaven and earth combine their powers, and the myriad entities are thereby sustained in their existence; cold and heat pass on in alternation, and the five phases are thereby completed. They are manifested in the five colors; they issue forth as the five tones. The stirring of tone and sound is just like odors in the world; in their varieties of good and bad, though they meet with muddying and mixing, they remain the selfsame in substance, without change—how could they alter their qualities owing to being liked or disliked or change their way of being owing to joy or sadness? When it comes to the assem-bling and sequencing of notes of the scale, whereby sounds and tones are made harmonious—this is something the human mind wishes for in the utmost de-gree, a focal point of emotions and desires. The ancients knew that emotions must not be allowed to run wild and that desires must not be indulged to the extreme, and therefore, following on the natural course of effects of this sort, in each case they instituted a restraining measure, so that sadness would not go so far as to cause harm or joy go so far as to provoke licentiousness.[12] They appointed names for things, each in keeping with its effects, so that each phenomenon had its designation. Weeping they called 'sad,' and singing they called 'joyful.' This in broad terms is how the matter stands.

ii. "However, 'Music! Music!—is it just bells and drums?' Sadness! Sadness!—is it just weeping? To speak of the matter in this way, 'jades and silks' are not the actuality of propriety and reverence, and song and dancing are not the driving force behind grief and sadness.[13] How shall we make this point clear? Different regions have disparate customs, and their singing and weeping are not the same. Supposing we were to employ such different modes in a way that crossed up these regional conventions—we would find some who would be cheered upon hearing 'weeping' and others who would grow despondent on hearing 'song.' Yet their emotions of grief and joy would remain the same. Now, when the effects are these shared inner responses, yet the expressions are these manifoldly divergent sounds—is this not proof of the inconstancy of tones and sounds?

iii. "Harmonized and sequentially arranged sounds and tones, however, are what most deeply stirs human beings—'the ones hard at work sing of their tasks, and delighted ones dance, miming their accomplishments.'[14] One who inwardly has a mournful and pained mind will be stirred to sad and pitiable words. Words are sequenced to form poems; sounds are sequenced to form tones. When these are mingled together in song, when people are gathered to hear them, their minds are moved by the harmonized sound while their feelings are stirred by the bitter words—and before their sighing has ceased, tears flow in welling streams. Now, the sad mind is concealed within and is manifested only after it encounters these harmonized sounds—the harmonized sound is without signification, yet the sad mind has that which serves as its determining force. That person whose sad mind has its own determining force but is expressed only following on the signless harmonious sound—what that person becomes aware of is 'sadness' and nothing more. How could this person know of that which 'blows across the myriad dissimilar things and causes them to cease on their own'?[15]

iv. "Local customs follow their own propensities, and in this manner, modes of governance come into being. Thus the scribes of the states, aware of the rights and wrongs of government and teaching and clearly grasping the prosperity or decline of their states' mores, presented veiled criticism of their superiors by singing and chanting from their emotional natures.[16] This is why it is said that 'the tone of the perishing state is sad and longing.'

v. "Now as for happiness, anger, sadness, and joy; liking, disliking, shame, and fear—all these eight things are the means whereby human beings interact with things and communicate their inner feelings; each has its distinct application that cannot be overstepped. Flavor is distinguished according to 'sweetness' and 'bitterness.' Now, suppose that I feel a fondness in my mind for A because he is worthy and have feelings of dislike for B owing to his stupidity. In such a case, the fondness or dislike ought to be attributed to me while the worthiness or stupidity ought to be attributed to the other—would it be permissible to call the one a 'fondness person' because of my fondness, or a 'dislike person' because of my dislike? Or of a flavor, to call it 'happiness flavored' because it makes me happy, or 'anger flavored' because it makes me angry?

vi. "Speaking of the matter in line with these illustrations, we see that the inner and outer are different classes of effects and that terms are distinguished according to whether they are applied to the object or the subject. In the case of sounds, one ought naturally to take 'good' and 'bad' as their primary criteria, and thus they have no connection with sadness or joy; in the case of sadness and joy, these are naturally expressed only because of the stirring of an inner emotion, and thus they are not attached to sounds. Once we have eliminated [errors relating to] both the name and the actuality,[17] then all this becomes manifest in itself. Moreover, when Master Ji went to Lu, he gathered poems and observed rituals as a means of distinguishing the 'Airs' and 'Odes'—how could it be that he determined his praise and blame based on the sounds alone?! And also, as for Confucius's hearing the *shao* music, he was astonished by its overall unity and therefore exclaimed about it—what need was there for him to rely on the sound to know Shun's virtue and only then to sigh over it? Here I've laid out one corner of the question, which should put you well on the way to understanding."[18]

2A.i. The guest from Qin refuted this, saying, "The various regions differ in their customs, and there are countless varieties in the modes of song and weeping—yet the inner states of sadness and joy cannot but become manifest. When the mind is stirred within and the sound emerges from the mind, though that mind be expressed through some alien accent or lodged in some incidental sound, those skilled in listening with discernment will generally in such cases indeed detect it, with no fear of mistake. Of old, Bo Ya plied his zither, and Zhong Ziqi knew what he was intent on; the clerk struck the lithophone, and Ziqi discerned that his mind was sad; the man from Lu wept in the morning, and Yan Yuan perceived that he was parted from his kin.[19] Do you believe that those few men borrowed wisdom from fixed tones or derived the efficacy of their judgments from musical patterns? When one's mind is grieved, then the form will be stirred accordingly; when one's inward feelings are mournful, then one's voice will be sad accordingly—this is a matter of natural response and something that is inescapable; it is just that only those of preternatural perceptiveness are able to detect these things minutely. For one who is able to do this, a profusion of sounds does not add to the difficulty; for one who is unable to do this, a dearth of sounds does not make it easier. So now it is not permissible to claim, simply because we ourselves have not encountered such an expert listener, that there is no perceptible principle within sound nor to claim, in view of the multiplicity of local customs, that sounds are without sadness or joy.

ii. "You also say that a worthy man ought not to be called 'liking,' or a stupid man 'disliking,' but granting this, we see that this 'liking' exists only when there is 'worthiness' and that 'disliking' arises only when there is 'stupidity'— it's only that the names are not to be used interchangeably. As for the arising of sadness and joy, these alike come about through particular causes—which is as much as to say that a sound may make me sad; a tone may make me joyful. Now if sadness and joy are brought about by sounds, then they alternate in their effects as actualities—how can we 'eliminate both the name and the actuality'?

iii. "And you also say that 'Ji Zha collected poems and observed rites to distinguish the "Airs" and "Odes" and that Confucius was astonished at the unity of the tones of the *shao* music and that this was the reason for which he exclaimed about it'—what tales are these? Moreover, Confucius glimpsed the countenance of King Wen when Music Master Xiang performed the zither piece;[20] Ziye recognized the tone of doomed state when Music Master Juan presented the melody[21]—do you think they rendered these judgments only after considering the lyrics or that they issued these evaluations only after having practiced rites? These both are instances of unique insights of wondrous perception; there was no need of lingering to make inquiries for days on end—already they had gained a comprehensive grasp of the auspicious or inauspicious portent of those sounds. And it was for just this reason that these events were preserved in the annals of antiquity as celebrated exempla. And now you, with your petty, new-fangled wisdom, constrain everything to the level of what you yourself have witnessed—is this not a slander to the ability of the worthies of the past to discern subtleties, and a betrayal of the Master's wondrous perception?"

2B.i. The host replied, "In your refutation you say, 'Though there be countless varieties in the modes of song and weeping . . . those skilled in listening with discernment will generally in such cases indeed detect it,' without 'borrowing wisdom from fixed tones or deriving the efficacy of their judgments from musical pattern,' and that Zhong Ziqi and his like are of this sort. This is as much as to say those whose hearts are grieved, though they chat and laugh and drum and dance; or those whose feelings are merry, though they beat their breasts and moan and sigh, will nonetheless be unable to master their outward forms as to conceal themselves or to trick a perceptive observer through deceptive resemblances. And thus you hold that even supposing there to be no fixed form for sounds and tones, we still ought to say that they possess sadness and joy.

ii. "You also say that Ji Zha listened to the sounds to know the manners of the many states and that Confucius glimpsed the countenance of King Wen when Music Master Xiang played the zither tune. Now, observe closely: if things be as you claim, this amounts to saying that the accomplishments and virtue of King Wen, and the phases of flourishing and decline of manners and customs, may all be figured forth in sound and tones and that the degrees of lightness and heaviness of sounds may be transmitted to later ages, such that the skill of Music Masters like Xiang and Juan is able to capture them in years to come. If things were like this, then the Three August Ones and the Five Emperors could have been preserved without break until this day—would it have been merely a matter of these few instances you cite? Now if this turns out in fact to be the case, then there must be some permanent measure in King Wen's zither tune, some fixed proportions in the tones of the *shao* and the *wu*, allowing for no admixture of extraneous variation or any incidental sound. And thus what you said just now about the inconstancy of sounds and tones or about Zhong Ziqi's ability to draw categorical inferences, stumbles on this point.

iii. "What, then, if tones and sounds *do* lack constancy and if Zhong Ziqi *did* rely on categorical inference—might this turn out to be so? In this event, then, [the stories about] Confucius's perception of the subtle or of Ji Zha's skill at listening are indeed erroneous. Such things are all the wild jottings of vulgar scholars, who concocted them after the fact in order to add mystery to these matters; wanting to make the world confused as to the way of sounds and tones, they did not speak of the generative principles involved. If we pursue the full implications of this instance, we see that to make this mysterious, wondrous, and difficult to know about; to regret one's failure to meet with an extraordinary listener in one's own age; and to sigh over one's fate, yearning for the ancients—is a means of greatly misleading later generations.

iv. "Now, in following categorical correspondences and distinguishing objects, we ought first to seek how things stand in terms of natural principle. Once the principles have been established, then and only then ought we to draw on ancient teachings, simply to shed light on them, and that is all. Now, you rely extensively on statements from the past for support of your discourse before you have gained a grasp of the matter in your own mind. If you continue on in this way, I fear that 'even one clever at calculation will be unable to keep track.'[22]

v. "In your refutation you also say, 'The arising of sadness or joy is like the feelings of like and dislike in their following from worthiness or stupidity; this shows that sounds make me sad and tones make me joyful. If sadness and joy arise from sounds, then they alternate in their states as actualities.' Now, the five colors have distinctions of beauty and ugliness, and the five tones have distinctions of good and bad—these are matters of the things in themselves. When it comes to liking or disliking or to being pleased or displeased, these are transformations of human feelings, principles underlying the actions of things—so much and no more. Yet these things all have nothing to do with the inner self; they merely form contingently owing to outer things. As for sadness and joy, these are naturally due to conjunctions of events that have first taken on structure within the mind; they simply manifest themselves following on the harmonious sounds. Therefore in my earlier discussion I elucidated the lack of fixed rules in how this comes about—now let me again borrow this occasion just to set our terminology straight: We do not say that the way in which sadness and joy are released through sound resembles the way in which liking and disliking arise from worthiness and stupidity. However, the way in which harmonious sounds stir the human mind *is* just like the way in which wine releases the human affections: the wine is distinguished based on criteria of 'sweet' and 'bitter,' whereas the drunken ones show its effects in terms of 'happiness' and 'anger.' Seeing cheer or despondency being released because of sounds, and saying that the sounds possess sadness or joy is just like seeing how pleasure or anger come about because of wine and saying that wine possesses some principle of pleasure or anger in it."

3A.i. The guest from Qin refuted him, saying, "The art of observing a person's air and taking readings of facial expressions is something in universal practice throughout the world.[23] When the mind alters within and the expression responds without, this is manifest and plain to see—and therefore, you, my dear fellow, do not cast doubt on it. Now, sound is itself simply agitated air:[24] the mind stirs in response to a stimulus, and the sound issues forth in keeping with that change; the mind has its alternations of vigor and weakening, and sound has its swellings and diminutions. All these processes are at work in the single person—why is it that alone in the case of sound, we ought to doubt them? Pleasure and anger are manifested through the indicators of the expression; sadness and joy ought likewise to take shape in the sound. Sound ought indeed to be said to possess sadness and joy—it is just that benighted persons are unable to discern it. And even though Zhong Ziqi and his like encountered inconstant sounds, they alone proved able to clearly perceive what it was they expressed.

ii. "Now, a blind man may face a wall without being aware of it, while Li Lou clearly perceives, down to its very tip, a downy autumn hair a hundred *xun* away.[25] To speak of things along these lines, the abilities of the clear-sighted and dim-sighted are indeed disparate! We must not cast doubt on Li Lou's sharp eyesight because we stubbornly cling to our own capacity of inches or feet, or cast suspicion on Zhong Ziqi's keen hearing because we cling to our ordinary listening ability, and say that all these things are wild jottings of the ancients."

3B.i. The host replied, "In your refutation you say, 'The mind moves in response to a stimulus, and the sound issues forth in keeping with this change; the mind has its alternations of vigor and weakening, and the sound has its swellings and diminutions. The inner states of sadness and joy must certainly take shape in the sound. Zhong Ziqi and his like, though encountering inconstant sounds, still clearly perceived what those sounds expressed.' If we had to make things as you say, then the full bellies of Zhuo and Zhi or the hunger on Mount Shouyang, the injustice done to Bian He or the sadness of Boqi, Xiangru's withheld anger or Buzhan's fearful reverence—all these myriad variations—if in each case you were to have the person send forth a song of a single verse, accompanied with the uncovering of the subtleties of a few strums of the zither, then Master Zhong and his like would gain a clear understanding of the inner states of each man.[26]

ii. "You hold that those who are adept at listening do not alter their thinking depending on whether the sounds are those of many people or of few and that those who clearly perceive inner states do not consider the larger or smaller as different—rather, for all the things that alike emerge from the single person, they make it their goal to discern what each betokens. Now suppose that this sound emerges from below—then ought Ziye and his like in this case as well to take pitch pipes in hand and blow reeds to ascertain its tone so as to know the flourishing or decline of the 'airs of the south,' or to distinguish the lewdness or propriety of the 'Odes' and 'Airs of Zheng'?[27]

iii. "Now as for the relation between eating spicy food and laughing wildly, or that between getting smoke in one's eyes and weeping with sadness—these have the shared effect of producing tears; yet if we had Yi Ya taste them, he would certainly not say that the tears of joy are sweet and those of sadness bitter—of this we may be sure. What is happening here? In the case of fluids in the flesh or sweat in the muscles, these are excreted when pressure is applied—and this process is not determined by joy or sadness. It is just as in the case of straining wine through a filter sack—though the kind of winepress used may differ, the wine's flavor is unchanged. Sounds, as well, are things emerging from this same body—why should they alone contain principles of sadness and joy in them?

iv. "Moreover, the *Xianchi*, the *Six Stalks*, the *Great Stanza*, the *Shao*, the *Xia*—these are the utmost music of the kings of old, the means whereby they 'moved heaven and earth and stirred ghosts and spirits.'[28] Now you insist on claiming that every sound or tone gives an emblem of its emitter's body and transmits his mind—this necessarily implies that this ultimate music could never be entrusted to the Music Masters but must require a sage to play its pipes and strings and that only then could its elegant tone be unimpaired. 'Shun commanded Kui: strike the stones, stroke the stones, and the eight tones were made to accord; spirits and humans put in harmony'[29]—speaking of it from this perspective, though the ultimate music relies on sages to create it, it is not necessary that the sage himself perform it. Why is this? Tones and sounds have their natural harmonies that do not rely on human affections; the tone that is 'made to accord' is formed with metal and stone chimes; the perfectly harmonious sound is achieved with the pipes and strings. That fine hair you speak of does indeed have a form that is there to be perceived, and that is why Li Zhu and the blind music master differ in their abilities. If you 'season water with water,' by what means will you distinguish them?"[30]

4A. The guest from Qin disputed this, saying, "Though there are points of obscurity in the several illustrations I have put forth, sufficient to provoke your attacks—nonetheless the main principle involved must have some application. As in the case of Ge Lu who knew, upon hearing the bellow of the bull, that its three calves had been taken as sacrifices; or of Music Master Kuang, who blew the pitch pipes and knew that the airs of the south were outmatched and that the Chu army would surely be defeated; or of Yangshe's mother, who heard the baby's cries and knew he would lead to the extermination of the family. All these several things were confirmed in ages of old and, for this reason, were recorded. If we follow the implications of such instances as these, then there will be no fate of prosperity or decline, no fair or ill omen, that is not present in sound. Now if you once more call such things baseless errors, then all our documents of the past will be useless trash—and if you want to claim that this is a generally valid argument, no one will be satisfied. If you can elucidate the basis for such occurrences and show how they come about, however, such that both your argument and the claims about such events are maintained, then I would like to hear this once more."

4B.i. The host replied, saying, "What I meant earlier by the one who was able to 'reply with the three other corners,' was someone who 'got the meaning and forgot the words,' and for this reason my preceding discourse was brief and not detailed.[31] Now that you have gone to the trouble of making these repeated and insistent refutations, how should I presume not to exhaust all I have to say on these matters? Now, that the ox from Lu should be able to know of the deaths, one after the other, of those sacrificial victims, to mourn that its three offspring had not survived, to feel pent-up grief over a course of years, and to vent its sense of injustice to Gelu—this would be a case in which it shared the same mind as a human's, differing only in its animal form. Again, this is something about which I feel doubt. Moreover, cattle are not humans, and there is no mode by which the two could communicate; if you say that all beasts with calls or cries are capable of this and that Gelu by his natural endowment alone was able to understand them, then this is a matter of grasping their speech and discoursing of their affairs, just as a translator transmits words from other languages. This would not be a matter of knowing their inner states by testing the sounds, so this would be beside the point for your refutation. If you say that those who know such matters are supposed to get to the meaning through direct contact with the thing in question, with nothing they do not know, then let us now begin with the easy cases.

ii. "Allow me to ask you: if a sage were suddenly to enter a barbarian region, would he know what they were saying? Someone refuting in the way you do must certainly say, 'He would.' And how are we to explain the principle based on which he would know this? Allow me to borrow from your refutation to establish a context within which we may clearly recognize the issues. Would he have dealings with them and, through those dealings, grow familiar with their speech? Or would he test their tone with pitch pipes and sounding reeds? Would he observe their air and collect visual cues so as to know their minds? If this latter is the case, then this is to say that knowledge of the mind comes about via the air and expression—even if they didn't speak at all, he would know them, so this method for knowing is not something we need speak of here. If he tests their tone by blowing pitch pipes, then supposing his interlocutor had his mind intent on a horse and said 'deer' by mistake, then we would still expect the percipient one to trace back from this word 'deer' to know the intended horse—this is to say that the mind is not attached to words and that some words are insufficient as proof of the mind. If we suppose he understands their speech through having dealings with them, this is the same as a child who learns speech from its teachers and only then understands—in this case, then, what is the value of the sage's perspicacity? Now, speech is not a naturally determinate thing: various lands have different customs, and same things often bear different designations—it is simply that words are adopted from convenience to demarcate and call those things to mind. Now, the sage has an exhaustive grasp of principles; what this means is that when there are natural relations to trace out, there are none, be they ever so subtle, that he does not see clearly. If the principle itself is deficient, then he will fail to perceive even things near at hand—therefore it is not possible to force the speech of disparate lands to become mutually intelligible. If we follow the implications of this conclusion, then may we not say that our proof that Gelu did not understand the cow's lowing is complete?

iii. "In your refutation you also say, 'Music Master Kuang blew the pitch pipes and knew that the airs of the south were overmatched and that there was much death in the sound of Chu.' This is also something about which I have doubts. Allow me to ask you, when Music Master Kuang was blowing the pitch pipes, do we say this was an air of Chu? Then at a distance of a thousand *li*, there was no way for the sound to carry. Or do we say that the wind recognized the state of Chu and came to enter the pipes? Then south of Chu are the states of Wu and Yue and, to its north, those of Liang and Song—without seeing its origin, by what means did he recognize it? In general, winds are produced only through the mutual agitation of yin and yang; with the reciprocal stirring of energies, which are released on contact with the earth—how could such a thing emanate from the court of Chu and come into Jin? Moreover, the yin and yang pitch pipes themselves are simply a means of distinguishing the nodal energies of the four seasons: when the time arrives, the corresponding energy is stirred up; when the pitch pipe responds, the ash is puffed away.[32] All these are matters of natural interdependencies, which do not rely for their effects on human action.

The upward-generated and downward-generated pitches are the means of balancing the harmony of the five notes and of setting in order the distinctions of hard and soft.[33] However, each pitch of the scale has its fixed sound, and even if we blow the *zhonglü* pipe in the winter, its tone will naturally be full and unblemished. Now when this unblemished pipe is blown with the breath of a man of Jin, how is the wind of Chu to be able to enter into it, to participate in making it swell or shrink? If Chu's winds are without form, and its sounds do not connect with the pitch pipes, then those in the place where the testing of principle is done will not rely on wind or pitch pipes—is this not so? Might it not be simply that Music Master Kuang was versed in lore and full of understanding and that he had his own way of knowing the signs of victory and defeat and that he attributed this knowledge to divine and subtle causes through a desire to give resolve to the minds of the masses, just as when Bo Changqian promised Duke Jing a long life span?[34]

iv. "Your refutation further states, 'Yangshe's mother heard the baby cry and knew that it would bring ruin to its family.' Once more I ask you, by what means did she know this? Was it that through a stroke of inspiration she intuited it on her own and, speaking at random, happened to get it right? Or was it that she had before heard a baby crying with a noise as great as this and that child had been bad, and that since this later sound of crying resembled that past sound of crying, she knew he would be the ruin of its family? If through a stroke of inspiration, she intuited it on her own and, speaking at random, happened to get it right, then this was not achieved through grasp of principles, and though it is said she heard the crying, she did not derive proof from the baby's sound. If because the sound she had heard before turned out bad, she knew that this later crying ought to come out bad as well, this is a matter of using the sound of A as a measure for assessing the crying of B. Now, the relation of sound to tone is just like that of the outer form to the mind: there are those who share an outward form whose inner states differ, as well as those whose appearances are different but whose minds are alike. How shall we make this clear? Sages are alike in mind and equal in virtue, yet their outward appearances are not the same. If their minds are the same and yet their forms differ, then how are we to speak of knowing the mind through observing the form? Moreover, as for the way in which agitated air from the mouth creates sound, in what way does this differ from the way in which flutes or pipes resound when they take in air? The goodness or badness of the sound of crying does not arise from the good or ill omen of the baby's mouth, just as the high or low notes of the lute or zither are not determined by the skill or clumsiness of the player. Someone who is able to discern principles and is good at conversation yet cannot make flutes and pipes tuneful and clear is just like the music master who can properly arrange the composition but cannot cause the instruments to necessarily be pure and harmonious ones. The instruments do not become well built because of the wondrously skilled music master; a flute does not become well tuned because of the player's fine intellect. In this way, we see that the relation of mind to sound is quite manifestly that of two separate things. And if they are indeed two separate things, then one who seeks out the inner state of things will not linger in observing the outward appearances, and one who seeks to divine the mind's intentions will not lend his ears to mere sound. That a percipient one should wish to know the mind by way of the sound—would this not be a roundabout approach? And now this mother of Jin who did not reach her judgment by verifying the truth but rather gave exclusive credence to a sound heard earlier as proof about the present-day cry—is this not a case of someone hitting on the right answer by accident in a former age, whom lovers of strange tales have subsequently made much of?"

5A. The guest from Qin refuted him, saying, "I hear that for defeated troops, to be unashamed of fleeing is a means of survival. My mind is not satisfied, but your words are difficult to respond to, so I will pass on to other remaining questions. Now, a person of mild and equable disposition, upon hearing *zheng*, flute, and *pipa*, grows physically restless and mentally exhilarated; contrarily, upon hearing the tones of lutes and zithers, he grows calm in body and reposeful in mind. And in the repertoire of a single instrument there are differences for each tune, and in each case the hearers' emotional state changes accordingly. When tunes of Qin are performed, then they sigh with yearning and are filled with grand emotion; when Qi or Chu melodies are played, then their feelings are steadied and their minds focused; when beguiling caprices are given free rein, they feel cheerful abandon and are satisfied in their desires—such is the multitude of the mind's transformations under the influence of sounds. If restlessness and tranquility arise through sounds, then why do you refuse them sadness and joy? Rather, you insist that 'the perfectly harmonious sound stirs in every way,' attributing grand unity to sounds while explaining the multifarious changes to human emotions—might it be that in grasping this latter case you have lost sight of the others?"

5B.i. The host replied, saying, "In your refutation you say, 'the *pipa*, the *zheng*, and the flute make people restless and agitated,' and also, 'the effects of each tune vary, and the emotions change correspondingly'—these are indeed ways by which we can constantly produce the same responses in people. The *pipa*, *zheng*, and flute produce closely spaced sounds at a large volume, and the music written for them is very changeable and has driving rhythms. These instruments play driving rhythms with a loud volume, and this is why such music causes the physical restlessness and mental exhilaration. This is like the way in which rattles and clappers strike the ear, and bells and drums startle the mind. Thus when one hears the sound of the battle drum, one thinks of ministers fit for military command; this, we may suppose, is because among sounds there are greater and lesser ones, and therefore in their effects on people we see these distinctions of wildness and quietness. The *qin* and *se* zithers are so constituted that the spacing between sounds is distant and the tone is soft; in its music there is little variation and the sound is clear. These instruments play sparse variations with a soft tone—if one does not attentively and calmly listen, then one will not fully catch the full effect of their pure harmony, and for this reason one's body grows quiet and one's mind reposeful. The differences in the effects of various compositions are just the same as with the tones of different instruments. In the compositions of Qi and Chu, there is a lot of repetition, and therefore the emotions are equalized; their transformations are wondrous, and therefore the thoughts are focused. The tones of those beguiling caprices collect the fine effects of all the instrumental sounds and assemble the harmonies of the five tones; their form is copious and their effects are broad, and therefore the mind is set in action following the many patterns; the five tones are brought together, and therefore there is cheerful abandon and gratification of desire. However, all these things are constituted in terms of single or multiple, loud or soft, pleasing or unpleasing, while human emotions respond in terms of restlessness or quiet, focus or distraction. To speak by analogy, when we wander through the sights of a big city's marketplace, our eyes are bewildered and our emotions run wild; when we pause contemplating the structure of a musical composition, our thoughts grow still and our demeanor grows formal. This tells us that the substance of sounds consists completely of characteristics such as slow or rapid, while the responses of the emotions also go no further than things like agitation and calm.

ii. "As for how different compositions differ in their effects and how the emotional response varies in accordance with these, this is just like the way in which flavors vary in their excellences, yet the mouth is able to recognize each. The five flavors have myriad distinct combinations, yet these reach their grand unity in the delicious; though the transformations of compositions be many, these also reach their grand unity in harmony. Deliciousness includes sweetness, and harmony includes joy; however, the emotions that follow a composition approach the realm of harmony, while the mouth that responds to deliciousness is removed from the bounds of sweetness—how could sadness or joy intrude here? However, the inner states of humans vary, and each draws guidance from what it is able to understand, in releasing what it holds within. If we speak of one who is of mild and equable disposition, in which sadness and joy are in just and equal balance, then neither will be released before the other, and thus in the end what will result is a state of restlessness or calm; if one is released before the other, there is a prevalent quality within, and such a disposition is no longer to be considered mild and equable. To speak of it in this way, the restlessness or calm is the effect of the sound; sadness or joy is the predominating factor in the hearers' inner states. One cannot claim, based on seeing such responses of restlessness or calm, that sadness or joy arises through sound.

iii. "Moreover, though sounds have their qualities of wildness or quiet, these wild and quiet sounds each have their own sort of harmony, and those things that are stirred by harmony are in every instance self-impelled. How shall we clarify this point? Let's say that there is a banquet hall filled with assembled guests, and as they're all a bit tipsy with wine, a zither plays. Some are delightedly cheered, while others despondently weep. It is not that the latter have been served sadness while joy has been conveyed to the former. The sound is unchanged from what it was before, yet these effects of cheerfulness and grief occur together—is this not an instance of 'blowing across the myriad dissimilar things'? Now, if sound has no determination with regard to pleasure or anger, it ought as well to have no determination with regard to sadness or joy, and thus both cheer and grief appear. If it relied on some fixed and one-sided tone, harbored some sound of uniform effect, and if the things it released and brought to light each accorded to these distinct qualities, then how could it comprehensively master the varied principles and give collective expression to the inner feelings of the multitude? To speak of it in this way, sound takes equable mildness as its basic medium yet is inconstant in the effects it stirs up in things; the mind and its concerns are determined by their expectations, and these predeterminations are released in response to stirring. This being the case, then, the relation between sound and the mind is one of things on quite separate tracks, which do not intersect with each other—how can one sully the Great Harmony with such qualities as cheer or grief or append such fictitious designations to it as sadness or joy?"

6A. The guest from Qin refuted this, saying, "In your discourse you state, 'Wild and quiet tones each have their own harmony, and those things that are stirred by harmony are in every instance released of themselves; for this reason when the zither is played for a tipsy audience, the effects of cheer and grief are brought about together.' This is speaking of the case when an imbalanced emotion is first built up within, so that those who harbor cheerful feelings will express these when encountering sad tones, while those who grieve inwardly will have these feelings stirred on meeting with joyful sounds. Now these sounds indeed ought to have their determinate qualities of sadness or joy, but the transformative power of sound operates slowly and is unable either to take effect all at once or to replace one emotion with its opposite. Imbalanced emotions are activated through contact with outer things, thus causing the responses of sadness and joy to happen at the same time. But even though these two emotions appear together, what does this take away from the fact that the sounds have their determinate principles?"

6B.i. The host replied, saying, "In your refutation you say, 'Sadness and joy do indeed have their fixed sounds, but imbalanced emotions cannot be shifted all at once, therefore those who feel moved with grief are sad when meeting with joyful sounds.' Supposing it were as you say and that sounds had their fixed qualities, then suppose we had 'The Deer Cry' performed repeatedly: this is a 'joyful' sound, and if we have a grief-filled person encounter it, even if the transformative power of sound operates slowly, it ought only to be unable to change him and make him cheerful right away—how could it make him all the more sad? Just as in the case of the flame of a single torch: though it is insufficient to warm a whole room, it ought not to further increase its coldness. Fire is not a cold-heightening thing, and music is not a tool for increasing sadness. The fact that cheer and grief are brought about together when we ply the strings in the high hall is simply because of the way in which perfect harmony releases what is pent up and conducts the emotions and therefore allows the things stirred up by outer stimuli to exhaust themselves.

ii. "Your refutation says, 'Imbalanced emotions arise upon contact with outer things, therefore causing the responses of sadness and joy at the same time.' Now those we call 'sad' will sometimes weep on seeing a desk or a walking stick and sometimes feel grief when looking at a carriage or on clothes—this is simply because they are stirred by how such objects linger after their owner is gone and feel pained that these personal effects are visible though the actual person is not to be seen. In all such cases there is a particular context underlying the way in which they encounter those things; it is not a case of sadness simply springing up there on the spot or of tears falling in the middle of a banquet. In the present case, where there is no desk or walking stick to bring about the stirring but one in which someone weeps upon hearing harmonious sounds, these emotions are not stirred by the harmony itself but, in each case, are released by themselves."

7A. The guest from Qin refuted him, saying, "In your discourse you said, 'When the zither is played for tipsy guests, then effects of cheer and grief occur together.' I wished to make this premise viable and therefore replied in terms of imbalanced emotions that are released through the stirring of outward things. Now let's take the mind out of our discussion and explain these things in terms of fully realized effects. Now, if the human mind is not cheerful, then it is grieved, and if not grieved, then it is cheerful: these are the great regions into which emotional tendencies are divided. However, weeping is the harmful effect of grief, while laughter is the effect of cheerfulness. Now I think we can say that as for people listening to the compositions of Qi and Chu, we observe only sad and tearful countenances and have never seen appearances of hilarity. This must necessarily be because the compositions of Qi and Chu take sadness as their basic substance, and therefore the things they stir up are in keeping with their measure—how could it be merely a matter of their having 'much repetition with scant variation' and thus 'bringing on uniform spirits and focused thoughts'? If indeed these compositions are able to bring about weeping, then if sound possesses sadness and joy, we may decisively conclude that we allow this to be the case."

7B. The host replied, saying, "Although human emotions are stirred to sadness and joy, sadness and joy each have their degrees. Moreover, the ultimate degrees of sadness and joy need not necessarily lead to the same effects. Now, with mild sadness the expression becomes discomposed, while with great grief comes weeping—this is the way of things with sadness. With mild cheerfulness the face shows pleasure, while with ultimate joy comes laughter—such are the principles of joy. How shall we clarify this? When those most dear to us are secure and happy, then we are pleased and at ease and feel a sense of self-satisfaction with things as they are. When they are in a dangerous crisis and only just make it through in the end, then we're clapping our hands before there's even time to begin dancing about with delight.[35] To speak of it in this way, then this later capering is not as good as that earlier satisfaction with things as they were—how could it be otherwise! When it comes to raucous laughter, though this arises from feelings of cheerfulness, it nonetheless comes about based on its own principles—it is not, any more than these other effects, a natural means for responding to sounds. This shows us that joy's response to sound takes self-satisfaction as its main element, while sadness's response to stirring takes shedding tears as its affair. Shedding tears is an action that can be detected, while with satisfaction there is a confluence of the spirit with no outward change. For this reason you observe the difference between the two cases without recognizing their similarity; you distinguish the externals but have not clearly perceived what lies within. If this is so, then can we believe that it is only with the compositions of Qi and Chu that raucous laughter does not appear as the effect of the sounds? Now you are not looking for joy in the realm of self-satisfaction but rather call the music of Qi and Chu basically sad owing to the absence of raucous laughter—is this not a matter of neither knowing sadness nor recognizing joy?"

8A. The guest from Qin refuted him, saying, "Confucius has the saying 'As for changing manners and transforming customs, there is nothing better than music.'[36] Supposing that things are as you claim in your discourse and that all the hundreds of varieties of sadness and joy are not in sound, then by what means exactly *does* this 'changing of manners and transformation of customs' come about? Moreover, the ancients were cautious about delicate and seductive airs and suppressed those sounds that enrapture the ears. Therefore he also said that one ought to 'banish the airs of Zheng and keep flatterers at a distance.' If this is so, then about these tones of Zheng and Wei, or those sounds in which they 'strike the ringing chimes to bring accord to gods and humans,' I make bold to ask, what are the ultimate degrees of flourishing and disrepair of these two types—the *Zheng* and the *Odes*—and through what process does that 'changing and transforming of manners and customs' come about? I wish to hear this once more, so that I may be enlightened on these points of doubt."

8B.i. The host responded to him, saying, "The person who spoke of 'changing manners and transforming customs' must surely have been addressing the aftermath of a period of decline and abuses. The kings of antiquity followed the precepts of heaven in bringing order to the creatures of the world; they unfailingly exalted simple and easily followed teachings and directed by means of governance free of artifice. The lord was quiet above, the ministers compliant below; mysterious transformation went on unimpeded, without anyone noticing; and heaven and humanity enjoyed a shared peace. Those classes of creatures who were withered and sere were dampened and nurtured with numinous liquid; within the Six Directions, all things were bathed in a great flow, which rinsed clean all dust and dirt. The masses of living things were at ease and free and, seeking out manifold blessings of their own accord, were in tacit accord with the Way, harboring sincerity and grasping right action without being aware how it all came about. Their harmonious minds were sufficient within them, and their harmonious air appeared outwardly. Therefore they sang to give accounts of their aspirations and danced to make manifest their feelings. Afterward ornamented these things with brilliant patterning: making it bright with the 'Airs' and 'Odes,' setting it to the sounds of the eight timbres, infusing it with the spirit of Great Harmony. They guided their spirit and breath, nourishing them and completing them; they received their dispositions and natures, bringing them to presence and illuminating them. They caused their minds to be in accord with principle; the energies of nature and their own voices responded to each other. They brought these things together in a meeting and mingling to bring to fruition the beauties of each. Therefore their feelings of joyful celebration appeared through the metal and stone chimes; what 'harbors vastness and sheds light on the grand' was manifest in tones and sounds.[37] Carrying on in this way, the ten thousand states would have shared manners, their fragrant blossoms burgeoning equally, with an aroma like the autumn thoroughwort. Word and deed would accord without conscious planning; affairs would be accomplished without deliberation; and all would be placidity and mutual affection as when one spreads brocade or lays out colored silks, the dazzling brilliance is beguiling. The grand way has no grander height than this; the legacy of great peace has no more manifest display than this. Therefore it is said, 'For changing manners and transforming customs, there is nothing better than music.'

ii. "However, music is so constituted that the mind is its primary medium. Therefore, the music that is without sound is the father and mother of the common folk. The joining and blending of the eight timbres are something people delight in and are also classified as 'music.' The changing and transforming of manners and customs, however, were never a matter of *this* sort of music to begin with. The harmonizing and sequencing of tones and sounds are something that human emotions cannot get enough of. For this reason the ancients, knowing that these emotions must not be allowed to run rampant, suppressed those aspects in which the emotions were liable to run away; knowing that desires cannot be cut off entirely, they built on the place from which the emotions arise.[38] Therefore they created rituals that could be followed and brought about a tractable kind of music.[39] The mouth does not exhaust flavors, and music does not take sound to its extreme: they took the measure of what was fitting from beginning to end and assessed the midpoint between the worthy and the fool, establishing for all a law and standard, so that the far and near would share the same manners, drawing on this endlessly. It is also a means for forming sincerity and trustworthiness and making manifest those things that cannot be altered, and therefore the town schools and the academies of cities and clans also follow it. They made it so that strings and bamboo flutes are maintained along with sacrificial boards and dishes; banners adorned with feathers and hair are employed along with the ceremonies of bowing and deference; proper speech and harmonious sounds ring out together. They made it so that when about to hear a certain sound, then one will certainly hear particular words; when about to look on a certain spectacle, then one will certainly perform a particular rite—just as the guests and host ascend and descend the hall, and only then does the exchange of toasts take place.[40] And with this the proper measure in speech and the right ordering of sounds, the due postures of deference and the fixed rhythms of motion and stillness—each is made reliant in turn on the other, so as to form together a single entity. Lord and ministers employ it at court, and ordinary gentlemen employ it within their families. Practicing it in youth and not slacking in adulthood; the mind grows secure in it and the inclination to it grows firm, as the pursuit of good transforms us day by day; and then we approach it with reverence and maintain it with . . . ,[41] persevering long without change; and then the transformative process is completed. This also was part of what the ancient kings intended by their use of music. Therefore at court banquets or diplomatic feasts, fine music must surely be included. For this reason, the scribes of the state collected signs of the flourishing and decline of manners and customs and entrusted them to the musicians to display them to the sounds of wind and string instruments, so that the one who spoke these things might be without blame while the one who heard these things might derive enough for their own self-correction.[42] This also was part of what the ancient kings intended by their use of music.

iii. "As for the sound of Zheng, this is the most wondrous of all the sounds. The way in which wondrous tones stir humans is just like the way in which sexual attractions confuse the will or like besotted lingering in drunken dissipation—by all these, the projects of one's life are easily brought to ruin.[43] Who, short of a perfect person, can control such forces? The former kings feared that the world would wander off in these ways without return and therefore set in place the eight timbres, avoiding excess in their sounds, and cut off the grand harmony, so that its transformations might not be taken to their utmost. They cast aside these lithe and lovely sounds, so that music might be 'joyful, yet not licentious': this is just like the way in which the grand broth is not seasoned, not taking to its extreme the flavor of the peony.[44] As for those crass and shallow vulgar customs, their sounds are not worth delighting in, nor are they something to be cheered by. As for when the rulers deviated from their way and the state lost its order, men and women eloping in licentious dissipation lacking all rule, the manners were changed owing to all this, and customs formed from these predilections. When they esteemed what their minds were intent on, the mass of folk were free to run wild in it; when they delighted in what they had grown accustomed to, by what means could they be punished? All this was set to harmonious sounds, which accompanied and fostered it. What they had inside was moved by the words; while their minds were stirred by the harmonious sound, the manners and customs were formed as a single entity, and the name was bestowed on this unitary thing. However, the sound itself that was so named does not strike on license or depravity: licentiousness and propriety alike are matters of the mind. With this, the basic substance of the 'Odes' and 'Airs of Zheng' may be observed."

[Dai Mingyang 戴明揚, *Xi Kang ji jiaozhu* 嵇康集校注 (Beijing: Renmin wenxue, 1962), 5.196–225]

NOTES

1. The expression appears in Dongfang Shuo's "Discourse of Master Nonesuch" (*Wuyou xiansheng lun* 無有先生論), in which it refers to the difficulty of speaking in front of a ruler. Here Wang Sengqian appropriates it to refer to the difficulties of the particularly medieval conversational genre of "pure conversation" (*qing tan* 清談) or "conversation about the Mysterious" (*xuan tan* 玄談).

2. Wang Bi (226–249) and He Yan (ca. 195–249) were founding writers, commentators, theoreticians—and conversationalists—of the school that eventually became known as "*xuan* studies." Ma Rong 馬融 (79–166) and Zheng Xuan 鄭玄 (127–200) were two of the most influential classicist scholars of the Eastern Han. Wang Bi wrote a general introduction to his commentary to the *Laozi* entitled the "Concise Exegetical Principles for the Subtle Points of the *Laozi*" (*Laozi weizhi lilüe* 老子微旨例略); the "*zhili*" referred to here may be to this work or to some other work or works in a similar vein.

3. *NQS* 33.598.

4. *Recent Anecdotes from the Talk of the Ages* (*Shishuo xinyu* 世說新語) is full of examples of this sort of conversational exchange and is often quite emphatic about the cultural, social, and political stakes involved, as it shows a special preference for stories of conversational exchanges that result either in a sudden rise from obscurity to prestige and high position or in public humiliation. For examples and discussion, see Jack W. Chen, chapter 21 of this volume.

5. Literally, "crossed the Yangzi," which means following the fledgling Eastern Jin court to Jinling in the aftermath of the Eight Princes' rebellion that ended the Western Jin and began the period of Northern–Southern division.

6. *Shishuo xinyu* 3/21.

7. Except where otherwise noted, the text adopted here follows the recommended readings in Dai Mingyang's collated edition. For ease of reference, the rounds of "refutation" and

"reply" are numbered 1 through 8 (with A designating the guest's "refutations" and B the host's "replies"), and the longer passages are subdivided with lowercase roman numerals. These smaller section subdivisions are intended solely as an aid in navigating the main steps in the arguments; they are not signaled in any way in the original text, and in many cases, one could doubtless make a case for dividing them differently.

8.   This is an abridged citation from a passage from the "Record of Music" in the *Record of Rites*; similar language also appears in the "Great Preface" to the Mao-school commentary to the *Classic of Poetry*. For more details, see the introduction.

9.   *Analects* 3/25.

10.   One of the most prominent anecdotes about "preternatural listening": Ji Zha visited the court of Lu and heard a suite of performances corresponding more or less to the sequence of songs in the *Classic of Poetry*, and he was able to discern on this basis the characters of the states and historical periods reflected in each piece. See *Zuozhuan* 左傳, Xiang 29.

11.   Literally, "one corner." The phrase stems from *Analects* 7/8. Here it serves both as a self-deprecatory comment by the host, who does not presume to cover the topic inclusively, and, at the same time, as a veiled challenge to the hearer, since in the original context the phrase is used to suggest that hearers who cannot get the other three corners by themselves are not worth talking to. Note that this connection with the *Analects* voice of Confucius is picked up again at the beginning of section 4B—not to the advantage of the "guest," it must be said.

12.   This echoes Confucius's comments on the first poem in the *Classic of Poetry* in *Analects* 3/20.

13.   These two sentences are constructed around an ingeniously skewed citation of *Analects* 17/11. Where the emphasis in the original context would seem to be more on the question of the inner sincerity of the participants in ritual and music, here Xi Kang borrows the language of the passage to point to the need to maintain a rigorous distinction between inner states and outward phenomena, along the way toward his argument in the following passage that any connections between these two are simply local conventions and not intrinsic connections.

14.   The first clause is a fragment from the Han-school commentary to the *Classic of Poetry* 165; Dai Mingyang cites a parallel text for the second clause, but the correspondence is not exact—at any rate, the traditions surrounding sagely music such as the *shao* and *wu* dances was that these gave typified representations of the character and accomplishments of the sage kings who initiated them.

15.   Citing *Zhuangzi* 2, "Qiwu lun."

16.   This is a succinct statement of the role of early "state scribes" (*guo shi*) in compiling the *Classic of Poetry*, as laid out in the "Great Preface."

17.   The text reads *ming shi ju qu* 名實聚去 (literally, "when both name and actuality are eliminated"), but we probably should understand "name" and "actuality" as referring to the two types of *errors* through which the mistaken notion that sound has sadness or joy comes into being, and which the "host" has just laid out in the preceding passages: (1) "name" (*ming*): the misleading sort of language in texts such as the *Record of Rites* that

seems to attribute emotion to sound (as critiqued in 1B.iv), and (2) "actuality" (*shi*): mistaken understandings of the relations between inner states and outer things (as critiqued in 1B.v). Thus *ming shi ju qu* would mean, in effect, "remove both obstacles of (misleading) language and (misconceived) actualities." Robert Henricks renders the phrase "when name and reality are kept apart," which does provide a basically viable sense for this passage (though at the expense of a rather strained rendering of the phrase), in *Philosophy and Argumentation in Third-Century China: The Essays of Hsi K'ang* (Princeton, N.J.: Princeton University Press, 1983), 76.

18. The closing phrase is drawn from the *Xici* section of the *Classic of Changes*: "one who understands, upon reading the line judgments, will be more than halfway there."

19. Bo Ya was a master zither player, and his friend Zhong Ziqi was a master listener, who could intuit what Bo Ya's mind was intent on has he played. For example, see *Liezi* 列子, chapter 5, "Tang's Question" 湯問. Another anecdote about Zhong Ziqi describes how he heard someone playing stone chimes at night and felt sad; upon inquiring, he discovered that the player was a prisoner who had been separated from his family. See *Lü shi chunqiu* 呂氏春秋, section 5, chapter 9, "Fine-Tuned Communication" (*Jing tong* 精通). The "Yan Yuan" chapter of *Kongzi jiayu* 孔子家語 records a story in which Yan Yuan hears the sound of someone crying and judges that it is the sound of someone parted from loved ones due to the resemblance of that sound to the earlier cry he had heard a bird make when its offspring were about to fly away forever.

20. *Han shi wai zhuan* 韓詩外傳, *juan* 5.

21. The story appears in *Han Feizi*, chapter 10, "Ten Faults" (*Shi guo* 十過). Duke Ling of Wei was traveling to Jin and, while passing near the Pu River, heard a zither playing new music at night. Duke Ling commanded his Music Master Juan 師涓 to reproduce the music. When Duke Ling later had Master Juan perform the music at the Jin court, the Jin Music Master Kuang—the "Ziye" referred to here—recognized it as an ill-omened musical emanation left over from the fall of the Shang dynasty.

22. The phrase is drawn from *Zhuangzi* 2, "Qiwu lun." Such casual citation of an ancient text, at exactly this moment as the "guest" is being taken to task for excessive dependence on ancient texts, is likely intended as ironic or gently humorous.

23. We may take the "guest" as referring here to the ordinary way in which we judge others' moods or personalities based on outward appearance and demeanor and also to the more formal science of physiognomy as reflected, for example, in the roughly contemporary *Treatise on Personality* (*Renwu zhi* 人物志) by Liu Shao 劉劭.

24. In its immediate context, we understand this clause as saying "the voice is an agitated kind of breath." The argument put forward here by the "guest," however, draws both on the range of *qi* to denote not only the "breath" but also the "air" or demeanor observed by the physiognomist, and on the range of *sheng* to denote both "voice" and "sound" more generally.

25. Li Lou, or Li Zhu, was a figure said to have preternaturally keen eyesight.

26. Zhuo and Zhi: two families referred to by Sima Qian as emblematic examples of rising from humble origins to prosperity. See *SJ* 129.3282. Hunger on Mount Shouyang: alluding to the renowned story of the brothers Bo Yi and Shu Qi, who refused to cooperate

with the Zhou after the fall of the Shang and eventually starved to death there. Bian He: the man from Chu who three times offered a wondrous piece of jade that looked outwardly like an ordinary stone. After having his feet cut off on the first two times that he was accused of insulting the king by submitting mere stone, Bian He finally saw his jade recognized. Boqi: there are a number of versions of Boqi's story, but all involve his being estranged from his father through the machinations of a bad stepmother and reconciled after a period of exile that often involves his singing songs. Xiangru: referring to the moment in the story of Lin Xiangru at which he holds the precious He jade at the Qin court, threatening to smash it and his own head if the king of Qin makes any move to take it. Buzhan: a man described in a citation from *Hanshi wai zhuan* who, when summoned to war, was too loyal to refuse but too physically cowardly to endure the fear and who thus died of terror on hearing the battle drums.

27. The host here employs a calculatedly indecorous image to reduce the guest's hyperbolic praise of the discerning listeners to absurdity: If master listeners like Music Master Kuang (the "Ziye" mentioned explicitly here) and Ji Zha (the listener obliquely alluded to by the comment about knowing the flourishing or decline of the "Odes" and "Airs of Zheng") can indeed discern the affairs of whole states from listening to a mere fragment of the song of a single person, and if sound, as mere "agitated air," is no different in kind from the other voluntary or involuntary responses or reactions that take place in a person's outward form and reveal the inner state (as suggested at the opening of the guest's refutation here), then why shouldn't we expect such master listeners to apply their skills to discern what is "expressed" in the breaking of wind?

28. This quotation is of a familiar phrase from the Mao-school "Great Preface."

29. This quotation, from the *Classic of Documents* (*Shang shu* 尚書), "Yao dian" chapter, is one of the key classical reference points for discussing music as a sagely institution.

30. That is, if visual cues and aural cues are really the same thing (as the guest suggests at 3A.i), then how are we to differentiate between the abilities of Li Lou and the blind music master (abilities whose basic incommensurability the guest emphasizes in 3A.ii)? The expression *yi shui ji shui* 以水濟水 derives from a speech in the *Zuozhuan* in which Yanzi, the wise minister of Qi, draws on analogies of cooking and music—in both of which arts it is a harmony of varied elements, rather than simple monotonous agreement, that makes for the highest accomplishment—to show that obsequious agreement is less valuable in a minister than proper dissent. See *Zuozhuan*, Zhao 20.

31. For the *Analects* reference, see note 11. Here the "host" combines this reference with *Zhuangzi* 26, "Wai wu."

32. This alludes to a traditional practice at court for monitoring the progress of the times of the year: it was said that each of the twelve pitch pipes would resonate with a particular period of the year's cycle. A film of reed ash was laid across the mouth of each pipe, and when a pipe's stage of the cycle arrived, a sympathetic energy would blow the ash out. Xi Kang does not cast doubt on this practice, but simply insists that this sort of correspondence is not to be conflated with actual musical sounds.

33. This refers to the derivation of all the pitches of a scale from a fundamental pitch via the circle of fifths. Since the pitch one-fifth higher than a given pitch k is $3/2k$, and that of

the pitch one-fifth lower is 2/3*k* (in terms of frequency; in terms of pitch pipe length *l*, the values would be 2/3*l* and 3/2*l*), notes may be iteratively derived either "upward" or "downward." Two pitches derived in the upward direction plus two pitches derived in the downward direction yields—transposing where necessary to put the notes in the same octave—the pentatonic scale.

34. The story appears in the *Yanzi chunqiu* 晏子春秋. Bo Changqian, after having built a reputation as a man of preternatural powers of foresight, uses this reputation to produce a "placebo" effect for the duke by predicting an extended life span for him.

35. *Bian wu* 抃舞 (clapping and dancing) is a quasi-proverbial expression for the height of joy. Xi Kang (or the host) here takes advantage of the association of the terms in this expression to invent this description of an even more extreme feeling of delight.

36. Once more in this final "refutation," the "guest" cites the language of the *Record of Music*. See also the use of this term in Xunzi's "Discourse on Music."

37. *Classic of Changes*, hexagram 2 (*kun* 坤).

38. That is, they founded the institution of music using some of the things that people naturally desire, only keeping in mind the need to keep these desires from going unchecked. This section on the complementary relationship between music and ritual is very reminiscent of Xunzi.

39. In the context, it seems we may take this "tractability" as referring to a kind of music that is both itself manageable and conducive to shaping manageable personalities.

40. Referring to the sequence of ritually specified acts specified on occasions of banqueting and musical performance, as in the case of the ritual banquet (*xiang yin jiu* 鄉飲酒) described by Xunzi in the end of "Discourse on Music."

41. As noted in Lu Xun's collated edition, one character is clearly missing here.

42. Again, citing the "Great Preface."

43. The sentence begins by drawing a comparison between the effects of unbridled music and those of unbridled sexual desire. As the sentence goes on to mention drunkenness, it is somewhat unclear whether this is to be taken as a further analogy or as suggesting simultaneous indulgence in all three dangerous pleasures. The latter possibility is certainly underwritten by a whole tradition of poetic evocations of banqueting as a site of alluring, if sometimes dangerous, sensual indulgence.

44. The mention of the peony here is particularly apt, as its root was praised as a fine flavor, while in its poetic associations it recalls the "licentious" exchanges between men and women in poems from the "Airs of Zheng," such as Mao 95, as Hendricks points out in *Philosophy and Argumentation in Third-Century China*, 105–6.

13. Poetry on the Mysterious

The Writings of Sun Chuo

PAUL W. KROLL

The first generation of men who reached maturity in the Eastern Jin—that is, those who were born shortly after the large-scale removal south of the Northern aristocracy or who had been young children during the exodus— grew into a different view of their political and geographical surroundings than that of their displaced fathers. It was this generation that established the norms of culture and literature that we now think of as typical of the dynasty and, indeed, held the stage during what were the most thriving decades of the Eastern Jin. No one better embodied the complications and tensions arising in the new literary and social environment than Sun Chuo 孫綽 (314–371),[1] who, by the midfourth century, was widely regarded as the foremost writer of the age.

Sun Chuo is now most noted in literary history as the dean of poets who wrote "verse on the mysterious [Dao]" (xuanyan shi 玄言詩). Before considering some of those poems, we will glance briefly at the personality behind them. Sun Chuo had many sides, and proper recognition of this fact will help us appreciate the world that he and other fourth-century men of letters inhabited. Indeed, according to our sources, Sun Chuo seems to have been both more and less than a man of letters. He appears in almost fifty entries in the Recent Anecdotes from the Talk of the Ages (Shishuo xinyu 世說新語), and judging from the opinions offered there by those who knew him, his contemporaries recognized and sometimes chided the inconsistent or, at least, varying nature of his personality. In this sense, if we can forgo our usual expectation of a consistency in historical characters that we do not demand of ourselves, Sun Chuo may emerge as one of the more vivid figures of early medieval times.

After an initial period of reclusion in his youth, he quickly made a name for himself in the circles of power, learning, and influence, occupying numerous official positions at court and in the provinces. Occasionally, he was criticized for the ways in which he sought favor, but this talent for self-promotion did not prevent him from gaining the respect and appreciation, at different times, of men such as Xie An 謝安 (320–385), Wang Xizhi 王羲之 (309–ca. 365), and the famous monk Zhi Dun 支遁 (314–366), all noted for their integrity and intelligence. In fact, Sun Chuo is credited as having introduced the latter two individuals to each other. He enjoyed the support of important political patrons but rarely took part in court controversies. The one significant mark he made in the political sphere was his successful opposition in 362 to the urging by Huan Wen 桓溫 to return the capital northward to Luoyang, which a Jin expeditionary force under Huan had earlier (but only temporarily) recaptured. Sun Chuo's persuasive memorial against this hazardous suggestion is quoted at length in his official biography, taking up most of that account. It is a very lucid and, in places, surprisingly vehement document from someone who was usually careful to avoid partisan disputes. Aside from this occasion, Sun's influence was felt mainly in the less parlous but more intellectually conspicuous sphere of literature.

During the first half of his career, Sun Chuo made his name and was much sought after as a writer of eulogies. Several of these compositions survive, including those for such prominent figures as Wang Dao 王導 (276–339), Yu Liang 庾亮 (289–340), and Yu Bing 庾冰 (296–344). Although Wang Dao and the Yu brothers were political rivals who played out their differences at the highest level of government, Sun's commemorations praise them equally. An interesting feature of Sun's eulogies is his penchant for inserting self-references into them, which was normally avoided in such compositions and for which he was sometimes criticized. Another unusual trait is his extensive use of landscape imagery in the verse passages that conclude the eulogies and cogently summarize the deceased's legacy.

When the occasion called for it, Sun Chuo was capable of expressing very fine distinctions in evaluating his contemporaries as well as men of the past. Many entries in *Recent Anecdotes from the Talk of the Ages* show him offering astute characterizations of conduct, quality, and literary style. Thus, of the famous Western Jin poets Pan Yue 潘岳 (247–300) and Lu Ji 陸機 (261–303), he said, "Pan Yue's writings are sumptuous, like draped brocade—there's no place in them that isn't good. Lu Ji's writings, on the other hand, are like pieces of gold in sand—every now and then you see a treasure."[2] Elsewhere, varying the metaphors, he says more pithily, "Pan Yue's writings are shallow but limpid. Lu Ji's are deep but weed choked."[3] Sun could be cutting, as when he opined about his contemporary, Yuan Qiao 袁喬 (312–347), "Those who don't know him don't recognize his ability, and of those who do know him no one has any use for him as a person," although on a different occasion he characterizes the same person as "washed and scoured; pure and alert."[4] Comparing himself with Xu Xun 許詢 (ca. 325–ca. 352), a younger friend who is often paired with Sun as a leading poet of *xuanyan* verse, he said in response to a question from his Buddhist teacher, Zhi Dun: "As far as exalted feelings and remoteness are concerned, your disciple has long since inwardly conceded Xu's superiority. But in the matter of a single humming or a single intoning of poetry, Xu will have to sit facing north."[5] The person in the place of honor traditionally sat facing south, as the emperor did; here, although Sun Chuo readily acknowledges Xu Xun's ascendancy in terms of temperament, he concedes nothing with regard to his skill in poetry. In making aphoristic judgments of these kinds, Sun Chuo—like many others whose remarks are similarly recorded—is self-consciously displaying his own analytical and verbal abilities. This was one of the minor intellectual pastimes of the Eastern Jin elite and testifies to the age's exceptional, perhaps overrefined, passion for artful language, which also is evident in other activities.

Sun Chuo's understanding of and attachment to Buddhist teachings was strengthened by his association with Zhi Dun, a monk in whom both elegance and eloquence combined and who was closely involved with many members of the Eastern Jin nobility. For Sun Chuo, as for Zhi Dun, being a Buddhist did not entail the denial of Confucian or Daoist teachings. In fact, in most of his writings Sun Chuo makes great efforts to find common ground among the three traditions. The best example of this is his extended exercise in Buddhist apologetics, "On Explicating the Way" (*Yudao lun* 喻道論), in which he seeks to place Buddhist thought and practice squarely within native Chinese usage. The Buddha, for instance, is identified in one passage as the "embodiment of the Dao" and, in another, as no different from Confucius himself. Elsewhere, the Confucian virtue of filial devotion is discussed deftly and at length as a conception perfectly exemplified by the very life of the Buddha. In a separate work, "On the Worthies of the Way" (*Dao xian lun* 道賢論), which exists only in fragments, Sun Chuo compares seven eminent Chinese monks with the famous Seven Sages of the Bamboo Grove. Interestingly, Zhi Dun is included here, matched with Xiang Xiu 向秀, who was admired for his subtle commentary on the *Zhuangzi* 莊子. Though they lived at different times, says Sun, these two shared the same "fondness for the Dao."

This blending of Buddhist and Daoist concepts and images can be seen in most of Sun Chuo's extant writings. It is manifest perhaps most tellingly in what is now his best-known poem, the "Rhapsody on Roaming the Tiantai Mountains" (*You Tiantai shan fu* 遊天台山賦). Included in the important sixth-century anthology *Selections of Refined Literature* (*Wen xuan* 文選), this is a long and gorgeous description of the poet's excursion to the Tiantai range (in present-day eastern Zhejiang), which gradually turns into a metaphorical account of a journey to mystical enlightenment. Sun Chuo's compelling use of the landscape in both its real and figurative guises as the immanent setting for transcendent experience has made this the unsurpassed model and masterpiece of all poems in the subgenre of mountain-ascent verse. Four English translations are currently available.[6]

Of his few remaining poems in the *shi* 詩 form, the two compositions preserved from Wang Xizhi's famous gathering at Lanting 蘭亭 in 353, another one on the Double-Three festival, and one called simply "An Autumn Day" (his only extant pentametric poem) are all well-crafted depictions of natural scenes. Another outstanding but virtually unknown example of his descriptive talent is the fragment that remains of his tetrametric "Inscription for Mount Taiping" (*Taiping shan ming* 太平山銘), in praise of a mountain northeast of the Tiantai range; it is translated in this chapter. Sun's appreciation of the significance of untainted landscape is attested in the opinion attributed to him, that unless one's spirit and feelings are in accord with the mountains and streams, one is unlikely to write well.[7]

Sun Chuo's use of landscape imagery, like that of many of his contemporaries, was, however, far from being simply a delight in description. Scholars of literature often speak of the rise of "landscape poetry" in the fourth century, but this overlooks the very different end to which natural imagery is being put by writers such as Sun Chuo. I noted earlier that landscape imagery is prominent even in some of the concluding verse sections of Sun's eulogies. Here and elsewhere the natural world is not depicted for its own beauty but is often used for symbolic purposes. This owes much to concepts of language current among the Jin literati, which posited a developing continuum from idea (*yi* 意) to image (*xiang* 象) and, finally, word (*yan* 言), each element suggesting more than—though never perfectly representing—what prompts it, but with the hope that one may ultimately let go of the merely expedient words and grasp the original idea (*de yi wang yan* 得意忘言). The poem "An Autumn Day," translated here, is a good example in which the carefully chosen sequence of natural images leads to a concluding statement that asserts the poet's harmony with the autumn landscape but also points up, by means of an allusion drawn from the *Zhuangzi*, the incapacity of words to express it adequately.

Notions such as these, regarding the complicated relations of mind, reality, and language were central to the particular form of discourse known as *xuanxue* 玄學, popular among scholars during the third century and through the middle of the fourth century. The term means "the study of the mysterious"—which is to say, of the Dao (*xuan* recalling here its usage in chapter 1 of the *Laozi* 老子). Starting with the young genius Wang Bi 王弼 (226–249) and his contemporary He Yan 何晏 (ca. 190–249) and developing through succeeding generations, *xuanxue* adepts made use of concepts taken from the *Laozi*, the *Zhuangzi* 莊子, and the *Classic of Changes* (*Yijing* 易經) to reinterpret classical texts and explore questions that we might now identify as involving semiotics, epistemology, and metaphysics. By Sun Chuo's time, some scholars were attempting to incorporate these concerns in both the style and the substance of poetry, the *xuanyan shi* (verse on the mysterious), noted earlier.

It is for such verse that Sun Chuo was most recognized by later scholars. Liu Xie 劉勰 (ca. 465–ca. 522), writing in the early sixth century, identifies *xuanyan* verse as the prevailing style of the Eastern Jin and Sun Chuo and Xu Xun as its most famous practitioners. However, this fashion went out of vogue within a few decades and gradually became a target of criticism. As a consequence, most of these poems were increasingly ignored and ultimately lost. In later eras. it became difficult to find examples of Sun Chuo's poetry in this style. From at least the tenth through the eighteenth century, only the handful of Sun's *shi* poems mentioned earlier seem to have survived, plus a poem to express his grief for his deceased parents and three other verse inscriptions for objects. His *xuanyan* poems were known only by hearsay. During the nineteenth and the first half of the twentieth century, various fragments of the *Wenguan cilin* 文館 詞林, a thousand-chapter anthology of literature compiled in the mid-seventh century by the scholar-official Xu Jingzong 許敬宗 (592–672) and long thought lost, came to light in Japan. As chance would have it, included among the mere twenty-seven chapters of this anthology that have been recovered was a chapter containing examples of *xuanyan* verse from the Eastern Jin, and four of those poems were by Sun Chuo. Two of these are translated here.

Both of the poems are in tetrametric form. The first of them, made up of nine stanzas, each of which follows a different rhyme, is a reply to a poem by Xu Xun, which no longer survives. Writing in the mid-340s to his young friend and fellow poet who is on his way to fill a junior position at the capital in Jiankang 建康, Sun Chuo begins by musing on the vicissitudes of fate, the continual shuffling of fortune, and the wisdom of not seeming to shine too brightly. Halfway into the poem, in the fifth stanza, he addresses Xu Xun directly, going on to praise the latter's talent and character and celebrating their friendship. This, says Sun, will not suffer, though their paths now diverge, for they shall continue to write to each other, though one may be in the capital and the other in the countryside. Much of the advice—or encouragement—in the poem, to both Xu Xun and himself, is couched in Daoist terms, and allusions to the classics also abound. The more important references are glossed in footnotes. Shared appreciation of such matters was an expected part of verse in this style, regardless of whether the ostensible topic of the poem is friendship, leave-taking, politics, or philosophy.

This is also the case with the second of Sun Chuo's *xuanyan* poems translated here, which is addressed to the famous figure Xie An. In many respects Xie An was the ideal Eastern Jin gentleman. Descendant of an aristocratic family and broadly learned in all fields, he possessed a casual charm and insouciant ease that permitted him to indulge his own whims and remain aloof from worldly trammels for most of his life—the very model of someone who had absorbed and put into practice the ideas emanating from the "study of the mysterious." At the time that Sun Chuo's poem to him was written, probably in 360, Xie An had finally emerged at age forty from his long and pointed avoidance of capital politics to accept a position under Huan Wen, the man who was then the dominant power at the Eastern Jin court. The first half of Sun's poem is marbled with natural imagery meant to recall Xie's reclusive life in the "eastern mountains" at the same time it describes and symbolizes the understanding of the Dao and detachment from mundane concerns that he has attained there. This is further complemented by an assortment of gnomic, sometimes paradoxical, statements reminiscent of the *Laozi*. In the concluding stanza, Sun Chuo associates himself with Xie in their mutual awareness of how best to adapt to the world's ways and directly implores the patronage of his now highly placed friend.

FURTHER READING

For studies on Sun Chuo's life, see Hachiya Kunio 蜂尾邦夫, "Son Shaku no shōgai to shisō" 孫綽の生涯と思想, *Tōyō bunka* 東洋文化 57 (1977): 65–100; Li Wenchu 李文初, "Dong Jin shiren Sun Chuo kaoyi" 東晉詩人孫綽考議, *Wen shi* 文史 28 (1987): 207–20; and Hasegawa Shigenari 長谷川滋成, "Son Shaku shōden" 孫綽小傳, *Chūgoku chūsei bungaku kenkyū* 中國中世文學研究 20 (1991): 74–91. Annotated Japanese translations of Sun's poetry and prose may be found in Hasegawa Shigenari, *Son Shaku shi yakuchū* 孫綽詩譯注 (privately published, 1990), and *Son Shaku bun yakuchū* 孫綽文譯注 (Higashihiroshima: Hiroshima daigaku kyōikugakubu kokugo kyōiku kenkyūshitsu, 1996). For a collection of brief essays on many matters pertaining to Sun Chuo's life and works, see Hasegawa Shigenari, *Son Shaku no kenkyū: risō no "michi" ni akogareru shijin* 孫綽の研究：理想の「道」に憧れる詩人 (Tokyo: Kyūko shoin, 1999). The reconstituted chapters of the *Wenguan cilin*, which include Sun Chuo's *xuanyan* verse, as well as some of his eulogies in longer versions than are recorded in the seventh-century encyclopedia *Yiwen leiju* 藝文類聚, have been published as *Ri cang Hongrenwen ben Wenguan cilin jiaozheng* 日藏弘仁文本文館詞林校證, ed. Luo Guowei 羅國威 (Beijing: Zhonghua shuju, 2001). For a translation of the "Yudao lun," see Arthur E. Link and Tim Lee, "Sun Ch'o's 'Yü-tao lun': A Clarification of the Way," *Monumenta Serica* 25 (1987): 207–20. Many references to Sun's role in fourth-century "gentry Buddhism" are in Erik Zürcher, *The Buddhist Conquest of China: The Spread and Adaptation of Buddhism in Early Medieval China*, 3rd ed. (Leiden: Brill, 2007); and Tsukamoto Zenryū, *History of Early Buddhism: From Its Introduction to the Death of Huiyüan*, trans. Leon Hurvitz (Tokyo: Kodansha International, 1985). On Xie An, see Jean-Pierre Diény, *Portrait anecdotique d'un gentilhomme chinois: Xie An, 320–385, d'après le Shishuo xinyu* (Paris: Collège de France, Institut des hautes études chinoises, 1993). In recent years, much has been published in Chinese on *xuanyan* poetry; two of the most useful books are Tao Shunzhi 陶順智, *Dong Jin xuanyan shipai yanjiu* 東晉玄言詩派研究 (Wuchang: Wuhan daxue chuban-she, 2003); and Hu Dalei 胡大雷, *Xuanyan shi yanjiu* 玄言詩研究 (Beijing: Zhonghua shuju, 2007).

Sun Chuo 孫綽

Inscription for Mount Taiping (fragment) 太平山銘

	Soaring skyward is Mount Taiping,	巋峩太平
	Surpassing in steepness Hua and Huo.[8]	峻�󠄀踰華霍
	Spiring ridges run every which way,	秀嶺樊縕
4	Its singular peak thrusting upright.	奇峰挺崿
	Above, it impinges on the bright-blue vapors;	上干翠霞
	Below, enfolds valleys leaved in red.	下籠丹壑
	An adept roams there in darkness,	有士冥遊
8	Ambling quietly round chosen haunts.	默往寄託
	His form impassive as a withered tree,[9]	蕭形枯林
	His mind shining in hidden silence.	映心幽漠
	"Having once come upon him,"[10]	亦旣覯止
12	May one placidly linger here long,	渙焉融滯
	Where a ridgepole hangs in halcyon-blue haze,	懸棟翠微
	And eaves fly on at the edge of the clouds.	飛宇玄際
	Here layered tors twist and turn,	重巒寒產
16	And winding streams gird like a belt.	廻溪縈帶
	Cloaked with deep-green pines,	被以青松
	It is freshened by pure-white rills.	灑以素瀨
	As drifting winds catch sweet scents,	流風佇芳
20	Wafted clouds tarry in thin mists.	翔雲停靄

[*Yiwen leiju* 8.145; *Quan Jin wen*, in *QW* 62.5a–b]

An Autumn Day 秋日

	Coldly chill is the moonlight of midautumn,	蕭瑟仲秋月
	While in a gusting gale, wind-borne clouds run high.	颼唳風雲高
	Dwelling in mountains, I feel the change of the seasons;	山居感時變
4	A distant visitor, I give rise to a drawn-out song.	遠客興長謠
	In a sparse grove, cool winds mount up,	疏林積涼風

And on bare mountain passes, thick mists collect. 虛岫結凝霄

As heavy dew soaks the courtyard trees, 湛露灑庭林

8   Clustered leaves forsake once-laden boughs. 密葉辭榮條

Touching a mushroom, I grieve for what falls first; 撫菌悲先落

And stroking a pine tree, envy what fades last.[11] 攀松羨後凋

Casting one's line in the wooded countryside,[12] 垂綸在林野

12   Friendships are fixed apart from court and marketplace. 交情遠市朝

So at peace, then, this heart of olden thoughts— 澹然古懷心

14   It is not very far from being "above the Hao."[13] 濠上豈伊遙

[Lu Qinli, XS 901–2]

In Answer to Xu Xun 答許詢

We look up, observing the greater designs, 仰觀大造

And downward to behold the things of time. 俯覽時物

When the trigger is tripped, mischance arises; 機過患生

4   Good and ill fortune press upon each other. 吉凶相拂

Wisdom is bedimmed by self-interest, 智伊利昏

And perception is twisted by feeling. 識由情屈

In the countryside one withers from the cold, 野有寒暑

8   While at court one is stifled by heat.[14] 朝有炎鬱

If when deprived you "shake with fear,"[15] 失則震驚

Succeeding, you'll surely be "undone by fullness."[16] 得必充詘

Haughty and high, the tall gateways, 戔戔高門

12   But specters will peer into their courtyards.[17] 鬼闞其庭

Imposingly handsome the ornate wheels, 弈弈華輪

But treacherous roads will overturn them. 路險則傾

When the front shaft shivers the axle, 前輈摧軸

16   The carriage bells will shake the grelots. 後鑾振鈴

Were a cohort of troops brawling to run off, 將隊競奔

Correction must fall on those in charge. 誨在臨頸

Men of insight are aware of first causes; 達人悟始

20   Setting self aside, one bequeaths honor. 外身遺榮

Bequeath honor, and honor endures; 遺榮榮在

Set self aside, and self stays intact. 外身身全

Impressive indeed those former teachers! 卓哉先師

24   Cultivating virtue, they attained to ease. 修德就閒

They relaxed on the breeze of mystery,[18] 散以玄風

Washed themselves in the clear stream;[19] 滌以清川

Another treading the raised floor,[20] 或步崇基

28 And another content in the garden in Meng.[21] 　或恬蒙園
　　With the Way complete and held to heart, 　道足匈懷
　　Spirit will settle in the Unimpeded.[22] 　神棲浩然

　　Alas for me, just a stripling![23] 　咨余沖人
32 Endowed with such imperfect qualities; 　稟此散質
　　Competence not even embracing the common, 　器不韜俗
　　Talents not standing out from the crowd. 　才不兼出
　　Pulling in my lapels, I profess sincerity, 　斂衽告誠
36 Dare to apologize for deficient qualities. 　敢謝短質
　　May the invisible cycle release me from emotion,[24] 　冥運超感
　　And visit me with mystic detachment. 　覿我玄逸
　　Let mind dwell in unmeasured infinity, 　宅心遼廓
40 Savoring and pondering marvelous oneness.[25] 　咀嚼妙一

　　There is a saying of Father Kong: 　孔父有言
　　"Those born later may be held in awe."[26] 　後生可畏
　　Dazzling and vibrant is Master Xu, 　灼灼許子
44 Conspicuously singular, one of a kind, 　挺奇拔萃
　　To be set against jade, compared with crystal, 　方玉比瑩
　　Matched with thoroughwort, equated to averoyne.[27] 　擬蘭等蔚
　　Imparting what he feels, he is the "master carpenter";[28] 　寄懷大匠
48 I look up to admire his bent for the far removed. 　仰希遐致
　　Were he raising a structure of a thousand fathoms, 　將隆千仞
　　He could never be short even one basketful.[29] 　豈限一匱

　　From when I "took you by the hand,"[30] 　自我提攜
52 We were "flash-and-flicker" in every direction.[31] 　倏忽四周
　　Allied in agreement to a single source, 　契合一源
　　Neatly knotted in a returning current. 　好結回流
　　Wading, we were sure to blend our tastes,[32] 　泳必齊味
56 And soaring we must roam together. 　翔必俱遊
　　Our joys mounted up with the times, 　懽與時積
　　Hence strengthening the ties that bound us.[33] 　遂隆綢繆
　　"A single day without seeing you," 　一日不見
60 I felt was the same as "three autumns."[34] 　情兼三秋

　　All the more so when your road now goes afar, 　矧乃路遐
　　As here we are come to a parting of the ways. 　致茲乖違
　　You shall take shelter in the western corner,[35] 　爾託西隅
64 While I persevere in this domain. 　我滯斯畿
　　Still and silent in a crooked alley,[36] 　寂寂委巷

Lorn and forlorn I close the door.	寥寥閉扉
A bleak wind swells in the nighttime,	淒風夜激
68 And hoary snow is whirling at dawn.	皓雪晨霏
Leaning on my low desk, I chant alone,	隱几獨詠
But who is there to regard this song?	賞音者誰

You bestowed on me a new poem,	貽我新詩
72 Uncanny in resonance, pure in its meaning,	韻靈旨清
Resplendent as shaken silk-brocade,	粲如揮錦
As sonorous as carnelian when it is tapped.	琅若叩瓊
Though happy now that life is known for a dream,	既欣夢解
76 I am yet ashamed not to have plumbed the depths.	獨愧未冥
Since displeasure lies in having a body,	慍在有身
Then pleasure must lie in forgetting this life.	樂在忘生
As for us, we are different from most:	余則異矣
80 There is no going away that will not be level.[37]	無往不平
If Truth were but always like this,[38]	理苟皆是
Why should one be tangled in feelings?	何累於情

Why should one be tangled in feelings?[39]	何累於情
84 Admonitions come from the men of old.	戒以古人
So remote, the graybeards and the one who nested,[40]	邈彼巢晧
A thousand years past, cut off from the dust.	千載絕塵
In the mountains one settled in "exalted retreat,"[41]	山棲嘉遯
88 And also there was one who shouldered firewood.[42]	亦有負薪
"Measuring our strength" and "holding to essentials,"[43]	量力守約
We dare to admire the men of former times.	敢希先人
Let us save up words of good counsel,	且戢讜言
92 Always to be "written on the ends of one's sash."[44]	永以書紳

[*Ri cang Hongrenwen ben Wenguan cilin jiaozheng*
157.57–58; *XS* 899–900]

Presented to Xie An 贈謝安

So far from us—in faintest antiquity,	緬哉冥古
Now so remote—those August Ones on high;	邈矣上皇
In the early times of Greatest Simplicity,	夷明太素
4 They knotted together the numinous guide-rope.[45]	結紐靈綱
Though there was no longer a unity,	不有其一
Could a twofold Truth not be manifest?[46]	二理曷彰
The hidden wellspring then flowed freely,	幽源散流
8 And the mysterious breeze exuded its scent.[47]	玄風吐芳

But when a scent is fanned, it fades away;　芳扇則歇
When the flow advances, it reaches far off.　流引則遠
The unhewn is spoiled through carving,[48]　朴以雕殘
12　And the fruit is preceded by the flower.　實由英前
The shortcut is prized by everyone,　捷徑交鶩
While the overgrown route by none is trod.　荒塗莫踐
But transcendently you rise to awakening;　超哉沖悟
16　Borne on the clouds, returning alone.[49]　乘雲獨反

As green pine trees shoulder snow,　青松負雪
White jade takes on a shimmer.　白玉經飆
A style too novel overwhelms clarity,　藻藻彌映
20　While plain substance will outdo splendor.　素質逾昭
Concentrating your spirit, sinking deep within,　凝神內湛
You leave as dregs not a single drop.　未釃一澆
And so, following your long-held likings,　遂從雅好
24　Loftily you advance to the nine empyreans.　高跱九霄

Bountifully rippling—your fathomless fountain;[50]　洋洋浚泌
Lush and luxuriant—your garden amid the hills.　藹藹丘園
In the courtyard no chance wheel-marks;　庭無亂轍
28　In your dwelling the sound of pure strings.　室有清絃
You never step beyond your borders,　足不越疆
And your talk strays not from the abstruse.[51]　談不離玄
Your mind leans on drifting clouds,　心憑浮雲
32　And your qi conforms to the Unimpeded.[52]　氣齊浩然

Looking up, you celebrate the lessons of the Way;　仰詠道誨
Downward, set about instructing the people.　俯膺俗教
Living consonant with Heaven, one is at rest,　天生而靜
36　But seduced by things, one grows impatient.　物誘則躁
Wholeness comes from embracing simplicity,　全由抱朴
While disaster comes from boring out openings.[53]　災生發竅
If perfection took refuge just in foreknowledge,　成歸前識
40　Who would be capable of silent enlightenment?[54]　孰能默覺
Unseen in the haze, the man in hiding;　曖曖幽人
He hoards his competence, conceals his brilliance.　藏器掩曜
Wading through the *Changes*, he understands　涉易知損
　　"diminution";[55]
44　Settling into the *Laozi*, he probes the "marvelous."[56]　棲老測妙

We retain alike a free-flowing manner,　交存風流
But are tied and tethered by karmic conditions.　好因維摯

	Since last we encountered each other,	自我不覿
48	Heat and cold have thrice returned.[57]	寒暑三襲
	When Emperor Wen of Han invited Jia Yi in,	漢文延賈
	He realized he couldn't advance him.[58]	知其弗及
	When young Dai Liang met Huang Xian,	戴生之黃
52	He couldn't help but humble himself.[59]	不覺長揖
	In company with you, I arrived at the abstruse,	與爾造玄
	But our tracks did not go in together.	跡未偕入
	Since you have spread your sounding wings,[60]	鳴翼既舒
56	I can but stand erect as a crane,	能不鶴立
	Preening my feathers, anticipating the wind,	整翰望風
58	Hoping to share your distant perch.	庶同遙集

[*Ri cang Hongrenwen ben Wenguan cilin jiaozheng*
157.58–59; *XS* 900–901]

NOTES

1. Sun Chuo's dates have been a subject of dispute. Those adopted here have been argued for, persuasively in my view, in Cao Daoheng 曹道衡, *Zhonggu wenxueshi lunwen ji* 中古文學史論文集 (Beijing: Zhonghua shuju, 1986), 309–12.

2. When quoting from *Recent Anecdotes from the Talk of the Ages* (*Shishuo xinyu*), I use Liu I-ch'ing [Liu Yiqing], comp., *Shih-shuo Hsin-yü: A New Account of the Tales of the World*, 2nd ed., trans. Richard B. Mather (Ann Arbor: Center for Chinese Studies, University of Michigan, 2002), 144 (item 4/84).

3. Liu I-ch'ing, comp., *Shih-shuo Hsin-yü*, 146 (item 4/89).

4. Liu I-ch'ing, comp., *Shih-shuo Hsin-yü*, 286 (item 9/65), 277 (9/36).

5. Liu I-ch'ing, comp., *Shih-shuo Hsin-yü*, 283 (item 9/54).

6. In chronological order, they are Richard B. Mather, "The Mystical Ascent of the T'ien-t'ai Mountains: Sun Ch'o's *Yu T'ien-t'ai-shan fu*," *Monumenta Serica* 20 (1961): 226–45, including an excellent prefatory study and copious notes; Burton Watson, *Chinese Rhyme-Prose: Poems in the Fu Form from the Han and Six Dynasties Periods* (New York: Columbia University Press, 1971), 162–71; Xiao Tong, comp., *Wen xuan, or Selections of Refined Literature*, vol. 2, *Rhapsodies on Sacrifices, Hunting, Travel, Sightseeing, Palaces and Halls, Rivers and Seas*, trans. David R. Knechtges (Princeton, N.J.: Princeton University Press, 1987), 243–53; and Stephen Owen, *An Anthology of Chinese Literature: Beginnings to 1911* (New York: Norton, 1996), 185–88.

7. Liu I-ch'ing, comp., *Shih-shuo Hsin-yü*, 254 (item 8/107).

8. Hua and Huo are two much more famous mountains, renowned as sites for reclusion.

9. In *Zhuangzi* 莊子2, a certain Ziqi of Nanguo, who would "lose himself" when at rest, is described by a visitor as looking at such times like a "withered tree," with a heart like "dead ashes."

10. Quoting a line from the *Classic of Poetry* (*Shijing* 詩經) 14, which speaks of a wife's longing to meet her lord.

11. The short-lived mushroom symbolizes things that decline quickly, while the pine, recalling a famous passage in the *Analects* 9/27, stands for endurance in adversity.

12. "Casting one's [fishing] line" in the wilds is a standard image for removing oneself from unseemly jostling for power.

13. A well-known passage in *Zhuangzi* 17 tells that when Zhuangzi and his friend Huizi were strolling on a bridge above the Hao River, Zhuangzi exclaimed over the "happiness of the fishes." Huizi questioned how Zhuangzi could know that the fish were happy. The argument that follows is resolved by Zhuangzi's final retort, "Let's go back to the beginning: you asked whence I knew of the fishes' happiness, thus already knowing that I knew. I know it just by being here above the Hao."

14. The cold and heat are largely, but not merely, figurative, indicating nearness to the ruler.

15. Quoting from the *Classic of Poetry* 263.

16. This alludes to a passage in the *Record of Rites* (*Liji* 禮記) that warns against being "undone by fullness in wealth and honor."

17. The tall gateways are those of the powerful, but their dominance never lasts long.

18. The air or aura of the Dao itself.

19. Like the legendary recluse Xu You, who washed out his ears in the Ying River when Emperor Yao offered to put him in charge of the government.

20. Although the phrase "raised floor" sometimes indicates a ritual platform, here it is an elegant term for a mountain path. I do not know which specific recluse of the past the poet has in mind.

21. This refers to Zhuangzi, who was said to have held a minor position in the "lacquer garden" in the state of Meng. Sun Chuo is here exploiting the literal meaning of the place.

22. Mencius once spoke of being good at "cultivating the unimpeded *qi*," which he defined as the *qi* that "unites rightness and the Way" and is able to fill, when unobstructed, the whole space between heaven and earth. See *Mengzi* 2A/2.

23. The term is conventionally humble; Sun was actually in his mid-thirties at this time.

24. The "invisible cycle" is the unavoidable round of fate, the permutations of which the poet wishes to accept without the usual interference of human emotions.

25. The all-enfolding unity of the Dao or, equally, of the Dharma.

26. A remark by Confucius (Father Kong) that begins his acknowledgment, quoted in the *Analects* 9/23, that it is always possible for the younger generation to surpass its elders. Sun Chuo here uses it to introduce his laudatory comments about Xu Xun.

27. The fragrant flowers of thoroughwort and averoyne were traditional images for personal virtue.

28. Recalling *Laozi* 74, in which one is warned that if he tries to hew wood in place of a master carpenter, he shall surely cut his own hand.

29. A passage in the *Classic of Documents* (*Shujing* 書經) cautions that "in making a mound of nine fathoms, the deed may be incomplete for just one basketful of earth." The image is also used by Confucius in *Analects* 9/18 to suggest the ceaseless effort that must be made in learning.

30. Quoting from the *Record of Rites*.

31. Another image from *Zhuangzi* 7, referring to what is or should be inseparable, just as were the lords of the North and South seas.

32. The image of wading is borrowed from *Classic of Poetry* 9 and joined with that of "blended tastes" taken from a passage in *Huainanzi* 淮南子 11 that speaks of harmonizing different flavors.

33. Recalling a line from the *Classic of Poetry* 118.

34. The *Classic of Poetry* 72 contains the couplet "A single day without seeing you, / Was like three autumns."

35. That is, in the capital, which lies to the west of Guiji where Sun Chuo and Xu Xun had become friends.

36. This conventional hyperbole is used to suggest the poet's loneliness.

37. The commentary to the *Classic of Changes* (*Yijing* 易經), hexagram 11, says that "there is no level that does not slope, no going away that does not return; be constant in adversity and there will be no blame." Sun Chuo suggests in this line that the two friends will surely meet again, so there is no reason to be sad.

38. "Truth" is *li*, the inherent pattern in things.

39. This reprise of the last line of the preceding stanza is a device to signal the concluding nature of this stanza.

40. Referring to the legendary recluse known as Chaofu, the "Nest Father," who reputedly made his dwelling in a tree and to the group of "Four Graybeards" who took to the hills in order to avoid the chaos at the end of the Qin dynasty.

41. The commentary to the *Classic of Changes*, hexagram 33, notes that "constancy in exalted retreat brings good fortune."

42. This recalls Zhu Maichen, from the Western Han dynasty, who lived in obscurity, toting firewood, but eventually was promoted to an official position.

43. The line joins together two admonitions, one negative from *Zuozhuan* 左傳, Yin 11, regarding the ill effects of not "measuring one's strength," and one positive from *Mengzi* 2A/2, in which Mencius says that "holding to essentials but extending liberality is a most excellent Way."

44. Just as Confucius's disciple Zizhang is said to have copied down the Master's good counsel on the ends of his sash, in *Analects* 15/5.

45. The era of "Greatest Simplicity" was, according to the *Classic of Changes*, the inauguration of unformed substance.

46. That is, the pattern of yin and yang.

47. The hidden wellspring and mysterious breeze picture the inexplicable creative and sustaining power of the Dao.

48. This entire stanza plays on the notions of alternation and the worth of the simple, so familiar from the *Laozi*. The particular image of the unhewn block appears often in the *Laozi*, representing original wholeness.

49. In saying that Xie An's lofty character, unlike that of the common run, "returns," Sun Chuo recalls the ideas that "return [or reversal] is the movement of the Dao" (*Laozi* 40) and that one should "return to the root." The reference to "awakening" in the

preceding line brings in a comparable Buddhist image, something we will see again later.

50. The image of the rippling fountain is taken from the *Classic of Poetry* 138, which describes the contentment of a recluse in his simple dwelling.

51. "Abstruse" translates the same Chinese word as "mysterious," which here would give the wrong connotation.

52. Compare line 30 of the preceding poem.

53. This refers to the story in *Zhuangzi* 7 that tells how the two lords "flash-and-flicker" (see line 52 of the preceding poem) sought to repay the hospitality shown them by their friend Huntun ("entire wholeness"); noticing that Huntun lacked the seven sense-openings that other men had, they bored one in him daily until he had them all, at which point Huntun died.

54. Foreknowledge is defined in *Laozi* 38 as "the flower of the Dao, the origin of witlessness" and is regarded as a mark of inferior virtue. The early *xuanxue* adept associates it in his commentary on this passage with those who spend their effort dealing with worldly affairs. "Silent enlightenment," which here refers to both the Buddhist concept of *nirvana* and the perfection of the Daoist sage, is more than this.

55. The *Classic of Changes*, hexagram 41, called "diminution," points to the ultimate benefits of curbing one's passions and desires.

56. The "marvelous" (or "subtle") is an image depicting the workings of the Dao. Compare line 40 of the preceding poem.

57. That is, three years have passed.

58. Although the brilliant young scholar Jia Yi 賈誼 (201–168 B.C.E.) was invited to speak privately and at length with the emperor, the latter realized that he must send Jia away from court because of the resentment and jealousy Jia occasioned in the ruler's older, established officials. Sun Chuo here identifies himself with Jia Yi.

59. When young, Dai Liang 戴良 (fl. 1–20) was arrogant about his abilities, but when he met Huang Xian 黃憲, a younger talent from his home district, he acknowledged Huang as his better. In this allusion, Sun Chuo plays Dai Liang to Xie An's Huang Xian.

60. Sun Chuo portrays Xie An's removal to the capital as a graduation to an even higher form of enlightenment, in keeping with the popular notion that the true sage can be aloof even at court.

14. The Art of Poetry Writing

Liu Xiaochuo's "Becoming the Number-One Person for the Number-One Position"

An important social change that is reflected in the literary production in the two centuries following the fall of Luoyang in 311 is the waning of hereditary families' influence over political and cultural matters at the southern court of Jiankang. The conflict between the "high clans" (shizu 世族) and the "cold gates" (hanmen 寒門) is evident in the reshuffling of social groups. From Liu Yu 劉裕 (363–422, r. 420–422) to Chen Baxian 陳霸先 (503–559, r. 557–559), all four founding emperors of the Southern Dynasties were commoners. Their sudden ascension to the top of the social pyramid encroached on the prestige and prerogatives of the old aristocratic class, which was not yet ready to accept a new hierarchical order. Ensuing contention between the "rootless" emperors and big-clan members during the fifth century was a manifestation of the power and terror of absolute rule. The deaths of the two highest-valued poets from the eminent Xie clan of Chen Commandery (in modern Henan), Xie Lingyun 謝靈運 (385–433) and Xie Tiao 謝朓 (464–499), speak volumes about this matter.

Nevertheless, the unchallenged dominance of the ruling house in political matters did not always extend to the cultural field, in which some Southern Dynasties emperors and military generals felt the most insecure. The art of writing poetry thus reemerged as an important site of competition for cultural prestige after a respite during the fourth century. At this time, personality evaluation centered on elegance and eloquence, as seen in numerous anecdotes in *Recent Anecdotes from the Talk of the Ages*. What once was a leisure art by which one could inadvertently flaunt one's highbrow taste had now become a studied art. For the youngsters of the Xie clan, what once was a means to display the wit and talent that came with elegant upbringing had now been transformed into a labored pursuit. The awareness that poetry was a particularly important symbol of culture drove almost everyone to acquire this cultural literacy. In his preface to *Grades of the Poets* (*Shipin* 詩品, or *Evaluations of the Poets* [*Shiping* 詩評]), Zhong Rong 鍾嶸 (468–518), after giving a historical and evaluative survey of *shi* 詩 (poetry), addressed his contemporaries about this obsession with writing poetry:

> As for men of letters and composers, none are not fond of this [art of *shi*]. Among contemporary gentry and commoners, this trend has reached a fervent pitch. Starting with children who have just started pursuing elementary studies, they wholeheartedly pursue it. Thereupon, producing mediocre sounds and using miscellaneous forms, each person writes as he pleases. This has even caused aristocratic youngsters to think it shameful should their literary attainment not be up to a certain level. Day and night they polish and revise, chanting and reciting.[1]

In addition to the fierce competition, Zhong Rong also pointed out the chaos in this somewhat blind pursuit. His disapproving attitude toward some literary productions evident in this passage was echoed by others like Pei Ziye 裴子野 (469–530) and Xiao Yi 蕭繹 (508–554). As a champion of classical learning, Pei Ziye lamented that "unrestrained writings impaired the classical form." In his *Master of the Golden Tower* (*Jinlou zi* 金樓子), Xiao Yi sighed over the fact that inferior writings had merely become a burden for those studying them.[2] The flourishing of literary production called for evaluative standards that were largely nonexistent.

Opinions on this matter as expressed in various essays by scholars and poets have led to a widely accepted belief that three schools can be identified according to their views of literature: the conservatives, the eclectic, and the progressive,[3] although the demarcation lines between these three groups were not always clear. For poets themselves, the most perceptible standards lay in the evaluations by those who read their works. An arbiter was often a patron or a potential patron. At the Liang court, in addition to Emperor Wu, Xiao Yan 蕭衍 (502–549), the three literary masters Shen Yue 沈約 (441–513), Fan Yun 范雲 (451–503), and Ren Fang 任昉 (460–508), who were the emperor's advisers in his early years, played the role of literary connoisseur. As they both explicitly and implicitly meted out praise or disapproval, they not only guided others in how to write poetry, but they also redistributed cultural capital, real and symbolic. This is because poetry—more so than other aristocratic arts such as calligraphy, chess, music, and painting—lay at the heart of the construction of a new social hierarchy. Unlike some previous studies claiming that the arts were the self-centered upper class's means of escape from the mundane world, poetry was actually an endeavor by all who tried to carve out a niche for themselves in the newly established social edifice.[4]

As John Timothy Wixted rightly observes, the obsession with evaluating men of letters in terms of their art of versification was the new form of characterology in vogue during the fourth and fifth centuries.[5] Having a decisive say in the production and consumption of such cultural symbols as poetry was of utmost importance to those who vied to hold office in the new order. As a result, poet and patron alike strove for such authority, and the whole process of poetic production and consumption became a serious quest for the cultural capital that used to be regarded as a leisurely pursuit. For example, the Liang Emperor Wu, albeit lenient and magnanimous in grave matters concerning his clansmen, subordinates, and writers, was never willing to budge or compromise when it came to the business of words.[6] Indeed, he refused to lose to the erudite Shen Yue in a counting match of allusions or references to early texts.[7]

The practice of allusion, an important part of the art of poetry, was thus a reflection of not only a person's mastery of the cultural lore, an indicator of upbringing and therefore social status, but also his skill in applying the established sources toward the end of affecting and influencing. Nonetheless, there was a trend toward obsession with the former rather than the latter—that is, an inordinate interest, especially among the newly minted upper class, in showing off one's knowledge of the books.

When the shaggy-looking Liu Jun listed more than ten textual references on the topic of "brocade quilts" (*jin bei* 錦被), the others in his company were at a loss for words, and "everyone in attendance was startled and the emperor's face, without his knowing it, lost color. After that, the emperor felt revulsion for Liu Jun and never again called him to be in the audience."[8] It is understandable that the emperor who had ascended the throne would prefer to monopolize the cultural field so as to enhance his legitimacy.

In this environment, talent alone could not warrant a favorable evaluation. Many poets who came to be admired in later ages were not recognized during their lifetime. Along with the anxiety to acquire and display talent was the urgency to quantify the assessment process. The flourishing of both literary milestones and miscellaneous works on the literary criticism of the period emerged from such needs. That the authors of two notable achievements—Zhong Rong's *Grades of the Poets* and Liu Xie's *The Literary Mind and the Carving of Dragons* (*Wenxin diaolong* 文心雕龍)—were themselves outside the recognized mainstream is instructive. Moreover, the title of Zhong Rong's *Grades of the Poets* betrays the motive to formulate a hierarchy of poetry fashioned on the system of "nine grades and equitable rectifiers" (*jiupin zhongzheng* 九品中正), instituted in the third century for selecting officials. Through their works, these two poets attempted to bring poetry to the forefront of personality valuation. Moreover, Zhong Rong based his work on an idea of Liu Hui 劉繪 (458–502), a member of the upstart Pengcheng clan: "The late Liu Hui of Pengcheng, style name Shizhang, a man of high critical acumen, became exasperated at this confusion and intended to compile a 'Gradings of Poets' for his generation. In conversation he set forth its general outline, but the work itself was never completed. Accordingly, I have been moved to write such a work."[9]

Without realizing this important work, Liu Hui died in 502. Among his ten sons and daughters, all of whom were proficient writers, the best known is Liu Xiaochuo 劉孝綽 (481–539). His biography History of the South (Nan shi 南史) offers the following about the Liu clan's literary achievement during the first half of the sixth century: "Xiaochuo, together with his brothers and sisters, sons and nephews, all were good at literary writing. It was unprecedented in recent history." According to the reckoning by Ma Baoji 馬寶記, the extant works by twelve writers belonging to the family amount to 185 poems and 81 prose works.[10] Thus the Pengcheng Liu clan became, arguably, the leading literary family during the sixth century, replacing the Wang and Xie families, who reigned during the previous 150 years.[11] The Liang Emperor Wu named Liu Xiaochuo the "number-one person," and Liu served as Crown Prince Zhaoming's leading poet and compiler. In order to understand how Liu Xiaochuo and his clan reached this dominant position in the literary and, to a great extent, the political arena in such a short period of several decades, we will next examine the key figures in the Liu family.[12]

Liu Xiaochuo's grandfather Liu Mian 劉勔 (418–474) was Master of Works in the Liu Song dynasty. Posthumously known as the Duke of Loyalty and Brightness 忠昭公, Liu Mian died while suppressing the rebellion of the Prince of Guiyang 桂陽王, Liu Xiufan 劉休範, in 474.[13] Liu Mian's eldest son Liu Quan (alternative pronunciation, Xun) 劉悛 (d. 496), who had fought together with his father and attained numerous merits in his own right, became an imperial in-law and had a close relationship with the Song Emperor Ming 宋明帝 (r. 466–472), Liu Yu 劉彧.[14] Even after the fall of the Song, Liu Quan continued to receive favorable treatment from the founding emperor of the succeeding Qi dynasty, Xiao Ze 蕭賾 (440–493, r. 483–493). The family's ties with the royal houses of Qi and Liang were deepened when Liu Quan's two daughters married Qi princes, and his three sons—Liu Ru 劉孺 (483–541), Liu Lan 劉覽 (fl. 485–530), and Liu Zun 劉遵 (488–535)—were selected by Xiao Yan at some point in their lives to serve Xiao Tong, the crown prince. Liu Mian's second son died early, and his surviving son, Liu Bao 劉苞 (482–511), joined his cousins at the Liang court. Among these Liu brothers, Liu Ru held the highest official post as the Minister of the Personnel Bureau (Libu shangshu 吏部尚書). The family's literary achievements were made possible mainly through the influence of Liu Xiaochuo's father, Liu Hui, who was the third son of Liu Mian and thus Liu Quan's younger brother.

Liu Hui was considered the most talented member of the family in literature and arts and was often called on to engage with family guests and visitors in conversation. When Xiao Ziliang founded his literary salon in the Western Residence, Liu Hui joined the group and served as a leader among the *arrivistes* (*houjin* 後進), which enabled him to become acquainted with Shen Yue, Fan Yun, and Xiao Yan.[15] As a man of quick wit and harboring an acute interest in literature, Liu Hui also won respect from well-known scholars such as Zhou Yong 周顒 (d. 485) and Zhang Rong 張融 (444–497). Liu Hui must have brought his eldest son, Liu Xiaochuo, along to the gatherings he attended, for a number of accounts speak of Liu Xiaochuo as a famed young prodigy among the Yongming poets. Wang Rong, Liu Hui's brother-in-law and Liu Xiaochuo's uncle, thus lavished praise on Liu Xiaochuo: "A'shi's [Liu Xiaochuo's nickname] literary talent is second to none in this world but me."[16] Fan Yun also made his own son, Xiaocai 孝才, a sworn brother with Liu Xiaochuo.[17]

Liu Xiaochuo's family background and personal reputation alone were not enough, however, to ensure a smooth career at the Liang court. He still needed to impress the emperor as well as powerful officials with his art of poetry, of which his use of allusion is, I believe, the most conspicuous aspect of his art. Liu's art is revealed in his poetry only through the painstaking annotation and analysis of allusions that he handled with care and delight. Indeed, Liu transformed a store of textual and historical antecedents into an art and therefore transcended the game of "who numerates the most allusions" that the Liang emperor found so delectable. Through a convincing display of his mastery of the art of allusion, Liu succeeded in persuading his superiors to grant him promotions, which eventually led him to be called the "number-one person" by the emperor himself.

The poems translated here speak to two noted occasions in which Liu allowed his art of poetry to work for his advancement at court. The first poem was written not long after his first official appointment as Assistant Editorial Director (*Zhuzuo zuolang* 著作佐郎) in the early years of Tianjian 天監 (502–520). In this poem, he addresses the important patron Ren Fang, who occupied an important position; the basic meaning is clear: Liu wanted to be transferred out of his current slot as assistant editorial director, which was one of eight assistants to the editorial director, an office established during the Wei to oversee the keeping of historical records.[18] Not of particular importance, this position was, nevertheless, where young men from aristocratic families began their careers. Many youngsters from the Wang clan—Wang Ying 王瑩, Wang Zhan 王瞻, Wang Changxuan 王長玄, and Wang Jun 王峻—all served as assistants, as did the sons of Shen Yue and Xu Mian. Given what we know about the Liu family and the environment in which Liu Xiaochuo grew up, it is not surprising that he became discontented with this position after some months there and thus made an appeal to Ren Fang. Ren Fang wrote a reply to Liu's poem, which is the second poem translated here. In this exchange of poems, the use of allusion reveals something subtle. On the one hand, the younger poet Liu Xiaochuo expresses subordination and deference to Ren Fang, but on the other hand, he aggressively urges his senior to grant him a promotion. The combination of this ritual propriety and practical bluntness, both necessary for a successful petition, can be executed poetically only through a skillful maneuvering of allusions that are readily recognizable yet necessitate contemplation for their real intent. In any case. Liu Xiaochuo was appointed Attendant (*Sheren* 舍人) at the court of Crown Prince Xiao Tong.[19] Even though this was a horizontal transition, the new position granted Liu proximity to the royal family, hence the emperor himself. Ren Fang evidently meant this to be a test for the bold young man. And Liu Xiaochuo, despite his less than desirable temperament, won over the emperor with his poetry while attending banquets.

On one such occasion when both Ren Fang and Shen Yue were present, Liu Xiaochuo composed seven poems, two of which survive. Xiao Yan highly praised both, which became the turning point in Liu Xiaochuo's career. About this matter, Liu's biography reads: "When Xiao Yan looked through his writings, he marveled at each one. From this point on, people inside and outside the court all changed their opinion [about Liu Xiaochuo]."[20] The two extant "Attending Banquet" (*Shiyan* 侍宴) poems are translated here. Their tone, reserved and modest, is noticeably different from the poem that Liu had written for Ren Fang. Here he bows to the imperial system of hierarchy and admits his own inferiority and humility. A conscious departure from Liu's earlier poem for Ren Fang, he now turns a "sparse tree" image into a "lush tree," which may be associated with a generous patron who offers shade and shelter to his guests. The second poem of "Attending Banquet" is a short, ten-line verse in which the poet subtly praises the emperor through allusions and images. Its deferential tone is in stark contrast to the self-assuring one in Liu's poem for Ren Fang. Even though both poems end with an allusion to reclusion, they convey different, contrastive tones. In the poem for Ren Fang, reclusion is depicted with amusement and pride as an elitist pursuit, but here the allusion to Bo Yi and Shu Qi, two martyr recluses of the Shang dynasty, is meant to arouse a different sentiment. The two virtuous brothers, refusing to become subjects of the Zhou King Wu 周武王, went into hiding in the Shouyang Mountain 首陽山, where they sustained themselves solely on "mallow and bean leaves" 葵藿 and eventually starved to death. Their tragic course has been a point of contention, and based on the two brothers' biography, Sima Qian raises a series of thought-provoking questions about their fates.[21] Liu Xiaochuo seems to also have doubts about this type of reclusion, which must have been disappointing to the Liang emperor.

The lesson here regarding allusions is that mere identification is not enough because a skilled poet uses allusion in such a way that the stories and references become an organic part of the poem, contributing to signification in ways both subtle and explicit. The art of speaking through poetry was what the court needed and valued, especially when such art—more than any other of its features—was the contended field of capital. Liu Xiaochuo certainly recognized this and played the game to his own advantage. Accordingly, he received a series of substantive appointments, among which Vice Director of the Imperial Library (*Mishu cheng* 秘書丞) was the most prestigious. When the emperor made this appointment, he remarked: "For the number-one position, the number-one person should be employed."[22] From then on, Liu Xiaochuo was firmly established at the Liang court, which shows us that the effectiveness of poetic language is not just learning or knowledge but how they are applied. Displaying what one knew no longer was sufficient; rather, one had to know *how* to display it. In this sense, the art of poetry is a revealing window onto the emerging new order.

FURTHER READING

For general studies of Six Dynasties poetry, see Kang-i Sun Chang, *Six Dynasties Poetry* (Princeton, N.J.: Princeton University, 1986); and Stephen Owen, *The Making of Early Chinese Classical Poetry* (Cambridge, Mass.: Harvard University Asia Center, 2006). For the most recent study of Liang dynasty culture and literature, see Xiaofei Tian, *Beacon Fire and Shooting Star: The Literary Culture of the Liang (502–557)* (Cambridge, Mass.: Harvard University Asia Center, 2007). For discussions of the use of allusions in classical Chinese poetry, see James Hightower, "Allusion in the Poetry of T'ao Ch'ien," *Japan Association of Overseas Studies* 31 (1971): 5–27; and Yu-Kung Kao and Tsu-Lin Mei, "Meaning, Metaphor, and Allusion in T'ang Poetry" *HJAS* 38, no. 2 (1978): 281–356. For court patronage and poetry at the Southern Qi court, see Cynthia L. Chennault, "Odes on Objects and Patronage During the Southern Qi," in *Studies in Early Medieval Chinese Literature and Cultural History: In Honor of Richard B. Mather and Donald Holzman*, ed. Paul W. Kroll and David R. Knechtges (Provo, Utah: T'ang Studies Society, 2003), 331–98.

Liu Xiaochuo 劉孝綽

Off Duty, Presented to Vice Censor-in-Chief
Ren Fang 歸沐呈任中丞昉

Walking out of the Golden Splendor Bureau,[23]	步出金華省
I looked back at the Received Brilliance Lodge.[24]	還望承明廬
Grand indeed is this land of Yuan and Luo;[25]	壯哉宛洛地
4 Wondrous sights fill the imperial city.	佳麗實皇居

Rainbows stretch over the flying gallery;   虹蜺拖飛閣

Thoroughwort and angelica cover limpid canals.   蘭芷覆清渠

A round pool reflects the lotus flowers;[26]   圓淵倒荷芰

8   The square mirror traces the image of hat pin and lapel.[27] 方鏡寫簪裾

Gone are the white clouds of summer on the peak;   白雲夏峰盡

Sparse are the leaves of green pagoda trees.   青槐秋葉疎

Since I joined in the honors bestowed by men,   自我從人爵

12   The "toad and hare" have waxed and waned many times.[28]   蟾兎屢盈虛

Skinned bamboos have in vain sweated;   殺青徒已汗

Yet the office of promotion has no further news.   司舉未云書

The "literary star" feels undeserved facing the official   文昌愧通籍
roster;

16   "Sima Xiangru" luckily has passed the exam.[29]   臨邛幸第如

You, my lord, are generous in your appreciation and favor;   夫君多敬愛

Even on a piece of useless timber, you freely lavish your   蟠木濫吹噓
praise.

At times, you may put aside the administrative work,   時時釋簿領

20   Ride your chariot and come to my home.   駟駕入吾廬

Although my speech can be called jade-like stone;[30]   自唾誠礦砆

It is no match for the fine jade of Fanyu.[31]   無以儷播璵

But I hope only for long-term leisure;   但願長閒暇

24   So I can ladle day-old wine and dine on roasted fish.   酌醴薦焚魚

A Poem in Reply to Liu Xiaochuo 答劉孝綽詩

When all waters gather together, they form billows;[32]   閱水既成瀾

One hides a boat in the gully, but unknowingly it is   藏舟遂移壑
moved away.[33]

This fine young talent of Luoyang,   彼美洛陽子

4   Throw me a poem harboring thoughts of autumn.   投我懷秋作

"Long respect" is close to a sincere comment;   久敬類誠言

"Lavish praise" seems to be words of ridicule.   吹噓似嘲謔

There you say summer clouds have ended;   兼稱夏雲盡

8   Again you mention that autumn trees are withered.   復陳秋樹索

Do you mean to console this man who sighs over old age?   詎慰耋嗟人

Uselessly sincere is this old man's promise.   徒深老夫託

An upright scribe gives forth both laudatory and   直史兼褒貶
derogatory comments;

12   Those in charge focus on criticism and condemnation.   轄司專疾惡

Nine setbacks mostly lead to a fine diagnosis;   九折多美疢

Without immediate effect, that is very likely good medicine.   匪報庶良藥

Make sure to polish your blade and tip;[34]   子其崇鋒穎

16   Spring hoeing encourages autumn harvest.[35]   春耕勵秋穫

Attending Banquet 侍宴

I

At this elegant banquet, many lofty men are invited;　清宴延多士

Among those holding honorable positions,　鴻漸溢微薄
　　there mingled this insignificant person.

Facing a strong wind, we go leave the Basil Tower;　臨飈出蕙樓

4　Gazing at stars, we climb up the Mushroom Gallery.　望辰躋菌閣

Its top cuts into the Milky Way;　上征切雲漢

Looking down, we see Luoyang, the capital of Zhou.　俛眺周京洛

Official residences are diversely disposed;　城寺鬱參差

8　Streets and thoroughfares run crisscross.　街衢紛漠漠

The imperial park gives forth chilly air at night;　禁林寒氣晚

It is almost autumn, but the leaves have not fallen.　方秋未搖落

The august mind values expression of intention;　皇心重發志

12　The emperor writes a poem, and we all follow suit.　賦詩追並作

Long have I been embraced by heaven's favor;　自昔承天寵

Here I receive honors bestowed by men.　於茲被人爵

My chosen words are not exquisite or elegant;　選言非綺紈

16　How could they match the golden　何以儷金艧
　　and indigo blue?

II

This hall is tall and towering;　茲堂乃峭嶠

Leaning on the railing, we face the serpentine pond.　伏檻臨曲池

Amid the trees, we see flowing water;　樹中望流水

4　Among the bamboos, we spot clusters of branches.　竹裏見攢枝

The banister is tall, yet sunlight cannot be blocked;　欄高景難蔽

Mountain nooks are deep, still clouds easily droop　岫隱雲易垂
　　over them.

Unexpectedly, I encounter this blissful blessing;　邂逅逢休幸

8　The vermilion procession pulls along the green rushes.[36]　朱蹕曳青規

Mountains and hills cannot answer;　丘山不可答

Only one himself knows about mallow and bean leaves.[37]　葵藿空自知

[Lu Qinli 逯欽立, *Pre-Qin, Han, Wei, Jin, and Southern and Northern Dynasties Poetry (Xian-Qin Han Wei Jin Nanbeichao shi* 先秦漢魏晉南北朝詩) (Beijing: Zhonghua shuju, 1983), 1825–26]

NOTES

1. Zhong Rong 鍾嶸, *Shi pin ji zhu* 詩品集注, ed. Cao Xu 曹旭 (Shanghai: Shanghai guji chubanshe, 1994), 54–58.

2. Xiao Yi 蕭繹, *Jinlou zi* 金樓子, "Liyan" 立言上, *SKQS* 4.15b.

3. Zhou Xunchu 周勛初, *Wei Jin Nanbeichao wenxue luncong* 魏晉南北朝文學論叢 (Nanjing: Jiangsu guji chubanshe, 1999), 230–53.

4. John Marney, *Liang Chien-wen Ti* (Boston: Twayne, 1976), 14.

5. John Timothy Wixted, "The Nature of Evaluation in the *Shih-p'in*," in *Theories of the Arts in China*, ed. Susan Bush and Christian Murck (Princeton, N.J.: Princeton University Press, 1983), 228–29.

6. Cao Daoheng 曹道衡, *Nanbeichao wenxue shi* 南北朝文學史 (Beijing: Renmin wenxue chubanshe, 2000), 11.

7. *LS* 13.243. See also Xiaofei Tian, *Beacon Fire and Shooting Star: The Literary Culture of the Liang (502–557)* (Cambridge, Mass.: Harvard University Asia Center, 2007), 97.

8. *NS* 49.1219–20.

9. Wixted, "Nature of Evaluation in the *Shih-p'in*," 227.

10. Ma Baoji 馬寶記, "Nanchao Pengcheng Liushi jiazu wenxue yanjiu" 南朝彭城劉氏家族文學研究, part 1, *Xuchang shizhuan xuebao* 許昌師專學報 18, no. 4 (1999): 35–38; part 2, *Xuchang shizhuan xuebao* 許昌師專學報 19, no. 3 (2000): 52–55, 35.

11. Cao Daoheng, *Nanbeichao wenxue shi*, 8.

12. For the Liu family history and lineage, see *NS* 39.1001–15. See also Zhou Weiyi 周唯一, "Pengcheng Liushi shiqun zai Qi Liang shitan zhi chuangzao yu yingxiang" 彭城劉氏詩群在齊梁詩壇之創造與影響, *Zhongguo wenxue yanjiu* 中古文學研究 61, no. 2 (2001): 20–24.

13. *SS* 86.2191–92.

14. *NQS* 37.649–54.

15. *NQS* 48.841–43.

16. *NS* 39.1010.

17. *NS* 39.1010.

18. Du You 杜佑, *Tong dian* 通典, annot. Wang Wenjin 王文錦 (Beijing: Zhonghua shuju, 1988), 736–37.

19. *LS* 33.480.

20. *LS* 33.480; and *NS* 39.1011.

21. *Records of the Historian (Shiji* 史記) 61.2127.

22. *LS* 33.480.

23. Golden Splendor Bureau refers to the Chancellery.

24. Chengming lu (Received Brilliance Lodge), built in the Western Han, was where officials stayed overnight for court business. Here it designates the Liang counterpart and signifies official employment at court.

25. Yuan Luo, the names of two famous towns in the north, Nanyang and Luoyang, is a reference to the Southern capital, Jiankang.

26. Compare Wang Yanshou, 王延壽 "Lu Lingguang dian fu" 魯靈光殿賦, in *Wen xuan* 11.513; Xiao Tong, comp., *Wen xuan*, or *Selections of Refined Literature*, vol. 2, *Rhapsodies on Sacrifices, Hunting, Travel, Sightseeing, Palaces and Halls, Rivers and Seas*, trans. David R. Knechtges (Princeton, N.J.: Princeton University Press, 1982), 270n.L.104, 271: "In a round pool on the square well, / Inversely planted are lotus."

27. *Zanju* 簪裾 (hat pin and lapel) refers to one's official attire. "Square mirror" is the receptacle used to catch dew on moonlit night in autumn. See *JTS* 23.887.

28. *Chantu* 蟾兔 (toad and hare) designates the moon.

29. Linqiong 臨邛, a town in Sichuan, is where Sima Xiangru and Zhuo Wenjun lived. Liu is comparing himself with the great Han *fu* writer.

30. Compare Wang Ziyuan 王子淵, "Si zi jiang de lun" 四子講德論, in Xiao Tong, *Wen xuan*, 51.2249.

31. Compare Cao Zhi, "Zeng Xu Gan" 贈徐幹, in Xiao Tong, *Wen xuan*, 24.1118: "If indeed one embraces jade-like goodness; / With time his goodness will become manifest."

32. Compare Lu Ji 陸機 (261–303), "*Fu* Lamenting the Passage of Time" (*Tanshi fu* 嘆逝賦), in Xiao Tong, *Wen xuan*, 16.725: "Water gathers to make a river; / It flows torrentially and time passes, just like that."

33. This line alludes to the *Zhuangzi*. See Guo Qingfan 郭慶藩 (1844–1896), comp., *Zhuangzi jishi* 莊子集釋 (1961; repr., Beijing: Zhonghua shuju, 1985), 243.

34. *Fengying* 鋒穎 (blade of a sword and tip of a brush) refers to one's talent and skill.

35. For the Chinese text, see *XS* 3:1598. Parts of the poem are found in *LS* 33.480; *NS* 39.1010; *Yiwen leiju* 藝文類聚 (Shanghai: Zhonghua shuju, 1965), 31.554; and *Wenyuan yinghua* 文苑英華 (Taibei: Yiwen yinshuguan, 1966), 240.4a.

36. *HS* 82.3378.

37. Jiang Yan 江淹, "Za ti-Chen si wang zeng you" 雜體陳思王贈友, in Xiao Tong, *Wen xuan*, 31.1456: "Being rich, one does not forget about poverty; / the way lies in mallow and bean leaves."

15. Six Poems from a Liang Dynasty Princely Court

XIAOFEI TIAN

The six poems discussed in this chapter were composed by Xiao Gang 蕭綱 (503–551), the then prince of Jin'an 晉安王, and his courtiers on the topic "Making Offerings in the Temple of the Han Exalted Emperor" (*Han Gao miao saishen* 漢高廟賽神). The temple was dedicated to the founding emperor of the Han dynasty, Liu Bang 劉邦 (r. 206–195 B.C.E.), and it was located in Xiangyang 襄陽 (in modern Hubei), the capital of the Yongzhou region. Xiao Gang, the third son of the Liang Emperor Wu (梁武帝, r. 502–549), served as the Governor of Yongzhou from 523 to 530, and these poems were composed during this period. Xiao Gang's staff members, some of the best-known Liang writers, wrote on the same topic at the command of the prince.

Xiangyang was part of the Hanzhong 漢中 area, which had been the Han founding emperor's fief before he ascended the throne. Temples dedicated to the Han founding emperor abounded in the upper reaches of the Han River throughout imperial China. However, *The Forest of Tales from the Tang* (*Tang yulin* 唐語林), an anecdotal collection compiled by Wang Dang 王讜 (fl. 1101–1110), claims that the temple at Xiangyang was originally called Temple of the Han Riverbank (Han gao miao 漢皋廟), established on the basis of an old legend about Zheng Jiaofu 鄭交甫 encountering two maidens by the side of the Han River, and that it was a mistake to identify it as the temple of the Han Exalted Emperor, also known as Han Gao miao 漢高廟.[1] In the Zheng Jiaofu story, the maidens turned out to be two goddesses and disappeared after presenting Zheng Jiaofu with a gift of large pearls. The pearls subsequently also vanished.[2] The *Commentary on the Classic of Waters* (*Shuijing zhu* 水經注) by Li Daoyuan 酈道元 (d. 527) notes that Han'gao 漢皋 is another name for Mount Wan 萬山. The worship of the Han River goddesses was related to a fertility ritual in early spring, which remains one of the most celebrated local festivals in Xiangyang, known as the Festival of Penetrating the Heaven 穿天節.

The poems by Xiao Gang and his courtiers were, however, written in the autumn. The Eastern Han writer Zhang Heng 張衡 (78–139) wrote in his "*Fu on the Eastern Metropolis*" (*Dongjing fu* 東京賦): "He goes on an autumn outing to reap a harvest." According to the *Wen xuan* commentary, "An autumn outing is called *yu*. This refers to the rite performed at the temple of the Exalted Emperor in autumn; at this time, myriad things have just ripened." Thus the young governor of Yongzhou may have been observing a long-established seasonal ritual, or he may even have appropriated the local "goddess cult" and transformed it into a state-sponsored public ritual, honoring not the river goddesses but a founding emperor of an earlier dynasty.

A few words need to be said about the significance of the Yongzhou region and its capital, Xiangyang, during the Liang dynasty. Situated on the frontier facing the Northern Wei, Yongzhou was the royal family's old power base: Xiao Gang's father, Emperor Wu, began his uprising in Xiangyang, with the support of the local great clans, and Lady Ding Lingguang 丁令光 (485–525), Xiao Gang's mother, was a native of Xiangyang. Throughout Emperor Wu's rule, the Yongzhou governorship was held primarily by close relatives of the royal family. In performing the ritual offerings to Han Gaozu, Xiao Gang was, first of all, acting as a royal prince, a proxy of the emperor, and a public official.

Writing poetry on the occasion is to celebrate and commemorate, to assert and confirm the right to make offerings as legitimate inheritors of the Han heritage. As the leader of the group, Xiao Gang sets the tone with his poem, describing the progress of the ritual from early morning to midday. His poem emphasizes the "communication" established between the spirit of the Han emperor and the Liang prince. Because he does not depict the actual activities in the temple in concrete detail as do some of the other poems in the series, the poem maintains an aura of ambiguity, which enhances the majesty and mystery of the spirit world. The focus of the poem is the third couplet: the absolute brightness of the moment embodies the full presence of the emperor's soul, who has descended because he is moved by the sacrifices performed by the prince. The divine presence is therefore a confirmation of the ritual's efficacy and political/moral propriety, thus reaffirming the state authority and the claim to imperial legitimacy of the Xiao-Liang ruling house.

The poem series furnishes a fine example of group composition on the same topic in a princely salon, as was the custom in the flourishing court culture of the period. In the many studies in Chinese, Japanese, and English of "literary groups" (*wenren jituan* 文人集團) in early medieval China, this concept is applied to a wide range of groups, which were sometimes formed more out of political necessity (such as "Twenty-Four Friends" [*Er shi si you* 二十四友], by the Western Jin minister Jia Mi 賈謐) than out of literary inclination. If we define a "literary group" more precisely as a group founded primarily on common literary interests and certain shared conceptions of literary style, then perhaps such literary groups properly began in the late fifth and early sixth centuries and centered on the princely establishment of the Prince of Jingling 竟陵王 (460–494) of the Qi dynasty and, decades later, on that of Xiao Gang. The key members of Xiao Gang's group were quite self-conscious about writing in a novel style, and their stylistic innovations were also readily recognized by their contemporaries. After Xiao Gang became the crown prince in 531 following his elder brother's untimely death, his and his associates' literary style was dubbed by their contemporaries "Palace Style Poetry" (*gongti shi* 宮體詩), with "Palace" referring specifically to the Eastern Palace, the official residence of the crown prince.[3]

Another characteristic that distinguishes the Southern Dynasties literary salons hosted by culturally sophisticated princes is that their members, though always subordinate to the prince, played a more active role in their interaction with him than ever before. This happened because of several factors. First, in most cases a prince began to acquire his own staff at a tender age and looked to his much older attendants as mentors. A good example is Xiao Gang's relationship with Xu Chi 徐摛 (474–551) and Yu Jianwu 庾肩吾 (ca. 487–551). Xiao Gang's staff members were well-known men of letters in their own right, unlike, for instance, the obscure contributors to the philosophical work *Huainanzi* 淮南子 compiled under the Prince of Huainan in the second century B.C.E. Instead, they were chosen from prominent gentry clans that wielded considerable power, which, if not always political, was social and cultural. Second, a prince who gathered a group of scholars and writers around himself during the Southern Dynasties was often an accomplished scholar and writer in his own right, in contrast with earlier princes, such as Prince Xiao of Liang 梁孝王 in the Western Han, who was a great patron of *fu* writers but was not known as one himself.

Xiao Gang, the leader of the Palace Style group, is also known by his posthumous title, Emperor Jianwen. He succeeded to the throne during a major rebellion by the Northern general Hou Jing in the summer of 549 and ruled under Hou Jing's power for two years before he was deposed and then murdered by Hou Jing's men. Xiao Gang's immense literary collection in one hundred scrolls was dispersed and lost after he died. Many of his writings that survived are found in encyclopedias, so many of them are only excerpts. Nevertheless, the total number of Xiao Gang's extant poems, more than 250, still far exceeds any other poet's surviving output from the period. In the age of manuscript culture, when the transmission of a text depended solely on hand copying, the survival of a rather large number of Xiao Gang's poems shows that there was apparently a great deal of interest in his work.

The other five poems discussed in this chapter were written by Liu Xiaoyi 劉孝儀 (484–550) and his cousin Liu Zun 劉遵 (488–535), Wang Taiqing 王臺卿, Xu Ling 徐陵 (507–583), and Yu Jianwu. All these poets were renowned literary personages in their day, with Xu Ling and Yu Jianwu worth special mention. Xu Ling was the son of Xiao Gang's mentor Xu Chi and is now best known for compiling the poetry anthology *New Songs of the Jade Terrace* (*Yutai xinyong* 玉臺新詠), one of the two anthologies that have survived more or less intact from early medieval China and the only extant single genre anthology from the pre-Tang period. This anthology is notable in that it was compiled for an upper-class female readership. Yu Jianwu was of the same generation as Xu Chi and was the father of Yu Xin 庾信 (513–581), the most famous late Southern Dynasties poet. The two father-and-son pairs were Xiao Gang's favorite courtiers and the main practitioners of the Palace Style Poetry, indeed so much so that the Palace Style was also dubbed the "Xu-Yu Style" (*Xu-Yu ti* 徐庾體) by their contemporaries. The poems discussed in this chapter are good examples.

Palace Style Poetry represents a new way of seeing the phenomenal world informed by the Buddhist concepts of meditative visualization and illumination. It focuses on temporal and spatial particularity, typically on small details. Moreover, its parallel couplets embody the intricate relationships among the things of this world, so that ideally in a parallel couplet, each line interacts with the other line in a dynamic way rather than simply forming a mechanical parallel with a repeated message.

The poem by Yu Jianwu provides a beautiful example of Palace Style Poetry. Unlike the other poems in the series, which invariably describe the temple grounds or the ceremonies in the temple, Yu Jianwu's poem, like Xiao Gang's, looks outward, mimicking the point of view not of the temple visitors but of the Han emperor, with the temple and the ritual hinted at in the opening couplet. A pathos that is worthy of the founder of a grand empire is anticipated in the second couplet, as it evokes the chaos and devastation marking the end of the glorious Han dynasty. The third couplet represents an expansive but rather bleak autumn scene.

The plain, an empty expanse, where autumn first stirs;	野曠秋先動
trees are tall; leaves wither early.	林高葉早殘

Instead of saying the autumn wind blows over the plain, swaying all the trees and grass, the poet simply states "autumn stirs," something vast, intangible, and yet made almost corporeal—and menacing—by being placed in the opposite position of the noun, "leaves," in the matching line. The fourth couplet is about the aftermath of the ritual:

Dust flies, riders disappear in the distance;   塵飛遠騎沒
the sun moves, half of the peak turns cold.   日徙半峰寒

The time is late afternoon, the sun is setting, but the sun moving away also parallels and thus figures the prince's departure from the temple. The spirit of the Han emperor is sinking into darkness and oblivion, just as the setting sun leaves half the peak cold and dark. This, of course, is also intended as a response to the fifth line of Xiao Gang's poem: "Sun in midheaven, mountains deprived of their shadows," which nicely captures the majesty of the "royal aura" of the ritual ceremony.

The structure of Yu Jianwu's poem, with two parallel couplets on scenery in between, is evocative of the structure of Tang regulated verse. The poet's investment of his creative energy in the two parallel couplets (usually on what the poet sees) later became a standard practice and was perfected to a high art in the Tang, a period that is still considered as Chinese poetry's golden age.

One last note of interest: when Xiao Gang was the Governor of Yongzhou, he celebrated the locale with a *yuefu* song series entitled "The Ditties of Yongzhou" (*Yongzhou qu* 雍州曲), which echoes his father Emperor Wu's *yuefu* song series "The Brass Hooves from Xiangyang" (*Xiangyang ta tongti* 襄陽蹋銅蹄), which commemorates his uprising against the Qi from Xiangyang. And yet during this period, any regional literary activity was a function of the entourage of the prince governor presiding over the region. In Xiao Gang's case, when he returned to Jiankang in 530, the key members of his salon—the Yus and Xus— were brought along with him; the practice of the Palace Style was continued in the capital area and became established as the prevailing style after Xiao Gang was made the crown prince. Regional literature in early medieval China is thus characterized by its continuity with the central court, as contrasted with its later development.

FURTHER READING

For a critical biography of Xiao Gang, see John Marney, *Liang Chien-wen Ti* (Boston: Twayne, 1976); and Xiaofei Tian, "Suppression of the Light: Xiao Gang, Prince and Poet," in *Beacon Fire and Shooting Star: The Literary Culture of the Liang (502–557)* (Cambridge, Mass.: Harvard University Asia Center, 2007), chap. 6. For a discussion of the Southern Dynasties princely establishment and its sociopolitical and literary significance, see Ishii Hitoshi 石井仁, "On Aides-de-Camp in the Southern Dynasties: Principally in the Forces of Chien-wen-ti of Liang" (Nanchō ni okeru zuifu-fusa: Ryō no kanbuntei shūdan o chūshin toshite) 南朝における隨府府佐: 梁の簡文帝集団を中心として, in *Shūkan tōyōgaku* 集刊東洋學 53 (1985): 34–49; and Wang Wenjin 王文進, "Zhoufu shuanggui zhi dui nanchao wenxue de yingxiang: Yi Jing Yong didai weizhu de guancha"

州府雙軌制對南朝文學的影響: 以荊雍地帶為主的觀察, in *Wenxue yu shehui*
文學與社會 (Taibei: Xuesheng shuju, 1990). For a study of the Six Dynasties
salon literature, see Morino Shigeo 森野繁夫, *Rikuchō shi no kenkyū: "Shūdan
no bungaku" to "kojin no bungaku"* 六朝詩の研究:"集団の文学"と"個人の文学"
(Tokyo: Daiichi gakushūsha, 1976).

Xɪᴀᴏ Gᴀɴɢ 蕭綱

Making Offerings at the Temple of
the Han Exalted Emperor 漢高廟賽神

Jade wheel locks are about to be released in the morning;	玉軑朝行動
The celestial gateway should be opening up as dawn breaks.[4]	閶闔旦應開
White clouds rise over the Cangwu plain,	白雲蒼梧上
Cinnabar vapors pour out from Xianyang.[5]	丹霞咸陽來
Sun in midheaven, mountains deprived of their shadows;	日正山無影
The city wall slanting, the Han River frequently twists and turns.	城斜漢屢廻
When we look at the watercourse, it resembles earth's veins;	瞻流如地脈
We gaze toward the peaks—they match the Heavenly Terrace.[6]	望嶺匹天台
To dispel this sorrow of late autumn,	欲祛九秋恨
Let us, for now, raise the cup filled with ten-thousand-cash wine.[7]	聊舉十千杯

[*Yiwen leiju* 藝文類聚 38.686; Lu Qinli 逯欽立, ed.,
Quan Liang shi 全梁詩, in *XS* 21.1943]

Lɪᴜ Xɪᴀᴏʏɪ 劉孝儀

Making Offerings at the Temple of the
Han Exalted Emperor, in Response to the Poem
by Emperor Jianwen[8] 和簡文帝賽漢高帝廟

Jade and silks are used to honor glorious rites;	珪幣崇明祀
Sacrifices and libations, to venerate an exalted deity.	牲樽禮貴神
A startling wind, as if he is making a stop in the temple;	風驚如集廟
Light breaks, as if he has manifested himself to us.	光至似來陳
Spirit carriage enters lingering;	徘徊靈駕入
With loud chanting, the songs are fresh.	叫咷倡歌新
Words offered are not for one's personal benefit;	將言非為己

Paying respect is in fact to pray for the folk.　　　　　致敬乃祈民
Having much talent and having many concerns—　　　　多才與多事
Have always been close neighbors in the past and present.　今古獨為鄰

[*Yiwen leiju* 79.1350; Lu, *XS* 19.1893]

LIU ZUN 劉遵

Making Offerings at the Temple of the Han Exalted Emperor, in Response to the Poem by Emperor Jianwen 和簡文帝賽漢高帝廟

Cutting the snake in half: his hegemonic accomplishments　分蛇淪霸跡
　　have vanished;
Holding a sword in hand—such manly majesty　　　　　　提劍滅雄威
　　is long gone.[9]
Only the space for making pure offerings still remains;　　空餘清祀處
Auspicious clouds are flying no more.[10]　　　　　　　　無復瑞雲飛
Immortal carriage shines on cinnabar grottos;　　　　　　仙車照丹穴
Rainbow skirts reflected in the azure foliage.　　　　　　霓裳影翠微
Cast a jade pendant to invite the maidens of Han River;　　投玦要漢女
Blow the pipes to summon the Consort of the Xiang.[11]　　吹管召湘妃
Fortunately we encounter the day of "harboring intense　　幸逢懷精日
　　feelings";
Happily we shall receive time off upon our return.[12]　　　豫奉沐休歸

[*Yiwen leiju* 79.1350; Lu, *XS* 15.1809]

WANG TAIQING 王臺卿

Making Offerings at the Temple of the Han Exalted Emperor, in Response to the Poem by Emperor Jianwen 和簡文帝賽漢高帝廟

Washing our hair with perfumes, we serve peppered wine;　沐芳事椒醑
Going out in our carriages, we follow the road to the House　駕言遵壽宮
　　of Long Life.[13]
Jasper Terrace protrudes sideways, connecting to the peak;　瑤臺斜接岫
Jade Hall rises up toward the skies.　　　　　　　　　　玉殿上凌空
Trees stretch out, casting shadows from the cliffs;　　　　樹出垂巖影
Bamboos guide the wind that circles the mountain.　　　　竹引帶山風
Long stairs make it difficult for the mist to pause;　　　　階長霧難歇
Windows are high, an easy passageway for the clouds.　　　窗高雲易通
One feels sad only that when goblets and vessels are　　　所悲樽俎撤
　　taken away,

The singing and tapping out of the rhythms have not
    yet come to an end.　　　　　　　　　　　　　按歌曲未終

                   [*Yiwen leiju* 79.1350; Lu, *XS* 27.2088]

Xu Ling 徐陵

Making Offerings at the Temple of the Han Exalted Emperor, in Response to the Poem by Emperor Jianwen 和簡文帝賽漢高帝廟

Mountain palace resembles the Ox Head;　　　　　　山宮類牛首
The Han Mound seems like the Dragon Watercourse.[14]　漢寢若龍川
In the jade goblet, there is no more autumn ale;[15]　玉盃無秋酌
From the metal lamp, night smoke is extinguished.　金燈滅夜煙
Cinnabar curtains press close upon the numinous mountain;　丹帷迫靈嶽
Onto the maroon mats descend a plethora of immortals.[16]　紺席下羣仙
In the empty hall echoes the sound of Lord Pei's harp;　堂空沛筑響
Her hair pins hanging low, Lady Qi dances with charm.[17]　釵低戚舞妍
Nothing, however, could surpass the fact that in
    the imperial temple　　　　　　　　　　　　何殊后廟裏
Zijian has composed a splendid poem.[18]　　　　　子建作華篇

      [*Yiwen leiju* 79.1350; Lu Qinli, ed., *Quan Chen shi*, in *XS* 5.2529]

Yu Jianwu 庾肩吾

Making Offerings at the Temple of the Han Exalted Emperor, in Response to the Poem by Emperor Jianwen 和簡文帝賽漢高帝廟

In the past he was in the folds of Tangshan,　　　　昔在唐山曲
Now we serve him on the altar of purple shells.[19]　今承紫貝壇
Little would he know that coming upon the riverbanks
    of Chu,　　　　　　　　　　　　　　　　寧知臨楚岸
No more would he gaze toward Chang'an.[20]　　　非復望長安
The plain, an empty expanse, where autumn first stirs;　野曠秋先動
Trees are tall; leaves wither early.　　　　　　　林高葉早殘
Dust flies, riders disappear in the distance;　　　塵飛遠騎沒
The sun moves, half the peak turns cold.　　　　日徙半峰寒
In vain do I try to measure up to your speedy yet
    polished composition,[21]　　　　　　　　　　徒然仰成誦
For it is truly difficult to find a talented man.[22]　　終用試才難

                [*Yiwen leiju* 38.686; *XS* 23.1989]

NOTES

1.   Wang Dang 王讜, *Tang yulin* 唐語林 (Shanghai: Shanghai guji chubanshe, 1978), 8.286.

2.   The legend appears in a citation from *Han shi neizhuan* 韓詩內傳 in the *Wen xuan* commentary on Guo Pu, 郭璞 (276–324), "Jiang fu" 江賦.

3.   For a detailed discussion of Palace Style Poetry, see Xiaofei Tian, *Beacon Fire and Shooting Star: The Literary Culture of the Liang (502–557)* (Cambridge, Mass.: Harvard University Asia Center, 2007), 211–59.

4.   The celestial gateway, Changhe, is the main portal of the Ziwei constellation. In the first couplet, as the prince and his entourage set out to make offerings in Han Gaozu's temple in the morning, he imagines (delicately indicated by the word *ying*) that the spirit of Han Gaozu is, too, getting ready to descend to enjoy the offerings made in his temple.

5.   The "white clouds" refer to a remark in *Zhuangzi* 莊子: "[The sage] feels weary of the world in a thousand years and will depart and become immortal. Riding the white clouds, he shall henceforth arrive at the land of the gods" (*Zhuangzi jijie* 莊子集解 12.103). It also echoes the song sung by the Queen Mother of the West to King Mu of the Zhou, which begins with the line "White clouds in the sky" and ends with the wish "May you never die, / and will be able to come back." Cangwu was where the legendary sage-emperor Shun died and was buried. See *SJ* 1.44. When Liu Bang was still a commoner, his wife could always find him, no matter where he went into hiding. When he asked her how she did it, she said it was because there were always unusual cloud vapors above where he was. See *SJ* 8.348. Xianyang was the Qin capital. Liu Bang's army, who used red banners because Liu Bang was believed to be the son of the Red Emperor, was the first of the rebel armies to enter Xianyang.

6.   The Heavenly Terrace refers to the Tiantai Mountain, a sacred mountain for Daoist adepts.

7.   The wine-cup of ten thousand cash is an allusion to a line in Cao Zhi's 曹植 (192–232) *yuefu* poem, "Song of the Renowned Capital" (*Mingdu pian* 名都篇): "Fine wine costs ten thousand cash for each gallon (*dou*)" 美酒斗十千. See *XS* 1:431. By the sixth century, Cao Zhi, the talented younger brother of Cao Pi 曹丕, the Wei emperor, had become a common reference to the "younger brother of the heir apparent," and the citation of Cao Zhi is therefore an allusion to Xiao Gang himself. Much irony is inherent in the gesture, since Cao Zhi came from none other than the family that deposed the last Han emperor and established the new successor dynasty.

8.   The title of the poem, like the titles of the other poems written by Xiao Gang's staff members on this occasion, was most likely added by the editors of *Yiwen leiju*, the earliest source of this poem, for Xiao Gang was certainly not yet emperor, let alone "Emperor Jianwen," when these poems were written.

9.   The first two lines refer to the story that when still a commoner, Han Gaozu once cut a white snake in half in a drunken fit. Later an old woman wept over the dead snake, saying that the son of the Red Emperor had slain the son of the White Emperor.

10.   "Auspicious clouds" refer to the cloud vapors over Gaozu's head.

11. The "maidens of the Han River" refer to the goddesses in the Zheng Jiaofu story. The Consort of the Xiang, the Goddess of the Xiang River, is celebrated in the "Nine Songs" (*Jiu ge* 九歌) of the *Lyrics of Chu* (*Chuci* 楚辭).

12. *Huaijing* 懷精 is an unusual phrase. In Wang Chong's 王充 (27–after 100) *Lun heng* 論衡: "Yu Rang planned to assassinate Zhao Xiangzi, and Xiangzi's heart felt trepidation; Guan Gao planned to assassinate Gaozu, and Gaozu's heart also felt trepidation. The two men harbored intense feelings [懷精], and so the two rulers were moved and shaken." See *Lun heng jiaoshi* 論衡校釋, comp. Huang Hui 黃暉 (Beijing: Zhonghua shuju 1990), 234. Guan Gao's 貫高 failed attempt at assassinating Gaozu occurred in 199 B.C.E. See *SJ* 8.387.

13. The House of Long Life is where sacrifices to deities are made. The first two lines echo "The Lord Within the Clouds" from the "Nine Songs": "We have bathed in orchid water and washed our hair with perfumes. . . . He is going to rest in the House of Long Life" 浴蘭湯兮沐芳 . . . 蹇將憺兮壽宮. The Han Emperor Wu also constructed a House of Long Life in Sweet Springs Palace.

14. Ox Head was the name of a hill to the southwest of Chang'an. The Dragon Watercourse may be a reference to the Dragon Head Aqueduct northeast of Chang'an. The underground aqueduct was dug in the Western Han, and since a set of "dragon bones" was discovered during the digging, the aqueduct was named Dragon Head. See *SJ* 29.1412.

15. "Jade goblet" may be a reference to an anecdote in *The Romance of Han Emperor Wu* (*Han Wudi gushi* 漢武帝故事): In 84 B.C.E.., someone was selling a jade goblet in the marketplace. A magistrate suspected that the jade goblet had been stolen from the imperial palace and was going to arrest the seller, who at this point suddenly vanished. The jade goblet turned out to be from the Maoling, Emperor Wu's mausoleum. The magistrate of the marketplace described the seller, whose appearance "resembled the deceased emperor" himself. "Autumn ale" refers to the *zhou* 酎 (a fine ale) used in autumn sacrifices to Gaozu's temple in the eighth month. See *HS* 5.137 and *HHS* 3.142.

16. "Cinnabar curtains" are often used to refer to the setting for the royal presence. According to the *Hanguan jiuyi* 漢官舊儀: "When making sacrifices to heaven, they set up a purple altar with curtains. Emperor Gaozu was treated as a match for Heaven in the rites, and his spirit tablet was placed in the hall facing west, within a maroon curtained enclosure and a set of maroon mats." See *Han guan liu zhong* 漢官六種, ed. Sun Xingyan 孫星衍, annot. Zhou Tianyou 周天游 (Beijing: Zhonghua shuju, 1990), 56.

17. Gaozu was a native of Pei 沛, and Lord of Pei 沛公 was Gaozu's title when he first rebelled against the Qin. Lady Qi was Gaozu's favorite concubine. The *Records of the Historian* 55.2047 records a story about Gaozu asking Lady Qi to perform a Chu dance while he himself sang a Chu song. According to *Xijing zaji* 西京雜記, she was skilled in playing the zither (*se*) and harp (*zhu*) and in performing the dance of "raising sleeves and bending waist" 翹袖折腰之舞.

18. Zijian was Cao Zhi's byname and was used as a standard reference to a talented prince who was the younger brother of the crown prince.

19. Tangshan, the Tang Hill, was the name of a hill to the northeast of Xiangyang. It was also the surname of one of Han Gaozu's concubines. Like Gaozu himself, Lady Tangshan was

a native of Chu and was skilled in Chu music. She was allegedly the composer of "The Air of the Inner Chambers" (*Fangzhong yue* 房中樂), which was renamed "The Air of Pacifying the World" (*Anshi yue* 安世樂) after Gaozu died. Here Yu Jianwu may be punning on the name Tangshan/Tang Hill, as well as on the double meanings of *qu*: "folds of a mountain" and "music." "The altar of purple shells" is a reference to "Lady of the Xiang River" in the "Nine Songs" of the *Chuci*.

20. Yongzhou, as we know, was in the old Chu territory. The second couplet evokes the famous lines from Wang Can's poem "Seven Sorrows" (*Qi ai shi* 七哀詩): "To the south I ascend the embankments of the Ba Mound, turning my head, I gaze at Chang'an from afar" 南登霸陵岸, 迴首望長安. The Ba Mound was the grave of Emperor Wen of the Han (Gaozu's son), and Wang Can was lamenting the devastation of the old Han capital during the civil war when he was leaving for the Chu region. These two lines mean that now that the Han is over, sacrifices are no longer made in Chang'an, but only back in Gaozu's home region.

21. What I have translated as "speedy yet polished composition" is literally "reciting everything by heart" 成誦在心, which was used by Yang Xiu 楊修 (175–219) in praise of Cao Zhi's remarkable talent in his letter to Cao Zhi. See *QW* 51.758. Here Yu Jianwu is using the reference to praise Xiao Gang's literary accomplishments.

22. "How difficult it is to acquire a talent!" is a lament by Confucius in the "Taibo" chapter of the *Analects*. Here Yu Jianwu is obviously talking about himself: he is not a talent, which proves that Confucius was right.

16. Pei Ziye's "Discourse on Insect Carving"

Pei Ziye 裴子野 (469–530) was an eminent historian and literary writer of the Liang dynasty.[1] He is best known now for his staunchly conservative views on literature, which are preserved in the essay "Discourse on Insect Carving" (*Diaochong lun* 雕蟲論). Pei was born into a prominent official family with a distinguished tradition of historical scholarship; his grandfather, Pei Yin 裴駰, wrote annotations for Sima Qian's *Records of the Historian* (*Shiji* 史記), and his father, Pei Zhaoming 裴昭明, served as an erudite in the Grand Academy (*Taixue boshi* 太學博士). Most famous of all was his great-grandfather, Pei Songzhi 裴松之 (372–451), who composed the major commentary to the *Record of the Three Kingdoms* (*Sanguo zhi* 三國志), as well as the now-lost *Annals of the Jin* (*Jin ji* 晉紀). Pei Songzhi was also ordered to compile the *History of the Song* (*Song shi* 宋史) but died before completing this project.

Pei Songzhi's unfinished *History of the Song* seems to have weighed heavily on Pei Ziye's mind. When the eminent poet Shen Yue 沈約 (441–513) finished his own history of the Song—which would be known as the *Song shu* 宋書—Pei Ziye was spurred to complete his great-grandfather's work. The *History of the Liang Dynasty* (*Liang shu* 梁書) records the following account:

In the beginning, Ziye's great-grandfather Songzhi received an imperial command during the Yuanjia reign [424–453] in the Song dynasty to finish compiling He Chengtian's *History of the Song*.[2] However, he died before completing it. Ziye long wanted to take up and complete his fore-bear's work. At the end of the Yongming reign [483–493] in the Qi dynasty, Shen Yue's *History of the Song* already was in circulation. Ziye revised and pared down the work, making the *Concise Account of the Song* in twenty fascicles. Its style of narration and its evaluative discussions were quite excellent. When Yue read it, he sighed, saying, "I cannot match this."[3]

Pei Ziye's *Concise Account of the Song* (*Song lüe* 宋略) serves not only as a tribute to his great-grandfather but also as a historiographic triumph over Shen Yue, who was criticized for his flowery style and lack of historiographic rigor by later critics such as Liu Zhiji 劉知幾 (661–721).[4] Unfortunately, Pei's revision of the *History of the Song* is no longer extant except for fragments and excerpts, including the "Discourse on Insect Carving."

The title by which Pei Ziye's discussion of literature is currently known is an allusion to a comment by the Han poet and philosopher Yang Xiong 揚雄 (53 B.C.E.–18 C.E.), who contemptuously referred to his youthful love of composing rhapsodies as mere "carving insect-characters and seal-script engravings" (*diaochong zhuanke* 雕蟲篆刻).[5] Note that Pei Ziye did not create the title "Discourse on Insect Carving." Instead, the earliest surviving text of the discourse is that found in the *Comprehensive History of Institutions* (*Tongdian* 通典) by Du You 杜佑 (735–812). Before quoting Pei Ziye, Du You provides a prefatory remark that ends with this statement: "Thus the empire admired how people laid ornament to their own words, and the art of insect carving was ascendant in the age."[6] By the time the piece was included in the collection *Fine Blossoms from the Garden of Letters* (*Wenyuan yinghua* 文苑英華), Du You's comment had become accepted as Pei's own preface, which then became the title for the "essay." Pei's argument begins by constructing the origins of poetry through the fourfold generic divisions and sixfold tropic schemes found in the Han dynasty "Great Preface" (*Da xu* 大序), attached to the Mao version of the *Classic of Poetry* (*Shijing* 詩經). Among other things, the "Great Preface" argued that poetry was the basis for kingly transformation, as its proper function was to represent the condition of the world and to articulate the moral aims of the gentleman. However, once poetry began to focus on the secondary aspects of literary ornament, it became a debased thing, no longer directed toward moral transformation but whose only purpose was what Pei calls *zitong* 自通, a phrase that conveys both the sense of making one's feelings known to the world and seeking to be known by the world.

At this point, Pei Ziye turns to the historical development of poetry following the *Classic of Poetry*. This is a narrative of poetry's failure, based on the moral abdication of poetry shown in its rhetorical excess, which itself reflects the desire of poets to express and promote themselves and to foreground the personal and subjective at the expense of illuminating ethical principles. Pei's narrative posits two origins for poetry, the first being the *Classic of Poetry* and the second, the *Lyrics of Chu* (*Chuci* 楚辭). If the *Classic of Poetry* represents the timeless principles of the sages, then the *Lyrics of Chu* is a decline into a compromised historical temporality in which the poet and his desire for recognition take precedence over moral transformation.

Despite periods when writers returned to the proper course of literary study and production, Pei sees the state of literature following the end of the Yuanjia reign (424–453) in the Song dynasty as one of increasing rhetorical extravagance and moral dissolution. It is interesting that Pei carefully limits his criticism to the Song, never once mentioning the Qi dynasty, which witnessed the true flourishing of the literary trends that he abhorred. Yet it is also clear that the discourse ends at a point after the Song, since he speaks of the Song's "lingering influence" (*yifeng* 遺風) and of the present time, which should heed the lessons of the past lest it, too, be remembered as an age of chaos.

The didactic moralism of the "Discourse on Insect Carving" prefigured the "restoring antiquity" (*fugu* 復古) poetics that took shape in the Sui and early Tang and fully emerged during the mid-Tang, in the aftermath of the An Lushan rebellion. To later literary scholars, Pei Ziye represented the countervoice of the Liang "Palace Style" (*gongti* 宮體) poets, even though the subjects of his criticisms were the poets of an earlier generation.

FURTHER READING

On the history of Pei Ziye and his family, see Zhou Zhengsong 周征松, *Wei Jin Sui Tang de Hedong Peishi* 魏晉隋唐的河東裴氏 (Taiyuan: Shanxi jiaoyu chubanshe, 2000). For studies of Pei Ziye and his literary thought, see Cao Daoheng 曹道衡, "Guanyu Pei Ziye shiwen de jige wenti" 關於裴子野詩文的幾個問題, *Wenxue yichan* 文學遺產 2 (1984): 107–12; Hayashida Shinnosuke 林田慎之助, "Pei Ziye 'Diaochong lun' kaozheng—guanyu 'Diaochong lun' de xiezuo niandai ji qi fugu wenxue lun" 裴子野《雕蟲論》考證—關於《雕蟲論》的寫作年代及其復古文學論, trans. Chen Xizhong 陳曦鐘, *Gudai wenxue lilun yanjiu congkan* 6 (1982): 231–50; and John Marney, "P'ei Tzu-yeh: A Minor Literary Critic of the Liang Dynasty," *Selected Papers in Asian Studies* 1 (1976): 161–71. Pei Ziye's "Diaochong lun" also is discussed and translated in Thomas Jansen, *Höfische Öffentlichkeit im frühmittelalterlichen China: Debatten im Salon des Prinzen Xiao Ziliang* (Freiburg im Breisgau: Rombach, 2000); Ping Wang, "Culture and Literature in an Early Medieval Chinese Court: The Writings and Literary Thought of Xiao Tong (501–531)" (Ph.D. diss., University of Washington, 2006); and Wu Fusheng, *The Poetics of Decadence: Chinese Poetry of the Southern Dynasties and Late Tang Periods* (Albany: State University of New York Press, 1998). Useful overviews of Pei Ziye's place in the historical context of the Liang dynasty can be found in Hayashida Shinnosuke, *Chūgoku chūsei bungaku hyōronshi* 中國中世文學批評史 (Tokyo: Sobunsha, 1979); and Xiaofei Tian, *Beacon Fire and Shooting Star: The Literary Culture of the Liang (502–557)* (Cambridge, Mass.: Harvard University Asia Center, 2007).

Pei Ziye 裴子野

Discourse on Insect Carving (*Diaochong lun* 雕蟲論)

In the ancient past, the "Four Beginnings" and "Six Principles" were combined for the composition of poetry.[7] Poetry was used both to portray the manners of the four quarters and to display the aims of the superior man, to encourage goodness, and to castigate evil—kingly transformation was based on this. Later writers, keeping their thoughts on branches and leaves [i.e., secondary or inessential aspects], multiplied ornaments and hoarded elegance, and used poetry to express themselves in order to make themselves known.

As for despondent sorrow [expressed through] florid perfume, the *Elegies of Chu* was the ancestor; and as for finely wrought beauty [depicted with] unrestrained excess, Sima Xiangru harmonized to such tones. From this point on, the sort to pursue echoes and shadows cast aside the critical essence and had nothing on which to hold; rhapsodies, lyric poems, songs, and odes numbered by the hundreds of sackloads, enough to fill five whole carts. Cai Yong viewed this as clownish entertainment,[8] while Yang Xiong regretted what he had done as a young man.[9] Now that sages no longer appear, who can distinguish between elegant music and the music of Zheng?[10] The tradition of pentasyllabic poetry emerged with Su Wu and Li Ling;[11] Cao Zhi and Liu Zhen strengthened the force of its influence;[12] and Pan Yue and Lu Ji made firm its branches and leaves.[13] Following the move south of the Yangzi, people acclaimed Yan Yanzhi and Xie Lingyun; their "embroidered finery extended even to sash and handkerchief" and was not employed for court occasions.[14] From the beginning of the Song through the Yuanjia reign, there was much focus on classics and histories,[15] but by the period of the Daming reign, they truly loved literature.[16] The outstanding verses of the greatest talents paled before those of the former worthies; waves and currents reinforced one another; and they grew even more pronounced.

From this point on, among youths from village lanes and young men of highborn leisure, none have not abandoned the "Six Principles," chanting and singing about feelings and emotions. Students have taken figurative language as a pressing matter, referring to classical scholarship as narrow and dull. In their dissolute writings, they smashed canonical models and instead took refinement as meritorious achievement. Nothing was set to pipes and strings, and they did not stop at the limits set by rites and morality.[17] Their minds were deeply focused on grasses and trees, and their most far-reaching interests extended only to wind and clouds. Their deployment of allegorical signification were superficial and their aims weak; [their works were] labored but without consequence and esoteric but without profundity. If one seeks its origins, it was indeed the lingering influence of the Song dynasty. If Ji Zha were to hear its tones, he would not consider them those of a flourishing state.[18] Li, who hastened across the chamber, would certainly not dare to do this.[19] Xun Qing once said that the sign of a chaotic age was that its literary writings were depraved and ornate.[20] How could the present situation not reflect this?

[The translation is based on the version of the text found in Du You 杜佑 (735–812), comp., *Tongdian* 通典, 5 vols. (Beijing: Zhonghua shuju, 1984), 16.389–90. I also have consulted the version found in Li Fang 李昉 (925–996) et al., comps., *Wenyuan yinghua* 文苑英華, 6 vols. (Beijing: Zhonghua shuju, 1966), 742.3873b–74a]

NOTES

1. For a biography of Pei Ziye 裴子野, see *LS* 30.441–44 and *NS* 33.865–71.

2. He Chengtian 何承天 (370–447) was one of the most learned scholars in the early medieval period. He began his official service during the Jin, serving as an erudite in the Grand Academy. A mathematician and astronomer, He is now best known for recalibrating the Song calendar, which he submitted in 444; it was promulgated two years later. For his biography, see *SS* 64.1701–11.

3. *LS* 30.442–43. A longer version of this exchange is found in *NS* 33.866.

4. Richard B. Mather, *The Poet Shen Yüeh (441–513): The Reticent Marquis* (Princeton, N.J.: Princeton University Press, 1988), 28.

5. Wang Rongbao 汪榮寶, annot., *Fayan yishu* 法言義疏, ed. Chen Zhongfu 陳仲夫, 2 vols. (Beijing: Zhonghua shuju, 1987), 3.2.45.

6. Du You 杜佑 (735–812), comp., *Tongdian* 通典, 5 vols. (Beijing: Zhonghua shuju, 1984), 16.4.389.

7. This refers to the discussion of the poetic techniques and genres of the *Classic of Poetry* (*Shijing* 詩經) as described in the "Great Preface" (*Da xu* 大序). The "Four Beginnings" are the four generic divisions of *feng* 風, *xiaoya* 小雅, *daya* 大雅, and *song* 頌. The "Six Principles" combine the three genres of *feng*, *daya*, and *song*, with the rhetorical devices of *fu* 賦, *bi* 比, and *xing* 興. For a translation and discussion of the "Great Preface," see Stephen Owen, *Readings in Chinese Literary Thought* (Cambridge, Mass.: Council on East Asian Studies, Harvard University, 1992), 37–49.

8. Cai Yong castigated the use of rhapsody composition as a criterion in the selection of officials in a sealed document he presented to the Han Emperor Ling 漢靈帝 (r. 168–189). See *HHS* 60B.1996. This is discussed in David R. Knechtges, "Court Culture in

the Late Eastern Han: The Case of the Hongdu Gate School," in *Interpretation and Literature in Early Medieval China*, ed. Alan K. L. Chan and Yuet Kueng Lo (Albany: State University of New York Press, 2010), 9–40.

9. This is a reference to the comment by the Han scholar Yang Xiong 揚雄 (53 B.C.E.–18 C.E.), as mentioned in my introduction.

10. The "music of Zheng" is a standard figure for lascivious customs. See, for example, *Analects* 15/10.

11. Su Wu 蘇武 (140–60 B.C.E.) and Li Ling 李陵 (d. 74 B.C.E.) are traditionally considered the authors of a body of ancient-style poetry (*gushi* 古詩). Few critics now believe this attribution, though they are still spoken of as the first identified poets to compose in pentasyllabic verse.

12. Cao Zhi 曹植 (192–232), son of Cao Cao and younger half brother of Cao Pi, was the most talented poet of the Jian'an period, and among his corpus is the first known pentasyllabic-poem cycle, "Poems Presented to Prince Biao of Baima" 贈白馬王彪詩. Liu Zhen 劉楨 (d. 217) was one of the Seven Masters of the Jian'an (*Jian'an qizi* 建安七子).

13. Here Pan Yue 潘岳 (247–300) and Lu Ji 陸機 (261–303) represent the poets of the Western Jin. Pan Yue is best known for his poems lamenting his dead wife, and Lu Ji wrote, among other pieces, a series of imitations of *gushi*.

14. Here Yan Yanzhi 顏延之 (384–456) and Xie Lingyun 謝靈運 (385–433) represent the poets of the Liu Song dynasty. The figure of embroidered sash and handkerchief is an allusion to Yang Xiong, who comments that "the learning of the present age, not only does it employ florid diction, but lacking restraint, it embroiders even sashes and handkerchiefs" 今之學也, 非獨為之華藻也, 又從而繡其鞶帨. See *Fayan yishu*, 10.7.222.

15. The period from the founding of the Liu Song in 420 to the Yuanjia reign (424–453) saw the presentation of Fan Ye's *Hou Han shu*, as well as the founding of four state academies: one each for Confucian scholarship, "learning of the Mysterious [Dao]" (*xuanxue* 玄學), historical studies, and literary learning.

16. The Daming reign (457–464) is not usually singled out as a period of great literary accomplishment, falling, as it did, between the Yuanjia reign, identified with the writers Bao Zhao 鮑照 (ca. 414–466), Xie Lingyun, and Yan Yanzhi, and the illustrious Yongming reign (483–494) of the Southern Qi dynasty. In *Grades of the Poets* (*Shipin* 詩品), Zhong Rong 鐘嶸 (ca. 468–518) criticized the literary works of this period as "practically the same as rote book copying" 殆同書抄. To be sure, Bao Zhao, who was much younger than Xie and Yan, was active during the Daming reign. Xie Zhuang 謝莊 (421–466) was another famous writer of the period. By singling out the Daming reign, Pei probably wants to mark a break from the Yuanjia reign, which he has already identified as a period steeped in classical learning, even though the literary trends under way in the Daming reign had begun in the Yuanjia reign.

17. This is an allusion to the "Great Preface," which, in describing the "changed" poetry of the Zhou's decline, states, "Thus the changed airs were produced from feelings, but they stopped at the limits set by rites and morality. That they were produced from feelings was the nature of the people; that they stopped at the limits set by rites and morality was the grace of the former kings."

18. This is a reference to an episode related in the *Zuozhuan*, Xiang 29. Ji Zha 季札 was Prince of Wu 吳, and when he visited the state of Lu 魯, he asked to have the classical music of the Zhou states performed for his inspection. His comments on each of the performances correlate the cultural production of a state with its political health. In particular, Ji Zha notes that the music of Zheng 鄭 and Chen 陳 reveal that the two states are doomed.

19. This is an allusion to *Analects* 16/13, in which Confucius's son Li 鯉, byname Boyu 伯魚, was intercepted by the Master and questioned about his studies. When asked whether he had studied the *Odes*, Li confessed that he had not. Confucius chastised him, and Li obediently retired to study the *Odes*. Here, the *Tongdian* reads *dun* 敦 instead of *gan* 敢.

20. This is a reference to Xunzi's "Discourse on Music" (*Yue lun* 樂論). However, when Xunzi speaks of *wenzhang*, he means "pattern and ornament," not "literature." See Wang Xianqian 王先謙, annot., *Xunzi jijie* 荀子集解, 2 vols. (Beijing: Zhonghua shuju, 1988), 14.20.385.

17. Classifying the Literary Tradition

Zhi Yu's "Discourse on Literary Compositions Divided by Genre"

WENDY SWARTZ

"Discourse on Literary Compositions Divided by Genre" (*Wenzhang liubie lun* 文章流別論; hereafter, "Discourse") by Zhi Yu 摯虞 (d. 311) is a rare early example of Chinese genre study. As with many texts from the early medieval period, it has not survived intact, and the received version has been pieced together from quotations found in several encyclopedias.[1] In what has remained, we may easily discern that Zhi Yu traces the origins, delineates the developments, gives the characteristics, and identifies examples of various literary genres. Of the particular examples he provides, Zhi Yu further evaluates their merits or demerits. According to an early mention in the *Jin shu* 晉書 by Fang Xuanling 房玄齡 (579–648) et al., Zhi Yu wrote "discussions" (*lun* 論) for each genre included in his *Anthology of Literary Compositions Divided by Genre* (*Wenzhang liubie ji* 文章流別集*;[2] hereafter, *Anthology*),[3] and the work that since the Liang dynasty has circulated independently by the title "Discourse" is most likely a collection of the various "discussions" attached to each of the genres represented in the *Anthology*.[4] Although the number of "discussions" or genres originally included in the *Anthology* and therefore in the "Discourse" is not known, the extant text covers twelve genres.[5]

Much of the scholarship on the "Discourse" has been about detective work: figuring out the distinction among the "Discourse," *Anthology*, and "Treatise on Literary Compositions Divided by Genre" (*Wenzhang zhi*, or *Wenzhang liu-*

bie zhi 文章流別志; hereafter, "Treatise"); extrapolating their contents; and deducing their relationships. Although we may regard the role of the "Discourse" in the original *Anthology* with little doubt, its relation to the "Treatise" has been much less certain. Part of the confusion stems from their listings in two early histories. Whereas the *Jin shu* lists the *Anthology* (which presumably included the "Discourse" in some form) and the "Treatise" as separate works, the *History of the Sui* (*Sui shu* 隋書) lists the "Discourse" and the "Treatise" as one work, distinct from the *Anthology*.[6] In addition, early citations of these works often used abbreviations, which ultimately spelled trouble because these titles shared mostly the same characters. Moreover, the content of the "Treatise" has puzzled readers, who have debated how to classify the work. Some scholars assert that it is a bibliographic catalog, and others believe it to be a collection of biographical notices.[7] Based on all the available evidence, both these positions can be correct: the *Sui shu* lists the "Treatise" under bibliographic catalogs, and the surviving fragments from this text offer biographical information about writers, which often includes bibliographical items.[8] Note that ostensibly bibliographic works may include writers' biographies. A contemporary example, *Zhuge shi ji mulu* 諸葛氏集目錄 by Chen Shou 陳壽 (233–297), is a catalog of the *Collected Works* by Zhuge Liang 諸葛亮 (181–234), even though the list was presented *with* the biography of the famed Shu minister in a single document.[9]

Zhi Yu's "Discourse" responded to an important development in the literary landscape of the first few centuries in China: the proliferation of literary genres and forms. One modern scholar tabulated forty-one genres that were recognized by Zhi Yu's time.[10] Zhi Yu's "Discourse" organizes this wealth of literary output by establishing a genealogy of genres, clarifying the distinctions among them, and (re)asserting paradigms for later writers to observe. Zhi Yu's discussion treated more genres than those mentioned in the works of other Wei and Jin critics, most notably the "Discourse on Literature" (*Lun wen* 論文) by Cao Pi 曹丕 (187–226) (eight genres) and "Exposition on Literature" (*Wen fu* 文賦) by Lu Ji 陸機 (261–303) (ten genres). All of Zhi Yu's known examples are drawn from the Classics to works dating from the end of the Han dynasty, resulting in a new kind of work: a comprehensive historical anthology organized by genre and interspersed with criticism. By the Western Jin,[11] anthologies of single genres were not uncommon, but an anthology of critically selected works illustrating various genres that offered a systematic overview of literary history would have stood out.

The "Discourse" played a defining role in not only genre study and anthology production but also traditional Chinese literary history and criticism more generally. This text rigorously performed what later became the dual tasks of traditional literary criticism: tracing the origin and tracking the development. It also provided specific models for various genres, along with instructive judgments on these particular works. The extant fragments reveal two salient aspects of Zhi Yu's literary thought: a highly reverential attitude toward the

Classics, which are posited as the source for a number of genres, and the importance of the constancy of the literary form (*ti* 體), which should remain stable even if the language used changes over time. The formal and ideological requirements of a particular genre should be evident in all its various realizations, regardless of era.

Certain of Zhi Yu's emphases underscore a classical bent as much as they reflect contemporary interests. For example, he appears to privilege the laud (*song* 頌), extolling it as the most excellent example of poetry. The laud is one of the three forms or subgenres in the *Shijing*, though it became a major genre in the Eastern Han under imperial patronage and flourished in the first several centuries of the Common Era. Also, Zhi Yu's regard of the four-syllable line, the dominant form in the *Classic of Poetry*, as the paradigmatic form of tonal standards was in tune with the preference of Jin dynasty writers of court music, who found that the rhythm of this form harmonized well with the sounds of bells and stone drums to produce stately music.[12]

Zhi Yu's work on genre study had tremendous influence on later anthologists and critics. His anthology inspired sequels, for example, *A Separate Version of Literary Compositions Divided by Genre* (*Wenzhang liubie bie ben* 文章流別別本) by Xie Hun 謝混 and *A Continuation of Literary Compositions Divided by Genre* (*Xu wenzhang liubie* 續文章流別) by Kong Ning 孔甯.[13] More important, the strength of Zhi Yu's judgment can be perceived in grand compilations such as *Selections of Refined Literature* (*Wen xuan* 文選) by Xiao Tong 蕭統 (501–531) and *The Literary Mind and the Carving of Dragons* (*Wenxin diaolong* 文心雕龍) by Liu Xie 劉勰 (ca. 465–ca. 522) in their generic classification and choice of examples. Despite its current fragmentary appearance, Zhi Yu's "Discourse" remains an invaluable testimony of a great attempt to take stock of a literary heritage and a major medieval work that involved anthology production, genre study, and literary history and criticism. In the following translation, each genre is marked by a separate paragraph after the opening. The text begins with general remarks on literature and an overview of the fundamental principles of poetry.

FURTHER READING

For an annotated modern edition of Zhi Yu's "Discourse," see Guo Shaoyu 郭紹虞, ed., *Zhongguo lidai wenlun xuan* 中國歷代文論選 (Shanghai: Shanghai guji chubanshe, 1979), 1:190–205. For an earlier English translation with annotations, see Joseph R. Allen III, "Chih Yü's Discussions of Different Types of Literature: A Translation and Brief Comment," in Joseph R. Allen III and Timothy S. Phelan, *Two Studies in Chinese Literary Criticism* (Seattle: Institute for Comparative and Foreign Area Studies, University of Washington, 1976), 3–36. The most comprehensive study to date of Zhi Yu and his works is Deng Guoguang

鄧國光, *Zhi Yu janjiu* 摯虞研究 (Hong Kong: Xueheng chubanshe, 1990). Recent articles include Mou Shijin 牟世金, "'Wenzhang liubie zhi lun' yuanmao chu tan" 《文章流別志、論》原貌初探, in *Zhongguo gudai wenlunjia ping zhuan* 中國古代文論家評傳 (Zhengzhou shi: Zhongzhou guji chubanshe, 1988), 351–61; and Li Zhi 力之, "Lun *Wenzhang liubie ji* ji qi yu 'Wenzhang zhi' de guanxi" 論《文章流別集》及其與 《文章志》的關係, *Shaoguan xueyuan xuebao, shehui kexue* 29, no. 5 (2008): 1–6. For a good recent monograph on genre study in the Wei, Jin, and Northern and Southern Dynasties, see Li Shibiao, 李士彪 *Wei Jin Nanbeichao wenti xue* 魏晉南北朝文體學 (Shanghai: Shanghai guji chubanshe, 2004).

ZHI YU 摯虞

Discourse on Literary Compositions Divided by Genre
(*Wenzhang liubie lun* 文章流別論)

Literary compositions are for the purpose of making known the phenomena that are above and below, to make clear the order of human relationships, to expound fully on the principles and nature of things,[14] and to investigate what is appropriate to the myriad things. Kingly beneficence flowed and the *Odes* flourished; accomplishments spread and hymns arose; virtuous service was established and inscriptions were made; the good pass away and dirges accumulate.[15] The supplicant and the scribe [*zhu shi* 祝史] set forth the statements [that issued from the court];[16] officials admonished the king's faults. In the *Rites of Zhou* [*Zhou li* 周禮], the Grand Preceptor of Music [*Taishi* 太詩] was in charge of teaching the Six Modes of Poetry [*liushi* 六詩]: Airs [*feng* 風], exposition [*fu* 賦], comparison [*bi* 比], stimulus [*xing* 興], Elegantiae [*ya* 雅], and Lauds [*song* 頌].[17] When affairs of a state are tied to the basis of a single individual, it is called an air. When speaking of the affairs of the empire and manifesting the customs of the four quarters, it is called an elegantia. Lauds praise the appearance of great virtue. Exposition is the term for displaying and setting forth something. Comparison is when words analogize things of the same kind. Stimulus is the language of being stirred. In later ages, many people wrote poems. Those works that speak of accomplishments and virtue are called lauds. The rest are collectively called poems.

Lauds are the most excellent examples of poetry. In antiquity when sagely emperors and enlightened kings accomplished deeds and established order, then the sounds of lauds arose. Thereupon, scribes recorded these pieces and musicians set to song these compositions in order to present them in the ancestral temples and announce them to the ghosts and spirits. Thus what the lauds praise is the virtue of sagely kings. And then pitch pipes were constructed.

[With their aid,] some later pieces adopted the form [*xing* 形] of lauds, while others, their music [*sheng* 聲]. Although they show a high degree of meticulousness, they do not possess the meaning of ancient lauds. In the past, Ban Gu 班固 wrote "Laud for Marquis Dai of Anfeng" 安豐戴侯頌*[18] and Shi Cen 史岑 wrote "Laud for Leading Out the Army" 出師頌[19] and "Laud for Empress Deng the Harmonious Light" 和熹鄧后頌*: these pieces are similar in form and meaning to the "Lauds of Lu" 魯頌,[20] yet the difference in language shows change from past to present. "Laud for Zhao Chongguo" 趙充國頌[21] by Yang Xiong 揚雄 is called a laud, but it resembles an elegantia. The language of "Laud for Xianzong" 顯宗頌*[22] by Fu Yi 傅毅 resembles that in the "Lauds of Zhou" 周頌 but mixes together the intent of the airs and elegantiae. The lauds "Guangcheng" 廣成[23] and "Shanglin" 上林* by Ma Rong 馬融 are purely in the form of today's poetic expositions [*fu* 賦], but to call them lauds would be far-fetched.

Exposition, the designation for display, is a type of ancient poetry. The poets of antiquity wrote from feeling but stopped within the bounds of ritual propriety.[24] Feelings were expressed in the form of words; the meaning of rites and of rightness was clarified by the matter described. Thus there is the genre of exposition, which is a means by which [a writer] avails himself of images and exhausts his vocabulary to set forth his intent. In past ages, those who wrote poetic expositions were, for example, Sun Qing 孫卿[25] and Qu Yuan 屈原,[26] who still rather demonstrated the meaning of ancient *Odes*. When it came to Song Yu,[27] then we find mostly the flaw of excessiveness. The expositions contained in the *Lyrics of Chu* [*Chuci* 楚辭] are the most excellent example of its kind. Thus Master Yang [Xiong] considered that there is no poetic exposition more profound than "Li Sao."[28] The works of Jia Yi 賈誼[29] are a match for those by Qu Yuan. In the exposition of ancient *Odes*, feelings and rightness were primary, whereas matter and things were secondary. In today's poetic expositions, matter and phenomena are fundamental, whereas rightness and correctness are supplementary. When feelings and rightness are primary, then the words are concise and the writing shows regulation. When events and phenomena are fundamental, then the words are rich and the language has no consistency. From this undoubtedly stem the superfluity and conciseness of writing as well as the difficulty and ease of language. When created images are exaggerated, they are removed from their actual kind. When lofty language is excessively strong, it opposes actual things. When the words of disputation are overly logical, they miss the actual meaning. When the ornate exceeds the beautiful, it is contrary to actual feelings. These four faults go against great principles and harm ethical teachings. It is because of this that Sima Qian 司馬遷 left out the frivolous discourse by Sima Xiangru 司馬相如,[30] and Yang Xiong disliked that "the poetic expositions of the rhapsodists [*ciren* 辭人] are beautiful but unrestrained."[31]

The *Classic of Documents* [*Shangshu* 尚書] states, "An ode speaks what is intently on the mind; a song makes words last." To speak of one's intent is called poetry. In antiquity, there were officials in charge of collecting odes, so that the king might know his merits and failings.[32] Ancient *Odes* were written in lines of three, four, five, six, seven, and nine syllables. Ancient poems in general take the four-syllable line as the paradigmatic form. Yet at times, there was a line or two of mixed length found among four-syllable lines. Later generations developed those lines of mixed length, from which they formed pieces of their own. Of three-syllable lines in ancient poetry, there is, for example, "In a flock are the egrets, the egrets go flying."[33] Han dynasty suburban altar hymns often use this form. Of five-syllable lines, there is, for example, "Who says the sparrow has no beak? How else would it pierce my roof?"[34] Comic pieces and songs of entertainment often use this form. Of six-syllable lines, there is, for example, "Meanwhile, I pour from the bronze flask."[35] *Yuefu* pieces also use this form. Of seven-syllable lines, there is, for example, "Flying to and fro are the yellow birds; they come to perch on the mulberry trees."[36] Comic pieces and songs of entertainment often use this form. Of nine-syllable lines in ancient poetry, there is, for example, "Far away at the running pool we draw water; we scoop it there and pour it here."[37] Lines of this length were not adopted in songs, and they thus are rarely used. Although the basis of poetry is feeling and intent [*qingzhi* 情志], its rhythm relies on set sounds. In any case, the four-syllable line is paradigmatic for the melody of elegant tones. The other poetic forms, though of varying cadence [that can readily be sung], are not tonally correct.

The "Seven Stimuli" 七發, written by Mei Sheng 枚乘,[38] uses the roles of [the visitor from] Wu and [the heir apparent of] Chu as the guest and the host, respectively. It first speaks of [the heir apparent's] "going by carriage and coming by palanquin and the resultant affliction of atrophy." And it speaks of "inner palaces and secluded chambers and the consequent ailment of chills and fevers," how "indulgence of sexual pleasures is the poison of peaceful living," and how "rich flavors and warm clothes are harmful in their excessiveness." And so "it is proper [for the heir apparent] to listen to the gentleman of his age speak of essential words and wondrous ways, which will enable him to channel his spirit and guide him to purge himself of his chronic ailment."[39] After setting forth these words in order to delineate clearly the path one should take, the work then argues for the pleasures of sex, music, leisure, and travel. These arguments failed to persuade. Thereupon, the work presented the joys in the explanations and discourses of sages and disputers, and suddenly his ailment was cured. This is corrective advice for the common ailment of the rich. Although the work contains highly exaggerated language, it does not do away with the purpose of criticism and advice. The development of this genre has been extensive, and so its guiding principles have changed; works of this genre generally have the error of excessive ornateness as shown by the rhapsodists. Cui Yin 崔駰,

after writing "Seven Reliances" 七依,[40] borrowed the words of Mister Nonexistent:[41] "Alas! Yang Xiong once said, 'Young children practice "carving insects" and "engraving seal characters,"' and then suddenly said, 'No grown man would do this.'"[42] Confucius disliked how petty words ruin the Way.[43] With this type of writing,[44] could not one say that meaning is lacking but eloquence is abundant? "Poetic exposition is supposed to criticize," but "I fear that these pieces instead encourage."[45]

Based on the "Forester's Admonition" 虞箴,[46] Yang Xiong wrote his "Admonitions for the Twelve Regions" 十二州 and "Twelve Official Admonitions" 十二官箴.[47] Since the admonitions for nine of the offices had missing parts, the Cui's [Yin and his son Yuan 瑗] in the following generations filled the gaps. Hu Guang 胡廣 then arranged the order of the topic headings and wrote commentaries for them. This compilation is entitled "Admonitions for Various Offices" 百官箴.[48]

Ancient inscriptions [ming 銘] were extremely concise, whereas today's inscriptions are verbose. Indeed, there is a reason for this. We have already discussed that the plainness and embellishment of writing have changed through time.[49] The inscriptions of high antiquity were inscribed in the steles of ancestral temples. Cai Yong 蔡邕 made an inscription for the Venerable Yang,[50] the language of which is exemplary and correct. This is the most excellent work from the waning years of the Han dynasty. The finest examples of inscriptions on instruments in later generations are "Cauldron Inscription" 鼎銘* by Wang Mang 王莽,[51] "Stool Inscription" 机銘* by Cui Yuan 崔瑗,[52] "Cauldron Inscription" 鼎銘* by Zhu Gongshu 朱公叔,[53] and "Inkstone Inscription" 硯銘 by Wang Can 王粲.[54] All these pieces commemorate deed and virtue. This is the purpose of imperial inscriptions on the official standard [jialiang 嘉量] and those of various lords and officials on the king's banner [taichang 太常], bells, and drums. Although what they say differs, the excellent virtue that is commemorated is the same. Li You 李尤[55] wrote inscriptions for mountains, rivers, capitals, towns, as well as for knives, brushes, tallies,[56] and carving blades. There is nothing for which he does not write an inscription; and so his writings have the flaw of prolixity. His works offer ideas and show embellishment,[57] and so his words are worth recording.

Examples of poetry, laud, admonition, and inscription all include works written in the ancient past, which may serve as models for later composition. Only the dirge [lei 誄] has no established form; thus there is much variation among its writers. Of those that appear in canonical texts, the dirge written by Duke Ai for Confucius in the Zuo Commentary 左傳 is notable.[58]

The lament [ai 哀] is a type of dirge. Cui Yuan, Su Shun 蘇順,[59] Ma Rong, and the like wrote laments. They are usually written for children who died young and others who died prematurely, unable to reach old age. During the Jian'an period [196–220], Emperor Wen 文帝 [Cao Pi 曹丕, r. 220–226] and the Marquis of Linzi 臨淄侯 [Cao Zhi 曹植, 192–232] each lost a young child, and they commanded Xu Gan 徐幹,[60] Liu Zhen 劉楨,[61] and others to write laments for them. The form of the lament, in which grief and pain are primary, can be traced to the language of sighs.

What is today called eulogy (*aice* 哀策) shows the purpose of ancient dirges.

[Yang Xiong's] "Defense Against Ridicule" 解嘲[62] shows great ease and superior magnanimity. [Ban Gu's] "Response to a Guest" 應賓[63] shows profound exemplarity and gentle elegance. Cui Yin's "Expressing Intent" 達旨[64] shows vigorousness and emotiveness. Zhang Heng's 張衡 "Response to a Reproach" 應間[65] shows delicacy and diligence. In both form and substance, there is none among the four that is not outstanding.[66]

In antiquity, there were steles [*bei* 碑] at the ancestral temples. Later ages erected steles at the tombs to display them to the thoroughfare. What we have recorded are the texts of the inscriptions.

Although prognostication texts [*tuchen* 圖讖] are not the standard of correct writing, we can nonetheless accept that there is significance in the "vertical and horizontal" and that a piece is made by its "back and forth."[67]

[Yan Kejun 嚴可均, ed., *Quan Jin wen* 全晉文, in *QW* 77.1905a–6a]

NOTES

1. I have used the standard edition found in Yan Kejun 嚴可均, ed., *Quan Jin wen* 全晉文, in *QW* 77.1905a–6a. For a different reconstruction with added quotations, see Deng Guoguang 鄧國光, *Zhi Yu janjiu* 摯虞研究 (Hong Kong: Xueheng chubanshe, 1990), 182–92.

2. An asterisk denotes that the work is no longer extant.

3. For the biography of Zhi Yu 摯虞, see *JS* 51.1427.

4. The "Sui shu jingji zhi" 35.1081 cites the bibliographic catalog *Qi lu* 七錄 by Ruan Xiaoxu 阮孝緒 (479–536) in the entry on Zhi Yu's *Anthology*, which distinguishes among the *Anthology*, "Discourse," and "Treatise"* (to be discussed).

5. The "Song zan" 頌贊 chapter of *Wenxin diaolong* 文心雕龍 by Liu Xie 劉勰 (ca. 465–ca. 522) makes a reference to *Liubie*, indicating that the "account" (*shu* 述), which Liu Xie refers to as "historian's judgments" (*zan* 贊), was among the original genres treated by Zhi Yu.

6. *JS* 51.1427; *History of the Sui* (*Sui shu* 隋書) 35.1082.

7. For a concise survey of advocates of each view, see Deng Guoguang, *Zhi Yu yanjiu*, 163–64.

8. *Sui shu* 33.991. Deng Guoguang collected nineteen quotations from the "Treatise" in *Zhi Yu janjiu*, 160–62.

9. *SGZ* 53.929–31.

10. Deng Guoguang, *Zhi Yu janjiu*, 239–42.

11. "Qi lin" 七林 by Fu Xuan 傅玄 and "Han ming chen zou shi" 漢名臣奏事 by Chen Shou 陳壽 are examples.

12. "Yue zhi" 樂志, in *JS* 22.684–5.

13. *Sui shu* 35.1082. The title of Xie Hun's work is probably *Wenzhang liubie bie ben*, and not *Wenzhang liubie ben*, as it is listed in the *Sui shu*. The character *bie* (separate) was likely mistakenly omitted from the phrase *bie ben* (separate version) in the transmission of the title. See Yao Zhenzong 姚振宗, *Sui shu jingji zhi kaozheng* 隋書經籍志考證, in *Xuxiu Siku quanshu* 續修四庫全書 (Shanghai: Shanghai guji chubanshe, 1995–2002), 40.120.

14. The phrase *qiongli jinxing* 窮理盡性 is drawn verbatim from the opening of "Explaining the Trigrams" (*Shuogua* 說卦) commentary to the *Classic of Changes* (*Yijing* 易經). It refers to how the sages thoroughly investigated natural patterns and principles in order to arrive at an understanding of fate, whose workings are variously represented in the *Classic of Changes*.

15. Dirge (*lei* 誄) is glossed by Zheng Xuan 鄭玄 in the *Record of Rites* (*Liji* 禮記, *juan* 19, "Zengzi wen," part 2) as "to pile up" (*lei* 累), which refers to how a dirge "piles up" and lists biographical information of the deceased subject. *Ji* 集, here rendered as "accumulate," reinforces this sense.

16. The supplicant, or invocator, says prayers and/or invokes gods and spirits. See Charles O. Hucker, *A Dictionary of Official Titles in Imperial China* (Stanford, Calif.: Stanford University Press, 1985).

17. Ruan Yuan 阮元, ed., *Zhou li zhushu* 周禮注疏, in *Shisan jing zhushu* 十三經注疏 (Beijing: Zhonghua shuju, 1980), 23/158a/, 796.

18. Ban Gu 班固 (32–92) is the author (along with his father, Ban Biao 班彪 [3–54], and sister Ban Zhao 班昭 [ca. 48–ca. 112]) of the *Han shu*. He was also well known as a *fu* writer. The Marquis Dai of Anfeng here refers to Dou Rong 竇融.

19. Shi Cen 史岑 (fl. early first century C.E.) was well known as a prose writer. "Laud for Leading Out the Army" 出師頌, collected in the *Wen xuan*, *juan* 47, celebrates the beginning of Deng Zhi's 鄧騭 campaign against the Western Qiang 羌 tribe. He was the elder brother of Empress Deng (81–121), the subject of "Laud for Empress Deng the Harmonious Light" 和熹鄧后頌*.

20. These three works resemble the "Lauds of Lu" 魯頌, one of the three subsections of the lauds in the *Classic of Poetry*, in that they celebrate the deeds and virtue of those other than the son of Heaven. The other two subsections, the "Lauds of Zhou" 周頌 and "Lauds of Shang" 商頌, are concerned strictly with the royal lines of Zhou and Shang.

21. Yang Xiong 揚雄 (53 B.C.E.–18 C.E.) was a leading *fu* writer of the Han before he famously renounced the genre for its inefficacy in moral suasion. "Laud for Zhao Chongguo" 趙充國頌 (*Wen xuan*, *juan* 47), a piece commissioned by Emperor Cheng (r. 33–7 B.C.E.), praises the famous Western Han general for successfully defending against a Western Qiang tribe, the Xianling 先零, during the reign of Emperor Xuan (r. 74–49 B.C.E.).

22. Of Fu Yi 傅毅 (d. ca. 90), "Laud for Xianzong," only four lines remain. See "Quan Hou Han wen," in *QW* 43.707a. According to his biography in *HHS* 80A.2613, based on the *Classic of Poetry* 266, "Hallowed Temple" (*Qing miao* 清廟), Fu Yi wrote this laud to praise the extraordinary deed and virtue of Emperor Ming 明 (r. 57–75), whose posthumous title is Xianzong.

23. Ma Rong 馬融 (79–166) was an important classicist who wrote many commentaries, including ones on the *Classic of Documents*, *Classic of Poetry*, *Classic of Changes*, *Record of Rites*, and the *Analects*, none of which have survived in whole. Ma Rong's "Guangcheng song," a remonstrance piece, is recorded in his biography in *HHS* 60A.1954–69.

24. Zhi Yu here draws from the "Great Preface" (*Da xu* 大序) to the *Classic of Poetry*: "That [mutated odes] emerged from feelings is the nature of the people; that they stopped within the bounds of ritual propriety shows the beneficent influence of the former kings."

25. This refers to Xun Qing 荀卿 or Xunzi 荀子 (Master Xun; fl. ca. 260 B.C.E.), a philosopher of the Confucian school whose name is the title of a rich body of writings, including a section called "Chapter on the *Fu*" (*Fu pian* 賦篇).

26. Qu Yuan 屈原 (343–277 B.C.E.) is the supposed author of a number of works (most notably, "Encountering Sorrow" [*Li sao* 離騷]) in the *Lyrics of Chu* (*Chuci* 楚辭), the second oldest and authoritative poetic anthology after the *Classic of Poetry* in premodern China. See also his biography in *SJ* 84.2481–91, which supplies most of the framework with which readers have interpreted his works.

27. Song Yu was a native of Chu who lived during the late Warring States era and is mentioned in Qu Yuan's biography in the *Records of the Historian* 84.2491 as a well-known rhapsodist after the time of Qu Yuan. Among the poetic expositions attributed to him are "Poetic Exposition on the Gaotang Shrine" (*Gaotang fu* 高唐賦) and "Poetic Exposition on the Goddess" (*Shennü fu* 神女賦), both collected in the *Wen xuan*.

28. Zhi Yu is quoting Ban Gu's appraisal in his biography of Yang Xiong in *HS* 87B.3583, which states that Yang Xiong deemed no poetic exposition (*fu*) to be more profound than "Li Sao."

29. The best-known poetic expositions by Jia Yi 賈誼 (200–168 B.C.E.) are "Condolence for Qu Yuan" (*Diao Qu Yuan* 弔屈原) and "Poetic Exposition on the Owl" (*Fu niao fu* 鵩鳥賦), both collected in the *Wen xuan*.

30. In the biography by Sima Xiangru 司馬相如 (179–117 B.C.E.) in *SJ* 117.3043, Sima Qian 司馬遷 (ca. 145–ca. 86 B.C.E.) notes that the extravagant diction and flights of fancy that characterize certain passages of Lord No-such's (Wu shi gong 無是公) and Sir Vacuous's (Zi xu 子虛) descriptions of hunting parks in "Shanglin fu" 上林賦 were found objectionable, and thus only the "essentials" were accepted by the emperor. Burton Watson argued that "Sima Qian seems to have quoted the entire poem, without omitting the passages that the emperor and his court found objectionable" (Sima Qian, *Records of the Grand Historian: Han Dynasty II*, trans. Burton Watson [New York: Columbia University Press, 1993], 284n.14).

31. In *Fa yan* 法言, Yang Xiong 揚雄 compares the poetic expositions (*fu*) by writers of odes (*shiren*) and those of rhapsodies (*ciren*), concluding that the former are both beautiful and exemplified standards. See Han Jing 韓敬, ed., *Fa yan zhu* 法言注 (Beijing: Zhonghua shuju, 1992), 27. Yang Xiong considered Qu Yuan to be continuing the tradition of *shiren*, whereas Jing Cuo 景差, Tang Le 唐勒, Song Yu, and Mei Sheng of subsequent eras represented *ciren*, who, for Yang Xiong, were excessively concerned with ornate language.

32. There are two different accounts of this point. According to Ban Gu in *HS* 24A.1123 and 30.1708, an official in charge of collecting poems (*da shi* 大師 or *cai shi zhi guan* 采詩之官) traveled to different states to gather public opinion of the ruler's governance. According to He Xiu 何休 (129–182), in his commentary to the *Gongyang zhuan* 公羊傳, Duke Xuan 15, there did not seem to be a special official in charge of collecting poems; rather, each state gathered poems from its inhabitants and presented them to the Zhou king.

33. *Classic of Poetry* 298, "Stalwart" (*You bi* 有駜), though the second line here is slightly misquoted.

34. *Classic of Poetry* 17, "Dew on the Road" (*Xing lu* 行路).

35. *Classic of Poetry* 3, "Cocklebur" (*Quan er* 卷耳).

36. *Classic of Poetry* 131, "Yellow Birds" (*Huang niao* 黃鳥).

37. *Classic of Poetry* 251, "Far Off We Draw Water" (*Jiong zhuo* 泂酌).

38. For a translation, see Hans Frankel, *The Flowering Plum and the Palace Lady: Interpretations of Chinese Poetry* (New Haven, Conn.: Yale University Press, 1976), 186–211.

39. Zhi Yu is loosely quoting from the opening and ending of the "Seven Stimuli."

40. "Seven Reliances" 七依 by Cui Yin 崔駰 (d. 92) is found in "Quan Hou Han wen," in *QW* 44.714a, in highly fragmented form. Based on what survives, this appears to be a poetic exposition narrating a dialogue between a guest and his noble host, in which the former uses food, banqueting, hunting, and music in his persuasion. Liu Xie in cites this piece as an example of erudition and elegance in *Wenxin diaolong*, chap. 14, "Za wen" 雜文.

41. This reference is unclear and has no apparent connection with the best-known Mister Nonexistent, the main fictional character in "Mister Nonexistent's Discourse" (*Feiyou xiansheng zhuan* 非有先生論) by Dongfang Shuo 東方朔 (b. ca. 160 B.C.E.), which illustrates how Mister Nonexistent persuades the king of Wu of the ways of good government.

42. From the opening passage in the "Wu zi" 吾子 chapter of *Fa yan*, in which Yang Xiong is likely referring to two of the six forms of calligraphy that children practiced. See *HS* 30.1721.

43. Confucius is quoted in the "Xiao bian" 小辨 chapter of *Da Dai li ji* 大戴禮記 as saying, "Petty words ruin rightness. Petty rightness ruins the Way."

44. I have emended the text from *cu* 簇 (cluster) to *zu* 族 (kin or kind). See Guo Shaoyu 郭紹虞, ed., *Zhongguo lidai wenlun xuan* 中國歷代文論選 (Shanghai: Shanghai guji chubanshe, 1979), 1:199.

45. Zhi Yu here combines two phrases: one from Yang Xiong's "Own Preface" (*Zixu* 自序), as quoted in HS 87B.3575, and the other from the opening passage in the "Wu zi" chapter of Yang Xiong's *Fa yan*.

46. When Xin Jia 辛甲 served as Grand Historian of the Zhou, he ordered all officials to submit admonitions to reprove the king's faults. The "Forester's Admonition" reminds the king to govern well by evoking the historical lesson of Yi Yi 夷羿, who spent his time hunting and eventually lost the throne he usurped from Yu's 禹 descendants. See *Zuozhuan*, Ai 4.

47. According to the "Biography of Hu Guang" in *HHS* 44.1511, the title is "Twenty-Five Official Admonitions."

48. In the biography by Hu Guang 胡廣 (91–172) in *HHS* 44.1511, Fan Ye 范曄 writes that nine of the admonitions were either lost or fragmentary; subsequently, Cui Yin, Cui Yuan 崔瑗 (78–143), and Liu Taotu 劉騊駼 added sixteen pieces, and Hu Guang wrote four.

49. I have emended the text according to the version in *Taiping yulan* 太平御覽. See Guo Shaoyu, ed., *Zhongguo lidai wenlun xuan*, 192.

50. "Stele Inscription for Defender-in-Chief Yang Ci" (*Taiwei Yang Ci bei* 太尉楊賜碑) by Cai Yong 蔡邕 (133–192), in "Quan Hou Han wen," in *QW* 78.893a–895a, is praised in the "Dirge and Stele Inscription" (*Lei bei* 誄碑) chapter of *Wenxin diaolong* as an exemplary piece by the great stele inscription writer.

51. Wang Mang 王莽 was the founder of the Xin 新 dynasty (9–23). For fragments of three of his stele inscriptions, see "Quan Hou Han wen," in *QW* 60.456b.

52. Either this piece is no longer extant or the title listed here represents a textual corruption, since there is an extant piece by Cui Yuan called "Staff Inscription" (*Zhang ming* 杖銘). See "Quan Hou Han wen," in *QW* 45.719a. The characters *wu* 杌 (or, in some texts, *ji* 机) and *zhang* 杖 are graphically similar enough to consider the strong possibility of a scribal error.

53. For the biography of Zhu Gongshu 朱公叔 (100–163), whose name is Mu 穆, see *HHS* 43.1461–74.

54. Wang Can 王粲 (177–217) was one of the Seven Masters of the Jian'an period, an apex in Chinese literary history. For his "Inkstone Inscription," see "Quan Hou Han wen," in *QW* 91.966a.

55. Li You 李尤 (fl. early to mid-second century C.E.) was recommended for office by Jia Kui 賈逵, who praised Li as having the style of Sima Xiangru and Yang Xiong.

56. I have followed the *Taiping yulan*, which has *fu* 符 (tally) instead of *ping* 平 (paperweight).

57. The phrases *taolun* 討論 and *runse* 潤色 are drawn from the *Analects* 14/8, in which Confucius says that Shishu 世叔 would comment (*taolun*) on a diplomatic treaty composed by Bi Chen 裨諶, and Zichan 子產 would embellish (*runse*) the text.

58. *Zuozhuan*, Ai 16.

59. The short biographical notice by Su Shun 蘇順 (fl. 100 C.E.) in *HHS* 80A.2617 lists mourning pieces such as dirges and laments as part of his œuvre. There are no extant examples of Su Shun's laments, though Yan Kejun has collected three of his dirges, mostly fragmentary, in "Quan Hou Han wen," in *QW* 49.744b.

60. Xu Gan 徐幹 (171–218) was one of the Seven Masters of the Jian'an period. There are no extant laments in his works.

61. Liu Zhen 劉楨 (d. 217) was one of the Seven Masters of the Jian'an period. There are no extant laments in his works.

62. "Defense Against Ridicule" was written to justify Yang Xiong's cosmological work, *Grand Mystery* (*Tai xuan* 太玄). For a translation, see David R. Knechtges, *The Han shu Biography of Yang Xiong (53 B.C.–A.D. 18)* (Tempe: Center for Asian Studies, Arizona State University, 1982), 46–52.

63. This most likely refers to "Bin xi" 賓戲, which is cited as such in the same passage as the other three works in the "Za wen" chapter of *Wenxin diaolong*. "Response to a Guest's

Chiding" (*Bin xi* or *Da bin xi* 答賓戲) was supposedly written to console the author himself for not having been promoted in years. See "Quan Hou Han wen," in *QW* 25.609b–10b.

64. I have emended the text from *lian* 連 to *da* 達. See Guo, ed., *Zhongguo lidai wenlun xuan*, 192. The "Za wen" chapter of *Wenxin diaolong* cites this work as "Da zhi." This work responds to mocking criticism of Cui Yin's choice of retirement. See "Quan Hou Han wen," in *QW* 44.712a–3a.

65. "Response to a Reproach" 應間 by Zhang Heng 張衡 (78–139) expounds on the author's views of service. He famously remarked, echoing Confucius's sentiments in *Analects* 15/32, that a gentleman frets not about low office or meager salary but is concerned instead with whether his virtue is great enough and his knowledge broad enough. See "Quan Hou Han wen," in *QW* 54.773b-4b.

66. The four works mentioned in this section are discussed in the "Za wen" chapter of *Wenxin diaolong* as "Responses to Questions" (*Duiwen* 對問), which is listed as a genre in the *Wen xuan, juan* 45.

67. The nearly parallel terms "vertical and horizontal" (*zongheng* 縱橫) and "back and forth" (*fanfu* 反覆) are enigmatic here. "Vertical and horizontal" immediately calls to mind the name for political strategists during the Warring States era, but that association seems irrelevant here. "Back and forth" may refer to the sartorial metaphor of apocryphal texts (*wei* 緯) as the woof. According to the etymological dictionary *Shiming* 釋名 (ca. 200) by Liu Xi 劉熙, "apocryphal/woof [*wei* 緯] means to hem in [*wei* 圍]; it goes back and forth, around and around, to form a text [*jing* 經]." See *Shiming shu zheng bu* 釋名疏證補 (Beijing: Zhonghua shuju, 2008), 6/20/221. David R. Knechtges suggested a more straightforward interpretation of the phrases: "Because one can accept that here and there are moral principles, these writings . . . end up creating a coherent work" (e-mail to author, October 21, 2008).

18. Zhong Rong's Preface to *Grades of the Poets*

STEPHEN OWEN

Grades of the Poets (*Shipin* 詩品) by Zhong Rong 鍾嶸 (ca. 468–518) is one of the classics of early medieval literary criticism and the earliest critical work devoted exclusively to classical Chinese poetry—that is, poetry after the *Classic of Poetry* (*Shijing* 詩經) and *Lyrics of Chu* (*Chuci* 楚辭). Although the work is not dated, Zhong Rong claims not to have included anyone still living, which places it securely in the last years of his life. It thus postdates the other extant monument of literary criticism of the age, *Literary Pattern in the Mind or Carved Dragons* (*Wenxin diaolong* 文心雕龍) by Liu Xie 劉協, probably from around the very turn of the sixth century, a book that Zhong Rong does not mention and may well not have known.

Although the number differs according to how one counts, the book offers brief critical comments on 123 poets writing in the five-syllable line (including one set of early anonymous poems). These are divided into three grades, with only eleven poets and the corpus of anonymous poetry occupying the highest grade. The fuller entries usually begin with a filiation with some earlier writer or corpus of texts, followed by a characterization of the poet's work.

The book also has three prefaces, here translated in their entirety, with the exception of the concluding list of poems that Zhong Rong particularly admired. Although early editions assign the three prefaces to the three grades, the placement of the prefaces in the original form of the book is highly uncertain.

There are other uncertainties as well. *Grades of the Poets* was probably not the work's original name. In most Tang sources and many later sources, it is known as *Criticism of Poetry* (*Shiping* 詩評), foregrounding the judgments themselves rather than the classification system. This is the proper name given to it in the "Bibliography" (*Jingji zhi* 經籍志) of the *History of Sui* (*Sui shu* 隋書), with a note that the book was also known as *Shipin*. Another question is the degree to which the judgments in the work are Zhong Rong's own. In the first preface, he tells us: "Recently Liu Hui of Pengcheng, a gentleman of exceptional taste, was distressed at such utter confusion and, wanting to make gradations of poets in current times, he orally set forth critical judgments, but a written version was never completed. I, Rong, was stirred and have written of it."

There are enough personal comments in *Grades of the Poets* (including this tribute to Liu Hui) to make Zhong Rong at least "an" author of the text, but the Chinese is, as often, ambiguous as to how much the book represents a written version of the judgments of Liu Hui, who had died in 502, and how much these are Zhong Rong's own judgments. The passage sets up some essential issues of the age: a vigorous contemporary debate on poetry that, upon seeing such debate as "utter confusion," leads to a desire for authoritative judgment that will transform contention into consensus. Most of all, we should note that this was a world of primarily oral discourse on literature; the few written critical texts that we have are only small remnants of that much larger discursive world.

Scholars often speak of "schools" or "factions" when describing the literary debates of the period and sometimes map intellectual positions onto social groups. The reality seems to have been far more complex, with good friends or members of the same social set sometimes divided by strong opinions. Zhong Rong certainly had strong opinions, his strongest animadversion being against the desire to legislate the rules of poetic euphony that had developed in the preceding decades. The preeminent theorist of rules of euphony and the grand man of letters for decades had been Shen Yue 沈約 (441–513), who, according to Zhong Rong's biography in the mid-seventh-century *History of the South* (*Nan shi* 南史), had rebuffed Zhong Rong's early attempts to seek recognition. Like all literary figures for the preceding eighty years, Shen Yue was placed no higher than the middle grade, but Zhong Rong's criticism of him was remarkably generous. By contrast, the most admired recent poet of Zhong Rong's day, Xie Tiao 謝朓 (464–499), was also ranked in the middle grade. Despite some grudging praise, it is clear that Zhong Rong viewed Xie Tiao's poetry with some contempt. In his youth, as a student in the academy, Zhong Rong had been a protégé of Wang Jian 王儉, the General of the Guards, and Xie Tiao had also been in Wang's service. Zhong Rong ends his entry on Xie Tiao as follows: "Xie Tiao frequently discussed poetry with me; his excitement and the twists and turns of his discourse surpassed his writing." We see two young men in the same social circle often talking about poetry—perhaps disagreeing, perhaps not. They must have been friends, or they would not have continued their discussions. But that did not prevent Zhong Rong from turning his fond memory of those discussions into a contemptuous summation of his judgment of Xie Tiao the writer. We see differing individual convictions that could lead to disagreement, but no "faction."

Description of the opinions of those with whom one disagrees are generally untrustworthy, and particularly so in medieval China. We thus should take Zhong Rong's account of contemporary values in poetry in his prefaces with a grain of salt. On a more profound level, however, those who disagree always share terms, and those terms are informed by common values. If there were a controversy of the "ancients" versus the "moderns," Zhong Rong would position himself as the champion of the "ancients," though he rejects the four-syllable line as simply too "ancient." However contemptuously Zhong Rong may have treated Xie Tiao, Xie Tiao was still placed in the middle grade. Cao Cao 曹操 (155–220), richly praised in the preface, appears in the lowest grade, with a characterization that should have thrilled any champion of the ancients: "Lord Cao's ancient directness has wonderfully chill and mournful lines." Yet Zhong Rong's third grade was the home for many remarkably undistinguished poets. Although convictions played an important role in Zhong Rong's judgments, those convictions had not ossified into an ideology that determined judgment.

If reading, composing, and discussing poetry came to play a larger role in premodern China than in most cultures, it was thanks to this period, which was the culmination of a craze for poetry that had been growing throughout the fifth century. In addition to new works, older poems were gathered, imitated, and discussed. In the fifth century we see the beginnings of a historical understanding of classical poetry, and by Zhong Rong's time, chronological sequence was the most fundamental taxonomical principle. An anthology or critical treatise might be divided first by genre or, as Zhong Rong did, by "grades," but within such divisions, works were always organized by chronology.

Zhong Rong's first preface begins with a statement of theory, defining the place of poetry in the natural order. This is not "theory" in any modern sense of the term but a series of commonplaces elaborated from earlier texts and largely shared with the discourse on music. In the context of Zhong Rong's times, these claims were not open to negation; they were what every educated person in his community knew to be true. If Zhong Rong had claimed that a poem was the creation of individual genius, working in complete independence of the poet's experience in the social and political world, such a claim would have been unacceptable to the point of being incomprehensible.

From nature, Zhong Rong moves to history, beginning in high antiquity. Although Zhong Rong later began the history of poetry in the five-syllable line after antiquity, here he follows a standard discursive trope of discourse on literature, which was meant to give a genre authority by tracing it back to high antiquity. The earliest critical statement on poetry in the five-syllable line was found in the theoretical treatise attached to the *Anthology of Literary Compositions*

Divided by Genre (*Wenzhang liubie ji* 文章流別) by Zhi Yu 摰虞 (d. 311). There Zhi Yu lists all the possible verse line lengths, giving examples of where such line lengths can be found in the *Classic of Poetry*. Since the *Classic of Poetry* has many irregular lines, this is nothing more than an affirmation that there is nothing new in verse. Zhong Rong does something very similar, finding five-syllable lines in various verses from antiquity, albeit allowing that the "form of poetry had not fully developed."

After this follows a version of the standard history of poetry as it was understood in Zhong Rong's day, concluding with Xie Lingyun, the last poet in the highest grade. Notes on filiation, a judgment that a given poet's work grew out of the work of an earlier poet, affirmed the continuity of poetic history against the "moderns," the advocates of rules of euphony, who stressed the radical novelty of their discoveries. It was also a peculiarly Southern Dynasties gesture, creating literary lineages as the counterpart of contemporary family lineages that conferred social value on an individual.

Different critics passed different judgments on particular writers and eras, but as with political historians, the primary focus of attention was on identifying phases of flourishing and decline. The critic's taste determined what was "flourishing" and what was "decline." For Liu Xie, the poets of the Western Jin were going downhill into frivolous rhetoric; for Zhong Rong, the Western Jin poets represented a splendid revival of poetry following a decline in the second quarter of the third century. Tracing the roller coaster of history in this section, Zhong Rong names all the poets in the highest grade but one, Ruan Ji 阮籍 (210–263). Ruan unfortunately made his appearance in an age that Zhong Rong had designated as "decline." Here, as often in *Grades of the Poets*, the general account of poetry in the prefaces can be at odds with the judgments of individual poets.

Zhong Rong follows this with something genuinely new, a defense of poetry in the five-syllable line, as opposed to poetry in the four-syllable line, which followed the model of the *Classic of Poetry* and possessed immense authority. Within the history of poetry in the five-syllable line, Zhong Rong's values are distinctly on the side of the "ancients," who were not, in fact, very ancient. To defend the form itself, however, Zhong Rong adopts the arguments of the proponents of the moderns. In a nutshell, recent poetry in the four-syllable line is prolix and vapid, while poetry in the five-syllable line has "the most savor" and is the most popular. Later in the third preface, when attacking rules of euphony, he uses "popularity" as a criterion for scorn.

After a return to conventional poetics, Zhong Rong turns to the current situation as he sees it, something like a contemporary "craze" for poetry. This is not a happy phenomenon in Zhong Rong's view, because we see young men showing off "commonplace sounds and impure norms of genre." From this generally lamentable state of poetic affairs, we progress to something still worse, which is contempt for earlier poetry in the five-syllable line because of incompetent admiration for Bao Zhao 鮑照 and Xie Tiao, the most respected poets from the preceding seventy years. Zhong Rong proceeds to what he sees as a chaos of judgment, a chaos needing correction, which was first addressed by Liu Hui 劉繪 (458–502) and then completed by Zhong Rong himself.

The brief passage on judgment is one of the most remarkable in the preface. Zhong Rong first invokes earlier systems of grading and categorization but immediately points out the mistakes. By contrast, he believes that his own systematic organization of poetry will make levels of skill as self-evident as skill in chess. We have come a long way from the conventional theory of the opening, in which poetry is the natural consequence of nature's capacity to stir human beings; now it is a "skill" (*ji* 技) like other skills, such as chess. The first preface concludes with the requisite praise of the current ruler, the Liang Emperor Wu.

The second preface takes up the issue of making references or allusions (*yong shi* 用事) in poetry. While Zhong Rong acknowledges that this practice is inevitable for public genres that seek precedents for arguments, it violates the immediacy of poetry. Zhong Rong considers this the bane of recent poetry, even though historical reference and allusion can be found in virtually every poet he includes.

Zhong Rong next turns to previous critical works on literature, in each case offering a term of praise and a term of blame, noting that none "offered graded evaluations." The distinction of his treatise is both graded evaluations and restriction to poetry in the five-syllable line.

The brief third preface is the most polemical, a direct attack on those who advocate rules of euphony for poetry. The loss of music, an old theme in criticism of the *Classic of Poetry*, returns here. Once poetry was sung and was naturally euphonic. The current desire to legislate euphony follows from the fact that poetry is no longer sung. The very popularity that justified poetry in five-syllable line becomes the term of contempt for rules of euphony that are "already fully present in the villages."

Liu Xie composed his far larger treatise in isolation from the literary debates of the Jiankang elite, though he knew of them. Sometimes he attempts to reconcile a disagreement, and sometimes he simply presents opposing sides of an issue at different points in a chapter. While not of the highest elite, Zhong Rong was more part of the elite community of discourse that Liu Xie describes from the wings. He was an aging polemicist, his ire directed against the hot issues of his somewhat younger years. Those to whom he showed contempt were as dead as those he praised without reservation. In the second decade of the sixth century, the issues in poetry were changing while Zhong Rong was still fighting the battles of his younger years. Nevertheless, this is one of our few precious written survivals of a lively world of discourse on literature.

Another annotated translation of the preface and entries on individual poets can be found in John Timothy Wixted, "The Literary Criticism of Yüan Hao-wen (1190–1257)" (Ph.D. diss., University of Oxford, 1976), app. A. Wixted's "The Nature of Evaluation in the *Shih-p'in* (Grading of Poets) by Chung Hung (469–518)" is included in *Theories of the Arts in China*, ed. Susan Bush and Christian Murck (Princeton, N.J.: Princeton University Press, 1983). The two best annotated editions are Cao Xu 曹旭, *Shipin jizhu* 詩品集注 (Shanghai: Shanghai guji chubanshe, 1994); and Wang Shumin 王叔岷, *Zhong Rong Shipin jianzheng gao* 鍾嶸詩品箋證稿 (Taibei: Zhongyang yanjiuyuan wenshizhe yanjiusuo Zhongguo wenzhe zhuankan, 1992). See also Zhang Bowei 張伯偉, *Zhong Rong Shipin yanjiu* 鍾嶸詩品研究 (Nanjing: Nanjing daxue chubanshe, 1999).

❖

Zhong Rong 鍾嶸

Grades of the Poets (Shipin 詩品)

FIRST PREFACE

As the ethers stir the things of the world into motion and as those things move human beings, so are our sentiments swayed and swept along, and these take form in dance and song.[1] In this way, they illuminate the Three Substances [Heaven, Earth, and Humankind] and cast a glow on the infinite variety of existing things. The spirits depend on dance and song to have sacrifices brought; the hidden beings rely on them to be informed.[2] To stir Heaven and Earth and to move the spirits and gods, nothing is more appropriate than poetry.[3] Long ago, the lyrics of the "South Wind" and the hymn of "Auspicious Clouds" were of far-reaching significance.[4] The "Song of Xia" went: "My heart swells within."[5] The Chu song went: "He gave me the name Proper Norm."[6] Although this genre of poetry had not fully developed, still these are the wellsprings of the five-character line. When we reach Li Ling in the Han, the category of the five-character line becomes fully manifest for the first time.[7] The "old poems" are so far from us they are unclear, and the times of their authors cannot be ascertained fully.[8] Yet when we examine the genre, they are obviously the work of the fiery Han and not the songs of the waning Zhou.[9] Poetic expositions by the likes of Wang, Yang, Mei, and Sima competed in splendor; yet their chants and songs are not now heard.[10] From Defender Li Ling down to the Fair Consort Ban, for an interval of almost a hundred years, since there was a woman here, there was only one person.[11] The influence of the poets of the *Classic of Poetry* was utterly lost.[12] During the two centuries in which the capital was in the east we have only Ban Gu's "On History," which is plain, wooden, and lacking adornment.[13] When we come down to the Jian'an reign [196–220], the lords Cao, father and sons, showed a devoted fondness for literary culture.[14] Pingyuan [Cao Zhi] and his brother were glorious as the main beams of letters.[15] Liu Zhen and Wang Can formed their wings.[16] In addition there were those who "clung to the dragon and rode the phoenix," while those made it to the level of attendant carriages can be reckoned as almost a hundred.[17] The height of pattern and substance in balance was fully achieved in those times. Thereafter things went downhill and grew feeble all the way to the Jin.[18] In the Taikang reign [280–289], three Zhangs, two Lus, a pair of Pans, and a Zuo burst forth in a revival and followed in the footprints of the former [Cao] princes; panache had not yet dissipated, and this too was a restoration of literature.[19] During the Yongjia reign [307–313], they prized the Yellow Emperor and Laozi and tended to esteem discussions of emptiness.[20] In the works of those times, conceptual principles outstripped eloquence, and they are bland and wanting in savor.[21] By the time we moved South of the River, their diminishing influence still was passed on.[22] The poems by Sun Chuo, Xu Xun, Huan, and Yu all were flat and normative, like the "Discourse on the Way and Virtue"; the affective force of the Jian'an was gone.[23] Earlier, Guo Jingchun had employed his superlative talents to transmute that form of writing; Liu Yueshi depended on his clear and adamantine temperament to complement and perfect its loveliness.[24] Nevertheless, others were many while they were few, and they could not budge this fashion. When it came to the Yixi reign [405–418], Xie Yishou continued them gloriously.[25] Early in the Yuanjia reign [424–453], there was Xie Lingyun; his talent was lofty and his eloquence fulsome, possessed of a rich allure in whose footsteps it is hard to follow; indeed, he encompassed and surpassed Liu [Kun] and Guo [Pu]; he overwhelmed Pan [Yue] and Zuo [Si].[26] Thus we know that [Prince] Si of Chen [Cao Zhi] was the eminence of the Jian'an, with Gonggan [Liu Zhen] and Zhongxuan [Wang Can] as his seconds; Lu Ji was the flower of the Taikang, with Anren [Pan Yue] and Jingyang [Zhang Xie] as his seconds; Xie Ke [Xie Lingyun] was the dominant figure of the Yuanjia, with Yan Yannian [Yan Yanzhi] as his second.[27] These are all the crowned heads of the five-syllable line, the glory of their ages in letters.

In the four-syllable line when the text is terse but the meaning broad, one has taken the Airs and Sao to emulate, and then one can achieve much.[28] But the four-syllable line generally suffers from the text being prolix and the meaning too little; thus few in this age practice it. The five-syllable line occupies the essential position in writing—among all the kinds of composition, this is the one with the most savor; thus it accords with the popular taste. Can there be any reason other than the fact that it is the most detailed and exact in referring to events, fashioning shapes, giving full expression of sentiment, and delineating things? Poetry has Six Principles: one is known as "affective image"; the second is known as "comparison"; a third is known as "exposition."[29] When the text is finished but there is further meaning, this is affective image.[30] To figure one's aims through things is comparison.[31] To directly write some matter and delineate things in words is exposition.[32] To extend these three Principles and use them with deliberation, giving them a frame of affective force and enriching them with rhetorical colors, making those who savor them have inexhaustible experience and those who hear them have their hearts moved—this is the perfection of poetry. If one uses comparison and affective image exclusively, the problem lies in [excessive] depth of intended meaning; when intended meaning is too deep, then the language stumbles.[33] If one uses only the form of exposition, the problem lies in meaning being ungrounded; when meaning is ungrounded, the text comes apart; completed as amusement and carried this way and that, the text has nothing to moor it and finds itself in the predicament of uncontrolled diffuseness.[34] When it comes to spring breeze and spring birds, autumn moon and autumn cicadas, summer clouds and sultry rains, and the intense cold of winters months—these are aspects of the four seasons that bring stirring in poetry.[35] At fine gatherings, one entrusts one's feelings to poetry in order to express affections; separated from others, one depends on poetry to express resentment. When it came to the subject of Chu leaving the realm[36] or the handmaiden of Han departing the palace,[37] sometimes the bones lay strewn in the northland's wilds; sometimes the soul went along with the flying dandelion puff;[38] sometimes one carried a pike for garrison duty abroad, and the atmosphere of killing dominated the frontier; the clothes of the traveler on the frontier were thin, while in her chamber the widow's tears were spent. And then a man may take off his pendants and leave the court, oblivious of return once he has gone; a woman may arch her brows and find favor, her second glance overturning a kingdom.[39] All these various situations can carry the human heart away—how can one give account of their significance except by presenting it in a poem, and how can one let one's feelings run free except by singing it out? Thus is it said: "By poems one may show conviviality and one may express resentment."[40] If one would have the poor and humble be at peace and those living in seclusion feel no woe, nothing is more esteemed than poetry.

For this reason, no writer or person of eloquence fails to adore it. Its influence is all the rage in the fashion of gentlemen these days. No sooner is a boy out of baby clothes and just entering primary school than he inevitably goes in headlong pursuit of it. At this point each person is showing off his commonplace sounds and impure norms of genre. We have reached the point that these lads who feed on the fat of the land are ashamed if their writing is not up to the mark; the whole morning is spent adding ornaments, and they are sonorously reciting their compositions at night's midpoint. Each in own estimation will claim striking lines, while in the judgment of others they ultimately fall flat.

Then there are those lightweight fellows who make fun of Cao Zhi and Liu Zhen for old-fashioned clumsiness. They think that Bao Zhao is the foremost figure of Fu Xi's time [high antiquity] and that Xie Tiao is in a class by himself in past and present.[41] Yet in taking Bao Zhao as their master, they never match "In the sunlight market and court are full"; in emulating Xie Tiao, they hardly get "Yellow birds cross past green boughs."[42] They give up a higher point of view to no effect, and they will never enter the literary tradition.

I, Rong, have watched nobles and gentlemen with tablets of office in their sashes. At leisure after broad-ranging discussions, they never fail to take up poetry as a topic of discussion.[43] Following their own personal likes, they are not uniform in their judgments. The waters of the Zi and Min flow together, red and purple confound each other, loud arguments rise in contention, and there is no standard to rely on.[44] Recently Liu Shizhang [Hui] of Pengcheng, a gentleman of exceptional taste, was distressed at such utter confusion, and wanting to make gradations of poets in current times, he orally set forth critical judgments, but a written version was never completed.[45] I, Rong, was stirred and have written of it.

Of old, men were considered in nine grades, and gentlemen were classified in seven categories; if we compare actuality and its guest [reputation], truly they often missed the mark.[46] When it comes to a skill such as poetry, things can be known self-evidently; and investigating each by its kind, it is virtually equal to [judging skill in] chess.[47] Our current emperor has been endowed with the supreme talent of innate knowledge, embodying profound and stored-up thought.[48] His own writing cleaves to sun and moon, and his learning investigates Heaven and Man.[49] Long ago in his noble excursions, he was already known as foremost.[50] Even more so now that the eight [stays] directions have been encompassed, the winds meander and clouds puff up.[51] Those who harbor jade stand shoulder to shoulder, and those who hold pearls follow in one another's footsteps.[52] Indeed, they look down on the Han and Wei without looking back; they have swallowed up the Jin and Song in their breasts. It is truly not a situation in which farmer songs or drover disputes can dare provide distinction of currents.[53] I hope that what I, Rong, now record will circulate among the villages and be equal to mere topics of casual pleasantries.

SECOND PREFACE

Within each category, I have made a rough chronological arrangement and have not organized the sequence by relative quality. Moreover, since these men are gone, their writings may be securely judged; in what I have now put into words, I have not put down those still alive.

Making parallel references in composition is now a matter of general discussion.[54] When it comes to things like official documents in managing the state, they should be endowed with broad knowledge of precedent; critiques and memorials giving account of virtue ought to give all the outstanding cases of those now dead. But when it comes to chanting one's feelings and nature, what value is there in making references?[55] "I long for you like the flowing water" is just what was before the eyes.[56] "On the high terrace much mournful wind" is also only what was seen.[57] "In the clear morning I climbed Longshou" has nothing to do with anything that happened in the past.[58] "Bright moonlight shines on drifts of snow"—did that come from the Classics or histories?[59] If you observe the finest phrases of past and present, most are not patched or borrowed; all follow from direct encounters. Yan Yanzhi and Xie Zhuang were extremely profuse and dense [in allusion] and transformed their age.[60] Thus in the Daming reign [457–464] and the Taikang reign [65–471], literary works became virtually the same as commonplace books.[61] More recently, Ren Fang and Wang Yuanzhang and others did not prize remarkable eloquence but instead competed to make novel references.[62] Among recent writers, this has gradually become the fashion. As a consequence, lines have no empty phrases and phrases have no empty words; they are a constricted patchwork, to the extreme harm of literature.[63] We seldom encounter anyone who is simply natural, with outstanding implications. Since eloquence has lost all nobility, they might as well add significant references; although they have given up on natural talent, for the time being they can show learning—isn't this, too, a principle?

Lu Ji's "Poetic Exposition on Literature" goes to the heart of the matter yet offers no critiques.[64] Li Chong's "Forest of Brushes" is remote but not incisive.[65] Wang Wei's "Great Treasure" is dense yet does not exclude.[66] Yan Yanzhi's "Discussion of Literature" is refined to the essentials yet hard to understand.[67] Zhi Yu's "Aims of Literature" is detailed yet broad and ample, and he may well be said to be one who understands.[68] When I consider these various masters, all tend to direct their discussions to the forms of literature and do not demonstrate judgments of relative quality. When it comes to Xie Lingyun's anthology of poems, he just took whatever poem he happened on.[69] In Zhang Zhi's [or Yin's] "Men of Letters," he just wrote down whatever piece of writing he happened on.[70] In what was recorded by all these eminent men, the significance was, in all cases, in questions of literature itself; they never offered graded evaluations. In what I have recorded here, I have limited myself to the five-syllable line.[71] Nevertheless, it encompasses past and present, virtually assembling [all] literary writing, and I rashly intend to distinguish the clear and muddy, to pick out fine points and flaws in regard to 120 men in all.[72] Those included in this tradition from origin to derivation may be declared men of talent. When it comes to the relative position of poets within these three grades, judgment is not at all fixed; and for amplifying changes in uniform norms, I would entrust this to those who know better.[73]

THIRD PREFACE

Cao and Liu of old are the sages of literary writing; Lu and Xie were talents who took their model from those two.[74] Their concentration and deep reflection will endure hundreds and thousands of years, yet we do not hear of distinctions between *gong* and *shang*, or discourses on the four tones.[75] Some claim that the former masters simply chanced not to notice these, but how could that be so?[76] Let me try to explain it: what were called poems and hymns in ancient times were all set to the music on instruments of metal and bamboo; and if indeed these were not in harmony with the five notes, there would have been no way to use them with the music.[77] Lines like "Set out ale in the high hall" or "The bright moon shines in the high mansion" are foremost in resonance.[78] Even though the text itself might not be polished, the lines of the three Wei rulers had a resonance that was set to song.[79] This is the real significance of tone and rhyme, and it is different indeed from the *gong* and *shang* that are spoken of these days. Since nowadays [poems] are not set to pipes and strings, what point is there in rules of sounds? In the Qi Wang Yuanzhang once said to me:[80] "*Gong* and *shang* were born together with the Two Orders, but writers from ancient times on did not know how to use them.[81] Only Yan Yanzhi spoke of the rules of pitch pipes and the harmony of tones, yet in fact he was in great error. I have seen only Fan Ye and Xie Zhuang as having particular understanding of it."[82] Wang always wanted to present a "Discourse on Understanding Music," but he died before he did so. Wang Rong started it; Xie Tiao and Shen Yue stirred the waves.[83] These three worthies were all scions of the nobility and discussed literature from youth, whereupon the common run of gentlemen admired them, devoting themselves to producing what was refined and dense; their crinkled patterns were fine and delicate, and they took as their sole aim to outdo one another. Thus they brought about many restrictions and prohibitions in writing, harming its genuine beauty. It is my opinion that the basis of fashioning a text is the capacity to recite it; it should not be lame or blocked. It is adequate as long as the clear and muddy sounds flow through, and it suits what comes easiest to the lips.[84] When it comes to "level," "rising," "falling," and "entering" tones, I suffer from incapacity. "Wasp waists" and "crane knees" are already quite well known in the villages.[85]

[Cao Xu 曹旭, *Shipin jizhu* 詩品集注
(Shanghai: Shanghai guji chubanshe, 1994)]

NOTES

1.   Giving poetry, dance, and music a ground in natural process was commonplace. *Qi*, here translated as "ethers," was a technical term of Chinese thought whose value lay in the breadth of its application rather than in its determinate precision. In this case, *qi* refers to the "ethers" of the cosmos, specifically manifest in the changing atmosphere of the seasons, whose effect on the things of the world in turn stirs human feelings. Feelings lack determinate physical substance but take on determinate form in song and dance.

2. This develops the "Three Substances." The "spirits" are specifically Heaven and the Earth Spirit, which are not only "illuminated" but provided with offerings accompanied by ritual hymns. The "hidden beings" are the spirits, presumably of the ancestors (representing Humankind), who are ritually informed of happenings in the world of the living, also to the accompaniment of ritual hymns.

3. This is a direct quotation from the "Great Preface" (*Da xu* 大序) of the *Classic of Poetry* (*Shijing* 詩經). Since the "hidden beings" is another term for the "spirits and gods" (*guishen* 鬼神), this recapitulates the three terms of the preceding periods.

4. Zhong Rong 鍾嶸 is citing from poems attributed to antiquity that are in five syllables, the form of poetry that he is discussing. "South Wind" is mentioned as the title of a song by the sage-emperor Shun in the "Record of Music" (*Yueji* 樂記) in the *Record of Rites* (*Liji* 禮記). The lyrics are quoted in the commentary by Zheng Xuan 鄭玄 to the *Record of Rites*. Two of the four lines have five syllables, but they are not the five-syllable line of later poetry. "Auspicious Clouds" is a song mentioned in the "Great Tradition of the *Shang shu*" (*Shangshu dazhuan* 尚書大傳). The lyric as preserved has no five-syllable lines, but given the vagaries of medieval transmission, Zhong Rong probably saw a version that had at least one five-syllable line.

5. *Shangshu zhushu* 6.11a (*SBCK*).

6. "Li sao," l.7.

7. Li Ling 李陵 (d. 74 B.C.E.) was a failed Western Han general, captive among the Xiongnu. At least by the early fifth century, a collection of parting poems was circulating under his name. Although the attribution is clearly false and was even doubted in the fifth century, if accepted (as Zhong Rong does here), Li Ling would be the earliest poet using the five-syllable line.

8. These are not the current anonymous "Nineteen Old Poems" but the larger corpus of fifty-nine that Zhong Rong refers to in his entry on the "Old Poems." That larger corpus certainly included most of the "Nineteen" and probably all of them.

9. The Han dynasty has the epithet "fiery" because fire was its dynastic element among the Five Phases. Cao Xu 曹旭 notes that even though the long Jian'an reign (196–220) belonged to the Han, Zhong Rong does not treat it as part of the Han but as belonging to the subsequent Wei, in *Shipin jizhu* 詩品集注 (Shanghai: Shanghai guji chubanshe, 1994), 10. The possibility of a pre-Qin date ("waning Zhou") for the anonymous "old poems," rejected here by Zhong Rong, is nowhere proposed in extant sources.

10. These are Wang Bao 王褒 (d. 61 B.C.E.), Yang Xiong 揚雄 (53 B.C.E.–18 C.E.), Mei Sheng 枚乘 (d. 140 B.C.E.), and Sima Xiangru 司馬相如 (179–117 B.C.E.), the acknowledged masters of the Western Han *fu*. Although the "Bibliography" of the *Han shu* does record the existence of "chants and songs" attributed to these masters of the *fu*, either they did not survive, or Zhong Rong was thinking only of poetry in the five-syllable line. In *Yutai xinyong* 玉臺新詠, an anthology compiled probably a few decades after Zhong Rong's *Grades of the Poets*, nine of the "old poems" are attributed to Mei Sheng. In his chapter "The Elucidation of Poetry" (*Mingshi* 明詩), in *Literary Pattern in the Mind or Carved Dragons* (*Wenxin diaolong* 文心雕龍), somewhat earlier than Zhong Rong, Liu Xie 劉勰

shows that he was aware of this attribution. Liu Xie does not indicate whether he credits this attribution, but Zhong Rong clearly does not.

11. "Fair Consort" (*jieyu* 婕妤) was a high harem rank. Fair Consort Ban lived in the reign of Emperor Cheng (32–7 B.C.E.) and was credited with a famous poem in the five-syllable line written on a fan. We are compelled to this interpretation, which excludes the woman author from the category of "person" by the exactly parallel phrasing in *Analects* 7/20. The original *Analects* passage does not do this but instead excludes a woman from the category of "able minister." By the way Zhong Rong has borrowed it, the passage does have the effect of excluding women from the category of "person."

12. *Feng* 風 here is both the continuing "influence" of the *Classic of Poetry* and poetry like the "Airs" (*feng*) in the *Classic of Poetry*.

13. This is the Eastern Han, from 25 to 220, even though Zhong Rong does not count the Jian'an reign, the last twenty-five years of that period. Zhong Rong has entries for four other Eastern Han poets in the five-syllable line, two of whom (Qin Jia and his wife, Xu Shu) are ranked in a higher grade than Ban Gu (32–92). We can resolve this discrepancy only speculatively. Of the five Eastern Han poets given entries (Qin Jia, Xu Shu, Li Yan, Zhao Yi, and Ban Gu), only Ban Gu had been mentioned by an earlier critic, Lu Jue 陸厥 (472–499). We can speculate that Zhong Rong composed the preface first and that the very dearth of Eastern Han poems he describes contributed to the rediscovery of the other poems.

14. The Caos were the father Cao Cao 曹操 (155–220), the elder son Cao Pi 曹丕 (187–226), and his younger brother Cao Zhi 曹植 (192–232). *Siwen* 斯文, here translated as "literary culture," was a resonant term for "culture" in general, usually cultural traditions received from the past. Zhong Rong sees this broader concept instantiated in Jian'an literary culture.

15. Cao Zhi was the count of Pingyuan. Cao Cao was ranked in the bottom grade; of the two brothers, Cao Zhi was in the top grade and Cao Pi was place in the middle grade. The Cao princes were the centers of patronage and influence, just as the Xiaos, emperor and princes, were in Zhong Rong's own day. Thus the Cao brothers are given priority here over Liu Zhen 劉楨 (d. 217) and Wang Can 王粲 (177–217), even though both were placed in the top grade, over the poetry of their patron Cao Pi.

16. In a mandala of power, the primary supporters of a central figure (here cultural rather than purely political) are the "wings."

17. By Zhong Rong's time, to "cling to the dragon and ride the phoenix" referred to those who rose to power with a ruler. Cao Cao was a de facto ruler, and Cao Pi was a de jure emperor; thus these images of political leadership were easily transferred to leadership in the world of letters. The same ambiguity of political and cultural leadership is carried on in the figure of "attendant carriages," which follow the ruler's coach as an entourage.

18. Zhong Rong is evidently immersed in his narrative of cultural history tied to the political world and is referring to the decline of the Wei dynasty toward the mid-third century. His story of decline and restoration omits all reference to Ruan Ji 阮籍, who is

given an entry in the top grade. The first period is taken verbatim from Sima Xiangru's "Discourse on the Feng and Shan Sacrifices" (*Fengshan wen* 封禪文).

19. According to the "Biography of Zhang Kang" in the *Jin shu*, the "three Zhangs and two Lus" were Zhang Kang 張亢 and his brothers Zhang Zai 張載 and Zhang Xie 張協 (d. 307), along with the two Lu brothers, Lu Ji 陸機 (261–303) and Lu Yun 陸雲 (262–303). See *JS* 55.43b (*SBCK*). Zhang Kang, however, was not at all known as a poet; and from Zhong Rong's perspective, the best candidate for the third Zhang would have been Zhang Hua 張華 (232–300), an important literary figure of the period who had an entry on Zhong Rong's middle grade. The "pair of Pans" were Pan Yue 潘岳 (247–300) and Pan Ni 潘尼 (ca. 251–ca. 311), while the solitary Zuo was Zuo Si 左思 (ca. 250–ca. 305). The immensely resonant term "former kings" (*qianwang* 前王) from the "Li sao" is easily appropriated here because of the Han imperial system, in which *wang*, once the "king," became a "prince" under the emperor. Even though Cao Pi became an emperor and posthumously elevated his father, at one time or another all three Caos had been *wang*, imperial "princes."

20. The fall of the Western Jin to various invading peoples from the North was commonly blamed on the interest in Daoism and "arcane discourse" (*xuanyan* 玄言)—that is, interest in abstract philosophical issues rather than the pragmatic needs of the polity. This interest had, in fact, been common throughout much of the third century and into the fourth. The history of poetry in the five-syllable line, with its famous poets of the Taikang era, mapped very poorly onto that conventional of politics and culture, forcing Zhong Rong to compress the era of Daoist interests into the Yongjia reign, when the Jin was breaking apart and just before the final loss of the North.

21. Zhong Rong earlier had described the poetry of the Jian'an as *binbin* 彬彬, the quality of "pattern and substance in balance." The most common terms for this binary were "substance" (*zhi* 質) and "patterning" (*wen* 文). Zhong Rong varies these terms to describe the failure of the poetry of "arcane discourse"; *li* 理, translated as "conceptual principles," is the abstract "order of things," baldly versified without literary grace (*ci* 辭 ["eloquence" or "diction"]). The result is a negative reworking of *Laozi* 35: "When the Way comes from the mouth, it is bland and wanting in savor."

22. "South of the River" refers to the Eastern Jin, the reestablishment of the dynasty in Jiankang, south of the Yangzi.

23. These were the poets of "arcane discourse" in the Eastern Jin: Sun Chuo 孫綽 (314–371), Xu Xun 許詢, Huan Wen 桓溫 (312–373), and Yu Liang 庾亮 (289–340). It is unclear whether the "Discourse on the Way and Virtue" refers to specific works by He Yan 何晏 (190–249) and other third-century intellectuals or is conceived as a categorical term for Neo-Daoist philosophical treatises. *Fengli* 風力, translated as "affective force," is yet another of the transforming compounds of *feng* in the preface. It appears first in "the influence (*feng*) of the poets of the *Classic of Poetry*" that was lost in the Western Han; it apparently returned in the Jian'an, because in the Taikang reign, the Jian'an "panache [*fengliu* 風流] had not yet dissipated"; but here in the Eastern Jin, "the affective force [*fengli* 風力] of the Jian'an was gone."

24. Guo Jingchun was the writer Guo Pu 郭璞 (276–324); Liu Yueshi was Liu Kun 劉琨 (271–318). These were rough contemporaries of the Eastern Jin poets of "arcane discourse" described previously. "Temperament" here is *qi* 氣, translated earlier as "ethers" in the context of operations of nature.

25. Xie Yishou was Xie Hun 謝混 (d. 412).

26. Here I read *chu* 初 with the *Liang shu* text, rather than *zhong* 中 with the 1320 edition. Xie Lingyun (385–433) was the only poet after the Western Jin whom Zhong Rong included in the top grade, a judgment anticipated here by the comment that it was hard to follow in his footsteps. Here and in the following paragraph of summation, even the top grade allows for a hierarchy of values; both Pan Yue and Zuo Si, surpassed by Xie Lingyun, were in the top grade.

27. Although Zhong Rong stopped his narrative of the history of poetry in the five-syllable line with Xie Lingyun, for symmetry he needs to provide him with at least one second, for which Xie's contemporary Yan Yanzhi 顏延之 (384–456) must serve. All the other "seconds" are placed in the top grade, but Yan Yanzhi ranks only in the middle grade.

28. The 1320 edition reads *yi* 易 for *yi* 意, which is the reading given in the *Liang shu* and several other sources. In the version using 易, the beginning of the passage reads: "In the four-syllable line the text is terse, but easy to extend." *Guang* 廣 (extend) may refer to either the dissemination of the text or the ability to see its "broader" significance. There has been debate on which reading is preferable, with Cao Xu, in *Shipin jizhu*, and most commentators preferring 易, to avoid an apparent contradiction with "the text being prolix and the meaning too little." There is, in fact, no contradiction; textual terseness and broad meaning was the ideal of the form, following the model of the *Classic of Poetry*; the problem for Zhong Rong lay in the way in which the form had been used in more recent times: poems made up of many long stanzas saying very little. Editors see this as a confusion of sounds, but in Middle Chinese the initials were quite distinct. In other words, the choice of 意 in Zhong Rong's *Liang shu* biography cannot have been caused by a confusion of sounds. The homophone substitution can have occurred only in Early Mandarin, probably to avoid what an editor saw as a contradiction with the following passage. There are only a few four-syllable line works in the *Lyrics of Chu* (Sao), and those were not emulated. Feng Sao 風騷 (the Airs and Sao) is here just a general term for ancient poetry, in this case the *Classic of Poetry*.

29. This is directly from the "Great Preface" to the *Classic of Poetry*, but giving only the three modes of poetic discourse and omitting the three sections of the *Classic of Poetry*.

30. Zhong Rong departs considerably from earlier definitions of *xing* (affective image). These often begin with the primary gloss *qi* 起 (to start up or rouse). Zheng Xuan 鄭玄 (127–200) glosses it as "to impute matters to things" 託事於物, and Kong Anguo 孔安國 (Western Han) explains it as "drawing a comparison and making association by kind" 引譬連類 (*Lunyu jijie yishu* 論語集解義疏, 179). Zhong Rong completely abandons both the functional "stirring" and the operational process of figural association, and concentrates solely on the aftermath, the capacity of an affective image to produce meaning that lasts after the text is read.

31. The definition of "comparison" is, with slightly different phrasing, identical to that given in "Comparison and Affective Image," in Liu Xie, *Literary Pattern in the Mind or Carved Dragons*.

32. The first period of Zhong Rong's definition of "exposition" (*fu* 賦) is entirely in keeping with the commentarial tradition. I have translated *yuyan* 寓言 as "lodged in words" because the compound is used in the second preface; *yuyan* is, however, often "parable," which is possible here. Although we do not usually associate parable with *fu* as a figure in poetry, parable was common in the *fu* genre, and Zhong Rong may consider parables in classical poetry also as *fu*.

33. This is a characteristically compensatory move in medieval Chinese critical discourse; a virtue carried to an extreme becomes a vice. The issue here seems to be obscurity.

34. Despite the introduction of parable as a possibility in exposition (parable having a message that governs representation), the purely descriptive aspect of exposition threatens this discursive mode with having no governing intent.

35. These are the particular cases of the opening statement of the preface, how the seasonal ethers affect things, which in turn move people to poetry.

36. This refers to the exile of Qu Yuan by the king of Chu.

37. This refers to the court lady Wang Zhaojun 王昭君, who was married to the ruler of the Xiongnu in 33 B.C.E.

38. This is the image of the soldier who died in the frontier campaigns of the Han, his soul left to wander without rest. These and subsequent images of the frontier soldier and his wife at home come from *yuefu* rather than the social reality of Southern writers.

39. "Overturning a kingdom" is the figurative capacity of an exceptionally beautiful woman with whom an emperor is infatuated.

40. *Analects* 17/9.

41. Here I have adopted the *Liang shu* reading of *qingdang* 輕蕩 in place of the standard reading *qingbo* 輕薄. Fu Xi was a legendary emperor of high antiquity. Chen Yanjie understood Bao Zhao 鮑照 as being "the foremost of Fu Xi's time" to be referring to his archaic plainness; in *Zhong Rong Shipin jianzheng gao* 鍾嶸詩品箋證稿 (Taibei: Zhongyang yanjiuyuan wenshizhe yanjiusuo Zhongguo wenzhe zhuankan, 1992), Wang Shumin 王叔岷 has demonstrated that this was not the view of Bao Zhao in the early sixth century. Instead, I believe that Zhong Rong is being ironic, suggesting that the "modern" style is so popular that Bao Zhao, writing only half a century earlier, seems like high antiquity. Xie Tiao is the highest standard. Note that Zhong Rong places both Bao Zhao and Xie Tiao in the middle grade.

42. The Bao Zhao line comes from "Becoming a Retainer in the World of Young Men" (*Dai jieke shaonian chang xing* 代結客少年場行), in *XS* 2:1267. In attempting to imitate Xie Tiao, these followers of modern fashion can barely equal a line from Yu Yan's 虞炎 "Resentment on the Stairs of Jade" (*Yu jie yuan* 玉階怨), in *XS* 2:1459.

43. Zhong Rong's name is added to the text from the *Liang shu* version. *Jin shen* 搢紳 is literally "stick in the sash," referring to the *hu* 笏, the tablet carried by those who attend court.

44. The waters of the Zi and Min rivers in eastern China were supposed to have distinct flavors; the ability to tell the two apart by taste was a touchstone of discrimination. I

have translated the line on red and purple as written, but it would have been understood in terms of its source in *Analects* 17/18, in which Confucius says: "I hate how purple confounds the red; I hate how the music of Zheng throws classical music into disorder." Note that the two allusions move from discrimination without value judgment to discriminating what is good and bad. I read *xuanye* 喧嘩 with *Liang shu* rather than *xuanyi* 喧議 of the received text; *xuanye* is the early attested compound. *Zhundi* 準的 was originally a "target" but was early extended to "standard," as translated here.

45. Liu Shizhang was Liu Hui 劉繪 (458–502), who appears in the bottom grade of the main body of the text, with a less favorable judgment than is suggested here.

46. In the "Table of Persons Past and Present" (*Gujin renbiao* 古今人表) in the *Han shu*, Ban Gu divided people into nine grades. The Wei Emperor Wen (Wen Wendi, Cao Pi, r. 220–226) organized this into a political system for ranking of talents for government office. The nine grades were subdivided into three large grades, each having three levels. It is on this tripartite division that Zhong Rong's own ranking system is based. *Seven Catalogs* (*Qi lue* 七略) by Liu Xin 劉歆 (ca. 53–23 B.C.E.), based on the organization of the imperial library first undertaken by his father, Liu Xiang 劉向 (77–6 B.C.E.), was a bibliographical organization of texts and not a hierarchical ranking based on a single standard. When paired with "actuality" (*shi* 實), "guest" (*bin* 賓) simply stands for "reputation," which may or may not be justified.

47. "Chess" is here the game *liubo* 六博, and *go* (surround chess). Gu Zhi notes that in contrast of overall grading of men's talents, skill in poetry is as clear as skill in chess.

48. Xiao Yan 蕭衍 (Liang Emperor Wu, r. 502–549).

49. The use of *li* 麗 is that of the *Classic of Changes* under the hexagram Li 離: "The sun and moon cleave to the heavens." Zhong Rong's statement is thus a variation on the standard hyperbole of literary praise, that someone's writing hangs in the heavens with the sun and moon. This common but highly specialized use of *li* had certainly picked up secondary associations from the far more common use of the term as "beautiful."

50. During the Southern Qi, Xiao Yan had been one of the "Eight Companions of the Prince of Jingling," the celebrated literary salon that included Shen Yue 沈約 (441–513) and Xie Tiao 謝朓 (464–499). This salon was an important venue in which tonal prosody was promulgated, a development in poetry deplored by Zhong Rong. The claim that Xiao Yan was the "foremost" in this group is a polite fiction.

51. This is a figure for the profusion of talents that follow the influence (*feng* [wind]) of the ruler. The rhetoric of universal rule was maintained, even in a regional polity like the Liang.

52. Zhong Rong maintains a fine balance between irony and celebration in this passage. "Harbor[ing] jade" and "hold[ing] pearls" is a figure for talent here presented as a fact, but it unmistakably echoes Cao Zhi's famous "Letter to Yang Dezu" (*Yu Yang Dezu shu* 與楊德祖書), in which the same figures are used for vain followers of those who merely believe they have such talents.

53. The obvious sense on the surface is that the sophistication of letters in the current day is beyond the capacity of the unsophisticated to judge. Given the following sentence, Zhong Rong may be modestly referring to his own critical judgments. Although he

includes a few Liang writers, this may be a way of staying out of current literary disputes. "Distinction of currents" (*liubie* 流別) is the term Zhi Yu 摯虞 (d. 317) had used in his *Anthology of Literary Compositions Divided by Genre* (*Wenzhang liubie ji* 文章流別集) with accompanying judgments in the late Western Jin. Since this was the foundational text for critical judgments, its use here is significant.

54. "Pairing references in composition" is a phrase taken from "Explanations of the Classics" (*Jing jie* 經解) in the *Record of Rites*. There it is "the teaching of the *Spring and Autumn Annals*" (*Chunqiu jiao ye* 春秋教也).

55. "Chanting one's feelings and nature" (*yinyong xingqing* 吟詠性情) is one of the canonical functions of poetry in the "Great Preface" to the Mao version of the *Classic of Poetry*. "Making references" (*yongshi* 用事) is sometimes translated as "allusion"; however, the scope is restricted to references to past persons and events.

56. Quoting Xu Gan's 徐幹 (170–217) "Chamber Longings" (*Shi si* 室思), in *XS* 1:376.

57. Quoting from the first of Cao Zhi's "Unclassified Poems" (*Za shi* 雜詩), in *XS* 1:456.

58. Wang Shumin found this line in a fragment of a poem by Zhang Hua 張華, cited in *Beitang shuchao* 北堂書鈔, in *XS* 1:622.

59. From a fragment of a poem by Xie Lingyun 謝靈運, "The Time of Year" (*Sui shi* 歲時), in *XS* 2:1181.

60. Yan Yanzhi 顏延之 and Xie Zhuang 謝莊 (421–466). Zhong Rong is here referring to the use of references.

61. I have taken *shuchao* 書抄 as the scholarly genre in which short passages from earlier works were arranged by categories. We might simply take it as "copying from books."

62. Ren Fang 任昉 (460–508) and Wang Rong 王融 (467–493).

63. "Empty" (*xu* 虛) here must mean "free of references." In later usage, *xu* referred to grammatical particles, whose use in poetry made it less dense. *Du* 蠹, translated as "harm," is the commonplace extended meaning of a word that, as a noun, is a "bookworm." Making "literature" the object of the verbal usage recalls the primary meaning as a noun.

64. There is much debate on the meaning of *bian* 貶. I have followed the simplest interpretation, that Lu Ji 陸機 criticized no particular authors in "The Poetic Exposition on Literature."

65. Li Chong's "Forest of Brushes" is lost except for a few passages. The precise sense of *shu* 疏, translated as "remote," is uncertain in this context; it could be "rough." In other cases, the first term describing a critic tends to be positive.

66. Wang Wei 王微 (415–453) appears in Zhong Rong's middle grade. The "Great Treasure" is not mentioned in his *Song shu* biography, though the "Bibliography" of the *Sui shu* does list a "Great Treasure" in ten scrolls without an author. The most likely sense of *cai* 裁 in this context is "to exclude"—that is, to show judgment by rejecting some works or authors.

67. Yan Yanzhi is not credited with any particular work of literary criticism, but Zhong Rong may have had access to texts no longer extant. I have treated this as the name of a work in parallel with the comments on the other critics; however, it may simply be his "discussions of literature."

68. Zhi Yu, the only earlier critic of whom Zhong Rong fully approves, compiled a critical work in conjunction with his *Anthology of Literary Compositions Divided by Genre*. The critical essays are apparently divided into "discussions" (*lun* 論) and "aims" 志. *Zhi* might be more simply translated as "account," but the praise of Zhi Yu's understanding that follows strongly suggests that this work commented on the "aims" of the authors. "Understands" is literally "understands language" (*zhiyan* 知言). This probably refers to the explanation of "understanding language" in *Mengzi* II A.2, which is the classic articulation of knowing a person by the way one speaks. Here it is extended to the critic's understanding of literary works and is strongly associated with knowing a person's "aims."

69. Xie Lingyun's poetry anthology appears under various names and in various sizes in the "Bibliography" of the *Sui shu*, which is characteristic of popular anthologies, expanded and excerpted at will by those who made copies. Xie Lingyun's anthology, confined to poetry, may have been a collection of his favorites. The variety of versions in which it survived, along with expansions and apparent continuations, suggest its popularity.

70. This is *Biographies of Men of Letters* (*Wenshi zhuan* 文士傳) in fifty scrolls, now lost.

71. As many commentators note, not all Zhong Rong's judgments are confined to poetry in the five-syllable line. The vast majority, however, are.

72. The use of *qing* 輕, translated as "rashly," is far from clear. I have taken the more common sense of *qing*, assuming that it is self-deprecatory. "To pick out fine points and flaws" 掎摭利病 is a slightly reformulated phrase from Cao Zhi's "Letter to Yang Dezu," significantly referring to the person who is a better critic than writer: "Liu Jixu's [Xiu] talents cannot equal the major writers, but he loves disparaging literary works, picking out fine points and flaws."

73. "Changes in uniform [norms]" (*bian cai* 變裁) is a literal translation, implying changes in judgment, linking this literary grading to changes in status of rank in the polity, made visible by the court uniform.

74. This accords with the comments on Cao Zhi and Liu Zhen in the main entries. Zhong Rong is clearly singling out Lu Ji and Xie Lingyun as preeminent in those who follow, though the precise weight of *ti er* 體貳, translated as "took their model from those two," is uncertain. The phrase, written as 體二, is used in the discussion of sages and followers in Li Kang's 李康 (third century) "Discourse on Fate" (*Yunming lun* 運命論). There Confucius is identified as the "perfect sage" (*zhi sheng* 至聖), with his two disciples Yan Yuan 顏淵 and Ran You 冉有 as "great worthies" (*da xian* 大賢). The later Confucians Meng Ke 孟軻 (Mencius) and Sun Qing 孫卿 (Xunzi) were said to *ti er*—that is, "to take their model from the two" (Yan Yuan and Ran You) or "to take their model from his [Confucius's] seconds." In Li Kang's essay, the significance is the same, but in Zhong Rong's usage, there would be a distinction between (1) taking both Cao Zhi and Liu Zhen as models and (2) taking Liu Zhen as a model who, in Zhong Rong's words, "stands out alone after [i.e., second to] Cao Zhi."

75. *Gong* and *shang* were notes in the pentatonic scale and commonly invoked in discussions of poetic euphony achieved through balancing of tones. Zhong Rong is writing in

the wake of decades of discussion of tonal rules of euphony, and he invokes great poets of an earlier era whose works did not observe such rules.

76. This refers to Shen Yue's 沈約 discussion of tonal rules in the "Biography of Xie Lingyun" in the *Song shu*. Shen argued that euphony in the Eastern Han and Jian'an poets came naturally and pre-reflectively but that such instincts were lost in the second half of the third century.

77. "Metal and bamboo" are metonymy for bells and pipes.

78. "Set out ale in the high hall" is a variant of the opening line of Cao Zhi's "Lay of the Harp" (*Kunghou yin* 箜篌引), in *XS* 1:424. "The bright moon shines in the high mansion" is the opening is the opening of Cao Zhi's "Many Sorrows" (*Qi ai shi* 七哀詩), in *XS* 1:458. *Yun* 韻, translated as "resonance," is also the term for "rhyme." While it is conceivable that Zhong Rong is referring specifically to the use of rhyme in these poems, it seems more likely that he is referring to a general euphony and perhaps to a sense that the sound of the word echoed the sound of the music. This would, of course, be purely notional in that the music was long lost.

79. The "three rulers" must be Cao Cao, Cao Pi, and Cao Rui 曹叡 (Emperor Ming, r. 226–239).

80. Wang Yuanzhang was Wang Rong 王融.

81. The "Two Orders" are Heaven and Earth. Wang Rong's claim is that the principles of music, hence of tonal balance, were grounded in Nature. Since the contemporary discourse on tonal euphony was based on antithesis and alternation, it corresponded to the kinds of processes that were believed to be at work in Nature.

82. Fan Ye (398–445) and Xie Zhuang are included in the lowest grade.

83. "Stir the waves" was a common figure for amplifying some cultural process.

84. "Clear" and "muddy" were the binary pair used to discuss euphony. In tones. this corresponds roughly to later "level" and "deflected" tones,

85. Two of Shen Yue's "Eight Faults" (*babing* 八病): "wasp waists" is the error of using words of the same tone in the second and fifth positions in a line, and "crane knees" refers to using the same tone at the end of the first and third lines.

19. Book Collecting and Cataloging in the Age of Manuscript Culture

Xiao Yi's *Master of the Golden Tower* and Ruan Xiaoxu's Preface to *Seven Records*

XIAOFEI TIAN

Literary and scholarly activities reached an unprecedented height in the early sixth century, coinciding with the rule of the Liang Emperor Wu (r. 502–549). Scholars from the Liang capital Jiankang in the late fifth and early sixth centuries had indeed "fixed" early Chinese literary history as we have it today by their anthology making, editorial decisions, and works of literary criticism. For this chapter, I have chosen two pieces of writing from the Liang to throw some light on one cultural activity in particular: book collecting and book cataloging.

The first piece was written by Xiao Yi 蕭繹 (508–555), the seventh son of the Liang Emperor Wu and the younger half brother of Xiao Gang 蕭綱 (503–551). He was enfeoffed as the Prince of Xiangdong 湘東王 at the age of six. Like his two elder brothers, Xiao Tong 蕭統 (501–531) and Xiao Gang, Xiao Yi was one of the most culturally refined of Emperor Wu's sons. He was an accomplished poet and painter and a major practitioner of the new style of writing espoused by Xiao Gang, and played an important role in the literary transformations taking place in the first half of the sixth century. Xiao Yi was also an avid reader and an insatiable book collector, owning one of the largest private book collections of the time. Xiao Yi took the throne after Xiao Gang was murdered by the rebel general Hou Jing in 552. Instead of ruling from the imperial palace complex at the capital city Jiankang, Xiao Yi chose, against the council of many of his advisers, to remain in Jiangling (in modern Hubei), the headquarters of

Jingzhou region where he had served as governor. After vanquishing Hou Jing's rebel army, one of the first things he did was to transfer whatever remained from the book collection from the Imperial Library to Jiangling and have a number of scholars and writers collate the books. By this time, the Liang empire was considerably weakened by the war, and Xiao Yi's failings as a leader contributed to the crumbling of the state. In the winter of 554, Jiangling was besieged by the Western Wei army. The city eventually fell, and Xiao Yi was captured and executed in early 555. He was granted the posthumous title Liang Emperor Yuan 梁元帝. Before Jiangling fell, Xiao Yi ordered that his huge book collection be burned. This act of destruction is regarded as the largest "bibliocaust" since that ordered by the First Qin Emperor. Ironically but perhaps not inappropriately, a great book lover turned out to be one of the greatest destroyers of books of all times.

The piece by Xiao Yi translated here, "Collecting Books," is a chapter from his *Master of the Golden Tower* (*Jinlouzi* 金樓子), a work that belongs to the tradition of Masters Literature (*zishu* 子書) but also subverts and permutes the tradition. *Master of the Golden Tower* no longer survives as a whole; what we have was reassembled by Qing dynasty scholars from the bits and pieces preserved in encyclopedias. It has fourteen chapters:

1. The Rise of the King 興王
2. Admonitions 箴誡
3. Imperial Consorts 后妃
4. Commands for Funeral Arrangements 終制
5. Admonishing My Sons 誡子
6. Collecting Books 聚書
7. The Two Nans and the Five Hegemons 二南五霸
8. A Discourse on Princedom 說藩
9. Establishing Words 立言
10. Writing Books 著書
11. Witticisms 捷對
12. Account of Anomalies 志怪
13. Miscellaneous Records 雜記
14. Self-Account 自序

In the chapter "Collecting Books," Xiao Yi traces the long history of his book collecting, beginning with his receipt of a gift set of Confucian Classics from his father at the age of six. He proceeds to describe the sources of his acquisitions over the years and, in doing so, documents his passion for books. Although book collecting did not begin with Xiao Yi and certainly did not end with him, this chapter represents the first extant writing on book collecting—or any kind of collecting—that we know of in Chinese literary history. The discourse on collecting became much more popular and common in later periods.

Except when receiving books as gifts or acquiring someone else's collection, Xiao Yi obtained most of his books by means of copying, as was typical of the age of manuscript culture. Hand copying a book was a practice continuing well into the twentieth century, but before the advent of printing, it was almost the only method of textual transmission (another method was making ink rubbings, but this was confined to stele inscriptions and was not a major means of textual dissemination). Although professional scribes could be hired, a prince like Xiao Yi most likely kept his own scribes on his staff.

Xiao Yi lovingly talks about the paper and ink used in book copying; in one case, he affectionately comments on the "minute and exquisite" calligraphy of the copyist. Here, however, we notice something "wrong." Xiao Yi had had problems with his eyes since the age of thirteen. He eventually lost all sight in one eye, and the other eye was so weak that he would often have his attendants read books aloud to him, sometimes throughout the night. How, then, could he possibly have read those small-size "pocket-treasure editions" with their "minute and exquisite" calligraphy? The answer is simple: he most likely could not and did not read them. This is not to deny that Xiao Yi was a voracious reader, but for the true collector, the pleasure of collecting always lies in the very act itself. Books, regardless of their content, become pure material objects to be touched and caressed. As Walter Benjamin, a book collector from another time and another culture, says in his essay about book collecting, "For a collector— and I mean a real collector, a collector as he ought to be—ownership is the most intimate relationship that one can have to objects. Not that they come alive in him; it is he who lives in them."[1] For such a "real collector," the number of books counts: Xiao Yi's collection included many identical copies of the same book, which accounts for the incredibly large number of "eighty thousand scrolls" (before he had the Imperial Library collection shipped to Jiangling). Furthermore, his having his book collection destroyed on the eve of his surrender to the Western Wei becomes, if not forgivable, at least more comprehensible when we understand his relationship to the collection. If he "lived in" the books, then the books must also die when his life ended. In this case, however, the book collector also happened to be an emperor, and the destruction is characterized by an irreconcilable conflict between the passion of a private person and the public interest.

Another intriguing thing about Xiao Yi's collection is that he stopped short of mentioning his largest hoard of books: the imperial collection, transported to his headquarters at Jiangling from the capital at Jiankang. This once again demonstrates the conflict between Xiao Yi's role as an emperor, who is supposed to be a public guardian of culture, and his self-perceived identity as a private collector, which we see in his *Master of the Golden Tower*.

In talking about booking collecting, Benjamin observes: "If there is a counterpart to the confusion of a library, it is the order of its catalogue." Cataloging is a way of sorting out and managing chaos, not just tidying up books strewn about on the floor, but also ordering and classifying knowledge. The second piece translated here is a preface to a book catalog compiled by Ruan Xiaoxu 阮孝緒 (479–536), a member of an illustrious noble clan and an imperial relative who nevertheless chose to remain a recluse all his life. This recluse was, however, engaged in an ambitious undertaking; that is, criticizing the imperial book catalog for its lack of comprehensiveness, he vowed to compile a catalog that included "all the books" in the Liang empire. With the aid of his friends and associates, Ruan Xiaoxu completed his project and wrote a preface to this book catalog, which he entitled *Seven Records* (*Qi lu* 七錄), in the year 523.

From Ruan Xiaoxu's preface, we learn that at the time many private book collections were so large that each of them had its own catalog: this was the first time in Chinese history that private book catalogs were mentioned. This observation shows the prevalence of book collecting among well-to-do gentry families and the widespread dissemination of texts and learning that owes its origin to the availability of cheaper paper. Against this larger background, Ruan Xiaoxu's undertaking was an individual passion that was representative of his age. While the imperial book catalog was still upheld as a standard to measure the existing private book catalogs, Ruan Xiaoxu's project demonstrates that a private individual felt just as entitled to the grand task of ordering the cultural capital of the state. To be sure, this was not something "anybody" could do in the stringently hierarchical society of the Six Dynasties, and Ruan Xiaoxu was a particularly privileged member of the elite because of his illustrious family background and his imperial kinship ties. Nevertheless, he was a lifelong recluse who was the very antithesis of the public man of the state, and he was solely responsible for the project he undertook as a private citizen, not as an official representative of any cultural institution. Thus in both Xiao Yi's and Ruan Xiaoxu's writings, we see a conflict between public and private discourses.

FURTHER READING

For a detailed study of the practice of book copying and textual transmission in this period, see Glen Dudbridge, *Lost Books of Medieval China* (London: British Library, 2000); and Xiaofei Tian, *Beacon Fire and Shooting Star: The Literary Culture of the Liang (502–557)* (Cambridge, Mass.: Harvard University Asia Center, 2007). For a modern typeset edition of *Master of the Golden Tower* with collation notes and annotations, see Xu Yimin 許逸民, *Jinlouzi jiaojian* 金樓子校箋 (Beijing: Zhonghua shuju, 2011). For a general discussion of *Master of the Golden Tower*, see Liu Yuejin 劉躍進, "Guanyu *Jinlouzi* yanjiu de jige wenti" 關於金樓子研究的幾個問題, in *Disanjie Wei Jin nanbeichao wenxue guoji xueshu yantaohui lunwenji* 第三屆魏晉南北朝文學國際研討會論文集 (Taibei: Wenshizhe chubanshe, 1998); Xiaofei Tian, "The Twilight of the Masters: Masters Literature (*zishu*) in Early Medieval China," *Journal of American Oriental Society* 126, no. 4

(2006): 1–22; and Zhong Shilun 鍾仕倫, *Jinlouzi yanjiu* 金樓子研究 (Beijing: Zhonghua shuju, 2004). For a discussion of the chapter "Collecting Books" in *Master of the Golden Tower*, see Wu Guangxing 吳光興, *Xiao Gang Xiao Yi nianpu* 蕭綱蕭繹年譜 (Beijing: Zhongguo shehui kexue chubanshe, 2006); and Zhao Lixin 趙立新, "*Jinlouzi* Jushupian buzhu" 金樓子聚書篇補注, *Zaoqi Zhongguo shi yanjiu* 早期中國史研究 1 (2009): 29–43. For a discussion of Ruan Xiaoxu as a recluse, see Alan Berkowitz, "Hidden Spoor: Ruan Xiaoxu and His Treatise on Reclusion," *Japan Association of Overseas Studies* 111, no. 4 (1991): 704–11. For a study of Ruan Xiaoxu's preface to *Seven Records*, see Cao Hong 曹虹, Guan Daoxiong 關道雄, and Zhang Hongsheng 張宏生, "Ruan Xiaoxu 'Qilu xu'" 阮孝緒七錄序, *Guji zhengli yu yanjiu* 古籍整理與研究 2 (1987): 147–57; and Jean-Pierre Drège, *Les bibliothèques en Chine au temps des manuscrits* (Paris: École française d'extrême-orient, 1991).

Xiao Yi 蕭繹

Master of the Golden Tower (*Jinlouzi* 金樓子)

COLLECTING BOOKS

When I was first enfeoffed and went to stay at the Western Quarters, His Majesty gave me a set of the Five Classics with a duplicate.[2]

When I was Magistrate of Langye, I was again granted books by His Majesty; I also had books copied privately for myself.[3]

When I was Magistrate of the eastern region [Kuaiji], I had people copy the *Records of the Historian, History of the Han, Account of the Three Kingdoms*, and *History of the Jin*.[4] I also had people copy the books owned by Liu Ru, the Minister of Personnel, and by Xie Yanyuan, the Senior Recorder for Comprehensive Duty.[5] I also sent people to Wuxing Commandery to copy out the books of Xiahou Tan, as well as the books of Yu Chan [fl. 500s], Superior Grand Master of the Palace.[6]

When I was Governor of Danyang, I had asked to borrow books from the collection of the crown prince.[7] I also approached the Marquis of Xinyu, the Marquis of Shanghuang, and the Marquis of Xinwu and copied some of the manuals for the game of *gewu*.[8]

When I was Governor of Yangzhou, I copied the imperial diaries owned by various gentlemen of Wu Commandery. I also acquired the imperial diary kept by Duke Jiansu, Xu Mian.[9]

When I was in Jingzhou, the Prince of Jin'an was Governor of Yongzhou, and I asked his permission to have his books copied.[10]

Before [——] went to the Shu region, I again had people copy [his] books.[11]

I also instructed a resident of Jingzhou, Zong Mengjian, to go to the capital and buy books there. I also acquired books from Bao Quan, my record keeper, who presented them to me.[12]

When Prince Yang of Ancheng died in Xiangzhou, I sent people to copy his books.[13]

I also copied books from Senior Nanjun Magistrate Liu Zhilin [478–549], Junior Nanjun Magistrate Liu Zhiheng, Yue Facai of Jiangxia, Administrative Aides Yu Qiao and Zong Zhonghui, Assistant Magistrate Yu Ge, and Buddhist Chief Fachi.[14] I copied everything in their family collections.

I also acquired commentaries and prefaces to various Buddhist sutras from Dharma Master Yan of the Zhaoti temple.[15] I again acquired books on yin–yang, divination, and necromancy from Dharma Master Tanzhi of the Toutuo temple.[16] A native of Jingzhou, Zhu Danyuan, presented me with some unusual books. I also copied books of the four categories from Master Jing of the Changsha temple.[17]

I also acquired five cases of the *History of the Han* of the Yuanjia reign [424–453] from Jiang Ge of Jiangzhou, three cases from Yao Kai, and four cases from Jiang Lu.[18] Together they form one volume, totaling twenty cases in 115 scrolls. They all were copied during the Yuanjia reign; the paper and ink used are exquisite.[19]

I also gathered about a thousand scrolls of the *History of the Latter Han*, as well as of the *Records of the Historian, Sequel to the Han Annals, Spring and Autumn Annals, Zhou Offices, Classic of Documents*, and various collections of Masters Literature from the Yuanjia reign. I also acquired the *Classic of Changes, Classic of Documents, Zhou Offices, Book of Ceremonials, Record of Rites, Mao Odes*, and *Spring and Autumn Annals*, one copy of each, written in minute calligraphy. I also asked Kong Ang to copy the *History of the Former Han, History of the Latter Han, Records of the Historian, Account of the Three Kingdoms, Jin Annals, Zhuangzi, Laozi, Emergency Prescriptions*, and *Lisao*, totaling 634 scrolls. They all fit into one headband box—the calligraphy is that minute and exquisite!

When I returned to the capital and was in change of defense at the Stone Fort, I had people copy out various metaphysical and Confucian commentaries.[20]

When I was Governor of Jiangzhou, I had people copy out the books of Administrative Adviser Xiao Ben, Record Keeper Liu Huan, and Office Manager Zhou Hongzhi.[21]

At the time Xiao Yue, the Marquis of Luoxiang, was defeated at Ancheng; I sent my administrative adviser, Wang Sengbian, to take his book collection.[22]

It also happened that Marquis Guang of Wuping came from Guangzhou, and I sent He Mian, Administrator of the Accounts Section, to copy his books.[23]

Then it happened that the Marquis of Hengshan was on his way to the capital from Yongzhou, and I copied his books as well.[24]

When Lan Qin, general of the Left Guard, returned from Nanzheng, I copied his books.[25] Many of Lan's books are from before the crossing of the River.[26]

Some of them were produced here [in the South]. They are quite novel and remarkable.

The Governor of Xiangzhou, Zhang Zuan, once gave me a batch of books, such as *Erya* with Fan Guang's annotations. The Magistrate of Yuzhang, Zhang Wan, gave me books such as the *Biographies of Eminent Monks*. The Magistrate of Boyang, Fan Xu, gave me books such as the *Strategies of the Warring States* with Gao You's annotations. The recluse Wang Zhenzhi gave me books such as the *Biographies of Noted Children*.[27]

I again copied books on calligraphy from Dharma Master Zhibiao of the Donglin temple.[28] Protector General Wei Rui gave me several scrolls [of model calligraphy] as a gift.[29] Yin Jun, Count Zhen, also gave me some.[30] Later I sent Fan Pu and Pan Puti to purchase pieces of model calligraphy; all the pieces they bought were by the two Wangs.[31] Clerk Yu Jiao has a great deal of old calligraphy pieces, which amount to more than five hundred scrolls; he left all of them with me.[32] My retainer Fang Zhuan also had about three hundred scrolls, which I kept.[33] Thereupon, I came into possession of various calligraphy pieces. I also acquired some from the monk Huijiao of Hongpu temple at Kuaiji.[34] When Marquis Ling of Linru came back from Yizhou, I obtained a huge batch from him.[35]

Later I acquired the book collections once owned by Yue Yanchun and Liu Zhilin, which amount to around five thousand scrolls.[36] I also acquired the book collections of the Prince of Nanping, of Governor Zhang of Yongzhou, of the Prince of Guiyang, and of Liu Zhiyuan.[37]

I am forty-five years old [forty-six *sui* by Chinese reckoning] this year, and I have been collecting books for forty years.[38] I have acquired eighty thousand scrolls of books.[39] The Prince of Hejian's book collection rivaled the Han imperial collection; I dare say that mine surpasses his.[40]

[*Jinlouzi jiaojian* 金樓子校箋, 515–50]

Ruan Xiaoxu 阮孝緒

Seven Records (*Qi lu* 七錄)

PREFACE

Sun and moon are constantly bright, and yet without light they cannot shine forth; Mount Song and Mount Hua nurture life, and yet without wind and clouds they cannot display their moving power. When the great sage is born, he follows the dictates of fate and becomes renowned, so as to help rectify the customs and correct the ways of the world. And yet without the Nine Hills, Three Mounds, and Five Canons, without the *Odes*, *Documents*, *Rites*, and *Music*, how could he accomplish the august feats and bring about the vast transformations?[41] Therefore, when the way of the Primitive Beginning was lost, the kingly Hao devised hexagrams; when the principle of tying knots on ropes to record events vanished, the regal Jie invented language. From that point on, people adopted various traditions to suit their different needs, but when the feats are accomplished and deeds are done, each has an account.

After the orthodox lineage was destroyed, music deteriorated and rites collapsed. The method of the former sages became like banners fluttering in the wind. Thereupon, Confucius [551–479] heaved a sigh, saying, "When the great Way was being carried out, the finest men of the Three Dynasties had partaken in it. Alas, I was born too late; nevertheless, I have my aspiration." Confucius's aspiration refers to his belief that ancient writings were still undamaged. So after returning to Lu, he finally began the enterprise of the Uncrowned King: he edited the *Odes* and *Documents*, fixed rites and music, instituted the Five Beginnings in *Spring and Autumn Annals*, and created the Ten Wings of the *Changes*.[42] After the Master departed from the world, the subtle words he spoke were almost extinguished; then, as his seventy-two disciples passed away one after another, the great principles were eventually abandoned. By the time of the Warring States period, customs were all diverse and policies all different; one hundred masters vied with one another, and nine schools of thought in turn rose and fell. Ying Zheng 嬴政 [First Qin Emperor, r. 221–210 B.C.E.] was so sick of the state of affairs that he burned the books and buried alive the Ru scholars, which was truly a disaster.

Only in the fourth year of the Han Emperor Hui's reign [191 B.C.E.] were the laws forbidding the possession of books finally done away with. Later on, there were book hoards of the Chamberlain for Ceremonials, the Grand Scribe, and Erudites outside the imperial court, and the libraries of Continuity Pavilion 延閣, Expansion Quarters 廣內, and the Chamber of Seclusion 祕室 inside [the court]. The way was opened for people to present books to the ruler, and the Office of Book Copying was established. By the time of the Han Emperor Cheng [32–7 B.C.E.], many titles were discovered to be lost, so the emperor sent out Receptionist Chen Nong 陳農 to look for them in the empire. He also commissioned Liu Xiang 劉向 [ca. 79–8 B.C.E.], as the Grand Master for Splendid Happiness, and his son Liu Xin 劉歆 [d. 23], courtesy name Zijun 子俊, to collate the books in the imperial collection. Every time they finished working on a volume, they would report to the throne. After Liu Xiang died, the emperor ordered Liu Xin to continue the project. The books housed in the Chamber of Warmth were then moved to the Tianlu Pavilion, and Liu Xin went through various tomes and presented the *Seven Catalogs* 七略 to His Majesty.

In the Latter Han, the Magnolia Terrace 蘭臺 was still used for storing books and documents, but new catalogs were being compiled at the Eastern Lodge 東觀 and the Hall of Benevolence and Longevity 仁壽閣. Collators Ban Gu 班固 [32–92] and Fu Yi 傅毅 [d. ca. 90] both were in charge of the imperial book collection. Ban Gu put together the "Bibliography" in the *History of the Han* based on the *Seven Catalogs*. Yuan Shansong 袁山松 [d. 401] recorded later titles in the "Bibliography" in his *History of the Latter Han*.

During the Wei and Jin dynasties, the number of books increased even more. The imperial collection was housed in the three pavilions of the Palace Library. Zheng Mo 鄭默 [213–280], Assistant in the Imperial Library of the Wei, revised the old catalogs. Contemporaries commented that vermilion and purple were finally distinguished from each other. The Director of the Imperial Library of the Jin, Xun Xu 荀勗 [d. 289], compiled a new catalog based on Zheng Mo's *Central Collection of the Classics*. Xun Xu's catalog comprised more than a dozen scrolls, but all the titles were classified into four categories.[43]

The imperial collection was nearly completely destroyed in the chaos breaking out during the reign of Emperors Hui 惠帝 [r. 290–306] and Huai 懷帝 [r. 307–313]. When the Jin royal house was reestablished south of the Yangzi River [317], hardly one volume out of ten survived. Although much recovery work was done, the books were left in a confused and messy state. Li Chong 李充 [d. ca. 350s], the Assistant Editorial Director of the Imperial Library, began to sort out the collection and revise the catalog. He adopted Xun Xu's four categories but switched the order of second and third categories.[44] He also omitted the name given to each category and simply listed them as A, B, C, and D.

Since then, bibliographers have been following Xun Xu's practice. Xie Lingyun 謝靈運 [385–433], Director of the Palace Library in the Song [420–479]; Wang Jian 王儉 [452–489], Vice Director; Xie Fei 謝朏 [441–506], Director of the Palace Library in the Qi [479–501]; and Wang Liang 王亮 [d. 510], Vice Director, all compiled catalogs of the new additions. While serving as Vice Director of the Palace Library, Yin Chun 殷淳 [403–434] compiled the Greater Catalog of the Four Categories of Books. Then again, Wang Jian followed the format of Liu Xiang's *Separate Records* 別錄 and produced the *Seven Accounts* 七志. The lost titles from the central court [of the Western Jin] were gradually recovered to a great extent, although there was still more than half missing.

At the end of the Qi, a fire caused by the rebels extended to the Palace Library, so that many titles were missing when the Liang was founded. His Majesty enjoined Ren Fang 任昉 [460–508], Director of the Palace Library, to undertake the task of collecting and restructuring. Books are stored in the Hall of Literary Virtue 文德殿, and academicians such as Liu Xiaobiao 劉孝標 [462–521] were instructed to collate them. The writings on necromancy were divided into a separate category, and Zu Xuan 祖暅, Court Audience Attendant, was commissioned to put together a catalog for it. The Quarters of the Imperial Secretariat 尚書閣 houses the classics, histories, and miscellaneous titles; the Park of Flowering Groves 華林園 accommodates the Buddhist scriptures and commentaries. Ever since the Jin royal house crossed the River, the imperial book collection has never reached the grandeur of today.

I have loved books since my early days and do not feel weary of them in adulthood. Due to my delicate health, I live in reclusion; no worldly matter ever interrupts my leisure. As soon as dawn breaks, the yellow silk book wrappers are opened; only in the wee hours do I put the scrolls back into their green cases. Yet I still could not exhaust books of the nine schools or those recorded in the *Seven Catalogs*, nor could I unlock all the mysteries and uncover all the secrets. When I checked my reading against the received bibliographies, I found many gaps in my knowledge. I therefore spent much time seeking hidden records and lost titles. If the residence of a prince or a member of the gentry has a large book collection that has been built up since the Song and Qi dynasties, I would make every effort to obtain a copy of its catalog. I encountered many titles this way: some I saw with my own eyes; some I became aware of through word of mouth. When I compared them with the Imperial Library catalog, I noticed that many titles were missing from it. Thereupon, I gathered together various catalogs to produce a new one. I combined all the secular writings, from the classics and histories to works on necromancy, into five catalogs, referred to as the *Inner Records*. Each of the religious writings, Buddhist and Daoist scriptures, occupies one catalog, collectively referred to as the *Outer Records*. Since there are all together seven records, I henceforth named my catalog the *Seven Records*.

In the past, Sima Zichang 司馬子長 [Sima Qian 司馬遷, ca. 145–ca. 86 B.C.E.] put in writing the events of several thousand years. Former worthies considered his diligence with sympathy, and his work was deemed good history; but it still was criticized for its choice of material. One could certainly find even more faults with my catalog, as it involved investigating into forty thousand scrolls of books, discussing each and every one of them and distinguishing their themes and purposes, not to mention that I am no comprehensive talent and lack broad learning. In my case, I do not have Ban Si's 班嗣 books, which were given him by the emperor himself;[45] nor am I like Huang Xiang 黃香 [fl. first century], who was granted access to the Eastern Lodge for browsing.[46] If I wanted to check something in a volume, I was inconvenienced by an inadequate library at home; when I had doubts and questions, I could find no one by my side to enlighten my darkness. It would be no wonder then that my catalog should contain many errors. I am afraid that it will become the very reason for my disgrace in the opinion of the later born. Nevertheless, for revisions and corrections, I shall wait for a fine gentleman to come along.

In the old days, when Liu Xiang collated books in the Imperial Library, he would compose a record after he had finished collating a title. In the record, he discoursed on the subject matter of the book and analyzed its errors; then he presented it to the throne. This is all recounted in his work. He then put together the various records and referred to it as *Separate Records*; this is the *Separate Records* we still have today. His son Liu Xin summed up its gist and produced the *Seven Catalogs*. The first catalog represents a recapitulation of the six catalogs and henceforth is simply named the *Summary of the Catalogs* 輯略. The second is the *Catalog of the Six Arts* 六藝略, then the *Catalog of the Masters* 諸子略, then the *Catalog of Poetry and Fu* 詩賦略, then the *Catalog of Military Strategies* 兵書略,

then the *Catalog of Necromancy* 數術略, then the *Catalog of Professional Methods* 方伎略.

Wang Jian's *Seven Accounts* changed the category of Six Arts to that of the Classic Canon 經典; then there is the *Account of the Masters* 諸子; then he renamed the *Catalog of Poetry and Fu* as the *Account of Literary Writings* 文翰; *Military Strategies* as *Martial Strategies*軍書; *Necromancy* as *Yin–Yang* 陰陽; and *Professional Methods* as *Techniques and Arts* 術藝. Because there are only six catalogs in the work by Liu Xiang and Liu Xin despite its title, Wang Jian added the *Account of Charts, Drawings, and Registers* 圖譜 to fulfill the number of "seven." Finally, he created a separate catalog of the titles missing in the *Seven Catalogs*, in the bibliography sections of the *History of the Former Han* and the *History of the Latter Han,* and in Xun Xu's *List of Central Collection of the Classics;* he also made a list of Buddhist and Daoist scriptures. Though these titles come right after the seven accounts, they do not constitute part of it.

My *Seven Records* represents a compromise between Wang and Liu. Wang thought that the term "Six Arts" was not adequate to distinguish the catalog of the classics and henceforth changed it to the *Classic Canon;* I have followed Wang's practice, and the *Record of the Classic Canon* [*Jingdian lu* 經典錄] occupies the first place in the *Inner Records.*

Both Liu and Wang attached various histories to the *Spring and Autumn Annals.* In Liu's time, there were very few works of historiography, so it was quite appropriate that those few works were appended to the *Spring and Autumn Annals.* Nowadays, various historical accounts and biographies are, however, many times more [numerous] than the works listed in the *Record of the Classic Canon.* If we still accept Liu's procedure, the section would become overcrowded and messy. Besides, poetry and *fu* in the *Seven Catalogs* are not incorporated in the "Poetry" category in the *Catalog of the Six Arts* but are placed in an independent catalog, precisely because there are too many titles of poetry and *fu.* I adhere to this principle by setting up a separate catalog: the *Record of Various Histories, Accounts, and Biographies* [*Zhong shi xu ji zhuan lu* 眾史序記傳錄], which comes after the *Record of the Classic Canon* in the *Inner Records.*

As for the term "Masters Literature," Liu and Wang show no divergence. Liu has a catalog of *Military Strategies.* Wang thought the word "military" [*bing* 兵] was too common and shallow, whereas "martial" [*jun* 軍] is profound and broad, so he changed "Military Strategies" to "Martial Strategies." In my humble opinion, in the ancient times there were phrases such as "military affairs," "military forces," "military maneuvers," and "military tactics," so "military" is in truth a general term for martial matters. I therefore changed "martial" back to "military." Since military works are, however, few, they do not quite merit a separate catalog, so I attached those titles at the end of the Masters Literature and named the third record in the *Inner Records* the *Record of Masters Literature and Military Works* [*Zi bing lu* 子兵錄].

Wang felt that the name "Poetry and *fu*" did not include other genres, so he changed it to "Literary Writings." In my humble opinion, one's literary writings are collectively known as a "collection." If the word "Writings" could be changed to "Collections," then the name would be especially unambiguous. Therefore, I place the *Record of Literary Collections* [*Wen ji lu* 文集錄] as the next in the *Inner Records*.

Wang found the term "Necromancy" too diffuse and miscellaneous, so he changed it to "Yin–Yang"; he also felt that the phrase "Professional Methods" was unsubstantiated in the classics, so he changed it to "Techniques and Arts." In my humble opinion, "Yin–Yang" seems to be a rather specialized term and not as comprehensive as "Necromancy"; "Techniques and Arts" mixes the Six Arts and necromancy and is not as clear and unmistakable as "Professional Methods." Therefore, I revert to Liu's categories and keep his original terms. However, techniques for the inner chambers and methods of seeking immortality are already classified under the *Record of Daoist Transcendence*, and medical prescriptions and manuals are not numerous enough to merit a separate catalog; therefore, I combined the *Catalog of Necromancy* and the *Catalog of Professional Methods* into one, which is entitled the *Record of Techniques and Professional Methods* [*Shu ji lu* 術伎錄]. It comes as the fifth in the *Inner Records*.

Wang Jian's *Account of Charts, Drawings, and Registers* is a new creation, which Liu Xin's *Seven Catalogs* does not have. Although Liu's *Catalog of Necromancy* contains calendar register, it is different from what we mean today by "registers." In my humble opinion, charts and drawings should be attached to the subject they illustrate, so I have listed each of them under the appropriate catalog. "Registers" are in fact annotations and accounts and should be referenced with historiographies. Therefore, I have appended them at the end of historical accounts and biographies.

The catalogs listed above all belong to the *Inner Records*.

The teachings of the Buddhists have in truth spread all over the Middle Earth. They are expounded, explicated, lectured on, and savored, possessing an equal status as the Confucian classics. Although Wang has recorded them, they do not constitute a legitimate part of the *Seven Accounts*. When we examine the principles and measure the reality, I am afraid Wang's practice is not quite appropriate. Thereupon, I have listed the *Record of Buddhist Laws* [*Fo fa lu* 佛法錄] as the first one of the *Outer Records*.

Works on Daoist immortals have had a long history. Liu placed "Gods and Immortals" at the end of the *Catalog of Professional Methods*, while Wang left Daoist scriptures outside the confines of the *Seven Accounts* altogether. I have now included the *Record of Daoist Transcendence* [*Xian dao lu* 仙道錄] as the second record in the *Outer Records*. Wang put the Daoist teachings before the Buddhist; now I have reversed the order and given precedence to the Buddhist. This is not only because our beliefs differ but also because the teachings are poles apart in their depths.

The *Inner* and *Outer Records* together make up the *Seven Records*. One hopes that all the hidden records and lost titles of the world have been included in this catalog. On the seventeenth day of the second spring month, in the fourth year of the Putong reign of the Liang [March 19, 523], I first began to give an account of this work at my residence in the Jinzhong District of Jiankang. Liu Yao 劉杳 [487–536] of Pingyuan, a man of the world, is an associate of mine, and I told him about my project. It turned out that Yao had been similarly inclined for a long time but had not had an opportunity to wield his brush. When he heard that I had already begun, he was pleased, understanding my intent all too well. He thereupon gave me all the extracts of books he had made and was truly instrumental in broadening my knowledge. This, I suppose, is very much like the case of Zheng Xuan 鄭玄 [127–200], who gave all his annotations of the *Spring and Autumn Annals* to a fellow scholar, Fu Qian 服虔, thereby contributing to the completion of the latter's work.

[Yan Kejun 嚴可均, ed., "Quan Liang wen" 全晉文, in QW 66.3345–46]

NOTES

1. Walter Benjamin, "Unpacking My Library: A Talk About Book Collecting," in *Illuminations* (New York: Schocken Books, 1969), 67.

2. Xiao Yi 蕭繹 was born on September 16, 508. He was made Prince of Xiangdong on September 3, 514, at the age of six. The Western Quarters was also known as Eternal Blessings Quarters 永福省, the name of a part of the living quarters in the imperial palace. The Five Classics are the *Classic of Poetry* (*Shijing* 詩經), *Classic of Documents* (*Shangshu* 尚書), *Record of Rites* (*Liji* 禮記), *Classic of Changes* (*Yijing* 易經), and *Spring and Autumn Annals* (*Chunqiu* 春秋).

3. Xiao Yi was made Magistrate of Langye 琅琊郡 in 517 and remained in this post until 518 or 519. The district capital was in Baixia 白下, a fortress city northwest of the Palace City (Taicheng 臺城).

4. Xiao Yi became Magistrate of Kuaiji 會稽 (in modern Zhejiang) in 519. He was eleven years old, and according to his memoir in *The Master of the Golden Tower* as well as the reminiscences of Yan Zhitui 顏之推 (ca. 531–591), he was deeply absorbed in reading dynastic histories at the time.

5. Nothing is known about Xie Yanyuan 謝彥遠. Liu Ru 劉孺 (483–541) came from the Liu clan of Pengcheng (in modern Jiangsu), which produced a number of famous writers in the early sixth century. Liu Ru served as Secretary under Xiao Yi in Kuaiji; the last office he held was Minister of Personnel.

6. Wuxing 吳興 Commandery included parts of Zhejiang and Jiangsu. Xiahou Tan 夏侯亶 (483–538) was a general, and Yu Chan 虞闡 was one of the compilers of the *Record of the Buddha* (*Fo ji* 佛記), commissioned by the Liang Emperor Wu and completed by 513.

7. Xiao Yi was made Governor of Danyang 丹陽 in 522. Danyang was the larger metropolitan area around the capital city, Jiankang 建康 (modern Nanjing). The crown prince

was Xiao Tong, Xiao Yi's eldest brother, whose library boasted thirty thousand scrolls of books.

8. The Marquis of Xinyu 新渝 was Xiao Ying 蕭暎 (d. 544), a cousin of Xiao Yi; the Marquis of Shanghuang 上黃 was Xiao Ye 蕭曄, Xiao Ying's younger brother. It is not known who the Marquis of Xinwu 新吳 in the Liang was, but presumably he was also a member of the royal family. *Gewu* 格五 is the name of a gambling game.

9. Xiao Yi was temporarily put in charge of Yangzhou in 526 when the final decision on the governorship was pending. Here Yangzhou is the region, not the city, of Yangzhou, which was called Guangling 廣陵 in the Six Dynasties. Wu Commandery included parts of Jiangsu and Zhejiang. Xu Mian 徐勉 (466–535) was an important minister in Emperor Wu's court, and Duke Jiansu 簡肅 was his posthumous title.

10. On October 26, 526, Xiao Yi was made Governor of Jingzhou, with its district capital in Jiangling (in modern Hubei). He was eighteen years old. His elder brother Xiao Gang was Governor of Yongzhou at the time.

11. This sentence may have some lacunae. Xiao Yi himself had never been to Shu (modern Sichuan), though his younger brother Xiao Ji 蕭紀 (508–553) was made Governor of Yizhou 益州 in Shu in 537. I suspect that Xiao Yi is referring to Xiao Ji. Xiao Ji was an aggressive contender for throne after Emperor Wu died and was deeply engaged in infighting with Xiao Yi in 553, the year when Xiao Yi was writing this chapter. He was killed in battle in the autumn; Xiao Yi excluded him from the family and even changed his surname to Taotie 饕餮, the name of a monster in Chinese mythology. Perhaps for this reason, Xiao Yi deliberately made the wording ambiguous.

12. Nothing is known about Zong Mengjian 宗孟堅. Bao Quan 鮑泉 was a talented writer and died in the Hou Jing rebellion in 552.

13. Prince Yang of Ancheng 安成煬王 was named Xiao Ji 蕭機. He was the eldest son of Emperor Wu's brother Xiao Xiu 蕭秀 (475–518), Prince Kang of Ancheng. The *History of the South* (*Nan shi*) says that "his family had a large book collection, and he was broad in learning and keen in memory" (52.1290).

14. Liu Zhilin 劉之遴 and Liu Zhiheng 劉之亨 were brothers, and each served as Magistrate of Nanjun 南郡. Yue Facai 樂法才 was a native of Jiangling. Yu Qiao 庾喬 was a member of the powerful local clan in the Chu region and served under Xiao Yi; he was noted for his arrogance regarding his elite gentry status. Nothing is known about Zong Zhonghui 宗仲回 or Fachi 法持.

15. Zhaoti temple 招提寺 was in Jiankang, north of the Stone Fort. Dharma Master Yan was Huiyan 慧琰.

16. Toutuo temple 頭陀寺 was in Yingzhou 郢州 (modern Hubei). It was celebrated in the inscription written by Wang Che 王巾 (d. 505), included in *Wen xuan*.

17. Changsha temple 長沙寺 was in Jiangling, the district capital of Jingzhou. Nothing is known about Zhu Danyuan 朱澹遠.

18. Jiang Ge 江革 (d. 535) was a famous minister in the Liang. Nothing is known about Yao Kai 姚凱. Jiang Lu 江祿 is an error for 江禄. He was on the staff of Xiao Yi in Jingzhou but had a fallout with Xiao Yi because of his arrogance. Xiao Yi hated him so much that he changed his courtesy name to Rongcai (Glorification of Wealth) because Jiang Lu

had amassed quite a fortune when he was in office. He was, however, a well-known book lover.

19. I have emended the opening sentence in this passage, "I also acquired five cases of *books from around* the Yuanjia reign from Jiang Ge of Jiangzhou," to "I also acquired five cases of the *History of the Han* [*Han shu*] of the Yuanjia reign [424–453] from Jiang Ge of Jiangzhou," as this better fits the context. The emphasis here does not fall on the *History of the Han*, which was not a rare item by any means, but on a copy of the *History of the Han* copied during the Yuanjia reign, an era that was clearly famous for its choice use of paper and ink. Xiao Yi also claims to have acquired the "*History of the Latter Han* from the Yuanjia reign" 元嘉後漢 in the following passage.

20. Xiao Yi was called back to the capital on August 27, 539. I follow Zhao Lixin's emendation of *yuan ru* 元儒 (leading Confucian scholars) to *xuan ru* 玄儒 (metaphysical and Confucian) in this sentence. See Zhao Lixin 趙立新, "*Jinlouzi* Jushupian buzhu" 金樓子聚書篇補注, *Zaoqi Zhongguo shi yanjiu* 早期中國史研究 1 (2009): 29–43.

21. Xiao Yi was made Governor of Jiangzhou in 540. Xiao Ben 蕭賁 (d. 549?) was on Xiao Ji's staff and offended Xiao Yi during the Hou Jing rebellion by criticizing Xiao Yi for not going to the rescue during the siege of the Palace City; he was subsequently executed by Xiao Yi under some other pretext. Liu Huan 劉緩 (fl. 540s) was a leading poet in Xiao Yi's entourage; his father was a cousin of the famous poet Jiang Yan 江淹 (444–505). Zhou Hongzhi 周宏直 was a nephew of the famous minister and man of letters Zhou She 周捨 (471–524).

22. This happened in February 542. Liu Jinggong 劉敬躬, a native of Ancheng, rebelled; Xiao Yue 蕭說, who was Administrator of Ancheng, abandoned the county and ran away. On March 3, Xiao Yi sent his general Wang Sengbian 王僧辨 to quell the rebellion, and Liu Jinggong was defeated within a month. Xiao Yue, Marquis of Luoxiang 羅鄉侯, was a member of the royal family.

23. The Marquis of Wuping was Xiao Mai 蕭勱, a member of the royal family (Emperor Wu's cousin's son). He had a book collection totaling thirty thousand scrolls. He was particularly fond of *Dongguan Han ji* 東觀漢記 and memorized it by heart. He was a close friend of Xiao Yi's, and he served as Governor of Guangzhou for a number of years and had an excellent reputation. Nothing is known about He Mian 何沔.

24. The Marquis of Hengshan was Xiao Gong 蕭恭 (d. 549), Emperor Wu's nephew. He was appointed Governor of Yongzhou in 535 and was called back to the capital (sometime between 542 and 547) when Xiao Xu 蕭續 (506–547), the Prince of Luling, filed a complaint about his subordinate Chen Baoyin 陳寶印. Xiao Gong later died in the siege of the Palace City during the Hou Jing rebellion.

25. Lan Qin 蘭欽 (ca. 403–544), a noted general, defeated the Western Wei army at Nanzheng 南鄭 (in modern Shaanxi) in 535.

26. The crossing of the River refers to the Jin court crossing the Yangzi River in 317 when the North fell under the control of non-Han peoples.

27. Zhang Zuan 張纘 (499–549) was Xiao Yi's brother-in-law and a close friend. Zhang Wan 張綰 (493–555) was the brother of Zhang Zuan. Fan Xu 范胥 (fl. 530s–540s) once served as the receptionist in charge of receiving the Eastern Wei emissaries. Nothing is

known about Wang Zhenzhi 王縝之, the author of the *Biographies of Noted Children* (*Tongzi zhuan* 童子傳), now lost except for one fragment; his name was written as Wang Tianzhi 王瑱之 in the *Sui shu* "Bibliography." Fan Guang 樊光 was a Han commentator of *Erya* 爾雅; some of the annotations of *Zhanguo ce* 戰國策 by Gao You 高誘 (fl. 205) are still extant. The *Biographies of Eminent Monks* (*Gaoseng zhuan* 高僧傳), written by the monk Huijiao 惠皎, is extant.

28. Donglin temple 東林寺 was in Mount Lu of Jiangzhou (modern Jiangxi). When Xiao Yi's older brother, Xiao Lun 蕭綸 (507?–551), was in Jiangzhou between 537 and 540, he associated with Zhibiao 智表.

29. Wei Rui 韋叡 (442–520) was a famous general.

30. Yin Jun 殷鈞 (posthumous title, Count Zhen 貞子, 484–532) was Xiao Yi's brother-in-law. His wife, the Princess of Yongxing, was the Liang Emperor Wu's eldest daughter.

31. Nothing is known about Fan Pu 范普 or Pan Puti 潘菩提. The Two Wangs are the father and son Wang Xizhi 王羲之 and Wang Xianzhi 王獻之, famous calligraphers of the fourth century.

32. Nothing is known about Yu Jiao 虞㒼.

33. A poem preserved in the early Northern Song compendium *Wenyuan yinghua* 文苑英華, *juan* 193, is attributed to a Fang Zhuan 房篆 of the Liang, which I suspect is the same Fang Zhuan here.

34. Huijiao once stayed at Hongpu temple 宏普 in Kuaiji.

35. The Marquis of Linru was Xiao Yuanyou 蕭淵猷 (d. 533), Emperor Wu's nephew. He served as Governor of Yizhou in the 520s.

36. Nothing is known about Yue Yanchun. It is claimed that Liu Zhilin was poisoned by Xiao Yi on July 15, 549, because Xiao Yi "was jealous of his talent" (*NS* 50.1252). This is rather suspicious. One wonders what exactly made Liu Zhilin's talent so special that Xiao Yi was jealous to the extent of having him murdered, since, after all, Xiao Yi was constantly surrounded by talented staff members.

37. The Prince of Nanping 南平王 was Xiao Ke 蕭恪 (d. 552), Xiao Yi's cousin. Governor Zhang of Yongzhou, Zhang Yongzhou 張雍州, refers to Zhang Zuan. Earlier in this chapter, Zhang Zuan is referred to as Governor of Xiangzhou, a post he assumed in 543. In 548, however, he was reappointed as Governor of Yongzhou right before the Hou Jing rebellion broke out. His replacement at Xiangzhou, Xiao Tong's son Xiao Yu, detained Zhang Zuan for personal grievances. Zhang Zuan escaped to Jiangling to join Xiao Yi, who then sent Zhang Zuan to Yongzhou to replace the then governor, Xiao Tong's third son, Xiao Cha. Xiao Cha refused to be replaced and eventually had Zhang Zuan killed in 549 during his infighting with Xiao Yi. Zhang Zuan had left all his possessions in Jiangling, including twenty thousand scrolls of books. The Prince of Guiyang 桂陽王 was Xiao Zao 蕭慥, son of Xiao Yi's cousin. He was executed by Xiao Yi in 552 during the Hou Jing rebellion. Nothing is known about Liu Zhiyuan 留之遠.

38. The year in which Xiao Yi wrote—or finished writing—the chapter was 553. Xiao Yi had taken the throne on December 13, 552, and decided to remain at Jiangling, his former Jingzhou headquarters, instead of returning to the capital city, Jiankang.

39. This number does not include the books (about eighty thousand scrolls) that Xiao Yi had his general Wang Sengbian transport to Jianling from the imperial library at Jiankang after Wang Sengbian retook Jiankang from the rebel Hou Jing.

40. The Prince of Hejian 河間 (r. 155–130 B.C.E.) was named Liu De 劉德; he was one of the sons of the Han Emperor Jing 漢景帝 (r. 156–141 B.C.E.), an active collector of ancient texts, and a lover of learning and scholarship.

41. Nine Hills, Three Mounds, and Five Canons are ancient titles long lost.

42. According to the *Records of the Historian* (*Shiji* 史記), Confucius returned to the state of Lu after years of wandering in 489 B.C.E., when he was sixty-three *sui* (sixty-two years old by Western reckoning). The Five Beginnings in the *Spring and Autumn Annals* refers to how the historian typically begins the account of the reign of a duke of Lu: "In the spring of the First Year, in the first month of the [Zhou] King's calendar, the duke took office."

43. The four categories are the Confucian Classics, Masters Literature, Historiography, and Literary Collections, in that order.

44. That is, Masters Literature and Historiography switched places.

45. Ban Si was a cousin of Ban Gu's father, Ban Biao 班彪; the two of them studied together. The *History of the Han* claims that they had books given to them from the imperial library. Once Huan Tan 桓譚, a famous writer, asked to borrow some books; Ban Si wrote back, turning him down. See *HS* 100A.4205–6.

46. In 84 C.E., the Han Emperor Zhang (r. 76–88) granted Huang Xiang free access to the Eastern Lodge 東觀, which housed the imperial book collection at the time, to read all the books he had not seen before. See *HHS* 80.2614.

PART IV

Imaging Self and Other

The early medieval period of China has often been described in the following terms: "rise of individualism," "growth of self-awareness," and "cult of the personality."[1] While there is no doubt that the social values and behavioral norms of the Han were seriously (and, incidentally, in some cases, comically) challenged in the Wei and Jin dynasties, it is equally certain that people living before this era had experienced self-awareness as unique individuals. One would not need to search far and wide for examples: Qu Yuan 屈原 (343–277 B.C.E.), who expressed in no uncertain terms a feeling of being different from others in "Encountering Sorrow" (*Li sao* 離騷), and Sima Qian 司馬遷 (ca. 145–ca. 86 B.C.E.), whose sense of a personal, unique enterprise led him to choose castration over an honorable suicide so that he might live to write the *Records of the Historian* (*Shi ji* 史記), for no other person would have been able to fulfill this task. In fact, the various acts of subverting established codes of conduct recorded in the literature of the period confirm that normative behavior had widened its scope and that nononformist attitudes had become popular among the gentry elite.

The chapters in part IV suggest other vantage points from which to consider the issues of selfhood, representation (of both oneself and other selves), and personality in the period: an expansion of models of behavior, the development both of elaborate systems of classifying such behaviors and of a sophisticated vocabulary for appraising character, and the experimentation with literary forms of self-representation. The past becomes comprehensible when it can be apportioned into distinct categories of types, endeavors, and attitudes. In addition, the past becomes meaningful when one can identify particular models of conduct, which may inform one's future actions. An act or behavior that can be classified more easily lends itself to be copied (or to serve as a warning).

China's history is told mainly through the lives of individuals, as Alan Berkowitz points out in chapter 20, which discusses a collection of biographical accounts of "high-minded men" (gaoshi 高士), a work by the reclusive scholar Huangfu Mi 黃甫謐 (215–282). The official dynastic histories devote much space to biographies of men. Some stand as individual or paired entries, and others grouped under categorical types such as scholars, humorists, abusive officials, and recluses. The biographies in either official works like dynastic histories or private scholarship like Huangfu Mi's *Accounts of High-Minded Men* (*Gaoshi zhuan* 高士傳) do not present individual lives in any chronological or comprehensive sense. Rather, historians tended to select only one or two characteristics to define the subject. Moreover, the specific traits highlighted usually illustrate the individual's type, if any. Typology therefore shapes significantly the biographies found under a given heading. In Huangfu Mi's *Accounts of High-Minded Men*, some of the characteristics shared by the various high-minded men are decline of office, show of independent will, and disregard for fame or profit. In a later set of biographies of recluses in the *History of Song* (*Song shu* 宋書, 488) by Shen Yue 沈約 (441–513), many subjects share, in addition to these traits, a love of nature and material self-sufficiency. The men in *Accounts of High-Minded Men* may possess the same desire for disengagement, but each often explains his own motivation or rationale by way of clever analogies and witty punch lines. These biographical accounts thus combine exemplarity and singularity: each subject exemplifies a type (i.e., high-minded men) through a unique story.

Charting a typography of human endeavors and behaviors was not only a feature of historical biographies but also a major aspect of the genre of "small talk" (*xiaoshuo* 小説), as in *Recent Anecdotes from the Talk of the Ages* (*Shishuo xinyu* 世說新語), a fifth-century collection of stories about people who lived from the Han dynasty to the Jin. In its earliest form, the genre of *xiaoshuo* was associated with local stories and gossip,[2] material that may have been useful for government agents but was deemed unsuitable to be included in histories of any kind. The subjects in *Recent Anecdotes*, however, belonged to a specific class of people—the intellectual elite—and many stories find at least some corroboration in historical or other estimable kinds of sources. *Recent Anecdotes* spawned so many imitations during the Tang and Song dynasties that it eventually became the first in a distinct genre bearing its name, "talk of the age genre" (*shishuo ti* 世說體). The stories in *Recent Anecdotes* are organized into thirty-six categories of abilities or behaviors, such as precocious intelligence (*suhui* 夙惠), appearance and manner (*rongzhi* 容止), and incivility and arrogance (*jian'ao* 簡傲). One scholar described the thirty-six categories as collectively representing the following aspects of personality: capacity (*de* 德), ability (*cai* 才), temperament (*xing* 性), and feeling (*qing* 情).[3] The historical figures in these anecdotes are intended to exemplify one particular trait, ability, or feeling according to the given categorical heading.

This interest in evaluating and classifying character traits can be traced to an early-third-century political work, *Treatise on Personality* (*Renwu zhi* 人物志), by a Wei dynasty official, Liu Shao 劉劭 (ca. 189–ca. 245). Although both the *Treatise* and *Recent Anecdotes* focus on the assessment and classification of human ability and attitudes, the former is guided by a pragmatic approach to personality, while the latter expresses an aesthetic appreciation for its subjects, as Jack Chen demonstrates in chapter 21. The basic issue underlying the *Treatise* is how the government may best utilize human talent. To achieve this end, this manual discusses in detail the various observable manifestations, types of personality, categories of abilities (*cai* 材), and official posts that best correspond to each ability. This approach developed from the philosophy associated with the School of Names (*mingjia* 名家), which was concerned with correctly matching substance and its designation. This principle would be applied to recruitment for the political bureaucracy: the study of names or ranks and their corresponding duties and rites, and the differences among the various names.

The way in which the literary vignettes in *Recent Anecdotes* are constructed point to an aesthetic interest in the personalities at play: the level of narrative detail, the sophistication of the descriptive language, the fully developed dialogues, and the snappy remarks all enable the complex, interesting, and dynamic aspects of the characters to enfold. In *Recent Anecdotes*, the performative element of human personality is put on display. Consider one of the best-known anecdotes, in the "Free and Uninhibited" (*Ren dan* 任誕) chapter, in which Liu Ling 劉伶 (d. after 265), one of the Seven Worthies of the Bamboo Grove and the author of "Hymn to the Virtue of Wine" (*Jiu de song* 酒德頌), flouts convention with great flair and brilliantly acts out a sense of freedom and lack of inhibition: "On many occasions Liu Ling, under the influence of wine, would be completely free and uninhibited, sometimes taking off his clothes and sitting naked in his room. Once when some persons saw him and chided him for it, Ling retorted, 'I take heaven and earth for my pillars and roof, and the rooms in my house for my pants and coat. What are you gentlemen doing in my pants?'"[4]

The attention given to individual personalities in *Recent Anecdotes* should not obscure the fact that many of its subjects shared a group identity centered on the cultural practice of "pure conversation" (*qingtan* 清談), in which participants discussed various metaphysical, ontological, and semiotic issues associated with the dominant intellectual current of "mysterious learning" (*xuanxue* 玄學). Moreover, numerous anecdotes in *Recent Anecdotes* show a common interest by the Wei and Jin gentry in the intricacies of human nature, character appraisal, and connoisseurship of human types. Likewise, these men were constantly aware that they themselves might be the objects of evaluation, hence the attentiveness to what they expressed and how they appeared. To a considerable extent, image and reputation made the man. Many of the individuals prominently featured in *Recent Anecdotes* are, in fact, best known as belonging to a certain group of a given era: the Seven Masters of the Jian'an period, the Seven Worthies of the Bamboo Grove (Wei–Jin transition),[5] Jia Mi's Twenty-Four Companions (Western Jin), and the Lanting Party (Eastern Jin).

Group identity is based mainly on shared concerns and activities, especially a keen sense of joint experience. In chapter 22, on literary communities, Ping Wang focuses on a later example from the court of the Liang crown prince, Xiao Tong 蕭統 (501–531), and traces the construction of the literary group's identity to the earlier models of Cao Pi 曹丕 (187–226) and the Seven Masters of the Jian'an period, and of Xiao Ziliang 蕭子良 (460–494) and the Eight Companions of Jingling. In one case, the occasions that inspired a collective feeling of pleasure in the moment and melancholy in the transience of things were group outings. In another case, scholarly group projects enhanced the sense of intellectual camaraderie. In Ping Wang's selection of poems, dating from an excursion to a Buddhist seminar in the mountains, the courtiers in Xiao Tong's group appear to try to distinguish themselves individually within the context of a common experience: each displays his skill in capturing the natural setting and import of the occasion and competes to outdo one another in offering praise of their patron.

Self-representation has a long tradition in China, and its earliest (and strongest) association was with poetry. As one scholar remarked, "In imperial China poetry was the form for the expression of the self and the mode of writing most closely identified with an individual, authorial voice."[6] The identification of a poem and an individual voice derived in great part from Han readings of the *Classic of Poetry* (*Shijing* 詩經) and the *Lyrics of Chu* (*Chuci* 楚辭), China's earliest anthologies of verse, which posited behind the composition of each song an author or specific historical event. This link was traced to the earliest pronouncement on poetry from the "Canon of Yao" (*Yao dian* 堯典) chapter of the *Classic of Documents* (*Shangshu* 尚書): "The poem speaks what is intently on the mind." The two literary examples of self-representation selected for this volume look beyond the genre of poetry and examine the experimentation with new or less developed genres for talking about oneself in the early medieval period.

The first example comes from Tao Yuanming 陶淵明 (365?–427), who significantly expanded the art of self-narration by inventing new modes. There is no precedent in Chinese literature for the scope of Tao Yuanming's autobiographical project: not only did he scrupulously document his life through poetry, but he also fashioned two distinct genres for imaging oneself. His "Biography of the Master of Five Willows" (*Wuliu xiansheng zhuan* 五柳先生傳), which I translated and discuss in chapter 23, is considered the earliest fictionalized autobiography, and his "Elegy for Myself" (*Zi jiwen* 自祭文) has no precedent, since elegies (*jiwen* 祭文; literally, "sacrificial piece") usually were composed for the deceased by another person. Moreover, Tao Yuanming often used the paratextual devices of the title to document time, place, and occasion, and the preface to guide the reader in interpreting his work. By extensively employing such devices, Tao became, in effect, the first editor of his own works.

The subject of the second example is Jiang Yan 江淹 (444–505), who edited his own collection of works and wrote an autobiographical preface to it. This *zixu* 自序 (his own preface or self-preface) can be traced to the last chapter of the *Records of the Historian* (*Shi ji* 史記) by Sima Qian, which is generally considered the original model for this genre. Sima Qian's autobiographical preface does not, however, provide a substantial account of his public or private life. Instead, most of the preface is an overview of the *Records of the Historian*, and much of the rest is devoted to quoting one of his father's essays, explaining his charge from his dying father to write the history and the importance of this achievement and expressing his own view of history, as embedded in his discussion of Confucius's *Spring and Autumn Annals* (*Chunqiu* 春秋).

In contrast, Jiang Yan's autobiographical preface, translated by Paul W. Kroll in chapter 24, offers a more comprehensive account of the writer's life: his early education and youthful ambitions, a chronological survey of his official career, and his inner desire for a quiet life. In Jiang Yan's account of himself, as with other autobiographical narratives, the author is compelled to explain or justify certain major decisions in his life. For Jiang Yan, it was his falling-out with his first major patron, Liu Jingsu 劉景素 (452–476); for Tao Yuanming, it was his withdrawal from office; and for Sima Qian, it was his choice of a humiliating castration over an honorable suicide. Self-representation thus requires a certain amount of self-interpretation, and self-interpretation is carried out with an eye on how the self will be represented.

The autobiographical impulse to leave a testimony of oneself and to shape how later readers will look at oneself suggests that the constitution of the self is not only knowing where one stands and how one is oriented but also imagining oneself standing at a future point, looking back, and asking and trying to answer the question, "How shall I be known?" It is, then, especially remarkable to find in the writings of Tao Yuanming and Jiang Yan a disavowal of concern for one's posthumous reputation and a rather casual attitude toward writing. In the preface to "On Drinking Wine, Twenty Poems," Tao Yuanming coolly tells us, "Once I am drunk I write a few verses for my own amusement."[7] Jiang Yan writes in his own preface, "When feeling fancy-free, I composed literary pieces to amuse myself." And later he dispassionately asks, "Why the need [for a man to] focus thoughts and labor hard to win fame that will live on? For this reason, from youth to when I was older, I have never written a book of my own and have a collection of only ten *juan*." The wonderful tension between the desire to direct the way in which one will be seen by a future audience and the claim of disinterest in posthumous fame creates fascinating characters like Tao and Jiang. Their constant awareness of their future readership implies a posturing (even in good faith), and their persistent efforts at self-expression suggest a genuineness (even in self-consciousness). As Kroll reminds us in his chapter on Jiang Yan, we would do well not to demand of those who lived in the past a consistency of motivation and simplicity of personality that we probably would not seek in ourselves. Only then can we enjoy the complexities and tensions that make these characters truly dynamic.

Representation evokes quite a different set of issues when the subject is a transcendent figure, one radically "other." In chapter 25, Eugene Wang presents a selection of texts on pictorial representation dealing with the "shadow image." This image refers to a pictorial representation of Śākyamuni Buddha in a mountain cave south of Nagarahāra (near modern-day Jalalabad, Afghanistan). The lore of the "shadow cave" tells how Buddha, responding to the plea of the dragon king to stay, supposedly leaped into the rock wall, where he is seen as a bright manifestation from afar, but fades into obscurity upon closer look. Scriptural accounts based on the translations by, for example, Kumārajīva 鳩摩羅什 (343–413) and Buddhabhadra 佛陀跋陀羅 (360–429) and the eyewitness reports of pilgrim monks like Faxian 法顯 (320?–420?) likely inspired the monk Huiyuan to build a replica cave on Mount Lu in 412. As Wang explains, the issues at stake were how to capture a figure transcending space and time and to effect the illusion of presence, one strong enough to facilitate the visualization of the Buddha. The chosen medium, painting, and a new pictorial technique, chiaroscuro, were part of the answer. A "shadow image" is a trace that shows what was there but, more important, affirms that it always is here. Painting, more so than other media whose focus is drawn to the physicality of the vehicle, offers an optical experience that reconciles "the illusionistic depth and the material surface" to render possible an oneiric vision of the Buddha. The contrast between the darkness of the cave and the shades of the pictorial image in the background, and the illumination of the "manifestation" in the foreground, as well as the continual shift of perspective that is required for viewing the "shadow image," create an optical effect of "half seeing and half imagining" the image. Wang describes the historical context, concrete goals, and theoretical concerns in the early development of a Chinese theory of images.

Wendy Swartz

NOTES

1.   See the influential volume edited by Donald Munro, *Individualism and Holism: Studies in Confucian and Taoist Values* (Ann Arbor: Center for Chinese Studies, University of Michigan, 1985), especially Ying-shih Yü, "Individualism and the Neo-Taoist Movement

in Wei-Chin China," 121–55, and Richard Mather, "Individualist Expressions of the Out-
siders During the Six Dynasties," 199–214.

2. Ban Gu 班固 described this genre as consisting of "street gossip and alley conversa-
    tions" (*jie tan xiang yu* 街談巷語) (*HS* 20.1745). For a concise account of the early history
    of the genre, see Kenneth Dewoskin, "Hsiao-shuo," in *The Indiana Companion to Tradi-
    tional Chinese Literature*, ed. William Nienhauser (Bloomington: Indiana University
    Press, 1986), 1:423–26.

3. Qian Nanxiu, *Spirit and Self in Medieval China: The Shih-shuo hsin-yü and Its Legacy*
    (Honolulu: University of Hawai'i Press, 2001), 9.

4. *Recent Anecdotes from the Talk of the Ages*, 23/6, in Liu I-ch'ing [Liu Yiqing], comp., *Shih-
    shuo Hsin-yü: A New Account of the Tales of the World*, 2nd ed., trans. Richard B. Mather
    (Ann Arbor: Center for Chinese Studies, University of Michigan, 2002), 402.

5. Scholars have questioned the reality of such a group, which is said to have gathered in a
    bamboo grove and carried out their antics there. As Mather points out, some of these
    Seven Worthies may have been friends, though he argues that the Seven Worthies was
    ultimately an idealized construction by the Northern émigrés almost a century later,
    who felt a nostalgic longing for their homeland and thus created this association to
    represent "the spirit of freedom and transcendence" of the seven men (Liu I-ch'ing,
    comp., *Shih-shuo Hsin-yü*, 399).

6. Mark Edward Lewis, *Writing and Authority in Early China* (Albany: State University of
    New York Press, 1999), 147.

7. James Hightower, *The Poetry of T'ao Ch'ien* (Oxford: Clarendon Press, 1970), 124.

20. Biographies of Recluses

Huangfu Mi's *Accounts of High-Minded Men*

ALAN BERKOWITZ

In China as elsewhere, accounts of individuals contribute to the construction of cultural memory. But readers of Chinese literature through the ages cannot help but be struck by the immediacy and fullness of the recounting of actions and words. Indeed, China's past has largely been expressed through its individuals, for of the roughly four thousand or so scrolls (*juan* 卷) of the twenty-five now standard dynastic histories, some two-thirds are extensive expositions of individuals or are grouped biographical accounts, and more than half of these are categorized biographies, that is, accounts of individuals whose lives reflect particular sectors of endeavor.

Since Han times at least, collections of categorized biographies were collated and likely circulated as independent works. While some of these concerned worthies of particular locales, from the outset most focused on the lives of extraordinary individuals. Perhaps the earliest compilations were *Arrayed Accounts of Transcendents* (*Lie xian zhuan* 列仙傳) and *Arrayed Accounts of Women* (*Lie nü zhuan* 列女傳), both attributed to Liu Xiang 劉向 (79–8 B.C.E.). Categorized biographies functioned as repositories for information about particular individuals and also as collections of representative examples of the subject matter. Moreover, since early times biographical accounts have played an important role in transmitting cultural values. By encapsulating exemplary behavior in the portrayal of personal conduct and endeavor, the lives of individuals could serve as inspirations (or sometimes as deterrents) for similar behavior. At the very least, the collective portrayal could serve as a definition of a notable human activity. In effect, categorized biographies and hagiographies are a rhetorical mode and thus necessarily reflect interpretive strategy. That is, whereas individual biographical accounts ostensibly recount what is notable in the lives of individuals, collections of categorized accounts also reflect the selective redaction of materials to suit the narrative context at hand, along with iconographic portrayal and literary convention. *Accounts of High-Minded Men* (*Gao shi zhuan* 高士傳) by Huangfu Mi 皇甫謐 (215–282) is a premier example of collective biography, and it formulated both the literary depiction of high-minded men (*gao shi* 高士) and this type of conduct as an enduring facet of Chinese society and culture.

The term "high-minded men" (*gao shi*; sometimes interpreted as standing for *gao de zhi shi* 高德之士 [men of lofty virtue] or *gao zhi zhi shi* 高志之士 [men of lofty will]) was one of many designations for a few extraordinary men recognized for forgoing the conventional life of the scholar-official, living instead in a highly individualistic and idiosyncratic manner that at the same time fit key cultural values. These individuals were known more generally as "men in reclusion" (*yinshi* 隱士 or *yinzhe* 隱者; literally, "hidden men" or "concealers") and sometimes also were known by such euphemistic appellations as "disengaged persons" (*yimin* 逸民), "scholars-at-home" (*chushi* 處士), and, owing to a common association of reclusion and living apart from society, "men of the cliffs and caves" (*yanxue zhi shi* 巖穴之士). The commonly used English words "hermit" and "recluse" are not equivalent, although they do capture some of the mystique that became associated over time with some abstract, imagistic aspects of the portrayal of life in reclusion. Although a few practitioners did live as recluses or hermits, the terms are not at all appropriate for most men living in reclusion. As a group, they were characterized as men of integrity and virtue who declined to serve in the imperial bureaucracy in an official capacity. As such, political principles and backgrounding often were assumed or were ascribed to the motivations for eschewing office and, likewise, to any consequent ramifications. Yet men in reclusion were venerated nonetheless as contributing to society as moral and ethical exemplars and, equally, as exponents of individualistic freedom that those bound to official position could never attain. Portrayed as uncompromising in conduct, unconventional in lifestyle, or unencumbered in mind-set and action, high-minded men were often seen as the idealized antithesis of the government official. Indeed, men in office occasionally would assume the persona of a man in reclusion and ponder this unfettered alternative in poetry and other literary compositions.

Indeed, the most immediate, pervasive, and compelling writings and artistic depictions of reclusion are those by scholar-officials. These include much of so-called landscape poetry and landscape painting through the ages; narrative, poetic, or figurative representations of men in reclusion, their ideals, and their lifestyle; literary reference to (or identification with) the great men in reclusion from past to present; and the accoutrements of reclusion. Men in reclusion often were portrayed as free spirits living in a simple, aesthetic, and ecological manner, which is why many cultural constants such as mountains and streams, fishermen and woodcutters, simple dress and unbound hair, and spare living conditions and an easy rapport with wild beasts were redolent with life in reclusion. During the early medieval period, the portrayal further began to include the idle joys of rural life and retirement, often combined with the company of wine and the seven-string fretless horizontal zither known as the *qin* 琴. But the vast majority of men in reclusion were by no means simple rustics. The assumption was that they were extraordinary individuals imbued with excellence and virtue, wisdom and forthrightness, and often extraordinary skills or arts. This is why they were repeatedly sought to serve in office (and why some aspiring officials found it expedient to emulate high-minded conduct) and why many sages' writings and esoteric traditions are attributed to men in reclusion. And while life in reclusion did not necessarily imply asceticism or withdrawal from the mundane world, several famous men of religion were also regarded equally as men in reclusion.

Huangfu Mi was a prominent authority on classical scholarship, literature, history, and the medical arts. He repeatedly rejected calls to assume an official position in the court bureaucracy, choosing to remain instead publicly "in reclusion." In this way, he exemplified in his own life the lives of the people in his *Accounts of High-Minded Men*, which served as an oblique yet potent defense for his chosen life path. Not responding to one's ruler's call to service often was seen as an implicit indictment of the present state of affairs and those in charge, and independence of action always was seen as a problematic challenge to autocracy. Huangfu Mi reasoned that high-minded men contributed to the well-being of the people in the local community and the world at large by serving as moral exemplars, ones who stood by their ideals, disdained avarice and personal gain, and inspired harmonious interactions among individuals. In particular, there was historical precedent: if these men were lauded in the great ages of the past for their ideals and their conduct, should ones like them now not also receive similar recognition for declining to serve in office?

Huangfu Mi was a learned scholar, and in other highly crafted and allusive writings he defended his position. He remained out of office throughout his life, and his *Accounts of High-Minded Men* has served as a foundational compendium of exemplary men in reclusion. It is significant that Huangfu Mi specifically excludes from his collected accounts worthy men like the legendary Bo Yi 伯夷 and Gong Sheng 龔勝 (68 B.C.E.–11 C.E.), both of whom committed suicide to preserve their virtue and integrity. Bo Yi and his younger brother Shu Qi 叔齊 are famous for refusing to eat the grain of the newly founded Zhou 周 dynasty and starving to death in the mountains. This was their resolute and conscientious objection to King Wu 周武王, whom they considered unfilial for failing to observe the mourning rites for his recently deceased father King Wen 文王 and instead waging war to overthrow his own dynastic sovereign. The Han official Gong Sheng retired from office at the advent of Wang Mang 王莽 (46 B.C.E.–23 C.E.), and subsequently starved himself to death when pressed to return to office in the capital, saying, "How could I with my single life serve two ruling houses?" One can imagine that Huangfu Mi did not wish to intimate that his rulers were unsuitable to serve and, even more, did not wish to advocate the precedent of righteous suicide as a suitable way to decline a ruler's summons to office.

Huangfu Mi's *Accounts of High-Minded Men* may not have been the first work to focus on preeminent examples of men in reclusion. Huangfu Mi himself refers to two predecessors in his "Preface," one by Liang Hong 梁鴻 (before 24–after 80) and the other by Su Shun 蘇順 (late first century–early second century). There is an ongoing scholarly debate about whether Huangfu Mi's work predated or followed a work by Ji Kang 嵇康 (223–262, also romanized as Xi Kang) called *Accounts of Sages, Transcendents, and High-Minded Men, with Encomiums* (*Shengxian gao shi zhuan zan* 聖仙高士傳讚, commonly also known as *Gao shi zhuan*). But Huangfu Mi's *Accounts* decisively set the model for the many subsequent works on the topic and, moreover, set the parameters for defining the nature of high-mindedness in the Chinese cultural tradition. Encompassed in these vignettes is the image of a pristine abhorrence of worldly taint, freedom from the constraints of the mundane world, as well as a high-spirited and determined individualism that exalted upholding one's integrity and personal values above all else. Certainly not all these stories are records of the actual actions of historical individuals, but they just as certainly reflect a mind-set that has resonated in traditional Chinese culture from early times to the present, whose articulation was formulated during the early medieval period, especially with the redaction and dissemination of famous accounts of high-mindedness through the ages.

The following representative selection of accounts is in rough chronological order, in the same way that they appear in Huangfu Mi's *Accounts*, and each account is translated in full. Note that some of the men were anonymous individuals, known only by a descriptive sobriquet derived from an anecdote about them that focuses on a polemic or a demonstration of virtue and integrity. Others are familiar individuals prominent in historical, philosophical, and expository literature. Exponents of values conventionally viewed as pertaining to the so-called Confucian or Daoist traditions are evident in Huangfu Mi's accounts. "Daoist" views seem to some extent to be more noticeable, but many of the men would be hard to relegate to just one of these classifications. This blurring of traditional characterizations underscores how reclusion as a deep-seated cultural value has itself imbued Chinese and other East Asian civilizations. This shows, too, that the characterization of values and conduct is both complex and fungible in regard to individuals. In any case, most of the accounts in this collection are greatly abridged treatments, even taking into account how much of the text has been lost through the years. (Many fragments from the *Accounts of High-Minded Men* that do not appear in the received collation can be found in commonplace books and commentaries.) Most of Huangfu Mi's accounts are derived from previous recountings in a wide range of classical writings. Some are spare and iconographic, but others contain information found nowhere else. Many of the individuals turn up in a broad array of sources, as well as in other collections of biographies of extraordinary men, including Daoist and other hagiographies. Although ostensibly they were hidden individuals, high-minded men have been conspicuous throughout the centuries and into modern times. Their stories convey cultural values and content, and some are patently inspirational; if nothing else, they may serve to, in the words of the Venerable Pang, bequeath peace.

FURTHER READING

For discussions of reclusion in Chinese culture, see Alan Berkowitz, *Patterns of Disengagement: The Practice and Portrayal of Reclusion in Early Medieval China* (Palo Alto, Calif.: Stanford University Press, 2000), and "Social and Cultural Dimensions of Reclusion in Early Medieval China," in *Philosophy and Religion in Early Medieval China*, ed. Alan K. L. Chan and Yuet-Keung Lo (Albany: State University of New York Press, 2010), 291–318; and Aat Vervoorn, *Men of the Cliffs and Caves: The Development of the Chinese Eremitic Tradition to the End of the Han Dynasty* (Hong Kong: Chinese University Press, 1990). On Huangfu Mi, see also Dominik Declercq, *Writing Against the State: Political Rhetorics in Third and Fourth Century China* (Leiden: Brill, 1998), 159–205.

HUANGFU MI 皇甫謐

Accounts of High-Minded Men (Gao shi zhuan 高士傳)

PREFACE

Confucius stated that "[King Wu of Zhou] called to office those disengaged persons, and the people turned their hearts toward him." Master Hongya 洪崖 established the Way of High-Mindedness during the age of the earliest emperors, and Xu You 許由 and Shanjuan 善卷 would not let down their resolve during the reigns of Tang 唐 and Yu 虞 [i.e., the idealized times of the legendary emperors Yao and Shun]. On account of this, in [the *Classic of*] *Changes* there are the implications of [gifts to worthy men consisting of] "bundled silk," and in [the

Record of] Rites there is the institution of [ritually bestowing] "dark-colored pe-
cuniary silks." The poets issued forth the song of "White Colt" [about the flight
of the worthy man from an unworthy court]; the Spring and Autumn [Annals]
extolled the integrity of Zizang 子臧 [who declined the throne on principle];
and according to the Monthly Ordinances of the Hall of Clarity, during the final
month of spring, one should "extend invitations to renowned gentlemen and
pay ceremony to worthy ones." This being the case, then, gentlemen who loftily
made renunciations were the ones promoted by the regal government, serving
the function of curbing corruption and quelling avarice.

Many are those [men in reclusion] who were omitted or passed over by the
historian [Sima Qian 司馬遷] and Ban [Gu] 班固 [in their comprehensive histories Records of the Historian and History of Han]. Liang Hong eulogized disengaged persons, and Su Shun classified high-minded men. Some, in also recording cases of letting down one's resolve, were indiscriminate and adulterated.
Others selected from the Qin and Han of recent times and did not reach back
to the distant past. Now, when we contemplate on these men, we especially
cherish what they have established; how much more so should we acclaim their
virtue and extol their deeds!

I, Mi, have selected from past and present the men of eight ages who themselves were not humbled by a king or a lord and whose reputations were not
dissipated by the passage of time, from [the time of] Yao down to the [present
times of the] Wei 魏, more than ninety men in all. All those who may [simply]
have held fast to their resolve in the manner of [Bo] Yi 伯夷 and [Shu] Qi 叔齊
[who starved to death in the mountains rather than associate with a ruler they
thought to be unworthy], whose chosen acts mayhap were like those of the two
Gong 龔 [Gong Sheng 龔勝, who starved himself to death rather than serve the
court of the "usurper" Wang Mang 王莽, and Gong She 龔舍, who often was
paired with Gong Sheng as a literary reference], I do not record.

Written by Huangfu Mi

CHAOFU 巢父 (THE NEST-DWELLER, TIME OF THE LEGENDARY EMPEROR YAO 堯)

The so-called Nest-Dweller was a "hidden man" [i.e., a man in reclusion] of the
time of [the legendary emperor] Yao. He lived in the mountains and did not pursue worldly gain. Old in years, he slept atop a tree in a nest he made, so people
of the time called him the Nest-Dweller. When Yao wished to cede his rule to
Xu You 許由, Xu You told this to the Nest-Dweller, who said, "Why do you not
hide yourself and keep your brilliance inside? It's as if you're no friend of
mine." He then pushed him down with a blow to the chest. Xu You felt mortified and could not compose himself, then went over to a clear and cold stream
and rinsed out his ears and wiped his eyes, saying, "In making him listen to

those covetous words, I have betrayed my friend." Thereupon he departed, and they did not see each other for the rest of their lives.

XU YOU 許由 (TIME OF THE LEGENDARY EMPEROR YAO)

Xu You, whose courtesy name was Wuzhong 武仲, was a man from Huaili in Yangcheng. He was a person who adhered to dutiful conduct and followed the path of uprightness. He would not sit at an inappropriate placement, would not eat inappropriate victuals. He later went into reclusion amid the marshes and fertile lands. When Yao wished to cede his rule to Xu You, he told Xu You, "When sun and moon have come out, yet one does not extinguish the candle's flame, then in providing illumination, is that not unavailing? When timely rain has fallen, yet one still irrigates and waters, then in providing moisture, is that not just making work? Now you, sir, are so well established that all under heaven is ordered; yet still I act as your surrogate. I regard myself as inadequate and request to convey the rule of the empire to you." Xu You replied, "As you have set order to the empire, the empire already is in good order; were I still to replace you, would I be doing it for a name? A name is the guest of reality; would I be doing it to be a guest? When the wren nests in the deep woods, it takes no more than a branch. When the mole rat drinks from the river, it does no more than fill its belly. Go home and desist, my lord! I have no use at all for the empire. Even when the kitchen man has not put order to the kitchen, the surrogate of the ancestors who is leading the sacrificial ceremonies certainly will not leap over the goblets and platters to replace him." He did not accept [the invitation] and escaped.

Nieque 齧缺 [Xu You's teacher] met up with Xu You and asked, "Where are you off to?" Xu You replied, "I'm escaping Yao." Nieque asked, "What are you referring to?" Xu You answered, "Now, Yao understands how worthy men benefit the empire, yet he does not understand how they cheat the empire. It is only people other than the worthies who understand this." Xu You thenceforth hid out plowing in the area of the central of the Five Sacred Peaks [i.e., Song shan], at the base of Ji Mountain on the northern bank of the Ying River. For the rest of his life he showed no desire to govern the empire.

Yao once again summoned Xu You to be the leader of the nine states. Xu You did not even wish to hear about it and rinsed out his ears on the bank of the Ying. Just then his friend, Chaofu [Nest-Dweller], was leading over his young calf to water it. Seeing Xu You rinsing his ears, he asked the reason. Xu You replied, "Yao wished to summon me to be the leader of the nine states. I loathed hearing his words and for this reason rinsed my ears." The Nest-Dweller said, "If you were to place yourself on a high cliff or in a deep vale, where roads used by men do not reach, who would be able to see you? You purposely flit about, wishing to be noticed, seeking your fame and renown. You have fouled my calf's mouth." He led his calf upstream to water it.

When Xu You died, he was buried at the top of Mount Ji. Also called Xu You's Mountain, it is located a bit more than ten *li* south of Yangcheng. Yao subsequently visited his grave and gave him the posthumous title of Lord of Ji Mountain 箕山公, and thus his spirit could receive sacrifices accessory to those provided to the Five Sacred Peaks. From generation to generation he has been presented with sacrificial offerings, and this practice continues until today.

PIQIU GONG 披裘公 (THE FUR-CLOAKED ELDER, SIXTH CENTURY B.C.E.)

The Fur-Cloaked Elder was a man from Wu. Jizi of Yanling 延陵季子 [i.e., Duke of Wu] went traveling and noticed some gold left behind on the road. He looked over to the Fur-Cloaked Elder and told him to take the gold. The Elder threw down his sickle, stared fixedly, waved him off, and said, "How lofty is your position in life, yet how base is your regard for people. In the fifth month [around July], I wear a fur cloak and carry firewood on my back; how at all could I be one who would pick up [other people's] gold?" Jizi was greatly surprised. When he apologized and asked for his name, the Elder said, "You, my man, are one who judges on the basis of outward appearance; how could you merit my telling you my name?"

LAOZI LI ER 老子李耳 (SIXTH CENTURY B.C.E.?)

Laozi, Li Er, courtesy name of Boyang 伯陽, was a man from Chen. He was born during the time of the Yin dynasty and served as principal historian for the Zhou. He was devoted to nourishing his vital essence and *qi*. He placed value on being receptive and did not make a show of himself. He transferred to the position of historian and conservator of the archives, where he remained for more than eighty years. The *Records of the Historian* says that it was for more than two hundred years. At the time he was known as a hidden princely man. He was given the posthumous appellation "Dan" [Long-Eared]. When Confucius went to Zhou, he visited Laozi. Recognizing him as a sage, Confucius took him as his teacher. Later, when the virtue of the Zhou declined, Laozi mounted a cart pulled by a black ox and entered the area of the Great Qin [i.e., the farthermost western-border regions], to go through the western pass. The guardian of the pass, Yin Xi 尹喜, had observed the ethereal emanations and knew of his arrival in advance. So, he posted a description, blocked the way, and waited for him. Finally, Laozi arrived as expected. Yin Xi compelled him to compose writings, so he wrote down the *Classic of the Way and Virtue* [*Daodejing* 道德經, or *Laozi* 老子] in more than five thousand words. Laozi is considered the patriarch of the lineage of Daoist teachings. Because he was old in years, his writing was known as the *Laozi* [*The Aged Master*].

LAOLAIZI 老萊子 (SIXTH CENTURY B.C.E.?)

The one known as Laolaizi was a man from Chu. Meeting a time when the world was in disorder, he fled from the world and farmed on the sunny side of Meng Mountain. Aster and reed served for his walls; tumbleweed and artemisia were used for his room. Branches and timber served for his bed; yarrow and mugwort were used for his mat. He drank from the streams and ate wild pulses; cultivating the mountains, he sowed and planted. Someone spoke of him to the king of Chu, and the king of Chu thereupon arrived by carriage at Laolaizi's gate. Laizi just then was weaving a basket. The king said, "I would humbly wish to trouble you, Master, with looking after the government." Laolaizi said, "I assent." The king departed. Laolaizi's wife returned from gathering wood and said, "Did you agree to it?" Laolai said, "It is so." His wife then said, "Your wife has heard that one who can feed you with wine and meat can follow up with whip and cane. One who can draw plans for you with office and salary can follow up with the executioner's ax. Your wife is someone who is unable to submit to the control of others." His wife then threw down her basket and departed. Laolaizi also followed his wife, and they stopped when they had reached Jiangnan [the territory south of the Yangzi]. They said, "The hairs and feathers of birds and beasts can be woven into clothing, and their leftover kernels are sufficient for food." Confucius once heard of their rationale, and furrowing his brows he took on a renewed countenance over it. Laolaizi composed writings amounting to fifteen rolls, which spoke of the utility of the lineage of Daoist teachings. No one knows how he came to his end.

YAN HUI 顔回 (ALSO KNOWN AS ZIYUAN 子淵, FL. EARLY SIXTH—LATE FIFTH CENTURY B.C.E.)

Yan Hui, courtesy name of Ziyuan, was a man from Lu. He was a disciple of Confucius. He was poor but he found joy in the Way. He withdrew to reside in the humble alleyways, sleeping with crooked elbow [for his pillow]. Confucius said, "Hui, you've come from a family that is poor, and you live in the most modest circumstances. Why do you not take an official position?" Hui replied, "I do not wish to serve in office. I possess fifty *mu* of land [a bit less than twenty acres] outside the city wall, sufficient enough to provide porridge and gruel, and ten *mu* of gardens inside the wall, sufficient enough to produce silk and hemp. Drumming out music [on the *qin*] in the modes of *gong* and *shang* is sufficient enough for my amusement. I internalize what I have heard from you, my Master, and this is sufficient for my happiness. For what would I wish to take up official service?" Confucius was moved and took on a renewed countenance and said, "Excellent! are Hui's convictions."

YUAN XIAN 原憲 (ALSO KNOWN AS ZISI 子思, EARLY SIXTH–LATE FIFTH CENTURY B.C.E.)

Yuan Xian, courtesy name of Zisi, was a man from Song. He was a disciple of Confucius and resided in Lu. His poor small hut had grass growing on its thatched roof, and his overgrown broken door had a mulberry tree for its central hinge. The tiny jar-mouth windows of the two rooms were shut with coarse cloth. It leaked from above and was damp from below, yet he sat with square posture and strummed his *qin* [zither]. When Zigong 子貢 [another of Confucius's disciples, also known as Duanmu Ci 端木賜], serving as grand councillor in Wei, passed the cultivated greens and pulses, in his harnessed quadriga linked with steeds, he entered the impoverished hamlet, where alleyways were too narrow for a carriage: he had come to visit Yuan Xian. Yuan Xian in leather cap and flat sandals, with a plant stalk as his cane, came to answer the door. Zigong said, "Ai, how distressed you are, my good sir." Xian said to him in response, "I, Xian, have heard that if one lacks wealth, it is called poverty. If one studies the Way yet is not able to put it into practice, it is called distress. As for me, Xian, I am impoverished but I am not distressed. Now, to go about with an eye to getting ahead in the world; to make acquaintances looking to build gainful associations; to use study to brag to others, and teaching to show off oneself; to use humaneness and righteousness to bring to bear evil doings; to use carriages and horses purely for ornament: these are things that I, Xian, could not bear to do." Zigong shrank back with a mortified look and, to the end of his life, was ashamed at the error of his words.

ZHUANG ZHOU 莊周 (ALSO COMMONLY REFERRED TO AS ZHUANGZI, FL. EARLY FOURTH–LATE THIRD CENTURY B.C.E.)

Zhuang Zhou was a man from Meng in the state of Song. When young he studied the *Laozi* and worked as a deputy officer in the Lacquer Garden [archives]. He subsequently left the world behind, freed himself from constraint, and no longer served in office. Of kings, lords, and men of consequence, not one could obtain his services in any particular capacity. King Wei of Chu 楚威王 sent his grandees with hundreds in gold to invite Zhuang Zhou to serve at court. Zhou just then was fishing on the banks of the Pu River; grasping his fishing cane, he did not pay them heed. He said, "I have heard that in Chu there is a sacred tortoise that has been dead for two thousand years. Wrapped and kept in a basket, it is stored in the temple hall. Would this tortoise prefer being regarded as precious, having his bones preserved without anything for it to do? Or would it prefer to be living and dragging its tail in the mud?" The grandees said, "It simply would rather drag its tail in the mud." Zhuangzi said, "Be off. I am just now dragging my tail in the mud." Someone else invited Zhou, with coins worth thousands in gold, to serve as prime minister. Zhou replied, "Do you not see the sacrificial ox used in the suburban sacrificial rites? It is clothed in patterned embroidery and fed grasses and pulses. At the moment it is led into the great temple, it wishes it were an orphan piglet, but can it get its wish?" To the end of his life, he did not serve in office.

THE ADEPT BY THE RIVER 河上丈人 (HESHANG ZHANGREN, FL. THIRD CENTURY B.C.E.)

It is not known from which state the one known as Heshang Zhangren came. He had a keen understanding of the arts of Laozi and did not disclose his family and personal names. He resided by the banks of the [Yellow] River and wrote *Commentary to the* Laozi *by Line and Section*, and for this reason he was known to the world as the Adept by the River. At the end of the Warring States period, when the feudal lords were vying with one another, all the eloquent strategists overcame one another with power and position. Only the Adept hid himself in reclusion, practicing the Way. He did not decline in health even when he aged. He passed on his vocation to Anqisheng and, with this, came to be considered as a patriarch of a lineage of Daoist teachings.

THE FOUR HOARYHEADS 四皓 (SI HAO, FL. EARLY THIRD–LATE SECOND CENTURY B.C.E.)

The so-called Four Hoaryheads were all from Zhi in He'nei [north of Luoyang, near modern Jiyuan xian, Henan] or, according to one source, from Ji [northeast of modern Xinxiang City, Henan, west of modern Ji xian]. The first was called Dongyuan Gong 東園公 [Elder of the Eastern Garden]; the second, Luli Xiansheng 用里先生 [Master from Lu Hamlet]; the third, Qili Ji 綺里季 [Younger One from Qi Hamlet]; and the fourth, Xia Huanggong 夏黃公 [Venerable Huang from Xia]. They all practiced cultivating the Way and refining themselves; if not for a higher purpose, they would be unmoved. During the time of the First Emperor of Qin, they perceived the tyrannical way of the Qin government and withdrew into the mountains of Lantian [around eighteen and a half miles southeast of the capital], composing a song, which goes:

Hazy so hazy, the high mountains;	莫莫高山
The deep valley twists and twines.	深谷逶迤
Fulgent, refulgent, the purple polypore:	曄曄紫芝
With it we remedy hunger.	可以療飢
The ages of Yao and Shun are distant,	唐虞世遠
Where might we find a home?	吾將何歸

Horses in fours, baldachins tall—	駟馬高蓋
The troubles they bring too great.	其憂甚大
Wealth and nobility may awe people,	富貴之畏人
but that can't compare with	不如
How being humble and poor frees the will.	貧賤之肆志

They then together set off into the Shangluo region [near Lantian], going into reclusion at Difei shan to await the settling of the world. When the Qin was overthrown, the Han Emperor Gao 高祖 heard of them and summoned them for office, but they did not go. They hid themselves deeply in the Southern Mountains; they refused to compromise themselves.

YAN ZUN 嚴遵 (ALSO KNOWN AS ZHUANG ZUN 莊遵 OR YAN JUNPING 嚴君平, FIRST CENTURY B.C.E.)

Yan Zun, courtesy name of Junping, was a man of Shu [modern Sichuan]. He lived in reclusion and did not serve in office. He often told fortunes in the Chengdu market. Daily, when he had earned the hundred in cash that would be enough to provide for himself, his prognosticating would cease, and he would let down his curtain [and close up shop] to occupy himself with writing. Yang Xiong 揚雄 [53 B.C.E.–18 C.E.] had followed him as his teacher when young and repeatedly praised his virtue. When Li Qiang 李強 [first century B.C.E.] became regional governor of Yizhou, he said in delight, "If I were to get Junping as a staff retainer, he would be all I would need." Yang Xiong replied, "If you go with full and proper ceremony, you might be able to see him in person, but you will not be able to get him to acquiesce." [Marshal of State] Wang Feng 王鳳 [d. 22 B.C.E.] sought to have associations with Junping, but he refused.

In Shu there was a wealthy man named Luo Chong 羅沖, who asked Junping, "For what reason do you not serve in office?" Junping answered, "I do not have the means to set forth." When Chong collected for Junping a cart and horse, clothing and food, Junping said, "I simply have an ailment; it is not that I am lacking. I have an excess, and you, sir, [have] an insufficiency. How could an insufficiency be of service to an excess?" Chong said, "I have ten thousand in gold and you are lacking even a picul-weight. Now you say you've got an excess—is that not erroneous?" Junping replied, "Not so. Previously I stayed in your home. When others had turned in, still you hustled and bustled without rest. Morning and night you are all ahurry, never ever having enough. Now, I do divinations as a profession; I do not even get out of bed, yet money arrives by itself. I still have a surplus of several hundreds, with dust on it an inch thick, and I do not know what to do with it. Is this not my having a surfeit and you not having enough?" Chong was greatly mortified. Junping said with a sigh, "What increases my goods harms my spirit; what makes my reputation destroys my self. It is for this reason that I do not serve." People of the time were won over.

THE OLD MAN FROM PENGCHENG 彭城老父 (PENGCHENG LAOFU, FIRST CENTURY B.C.E.–FIRST CENTURY C.E.)

The one referred to as the Old Man from Pengcheng was a hidden man [i.e., man in reclusion] from Chu. Seeing the dynastic house of Han in decline, he hid himself away and cultivated the Way, not working toward reputation or gain. At the time when the Old Man was over ninety years of age, [the usurper] Wang Mang 王莽 summoned to court [in 11 C.E.] the former imperial household grandee Gong Sheng 龔勝 [68 B.C.E.–11 C.E.], wishing to appoint him to the office of academic chancellor for the preceptors and companions of the heir designate. Gong Sheng felt shamed at the idea of serving two ruling houses, and when Mang pressed him, Sheng forthwith stopped eating and died. Mang's emissaries, as well as officials from the grand administrator of the commandery on down who gathered for the burial, numbered in the several hundreds. The Old Man was distressed that Sheng had come to disaster on account of his renown. So it was that he came in alone and wailed over Sheng in a terribly grievous manner. Soon he said, "Alas! Incense burns itself up on account of its fragrance; lamp oil depletes itself on account of its brightness. Master Gong in the end cut off prematurely his heavenly appointed years—he was no disciple of mine." His weeping then ended, and he left the crowd in a hurry. No one knew his identity.

LIANG HONG 梁鴻 (BEFORE 24–AFTER 80)

Liang Hong, courtesy name of Boluan 伯鸞, was a man from Pingling in Fufeng. Encountering a disordered age, he received training at the imperial academy, where he did not follow the vogue in the punctilious annotation of the Classics. When his studies were completed, he went to herd swine in the imperial hunting preserve. It happened that an unattended fire spread to another man's lodge, so Hong paid a visit to the man whose lodge had been burned down, to inquire about his losses. He repaid them entirely with his swine. When the owner of the lodge thought that it was still insufficient, Hong further personally went to reside there, where he proved to be an assiduous laborer. Neighborhood elders noticed that Hong was not an ordinary person, and rebuking the owner, they praised Hong as an honorable man. With this, the owner for the first time gave him respect and found him exceptional and returned every one of his pigs. Hong did not accept them and left to return home to his native place of residence.

The influential families admired his lofty integrity, and many wished to give [him] their daughters in marriage. Hong refused them all and did not choose any for his wife. A family named Meng 孟 from his same *xian* district had a daughter who was robust and unbecoming; they had selected matches for her, but she did not marry. When her parents asked her the reason, the daughter said, "It is my wish to get a worthy man like Liang Boluan." Hong heard about this and married her. When they were married, she entered his gates adorned for the first time with finery. For seven days Hong gave her no response. His wife then knelt and implored Hong, and Hong said, "I sought someone who dressed in a greatcoat of fur and coarse attire, one with whom I could live secluded deep in the mountains. But now you are clothed in fine silk damask and have applied cosmetic powder and kohl: how could this be what I wished for?" His wife said, "It was simply to observe my good man's will. Your wife, of course, has the attire for living in seclusion." She then changed her coiffure to a coiled bun and put on homespun attire and presented herself ready for manual labor. Hong was greatly pleased and said, "This truly is the wife of Liang Hong, one who is capable of attending to me!" He gave her the courtesy name of Deyao Meng Guang 德曜孟光 [Meng Guang of Resplendent Virtue].

After a while, they together entered into the Baling Mountains, making their living farming and weaving. Hong recited the [Classic of] Poetry and the [Classic of] Documents and found enjoyment in playing the qin [zither]. He looked up to and admired the high-minded men of former ages and so composed eulogies for twenty-four men, beginning with the Four Hoaryheads [Si hao]. Subsequently he headed east out through the pass, and when passing by the capital region, he composed "Song with Five Ai!s." The Suzong emperor 蕭宗 [Emperor Zhang 章帝, r. 75–88] sought out Hong but did not find him. Hong then changed his surname to Yunqi 運期 and his personal name to Yao 耀 and took the courtesy name of Houguang 侯光; he lived in the vicinity of Qi and Lu [in the area of modern Shandong] with his wife and children.

After a while he left again, going to Wu [in the southeast], where he lived under the aegis of [the landowner] Gao Botong 皋伯通, where he worked hulling grains for others. Each time he returned home, his wife would prepare his food and present his food tray raised to the level of her eyebrows [in deep respect]. When Botong looked into this, he found Hong to be exceptional and immediately lodged him in his house. Hong shut himself off in seclusion and composed writings totaling more than ten sections.

When he became ill, he informed his patron, "In the past, Jizi of Yanling was buried away between Ying and Bo and did not return to his native home. Take care not to ask my children to hold to mourning ritual and return me home." When he passed away, Botong and his associates sought out a grave site for him beside the tomb of [the local hero] Yaoli 要離 of Wu.

HAN KANG 韓康 (FL. CA. 147–167)

Han Kang, courtesy name of Boxiu 伯休, was a man from Baling in Jingzhao [outside the capital of Chang'an]. He often roamed the famous mountains in search of medicinal plants, which he sold in the Chang'an market. For more than thirty years. he would not haggle over prices. Once a girl was buying some simples from Kang, and she became angry when Kang held to his price.

She said, "Be you, man, Han Boxiu, and so no second price?" Kang said with a sigh, "I had desired to avoid a reputation, but now even little girls all know of me. Of what use could even medicines be?" So he ran off into the Baling Mountains. He was repeatedly summoned for postings as an erudite and in the imperial conveyance bureau, but he never went. During the time of Emperor Huan 桓帝 [r. 146–167], he was offered an appointment with full ceremonial offerings of bolts of dark silk and a comfortable carriage. An envoy with the imperial proclamation in hand met up with Kang, and Kang had no recourse but to feign acceptance. He excused himself from the comfortable carriage and rode alone in a brushwood cart. He went forth one dawn before the others and arrived at a way station, where the station head was just then sending out men and oxen to repair the roads and bridges because Master Han, Recipient of Imperial Summons, was due to pass by. Seeing Kang's brushwood cart and his cloth turban, he took Kang for an old peasant and requisitioned his ox. Kang immediately released it from its yoke and gave it to him. After a while the envoy arrived, and because the old man whose ox had been requisitioned was in fact the Recipient of Imperial Summons, the envoy wished to petition to have the station head executed. Kang said, "This is the result of an old man giving it up; what is the crime of the station head?" The envoy then desisted. Subsequently, along the way Kang ran away into hiding. He died in old age.

XU ZHI 徐穉 (97–168)

Xu Zhi, whose courtesy name was Ruzi 孺子, was a man of Nanchang in Yuzhang. When [he was] young, his classical learning and his conduct were the most exalted in Nanzhou. During the time of Emperor Huan [r. 146–167], Chen Fan 陳蕃 [d. 168] of Ru'nan was serving as grand administrator of Yuzhang and accordingly recommended Xu Zhi to the court. From this moment on, Zhi was put forward five times [in the categories of] Filial and Incorrupt or Worthy and Excellent, but he did not accede to any of them. He was repeatedly summoned for appointment in the offices of the Three Dukes, but he did not proceed; never once did he answer to their decrees. Yet when one of them died, he would personally go and mourn. The Grand Administrator, Huang Qiong 黃瓊, also had summoned Zhi earlier, and when Qiong died [in 164] and was returned home for burial in Jiangxia, as soon as Zhi heard, he picked up a satchel and traveled more than thirty li by foot from Yuzhang to Qiong's tomb in Jiangxia, where he offered sacrificial libations and wept for him. Later he refused three summonses from the imperial offices and subsequently died in old age.

GUAN NING 管寧 (158–241)

Guan Ning, courtesy name of You'an 幼安, was a man from Zhuxu in Beihai. At the close of the reign of Emperor Ling 靈帝 [r. 167–189], because the central states had at that moment fallen into turmoil, Ning and his friend Bing Yuan 邴原 [d. 217] crossed the sea to reside under the auspices of Gongsun Du 公孫度 [d. 204], the Grand Councillor of Liaodong, who greeted them with the ceremonial respect of having no one else present in his offices. Later, when the troubles in the central states were somewhat settled, many people returned southward to their home. Only Ning did not return. During the Huangchu period 黃初 [220–226], Hua Xin 華歆 [157–231] recommended Ning for imperial office [in 223]. Ning knew that Gongsun Yuan 公孫淵 [d. 238] was certain to cause disturbances [in Liaodong], so using the imperial summons as his reason, he took his leave and returned home. Ning was appointed to the position of Grand Palace Grandee, but he vehemently declined to accede to the office. All in all, Ning received imperial summons and appointment ten times and ceremonially [received] the bestowal of carriage and clothing four times. He always sat on the same wooden couch [kneeling in proper posture], and after fifty-five years of never once sitting with splayed legs, the places on the couch where he positioned his knees were worn through. He always wore a cloth skirt and a raccoon-dog fur jacket; only when he would offer sacrifice to his ancestors would he wear an old formal cloth garment and wear a cloth turban on his head as well. The Liaodong government had his likeness painted in the prefectural offices, giving it the title the "Worthy One."

ZHENG XUAN 鄭玄 (127–200)

Zheng Xuan, courtesy name Kangcheng 康成, was a man from Gaomi in Beihai. His eighth-generation ancestor Chong 崇 [late first century B.C.E.] worked in the Secretariat during the Han. When young, Xuan was fond of study. He was more than eight *chi* in height, with long and beautiful whiskers and eyebrows, and his physical aspect and countenance were exceedingly arresting. He was highly proficient in the *Classic of Filial Piety* [*Xiao jing* 孝經] and the *Analects* [*Lunyu* 論語], and he was likewise expert on *Mr. Jing's* [*Yijing*] *Jing shi* [*Yijing* 京氏 [易經], the *Gongyang Commentary* to the *Spring and Autumn Annals* [*Gongyang Chunqiu* 公羊春秋], the *Three Standards Calendrical System* [*San zheng li* 三正曆], the *Nine Chapters on the Mathematical Arts* [*Jiu zhang suan shu* 九章算數], the *Offices of Zhou* [*Zhou guan* 周官], the *Record of Rites* [*Liji* 禮記], and *Mr. Zuo's Commentary on the Spring and Autumn Annals* [*Zuo shi Chunqiu* 左氏春秋]. Generalissimo He Jin 何進 [d. 189] summoned Xuan for office, and when both the province and the district coerced him, he had no recourse but to pay a visit to Jin. Jin set out a low table and armrest for formal ritual reception [of respected elders] in order to receive Xuan, but Xuan came to see Jin wearing an [informal] cloth turban; he stayed one night and then ran off. The imperial offices summoned him more than ten times in all, but he never acceded.

PANG GONG 龐公 (FL. LATE SECOND CENTURY C.E.)

The one known as Venerable Pang [Pang Gong] was a man from Xiangyang in the Southern Commandery. He lived to the south of the Xian hills and never once entered the city compound. He and his wife treated each other with the respect accorded a guest. The Inspector of Jingzhou, Liu Biao 劉表 [142–208; post held from 190 to 195], repeatedly had extended invitations to him but could not get him to comply. So he personally went to inquire after him and said, "How could preserving intact a single person compare with preserving intact all under heaven?" Venerable Pang laughed and said, "The wild goose and the gray crane nest atop the tall forests and in the evening have their place to perch. The turtle and the alligator make their dens at the bottom of the deepest abyss and at night have their place of lodging. Now, the choice of what to adopt and what to reject, when to act and when to refrain from action, likewise are the nest and den of a man. As such, each but finds his place to perch or lodge; it is not all under heaven that he would hold for his own." With this, he excused himself to till the knoll while his wife and children weeded ahead [of him]. Liu Biao pointed to them and asked, "If you, sir, would dwell in hardship amid the furrowed fields and not consent to office and emolument, then what will your descendants have to bequeath to their posterity?" Venerable Pang replied, "People of the world all bequeath them peril; today I alone bequeath them peace. What I bequeath might be different, but it is not that I pass down nothing." Biao heaved a sigh and departed. Later, leading his wife and children, Venerable Pang climbed Deer Gate Mountain [Lumen shan], where he gathered medicinal plants, never to turn back.

[*Gaoshi zhuan* 高士傳, in *SBBY* (based on a *Han Wei congshu* 漢魏叢書 edition); also in *Gujin yishi* 古今逸史 (reprint of Ming edition)]

21. Classifications of People and Conduct

Liu Shao's *Treatise on Personality* and Liu Yiqing's *Recent Anecdotes from the Talk of the Ages*

JACK W. CHEN

Both the *Treatise on Personality* (*Renwu zhi* 人物志) and *Recent Anecdotes from the Talk of the Ages* (*Shishuo xinyu* 世說新語) emerged from the early medieval practice of evaluating character traits and personalities (*renlun jianshi* 人倫鑑識).[1] Many scholars have noted that in the early medieval period, philosophical and literary subjectivity, as well as personal selfhood and self-consciousness, began. Nevertheless, even though there may have been much interest in the concept of the person, as opposed to normative social roles, it is difficult to say whether this constituted an authentically free notion of selfhood or was merely an expansion of typological models.

Systematized character evaluation can be traced to the Han dynasty, when the state began to consider personal morality as a criterion for recommending and selecting candidates for political office. The *Comprehensive History of Institutions* (*Tongdian* 通典), compiled by Du You 杜佑 (735–812), records that the interest in recruiting virtuous, talented men from all over the empire began with Han Gaozu 漢高祖 (r. 202–195 B.C.E.). By the time of the Han Emperor Wu 漢武帝 (r. 141–87 B.C.E.), the government began to announce the criteria for recruitment, seeking men who were "worthy and excellent" (*xianliang* 賢良) and "square and proper" (*fangzheng* 方正), men of "plain speech" (*zhiyan* 直言) and "unstinting remonstrance" (*jijian* 極諫).[2] Emperor Wu singled out the category of "filial and incorrupt" (*xiaolian* 孝廉) for particular emphasis, ordering that all the commanderies submit one candidate in this category.[3] Although these characterological classes were expanded in the Eastern Han to include other, less ostensibly Confucian categories—such as "unique conduct" (*duxing* 獨行), "lofty integrity" (*gaojie* 高節), and "pure and untainted" (*qingbai* 清白)—the category of *xiaolian* remained the most prominent.[4]

TREATISE ON PERSONALITY

If the Han state created categories by which to classify and grade its potential officials, intellectuals of the period following the Han themselves began to form categories for understanding different personality types and abilities. The first text translated here, the *Treatise on Personality*, was written by Liu Shao 劉劭 (third century).[5] According to his biography in the *Record of the Three Kingdoms* (*Sanguo zhi* 三國志), Liu Shao was a minor official during the last reign of the Han but rose during the Wei dynasty to assume the duties of Secretarial Court Gentleman (*shangshu lang* 尚書郎) and, under the Wei Emperor Ming 魏明帝 (r. 226–239), was promoted to governor of Chenliu (in modern-day Henan) and ultimately Cavalier Attendant-in-Ordinary (*Sanqi changshi* 散騎常侍). In the Jingchu reign (237–239), Liu was commanded to create procedures for examining candidates for metropolitan offices.[6] While Liu's proposal is no longer extant, his *Treatise on Personality* survives as valuable documentation of how the state might be imagined as viewing the selection and employment of talented men.

The *Treatise*'s textual history is fairly straightforward. It is mentioned in Liu Shao's biography, which would have been written and presented by 297, when the *Record of the Three Kingdoms* was completed. Although Liu Shao himself probably considered his work to be in the intellectual lineage of Confucius, the bibliography of the *History of the Sui* (*Sui shu* 隋書) assigns it to the category of the School of Names (*mingjia* 名家), where it is found in all subsequent dynastic bibliographies.[7] However, while Liu's work may be seen as an extension of philosophical concerns in the School of Names (i.e., the analysis of how language matches reality), his treatise is much more practical in many ways, focusing on how best to recognize and use particular personality types. That is, this is a work of eminently useful philosophy, looking to bring order to the world of human talents so that they could be properly employed by the sovereign.

I should note that the translation of *renwu* 人物 as "personality" is far from perfect. In a sense, Liu Shao is describing what in English would be called "personhood," but in the original sense of person as *persona* (i.e., "role"). I use the word "personality" to recall the sense of persona and also to indicate Liu's actual interest in the psychological delineation of abilities from character traits.

In the first chapter of the *Treatise on Personality*, Liu Shao discusses the basis of human nature, beginning with the endowments in each person of yin and yang and of the Five Phases (*wuxing* 五行). The endowment of yin and yang make up a person's intellect in the respective faculties of theoretical and practical knowledge. After this, he turns to the Five Phases—wood, metal, water, earth, and fire—which are what constitute a person's physical form. Wood becomes bone; metal becomes muscle and connective tissue; fire becomes breath; earth becomes flesh; and water becomes blood. Each of these in turn has a primary capacity (*cai* 才), though Liu Shao is not consistent here in correlating these capacities with the five physical aspects that engender them. What is clear is that bone engenders humaneness (*ren* 仁), breath engenders propriety (*li* 禮), and muscle engenders righteousness (*yi* 義). He also states that the corporeal body (*ti* 體), probably meaning "flesh," engenders trustworthiness (*xin* 信). However, where he should have blood, he instead mentions "aspect" (*se* 色), which engenders wisdom (*zhi* 智). These he calls the "Five Constants" (*wuchang* 五常) and argues that all of them are discernible in people's manners and appearance.

Only in the sage, however, are the Five Constants fully and perfectly realized and in harmonious balance—what Liu Shao calls the Centered Mean (*zhongyong* 中庸). In those men who fall short of the sagely ideal, the qualities of the Five Constants are incomplete, therefore requiring evaluation as how a deficit in one quality affects the personality. The categories that he provides for evaluation are the Nine Marks (*jiuzheng* 九徵). Liu Shao divides all men into three grades based on their possession of the Nine Marks. Again, the sage is the highest grade, as he possesses all nine of these marks in perfect harmony. The next grade is the person who possesses some part of all these nine aspects—this is a person of "virtuous conduct" (*dexing* 德行). The last grade is a person who possesses only one of the nine aspects. This is a person of "partial ability" (*piancai* 偏才) and, for Liu Shao, is not worth discussing. From the Nine Marks, Liu Shao goes on to delineate the twelve aspects of the second grade of men—those of "virtuous conduct" who fall short of sagely perfection yet are nonetheless superior to the lowest grade. He then explains how each type may be used and what the limitations of each are, providing a more formal taxonomy of these twelve categories and citing historical examples to illustrate his points. His use of these examples thus presents the work as a system of historicizing categorization rather than as an abstract discussion of psychology.

Throughout the treatise, Liu Shao distinguishes between the ruler, who is able to encompass all talents and evaluate their worth, and the individual talents that find employment by the state. Just as each individual talent is partial, the man who possesses that talent has only a partial perspective on the entire range of talents.

There is one complete translation of the *Treatise on Personality* into English with a detailed introductory study: Liu Shao, *The Study of Human Abilities: The Jen wu chih of Liu Shao*, trans. John K. Shryock (New Haven, Conn.: American Oriental Society, 1937). For translations into modern Chinese, see Fu Junlian 伏俊璉, *Renwu zhi yizhu* 人物志譯注 (Shanghai: Shanghai guji chubanshe, 2008); and Wu Jiaju 吳家駒, trans. and ed., *Xinyi Renwu zhi* 新譯人物志 (Taibei: Sanmin shuju, 2003). An important discussion of the work is by Tang Yongtong 湯用彤, "Du *Renwu zhi*" 讀 (人物志), in *Tang Yongtong quanji* 湯用彤全集, vol. 4 (Shijiazhuang: Hebei renmin chubanshe, 2000).

Liu Shao 劉劭

Treatise on Personality (*Renwu zhi* 人物志)

PREFACE (*ZIXU* 自序) (EXCERPT)

Regarding what is excellent in sages and worthies, nothing is more excellent than intelligence; and regarding what is to be valued in intelligence, nothing is more valuable than being able to make discernments among men. If one indeed has the knowledge to discern among men, then the numerous kinds of abilities would gain rank, and the various undertakings would flourish and succeed.

CHAPTER 1. THE NINE MARKS (*JIUZHENG* 九徵) (EXCERPT)

The most valuable of the substantive qualities and capabilities of men are balance and harmony. The qualities of balance and harmony necessarily reside in unseasoned blandness and flavorlessness, thereby making it possible to blend and form the five capacities and, in the course of its transformations, follow normative patterns. Therefore, in observing men and investigating their substantive qualities, one must first investigate them in an unseasoned state and only afterward seek after their qualities of astute intelligence. Astute intelligence is the essence of yin and yang. When yin and yang are pure and in harmony, there is insight within and clarity without. Because the sages are radiantly enlightened, they possess both these excellent [qualities] at the same time, knowing what is subtle and what is manifest. If one is not a sage, one cannot pursue both. Thus a gentleman who has clear understanding may grasp the trigger of the action but be unaware of more profound considerations; and a person who has profound considerations may know the principles of quiescence but have difficulty acting with haste. It is like fire or the sun shining outward but being able to make visible what is inward, and metal or water illuminating inward but cannot cast light outward. The significance of these two may perhaps be considered the distinction between yin and yang.

The distinctions among the Five Constants are arrayed as the Five Virtues. Thus the virtue of wood is to be gentle yet upright and pliant yet resolute. The virtue of metal is to be hard and solid, potent and resolute. The virtue of water is to be honest and respectful, reasonable and reverent. The virtue of earth is to be magnanimous yet strict, gentle yet principled. The virtue of fire is to be sparing yet fluent, illuminating and purifying. Although transformations of substances are without limit, they nonetheless depend on these five substances. Therefore, the marks of hardness and pliancy, illumination and fluency, and integrity and resoluteness, are manifest in form and appearance, perceptible in voice and expression, and produced in feeling and evocation, each conforming to its outward appearance.

Therefore it is said that when things are produced, they have forms and that forms have spirits and essences. If one is able to discern essences and spirits, then one can exhaustively comprehend principle and human nature. What fully explains human nature are the marks of the Nine Substantive Qualities. In this way, then, the substantive quality of balance or imbalance resides in the spirit; the fact of illumination or benightedness resides in the essence; the disposition of courage or cowardice resides in the muscles; the roots of strength or weakness resides in the bones; the determination of rashness and tranquillity resides in the breath; the feelings of sorrow and delight reside in the aspect; the forms of decline and robustness reside in the manner; the actions of improper and proper conduct reside in the appearance; and the condition of slowness or swiftness resides in speech.

CHAPTER 2. DIFFERENTIATIONS OF SUBSTANCE
(*TIBIE* 體別) (EXCERPT)

Thus those who strive unyieldingly violate [the Central Mean], while those who are conventionally bound will not reach it. Both the unyielding striver and the conventionally bound go against the middle position and therefore have some measure of excellence but also some deficiencies in normative principle.

1. Therefore, if a person is severe and upright, hard and resolute, his capacity will reside in rectification and correction, but his deficiency will be enthusiasm for exposing the faults of others.[8]

2. If he is pliant and conforming, peaceful and empathetic, his fine points will be his magnanimity and tolerance, but his deficiency will be a lack of decisiveness.

3. If he is virile, fierce, heroic, and robust, his abilities will reside in bold audacity, but his deficiency will be a surfeit of jealousy.

4. If he is refined and decent, vigilant and cautious, his excellence will be respectful deference, but his deficiency will be a surfeit of suspicion.

5. If he is forceful and exemplary, firm and unyielding, his function will reside in acting as a pillar of support, but his deficiency will be single-minded stubbornness.

6. If he can discuss and argue with analytical and deductive reasoning, then his abilities will reside in the explication of difficult problems, but his deficiency will be a lack of stability and discipline.

7. If he is charitable and generous to all, his greatness will be the broad reach of his associations, but his deficiency will be murkiness and taint.

8. If he has purity of principle and is incorruptible, his integrity will reside in frugality and steadfastness, but his deficiency will be conformity and close-mindedness.

9. In his actions, if he is unaffected and without constraints, his achievements will be advancement and ascension, but his deficiency will be negligence and inattention to detail.

10. If he is profound and tranquil, shrewd and crafty, his essence will reside in obscure subtleties, but his deficiency will be a slowness to act.

11. If he is honest and candid, straightforward and forthright, his quality will be a heartfelt sincerity, but his deficiency will be a lack of subtlety.

12. If he has much wisdom and an ability to suppress his feelings, he will be able to weigh tactics and strategies, but his deficiency will be equivocation.

CHAPTER 3. CATEGORIZING VOCATIONS
(*LIUYE* 流業) (EXCERPT)

There are twelve vocations of these human categories; the exemplar of purity, the jurist, the strategist, the minister of state [literally, "limb of the state"], the man of capacious ability, the moralist, the man of efficacy, the wise man of ideas, the literary man, the scholar, the rhetorician, and the hero.

1. Now, the man whose virtuous conduct is lofty and sublime, whose manner and deportment could be used as a model—this is what is called the exemplar of purity; it is the category of Ji Zha and Yan Ying.[9]

2. The man who establishes laws and institutions, strengthening the state and enriching the people—this is what is called the jurist; it is the category of Guan Zhong and Shang Yang.[10]

3. The one whose thoughts can penetrate the transformations of the Way, whose tactics and plots are marvelous and sublime, this is what is called the strategist; it is the category of Fan Li and Zhang Liang.[11]

4. One who possesses these three capacities at the same time, in whom the three capacities are complete, his virtue would be sufficient to advance the customs and manners of the world; his laws would be sufficient to govern all under Heaven; and his strategies would be sufficient to plan victory before the ancestral temple. This is what is called the minister of state; it is the category of Yi Yin and Lü Wang.[12]

5. One who possesses the three capacities at the same time, but in whom all the three capacities are minimal, his virtue would be sufficient to lead one state; his laws would be sufficient to govern a city-state; and his strategies would be sufficient to weigh what is appropriate to the situation. This is what is called the man of capacious ability; it is the category of Zichan and Ximen Bao.[13]

6. One may possess the three categories at the same time but in different measure; each also has its category. One who belongs to the category of pure exemplar but lacks expansive empathy—such a man enjoys sneering and fault-finding even as he draws distinctions between right and wrong. This is what is called the moralist; it is the category of Zixia and his ilk.[14]

7. One who belongs to the category of jurist but not be able to think of new ideas or make long-term schemes yet is able to perform the responsibilities of a single office, implementing ideas with crafty intelligence—this is what is called the man of efficacy; it is the category of Zhang Chang and Zhao Guanghan.[15]

8. One may belong to the category of strategist but not be able to create institutions or bequeath rules yet still be able to weigh how best to meet vicissitudes. He has a surfeit of judgment and wisdom but a deficit of public-minded uprightness. This is what is called the wise man of ideas; it is the category of Chen Ping and Han Anguo.[16]

9. In general, all the preceding eight vocations have as a basis the three capacities of virtue, law, and strategy. Therefore, despite the kinds of distinctions as between waves and currents [i.e., in terms of primacy], they all are capacities of governing affairs. Now, one who is able to compose essays and write accounts, this is what is called the literary man; it is the category of Sima Qian and Ban Gu.[17]

10. One who is able to transmit the achievements of the sages but is not able to handle affairs and implement policies, this is what is called the scholar; it is the category of Master Mao and Master Guan.[18]

11. One whose arguments do not concern the Way but whose statements and responses have Heaven-endowed fluency—this is what is called the rhetorician; it is the category of Yue Yi and Cao Qiusheng.[19]

12. One whose courage and might exceed [those of] the common herd and whose talents and strategies surpass [those of] other men—this is what is called the valiant hero; this is the category of Bai Qi and Han Xin.[20]

These twelve capacities all describe the responsibilities of officials; the virtue of the ruler is not mentioned among them. The one who possesses the ruler's virtue is astutely intelligent and has the quality of unseasoned blandness; he is able to assemble and direct the host of capacities and does not himself take on these responsibilities. Therefore, when the way of the ruler is established, each of the twelve capacities will have its own responsibility.

CHAPTER 7. HAVING KNOWLEDGE OF MEN (*JIESHI* 接識) (EXCERPT)

From the very beginning, it has been extremely difficult to discern among men. Nevertheless, many scholars believe themselves capable of discerning among men. Therefore, when they use themselves as a measure when observing other people, they believe that they are capable of making discernments. However, when one observes other people investigating people, then one decides that they have no knowledge of this. Why is this so? It is because they can know the excellent [qualities] of those who are similar to themselves but sometimes miss the excellent [qualities] of those who do not have the same abilities.

[Li Chongzhi 李崇智, ed., *Renwu zhi jiaojian* 人物志校箋
(Chengdu: Ba Shu shushe, 2001)]

RECENT ANECDOTES FROM THE TALK OF THE AGES

The collection of anecdotes that make up *Recent Anecdotes from the Talk of the Ages* may be read as a textual representation of the political, intellectual, and cultural life of Chinese elites from the end of the Han dynasty to the end of the Jin dynasty. It was compiled by (or in the name of) Liu Yiqing 劉義慶 (403–444), a prince of the royal Song house and the nephew of the dynastic founder Liu Yu 劉裕 (365–422). While the collection is often cited as the main surviving record of "pure conversation" (*qingtan* 清談), a cultural practice prevalent in the Wei–Jin period, it also can be seen as an attempt to categorize human behavior in a way that both recalls and diverges from Liu Shao's work.

Recent Anecdotes from the Talk of the Ages consists of thirty-six chapter headings, each describing a character attribute, behavior, or activity. Some of the most famous historical and cultural figures of the time appear in its 1,130 anecdotes, including Cao Cao 曹操, Cao Pi 曹丕, Ruan Ji 阮籍, Xi Kang 嵇康, Lu Ji 陸機, Wang Xizhi 王羲之, Xie An 謝安, and Gu Kaizhi 顧愷之. The historical reliability of the work is often debated, although the commentary by Liu Jun 劉峻 (458–521/522) helps clear up and corroborate some of the details. In any case, traditional readers probably would not have viewed the work as primarily one of history. Traditional bibliography places the collection under the philosophical rubric of "small talk" (*xiaoshuo* 小說) rather than either history or literature.[21] What *xiaoshuo* meant was not the later sense of "fiction" but what

Han bibliographers understood as "local sayings" or "street gossip" and what the Sui bibliographers began to see as anecdotal materials and narrative writings that lacked historiographic reliability. There was a certain sense of miscellany or hodgepodge in how the *xiaoshuo* category was conceived, and in regard to *Recent Anecdotes from the Talk of the Ages*, what is clear is that the selection and arrangement of anecdotes seem to suggest a purpose other than a purely factual recording or imaginative representation.

Another ongoing debate over the reading of *Recent Anecdotes from the Talk of the Ages* pertains to its relationship to Confucian and Daoist moral values. Many of the categories in the collection, however, cannot be identified as primarily Confucian or Daoist, and in many ways, it is more useful to think of the work as a taxonomy of attitudes and behaviors, a gathering of historical exemplars, or illustrative examples from history. Then *Recent Anecdotes from the Talk of the Ages* can be seen as developing the historicizing taxonomies of Liu Shao's *Treatise on Personality*. At the same time, the difference between the two works is in *Recent Anecdotes from the Talk of the Ages'* aesthetic interest in its subjects, the way in which a particular theme is introduced in one anecdote and then repeated and complicated in other anecdotes. This rhetorical arrangement is found not only within individual chapters but often across chapters. The first four selections of the following translation deal with Hua Xin 華歆 (157–231), byname Ziyu 子魚. Hua Xin served as a member of the Secretariat during the Han and was elevated to Censor in Chief (*Yushi daifu* 御史大夫) under Cao Cao. After Cao Pi ascended the throne, Hua was made Counselor in Chief (*Xiangguo* 相國). Although Hua Xin was a prominent political figure, he was hardly an interesting intellectual figure. Nevertheless, in reading through four of the five anecdotes that concern him, we may see why the anecdotes can be read sequentially and what the juxtaposition of the anecdotes tells us about the figures involved.

FURTHER READING

For other modern critical editions of *Recent Anecdotes from the Talk of the Ages*, see Xu Zhen'e 徐震堮, ed., *Shishuo xinyu jiaojian* 世說新語校箋, 2 vols. (Beijing: Zhonghua shuju, 1984); and Zhu Zhuyu 朱鑄禹, ed., *Shishuo xinyu huijiao jizhu* 世說新語彙校集注 (Shanghai: Shanghai guji chubanshe, 2002). The standard translation into English is Liu I-ch'ing [Liu Yiqing], comp., *Shih-shuo Hsin-yü: A New Account of the Tales of the World*, 2nd ed., trans. Richard B. Mather (Ann Arbor: Center for Chinese Studies, University of Michigan, 2002). There are several translations into modern Chinese, including Liu Shizhen 劉士鎮 and Liu Kaihua 劉開驊, trans. and eds., *Shishuo xinyu quanyi* 世說新語全譯 (Guiyang: Guizhou renmin chubanshe, 2008); and Zhang Weizhi 張撝之, trans. and ed., *Shishuo xinyu yizhu* 世說新語譯注 (Shanghai: Shanghai guji chubanshe, 1996). Secondary studies include Wai-yee Li, "*Shishuo xinyu* and the Emergence of Aesthetic Self-Consciousness in the Chinese Tradition," in *Chinese Aesthetics: The Ordering of Literature, the Arts, and the Universe in the Six Dynasties*, ed. Zong-qi Cai (Honolulu: University of Hawai'i Press, 2004), 237–76; Nanxiu Qian, *Spirit and Self in Medieval China: The Shih-shuo hsin-yü and Its Legacy* (Honolulu: University of Hawai'i Press, 2001); and Zhou Yiliang 周一良, "*Shishuo xinyu* he zuozhe Liu Yiqing shenshi de kaocha" 世說新語和作者劉義慶身世的考察, in *Wei Jin Nanbeichao shi lunji xubian* 魏晉南北朝史論集續編 (Beijing: Beijing daxue chubanshe, 1991).

Liu Yiqing 劉義慶

Recent Anecdotes from the Talk of the Ages
(*Shishuo xinyu* 世說新語) (excerpts)

I. ON VIRTUOUS CONDUCT (*DEXING* 德行)

10. Hua Xin treated his sons and younger brothers with extreme meticulousness. Although they might be in the private chambers of their own house, he would be as strict as if he were following court ritual regulations. Chen Yuan-fang [Chen Ji] and his younger brother Chen Chen embraced the path of unconstrained affection.[22] Nevertheless, inside these two sets of gates, neither side lacked for harmonious delight and tranquillity.

11. Guan Ning and Hua Xin were together hoeing vegetables in the garden when they saw on the ground a piece of gold.[23] Guan continued hoeing as if the gold were no different from a tile or stone, but Hua picked it up and only then threw it away. On a different occasion, they were sharing a mat while reading when a distinguished personage riding in a lavish carriage passed by the gate. Ning continued reading as before, but Xin dropped his book and went out to see. Ning then cut the mat in half and said, "You are no longer my friend."

12. Wang Lang was always extolling Hua Xin for his powers of understanding.[24] On the day of the Year-End Sacrifice, Xin had the custom of gathering his sons and nephews for a feast. Wang imitated him. Someone told this story to Zhang Hua, and Zhang said, "For Wang imitating Hua, it was always a matter of surface appearances, and thus Wang would just end up more unlike him than before."[25]

13. Hua Xin and Wang Lang were together sailing in a boat and fleeing the political upheavals. A person wanted to go with them, but Xin refused him. Lang said, "Fortunately, there is still room in the boat, so why couldn't we let him join us?" Later, when the rebel troops were in pursuit and about to overtake them, Wang wanted to throw out the man they had picked up. Xin said,

"This is exactly why I originally had doubts about this. Since we have already given in to his pleading, how can we abandon him during an emergency?" And so they brought him along, rescuing him, just as before. Based on this, the world has evaluated the relative merits of Hua and Wang.

The question of judgment is inherent in the anecdotes of the collection, and even those who have the good judgment to admire the moral qualities of a friend may themselves be lacking. One of the most celebrated figures in *Recent Anecdotes from the Talk of the Ages* is Ruan Ji 阮籍 (210–263), byname Sizong 嗣宗. Ruan Ji was perhaps the greatest poet of the age as well as a talented musician. He was one of the Seven Sages of the Bamboo Grove and took a principled (as well as pragmatic) stance against involvement in the ruthless world of Jin politics. He makes nearly twenty appearances in the collection. Ruan Ji's first appearance is worth noting, as the passage thematizes and complicates the question of public recognition and reputation that runs throughout the pages of the book. He is the object of praise by a prince, and yet what he is being praised for is his own refusal to participate in the culture of appraisal.

15. Sima Zhao, Prince Wen of the Jin, praised Ruan Ji for his absolute discretion, saying that every time he spoke with him, Ruan's words were always mysterious and remote, never once praising or criticizing another's character.[26]

The question of character evaluation can also be seen in the two anecdotes about Wang Rong 王戎 (234–305), the youngest of the Seven Sages. Wang suffers in reputation because of his later decision to serve Sima Zhao, becoming Director of State Affairs (*Shangshu ling* 尚書令) and, later, Minister of Education (*Situ* 司徒). In his biography in the *Jin shu*, Wang also was acclaimed for possessing "the ability to recognize human character types" (*renlun jianshi* 人倫鑑識).

16. Wang Rong once said, "I have dwelled with Xi Kang for twenty years, and never once have I seen on him an expression of either delight or vexation."[27]

17. Wang Rong and He Qiao met with the "great bereavement" [the death of a parent] at the same time, and both were praised for their filiality.[28] Wang was reduced to "chicken bone"–like thinness and kept to his bed. He wept and cried while completing the ritual observances. Emperor Wu said to Liu Yi, "Have you been observing the behavior of Wang and He? I have heard that He's sorrow and suffering exceeds ritual observance, causing people to worry about him."[29] Yi said, "Although He Qiao he has completed all ritual observances, he has suffered no injury to spirit or health. Although Wang Rong did not complete the observances, his sorrow brought such devastation that his bones stick out. I consider that He Qiao exemplifies filiality while alive but that Wang Rong exemplifies filiality unto death. Your Majesty should not worry about Qiao but, instead, about Rong."

II. ON SPEECH (*YANYU* 言語)

It is said that *Recent Anecdotes from the Talk of the Ages* is the primary source for the practice of "pure conversation" (*qingtan* 清談), which developed out of the political practice of "pure criticism" (*qingyi* 清議) of the late Han. But whereas the practitioners of "pure criticism" sought to evaluate the moral character of potential candidates for office, those of "pure conversation" seemed to be engaged in a rarefied game of wit and skill. The stakes might be only one's reputation or dignity, but these are not always low stakes.

1. Bian Rang appeared before Yuan Lang and seemed ill at ease.[30] Lang said, "In the past, when Yao summoned Xu You, Xu You betrayed no anxiety.[31] Why are you, sir, 'putting on your clothes upside down'?"[32] Rang replied, "Your Excellency has just taken up the post, and the virtue of Yao has not yet been manifested. This is why this lowly person is 'putting on his clothes upside down.'"

IV. ON LITERARY LEARNING (*WENXUE* 文學)

In many ways, the practice of "pure conversation" was agonistic, and the participants entered an exchange as if they were in combat. Here, two of the most famous figures in the "mysterious learning" (*xuanxue* 玄學) movement meet for the first time, with humiliating results for one.

6. He Yan was the Minister of Personnel and had much influence and prestige. Guests who came to converse with him often filled all the seats in his hall. Wang Bi, who was not yet of capping age [not yet twenty years], went to see him. Yan had heard of Bi's reputation, and so he selected some of the successful theses from past conversations and said to Bi, "These theses I consider to be unsurpassable. Would you like to discuss them further?" Bi thereupon raised his disputations, and the entire audience considered that Yan had been defeated. At that point, Bi himself assumed the roles of both guest and host in argument, reversing roles for several bouts. This was something that no one in the audience could equal.

Despite the fluidity of Wang Bi's performance, the position that one took in argument was not supposed to be completely divorced from one's personal beliefs and views. Skill in argument was not supposed to be utter sophistry but was supposed to reflect the uniqueness of one's ideas and abilities. The exigency of a triumphant performance, however, sometimes could take priority over originality of thought, as in the following anecdote about the rival Buddhist masters Yu Fakai 于法開 (ca. 310–370) and Zhi Dun 支遁 (314–366). It is useful to know that Yu Fakai came to be considered the head of the "School of Stored Consciousness" (*shihan zong* 識含宗), which argued that phenomenal reality is like the stored images of dreaming but that true reality is emptiness. Zhi Dun, the creator of the "Matter as Such doctrine" (*jise yi* 即色義), argued that true reality is found in material phenomena, and thus there is no actual distinction between emptiness and material reality.

45. At the beginning, Yu Fakai competed over the primacy of his reputation with Zhi Dun, but later, public feeling gradually favored Zhi. In his heart, Yu was distressed and thereafter concealed his traces at the foot of the mountains of Shan Prefecture.[33] He sent a disciple to go to the capital, ordering him to pass through Kuaiji. At this time, Zhi was engaged in lecturing on the *Shorter Prajñāpāramitā Sutra*. Fakai prepared his disciple by saying, "When you arrive, Zhi Dun should be in the midst of discussing such-and-such a section in his lecture." He accordingly instructed the disciple how to attack with disputations for several tens of bouts, saying, "In the past, these are the points for which Zhi's arguments were not sound." The disciple, as directed, went to pay a visit to Zhi Dun. Zhi was indeed in engaged in lecturing on the particular passage, and so the disciple carefully proceeded to relate Fakai's ideas. The argument went back and forth for quite some time, but in the end, Zhi was defeated. In a sharply bitter voice, Zhi cried, "Why should you, sir, have come here bearing another man's commission?"

VI. ELEGANCE AND DIGNITY (*YALIANG* 雅量)

Although *Recent Anecdotes from the Talk of the Ages* is a categorized work, sorting historical anecdotes into typological traits, activities, and behaviors, it also is a work profoundly concerned with irreducible natures and personalities, anticipating the very idea of selfhood.

2. When Xi Kang was about to be executed in the Eastern Market, his spirits and manner did not change. Taking out his zither, he plucked its strings, playing "Guangling Melody."[34] When the tune ended, he said, "Yuan Zhun once asked to learn this melody, but I was jealously stubborn and would not share it with him. On this day, 'Guangling Melody' will be lost forever!"[35] The three thousand students of the Grand Academy submitted petitions, pleading to make Xi Kang their teacher, but this was not granted. Not long after, Sima Zhao felt regret for this.

What often seems to be valued implicitly by the selection and narration of anecdotes is not only the rigidly unchanging character but also the one that is indifferent to the prospect of promotion, good fortune, and advantage. It has been remarked that much of "pure conversation" was concerned with explicating Daoist philosophy. The *Zhuangzi*, in particular, was valued for its advocacy of maintaining a natural equanimity regarding the vicissitudes of life. The intellectual argument would become an ethical one, a vision of how to live life. The following anecdote is about Wang Xizhi 王羲之 (309–ca. 365), the most famous calligrapher in Chinese history.

19. When Chief Defender Chi Jian was in Jingkou, he sent one of his trusted stewards to give a letter to Chief Counselor Wang Dao, asking for a son-in-law.[36] The counselor told Chi's messenger, "Go to the eastern wing and choose whomever you like." The steward returned and reported to Chi, saying, "All the young masters of the Wang household can be considered fine. When they heard that someone had come seeking a son-in-law, they all put on distinguished airs. Only one fellow lay on the eastern bed with his belly showing, as if he had not heard." Lord Chi said, "He's precisely the one I want!" When he paid his visit, it turned out to be Wang Xizhi, and he accordingly gave his daughter to him in marriage.

One of the most famous examples of this equanimity concerns Xie An 謝安 (320–385). At the time, Xie's nephew Xie Xuan 謝玄 (343–388) was in charge of defending the Eastern Jin against the invasion of Fu Jian 苻堅 (338–385), Emperor Xuanzhao 宣昭 (r. 357–385) of the Former Qin. Xie An's younger brother Xie Shi 謝石 (327–388) was also present. The Eastern Jin forces were massively outnumbered by those of Fu Jian, who had unified Northern China and was now seeking to annex the South.

35. Lord Xie was playing chess with someone when suddenly a letter arrived from Xie Xuan, who was at the Huai River. Xie glanced through the letter and, without a word, leisurely turned back to the chessboard. When his guests asked whether the news from the Huai River was good or bad, he replied, "My boys have crushed the thug." In expression and comportment, he acted no differently than usual.

VII. ON KNOWING AND EVALUATING (*SHIJIAN* 識鑒)

The power of recognizing human abilities and character traits has its own section in *Recent Anecdotes from the Talk of the Ages*. The following anecdote is an evaluation of the character of the great warlord Cao Cao 曹操 (155–220), though this differs from the famous version preserved in the *Record of the Three Kingdoms*.

In his youth, Lord Cao met with Qiao Xuan.[37] Xuan told him, "The empire is currently in disorder, and the throngs of heroes contend like tigers with one another. The one who will set things into rule and order—is that not you, sir? [Even though] you will truly be a hero in an age of disorder, [you will be] a treacherous thug in a well-governed one. I regret bitterly that I already am old and will not see you rise to wealth and power. I will entrust the welfare of my sons and grandsons to you."

VIII. APPRECIATION AND PRAISE (*SHANGYU* 賞譽)

In Qiao Xuan's evaluation of Cao Cao, there is still the Han interest in correlating moral character and public function. In the following example, Wang Rong characterizes (*mu* 目) the person of Shan Tao 山濤 (205–283), another of the Seven Sages, and one who, like Wang, eventually went to serve the Simas.

10. Wang Rong characterized Shan Tao as follows: "Like uncarved jade or unrefined gold, people all admire how precious he is, but no one knows how to name his capacity."

Characterization may have sought to crystallize the essence of another person in a few well-chosen words, but the poetic nature of those words often indicated the virtuosic skill necessary both to make the characterization and to understand it. The following example deals with the monk Śrīmitra (Gaozuo daoren 高坐道人, fl. ca. 310–340).

48. People of the time wanted to characterize Śrīmitra but could not. Huan Yi asked Zhou Yi about it, and Marquis Zhou said, "He could be called 'transcendent and bright.'"[38] Lord Huan said, "His spirit reveals itself from within the deep."

IX. GRADATIONS OF EXCELLENCE (*PINZAO* 品藻)

While the most memorable character evaluations tended toward an aesthetic remove, some that also portray the reactions of those being evaluated point to the underlying differentials of power and prestige. Wen Qiao 溫嶠 (288–329), byname Taizhen 太真, was Governor of Jiang Province and a leading general of the Eastern Jin.

25. When the age evaluated Wen Qiao, he was ranked the highest of the second grade of men who crossed the Yangzi. When the famous fellows of the time came together to talk about personalities and were just about to finish with the first grade, Wen always turned pale.

XIV. APPEARANCE AND CONDUCT (*RONGZHI* 容止)

The ability to evaluate other people is grounded in the attempt to grasp the true nature of the person being evaluated, to see past appearances and to understand what is really taking place. Again, the act of evaluation is often reflective, demonstrating the worth of the subject as well as the virtuosity of the evaluator.

36. Xie Xuan said this of his uncle Xie An: "When roaming in leisure, he indeed has no need of high-toned chanting. He only need solemnly sit, pinch

his nose, and let his eyes drift all around, and then he naturally has the appearance of one dwelling in the hills and marshes."

XXIII. THE FREE AND UNINHIBITED (RENDAN 任誕)

It has often been noted that the rise of individualism can be found in the Wei–Jin period, though often what is seen as evidence might be considered anticonventionalism rather than authentic individuality.

2. When Ruan Ji was mourning the death of his mother, he was among the guests of Prince Wen of Jin, helping himself to wine and meat. Metropolitan Commandant He Zeng was also present and said, "Your Lordship rules the empire through filial devotion, yet Ruan Ji, in a period of heavy mourning, appears among the lord's guests drinking wine and eating meat—it would be appropriate to banish him beyond the seas in order to rectify the instruction of popular customs."[39] Prince Wen said, "Ji, as emaciated and worn as he is—and you still are unable to empathize with him? Why is this? Moreover, to drink wine and eat meat when one is ill certainly accords with mourning observances!" Ji went on eating and drinking without pause, his spirits and expression entirely self-composed.

XXV. SCORNING AND SNEERING (PAITIAO 排調)

To be sure, even masters of self-possession may find themselves on the receiving end of a witticism and thus the momentary loser of a verbal exchange. Wang Rong's response to Ruan Ji is significant not only as a snappy rejoinder but also as a double comment on both Ruan Ji's lapse into conventionalism and the connoisseurly elitism inherent in regimes of wit.

4. Xi Kang, Ruan Ji, Shan Tao, and Liu Ling were in the bamboo grove drinking heavily.[40] Afterward, Wang Rong came over. Ruan Ji said, "That vulgar character has once again come to ruin a person's mood." Wang Rong laughed, saying, "You people's mood—is it indeed something that can be ruined?"

XXXV. ON BESOTTED DELUSION (HUONI 惑溺)

Women make occasional appearances in the *Recent Anecdotes from the Talk of the Ages*, though they are far from prominently featured. This last passage takes up the interesting question of whether adherence to normative roles should take precedence over the expression of true feelings and intimacy. Its inclusion in the chapter "On Besotted Delusion" suggests one reading, yet the story itself remains ambiguous.

6. Wang Rong's wife often addressed him with the familiar pronoun *qing*. Rong said, "For a wife to address her husband with *qing* is not reverent according

to ritual etiquette. In the future, don't do this again." His wife said, "I am intimate with you; I love you; this is why I call you [*qing*] *qing*. If I don't call you [*qing*] *qing*, who else would have the right to call you [*qing*] *qing*?" Thereafter, Wang let her do as she wanted.

[Yang Yong 楊勇, ed., *Shishuo xinyu jiaojian* 世說新語校箋, 4 vols.
(Beijing: Zhonghua shuju, 2006)]

NOTES

1. In translating the title for *Shishuo xinyu*, I decided not to follow the now-conventional translation by Richard B. Mather, who rendered it as *Shih-shuo Hsin-yü: A New Account of the Tales of the World*, 2nd ed. (Ann Arbor: Center for Chinese Studies, University of Michigan, 2002). The phrase *shishuo* is more accurately translated as "talk from successive ages," whereas *xinyu* is closer to "recent sayings." However, I have taken the liberty of rendering *yu* as "anecdotes," since "sayings" in English denote proverbs or adages rather than the kind of anecdotal literature found in the text. The last issue is whether the relationship between *shishuo* and *xinyu* should be coordinate ("and") or genitive ("of"). Although there is no definitive answer, I have chosen a genitive rendering based on the assumption that the phrase *shishuo* likely invoked the title of an earlier Han dynasty work, titled simply *Shishuo*, and that *xinyu* is used to distinguish this later work from the Han text.

2. Du You 杜佑, comp., *Tongdian* 通典, 5 vols. (Beijing: Zhonghua shuju, 1984), 13.1.310.

3. *HS* 6.160, 167.

4. *HHS* 61.2042. For a discussion of this, see John Makeham, *Name and Actuality in Early Chinese Thought* (Albany: State University of New York Press, 1994), 100–103.

5. Note that Shao 劭 sometimes is written 邵.

6. For the biography of Liu Shao 劉劭, see *SGZ* 21.617–20. Liu's role in creating the metropolitan exams is mentioned also in *Tongdian* 14.327, 15.367.

7. *Sui shu* 34.1004.

8. The numbering is provided for the sake of clarity and is not in the original text.

9. Ji Zha 季札, a prince of Wu, lived during the Spring and Autumn period in the sixth century B.C.E. He declined the throne of Wu, as it would mean usurping the primogeniture of his elder brother, and instead traveled throughout the states. Yan Ying 晏嬰 (d. 493 B.C.E.) was a minister of Qi and traditionally considered the author of the *Spring and Autumn of Master Yan*. Both Ji and Yan were famed for their high moral standards and conduct.

10. Guan Zhong 管仲 (d. 645 B.C.E.) was the prime minister of Duke Huan of Qi 齊桓公 (r. 685–643 B.C.E.) during the Spring and Autumn period. Guan's political reforms reorganized the state by centralizing authority, and as a result, Duke Huan was able to become hegemon. Shang Yang 商鞅 (d. 338 B.C.E.) was a minister of Qin whose agricultural reforms and anti-merchant policies strengthened the state's control over the economy.

11. Fan Li 范蠡 served Goujian 勾踐 (r. 496–465 B.C.E.), King of Yue, at the end of the Spring and Autumn period and helped destroy the state of Wu, after which he retired. Zhang Liang 張良 (d. 187 B.C.E.) was the primary strategist of Liu Bang 劉邦 (256 or 247–195 B.C.E.), who reigned as Han Gaozu 漢高祖 (r. 202–195 B.C.E.).

12. Yi Yin 伊尹 was the great minister of Cheng Tang 成湯, king and founder of the Shang dynasty. Lü Wang 呂望 was an adviser to King Wu 武王 (r. 1046–1043 B.C.E.) of the Zhou dynasty during the conquest of the Shang.

13. Zichan 子產 (581–521 B.C.E.) was the prime minister in the state of Zheng, serving for more than forty years. Ximen Bao 西門豹 (fl. third century B.C.E.) was a magistrate during the Warring States period. He was famous for ending the cult of the River Earl 河伯, which required the regular sacrifice of maidens.

14. Zixia 子夏 (b. 507 B.C.E.), a famed disciple of Confucius, is traditionally credited with writing the *Gongyang Tradition* and the *Guliang Tradition*.

15. Zhang Chang 張敞 (d. 48 B.C.E.) was a famed official under Han Xuandi 漢宣帝 (r. 74–48 B.C.E.). He was appointed as governor of the capital region, holding the post for a remarkable nine years and suppressing violence and crime during his tenure. Zhao Guanghan 趙廣漢 (d. ca. 65 B.C.E.) was also famed for his long tenure as governor of the capital region under the reign of Han Xuandi. Zhao Guanghan was sentenced to death after attempting to impeach high-ranking government ministers and crossing members of the influential Huo family.

16. Chen Ping 陳平 (d. 178 B.C.E.) first served Xiang Yu 項羽 (232–202 B.C.E.) and then Liu Bang, becoming minister after the founding of the Han. He was famed for his cunning, and though he served under Empress Lü 呂后 (241–140 B.C.E.), he was instrumental in ensuring the defeat of her family's attempt to change the dynasty. Han Anguo 韓安國 (d. 127 B.C.E.) won notice for his participation in the pacification of Wu and Chu and later for his advocacy of maintaining treaties with the Xiongnu.

17. Sima Qian 司馬遷 (ca. 145–ca. 86 B.C.E.) completed the *Records of the Historian*, a project begun by his father. Ban Gu 班固 (d. 92) was the main author of the *Han shu*.

18. Master Mao 毛公 refers to Mao Heng 毛亨, the Western Han commentator of the *Classic of Poetry*. There was also a Master Mao the Younger, which refers to another *Poetry* specialist by the name of Mao Chang 毛萇. Master Guan 貫公 received instruction in the *Chunqiu Zuozhuan* 春秋左傳 from the famed writer and scholar Jia Yi 賈誼 (200–168 B.C.E.)

19. Yue Yi 樂毅 is best known as the general of Yan during the Warring States period who brought about the military defeat of Qi. Cao Qiusheng 曹丘生 was a skilled debater who lived during the reign of Han Wendi 漢文帝 (r. 180–157 B.C.E.).

20. Here, Liu Shao uses the phrase *xiaoxiong* 驍雄 instead of *xiongjie* 雄傑, the phrase he used in introducing the twelve categories. Bai Qi 白起 (d. 258 B.C.E.) was a general of Qin during the Warring States noted for both his skill with weaponry and his homicidal tendencies. Han Xin 韓信 (d. 196 B.C.E.) was the chief general of Liu Bang's army and famed for his strategic abilities. Both Bai Qi and Han Xin were eventually put to death by the regimes they served.

21. See, for example, *Sui shu* 29.1011.

22. Chen Ji 陳紀 (ca. 130–200), byname Yuanfang 元方; his younger brother Chen Chen 陳諶; and their father, Chen Shi 陳寔 (104–187), were known as the "Three Gentlemen" (*sanjun* 三君) and were famed for their high standards of morality.

23. Guan Ning 管寧 (158–241) traced his lineage back to the famed Spring and Autumn minister Guan Zhong 管仲. He fled the tumult at the end of the Han dynasty and refused to accept office under the Wei, despite the entreaties of both Wendi and Mingdi.

24. Wang Lang 王朗 (d. 228) was the Governor of Kuaiji under the Eastern Han, and after the founding of the Wei, he served in a number of high-ranking positions in the central government.

25. Zhang Hua 張華 (232–300) was a leading figure in both Jin politics and letters. His strategies helped Jin Wudi conquer Wu, and afterward he served in a number of influential positions in the court.

26. Sima Zhao 司馬昭 (211–265) was the second son of Sima Yi 司馬懿 (179–251) and the enfeoffed prince of Jin. He was responsible for the death of Cao Mao 曹髦 (241–260), the Wei puppet-ruler set on the throne by the Sima clan. Sima Zhao intended to take the throne himself but died before realizing his plan.

27. Xi Kang 嵇康 (223–262) is, with Ruan Ji 阮籍, the most prominent of the Seven Sages of the Bamboo Grove. He had close ties through marriage to the Wei royal house and thus devoted himself to literary pursuits and Daoist self-cultivation techniques after the rise of the Sima clan. He was famed for his poetry, musical abilities, and philosophical essays.

28. He Qiao 和嶠 (d. 292) began in the employment of Emperor Wu while the emperor was still crown prince, and rose to become Director of the Secretariat. His biography in the *Jin shu* notes that He Qiao possessed the ability "to evaluate human categories" (*li renlun* 理人倫).

29. Liu Yi 劉毅 (ca. 210–285), byname Zhongxiong 仲雄, was descended from the Han imperial clan. He served in the Secretariat and as Chancellor of the National University (*Guozi jijiu* 國子祭酒) and was valued by Wudi for his unyielding criticisms and honesty.

30. Bian Rang 邊讓 (d. ca. 196–220), byname Wenli 文禮, served as the Governor of Jiujiang but quit his post during the tumult of the Han's last decades. He was a literary writer known for his rhapsodies, one of which is included in his biography in the *Hou Han shu*. In the end, he was killed for slandering Cao Cao 曹操. Yuan Lang 袁閬 (fl. second century), byname Fenggao 奉高, does not seem to have ever held a high official position. The *Hou Han shu* notes only that Yuan served in the Labor Section (*gongcao* 功曹) of Runan.

31. The allusion is to the sage-king Yao, who sought to offer the throne to the moral exemplar Xu You 許由. But Xu You, upon hearing of this, fled and went into hiding.

32. This is a quotation from "The East Is Not Yet Bright" 東方未明 (no. 100) in the *Classic of Poetry*, a poem that describes the haste of an official summoned to morning court.

33. This refers to Mount Sheng 嵊 in modern Zhejiang Prefecture.

34. "Guangling Melody" dates back to the Han dynasty. In his "Rhapsody on the Qin" 琴賦, Xi Kang mentions the title.

35. Yuan Zhun 袁準 (fl. 265–274), byname Xiaoni 孝泥, held only low official posts through-out his life, devoting himself to other pursuits. He was famed for his moral rectitude.

36. Chi Jian 郗鑒 (269–339) and Wang Dao 王導 (276–339) were two of the most influential men of the early Eastern Jin.

37. Qiao Xuan 橋玄 (fl. second century), famed for his scholarship on the *Record of Rites*, held such prestigious offices as Minister of Works (*Sikong* 司空) and Minister of Education.

38. Huan Yi 桓彝 (275–328) and Zhou Yi 周顗 (269–322) were high-ranking officials in the Eastern Jin central government. Zhou Yi was also famed for his drunkenness while in office.

39. He Zeng 何曾 (199–278), a prominent official during the Wei, was part of the Sima fac-tion. He had a reputation for leading an extravagant life and for being jealous of others.

40. Liu Ling 劉伶 (d. ca. 265), one of the Seven Sages, was famed for his love of wine.

22. The Literary Community at the Court of the Liang Crown Prince

PING WANG

The court's patronage of men of letters can be traced back in Chinese history as early as the third century B.C.E. in the state of Chu (part of modern Hubei and Hunan Prefectures, south of the middle reaches of the Yangzi River). King Xiang of Chu 楚襄王 (297–263 B.C.E.) is said to have surrounded himself with notable literary figures such as Song Yu 宋玉, Tang Le 唐勒, and Jing Cuo 景差, who were "fond of words" and famous for writing in a genre known as *fu*.[1] Although all three men were said to be disciples of Qu Yuan 屈原, Song Yu excelled among the group, and two dozen *fu* attributed to him are still available to us. Many of these pieces start with a self-referential description of the court composition scene of competition for the royal patron's verbal and material award.[2]

During the earlier Han dynasty, literary activities flourished at the princely courts of Liu An 劉安, better known as the Prince of Huainan 淮南王 (179–122 B.C.E.), and Liu Wu 劉武, also known as the Prince of Liang 梁王 (d. 144 B.C.E.). Later, many of the writers employed at these princely residences came to the capital and served under the Han Emperor Wu (r. 140–87 B.C.E.). The illustrious career of Sima Xiangru 司馬相如 (179?–117 B.C.E.), one of best-known writers in premodern China, followed such a path. Sima Xiangru's piece on the imperial park, praising the might and magnificence of the Han imperial house through his superior command of literary language and nimble rhetoric, is an exemplary work of the genre *fu*.[3] Despite their success at writing, literary men like Sima Xiangru and, later, Yang Xiong 揚雄 (53 B.C.E.–18 C.E.) expressed great discontent with the limited practical and political role they and their writing served for the state. Their attempts to advise on policy were rarely taken seriously. Instead, writers were sometimes ranked with court jesters and comedians, whose main task was to divert and please the emperor. Deeply frustrated, Yang Xiong vowed to do away with *fu* writing, which he had come to see as a childish practice with no evident utility.

Indeed, writing that had a particular court function—such as edicts, petitions, memoranda, proclamations, admonitions, and even dirges and tomb inscriptions—had privileges denied to the equivalent of "pure literature." Beginning in the third century, literary men were, first and foremost, skilled drafters of official documents, and it was for this that they were hired, even though they were valued by posterity for their poetry. For example, the court of Cao Cao 曹操 (155–220) gathered many proficient writers of the day, among whom the most famous were Kong Rong 孔融 (153–208), Xu Gan 徐幹 (170–217), Wang Can 王粲 (177–217), Chen Lin 陳琳 (160?–217), Ying Yang 應瑒 (170?–217), Liu Zhen 劉楨 (170?–217), and Ruan Yu 阮瑀 (170?–212)—referred to as the Seven Masters of Jian'an (*Jian'an qizi* 建安七子) by Crown Prince Cao Pi 曹丕 (187–226). Cao Pi gives an account of these gatherings in a letter written in 212:

> I often reminisce about our past excursions in Nanpi. They were indeed unforgettable. We wonderfully contemplated the Six Classics and loitered among the Hundred Philosophers. Pellet chess was set up from time to time, and we would always finish with *liubo*.[4] Lofty conversation gladdened the heart, and the mournful music of zithers was pleasing to the ear. We galloped in the fields to the north and feasted in the lodges to the south, floated sweet melons on clear springs, and sank red plums in cold water. When the white sun disappeared, we carried on by the bright moon. Riding together we roamed the rear gardens. The carriage wheels moved slowly, and the entourage was silent. Cool breezes arose in the night, and a sad reed whistle softly moaned. Happiness left and sorrow emerged in its stead, leaving us woeful and melancholic. I would look around and comment that such joy would not last. You and everybody else thought I was right.[5]

Cao Pi's nostalgic account appealed strongly to patrons of later times, who not only carried out the same activities recorded here but also tried to outdo their predecessor. Cao Pi's account is a model and milestone in the history of the literary patronage in early medieval times. What is of interest here goes beyond the many salon activities, which ranged from serious textual studies and discussions to leisurely gaming and roaming. But it is the laying bare of a sentimental yearning for an idealized past and lamenting over time that is most affecting. Every aspect of the recorded events is filtered through the retrospective lens and affectionate tone of the Crown Prince of Wei, who had just lived through a plague that took the lives of many members of his court. Such a tragic loss would have made meaningless any differences and distinctions and reflected on the group's shared experience. Cao Zhi's contemplation of the ephemeral nature of human existence enveloped his memory of the group in a shroud of sadness and found resonance in the remembered activities. There, sad music and nature prompted the writers to lament the sorrowful fate of humankind. It is the same sentiment that reminded them of Cao Pi, and the key to their group identity is that shared moment of human empathy and literary sensitivity. Even though the excursions that Cao Pi described may not have been planned for the purpose of literature, they were made meaningful and memorable when literary expressions became the only appropriate medium for commemorating the group's experience.

The passage in Cao Pi's letter, frequently alluded to in practice and writing, may have been the first time that "literary group" and "literary patronage" were defined. Educated men gathered together for all kinds of reasons, and what made their gathering literary was the sense of camaraderie infusing their poetry. During the late fifth and early sixth centuries when members of the imperial court engaged men of talent and/or status for various projects and occasions, their poetic reports seldom failed to recall the same collective consciousness of time and human fate as expressed in Cao Pi's letter. The names of the Seven Masters and their Cao family patrons, the ambience of their excursions, their activities, and their conviviality were imitated by generations to come, especially during the Qi 齊 (479–502) and Liang 梁 (502–557) periods.

It is during these two Southern dynasties that we encounter a major revival of literary courts and, we could argue, that as a result, the art of poetry became important. Almost all the patrons of these literary courts were members of the Xiao clan, of which the best known is Xiao Ziliang 蕭子良 (460–494), whose group is known as the "Eight Companions of Jingling," Jingling being the name of the Qi prince's commandery.[6] *The History of Southern Qi (Nan Qi shu* 南齊書) gives an account of Xiao Ziliang's salon:

Ziliang had been pure and high-minded since he was young. He treated gifted men with courtesy and was fond of men of integrity. Always trusting, he was completely devoted to his guests. Men of learning and talent in the realm all came to gather at his court. He was fond of hosting grand gatherings. In the summer, when guests arrived, he would put out melons, beverages, and compote for them. To establish civil cultures, literary writings by aristocratic lads as well as court dignitaries were, in all cases, issued for instructional purposes or compiled as records. They engaged in literary and moralistic writings. The works by aristocratic lads and court dignitaries were all collected. In the fifth year [of the Yongming reign, i.e.,

487] . . . the prince moved to his villa at Jilong [Chicken Cage] Mountain. There he gathered scholars to copy the Five Classics and philosophical works of the hundred schools, and they compiled a thousand-*juan* work called *Essential Digest in Four Categories* [*Sibu yaolue* 四部要略] following the format of the imperial survey [*huanglan* 皇覽]. He summoned famous monks to lecture on the Buddhist dharma and expound on new chants for the sutras. Such a grand gathering of both monks and laymen was unprecedented since the establishment of the court in the south.[7]

Although preoccupied with scholarly and religious activities, almost all the members of Xiao Ziliang's salon were skilled in poetry. Indeed, sometimes literary talent served to secure one's membership:

Ziliang, prince of Jingling, opened up his Western Residence and summoned literateurs. [Wang] Sengru, together with imperial academy students Yu Xi, Qiu Guobin, Xiao Wenyan, Qiu Lingkai, Jiang Hong, Liu Xiaosun, all joined the salon for their excellence in literary diction. . . .

Ziliang, Prince of Jingling, used to gather scholars at night to write poems [within a length of time measured] in notches on candles. For a poem with four rhyming couplets, they would carve a notch of one inch. Wenyan said, "What is so difficult about composing a poem within the time it takes to burn one inch of the candle?" Then, together with Lingkai and Jiang Hong, they struck a bronze bowl to establish the rhyme. As soon as the sound faded, the poem was finished. And it was quite readable.[8]

During the Liang dynasty, Crown Prince Xiao Tong 蕭統 (501–531), most famous for his compilation of the *Wen xuan*, China's best-known literary anthology, also hosted scholars and writers at his court. The scale of his salon was reportedly unprecedented:

By nature, [the prince] was generous and amiable. Seldom did he show intense moods of happiness or anger. He attracted and brought in talented and learned men, whom he unfailingly appreciated. Often they deliberated on the Classics. Sometimes he discussed historical questions with the scholars. At leisure, they usually composed writings. At the time, there were nearly thirty thousand scrolls of books in the Eastern Palace. Famous men of the time were all gathered there. Literature had not flourished to this extent since the Jin and Song dynasties.[9]

Like Cao Pi and earlier literary patrons, Xiao Tong and his group wrote commemorative pieces about their excursions, some of which have a religious strain.

In the autumn of 521, the monk Zhizang 智藏 (458–522) hosted a Buddhist convention at the Kaishan temple and lectured on the *Nirvana Sutra*. Xiao Tong and his entourage made an excursion to Mount Zhong in order to attend this lecture, about which poems were written. Even though the occasion was Buddhist, the poems concentrate on describing the landscape and thus treat this event mainly as a group outing. In discussing these and similar poems by the Liang royal house, Cynthia Chennault explains "how landscapes are made Buddhist" and believes that a key feature is the "mention of Buddhist concepts, and also the transposing of Buddhism's sacred sites onto the Chinese landscape."[10] These poems do use some Buddhist terms and locales, and yet they also describe other topics, for example, literary companionship. The many allusions to Cao Pi's letter and the Jian'an writers underscore the convivial gathering and self-reflective versification. In other words, this is a literary event, or at least it was recorded and remembered as such.

The prince left us two poems regarding this event, one on the early-morning journey to the mountain and the other written at the conclusion of the lecture. Four members of his entourage wrote poems responding to his second poem, one of which was written by the senior official Lu Chui 陸倕 (470–526), a former member of the Eight Companions of Jingling. Lu Chui was a member of the renowned Lu family of Wujun 吳郡 and, as one of the best writers of his day, was acclaimed for his poem "On the One Who Appreciates Me" (*Gan zhiji fu* 感知己賦) and two imperial commissioned inscriptions: On the New Clepsydra (*Xin louke ming* 新鏤刻銘) and On the Stone Gate (*Shi que ming* 石闕銘).[11] Lu Chui served at the crown prince's court on and off for nearly two decades. Six of eleven couplets of Lu Chui's poem are a laudatory description of the geographical location of Mount Zhong and the Kaishan temple. The formality of the poet's referring to the Southern capital by the names of the Northern locales puts in perspective the significance of the crown prince's visit and thus gives the destination meaning rather than vice versa. That is, the poet makes the prince's excursion sound like an imperial inspection rather than a religious pilgrimage. The actual religious event is elided in favor of the context and the following banquet where the prince and his companions participated in a literary composition.

Also present on this occasion was Xiao Zixian 蕭子顯 (489–537), an imperial relative of the former Qi dynasty and a historian who drafted the history of the Southern Qi. Xiao's monograph on "literary writers" (*wenxue* 文學) is an important work of literary criticism,[12] whose view of writing is similar to Xiao Tong's. Xiao Zixian states how versification can express sentiment:

Looking back on my life, I was rather fond of writing. Although I have not achieved a name for myself, having the intention is enough. Ascending high, we gaze afar; arriving at the riverbank, we see friends off; wind stirs up on a spring morning; the moon shines on an autumn night. There are

early geese and young orioles, blooming flowers and fallen leaves. . . .
These all are occasions about which I cannot keep myself from writing.[13]

Xiao Zixian's matching poem gives a scenic description of the capital, the
mountain, the journey of the prince's entourage, and a view of the capital's suburbs. The poem keeps the same rhyme as Lu Chui's poem—that is, the *geng* 庚
rhyme in the level, or first, tone. Xiao Tong's original poem has a slightly different rhyme—the *geng* 梗 rhyme in the *shang*, or third, tone.

The other two poems, in different rhymes, were written by two brothers
from the Pengcheng Liu family, Liu Xiaochuo 劉孝綽 (481–539) and Liu Xiaoyi
劉孝儀 (484–550). Like the other poets participating in the event, the Liu brothers do not emphasize what might have been the actual purpose of this trip—to
learn about Buddhist teachings—but instead focus on the trip to the mountain
and the banquet on the outskirts of the capital. Taken together, these poems
suggest a picture very similar to what Cao Pi wrote in his letter about literary
groups and patronage. Even though writing poetry seldom seems to be the actual function of a group activity, it always turns out to be the means and end in
the commemoration of whatever event it was in the first place.

FURTHER READING

For an introduction to early medieval literary groups, see Hu Dalei 胡大雷,
Zhonggu wenxue jituan 中古文學集團 (Guilin: Guangxi shifandaxue, 1996); and
Morino Shigeo 森野繁夫, *Rikuchō shi no kenkyū* 六朝詩の研究 (Tokyo: Daiichi
gakushusha, 1976), chaps. 1–3.

Xiao Tong 蕭統

On the Buddhist Convention Held at
Kaishan Temple 開善寺法會詩

The resting crow has not yet soared;	栖烏猶未翔
I ordered my chariot to set out from my mountain villa.	命駕出山莊
Twining and twisting, we ascend the horse ridge;	詰屈登馬嶺
4 Winding and bending, we enter the goat gut switchback.	迴互入羊腸
Gradually we can see the plain with luxuriant vegetation;	稍看原藹藹
After a while, dark blue peaks are in sight.	漸見岫蒼蒼
Falling stars are buried among distant trees;	落星埋遠樹
8 New fog arises with the morning sun.	新霧起朝陽
In the shaded pond, there swim morning geese;	陰池宿早雁

Cold wind urges on the night frost.　　　　　　　寒風催夜霜

This location is indeed serene and secluded;　　　兹地信閑寂

12　Quiet and spacious, there is only the dharma retreat.　清曠唯道場

On the jade tree, there is colored glass resembling water;[14]　玉樹瑠璃水

Feather canopies cover couches scented with crocus.[15]　羽帳鬱金床

Purple pillars are made of coral;　　　　　　　　紫柱珊瑚地

16　Divine screens are decorated with luminous pearls.　神幢明月璫

Holding onto lichen, we descended the stone steps;　牽蘿下石磴

Grasping cinnamon branches, we climbed the pine ridge.[16]　攀桂陟松梁

The gully is slanted, and the sun is about to hide;　澗斜日欲隱

20　Mist rises, and the building is half concealed.　　　煙生樓半藏

How distant and far is a thousand years?　　　　　千祀終何邁

A hundred generations all come to pay homage to　百代歸我皇
　　our emperor.

The divine power shines through without limit;　　神功照不極

24　The wise mirror is clear without equal.　　　　　睿鏡湛無方

The dharma wheel brightens the dark room;　　　法輪明暗室

Across the ocean of Buddha wisdom, boats of　　慧海渡慈航
　　mercy are ferried.

My roots to the world have long lacked cleansing;[17]　塵根久未洗

28　They wish to be moistened by the bestowed luster of dew.　希霑垂露光

Xiao Tong

Lecture Dismissed at Mount Zhong 鍾山解講詩

At clear dawn, we leave the Vista Garden;[18]　　　清宵出望園

In the morning, we arrive at Mount Zhong.　　　詰晨屆鍾嶺

Wheels about to move, literary companions mount　輪動文學乘
　　carriages;

4　Bell rung, guests follow quietly.　　　　　　　　笳鳴賓從靜

The sun has risen, yet cliffs still block the light;　曒出岩隱光

The moon has fallen into the shadows of the grove.　月落林餘影

Twisting and twining, the eight cinnamon　　　　糾紛八桂密
　　trees densely grow;

8　Rugged and rough, the road to the Second City is now　坡陀再城永
　　far away.[19]

I am fond of mountains and rivers;　　　　　　　伊予愛丘壑

Ascending high, I have reached the lofty site.　　登高至節景

Into the distance, I see a thousand chambers;　　迢遞觀千室

12　Meandering and extending, there are thousands　迤邐觀萬頃
　　of acres of land.[20]

The current gathering has now come to closure;	即事已如斯
Once again, we roam this splendid place.	重茲遊勝境
Essential principles have already been expounded;	精理既已詳
16 Mystic words also have been displayed.	玄言亦兼逞
Now I realize that the patchouli-belted person,	方知蕙帶人
Has made the "noisy marketplace" his easy hideout.	囂虛成易屏
Roaming my gaze, I have not yet enjoyed myself completely;	眺瞻情未終
20 But the Dragon Mirror[21] has quickly galloped away.	龍鏡忽遊騁
It is not that I take pleasure in dallying and roaming;	非曰樂逸遊
My true intention is to know the recluse.[22]	意欲識箕潁

LU CHUI 陸倕

Matching the Crown Prince's "Lecture Dismissed at Mount Zhong"

Mount Zhongnan neighbors the Han watchtower;	終南鄰漢闕
Its high palm spans the old Zhou capital.[23]	高掌跨周京
This ridge eclipses all other peaks;	復此虧山嶺
4 Arching high, it squats by the imperial city.	穹窿距帝城
Facing the thoroughfare, a pearly lodge is open;	當衢啟珠館
Looking downward, a mansion is constructed in the mountain.	臨下搆山楹
Gazing southward, one sees as far as the banks of the Huai;	南望窮淮淑
8 Peering north, the vast ocean is in sight.	北眺盡滄溟
[Long] are the covered walkways where one must halt midway;	步檐時中宿
Flights of stairs ascend on high.	飛階或上征
Carved lattices have patterns of clouds;	網户圖雲氣
12 Niches on the wall have paintings of divine beings.	龕室畫仙靈
Our vice lord is concerned about the worldly net;	副君憐世網
He widely summons and gathers men of outstanding talent.	廣命萃人英
The dharma lecture has now finished;	道筵終後說
16 The prince's carriage appears at the outskirts.	鑾轡出郊坰
The sound of pipes echoes among the cloud-covered peaks;	雲峰響流吹
The pine fields reflect fluttering banners.	松野映風旌
His discerning mind praises fine virtue;	睿心嘉杜若
20 His divine composition stands out among jade and jasper.	神藻茂琳瓊
He declines praise of his quickness in finishing first;	多謝先成敏
He merely distributes honors to those who follow.	空頒後乘榮

Xiao Zixian 蕭子顯

Matching the Crown Prince's
"Lecture Dismissed at Mount Zhong"

	The Song marchmount formed the foundation for our old capital;	嵩岳基舊宇
	Coiling dragon spans the southern capital.	盤嶺跨南京
	His discerning mind cherishes the Buddhist temple;	叡心重禪室
4	His roaming carriage ascended the storied peaks.	遊駕陟層城
	Golden chariots slowly start;	金輅徐既動
	Dragon steeds gallop and neigh.	龍驂躍且鳴
	Before the dust is about to settle in the rear;	塗方後塵合
8	The road far ahead has already been cleared with ringing bells.	地迴前笳清
	Sinuously snaking, terraces and pavilions lean against each other;	邐迤因臺榭
	Diversely disposed, plumes and pennants rest together.	參差憩羽旌
	Its height reaches that of Langfeng;	高隨閬風極
12	Its form matches that of primal heaven.[24]	勢與元天并
	The morning fog has lifted, and a pine grove extends into the distance;	氣歇連松逺
	Clouds ascend and autumn fields are flat.	雲昇秋野平
	Connected and conjoined are the houses in the city;	徘徊臨井邑
16	Inside and outside are the Huai River and the ocean, respectively.	表裏見淮瀛
	Praying for *phala*, one honors the eternal reality;	祈果尊常住
	Desiring dharma wisdom, one resides in nirvana.	渴慧在無生
	For a moment, halt your chariot on this stone path;	暫留石山軌
20	So as to understand the genuine essence of fragrance.	欲知芳杜情
	Bowing and saluting, they offer felicitations;	鞠躬荷嘉慶
	Gazing upon the road, we hear songs of praise.	瞻道聞頌聲

Liu Xiaochuo 劉孝綽

Matching the Crown Prince's
"Lecture Dismissed at Mount Zhong"

	Riding on a crane, his majesty flies over the Yi River;	御鶴翔伊水
	Spurring on his horse, he departs the capital.	策馬出王田
	My lord roams to this Divine Vulture Peak;[25]	我后遊祇鷲
4	Compared with previous times, this is indeed more glorious.	比事實光前
	The turquoise canopy is bathed in morning sun;	翠蓋承朝景

Cinnabar banners trail in the dawn mist. 朱旗曳曉烟
Awnings of the tower wreathe the craggy valley; 樓帳縈巖谷
8 Streams of red silk shine through forest paths. 緹組曜林阡
At this place where we ascend the heights, 況在登臨地
It has reached the season of autumn. 復及秋風年
On tall branches, summer leaves have changed their color; 喬柯變夏葉
12 In the secluded gulley, cool spring water is clean. 幽澗潔凉泉
Having halted our carriages, we sit at the lecture; 停鑾對寶座
Discussions and debates please both men and devas. 辯論悦人天
Dousing the dust depends on drops of ocean water; 淹塵資海滴
16 Illuminating darkness relies on the lighting of the lamp. 昭暗仰燈然
The dharma companions have already departed; 法朋一已散
The sound of the bell solemnly announces our return. 笳劍儼將旋
By chance, we meet this generous hospitality; 邂逅逢優渥
20 Riding along are talented and worthy companions. 託乘侶才賢
Although we write together under the same command, 摛辭雖並命
I regret that my piece is the least accomplished. 遺恨獨終篇

Liu Xiaoyi 劉孝儀

Matching the Crown Prince's "Lecture Dismissed at Mount Zhong"

Shao music is played in front of the Eastern Palace;[26] 韶樂臨東序
Now our carriages set out from the Western Garden.[27] 時駕出西園
Although the excursion to probe the ultimate 雖窮理遊盛
  truth is splendid,
4 Yet we hear the din of the profane world. 終爲塵俗喧
What is it like to promulgate the seven degrees 豈如弘七覺
  of enlightenment?
Urging on our carriage, we will pry open the four gates.[28] 揚鑾啓四門
Night air purifies the sound of panpipes; 夜氣清簫管
8 In early morning, our retinue brightens the suburban plain. 曉陣爍郊原
A mountain breeze flutters colorful banners; 山風亂采旄
The early sun shines on the carved carriage crossbar. 初景麗文轅
The forest opens up, and ahead we ride along; 林開前騎騁
12 On a zigzagging path, feathered pennants gather. 逕曲羽旄屯
On the misty cliffs drift greenish hues; 煙壁浮青翠
Stony shallows resound as if in fleet flight. 石瀬響飛奔
Turning our carriage, we descend from the layered gallery; 迴輿下重閣
16 Taking to the road, we visit the source of truth. 降道訪眞源
Our discourse on emptiness bubbles up like a spring; 談空匹泉涌
Our woven compositions surpass the intricacy of brocade. 綴藻邁絃繁

Trivial men make mistakes in their encounters;   輕生逢遇誤

20 Together we become a group of dragon birds.   竝作羣龍鵷

Looking at myself, I have already exchanged cups with you;   顧已同偏爵

Why do I again pour from the roadside goblet?   何用把衢樽

[Yu Shaochu 俞紹初, *Zhaoming taizi ji jiaozhu* 昭明太子集校註
(Zhengzhou: Zhongzhou guji, 2001), 29–32; 32–34 and *XS* 3:1796;
35 and *XS* 3:1775; 35 and *XS* 3:1818; 36 and *XS* 3:1829; 36 and *XS* 3:1893]

NOTES

1. Sima Qian 司馬遷, *Records of the Historian* (*Shiji* 史記) 84.2491.

2. Gao Qiufeng 高秋鳳, *Song Yu zuopin zhenwei kao* 宋玉作品真偽考 (Taibei: Wenjin chubanshe, 1999).

3. David R. Knechtges, "The Emperor and Literature: Emperor Wu of the Han," in *Court Culture and Literature in Early China* (Aldershot: Ashgate, 2002), 51–76.

4. For the game *liubo*, see Yang Lien-sheng, "A Note on the So-Called TLV Mirrors and the Game Liu-po," *HJAS* 9, nos. 3–4 (1947): 202–6, and "An Additional Note on the Ancient Game Liu-po," *HJAS* 15, nos. 1–2 (1952): 124–39.

5. *Wen xuan* 文選 (Shanghai: Shanghai guji, 1986), 42.1895. The translation is by Robert Joe Cutter, with minor modifications, "Cao Zhi's Symposium Poems," *CLEAR* 6 (1984): 1–32.

6. On the Yongming poets and the Eight Companions of Jingling, see He Rong 何融, "Qi Jingling wang Xidi ji qi xueshi kaolüe" 齊竟陵王西邸及其學士攷略, *Guowen yuekan*, March 10, 1949, 22–25; Nie Dashou 聶大受, "'Jingling bayou' wenxue jituan de xingcheng ji qi tedian" '竟陵八友'文學集團的行成及其特點, *Shandong daxue xuebao* 2 (1998): 24–29, 37; Ami Yūji 網祐次, *Chūgoku chūsei bungaku kenkyū: Nan Sei Eimei jidai o chūshin to shite* 中國中世文學研究: 南齊永明時代お中心として (Tokyo: Shinjusha, 1960); and Liu Yuejin 劉躍進, *Yongming wenxue yanjiu* 永明文學研究 (Taibei: Wenjin chubanshe, 1992).

7. *NQS* 40.694–98.

8. *NS* 59.1463.

9. *LS* 8.168.

10. Cynthia L. Chennault, "Representing the Uncommon: Temple Visit Lyrics from the Liang to Sui Dynasties," in *Interpretation and Literature in Early Medieval China*, ed. Alan K. Chan and Yuet-keung Lo (Albany: State University of New York Press, 2010), 189–222.

11. For the biography of Lu Chui 陸倕, see *LS* 27.401–3.

12. *NQS* 52.907–9; Zhou Xunchu 周勛初, "Liangdai wenlun sanpai shuyao" 梁代文論三派述要, in *Wei Jin Nanbeichao wenxue luncong* 魏晉南北朝文學論叢 (Nanjing: Jiangsu guji chubanshe, 1999), 230–34.

13. *LS* 35.512.

14. *Liuli* is a type of colored glass with a crystalline quality that was often compared to water.

15. Bertold Laufer identifies as a crocus the *yujin* that was offered to the Buddha, in *Sino-Iranica: Chinese Contributions to the History of Civilization in Ancient Iran, with Special Reference to the History of Cultivated Plants and Products* (Chicago: University of Chicago Press, 1919), 317.

16. For the phrase *pangui* 攀桂, see "Zhao yin shi" 招隱士, in *Chu ci buzhu* 楚辭補註, annot. Hong Xingzu 洪興祖 (Taibei: Da'an, 1995), 376.

17. Here *chengen* 塵根 refers to the *liuchen* 六根 (the dusty roots of six senses): 眼根 (eye, or *cakṣurindriya*), 耳根 (ear, or *śrotrendriya*), 鼻根 (nose, or *ghrāṇendriya*), 舌根 (tongue, or *jihvendriya*), 身根 (body, or *kāyendriya*), and 意根 (mind, or *manaīndriya*).

18. Zhongshan 鍾山, also known as Zhongfu 鍾阜 or Jiangshan 蔣山, cited in the title of the poem, is in the northeast suburb of Nanjing City.

19. Zaicheng (Second City) is another name for the Hanging Garden, which is the second highest peak of Mount Kunlun.

20. *Qing* is a unit of area equal to 6.6667 hectares, or 16.5 acres.

21. The term "Dragon Mirror" refers to the sun.

22. Here 箕穎 (Ji Ying) refers to Ji Mountain 箕山 and Ying River 穎水, places in modern Henan where the famous recluse Xu You 許由 went into hiding.

23. Mount Hua is located in the vicinity of the Han capital, Chang'an. One of its peaks is called Xianren zhang 仙人掌 (Immortal's Palm).

24. These two lines describe the mountain in exaggerated terms. Langfeng is another peak on Mount Kunlun.

25. Divine Vulture (Ling jiu 靈鷲) is the famous Gṛdharakūṭa (Vulture Peak) in Rājagṛha, India. This is where the Buddha preached the *Perfection of Wisdom Sutras* (*Prajñāpāramitā-sūtras*) and the *Lotus Sutra* (*Saddharmapundarīka-sūtra*).

26. *Shao* or *jiushao* 九韶 music is the music praising the virtues of Shun.

27. Cao Cao built a garden called Western Garden in his capital, Ye, for naval training. The name Western Garden refers to Xiao Tong's Hanging Garden.

28. The four city gates are the gates of the city of Kapilavastu through which Prince Siddhārtha passed on four separate excursions, when he saw for the first time the four distresses of human condition: disease (through the East Gate), old age (through the South Gate), death (through the West Gate), and deliverance (through the North Gate).

23. Self-Narration

Tao Yuanming's "Biography of the Master of Five Willows" and Yuan Can's "Biography of the Master of Wonderful Virtue"

WENDY SWARTZ

The "Biography of the Master of Five Willows" (*Wuliu xiansheng zhuan* 五柳先生傳) by Tao Yuanming 陶淵明 (365?–427) is generally considered the first fictionalized autobiography in China. Written in the third person, the autobiography describes the personality and habits of the so-called Master of Five Willows. Although Tao Yuanming's experimentation with methods of self-narration verges on play when he uses a fictional rather than a documentary mode to narrate his own life, since its earliest reception, the "Biography of the Master of Five Willows" has been read unequivocally as a genuine testimony.[1] Two factors may have led to this understanding:

1. Tao Yuanming exhibits a consistently strong autobiographical impulse in his work, leading one modern scholar to remark that "there is the 'I' in each of [Tao's] works."[2] Tao wrote detailed poetic accounts of his daily life, made extensive use of paratextual devices such as explanatory prefaces and titles, and even wrote his own funerary elegy, normally written by another for the deceased, as though he wished to have the last word about himself. The portrait drawn in the "Biography of the Master of Five Willows" accords with the dominant self-image in his other works: a complacent gentleman who made a principled withdrawal from office, choosing integrity and poverty over rank and riches, and who lived as a sociable recluse-farmer, engaging in all aspects of the mundane.

2. There is a well-known literary precedent of using the biography of a fictional character to express oneself. The "Biography of Master Great Man" (*Daren xiansheng zhuan* 大人先生傳) by Ruan Ji 阮籍 (210–263) has been traditionally regarded as an account of an idealized man who reflects the author's own thoughts and interests. Ruan Ji's work, which is devoted as much to expounding Daoist philosophy as to depicting a character, lies somewhere between a discourse (*lun*) and a biography (*zhuan*), so it differs from Tao Yuanming's work, which focuses on the person.

The traditional Chinese understanding of autobiography is considerably broader and looser than the Western conception. In the West, an autobiography generally is a first-person narrative recounting one's life experiences and meditating on one's course and development, whereas in China, an autobiography may be any snapshot of a life story (e.g., a glimpse into one's inner life, a response to a certain situation, or a record of one's activities). Traditional Chinese autobiographical accounts tend to present a static, completed picture of the subject rather than transformations and realizations that shape the subject. Moreover, autobiographical accounts, beginning with "Own Preface" (*Zixu* 自序) by the Grand Historian Sima Qian 司馬遷 (ca. 145–ca. 86 B.C.E.), which forms the last chapter of his monumental *Records of the Historian (Shiji* 史記), often borrowed from the conventions of historical biographies. Examples are the use of third-person narration in the voice of the historian to create a semblance of objectivity; the inclusion of the subject's name, clan, and birthplace; and details of his education and career. The Tang historiographer Liu Zhiji 劉知幾 (661–721) considered the information about the subject's name and birth to be the basic defining feature of self-narration (*zixu* 自敘). Accordingly, the "Biography of the Master of Five Willows" follows certain formal norms of Chinese historiography and autobiography, yet it also playfully surprises the reader's expectations.

The biography begins by addressing the subject's name and birth, which are unknown. This negative information is as much a suggestion of the subject's otherworldliness as the author's dismissal of information regarded by historians as crucial to a subject's identity and constitution. As one modern scholar noted, "We do not know his name" and "We do not know from where he comes" are discursive openers commonly found in the biographical notices in *Biographies of Immortals (Liexian zhuan* 列仙傳), traditionally ascribed to Liu Xiang 劉向 (79–8 B.C.E.), and *Biographies of Divine Immortals (Shenxian zhuan* 神仙傳), ascribed to Ge Hong 葛洪 (283–343).[3] This type of play makes an outlandish turn as the subject's makeshift designation is revealed: Master of Five Willows, a name without any substantive meaning, like Ruan Ji's "Master Great Man," and one that can only be regarded as arbitrary.

The narrator-historian introduces the subject as a reclusive gentleman who has absolutely no ambition in either career or learning. Instead, his motivation to study is rooted in a certain delight in comprehension, rather than in the production of laborious exegesis (*zhangju zhi xue* 章句之學; literally, "the study of chapter and verse") or in the search for exact meaning, which were the common practices of Han scholars. According to this portrayal by the narrator-historian, he is as sociable and easygoing as he is private and introverted. He engages with relatives and friends but remains free in his comings and goings. The equanimity suggested by the ease with which he relinquishes an opportunity to drink is made prominent in a passage that juxtaposes a description of his extreme poverty and a statement of his extraordinary complacency. The images of want are borrowed from classical portrayals of poor scholars: *huandu* refers to the cramped quality of the scholar's habitat in the *Record of Rites* (*Liji* 禮記); *danpiao* and *lükong* call to mind the laudatory descriptions of Yan Hui in the *Analects* (*Lunyu* 論語) as someone who happily lived on "a bowl of rice and a ladle of water" in "dire poverty"; and "yet he was complacent" (*yan ru ye* 晏如也) is a phrase previously used by Ban Gu 班固 (32–92), author of the *History of the Han* (*Han shu* 漢書) to describe the impoverished scholar Yang Xiong 揚雄 (53 B.C.E.–18 C.E.).[4] The extended description of the master's poverty in this passage abruptly ends with "yet he was complacent": he may be poor, but more important, he finds contentment in the simple life of writing and reading, and drinking with relatives and friends.

This happy acceptance of poverty gains further significance by being linked to a preservation of principle and integrity in the appraisal appended to the text, in which Tao Yuanming judges the subject of the biography according to the conventions of the genre in the *Records of the Historian* and the *History of the Han*. The words of Qian Lou's wife were originally used to characterize her husband, a recluse of exalted principles and unbending integrity celebrated in the fourth of Tao Yuanming's seven poems "In Praise of Impoverished Gentlemen" (*Yong pinshi* 詠貧士).[5] The narrative distance inherent in using a fictional third-person biography to present an autobiography is increased by quoting the words of a third party to describe the Master of Five Willows, who is supposed to represent the author himself. Despite this play with historiographic conventions and narrative techniques, the reader still understands (and is meant to understand) the picture Tao Yuanming has drawn of himself.

Tao Yuanming's autobiography produced his "life" as much as his life produced his autobiography. As Paul De Man wrote in his influential and provocative essay "Autobiography as De-Facement" (1979),

> We assume that life *produces* the autobiography as an act produces its consequences, but can we not suggest, with equal justice, that the autobiographical project may itself produce and determine the life and that whatever the writer *does* is in fact governed by the technical demands of self-portraiture and thus determined, in all its aspects, by the resources of his medium?[6]

Tao Yuanming's self-image is a literary construct built on generic conventions and already established vocabularies of reclusion and poverty, as well as on an interest in altering them and creating a new model of self-narration. The "Biography of the Master of Five Willows" inspired many imitations in later centuries. Following my translation of the "Biography of the Master of Five Willows" is an interesting example written about half a century later: "Biography of the Master of Wonderful Virtue" (*Miaode xiansheng zhuan* 妙德先生傳) by Yuan Can 袁粲 (421–478), which also is an autobiographical account written as a biography of a fictional character. This work is a tale within a tale. After describing the Master of Wonderful Virtue, the biography tells a story told by the master, one in which the famous lesson by the truculent, slandered official Qu Yuan 屈原 (343–277 B.C.E.) is ironically inverted: "All men are drunk; I alone am sober. . . . How can I submit my lustrous purity to the dirt of the vulgar world?"

FURTHER READING

For discussions of Tao Yuanming's autobiographical mode in English, see Kang-i Sun Chang, "T'ao Ch'ien," in *Six Dynasties Poetry* (Princeton, N.J.: Princeton University Press, 1986), 3–46; Stephen Owen, "The Self's Perfect Mirror: Poetry as Autobiography," in *The Vitality of the Lyric Voice: Shih Poetry from the Late Han to the T'ang*, ed. Shuen-fu Lin and Stephen Owen (Princeton, N.J.: Princeton University Press, 1986), 71–102; and Wendy Swartz, "Interlude: Tao Yuanming's Autobiographical Project," in *Reading Tao Yuanming: Shifting Paradigms of Historical Reception (427–1900)* (Cambridge, Mass.: Harvard University Asia Center, 2008), 130–44. For a recent study of Tao Yuanming's autobiographical writings, see Wang Kuo-ying 王國瓔, "Tao Yuanming shi zhong 'pian pian you wo'—Lun Tao shi de zizhuan yiwei" 陶淵明詩中「篇篇有我」—論陶詩的自傳意味, in *Wang Shumin xiansheng xueshu chengjiu yu xinchuan yantaohui lunwen ji* 王叔岷先生學術成就與薪傳研討會論文集 (Taibei: Taiwan daxue zhongguo wenxue xi, 2001). For a general survey of autobiography in traditional China, see Kawai Kōzō 川合康三, *Chūgoku no jiden bungaku* 中國の自傳文學 (Tokyo: Sobunsha, 1996).

Tao Yuanming 陶淵明

Biography of the Master of Five Willows 五柳先生傳

We do not know where this master is from, nor do we have details of his family name or byname. Beside his house stand five willow trees, and thus he was so called. Quiet and of few words, he did not yearn for honor or profit. He was fond of reading but did not seek explanation to the utmost. Whenever he read something that met with his intentions, he became so delighted that he forgot to eat. By nature he loved wine, but his family was poor so he usually could not get it. His relatives and friends, knowing that this was the case, sometimes would set out wine and invite him. Whenever he went to drink, he would drink his fill—his expectations were to get drunk. Once drunk, he would withdraw, never regretting that he had to go. His house, surrounded by a thin wall, was desolate and did not shield him from wind and sun. His short, coarse robe was torn and patched. His bowl and ladle were often empty. Yet he was complacent. He constantly amused himself with writing, in which he expressed his own ideals. He forgot about gain or loss, and he lived in this way to the end.

The Appraisal: Qian Lou's wife had a saying, "He was not distressed by poverty or low station, nor was he anxious for wealth and rank."[7] Examining these words, may we not say that he is of the same kind? He delighted himself by drinking wine and writing poetry. Was he not living in the time of [the ancient rulers] Mr. Wuhuai or Mr. Getian?

[Yuan Xingpei 袁行霈, ed., *Tao Yuanming ji jian zhu* 陶淵明集箋注
(Beijing: Zhonghua shuju, 2003), 502]

YUAN CAN 袁粲

Biography of the Master of Wonderful Virtue 五柳先生傳

There was a Master of Wonderful Virtue, who was a man of the state of Chen. His spirit was profound and hollow; his air pure and luminous. He was by nature filial; his actions compliant. His life in seclusion was carefree; his livelihood simple. He had inherited the way of [the ancient sage-king] Shun.

Since his childhood, the master had been plagued by numerous ailments and was lazy by nature, never striving for anything. Regarding the discourses of the nine schools and hundred philosophers, as well as the art of carving dragons and discussing heaven [associated with the Warring States rhetoricians Zou Shi and Zou Yan, respectively], he broadly understands their general points but does not use them to make a name for himself.

His family was poor and therefore he went into office, but this was not his desire. He obscured his sounds and tracks and concealed his thoughts and behavior. Thus, of his longtime friends, some grew distant; he is not known to the common observer. At his residence, the straw-mat door was often closed; the "three paths" [of the Han scholar Jiang Xu, who retired after Wang Mang usurped the throne] were cleared open. Although Master Yang Xiong was solitary, and the old man Yan Zun [courtesy name, Junping; a diviner by trade who studied the *Laozi*] traceless, they do not surpass the Master of Wonderful Virtue. He cultivated himself and satisfied his intent. To the end, he never achieved anything by which he could be known.

He had told those around him that "there once was a kingdom and in the kingdom a body of water, called the Spring of Madness. Of the people in the kingdom who drank from this spring, none was not mad. Only the king, who dug a well to draw his own water, did not become afflicted. Since all the people were mad, they considered the ruler's lack of madness to be madness. Hence they plotted together, seized the king, and treated his illness of 'madness' with moxibustion, acupuncture, and medicinal herbs— there was none that was left out. The king could not bear the suffering; hence he went to the spring, drew water, and drank it. After drinking it, he became mad. The king and his subjects, high and low—their madness appeared to be the same and all were now happy. As long as I am not mad, it is difficult to stand alone. Like the rest, I shall try to drink this water."

[Yan Kejun 嚴可均, ed., *Quan Song wen* 全宋文, in *QW* 44.2682a]

NOTES

1. Shen Yue 沈約 cites this work as Tao Yuanming's 陶淵明 autobiography. See *SS* 93.2286. See also Xiao Tong 蕭統, "Tao Yuanming zhuan" 陶淵明傳, in *Quan Liang wen* 全梁文, in *QW* 20.3068b–69a.

2. Wang Kuo-ying 王國瓔, "Tao Yuanming shi zhong 'pian pian you wo'—Lun Tao shi de zizhuan yiwei" 陶淵明詩中「篇篇有我」—論陶詩的自傳意味, in *Wang Shumin xiansheng xueshu chengjiu yu xinchuan yantaohui lunwen ji* 王叔岷先生學術成就與薪傳研討會論文集 (Taibei: Taiwan daxue zhongguo wenxue xi, 2001), 299.

3. Kawai Kōzō 川合康三, *Chūgoku no jiden bungaku* 中國の自傳文学 (Tokyo: Sobunsha, 1996), 78.

4. Tao Yuanming has combined two descriptions of Yan Hui's poverty in the *Analects* 6/11 and 11/19.

5. The description of Qian Lou by his wife as recorded in *Lienü zhuan* is slightly different from that cited in Tao's text; "'anxious' [*jiji* 汲汲] for wealth and rank" appears here in place of "'happy' [*xinxin* 忻忻] for wealth and rank." See Liu Xiang, *Lienü zhuan*, in *SBBY* 2.8a.

6. Paul De Man, *The Rhetoric of Romanticism* (New York: Columbia University Press, 1984), 69 (italics in the original).

7. Most recent editions of *Tao Yuanming ji* have emended this passage by changing "Qian Lou" to "Qian Lou's wife," which appears as a variant in the Northern Song Jiguge edition and Zeng Ji's 曾集 1192 edition. This variant is supported by a passage from her biography in Liu Xiang's *Lienü zhuan*.

24. On Political and Personal Fate

Three Selections from Jiang Yan's Prose and Verse

PAUL W. KROLL

Jiang Yan 江淹 (444–505, byname Wentong 文通) is remembered today mainly for two compositions in the *fu* 賦 form—the "Rhapsody on Regret" (*Hen fu* 恨賦) and the "Rhapsody on Separation" (*Bie fu* 別賦)—and a set of thirty *shi*-poems imitative of various earlier poets (*Zati sanshishou* 雜體三十首). These works were included by Xiao Tong 蕭統 (501–531) in his anthology *Wen xuan* 文選, whose great influence has ensured their recognition to this day. Jiang Yan was also the author of many other fine works in verse and much official prose and during his life was a prominent figure in three successive dynasties: the Song (421–479), Qi (479–502), and Liang (502–557). His career and writings open a particularly revealing window on both the court and literary culture in the second half of the fifth century.

Hailing from a minor branch of a once important clan, Jiang Yan had an early aptitude for literature but was not a noted prodigy. Although his father died when Jiang was twelve years old and he passed his adolescence in straitened circumstances, the family's lingering prestige—as well as Jiang's own scholarly abilities—may have contributed to his selection seven years later (463) as a tutor and secretary for one of the Song imperial princes. This position was not quite as important as it may sound, for the prince in question was but the eleventh son of the reigning emperor and only eight years old. However, this brought Jiang Yan to the attention of other members of the ruling Liu 劉 family, and his growing involvement with affairs at court thereafter largely determined his future.

The course of his career from 464 to the early 480s is described in some detail by Jiang himself in the preface to his collected works, translated here, which also served as the basis for his official biographies in the *History of Liang* (*Liang shu* 梁書) and the *History of the South* (*Nan shi* 南史).[1] There were two personal associations of critical importance for Jiang Yan. The first was with Liu Jingsu 劉景素, the eldest grandson of the Song Emperor Wen 宋文帝 (r. 424–454). Although he was not in the direct line of imperial succession, Liu Jingsu had a princely establishment of some note and a particular interest in literature. From his teens onward, he occupied a succession of different governmental posts, sometimes near to and sometimes farther from the capital. Jiang Yan entered Liu Jingsu's service in late 466, when the prince was fourteen and Jiang, twenty-two. On brief occasions thereafter, Jiang was seconded to other princes, but Liu Jingsu remained his chief patron for the next eight years.[2] The two young men were closely tied and on "the most familiar of terms" until the death of Emperor Ming 明帝 in the summer of 472 awakened Liu Jingsu's imperial aspirations. Because Jiang Yan was not a full-throated supporter of Liu Jingsu's increasingly focused ambitions, a growing coolness set in. This was not eased by Jiang's composition in 474 of a set of fifteen monitory poems that expressed by means of subtle indirection his doubts about the path that Liu Jingsu was pursuing. Shortly afterward, a dispute regarding Jiang Yan's own desire to assume prefectural authority in Donghai 東海 led to his effective banishment, as the Magistrate of Wuxing 吳興 District in Jian'an 建安 Commandery, far off in the interior of Fujian.

Although now Jiang Yan was no longer able to participate in the important events at court (which ultimately led to the demise of the Song), he remained safe from the deadly strife that carried off many of his contemporaries, including Liu Jingsu in 476. But the two and a half years that Jiang Yan spent rusticated in Jian'an Wuxing, from the autumn of 474 to early 477, were the most productive of his literary career. During this time, he wrote the majority of his extant verse, composing *fu* and *shi* on a wide variety of subjects. Often, as with the "Rhapsody on Regret" and the "Rhapsody on Separation," these carried a flavor of resigned optimism or melancholic acceptance.

The second key figure in Jiang Yan's career was Xiao Daocheng 蕭道成. He emerged from the turmoil of the mid-470s as the most successful political and military power at court. Over several years, he orchestrated the end of the Song dynasty and the abdication in 479 of the final Song ruler to himself as the founding emperor of the Qi dynasty (to be known posthumously as Qi Gaodi 齊高帝). In the summer of 474, not long before Jiang Yan's break with Liu Jingsu and removal to Fujian, Xiao Daocheng summoned Jiang to compose on behalf of the court a formal response to the claims of Liu Xiufan 劉修范, a prince who had openly rebelled. Xiao Daocheng remembered this good service when he eventually took de facto control of the court in 477, and he called Jiang Yan to his side. After Jiang's return to court, his star continually rose. He was the author of most of the official documents surrounding Xiao Daocheng's ascension to emperor. Thereafter, he remained a trusted Qi official, gathering to himself a succession of increasingly important positions throughout the dynasty's brief thirty-one-year tenure, though he never exercised major political power.

When the Liang dynasty replaced the Qi in 502, Jiang Yan retained and even added to his honors. At that time, he was ennobled as the count of Liling 醴陵伯, but by then his age had effectively removed him from immediate influence at court. He was, however, respected along with Shen Yue 沈約 (441–513) as a rare individual to have served three successive dynasties with integrity and distinction. In 505, when he died, he was granted the posthumous title Exemplary Count (*Xianbo* 憲伯).

Jiang Yan had little to do with the celebrated experiments in tonal prosody that occupied certain poets during the Yongming (483–493) period. Indeed, of his extant poems—some 26 *fu* and more than 130 *shi*—the great majority were written before 477 when he was drawn into Xiao Daocheng's orbit. The bulk of his writing after that date exists in the form of various official documents. The decline in Jiang Yan's verse output as his years and honors accrued gave rise to a famous anecdote, current soon after his death and possibly while he was still alive: Guo Pu 郭璞 (276–324), a great poet of the Jin dynasty, is supposed to have appeared to Jiang Yan in a dream sometime in the mid-490s and to have demanded from him the return of the "writing brush of many colors" 五彩之筆 that Guo had lent to Jiang at an earlier time.[3] After this, the story goes, "Master Jiang's genius dried up" 江郎才盡. The anecdote is well known, thanks largely to the telling of it by Zhong Rong 種嶸 in his *Grades of the Poets* (*Shipin* 詩品). But considering that there could have been only one witness to the dream and that *he* would be unlikely to spread such a deflating tale, there is no reason to put any credence in it.

In 483 or possibly 484, Jiang Yan compiled a collection of his verse and prose writings. He prefaced this with a lengthy autobiographical narrative, translated here. This account is revealing not only as a commentary on the affairs of his time but also, in its closing paragraphs, for Jiang's ironically worded statement of his aims and ideals. The latter owes something to literary tradition and an expectation to adopt a pose of fundamental detachment, but it should not be dismissed as rhetoric only. We do well to allow those who lived in the past the same measure of complexity and even contradiction in temperament that we accept in ourselves.

The second selection translated here is one of the more poignant pieces of early medieval poetry that has come down to us, a *fu* on the death of Jiang Yan's infant son, who died before completing his first year of life. If this was in 474, as some scholars think, it would have been during the time of Jiang Yan's final break with Liu Jingsu and shortly before his banishment to Jian'an Wuxing. It

also is possible that this loss occurred during the Fujian exile; there is no con-
clusive evidence. Here the form of the *fu* gives Jiang the scope and framework
to express a personal grief that cannot be contained otherwise. Afterward, even
more sadness was to descend on Jiang Yan, as his wife—so touchingly referred
to in this *fu*—passed away as well. These deaths compounded the loss already
felt by Jiang Yan of his dearest friend, the young man named Yuan Bing 袁炳
(also mentioned in the preface), whose unexpected, early death had shaken Jiang
just a year or two earlier.

There was, therefore, plentiful disappointment of both a personal and a professional nature to accompany Jiang Yan in the wilderness of central Fujian.
The numerous *shi* and *fu* he composed during his time there include works of
great descriptive and emotional depth. In many of them, Jiang Yan seems to
find a difficult accommodation with the remote physical place in which he now
resides. In this setting, the "North" to him no longer means, as it always had before, the traditional Chinese heartland that had been lost to northern barbarians
since 317 but, rather, the Jiangnan 江南 region ruled by the Song regime, which
he hopes someday to see again. Among Jiang's celebrations of local flora and
fauna, an attractive example is the third selection translated here, a small *fu* on
the halcyon (white-throated) kingfisher (*Halcyon smyrnensis*). For centuries,
the beautiful little kingfisher, native to southeastern China, was hunted for its
iridescent turquoise-blue plumage, which was used to decorate sundry objects
of luxury decor (hair ornaments, coverlets, carriage canopies, and the like). For
Jiang Yan, it suggests how anything of value will be snared and ultimately destroyed by the court. Jiang Yan presents the bird through a summery haze of
humid carmine, employing virtually every shade of red (the symbolic color of
the South) to be found in the Chinese spectrum and lexicon.[4]

FURTHER READING

The best editions of Jiang Yan's works are *Jiang Wentong ji huizhu* 江文通集彙註
(Beijing: Zhonghua shuju, 1984) (cited as *JWTJHZ*), which includes the commentary of Hu Zhiji 胡之驥 (fl. 1598); and *Jiang Yan ji jiaozhu* 江淹集校註, ed.
and annot. Yu Shaochu 俞紹初 and Zhang Yaxin 張亞新 (Zhengzhou: Zhongzhou chubanshe, 1994) (cited as *JYJJZ*). *Jiang Liling ji* 江醴陵集 (cited as *JLLJ*),
collected in Zhang Pu 張溥 (1601–1641), *Han Wei Liuchao baisan mingjia ji* 漢魏
六朝百三名家集, should also be consulted. Cao Daoheng 曹道衡 has published
several articles, together amounting to a substantial monograph, on Jiang Yan.
These are the best studies available of Jiang's life and work and include Cao's
chapter on Jiang Yan in *Zhongguo lidai zhuming wenxuejia pingzhuan* 中国历代
著名文学家评传, ed. Lü Huijuan 呂慧鵑 et al. (Ji'nan: Shandong jiaoyu chubanshe, 1983), 1:503–25; "Jiang Yan zuopin xiezuo niandai kao" 江淹作品写作年代考,
Yiwen zhi 艺文志 3 (1985): 55–97; and "Jiang Yan ji qi zuopin" 江淹及其作品 and

"Lun Jiang Yan shige de jige wenti" 论江淹诗歌的几个问题, in Cao Daoheng, *Zhonggu wenxueshi lunwen ji* 中古文学史论文集 (Beijing: Zhonghua shuju, 1986), 257–66, 267–87, among others. Ding Fulin 丁福林 has also published several important articles, some of which culminated in *Jiang Yan nianpu* 江淹年谱 (Beijing: Fenghuang chubanshe, 2007), the most recent chronological biography of Jiang Yan. Disagreement remains about the dating of some of the poems. Xiao Hezi 蕭合姿, *Jiang Yan ji qi zuopin yanjiu* 江淹及其作品研究 (Taibei: Wenjin chubanshe, 2000), contains many helpful observations. The early article by Takahashi Kazumi 高橋和己, "Kō En no bungaku" 江淹の文學, in *Yoshikawa hakushi taikyū kinen: Chūgoku bungaku ronshū* 吉川博士退休紀念：中國文學論集 (Tokyo: Chikuma shobō, 1968), 253–70, is still useful. In English, John Marney, *Chiang Yen* (Boston: Hall, 1981), is now outdated, and the translations are unreliable. Fully annotated and accurate translations of the "Rhapsody on Regret" and the "Rhapsody on Separation" are in Xiao Tong, comp., *Wen xuan, or Selections of Refined Literature*, vol. 3, *Rhapsodies on Natural Phenomena, Birds and Animals, Aspirations and Feelings, Sorrowful Laments, Literature, Music, and Passions* trans. David R. Knechtges (Princeton, N.J.: Princeton University Press, 1996), 193–200, 201–9. The thirty "Zati" poems have attracted more attention recently. See, especially, Nicholas Morrow Williams, "The Brocade of Words: Imitation Poetry and Poetics in the Six Dynasties" (Ph.D. diss., University of Washington, 2010), which, in addition to the "Zati" poems, has much of interest to say about Jiang Yan throughout. There are also perceptive comments in Brigitta A. Lee, "Imitation, Remembrance, and the Formation of the Poetic Past" (Ph.D. diss., Princeton University, 2007). For German translations of the "Zati" poems, see Erwin von Zach, *Die chinesische Anthologie: Übersetzungen aus dem* Wen hsüan (Cambridge, Mass.: Harvard University Press, 1958), 582–605.

Jiang Yan 江淹

His Own Preface 自序[5]

I, Yan 淹, with the byname Wentong 文通, hail from Kaocheng 考城 in Jiyang 濟陽.[6] In childhood, I was heir to the family heritage, and in my sixth year I could compose verse. But at thirteen, I was left fatherless and thereafter was far from receiving any teachings when crossing the courtyard.[7] As I grew, I read widely in all sorts of books but did not trouble with "chapter-and-verse" learning,[8] preferring instead to focus my attention on belles lettres. What I produced for chanting aloud amounted to roughly 200,000 words, with a pronounced fondness for the unordinary and a deep immersion in far-ranging information. I always aspired to the likes of Sima Zhangqing 司馬長卿 and Liang Boluan

梁伯鸞[9] but was never able to bring it off fully. Of those with whom I had a spiritual association there was Yuan Shuming 袁叔明 of Chenliu 陳留,[10] and only him.

At the age I was capped,[11] I was appointed to instruct in the Five Classics Liu Zizhen 劉子真, Prince of Shi'an 始安王 under the Song 宋 regime,[12] more or less imparting to him just the general sense. I then served as an attendant 從事 to the Prince of Xin'an 新安王[13] in Xuzhou South 南徐州[14] and was honored with an invitation to court. Upon the demise of Xin'an, my name came to Liu Jingsu 劉景素, Prince of Jianping 建平王,[15] who treated me on the most familiar of terms. But being young, I was careless and unworldly and incurred the malice of certain men of the world. And so I was falsely accused of accepting a bribe. As I was facing the penalty for this crime, I sent up a letter to show my thoughts, with the result that I was then set free.[16]

Afterward, I was recommended for the *xiucai* 秀才 examination by the Prince of Guiyang 桂陽王 in Xuzhou South.[17] My responses earned the highest grade, and I was then transferred to serve as Right Attendant-in-Ordinary 右常侍 to the Prince of Baling 巴陵王[18] and then as Superintendent of Records 主簿 to the Prince of Jianping.[19] The latter treated me as an honored guest for a great many years and regularly met with me out of a shared interest in literature.

However, the decline of the Song was fraught with trouble, and difficulties afflicted the ancestral house. The prince at first wished to send out a call-to-war mustering the soldiers of the empire in quest of a new morning's fortune.[20] In an offhand manner, I tried to make known my objections, speaking of the reversals of human affairs, often along the lines of "If Your Excellency seek not the stability of the ancestral shrine but trust instead to the schemes of those around you, we will once more see the wild deer in frost and dew sheltering by the Gusu terrace."[21] In the end, he did not agree and began to have doubts about me. When the prince moved his headquarters to Zhufang 朱方,[22] I was made Consultant to the Garrison 鎮軍參事 and deputed to be Subprefect 丞 of Donghai Commandery 東海郡.[23] It was then that the prince and his reckless adherents laid plans day and night. I realized that the trigger to disaster was about to be tripped and thereupon presented fifteen *shi*-poems roughly illustrating the principles of fate that they might serve for indirect criticism.[24] But the prince did not then understand and, in his anger,[25] expelled me to be Magistrate of Wuxing 吳興 in the Jian'an region.

This land lies beyond the mountain range of the southeast and is an old-time territory of Min 閩 and Yue 越.[26] In it there are deep-blue rivers and sun-flushed mountains, rare trees and numinous plants, everything I have been most partial to my whole life—and I did not mind how distant was the road that took me there. Amid the mountains, I was free of official tasks and had the books of the Way as my companions. I would go out walking alone, my heart drifting off, sometimes oblivious of returning home at dusk of day. When feeling fancy-free, I composed literary pieces to amuse myself.

I was in this place for three years until, finally, Zhufang was quashed.[27] Returning again to the capital, I beheld the world's way benighted. So, maintaining a resolve to live at ease, I did not mix with those in charge. But soon, the august emperor began doing great deeds amid the Four Seas.[28] Hearing of me, he sent a summons calling me to him. I was made Director of the Board of Military Equipage in the Secretariat 尚書駕部郎 and Aide-de-camp to the Duke of Jingling, General of Cavalry on the Alert 驃騎竟陵公參軍事.[29]

Just at the time Shen Youzhi 沈攸之 took up arms in western Chu 楚,[30] the people were fearfully on edge. On one occasion, Gaodi 高帝[31] turned to me and asked, "Why is it, say you, that everyone is in such a panic?" I replied, "In times past Xiang Yu 項羽 was strong and Liu Bang 劉邦 weak; Yuan Shao's 袁紹 troops were legion and Cao Cao's 曹操 few. But Yu, though he commanded the feudal lords, in the end suffered disgrace from a single sword; and Shao, though he bestrode four provinces, finally turned tail, a caitiff.[32] This is exactly what is meant by the phrase 'It depends on one's virtue, not on the cauldrons.'[33] So, my lord, you needn't be anxious over it." The emperor said, "I've heard words of this sort many times. Please spell it out for me." I said, "My lord, you are a valiant warrior with exceptional skill in strategy—advantage number one. You are generously accommodating and you have a humane feeling for others—advantage number two. You are able to exploit your qualities to the utmost—advantage number three. The people look to you as though returning home—advantage number four. You defer to the Son of Heaven and punish defiant rebels—advantage number five. As for Shen Youzhi, though his resolve is keen, his competence is slight—disadvantage number one. He has an air of impressiveness but nothing of graciousness—disadvantage number two. His fighting men have lost heart—disadvantage number three. His court officials are not cared for closely—disadvantage number four. His troops are strung out several thousand *li* but have not even the shared loyalty of thieves to help one another in distress—disadvantage number five. Therefore, though the wolves and dholes number ten myriads, in the end they all will be taken by us." The emperor smiled and said, "Your speech, sir, goes too far!"

During this time, all the military documents, memorials, and records were prepared in draft form by me. Right up to when he became overlord of the capital district,[34] I continued to be in charge of brush and quill. Upon the establishment of his ministerial offices,[35] I remained as Secretarial Aide-de-camp 記室參軍事. When it came to the Prince of Qi's ceding all implements of the Nine Bestowals,[36] this, along with sundry other texts and memorials, were all written by me. After the imperial abdication was accepted, I was made Secretarial Aide-de-camp to the General of Cavalry on the Alert, Prince of Yuzhang 豫章王.[37] I wielded the magistracy of Dongwu 東武, played a role in handling imperial rescripts, and also oversaw the state history. These were not long-held goals of mine, but I was not permitted to decline them. Subsequently, I was promoted to Gentleman Cavalier Attendant 散騎侍郎 and Deputy Director of the Palace Secretariat 中書侍郎.[38]

Once I remarked that to be happy in this life, a man must be at ease with his own inborn nature—why then need he focus thoughts and labor hard to win fame that will live on after his death? For this reason, from youth to when I was older, I have never written a book of my own and have a collection of only ten *juan*. I expect, however, that this will suffice.

I have thought it important that learning not be for the sake of impressing others and that relationships not be contracted carelessly. Further, I place profound faith in the Indic texts on conditioned karma and am particularly fond of Laozi's teachings of purity and quietude. As to official service, what I hoped for did not extend to the two-thousand-bushel stipend of the highest ministers; given resources from plowing in the summer and spinning in the winter, I could hide away. For I have always preferred to reside inconspicuously in a simple dwelling, cut off from human affairs. Let there be red-leaved trees for an orchard and virid water for a pool, on the left adjoining wild moors, on the right bordering a marshy fen. When green springtime follows the year's turning, I'll wend my way to the level shore; and in the limpid sunlight of unsullied autumn, I'll pour a cup alone in my empty room, with three or four serving-girls or a few beauties from Zhao. Otherwise, let me wander at will through the classics and chronicles, play the zither, and recite poetry. And in the brief space of the morning dew, let me forget the near approach of old age. This is everything I have learned, nothing more.

[*JWTJHZ* 10.378–81; *JYJJZ* 289–95; *JLLJ* 2.36b–39b;
Quan Liang wen, in *QW* 39.10a–11b; excerpts in *Yiwen leiju* 55.994–95]

Fu Lamenting My Beloved Son 傷愛子賦

Jiang Qiu 江芃, byname Yinqing 胤卿, was my second son. He seemed a wondrous prodigy when born and would surely have the most admirable qualities. Alas! that only woe awaited and he was gone before the year. The grief has left me weak-kneed and bewildered. Hence I wrote this text:

In the pallid shimmer of autumn's aura,	惟秋色之顥顥
My heart is twisted in knots as grief mounts up;	心結縞兮悲起
Heaped with heartache, sick at heart, heart-stricken, disheartened,	曾燗憐之慘悽
I hurt for my dear son who was like a pearl in one's hand.	痛掌珠之愛子
Forlorn and worn, it shows on my body without,	形悾悾而外施
And my heart, pierced and pitted, is wizened within.	心切切而內圮

4

Though sun and moon be dissolved, this anguish will not be quenched;	日月可銷兮悼不滅
8 Though stone and metal be melted down, when will these thoughts end?	金石可鑠兮何已
Spreading far, the glittering sheen of our forefather,	緬吾祖之赫羲
To us, distant children of that sovereign Gaoyang.[39]	帝高陽之玄冑
Alas! for the decline and fall of a withering ancestral line;	惜衰宗之淪沒
12 I now fear that our house will be added to no more.	恐余人之弗構
I had wished for blessings to descend from the Three Powers above,[40]	覬三靈之降福
Yearning for a young son to come forth and thrive.	竚弱子之擢秀
What cruelty is it then, oh Yinqing,	酷奈何兮胤卿
16 How it befell that Heaven did not watch over you.[41]	那逢天兮不祐
You were given form in the greening springtime,	爾誕質於青春
As the stars of Sheti shone in the earliest month,[42]	攝提貞乎孟陬
Indicating you should be aligned with past exemplars,	謂比方於右列
20 Presaging you to bloom as did former worthies,	望齊英於前修
To fare along the admired tracks of those who proceeded on high,	滯高行之美跡
To enlarge the pure counsel of those whose deeds prospered.	弘盛業之清猷
But then when the white dew cloaked all the hundred plants,	白露奄被此百草
24 You withered away just like paulownia and catalpa.[43]	爾同凋於梧楸
I recall when summer's light was in its season,	憶未明之在節
How priceless it was seeing your precocious ways.[44]	顧岐嶷之可貴
Now glimpsing the brazier and curtain saddens me much,	睨鑪帳而多怊
28 And to glance at your door and window I need to be calmed.	瞻戶牖而有慰
Oh, in the hushed stillness that now is here,	奚在今之寂寞

Even vague seemings of voice or semblance
    are missing. 失音容之髣髴

As your sister sniffles with weeping eyes, 姊目中而下泣

32   Your brother moans while swallowing his tears. 兄嗟秀而飲淚

To make wood and stone feel, I raise a lament; 感木石而變哀

Provoked on every side, I break down sobbing. 激左右而隕欷

My most dear thing, as though snatched from
    my sleeve— 奪懷袖之深愛

36   You were the lovely boy come from your mother. 爾母氏之麗人

I shed tears of blood onto the loamy earth below, 屑丹泣於下壤

Send my painful plaint to the autumn sky
    up above. 愫懸憂於上旻

Contemplating clues that went nowhere,
    I beat my breast;[45] 視往端而撫慄

40   Stepping on threads that remain is anguish
    most bitter. 踐遺緒而苦辛

Who can keep me from following out this deep
    torment? 就深悼而誰弭

And how to say one will surrender to your
    thwarted fate? 歸末命兮何陳

Of good fortune for my own self I have had
    more than my share 我過幸於時私

44   Even to holding office by the banks of the Jiang.[46] 受守官於江潯

But my grief nearing nightfall becomes
    unbearable, 悲薄暮而增甚

And longings in the pale-gold twilight cannot
    be checked. 思繡黃而不禁

As the moon replaces the sun, light is still shed; 月接日而為光

48   As rose-mists join with clouds, darkness
    is forming. 霞合雲而成陰

A haze enfolding, encaging, swathes the trees, 霧籠籠而帶樹

And moonlight wanly white frames the grove. 月蒼蒼而架林

Ah!—what can be done for my frail boy? 嗟奈何兮弱子

52   I would search him out through a hundred trials, 我百艱兮足尋

Look till my slender sash grows loose at nighttime, 驗纖帶之夜緩

Seek till unkempt sidelocks are tinged gray in
    the morning. 察葆鬢之朝侵

It is true that man's life, as it is in this world, 惟人生之在世

56   Has few lasting pleasures but a plenitude
    of distress. 恆懽寡而戚饒

Even for ten centuries of empty afterlife fame,　　雖十紀之空名
Could one be prevailed on to trade his hundred　　豈百齡之能要
　　years?
Swiftly the red glow wanes into nighttime,　　迅朱光之映夜
60　　Heavy the white dew thickens in the morning.　　湛白露之凝朝
Point toward *this* metaphor to find a way out,　　指玆譬而取免
And draw out this truth to release yourself.　　排此理以自銷

It being so,　　然則
The delights of life—they are family　　生之樂兮親與愛
　　and dear ones,
64　　Whether nearer or farther—older or younger.　　內與外兮長與稚
I lament my frail boy in the deepening dark,　　傷弱子之冥冥
Ever mourning him so alone in the shrouded　　獨幽泉兮而永閟
　　underworld.
But let me not offend spirits chthonic or celestial,　　余無愆於蒼祇
68　　Nor do I make reproof of the bountiful earth.　　亦何怨於厚地
I put my faith in Śākya's law of divine effect,　　信釋氏之靈果
Take refuge in the sweeping efficacy of the　　歸三世之遠致
　　Triple World.[47]
I pray we shall together mount to that Pure Kṣetra,[48]　　願同升於淨剎
72　　Leaving the habits of this world of dust　　於塵習兮永棄
　　behind us forever.

> [*JWTJHZ*, "Yiwen," 383–84; *JYJJZ* 151–52; *JLLJ* 1.12a–13b;
> *Quan Liang wen*, in *QW* 33.10b–11a; *Guang Hongming ji*
> 廣弘明集, T2103.29:342b–c]

Fu on the Halcyon Kingfisher 翡翠賦

The rare beauty of these two birds[49]　　彼二鳥之奇麗
Lives in golden isles and the hills of flame,　　生金洲與炎山
Glinting in the pure white vapors over mounds　　映銅陵之素氣
　　of bronze,
4　　Bathing in the crimson spring of deep-blue ledges,　　濯碧磴之紅泉
There where boulders like folds of brocade　　石錦質而入海
　　lead into the sea,
And clouds of filigree shape move out into the sky,　　雲綺色而出天
Where cliffs sweltering and steep occlude the sun,　　峰炎巖而蔽日
8　　And trees staid and shaded lean over a spring.　　樹靜瞑而臨泉

Auroras, laden or light, form there a prism of color　　霞輕重而成彩
And the leavings of mist make up lingering threads.　　煙尺寸而作緒
Where humid breezes gathering make billows swell,　　熱風翕而起濤

12 Reddening cinnabar vapors build up
summer's heat. 丹氣赫而為暑

There they confront lamias and dragons of
the scouring flow, 對滌流之蛟龍

Pushing through the blur and rain of spattering
showers. 衝汶漻之霧雨

They dazzle green leaves in winter's hill-gaps 耀綠葉於冬岫

16 And mirror blooms of vermilion on chilly islets. 鏡朱華於寒渚

Drawing in their proud nature and docile heart, 斂惠性及馴心

They rear up on pinions of carmine, plumes of
bice-blue. 騫頹翼與青羽

But their fate is finally cut short by hunting men 終絕命於虞人

20 Who stuff the Royal Storehouse with southern
treasures. 充南琛於祕府

There they complement precious screens as
shining trimmings, 備寶帳之光儀

Are presented as gorgeous adornments
to lovely women. 登美女之麗飾

Mingled with white jade to form a fine pattern, 雜白玉以成文

24 Or interleaved with purple gold to give color, 糅紫金而為色

They are first of marvelous tints in the five
great cities,[50] 專妙綵於五都

Take highest place of perfect splendor amid
the eight points.[51] 擅精華於八極

While their prized forms are propagated on
bamboo and silk, 傳貴質於竹素

28 Their deep-hidden voice is dulled to all
and sundry.[52] 晦深聲於百億

Ah, alas! 嗟乎

Swallow and sparrow come to woe by nesting in
the roof-beams of halls, 燕雀以堂構貽

Duck and fowl come to grief out of desire for rice
and millet. 雞鶩以稻粱致憂

Since their affections and penchants are for
snaffling benefits, 既衒利之情近

32 They thus have no way of escaping
from harm. 又遁害之無由

And now 今乃

Keeping close by its far-off shores of ruddy fire, 依赩火之絕垠

The halcyon comes from the corded isles of
the Red District,[53] 出赤縣之紘州

	So that far from men's tracks it may stand alone	追人跡而獨立
36	And cling to the sky's edge as though to a confidant.	攬天倪而為儔
	Yet in the end it will be caught like geese on the river,	竟同獲於河雁
	Shown no more fellow feeling than the gulls by the sea.[54]	不俱恕於海鷗
	One's inborn fate is certain to be what it shall be;	必性命兮有當
40	Who can make it conform with what he would seek?	孰能合兮可求

[*JWTJHZ* 2.81; *JYJJZ* 211–13; *JLLJ* 1.34b–35a;
Quan Liang wen, in *QW* 34.6b–7a; *Yiwen leiju* 92.1609 (excerpt)]

NOTES

1. *LS* 14.247–51; *NS* 59.1447–51.

2. He even effected Jiang Yan's release from a brief imprisonment in autumn 467, after Jiang had been implicated in a crime involving the Magistrate of Guangling 廣陵. The plea that Jiang Yan wrote from prison is a model of self-justification and protest, wrapped in historical allusions, and is recorded in his official biographies.

3. An alternative version of this tale identifies the spirit of the poet Zhang Xie 張協 (d. ca. 307) as coming to retrieve a length of polychrome damask, which Jiang Yan returns to him in tatters and Zhang Xie then gives to Jiang's lesser contemporary, Qiu Chi 丘遲 (464–508).

4. For more on the bird, see Paul W. Kroll, "The Image of the Halcyon Kingfisher in Medieval Chinese Literature," *Journal of the American Oriental Society* 104 (1984): 237–51. The current translation of Jiang's *fu* supersedes the one included in that article.

5. This was the preface to the first collection of his writings, in ten *juan*, probably compiled in 483 or 484.

6. In extreme eastern He'nan. Jiang Yan, as is customary, identifies the place of his ancestors' official registry, not his birthplace.

7. See *Analects* 16/13, the famous incident regarding Confucius instructing his son.

8. That is, with the minutely detailed commentaries to classical texts.

9. These are the great writer of *fu*, Sima Xiangru 司馬相如 (179–117 B.C.E., byname Zhangqing), and Liang Hong 梁鴻 (byname Boluan), a poor but upright fellow of the mid-first century who was said to have secluded himself and his wife in the mountains, where they saw to their own needs and he read and wrote for his own amusement. Liang Hong is referred to admiringly by Jiang Yan often in his writings. Note that Liang, too, was orphaned young and also "read widely . . . but disregarded chapter-and-verse scholarship" (*HHS* 83.2765).

10. Yuan Shuming's personal name was Bing 炳. He was clearly a special friend. See also Jiang's "Letter in Response to Yuan Shuming" 報袁叔明書 (*JWTJHZ* 9.346–49; *JYJJZ*

235–37; *JLLJ* 2.13a–15a; Taiping Chang and David R. Knechtges, trans., "Jiang Yan: Letter in Response to Yuan Shuming," *Renditions* 41–42 [1994]: 25–31), in which Jiang avers his desire to live in reclusion, and the two works he composed on Yuan's early death at twenty-eight (probably in 473 or 474): "Account of My Friend Yuan" 袁友人傳 (*JWTJHZ* 10.377; *JYJJZ* 245–46; *JLLJ* 2.36a–b) and "*Fu* Lamenting My Friend" 傷友人賦 (*JWTJHZ* 2.68–72; *JYJJZ* 141–42; *JLLJ* 1.10b–12a).

11. In his twentieth year, sometime in 463.

12. Liu Zizhen was aged eight at this time. He was the eleventh son of the reigning emperor, Liu Jun 劉駿 (Xiaowudi 孝武帝, r. 454–464). Following the ascension of Liu Yu 劉彧 (Emperor Ming 明帝, r. 466–473) in 466, he was forced to commit suicide.

13. This was Liu Ziluan 劉子鸞, eighth son of Emperor Xiaowu, by his consort née Yin 殷, and the emperor's favorite. He was ten at this time (464) and was killed a year later by the new (and himself short-lived) ruler, Liu Ziye 劉子業 (Emperor Qian Fei 前廢帝, r. 465).

14. Many places under the control of the Southern Dynasties were renamed to recall familiar places in the North, differentiated by the adjective "South" (cf. New York, New Orleans). Xuzhou South was an important city on the south bank of the Yangzi, about fifty miles downstream from the capital, Jiankang 建康, roughly where present-day Zhenjiang 鎮江 is.

15. Liu Jingsu was Jiang Yan's first great patron, who supported him for nearly a decade, though the relationship later deteriorated, as we shall see. He was the eldest grandson of Liu Yilong 劉義隆 (Emperor Wen 文帝, r. 424–454), but no longer in the direct line of succession. He was fourteen at this time.

16. Jiang Yan had been put in prison. His letter of complaint and soul-baring to Liu Jingsu is included in the *Wen xuan* (39.1786–91) and his official biographies.

17. This prince was Liu Xiufan 劉休范, born in 448, the eighteenth son of Wendi.

18. This was in the fall of 467. The Prince of Baling, Liu Xiuruo 劉休若 (b. 448), was the nineteenth son of Wendi. At this time, he was serving as Prefect of Yongzhou 雍州刺使, with his headquarters in Xiangyang 襄陽. Cao Daheng has argued convincingly that it was on the way upstream to join Liu Xiuruo in Xiangyang that Jiang Yan wrote his poem "Wang Jing shan" 望荊山. The position of Attendant-in-Ordinary was a senior staff posting with no specified duties. A variant text makes Jiang the left 左 *changshi*.

19. Thus returning to the employ of his first patron, Liu Jingsu.

20. That is, Liu Jingsu wished to advance his own claim to the throne.

21. Here Jiang Yan is recasting the words of Wu Bei 伍被 when the latter was cautioning Liu An 劉安, King of Huainan 淮南王, against imperial aspirations during the reign of the Han Emperor Wu. See *Records of the Historian* [*Shiji* 史記] 86.3085. Wu Bei himself cited words attributed to Wu Zixu 吳子胥 when advising King Fuchai 夫差 of Wu several centuries earlier not to attack his archrival Goujian 句踐 of Yue 越 ("Your servant foresees the wild deer roaming by the Gusu terrace"). Fuchai did not heed the advice and ended up losing his kingdom and his life. In his remonstrance with the King of Huainan, Wu Bei added the statement that he foresees thorns and brambles growing in the palace grounds and dew soaking the clothes of Liu An's officials. Of course, Liu An,

too, refused to listen and met a traitor's end. Jiang Yan's "offhand" comments to Liu Jingsu are thus laden with historical caution.

22. This was in 471. The prince was then Governor of Xuzhou South. Zhufang was the old name for Dantu 丹徒, a smaller county seat just east of Xuzhou South. Liu Jingsu's move there seems to have been designed to give him some breathing space to plan his coup.

23. Donghai (South) Commandery was attached to Xuzhou South.

24. These are Jiang Yan's group of poems "In Imitation of Ruan Ji" (*Xiao Ruan Gong shi* 效阮公詩十五首), written in 474.

25. Jiang Yan does not mention another reason for the prince's anger, which is recorded in the official histories. This was the dispute that occurred when the Prefect of Donghai took a leave of absence for mourning purposes. Jiang Yan expected to be made acting prefect, and when Liu Jingsu refused to appoint him (probably because of the growing tension between them on larger issues), Jiang protested. The prince regarded this as insubordination and referred the case to the Board of Appointments; he was then permitted to rusticate Jiang.

26. This is not to be confused with the better-known Wuxing, more desirably located just south of Lake Tai in Zhejiang. In texts, this place is usually specified, as by Jiang Yan in the preceding sentence, as "Jian'an Wuxing." It was in north-central Fujian, far in the hinterlands, near the site of present-day Pucheng 浦城.

27. That is, until Liu Jingsu's bid for power was defeated and he was killed, in the summer of 476.

28. Jiang is referring anachronistically to Xiao Daocheng, who emerged in these years as the chief defender of the royal house against various threats but gradually engineered a change in dynasties, ascending the throne himself (hence "august emperor") in 479 as the first emperor of the Qi 齊 (r. 479–482).

29. The title held by Xiao Daocheng in 477.

30. Shen Youzhi was a former friend and colleague of Xiao Daocheng. As governor of the strategic province of Jingzhou 荊州, he opposed Xiao's control of the emperor and rebelled in the spring of 477. He was defeated and killed a few months later.

31. Here Jiang Yan uses, anachronistically, Xiao Daocheng's posthumous temple-name as emperor.

32. Jiang is recalling two historical situations that he wishes to see as analogous to the present: the clash between the warlords Xiang Yu and Liu Bang, which resulted in the latter's establishment of the Han dynasty, and the important battle of Guandu 官渡 in 200, which shifted the balance of power at the end of the Han to the benefit of Cao Cao, who was "protecting" the last Han emperor in the same way Xiao Daocheng was defending the Song monarch.

33. *Zuozhuan*, Xuan 3. When the impertinent Viscount of Chu 楚子, visiting the imperial capital, asked about the sacred cauldrons, whose size and weight were reputed to fluctuate according to the strength of the royal house, the minister Wangsun Man 王孫滿 instructed him that it was not the condition of any symbolic object, such as the cauldrons, but the moral power or virtue of the ruler, that mattered most.

34. I am uncertain how to render the phrase 東霸城府. It may indicate Xiao Daocheng's taking control of Dongfu 東府, directly south of Jiankang, which occurred in early 478. Or it may follow from the designation of the 霸門 (or 霸城門) as the northernmost gate in the eastern wall of Han-time Chang'an.

35. In the late spring of 479, Xiao Daocheng was made Minister of State 相國.

36. The Nine Bestowals was an old ritual that had become part of the elaborately choreographed schedule of (usually triple) refusals and reluctant acceptances of increasing honors that led ultimately to the Song emperor's surrendering his throne to Xiao Daocheng.

37. This was Xiao Ni 蕭嶷, Xiao Daocheng's second son. He received this title in 479. He played an important role in establishing the dynasty and, following Daocheng's death in the summer of 482, remained loyal to his older brother Xiao Yi 蕭頤, who succeeded to the throne (Qi Emperor Wu 齊武帝, r. 482–493).

38. Jiang Yan received these promotions in 480, and they are the last titles he mentions in the preface. His next appointments were not until 485. Since Xiao Daocheng died in 482 and was canonized as Gaodi, the title by which Jiang refers to him in the preceding paragraph, we may date this text somewhere between late 482 and early 485.

39. Jiang Yan claims that his clan descends, like that of Qu Yuan 屈原 (see the opening lines of "Li sao") from Gaoyang 高陽, known also as Zhuanxu 顓頊, the legendary god-king of Chu.

40. That is, sun, moon, and stars; or the gods of Heaven, Earth, and Man.

41. In addition to the cruel trick that Heaven seems to have played, note that the boy's by-name, Yinqing, meaning "Heritor-Minister" and bespeaking his father's great hopes for him, is a name that now seems quite ill-starred.

42. Quoting exactly from "Li sao" regarding the time of Qu Yuan's birth.

43. These two lines are closely calqued on a couplet from the "Jiu bian" 九辯, in the *Lyrics of Chu* (*Chuci* 楚辭).

44. See *Classic of Poetry* (*Shijing* 詩經) 245, regarding the infant Hou Ji 后稷.

45. "Clue" (*duan* 端) is being used in its original sense of the end-tip of a ball of thread (parallel to *xu* 緒 in the next line), from which the common connotation derives and which is most appropriate here.

46. That is, in the capital area of Jiankang 建康 and its wider environs, along the lower Yangzi.

47. Referring to Śākyamuni Buddha and the karmic law of cause and effect, and to the "Triple World" (past, present, future) in which karma operates.

48. A *kṣetrā* 刹 is a Buddha realm, here specifically the "Pure" 淨 Land, Sukhāvatī, of Amitābha in the west.

49. By referring to the "two" halcyons, Jiang Yan is following the old practice of seeing the *fei* and *cui* as a pair of complementarily matched birds, the former having red plumes and the latter having blue plumes. Compare the traditional definition of the *feng* 鳳 as the "male" phoenix and the *huang* 凰 as the "female." The pleonastic term "halcyon kingfisher" renders the binome *feicui*; either "halcyon" or "kingfisher" by itself suffices for *cui* when it appears alone.

50. The classical "five metropolises" include the capitals Chang'an 長安 and Luoyang 洛陽. Scholars disagree over the identification of the other three, but it matters little.

51. That is, amid the eight points of the compass-rose.

52. The kingfisher has often been described in literature ("on bamboo and silk"), and its distinctiveness has now become all too common.

53. The "corded isles" refers to China's farthermost territories. The "Red District" is an old designation of the Chinese empire and may be thought of here as specifically the Southern regions.

54. See the famous story in *Liezi jishi* 列子集釋 (Beijing: Zhonghua shuju, 1979) 2.67–68.

25. The Shadow Image in the Cave

Discourse on Icons

EUGENE WANG

Buddha images appeared in China as early as the Han dynasty (206 B.C.E.–220 C.E.), according to some accounts, but it was not until around 400 C.E. that the making of Buddhist images became a widespread practice there. The movement was accompanied by serious theoretical inquiries into the nature of images, and the body of writings inspired by a shadow image in a proverbial cave best epitomized this new interest.

At the same time, around 400, the lore of the "Shadow Cave," allegedly located in the region of Nagarahāra (west of present-day Jalalabad, Afghanistan), was circulating in China. The interior wall of the hillside grotto was said to display a "[Śākyamuni] Buddha's shadow image" 佛影 or reflection,[1] visible from a distance and invisible upon closer look. It apparently captured the Chinese imagination, for the Chinese monk Faxian 法顯 (ca. 337–ca. 422) visited the cave in 402, followed by other Chinese monks around 520 and thereafter. Faxian's report is corroborated by the contemporary Chinese translations of Buddhist texts, most notably those by Kumārajīva 鳩摩羅什 (343–413) and Buddhabhadra 佛陀跋陀羅 (359–429).[2]

Born in Kuchā, Kumārajīva studied in Kashmir and Kashagar and established his reputation as an eminent Buddhist master and a specialist in mantic arts. Brought to northwestern China in 383, he arrived in Chang'an in 402, where his authority in Buddhism remained unrivaled until the arrival of Buddhabhadra.

A master of meditation from Kapilavastu in northern India, Buddhabhadra arrived in Chang'an in 406. His translation of the *Sutra of the Oceanic Samādhi of Visualizing the Buddha* (*Guanfo sanmei hai jing* 觀佛三昧海經) contains the most comprehensive account of the Shadow Cave.[3] Skeptical about its status as a translated Indian sutra, modern scholars are inclined to regard it as an apocryphal text mixing Chinese and Indian elements.[4]

A fallout between Buddhabhadra and the Buddhist establishment in the North headed by Kumārajīva led to the exile of Buddhabhadra to the South, and his visit to Mount Lu was instrumental in the making of a shadow cave there. On Mount Lu, Huiyuan 慧遠 (334–416), an eminent Chinese Buddhist scholar, led a faithful community in the mountain retreat that practiced Buddhist meditation. Buddhabhadra may have informed Huiyuan about the details of the Shadow Cave in Nagarahāra. Likely inspired by the proverbial shadow image, Huiyuan and his followers constructed a replica cave on a hillside of Mount Lu. A Buddha image painted in delicate colors on a piece of silk was hung on the interior wall of the cave as the "Shadow Image."

Although the replica cave no longer exists as such, the effusive hymns that Huiyuan and his followers wrote in response to the shadow image are just as significant. Together with the contemporary accounts of the Shadow Cave at Nagarahāra, they form a cogent body of what amounts to the Chinese theory of images "before the era of art."[5]

Canonical Chinese art theory typically favors texts that speak to our modern notion of "art" involving aesthetic principles and creative processes, and it tends to prioritize the agency of individual artists as world-making forces. In early medieval China, however, the notion of "art" that owes its existence to the originality of creative artists had relatively little currency. The efficacy of images was the primary concern; perception trumped creation. Therefore, the writings on the Shadow Image are chosen here over the better-known works of "art theory," on the grounds that the theory of images better captures the cultural dynamics of the time.

The medium of representation remains at the forefront of this period. To Huiyuan and his contemporaries, the Buddha's presence amounts to an apparition accessible largely as a dream image or a reflection in a mirror. To this end, a shadow image in a cave provides the best possible medium to materialize the Buddha's accessibility. The imaginary scenario of a Buddha leaping into the grotto wall and staying on it as an *image* amounts to an ideal model of representation. The situation then points to the Buddha *image* as a *medium*. Here, "medium" has two senses. On the one hand, it denotes the material support of an image, in the sense of a pictorial and sculptural medium. On the other hand, it suggests a stopgap, an abode, or a vehicle that hosts the otherwise transcendent being, such as a buddha. The text does not pretend that the image on the wall *is* the Buddha. It is merely the Buddha's shadowy reflection that signals both his *presence* and his *absence*. The Buddha *was* here but has now departed. The shadow image on the wall is a trace of that erstwhile presence, what *used to be* but *no longer is* here. The shadow image is therefore a model of all visual representations of the Buddha: the material support—the configuration on the rock surface—is a medium in the same way that a human being can act as a medium of which a deity may take possession. Once possessed, he is beside himself. Likewise, once the wall surface is believed to host a spiritual being, it is seen as more than just a wall.

This image-as-medium theory spoke to a society caught up with both traditional concerns involving ancestral spirits and new glimpses into an alternative mode of existence as Buddhism gained popularity. The vexed relationship between body and spirit became increasingly a point of contention. The traditional Chinese scheme of human body and spirit regards human life as a combination of two parts: heaven endows one part with a certain animating spirit, and earth gives the other part a bodily frame. Both the spirit and the body are made of pneuma or vapor, their difference lying in the varying degrees of refinement. Dispersion of the pneuma or vapor means death, the cessation of the individual existence. That is, what follows in the hereafter is often lost in a nebula.

This idea did not square with the Buddhist notion of transmigration and reincarnation that was newly gaining ground in early medieval China. One potent metaphor inherited from the early Chinese discourse on human life was the dependence of fire on burning wood.[6] The body is to the spirit what wood is to fire. The fire ("spirit") is extinguished when the log ("bodily form") burns out. To argue for the continued existence of the postmortem spirit, therefore, Huiyuan and his contemporaries reinvented the wheel. They envisioned the "spirit" 神 (*shen*) as capable of inhabiting different bodies. To them, the "spirit" meant the de-individualized World Soul permeating the universe, ready to lodge in any medium and manifest itself. They thereby gave an ingenious twist to the same fire–wood analogy: the fire and the wood need not be in a fixed one-to-one relationship. Instead, the fire can continue to burn and avoid extinction by moving to a different log.

The flexible unlinking and relinking of the spirit and bodily form informed the image theory fashioned by Huiyuan and his contemporaries. The invisible World Soul or spirit (*shen*) roams around in the numinous realm. The human-made image is a physical medium that allows the spirit to inhabit it. Much as the physical medium of the image has a fixed form, it amounts to a placeholder that allows for the arrival and departure of the invisible "spirit." The image thus conceived makes the potential problems of idolatry or iconolatry a moot issue in the Chinese context. The image commands attention and reverence not because of its inherent special property but because of its role as a medium to be possessed and inhabited by the spirit. Without the lodging spirit, it is purely physical stuff.

The theory provides a convenient solution to the dilemma faced by the Chinese Buddhist community. For the Chinese to feel connected to a supernatural god that never set foot on Chinese soil, such a medium, with both noumenal and phenomenal properties, effectively reconciles the fiction of presence and the reality of absence. That is, it serves as a refutation of the hard-nosed empirical quest for the verity of the Buddha's existence on Chinese land.[7]

The pictorial medium best reifies this image theory. Buddha images recorded in early historical sources appear to be mostly freestanding statues,[8] and the widely circulated early medieval image lore also gravitated toward the medium of sculptural icons.[9] But the physicality of freestanding Buddhist statues made of bronze, wood, or clay was susceptible to skepticism about whether the statues could truly embody divinity.[10] It certainly did little to assuage the anxiety or subdue the bewilderment felt by the medieval Chinese about the nature of the disembodied beings transcending time and space and being manifested to the living in bodily forms. Painting, by contrast, can have it both ways. It has the efficacy of conjuring up the visual illusionism of a presence, and at the same time, it remains a physically impenetrable surface. Painting therefore became a compelling medium with which the medieval Chinese could come to terms with the elusiveness of the "body" of the eternal Buddha and the bodhisattvas.

The "shadow of the Buddha" strongly suggests a model of painting. Although primarily a spatial structure, the center of gravity of the Shadow Cave is the luminous reflection on the wall or an image registered on a flat surface. Faxian, the first known Chinese pilgrim to visit the cave in Nagarahāra, noted that "the kings of the neighboring countries sent skillful painters to copy the Buddha's shadow, but to no avail."[11] Consequently, Huiyuan's construction of the mountainside shrine to replicate the Shadow Cave was oriented toward a painted image.[12]

The eulogies on the "shadow of the Buddha" by Huiyuan and his followers therefore established a model of perceiving and conceptualizing the pictorial medium. They registered an interest in a new pictorial mode, as opposed to the traditional surface-oriented curvilinear painting. Chiaroscuro, a formal quality that had hitherto held little interest to the Chinese, now appeared to be of primary concern to Huiyuan's circle. Much was invested in indistinct optical and atmospheric conditions such as "darkness," "dimness," "obscurity," and "void" to offset the luminous forms of "manifestations." Attention was drawn to the interplay between background and foreground, "darkness and light," brilliance and obscurity. There was a decided interest in visual illusionism.

In grappling with the ontological implications of the shadow image, Huiyuan and his contemporaries were in fact finding ways of coming to terms with the formal property of a new type of pictorial form thriving on unstressed edges rather than on stressed ones, as well as formulating their own perceptions of such images. Their responses show a clear awareness of the dual qualities of the pictures of this kind: the illusionistic depth and the material surface. The pictorial images, as the poet Xie Lingyun 謝靈運 (385–433) puts it, "manifest appearances if looked from afar, and become smudges once one comes close [to them]. They are neither substance nor void."[13] In other words, they are neither entirely a palpable surface nor a real space. This motif is reiterated in medieval accounts of the shadow image, which insist on the distinction between the success of viewing the image from afar and the failure to do so if examining it up close to the wall. The spectator's shuttle back and forth in relationship to the wall is tantamount to the proper steps taken to obtain the desired illusionistic effect in viewing murals: moving close, one sees only the material surface; stepping back, one sees the figures being pictured. By extension, the yearning for such an image entailed the actual making of pictures in this manner, which required the painter to step back to enact the experience of his implied spectator. The perceptual experience involved here is what modern theorists describe as the "twofoldness" of the "seeing in." One is "visually aware of the surface" one looks at, and one discerns something standing in front of oneself and receding behind the wall's surface.[14]

The beholder's share and the optical experience are key aspects of this image theory. It is notable that the alleged efficacy of the image depends on the topography of the grotto. A comparison of the accounts of the same topography by Buddhabhadra and by the Chinese authors reveals shared concerns as well as different interests. Buddhabhadra's story of the cave is animated by a narrative description of Buddha's dramatic subjugation of the dragons in the cave. The allegorical scenario of the transcendent Buddha taking over the lair of a local *naga* (dragon) is a familiar narrative scenario in the Indian tradition. It enacts the symbolic process of localizing the translocal Buddha.[15] The Chinese authors, however, had little use for it but were instead drawn to the optical theater facilitated by the grotto setting. The interiority creates a condition of sensory deprivation inducive of a heightened state of "viewing," which amounts to the half seeing and half imagining of an image.

The purpose of such an illusionism is to facilitate the contemplative visualization of the Buddha. The key meditation guide for Huiyuan and his contemporaries was the *Banzhou sanmei jing* (*Pratyutpanna Sutra*), which offers instructions for ways of obtaining a vision "as if [all buddhas] were standing before one's eyes." The devotee is advised to concentrate and work himself into a trance so that he may obtain a dreamlike vision of the Buddha analogous to "a reflection in the mirror." The hallucinatory mode of perception and oneiric quality of the vision are encouraged. Such a visual encounter reinforces the illusionism of presence and fosters the sense of the image inhabiting a virtual realm that transcends the quotidian plane of experience and constraints of time and space. The way that Huiyuan and his peers conceived of the painted icons as "the Buddha's shadow" is resonant with this teaching. The numinous realm ("the Void") in which "the Buddha's shadow" lodges takes on properties of virtual and spatial illusionism that allow the devotee's mind to enter, dwell, and roam: "Deeply cherish the mystic refuge and, at night, think of letting your spirit roam."[16]

A dialectic notion of image emerges from this penumbra of perceptual experience. The shadow image has two inextricably linked properties. It resides in both the physical medium of the painting on the wall and the mind's eye of the beholder. It is both a physical trace and a mental image, visible and invisible, present and absent. The shift in locales or domains in the *Sutra of the Oceanic Samādhi of Visualizing the Buddha* therefore comes as no surprise: the instruction on visualization starts with the proverbial physical grotto in the distant land with its shadow image; it then careens to the imaginary cave conjured up in the practitioner's mind. As the instruction coaxes the mind into the cave, it also places the cave in the mind, with the elusive shadow image oscillating between the cave and mind. The physical cave thus gives way to the cave as a mental topography for the visualizer.

Much as the Shadow Cave provides a new model of perception, Huiyuan and his contemporaries also relied on cognitive frameworks and habitual imaginary resources drawn from their own tradition. The long-standing notion of a shadow as an energetic-ethereal extension of the body from which it can be disengaged certainly availed itself to the medieval imagination. Furthermore, there was no lack of Chinese precedents of shadow images. The most illustrious case is the shadow image conjured up by a Han magician, repeatedly described in Han sources and then elaborated in a fourth-century source.[17] Pining for his departed consort Lady Li, the Han Emperor Wu (r. 141–87 B.C.E.) is said to have repeatedly dreamed of her in his sleep. He sought help from a magician named Shao Weng, who had a statue carved out of a dark stone obtained from the sea. The statue was then placed behind a gauze curtain as a shadow image. When the emperor asked if he could take a close-up view, Shao explained that the image was comparable to a "dream one had during a noon nap." It could be viewed only from a distance instead of at close range.[18]

The fourth-century inflection of the Han story anticipates Huiyuan's shadow image. The oneiric quality of the image resulting from the light projection, the distant viewing, and the inaccessibility are precisely the motifs attending the Buddha's image in the proverbial shadow cave. The narrative context of Shao Weng's shadow image provides another layer of relevance: after all, the projected shadow image of Lady Li was a device to register the presence of an absence, the illusive manifestation of the deceased's likeness. The medium of the shadow image on a curtain projected from a statue speaks further to the complicity of the corroborative role of the mind in creating the image.

FURTHER READING

For studies of the shadow image in the proverbial Shadow Cave, see Alexander Soper, "Aspects of Light Symbolism, Part 1," *Artibus Asiae* 12 (1949): 252–83; "Part 2," *Artibus Asiae* 12 (1949): 314–30; "Part 3," *Artibus Asiae* 13 (1950): 63–85, and *Literary Evidence for Early Buddhist Art in China* (Ascona, Switzerland: Artibus Asiae, 1959), 265–68; Erik Zürcher, *The Buddhist Conquest of China: The Spread and Adaptation of Buddhism in Early Medieval China* (Leiden: Brill, 1972); Marylin Martin Rhie, *Early Buddhist Art of China and Central Asia: The Eastern Chin and Sixteen Kingdoms Period in China and Tumshuk, Kucha, and Karashahr in Central Asia* (Leiden: Brill, 1999–2002), 2:112–37; and Eugene Wang, *Shaping the Lotus Sutra: Buddhist Visual Culture in Medieval China* (Seattle: University of Washington Press, 2005), 245–55. For textual studies of the *Sutra of the Oceanic Samādhi of Visualizing the Buddha* (*Guanfo sanmei hai jing* 觀佛三昧海經), which contains the most comprehensive account of the Shadow Cave and the issue of its authorship, see Nobuyoshi Yamabe, "*The Sutra on the Ocean-Like Samadhi of the Visualization of the Buddha*: The Interfusion of the Chinese and Indian Cultures in Central Asia as Reflected in a Fifth Century Apocryphal Sutra" (Ph.D. diss., Yale University, 1999); and Jinhua Chen 陳金華, "Fotuobatuo gong Huiyuan gou foyingtai shi zaikao" 佛陀跋陀共慧遠構佛影臺事再考, in *Guoxue yu foxue: Lou Yulie jiaoshou qizhi jinwu songshou wenji* 國學與佛學樓宇烈教授七秩晉五頌壽文集, ed. Li Silong 李四龍 (Beijing: Jiuzhou chubanshe, 2009), 55–64, and "Meditation Tradition in Fifth Century Northern China: With a Focus on a Forgotten 'Kashmiri' Meditation Tradition Brought to China by Buddhabhadra (359–429)," in *Across Asia: Networks of Material, Intellectual, and Cultural Exchange*, ed. Tansen Sen (Singapore: Institute of Southeast Asian Studies, 2010), 1–27. See also a related article, Jinhua Chen, "Buddhabhadra's (359–429) Connection with Huiyuan (334–416) in Transplanting the Nagarahāra Image-cave to China: A Reexamination," in *Chūgoku Indo shūkyōshi, tokuni Bukkyō shi ni okeru shomotsu no ryūtsū denpa to jinbutsu idō no chiiki tokusei* 中国印度宗教史とくに仏教史における書物の流通伝播と人物移動の地域特性, ed. Funayama Toru 船山徹 (Kyoto: Institute for Research in Humanities, Kyoto University, 2011), 177–91. For a modern investigation of the Shadow Cave in Central Asia, see E. Caspani, "The Cave of the Shadow of the Buddha at Nagarahāra," *Journal of the Royal Asiatic Society of Bengal* 11 (1945): 47–52. For Huiyuan's theoretical reflections on Buddhahood, body, and spirit, see Walter Liebenthal, "Shih Hui-yüan's Buddhism as Set Forth in His Writings." *Journal of the American Oriental Society* 70, no. 4 (1950): 243–59.

Faxian 法顯

The Record of Faxian 法顯傳 (excerpt)

Half *yojana* or so south of the Nagarahāra city is a rock cavern amid rolling hills, facing southwest. Here the Buddha left his shadow. Inside the cave, one views the [shadow] as if it were the Buddha's true form, a radiant golden image in full splendor. Upon close inspection, one finds the image fading into a tantalizing obscurity. Kings of various regions have sent skillful painters to make copies of the image, but none succeeded. People of the land say: The Thousand Buddhas all must have left their shadows here.[19]

[*Faxian zhuan*, T 51:859a]

BUDDHABHADRA 佛陀跋陀羅

Sutra of the Oceanic Samādhi of Visualizing the Buddha 觀佛三昧海經 (excerpt)

GUANFO SANMEI HAI JING (SKT. BUDDHA-DHYĀNA-SAMĀDHISĀGARA-SŪTRA)

At that time, the dragon king knelt down, with his palm closed, pleaded with the World-Honored One: "It is my wish that the Thus-Come One [Tathāgata] reside here for eternity. If the Buddha is absent, I may entertain evil thoughts that would prevent me from attaining the supreme enlightenment. It is my devout wish that the Thus-Come One leave his spirit here and turn his thought here forever." Thus he pleaded three times in earnest, unceasing. At that time, the Brahman king came again to pay homage to the Buddha with closed palms and enjoined the Buddha to stay: "We wish that the World-Honored stay, not just for this small dragon, but for the masses of the sentient beings of the future generations." Thus the kings of the Brahman heaven pleaded in the tens and thousands in a uniform chorus.

At that time, the Thus-Come One smiled. His mouth issued tens and thousand radiant rays populated by countless Buddha manifestations, each attended by zillions of bodhisattvas. Then the dragon king in the pond presented a Seven-Treasure Tower to the Buddha: "Please, Lord, accept this tower of mine." The World-Revered told the dragon king: "The tower is unnecessary. You may give me the ogres' grotto." Then the Brahman king and his princes first entered the cave. The dragon king festooned the cave with a variety of treasures. The Buddha told Ananda: "Go and request the dragon king to sweep clean the grotto." Upon hearing this, all the celestial kings hastened to take off their precious garments to sweep the cave. The Thus-Come One recollected his bodily radiance, the myriad Buddha manifestations, and all into his head excrescence [Skt. *uṣṇīṣa*]. Bidding all the monks to stay outside the cave, the Buddha alone went in and spread his sitting mat. In doing so, he turned the rocky hill into a Seven-Treasure [Mountain]. The ogre and the dragon then produced five caves for the Buddha's four disciples and the Venerable Ananda.

At that time, the World-Honored One sat in the dragon king's cave without changing his spot. At the king's request, he entered the city of Nagarahāra. Gṛdhrakūṭa, Śrāvastī kingdom, the city of Kapilavastu, and other populated places all have the sightings of the Buddha. The space is filled with countless Buddha manifestations on lotus thrones. All the world is filled with Buddha manifestations. Overjoyed, the dragon king made a great vow: "May I have the Buddhas in my future lives." At the king's request, the Buddha spent seven days thus. The king sent a man riding on an eight-thousand-league elephant, carrying with him offering paraphernalia to visit all the kingdoms to support the monks. There are sightings of the Buddha everywhere. The messenger reported back to the king: "Not only does this kingdom have the Buddha, so do all other kingdoms. Moreover, in all these kingdoms, the Buddhas all preach the [doctrine of] suffering, emptiness, inconstancy, nonself, and the Six Perfections."[20] Upon hearing this, the king had the epiphany, realizing that all things are beyond birth and decay.

Then the World-Honored One exited the grotto on his supernatural feet and roamed with the monks. Recalling his former lives as a bodhisattva, [the Buddha took the monks to visit] the place where he had given away his two sons, the spot where he had forfeited his life to feed the hungry tigress, the site where he had donated his head, the location where he had had his body maimed to light up a thousand lamps, the venue where he had gouged out his eyes for charity, and the venue where he had allowed his flesh to be cut in order to ransom the dove. The dragons followed the Buddha's steps in all these stops. Then, learning that the Buddha had gone back to his home state, the dragon king broke into tears and said: "World-Honored One, pray thee, stay for eternity. Why do you abandon me so that I do not see the Buddha? I may commit crimes and relapse into evil ways." The World-Honored One then consoled the dragon king: "I accept your request to sit in your cave for a thousand and five hundred years." At this, all the junior dragons closed their palms and crossed their arms, and pleaded with the Buddha to return to the cave. The dragons then saw the Buddha sitting in their grotto. From his body, water shot up and fire issued down, creating eighteen kinds of transformations. The sight of this reinforced the junior dragons' conviction in following the [Buddhist] way. Śākyamuni Buddha then leaped into the rock [wall] where it appeared as a bright mirror that reflected one's visage. The dragons all saw the Buddha inside the rock and manifested outward [on the rock surface]. At this, the dragons all clasped their hands and rejoiced. They could constantly see the Buddha Sun without going out of the pond.

At that time, the World-Honored One sat with legs crossed inside the rock. The way the sentient beings saw [the image], they could catch sight of it only at a distance. Drawing closer, they could not see it. Celestials in the tens and thousands made their offerings to the Buddha's image, which in turn preached the dharma law. With their palms closed, the kings of the Brahman heaven venerated [the image], and praised it in verse:

Thus-Come resides in the grotto,	如來處石窟
Having leaped into the rock.	踊身入石裏
Like the sun unblocked,	如日無障礙
Full golden light and all the marks.	金光相具足
I hereby pay my homage,	我今頭面禮
O, Śākyamuni, the world-saving Lord.	牟尼救世尊

At that time, the World-Honored One conjured up five hundred treasure carriages. The Buddha in each carriage split into five hundred bodies. The treasure carriages moved and turned in the air with total ease, their drums and spokes illuminated with tens and thousands of radiant rays, each showing myriad Buddha manifestations. Neither moving nor turning, the Buddhas arrived in the Kapilavastu. Sitting on lion thrones, the Buddhas appeared to have entered the perfect absorption [samādhi]. Each pore had a Buddha exiting and a Buddha entering. They filled up the entire space—those Buddha manifestations, sitting cross-legged. This is called the state of the seated Buddha. After the Buddha's extinction, all Buddhist disciples should heed this. To know the seated Buddha, one should visualize the Buddha's shadow. To do so, one first visualizes a Buddha image through the mental conception of [a statue of] one zhang and six [in height], sitting with crossed legs on a grass mat.[21] One invites the statue to be seated and sees to it that it indeed does so. One then conceives a grotto, one zhang and eight chi in height and twenty-four in depth, made of resplendent rocks.[22] Having formed this thought, one indeed sees a seated Buddha in the air, whose feet are raining flowers. One then thinks of entering the grotto. Having entered, one rehearses the thought of the grotto as a seven-treasure mountain. With the formation of this thought, one once again sees the Buddha statue leaping into the rock surface, which appears transparent like a bright mirror. Succeeding in this conception, one then contemplates the Buddha's thirty-two distinguished features in the foregoing manner. Each feature ought to be made distinct in one's visualization. Having formed this thought, one then sees myriad Buddha manifestations, sitting cross-legged on big precious flowers, their radiant bodies illuminating all. Each seated Buddha's pores rain incalculable seven-treasure canopies whose tops anchor tens and thousands of banners each. Even the smallest of the banners is the size of Mount Sumeru. Each treasure banner contains hundreds and thousands of Buddha manifestations, all leaping into the navel of the Buddha shadow of this grotto. Once this thought presents itself, it is what is said about the Buddha's heart. This is the proper mode of visualization. Any departure from this is a devious mode. This way of visualizing the Buddha shadow after the Buddha's extinction is called the true vision of the seated Buddha, which is tantamount to seeing the Buddha body. [This vision] can eliminate the crimes accumulated in life-and-death cycles of hundreds and thousands of eons. If one fails to have this vision, one should enter the stupa tower to contemplate all the seated images. Seeing the seated images, one repents one's sins of karmic hindrances. The person's visualization of the Buddha image earns him causes of good destiny in anticipation of Maitreya's arrival. He then sees Maitreya sitting cross-legged under the dragon-flower trees from the very beginning. Having seen this, he is overjoyed. He thus accomplishes the three resolves,[23] and all his wishes are met.[24]

[*Sutra of the Oceanic Samādhi of Visualizing the Buddha* 觀佛三昧海經, *T* 15:680c–681c]

Monk Shi Huiyuan 釋慧遠 of Jin

Inscription on Buddha's Shadow 佛影銘

Buddha's Shadow is located in the stone chamber of ancient immortals in the south mountain of the west Nagarahāra kingdom.[25] If one follows the footpath across the Flowing Sand, it is 15,850 *li* from here. Previous accounts have elaborated on the manifestations of its miraculous responses.

Entrenched in superficial habits, one is unlikely to acquire the rare Word.[26] Following the mundane routine to while away time, one rarely harbors transcendent sentiments. Therefore, worldly thoughts fall short of metaphysical aspirations; the firmament net caps the inspired ideals. If one chooses to spend one's lifetime thus, how can one possibly have a chance for change?[27] If one is content with life as such, then enlightenment is forever out of reach. Thus determined, I work day and night, forgoing meals.[28] My feeling [for the Buddha] has grown by the day. Purifying my thoughts deep in the night, my inner thought harmonizes with the Buddha mind. I have therefore gratefully received the Buddha's myriad blessings.[29] Thrice I was able to see the compassionate [visage] of the unattached [Buddha]; accordingly, I have been searching for the reasons behind the dharma body's manifestations [and come to appreciate that] divinity shows but does not speak; the Buddha's manifestation does not hinge on how we feel; his compassion does not necessarily stem from our causal conditions—we will feel it through quiet meditations.[30] The sun and moon hang in the sky, ever so bright. Accordingly, myriad things flourish; sentient beings all go by them. All are delighted in being bathed in luminance from the high, little aware that here lodges the [divinity's] ever varying adaptations to [myriad things].[31] The discourse on the scheme of things can only go thus far. One may wish to measure the depth of the mystical universe so as to speak of its ways. However, its seeming existence is ultimately ineffable. Why do we say so? The dharma body has its way of setting things in motion. Instead of driving them, it signals itself through them. Instead of diagramming their end, it intimates the finality. It models the metaphysical on the surface of the myriad transformations. Its destiny resides in the unnamable. If one speaks of its lodging, then the Way is everywhere. Therefore the Thus-Come One [Tathāgata] may obscure his former traces on elevated altars or manifests himself in the living world as a definite body. He either singularly hails from the unfathomable noumenal realm or avails himself [to the beholder] in the domain of the phenomenal existence. Accordingly, the noumenal singularity amounts to his bodily frame; his interactive relationship [with the beholder] amounts to a shadow. Consider the profound implication of this—does his existence depend or not depend [on our perception]?[32] The way I see it: this is a matter of mediated or direct experience. The dharma body ultimately comes down to nonduality. Where do we draw the dividing line between its bodily frame and its shadow image? Those seeking the Way nowadays all depict the [image] of the divine body as if it were in a distant past. Little do they realize that the divine response is right here. Even though they know the supreme transformation takes no specific bodiless form, they still gauge his physical traces through his whereabouts [literally, movement and arrest]. Is this not misguided?

I, [Hui]yuan, used to seek out the late master and attended him for years.[33] Even though I was enlightened by the generous teaching and immersed myself in the Buddhist sutras, every now and then I have always pictured in my mind the Buddha's miraculous deeds to solidify my conviction. From the encounter with the itinerant monk from the Western Region, I learned about the Buddha Shadow [Image]. However, my informer was vague on this. Later, a meditation master from Kaśmīra, a *vinaya* monk of the south state, confirmed what I heard on the basis of his own visit to the site. I pressed them more on the matter and found that many miracles had been verified. The divine Way is unfathomable except through its lodging in images. The insight results from prolonged contemplation instead of a momentary impulse. I have thus come to believe firmly in the truthfulness of what I have been told and share the same conviction.[34] I have therefore convened a group of like-minded [people], and together we shall broadcast the Buddha's true flavor. In a worthy effort to spread the joy of inclusionary wholesome practice, we have thus made the picture. I hereby make the inscription:

I

Boundless is the Great Image,	廓矣大象
Its principle and mystery remains ineffable.	理玄無名
[Buddha's] body and spirit have merged into evolving nature,	體神入化
His shadow cast, his body gone.	落影離形
His lingering light brightens the layered peaks,	迴暉層巖
Illuminating the hillside pavilion.	凝映虛亭
Residing in obscurity, the image does not dim;	在陰不昧

The darker its location, the brighter its radiance.　處暗逾明
Gracefully it walks,[35] in a cicada-like transcendence,　婉步蟬蛻
Commanding the audience of myriad spirits.　朝宗百靈
Manifestly responsive in different ways,　應不同方
It remains traceless and obscure.　跡絕而冥

II

Murky and nebulous is our vast cosmos,　茫茫荒宇
Nothing here persuades and inspires [us].　靡勸靡獎
Bland and light touches suffice to bring out Buddha's
　visage,　淡虛寫容
Out of nowhere is born the image .　拂空傳像
Displaying [the Buddha's] marks, its frame is subtle,　相具體微
Its transcendent manner is self-apparent.[36]　沖姿自朗
The white tuft of hair [between the Buddha's eyebrows]
　radiant,　白毫吐曜
Bright even in the deep night.　昏夜中爽
Deep contemplation solicits its response,　感徹乃應
Utter devotion causes it to resonate.　扣誠發響
As the lingering echo in the valley, it remains　留音停岫
Apprehensible only to the cleansed mind in quietude.　津悟冥賞
Contact with it produces epiphany,　撫之有會
The achievement outgrows all that past.　功弗由曩

III

Turning around, [one may] instantly forget reverence.　旋踵忘敬
Thereby forgoing contemplation and cognitions.　罔慮罔識
The Three Luminaries [sun, moon, stars] may thus
　be obscured.　三光掩暉
Myriad appearances reduced to one appearance.　萬象一色
A dark haze envelops the courtyards;　庭宇幽藹
One loses the way to return.　歸塗莫測
Buddha enlightens us by means of calm,　悟之以靜
And rescues us with power.　挹之以力
Now this zephyr of wisdom has grown distant,　惠風雖退
Only the worldly dust settles there.　維塵攸息
Without this mystic mirror,[37]　匪伊玄覽
How can this dust be swept from afar?　孰扇其極

IV

The precious sound reaches afar,	希音遠流
Now to the east it casts regard.	乃眷東顧
Delighting in the trend and aspiring to the Way,	欣風慕道
We revere and follow the bright moon.	仰規玄度
Its wonder hangs on the tip of the brush,	妙盡毫端
As its subtlety courses along the light silk.	運微輕素
Light and delicate are the colors deployed,	託采虛凝
They fairly illuminate the nocturnal fog.	殆映宵霧
Images register the [divine] trace,	跡以像告
Resonant with profound conceptions.	理深其趣
The extraordinary revelations open up one's mind.	奇興開襟
The auspicious wind guides the way.	祥風引路
The pure vapor encircles the lofty chamber.	清氣迴於軒宇
Opacity and clarity merge before the dawn,	昏明交而未曙
[The image] appears to mirror the divine visage,	彷彿鏡神儀
Vaguely discernible as if face to face.	依俙若真遇

V

Inscribing and picturing the [shadow image],	銘之圖之
What do we seek after all?	曷營曷求
If spiritual beings hear this,[38]	神之聽之
They would heed this endeavor.	鑒爾所修
We wish to use the practice of this world,	庶茲塵軌
To reflect the mystic stream yonder.	映彼玄流
The spirit pond purifies our heart—	漱情靈沼
Drinking from it makes one lithe and lissome.	飲和至柔
It illuminates the void and responds to simplicity,	照虛應簡
Rounding up the seat of wisdom.	智落乃周
Profound is our reverie, lodged in nebulae,	深懷冥託
Oneiric yearnings power out-of-body roaming.	宵想神遊
All our lives are condensed into this one encounter,	畢命一對
That frees us once for all from myriad vexations.	長謝百憂

On the first day of the fifth month, the *renzi* year [412], Jinxi the eighth year of Jin, together we set up this platform. We have made an image in our mountain, in which we lodge our sincerity. Even though this image is man-made, its merit is unsurpassed. When the Year Star reached the Stellar Sequence,[39] Chifengnuo pointed to the ruin of the Great Yin [i.e., the twelfth year of the Jovian cycle].[40] On the third of the ninth month, I have carefully gone through others' texts. Hereby they are inscribed on stone. From the day when the project was planned and commenced, people's sincerity has multiplied. The *sanga* and the laity all have delighted in the endeavor, as their contact with the leftover trace speak to them directly. Our feelings have welled up from the within; thereby we have become tireless. All the guests who took up the brush eulogized in harmony. Our thoughts all turned to the goal ahead. The image is based on what we have heard variously. We hope it will serve as a template for future wisdom-seekers.[41] Therefore we have gathered people of the time at the shadow image in an assemblage of the Great Pervader.[42] This is indeed beyond what the conventional wisdom can expect.[43] Standing still and marveling at the distant Buddha, we have already transcended the spirit realm.

[*T* 52:197c–98b; the *Gaoseng zhuan* also contains
the inscription, *T* 50:358–59]

Xie Lingyun 謝靈運

Inscription on Buddha's Shadow (with Preface) 佛影銘 (并序)

The great compassionate Buddha blesses beings through sympathetic sentience. The causes of his communication with the beings vary. These are less amenable to being registered in forms, as they are better deduced conceptually. Much of this has been documented and discussed in scriptures and commentaries. Though things of the world come and go,[44] the [dharma] way of the images endures. Lamenting the way of the world, our Buddhist faith has grown by the day. The Buddha's Shadow, as reported in detail by the monk Faxian, who has arrived from Jetavana,[45] is truly marvelous and extraordinary. Fixed on the stone wall of a grotto, the image appears to be there, with its elegant visage and manners, complete in all the marks and features. Its manifest cycle is beyond our grasp, yet its calm repose remains constant. Having heard about it with delight, the dharma master of Mount Lu [Huiyuan] excavated a quiet dark chamber out of a grotto to joyfully involve others in [his wholesome image-making practice].[46] Nestled in a steep hill to the north, it fronts a rapid to the south. He made an image based on proportions given to him and decorated it with green colors. All this is not done for mimetic verisimilitude but to convey his deepest feelings. Monk Daoping came all the way to convey [Huiyuan's] request for a votive text to be inscribed [on the rock at the cave site]. The intent behind the stone inscription is to spread virtues, though it can hardly match the magnitude of the Buddhist way. Likewise, my shallow thinking and skin-deep learning can hardly capture [Master Huiyuan's accomplishment]. [Huiyuan's image-making] event is already a thing of past. However, it has always stayed on my mind. I therefore exhaust whatever meager talent I have to fulfill my long-cherished wishes. The plenitude of the mystery and wonder is hard to capture in depiction. We hope that our sincere intent can touch the sentient beings. The flying owls can be expected to reform their ways.[47] The *icchantikas* will find their salvation path on their own.[48] All shall seek the Pure Land and brighten at the site of practice. The Buddha does not fail me; our uttermost effort will be rewarded. Wielding the brush to express in words, my feelings grow, and I can only sigh.

The sentient beings defile and afflict one another,	群生因染
All caught in the Six Paths.	六趣牽纏
The Seven Consciousnesses arise in succession;[49]	七識迭用
The transmigration among the Nine Abodes unceasing.[50]	九居屢遷
The Five Aggregates are overworked,[51]	劇哉五陰
The Four Worldly Senses wearing thin,[52]	倦矣四緣
Driving the wheel of existence.	遍使輪轉
The root of suffering causes us to trip along,	苦根迭遭
Tripping along we go,	迭遭未已
All because of the turning of the wheel.	輪轉在己
The Four Worldly Senses are like thin clouds,	四緣雲薄
The Five Aggregates are enflamed.	五陰火起
Full of activities, this enlightened being.	亹亹正覺
Perfect and well reasoned,	是極是理
It remains active, with tranquillity undisturbed.	動不傷寂
Moving, without disrupting the stillness.	行不乖止
You dawn on us through our protracted dreams,	曉爾長夢
And correct our transgressions	貞爾沈詖
Let my spiritual illumination,	以我神明
Round off your divine intelligence.	成爾靈智
That I have no self,	我無自我
Is thus derived from the above	實承其義
You have no self either,	爾無自爾
Thereby dispelling the falsehood.	必祛其偽
Pretensions have their various ways;	偽既殊塗
Meanings have their loose ends.	義故多端
Through sound they become rhymes,	因聲成韻
Through forms they acquire visages.	即色開顏
Viewing the shadow image makes cognition easy;	望影知易
Searching for the voice no longer difficult.	尋響非難
Beyond the form and sound,	形聲之外
There is still something to behold.	復有可觀
Looking afar, the image takes shape;	觀遠表相
Viewed close-up, it is all but an optical blur.	就近曖景
Neither substance nor emptiness,	匪質匪空

It is at once inscrutable and unfathomable.	莫測莫領
Backing against the hill, it illuminates the woods;	倚巖輝林
Fronting a pond, it mirrors the well.	傍潭鑒井
Across space it conveys the verdure;	借空傳翠
Sparking and radiating, it brings in light.	激光發冏
Its gold thrives on dim surroundings,	金好冥漠
Its white tuft of hair shines in dark obscurity.	白毫幽曖
O sun, O moon,[53]	日月居諸
Why should I have this stirred thought?	胡寧斯慨
It is all because of this eminent monk,	曾是望僧
In all earnestness, attends the [image]	擁誠俟對
Following the venerable style and time-honored convention,[54]	承風遺則
He brings the elusive image to the broad daylight.	曠若有概
With reverence he pictures the trace of [the Buddha],	敬圖遺蹤
Chiseling and piercing the hillside.	疏鑿峻峰
Arcaded walks stretch around.[55]	周流步櫚
Secluded is the chamber	窈宛房櫳
The rippling waves reflect the stair ways	激波映墀
The moon is thus included in the window frame.	引月入窗
Clouds depart, skirting the hilltop.	雲往拂山
Winds arrive, passing the pine trees.	風來過松
Exquisite is the topography.	地勢既美
Faithful is the image.	像形亦篤
The reserved colors brings forth a floating appearance,	采淡浮色
Sustained gaze prompts deep contemplation,	詳視沈覺
The [Buddha] appears to border on distinction and absence;	若滅若無
It nevertheless exists through the simulation and emulation.	在摹在學
Its pure and crystal essence	由其潔精
Resonates with distinct holiness	能感靈獨
Sincerity amounts to transcendence;	誠之云孚
Munificence likewise steadily flows	惠亦孔續
Ah, you who practice the Way	嗟爾懷道
Take care not to relax your guard.	慎勿中惕
There is the youthful waywardness	弱喪之推
And the *icchantika*'s bondage.	闡提之役
Now we have seen the returning route	反路今睹
The view here dispels ignorance.	發蒙茲覿
It inspires the heart,	式厲厥心
While time goes on and things change.	時逝流易
I venture here to inscribe this in view of the spirit cosmos.	敢銘靈宇
In reverence I inform the fellow staff holders.	敬告振錫

[*T* 52:199b–c]

NOTES

1. Alexander C. Soper translated the term 影 as "shadow," in "Aspects of Light Symbolism in Gandhāran Sculpture, Part 1," *Artibus Asiae* 12, no. 3 (1949): 252–83, esp. 273. Other scholars have argued for different translations. Erik Zürcher, who initially also phrased it as "shadow," later preferred "reflection," in *The Buddhist Conquest of China: The Spread and Adaptation of Buddhism in Early Medieval China* (Leiden: Brill, 1972), 242; see also Zürcher to Marylin Rhie, January 2, 2001. Marylin Martin Rhie chose to render it as "reflection" image, in *Early Buddhist Art of China and Central Asia*, vol. 2, *The Eastern Chin and Sixteen Kingdoms Period in China and Tumshuk, Kucha, and Karashahr in Central Asia* (Leiden: Brill, 2002), 113. Jinhua Chen opted for "image" as the word to translate 影 in this context, in "Meditation Tradition in Fifth Century Northern China: With a Focus on a Forgotten 'Kashmiri' Meditation Tradition Brought to China by Buddhabhadra (359–429)," in *Across Asia: Networks of Material, Intellectual, and Cultural Exchange*, ed. Tansen Sen (Singapore: Institute of Southeast Asian Studies, 2010), 1–27, esp. 122.

2. Kumārajīva translated the *Mahāprajñāpāramitā-śāstra* 大智度論 (*Da zhi du lun*) between 402 and 405. See *Taishō shinshū daizōkyō* 大正新修大藏經, ed. Takakusu Junjirō 高楠順次郎 and Watanabe Kaigyoku 渡邊海旭 (henceforth abbreviated as *T*) (Tokyo: Taishō issaikyō kankōkai 大正一切經刊行會, 1924–1932), 25:57c–756b. The work is attributed to the authorship of Nāgārjuna 龍樹 (150–250), an influential Indian Buddhist logician.

3. *T* 15:654–79. There is no surviving original Indian text. The reconstructed title is *Buddha-dhyāna-samādhisāgara-sūtra*, or *Buddhānusmṛti-samādhi-sāgara-sūtra*.

4. A number of Japanese scholars regard the text as a conglomerate of Indian and Chinese traditions. Yamabe Nobuyoshi even questions Buddhabhadra as the "translator" of the text. For a scholarship review and the most recent study of this issue, see Yamabe Nobuyoshi, "*The Sutra on the Ocean-like Samadhi of the Visualization of the Buddha*: The Interfusion of the Chinese and Indian Cultures in Central Asia as Reflected in a Fifth Century Apocryphal Sutra" (Ph.D. diss., Yale University, 1999).

5. Here I am taking cues from Hans Belting, "Image, Medium, Body: A New Approach to Iconology," *Critical Inquiry* 31, no. 2 (2005): 302–19.

6. Authors holding this position include Huan Tan 桓譚 and Wang Chong 王充. See Huan Tan, *Xinlun* 新論, "Body and Spirit" 形神; and Wang Chong, *Lunheng*, "Chapter on Death" 論死篇.

7. Eugene Wang, *Shaping the Lotus Sutra: Buddhist Visual Culture in Medieval China* (Seattle: University of Washington Press, 2005), 245–47.

8. Omura Seigai 大村西崖, *Shina bijutsu-shi: Chōsōhen* 支那美術史彫塑篇 (Tokyo, 1922), 116–32.

9. *Gaoseng zhuan*, in *T* 50:352b, *T* 50:358c; *Guang Hongming ji*, in *T* 52:202.

10. Buddhist apologetic literature often cites the opponents' charge about the unreliability of the "clay and wood" to stand for Buddhahood and includes arguments in defense of their symbolic functions. See, for example, *T* 52:175a.

11. *Gaoseng Faxian zhuan*, in *T* 51:859a.

12. Huiyuan's eulogy on the "shadow of the Buddha" includes the line: "Its wonder hangs on the tip of the brush / As its subtlety courses along the light silk. / Colors reside in the virtuality. This leads Zürcher to conclude that the image was "a painting on silk and not a mural" (*Buddhist Conquest of China*, 224).

13. Xie Lingyun, "Foyingming," in *T* 52:199c.

14. Richard Wollheim, *Painting as an Art* (Princeton, N.J.: Princeton University Press, 1987), 46.

15. Richard Cohen, "Nāga, Yakṣiṇī, Buddha: Local Deities and Local Buddhism at Ajanta," *History of Religions* 37, no. 4 (1998): 360–400.

16. Cohen, "Nāga, Yakṣiṇī, Buddha," 243.

17. *HS* 97.3952; 25.1219; *Records of the Historian*, 28.1387; Gan Bao 干寶 (fl. 317–322), *Soushen ji* 搜神記, in *Han Wei Liuchao biji xiaoshuo daguan* (Shanghai: Shanghai guji, 1999), 292; Wang Jia 王嘉, *Shiyi ji* 拾遺記, in *Han Wei Liuchao biji xiaoshuo daguan*, 525.

18. Wang Jia, *Shiyi ji*, 525.

19. For alternative translations, see James Legge, *A Record of Buddhist Kingdoms Being an Account by the Chinese Monk Fa-hien of His Travels in India and Ceylon (A.D. 399–414) in Search of Buddhist Books of Discipline* (Oxford: Clarendon Press, 1886), 39; and Rhie, *Early Buddhist Art of China and Central Asia*, 2:127.

20. The Six Perfections 波羅蜜 (*pāramitās*) are charity 布施 (*dāna*), precept abiding 持戒 (*śīla*), forbearance 忍辱 (*kṣānti*), zealous effort 精進 (*vīrya*), meditation 禪定 (*dhyāna*), and wisdom 智慧 (*prajñā*).

21. Without the subject, the ambiguous line could be taken to mean either the Buddha or the practitioner sits cross-legged. On the basis of the semantic overflow, the first alternative is probably the stronger reading.

22. A literal translation would be "pure and white rocks" 清白石, or, alternatively, according to different editions, "blue-and-white stone" 青白石. See *T* 15:681n.16.

23. The phrase "three resolves" is defined variously. One possible glossing concerns the three assured ways of reaching the Pure Land: (1) perfect sincerity, (2) deep resolve, and (3) resolve on demitting one's merits to others. See *Foguang da cidian* 佛光大辭典, ed. Ciyi 慈怡 (Gaoxiong: Foguang chubanshe, 1989), 532.

24. *Guanfo sanmei haijing*, in *T* 15:680c–81c.

25. Nagarahāra is an ancient kingdom and city on the southern bank of the Cabool River about thirty miles west of Jalalabad. See William E. Soothill and Lewis Hodous, *A Dictionary of Chinese Buddhist Terms* (Taibei: Foguang, 1994), 247.

26. The phrase 稀世之間 is considered a variance of 稀世之聞 in the *Taishō* edition. See *T* 52:197n.35.

27. The character 過 is corrected as 遇, making possible the reading of "how can one have a chance for change?" See *T* 52:197n.36.

28. Variations of 忘寢 are 忘寢食 and 忘食. See *T* 52:197n.37.

29. The phrase 思澤 is rendered as 恩澤 in one edition. See *T* 52:197n.39. Here I follow the latter.

30. If we follow the one edition that renders 宴懷 as 冥懷 (*T* 52:197n.42), the line would read: "we will feel it through calm meditations."

31. The phrase 曲成 is a shorthand reference to the idiom 曲成萬物 in the *Great Treatise on Classic of Changes*: "[A sage] properly encompasses the transformations of heaven and earth; with flexibility, he unfailingly rounds off the myriad things." See *Duanju Shisanjing jingwen* 斷句十三經經文 (Taibei: Taiwan Kaiming, 1991), 22.

32. Here Huiyuan borrows the notions of "that for which one waits" 有待 from the *Zhuangzi*: "The same holds true for myriad things. They have that for which they wait, whereby they die; they have that for which they wait, whereby they live" (*Zhuangzi jishi* 莊子集釋, comp. Guo Qingfan 郭慶藩 and annot. Wang Xiaoyu 王孝魚 [Beijing: Zhonghua shuju, 1995], 707). He also borrows the concept of "independence" 無待 from the traditional Chinese classical language.

33. The "late master" refers to Dao-an.

34. I follow the "Three Editions" and the "Old Song edition" (1104–1148) (in the Library of the Imperial Household of Japan) by choosing the variant 信 (conviction) instead of 位 in the *Taishō* edition. See *T* 52:198n.2.

35. This suggests the image as a standing Buddha. Huiyuan describes the "one *zhang* and six–tall Golden Image at Xiangyang" in similar terms: "It takes divine steps to respond to its contemporaries" or "it takes graceful steps" (*Jin Xiangyang zhangliu jinxiang xu* 晉襄陽丈六金像讚序, in *T* 52:198bc).

36. The *Guang hongming ji* version gives 中姿, while the *Gaoseng zhuan* version has 沖姿. The phrase 沖姿 makes more sense.

37. On the notion of "mystic vision" 玄覽, see Wang, *Shaping the Lotus Sutra*, 292–310.

38. The line "spirit beings shall hearken to you" derives from the *Classic of Poetry* (*Shijing* 詩經). The "Xiao Ming" in the "Minor Odes of the Kingdom" 小雅 contains the line: "Quietly fulfill the duties of your offices, / Associating with the correct and upright. / *So shall the Spirits hearken to you, / And give you good*" (James Legge, *The Chinese Classics*, vol. 4, *The She King or the Book of Poetry* [Hong Kong: Hong Kong University Press, 1970], 366). "Felling the Trees" 伐木 of the "Minor Odes of the Kingdom" in the *Classic of Poetry* contains the line: "*Spiritual beings will then hearken to him; / He shall have harmony and peace*" (Legge, *Chinese Classic* 4:254).

39. The Year Star (*suixing* 崴星 [i.e., the planet Jupiter]) reaching the Stellar Sequence (*xingji* 星紀), the initial Jupiter station.

40. The Great Yin (*taiyin* 太陰) is an invisible counter-Jupiter, "an imaginary counterorbital asterism" to track the actual motions of the Year star. See John S. Major, *Heaven and Earth in Han Thought: Chapters Three, Four and Five of the Huainanzi* (Albany: State University of New York Press, 1993), 74. Chifenruo 赤奮若 is the name of the twelfth year when the counter-Jupiter, or Great Yin, reaches twelfth chronogram in the scheme of twelve chronograms of the Jovian cycle. According to "The Treatise on the Pattern of Heaven" in the *Huainanzi* 淮南子, "When the Great yin is in *chou*, the year is called *Chifenruo*" (Major, *Heaven and Earth in Han Thought*, 122).

41. The phrase 重軌 in the line 庶來賢之重軌 contained in the *Taishō* edition here is puzzling. One possible alternative is "halo" 重暉, which appears in the early-fifth-century

inscription on the shadow image in cave 169 of Binglingsi: 神儀重暉. For a photograph of the inscription, see Gansusheng wenwu gongzuodui 甘肅省文物工作隊 and Binglingsi wenwu baoguansuo 炳靈寺文物保管所, eds., *Zhongguo shiku Yongjing Binglingsi shiku* 中國石窟永靖炳靈寺石窟 (Beijing: Wenwu, 1986), pl. 28.

42. Through the notion of the Great Pervader 大通, Huiyuan alludes to the account of a seated meditation in the *Zhuangzi*:

A third day, Hui again saw [the Master], and said, "I am making progress." "What do you mean?" "I sit and forget everything." Zhongni changed countenance, and said, "What do you mean by saying that you sit and forget [everything]?" Yan Hui replied, "My connection with the body and its parts is dissolved; my perceptive organs are discarded. Thus leaving my material form, and bidding farewell to my knowledge, I am become one with the Great Pervader. This I call sitting and forgetting all things." Zhongni said, "One [with that Pervader], you are free from all likings; so transformed, you are become impermanent. You have, indeed, become superior to me! I must ask leave to follow in your steps."

See Chen Guying 陳鼓應, *Zhuangzi jinyi jinzhu* 莊子今譯今注 (Beijing: Zhonghua shuju, 1983), 207; and James Legge, trans., *The Sacred Books of China: The Texts of Taoism* (Oxford: Clarendon Press, 1891), 257.

43. Here the phrase 悲現 in the *Taishō* edition does not quite make sense. I therefore follow the alternative version in the "Three Editions" (Song, Yuan, Ming) as 非理. See *T* 52:198cn.18.

44. Here the phrase 舟壑緬謝 is derived from the expression "store the boat in the ravine" 藏舟於壑 in the *Zhuangzi*:

We store our boat in the ravine, our fishnet in the marsh, and say it's safe there; but at midnight someone stronger carries it away on his back, and the full ones do not know it. The smaller stored in the bigger has its proper place, but still has room to escape; as for the whole world stored within the world, with nowhere else to escape, that is the ultimate identity of an unchanging thing. (Chen Guying, *Zhuangzi jinyi jinzhu*, 178)

This translation follows A. C. Graham, *Chuang-Tzu: The Inner Chapters* (Indianapolis: Hackett, 2001), 86. The metaphor "boat and ravine" therefore refers to the changing circumstances of the world.

45. Jetavana 祇園, a park near Śrāvastī, is said to have been obtained from Prince Jeta by the elder Anāthapiṇḍika, in which monastery buildings were erected, and have been the favorite resort of Śākyamuni. It is said to have been destroyed by fire two hundred years later, rebuilt smaller five hundred years after, and again burned down a century later; it was rebuilt on the earlier scale thirteen years afterward, but a century later, entirely destroyed. See Soothill and Hodous, *Dictionary of Chinese Buddhist Terms*, 310. In this context, it simply stands for India. Xie Lingyun was in the capital city, Jiankang, where Faxian spoke about the shadow image.

46. The term 隨喜 in the Buddhist discourse more specifically means "to rejoice in the virtuous behavior of others."

47. The "flying owls" 飛鴞 alludes to the "Panshui" 泮水 piece in "Praise Songs of Lu" 魯頌
of the *Classic of Poetry*:

They come flying on the wing, those owls,	翩彼飛鴞
And settle on the trees about the college;	集于泮林
They eat the fruit of our mulberry trees,	食我桑黮
And salute us with fine notes.	懷我好音
So awakened shall be those tribes of the Huai;	憬彼淮夷
They will come presenting their precious things,	來獻其琛
Their large tortoises and their elephants' teeth,	元龜象齒
And great contributions of the southern metals	大賂南金

See Legge, *Chinese Classics*, 4:620 (transliteration adapted to *pinyin*).

48. The phrase "chanti" 闡提 is an abbreviation of "yichanti" 一闡提, a Chinese transliteration of the Sanskrit word *icchantika*. In general, it refers to a class of beings incapable of
reaching enlightenment on their own. The *Fanyi mingyi ji* 翻譯名義集, for instance,
defines an *icchantika* as a shameless, unfriendly, and unrepentant person lacking faith
in cause and effect, karmic retribution, blind to present and future, and indifferent to
Buddha's moral teaching. See *T* 54:1084a. However, an alternative view, such as voiced
in the Dharmakṣema 曇無讖 (385–433) version of the Mahāyāna *Mahāparinirvāṇa-sūtra*
and the *Laṅkâvatāra-sūtra*, argue that no one, not even the *icchantika*, is barred from
Buddhist enlightenment and eventual salvation.

49. The Seven Consciousnesses are in action in succession. According to Buddhist teaching, the base consciousness, or *ālaya-vijñāna* 阿賴耶識, generates seven consciousnesses: the mentation (*manas*) consciousness 末那識, the thinking consciousness 意識,
and the five (i.e., visual 眼識, auditory 耳識, olfactory 鼻識, gustatory 舌識, and tactile 身
識) consciousnesses 五識 associated with the five sense organs of eyes, ears, nose,
tongue, and skin, corresponding respectively to form, sound, smell, taste, and touch.
These seven consciousnesses are believed to cause the afflictions. See Xuanzang, trans.,
Yuqie shidi lun 瑜伽師地論 (*Yogâcāra-bhūmi-śāstra*), in *T* 30:292c; *Chengweishilun* 成唯
識論 (*Vijñaptimātratāsiddhi-śāstra*), in *T* 31:2a.

50. The Nine Abodes 九居 refer to the nine celestial habitats (Skt. *navasu attvāvā*) for sentient beings, arranged in an ascending order, as defined in the *Dīrghâgama* 長阿含經.
These are (1) the human and deva heavens 天及人天, with mixed bodies and thoughts
in the realm of desire (or world of five senses); (2) the three brahma heavens 梵光音天,
with mixed bodies but uniform thinking, the first of the four *dhyāna* heavens; (3) the
three pure heavens of light 光音天, with identical bodies and different thoughts; (4) the
three pervasively pure heavens 遍淨天, inhabited by identical bodies and thoughts; (5)
the thought-free heaven 無想天, the highest of the four *dhyāna* heavens; (6) the boundless space 空處, the first of the formless realms; (7) the space of boundless thought
識處; (8) the space of nothingness 不用處; and (9) the space beyond thought and non-

thought 有想無想處, the fourth of the formless heavens. See *Chang a'han jing* 長阿含經 (*Dīrghâgama*), in *T* 1:56b.

51. The Five Aggregates 五陰 refer to the five components of a sentient being, especially a human being. According to the Buddhist view, an intelligent being possesses (1) physical body with five senses, that is, "form" 色 (*rūpa*); (2) "feelings" 受 (*vedanā*); (3) "ideas" 想 (*samjñā*); (4) "impulse" 行 (*samskāra*); and (5) "discriminating cognition" 識 (*vijñāna*). See Rupert Gethin, *The Foundations of Buddhism* (Oxford: Oxford University Press, 1998), 31; and Soothill and Hodous, *Dictionary of Chinese Buddhist Terms*, 126.

52. The term *siyuan* 四緣 here does not yet have the sense of the "four conditions" 四緣 of the Yogâcāra discourse, made available through Xuanzang's translation in the seventh century—that is, the "causal conditions" 因緣 (*hetu-pratyaya*), "equally antecedent conditions" 等無間緣 (*samanantara-pratyaya*), "object-dependent conditions" 所緣緣 (*ālambana-pratyaya*), and "peripheral and contingent conditions" 增上緣 (*adhipati-pratyaya*). See *Yogâcārabhūmi* 瑜伽師地論, translated by Xuanzang 玄奘 between 646 and 648, in *T* 30.583bc. Instead, the term used by Xie Lingyun means "four worldly senses" 四塵—that is, the senses of form 色塵, odor 香塵, taste 味塵, and touch 觸塵 integral to the defiled and polluted earthly experience. Xie Lingyun's use of "Four Worldly Senses" 四緣 in tandem with "Five Aggregates" 五陰 corresponds closely to Yan Zhitui's 顏之推 (531–ca. 595) use of "four worldly senses and five aggregates" 四塵五陰 in his discussion of Buddhist terminology, in "Jiaxun guixin pian" 家訓歸心篇, in *Guang hongming ji* 廣弘明集, comp. Daoxuan 道宣, in *T* 52:107b.

53. The expression 日月居諸 is a variation of the refrain "O sun; O moon," repeated three times in "Sun and Moon" 日月 from the "Odes of Bei" 邶風 of the "Lessons from the States" 國風 in the *Classic of Poetry*. See Legge, *Chinese Classics*, 4:44–46.

54. The phrase 承風遺則 here alludes to a line in the "Far-Off Journey" 遠遊, a second-century B.C.E. work included in the *Lyrics of Chu*: "I heard how once Red Pine had washed the world's dust off: / I would model myself on the pattern he had left me." This translation follows David Hawkes, *The Songs of the South: An Anthology of Ancient Chinese Poems by Qu Yuan and Other Poets* (New York: Penguin Books, 1985), 194.

55. Here the line 周流步欄 is a variation on 步欄周流, as in the "Sir Vacuous" 子虛賦 by Sima Xiangru 司馬相如: "Arcaded walks stretching such distances / That their lengths cannot be traversed in a single day" (*SJ* 117.3026; Sima Qian 司馬遷, *Records of the Grand Historian: Han Dynasty II*, trans. Burton Watson, rev. ed. [New York: Columbia University Press, 1993], 274).

PART V

Everyday Life

Like the culture, economy, politics, social institutions, and religions of early medieval China, everyday life came under the influence of sociopolitical turmoil, the frequent and extensive deracination of people, as well as the introduction of foreign ideas and practices. Changes were often rapid and drastic. The responses to them varied, some of which were as sweeping, disruptive, and vehemently resistant as the changes themselves. The efforts of Emperor Xiaowen of the Northern Wei to sinicize the elite by prohibiting Xianbei clothing and language is one such example. While these measures were intended to address a reality in which people of different cultural and ethnic backgrounds lived side by side, they in turn created new challenges. Nonetheless, studies of how people lived in this tumultuous period have traditionally focused on material culture, and scholars have drawn information from sources produced by literate elites. Even though new archaeological finds have greatly expanded our knowledge of the material culture, the ways in which people carried out their day-to-day life remain unclear. The question then becomes: Could we approach this in another way?

History is neither the totality of the past nor the sum of all its parts but a representation of the historical subject under study. Using what Michel de Certeau called the "procedures of everyday creativity,"[1] we may illuminate the ways of life following different individuals as they interpreted their surroundings and navigated day-to-day living. Everyday life, as Certeau pointed out, was an exercise of choice, even for those who did not have many. People lived from day to day using the resources that were available to them, and the ways in which they used these resources are as informative as the actual resources themselves. Exploring how people as individuals or members of a group "consumed" material *and* culture in their daily living and how that consumption shaped their surroundings could provide valuable insight. Moreover, people often used their resources in unintended ways and to serve purposes not anticipated by the original makers. A close examination of the ways and means therefore leads to a more thorough understanding of everyday life as expressed in the creation and recreation of early medieval material culture while fully recognizing the importance of human agency.

The "procedures of everyday creativity" referred not only to the use of material culture but also to the less tangible but nevertheless integral modes of thoughts and behaviors. Through concepts, discourses, ways and customs, and religious practices, people interpreted their surroundings, negotiated their place in society, constructed and represented their identity, dealt with challenges, and gave meaning to their lives. The concept of everyday life, with its emphasis on the creative process that each individual continuously (though not always consciously) engages while living his or her life, is different from the concept of daily life. That is, the focus of everyday life is the use of the object (material or immaterial), whereas the focus of daily life is the object in use. Accordingly, the two introductions and the entries in part V, with their attention to both concepts, present a more nuanced picture of what it was like living in early medieval China.

Shi Chong 石崇 (249–303), the Western Jin literatus famous for his enormous wealth, delighted in awing friends and spectators with the hedonistic luxuries that filled his everyday life. His voracious consumptions helped him build and maintain the persona of someone who was living ostentatiously, and unabashedly so. Moreover, he was not content with simply being the subject of talk around town. Instead, he used his considerable literary talent to subvert the idea and practice of quietude, spontaneity, and simplicity that his contemporaries prized. In his writings, some of which are translated here by David R. Knechtges, Shi Chong makes plain that his carefree abandonment and disengagement from worldly affairs were possible because of his wealth, and not in spite of it. By listing all those who attended his fashionable garden party, thus implicitly creating a wall of shame, Shi Chong subtly lampoons the cultural elite and its hypocrisy. In a manner that only enhances his flamboyant persona, he describes the many features (man-made as well as natural) of his estates and the merrymaking they occasioned for him and his guests. As if daring the reader to disapprove, he exposes all his own vulgarity to expose the vulgarity in others, who happily consume the material pleasure he feeds them, and he also recounts the countless anecdotes concerning his personality and lifestyle. He was, in this sense, an heir to the Seven Sages of the Bamboo Groove and their iconoclastic spirit. Shi Chong's story is one of consuming and being the object consumed while generating the tantalizing details of the lives of the ultrarich.

As in many other premodern societies, the year and the seasons imposed a rhythm on life in early medieval China. Nature served as the framework in which people identified and explained proper ways and customs. "Rhapsody on Pasta" by the Western Jin scholar Shu Xi 束皙 (263–302), introduced and translated here by David R. Knechtges, is an excellent example. After deducing the recent origin of pasta (*bing* 餅) and introducing the wide variety of noodles that was available, Shu Xi moves on to pairing a particular kind of pasta with each season. The thought that led to this pairing was straightforward and commonsensical: making and eating the kind of pasta that is best served hot when the weather is cold, and vice versa. These pairings ultimately set the stage for the one pasta that cannot be paired because it is served all year-round: boiled dumplings. Shu Xi then devotes the rest of the rhapsody to celebrating the experience of consuming boiled dumplings, the experience of loving the idea of them, appreciating the ingredients that went into making them, and relishing the sensations of eating them.

In the *Record of the Year and Seasons of Jing-Chu* (*Jing-Chu suishiji* 荆楚歲時記) by Zong Lin 宗懍 (498/502–561/565), introduced and translated by Ian Chapman, Nature provides a framework for interpretation that is both descriptive and prescriptive. The *Record*'s authors recount in detail the annual festival program in a calendrical sequence and explain the origin of each way and custom by reviewing and citing relevant passages from earlier sources. Such a practice is indicative of one approach to identifying the origins of current practices described in texts written in and about the past. Here the authors use Nature and these earlier texts to show the continuity of beliefs and practices, making the *Record* more than a litany of festivals. Describing and prescribing them thus reinforces the continuity of the Jing-Chu way of life.

The "procedures of everyday creativity" also suggest a way for the oppressed to undermine the power of their oppressors. The oppressed can do this not by rejecting or altering the rituals, representations, and laws imposed on them but by using them in ways their oppressors do not anticipate. It is a tactic that the oppressors cannot prevent, as it is they who have made this possible.[2] Jen-der Lee's chapter, "The Epitaph of a Third-Century Wet Nurse," and Jessey Choo's chapter, "Adoption and Motherhood: The Petition Submitted by Lady [neé] Yu," are both good examples. Xu Yi, whose background is unknown, became relatively prominent at court as the wet nurse for Empress Jia of the Western Jin dynasty. She was commemorated in her epitaph with praise usually lavished on highborn ladies, albeit at the expense of her charge's mother, Lady Guo. The latter lost all her children before Xu Yi arrived in her household as a wet nurse. Her assumption of the mother's role, one that the society highly valued, gave

Wet Nurse Xu an opportunity to transcend her humble background and raise the social station of her own family. As Lee points out, the possibility that someone like Xu could mother a child on behalf of another and use this role for her own ends made early medieval moralists and intellectuals very uneasy. Their ambivalence only underscores the power of this role. In Choo's chapter, the act of mothering was as crucial to Lady Yu as it was to Wet Nurse Xu Yi. After losing her adopted child to his birth mother, Lady Yu demanded that the child be returned to her on the grounds that it was she who performed all the mothering duties. That is, she maintained that raising a child was at least as, if not more, important as giving birth to it. She supported her position with her formidable knowledge of the Histories and the Classics. Indeed, her use of relevant passages and precedents was so ingenious and persuasive that even those who disagreed with her found it difficult to refute her argument.

Family Instructions of Mr. Yan (Yanshi jiaxun 顔氏家訓), by Yan Zhitui 顔之推 (531–after 591), some sections of which are translated here by Albert E. Dien, contains practical advice on how to live one's everyday life. It illustrates the kind of resourcefulness that Yan possessed and wanted to pass on to his descendants. Much of this resourcefulness resulted from his marginality as a Southerner who spent most of his life in the North. Yan was often one of the few Han Chinese who served in a court dominated by non-Han people. According to Family Instructions, he never accepted without question the normative values and practices of either the North or the South. Rather, he chose carefully among them, and by doing so, he set himself and his family apart from the rest. By creatively exploring marginality and the pluralities it engendered, he managed to find his own space without ever leaving the place in which he was forced to live. In this way, Yan survived the political vicissitudes that many of his fellow courtiers (Han and non-Han) did not. Based on the lessons he learned from his life experience, he demonstrates in Family Instructions the effectiveness of the "procedures of everyday creativity" and cements his identity as the consummate survivor. The work served as the ultimate testimony of his ingenuity.

Everyday life is a continuing process of making choices, with both the choices and the people who make them determining the characteristics unique to an age. Shi Chong's writings on his estates reveal not only the elite material culture but also how Shi Chong used his wealth and ostentation to build his own personality cult. The cyclical passage of time was the dominant way of thinking about the organization of day-to-day living. But intellectuals like Shu Xi and the authors of the Record of the Year and Seasons of Jing-Chu often skewed this thinking to support their interpretation of an experience. By presenting boiled dumplings as a food item not affiliated with any season, Shu Xi makes them extraordinary. By describing contemporary ways and customs and linking them to recorded precedents, the authors of the Record of the Year and Seasons of Jing-Chu emphasize the importance of continuity in life. Motherhood was as important in the early medieval period as in any other period. As both Xu Yi's and Lady Yu's cases show, bringing up a child was valued more highly than giving birth to a child. Accordingly, those who took care of a child could lay claim to credit traditionally given only to birth mothers. *Family Instructions* is a product of someone whose everyday life was colored by his permanent displacement from his native land. Yan Zhitui, its author, turned the marginality resulting from this displacement into a tool of self-defense and self-definition. Together these cases provide us with some hints of the pathos of early medieval China.

Jessey J. C. Choo

The Six Dynasties period has traditionally been considered the Dark Age of China, like that of the European Middle Ages, when China fell away from the ideal of being united under the rule of a single dynasty. Geography is an important determinant in lifestyles, and the differences between the North and the South during this period were as much influenced by climate and terrain as by the political situation that separated the two regions. The Qinling-Nanshan Mountains effectively divide the North and South. The relatively dry loess deposits, laid down by winds blowing in from the north, stop at that mountain barrier, while the moisture-bearing winds of the monsoon season drop most of the rain to the south of those mountains. The north is colder and drier and has to rely more on dry-farming techniques. The south has adequate water, although the soils, leached out to a greater degree than those of the north, require more fertilizer. Moving from north to south, the colder climate requires the planting of spring wheat, since the seed will not survive the winter cold. Millet and barley are also planted in this zone, and the southern reaches of animal husbandry overlap here. In the zone between north and south, one of the main crops is winter wheat, a softer wheat, which, because it slowly matures over the winter, has a shorter growing season in the spring, enabling a second, summer crop of various sorts. Because of the numerous waterways and the greater supply of water, rice is the main crop in the south; with justice this was called the land of fish and rice. The subtropical far south, where three crops a year are possible, did not achieve its full potential until after the Six Dynasties period.

FOOD AND WINE

More than any other aspect of life at that time, food reveals the differences between the North and the South. *Essential Techniques for the Common People* (*Qimin yaoshu* 齊民要術, ca. 540) by Jia Sixie 賈思勰 (dates unknown) provides a detailed account of agricultural practices and foodstuffs, primarily in the North where Jia had served as an official. During the Six Dynasties period, the North increasingly relied on wheat, but millet, barley, sesame, and soybeans also were staples. Jia mentions eighty-six varieties of nonglutinous millet alone, an everyday food eaten mainly as a gruel or congee. Other varieties were used to make wine. Soybeans were used for making fermented pastes and sauces, and their sprouts were eaten as well. Wheat flour increasingly was used to make a wide variety of pastas, unleavened and raised, fried, baked, steamed, and boiled, including both early forms of noodles and dumplings. The importance of these foodstuffs is vividly displayed in the Jin poem on pasta, translated and annotated in part V by David R. Knechtges.

A wide variety of fruit was available. *Essential Techniques* lists jujubes, peaches, plums, apricots, pears, apples, persimmons, and pomegranates. *A Record of Buddhist Monasteries in Luoyang* (*Luoyang qielanji* 洛陽伽藍記), a nostalgic memoir written in 547 by Yang Xuanzhi 楊衒之 (dates unknown), a former resident, is a valuable source on life in Luoyang during the short years before 534 when it was abandoned once more. The memoir also claims that all the monasteries in the city had fruit trees.[3] There seemed to be as many varieties of vegetables available as in modern times. *Essential Techniques* describes thirty-one, of which about twenty are still grown. These include various sorts of melons, Chinese cabbage, eggplant, spinach, lettuce, ginger, spices like coriander, and mustards. Many were foreign imports, some of whose names were still marked by the word *hu*, here meaning the West in general; these included peppers, carrots, and walnuts.

The cuisine at this time offered a wide range of ways of processing fruit, such as drying, pickling, and pressing. Various sorts of fermentations were used to prepare sauces, pickles, and dairy products. Both anecdotes and *Essential Techniques* testify to the popularity of dairy products in the North, perhaps under the influence of the northern nomadic neighbors. *Essential Techniques* has careful instructions for producing a kind of liquid yogurt or buttermilk, made from cow's or goat's milk, as well as cheese products.

The differences in the cuisine of the North and South become most apparent in the expression of opinions by the champions of one region or the other. For example, when the famous Southern literatus Lu Ji 陸機 (261–303) first came to Luoyang, he was served some yogurt and asked what Southern dish could measure up to it. Lu responded with two dishes, salted black-bean sauce from Jiankang 建康 (present-day Nanjing) and water-lily soup from Jiangsu. The latter is prominently mentioned in *A Record of Buddhist Monasteries in Luoyang* in a tirade by a Northerner deprecating Southern taste. Among the dishes so listed are the seeds of tares and darnel, crab roe, water chestnuts, lotus roots, frog soup, oyster stew, and, to top it off, betel nuts (to be chewed).

Wine was an important part of the diet. *Essential Techniques* provides detailed information on eight different fermenters or starters to be added to a variety of grains and lists some forty different alcoholic beverages. Grape wine was available in shops run by Western merchants, but neither wine nor the distilled *baijiu* 白酒 had yet become popular. That tea was a Southern beverage is clear from an anecdote about the Southerner Wang Su 王肅 (464–501), who had fled to the North after an unsuccessful rebellion and who maintained a diet of carp broth and tea, avoiding the more common mutton and yogurt of the North.[4] At that time, tea was made into cakes, chunks of which would be boiled in water with flavorings of orange peel, mint, ginger, and even scallions added. This style changed during the Tang to tea in a powdery form that, when added to boiling water, was stirred to create a foam, like the modern Japanese *mocha*.

By the end of the Six Dynasties period, with such staples as noodles, soy sauce, and tofu all in their early stages of development, Chinese cuisine as one finds it today was already in place. In time, some Southern elements became more important in the North, and the reliance on milk products faded, to be revived only in recent years, but by and large the cuisine was not that different from the modern one.

CLOTHING

The higher the status, the more clothes a person wore. During this period, male commoners, those who worked in the fields or as servants, wore a jacket that extended to the waist or the knees, with the lapels crossing to the right, full sleeves, and belted. Beneath the jacket were full trousers with slightly tapered cuffs. The trouser legs might be bound just below the knees to facilitate movement. Men wore a flat cap or had their hair gathered in a topknot. Women wore a similar jacket and either trousers or a long skirt. They wore their hair in either a chignon or buns. Both men and women of slightly higher status, perhaps attendants in a wealthy household, wore robes with long, flowing sleeves, which were less convenient for doing ordinary tasks. A trace of undergarment appeared where the robe's lapels crossed. Only the men wore a perky pillbox-shaped cap with a bow set in the middle, called a *pingshangze* 平上幘. The women wore their hair in a variety of hair styles, often in two buns, or they wore caps. Officials wore robes of the same style, perhaps requiring more fabric, and a tall semitransparent hat called a *longguan* 籠冠 (basket hat), probably made of lacquered horsehair, like the traditional Korean hat. In tomb inventories, this hat is associated with "scarlet robes," apparently an ensemble for officials, but women of high status are also seen with this basket hat. One variant of the gown was called a "loose robe and broad girdle" (*baoyi bodai* 褒衣博帶), a Northern innovation that became very popular and even replaced the Indian-style attire for the Buddha.

The Northerners who ruled in the North introduced a number of clothing styles into China. One was a caftan with somewhat tight sleeves and less overlap than the traditional gown. When closed, the collar was round and a bit snug; when open, it revealed an undershirt. The trousers worn with this were tucked into boots. This ensemble remained a favorite at court in the early years of the Tang, since the royal family considered themselves closely akin to those who had come off the steppes to rule northern China.

ARCHITECTURE AND FURNITURE

Many tombs of this period have been excavated and reported in the archaeological journals, but very little remains of the architecture above ground. Nevertheless, from what does remain and from various depictions and written sources, we do know a little. Although buildings in this period included those with weight-bearing walls, the major development was in the timber-frame structure, based on the principle of post-and-lintel architecture, which we see in China today. The walls bear no weight and basically are screens to shield the interiors. Over the duration of the Six Dynasties, there was an increasing emphasis on the roof, on the greater depth of the eaves, and on more complex bracket systems. Brick was used only for pagodas above ground and for tombs under it.

The roofs are perhaps the most distinctive feature. They were made of tile and came in three styles: (1) the gable (upside-down V in cross section), (2) the hip (slanted sides), and (3) the hip and gable, a combination of the first two and the most widely used during this period. The rafters were supported by brackets resting on pillars, the rafters decreasing in length as the building rose in height, so that the sides of the roof slanted, culminating in a ridgepole. The ends of the ridge might have an upward curve and, over time, became more ornate.

There were two basic types of columnar construction during this period. In the first, the columns rose to the roof, were of varying heights to accommodate the slanting roof, and were tied together by crosspieces to provide stability. This type was more typical of the South. The second, which was found in the North and eventually became the principal construction, relied more on the crosspieces, with short posts supporting the next layer above until the final post, called the "king post," which held the ridgepole. This post did not require lumber of the lengths employed in the first style, which may explain its eventual adoption in both the North and the South. Outbuildings included granaries, with the entrance high up and reached by a removable ladder to prevent robbery, and outhouses. Models of the latter consist of a simple room reached by stairs, with a pigsty below.

The general instability of the period required protection, especially on the estates in the countryside. A model of one such compound was surrounded by a wall that had two entrances. The one in front had a gate tower; that at the rear had no gate tower. Atop each corner of the wall were towers from which archers could repel any attackers. Inside the compound were two halls, front and rear, with three other buildings on each side. From the model, it appears that all these buildings had weight-bearing walls, but with the same tiled roofs as described earlier.

The ordinary home in the early Six Dynasties period may have closely resembled the traditional Japanese style. People sat on mats laid over a rougher one that made up the flooring. During this period, a low platform raised on legs became popular, especially in upper-class households. Called a *chuang* 牀 (couch), it was where one took one's ease, ate, read or wrote, and met guests. It was large enough to accommodate such furnishings as armrests, spittoons, braziers, and vessels for eating and drinking. It might have screens on the sides and back and perhaps a canopy over the top to conserve heat. Curtains, fastened with ties, could be drawn across the front for privacy. In this way, it developed into the traditional bed of the later premodern period. Smaller platforms suitable for a single person, called *ta* 榻 (benches), were also common. In tomb murals, the deceased is often depicted seated on a *ta*, facing the entrance, as he would have been to greet a guest. Especially for these smaller *ta*, dishes and other objects would have been placed on low tables to the side or even on the floor within reach, since these benches were only 4.5 to 11 inches off the floor. Yan Zhitui described the scions of the Liang dynasty royal family: "There was not one of them who did not perfume his garments, shave his face, use powder and rouge, ride in a carriage with long awnings, wear high-teeth clogs, sit on square cushions like a chess board, [and] lean on soft, silk bolsters arranged with curios and trinkets on each side, going in and out gracefully, looking like deities."[5] The cushions and bolsters would have been placed on just such couches and benches.

Other items of furniture would have included chests, wardrobes, and baskets, but since these were of perishable materials and seldom featured in the tomb murals, not much can be said about their appearance. We have more information about the kitchen. Scenes of preparing food can be found in the tomb murals, and the ceramic vessels that held provisions for the deceased are found in almost every tomb. Models of stoves are among the most numerous of such grave goods. The Northern-style stove is rectangular with a stepped pyramid in front, while the Southern-style oven is boat shaped, square at the front with the pointed prow in the rear. Both have a door for adding fuel at the front, a hole or chimney at the rear for the smoke, and one or two holes on the top surface to hold pots, kettles, or steamers over the fire.

CITIES AND CAPITALS OF THE NORTH AND SOUTH

The cities of the Six Dynasties, as in most periods of Chinese history, were walled, but little of what was within the walled-in areas has survived because of the nature of the architecture. Textual sources offer the most information. In the largest cities, those that served as capitals during this time, the shape usually was rectangular. The palace area also usually moved from the southern part of the city to the north, with the boulevard that led from the southern gate of the city to the southern main gate of the Palace City, thereby becoming the city's main axis, in other words, becoming the pattern followed in the urban planning of later periods. Between 493 and 534, planned cities like Luoyang resembled a checkerboard, although this was not always possible. Jiankang was already a city when chosen as the capital of the Southern dynasties and was hemmed in by a lake and mountains. Although the streets were winding, the area of the imperial city and the area around it were more regularized. Over time, a variety of building programs resulted in an evermore extravagant palace complex, to the point that the grounds were surrounded by triple walls, evidence of growing insecurity. The city walls, made of bamboo barricades, remained until the late fifth century when earthen walls, perhaps faced with brick, were erected. A grand imperial way led south to the Qinhuai River, crossed by the Scarlet Bird Pontoon Bridge. The low mountains, the lakes, and the Yangzi River, which formed a bowl in which the city was located, proved to be inadequate security, and natural defenses and the city suffered as a result.

In its early years, Pingcheng 平城, the capital of the Northern Wei, resembled an enlarged latifundium with a villa at its center. It was a combined palace and military headquarters, surrounded by fields worked by peasants brought in from other, conquered territories. The buildings were made of brick or pounded earth, and the complex was the center of much economic activity. Palace workshops employed slaves to weave silk, raise animals, brew liquor, and tend extensive vegetable gardens, to supply the palace and also to sell in markets. Huge storehouses held grain and arsenals held arms. The population of the city lived in wards south of the palace, with their own walls and gates, each holding from sixty or seventy to four hundred or five hundred families, an arrangement that enabled the administration to maintain control over them.

When Luoyang was rebuilt in 493 to accommodate the new capital of the Northern Wei, the general layout of Pingcheng appears to have been followed, although the available area between the Mang Hills 邙山 and the Luo River 洛水 forced the city to expand to the east and west, turning its rectangular shape on its side. There was an inner city, containing the palace and government offices, and an outer city, where the majority of the population and the workshops and markets were located. Each of these cities was surrounded by a wall. The outside city was divided into 220 walled wards, each with four gates that were closed at night and crisscrossed by internal streets and lanes. The size of the individual wards depended on the number of households and large estates included, and natural features. These wards, each with its own name, were independent neighborhoods with their own markets and temples. Luoyang had two large markets, one on each side of the city. Around them were wards largely dedicated to specific crafts. For example, north of the western market was Fengzhong Ward, whose shops specialized in coffins and funerary accessories.

Others were known for their specialization in music, breweries, butchers, various crafts, and merchants. Foreigners, including those who had fled from the South, were placed in the southern suburbs.

In *A Record of Buddhist Monasteries in Luoyang*, Yang Xuanzhi describes in vivid terms the enormous wealth that was concentrated in this capital city. In the early years after the move to Luoyang,

> princes and nobles of the imperial clan, princesses, and the Emperor's relations through marriage seized for themselves the wealth of mountains, seas, forests, and rivers. They competed in building gardens and mansions, boasting to each other of their achievements. They erected splendid gateways, sumptuous houses whose doors connected one with the next, flying passageways to catch the breezes, and high buildings shrouded with mist. Tall towers and fragrant terraces were built in every home, and each garden had flowering copses and twisting pools. They were all verdant with peach in summer and with bamboo and cypress in winter.[6]

We need, of course, to discount some of this as written by one who was recalling with much sadness the past glories of that ruined city.

SOCIAL CLASSES

The Six Dynasties period is often said to be one of powerful aristocratic clans. In fact, such a characterization is misleading and resembles the entity called the Holy Roman Empire, which was not holy, Roman, or an empire. Rather, this period should be seen as one in which status was achieved primarily through holding office in the imperial bureaucracy and through literary learning, based on the Classics and demonstrated by an ability to write well and even compose poetry when the occasion demanded. Family status rose with the number of successful officeholders, who, of course, made it easier for members of those families to rise in rank as well. With appointments came such privileges for the family as exemption from corvée duty and payment of taxes. High officials sometimes earned the right to appoint junior members of their family to low-ranking offices, although they did not earn the family any credit. A line that did not produce officials sank in status to that of commoners. Some families had such an excellent record that they could coast for a few generations on past accomplishments, a matter of frustration for the court, which desired to be the arbiter of who had earned such prestige and status. The situation in the South was somewhat special because the imperial court relied on the services of émigrés of distinguished families to maintain its claim to legitimacy. The term "aristocratic" is apt only in the sense of the hauteur and fine manners with which such privileged individuals carried themselves. There was no inheritance by blood, and any power they may have possessed was not based on their personal holdings but derived from their capacity as officers of the state and thus ultimately from the state itself. Finally, we may speak of lineages or, better, families in this period, but not of clans as commonly defined in the anthropological literature, that is, a corporate group claiming a common ancestor that owned communal property, pooled resources, offered mutual aid, and accepted direction by an elder or patriarch. The word "clan" is often used too loosely, even in reference to modern China.

The position of the privileged class of officials and literati was not necessarily secure. This was a society in which, except for some outstanding Buddhist monks, status and prestige could be gained only through excellence in letters. Yet this class served an imperial power with no institutional restraints on the exercise of its will, except as the ruler permitted. It is true that the officials who disagreed with any verdict were punished, but the point is that the imperial court had to demonstrate its adherence to the law. Not to do so would be to cause its own officials to become disaffected; the regime depended on the adherence of these officials, as representatives of their class, to be held as the legitimate rulers of the realm.

The chapter by Jessey Choo reveals some aspects of the practice of law in that age while also touching on other aspects of the society such as adoption, the rights of women of elite status, and how one might obtain redress of perceived wrongs by petition to the imperial court. Lady Yu, childless and now a widow, had raised a son of a brother of her husband. Her husband later took a concubine by whom he had a son who was then considered the heir. Yan Zhitui, in a chapter in his *Family Instructions*, mentions that in southern China, children of concubines were given full status in society. Evidently, in the case at hand, at the age of twenty the adopted son opted to return to his birth mother, and Lady Yu's petition, which was not successful, asked the government to require that the son be returned to her. While we can only speculate about the interpersonal relations in that household and why Lady Yu was so desperate to retrieve her son, the legal process involved is fascinating, especially regarding the basis on which the son could be commanded to return and why the government was involved in a familial controversy.

Below the officials and literati in social status were the commoners, who were the craftsmen and merchants in the cities and the rural landowners and peasants in the countryside. Some of the merchants at this time were quite wealthy. Yang Xuanzhu talks about one named Liu Bao, who lived in Luoyang, in a ward to the east of the western market.

> He had a station in all the leading centers of the provinces and prefectures and kept ten horses in each of them. He [observed] the movements of the prices of salt, grain, and other commodities everywhere; he traded

wherever boat or cart could go or foot could tread. Thus the goods from the whole area within the seas were assembled in his establishments. His property was comparable to a copper-bearing mountain, his wealth to a cave of gold. The scale on which his house was built exceeded the proper limits, and its pavilions and towers soared up through the clouds. His carriages, horses, clothes, and ornaments were like those of a prince.[7]

In the countryside one also hears of extensive estates. One of the most famous was that of Shi Chong, whose family had close ties to the ruling Sima of the Jin and who used his official posts to acquire the enormous wealth with which he maintained famed estates, the subject of another chapter by David R. Knechteges in part V. In contrast, Yan Zhitui, who disapproved of excesses and urged his sons to keep a low profile in order to survive the turbulent times, believed that a family of twenty persons should be satisfied with no more than twenty male and female slaves and ten *qing* of land, perhaps some 170 acres. The house should be good enough to protect from the weather, a carriage and horse for transportation, and a reserve of some ten thousand coins for use in the event of an emergency.[8] It was the ambition of the landed gentry to educate promising youngsters to qualify for office in the bureaucracy. Those sent off to the city would establish themselves there. Then that branch of the family could protect the interests of their rural kinsmen, and the family would survive if the family branch met with disaster in the dangerous game of politics at the center. Shi Chong, wealthy and influential as he may have been, was executed for his role in court politics, underscoring the reality of Yan's concern for survival.

The plight of the peasants varied over time and space. In the North, during the period of greatest hostilities, they flocked to the larger estates for protection, becoming dependents of the local magnate. In some cases, when the land changed ownership, they became, in effect, serfs considered to be attached to the land. In an attempt to move these peasants back onto the tax rolls and lessen the power of the landowners, a policy called the *juntian* 均田 (equal land allocation), promulgated by the Northern Wei in 485, provided forty *mou* per adult male and twenty for each female, all subject to readjustment as the situation changed. This amount was about one-eighth of that suggested by Yan Zhitui, though additional land granted to the peasants for planting mulberry trees and such would have eased the ratio a bit. Peasants, whatever their hardships, were considered to be the foundation of the state. The situation of those of lesser status was complicated and even less pleasant.

Those with special skills, whether as craftsmen or musicians, were prized for what they could contribute to the state. During the early wars of the Six Dynasties period, artisans in the subdued populations were brought to the capital as booty and enrolled in a special category as service households. This was a hereditary status of those who worked for the state and supplied all its needs, from silks to swords. During the conquests of the Northern Wei, these households swelled into the thousands. Later, as that source dwindled, convicts were assigned to this category as required. These service households had their own registers and were strictly controlled by the state; no release was possible even for subsequent generations. In time, the required service was lessened, and the households could begin to spend part of their time working on their own account. Despite a number of imperial edicts in the late sixth century to abolish the system and to integrate these households into the general population, this practice continued into the Tang.

At the lowest rung were the slaves, government and private. It was common practice for conquered populations to be enslaved. For example, the capture of Jiangling, the capital of the Liang in 554, brought thousands to Chang'an; we have a firsthand description of that harrowing trek. Slaves also were often distributed as gifts to notables as rewards for service to the state. Sources of private slaves included kidnapping, purchase during famines, and capture of border people, who often were made into eunuchs. Because slaves were a form of property, they had no legal recourse for mistreatment. Owners had complete liberty to beat, torture, or even kill them. Shi Chong, mentioned earlier, had a slave musician at a reception killed in front of the audience for missing a note. Another time, when he pressed a drink on a guest who refused, he then ordered that the slave girls offering the drink be killed in succession if the guest continued to refuse. Despite the ensuing slaughter, the guest still refused, claiming that it was no business of his if Shi Chong wanted to dispose of his property in that fashion.[9] Apart from the gorgeously dressed slave girls and concubines with whom the wealthy wanted to impress their peers, and cooks and household servants, the less fortunate slaves were used in agriculture, herding, and the salt and iron mines. In addition to various means of manumission and occasional edicts, slaves might automatically be freed on reaching old age.

MARRIAGE AND FAMILY

In a society as stratified as that of the Six Dynasties, the choice of marriage partners was a matter of great concern to both the parties and the state. The Northern Wei had strict regulations against marriages between the elite (i.e., those who were connected with the officialdom) and the commoners. That concern may well have driven the system of segregated wards in Luoyang between 499 and 534. But even within any one class, there were subtle gradations that had to be worked out. Yan Zhitui was critical of the current practice of bargaining, the price for the bride being determined by the differences in rank of the fathers and grandfathers on the two sides. Yan also compared the taking of concubines in the North and South. In the South, the practice was seen as a matter of convenience after the wife's death, but in the North, because children born of a concubine were held in such low esteem, remarriage was the custom. Remarriage, however, led to disruptions in the family, according to Yan, as stepmothers were likely to treat their stepchildren badly.

Yan also contrasted the role of women in the two regions. Women in the South rarely left the home and had little social intercourse with others. Northern women, on the contrary, were very active outside the home, involving themselves in all aspects of the family and their husband's career. As Yan observed, "Their carriages and equipages block the lands and crossroads, and their silks and gauzes fill the bureaus and offices. They seek offices on behalf of the sons and make pleas about grievances for their husbands. This, then, is the custom inherited from [the old capital of the Northern Wei] at Heng 恆 and Dai 代, [reflecting the influences of the Xianbei rulers]." Women on their own had little or no way to better their position in society except through a advantageous marriage. Serving as a wet nurse, however, could provide such an opportunity. In the North, a woman named Lu Lingxuan 陸令萱 (d. 577), who had been made a palace slave when her husband was executed for plotting rebellion, became the wet nurse of a prince and then a close friend of his mother, Empress Hu 胡. When the prince, Gao Wei 高緯 (557–577), came to the throne, the wet nurse's son became a close companion of the new emperor. She adopted one of the imperial concubines and then manipulated the harem so that her adopted daughter became the imperial consort, thus gaining her the title of *Taiji* 太姬, or Mother of the Empress. In this way, the wet nurse and her son took control of the court. But because of these and other irregularities, she was given some blame for the fall of the dynasty in 577. The case of Xu Yi, an imperial wet nurse during the Jin dynasty, discussed here by Jen-der Lee, is not as dramatic but is perhaps more typical of the practice. Her instance also demonstrates the honored status accorded these women and how it gave them access to positions of status and higher social standing for their own offspring. The relationship between the wet nurse and the infant that Xu Yi helped raise was enhanced by the importance of filial piety during this period.

Filial piety was a matter of great concern in the North and the South, and its observances were much in evidence even after the death of a parent. North and South differed in how one expressed condolences, but in both areas expressions of grief and sorrow were important. It could be carried too far, as in the case of a person who used a castor bean to irritate his skin as if caused by tears; he was greatly disgraced when the ruse was discovered.[10] Likewise, those who showed no sign of mourning even after the mourning period was over were not respected. Delicacy in these matters extended to friends taking great care to observe the avoidance of the names of their deceased friends or parents. Filial piety even came to be one criterion in evaluating fitness for appointment to office, and the *Classic of Filial Piety* (*Xiaojing* 孝經), one of the Confucian Classics, came to be placed in some tombs as a part of the funereal offerings.

LOCAL CUSTOMS AND FESTIVALS

During the Six Dynasties, as at any period and any place elsewhere in the world, the year was marked by seasonal customs and activities designed to avert bad fortune and to obtain blessings for the future. An important source of information for this period is the *Record of the Year and Seasons of Jing-Chu* by Zong Lin, who grew up in Jiangling, the most important urban center of the Jing-Chu region (approximately the modern central Yangzi prefectures of Hubei and Hunan). His work is a terse description of seasonal customs and activities in Jiangling as Zong Lin had experienced them for much of his life. Additional information is contained in the commentaries added by others soon after the work was compiled.

All through the year, special events and activities were held, designed to ward off evil influences, poisonous ethers, ghosts, and all sorts of other dangers. Among the events and activities that Ian Chapman describes was the fourteenth day of the eighth month, when people made a red spot, called "heavenly moxa" (*tianjiu* 天灸), on children's foreheads, which was meant to prevent illness. They also used colored brocade to make "bright-eyed" (*yanming* 眼明) bags to exchange as presents. On other dates, special foods were eaten, such as glutinous rice dumplings wrapped in bamboo leaves (*zong* 粽), which had no special apotropaic significance. The eighth day of the twelfth month was another important occasion. On this, the La 臘 day, villagers beat waisted drums, wore a cap called the Duke Hu head (*Hugong tou* 胡公頭), made Vairocana *vajras* (thunderbolts) in order to drive away pestilence, and washed and bathed in order to turn away sin and retribution. This obviously combined a traditional local custom with an infusion of Buddhist beliefs.

Buddhist celebrations were held all through the year. The eighth day of the second month was Buddha's birthday and also the time when Sakyamuni attained enlightenment. Faithful, almsgiving households observed the eight prohibitions concerning abstinence rules and set out the wheel, precious canopy, and various lamps. At dawn, carrying incense and flowers, they circumambulated the city, calling it "making a progression about the city." In Luoyang, this occasion apparently was celebrated on various days of the month, giving some temples their own day. On the fourth day of the fourth month, an image of the Buddha atop a six-tusked elephant, made entirely of the gold and jewels normally kept in the Changchu temple, was paraded through the city, accompanied by sword swallowers and fire breathers, men on stilts, rope walkers, and many other performers. The crowds grew so dense that some people were trampled to death. On the seventh day of that month, all the statues in the capital were brought to the Jingming temple, south of the city wall, and on the next day, they were brought to the palace, where the emperor scattered flowers on them. The incense gathered like a fog; the golden canopies dazzled in the sun;

and huge crowds and a multitude of entertainers abounded. These activities centering on the Buddha were but a small part that Buddhism played in daily life in this period.

From the end of the Han and early Six Dynasties when Buddhism first entered China, religion grew increasingly important. Initially the image of the Buddha appeared as a part of the décor on ceramic vessels and mirrors, more or less as one of many symbols of good fortune, but as the image took hold, it became an integral part of the society. The numbers are impressive. By the early sixth century, Luoyang alone had more than thirteen hundred Buddhist establishments: temples, monasteries, nunneries, and shrines. During the Northern Qi (550–577), as much as 10 percent of the population seems to have been Buddhist clerics, along with forty thousand temples. Buddhism also formed an integrative bond among the society's various strata. Despite two short periods of persecution, the religion flourished and made important contributions to the culture. Indeed, much of the art of this time was inspired by Buddhism. There are anecdotes about the efficacy of Buddhist shrines kept in the homes, and many votive epitaphs testify to the people's devotion. The monks in their religious robes and begging bowls must have been a common sight in the streets of that time. Buddhism not only brought solace and hope for an afterlife but also added an impalpable aura to day-to-day life as news of mysterious occurrences involving buddha figures spread among the population: a buddha figure was said to weep soon after terrible things happened, or someone did not fulfill a vow to a buddha and death struck his family. These events formed yet another layer to the common feeling at the time that other worldly beings were a constant presence in one's life.

We may also see a reflection of the role of Buddhism and other beliefs in the life of the people in the chapter "Final Arrangements" by Yan Zhitui, translated here. Yan's instructions for his burial demonstrates the amalgam of Buddhist, Confucian, and folk customs that had emerged in this period. Some of the objects he wished placed in his tomb would protect him from underworld threats. Other items would help his spirit find its way to the other world, while observances at graveside were Buddhist. But overall, regrets stemming from his inability to have fulfilled his duty as a filial son in providing an adequate burial for his mother moved him to insist that his own burial arrangements be simple. We see here how the various traditions—Confucian, Buddhist, and folk—intertwined to become the social and cultural practices that informed the lives of the people of the Six Dynasties period.

A survey of the Six Dynasties' many facets—material, social, cultural, and political—demonstrates that life in this period was as full and complex as that of any other period, including our own. Just as our image of Europe's Dark Ages has given way to a more insightful and sensitive analysis, revealing its many contributions to the ages that followed, so the Six Dynasties in China has attracted growing attention as a subject worthy of study. Its contributions in literature, the arts, religion, and many other fields have proved to be of importance in their own right, as well as being the foundation on which the developments in the Tang and later periods rested.

Albert E. Dien

NOTES

1.   Michel de Certeau, *The Practice of Everyday Life*, trans. Steven Rendall (Berkeley: University of California Press, 1984), xiv.

2.   Certeau, *Practice of Everyday Life*, xiii.

3.   W. F. J. Jenner, *Memories of Loyang: Yang Hsüan-chih and the Lost Capital (493–534)* (Oxford: Clarendon Press, 1981), 217.

4.   Jenner, *Memories of Loyang*, 215.

5.   Yen Chih-t'ui [Yan Zhitui], *Family Instructions for the Yen Clan: Yen-shih Chia-hsun*, trans. Ssu-yu Teng (Leiden: Brill, 1968), 303.

6.   Jenner, *Memories of Loyang*, 241–42.

7.   Jenner, *Memories of Loyang*, 237.

8.   Yen Chih-t'ui, *Family Instructions*, 127.

9.   Liu I-ch'ing [Liu Yiqing], comp., *Shih-shuo Hsin-yü: A New Account of the Tales of the World*, trans. Richard B. Mather (Minneapolis: University of Minnesota Press, 1976), 458.

10.   Yen Chih-t'ui, *Family Instructions*, 110.

26. Dietary Habits

Shu Xi's "Rhapsody on Pasta"

DAVID R. KNECHTGES

Among the many foods of the Chinese culinary tradition, the most memorable are the delectable dumplings, stuffed buns, and noodles. During the Six Dynasties period, these types of foods were all included in the generic category of *bing* 餅. Although there are various anecdotal accounts of *bing* from Han times on, the most detailed is a poem, "Rhapsody on Pasta" (*Bing fu* 餅賦), by the Western Jin scholar Shu Xi 束皙 (263–302).[1] Shu Xi was a native of Yuancheng 元城 (east of modern Daming 大名, Hebei), which was the administrative seat of Yangping 陽平 Commandery. Shu Xi was reputed to be a descendant of the famous Han scholar Shu Guang 疏廣, who served as grand tutor to Liu Shi 劉奭, the future Emperor Yuan (r. 48–33 B.C.E.). At the end of Wang Mang's reign (ca. 23) Shu Guang's great-grandson Shu Mengda 束孟達 changed the family name to Shu 束.

Shu Xi's grandfather and father were men of good reputation who had served as governors. In his youth (ca. 282), Shu Xi attended the national university in Luoyang where he attracted the attention of the scholar Cao Zhi 曹志 (d. 288). Shu Xi soon returned to Yuancheng, where he declined the nominations that he received from the local administration for being filial and incorrupt and an outstanding talent. Shu Xi's elder brother Shu Qiu 束璆 had married the niece of the powerful military man Shi Jian 石鑒 (d. 294). After Shu Qiu divorced her, Shi Jian held a grudge against the Shu family, thus preventing Xi and Qiu from serving in office until Shi Jian died in 294. During this period, Shu Xi continued to reside in Yuancheng. He wrote a lament for Wei Heng 衛恒 (d. 291), the eldest son of the minister Wei Guan 衛瓘 (220–291), who was killed along with his father in 291.[2] Shu Xi also wrote a long "hypothetical discourse," "Justification for Living in Reclusion" (*Xuan ju shi* 玄居釋), to defend his decision to avoid government service.[3]

Shu Xi must have circulated copies of his discourse, for it came to the attention of Zhang Hua 張華 (232–300), who in 294 arranged for Shu Xi to be appointed to the staff of the Minister of Works, the Prince of Xiapei 下邳, Sima Huang 司馬晃 (d. 296). When Zhang Hua became Minister of Works in 296, he appointed Shu Xi to the police section. Within six months, Shu Xi moved to the post of Assistant Editorial Director (*Zuo zhuzuo lang* 佐著作郎), in which he set to work compiling the imperial annals and monographs for a history of the Jin. While still holding this post, he was appointed *boshi* 博士 (erudite, professor, academician). In 279, a large cache of bamboo documents was discovered in a Zhou dynasty tomb located in Ji 汲 Commandery near modern Ji County, Henan. These texts, known as the "Ji Tumulus Texts" (*Ji zhong shu* 汲冢書), include the *Bamboo Annals* (*Zhushu jinian* 竹書紀年), *Account of the Travels of Emperor Mu of Zhou* (*Mu Tianzi zhuan* 穆天子傳), versions of the *Classic of Changes* (*Yijing* 易經), and a collection of fabulous tales.[4] In 298, Shu Xi was commissioned to edit these texts, a task that had been begun by his friend Wei Heng. Shu Xi's final post at the Jin court was that of Secretarial Court Gentleman (*Shangshu lang* 尚書郎). In the year 300, he resigned from office and returned to his home in Yuancheng, where he taught a large number of students. He died around 302, and his disciples and friends erected a stele in his honor by his grave.

Shu Xi was a skilled *fu* writer. In addition to the "Rhapsody on Pasta," portions of five other *fu* survive: "Rhapsody on My Impoverished Family" (*Pin jia fu* 貧家賦),[5] "Rhapsody on Reading Aloud" (*Du shu fu* 讀書賦), "Rhapsody on Nearby Roaming" (*Jin you fu* 近遊賦), "Rhapsody on the Encourager of Agriculture" (*Quan nong fu* 勸農賦), and "Justification for Living in Reclusion," mentioned earlier. Shu Xi wrote all of these pieces in Yuancheng during the period when Shi Jian prevented him from taking office. Some of his contemporaries condemned two of these pieces, "Rhapsody on the Encourager of Agriculture" and "Rhapsody on Pasta," for their "vulgarity." This was probably because Shu Xi employs a subtle humor and writes on rather mundane topics, and thus he has been considered one of the early writers of the so-called vernacular *fu* (*sufu* 俗賦).

The word *bing* in the title of Shu Xi's *fu* has a complicated history. Although in modern Chinese it designates flat or round cakes, in Shu Xi's period it had a much broader meaning and included a large number of foods made from dough, especially wheat dough. The Chinese were later than most civilizations in applying the process of fermentation to the making of leavened dough. In fact, they did not begin making dough out of wheat flour until the Warring States or early Han period,[6] probably because the process of flour milling was not widely understood in China until then. Berthold Laufer, writing in 1900, even claimed that the flour mill, which is found in Han archaeological sites, was an importation from the West.[7] Joseph Needham cautiously speculated that the rotary mill, or quern, may have originated in the Middle East and reached China around the Han period.[8]

The earliest occurrence of the word *bing* in a Chinese text is in the *Mozi* (ca. 400–ca. 300 B.C.E.).[9] Although in this passage the word clearly indicates some type of food, there is not enough context to ascertain how it was made. *Bing* also appears in the *Ji jiu pian* 急就篇, a Western Han dynasty word list attributed to Shi You 史游 (fl. 48–33 B.C.E.), together with three other food terms: *er* 餌 (rice cake), *mai fan* 麥飯 (cooked barley/wheat), and *gan dou geng* 甘豆羹 (sweet bean porridge). Yan Shigu 顏師古 (581–645), the Tang commentator to this work, which was intended mainly as a primer for children, says these all are "foods of rural people and peasants." He explains that *bing* was made by mixing flour in water and steaming it.[10] The word *bing* also occurs in another lexicon of the same period, the *Fangyan* 方言 of Yang Xiong 揚雄 (53 B.C.E.–18 C.E.), which says "*bing* is called *tun* 飩."[11] *Tun* is very likely an abbreviated form for *huntun* 餛飩 (wonton).[12]

Bing is given a definition in the *Explaining Simple and Analyzing Compound Characters* (*Shuowen jiezi* 說文解字), compiled around 100, which defines it as a *ci* 餈 made of wheat flour.[13] A *ci* actually is a boiled pastry made of rice or millet flour. The compiler of the *Explaining Simple and Analyzing Compound Characters* perhaps simply distinguished between the two names based on the ingredients used to make them. A more helpful explanation of *bing* appears in the late Eastern Han lexicon *Terms Explained* (*Shi ming* 釋名) by Liu Xi 劉熙 (fl. late second century), which gives a paronomastic gloss on 餅 as *bing* 并 (to combine). It explains that flour is mixed in water, causing it to *hebing* 合并 (coalesce). It then mentions various kinds of *bing*, all of which are named according to their shapes: *hu bing* 胡餅 (foreign *bing*), *zheng bing* 蒸餅 (steamed *bing*), *tang bing* 湯餅 (*bing* boiled in broth), *he bing* 蝎餅 (*bing* shaped like a scorpion), *sui bing* 髓餅 (marrow *bing*), *jin bing* 金餅 (metal-shaped *bing*, golden ingots),[14] and *suo bing* 索餅 (string-shaped *bing*).[15] The scholarly consensus is that *hu bing* is a type of bread; *tang bing* is noodles; *zheng bing* is steamed dough; *he bing* (or perhaps *xie bing* 蝎餅) is deep-fried dough with a large head and pointed end like that of a scorpion;[16] *sui bing* is a baked mixture of wheat flour, water, marrow, and honey; and *suo bing* is a type of noodle (compare Italian spaghetti from *spago* [string]). Thus, already by the end of the Later Han dynasty, the term *bing* encompasses a wide range of doughy concoctions that most food historians regard as the equivalent of the Western word "pasta."

Shu Xi's "Rhapsody on Pasta" has provided even more important information about the early medieval Chinese notion of *bing*. Shu Xi begins the poem with a brief introduction in which he traces the origins of *bing*. He first tells us that even though the *Record of Rites* (*Liji* 禮記) mentions that the supreme ruler ate wheat during the second month of spring and that wheat was used as a cooked grain food, it does not mention *bing*. Thus Shu Xi concludes that *bing* was a recent invention. The reason that he mentions wheat is that although some types of *bing* were made from the flour of other grains, mainly millet and rice, by Shu Xi's time, the main ingredient of *bing* was wheat flour. For example, the *Separate Biography of Zhuge Liang* (*Zhuge Ke biezhuan* 諸葛恪別傳, third century) mentions a banquet given by the Wu ruler Sun Quan 孫權 (182–252) in honor of the Shu emissary Fei Hui 費禕 (d. 253). In the middle of the banquet, Fei Hui suddenly "ceased eating his *bing*, requested a brush, and composed a *fu* on wheat,"[17] presumably because he was served a plate of *bing* made from wheat flour.

In the opening lines of the piece proper, Shu Xi enumerates the names of various types of *bing*. Some of the names, such as piglet's ear and dog's tongue, which are not otherwise known, probably were derived from the shape of the pasta. Several of the names, such as *angan* 安乾 and *butou* 餢飳, may be foreign words. Indeed, Shu Xi even says that some of the preparation methods originated in alien lands.

Shu Xi also mentions that some of the names come from "villages and lanes." This probably means that certain types of *bing* have humble origins. In Han sources, *bing* seems to have been favored by all levels of society, as there even are references to emperors eating *bing*. For example, before he became emperor, Emperor Xuan 宣帝 (r. 73–48 B.C.E.) purchased *bing* in the marketplace,[18] and the young Emperor Zhi 質帝 (r. 146) died after eating poisoned *bing*.[19] In the Former Han, there was a central government office called *tang guan* 湯官 (literally, "boiled-food officer") whose primary responsibility was to provide boiled pasta for the emperor and his entourage.[20]

There were also *bing* vendors, a subject about which Françoise Sabban has written.[21] When Wang Mang 王莽 first established the Xin dynasty, he granted the *bing* seller Wang Sheng 王盛 a noble rank.[22] During his flight to escape the wrath of a powerful court eunuch, the famous scholar Zhao Qi 趙岐 (d. 201) took up selling *bing* in the marketplace.[23]

Shu Xi associates a type of *bing* with each season. For the beginning of spring, the most appropriate pasta is *mantou* 曼頭, the stuffed bun commonly called *baozi*. Shu's poem has the earliest mention of it in Chinese literature. For the next season, summer, Shu Xi recommends something called *bozhuang* 薄壯, which literally means "thin and strong." I suspect that it is a type of pancake. In the autumn, one should eat what Shu Xi calls *qisou* 起溲 (rising soak), which may be a leavened bread.

In the final season, winter, the best thing to eat is *tang bing*, which must be boiled noodles, which were made with unleavened dough. The basic technique was to mix flour and water to make dough that was kneaded into strips or pulled in the fashion of the modern "thrown noodle." The *Essential Arts of the Common People* (*Qimin yaoshu* 齊民要術), which devotes an entire chapter to the techniques of making *bing*, mentions several kinds of boiled noodle. One, which has the un-Chinese sounding name of *botuo* 餺飥, used dough made of flour blended with a meat stock. The dough was kneaded into thumb-size clumps, which were then soaked in water and pressed into thin strips on the side of a plate. Another type of noodle, the *shui yin* 水引 (literally, "water pull"), was made of flour blended with a meat stock. The dough was kneaded or perhaps pulled into thin one-foot-long pieces of pasta as thin as the leaves of chives.[24] Although most scholars consider *botuo* a variety of *tang bing*, H. T. Huang judged it to be "gluten in the form of ribbons."[25]

During the Six Dynasties period, boiled noodles were eaten during the summer festival known as the Day of Concealment (*furi* 伏日), which was held on the third *geng*-day after the summer solstice—that is, between July 13 and 22. The custom of eating boiled noodles can be documented as early as the Wei dynasty. There is a famous story involving He Yan 何晏 (d. 249), who served at the court of the second Wei emperor, Ming 明 (r. 227–239). Because He Yan's complexion was exceedingly white, the emperor suspected him of applying powder. On one summer day, he induced him to perspire by giving him a bowl of boiled noodles. After He Yan ate the noodles, he did indeed begin to sweat profusely, so much so that he had to wipe himself with his vermilion robe. As he wiped his face, his complexion turned a glistening white.[26]

The *bing* that Shu Xi describes in the most detail is the *laowan* 牢丸, a dumpling stuffed with meat. The word probably means "kneaded dough balls." Unlike the other types of *bing*, which were reserved for a particular season, the *laowan* was appropriate for all seasons. The *laowan* probably was a predecessor of the *jiaozi* and wonton. Shu Xi tells us that the wrapper is made of wheat flour blended with a meat stock. Into the wrapper goes a filling consisting of minced lamb, pork, sliced ginger, and onions, which was flavored with cinnamon, fagara (*huajiao* 花椒), thoroughwort, salt, and bean relish. The dumplings are cooked in a bamboo steamer. Shu Xi describes how the cook quickly turns out one dumpling after another and drops them into the steamer. As the dumplings quickly cook in the steam, the filling swells in the wrappers to the point that they seem about to burst. The enticing aroma of these delectable delicacies wafts into the streets, causing people passing by to drool and salivate. Shu Xi then describes how the dumplings are eaten. As with modern *jiaozi*, the diners dip them, using chopsticks, in a sauce. The sauce they used is the ancient meat sauce called *hai* 醢, which was made of a mixture of meat, ferment, and salt that was steeped in ale and allowed to ferment. At the end of the *fu*, Shu Xi portrays the dumpling eaters as a pack of ravenous beasts that devour the dumplings so rapidly the cook cannot turn them out fast enough.

FURTHER READING

For studies of Shu Xi, see Matsuura Takashi 松浦崇, "Soku Seki no kokkei bungaku" 束皙の滑稽文學, in *Furuta kyōju taiken kinen Chūgoku bungaku gogaku ronshū* 古田教授退官記念中國文學語學論集, ed. Furuta Keiichi kyōju taikan kinnen jigyōkai 古田敬一教授退官紀念事業會 (Hiroshima: Furuta Keiichi kyōju taikan kinnen jigyōkai; Tokyo: Tōhō shoten hatsubai, 1985), 82–98; Satake Yasuko 佐竹保子, "Soku Seki no bungaku" 束皙の文學, *Shūkan Toyōgaku* 76 (1996): 42–60, and "Soku Seki" 束皙, in *Seishin bungakuron: Gengaku no kage to keiji no akebono* 西晉文學論: 玄學の影と形似の曙 (Tokyo: Kyūko shoin, 2002), 208–49; and Dominik Declercq, "The Perils of Orthodoxy: A Western Jin 'Hypothetical Discourse,'" *TP* 80 (1994): 27–60. On *bing*, see Aoki Masaru 青木正兒, "Aibin yowa—Nambokuchō izen no bin" 愛餅餘話—南北朝以前の餅, in *Aoki Masaru zenshū* 青木正兒全集, 10 vols. (Tokyo: Shunjūsha, 1969–1975), 9:425–60, and *Zhonghua mingwu kao* 中華名物考, Chinese trans. Fan Jianming 范建明 (Beijing: Zhonghua shuju, 2005), 242–52; Françoise Sabban, "De la main à la pâte: Réflection sur l'origine des pâtes alimentaires et les transformations du blé en Chine ancienne (IIIᵉ siècle av. J.-C.–VIᵉ siècle ap. J.-C.)," *L'Homme* 113 (1990): 102–37; Qiu Pangtong 邱龐同, "Han Wei Liuchao miandian yanjiu" 漢魏六朝麵點研究, *Zhongguo pengren* 2 (1992): 12–13 and 3 (1992): 6–8; Françoise Sabban, "Quand la forme transcende l'objet: L'histoire des pâtes alimentaires en Chine ancienne premier acte (IIIᵉ siècle av. J.-C.–IIIᵉ siècle ap. J.-C.)," *Annales: Histoire sciences sociales* 55, no. 4 (2000): 791–824; H. T. Huang, *Science and Civilisation in China*, vol. 6, *Biology and Biological Technology*, part 5, *Fermentations and Food Science* (Cambridge: Cambridge University Press, 2000), 466–91; and Silvano Serventi and Françoise Sabban, *Les pâtes: Histoire d'une culture universelle* (Arles: Actes sud, 2001), 339–422; *Pasta: The Story of a Universal Food*, trans. from the Italian by Antony Shugaar (New York: Columbia University Press, 2002), 271–344.

SHU XI 束皙

Rhapsody on Pasta (*Bing fu* 餅賦)

According to the *Record of Rites*, during the month of midspring, the Son of Heaven ate wheat.[27] In the bamboo offering baskets used in the morning sacrificial services, wheat was used to make the cooked grain food,[28] but the "Inner Regulations" of the *Record of Rites* does not mention *bing* among the various foods. Although we find reference to the eating of wheat, nothing is said about *bing*. The making of *bing* certainly is of recent origin.

As for such things as *angan* and the ring stick,[29]
    such varieties as piglet's ear and dog's tongue,
    or sword bands, tray offerings,[30]
    butou, and marrow pancake,[31]
    some of these names originate in the villages and lanes,
    and some of the methods for making them come from alien lands.

At the beginning of the three spring months,
    When yin and yang begin to converge,
    And the chilly air has dispersed,
    When it is warm but not sweltering,
    At this time for feasts and banquets
    It is best to serve *mantou*.[32]

When Wu Hui governs the land,[33]
    And the pure yang spreads and diffuses,
    We dress in ramie and drink water,
    Cool ourselves in the shade.
    If in this season we make pasta,
    There is nothing better than *bozhuang*.[34]

When the autumn wind blows fierce,[35]
    And the great Fire Star moves west,[36]
    When sleek down appears on birds and beasts,
    And barren branches appear on trees,
    Dainties and delicacies must be eaten warm.
    Thus, leavened bread may be served.[37]

In dark winter's savage cold,
    At early-morning gatherings,
    Snot freezes in the nose,
    Frost forms around the mouth,
    For filling empty stomachs and relieving chills,
    Boiled noodles are best.

Thus, each kind is used in a particular season,
    Depending on what is apt and suitable for the time.
    If one errs in the proper sequence,
    The result will not be good.

That which
    Through winter, into summer,
    Can be served all year round,

And in all four seasons freely used,
In no respect unsuitable,
Can only be the boiled dumpling.[38]

And then, twice-sifted flour,[39]
Flying like dust, white as snow,
Sticky as glue, stringy as tendons,
Becomes moist and glistening, soft and lustrous.

For meat
There are mutton shoulders and pork ribs,
Half fat, half skin.
It is chopped fine as fly heads,
And strung together like pearls, strewn like pebbles.
Ginger stalks and onion bulbs,
Into azure threads are sliced and split.
Pungent cinnamon is ground into powder,
Fagara and thoroughwort are sprinkled on.
Blending in salt, steeping black beans,
They stir and mix all into a gluey mash.

And then, when the fire is blazing and the hot water is bubbling,
Savage fumes rise as steam.
Pushing up his sleeves, dusting off his coat,
The cook grasps and presses, pats and pounds.
Flour is webbed to his finger tips,
And his hands whirl and twirl, crossing back and forth.
In a flurrying frenzy, in a motley mixture,
The dumplings scatter like stars, pelt like hail.

Meat does not burst into the steamer,
And there is no loose flour on the dumplings.
Lovely and pleasing, mouthwatering,
The wrapper is thin, but it does not burst.
Rich flavors are blended within,
A plump aspect appears without.
They are as tender as spring floss,
As white as autumn silk.
Steam, swirling and swelling, wafts upward,
The aroma swiftly spreads far and wide.
People strolling by drool downwind,
Servant boys, chewing air, cast sidelong glances.
Vessel carriers lick their lips,

Those standing in attendance swallow drily.
And then they dip them in black meat sauce,
Snap them up with ivory chopsticks.
Bending their waists, poised like tigers,
They sit knee to knee, leaning to one side.
Plates and trays are no sooner presented than everything is gone;
The cook, working without stop, is hurried and harried.

Before his hands can turn to another course,
Additional requests suddenly arrive.
With lips and teeth working smoothly,
Their taste is keen, their palate sharp.
After three steamer-baskets,
They go on to another course.[40]

[The base text used for this translation is Sun Xingyan 孫星衍
(1753–1818), ed., *Xu Guwen yuan* 續古文苑 (Taibei:
Dingwen shuju, 1973), 2.124–27]

NOTES

1. Scholars disagree on Shu Xi's dates. I have followed the dates established by Cao Dao-heng 曹道衡 and Shen Yucheng 沈玉成, *Wei Jin Nanbeichao wenxue shiliao congkao* 魏晉南北朝文學史料 (Beijing: Zhonghua shuju, 2003), 153.

2. For the extant fragments, see Yan Kejun 嚴可均, "Quan Jin wen" 全晉文, in *QW* 87.8a.

3. For the text, see *JS* 51.1428–30. For a translation and study, see Dominik Declercq, "The Perils of Orthodoxy: A Western Jin 'Hypothetical Discourse,'" *TP* 80 (1994): 27–60.

4. For a detailed account of these texts, see Edward L. Shaughnessy, *Rewriting Early Chinese Texts* (Albany: State University of New York Press, 2006), 131–84.

5. For the Chinese texts of these four works, see Yan Kejun, "Quan Jin wen," 87.1–2. For a translation of "Pin jia fu," see David R. Knechtges, "Early Chinese Rhapsodies on Poverty and Pasta," *Chinese Literature* 2 (1999): 112–13. For a translation of "Quan nong fu," see Lien-sheng Yang, "Notes on the Economic History of the Chin Dynasty" (1945), in *Studies in Chinese Institutional History* (Cambridge, Mass.: Harvard University Press, 1961), 146.

6. Joseph Needham, *Science and Civilisation in China*, vol. 4, *Physics and Physical Technology*, part 2, *Mechanical Engineering* (Cambridge: Cambridge University Press, 1965), 182. On the history of fermentation in China, see H. T. Huang, *Science and Civilisation in China*, vol. 6, *Biology and Biological Technology*, part 5, *Fermentations and Food Science* (Cambridge: Cambridge University Press, 2000).

7. Berthold Laufer, *Chinese Pottery of the Han Dynasty* (Leiden: Brill, 1909), 15–35.

8. Needham, *Science and Civilisation in China*, 4:191. For further discussion, see Huang, *Science and Civilisation in China*, 6:463.

9. *Mozi, SBBY* 11b.

10. *Ji jiu pian, SBCK* 30b.

11. The received text reads *tuo* 飥 for *tun* 飩. However, Qing and modern scholars have conclusively shown that the original *Fangyan* reading was *tun* 飩. See Hua Xuecheng 華學誠 et al., *Yang Xiong Fangyan jiaoshi huizheng* 揚雄方言校釋匯證 (Beijing: Zhonghua shuju, 2006), 986–87.

12. On the history of *huntun*, see Huang, *Science and Civilisation in China*, 6:478–80.

13. Ding Bubao 丁福保, ed., *Shuowen jiezi gulin* 說文解字詁林, 12 vols. (1928; repr., Taibei: Shangwu yinshuguan, 1959), 5B.2185a.

14. This may be a term for small pieces of silver or a type of metal ingot.

15. Wang Xianqian 王先謙, ed. and comm., *Shiming shuzheng bu* 釋名疏證補 (Shanghai: Shanghai guji chubanshe, 1984), 4.18a–19a.

16. Miao Qiyu 繆啟愉, ed. and comm., and Miao Guilong 繆桂龍, coll., *Qimin yaoshu jiaoshi* 齊民要術校釋 (Beijing: Nongye chubanshe, 1982), 514n.12.

17. *SGZ* 64.1430.

18. *HS* 8.237.

19. *HHS* 34.1179, 53.2085.

20. *HS* 19A.731.

21. Françoise Sabban, "De la main à la pâte: Réflection sur l'origine des pâtes alimentaires et les transformations du blé en Chine ancienne (IIIe siècle av. J.-C.–VIe siècle ap. J.-C.)," *L'Homme* 113 (1990): 114–15.

22. *HS* 99B.4100.

23. *HHS* 64.2122.

24. *Qimin yaoshu jiaoshi*, 510.

25. Huang, *Science and Civilisation in China*, 6:499.

26. Zhou Lengqie 周塄伽, *Pei Qi Yulin* 裴啟語林 (Beijing: Wenhua yishu chubanshe, 1988), 17–18. A version of it is recorded in *Recent Anecdotes from the Talk of the Ages* (*Shishuo xinyu* 世說新語), 14/2.

27. *Record of Rites* (*Liji zhushu* 禮記註疏), "Monthly Ordinances" (*Yue ling* 月令), *SSJZ* 15.3a.

28. The *Rites of Zhou* (*Zhouli* 周禮) mentions boiling wheat to make a cereal that was used in the early morning offerings. See *Zhouli zhushu* 周禮 注疏, *SSJZ* 5.22a.

29. The *angan* 安乾 and *junü* 粔籹 seem to be types of ring pastry, *gao huan* 膏環. Little is known about *angan*; I suspect that it is a transcription of a foreign word. The *junü* may have originated in the South before the Han dynasty. The same name, written 居女, appears on a list of foods recorded on bamboo slips discovered in Mawangdui Tomb no. 1. See Hunan sheng bowuguan 湖南省博物館 and Zhongguo kexueyuan kaogu yanjiusuo 鍾國科學院考古研究所, *Changsha Mawangdui yihao Han mu* 長沙馬王堆一號漢墓, 2 vols. (Beijing: Wenwu chubanshe, 1973), 2.140. Jia Sixie 賈思勰 (fifth century) says it was made by steeping glutinous rice flour in a honey–water mixture until it had the consistency of noodle dough. Balls of dough were then kneaded into eight-inch lengths, which were then joined end to end in the shape of a ring and fried in oil. See *Qimin yaoshu jiaoshi*, 509.

30. These are otherwise unknown. Silvano Serventi and Françoise Sabban note the similarity to such Italian pasta names as *lingue de passero* (sparrow tongues) and *orecchiette* (auricles) in *Pasta: The Story of a Universal Food*, trans. from the Italian by Antony Shugaar (New York: Columbia University Press, 2002), 279.

31. The *butou* 餶[食+主] may also be a foreign word. It is a type of fried pasta made from leavened dough that is first rolled into balls, soaked in water, and then allowed to dry. The dry balls of dough are rolled out on the hand and deep-fried. See Huang, *Science and Civilisation in China*, 6:510. Huang suggests that this may be the precursor of the modern *youtiao* 油條. The *suizhu* 髓燭 may be another name for the *sui bing* 髓餅 (marrow pancake). Marrow grease, honey, and flour were combined to form a half-inch-thick and six-to-seven-inch-wide pancake that was baked in an oven.

32. *Mantou* 曼頭 here refers to the stuffed bun now called *baozi* 包子.

33. Wu Hui 吳回, god of fire, was the younger brother of Zhurong 祝融, god of the south and summer. See *Shanhai jing* 山海經, *SBBY* 16.7a.

34. This is not otherwise known, but I suspect that it is a type of thin pancake.

35. Literally, "when the wind of the *shang* note has turned fierce." The *shang* 商 note of the Chinese pentatonic scale is correlated with autumn.

36. The great Fire Star (*Da huo* 大火) is Antares, whose westward movement indicates the beginning of autumn.

37. "Leavened bread" is my tentative translation for *qi sou* 起溲 (literally, "leavened and soaked").

38. The *laowan* 牢丸 is another name for the dumpling commonly called a wonton.

39. I follow the *Chuxue ji* version that reads "flour" 麵 for "barley porridge" (*qu* 麩), which makes no sense here. See Xu Jian 徐堅 (659–729), *Chuxue ji* 初學記 (Beijing: Zhonghua shuju, 1965), 26.643–44.

40. A full text of the "Rhapsody on Pasta" does not survive. Long extracts from it have been preserved in the following sources: Yu Shinan 虞世南 (558–638), *Beitang shuchao* 北堂書鈔 (Taibei: Wenhai chubanshe, 1965), 184.14b–16a; Ouyang Xun 歐陽詢 (557–641), *Yiwen leiju* 藝文類聚 (Beijing: Zhonghua shuju, 1965), 72.1241; Xu Jian, *Chuxue ji*, 26.643–44; and Li Fang 李昉 et al., comps., *Taiping yulan* 太平御覽 (Beijing: Zhonghua shuju, 1963), 860.5b–6a. All the fragments can be found in Yan Kejun, ed., "Quan Jin wen," in *QW* 87.2b–3a.

27. The Epitaph of a Third-Century Wet Nurse, Xu Yi

JEN-DER LEE

ower-class women have been employed to breast-feed and rear upper-class children in societies around the world,[1] and the consequent blurring or crossing of class and gender boundaries that this practice entails has frequently invited critical evaluation by contemporary moralists and intellectuals. But the specific issues that such debates raise with respect to gender, status, and social advancement through the female body have provided historians with many insights into broader aspects of politics and culture.[2] Historians studying ancient and medieval Europe have investigated various facets of wet nursing, ranging from the sexual regulations of wet nurses in Roman Egypt and a slave-made-nurse's unspoken decision to spare her milk for infant slaves to the wet nurses' quasi-maternal role and its impact on family relations in fourteenth- and fifteenth-century Florence.[3]

In China, although wet nurses also are mentioned in various documents, the topic has received little attention. Scholarly works on the late imperial period, including discussions of medical opinions on breast-feeding and research on charitable institutions such as foundling homes, mention in passing the practice of wet nursing.[4] But wet nurses are not the focus of these studies, and the earlier history of wet nursing has not been explored. To examine the lives of this particular group of women and to put their stories into the context of early medieval China, we must search through all kinds of material, including standard histories, literary collections, liturgical documents, medical texts, and archaeological discoveries. What I introduce and translate here is just one of these rare and precious records, the epitaph of a Jin dynasty empress's wet nurse, whose life story reveals much about the selection, duties, rewards, influence, and contemporary evaluations of wet nurses. Since wet nurses were often one of the most important marginal figures in aristocratic households, they are promising subjects for research into such topics as the history of family relations, women's medicine, social mobility, and the politics of the body in early medieval China.

The epitaph for the wet nurse of Empress Jia Nanfeng 賈南風, Xu Yi 徐義, was excavated in Luoyang, the Western Jin capital, in the early 1950s. According to the archaeological reports, Xu Yi's tomb was one of the largest of the group excavated, and her epitaph was one of three found at the site.[5] The epitaph was inscribed, and her body buried, in 299, nearly one year after her death. Although there is no name at the end of the epitaph to indicate its author, the fact that Wet Nurse Xu died at home and that the empress sent a representative to offer sacrifice in the family funerary hall, as well as the phrase "the adoration of her offspring was severed and they could no longer wait upon her . . . thus a song was composed," all confirm that the text was overseen and approved by her children, if not entirely written from their viewpoint.

The epitaph notes that before Nanfeng's birth, Empress Jia Nanfeng's mother, Lady Guo Huai 郭槐, "lost each of her children shortly after they were born." According to records given in *Recent Anecdotes from the Talk of the Ages* (*Shishuo xinyu* 世說新語) and the *History of the Jin* (*Jin shu* 晉書), this was because she murdered their wet nurses. When Guo saw her husband Jia Chong 賈充, one of the most powerful officials who helped found the dynasty, touching her newborn son while the infant's wet nurse was holding him, Guo killed the nurse out of suspicion; the baby would not take another woman's milk and died of sorrow. This kind of incident happened twice, the accounts say, and Jia Chong was thus deprived of male offspring.[6] Guo resented the wet nurses as if they were her husband's concubines, and her jealousy indirectly caused the death of her own sons. Even so, the epitaph shows that nonetheless, Guo appointed Xu Yi when Nanfeng and her sister were born, an indication of how common it was for the aristocracy to employ wet nurses.

Xu Yi is said to have "married into the Xu family," a commoner's household, suggesting that her birth family name was unknown. But despite her apparently obscure origin, Xu Yi was still praised for "disregarding her own honorable genealogy" when she decided to nurse the Jia sisters, indicating that wet nurses often came from a status lower than that of commoners. That Guo was never legally charged for her crimes of murder also illustrates the difficulty that wet nurses might face in securing legal protection. The third-century debates over whether or not one should mourn for one's deceased wet nurse reflect the fact that, unlike ancient times when presumably the lower aristocratic wives would be designated to breast-feed their superiors' babies, wet nurses in medieval China were often chosen from the household slaves. This practice caused problems among intellectuals in interpreting the Classics, which state that one should honor one's wet nurse with three months' mourning after her death.[7] Related arguments reveal the changes that occurred over time, in both the selection of wet nurses and the perception of a woman's status in an aristocratic household.

According to Xu Yi's epitaph, she was a mild-mannered person experienced in child rearing. Since she died at the age of seventy-eight in 298, we know that she already was thirty-eight years old when she started nursing the Jia sisters in 258. Indeed, she may have been appointed to the task because of her experience and may have escaped Guo's jealousy because of her advanced age.[8] Medical texts from this period advised the family to select women of mild temperament and healthy stature and to regulate their sexual activities and alcoholic consumption to ensure the quality of their milk.[9] Although no such details were recorded in Xu Yi's epitaph, her discretion and discipline were indeed emphasized. Her duties were nursing and tending to the Jia sisters while they were infants, guiding and watching over Jia Nanfeng when she became the imperial consort, and aiding Nanfeng in palace political struggles. According to the *Jinshu*, Jia Nanfeng conspired to oust Empress Yang and her father from political power. From another angle, however, the epitaph depicts the precarious court politics in which the conspirator had to activate all her human resources to avoid danger and carry out her plan.[10]

The epitaph portrays Xu Yi as a woman whose talents were greatly admired and whose contributions were too significant to be overlooked. After the political incident, not only was she invested with the title Lady of Fairness (*Meiren* 美人), but her son was promoted in officialdom. The appointment of Wet Nurse Xu's son to various offices by the emperor shows how wet nursing could open a path to upward social mobility for children of inferior households. Contemporary documents suggest that sometimes the master would adopt the wet nurse's sons, thus giving them an even greater opportunity for political advancement.[11] This practice, however, together with giving noble titles to loyal imperial wet nurses, did not escape criticism. Based on private relations and through unofficial channels, wet nurses' influence was usually considered sinister. As a result, the investiture of slave "mothers" to noble ranks was often linked as a bad omen with whatever natural disasters the empire suffered at the time, and the practice consistently drew reproach from concerned officials.

Since epitaphs were often filled with praises out of respect for the deceased, we would not expect to find such criticism there. We do not know whether Xu Yi was ever blamed by her contemporaries for Jia Nanfeng's infamous behaviors. According to the inscription, though, she was treated very well by her prestigious nursling throughout her life. Jia Nanfeng sent imperial doctors to care for Xu Yi and to provide her with the most nutritious diet when she fell ill, and she expressed her deepest sorrow when she passed away. Although no mourning service was mentioned, the imperial sacrifices and the lavishness of her burial testify to the favor and status that Xu Yi was able to accumulate through her wet-nursing career.

The study of wet nurses touches on women's occupations and social mobility, contemporary conceptions of mothering and women's bodies, and also the development of gynecology. As mentioned earlier, previous studies have analyzed the practices and meanings of wet nursing in late imperial China. Wet Nurse Xu's epitaph extends our knowledge and understanding of this significant institution back to early medieval China. In contrast to the medieval European custom in which newborns were sent away into the countryside to live with contracted wet nurses, premodern Chinese brought wet nurses into their homes, where they were closely supervised. Some scholars suggest that this may have helped reduce infant mortality in China, but these live-in wet nurses may also have caused unexpected problems for their masters' families. Originally a maidservant or a commoner at best, a wet nurse might continue to serve in her master's family after her nursling grew up. Indolent wet nurses were whipped, and distrusted ones were sometimes executed. Most wet nurses, however, became famous for their loyalty to and intimacy with their nurslings, which brought them and their families both material and honorary rewards. It was these rewards that provoked criticism from contemporaries.

Early medieval moralists and intellectuals criticized wet nursing not because upper-class women disregarded breast-feeding as the obligation of motherhood and not because lower-class women produced inferior milk and emotions that might corrupt their charges. Instead, the principal reason that scholar-officials objected to the institution was the shattering of conventional gender and status boundaries that would result if a former wet nurse were given an aristocratic title or if her former nursling carried out official mourning rituals for her. Court bureaucrats objected to the fact that political danger could arise if powerful men confided in and were influenced by these women, to whom they felt they owed their lives. Proponents of mourning honors for wet nurses insisted that whatever her origins, a rumu 乳母 (literally, "milk mother") did carry the name of "mother" and substantiated her motherly merits with her milk. Opponents, however, rejected the idea that milk and maternal care could raise a lower-class woman to the status of the "mother" of an upper-class infant.

Defining the status of different women in a patriarchal household was an important aspect of the Confucianization of early medieval China. In this regard, the North sometimes appears to have moved less rapidly than the South. In codifying classical family ethics during this period, Confucian scholars felt that a woman's status should be determined solely on the basis of her relationship to the master of the house. Another piece of source material translated in this collection shows that such an assertion—which in many cases was followed by Southern ruling houses—caused serious debates and sometimes denunciation in the Northern imperial courts.[12] Xu Yi's epitaph suggests that, given all the favors she enjoyed and the awards she received from the Jin imperial authority, whether inner court titles or material resources, she was not seen as having challenged the boundary between master and servant. Is this the reason why we find no contemporary criticism of Wet Nurse Xu, or is it simply that the Jin officials, unlike their counterparts in the Eastern Han, had no interest in blaming wet nurses for political problems? We need more sources to answer this question.

Moreover, even though the bond between a wet nurse and her charges was often depicted as a kind of mutual devotion, the reality was perhaps more complicated in view of the frequent political struggles in early imperial courts. Once a woman, slave or servant, was appointed as the wet nurse of an aristocratic newborn, she would be forced to ignore her own children in the interests of her master's, although she was given an opportunity to promote her family and herself by means of her female dispositions of milk and maternal care. But since history was never written by lower-class women, the true emotions and thoughts of wet nurses are probably forever beyond our grasp.

FURTHER READING

For a detailed analysis of Xu Yi's epitaph and a longer discussion of the institution of wet nursing in medieval China, see Jen-der Lee, "Wet Nurses in Early Imperial China," *Nan Nü: Men, Women and Gender in Early and Imperial China* 2, no. 1 (2000): 1–39. On wet nurses in late imperial China, see Angela Ki Che Leung, "L'accueil des enfants abandonnés dans la Chine du bas-Yangzi aux XVIIᵉ et XVIIIᵉ siècles," *Études chinoises* 4, no. 1 (1985): 15–54, and *Shishan yü jiaohua: Ming Qing de cishan zuzhi* 施善與教化: 明清的慈善組織 (Taibei: Lianjing chubanshe, 1997), esp. 71–102. See also Ping-chen Hsiung, "To Nurse the Young: Breastfeeding and Infant Feeding in Late Imperial China," *Journal of Family History* 20, no. 3 (1995): 217–38, and *A Tender Voyage: Children and Childhood in Late Imperial China* (Stanford, Calif.: Stanford University Press, 2005). For women's roles in domestic health care in medieval China, see Jen-der Lee, "Gender and Medicine in Tang China," *Asia Major* 16, no. 2 (2003): 1–32.

Epitaph of Xu Yi 徐義

[front] Epitaph of the Lady of Fairness [*Meiren* 美人], Xu Yi, wet nurse for Empress Jia of the Jin dynasty. The name of the Lady of Fairness was Yi, and she was from Dongwu 東武 County of Chengyang 城陽 Prefecture.[13] Her ancestors resided along the sea. After her parents and siblings died in local disturbances,

she drifted to the area north of the Yellow River, where she settled and married into the Xu family of Dayuan 大原.[14] The virtuous stature of the Lady of Fairness surpassed [that of] King Wen's mother; her spotless standing was comparable to [that of] Lady Bo 伯姬.[15] She was calm and elegant. Her management of the house was better than that of a benevolent man. She watched over all the areas without stepping down out of the hall. She took care of her children with wise guidance; her teaching was harsher than a severe father's, while her grace was grander than the spring sun. Her bright perception was known by those far and near; her generosity in reception and provision was praised by her neighbors. People sang about her, and families followed her [examples].

The Jin Dynasty's Late Palace Attendant, Acting Grand Guardian of the Heir Apparent, Grand Steward, and Duke Wu of Lu, [that is,] Master Jia [Chong], was from Pingyang 平陽. The master came from an eminent lineage [but] had few descendants [because] his wife Lady Guo, Countess Yicheng 宜城, had lost each of her children shortly after they were born. The Lady of Fairness had a loyal and faithful mind and decided to serve for the fortune [of the Jia family], disregarding her own honorable genealogy, beginning in the third year of the Ganlu era [258], to attend to Empress Jia and [her sister], the wife of the late Cavalry General Master Han of Nanyang 南陽. The Lady of Fairness nursed the babies, taking care of them as a tender mother and loving them more than a birth parent would. [When they wet the bed,] she would move the babies to the dry part and sleep on the wet spot herself. She [cared for them,] regardless of the icy weather, and she chewed delicacies to feed them, so much so that she hardly slept soundly, and she loved them from the bottom of her heart. If not for her meritorious words, they would have had no helping guidance. She taught them to stay in the inner chambers and play in the hall without displaying their voices and faces to the exterior.

The empress [Jia Nanfeng] was physically upright and thriving, her virtue wonderful and great. When she was thirteen, Emperor Wu thought that Master Jia had served the official administration and the imperial family very well and sent Chen Huang 陳惶, Viscount of Sikuai 泗澮子, also Chamberlain for the imperial clan, to betroth her as the consort of the heir apparent in the first month of the sixth year of the Taishi era [270]. The consort, at a young age, was entrusted to the prince's harem. The Lady of Fairness followed the consort into the palace in order to serve her there and was given official dresses and hats by the emperor. The consort behaved properly, as if she were a guest, when she had an audience with the emperor. She refrained from speech, meals, rest, travels, and music unless the Lady of Fairness also enjoyed them. Their affection was like that of parent and child. On the twenty-fourth day of the fifth month of the third year of the Dakang era [282], Emperor Wu invested [Xu Yi] with the title of Lady of Talents and appointed her son, Lie 烈, as an administrator in the Ministry of Education. On the twenty-second day of the fourth month of the first year of the Daxi era [290], Emperor Wu passed away. The heir apparent was enthroned as Emperor [Hui]. The Lady of Fairness began to serve in the imperial palace and was invested with the title Lady of Virtue. On the ninth day of the third month of the first year of the Yongping era [291], the treacherous Grand Mentor Yang Jun 楊駿 claimed to receive inner orders to raise the army and plotted treason. [His daughter] Empress Dowager Yang summoned Empress Jia to her side with the intention of doing evil. At the time, all the palace servants were frightened, afraid that death was unavoidable and destruction was imminent. The Lady of Fairness produced some excuses and thus saved the empress from the situation. After the principal criminal Jun was executed, the emperor, appreciating the contribution [of Wet Nurse Xu], bestowed on her the title of Lady of Fairness in the first year of the Yuankang era [291], granting her one thousand bolts of silk and twenty servants. The titles and the gifts were abundant. The empress commended her for taking care of all kinds of tasks and entrusted her with intimacy. Her cuisine was the same as that of the imperial concubines, and she enjoyed special favors. In the second month of the fifth year of the Yuankang era [295], the emperor decreed the investment of the son of the Lady of Fairness, Lie, as Battalion Commander of the Heir Apparent. Promotions and honors accumulated exceptionally; truly [the Lady of Fairness and her son] have benefited from the grace of the great Jin dynasty.

In the seventh month of the seventh year of the Yuankang era [297], the Lady of Fairness fell seriously ill and returned home from the palace to recuperate.

[back] The emperor and the empress cared for her, sending the imperial gatekeepers to ask after her health every day and commanding the palace doctors, the Commandant in Chief of Chariots [and] Marquis of Guanzhong Cheng Ju 程據, Liu Xuan 劉琁, and others to examine her at her house. They provided imperial medicine and a variety of foods. The Lady of Fairness received every kind of precious victuals in the empress's dietary. Her illness grew increasingly severe over the year, and she died at the age of seventy-eight, on the twenty-fourth day of the fourth month of the eighth year [of the Yuankang era, 298]. The empress could not help but cry and wail in lamentation. [The empress] granted [the Lady of Fairness] burial vessels and dresses, sent the Director of Palace Women, Song Duanlin 宋端臨, to personally oversee the funeral, and granted five million coins as well as five hundred bolts of silk for the funeral service. The emperor sent Gentleman of the Interior Zhao Xuan 趙旋 as a representative to offer the three sacrifices. The empress sent Concurrent Aide of the Private Storehouse, Receptionist, [and] Leader of the Court Gentlemen Attendants at the Palace Gate Cheng Gongbao 成公苞 to offer the small sacrifice in the family funeral hall.[16] On the fifth day of the second month of the ninth year, [the Lady of Fairness] was buried, forever covered deep down under the ground. The adoration of her offspring was severed, and they could no longer wait on her. Alas! What sadness it was!

Thus a song was composed, saying:

How tranquil the Lady of Fairness was, her virtue surpassed [that of] Er 娥 and Ying 英.[17] She was like the woman from Qi who ascended to the purple hall.[18] Her experience reached the imperial realm and extended to two palaces. She served the imperial household, supporting it faithfully. She was edifying and insightful, and her politics was good and clean. With all her authority, the empress listened to the Lady of Fairness. People both far and near admired and relied on her, singing songs to expand her fame. She was supposed to enjoy boundlessness and live to eternity. But Heaven had no sympathy, and she died at a young age. Her spirit was dispersed and gone, and she was covered deep down under the ground. What an everlasting pain! Not to be seen [again] in a thousand years! Crying out loud like cutting until the five viscera collapse.

This song was composed separately to finish the plain epitaph.

["Jin Jiahuanghou rumu meiren Xushi zhiming"
晉賈皇后乳母美人徐氏之銘, in Zhao Chao 趙超,
Han Wei Nanbeichao muzhi huibian 漢魏南北朝墓誌彙編
(Tianjin: Gujichubanshe, 1992), 8–10]

NOTES

1. Part of this introduction is based on material from Jen-der Lee, "Wet Nurses in Early Imperial China," *Nan Nü: Men, Women and Gender in Early and Imperial China* 2, no. 1 (2000): 1–39.

2. More than one hundred articles have been published on the history of wet nursing in Europe and America. See Valerie Fildes, *Wet Nursing: A History from Antiquity to the Present* (New York: Basic Blackwell, 1988), app.

3. For Roman wet nursing, see Keith R. Bradley, "Sexual Regulations in Wet-Nursing Contracts from Roman Egypt," *Klio* 62 (1980): 321–25. Bradley also discusses the impact of wet nursing in Roman social relations in "Wet-Nursing at Rome: A Study in Social Relations," in *The Family in Ancient Rome: New Perspectives*, ed. Beryl Rawson (London: Croom Helm, 1986), 201–9. Sandra R. Joshel explores nineteenth-century American documents on female slaves and nursing decisions, seeing similarities with the situation in ancient Rome, in "Nurturing the Master's Child: Slavery and the Roman Child-Nurse," *Signs* 12 (1986): 3–22. For wet nursing in medieval Florence, see Christiane Klapisch-Zuber, "Blood Parents and Milk Parents: Wet Nursing in Florence, 1300–1530," in *Women, Family, and Ritual in Renaissance Italy*, trans. Lydia G. Cochrane (Chicago: University of Chicago Press, 1985), 132–64.

4. For instance, Angela Ki Che Leung discusses the difficult recruitment and limited allowance of wet nurses in foundling homes in "L'accueil des enfants abandonnés dans la Chine," *Études chinoises* 4, no. 1 (1985): 15–54, and *Shishan yu jiaohua: Ming-Qing de cishan zuzhi* 施善與教化: 明清的慈善組織 (Taibei: Lianjing chubanshe, 1997). Ping-chen

Hsiung describes the selection of wet nurses in wealthy families in "To Nurse the Young: Breastfeeding and Infant Feeding in Late Imperial China," *Journal of Family History* 20, no. 3 (1995): 217–38, and *A Tender Voyage: Children and Childhood in Late Imperial China* (Stanford, Calif.: Stanford University Press, 2005). Both pieces deal with late imperial China.

5. According to the archaeological report, the excavation was carried out from the spring of 1953 to September 1955, and fifty-four Jin tombs were discovered. Among them, Xu Yi's tomb was almost 17 feet wide and about 40 feet deep, with a tomb alley nearly 123 feet long, testifying to the status of the tomb's occupant. See Jiang Ruoshi 蔣若是 and Guo Wenxuan 郭文軒, "Luoyang Jinmu de fajue," 洛陽晉墓的發掘, *Kaogu xuebao* 考古學報 1957, no. 1 (1957): 169–86.

6. The first incident was recorded in *Recent Anecdotes from the Talk of the Ages* (*Shishuo xinyu* 世說新語) 35/3. The second incident was recorded in *JS* 40.1170.

7. The three-month mourning was prescribed in the *Etiquette and Rituals* (*Yili* 儀禮), *SSJZ*, 33.8b. The debates were recorded in Du You 杜佑 (734–812), *Comprehensive History of Institutions* (*Tongdian* 通典) (Beijing: Zhonghua shuju, 1988), 92.2512.

8. Traditional Chinese medical texts often describe a woman's life according to her fertility, starting from her first menstruation at fourteen to her menopause at forty-nine. A preliminary survey of women's epitaphs in early medieval China suggests that the average life expectancy of women was about fifty-five years, so a thirty-eight-year-old woman would most likely be considered middle-aged. For a medical discussion of women's fertility and life span, see Lee Jen-der 李貞德, "Han Tang zhijian qiuzi yifang shitan—Jianlun fuke lanshang yu xingbie lunshu" 漢唐之間求子醫方試探—兼論婦科濫觴與性別論述, *Bulletin of the Institute of History and Philology, Academia Sinica* 中央研究院歷史語言研究所集刊 68, no. 2 (1997): 283–367. On gauging women's life expectancy through the survey of epitaphs, see Jen-der Lee, "The Life of Women in the Six Dynasties," *Funü yü liangxin xuekan* 婦女與兩性學刊 (Taibei: Women's Research Program, National Taiwan University) 4 (1993): 47–80.

9. The *Xiaopinfang* 小品方 by Chen Yanzhi 陳延之 of the Liu-Song period (420–479) was the first of the surviving medical texts to mention the qualities required of wet nurses. Similar ideas were reiterated by Sun Simiao 孫思邈 (581–682) and Cui Shi 崔氏 (presumably Cui Zhiti 崔知悌, d. 681). See Chen Yanzhi (ca. fifth century), *Xiaopinfang*, cited in Yasuyori Tanba 丹波康賴 (912–995), *Ishinpo* 醫心方 (982; repr., Taibei: Xinwenfeng chubanshe, 1982), 25.17a–b; and Sun Simiao, *Beiji qianjin yaofang* 備急千金要方 (Taibei: Hongyeh bookstore, reprint of Edo copy of Song edition), 5.74. The advice given by Cui Zhiti is cited in Wang Tao 王燾 (670–755), *Waitai miyao* 外台秘要 (reprint of Song edition, Taibei: Guoli zhongguo yiyao yanjiusuo, 1964), 35.980b.

10. For Jia Nanfeng's conspiracy, see *JS* 31.955.

11. For examples, see *BS* 49.1809–10.

12. Jen-der Lee, chapter 9 of this volume.

13. Zhao Chao 趙超, *Han Wei Nanbeichao muzhi huibian* 漢魏南北朝墓誌彙編 (Tianjin: Guji chubanshe, 1992), 8–10, includes this epitaph but mistakes her original place as Chengyang Dongwucheng 城陽東武城人也. I changed this in accordance with the origi-

nal image of the epitaph published in *Kaogu xuebao* 考古學報 1 (1957): 182. According to *JS* 14.424, Dongwucheng 東武城 was located in Qinghe Commandery in Ji Region 冀州 清河郡, but Dongwu was a county administrative unit belonging to Chengyang Commandery in Qing Region 青州城陽郡, according to a statement elsewhere in the same work. See *JS* 15.450. Paragraph breaks in this translation were added for clarity and are not in the original.

14. Dayuan 大原 should have been Taiyuan 太原, which belonged to Bing Region 并州. See *JS* 14.415, 14.428.

15. Lady Bo 伯姬 of the Spring and Autumn period is said to have been so virtuous that she refrained from stepping out of the hall without a chaperone even when the hall was on fire, and she burned to death. See Liu Xiang 劉向 (77–6 B.C.E.), *Lienü zhuan* 列女傳 (Taibei: Zhonghua shuju, reprint of *Sibu beiyao* edition, 1983), 4.1b–2a.

16. Not like the Three Sacrifices 三牲祠—of a bull, a goat, and a pig—the small sacrifice 少牢 entailed only a goat and a pig and often was categorized as the prince's, instead of the emperor's, sacrificial ritual.

17. Er means Erhuang 娥皇, and Ying means Nüying 女英. They were the two daughters of the ancient sage-king Yao 堯 who later became the wives of his successor, Shun 舜. For their virtuous stories, see Liu Xiang, *Lienü zhuan*, 1.1a–2a.

18. Here the epitaph writer was probably referring to the virtuous queen of King Xuan of Zhou, who was originally from the Qi kingdom. Purple palace or purple hall was often used to designate the imperial palace. For her story, see Liu Xiang, *Lienü zhuan*, 2.1a–b.

28. Festival and Ritual Calendar

Selections from *Record of the Year and Seasons of Jing-Chu*

IAN CHAPMAN

The lone bird in flight is an enduring image of Six Dynasties poetry and philosophy, and it is often with nonconformist or elitist sentiments that we associate this period's cultural creativity. Yet the "vulgar" crowd, of high or low status, was also a busy innovator, and often its creations were of lasting influence. One text to embrace the common was *Record of the Year and Seasons of Jing-Chu* (*Jing-Chu suishiji* 荆楚歲時記). This annotated festival calendar of the mid-sixth to the early seventh century not only charted important changes in religion, ritual, food, and entertainment—and in particular the formation of a new "canon" of major festivals—but also redefined popular celebration itself as a discrete cultural form that mediated social, regional, and sectarian differences.

Record of the Year and Seasons of Jing-Chu sets out, in calendrical sequence, an annual program of festival customs. Each entry combines direct narrative with textual citations, the latter serving to contextualize and elaborate on the former. These two elements form a text–commentary structure familiar to readers of classical hermeneutics. In fact, the work is a collaboration between an "author" and a "commentator," although surviving editions conflate their contributions. Zong Lin 宗懍 (498/502–561/565), a native of the mid-Yangzi "Jing-Chu" area highlighted in the title,[1] composed a work in the mid-sixth century possibly entitled *Record of Jing-Chu* (*Jing-Chu ji* 荆楚記).[2] This itself had a

text–commentary structure, including citations from other works.[3] Du Gongzhan 杜公瞻 (fl. 590), whose family was from the northeastern area of Boling
博陵 (modern Hebei), added extra commentary comprising more citations,
some original observations (often comparing his native "North" with Zong's
Chu), and probably the occasional custom not mentioned by Zong.[4] It was possibly Du Gongzhan's annotated version that acquired the now familiar title
Record of the Year and Seasons of Jing-Chu.[5] Du's additions drew extensively on
a separate seasonal observance calendar completed by his uncle Du Taiqing
杜臺卿 (b. ca. 536) around 581, itself strongly influenced by the *Record of Jing-
Chu*, titled *Precious Canon of the Jade Candle* (*Yuzhu baodian* 玉燭寶典).[6]

Extant versions of *Record of the Year and Seasons of Jing-Chu* differ quite dramatically.[7] Most scholars believe that all are Ming and Qing dynasty assemblages of quotations in other texts and that no complete edition survived after
the Song dynasty.[8] The Japanese scholar Moriya Mitsuo has refuted this, however, arguing that a 1615 edition is in fact a received, if imperfect, version.[9] Because of the problems with both hypotheses, the issue must be considered un-
resolved.[10] It is clear, however, that all the extant editions have substantial
problems, which comparison with early citations can only partly offset.

Part of the importance of *Record of the Year and Seasons of Jing-Chu* lies in its
documentation, albeit selectively and often at a remove of some centuries, of
major changes in popular ritual and religion that began in the late Han and
continued throughout the Six Dynasties. The most obvious change in festival
life was the emergence of an entire roster of new occasions. Many of the iconic
popular celebrations of Chinese tradition, such as the lunar New Year (first day
of the first month),[11] Yuanxiao 元宵 (Lantern, fifteenth day of the first month),
Qingming 清明 (Grave Sweeping, April 4–6),[12] Yu Fo 浴佛 (Buddha's Birthday,
fourth day of the eighth month), Duanwu 端午 (Dragon Boat, fifth day of the
fifth month), Qixi 七夕 (Seventh Night, seventh day of the seventh month),
Yulanpen 盂蘭盆 (Ghost, fifteenth day of the seventh month), and Chongyang
重陽 (Double Ninth, ninth day of the ninth month) festivals,[13] took form during
this period, though they continued to evolve and were joined by others. Changing calendrical conventions partly inspired their rapid and roughly synchro-
nous rise. In the late Han, numbered days of lunar months began to supplant
the sexagenary "heavenly stem and earthly branch" (*ganzhi* 干支) day-counting
system in less formal contexts. New ways of reckoning time produced new sacred days.[14] Especially important were the duplicated odd prime—that is, *yang*
陽—numbers below ten (first day of the first month, third day of the third
month, fifth day of the fifth month, seventh day of the seventh month, and
ninth day of the ninth month) and new and full moons (the first and fifteenth
days of the lunar month). New religions also introduced new ritual days. Many
Buddhist occasions, for example, fell on the eighth day of the month, the first of
the six monthly days of lay precept observance. *Ganzhi* festival days, such as the
she 社 (soil god altar) sacrifices and the end-of-year La 臘, survived into the Six

Dynasties and beyond but eventually became numeric-day festivals. Han dynasty solar calendar festivals, especially the solstices and equinoxes, proved durable, and with the Cold Food–Qingming festival complex saw a new addition. New days could host old activities, and vice versa. Customs often migrated from an old sacred day to a nearby new one—for example, from the summer solstice to Duanwu (both in the fifth month) or from the twelfth-month La festival to New Year's Day (first day of the first month). Numerous new practices came from Buddhism, Daoism, and the myriad local deity cults, as well as through increased contact with Central Asian and Yangzi delta cultures. Political fragmentation created a plurality of elite cultures, each responding to different regional influences.

Record of the Year and Seasons of Jing-Chu preserves some of the earliest reliable accounts of new festivals and observances. It documents four Buddhist occasions (eighth day of the second month, eighth day of the fourth month, fifteenth day of the fourth month, and fifteenth day of the seventh month) but, interestingly, no Daoist ones.[15] Moreover, it attempts to trace origins, though even in the sixth century, this proved exceedingly difficult. Zong and Du both quote contemporary etiology tales—some revealing interesting new heuristics, such as explaining festivals as death anniversaries—and combed the historical record for clues. They were willing to entertain the possibility, distasteful to many contemporaries, that high-society customs may have had humble beginnings.

Record of the Year and Seasons of Jing-Chu not only described change but itself exerted a lasting influence. One measure of this is its frequency of citation in Tang-Song compendia of seasonal observances, in encyclopedias, and elsewhere, surely higher than for any other nonclassical text. More remarkable is the reproduction in metropolitan calendars of most of the *Record*'s ostensibly provincial festival roster, despite evidence of regional variation.[16] Yet the *Record*'s greatest legacy may have been helping shape the imagination of festivals in subsequent literati writings up to the present.

To contextualize this, we should look at the *Record*'s predecessors. Zong Lin's work cut across two textual traditions, observance calendars and geographic writing, adapting a classical, universalist template to a vernacular, local milieu.[17] A number of calendars survive from the Warring States and Western Han that link the months of the seasons with cosmological cycles, terrestrial phenomena, and human activities. The last include ritual, governance, agriculture, construction, diet, and clothing.[18] One such calendar, "Monthly Ordinances" (*Yueling* 月令), was enshrined in the classical canon and read aloud as a court ritual.[19] These works were prescriptive and related largely to the state. But beginning in the late Han, writers began to adapt the model to other social settings. *Monthly Ordinances for the Four Walks of Life* (*Simin yueling* 四民月令) by Cui Shi 崔寔 (ca. 103–ca. 170) advised the landed patriarch when to conduct economic, social, and religious activities. *Record of Local Folkways* (*Fengtu ji*

風土記, ca. 236–ca. 297) by Zhou Chu 周處, on folk customs of the lower and mid-Yangzi regions, formed a link between calendars and geographic writing. Many of the work's surviving fragments concern seasonal observances, and there is some evidence that this material was arranged as a calendar.[20] Whereas earlier calendars prescribed universal norms for rulers or patriarchs, Zhou presents his writing as describing local practices shared across social strata.

Zong Lin adapted Zhou Chu's folk-calendar concept and some of his actual content as the basis for an entire work. What set the *Record of Jing-Chu* apart even from the *Record of Local Folkways* was its almost exclusive preoccupation with festival days. Gone are most of the references to work or weather cycles. Moreover, Zong eschewed repetition to establish a set of unique and essential observances for each occasion. The calendar was not complete as it stood, however. Du Gongzhan's commentary, with its repeated affirmations that Chu customs were "now" shared in the North, made explicit a conclusion that Zong himself hinted at in his choice of customs and textual citations: that Chu belonged to an extensive and evolving "imperial" cultural community. This putative community, the work seems to imply, had its origins mainly in the northern capitals of antiquity. After the fourth-century nomadic invasions, its center moved south with the Jin court to the Wu-Yue and, to a lesser extent, Chu areas. In the late sixth century, with Northern hegemony resurgent, it had spread north again. Although this would be an unremarkable narrative of *high* culture, its application to vernacular culture was novel. Jing Region was in fact a demographic and cultural conduit between north and south,[21] making it an ideal vantage point for observing such exchanges. Yet Zong's and Du's personal experiences of the imperial reunification process, which extended from 554 to 589, are also likely to have colored their outlook. Zong, a high official under the Liang Emperor Yuan (r. 552–554), had been instrumental in making Jiangling 江陵, the administrative seat of Jing Region, the dynastic capital in 552.[22] In 554, the northwestern state of Western Wei (535–557) captured the city, removing Zong and many others to its capital, Chang'an.[23] Members of Du Gongzhan's family had likewise been officials of a state annexed to Chang'an rule after the Northern Zhou conquered their native Northern Qi in 577. Gongzhan himself served the Sui as the District Magistrate of Anyang 安陽, the area of the former Northern Qi capital, Ye.[24]

The first text to emulate the *Record of Jing-Chu*, a quarter century after its composition, was Du Taiqing's *Precious Canon of the Jade Candle*. Du regrounded his calendar in classical traditions by beginning each month's chapter with quotations from "Monthly Ordinances" and other canonical works. He followed these with a section on contemporary observances, drawing on materials similar to those in Zong's work. In a return to the universalism of early calendars, he presented these as shared throughout an empire then close to reunification. The encyclopedia *Classified Assemblages of the Arts and Letters* (*Yiwen leiju* 藝文類聚, 624) incorporated a similarly universalist festival calendar in a section titled "The Year and Seasons" (*Suishi* 歲時).[25] The chief compiler, Ouyang Xun 歐陽詢 (557–641), was, like Zong Lin, a Chang'an-based Chu émigré.[26] The *Classified Assemblages'* calendar excludes Buddhist festivals and cites extensively from verse writings but otherwise owes much to the *Record of the Year and Seasons of Jing-Chu*. Zong's text bequeathed to later festival calendars the following premises: a festival is a discrete cultural form that can be discussed largely independently of agricultural or other cycles; the writer's goal is to establish the trademark customs of an occasion, hence he omits repetitive routines of feasting, ancestral sacrifice, and social visits; items worthy of note include deity offerings, apotropaic techniques, decorations, foods, and entertainments, whereas rowdy or licentious behaviors are off limits; and the investigation of origins must rely on textual records, though it might take into account oral traditions. Perhaps most important, writings of this type presuppose a medial cultural space between high and low cultures, in which people of different class, gender, locale, and sectarian affiliation act synchronously.

The pieces translated here convey both the variety of seasonal observances in the late Six Dynasties and the methods and concerns of the writers. The selection includes both relatively new festivals appearing in the late Han or early Six Dynasties and more established, though diverse and ever changing, celebrations.

FURTHER READING

An early bibliographic study of *Jing-Chu suishiji* is Wada Hisanori 和田久德, "*Keiso saijiki* nitsuite" 荊楚歲時記について, *Tōa ronsō* 東亞論叢 5 (1941): 397–437. Moriya Mitsuo 守屋美都雄, *Chūgoku kosaijiki no kenkyū; shiryō fukugen o chūshin to shite* 中國古歲時記の研究; 資料復元を中心として (Tokyo: Teikoku shoin, 1963) collects textual recompilations and bibliographic studies, based on numerous earlier articles, of *Jing-Chu suishiji* and several other observance calendars from the late Han to the Song. Moriya also published various annotated Japanese translations of *Jing-Chu suishiji*, the latest of which is *Keiso saijiki* 荊楚歲時記, ed. Nunome Chōfū 布目潮渢 and Nakamura Hiroichi 中村裕一 (Tokyo: Heibonsha, 1978). An alternative (and more interpretive) Japanese translation is that of Muramatsu Kazuya 村松一弥 and Baba Eiko 馬場英子, *Keiso saijiki* 荊楚歲時記, parts 1–3, *Higashi Ajia no kodai bunka* 東アジアの古代文化 2 (1974): 172–87; 3 (1974): 174–88; 1 (1975): 166–81. Helga Turban produced a study and German translation of the text in her dissertation, "Das *Ching-Ch'u sui-shih chi*, ein chinesischer Festkalender" (University of Munich, 1971). Wang Yurong 王毓榮, annot., *Jing-Chu suishiji jiaozhu* 荊楚歲時記校注 (Taibei: Wenjin chubanshe, 1988), contributes valuable data on the editions' textual variations. Xiao Fang 蕭放 moved from the bibliographic focus of earlier scholarship to address interpretive issues, most notably in his monograph *Jing-Chu suishiji yanjiu: jianlun chuantong Zhongguo minzhong shenghuo de shijian gainian* 荊楚

歲時記研究: 兼論傳統中國民眾生活中的時間觀念 (Beijing: Beijing shifan daxue chubanshe, 2000). A bibliographic study of the text by Andrew Chittick will appear in *Early Medieval Chinese Texts: A Bibliographic Guide*, ed. Albert E. Dien (Leiden: Brill, forthcoming).

Scholarship on the individual festivals that *Jing-Chu suishiji* describes is too voluminous to begin listing. But I refer readers to a few monographs that address a wide range of such festivals. On festivals before the Six Dynasties, see Marcel Granet, *Fêtes et chansons anciennes de la Chine* (Paris: Leroux, 1919); and Derk Bodde, *Festivals in Classical China: New Year and Other Annual Observances During the Han Dynasty, 206 B.C.–A.D. 220* (Princeton, N.J.: Princeton University Press, 1975). Other studies trace the development of festivals over a broad time span but include much material on the Six Dynasties. These include Nakamura Takashi 中村喬, *Chūgoku saijishi no kenkyū* 中国歲時史の研究 (Kyoto: Hōyū shoten, 1993), based largely on his *Chūgoku no nenchū gyōji* 中國の年中行事 (Tokyo: Heibonsha, 1988–1990); Yang Lin 楊琳, *Zhongguo chuantong jieri wenhua* 中國傳統節日文化 (Beijing: Zongjiao wenhua chubanshe, 2000); Chang Jianhua 常建華, *Suishi jieri li de Zhongguo* 歲時節日裏的中國 (Beijing: Zhonghua shuju, 2006); and Nakamura Hiroichi 中村裕一, *Chūgoku kodai no nenchū gyōji* 中国古代の年中行事 (Tokyo: Kyūko shoin, 2009–2011). A general English-language study is Wolfram Eberhard, *Chinese Festivals* (New York: Schuman, 1952).

Record of the Year and Seasons of Jing-Chu
(*Jing-Chu suishiji* 荊楚歲時記)

FIRST DAY OF THE FIRST MONTH[27]

The first day of the first month is the day of three primes.[28] The month is termed the "tip month."

    Records of the Grand Historian [*Shiji* 史記] refers to the first month as the "tip month."[29] *Commentary* to the *Spring and Autumn Annals* [*Chunqiu zhuan* 春秋傳][30] says: "One must tread the tip at the commencement."[31]

One arises with the crowing of the cock.

    Apocryphon to the Zhou Book of Changes: Penetrating Interpretations of the Hexagrams [*Zhou Yi weitong guayan* 周易緯通卦驗][32] says: "The cock is a *yang* 陽 bird and keeps watch over the four seasons for humans. It is thanks to it that people can raise their heads, fasten their belts, and straighten their clothes [each morning]."

    The "Norms for Domestic Life" [*Neize* 內則] chapter of the *Record of Rites* [*Liji* 禮記] says: "The son serves his parents; the wife serves her parents-in-law. At first cock-crow, all wash their hands, rinse their mouths, comb and tie up their hair, and insert hatpins." Hence this is a normal routine and not peculiar to this day. But on the morning of New Year's Day, one celebrates the living and mourns the departed. For officials there are court felicitations, in the private sphere there are sacrifices. The paying of sincere respects, followed by the return to usual stations, should be earlier than on other days. It is these things that set [this day] apart from the ordinary.

One begins by exploding bamboo in front of the hall, to repel mountain goblins and evil demons.[33]

Classic of Divine Marvels [Shenyi jing 神異經][34] says: "In the western mountains dwells a type of person slightly more than a chi tall, with a single foot. It is not by nature afraid of humans. If riled, it makes a person go hot and cold. It is called the 'mountain goblin.' {People} put bamboo into a fire, and it loudly bangs and pops, causing the mountain goblin to flee in fright." The Classic of Black and Yellow [Xuanhuang jing 玄黃經][35] refers to it as the "fierce mountain demon." Common folk believe that hall torches gave rise to the customs of exploding bamboo and burning grass and that households and principalities should not usurp the prerogatives of the king.[36]

To the gate is affixed a painting of a chicken, or a carving in the five colors and a wild chicken. One makes a board of peach wood and attaches it to the door; this is called the "wood of immortality." One draws images of the two gods and fixes one each side of the door. On the left is Shenshu 神荼, on the right Yulü 鬱壘, commonly known as the gate gods.

Zhuang Zhou 莊周[37] says, "Some hang a chicken from the door, suspend a reed rope above, and insert a peach talisman at the side. The hundred demons[38] are afraid of this." In the Wei dynasty, a person put the following question to Court Gentleman for Consultation Dong Xun 董勛:[39] "Nowadays, on the first day of the first and last months of the year, one arranges before the gate a fire, a peach-wood spirit effigy, a straw rope, and the wood of the pine and cypress. One kills a chicken and attaches it to the entrance, to drive out pestilences. Is this in accordance with ritual propriety?" Xun replied, "It is. In the twelfth month one scours the house to drive out pestilences, smears blood on the gates and doors, and makes expurgatory sacrifices of dismembered chickens.[40] The Han dynasty's ruling phase was fire, hence one made [a fire] to assist the airs [qi 氣] of this phase.[41] Demons are afraid of peach wood, so a human head carved in peach wood helps keep them in check. Peach wood is a portent of immortality.'

Also, peach embodies the essence of the five phases and can control the hundred demons. It is called the "wood of the immortals."

Illustrations of Far-Flung Lands [*Kuoditu* 括地圖][42] says, "On Peach Capital Mountain there is a great peach tree with a girth of three thousand leagues. Atop it is a golden chicken, which crows when the sun begins to shine. Below are two gods, one named Yü 鬱, the other Lü 壘. Each holds a reed rope and watches out for inauspicious demons. If they catch one, they kill it." There is no mention of the name Shenshu. Ying Shao's 應劭 *Comprehensive Customs* [*Fengsu tong* 風俗通][43] says, "The *Book of the Yellow Emperor* [*Huangdi shu* 黄帝書] states that in high antiquity there were two brothers named Shenshu and Yülü. They lived beneath a peach tree on Mount Dushu 度朔山 and kept watch over the hundred demons. If a demon wantonly harassed a person, they would snare it with a reed rope and feed it to tigers." In imitation of this, on the night before the La rites, district officials carve a peach figurine, suspend a reed rope, and paint tigers on the gates.[44]

Young and old all don the correct dress and headwear and offer obeisance and felicitations in the correct order. One drinks wines flavored with pepper or biota, peach soup,[45] and *tusu* wine 屠蘇酒.[46] One eats teeth-gluing toffee. One serves plates of the five pungent vegetables and takes *fuyu* powder 敷于散[47] and ghost-repellant pills. Each person eats a chicken egg. The order for drinking wine is from the youngest upward. After the Liang dynasty obtained all-under-heaven, people abstained from nonvegetarian foods. From that time on, the people of Jing ceased eating chicken eggs, in accordance with this norm.[48]

Monthly Ordinances for the Four Walks of Life [*Simin yueling* 四民月令][49] says, "The day after the La rites is known as Little New Year [*xiaosui* 小歲]. One pays respects and felicitations to the ruler and one's kin and drinks pepper wine, with the youngest drinking first. Pepper is the essence of the Jade Balance Star; imbibing it makes the body light and resistant to aging. Biota is a medicine bestowing immortality." "Pepper Flower Inscription" [*Jiaohua ming* 椒華銘] by Chenggong Zian 成公子安[50] says, "[At] the beginning of the year, first day of the first month, it is precious in flavor and purges the hundred diseases." It is thus apparent that the Little New Year was used in the Han, while New Year [*yuanzheng* 元正] was used in the Jin. *Canonical Studies* [*Dianshu* 典術][51] says, "The peach is the essence of the five phases. It brings evil airs into submission and controls the hundred demons." Dong Xun says, "There is the popular New Year custom of serving and drinking pepper wine. Pepper is naturally fragrant and can also be used as a medicine. Hence on this day, one picks pepper flowers to offer to one's superiors as a drink. One may consider this a rite of our era." Also, the magistrate of Haixi 海西 asked Dong Xun, "When the common people drink wine on New Year's Day, they have the youngest [people] drink first. Why is this?" Xun said, "According to folklore, the young gain a year, so they drink first to celebrate; the old lose a year, so they drink last."

Zhou Chu's 周處 *Record of Local Folkways* [*Fengtu ji* 風土記][52] says, "On New Year's Day one prepares plates of the five pungent vegetables. On the first day of the first month, the five piquant vegetables refine the [body] form. Note: The five pungent vegetables are for releasing the airs of the five viscera. They are garlic, leeks, garlic chives, mustard, and coriander. As Zhuangzi 莊子 said, 'In the first month, in spring, one drinks wine and eats shallots to open up the five viscera.'" *Reflections of the Court Dietitian* [*Shiyi xinjing* 食醫心鏡][53] says, "One eats the five pungent vegetables as protection against virulent airs." *Fuyu* powder comes from the "Alchemic Transformation" [*Lianhua pian* 煉化篇] chapter by Ge Hong 葛洪.[54] It is made by producing a powder from biota seeds, hemp seeds, asarum, dried ginger, aconite, and the like. One takes it with fresh well-water drawn in the morning. The preface to *Prescriptions of the Celestial Physician* [*Tianyi fang* 天醫方][55] says, "Liu Ciqing 劉次卿[56] from Jiangxia 江夏 was a ghost seer. He went to the market on New Year's Day and observed a student enter the market. The ghosts all avoided him. Liu asked the student, 'How did you do that? What art do you possess?' The student replied, 'I myself have no such art. On the day I left home, our family preceptor wrapped a medicinal ball in a red sachet and told me to attach it to my shoulder to ward off evil airs.' So Liu borrowed the medicine from the student and went to the spot where he had seen various ghosts. The ghosts all took flight. Hence the custom became widespread. The method is to take two taels of Wudu 武都 realgar and cinnabar powder, mix with wax, and knead into a pellet. On New Year's Day, males should wear one on the left and females wear one on the right." Zhou Chu's *Record of Local Folkways* says, "On New Year's Day one should swallow a raw egg. This is called refining the form." "Teeth-gluing" [toffee] is probably called this, since it makes [the teeth] firm and tight; here "glue" means to set firm. Today, Northerners do the same.

. . .

One also ties a string of cash to the end of a staff, then throws it onto a heap of manure, saying, "May wishes be granted."

Record of Marvels [*Luyi ji* 錄異記][57] says, "There was a merchant named Qu Ming 區明 {or Ou Ming 區明, according to one version}. While he was crossing Lake Pengze 彭澤湖, a horse and carriage emerged, with a figure who identified himself as the Lord of the Blue Lake 青湖君. He asked Ming to stop by his residence and received him there with great cordiality. He asked him if there was anything he required. Someone had advised Ming to ask for nothing but 'wishes granted' [*ruyuan* 如願]. So when the question came, Ming replied as he had been instructed. The Lord of the Blue Lake was most sad to part with this 'wishes granted' but reluctantly agreed. It turned out this was the name of a serving girl. The Lord of the Blue Lake said to Ming, 'Take her home with you. If there's anything you want, then {go straight to} Wishes {Granted}, and you will receive it without fail.' From then on, whenever the merchant desired anything, Wishes Granted promptly provided it. Thus within a few years he had grown very rich. Then one New Year's Day, Wishes Granted was late rising, and the merchant beat her with a staff. Wishes {Granted stuck her head} in manure and slowly sank and disappeared. Thereafter, the merchant's family gradually grew poor." Today, on the evening of New Year's Day, Northerners stand beside a heap of manure and have someone strike the heap with a staff. This addresses phantom pains.[58] One also fastens string to a figurine and throws it into the manure, saying "May wishes be granted." The meaning of this similarly derives from the story of Wishes Granted.

COLD FOOD (*HANSHI* 寒食) FESTIVAL

On the 105th day after the winter solstice, there are turbulent winds and heavy rains. This day is known as [the] Cold Food [festival]. Fire is prohibited for three days. One makes malt syrup and barley gruel.

This falls two days before Qingming. Sometimes it is 106 days after the winter solstice. Jie Zitui 介子推 was consumed by fire on the fifth day of the third month. The people of the land mourned him. In his honor, they abstained from lighting fires each year at the end of spring, calling this the "smoke ban." Rain and hail would ravage the fields of any violators. *Records of the Ye Court* [*Yezhong ji* 鄴中記] by Lu Hui 陸翽 says, "On the three {days} of Cold Food one {makes} malt syrup and curd,[59] boils sticky rice and barley to make curd, and pounds apricot kernels to boil as gruel." *Precious Canon of the Jade Candle* [*Yuzhu baodian* 玉燭寶典] says, "Today everyone makes barley gruel and grinds apricot kernels to make a curd; one moistens it with malt syrup." "A Sacrifice to Zitui" [*Ji Zitui wen* 祭子推文] by Sun Chu 孫楚[60] says, "A plate of cooked millet, a bowl of syrup and curd, and sweet water from a pure spring—all to fill my lord's kitchen." This is the forerunner of the apricot curd and barley gruel eaten at the Cold Food festival today.

Folklore has it that Jie Tui's body was burned, hence there is the prohibition of the dragon taboo. All say that in this month, his spirit does not take kindly to the lighting of fires. In the Later Han, Zhou Ju 周舉 was the Inspector of Bing Region 并州. He posted a notice in Jie Tui's shrine, saying that to eat only cold food for a month in the middle of spring was more than the elderly and infants could bear.[61] Today it lasts three days only, from the 104th to the 106th day after the winter solstice. *Zither Tunes* [*Qin cao* 琴操][62] says, "Duke Wen of Jin 晉文公 and Jie Zisui 介子綏 went into exile together. Zisui cut off the flesh of his thigh to feed Duke Wen. When Duke Wen reclaimed his kingdom, Zisui alone went unrewarded. Zisui composed the Dragon-Snake song and withdrew into reclusion. Duke Wen begged him [to return to serve at court,] but he refused to emerge. Hence [Duke Wen] set fire to the trees around him [to smoke him out]. Zisui died clutching a tree. Duke Wen mourned him and decreed that no one was to light a fire on the fifth day of the fifth month." Zhou Ju's notice, the "Enlightened Justice Decree" [*Mingfa ling* 明罰令] of the Wei Emperor Wu,[63] and Lu Hui's *Records of the Ye Court* all state that the extinguishing of fires for Cold Food originates with Zitui. The "Zisui" mentioned in *Zither Tunes* is Tui. This text also gives the date as the fifth day of the fifth month, which differs from today's date. These all are the legacy of folklore. According to *Zuo's Commentary* [*Zuozhuan* 左傳] and *Records of the Grand Historian*, there was no such thing as the burning of Jie Tui. The "Master of Fire" [*Sixuan shi* 司烜氏] entry in the *Rites of Zhou* [*Zhou Li* 周禮][64] says, "In the middle month of spring, with a wooden bell-clapper he proclaims a fire prohibition throughout the kingdom." The commentary says, "This is to prepare for the extinguishing of fires in the final month of spring."[65] Today, the Cold Food festival is timed according to the divisions of the solar calendar. It falls at the end of the middle month of spring [i.e., the second month], while Qingming is at the beginning of the third month. However, the fire prohibition most likely dates back to the old Zhou dynasty regime.

. . .

There is cockfighting, the carving of chicken eggs, and fighting for chicken eggs.

Precious Canon of the Jade Candle says: "During this festival, in cities especially there is much cockfighting. *Zuo's Commentary* mentions fighting between the cocks of Ji and Hou;[66] the custom goes back a long way. In the great houses of antiquity, food was called 'painted eggs.'[67] In our time, one still colors eggs with indigo, madder, and other dyes, engraves them, and exchanges them as gifts or places them in sacrificial vessels. *Guanzi* 管子 says, '[Let people] engrave eggs, only to boil them.'"[68] This is to release that which is stored and scatter [it among] the myriad things. "Rhapsody on the Southern Capital" [*Nandu fu* 南都賦][69] by Zhang Heng 張衡 says, "Spring eggs, summer bamboo shoots, autumn leeks, winter rape turnips."[70] These enrich flavor. As for fighting for eggs, the origin of this is unknown. The *Book of Dong Zhongshu* [*Dong Zhongshu shu* 董仲舒書] says, "It is as if the heart resides in an egg; it is the body's internal organ."[71] It leans against [the body's] hardness, which is akin to the principle of fighting.

FIFTH DAY OF THE FIFTH MONTH

The fifth day of the fifth month is known as the Orchid Bath festival [*Yulan jie* 浴蘭節]. People from the four walks of life all play at "treading the hundred herbs" [*ta baicao* 踏百草]. One picks argy wormwood, fashions it in the shape of a person, and hangs it on the door to expel toxic airs. One floats sweet flag, carved or cut into pieces, in wine.

Dai the Elder's Record of Rites [*Da Dai li* 大戴禮][72] says, "On the fifth day of the fifth month, gather orchids for washing the hair and bathing."[73] *Lyrics of Chu* [*Chuci* 楚辭][74] says, "We bathe in orchid-scented hot water and wash our hair with fragrant flowers."[75] Today this is called the Orchid Bath festival, or Duanwu 端午. "Treading the hundred herbs" has given rise to today's game of "competing [to pick] the hundred herbs." Zong Ze 宗則, byname Wendu 文度,[76] used often pick argy wormwood on the fifth day of the fifth month before the crow of the cock. He would gather plants with humanlike features that he saw. They proved highly effective in moxibustion. *Shi Kuang's Divination* [*Shi Kuang zhan* 師曠占][77] says, "In a year of much disease, the 'herb of disease' grows first. This refers to argy wormwood." Today, people fashion argy wormwood into the shape of a tiger, or they cut colored paper into the shape of a small tiger and attach it to a wormwood leaf to wear on their person.

On this day there are the races to cross [the river]; one picks various medicinal herbs.

According to folklore, the river races of the fifth day of the fifth month are held on the day Qu Yuan 屈原 drowned himself in the Miluo River 汨羅.[78] His death place inspires sorrow in people, so they marshal boats [as if] to rescue him. One uses a type of large boat, favored for its lightness and ease of movement, called the "flying mallard." It serves both as water cart and water horse. Regional commanders, gentry, and commoners all line the riverbank to watch. The people of Yue indeed use the boat as a cart and the oar as a horse. "Cao E Stele" [*Cao E bei* 曹娥碑][79] by Handan Chun 邯鄲淳 says: "On the fifth day of the fifth month, [Cao E's father Cao Xu 曹盱] was performing the greeting ritual for [a sacrifice to] Lord Wu [Zixu] 伍子胥.[80] As he moved upstream against the waves, he was swallowed by the water." [Boat racing] is a custom of Eastern Wu also. Zixu is the correct antecedent; it has nothing to do with Qu Ping 屈平.[81] *Yue Region Biographies* [*Yuedi zhuan* 越地傳][82] says it originated with the king of Yue, Gou Jian 勾踐.[83] There is no way to substantiate this. On this day, people compete to collect medicinal herbs. "Lesser Calendar of the Xia" [*Xia Xiaozheng* 夏小正][84] says: "On this day, gather medicinal herbs for expelling toxic airs."

One fastens threads of five colors to the arm. This is called a "weapon averter." It wards off illness and plague. There are also bracelets and other woven objects, which are exchanged as gifts. One takes mynah birds and teaches them to talk.

　　Apocryphon to the Classic of Filiality: Covenant of Divine Assistance [*Xiao jing yuanshen qi* 孝經援神契][85] says, "In the middle month of summer the silk cocoons first appear. The women dye and boil [the raw silk]; each has her tasks." The sun, moon, stars, birds, and animals all provide patterns, for either embroidery or metal engraving. One presents one's handiwork to a person one reveres. [Colored threads fastened to arms] are variously called "longevity threads," "life-prolonging threads," "weapon-averting ties," "five-colored threads," and "vermilion cords" {one version has "cords of a hundred"}; there are many names. Or one can arrange the colors red, blue, white, and black according to the four directions, with yellow at the center.[86] This is called a "fold of the directions," which is sewn to the center of the chest to show off a woman's sericultural skills. A poem says, "He clasps a pair of bracelets about my arms."[87] This refers to the same practice. Someone once asked the method for warding off the five weapons. The Master Who Embraces Simplicity [Baopuzi 抱朴子][88] said, "On the fifth day of the fifth month, make a red spirit-talisman and wear it in front of the heart." This is the same as today's hairpin talismans. In this month, the mynah bird chick's down and feathers have just grown. The popular custom is to climb up to a nest and remove the chicks as pets. You must clip off the tip of their tongue before teaching them to speak.

SUMMER SOLSTICE (*XIAZHI* 夏至)

On the node of the summer solstice, one eats *zong*.[89]

　　Zhou Chu's *Record of Local Folkways* calls this "horned millet."[90] People all make tubular *zong* from young bamboo. They insert chinaberry leaves [into the hair] and fasten [threads of] five colors to the arm, called "longevity threads."[91]

FIFTEENTH DAY OF THE SEVENTH MONTH

On the fifteenth day of the seventh month, monks, nuns and laypeople all lay out bowls to make offerings to the various buddhas.[92]

　　The *Yulanpen Sutra* [*Yulanpen jing* 盂蘭盆經][93] says: "[Yulanpen offerings bring] merit to seven generations [of forebears]. Banners and flowers, song and drums, fruits and foods all send them on their way." This is most likely the origin. The scripture also says, "Mulian 目連[94] saw that his deceased mother had been reborn among the hungry ghosts. He filled a bowl with rice and made an offering of it to her. But before the food could enter her mouth, it turned to flaming coals, so she could not eat it. Mulian let out a great cry and raced back to tell the Buddha. The Buddha said, 'Your mother's sins are grave. They are more than you alone can contend with. What is needed is the awesome spiritual power of the assembled monks of the ten directions. On the fifteenth day of the seventh month, for the sake of your parents of seven generations now in adversity, you must prepare foods of the hundred flavors and fruits of the five varieties, place them in a bowl, and offer them to those of great virtue of the ten directions.' The Buddha ordered the assembled monks to offer prayers for the donor's parents of seven incarnations, to meditate and concentrate, and then to receive food. At this time, Mulian's mother gained release from all the sufferings of a hungry ghost. Mulian said to the Buddha, 'Future disciples of the Buddha who are filial in conduct should also make *yulanpen* offerings.' The Buddha said, 'Perfect!'" Hence later generations have continued the practice, adding all kinds of embellishments. There is the engraving of wood, carving of bamboo, melting of wax,[95] and cutting of colored [paper] in the shapes of flowers and leaves, taking exquisite craftsmanship to its limits.[96]

NINTH DAY OF THE NINTH MONTH

On the ninth day of the ninth month, people of the four walks of life venture into the wilds[97] to drink and feast.

Du Gongzhan says: It is not known just when the banquet of the ninth day of the ninth month first began, but it remained unchanged from the Han to the Song.[98] Today, Northerners also view it as an important festival. One wears a girdle of evodia,[99] eats pastries, and drinks chrysanthemum wine, said to bring longevity. In recent times, banquets have always been held in a terrace pavilion. Also, *Sequel to Qi Xie's Records* says: "Huan Jing 桓景 of Runan 汝南 studied with Fei Changfang 費長房.[100] Changfang said to him: 'On the ninth day of the ninth month, disaster will strike your family. Have your family members immediately sew a pouch, fill it with evodia, and fasten it to the arm. Climb a mountain and drink chrysanthemum wine. In this way, the calamity can be averted.' Jing did as he was told, taking his whole family to climb a mountain. Returning that night, they found their chickens, dogs, cattle, and sheep had all dropped dead. When Changfang heard of this, he said: 'They can act as surrogates.' Today on the ninth day, people ascend to a height and drink wine, and women wear evodia pouches. This is probably the origin."

WINTER SOLSTICE (DONGZHI 冬至)

On the winter solstice, one measures the sun's shadow and makes red bean soup to ward off plague.

Gonggong 共工[101] had a ne'er-do-well son, who died on the winter solstice and became a pestilent ghost. He is afraid of small red beans. Hence on the day of the winter solstice, one makes red bean soup to drive him away. Also, in the Jin and Wei dynasties, in the palace they would use red threads to measure the sun's shadow. After the winter solstice, the shadow {would grow longer by the length of a thread}.

[Translated mainly from the 1615 Baoyangtang Miji 寶顔堂秘笈 edition, ed. Chen Jiru 陳繼儒, Xiang Linzhi 項林之, and Chen Gaomo 陳皋謨; reproduced in facsimile in *Suishi xisu ziliao huibian* 歲時習俗資料彙編 (Taibei: Yiwen yinshuguan, 1970), 30.1–59)]

NOTES

1. The combination "Jing-Chu" first appears in the *Classic of Poetry* (*Shijing* 詩經) song "Yinwu" 殷武, in the "Shang song" 商頌 section. Jing was one of the nine provinces (*jiuzhou* 九州) mentioned in the "Yu gong" 禹貢 chapter of the *Classic of Documents* (*Shangshu* 尚書), named after Mount Jing 荊山. The mountain's proximity also led to the title Jing being adopted as the name of a state established in the Western Zhou. This state later came to be known as Chu. Jing and Chu came to be used interchangeably or in combination. In the Southern Dynasties, "Jing-Chu" denoted a broad geographic domain with perceived historic and cultural coherence. See Wang Jianhui 王建輝 and Liu Senmiao 劉森淼, *Jing-Chu wenhua* 荊楚文化 (Shenyang: Liaoning jiaoyu chubanshe, 1992), 1–4; and Xiao Fang 蕭放, *Jing-Chu suishiji yanjiu: jianlun chuantong Zhongguo minzhong shenghou de shijian gainian* 荊楚歲時記研究: 兼論傳統中國民眾生活中的時間觀念 (Beijing: Beijing shifan daxue chubanshe, 2000), 14–34.

2. Zong Lin's authorship is not directly attested in bibliographic records until the early to mid-eighth century but seems reliable based on internal textual and circumstantial evidence. See Yu Jiaxi 余嘉錫, *Siku tiyao bianzheng* 四庫提要辨證 (Taibei: Yiwen yinshuguan, 1965), 436–38; Wada Hisanori 和田久德, "*Keiso saijiki* ni tsuite" 荊楚歲時記につい て, *Tōa ronsō* 東亞論叢 5 (1941): 405–7; and Moriya Mitsuo 守屋美都雄, *Chūgoku kosaijiki no kenkyū; shiryō fukugen o chūshin to shite* 中國古歲時記の研究; 資料復元を中心として (Tokyo: Teikoku shōin), 50–61. Wada ("*Keiso saijiki* ni tsuite," 400) and Moriya (*Chūgoku kosaijiki no kenkyū*, 61–68) argue that *Jing-Chu ji* was the likely title of Zong's original: Du Taiqing 杜臺卿, cites it consistently by this name in *Precious Canon of the Jade Candle* (*Yuzhu baodian* 玉燭寶典, ca. 581). There is no solid evidence regarding the time of composition, but some scholars believe (not always on good grounds) it most likely that Zong compiled the text after his removal to Chang'an—that is, between 554 and 565. See Xiao Fang, *Jing-Chu suishiji yanjiu* 5.154; Li Yumin 李裕民, "Zong Lin jiqi *Jing-Chu suishiji* kaoshu" 宗懍及其《荊楚歲時記》考述, in *Jing-Chu suishiji* 荊楚歲時記, ed. Song Jinlong 宋金龍 (Taiyuan: Shanxi renmin chubanshe, 1987), 10; and Ian D. Chapman, "Carnival Canons: Calendars, Genealogy, and the Search for Ritual Cohesion in Medieval China" (Ph.D. diss., Princeton University, 2007), 59–66. Moriya (*Chūgoku kosaijiki*

no kenkyū, 61–66) convincingly refutes Wada's ("*Keiso saijiki* nitsuite," 406–7) rationale for dating the text to 547 to 549.

3. Moriya, *Chūgoku kosaijiki no kenkyū*, 72–75.

4. Moriya, *Chūgoku kosaijiki no kenkyū*, 79. Wada dates Du Gongzhan's commentary to around 605 to 616, in "*Keiso saijiki* nitsuite," 410; but this is a speculative estimate based on references to his father and son and on a preface in Du's own name, dated 611, for the encyclopedia *Bianzhu* 編珠. The bibliographic chapter of the *History of Song* (*Song shi* 宋史, 1345) is the first to list *Bianzhu*, crediting Du as the compiler, but refers to it as a lost work. Gao Shiqi 高士奇 (1645–1704) purportedly rediscovered the first two of its four *juan*. See Li Xueqin 李學勤 et al., eds., *Siku dacidian* 四庫大辭典 (Changchun: Jilin daxue chubanshe, 1996), 2034. Given the doubts about *Bianzhu*'s authenticity, the only firm indication we have regarding Du Gongzhan's dates is that he died while serving as District Magistrate (*Ling* 令) of Anyang 安陽, as recorded in *Sui shu* 58.1421–22. According to *Sui shu* 30.847, Anyang was reinstated as a district in 590, so Du must have died after then.

5. Moriya, *Chūgoku kosaijiki no kenkyū*, 68–72.

6. For a short biography of Du Taiqing, see *Sui shu* 58.1421. *Yuzhu baodian* is an annotated calendar of classical and vernacular seasonal observances that he compiled and submitted to the throne shortly after 581. It survives as an incomplete Japanese manuscript, probably dating from the fourteenth century. See Niimi Hiroshi 新美寛, "*Gyokushoku hōten* ni tsuite" 玉燭寶典について, *Tōhō gakuhō* 東方學報 13, no. 3 (1943): 73–98.

7. Wada, "*Keiso saijiki* nitsuite," 415–22; Moriya, *Chūgoku kosaijiki no kenkyū*, 99–111; Wang, *Jing-Chu suishiji jiaozhu*, 4–7.

8. Chen Yurong 陳運溶 proposed this in the preface to his 1900 edition of *Jing-Chu suishiji*, in *Lushan jingshe congshu*, ser. 1, "Reconstituted Texts" 麓山精舍叢書, 第一集: 輯佚, cited in Wada, "*Keiso saijiki* nitsuite," 423. Wada (423–26) also provided an elaboration.

9. This is the Baoyantang Miji 寶顔堂秘笈 edition. A facsimile is reproduced in *Suishi xisu ziliao huibian* 歲時習俗資料彙編, vol. 30 (Taibei: Yiwen yinshuguan, 1970). Most scholars view this as the best of the extant editions. For Moriya Mitsuo's argument that it is in fact a received edition, see "*Keiso saijiki* no shoshigaku teki kenkyū (II)" 荊楚歲時記の書誌學的研究 (下), *Tōyō gakuhō* 36, no. 4 (1954): 75–110, and *Chūgoku kosaijiki no kenkyū*, 93–129. Chinese scholars rarely mention, and are yet to seriously appraise, Moriya's thesis.

10. For a summary and discussion of this debate, see Chapman, "Carnival Canons," 87–115.

11. I denote solar calendar dates by their Gregorian calendar equivalents. All other numerical dates in this chapter refer to lunar calendar dates. In the Han, the first day of the first month was mainly an official celebration; Derk Bodde terms it the "official new year." The "popular" equivalent was the La, held in the twelfth month, which Bodde follows contemporary usage in calling the "people's New Year." On these and three other Han "New Year" occasions, see Derk Bodde, *Festivals in Classical China: New Year and Other Annual Observances During the Han Dynasty, 206 B.C.–A.D. 220* (Princeton, N.J.: Princeton University Press, 1975), 45–220.

12. Qingming (Clear and Bright) is one of the twenty-four periods into which the traditional Chinese solar calendar is divided. The day of its commencement, also known as Qingming, fell two days after the Cold Food festival. Until the Song dynasty (960–1279), the Cold Food was the more important of the two occasions. Only in the Tang dynasty did grave sweeping become commonly associated with the Cold Food festival; it later became the central observance of the Qingming festival. Also in the Song, the Qingming festival incorporated Shangsi, a major festival from the Eastern Han to the Tang. See Lao Gan 勞榦, "Shangsi kao" 上巳考, *Zhongyang yanjiuyuan minzuxue yanjiusuo jikan* 中央研究院民族學研究所集刊 29, no. 1 (1970): 248.

13. Here I list common Chinese and English names for these festivals, but in most cases the latter is not a direct translation of the former.

14. On *ganzhi* and month-day festival date systems, see Lao Gan, "Shangsi kao," 245–48.

15. *Jing-Chu suishiji* identifies these dates with Buddha image processions, Buddha image bathing, the beginning of the summer monastic retreat, and the Yulanpen festival, respectively. At this time, the fifteenth day of the seventh month also was emerging as an important Daoist ritual occasion, known as Zhongyuan 中元 (Central Prime), but *Jing-Chu suishiji* makes no mention of this. Its entry on the fifth day of the fifth month cites *The Master Who Embraces Simplicity* (*Baopuzi* 抱朴子) on the use of talismans, but scholars disagree as to whether this text belongs to "Daoist" traditions, and certainly talismans were not uniquely Daoist.

16. This conversely raises the question of how "regional" *Jing-Chu suishiji*'s roster was in the first place. See Chapman, "Carnival Canons," 69–78.

17. Andrew Chittick traces the broader emergence of "local writing" in the Six Dynasties in "The Development of Local Writing in Early Medieval China," *Early Medieval China* 9 (2003): 35–70.

18. These include (1) "Xia xiaozheng" 夏小正, in *Da Dai li jij* 大戴禮記; (2) various sections of *Guanzi* 管子, including "Sishi" 四時, "Wuxing" 五行, and "Youguan" 幽觀; (3) various sections of *Yi Zhou shu* 逸周書, including "Zhou yue jie" 周月解, "Shixun jie" 時訓解, and "Yueling jie" 月令解; and (4) a calendar preserved, with slight variations, in the twelve-monthly "*ji*" 紀 of *Lüshi chunqiu* 呂氏春秋, as the "Shize" 時則 chapter of the *Huainanzi* 淮南子, and as the "Yueling" 月令 chapter of the *Liji* 禮記.

19. For a summary of the rite from the Han to the Tang, see Du You 杜佑 (735–812), *Tongdian* 通典 (Beijing: Zhonghua shuju, 1988), 70.1922–26.

20. In two surviving citations, Zhou Chu links months with musical pitches: *wushe* 無射 for the ninth month, and *huangzhong* 黃鍾 for the eleventh month. See *Beitang shuchao* 北堂書鈔 (ca. 630), in *Tangdai sida leishu* 唐代四大類書 (Beijing: Qinghua daxue chubanshe, 2003), 1.55.716b; and *Yuzhu baodian*, 2.578). This is a common feature of Warring States and Western Han observance calendars. It seems likely that Zhou's work had similar entries for each month.

21. Xiao, *Jing-Chu suishiji yanjiu*, 14–22.

22. Jiangling was in the area of modern Jingzhou City, Hubei Province.

23. See, for example, *NS* 8.244; *LS* 41.584; *ZS* 42.759–60; and *BS* 70.2434–35.

24. *Sui shu* 58.1421–22; *BS* 55.1990.

25. Later festival calendars often included the word *suishiji* in their titles. Moriya argues that this convention began with *Jing-Chu suishiji*, pointing out that although this was not Zong Lin's original title, the word *suishi* appears in a preface he attributes to Zong, in *Chūgoku kosaijiki no kenkyū*, 69–70. Other scholars have argued the reverse: that the title of *Jing-Chu suishiji* followed a convention established in encyclopedias.

26. Ouyang Xun's family was from Linxiang 臨湘, an area historically (and currently) also known as Changsha. He was yet another to see his home state swallowed in the Chang'an-centered unification process. See *JTS* 189.4947.

27. All the headings are mine. Indented paragraphs in the translation correspond to similarly indented "commentary" sections in the source text (the 1615 Miji edition). However, I have broken long commentary sections into smaller paragraphs. Curly brackets enclose editorial emendations and annotations in the source text, and square brackets indicate text that I have inserted, usually to compensate for the lower tolerance for elision of English but occasionally to supply essential contextualizing details (e.g., as provided elsewhere in a fuller rendition of a quoted passage). The translation sometimes follows variants in other editions or citations, but space does not permit noting all such instances. I have consulted the annotations (and Japanese translations, for the first two) of Moriya Mitsuo, *Keiso saijiki* 荊楚歲時記, ed. Nunome Chōfū 布目潮渢 and Nakamura Hiroichi 中村裕一 (Tokyo: Heibonsha, 1978); Muramatsu Kazuya 村松一弥 and Baba Eiko 馬場英子, *Keiso saijiki* 荊楚歲時記, parts 1–3, *Higashi Ajia no kodai bunka* 東アジアの古代文化 2 (1974): 172–87; 3 (1974): 174–88; 1 (1975): 166–81; and Wang Yurong, 王毓榮, annot., *Jing-Chu suishiji jiaozhu* 荊楚歲時記校注 (Taibei: Wenjin chubanshe, 1988).

28. *TPYL* 29.267b cites a similar passage from *Yuzhu baodian* (not found in the latter's extant edition), which glosses the three primes (*sanyuan* 三元) as "the prime [i.e., first] of the year, the prime of the season, and the prime of the day." Hu Sanxing's 胡三省 commentary to *Zizhi Tongjian* 140.4392 cites a slightly different gloss from the same text: "the prime of the year, the prime of the month, and the prime of the season." The term as used here differs from the Three Primes of Daoist usage, which refers to three days (typically the fifteenth day of the first, seventh, and tenth months) on which the celestial officials of Heaven, Earth, and Water, respectively, conduct inspections on earth.

29. In the *Records of the Historian* (*Shiji* 史記), the "Monthly Table [of Events] for the Transition from Qin to Chu" (*Qin-Chu zhiji yuebiao* 秦楚之際月表) uses *duanyue* 端月 (tip month) to indicate the first lunar month for events relating to Qin, but the conventional *zhengyue* 正月 for events in other regions during the civil war at the end of the Qin dynasty. The commentary of Sima Zhen 司馬貞 (d. 720) explains that this was to avoid a Qin imperial taboo on the character *zheng*. See *Shiji* 16.766. The *Shiji*'s biography of the First Emperor notes that he was born in the first month (*zhengyue*) and given the name Zheng 政. The commentary of Zhang Shoujie 張守節 (eighth century) claims that the time of birth, which he gives as the first day of the first month, inspired the name Zheng. See *Shiji* 6.223.

30. This refers to *Zuo's Commentary* to the *Spring and Autumn Annals* (*Chunqiu Zuozhuan* 春秋左傳), Duke Wen 1.

31. *Yuzhu baodian*, vol. 1, *Suishi xisu ziliao huibian*, 78–79, cites Fu Qian's 服虔 (d. 184–189) commentary to the *Zuozhuan*: "This is to step on the very beginning point; it is saying that in creating a calendar, one must tread the marking points and establish the first month as the commencement." It is an exhortation to establish the very beginning point (according to what criterion is unspecified) as the commencement of the calendrical year. In *Zuozhuan*, the comment is part of a series of instructions for creating calendars offered in response to an inappropriate intercalation.

32. This work has a commentary attributed to Zheng Xuan 鄭玄 (127–200); it survives only in fragmentary form. Many surviving entries link the hexagrams to seasonal cycles. For a relatively extensive compilation, see Yasui Kōzan 安居香山 and Nakamura Shōhachi 中村璋八, eds., *Chōshū isho shūsei* 重修緯書集成 (Tokyo: Meitoku shuppansha, 1971–1992), 1:part 2, 23–84.

33. On mountain goblins (here, *shansao* 山臊, also rendered *shanxiao* 山魈) in early and medieval China, see Richard von Glahn, *The Sinister Way: The Divine and the Demonic in Chinese Religious Culture* (Berkeley: University of California Press, 2004), 78–97.

34. This is a geographically organized "anomaly account" (*zhiguai* 志怪) collection combining a main text traditionally attributed to Dongfang Shuo 東方朔 of the Western Han and a commentary attributed to Zhang Hua 張華 (232–300); both attributions are now contested. More recently, scholars have dated the text to the late second century. See Robert F. Campany, *Strange Writing: Anomaly Accounts in Early Medieval China* (Albany: State University of New York Press, 1996), 43–45. But Li Jianguo believes that a late Western Han date for the main text is plausible. See "Shenyi jing yijuan," in *ZGXZ, wenyan juan* 文言卷, 384b.

35. According to Li Jianguo, this is one of only three surviving fragments of this work, all cited in the commentary to *Shenyi jing*. See "Xuanhuang jing," in *ZGXZ, wenyan juan*, 560–61. The black and yellow of the title refer to heaven and earth, respectively.

36. "Hall torches," arrayed at royal palaces and noble residences to welcome evening banquet guests, figure frequently in the classics and sometimes in Six Dynasties literati writings. The "Suburban Single-Bull Sacrifices" (*Jiaotesheng* 郊特牲) chapter of the *Liji* remarks that "[the use of] hall torches in a hundred [households] began with Qi Duke Huan." Zheng Xuan's commentary unpacks the veiled criticism: "This is a usurpation of the Son of Heaven" (*Liji zhengyi, SSJZ* 25.485b).

37. Zhuang Zhou is the putative author of *Zhuangzi*, presumed to have lived in the fourth century B.C.E. See H. D. Roth, "Chuang tzu," in *Early Chinese Texts: A Bibliographical Guide*, ed. Michael Loewe (Berkeley: Institute of East Asian Studies, University of California, 1993), 56. The cited text is not found in extant editions of *Zhuangzi*.

38. "Demon" translates the term *gui* 鬼, which can also refer to "ghost." Throughout the translation, I choose one term or the other according to the context, but in some cases both may be implied.

39. "Wei" here refers to the Cao-Wei (220–265). Little is known about Dong Xun. In several other Six Dynasties texts (e.g., *WS* 104.2325), his official title is given as Jin Dynasty Court Gentleman for Consultation (*Yilang* 議郎). Either he held the same office under two dynasties, or at least one version is incorrect. He appears in the historical

record almost solely in connection with his work *Questions on Rites and Customs* (*Wen lisu* 問禮俗), sometimes known as *Answers to Questions on Rites and Customs* (*Dawen lisu* 答問禮俗). Six Dynasties texts cite it as an authority on contemporary customs.

40. Chickens were attributed with apotropaic powers, hence were hung or depicted at entrances to communities and households at certain times of year. Moriya lists numerous references to this in pre-Qin to Six Dynasties sources, in *Keiso saijiki*, 11–13n.1.

41. The translation here follows the phrasing in *TPYL* 29.266a–b. The Miji text of *Jing-Chu suishiji*, the only extant edition to include this sentence, gives the character *han* 漢 as 熯 (parched). The translation would then read: "Parchedness and fire are abroad, hence one makes [a fire] to assist the phase's airs." Both variants present difficulties. Fire was indeed the governing phase of the Eastern Han dynasty, according to the theory that each dynasty corresponded to one of the five phases. But the exchange quoted here purportedly took place under its successor, the Wei, which identified itself with the earth phase. It is possible that Dong offers a historical explanation for the custom. In the other variant, "parchedness and fire" would refer specifically to the twelfth and possibly first months and thus be at odds with both climate and five phases theory: fire presided over the summer months, while the twelfth and first months were the preserve of water and wood, respectively. The "Han dynasty" reading seems preferable.

42. This work of unknown authorship, probably dating from the late Western or early Eastern Han, relates the mythology and strange phenomena of various locales. See Campany, *Strange Writing*, 42–43; and Li Jianguo, "Kuoditu," in *ZGXZ, wenyan juan*, 216–17. For other fragments, see Wang Mo 王謨, *Han Tang dili shuchao* 漢唐地理書鈔 (Beijing: Zhonghua shuju, 1961), 50–52.

43. Ying Shao (ca. 140–before 204) composed this text, also known as *Comprehensive Discussion of Customs* (*Fengsu tongyi* 風俗通義), between 197 and 204. See Michael Nylan, *Feng su t'ung i*, in *Early Chinese Texts*, ed. Loewe, 105–12. A passage similar to that cited here appears in extant editions—for example, Wang Liqi 王利器, ed. and annot., *Fengsu tongyi jiaozhu* 風俗通義校注 (Beijing: Zhonghua shuju, 1981), 8.367.

44. Peach wood, the gate gods Shenshu and Yülü, reed (or rush) ropes, and tigers are similarly interlinked in Han dynasty accounts of exorcisms at the La festival toward the end of the year. See Bodde, *Festivals in Classical China*, 127–38. This is one of several examples of festival customs being transposed from one Han festival to a different Six Dynasties festival. In this case, the transfer from La in the twelfth month to New Year's Day in the first month reflects the latter's gradual replacement of the former as the chief "new year" celebration, at least among higher social echelons.

45. Moriya suggests that biota seeds were used in wine to extend longevity and points to a citation in *TPYL* 954.4367b from a "transcendence scripture" (*xian jing* 仙經, usually a generic term for Daoist scriptures): "Imbibing biota seeds gives a person long life" (*Keiso saijiki*, 23n.2). However, this is the only reference to life-prolonging properties (as opposed to merely toasting a long life) among *TYPL*'s many quotations regarding cypresses. Moreover, its date is uncertain.

46. Ge Hong, 葛洪 (ca. 283–ca. 330), *Zhouhou beiji fang* 肘後備急方, in *Zhongguo yifang dacheng sanbian* 中國醫方大成三編 (Changsha: Yuelu shushe, 1994), 4:8.165b, contains a

recipe that it attributes to Hua Tuo 華佗 (of the Cao-Wei dynasty). The late Tang festival calendar *Suihua jili* recounts a popular legend claiming that *tusu* originally referred to the thatched hut in which the wine's inventor lived. See *Suishi xisu ziliao huibian*, 3:1.21. Li Xianzhang 李獻璋 links such explanations to the fact that in Han and Six Dynasties sources, *tusu* referred to the flat roofs of wooden boards popular among the Di and Qiang peoples to China's west, in "Tosoin shūzoku kō" 屠蘇飲習俗考, *Tōyōshi kenkyū* 東洋史研究 34, no. 1 (1975): 59–91. However, he proposes that *tusu* wine actually drew its name from two other Western sources. First, *tusu* was the name of a health-promoting grape beverage brought to China by Western travelers (similar words for "grape" exist in Tibetan and Sanskrit). In China, the name was adopted for a medicinal wine. Second, the Chinese transliteration of the Buddhist Tuṣita heaven, invoked in imprecations for good health, included the syllables *tusu* (rendered in the same or homophonous characters).

47. The literal meaning of this concoction's name is uncertain.

48. The Liang Emperor Wu ordered Buddhist monks and nuns to abstain from alcohol and meat, for reasons set out in his "On Abstaining from Wine and Meat" 斷酒肉文 (ca. 517–523), in Daoxuan's 道宣 *Guang Hongming ji* 廣弘明集, *juan* 26, *T* 2103, 52.294b–98c.

49. This is a calendrically sequenced guide to the seasonal activities of a rural household, touching on agricultural, animal husbandry, ritual, clothing, cuisine, medicine, and folk customs. The work, composed in the mid-second century c.e. by Cui Shi 崔寔, survives mainly through extensive citations in *Yuzhu baodian*, *Qimin yaoshu* 齊民要術, and the various encyclopedias. Some citations of this passage (e.g., *TPYL* 29.267a) give the date as New Year's Day rather than the day after La. For a full translation of the text, see Cho-yun Hsu, *Han Agriculture: The Formation of Early Chinese Agrarian Economy, 206 b.c.–a.d. 220* (Seattle: University of Washington Press, 1980), 215–28.

50. Byname of the Western Jin literatus Chenggong Sui 成公綏 (231–273).

51. The bibliographic treatise of the *Sui shu* (34.1042), which lists the work in its medical category, names the author as the [Liu] Song Prince of Jianping 宋建平王. Both Liu Hong 劉宏 and his son Liu Jingsu 劉景素 held this title. The work is not mentioned in the biographies of either father or son, in *Song shu* 72.1858–68. Okanishi Tameto 岡西為人 believes that Liu Hong was the author, as discussed in *Song yiqian yiji kao* 宋以前醫籍考 (Taibei: Nantian, 1977), 548. *TPYL* 808.3724b and some later bibliographies attribute the work to Wang Jianping 王建平, which may be a corruption of "Prince of Jianping."

52. Zhou Chu (ca. 236–ca. 297) served as an official in the lower Yangzi state of Wu (220–280) and also under its northern conqueror, the Jin. He took an interest in observing and sometimes reforming the local customs of areas to which he was dispatched. See *JS* 58.1570. *Record of Folkways* survives only in quotations. For a study of the work and compilation of its fragments, see Moriya, *Chūgoku kosaijiki no kenkyū*, 24–47, 295–312.

53. Okanishi equates this work with the similarly titled *Shiyi xinjian* 食醫心鑒, by the Tang author Zan Yin 咎殷, in *Song yiqian yiji kao*, 1340–41. *Expanded Record of the Year and Seasons* (*Suishi guangji* 歲時廣記, thirteenth century; *Suishi xisu ziliao huibian*, vols. 4–7, 5.175) attributes the same quotation to *Sun zhenren shiji* 孫真人食忌 (see Okanishi, *Song yiqian yiji kao*, 1337), presumably by Sun Simiao 孫思邈 (ca. 581–ca. 682). The lives

of Sun and *Jing-Chu suishiji* commentator Du Gongzhan would have overlapped some-what, but it is probable that this quotation is a later interpolation.

54. This chapter does not appear in extant editions of Ge Hong's works.

55. *Yuzhu baodian* 1.85 cites this title as *Da yifang* 大醫方. In "Tosoin shūzoku kō," 63, Li Xianzhang suggests that this may be a corruption of *Taiyi fang* 太醫方 (*Prescriptions of the Supreme Physician*), and points to the title *Chenshi Taiyi fang* 陳氏太醫方 (*Mr. Chen's Prescriptions of the Supreme Physician*) in the bibliographic section of *Tongzhi* 通志 (twelfth century). Other editions of *Jing-Chu suishiji* attribute the quotation to "*fang*," presumably indicating an unspecified pharmacological work. See Wang, *Jing-Chu suishiji jiaozhu*, 34–35

56. Li Xianzhang identifies him as Liu Juanzi 劉涓子 of the Jin dynasty, author of *Prescriptions of [Huang Fu] Gui (Gui yifang* 鬼遺方), in "Tosoin shūzoku kō," 63.

57. Also known as *Luyi zhuan* 錄異傳, this is an anomaly account collection of unknown authorship. Li Jianguo dates it to the Liang or Chen dynasty. See *Luyi zhuan*, in *ZGXZ*, *wenyan juan*, 274a. Another version of the tale appears in Gan Bao 干寶, *Soushen ji* 搜神記, *Han Wei Liuchao biji xiaoshuo daguan* 漢魏六朝筆記小說大觀 (Shanghai: Shanghai guji, 1999), 307–8. Du Guangting 杜光庭 wrote a different work also titled *Record of Marvels* (*Luyi ji* 錄異記) between 921 and 925. See *DZ* 591; and Franciscus Verellen, "*Luyi ji*," in *The Taoist Canon: A Historical Companion to the Daozang*, ed. Kristofer Schipper and Franciscus Verellen (Chicago: University of Chicago Press, 2004), 420–21.

58. Literally, "answers false (or borrowed) pains" 荅假痛. The meaning is somewhat obscure. *TPYL* 29.266b has "cures lower back pain" 治腰痛.

59. Moriya cites *Qimin yaoshu* in suggesting that 醴, usually a sweet wine, here probably refers to malt sugar syrup, in *Keiso saijiki*, 100. He also believes that "curd" refers specifically to the apricot kernel curd mentioned later.

60. Sun Chu (d. 293) was a literatus-official who served under the Wei and Western Jin dynasties.

61. Zhou Ju's biography in the *HHS* 61.2024 gives the season as the "the dead of winter." The commentary to the *Hou Han shu* commissioned by Li Xian 李賢 (ca. 653–684) offers the following explanation of the "dragon taboo" mentioned in Zhou's biography: "The Dragon Star lies in the wood position; in spring it appears in the East. The Heart [Asterism] is the Great Fire [Asterism]. A fear of fire prevails, hence there is a prohibition on fire." For more on the astrological dimensions of the prohibition, see Moriya Mitsuo, "Kanshoku kō" 寒食考, in *Wada hakushi kanreki kinen Tōyōshi ronsō*, ed. Wada Hakūshi kanreki kinen Tōyōshi ronsō hensan iinkai 和田博士還曆記念東洋史論叢編纂委員会 (Tokyo: Dainihon yūbenkai kodansha, 1951), 754–61; for a nonastrological explanation, see Donald Holzman, "The Cold Food Festival in Medieval China," *HJAS* 46, no. 1 (1986): 55–56.

62. This work, usually attributed to Cai Yong 蔡邕 (ca. 132–192), recorded the composers of various zither tunes, the stories behind their titles, and often the lyrics.

63. A section of this text, which decrees the festival's prohibition, is quoted in *Yuzhu baodian* 2.187 and *Yiwen leiju* 4.62. Cao Cao 曹操 (155–220) was posthumously given the title of Emperor Wu after his son Cao Pi 曹丕 established the Wei dynasty in 220.

64. Officially designated a Classic during the reign of Wang Mang (9–23), this text has, at different times, been attributed to the Duke of Zhou and the "forger" Liu Xin 劉歆 (49 B.C.E.–23 C.E.); modern scholars have argued that it existed in some form by the second century B.C.E.. It claims to describe the bureaucratic structure of the Western Zhou. See William G. Boltz, "Chou li," in *Early Chinese Texts*, ed. Loewe, 24–29.

65. The commentary is that of Zheng Xuan, *Zhou li zhushu* 周禮注疏, *SSJZ* 36.555a.

66. *Zuozhuan*, Zhao 25. The broader narrative concerns animosities between Ji Pingzi 季平子 and Hou Zhaobo 邱昭伯. James Legge's translation reads, "'The cocks of Ke [-sun] and the [Head of the] How [family] were in the habit of fighting. Ke-sun sheathed the head of his cock, on which How-she put metal spurs on his" (*The Chinese Classics* [Hong Kong: Lane, Crawford, 1872], 5:710a).

67. *Yuzhu baodian* 2.197 attributes this line to Cao Zhi's 曹植 (192–232) poem "Poetic Rhapsody on Cock-Fighting" (*Douji shifu* 鬥雞詩賦). It is unfortunately now lost, making it difficult to explore further this intriguing statement.

68. *Guanzi* is a political-philosophical work possibly compiled by Liu Xiang around 26 B.C.E. "Guanzi," or Master Guan, refers to the statesman Guan Zhong 管仲. See W. Allyn Rickett, "Kuan tzu," in *Early Chinese Texts*, ed. Loewe, 244–51. See also Rickett's translation of the relevant section of the original in *Kuan-tzu: A Repository of Early Chinese Thought* (Hong Kong: Hong Kong University Press, 1965), 311.

69. This poem was composed around 110. See Xiao Tong, comp., *Wen xuan, or, Selections of Refined Literature*, vol. 1, *Rhapsodies on Metropolises and Capitals*, trans. David R. Knechtges (Princeton, N.J.: Princeton University Press, 1982), 311. Zhang Heng (78–139) eulogizes Nanyang 南陽, his own native place and that of the Eastern Han founder, Emperor Guangwu (r. 25–57). The latter connection gave the city a privileged imperial status, hence Zhang's reference to it as a "capital."

70. Here I follow Knechtges's translation of the relevant line of the *Wen xuan* version of Zhang's rhapsody, which *Jing-Chu suishiji*'s citation matches, in *Wen xuan* 1:323.

71. Dong Zhongshu (179–104 B.C.E.) was a court erudite under the Han emperors Jing and Wu. It is unclear which of his works this refers to. Wang Chong 王充 quotes a similar phrase with reference to Dong: "[He] held that the heart is like a round egg, being the body's internal organ; and that the pupil is like a bean, being the body's light" ("Balanced Discourses," in *Lun heng jiaoshi* 論衡校釋, comp. Huang Hui 黃暉 [Beijing: Zhonghua shuju, 1990], 604–5).

72. This compilation of ritual writings is traditionally attributed to, and named for, Dai De 戴德 (first century B.C.E.). De is known as the Elder Dai to distinguish him from his nephew Dai Sheng, purported compiler of the *Liji* (see note 36). Scholars have traditionally viewed their respective *Liji* as drawing on a single corpus of transmitted or recovered materials. For a refutation of most of these assumptions, see Jeffrey K. Riegel, "Ta Tai Li chi," in *Early Chinese Texts*, ed. Loewe, 456–57.

73. This is from the "Xia xiaozheng" chapter. The extant *Da Dai liji* includes this prescription in its program for the fifth month but makes no mention of a specific day. See Wang Pingzhen 王聘珍, ed. and annot., *Da Dai liji jiegu* 大戴禮記解詁 (Beijing: Zhonghua shuju, 1983), 2.39.

74. This term originally referred to a corpus of verse writings from the Chu region but was later more narrowly associated with those anthologized in Wang Yi 王逸, *Chuci zhangju* 楚辭章句 (early second century C.E.). See David Hawkes, "*Chu tz'u*," in *Early Chinese Texts*, ed. Loewe, 48–55.

75. This line is from "The Lord in the Clouds" (*Yunzhong jun* 雲中君), the second of the Nine Songs (Jiu ge 九歌), traditionally attributed to Qu Yuan (ca. 340–278 B.C.E.). The extant *Jing-Chu suishiji* citation breaks this line differently from standard editions of the *Lyrics of Chu* (*Chuci* 楚辭), in which "flowers" begins a new line. David Hawkes translates the *Chuci* line as "We have bathed in orchid water and washed our hair with perfumes" (*The Songs of the South: An Ancient Chinese Anthology of Poems by Qu Yuan and Other Poets* [Harmondsworth: Penguin, 1985], 103).

76. Zong Ze was presumably an elder relative of Zong Lin. It may be the Zong Ce 宗測 whose biography appears in *NQS* 54.940, though the latter source gives a different byname. See Moriya, *Keiso saijiki*, 147–49n.7.

77. Shi Kuang is mentioned in various texts from the Warring States onward as a master of music and esoteric learning who served at the Spring and Autumn period court of Jin Duke Ping. A number of works incorporate his name in the title, though this text is rarely cited. See Li Jianguo, "Shi Kuang liupian," *ZGXZ, wenyan juan*, 388b; and Moriya, *Keiso saijiki*, 148–49n.8.

78. According to the *Shiji* 84.2481–91, Qu Yuan drowned himself in the Miluo River in despair after being sent into exile following the execution of Chu King Huai by the Qin, an outcome that Qu had warned against. A reliably testified association between Qu Yuan and Duanwu ritual appeared only in the Six Dynasties, perhaps as late as the sixth century. See Chapman, "Carnival Canons," 223–24. As we see later in this entry, Zong Lin (or Du Gongzhan) rejects the link.

79. A version of this stele, reinscribed in the Song, is collected in *Guwen yuan* 古文苑, in *SBCK* 102:19.14b–16b. This and Cao E's biography in *Hou Han shu* 84/2794–95 tell of how in 143 C.E. she plunged into the river to retrieve the body of her father, Cao Xu, after he drowned while sacrificing to Wu Zixu. She miraculously appeared with his body five days later, albeit drowned herself. In 151, a local official memorialized the throne requesting recognition of her filial piety and commissioned the stele.

80. Wu Zixu, like Qu Yuan, took his own life after seeing his ruler ignore loyal advice. However, his suicide, around 484 B.C.E., was forced on him by the reckless King of Wu, Fu Chai. The latter discarded Wu's body in the river, after which he became a vengeful water god. See *Shiji* 66.2179–80; and *Wu-Yue chunqiu jijiao huikao* 吳越春秋輯校匯考 (Shanghai: Shanghai guji, 1997), 10.169.

81. Qu Yuan's given name was Ping.

82. *Taiping Yulan* and various observance calendars occasionally cite this text but give no author or time of composition.

83. Gou Jian led Yue in an invasion of Fu Chai's Wu, an outcome that Wu Zixu had warned against.

84. Now a chapter in *Da Dai Liji* (see note 73), this is a calendar combining descriptions of astral and terrestrial seasonal cycles and prescriptions for human activity. A main text

and commentary are now intertwined. It was one of several such calendars in circulation in the late Warring States and Han, the most influential of which was that found in *Lüshi chunqiu*, *Huainanzi*, and *Liji* (the *Liji* terms it "Yueling" 月令 [Monthly Ordinances]).

85. The bibliographic treatise of *Sui shu* 32.940 names Song Jun 宋均 (d. 76 C.E., presumably the one whose biography appears in *HHS* 41.1411–14) as providing a commentary to this and many other "apocrypha" of the classics. For surviving text, see Yasui and Nakamura, *Chōshū isho shūsei*, 5:21–60.

86. This reproduces the cosmological correlations between direction and color in the five phases theory: east / blue, south / red, center / yellow, west / white, north / black.

87. The poem appears to be "Pledging Affection" 定情詩, attributed to Fan Qin 繁欽 of the late Eastern Han. The earliest extant complete version is in *Yutai xinyong* 玉臺新詠, *juan* 1, in Anne Birrell, trans., *New Songs from a Jade Terrace: An Anthology of Early Chinese Love Poetry* (Boston: Allen & Unwin, 1982), 51–53.

88. This refers to Ge Hong 葛洪 (ca. 283–ca. 330), who penned a long work of this name.

89. *Zong* is a delicacy consisting of sticky rice wrapped in a leaf of one kind or another. Later it became an archetypal Duanwu (fifth day of the fifth month) delicacy. Already by this period, many former summer solstice customs had migrated to the fifth day of the fifth month; this one would soon follow.

90. *Yuzhu baodian* 5.344 cites an explanation in Zhou Chu's text that this "horned millet" was actually made by wrapping sticky rice in wild rice (*gu* 菰) leaves.

91. *Yuzhu baodian* 5.353 cites a more detailed, if slightly repetitive, version of this passage from Zong Lin's original *Record of Jing-Chu*:

> The people cut down new bamboo shoots to make tubular *zong*. They insert chinaberry leaves in their hair, and throw cords of five colors into the river to ward off the danger of fire. Some gentlewomen [or gentlemen and ladies] insert chinaberry leaves in their hair, and fasten colored threads to their arms; these are called "longevity cords."

92. Several encyclopedia citations of this passage give "various temples" 諸寺 or "various temples and monasteries" 諸寺院. See Wang, *Jing-Chu suishiji jiaozhu*, 199. All the extant versions of *Jing-Chu suishiji* give "various Buddhas" 諸佛.

93. Opinion differs on whether this text originated in India or China and on its time of composition. See *T* 685, 16:779–80. A late-sixth-century source credits Dharmarakṣa 竺法護 (265–313) as the translator, but the scripture itself is not well testified until earlier in the same century. For a discussion and full translation of the text, see Stephen F. Teiser, *The Ghost Festival in Medieval China* (Princeton, N.J.: Princeton University Press, 1988), 48–56.

94. Mulian (Skt. Maudgalyāyana) was a disciple of the Buddha.

95. The text, consistent in various editions and citations, literally says "malt-syrup wax" 飴. Syntactic parallelism suggests that the word preceding "wax" should be a verb. I follow Muramatsu and Baba's Japanese translation in reading the expression as "melt wax" (*Keiso saijiki*, part 3, *Higashi Ajia no kodai bunka* 1 [1975]: 178). The phrasing is unusual

but presumably implies that wax gains the consistency of a syrup before being molded or applied in decorative patterns.

96. For a translation of this entry, see also Teiser, *Ghost Festival in Medieval China*, 56–57. My translation draws substantially on his.

97. For town dwellers, this would mean excursions into the surrounding countryside, on this occasion especially into the hills; for villagers, if applicable, it might mean journeying beyond settled or cultivated areas.

98. This sentence is unique in the text in citing the commentator, Du Gongzhan, in the third person; Moriya identifies it as an interpolation, in *Chūgoku kosaijiki no kenkyū*, 362n.3. Wada also points out that the phrase "from the Han to the Song" is anomalous, in "*Keiso saijiki* ni tsuite," 409. "Song" could refer to the Liu Song (420–479), but it is unclear why Du would not have extended the frame of reference to his own day, more than a century later. Both *TPYL* 32.282a and *Suishi guangji* 34.1070 have "ever since the Han," making no mention of the Song.

99. The original term is *zhuyu* 茱萸, which may refer to different plants, typically either *Tetradium ruticarpum* (*Euodia ruticarpa*; Ch. *Wu zhuyu* 吳茱萸, Eng. evodia) or *Cornus officinalis* (Ch. *shan zhuyu* 山茱萸, Eng. Japanese cornel dogwood).

100. For a biography of Fei Changfang, see the "mantics" (*fangshi* 方士) section of *Hou Han shu* (82b.2743–45). With the aid of a deity and talisman assigned him by his Transcendent mentor, he was able to cure illness and suppress demons. The latter finally killed him when he lost his talisman.

101. The "Shun dian" 舜典 chapter of *Shangshu* refers to Gonggong as an official at the court of Shun, whom the latter sent into exile. See *Shangshu zhengyi*, *SSJZ*, 3.128. He unsuccessfully battled Zhuanxu for the emperorship, and then caused part of heaven and earth to collapse when he angrily crashed his head against Mount Buzhou, according to the "Tianwen xun" 天文訓 chapter of *Huainanzi* 淮南子, in *Huainan honglie jijie* 淮南鴻烈集解, ed. Liu Wendian 劉文典 (Beijing: Zhonghua shuju, 1989), 80. The commentator Gao You 高誘 (fl. 205–212) variously describes Gonggong as an official title and a heavenly deity with human face and snake's body, in *Huainan honglie jijie*, 4.80, 154.

29. Custom and Society

The Family Instructions of Mr. Yan

ALBERT E. DIEN

The Family Instructions of Mr. Yan (*Yanshi jiaxun* 顏氏家訓) by Yan Zhitui 顏之推 (531–after 591) is divided into twenty sections, each of which deals with a specific topic. These include the education of children, the relations between brothers, supervision of the family, personal conduct, literature, the dangers of the military career, care for one's health, a defense of Buddhism, and directions for the author's funeral and tomb. The format is a general statement, with relevant citations from the Classics, some sage judgments, and a few anecdotes, often from personal experience, that bear out the validity of the advice. At times, there is little evidence of organization within a section, giving the impression that a number of notes may have been simply filed under a general heading.

The reason that Yan gives for writing the *Instructions* was that he wished his sons to carry on the family patrimony. The disorders of the time and the resultant dislocations endangered the transfer of family tradition from one generation to the next. Without that tradition with its social and intellectual underpinnings that formed the way of life that made possible maintenance of elite status, Yan was concerned that his sons would sink into the commoner class. He had observed that the more personal the source of advice and admonitions was, the more effective it tended to be. For example, in training children, the maidservants had more influence than did advice from teachers and friends, and in resolving conflicts between brothers, the words of the widowed mother had more relevance than the doctrines of Yao and Shun. Thus Yan felt that as the paterfamilias, what he had to say might well be given more weight than would counsel from other sources. As a result, the *Instructions* touches on many aspects of life about which Yan wished his descendants to be informed.

In keeping with the turbulence of the times and the dangers inherent in holding office, Yan's emphasis is on moderation. That is, one should be punctilious in matters of behavior, ritual, and command of the language written and spoken, but advancement to high office invites disaster. One should be accomplished in the arts, for example, in playing an instrument, painting, and calligraphy, but conspicuous skill brings with it the possibility of being reduced by imperial command to becoming a mere performer.

The *Instructions* have continued to be read through the ages. One possible reason is that Yan himself was a member of a governing elite, and what he had to say remained meaningful to those of that class. Yan and his peers maintained their positions by their achievements in classical learning, literary skills, and abilities to serve in the civil bureaucracy. His book was designed to pass on information that would enable his descendants to maintain a similar status in their own times. From the Tang period on, the number of persons in a similar situation rose as entry into officialdom through the civil service examinations became increasingly important. Thus Yan came at the beginning of developments that were to provide an audience for a work like the *Instructions*. Another reason for the book's popularity is that the *Instructions* is a personal document, delving into areas of experience not usually discussed in the formalized vehicles of expression used in Yan's day. From it, one gains the impression that Yan must have been a person with high standards of conduct, integrity, and scholarship. Thus the *Instructions* was the sort of edifying and moralizing book that one could give to children to influence their conduct and perhaps prepare them to fulfill positions in the bureaucratic structure of the state. The clear style of writing and interesting contents of Yan's book ensured its continuing popularity.

The tradition of presenting one's offspring with some well-chosen words is an old one in China; Confucius's urging his son to study the *Odes* is an early example. In the Han period, we find many such examples in the biographies of eminent men or ascribed to them. Dongfang Shuo 東方朔 (fl. 130 B.C.E.), Liu Xiang 劉向 (79–8 B.C.E.), Ma Yuan 馬援 (14 B.C.E.–49 C.E.), and Zheng Xuan 鄭 玄 (127–200) are some that may be mentioned. Wang Mang, too, is said to have written such a document in eight sections. These statements are usually "admonishments" (*jie* 戒), telling the younger progeny how to behave. That by Ma Yuan, for example, tells his nephews, among other things, to treat the errors of others just as they would the names of their parents: these may be heard but not spoken.

Wang Chang 王昶 (d. 259) of the Three Kingdoms period wrote a typical example of such a letter to his sons and grandsons. A portion of it reads as follows:

As for the Way of a man acting as a son, there is nothing greater than valuing one's person and preserving whole one's conduct in order to make illustrious one's father and mother. Man knows the good of these three, and yet why is it there are those who may endanger their person and break up the family, thus falling into the misfortune of extermination and loss? It proceeds from one taking as one's prototype and practices that which is not this Way. As for filial piety and respect, they are the primary ones of the Hundred Behaviors and the basis of establishing one's person. If one has filial piety and respect, then the ancestral clan can be at ease; if one has benevolence and righteousness, then the village and one's group value one. These behaviors are completed inwardly while one's fame is manifested outwardly. If a person is not diligent in extending his behavior but turns from the basic to chase after the trifles, then he will fall into evanescent splendors, into forming cliques. If [he desires] the evanescent splendors, he will be implicated with the empty and false, and if he is a part of a clique, he will have the distress of [a partial viewpoint of] these and those. The warnings of these two are obvious and manifestly clear, yet those who follow the overturned vehicle are a growing host, and those who chase after trifles are many. All stem from the reason that they are moved by the fame of the moment or are blinded by the profit before their eyes.[1]

The letter by Tao Yuanming 陶淵明 (365?–427) was meant to "instruct" (xun 訓) his sons, and both jie and xun came to be used interchangeably. In the growing number of such works that came to appear in the Six Dynasties period, there appears not only a concern for the moral well-being of the younger generation but also more attention paid to the social patterns of behavior, and the discussion shifts from general principles to more specific details. This probably reflects the gradual utilization of these tracts not so much to inculcate general moral principles as to pass on family traditions of behavior in danger of being lost because of the uprooting of families and social disorder.

One of the earliest of these instructions to appear as an independent work rather than as a letter was the *Courtyard Announcement* (*Tinggao* 庭誥) of Yan Yanzhi 顏延之 (384–456), but only small fragments have survived. In the sixth century, there is the *Pillow Book* (*Zhenzhongpian* 枕中篇) by Wei Shou 魏收 (506–572), written in a highly literate style, advocating that his nephews follow a pattern of moderation, humility, and flexibility in order to survive. *Instructions for the Youth* (*Youxun* 幼訓) by Wang Bao 王褒 (fl. 554), of which the first chapter has survived, was written after Wang was taken to Chang'an following the victory of the northern forces of Western Wei over the Liang in 554. What survives is interesting as an example of the syncretic tendencies of that period:

Tao Shiheng has said, "Formerly Great Yu was not stingy about a jade *bi* a foot [in diameter,] but he valued an inch of the shade [of time]."[2] The literary gentle, how can he not recite books; the martial gentle, how not [be able to ride a] horse or shoot? If, then, in the long nights of the dark winter and in the long-lasting days of [summer's] vermilion brightness, he is circumspect in his dwelling place and respectful within his walled cubit, when inside his doorway he is without miscellaneous and variegated [activities], and when sitting, he has no calling out or clamor but uses these [intervals] to seek learning, then he is a disciple of Zhongni [i.e., Confucius], and if he uses these [intervals] to compose letters, then he is [one who will] ascend the dais, as did Young Jia.[3]

In ancient times, the bowls and basins had inscriptions; the benches and canes had admonishments. In advancing or withdrawing, one complied with them, in looking up or down, one saw them. A poem of King Wen says, "None do not have a start, but few are able to have a [successful] end."[4] In establishing one's person and carrying out the Way, the end and the beginning should be as one. "Being tense and abrupt is necessary [only] in this"; these are the words of the Masterly Sage.[5]

The Confucian school [*rujia* 儒家] then has the honored and debased, degrees and differences [in status], good fortune and bad, and a descending [order] and pairing off [of ritual due]. The ruler facing south and the vassal facing north accord with the rectitude of heaven and earth. For the cauldron and stands to be single, and the sacrificial splint-baskets and platters to be paired, [they must] accord with the rectitude of the [forces of] yin and yang. [Adherents of] the Daoist school, then, dissolve the connection with their limbs and bodies and discard intelligence and brightness, disregard rectitude and cut off benevolence; they separate themselves from their material form and remove themselves from knowledge.[6] The rightful duty of the Sakya [i.e., the Buddhists] is to experience bitterness, to stop short one's practices, to prove extinction and to comply with the Way, to understand the cause and to distinguish the effects [of karma]; then suddenly the mortal becomes a sage. Although this teaches degrees and differences, its rectitude reverts to drawing and leading out [the talents of a person]. Since I started in my youthful study, coming to [now when I] understand [my heavenly] fate [i.e., at the age of fifty], I have honored the teachings of the Duke of Zhou and of Confucius but also conjoined this with complying with the talk of Laozi and Sakya. [From my time on] the Left [Bank] of the Jiang [i.e., the area south of the Yangzi] on, this apportioned task has not declined, and it is my will that you be able to cultivate it.[7]

From the writings of Yan Zhitui emerges a pattern of behavior for an official that is somewhat different from what had marked the earlier works of this

genre. For Yan, the traditional ideal of the Confucian official who put the welfare of the state above his own and who believed in the effectiveness of moral
persuasion was replaced by the figure of the competent and devoted bureaucratic functionary who assumed no part in setting policy or in reproaching the
ruler, unless that duty was clearly a responsibility of his office.

Like Wang Bao, Yan wrote his *Instructions* in order to ensure that his sons
and later descendants would carry on the family patrimony. The disorders of
the time and the dislocation of the family endangered the transfer of family
traditions from one generation to the next. These traditions formed a social and
intellectual complex that formed a way of life that Yan wished to preserve, in
large part because it ensured the success of his progeny in maintaining their
status above that of the commoners, with the requirement to pay taxes and provide corvée labor, service in the army, and the loss of other privileges that such
a downgrade would entail.

Because Yan had traveled through many parts of China, he was able to bring
to his discussions many examples and comparisons of what he had seen. This
is especially true in regard to social customs, which led Étienne Balazs to remark that the *Instructions* were an "ouvrage précieux pour ses nombreux ren-
seigments sur les moeurs et la civilisation du VIe siècle."[8] Thus the *Instructions*
has been cited in modern studies as a source of information on social customs
and also for its linguistic and philological information.

Satō Ichirō wrote a provocative article emphasizing the social context of the
Instructions.[9] He points out that Yan Zhitui's time was a transitional period
when the aristocratic society was moving to one in which, by means of examination, officials were selected from the smaller landowners. Yan's emphasis on
education as a practical preparation for office and his placing limits on property
and position suited this growing class. This social group also gravitated toward
the nuclear family rather than the extended family. This is especially evident
in the taxation system, which changed from one based on the larger household
in the early Six Dynasties period to one based on the nuclear family—that is,
husband, wife, and children—in the latter part of the period and, finally, in the
Sui Tang, to one based on individuals. Satō then cites Yan's emphasis on the
immediate family and the stress on stability within this smaller unit. From
Buddhism, Yan derived the importance of the ego and of the individual, which
also affected Yan's attitude toward the family structure.

Yan's attitudes toward the importance of childhood education were influenced
by his own experiences. Orphaned at nine, he was brought up by an elder brother.
In looking back, he contrasted the careful instruction and devotion to proper
conduct that he remembered of his parents, to the indulgent, undemanding love
of his brother. As a result of his upbringing, "although I read the *Ritual* [*Liji*]
and *Zuozhuan*, I had little love for composition, and I tended to be modeled and
tainted by ordinary persons. I had reckless desires and frivolous words and was
careless in my behavior." The same fault is ascribed to him in his biography, and
an incident is related there of his being found intoxicated when he should have

been on duty, thus causing him to lose his official position. Yan says that he realized the faults of his character and strove to improve himself but that this was extremely difficult: "After thirty, excessive transgressions were rare in me. Still, in each instance, my heart is always an enemy to my mouth, and my nature struggles with my emotions. In the evening I realize the mistakes of the day, and today I regret the errors of yesterday. I pity myself that being without instruction I have come to this." It was to this unfortunate experience in his upbringing that he blamed his own flaws, and one reason that Yan wrote the *Instructions* was to warn against the pitfall of indulgence in child rearing. Behind this lies the admonition that a person must firmly controlled his natural tendencies.

FURTHER READING

Albert E. Dien, *Pei Ch'i shu 45: Biography of Yen Chih-t'ui* (Bern: Herbert Lang, 1976), provides information on the vicissitudes in Yan's career that were a major factor in forming the attitudes apparent in his writings. Albert E. Dien presents Yan Zhitui's involvement in one especially perilous incident and helps us understand why he advised his sons to avoid too much prominence in those insecure times, in "Yen Chih-t'ui (531–591+): A Buddho-Confucian," in *Confucian Personalities*, ed. Arthur F. Wright and Dennis Twitchett (Stanford, Calif.: Stanford University Press, 1962), 44–64. A full translation of his manual is Yen Chih-t'ui [Yan Zhitui], *Family Instructions for the Yen Clan: Yen-shih Chia-hsun*, trans. Ssu-yu Teng (Leiden: Brill, 1966). A comparison with D. C. Lau, trans., "Advice to My Sons," *Renditions* 1 (1973): 94–98, a translation of section 2 of *Yen-shih chia hsun*, provides some insight into the difficulty of rendering this text. The history of this period is a complex one, and a good introduction to some of the events through which Yan lived may be found in John Marney, *Liang Chien-wen Ti* (Boston: Twayne, 1976); and Scott Pearce, "Who, and What, Was Hou Jing?" *Early Medieval China* 6 (2000): 49–73. For some insight into the society of the time, Keith N. Knapp, *Selfless Offspring: Filial Children and Social Order in Early Medieval China* (Honolulu: University of Hawai'i Press, 2005), helps us understand the way in which the stress on filial piety permeated so many aspects of life.

YAN ZHITUI 顏之推

The Family Instructions of Mr. Yan (Yanshi jiaxun 顏氏家訓)

SECTION 5. MANAGEMENT OF THE FAMILY (EXCERPT)

Transformative changes work their way from those who are above to those below and extend from those who come before to those who come after.[10] Therefore, if the father does not have parental love, the son will not be filial; if the elder brother is not friendly, then the younger brother will not be respectful; if the husband is not dutiful, then the wife will not be compliant. In those cases when the father is loving and yet the son is rebellious, the elder brother friendly and yet the younger brother is haughty, the husband dutiful and yet the wife is overly assertive, then these are, by nature, malignant people who are kept in order by [the threat of] punishment and execution and are not influenced by instruction or guidance.

When the whip and indignation are dispensed with inside the home, then the faults of the youngsters immediately appear. "If the punishments are not properly awarded, the people do not know how to move hand or foot."[11] Leniency or severity in the management of a household is like the administration of a state.

Confucius said, "Extravagance leads to insubordination, and parsimony, to being miserly. It is better [for the child] to be miserly than to be insubordinate."[12] He also said, "Though one has the abilities as admirable as those of the Duke of Zhou, if it causes him to be arrogant or penurious, the rest are not worth considering."[13] Thus, then, one may be parsimonious but not penurious. Being parsimonious refers to being frugal and straitened and yet doing what is ritually correct. Being penurious refers to [acting] impoverished and harried and not being empathetic [toward others]. Today if someone makes a donation, then he tends to be extravagant, and if he is thrifty, then he tends to be penurious. If one can make donations and not be extravagant or be parsimonious and not be penurious, then these are proper.

The basic activity of the people is sowing and harvesting in order to eat and using the mulberry tree and hemp to dress themselves. The stores of vegetables and fruit are those produced in the gardens and orchards. The provisions of chickens and pigs are those bred in the roosts and pens. Coming to the ridgepoles and eaves, utensils and implements, firewood and tinder, and tallow candles, all are from materials that are planted and grown. Those able to maintain their calling, even if they bolt the doors, would still have enough of what it takes to live; the household would lack only a brine well. At present, the general custom [of people] in the north is to be parsimonious in their person and to make economical expenditures in supplying [themselves with] clothing and food. South of the Yangzi [people] are extravagant and wasteful and, to a large extent, do not come up to this [standard].

. . .

The wife is in charge of the inner larder and should dispense wine, food, and clothing in accordance with the customary rules.[14] Just as in the state where [women] cannot be employed in preparing policy, so in the household, they cannot be employed to cope with concerns. If they are intelligent and bright, have talent and prudence, and understand ancient as well as modern affairs, then it is fitting and proper that they support and assist their husband

and aid him in his inadequacies. Then the hen will certainly not be crowing at daybreak as a prelude to disaster.

East of the Yangzi [i.e., in the South], women mix socially hardly at all. Even among families related by marriage, there may be no personal interaction for ten or more years, only making inquiries by messenger and sending gifts, becoming rather painstaking in this. According to the manners and customs of the Ye area [i.e., the North], it is the women alone who maintain the gates and doors [of the home]. They dispute and bring litigation about wrongs and rights; they go out to pay calls and meet and welcome [guests]. Their carriages and equipages block the lanes and crossroads, and their silks and gauzes fill the bureaus and offices. They seek official offices on behalf of their sons and make pleas about grievances for their husbands. This, then, is the custom inherited from [the old capital of the Northern Wei] at Heng 恆 and Dai 代, [reflecting the influences of the Xianbei rulers].[15]

The southern areas are poor and plain, and yet [the people there] always attend to outward ornamentation. They must so prize conformity and being well ordered in their vehicles and equipages that the members of the household, the wives and children, cannot avoid hunger and cold. The affairs of the people north of the [Yellow] River proceed more from domestic considerations. The silks and gauzes, the golden and feathered [ornaments,] cannot be done away with, but they make do with the minimum of lean horses and debilitated slaves. In the courtesy between husband and wife, sometimes [they even address each other as familiarly as] "thou" and "thee."

For the matrons north of the [Yellow] River, the business of weaving the fabrics and making the ribbons and cords, and the labor of figured needlework designs, elegant embroideries, and gauzes and thin silks are much superior than [in the area] east of the Yangzi.

. . .

It is in the nature of matrons generally to show favor toward their son-in-laws but to be cruel to the wives of their sons. If they favor their sons-in-law, their own sons will become resentful. And if they are cruel to their daughters-in-law, then calumny by their daughters will emerge. Thus, then, these women, whether moving [to a husband's residence] or remaining [at home,] are held at fault, but it is really the mothers who cause it. So, there has come to be a proverb, "Lonely and desolate [as the auntie[16] dining." This is repayment in turn [for their attitude toward their daughters-in-law]. Can one not take warning from this!

[Our ancestor] the Pacificatory Baron[17] made the rule that the families of the bride and groom should be a simple match. In arranging marriages in recent times, daughters have been sold for gain, or wives bought in exchange for silk cloth. One contrasts and measures the [status] of fathers and grandfathers and calculates and compares ounces and drams. Their demanding more and countering with less does not differ from the marketplace. Sometimes, then, there is a rustic son-in-law inside the doors or a haughty wife usurping the rooms. In coveting splendor and seeking gain, embarrassment and shame, on the contrary, are brought in. How can one not be careful!

Borrowed records and documents of others all must receive love and care. If they previously had parts lacking or damaged, then they ought to be repaired and put into order. This is one of the many actions [expected] of the gentle grandee. Jiang Lu 江錄 of Jiyang 濟陽,[18] when he had not yet finished reading a book, even if there were something pressing and urgent, it had to wait until he had rolled up and tied [the scrolls] and made them well ordered and regular, and only then would he arise. Therefore [books in his care] were without injury or loss, and others did not object when he sought to borrow them. Some leave their tables and benches in great disorder, separating and scattering the sections and sequences of the books. These are often stained by the children or maids and concubines of the household, or ruined or damaged by wind and rain or insects and rodents. This, in truth, is a moral defect. Each time I have read a book written by a sage, I have never but been solemn and respectful toward it. If some old piece of paper has the text or commentary of the Five Classics, or the names of the paragons, I do not dare misuse it.

In my household, we avoided mentioning the sorcerer's and shaman's prayers and making requests [of the gods]. We made no prayers with talismantic inscriptions or oblations.[19] All of you have seen this. Do not spend anything on the weird and absurd.

SECTION 11. TAKING UP RESPONSIBILITIES

In regard to the gentleman's role in his times, he places value in his having something to offer to matters [of the world], not just wide-ranging talk or impractical discussions, with a *qin* lute to his left and a book to his right, so as to waste the salary and position he receives from his ruler. In general, there are no more than six ways in which a state makes use of ability. The first is as officials at court, drawing on their thorough understanding of administrative matters and mastery of wide erudition. The second is as literary and scribal officials, drawing on their composing of regulatory documents and not being unmindful of precedents. The third is as military officers, drawing on their decisiveness in grasping strategies and forcefulness in carrying out drills. The fourth is as frontier officials, drawing on their thorough familiarity with the customs [of those areas] and their unsullied love of those people. The fifth is as officials used as envoys, drawing on their understanding of vicissitudes and their following what is [an] appropriate [course] and "not disgracing his prince's commission."[20] The sixth is as officials in charge of construction, drawing on their efficacy as engineers and regulators of expenses and their knack for drawing up plans. These, then, are all what those who have diligently studied and who take care with their conduct are able to provide. Men differ in their dispositions;

how could it be asked that anyone would be commendable in all six pursuits? But one ought to be completely aware of one's leanings, and if able to maintain one office, then one would have no cause for shame.

I have seen literary gentlemen in this age who can rank [works of] the past and of today as easily as pointing to the palm of their hands, but when it comes to being tested and employed, most do not have that for which they are fit. Having lived in a time of tranquillity, they know nothing of the misfortune of loss and disorder; having served at court, they know nothing of the anxieties of the battle line. Holding on to what they derive from their emoluments, they know nothing of the bitterness of tilling and sowing; acting carelessly as superiors to the functionaries and people, they know nothing of the drudgery of corvée labor. Therefore they have difficulty in responding to their time or in carrying out any duties.

When the Jin court moved to the south [in 317], to a large extent they relied on the gentle lineages, and therefore those with caps and sashes [i.e., the officials] who had talent and capabilities were singled out to hold positions ranging from director [of a department] and chief administrator [of an office] down to secretarial court gentleman and secretariat drafter. The rest of the literary gentles, for the most part, were blowhards and frivolous, not taking part in the responsibilities of the time. For slight errors, moreover, they were spared from being lashed. So they therefore were placed in the pure and high [offices][21] and thus shielded from their shortcomings. As the clerks, scribes, and lectors in the offices and halls, or scribes and the document clerks [on the staffs] of the various princes, all comprehended and were well trained in the practices of being a functionary; they handled competently what were required at any time. Since they were lowborn and could be lashed and reproved [for any transgressions], they therefore were often employed, and in general [the court] made use of whatever it was in which they excelled. People often do not take stock of themselves, and everyone resented that Emperor Wu of the Liang and his son[22] were fond of these lowborn men and kept at a distance the gentle grandees. This is indeed the eye not being able to see its eyelashes.

The gentle grandees of the Liang were all fond of long robes and broad sashes, large headgear, and high clogs. When they went out, they rode vehicles, and when they came inside, they were supported and waited on. There were none who rode horseback within the city environs. Zhou Hongzheng 周弘正 was cherished by the Prince of Xuancheng 宣城, who gave him a small horse.[23] He customarily rode it, and the whole court considered this to be profligate behavior. It even reached the point that if a Secretariat Court Gentleman [*Shangshu lang* 尚書郎] rode a horse, he would be impeached. By the time of the Hou Jing 侯景 disorders,[24] the skin [of the officials] was tender and their bones soft; they were unable even to walk, their bodies wasted and breath weak, unable to bear the heat or cold. Those who are terrified of being condemned to death are often like this. Wang Fu 王復, who was Magistrate of Jiankang 建康, by nature was bookish and gentle and had never once ridden a horse.[25] When he saw a horse snorting and galloping, he always shook in terror and would say to others, "This is really a tiger, why is it called a horse?" Their habits and customs had come to this pass.

Men in former times wanted "to understand the painful toil of sowing and reaping";[26] this in general is the way of valuing grain and attending to what is fundamental. Food is the heaven of the people [i.e., of the utmost importance], for if the people do not eat, they do not live. If there is no grain for three days, a father and son cannot survive. Plowing and planting, weeding and hoeing, cutting and reaping, loading and piling up, flailing, and winnowing and sifting, those are the various steps in getting the grain into the granary. How can one treat lightly agricultural affairs and place value on the petty trades? The court gentles of south of the Yangzi, relying on the renewal of the Jin, crossed to the south and wound up becoming dependents [of the Eastern Jin]. By now, it has been eight or nine generations, and they have not yet worked a field but rely entirely on their official salaries for sustenance. If there is something [to be done], they entrust it to their servants to carry out; they have never set eyes on a clod of earth being raised nor the weeding of a clump of sprouts; they do not know in what month one ought to begin or in what month one ought to harvest; how can they understand the other requirements of the world? Therefore, in carrying out their official duties, they do not see it through; in regulating their household, they do not manage. This all stems from an excess of leisure and idleness.

SECTION 13. BE CONTENT

The *Record of Rites* says, "Desires should not be indulged; the will should not be gratified to the full."[27] We can reach to the farthermost parts of the cosmos, but we do not know the breadth of man's nature. We can only reduce our desires and know where to stop in order to establish our limits. Our forefather, the Pacificatory Baron, admonished his sons and nephews, "Your family is a household of scholars, and for generations we have had no affluence or honor. Hereafter, in taking office, do not exceed [posts with a salary of] two thousand piculs. In marriage alliances, do not covet [a bride from] a powerful family." My whole life I have taken to heart what I consider to be these celebrated words.

The ways of heaven and earth, of ghosts and spirits, abhor any excess. One can avoid harm by being modest and self-effacing. In life, clothing should be adequate [only] to provide against the cold dew, and food adequate to block hunger and want. If in what relates to the interior of one's body, one tends toward not being wasteful and extravagant, then on one's exterior would one want to go to the extreme in arrogance and pride? King Mu of the Zhou [1001–945 B.C.E.], the First Emperor of the Qin [r. 221–210 B.C.E.], and Emperor Wu of the Han [r. 140–87 B.C.E.], whose wealth consisted of all within the Four Seas and who were honored as Sons of Heaven,[28] "had no idea of calculating where they should stop,"[29] and still they came to ruin and embranglement. How much more so would it be for a gentle and commoner?

Normally for a family of twenty individuals, the male and female slaves should not exceed twenty at most; ten *qing* of arable land, the buildings just able to shelter from wind and rain; vehicle and horse barely enough for a whip; [and] a cache of several ten thousands [of coins] intended for some unanticipated event, whether auspicious or baleful. If more than this, disperse [the excess] by honorable means. If [the family] has not achieved [that goal], do not seek it by iniquitous ways.

Holding office is praiseworthy and honorable, but one should not go beyond occupying a middle rank, with fifty persons ahead of one and fifty behind; this will ensure that one escapes shame and disgrace and avoids falling into danger. If the [offered] position is higher than this, then one ought to decline with thanks and retire to one's own courtyard. I recently acted as Attendant Worthy at the Yellow Gate [*Huangmen shilang* 黃門侍郎], at which point I could have retired.[30] At the time, the dependent lineages were in dread of being slandered. I thought of carrying out a plan, but there was no time.[31] Ever since the destruction and disorder [attendant on the collapse of the Northern Qi dynasty], I have seen those who took advantage of the opportunity to acquire riches and honors. At daybreak they held the levers of power, but by nightfall [their bodies] filled the pits. At the start of the month, they were pleased [to be like] Zhuo [Shi] 卓氏 and Cheng [Zheng] 程鄭,[32] but by midmonth, they wept [that they were not like] Yan [Hui] 顏回 and Yuan [Xian] 原憲.[33] These were not just five or ten people. Take heed, take heed.

SECTION 20. FINAL ARRANGEMENTS

Death is man's common portion and cannot be evaded. When I was nineteen, there came the bereavement and disorder of the Liang house.[34] At that time I was given the naked blade to become a line trooper several times over, but I fortunately received more than my share of good fortune and so have been able to survive until now. Someone in the past said, "By fifty, one no longer dies prematurely."[35] I am already over sixty; therefore in my heart I am satisfied and I do not brood over the years remaining. Earlier I was ill and am ever suspecting the end to be near. I write what I have habitually kept in my heart to serve as a precept for you.

Neither my deceased father nor my mother has yet been returned to the old home at Jianye 建鄴.[36] They are temporarily buried at the eastern outskirts of Jiangling 江陵.[37] At the end of the Chengsheng period [552–554], I had already reported [that I wished] to go to Yangdu 揚都, as I wanted to carry out the move from their temporary resting places.[38] The bricks were already being fired in a small suburb north of Yang Prefecture but just then my native state was engulfed and I was swept away like this; for several decades I have been cut off from returning to that for which I yearn. Now although [the country] has been united, our family resources are exhausted, so how can we manage the expenses of such an undertaking? Further, Yangdu is befouled and in ruins, without anything remaining.[39] I do not yet have a plan to return to those low-lying marshes. I censure and upbraid myself; [this sorrow] pierces my heart and is engraved in the marrow [of my bones].

One might say that I and my brothers ought not to serve in office [until proper arrangements are made for our parents], but our family is in decline and our kinsmen lone and weak; within the Five Degrees [of mourning], there is not one person at our side. We are cast out and homeless in a strange community and without any further resources or protection. If you all were to sink and be swallowed up in menial service, it would shame the previous generations. Therefore I have put on a brave face and have gone out into society, not daring to falter or to fail. Together with this are the strictness and severity of the administration of the north, and so there is absolutely none who may hide away or retire.

Now old in years and ill, if I were suddenly to die, how could I seek for a full ritual? On the same day, one need only to extend the limbs and bathe [the corpse]. Do not bother [to seek] the return of the animus, and use ordinary clothes to dress [the corpse for burial]. When my deceased mother was abandoned, the world at that time was barren and in need; the family's prospects were bleak and exigent; and we brothers, elder and younger, were immature and weak.[40] The coffin and grave goods in general were simple and skimpy, and there were no bricks inside the grave. I would have a pine coffin of two inches [cun 寸], but aside from clothes and cap, let there be nothing more. On the coffin platform, place the seven-star board [qixingban 七星板].[41] As for things like wax, the crossbow claw, the jade shoat, or tin figures,[42] all must be set aside, and the provision containers and numinous utensils [mingqi 明器][43] therefore are not to be provided. As for an epitaph or tomb inscription and the pendant streamers, these are out of the question.

Convey my body in a turtle-shell vehicle [i.e., hearse], and after lowering it into the ground, level the earth without a mound. If you fear that you will not know the portentous area when you come to make obeisance and sweep, you may build a stretch of low wall on all four sides in order to mark it for yourselves. For the spirit's banquet, do not set out pillows and tables; for the new and full moon, at the [first and second] anniversary services and the [third anniversary] sacrifice, you may put down plain congee, clear water, and dried jujubes. Do not have sacrificial offerings of wine, meat, cakes, or fruit. If relatives and friends come to sprinkle libationary wine, prevent them one and all. If any of you were to disobey my wishes, it would exceed [what I could do for] my deceased mother, and you would then drag down your father to be unfilial: how would this rest well with you?

The merit and virtue [to be gained from] those Esoteric Codes [i.e., the Buddhist scriptures] are to be pursued to the limits of your strength, but you are not to rip open or exhaust life's resources, bringing [suffering from] cold or starvation. The Duke of Zhou[44] and Confucius taught [us] about the offerings and sacrifices of the four seasons, for they desired men not to cut off [the memory of their deceased] parents and not to neglect the Filial Way. Though one searches through the Esoteric Codes, there is nothing to add to this. But if one kills to carry out [these offerings], on the contrary one would increase one's sinful ties. If one would repay that boundless kindness [of parent to child] or [alleviate] the grief at the frosted dew [when one dwells on the memory of one's parents], there are the periodic abstinence offerings and the Ullambana[45] in the middle of the seventh month, when I will look for you.

On Confucius's burying his parents: "[He] said, 'I have heard that the ancients made graves [only] and raised no mounds over them. But I am a man who will be [traveling] east, west, south, and north. I cannot do without something by which I can remember the place.' For this he [resolved to] raise a mound [over the grave] four feet high."[46] Thus, then, in carrying out the Way in accordance with their times, perfect gentlemen have also had occasions when they did not observe [the practice of] mounded graves. How much more might this be so under pressure of crises. I now am a wayfaring dependent, my body like a floating cloud. In the end I do not yet know what place will be my burial site, only that wherever my breath comes to a stop, then there I will be interred.

All of you ought to consider it your duty to take on our entailed task and to make your names known, and you should not look to or hanker for the decaying glebe,[47] lest you draw on yourselves going under and being lost.

[Zhou Fagao 周法高, coll. and comm., *Yanshi jiaxun huizhu*
顏氏家訓彙注, monograph no. 41 (Taibei: Academia Sinica,
Institute of History and Philology, 1960)]

NOTES

1. *SGZ* 27.744–45.

2. Tao Shixiang was Tao Kan, who has a biography in *JS* 66.1768–79. His statement, in *Wenxuan* 52.10a, is taken from *Huainanzi* 1.10b.

3. For the use of literary skills by Jia Yi 賈誼 (200–168 B.C.E.) to obtain high office, see *HS* 30.1756.

4. *Classic of Poetry* (*Shijing* 詩經) 18.1b.

5. *Xunzi* 13.10a, which has Way (*dao* 道) for "words."

6. *Zhuangzi*, "Dazongshi"; James Legge, *The Texts of Taoism* (New York: Julian Press, 1959), 257.

7. The first chapter, all that survives of this work, is included in the biography of Wang Bao 王褒 in *LS* 41.583–84.

8. Étienne Balazs, *Le traité économique du "Souei-chou"* (Leiden: Brill, 1953), 211.

9. Satō Ichirō, "Gansi-kakun shōron," *Tōkyō shinagakuhō* 1 (1955): 192–205.

10. "Transformative change" (*fenghua* 風化; literally, "windlike changes") harks back to the idea that just as the wind bends the grass, so superiors influence inferiors, a theme found in the *Classic of Documents* (*Shangshu* 尚書), *SSJZ* 18.11a; James Legge, *The Shoo King, or The Book of Historical Documents* (Hong Kong: Legge, preface dated 1865), 539; and the *Analects* 12/8b; James Legge, *The Analects of Confucius* (Oxford, 1893), 259.

11. *Analects* 13/2a; Legge, *Analects of Confucius*, 264.

12. *Analects* 7/12a; Legge, *Analects of Confucius*, 207.

13. *Analects* 8/4b; Legge, *Analects of Confucius*, 212.

14. Mencius's mother, quoted in Liu Xiang 劉向 (77–6 B.C.E.), *Lienü zhuan* 列女傳 5.17a, expresses the same sentiment.

15. Dai refers to Dai Commandery, established by the Northern Wei near modern Datong 大同, Shanxi. Heng Prefecture was the larger administrative unit, centered at the same place. This was the capital of the Northern Wei until the court was moved to Luoyang in 493.

16. "Auntie" (*agu* 阿姑) is the term used by a woman for her mother-in-law.

17. The Pacificatory Baron 靖侯 was the imperially awarded posthumous name of Yan Han 顏含 (ca. 260–ca. 350), the eighth-generation ancestor of Yan Zhitui. The reference is to his refusal to enter into a marriage alliance with the family of Huan Wen 桓溫 because the latter was too important a person. See *JS* 88.2287. One may conjecture how much Han's view was motivated by a story current in his time and now to be found in *Recent Anecdotes from the Talk of the Ages* (*Shishuo xinyu* 世說新語) that Wang Hun 王渾 took a girl of the Yan family as a concubine rather than a wife because of the disparity in their social standing. See Liu I-ch'ing [Liu Yiqing], comp., *Shih-shuo Hsin-yü: A New Account of the Tales of the World*, trans. Richard B. Mather (Minneapolis: University of Minnesota Press, 1976), 471.

18. For a biography of Jiang Lu 江錄, see *NS* 36.944–45. While his dates are not given, an elder brother lived from 473 to 525. See *LS* 21.333. Jiyang was near the modern Dingtao 定陶 in southwestern Shandong.

19. For an instance of Daoist oblations (*zhangjiao* 章醮) to seek good fortune and assistance, see *Sui shu* 36.1137.

20. *Analects* 13/20; Legge, *Analects of Confucius*, 271.

21. These were highly prestigious offices, usually without any onerous duties, reserved for the highest elite.

22. Emperor Wu (r. 502–549) and his son, Emperor Yuan (r. 552–554).

23. Zhou Hongzheng (487–565) was a child prodigy whose major interest was in Daoist texts. Despite his characterization here, his biography in *CS* 24.305–10 cites his willingness to stand up for his principles even in opposition to imperial actions. The Prince of Xuancheng during the Liang was Xiao Daqi 蕭大器 (523–551), the eldest son of Xiao Yan 衍, founder of the Liang dynasty. According to Xiao Daqi's biography in the *Liang shu* 8.172, he was given that title in 532. The horse, termed here "Under the Fruit [Tree] Horse," is explained to mean that rider and horse could pass under the branches of a fruit tree.

24. Hou Jing (d. 552), a renegade general, seized Jiankang, the capital of Liang, in 549 but failed in his attempt to replace that dynasty.

25. There is no biography of Wang Fu in the standard histories.

26. *Classic of Documents* 16.9a; Legge, *Shoo King*, 464.

27. *Record of Rites* (*Liji* 禮記) 1.5b; James Legge, *The Lĭ Kĭ: The Sacred Book of China: The Texts of Confucianism*, Sacred Books of the East (Oxford: Clarendon Press, 1879–1885), 1:62.

28. This is a rephrasing of a passage in *Mencius* 9A.2b; James Legge, *The Life and Works of Mencius* (Hong Kong, preface dated 1861), 344.

29. *Zuozhuan* 20.19a; James Legge, *The Ch'un-ts'ew with the Tso Chuen* (Hong Kong, preface dated 1872), 283.

30. The holder of the post of Attendant Worthy at the Yellow Gate (*Huangmen shilang* 黃門侍郎) was concerned with the remonstrance and control of the officials attending the emperor. For a discussion of Yan's tenure in this office, see Albert E. Dien, *Pei Ch'i shu 45: Biography of Yen Chih-t'ui* (Bern: Herbert Lang, 1976), 120n.41.

31. At a critical time in the invasion of the Northern Qi state by the Northern Zhou in 576/577, Yan offered a plan to allow the emperor to flee to safety, but others betrayed the emperor, who was then captured. Those who had gone over to the Northern Zhou initially were rewarded but then were put to death. For further details, see Dien, *Pei Ch'i shu 45*, 14–15. On the reasons why the Chinese officials at the court were fearful, see the discussion of the events of 573 in Albert E. Dien, "Yen Chih-t'ui (531–591+): A Buddho-Confucian," in *Confucian Personalities*, ed. Arthur F. Wright and Dennis Twitchett (Stanford, Calif.: Stanford University Press, 1962), 61–62.

32. These were both extremely wealthy people of the Han dynasty. See Nancy Lee Swann, *Food and Money in Ancient China: The Earliest Economic History of China to A.D. 25* (Princeton, N.J.: Princeton University Press, 1950), 411–12, 453.

33. Yan Hui and Yuan Xian were disciples of Confucius. The pair had been cited by Wang Fu 王符 (ca. 78–163) in his *Qianfu lun* 潛夫論 as having come from extremely poor backgrounds and as examples of why one could not use economic status to judge the worth of a person. See *Qianfu lun*, sec. 4, 1.7a, ed. *Baizi quanshu* (Taibei: Gujin wenhua chubanshe, n.d., photolithograph of the Chongwen shuju, 1875 ed.), 3:1909.

34. This refers to the coup of Hou Jing in 549 and the death of Emperor Wu as a prisoner in his own palace.

35. This statement is ascribed to Liu Bei 劉備 (161–223), ruler of Shu in the Three Kingdoms period. See *SGZ* (*Shu*), 32.891.

36. Jianye, the modern Nanjing, was established in 211 as the capital of the Wu state. In 313, because of an imperial taboo, the name was changed to Jiankang. Yan is being archaic here in using the older name.

37. Jiangling, in the mid-Yangzi area, served as the capital of Liang under Emperor Xiaoyuan from 552 to the fall of the state in 554. Yan served there at the royal court.

38. Yangdu refers to Jiankang, which had the alternative name of Yang Prefecture.

39. After the conquest of the Chen state by the Sui in 589, the city was leveled.

40. Yan was nine when his father died in 539. There is no information about when his mother died, but she also probably died when he was young.

41. The seven-star board represents the Big Dipper or Ursa Major, which was the vehicle, as it were, by which the spirit entered Heaven.

42. The purpose of the wax is not clear, but large quantities, as much as 200 to 1,000 *jin*, were awarded by the throne on the death of a high official. The crossbow part was a relic of the past practice of placing a whole crossbow in the grave. It may have been a symbol of defense against underground demons but may also have been a charm, since the word for the mechanism, *ji* 機, is a close homonym for the word *ji* 吉 (good fortune). The purpose of the jade shoat (*yu tun* 玉豚), now called "stone pig" (*shi zhu* 石豬) by archaeologists, has long been debated. Again, I believe its significance is that a homonym, *tunxi* 窀穸, is a euphemism for the grave. The point would be to remind the spirit that its proper place was the grave. Tin men (*xiren* 錫人) are most probably connected to folk Daoism; apparently, the figure was to stand in for the deceased and to perform any tasks assigned to the deceased in the other world.

43. Numinous utensils refer to those grave goods made especially to be placed in the tomb.

44. The Duke of Zhou—the brother of Wu Wang, the founder of the Zhou dynasty, and the regent for his nephew Cheng Wang until the latter gained his majority—was venerated by Confucius as a paragon of virtue.

45. The Ullambana festival is the day when offerings are made to the Buddhist deities and prayers read to release from purgatory the souls of the dead.

46. *Record of Rites* 6.7a; Legge, *Lǐ Kǐ*, 123.

47. The term *xiurang* 朽壤 occurs in the *Zuozhuan* 26.9a; Legge, *Ch'un-ts'ew with the Tso Chuen*, 357, where the collapse of a mountain due to such decayed soil is noted, and a wagon drover encountered on the road advised the ruler to respond by making proper sacrifices with all possible haste and humility. The point here is that Yan's children should not wait for the remote possibility of gaining notice due to some happenstance.

30. Adoption and Motherhood

"The Petition Submitted by Lady [née] Yu"

JESSEY J. C. CHOO

Adoption was not uncommon in early medieval China, where the practice of ancestral worship required that each married couple produce a male heir. "The Petition Submitted by Lady [neé] Yu in the Fifth Year of the Xianhe Reign of the Eastern Jin Emperor Cheng [330 C.E.]" (*Dong-Jin Chengdi xianhe wunian Sanqi cilang Qiao He qi Yushi shangbiao* 東晉成帝咸和五年散騎侍郎賀喬妻于氏上表) documents a complex case of adoption and its effects on an aristocratic family. The petition directly touches on a number of issues of interest to historians, such as divorce, child custody, motherhood, patrilineal principles and their implementation through law and ritual, and, most important, the nature of adoption. The petition also presents an opportunity for historians to assess the level of aristocratic women's classical education.

Lady Yu (Yu shi 于氏) was the childless wife of He Qiao 賀喬, the Gentleman Cavalier Attendant (*Sanqi cilang* 散騎侍郎) to the emperor. After being abandoned by her adopted son, she petitioned the throne to act on her behalf and order his return. She first outlined in her petition the circumstances that had led to the adoption and subsequent abandonment. She then presented her arguments for her adopted son's return. The emperor forwarded the petition to three departments that had jurisdiction over this matter and instructed them to arrive at a verdict based on legal and ritual traditions. They ruled against Lady Yu. The court asked for three opinions, those of the offices of the Chamberlain for Ceremonials, the Chamberlain for Law Enforcement, and the Erudite of Ritual and Law. Although the governor's opinion was not sought, he submitted one anyway. Each of the opinions was appended to the petition. Du You 杜佑 (735–823), a prominent statesman and historian in the Tang dynasty (618–907), included this case in its entirety in his encyclopedia of institutional history, *Comprehensive History of Institutions* (*Tongdian* 通典). The chapter in which he cites this case, along with another one, is devoted to adopting an heir. Even though Du You did not comment on the cases, he hints at his interpretations in his headings for them: "The Discussion About Adopting a Nephew as the Heir and Then Having a Child of One's Own" (*Yang xiongdizi weihou hou zishengzi yi* 養兄弟子為後後自生子議) for Lady Yu's case, and "The Discussion About Adopting Someone with a Surname Different from the Heir's" (*Yixing weihou yi* 異姓為後議) for the other. The subtlety of these headings becomes apparent in the following summary and discussion of the cases.

Lady Yu stated that the adoption came after her birth family had repeatedly demanded a divorce, citing the couple's prolonged childlessness. She, however, insisted on staying with her husband, thereby defying the expressed wish of her elder brother. Her mother-in-law, Lady [née] Bo (Bo shi 薄氏), sided with her, attributing Lady Yu's childlessness to Fate (*ming* 命). Lady Bo then ordered her son, He Qiao, to attempt with several concubines to produce an heir for his line. He Qiao's elder brother, He Qun 賀群, also was eager to help and gallantly promised to let Lady Yu adopt a son born to him and his wife, Lady [née] Tao (Tao shi 陶氏). With the help of her in-laws, Lady Yu saved her marriage.

Lady Tao soon gave birth to a son, who was handed over to Lady Yu almost immediately. To ensure that the baby would grow up believing that Lady Yu was his mother, He Qun went so far as to discourage his wife from picking up the baby and to punish any servants who revealed his true parentage. But the baby died a few months later, leaving his adoptive mother devastated. When Lady Tao again bore a son, he too was given to Lady Yu. This time, the baby lived and was named He Shuai 賀率. Up to now, Lady Yu's husband had been conspicuously missing from the scene. In fact, the petition says nothing about his responses to the divorce proceedings or the adoption, so whether he had an opinion about these issues remains unclear. Within a year of the adoption, however, he fathered a son with one of the concubines, and it was the birth of his own child that created the dispute that led He Shuai to abandon Lady Yu after he reached majority.

When He Shuai was six, He Qun died, after which his true parentage became the subject of street gossip. The prevailing view was that the couple no longer needed an adopted son to serve as their heir, since He Qiao had his own. The child should therefore be returned to his birth parents. Lady Yu disagreed, insisting that He Shuai was given to *her* for the sole purpose of preserving her marriage and that he was never intended to be her husband's heir. He Shuai did not react well to the gossip and eventually returned to his birth mother.

Soon after, when He Qiao was dying, he assured his wife that he agreed with her. But he died before he could explain to everyone the circumstances behind the adoption. Lady Yu thus petitioned the throne to have Shuai returned to her and to silence the dissenters.

Lady Yu argued that He Shuai was not her husband's heir, using a close reading of the relevant passages in all three of the *Rites*, demonstrating her formidable learning. She hoped to make the case that he was solely *her* adopted son. She further argued that in terms of mothering, child rearing was a far more intensive experience and a far bigger responsibility than childbearing. She cited an impressive array of examples drawn from the Classics and dynastic histories to drive home this point. In her eyes, she was no less entitled to He Shuai's filial devotion than was Lady Tao, his birth mother. She even referred to Confucius to plead her cause. The very same quotation was later used by Tang Empress Wu Zetian 武則天 (r. 690–705) in her argument for lengthening the mourning period for mothers to be equal to that for fathers.[1] Both women's arguments were predicated on the commonly accepted belief that child rearing was at least as important and demanding as childbearing.

The justices for this case did not rule in favor of Lady Yu. Although none of them disagreed with her argument that He Shuai was greatly indebted to her for her efforts in raising him, most of them ignored her emotional plea, stating that these arguments were completely beside the point. They found no ritual or legal principles that supported a woman's right to adopt. Furthermore, they maintained that contemporary custom and law recognized only those adoptions that served to secure a male heir and continue the patrilineal line. The majority opinion thus sided with He Shuai and agreed with his decision to return to his birth mother. Du You also agreed with this opinion, as he labeled this as a case about who was the heir rather than who had the rights of a mother.

The case of Lady Yu contributes greatly to our understanding of divorce, motherhood, adoption, and the law of inheritance in early medieval China. It suggests that both the husband's and the wife's families could use childlessness as grounds for divorce. But they could get around these grounds by securing a male heir through a concubine or adoption. This fits with the view postulated in the *Rites* that motherhood was derived from a social act, marriage, rather than a biological act, childbirth.[2] Women did not have any independent parental rights. The moment that He Qun gave the babies to Lady Yu to adopt, his wife Lady Tao lost her title and rights as their mother. When He Qiao died and was succeeded by his own son, the succession effectively voided Shuai's adoption, leaving Lady Yu without the title of, and claims as, his mother.

The alignment of marriage and parental rights could also help women, as it encouraged the primary wife to raise all her husband's children as her own, by assuming motherly privileges over the birth mother(s). Her position as *the* mother would be irrefutable if the child's birth mother were her social inferior.

Consequently, when Lady Yu asserted that child rearing was just as important as childbirth, if not more so, the justices did not dispute this claim. In short, both the petition and the outcome demonstrate the extent to which these "Confucian" patrilineal principles were observed by the aristocrats of the Eastern Jin.

Nonetheless, it is noteworthy that the one justice who sided with Lady Yu was the Erudite of Ritual and Law (*Lilü boshi* 禮律博士). He agreed with Lady Yu's understanding of the ritual technicality associated with the terms of adoption and with her use of past cases in which emotion (*qing* 情) served as the basis for implementing ritual (*li* 禮). Despite his low court rank compared with that of the other justices—which perhaps was the reason why he was ignored—his opinion was one shared by other learned scholars. The case thus serves as a window into the process by which the Classics were adapted to modern customs and practices. The classical form was not observed, however, at the expense of what was practiced. Moreover, the traditional interpretation could be cited to justify the natural outpouring of emotion.

Lady Yu was not the only woman whose petition to the throne was recorded in history. An earlier example was Tiying 緹縈, a daughter of the famed physician Chunyu Yi 淳于意, who persuaded the Western Han Emperor Wen 西漢文帝 (r. 180–157 B.C.E.) to overturn her father's harsh sentence.[3] Another example was Empress Wu, mentioned earlier, who persuaded her husband, Emperor Gaozong 高宗 (r. 649–684), to lengthen the mourning period that a son observed for his mother. Lady Yu's and Empress Wu's petitions, in particular, are filled with references to the Classics and their commentaries. Medieval historians frequently reported the erudition of numerous highborn ladies. Most of these women were celebrated because they used their learning to educate their children.[4] Indeed, there is little room to doubt that Lady Yu had written her own petition. The fact that one justice chided her for what, according to him, were misinterpretations of the *Rites* more or less confirms her authorship. The misogynist undertone of his opinion and the numerous accounts of learned mothers reveal a general attitude toward the proper application of women's learning, that it was far better for women to focus on their children than on composing petitions.

FURTHER READING

For information on adoption in periods earlier than the Six Dynasties, see Miranda Brown and Rafe de Crespigny, "Adoption in Han China," *Journal of the Social and Economic History of the Orient* 52, no. 2 (2009): 229–66. Ann Waltner provides a detailed study of adoption in late imperial China in *Getting an Heir: Adoption and the Construction of Kinship in Late Imperial China* (Honolulu: University of Hawai'i Press, 1990). Taiwanese scholar Cheng Ya-ju 鄭雅如 also has discussed this case at length in her monograph *Qinggan yu zhidu: Wei Jin shidai de muzi guanxi* 情感與制度: 魏晉時代的母子關係 (Taibei: National Taiwan University, 2001). Cheng also looks at the definition of mother and son in the social and legal practices of the Six Dynasties in "Zhonggu shiqi de muzi guanxi—Xingbie yu Han Tang zhijian de jiatingshi yanjiu" 性別與漢唐之間的家庭史研究, in *Zhongguo shi xinlun* 中國史新論, *Xingbeishi* 性別史, ed. Lee Jender 李貞德 (Taibei: Academia Sinica, 2009), 135–90.

❖

Du You 杜佑

The Discussion About Adopting a Nephew as the Heir and Then Having a Child of One's Own (Eastern Jin)

In the fifth year of the Xianhe 咸和 reign [330 C.E.], the wife of the Gentleman Cavalier Attendant He Qiao, née Yu, presented a petition to Emperor Cheng 成帝 of the Eastern Jin dynasty, stating:

When I first married into the He clan, I was childless. My maternal brother, Qun 群, who used my committing [one of] the Seven Outs [*qichu* 七出][5] as an excuse, repeatedly requested the He clan for my return. My mother-in-law Lady [née] Bo witnessed [the event] and took pity. [She reasoned] that there was no cause for divorce, since [my] childlessness was destined by Heaven and the [purpose of] marriage was to unite the two clans. She therefore ordered my husband, Qiao, to take several concubines. Qiao's second older brother, Qun,[6] who pitied my position and sympathized with my aspiration, told our relatives on several occasions that "New Bride[7] Yu was unfortunately childless. If my New Bride Tao has a male child, I shall give her the one that comes after." After Lady [née] Tao gave birth to two boys, Cheng and Fu, she became pregnant with another child, Hui. Qun appealed to Lady Bo that "if it is a boy, I request that you will give him to the New Bride [Yu]." I respectfully accepted what was to be bestowed on me and was thankful. I made clothes for the baby, anticipating his birth. On the day Hui was born, immediately after he was washed and his umbilical cord was cut, I took him home. I took medicine to induce lactation in order to breastfeed him. From time to time, Lady Tao would pick up the child and hold him. Qun always reprimanded her and stopped her from doing this. Whenever a maid or a servant gossiped about the story of [the child's] parentage, Qun would chastise her or him. [He] sincerely wished that the child would devote his love solely to me and be removed from his obligation to the one who bore him. [After] a hundred days or so, Hui died, not having the destiny [to live longer]. I was devastated and became haggard because of it. My mother-in-law and relatives, both old and young, came to pity me even more. Qun yet again gave me a son of his—Shuai—and entrusted me with his upbringing. I thus devoted all my thoughts and exhausted all my strength [to raise Shuai], just as I did with Hui. This is why even when Shuai became cognizant of the world, he did not know that he was not my [natural] son. More than a year after Shuai was born, Qiao's concubine [née] Zhang gave birth to a son, Zuan. At the time, Qun was still alive and well. [He] did not find [the situation] problematic. The original motivation for Lady Bo and Qun to give Shuai to me was not just to ensure the continuation of Qiao's line but also to preserve my position [in the He clan]. I could continue to perform the Zheng and Chang rituals[8] for the He clan because I kept Qun's trust. When Shuai was six years old and Zuan five, Qun passed away, after which the gossips were let loose, and Shuai began to hate that he was not my natural son. While Shuai was growing up, he paid respect to the kindred of my birth family within the nine degrees as if they were his maternal kin. Some scandalmongers reasoned that since Qiao had Zuan, Shuai could not continue to be my son. If he stayed, he would then allow himself to become an adopted heir [*renhou* 人後].[9] A year later, he returned to Lady Tao. Qiao was bedridden with illness at the time and told [me], "[This is the arrangement] made by my mother and older brother when they were alive. How could those who casually discuss it on the street understand the situation behind it? I shall discuss with those inside and outside the clan and set the record straight." But soon, he too passed away. Shuai was still young and did not understand the significance. Swayed by frivolous talk, he did not know what was appropriate. I am but a woman whose command of the Classics and *Rites* is limited, though I was told by my late mother-in-law that I should raise Shuai to be my son and not a so-called adopted heir. Fate has granted me little, and I am forsaken. I exhausted the emotions and strength of my youth [in bringing up Shuai]. I am being abandoned in my old age without being repaid for my efforts in fostering and educating him.[10] How could the heart of a woman not murmur with resentment? I respectfully present the six issues and the ten questions that trouble me, as follows:

What the *Rites* refer to as an adopted heir is not [simply] an adopted son. The world does not thoroughly comprehend the meaning of the *Rites* and has always confused the two, thus coming to conclusions that are gravely mistaken. "Heir" is a term that shall not be generally applied [to any adopted son]. It is used only for the period between the death [of the adopted parent] and the burial. It does not apply to those adopted when alive. Why do people nowadays confuse those who are adopted before the death of the parent with those who became the heirs only afterward? This is the first issue that troubles me.

The gossipmongers believe that because Qiao had his own child, Zuan, he would not object to Shuai's returning to whence he came. This view mistakes the *Rites*' meaning of "being an heir." *The Commentary* [to the *Classic of Etiquette and Rituals*] states, "What kind of heir is an adopted heir? The one who inherits the main line of the patrilineal descent"[*dazong* 大宗].[11] Since Qiao himself was not an heir to the main line and Shuai was not his heir, what difference did Zuan's existence make? This is the second issue that troubles me.

A child of the subsidiary line [*xiaozong* 小宗] should be brought in to inherit the main line because if the main line becomes extinct, there will be no basis on which to determine the seniority and closeness of blood relations. The practice of having an adopted heir carry on the main line is therefore institutionalized to ensure that the deference will remain unchanged, even after a hundred generations.[12] Why do the gossips compare a nephew with a child of a clansman who is made to inherit the main line? This is the third issue that troubles me.

When [a boy] becomes an adopted heir, the degree to which he mourns for his [birth] parents is lessened by one.[13] This is in accord with human nature. When he obeys the order of his [birth] parents and leaves his [natural] family for another, is he not different from those who are raised by their adopted families from infancy? The latter does not know the parents who gave birth to them but those who brought him up. We have a saying: "When a yellow hen lays an egg and a black hen hatches it, the chick knows only that it is the offspring of the black, and not the yellow, hen." The saying may be simple, but it helps explain which is more profound. How could the gossips compare an heir installed through the rites of adoption with an adopted child? This is the fourth issue that troubles me.

The *Commentary* to the *Classic of Etiquette and Rituals* states that "the adopted heir shall behave like a natural son toward his adoptive father's grandparents, wife, and wife's parents, brothers, and their children."[14] The one-who-is-like-a-son [*rou zi* 若子] has the ritual [*yi* 義][15] but not the emotional [*en* 恩] obligations of a son; thus it is said that an adopted heir is different from an [adopted] son. Why do the gossips give the ritual obligations of an adopted heir primacy over the emotional obligations of an adopted son to those who nurtured him? This is the fifth issue that troubles me.

The adoption of an heir occurs only when the main line has no heir and when the clansmen have chosen a son among the subsidiary lines as the successor. Some of our contemporaries believe that because [a child] who becomes an adopted heir cannot succeed his own parents, he permits himself to stay adopted for either the noble title or wealth. Such an action is not based on humaneness and righteousness and therefore should be detested. This was not the situation with Shuai: he was designated as the heir because he is the eldest son of a wife [*dizhang* 嫡長] before the son of a concubine [*shushao* 庶少] was born. Why is he laughed at because of this? This is the sixth issue that troubles me.[16]

I have also heard that the benevolence of the parents toward their child is half in bearing it and half in raising it. How could the [shared] breath between the fetus and the womb weigh more than the contribution of nurturing the child? Confucius said that "a child is completely dependent on the care of his parents for the first three years of his life—that is why he should mourn them for three years."[17] The *Classic of Poetry* states:

O my father, who begat me!	父兮生我
O my mother, who held me!	母兮鞠我
Ye patted me, ye fed me,	拊我畜我
Ye raised me, ye nurtured me,	長我育我
Ye cared for me, ye always returned for me,	顧我復我
Went in and out [of the room] cuddling me close to your breast.	出入腹我
The virtue that I want to repay	欲報之德
is as boundless as the Heaven.[18]	昊天罔極

Passages such as these praise the work of raising a child. The body of the mulberry insect is transformed by the wasp.[19] The clan of Ban [meaning "patterns"] was named so as to commemorate the tiger that suckled its primogenitor.[20] Based on these examples, it appears that the obligations to one who suckled are greater than those to the one who begat. Even though Shuai received his four limbs from Lady Tao, he grew his hair and skin under my watch. I placed him in the dry while I myself took the damp, tasking my muscles and exhausting my energy for twenty some years until he became an adult. How could he forget my contribution to his upbringing because of the difference in names? This is the first question that I have.

The most intimate human relations—between father and son, older and younger brothers, and husband and wife—are one. This means that father and son are like the head and toes; older and younger brothers are like the four limbs; husband and wife are like the two halves.[21] Because these are relations of one body [*yiti* 一體], it is said, "The sons of one's brothers are the sons of one's own."[22] One thus raised [*zi* 字] them [as one's own]. How could our closeness, as of one body, be taken as analogous to the remoteness between distant clansmen? How could the reality of being nurtured be matched in name to being adopted as an heir? This is the second question that I have.

A child shall treat his parents equally. Whence comes the reason for someone to abhor the affection of the mother in respect for the father, to forgo the benevolence of the mother to take up the cause of the father, or to replace the rites due the mother in following the command of the father? To respect the command of the father is an excuse for these actions. When his heir [to the throne] is elected by a mob, without distinguishing between the sons of a wife and a concubine, the command of the king is limited by that of his subjects. [A child treats] "the *ci* mother [*cimu* 慈母] like his mother" in life and death without remiss because he carries out the command of his father.[23] The reasons that I am the mother of Shuai are that it is the command of Qun, that he is a nephew [*youzi* 猶子][24] of Qiao, and that he owes me gratitude for nurturing him. With these three provisions, how could he now discard them? This is the third question that I have.

Zhuge Liang 諸葛亮 [181–234][25] was childless. He took the son, Qiao 喬, of his older brother, Jin 謹, as his own. Qiao's courtesy name was originally Zhongshen 仲深 [meaning Shen, or "secondborn"]. When Liang had a son named Zhan 瞻, he made Qiao his heir and renamed him Posong 伯松 [meaning Song, or "firstborn"]. He did not send Qiao back when he had Zhan. This was because "the sons of one's brothers are the sons of one's own."[26] Chen Shou 陳壽 said: "After Qiao died, Zhuge Ke 諸葛恪 was executed and his line was extinguished. Liang, having had heirs, sent Qiao's son, Pan 攀, to continue the ancestral rituals for Jin and his line."[27] He wanted to make it clear that had Ke not died without an heir, Pan was not to return. Liang was virtuous and Jin upright. The brothers who carried themselves as such would not put their descendants in a position in which they could not fulfill their ritual obligation and thus neglect the rites for a hundred generations, or would they? This is the fourth question that I have.

The [Zuo] Commentary to the Spring and Autumn Annuals states that "Dai Wei 戴嬀, a woman of Chen 陳, gave birth to Duke Huan 桓公, whom Zhuang Jiang 莊姜 took as [her] own child."[28] The phrase "as [her] own child" [weijizi 為己子] here means that she took and raised the child. The [Gongyang] Commentary [to the Spring and Autumn Annuals] states that "the one who is an adopted heir is the son of his adoptive parents."[29] This means that the adopted heir should go to [reside with] his adoptive parents and succeed them. The one who takes and names the child is the mother. The one who goes to [reside with] and succeeds is the child. The mother should have motherly benevolence like that of the wasp who raises the mulberry insect. The child should have the same ritual obligations as a child of the adopted heir who succeeds the main line. If [there is] one [who] could differentiate between a child who is taken "as [her] own child" and a child who is adopted as the heir, then we could then discuss how the rites should match these situations. The obligations are parallel: [a child treats] the adoptive father like a father [youfu 猶父]; the father is like a mother [youmu 猶母]. Zhuang Jiang could take Dai Wei's son as her son because they had the same husband; a man could take his brother's son as his son because they had the same grandfather. Such are the expressions and their examples. How could the gossips not look them up? This is the fifth question that I have.

[The minister under the Han Emperor Wu] Dong Zhongshu 董仲舒 [179–104 B.C.E.] was revered by his generation as the most unadulterated ru 儒 [scholar]. Whenever a dispute erupted over a difficult issue at the Han court, messengers were sent to visit [Dong], who could discern the heart of the case in a few words.[30] Once there was this confusing case:

A had no child. He raised as his own an orphan, B, whom he picked up from the street. After B became an adult, he committed a murder.

Someone reported [to the authorities] that A was hiding B [from the authorities]. How should A be charged?

Zhongshu reasoned:

> A had no child. He raised and nurtured B. Even if they were not natural parent and child, no one could contest this fact. The *Classic of Poetry* states that "the mulberry insects had children, and the wasps raised them." The *Spring and Autumn Annuals* says: "Fathers [should] cover for their sons."[31] Thus it was appropriate for A to cover for B.[32]

The verdict was that A should not be punished for B's crime. The *Rites* clearly forbids the adoption of an heir with a different surname.[33] Given Zhongshu's erudition, this rule could not be unknown to him. Thus we know that those who have heirs do not adopt but that those who are adopted are not [necessarily] heirs.[34] How could people not attend to the difference? This is the sixth question that I have.

There is another case:

> A has a son, named B, who was given to C in adoption. B reached adulthood in the care of C. [One day], A, who was drunk, told B, "You are my son." B was enraged and thrashed A twenty times. A could not suppress his anger at B, who was originally his son, and brought a lawsuit [against B] to the county magistrate.

Zhongshu judged:

> Even though A begot B, since he could not raise him and gave him up to C, their mutual obligations had ended. [Thus] even if B thrashed A, he should not be punished.[35]

[As shown in the first case,] when one adopts a child from the street, [he and the child] are considered to be father and son. [As shown in the second case,] when an adopted child vilifies his birth parent, he is not punished [for being unfilial]. This is a clear case in which the birth parents are stripped of their rights, is it not? How could the gossips not understand the meaning of an adopted son and mistakenly call him an adopted heir? This is the seventh question that I have.

Qin Jia 秦嘉 of the Han dynasty died young. His wife, Xu Shu 徐淑, adopted and raised a son. After Shu died, the son returned to his birth parents. Learned scholars [*tongru* 通儒] of the court altered his birthplace [in the tax registry] and relisted him as Shu's adopted son and the carrier of the Qin clan's ancestral rites.[36] [The learned scholars] did not object to [the adoption], even though the child had a different surname, [so] why should [anyone] object when the child [in question] was the son of a brother? This is the eighth question that I have.

Zhou Yi 周逸 of the Wu dynasty [229–280], known for his erudition in things past and present, was born to a man surnamed Zuo 左 and was adopted by a man surnamed Zhou. The latter then had his own son. Those who were ignorant also derided Yi, which he repudiated by citing past and contemporary precedence. He died without ever reclaiming his original surname.[37] [How could] those who were knowledgeable accept his action as appropriate [if it were not?] This is the ninth question that I have.

The following five stipulations are not for the expression of human emotions: First, the adopted heir observes full mourning for his adopted father and only one year of mourning for his birth father.[38] Second, a married daughter observes mourning for her parents in a lesser degree [than does an unmarried daughter].[39] Third, the heir does not observe mourning for his mother if she is divorced from his father.[40] Fourth, the son of a feudal lord and a concubine cannot observe mourning for his birth mother.[41] Fifth, the heir to the throne cannot observe mourning for his birth mother [if] she is a concubine.[42] The *Rites* refers to these cases as when ritual obligations outweigh the bonds of gratitude and thus establish the heavenly principle [*jiewen liyan* 節文立焉]. Those who willfully allow their emotion to lead their actions are following the way of barbarians. The problem remains that people who do not understand the nuances of the articles in the *Rites* and do not differentiate the subtlety of love and obligations have confused the greatest principles of human relations. This is why the Han Emperor Ai [r. 27–1 B.C.E.], being a feudal prince, was able to succeed the Son of Heaven.[43] He then elevated his birth parents, thinking that he had understood what the Duke of Zhou meant by revering one's father, without realizing that it greatly contradicted the statutes of the state.[44] When a child dies before being named, the parents do not weep for him. When a child dies after being named, the parents weep but do not put on mourning clothes for him. The degree to which the parents could mourn for the three premature deaths [*sanshang* 三殤] of their children varied from none to that of *qi* 齊 and *zhan* 斬.[45] Born of the same parents, siblings are of one body; yet the older children are treated differently from the younger in such gradations. Nowadays there are those who bear children and kill them without any attempt to raise them. A gentleman [who has done it] is not accused of being cruel. The authority does not exact punishment [from the parents] for killing their child. The six relations do not observe the mourning codes [for the murdered child]. The guests do not pay condolences. Is this not because [the child] has just been born and is not quite a human being? There are parents who bear and kill their children like this. There are parents who bear and abandon their child for others to rear. They then reclaim their child, saying to him, "You are originally mine." How can [they think that] the credit for being the birth parents is equal to the merits of raising and nurturing? This is the tenth question that I have.

It was decreed that the offices of the Chamberlain for Ceremonials [*Taichang* 太常],[46] the Chamberlain for Law Enforcement [*Tingwei* 廷尉],[47] and the Erudite of Ritual and Law each submit their judgment based on precedence.

The judgment of Erudite [of Ritual and Law] Du Yuan 杜瑗[48] states:
The so-called adopted heir is someone who will carry on the ancestral sacrifice after the passing [of the adoptive father] and is different from someone who is adopted before his passing. Thus, the term is not used

when the adoptive father is still alive. Since Shuai is designated as Qiao's heir, he shall therefore behave toward his adoptive parents as if [he were] their son [youwuzi 猶吾子]. When Qun was still alive, he promised [to give up Shuai] out of genuine compassion [for Lady Yu]. The conditions for considering [Shuai] as the couple's son have thus been met. It is regrettable that ignorant gossips would equate Shuai with an adopted heir and cause him to hurt the feelings of, and abandon his duties toward, [his adopted mother]. In the past, Zhao Wu 趙武 lived because of the help of Cheng Ying 程嬰. When Ying died, Zhao mourned him for three years [i.e., treating Ying as his father].[49] These two had different surnames and ritual obligations [to each other], and yet they behaved as such. How could he [i.e., Shuai], who is a blood relation to and has been raised and nurtured by [Lady Yu], not repay her in life and death?! All the evidence that Lady Yu provided is well supported. Her rights cannot be deprived.

The judgment of the Clerk to the Chamberlain for Law Enforcement [Tingshi 廷史], Chen Xu 陳序:[50]

The Code states: "The line of a man who died childless can be continued through adoption as long as the adopted does not [do this to] avoid corvée duties. No more than one [child per line] is permitted." The Code states: "One adopts a male child and then begets one. The adopted child, including those adopted by eunuchs [yanren 閹人] who are not from blood relations, should establish a separate household." Based on the fact that Qiao had his own son Zuan, Shuai should establish a separate household.

The judgment of the Imperial Secretary [Shangshu 尚書], Zhang Kai 張闓:[51]

The account memorialized by Qiao's wife, Lady Yu, is different from the deposition given by Qun's wife, Lady Tao. Tao states:

Qiao's wife was childless. My husband Qun commanded our youngest son Shuai to become Qiao's heir. One year later, Qiao's concubine Zhang gave birth to Zuan. The late Cavalry General [Piaoqi jiangjun 驃騎將軍] Gu Rong 顧榮[52] said to Qun that "since Qiao had a son, it is better to have Shuai return." [Gu] asked whether [Shuai] had been given [to Qiao] as the adopted heir.

The late Grand Minister of Works [Sikong 司空] He Xun 賀循[53] took his nephew [congzi 從子], Hong 紘, as his son. His effort in raising and nurturing [Hong] was comparable to [what Lady Yu did for] Shuai. Xun later begot a son and sent Hong back to his birth parents. Even if Shuai desired to stay with Qiao, he should be sent back. Lady Yu argued that she adopted Shuai as her own son and not as the adopted heir of her husband. She presented six issues and ten questions in order to demonstrate that "the adopted heir" is not a term to be used when the adoptive father is still alive. [She argued that] when the adoptive father is alive, the adopted son shall be referred to as the eldest child of the wife; when the adoptive father is dead, only then can the adopted child be called the adopted heir. Different terms should be used in life and death. [She] also argued that "one could raise a child of another without adopting him as the heir." In which Classic did she find an argument for this? The term was not created frivolously; it is there for a reason. There has been no such a case since antiquity. Nowadays when people adopt a child, they are adopting an heir. Moreover, Lady Yu states: "Those who become adopted heirs are chosen by their clansmen from a subsidiary line. It is different from Shuai's being designated as the heir because he was [considered] the eldest son by the wife and because [Qiao's] younger son was born to a concubine. Yet, he was [similarly] laughed at." This is precisely why Shuai should be removed rather than stay. Had Shuai given precedence to his insignificant duties as an adopted son over the great debts he owes to his birth parents, he would have made a momentous mistake. Lady Yu knows that the *Rites* does not have provisions for an adopted child. Therefore, she has attempted to skew the contemporary view of adoption by referring to a wide range of cases that are not comparable [to this case]. How could she argue that Shuai became her son through adoption while at the same time try to avoid the laughter that he would receive as an adopted heir?

The judgment of the Governor [*Yin* 尹] of Danyang,[54] Chen Mo 臣謨:[55]

My review of the memorial that [Lady Yu] submitted: While it refers to a wide range of precedents, her reasoning does not reflect the correct meaning of the *Rites*. It could be said that these all are forced arguments. Your humble servant reviewed the judgment issued by Imperial Secretary Kai and finds its language clear and fair, its reasoning concise and attuned to the Classics. [The judgment] should be revered as an exemplary model of our generation. My humble opinion is that [Your Majesty] should rule as Kai [suggests].

[Du You, *Tongdian* (Beijing: Zhonghua shuju, 1988), 69.1907–15]

NOTES

1. The Tang court adopted the empress's petition and decreed that a child must mourn his or her parents for the same length: three years. See *JTS* 27.1023. This well-known quotation also appears in numerous Buddhist sutras and commentaries concerning the repayment of parental kindness. One of the contemporary and best-known examples is the *Hymn and Explanation of the Yulanpen Sutra (Yulan pen jing zanshu* 盂蘭盆經讚述), *T* 687, 16:780c–81a.

2.   *Etiquette and Rituals* (*Yili* 儀禮), in particular. See *Yili zhushu* 儀禮註疏, *Shisanjing zhushu zhengliben* 十三經注疏整理本 (*SZZ*) edition (Beijing: Beijing Daxue chubenshe, 2000), 11.652–55.

3.   "Biography of Taicang Gong," in *SJ* 105.2795.

4.   Noted examples include Lady [née] Yang 羊氏, the mother of poet Xiahou Zhan 夏侯湛 (ca. 245–290), and Lady [née] Zhang 張氏, the mother of statesman Zhong Hui 鐘會 (225–264), both of whom taught their sons the Classics. See "Biography of Xiahou Zhan," in *JS* 55.1497; and "Biography of Zhong Hui," in *WS* 28.785.

5.   The Seven Outs (*qichu* 七出) refers to the seven conditions under which a man could divorce his wife. These are if the wife is (1) disobedient to her parents-in-law (*bu shun mu fu* 不順母父), (2) childless (*wuzi* 無子), (3) nymphomaniac (*yinpi* 淫僻), (4) sickly (*e ji* 惡疾), (5) jealous (*duji* 妒疾), (6) gossipy (*duokoushe* 多口舌), or (7) larcenous (*qiedao* 竊盜). However, the Seven Outs must be exercised within the perimeter set by the Three Stays (*sanbuqu* 三不去). Aimed to protect the wives from faithless husbands, the Three Stays maintain that a wife could not be divorced if she has (1) no home to return to (*wusuogui* 無所歸), (2) completed her mourning obligation to her parents-in-law (*yugong gen sannian zhi sang* 與共更三年之喪), or (3) married her husband before he became wealthy and prominent (*xian pingjian hou fugui* 先貧賤後富貴). See *Kongzi jiayu* 孔子家語, chap. 26, "Exposition of Life" (*Benming jie* 本命解).

6.   Lady Yu's maternal brother and brother-in-law were both named Qun.

7.   "New bride" (*xinfu* 新婦) was the deprecation used when a man referred to his wife in an address to his social superiors.

8.   *Zhengchang* 烝嘗 originally referred to the autumn and winter sacrifices to the ancestors. The compound came to be used for ancestral rites of all seasons. It was the wifely duty to prepare and assist the ancestral sacrifice of her husband's clan.

9.   *Renhou* 人後 literally means "heir." The term was used only in cases of adoption. See *Yili zhushu* 11.669.

10. Lady Yu alluded to the lines in the *Classic of Poetry* (*Shijing* 詩經) 196, "Xiaowan." In these lines, wasps (*guoying* 蜾蠃) are said to carry off the children of mulberry insects (*mingling* 螟蛉) to raise as their own, and people are advised to teach their children by providing them with good models (*shigu* 式穀).

11. Lady Yu was quoting from the *Yili zhushu* 11.669. Each article is often followed by a comment that further clarifies the meaning of the article through a series of questioning and answering. What Lady Yu quoted here is the commentary that highlights the difference between the main and the subsidiary lines of the patrilineal descent and the primacy of the main line to claim an adopted heir from a subsidiary line when necessary.

12. Here Lady Yu was referring to the patrilineal principles laid out in the *Record of Rites* (*Liji* 禮記), which clearly defines an heir is the eldest son born to a man and his wife. This line he passes on to his and his wife's eldest son is the main line. His other brothers, whether or not they have the same mother, begin their own lines. While each of these lines is subsidiary to the eldest son's, each passes on from father to the eldest son just as his does and could itself serve as the main line from which further subsidiary lines splinter. While the eldest son's line indefinitely remains at the center, the lines of

his brothers from the sixth generation on become so removed that they can no longer be included in his clan. These principles are particularly important when determining the right to inherit the throne. Those in the main line are the rulers; those in the subsidiary lines are their subjects; but those in the subsidiary lines and five times removed from the main line are no longer members of the royal clan. See *Liji zhengyi* 禮記正義, *SZZ* 15.1122; compare the subcommentary to the adopted heir's ritual obligations toward his own parents in the *Yili zhushu* 11.669.

13. Lady Yu here again referred to an article in the *Yili zhushu* 11.668–69 that explains the adopted heir's ritual obligations toward his own parents.

14. Lady Yu referred to the article in the *Yili zhushu* 11.642 that defines the candidacy for the adopted heir and his ritual obligations to his adoptive parents. The commentary to this article stresses in particular the importance of the adopted heir to act toward, and be treated by, adoptive parents like a natural son. Since her interpretation flew directly in the face of the article she quoted, she might have been influenced by other commentaries or traditions now no longer extant.

15. *Yi* is a particularly difficult term to render in English in part because throughout its long history, it had acquired a variety of meanings by the time of Lady Yu. Chen Jo-shui 陳弱水 points out that it was a term that carried the connotations of both ritual and propriety and thus should be understood as the performance of ritual principles that re-affirmed the human relation and social order, in "A Discussion of the Three Principles of 'Yi'" (*Shuo "yi" zhi sanze* 說「義」之三則), in *Gonggong yishi yu Zhongguo wenhua* 公共意識與中國文化 (Taibei: Lianjing chubanshe, 2005), 183–230.

16. Lady Yu tried yet again, this time from another angle, to argue that Shuai was not an adopted heir. She admitted here that he was briefly the heir—as the eldest son of the wife—before Zhun was born. However, she insisted that the situation that led Shuai to become the heir was different from those that led a person to become an adopted heir. Her basis is still the article in *Yili zhushu* 11.668–69 that explains the adopted son's ritual obligations to his natural parents.

17. This quotation comes directly from the *Analects*. Confucius criticized Zaiwo because the latter felt that three years was too long a period to mourn for one's parents. See *Lunyu zhushu* 論語註疏, *SZZ* 17.275. The *Record of Rites* 38.1820 quoted Confucius verbatim.

18. Lady Yu here quoted lines from the *Classic of Poetry* 202 (Liao E).

19. See note 10.

20. The Ban clan descended from Ziwen 子文, who was the Chief Minister (*Lingyin* 令尹) of the Chu 楚 state during the reign of King Cheng 成王 (r. 671–628 B.C.E.). He was a child resulting from an extramarital affair and was thus abandoned. A tigress suckled him until Yunzi 邧子 found him. See *Chunqiu Zuozhuan zhushu* 春秋左傳註疏, *SZZ*, Xuan 4, 21.701–2.

21. Here Lady Yu paraphrased *Yili zhushu* 30.662–63.

22. *Liji zhengyi* 8.262.

23. *Yili zhushu* 30.654. A *ci* mother is a concubine who looks after another concubine's child on the order of the father because the child is motherless. Yet, Lady Yu cited this quotation to emphasize that it is the father's command that decides which woman the

child should treat as his mother. She ignored the fact that she was a wife and therefore could never be a *ci* mother.

24. This refers to the notion, mentioned earlier, that "the sons of one's brothers are sons of one's own." See *Liji zhengyi* 8.262.

25. Zhuge Liang 諸葛亮, the celebrated chief minister to Liu Bei, the ruler of the Shu kingdom, has a lengthy biography in *SGZ* 35.911–31.

26. Lady Yu quoted this line from the *Record of Rites* yet again. See *Liji zhengyi* 8.262.

27. Lady Yu's quotation here is not exactly what is recorded in the "Biography of Zhuge Liang." See *SGZ* 35.931–32. It is possible that she worked from a different text.

28. *Chunqiu Zuozhuan zhushu*, Yin 3, 3.91.

29. *Chunqiu Gongyangzhuan zhushu* 春秋公羊傳註疏, *SZZ*, Cheng 15, 3.91.

30. Lady Yu may have been alluding to the comments on Dong Zhongshu 董仲舒 by Ban Gu 班固. See *HS* 56.2525. It is, of course, possible that she based this on other texts or traditions.

31. *The Spring and Autumn Annuals* here is only a substitute for all the Classics. Dong Zhongshu pioneered the method in which the Classics served as guides for judicial deliberations, known as "adjudicating using the *Spring and Autumn Annuals*" [*Chunqiu jueyu* 春秋決獄]. The quotation is in fact from the *Analects*, in which Confucius explains that "fathers cover up for their sons and sons cover up for their fathers" was what his people considered to be "uprightness" (*zhi* 直). See *Lunyu zhushu* 13.201. The same principle is also reflected in the discussion on "covering up for one's superior" (*wei zun zhe hui* 為尊者諱) in the *Chunqiu Gongyangzhuan zhushu*, Min 1, 9.224.

32. We may never know in which text Lady Yu found this case allegedly judged by Dong Zhongshu, since what is preserved in the *Comprehensive Institutions* (*Tongdian* 通典) through the record of Lady Yu's case are the only fragments that have survived. According to the *Treatise on Scholarship* (*Yiwen zhi* 藝文志) in the *Han shu*, there existed a collection of case files bearing the title *The Judgments of Gongyang [Erudite] Dong Zhongshu* (*Gongyang Dong Zhongshu zhiyu* 公羊董仲舒治獄), in sixteen chapters. See *HS* 30.1714. The may be the text that Lady Yu consulted.

33. It is not clear which article in the *Rites* Lady Yu referred to. According to the *Comprehensive Institutions* 69.1914–16, a number of surviving sources compiled before the Eastern Jin mentioned such a prohibition. Most of these accounts interpreted the prohibition against adopting an heir with a different surname according to the principle that "the [ancestral] spirits would not receive offerings from those outside the clan; [thus] people do not sacrifice to those not of their clans."

34. The argument Lady Yu tries to make here is that because he had raised him, A could shield B from the authorities as any father could, even though B was not his heir. In other words, an adoptive parent could claim parental privileges even when the adopted child is not the heir.

35. For the history of the source, see note 32. It is also difficult to know on which of the Classics Dong Zhongshu based this verdict.

36. Qin Jia 秦嘉 and his wife, Xu Shu 徐淑, were renowned for the parting poems that they exchanged. When Qin Jia was leaving for the capital to report for official duties, Xu Shu

was recovering from an illness at her parents' house, so they were unable to say farewell in person. Qin Jia served as Gentleman of the Palace Gate (*Huangmen lang* 黃門郎) to Emperor Huan 桓帝 of Han (r. 147–167). The fact that he died soon after he reached the capital gives these poems an unusual poignancy. *New Songs from the Jade Terrace* (*Yutai xinyong* 玉臺新詠; completed around the mid-sixth century) is the earliest of the surviving poetry anthologies to include these poems. What Lady Yu recounts here does not appear in any other of the surviving records. This account may have been another case tried in the Han court using the method of "adjudicating using the *Spring and Autumn Annals*," as Lady Yu stated that it was decided by "learned scholars." Sources written after Lady Yu's case maintain that Xu Shu fiercely resisted the pressure to remarry. The *TPYL* includes a letter that Xu Shu allegedly wrote to her brothers repudiating the legal actions they undertook to force her to remarry, in which she claimed to have two children—a boy and a girl—presumably by Qin Jia. If Xu Shu indeed adopted a son and cited him in her refusal to remarry, as these fragmented sources seem to indicate, then her case would be the closest legal precedence for Lady Yu's case.

37. No other surviving source mentions a scholar named Zhou Yi who lived during the Wu dynasty.

38. His first ritual obligation is to his adopted parents. See *Yili zhushu* 11.669.

39. Her first ritual obligation is to her husband's clan. See *Yili zhushu* 11.671–73.

40. The heir assumes the same ritual obligation as his father regarding his divorced mother. See *Yili zhushu* 11.659–60.

41. The son of a feudal lord belongs to a different social class from that of his concubine mother. Just as his father does not observe mourning for concubines, he also does not. See *Yili zhushu* 11.733–35.

42. A king observes ritual obligations only to his royal ancestors. See *Yili zhushu* 11.733–35.

43. Emperor Ai was originally a feudal prince. His father, Prince Gong of Dingtao 定陶恭王, was the son of an imperial concubine and a younger half brother of Emperor Cheng 成帝 (r. 51–7 B.C.E.). Emperor Cheng had no sons, so he designated his nephew as the crown prince. When Emperor Ai ascended the throne, he immediately elevated his own parents, who were known as Emperor and Empress Gong.

44. The Duke of Zhou was known to show his filial respect to his father, King Wen of Zhou, by pairing the ritual offerings to him with those to Heaven. See *Xiaojing zhushu* 孝經註疏, *SZZ* 5.33–38. Lady Yu suggested that what Emperor Ai did was wrong, since his ritual obligations were to his adopted father and his birth father was not a Son of Heaven.

45. A father names his children three months after they are born. The three premature deaths (*sanshang* 三殤) refer to children who die between the ages of eight and eleven (known as *xiashang* 小殤), between twelve and fifteen (*zhongshang* 中殤), and between sixteen and nineteen (*zhangshang* 長殤). The age at which the child dies determines the length and manner in which the parents should mourn. If the child dies before reaching the eighth year, the parents may weep a day for every month that he or she lived but should not wear mourning clothes. If a child dies between the ages of eight and nineteen, he or she is mourned by the parents and relatives based on their relative stations. For example, a father mourns the death of his eldest son in the same length and fashion

as he would be mourned by him, by wearing the *zhan* mourning clothes for three years. A mother mourns the death of her eldest son in the same length and fashion as she would be mourned by him, by wearing the *qi* mourning clothes for three years. See *Yili zhushu* 11.692–94, 11.640–41, and 11.655.

46. The Chamberlain for Ceremonials was the most eminent of the group of central government officials known collectively as the Nine Chamberlains (*Jiuqing* 九卿). His office was in charge of great state sacrificial ceremonies, particularly those involved in worshipping imperial ancestors.

47. The Chamberlain for Law Enforcement was one of the Nine Chamberlains. His office made judicial recommendations on complicated cases forwarded by local administrations.

48. There is no biography for Du Yuan 杜瑗 in the official history of the Jin dynasty. He was, however, the Governor of Jiaozhi 交趾 during the reigns of Emperors Xiaowu and An (372–418). See *JS* 10.231 and 10.251.

49. The story of Zhao Wu 趙武 and Cheng Ying 程嬰 took place during the reign of Duke Jing of Jin 晉景公 (r. 599–581 B.C.E.). The Zhaos had served at the Jin court for generations. In the year 597 B.C.E., the Zhao clan was exterminated in a military coup led by their political rivals. Zhao Wu was a posthumous child. Cheng Ying, a retainer and close friend of Zhao Wu's father, risked his life to raise and protect Wu. When the truth about the coup came to light fifteen years after the event, those who engineered it were themselves exterminated, and Zhao Wu was restored to his ancestral fief. When Zhao Wu reached maturity, Cheng Ying judged that he had fulfilled his promise to his good friend and liege and decided to follow him in death by committing suicide. After Cheng's death, Zhao Wu mourned him as he would for his father. For many generations, Zhao Wu's descendants continued to sacrifice to Cheng Ying every year in the spring and autumn. See *Records of the Historian* 43.1783–85.

50. Chen Xu 陳序 was most likely substantiating evidence for the argument set forth by the office of the Chamberlain for Law Enforcement. There is no information about Chen Xu in the official histories.

51. Zhang Kai 張闓 had served as imperial secretary before he became the Chamberlain for Law Enforcement. He must have written the judgment while in this position, although the *Tongdian* lists his previous title. For the official biography of Zhang Kai, see *JS* 76.2018–19. He was a prominent statesman active during the reigns of Emperors Yuan (r. 317–322) and Ming (r. 322–325). He died sometime after year 327. He was well acquainted with both Gu Rong 顧榮 and He Xun 賀循, whom he mentions in his judgment, having been their junior colleague.

52. The Cavalry General was one of the generals who shared the command of an active campaign. It was also a title often bestowed on courtiers who had enjoyed imperial favor. For the official biography Gu Rong (d. 322), see *JS* 68.1811–15. He was an eminent statesman who participated in some of the most important events leading to the founding of the Eastern Jin dynasty. He had a long political career, serving Emperors Ming and Yuan. Cavalry General was one of his posthumous titles.

53. For the official biography of He Xun (d. 319), see *JS* 68.1824–31. He was an eminent statesman active during the reigns of Emperors Ming and Yuan. He participated in many events leading to the founding of the Eastern Jin dynasty and served under Gu Rong for a time. He was respected as the foremost expert on rituals and contributed to the court debate on how Emperors Hui 惠帝 (r. 290–301) and Huai 懷帝 (r. 306–313) should be revered in the worship of imperial ancestors, because they were brothers rather than father and son. He Xun was also an older contemporary of Zhang Kai, whom he helped in a real-estate dispute. He was a senior clansman of He Qun and He Qiao.

54. Danyang is in modern-day Zhejiang Prefecture, and its jurisdiction includes the metropolitan area in which the capital city, Jiankang 建康, was located. The office of Governor of Danyang was created during the reign of Emperor Yuan.

55. Chen Mo 臣謨 most likely had a say in this case because it took place in the area under his jurisdiction. He served as Chamberlain for Ceremonials. Although there is no official biography of him in the *Jin shu*, we know that after he was Governor of Danyang, he was promoted to various prestigious offices and ended his career as one (*situ* 司徒) of the Three Dukes (*Sangong* 三公) during the reign of Emperor Kang 康帝 (r. 342–344). See the reference to him in the "Biography of Yin Hao" 殷浩傳, in *JS* 77.2046.

31. Estate Culture in Early Medieval China

The Case of Shi Chong

DAVID R. KNECHTGES

Already in the Western Jin period, wealthy persons created large gardens on their private estates. The most famous garden owner of this period is Shi Chong 石崇 (249–303),[1] whose Golden Valley Garden (Jingu yuan 金谷園) was the most lavish country estate in the Luoyang area, if not the entire realm.[2] Shi Chong was the youngest of the six sons of Shi Bao 石苞 (d. 273), a wealthy and powerful supporter of the Sima clan at the end of the Wei dynasty. When Shi Bao was on his deathbed, he distributed his property to all his sons except Chong, on the grounds that he had the ability to make a fortune on his own. At about age twenty-five (ca. 274/275), Shi Chong obtained his first official post, that of prefect of Xiuwu 修武 (modern Xiuwu, Henan), where he earned a reputation as a capable administrator. A year or so later, he went to the capital, where he served as Cavalier Attendant-in-Ordinary.

Around 278, Shi Chong took up the post of Governor of Chengyang 城陽 (equivalent to the southeastern portion of the Shandong Peninsula), located in the area of Qingzhou. In 280, he led an army to victory over forces from Wu and was rewarded with the noble title of Marquis of Anyang Township 安陽鄉. Soon thereafter, he resigned his post on grounds of illness. Two years later (282), however, he took up a position at court as Gentleman of the Palace Gate. In this capacity, he was in charge of transmitting court documents. After his elder brother Shi Tong 石統 was pardoned for having offended the Prince of

Fufeng 扶風, Sima Jun 司馬駿 (232–286), some court officials wanted to have Shi Tong punished because his younger brother Chong failed to thank the emperor for his mercy. Chong addressed the throne with a petition in defense of his brother, and no more was made of the matter.[3]

In the late 280s, Shi Chong rose to the positions of Cavalier Attendant-in-Ordinary and Palace Attendant. According to his biography in the *Jin shu*, "Because Chong was the son of a meritorious official and he had a capacity as a good administrator, Emperor Wu held him in high regard."[4] In 290, Emperor Wu died. Grand Tutor Yang Jun 楊駿 (d. 291) served as regent for the young Emperor Hui 惠 (r. 290–306). Shi Chong and He Pan 何攀 presented a petition to Emperor Hui protesting the excessive rewards given to Yang Jun and his cohorts. After his advice was rejected, Shi Chong was sent out to Jingzhou 荊州 (modern Hubei and Hunan) as inspector. He also held the military titles of Gentleman General of the South and Colonel in Charge of the Southern Man. While in Jingzhou, Shi Chong extorted money and goods from traveling merchants and in this way amassed a large fortune,[5] becoming one of the wealthiest men of his time. But he may have acquired wealth even earlier. According to the "Treatise on Food and Money" in the *Jin shu*, when the Jin conquered Wu in 280, the invading armies "took millions in cash, depleted the resources of the Three Wu regions, and took control of the resources of Shu that had been accumulated over a thousand years. . . . Thereupon, Wang Kai [王愷], Wang Ji [王濟], Shi Chong, and others competed in boastful displays. The splendor of their conveyances, apparel, and eating vessels rivaled that of the imperial court."[6]

Wang Kai, the younger brother of Empress Wenming 文明, wife of Emperor Wu's father, Sima Zhao 司馬昭 (211–265), was a wealthy man who competed with Shi Chong in displays of ostentation. Cao Daoheng and Shen Yucheng point out that Shi Chong was already competing with Wang Kai some years before he went to Jingzhou, and thus he must have acquired his riches in 280 when he participated in the expedition against Wu.[7]

The *Sequel to the Treatise on Literature* (*Xu Wenzhang zhi* 續文章志), a work of the early fifth century, says the following about the extent of Shi Chong's riches:

Shi Chong's assets and property amounted to many tens of thousands of gold pieces, and his dwellings, conveyances, and horses presumptuously emulated those of the royal house. His kitchen produced the best delicacies of water and land. His concubines numbered in the hundreds, and they all were draped in silks and embroideries and had ear ornaments made of gold and kingfisher plumes. The artistes of his string and pipe orchestra were the elite of the time. In constructing pavilions and digging ponds, he fully exercised all manner of human ingenuity. He competed with members of the consort clan such as Wang Kai and Yang Xiu in displays of extravagance.[8]

Although this figure may be an exaggeration, one source says that Shi Chong kept on his estate several thousand female servants and entertainers.[9] According to one near contemporary account, Shi Chong's privy was more like a large bedroom. It was decorated with scarlet curtains and was equipped with a large bed, cushions, and mats. Maidservants were stationed there to help guests with their ablutions.[10]

Throughout the 290s, Shi Chong maintained a close friendship with Jia Mi 賈密 (d. 300), the nephew of Empress Jia 賈 (d. 300), who was the real power behind the throne during the reign of Emperor Hui (r. 290–306). Shi Chong was a member of Jia Mi's literary coterie known as the Twenty-Four Companions of Jia Mi. The group included many of the most prominent writers of the time, including Pan Yue 潘岳 (247–300), Lu Ji 陸機 (261–303), and Zuo Si 左思 (250–305). In 300, both Shi Chong and Pan Yue were arrested for their alleged participation in a plot against Sima Lun 司馬倫 (d. 301), who had assumed de facto control of the imperial court. Both Pan Yue and Shi Chong were executed in the marketplace.

Shi Chong actually had two estates, the more famous Golden Valley Garden located on the Jingu Brook 金谷澗 northwest of Luoyang,[11] and the second estate north of the Yellow River in the area of Heyang 河陽.[12] In 296, Shi Chong hosted a large party at Golden Valley attended by high officials and prominent men of the area who gathered there to pay tribute to Shi Chong and another official who was about to depart for Chang'an. Thirty of the participants composed poems, and Shi Chong wrote a preface to the poems in which he describes the estate. He gives the location of his villa as ten li (2.5 miles) from the Luoyang city wall in the outskirts of Henan Prefecture, thus placing it in the northwestern suburbs of the capital. The garden was not simply a pleasure park but seems to have had an agricultural and economic function. Shi Chong mentions that his fields extended for ten qing (121 acres). He also had an orchard, a bamboo grove, fishponds, and an herb garden, as well as chickens, pigs, geese, ducks, and two hundred goats. Shi Chong's estate must have been a thriving economic unit, for it had thirty sites where water mills were installed. He also owned more than eight hundred slaves. Beginning in the third and fourth centuries, ownership of water mills, fields, and slaves was an indication of great wealth.[13]

Shi Chong used the Golden Valley Garden to entertain guests. At the gathering in 296, the guests roamed about the estate, climbing hills to look at the view or sitting together at the edge of a stream. They listened to music played by zithers and mouth organs (sheng 笙). Each person was obliged to compose a poem, and whoever could not write a poem had to drink three dou (6.5 quarts) of wine. The only complete poem that survives is by Pan Yue, "Poem Written for the Jingu Gathering" (Jingu ji zuo shi 金谷集作詩).[14] Shi Chong's "Preface to the Jingu Garden Poems" 金谷園序 is translated here, followed by Shi Chong's description of his other estate in Heyang. He portrays his Heyang estate in the

"Preface to the 'Song of Longing to Return'" as a refuge from the troubles and burdens of service at the court. In contrast to the preface to the Golden Valley gathering, this does not seem to be a place of large social gatherings but a refuge from the turmoil and annoyances of court life. It is also a place where he engages in Daoist macrobiotic practices, such as performing breathing exercises and ingesting various herbs and elixirs. Both the preface and the song are translated here as well.

FURTHER READING

For a biography of Shi Chong and general discussion of his writings, see Hellmut Wilhelm, "Shih Ch'ung and His *Chin-ku-yüan*," *Monumenta Serica* 18 (1959): 315–27. For a discussion of Shi Chong's role in the social and political environment of the Western Jin, see Zhang Aibo 張愛波, "Shi Chong renge lun" 石崇人格論, in *Xi Jin shifeng yu shige—Yi "Ershisi you" yanjiu wei zhongxin*, 西晉士風與詩歌—以"二十四友"研究為中心 (Jinan: Qi Lu shushe, 2006), 248– 62. On the gathering at the Golden Valley Garden, see Zhang Jinyao 張金耀, "Jingu youyan renwu kao" 金谷游宴人物考, *Fudan xuebao* (Shehui kexue bao) 2 (2001): 128–31. On the Golden Valley gathering preface and its relationship to the Lanting preface by Wang Xizhi, see Kōzen Hiroshi 興膳宏, "Seki Sū to Ō Gishi—Rantei no jo gaisetsu" 石崇と王羲之—蘭亭序外說 (1973), in Kōzen Hiroshi, *Ransei o ikiru shijintachi: Rikuchō shijin ron* 亂世を生きる詩人たち: 六朝詩人論 (Tokyo: Kenbun shuppansha, 2001), 325–41; Chinese translation in Kōzen Hiroshi and Peng Enhua 彭恩華, trans., *Liuchao wenxue lungao* 六朝文學論稿 (Changsha: Yuelu shushe, 1988), 171–82; and Liu Qinghua 劉慶華, "Cong 'Jinggu shi xu' 'Lanting ji xu' kan Liang Jin wenren de shengchun xuanze yu wenxue xuanze" 從《金谷詩序》《蘭亭集序》看兩晉文人的生存選擇與文學選擇, *Guangzhou daxue xuebao* (Shehui kexue ban) 5, no. 3 (2006): 91–96. On estates of the Western Jin period, see Ma Lianghuai 馬良懷, "Han Jin zhi ji zhuangyuan jingji de fazhan yu shidafu shengcun zhuangtai zhi guanxi" 漢晉之際莊園經濟的發展與士大夫生存狀態之關係, *Zhongguo shehui jingji shi yanjiu* 4 (1997): 7–15; and Zhou Weiquan 周維權, *Zhongguo gudian yuanlin shi* 中國古典園林史 (1999; repr., Beijing: Qinghua daxue chubanshe, 2003), 105–11.

SHI CHONG 石崇

Preface to the Jingu Garden Poems 金谷園序

In Yuankang 6 [296],[15] I left the office of Chamberlain of the Imperial Stud as an emissary, and I was given credentials authorizing me to supervise military affairs in Qing and Xu [modern Shandong, northern Anhui and Jiangsu] with the title General of Caitiff Campaigns. I have a villa on Jingu Creek on the outskirts of Henan County. It is ten *li* [2.5 miles] from the city wall, and it has ten *qing* [121 acres] of fields. The terrain is both high and low, and there are limpid springs, lush groves, diverse fruit trees, bamboo, cypress, and medicinal herbs. Two hundred head of goats and such creatures as chickens, pigs, geese, and dogs are all fully supplied. There also are water mills, fishponds, caves in the ground, and all things to please the eyes and gladden the heart. Chancellor and General of the Western Campaigns Wang Xu was about to return to Chang'an,[16] and thus I and various distinguished gentlemen escorted him to the creek. Day and night we roamed and feasted, frequently shifting our sitting places. Sometimes we climbed to a high place and looked down; other times we sat together at the edge of a stream. Occasionally, seven-stringed and twenty-five-stringed zithers, mouth organs, and bamboo zithers joined us in the carts and were played together on the road. When we halted, I had each one take turns performing with the orchestra. Then each person composed a poem in order to express his feelings. Whoever could not do so paid a penalty of drinking three *dou* [6.5 quarts] of ale. I was moved by the impermanence of human life, and I was fearful of not knowing when someone might "wither and fall." Thus I have recorded the official titles, names, and ages of those who were present. Following this information, I have copied the poems. I hope someone of a later time who is interested will read them.

There are all together thirty persons. Su Shao,[17] age fifty, of Wugong in Shiping, Tutor to the Prince of Wu, Court Gentleman for Consultation, Marquis Within the Pass, was at the top of the list.

> [The longest portion of the text is found in the commentary
> to *Shishuo xinyu* 9/57. See Yu Jiaxi, *Shishuo xinyu jianshu*
> (Shanghai: Shanghai guji chubanshe, 1993), 529. There are
> two reconstructed texts: Yan Kejun 嚴可均, "Quan Jin wen" 全晉文,
> in QW 33.13a; and Sun Xingyan 孫星衍, *Xu Guwen yuan* 續古文苑
> (Taibei: Dingwen shuju, 1973), 11.634–44]

SHI CHONG 石崇

Preface to the "Song of Longing to Return" 思歸引序

In my youth I had great ambition and wished to far outdistance the common folk. After being capped [at age twenty], I advanced to the court, where I spent twenty-five years in office. At age fifty, I was dismissed from my post because of a certain matter.[18] In my later years, I was all the more engaged in carefree abandon, and I was quite fond of woods and meres. I then retired to my villa in Heyang. This is how my dwelling is laid out:

The rear is blocked by a long dike, and the front overlooks a limpid water-way. Cypress trees nearly number ten thousand, and flowing water circles beneath the house. There are towers and pavilions, ponds and pools, where I raise fish and birds. My family long has been practiced in the musical arts, and we have not a few singers from Qin and Zhao. When I went out, I went sightseeing, fowled, and fished, and when at home, I had the pleasures provided by zither and books. I was also fond of ingesting elixirs and performing breathing exercises. My goal lay in attaining immortality, and I proudly assumed the manner of soaring the clouds. However, I suddenly again have become entangled in worldly affairs,[19] and I now loiter and linger in the official ranks. Distressed by the annoyances and corruption of the human world and constantly longing to return home, I heave long sighs. I have read through various musical pieces and found the "Song of Longing to Return." Presumably the ancients' feelings are the same as ours today, and thus they composed this tune. This tune has music but no lyrics. Now I have composed lyrics in order to relate my feelings. I regret that there is no accomplished musician who can compose new music and convey the tune by means of strings and reeds.

The following is the "Song of Longing to Return," which has been transmitted under Shi Chong's name:

[Singing?] the tune of "Longing to Return,"	思歸引
I return to Heyang.	歸河陽
Lending me their wings,	假余翼
The swan and crane soar on high.	鴻鶴高飛翔
I traverse the hills of Mang,[20]	經芒阜
I cross the Yellow River bridge.	濟河梁
I gaze upon my old lodges	望我舊館
And my heart rejoices.	心悅康
The waters of the limpid sluiceways pulse,	清渠激
Fish dart to and fro.	魚傍徨
Wild geese startled by backward-flowing waves,	雁驚溯波
Swim together in flocks.	羣相將
All day I gaze around	終日周覽
And my joy is beyond compare.	樂無方
I climb a cloud-capped pavilion,	登雲閣
Where arrayed are ladies like the Ji and Jiang.	列姬姜
They play strings and reeds,	拊絲竹
Tap tunes to *gong* and *shang*.	叩宫商
Feasting at a scenic pond,	宴華池
We drink from jade goblets.[21]	酌玉觴

[*Wen xuan* 45.2041]

NOTES

1. For a biography of Shi Chong 石崇, see *JS* 33.1004–8. For an annotated translation, see Hellmut Wilhelm, "Shih Ch'ung and His *Chin-ku-yüan*," *Monumenta Serica* 18 (1959): 315–27.

2. For a good account of the Jingu yuan, see Wang Duo 王鐸, "Dong Han, Wei Jin he Bei Wei de Luoyang yuanlin" 東漢, 魏晉和北魏的洛陽園林, *Zhongguo gudu yanjiu* 7 (1991): 117–20.

3. For a text of the petition, see *JS* 33.1005.

4. *JS* 33.1006.

5. *JS* 33.1006; Yu Jiaxi 余嘉錫, ed. and comm., *Shishuo xinyu jianshu* 世說新語箋疏 (Shanghai: Shanghai guji chubanshe, 1993), 30.877.

6. *JS* 26.783.

7. *Zhonggu wenxue shiliao congkao* 中古文學史料叢考 (Beijing: Zhonghua shuju, 2003), 121. Lu Kanru dates the competitions between Shi Chong and Wang Kai from 286 while Emperor Wu, who provided luxury goods to Wang Kai, was still alive, in *Zhonggu wenxue xinian* 中古文學繫年 (Beijing: Renmin wenxue chubanshe, 1985), 2.716–17.

8. Yu Jiaxi, *Shishuo xinyu jianshu*, 882.

9. This is from a near contemporary account by Wang Jia 王嘉 (d. ca. 390). See Qi Zhiping 齊治平, ed., *Shiyi ji* 拾遺記 (Beijing: Zhonghua shuju, 1981), 9.214.

10. Zhou Lengqie 周楞伽, ed. and comm., *Pei Qi Yulin* 裴啟語林 (Beijing: Wenhua yishu chubanshe, 1988), 43–44.

11. The Jingu Creek was a tributary of the Gu River 穀水, which flowed east of Luoyang. The site of Shi Chong's estate has been located in the southern foothills of the Beimang Mountains near modern Mengjin 孟津, Henan. See Zhang Shiheng 張士恆, "Jingu yuan yizhi kao yi" 金谷園遺址考異, *Mengjin shihua* 孟津史話 (Mengjin: Mengjin xian zhi zongbian shi, 1988), cited in Wang Duo, "Dong Han, Wei Jin he Bei Wei de Luoyang yuanlin," 119n.1.

12. Heyang was located north of the Yellow River, northwest of modern Meng 孟 County, Henan. This estate is often confused with the Jingu estate. However, Shi Chong makes a clear reference to the Heyang estate in his "Preface to the 'Song of Longing to Return'" (*Si gui yin xu* 思歸引序), in *Wen xuan* 45.2041: "I then retired to my villa in Heyang." The *Jin shu* of Wang Yin in the commentary to *Shishuo xinyu jianshu* 36/1 also says that at the time of Shi Chong's execution, his home was north of the Yellow River. This must refer to Heyang, which was on the north bank of the Yellow River. It could not be Jingu, which was south of the Yellow River in the northwestern suburbs of Luoyang. For a more detailed discussion, see David R. Knechtges, "Jin-gu and Lan Ting: Two (or Three) Jin Dynasty Gardens," in *Studies in Chinese Language and Culture: Festschrift in Honour of Cristoph Harbsmeir on the Occasion of His 60th Birthday*, ed. Christoph Anderl and Halvor Eifring (Oslo: Hermes Academic Publishing, 2006), 395–406.

13. Lien-sheng Yang, *Studies in Chinese Institutional History* (Cambridge, Mass.: Harvard University Press, 1963), 130.

14. *Wen xuan* 20.977–78.

15. The *Shui jing zhushu* (水經注疏) 16.1384 reads Yuankang 7 (297). Virtually all scholars accept the date of Yuankang 6 as authoritative.

16. Wang Xu 王詡, courtesy name Jiyin 季胤, was a native of Langye. The *Genealogy of the Wang Clan* (*Wangshi pu* 王氏譜) says that Wang Xu was a younger brother of Wang Yifu 王夷甫 = Wang Yan 王衍 (256–311). See Yu Jiaxi, *Shishuo xinyu jianshu* 14.612.

17. Su Shao 蘇紹 (247–300) was the grandson of Su Ze 蘇則 (d. 223), who served as Palace Attendant under Cao Pi after the founding of the Wei dynasty. Su Shao's father, Su Yu 蘇愉, was known for his loyal devotion and his wise advice. Shi Chong was married to Su Shao's elder sister, and an elder sister of Shi Chong was married to Su Shao. See Yu Jiaxi, *Shishuo xinyu jian shu* 9.529.

18. Shi Chong must be referring to the dismissal from his position as Supervisor of Military Affairs in Xuzhou and Qingzhou for having insulted Wang Dan during a drinking bout. See *JS* 33.1006. Shi Chong began his official career around age twenty-five, and he was about age fifty when he was dismissed from his position in Xuzhou and Qingzhou.

19. This refers to Shi Chong's appointment as Chamberlain for the Palace Garrison.

20. The Mang Hills are the mountains located directly north of Luoyang.

21. Ouyang Xun 歐陽詢 (557–641), *Yiwen leiju* 藝文類聚 (Beijing: Zhonghua shuju, 1965), 42.765; *Yuefu shiji* 樂府詩集 (Beijing: Zhonghua shuju, 1979).

PART VI

Relations with the Unseen World

Most religious texts portray aspects of a normally unseen world of divine beings, spiritual presences, or numinous zones that are argued to impinge somehow on human life. From among the enormous number of such texts that have come down to us from early medieval China, the seven chapters in part VI present all or part of a dozen or so. They represent a range of textual genres, religious traditions, communal concerns, and persuasive goals. Taken as a whole, they constitute a strong body of counterevidence to a pervasive tendency among some Sinologists to see traditional China as essentially secular or agnostic in orientation.

The selections from *Declarations of the Perfected* (*Zhen'gao* 真誥) translated by both Stephen Bokenkamp and Gil Raz represent one of the most intimate genres of religious writing in China: first-person accounts of divine epiphanies, recording in precise detail the names, titles, visual appearance, and—often at great length—speech of celestial deities claimed to have visited a highly literate spirit-medium. The burial instructions written for his descendants by Huangfu Mi 皇甫謐 (215–282), translated by Keith Knapp, are of interest as an example of a family document that was received and circulated much more widely on account of its literary value and ideological stance. Several selections—the miracle stories translated by Knapp (recorded to demonstrate the power of filial piety), the accounts of self-immolating monks translated by James Benn, and the records of anomalous events translated by me—represent a widespread and important genre of writing that, as this array of selections shows, was put to various ideological uses: the third-person narrative record of particular historical cases. Such texts, constituting a sort of unofficial historiography, preserved and disseminated a collective memory of unusual events in which some notable interaction had occurred between the unseen world and the human community. Another genre represented here (in parts of the material translated by Knapp, Benn, and Raz) is the essay, in which an author sets out to persuade readers of the truth or prestige of one or another religious stance based on a combination of argumentative devices. These devices included the appeal to historical cases, esoteric gnosis, scriptural authority, the example of teachers or sages, and personal testimony. Some of the texts introduced in part VI are performative in the technical sense that through the very act of copying, receiving, or distributing them, they were claimed to bring about results they describe. Documents buried with the deceased occupants of tombs and directly addressed to divine beings in the afterlife bureaucracy, a selection of which is translated by Timothy Davis, are clearly of this type. The Lingbao scripture translated by Clarke Hudson is as well, insofar as it is a text whose content is largely taken up with directives for its own copying and transmission and with promises of the benefits of these activities. The text translated by Hudson also is of interest as a scripture that presents itself (almost certainly fictively) as a commentary on another scripture. The commentarial genre is exemplified, too, in the comments by Tao Hongjing 陶弘景 (456–536) on *Declarations of the Perfected* (as translated by Bokenkamp and Raz).

These texts portray a remarkable spectrum of human and non- or superhuman actors. Their human protagonists range from pointedly ordinary (if mostly socially elite) persons, as in the anomaly accounts and miracle tales translated by me from *Records of the Hidden and Visible Worlds* (*Youming lu* 幽明錄), to those singled out for their high virtue, as in the filial piety narratives translated by Knapp; fierce religious dedication, as in the self-immolators memorialized by Huijiao 慧皎 (497–554) in *Biographies of Eminent Monks* (*Gaoseng zhuan* 高僧傳) in a passage translated by James Benn; or rare ability to see and interact directly with celestial spirits, as in the case of Yang Xi, the spirit-medium who is the main scribal persona in *Declarations of the Perfected*, or indeed the other spirit-mediums mentioned more fleetingly in other texts excerpted here. Perhaps we might see the entire community of living persons as the social actor whose fears are reflected and whose wishes are enacted in the tomb documents presented by Timothy Davis. In contrast, depicted in our texts as responding to this array of human actors, is an even larger array of other beings. Near the top of this crowded, hierarchically organized cosmos are such august personages as buddhas, bodhisattvas, a more or less anthropomorphized Heaven, gods of the directions, the Great One or Taiyi, the Queen Mother of the West, and the Perfected Ones of the newly revealed celestial zones known as

Upper Clarity. At its middle levels are many types of auspicious beasts, officers of the unseen bureaucracy, gods of particular places on the landscape, once-human heroes now divinized, and protective spirits residing in one's own body. The lower levels of this cosmic pyramid teem with untold numbers of ancestors, ghosts of the dead (i.e., lingering spirits of other people's ancestors), household gods, demons, sprites, and goblins, some of them at least initially specific to one or another of the relatively recently introduced religious traditions, and others having been fixtures of the common religious landscape for many centuries.

Our texts both portray and enact an equally large array of interactions between human and other beings. Some spirits harm, some help; their beneficence or malevolence may or may not depend on prior human actions or intentions, depending on which text we are reading. Some divine beings reveal or instruct; some demand sacrificial offerings. Some appear to many; others to only a select few. Some ghosts and ancestors provide assistance to living persons; others request assistance from the living. People command some spirits and beseech others; some divine figures beckon to be emulated by people, while others inspire mostly wonder, awe, or fear. Some of the texts represented here seek to regularize the riotous field of relations between humans and their nonhuman counterparts in the cosmos—whether by imposing a network of protocols, issuing demands backed by legal precedent, or arguing inductively based on the weight of collected examples that the denizens of the spirit world tend to operate in certain regular patterns structured by principles such as moral reciprocity, karma, and the law of "stimulus–response" (ganying 感應). The one sort of response to non- or superhuman beings that these texts do not broach is indifference: even the Confucian texts presented by Knapp—representing a tradition often claimed to be strictly agnostic on the question of the existence of spirit-beings—urge a view of the unseen world as alive with the presence of spirits.

At the same time that religious texts assert, depict, and enact various things regarding the world of spirits and other nonhuman beings, they also argue with one another. Their authors (and usually their readers, too) operate with the awareness that other texts emanating from other communities or traditions or, quite often, from different elements of the same tradition, or both, take certain positions, and they craft their own texts partly as responses. This sort of inter- and intrareligious contestation shows up explicitly in some of the following selections, but in others it is only implicit. The tomb texts studied by Davis are an example of merely implicit contestation. In the background to such performative texts were other, conflicting assertions about the dead (including the assertion that they do not exist in any form that would allow them to suffer harm at the hands of other dead persons or impinge menacingly on the living community), as well as other ways of dealing with the dead (including the mediation of spirit-mediums, the provision of special offerings, and/or the refurbishment of tomb sites as ways of quelling disturbances by the unquiet dead), to which these texts were being offered as alternatives or supplements. Similarly, the passages from *Declarations of the Perfected* are, implicitly, responses to other Daoist alternatives of which the makers and readers of these texts were well aware. Raz's contribution, however, reveals more explicit (albeit subtly waged) competition among rival techniques and lineages whose very similarity to one another only raised the stakes. It also shows how such competition was sometimes carried out intertextually. In talking about numinous landscapes, these texts also talk about much else, most notably the superiority of their favored techniques and lineages over others. Similarly, the scripture translated by Hudson makes clear—not in directly polemical argumentation but through the only slightly less direct mechanism of detailed prescriptions for ritual protocol—that its authors were concerned (among other things) with asserting the superiority of this and other Lingbao scriptures over older sorts of Daoist texts as well as Buddhist sutras. The protocols make it quite plain, without ever needing to state it, that it is the Lingbao scriptures that are to be regarded as most worthy of reverence.

Robert Ford Campany

32. Biographies of Eight Autocremators and Huijiao's "Critical Evaluation"

JAMES A. BENN

In this selection of early medieval hagiographical material, the theme of "relations between humans and nonhuman others" is exemplified by dealings not with the demons and deities of traditional China but with a set of actors relatively new to the Chinese religious scene: the buddhas and bodhisattvas of the *Lotus Sutra*. As we shall see, such interactions between human devotees and the heroes found in Buddhist literature translated from Indian sources did not drive out other kinds of relations with nonhuman beings. Signs that had roots in the much larger world of medieval religion and culture—dragons, golden deer, miraculous images, and various omens and portents such as falling stars and purple vapor—appear in these accounts, too.

Since around the end of the fourth century c.e., some Chinese Buddhists have drawn inspiration from a scripture known as the *Lotus Sutra* (Skt. *Saddharmapuṇḍarīka-sūtra*, Ch. *Miaofa lianhua jing* 妙法蓮華經) for a particular style of religious practice that involves burning the body in homage to and emulation of the text. Chinese sources usually refer to this incineration of the body as "autocremation" (*zifen* 自焚 or *shaoshen* 燒身). Autocremation is one manifestation of a broader range of Buddhist practices that involve making a gift of the body (e.g., feeding oneself to hungry animals or humans, jumping from cliffs or trees, or drowning oneself), which are termed "self-immolation" (variously *sheshen* 捨身, *wangshen* 亡身, or *yishen* 遺身). The best-known example of Buddhist self-immolation in recent times is that of the Vietnamese monk Thích Quang Đu'c (1897–1963), whose public autocremation in downtown Saigon in 1963 was captured in a series of dramatic photographs that have been widely reproduced.

Early medieval accounts of autocremation, such as the biographies translated here, tell of monks chanting the *Lotus Sutra* as they burned or deliberately imitating the model of the bodhisattva Medicine King (Skt. Bhaiṣajyarāja, Ch. Yaowang 藥王), who is depicted in the scripture as burning himself in a selfless and heroic manner. The biographies of autocremators make frequent allusions to the way in which the Medicine King carefully prepared his body to be burned. They also draw parallels between their subjects and the bodhisattva's story, with particular attention to his devotion to the *Lotus Sutra* and the relics of his teacher, the miraculous response of the universe to his extreme act of devotion, and the joyous approval of those who witnessed it.

The *Lotus Sutra* provided not only the template for autocremation, by showing readers how and why it might be performed, but also the liturgy. Self-immolators chanted the chapter about the Medicine King as they enacted it, thus making the scripture into a kind of performative speech. But although they drew on the sutra for inspiration, the biographies of self-immolators are by no means formulaic and repetitive; rather, in their variety, they make explicit some aspects of self-immolation that are only suggested by the scripture, such as the power of the act to convert people to Buddhism and to save sentient beings.

The *Lotus Sutra* tells us that the Medicine King was so inspired by the sutra's teaching that he wished to attain buddhahood, which he aimed to do by cultivating austerities. Having practiced diligently for twelve thousand years and attained an advanced level of meditation, he resolved to make offerings (Skt. *pūja*, Ch. *gongyang* 供養) to the buddha who had taught him and to the *Lotus Sutra*. First, he began meditating and magically produced a rain of flowers and incense. But he considered this offering to be inferior to the donation of his own body. The *Lotus Sutra* then describes his preparations in a way that was to echo through later accounts of autocremation in China:

Straightway then he applied [to his body] various scents, candana, *kunduruka*, *turuṣka* [two kinds of frankincense], *pṛkkā* [trigonella], the scent that sinks in water, and the scent of pine-tar; and he also drank the fragrant oils of campaka-flowers. When a thousand two hundred years had been fulfilled, he painted his body with fragrant oil and, in the presence of the Buddha Pure and Bright Excellence of Sun and Moon [Candrasūryavimalaprabhāsaśrī], wrapped his body in a garment adorned with divine jewels, anointed himself with fragrant oils, with the force of supernatural penetration took a vow and then burnt his own body.[1]

Thus the sutra describes how the bodhisattva doused himself in fragrance, drank scented oil, and wrapped his anointed body in an oil-soaked cloth. He made a vow (presumably stating his intention and identifying the recipients of the donation of his body) and then ignited himself. The light of his burning body reached innumerable other world systems. The buddhas of these realms were much impressed and praised his autocremation as "a true dharma offering to the Thus Come One." The enthusiasm of the buddhas for the Medicine King's autocremation was an element of the chapter that caught the attention of his Chinese imitators, who regarded it as an unequivocal endorsement of self-immolation.

By burning their bodies as prescribed by this chapter of the *Lotus Sutra*, Chinese monks (and nuns, too, although I have not translated any of their biographies here) took on the role of the devoted bodhisattva.[2] Some were careful to mimic his consumption of incense and oil and the wrapping of the body in oil-impregnated cloth that preceded his autocremation; some burned themselves in front of stupas or images or before large audiences. Evidence of their success in emulating his example was manifested, if not by the "world system shaking in six ways," then at least by lights and signs in the sky, by miraculous trees growing in their cells or at the site of the act, by dreams and portents, and by their relics.

The biographies often choose to highlight the sense of awe experienced by those who witnessed acts of autocremation, but we know from other sources that there were a variety of reactions to such performances. There were voices of criticism and revulsion from the community at large as well as from within the Buddhist establishment, as we learn from one of the biographies, when the monks of one monastery heard of their companion's intention to burn himself: "some castigated him, while others praised him." Some people considered that self-immolation was no more than suicide: an inauspicious death that was not capable of generating merit. Others claimed that the model of the bodhisattva Medicine King was appropriate only for laypeople to imitate and that monastics, whose vows included not killing, should not offer their bodies. By doing so, they would destroy an opportunity for laypeople to acquire merit through donations to the monastic community, which is considered a major "field of merit" in the Buddhist tradition. It was even asserted that killing oneself also meant terminating the lives of the many minuscule parasites (the so-called eighty thousand worms) that inhabit the human body.

As we shall see, autocremation in China could often take the form of a well-advertised performance, ritually staged in front of an emotional audience. The fact that some monks occasionally had to resort to more furtive ways of offering their bodies suggests that self-immolators were sometimes faced with active opposition to their plans.

Chinese Buddhists seemed to understand that self-immolation operated according to the mechanism of "stimulus–response" or "sympathetic resonance" (*ganying* 感應), a paradigm that was all-pervasive in every aspect of medieval thought.[3] The miracles that occurred before, after, and during the acts of auto-cremation described here indicated that these actions were stimulating (*gan*) a response (*ying*) from the cosmos, thus proving that autocremation was effica-cious and hence "right." Far from being a disrupting force, self-immolation could thus be interpreted as an act that was completely in harmony with the universe in which medieval people lived.

The paradigm of *ganying* offers us a way to make sense of the materials here. But in order to apply this model, we need to bear in mind that *ganying* can oper-ate at several levels simultaneously. First, in human society, interactions be-tween inferior and superior (typically between rulers and their subjects) are predicated on the rulers responding to the needs of their people. This aspect of *ganying* may help us understand why emperors and officials treated autocrema-tors with such reverence in death: they could not afford to ignore or disparage the sincerity of their actions, lest they be seen as violating the cosmic and hu-man order.

Second, *ganying* determines the relationship between the realm of humans (*ren* 人) and heaven (*tian* 天). It is understood that human actions and emotions can and do cause cosmic response and transformation. Acts that are the most sincere because they are selfless—acts such as self-immolation—cause the cos-mos to respond in accordance with the petitioner's intention. We see examples of this in accounts of self-immolators who burned themselves to bring rain or to end famine or other human disasters.

Third, the relationship between beings and the Buddha was conceived of in China as one determined by *ganying*. In Mahayana sutras such as the *Lotus*, Chinese Buddhists found the idea that buddhas and bodhisattvas were capable of assuming different forms and manifesting among humans in response to their needs. Thus there are frequent hints, and sometimes overt declarations, that self-immolators were in fact advanced bodhisattvas who had manifested in order to teach the dharma in a way appropriate to the age. But self-immolation also offered a way of becoming a buddha, a response to the stimulus of the self-less offering that was promised in the *Lotus* and other Mahayana texts.

I have translated seven biographies of monks who burned themselves in emulation of the Medicine King. The first six are from an important collection of monastic biographies, *Biographies of Eminent Monks* (*Gaoseng zhuan* 高僧傳), compiled by the monk Huijiao 慧皎 (497–554). These biographies are found, together with those of other self-immolators, in the "self-immolation section" (*wangshen pian* 亡身篇), one of ten rubrics covering the religious specialties of monks under which Huijiao organized his collection. The last biography is from *Biographies That Broadly Extol the Lotus* (*Hongzan fahua zhuan* 弘贊法華傳), compiled by Huixiang 慧祥 (d. after 667), a collection of biographies of devo-tees of the *Lotus Sutra* in which self-immolators are again grouped together.

After the biographies, I also have translated Huijiao's "critical evaluation" (*lun* 論) from the self-immolation section of *Biographies of Eminent Monks*.

The first biography is that of Fayu 法羽 (d. 396), who is the earliest known autocremator. His premeditated and publicly staged performance may have been based on the kinds of devotion that he had worked on in his earlier career. The biography notes that his master was particularly diligent in the practice of austerities and the cultivation of *dhūta* (*toutuo* 頭陀) in which he trained his disciple. The term *dhūta*, which literally means "to cast off," denotes ascetic practices such as eating only once a day, sleeping in the open, and not lying down to sleep—all of which were designed to free one from attachment to one's body. In these early medieval biographies, self-immolators are often described as having been trained in *toutuo*, which suggests an association with these particular modes of physical practice. But the term *toutuo* probably does not refer strictly to the standard lists of twelve or thirteen ascetic practices known from the canonical sources, since it often seems to be used in the larger and vaguer sense of "austerities" in general.

The biographies show that the autocremation of a monk could be advertised, thus drawing huge crowds and large amounts of donations. Why would laypeople want to witness an autocremation or to give alms on that occasion? Clearly, self-immolation was thought of as an act capable of generating large amounts of religious merit. The laity gave material goods in the expectation of seeing spiritual rewards at a later date. They wanted to be present at the offering itself so that they could form good karmic connections with the autocremator, who was thought to be accelerating along the bodhisattva path toward buddhahood. The biographies stress the diversity of the audience: aristocrats, commoners, monastics, and laity all came to witness the astonishing deeds of autocremators.

Preparations for autocremation could be quite elaborate and time-consuming, even lasting for several years. Huiyi, for example, changed his diet, first "abstaining from cereals," later consuming oil of thyme, and finally eating only pills made of incense. The biography stresses that although this diet made him physically feeble, he was still able to exercise sound judgment. In the biographies of Huiyi, Sengqing, and Faguang, we find abstention from grain paired with the ingestion of oil and incense, thus preparing the body as a suitably fragrant offering to the Buddha and mimicking the Medicine King's preparation for autocremation in the *Lotus Sutra*. But Huiyi's consumption of hemp and sesame also echoes the ingestion of elixirs by the transcendents described in texts such as *Biographies of Divine Transcendents* (*Shenxian zhuan* 神仙傳) by Ge Hong 葛洪 (284–363).[4] The procedure has much in common with the dietary practices adopted by Huiyi's Daoist contemporaries. Especially noteworthy is the presence of "incense pills" in Buddhist materials, as Daoist texts called for the similar making of pills and pellets out of mineral and vegetable drugs.[5]

The miracles associated with some acts of autocremation (the appearance of miraculously intertwined firmiana trees, Sengming's fingernail relic, apparitions of flowers, magical water, mobile images, and so on) do not map precisely onto any episodes recounted in the *Lotus Sutra* chapter. Rather, they emerged out of a larger world of the medieval Chinese imagination in which the *Lotus Sutra* was but another element alongside others, with antecedents both Buddhist and indigenous. We can see, for example, that the merit of Sengming's self-immolation was shared tangibly with others, in the form of the magic water from the pond. His ability to heal also hints at his identification with the Medicine King. Thus we observe a tendency to extrapolate from the *Lotus Sutra* and to make explicit in practice themes and ideas that are only hinted at in the text.

Read together, these biographies demonstrate the range of religious imagination that was brought to bear on the question of how to interact with buddhas and bodhisattvas and how, ultimately, to become like them. They show one of the ways in which medieval Chinese incorporated the richness and complexity of Buddhist cosmology into a religious landscape that was already teeming with life, both human and nonhuman. The critical evaluation by Huijiao shows some of the ways in which the Buddhist institution in medieval China made sense of the extreme actions of some of its members.

FURTHER READING

The foundational studies of self-immolation in medieval China were written in the 1960s by Jacques Gernet, "Les suicides par le feu chez les bouddhistes chinois de V^e au Xe siècle," *Mélanges publiés par l'Institute des hautes études chinoises* 2 (1960): 527–58; and Jan Yün-hua, "Buddhist Self-Immolation in Medieval China," *History of Religions* 4 (1965): 243–65. While somewhat dated, these remain significant works of scholarship. Jean Filliozat wrote an article in response to Gernet in which he discussed some of the Indian antecedents to the practice: "La mort voluntaire par la feu et la tradition Bouddhique indienne," *Journal asiatique* 251 (1963): 21–51. The most extensive study of Chinese Buddhist self-immolation is now James A. Benn, *Burning for the Buddha: Self-Immolation in Chinese Buddhism* (Honolulu: University of Hawai'i Press, 2007). I have also published a detailed study of a single case of autocremation, James A. Benn, "Written in Flames: Self-Immolation in Sixth-Century Sichuan," *T'oung Pao* 92 (2006): 117–72, and I discuss self-immolation in the context of apocryphal Chinese Buddhist scriptures in "Where Text Meets Flesh: Burning the Body as an 'Apocryphal Practice' in Chinese Buddhism," *History of Religions* 37 (1998): 295–322.

THE PSEUDO-QIN 偽秦 MONK FAYU 法羽 (CA. 352–396) OF PUBAN 蒲坂

Fayu was from Jizhou 冀州.[6] At fourteen, he left home and became a disciple of Huishi 慧始 [dates unknown]. [Hui]shi established a practice of austerities and the cultivation of *dhūta*. [Fa]yu, being energetic and courageous, deeply comprehended this method. He constantly aspired to follow the traces of the Medicine King and to burn his body in homage [to the Buddha]. At that time the illegitimate Prince of Jin 晉, Yao Xu 姚緒 [fl. late fourth century], was occupying Puban.[7] [Fa]yu informed Xu of his intention. Xu said, "There are many ways of entering the path; why do you choose only to burn your body? While I dare not firmly oppose it, I would be happier if you would think twice." But Yu's intention was resolute. Next he consumed incense and oil; he wrapped his body in cloth and recited the "Chapter on Abandoning the Body" [*Sheshen pin* 捨身品]. At its conclusion, he set fire to himself. The religious and laity who witnessed this were all full of grief and admiration. At the time he was forty-five years old.

[*Gaoseng zhuan* 50.404c11–18]

THE SONG MONK HUISHAO 慧紹 (424–451) OF ZHAOTI SI 招提寺 IN LINCHUAN 臨川[8]

Huishao's family [of origin] is unknown. When he was a child and his mother gave him fish or meat to eat, he vomited immediately, but he ate vegetables with no hesitation, and thereafter his diet was completely vegetarian. At seven, he left home and became a disciple of Sengyao 僧要 [dates unknown]. He was zealous and exemplary in his practice of austerities. Later, he followed [Seng]yao to Zhaoti si in Linchuan, where he secretly nurtured the idea of burning his body. He hired some people to cut firewood, which he had stacked up in the East Mountain [Dongshan 東山] grottoes to a height of several meters.[9] In the middle [of this pyre] he opened a niche just large enough for his own body.[10] Then he returned to his monastery to say farewell to [Seng]yao. [Seng]yao begged him not to go through with his plan.

On the day of the autocremation itself, he held a great ceremony for the eight precepts [*baguan* 八關] on East Mountain.[11] He said good-bye to his good friends. That day the whole region came flocking. The crowds of people, carts, horses, and those bringing offerings of gold and jewels were incalculable. During the first part of the night, religious ceremonies were performed, and [Hui]shao himself took part in the procession of incense.

After the offering of incense, he took a torch and set fire to the firewood. He got inside the niche, sat down, and began to recite the chapter on the "Original

Acts of the Medicine King" [*Yaowang benshi pin* 藥王本事品].[12] The crowd could now no longer see [Hui]shao but realized that he had already left them. Their prostrations not yet complete, they turned to where the firewood was. Although the firewood was completely aflame, the crowd could still hear the sound of his recitation. When the fire reached his forehead, they heard him chant "one mind" [*yixin* 一心], and with those words he passed away.[13] Then the whole assembly saw a star the size of a dipper descend straight into the smoke and suddenly rise into the sky. The witnesses all declared that this was [an emissary of] the Celestial Palace 天宮 come to fetch [Hui]shao.[14] Only after three days was the firewood completely burned out.

Just before the time of his death, [Hui]shao had told his fellow-disciples, "A firmiana tree [*wutong* 梧桐] will grow in the spot where I burn my body. Don't let anyone cut it down." Three days later one indeed sprang up there. [Hui]shao's autocremation took place in the twenty-eighth year of the Yuanjia period [451]. He was twenty-eight years old. [Hui]shao's master Sengyao was also pure and reverent, elegant and virtuous. He died at that monastery at the age of 160.

[*Gaoseng zhuan* 50.404c19–405a7]

THE SONG MONK HUIYI 慧益 (D. 463) OF ZHULIN SI 竹林寺 IN THE CAPITAL

Huiyi was from Guangling 廣陵.[15] When he was young, he left home and followed his master to Shouchun 壽春.[16] During the Xiaojian period of the Song [454–456] he arrived in the capital [Jiankang 建康] and resided at Zhulin si 竹林寺. He diligently practiced austerities, and he vowed to burn his body. When his fellow monks heard of this, some castigated him while others praised him. In the fourth year of Daming [460], he began by abstaining from cereals [*queli* 卻粒] and ate only sesame and wheat. In the sixth year, he stopped eating wheat and consumed only oil of thyme.[17] Sometimes he also cut out the oil and ate only pills made of incense. Although the four gross elements [of his body] became feeble, his spirit was clear and his judgment was sound.

Emperor Xiaowu 孝武 [r. 454–464] had a profound regard for Huiyi and respectfully inquired [as to his intentions]. He dispatched his Chief Minister Yigong 義恭, Prince of Jiangxia 江夏 [413–465], to the monastery to reason with him.[18] But [Hui]yi would not go back on his vow. On the eighth day of the fourth month of the seventh year of the Daming reign period [May 11, 463], he prepared to burn himself.

He set up a cauldron full of oil on the southern slope of Zhong shan 鐘山.[19] That morning, he mounted an oxcart drawn by humans and was going from the monastery to the mountain. But then he realized that the emperor was not only the foundation of the people but also the patron of the three jewels [*sanbao* 三寶].[20] He wanted to enter the palace under his own strength, but when he reached the Yunlong gate 雲龍門, he could no longer proceed on foot. He sent a messenger to say, "The man of the Way, Huiyi, who is about to abandon his body, is at the gate and presents his farewells. He profoundly hopes that the Buddha dharma may be entrusted [to his majesty]." When the emperor heard his message, he was upset and immediately came out to meet him at the Yun-long gate. When [Hui]yi saw the emperor, he earnestly entrusted the Buddha dharma to his care, then he took his leave. The emperor followed him. Princes, concubines, empresses, religious, laity, and officials flooded into the valley. The robes that they offered and the treasures that they donated were incalculable.

Huiyi now entered the cauldron, lay down on a little bed within it, and wrapped himself in cloth. On his head he added a long cap, which he saturated with oil. As he was about to apply the flame to it, the emperor ordered his chief minister to approach the cauldron and to try to dissuade him. [Yigong pleaded], "There are many ways to practice the path; why must you end your life? I wish you would think again and try a different track." But Huiyi's resolve was un-shakable and he showed no remorse. He replied, "This feeble body and this wretched life, how do they deserve to be retained? If the mind of Heaven and the compassion of the sage [i.e., the emperor] are infinite, then my wish is merely that twenty people [be allowed to] leave home." An edict ordering these ordinations was immediately issued.[21] [Hui]yi took up the torch in his own hand and ignited the cap. With the cap ablaze, he cast away the torch, put his palms together, and chanted the "Chapter on the Medicine King." As the flames reached his eyebrows, the sound of his recitation could still be clearly dis-cerned. Reaching his eyes, it became indistinct. The cries of pity from the rich and poor echoed in the dark valley. They all clicked their fingers [in approval]; they intoned the name of the Buddha and cried, full of sorrow.

The fire did not die down until the next morning. At that moment, the em-peror heard the sound of pipes in the air and smelled a strange perfume that was remarkably fragrant. He did not return to the palace until the end of that day. In the night he dreamed that he saw Huiyi, who came striking a bell. Again [the monk] entrusted to him the Buddha dharma. The next day, the em-peror held an ordination ceremony. He ordered the Master of Ceremonies to give a eulogy for the funeral service. At the place of the autocremation was built Yaowang si 藥王寺 in an allusion to [Huiyi's recitation of] the "Original Acts."

[*Gaoseng zhuan* 50.405b2–c1]

THE SONG MONK SENGQING 僧慶
(437–459) OF WUDAN SI 武擔寺 IN SHU 蜀

Sengqing's surname was Chen 陳, and he was from Anhan 安漢 in Baxi 巴西.[22] His family had been members of the Way of the Five Pecks of Grain [*wudoumi dao* 五斗米道] for generations.[23] When [Seng]qing was born, he awakened [to the truth] on his own. At thirteen, he left home and resided at Yixing si 義興寺. He cultivated chastity and wished to see the Buddha. He began by sacrificing three fingers and finally vowed to burn his body. Gradually he stopped eating grains and consumed only fragrant oil. On the eighth day of the second month of the third year of the Daming period [March 27, 459], west of Wudan si 武擔寺, at the walls of Shu 蜀, facing an image of Vimalakīrti [Jingming 淨名] that he had made himself, he burned his body in homage.[24] Prefect Zhang Yue 張悅 [fl. mid-fifth century] personally came and witnessed it.[25] [No matter whether] religious or lay, traveler or resident, everyone left the city empty [and went to attend the autocremation]. Passing clouds gathered and a heavy rain was falling gloomily when suddenly the sky cleared and fine bright weather returned. [The witnesses] saw something like a dragon come out of the pyre and leap into the sky. At the time [Sengqing] was twenty-three. The Governor of Tianshui 天水, Pei Fangming 裴方明 [fl. mid-fifth century], had his ashes gathered and erected a stupa for them.[26]

[*Gaoseng zhuan* 50.405c2–10]

THE QI 齊 MONK FAGUANG 法光
(447–487) OF LONGXI 隴西

Faguang was from Longxi in Qinzhou 秦州.[27] While he was still young, he had faith. When he was twenty-nine he left home. He diligently practiced *dhūta* and did not wear silk.[28] He refrained from the five grains and ate only pine needles. Later he vowed to burn his body, and from then on he ate pine resin and drank oil for half a year. On the twentieth day of the tenth month of Yongming of the Qi 齊 [November 21, 487], in Jicheng si 記城寺 in Longxi 隴西 [in present-day Shaanxi], he piled up firewood to burn his body in fulfillment of his former vow. As the flames reached his eyes, the sound of his recitation could still be heard. When it reached his nose, it became indistinct. He passed away peacefully. He was forty-one years old.

At the same time, around the end of the Yongming reign period [483–493], in Shifeng 始豐 District there was a *bhikṣu* called Facun 法存, who also burned his body in homage.[29] The Prefect of the commandery, Xiao Mian 蕭緬 [456–491], sent the *śramaṇa* Huishen 慧深 to erect a stupa for his ashes.[30]

[*Gaoseng zhuan*50.405c11–18]

THE QI MONK TANHONG 曇弘
(CA. 400–455) OF XIANSHAN 仙山 IN JIAOZHI 交趾

Tanhong was originally from Huanglong 黃龍.[31] When he was young, he practiced the precepts and mastered the Vinaya. During the Yongchu reign period of the Song 宋 [420–422], he wandered south and ended up at Tai si 臺寺. Later he also went to Xianshan si 仙山寺 in Jiaozhi 交趾.[32] There he recited the *Wuliangshou jing* 無量壽經 and *Guan wuliangshou jing* 觀無量壽經, and he consequently vowed to be reborn in the Pure Land [Anyang 安養].[33] One day in the second year of Xiaojian [455], he gathered up firewood on the mountain, then secretly entered [the pyre] and set fire to himself. His disciples rescued him and carried him back, although half his body had already been consumed by fire.

After a month, he showed some slight signs of improvement. But, later, one day when a nearby village held an assembly [*hui* 會] and invited all the occupants of the monastery, [Tan]hong again went into the valley to burn himself. By the time the villagers reached him he was already dead, so they added firewood to build up the fire, which did not burn out until the next day. That day, the villagers had seen [Tan]hong, his body golden in color, heading west riding a golden deer. He was in such a hurry that the villagers had no chance to exchange greetings with him. Not until then did the religious and laity realize [the meaning of] this miraculous event [*shenyi* 神異]. Together they gathered the ashes and bones and erected a stupa for them.

[*Gaoseng zhuan* 50.405c19–28]

THE LIANG 梁 MONK SHI SENGMING 釋僧明 OF SHIMEN SI 石門寺

Sengming's family name is unknown. His practice of the precepts was pure and correct, and *dhūta* was his specialty. He lived on Shimen shan, in Zhaoyi District 招義 in Haozhou 濠州.[34] On a rock on the peak of the mountain, he piled up bricks and constructed a heavenly palace of Maitreya and also made an image of Maitreya. He constantly recited the *Lotus* and deeply sought the marvelous meaning. When he recited, he always heard out of thin air the sound of fingers snapping and a voice saying "Excellent!" During the Tianjian period [502–519], he asked Emperor Wu of the Liang 梁武帝 for permission to burn his body. He did so repeatedly, on several occasions. When he heard it was permitted, on the rock in front of the Maitreya palace, he followed his earlier intention.

His body was completely reduced to ashes, leaving only one fingernail. The ground surrounding the site of the autocremation sank four or five feet and formed a pond. Two or three days later, flowers bloomed in it. Bright and luxuriant, they were unmatched in beauty. All those who drank the water were cured of disease. His disciples gathered up his ashes and made them into an image and also carved a smaller wooden image. They burned the nail relic again, took the ashes, and made a paste that they smeared on the image. It started moving, and wherever it went, flowers bloomed as large as pear or jujube trees. There were more than a hundred thousand of them. An inscription on a pagoda records all this in detail.

Also in Jiaozhou 交州, in Pinglu District 平陸縣, there was a layman whose personal and family names have been lost.[35] Because he chanted the *Lotus*, he aspired to the traces of the Medicine King. After he burned himself, the earth there swelled up in the shape of a human body. His father dug up the mound and, in it, found a golden statue as big as a man. He wanted to raise it so that it stood upright, but suddenly it disappeared.

[*Hongzan fahua zhuan* 51.24b27–c12]

HUIJIAO 慧皎

Critical Evaluation

Whoever possesses form values his body. Whoever thinks and feels treasures his life. For this reason, people eat fat, drink blood, ride sleek horses, and wear fine clothes in order to make themselves comfortable and feel pleasant.[36] People eat medicinal herbs and swallow elixirs, guard life, and nourish nature [yang-xing 養性] in order to extend their lives. This reaches a point that, out of stinginess, people would not pluck out a single hair even to benefit all under heaven or, out of meanness, they would not give up a single meal even to ensure [someone else's] survival.[37] This is terrible indeed! But here are people who possessed far-reaching awareness and penetrating vision. They offered themselves to feed others.[38] They innately realized that the three realms are merely a dwelling place during the long night and awakened to the fact that the four forms of birth are dreamlike and illusory spheres, that the essence [jing 精] and the spirit [shen 神] move rapidly like the wings of a gnat, and that the physical form and the skeleton are confined like jars of grain.[39] Therefore, they pay not the slightest heed to their bodies, from the crown of their head to their feet.[40] States and cities, wives and children, have been given away as though they were bundles of grass.[41] The current comment concerns these men.

Only for a duck did Sengqun abstain from water and give up his body; Sengfu stopped to help a mere boy, slicing open his own belly so that his life could be saved.[42] Fajin sliced his flesh in order to feed people, and Tancheng fed himself to a starving tiger. They all excelled in the way of aiding everyone [jianji zhi dao 兼濟之道].[43] These are cases of benefiting beings while being oblivious to oneself [wangwo liwu 忘我利物]. In the past, a prince discarded his body and the merit extended for nine kalpas.[44] [King Śibi] sliced his thigh and exchanged [the flesh] for a bird, astonishing sentient beings throughout the trichiliochosm.[45] People like this [i.e., bodhisattvas] have already become transcendent and have reached the ultimate.

Next then are [the cases of] Fayu up to Tanhong. They all reduced their bodies to ashes, discarding that which is treasured and loved. Some did it as a heartfelt aspiration for the Pure Land [Anyang 安養]; for others it was due to a vow to be reborn in Tuṣita Heaven [Zhizu 知足].[46] Thus a double firmiana appeared within a cell, or a single stellar mansion appeared in the sky.[47] These auspicious omens were brilliant and outstanding and appeared time after time.[48] But the teachings of the sage are not all the same; there are indeed differences between what is permitted and what is forbidden. If one performs great expedients for the good of sentient beings, acts in accordance with the times, and demonstrates myriad benefits [in the world], then [such actions] are not prohibited by the teachings. As the scripture says, "If you can burn a finger of your hand, or a toe, this greatly exceeds the gifts of whole states and walled cities."[49] But for ordinary monks who have left home, it is fundamental that they attract sentient beings with their "awe-inspiring deportment" [weiyi 威儀]; if they damage the body, they destroy the marks [Ch. xiang 相, Skt. lakṣaṇa] of a field of merit [Ch. futian 福田, Skt. puṇyakṣetra].[50]

Investigating this in order to discuss it, one finds that there are advantages and disadvantages. The advantages lie in being oblivious to the self [wangshen 忘身]; the disadvantages lie in breaking the precepts. This is why Nāgārjuna says, "Bodhisattvas who are new to practice are not able to practice fully all the perfections [Ch. du 度, Skt. pāramitās] simultaneously."[51] Some fulfilled the perfection of charity [Ch. tan 檀, Skt. dāna] but went against filiality [xiao 孝], such as the prince who gave himself to the tiger. Some fulfilled the perfection of wisdom but went against compassion, such as those who required others to give up food, and so on.[52] These all come from practices that are not yet completely perfected, so they are all unbalanced.

Also, the Buddha has said, "The body has eighty thousand worms, which share the same qi 氣 as the human being. When a person's life is over, the worms all die along with it."[53] This is why, after the death of an arhat, the Buddha permitted the burning of the body. But now we have people who burn themselves when they are not yet dead, and in some cases there may be a disadvantage as far as the life of the worms is concerned. In speaking of this, some might say, "If arhats are worthy of entering flames, what is so unusual about an ordinary person doing likewise?" Others might say, "Those who enter flames have previously already cast away their lives, and using their spiritual and intellectual powers, only then do they burn themselves." This being so, bodhisattvas who have attained the stage of the clan [Ch. xingdi 性地, Skt. gotrabhūmi] also have not yet escaped receiving a physical body as karmic retribution.[54] Some on occasion cast their bodies into a mass of flames. Others on occasion split up their bodies and divided them among people.[55] So we should know that in the discussion on killing worms, our investigation has not been completely detailed.[56]

Now, the three poisons and the four inverted views are the root of saṃsāra, while the seven factors of enlightenment and the eightfold path are the necessary way to true nirvana.[57] Surely it is not the case that it is necessary to burn the body to escape suffering? But if [bodhisattvas] are at the stage close to [the perfection of] forbearance [ren 忍], then they condescend to mingle their traces with ordinary people. Some on occasion have cast away their bodies for the benefit of beings. Then the words of my discussion do not apply to them. But when it comes to followers who are ordinary people, because their study has not been extensive, ultimately they have not realized that one should spend one's whole life practicing the Way. Why have they thrown away their bodies and lives? Some wished to be famous for a moment, others that their fame might be transmitted for ten thousand generations. But at the point when the fire reached the firewood, remorse and fear [within their minds] began to reinforce each other. As they had broadly publicized [their intention to burn themselves], they were ashamed of compromising their integrity, and they had to resolve to go through with their autocremation, vainly inflicting ten thousand sufferings on themselves. These cases are not discussed under the rubric of *yishen*.

The eulogy [*zan* 贊] says:[58]

> If a person can stiffen his will [*zhi* 志], then metal and stone cannot be considered hard.[59]
>
> Melting away what others consider important, they sacrificed it for that precious city,
>
> With its luxuriant vegetation and aromatic firmiana trees, and its fine floating purple buildings.
>
> Mounting the smoke with glittering colors, spitting out tallies, and bearing auspicious omens.
>
> They remain noble for a thousand years; their reputation is transmitted for ten thousand generations.
>
> [*Gaoseng zhuan* 50.405c29–406b13]

NOTES

1. Leon Hurvitz, *Scripture of the Lotus Blossom of the Fine Dharma* (New York: Columbia University Press, 1976), 294–95.

2. I discuss early medieval biographies of female autocremators in James A. Benn, *Burning for the Buddha: Self-Immolation in Chinese Buddhism* (Honolulu: University of Hawai'i Press, 2007), 42–45.

3. The most comprehensive discussion of *ganying* is now found in Robert H. Sharf, *Coming to Terms with Chinese Buddhism: A Reading of the Treasure Store Treatise* (Honolulu: University of Hawai'i Press, 2001), 77–133.

4. On this collection, see Robert Ford Campany, *To Live as Long as Heaven and Earth: A Translation and Study of Ge Hong's Traditions of Divine Transcendents* (Berkeley: University of California Press, 2002).

5. See, for example, *Taishang lingbao wufuxu* 太上靈寶五符序 (*DZ* 388, 2.2b–3a), which describes how to make pills out of the "five wonder-plants" (pine resin, sesame, pepper, ginger, calamus), in *The Taoist Experience: An Anthology*, ed. Livia Kohn (Albany: State University of New York Press, 1993), 152–53.

6. Jizhou was northeast of present-day Lucheng District in Shanxi.

7. Yao Xu was a paternal uncle of the Tibetan ruler Yao Xing 姚興, known as Emperor Wenhuan huangdi 文桓皇帝 of the Later Qin 後秦, which ruled North China from 384 to 417. See *JS* 117–18.2975–3006.

8. Linchuan was a commandery in Yangzhou 楊州 and was located just west of present-day Linchuan. Zhaoti si is not known from other sources.

9. The East Mountain referred to here is presumably not the mountain of that name near present-day Fuzhou, but a mountain in or close to Yangzhou.

10. *Kan* 龕 originally designated the niche for an image. By the tenth century, it had come to mean "coffin," perhaps partly by association with autocremators, in whose biographies the term is often used, as here, to designate the space within the pyre. For a Song definition of the term, see *Shishi yaolan* 釋氏要覽 (*Essential Readings for Buddhists*), comp. Daocheng 道誠 (fl. 1017), *T* 2127, 54.307c.

11. The eight precepts commonly taken by laypeople are (1) not to kill; (2) not to steal; (3) not to engage in ignoble (sexual) conduct; (4) not to lie; (5) not to drink alcohol; (6) not to indulge in cosmetics/jewelry, dancing, or music; (7) not to sleep on fine beds; and (8) not to eat after noon.

12. Fascicle 6 in Kumārajīva's translation of the *Lotus*, *Miaofa lianhua jing* 妙法蓮花經 , *T* 262, 9.52a–55a; and fascicle 9 in Dharmarakṣa's translation, *Zheng fahua jing* 正法花經, *T* 263, 9.125a–127a.

13. Kumārajīva's translation of the *Lotus* contains the phrase *yixin qiufo* 一心求佛 (seek the Buddha with a unified mind [9.53a25]); Dharmarakṣa's version contains the phrases *yong yixin gu wuyou kuhuan* 用一心故無有苦患 (employ the one mind and there will be no suffering [9.125b25]), and *dang yixin si* 當一心思 (one ought to think with a unified mind [125c25]).

14. "Celestial Palace" perhaps implies the Pure Land, or else Tuṣita Heaven, where the future Buddha, Maitreya, currently resides.

15. Guangling was close to present-day Yangzhou in Jiangsu.

16. Shouchun is present-day Shou District in Anhui.

17. The Three editions and the Palace edition read 酥油 (butter) for 蘇油 (oil of thyme), but since this compound seems not to be attested before the late seventh century, this reading is less likely. See *Gaoseng zhuan* 405n13.

18. Liu Yigong 劉義恭 was the fifth son of Emperor Song Wudi 宋武帝 (r. 421–422).

19. Zhong shan (Bell Mountain), now known as Zijin shan 紫金山, is northeast of the Song capital, close to the Yangzi River.

20. The three jewels are the Buddha, Dharma, and Saṃgha.

21. Elsewhere, the *Biographies of Eminent Monks* records that a monk named Fajing 法鏡 was one of those twenty monks who was ordained as a consequence of Huiyi's autocremation. See *Gaoseng zhuan* 50.417b24.

22. Baxi was north of present-day Nanchong District in Sichuan.

23. The "Way of the Five Pecks of Grain" was a somewhat pejorative term for the Way of the Celestial Masters (Tianshi dao 天師道), founded in Sichuan after Zhang Daoling 張道陵 received a revelation from Laozi in 142 C.E.

24. Shu refers to present-day Chengdu, Sichuan. The biography of Daowang 道汪 (d. 465) records that in late 464 or 465 he became the abbot of Wudan si. He had been active in Chengdu for some time before becoming the abbot, and it is likely that he knew Sengqing. See *Gaoseng zhuan* 50.371c.

25. Zhang Yue's appointment as Prefect of Yizhou in 456 is noted in *SS* 6.119. See also *SS* 84.2131. He was also a patron of Daowang. See *Gaoseng zhuan* 50.371c18–20.

26. Tianshui is present-day Tianshui District in Gansu. For a biography of Pei Fangming, see *SS* 45.1382–84.

27. Present-day Longxi, between Lanzhou and Tianshui in Gansu.

28. On the ascetic practice of avoidance of silk for monks' robes, see John Kieschnick, "The Symbolism of the Monk's Robe in China," *Asia Major*, 3rd ser., 12 (1999): 9–32.

29. Shifeng is present-day Tiantai in Zhejiang.

30. Xiao Mian was a nephew of the Qi Emperor Gaodi 高帝 (r. 479–482). For his biography, see *NQS* 45.794–95. The monk Huishen is not known from other sources.

31. Huanglong is in present-day Chaoyang, Liaoning.

32. Jiaozhi is the present-day Tonkin region in the north of Vietnam.

33. The sutras he recited are the *Sutra of Immeasurable Life*, T 360; and the *Sutra on the Contemplation of the Buddha of Immeasurable Life*, T 365.

34. Zhaoyi is present-day Fengyang District in Anhui.

35. Jiaozhou is present-day Cangwu District in Guangxi.

36. "Riding sleek horses and wearing fine clothes" alludes to *Analects* 6/4: "The Master said, 'When Chi was proceeding to Qi he had fat horses to his carriage and wore light furs. I have heard that a superior man helps the distressed but does not add to the wealth of the rich'" (James Legge, *The Chinese Classics: With a Translation, Critical and Exegetical Notes, Prolegomena, and Copious Indexes* [1935; repr., Taibei: SMC, 1991], 1:185–86).

37. "Pluck out a single hair" is from *Mencius* 13.26: "Mencius said, 'The principle of the philosopher Yang was—"Each one for himself." Though he might have benefited the whole kingdom by plucking out a single hair, he would not have done it'" (James Legge, *The Works of Mencius* [New York: Dover, 1970], 464).

38. I have emended *zhan* 瞻 (look up at) and translated it here as *shan* 贍 (offer).

39. It is possible that *gu* 穀 (grains) is an error for *ke* 殼 (shell), thus "the outer shell of a jar" rather than "jars of grain." The three realms (*sanjie* 三界) are the realm of desire (*yujie* 欲界), the realm of form (*sejie* 色界), and the realm of formlessness (*wusejie* 無色界). The "long night" (*zhangye* 長夜) refers to saṃsāra. The four forms of birth (*sisheng* 四生) are *taisheng* 胎生 (*jarāyu-ja*), or birth from the womb (humans, animals); *luansheng* 卵生 (*aṇḍa-ja*), or birth from the egg (birds); *shisheng* 濕生 (*saṃsveda-ja*), or birth from moisture (insects); and *huasheng* 化生 (*upapādu-ja*), or birth by transformation (those who dwell in the heavens and hells).

40. This allusion is to the *Mencius*: "The philosopher Mo loves all equally. If by rubbing smooth his whole body from the crown to the heel, he could have benefited the kingdom, he would have done it" (Legge, *Works of Mencius*, 464–65). According to Mencius, both Yangzi and Mozi went too far—one to the point of selfishness, the other to the point of indiscriminate love—but Huijiao appears to side with Mozi here. My thanks to Chen Jinhua for pointing out where Huijiao's sympathies lay in this case.

41. This allusion is to the *Lotus Sutra*, which extols self-immolation thus: "Even if one were to give realms and walled cities, wives and children, they would still be no match for it. Good man, this is called the prime gift. Among the various gifts, it is the most honourable, the supreme. For it constitutes an offering of Dharma to the thus come ones" (T 262, 9.53b; Hurvitz, *Scripture of the Lotus Blossom*, 295). On the offering of children, see also Hubert Durt, "The Offering of the Children of Prince Viśvantara/Sudāna in

the Chinese Tradition," *Journal of the International College for Advanced Buddhist Studies* 2 (1999): 147–82.

42. On Sengqun, Sengfu, and other self-immolators mentioned by Huijiao, see Benn, *Burning for the Buddha*, 19–53, 205–9. I follow the Yuan and Ming editions here in reading *zhi* 止 (stop) for *xin* 心 (mind).

43. This allusion is to the *Mencius*: "When the men of antiquity realized their wishes, benefits were conferred on them by the people. If they did not realize their wishes, they cultivated their personal character, and became illustrious in the world. If poor they attended to their own virtue in solitude; if advanced to dignity they made the whole kingdom virtuous as well" (13.9; Legge, *Works of Mencius*, 453).

44. This reference is to the Buddha in a former life, when as Prince Mahāsattva, son of King Mahāratha, he offered his body to a tigress. His self-sacrifice accelerated his bodhisattva career, shortening it by nine kalpas. This popular *jātaka* is discussed in Benn, *Burning for the Buddha*, 25–27.

45. This reference is to the *jātaka* of King Śibi, who gave his flesh in exchange for a pigeon. On the sources, see Étienne Lamotte, *Le traité de la grande vertu de sagesse de Nagarjuna* (*Mahāprajñāpāramitāśāstra*) (Louvain-La-Neuve: Université de Louvain, Institut orientaliste, 1944–1981), 1:143n.1. For a discussion of the story, see Reiko Ohnuma, "The Gift of the Body and the Gift of the Dharma," *History of Religions* 37, no. 4 (1998): 323–59.

46. Anyang is one of the Chinese names used for Sukhāvatī, the Pure Land of Amitābha. Zhizu, usually rendered Doushuai tian 兜率天, is Tuṣita Heaven, fourth of the six heavens in the realm of desire and the place whence the future Buddha Maitreya will descend. Although technically not a "Pure Land," a number of medieval Chinese Buddhists vowed to be reborn there. See, for example, the biography of Daoan 道安, in *Gaoseng zhuan*, 50.358c21.

47. The text here reads *guan* 舘 (mansion, celestial constellation) rather than the Chinese for "star."

48. The double firmiana and the appearance of a star refer to the biographies of Sengyu and Huishao, respectively.

49. *Lotus Sutra*, T 262, 9.54a13–14.

50. A field of merit is an object or a person to whom one should direct religious practice in order to accumulate merit. The most important are the three jewels of Buddha, Dharma, and Saṃgha. The body of a monk as a field of merit is obviously intended here.

51. This appears to be a paraphrase of *Da zhidu lun*, T 1509, 25.179c25–26: 若新行菩薩. 則不能一世一時遍行五波羅蜜.

52. I suspect that there is a reference here to a *jātaka* in order to parallel that of Prince Mahāsattva, but so far the allusion escapes me.

53. This is perhaps a paraphrase of a passage in *Shisong lü* 十誦律, T 1435, 23.284a–b.

54. During the second stage of the bodhisattva career, in which the practitioner determines his future path, he performs the practices of the *śrāvaka*, *pratyekabuddha*, or the bodhisattva.

55. I follow the Three editions and the Palace edition here in reading *ti* 體 for *hai* 骸 (skeleton).

56. I follow the Three editions and the Palace edition here in reading *mo* 莫 for *jing* 竟.

57. The three poisons are greed, hatred, and delusion. The four inverted views are that existence is permanent, joyful, possessed of a self, and pure. The seven factors of enlightenment are (1) *zefa* 擇法, correctly evaluating the teaching; (2) *jingjin* 精進, making effort at practice; (3) *xi* 喜, rejoicing in the truth; (4) *qing'an* 輕安, attaining pliancy; (5) *nian* 念, keeping proper awareness in meditation; (6) *ding* 定, concentrating; and (7) *xingshe* 行捨, detaching all thoughts from external things. The eightfold path consists of (1) right view, (2) right thought, (3) right speech, (4) right action, (5) right livelihood, (6) right effort, (7) right mindfulness, and (8) right concentration.

58. Like the *lun*, the *zan* (historical judgments in verse that appear appended to eight of the ten *lun* in the *Gaoseng zhuan*) derive from the conventions of earlier secular historiography. Fan Ye 范曄 (398–445) first gave these verses the name *zan* and added them to the end of his critical evaluations in *Hou Han shu*. See Arthur Wright, "Biography and Hagiography: Hui-chiao's Lives of Eminent Monks," in *Silver Jubilee Volume of the Zinbun-Kagaku-Kenkyusyo* (Kyoto: Kyoto University, 1954), 391.

59. That is, if one is determined, one can break even metal and stone.

33. Divine Instructions for an Official

STEPHEN R. BOKENKAMP

During the years 363 to 370, Yang Xi 楊羲 (b. 330), a medium employed by a Southern gentry family, began to receive visits from a group of deities descended from the Heavens of Upper Clarity (Shangqing 上清).[1] In addition to instructing him in ways more advanced than those known to other Daoists, these deities ministered to the spiritual needs of the Southern family that Yang served, answering such questions as "What is the fate of my ancestors in the spirit world?" "Which deities and practices are to be trusted?" "What must I do to better both my worldly and my posthumous destiny?" And as we shall see, Yang was presented with even more pressing personal questions. Before long, other aristocratic families came to address their own questions to Yang.

Thanks to Yang's literary skill and the satisfying answers he provided, a corpus of the poetic and prose transcripts of his visions and many of the scriptures he received from the deities came to be treasured by later Daoists. Among the beneficiaries was Tao Hongjing 陶弘景 (456–536), a member of a prominent Southern lineage who served the emperor as spiritual master and scholar. It was Tao who collected the fragments of Yang Xi's writings into the *Declarations of the Perfected* (*Zhen'gao* 真誥), on which the translation here is based.

The "Perfected" or "True Ones" (*zhenren* 真人) of the title refers to the class of deity that appeared to Yang. These deities, of the Heaven of Upper Clarity, distinguished themselves from the Transcendents (*xian* 仙) of earlier Chinese tradition. The term *zhenren*, which finds its source in the *Zhuangzi* and other texts, denotes that these are fully realized beings, possessed of incorruptible and fully etherealized immortal bodies. The Transcendents, Yang's informants reported, were of less durable physical constitution and populated lower heavens or inaccessible mountain peaks. Some of the Transcendents have, as the Perfected are fond of pronouncing, "not even achieved escape from death." A number of the Perfected, by contrast, far from having to worry about death, had never been human. Instead, these Perfected were stellar deities or female inhabitants of the mythical Kunlun Mountain in the West, where they served in the court of the Queen Mother. Other Perfected had once been human. Their careers are carefully mapped out in the text for the edification of those who might aspire to this status.

The Perfected who appear in the translations here are

- The Lady of the Left of Purple Tenuity, Wang Qing'e 王清娥, the twentieth daughter of the exalted ancient deity, the Queen Mother of the West
- The Perfected Consort of Nine Flowers of the Upper Palaces of Purple Purity, Lady An 安妃, a disciple of the Queen Mother of the West who had been promised to Yang Xi in spirit marriage
- The Lady of the Southern Marchmount, Director of Destinies of the Higher Perfected, Wei Huacun 魏華存, who during her human life had been one of the first Libationers of Celestial Master Daoism to come to the Jiangnan region. She has now ascended and serves as Yang Xi's divine teacher
- The Perfected of Purple Solarity, Zhou Yishan 周義山
- The Perfected of Pure Numinosity, Lord Pei 裴君
- Mao Gu 茅固, the Central Lord of Mount Mao, where Yang Xi often resided as he received his revelations
- Mao Zhong 茅衷, the Younger Lord of Mount Mao
- Wang Ziqiao 王子喬, a popular transcendent figure from the Han dynasty, now presented as the Perfected of Mount Tongbo

From the inclusion in this list of such popular ancient figures of the Transcendent cults as Wang Ziqiao, now reconfigured as Perfected, we stand to learn something of how Yang Xi constructed his teachings to augment their allure. Readers will want to pay particular attention to the deference with which Wang Ziqiao treats the central figures of Yang's revelations in the fragments translated here.

One sign of the elevated status of the Perfected is that, unlike the Transcendents of earlier scripture, these beings might not come into physical contact with the mundane world, even to the slight extent of handing over a writing or charm. Yang is told that the deities who descend to him may not express themselves in debased human writing. He is thus to act as an intermediary, writing out their words in his own excellent calligraphy. At the same time, the Perfected are particularly careful that he transcribe their words correctly. After each transmission, they look over what he has written and then "present" it to him as if they had written it themselves.

But we will not learn much more about these deities in the passages translated here. Instead, the exchanges granted to Yang Xi, who himself only seldom speaks, concern the problems of Yang's patron, Xu Mi 許謐 (303–373), a minor official at the imperial Jin court. As we shall see, Xu Mi was interested in certain features of Yang's revelations more than in others. In fact, the *Declarations of the Perfected* as a whole can be read as Yang Xi's efforts to convince Xu and his male family members and colleagues of the importance of leaving the workaday world of court and society to pursue the disciplines of self-perfection. Among the enticements that Yang and his Perfected offered were the prospect of merging, through nonsexual means, with a Perfected woman of tender age. Xu Mi was even told who his celestial bride was to be and was warned repeatedly to give up traditional Celestial Master methods of "merging qi" (*he qi* 和氣) intercourse without the exchange of fluids, to prepare himself for this higher form of union.[2] Also, as we will see, Xu Mi was told what rank he was to fill in the heavens upon his apparent "death." According to the documentary evidence we have, Xu Mi spent little ink inquiring about these things. His most immediate concerns lay elsewhere.

Xu Mi's reluctance was due not only to his attachment to official office. Xu was more than sixty years of age when these revelations took place; his wife had passed away; and his health was failing. He thus became particularly interested in what the Perfected characterized as "minor transcendent arts"—the restoration of sharp sight and hearing and the ability to turn white hair to black, thereby restoring lost youth—rather than the more exalted abilities promised by the Perfected.

The first fragments translated here were, according to Tao Hongjing, written by Yang Xi to show to Xu Mi. They date to 364, when Yang and his Perfected first approached Xu Mi with his glorious prospects. Already, though, we find that the Perfected must reassure Xu Mi that his human failings can be corrected.

The second translation comes from a collection of revealed materials that Xu Mi copied out into booklet form. In fact, the section of the *Declarations* from which this was taken contains several such collections of transcriptions. Issues of physical health occupy by far the greater space in these pamphlets, as indeed such questions must have occupied the mind of Xu Mi.

In line with the science of his day, Xu Mi understood his failing health to be the result of the weakening and departure of spirits that were responsible for the orderly functioning of his body. Within each person there were, for example, three *hun* 魂, a sort of light, ethereal "soul" whose wanderings were responsible for dreams or the gradual memory loss of senility. There were also seven *po* 魄, earthbound "souls," which were in charge of physical functions. Of particular concern to Xu Mi was his failing eyesight, the responsibility of spirits called "lads" or, in English, "pupils."

To understand these fragments, modern Western readers should also be aware that the ancient Chinese believed that vision and hearing were interactive processes. That is, sharp sight required the emission of beams of light from the eyes to meet the physical forms that could then be apprehended. This was accomplished by the deity of the eyes. The ears similarly emitted qi, though the gods making this possible could not be so easily detected.

FURTHER READING

For more on Yang Xi's relations with Xu Mi and on Tao Hongjing's editorial procedures, see Stephen R. Bokenkamp, *Ancestors and Anxiety: Daoism and the Birth of Rebirth in China* (Berkeley: University of California Press, 2007). For general accounts of the Shangqing scriptures, see Kamitsuka Yoshiko 神塚淑子, *Rikuchō dōkyō shisō no kenkyū* 六朝道教思想の研究 (Tokyo: Sōbunsha, 1999); and Isabelle Robinet, *La révélation du Shangqing dans l'histoire du taoïsme*, 2 vols. (Paris: École française d'extrême-orient, 1984). Some of Robinet's insights into the nature of Yang Xi's Shangqing scriptures are available in English in her *Taoist Meditation: The Mao-Shan Tradition of Great Purity*, trans. Julian F. Pas and Norman J. Girardot (Albany: State University of New York Press, 1993). For an account of the composition, social position, and diffusion of Yang Xi's writings, see Michel Strickmann, "The Mao-shan Revelations: Taoism and the Aristocracy," *T'oung-pao* 63 (1977): 1–63; and for insights into the Daoism of Tao Hongjing, see Strickmann, "On the Alchemy of T'ao Hung-ching," in *Facets of Taoism: Essays in Chinese Religion*, ed. Holmes Welch and Anna Seidel (New Haven, Conn.: Yale University Press, 1979), 123–92. Strickmann's most comprehensive work on the revelations granted to Yang Xi, however, remains *Le taoïsme du Mao chan: Chronique d'une révélation* (Paris: Collège du France, Institut des hautes études chinoises, 1981). Wang Jiakui 王家葵, *Tao Hongjing congkao* 陶弘景叢考 (Ji'nan: Qilu shushe, 2003), gives the most comprehensive account of the life and scholarship of Tao Hongjing. Yoshikawa Tadao 吉川忠夫, *Rikuchō dōkyō no kenkyū* 六朝道教の研究 (Tokyo: Shunjūsha, 1998), despite its general title, is a collection of essays on the *Zhen'gao* by those who participated in the famous Kyoto reading circle on the text. The only complete translation of the *Zhen'gao* in any language, representing the culminating product of the same reading group, is Yoshikawa Tadao 吉川忠夫 and Mugitani Kuniō 麥谷邦夫, trans., *Shinkō kenkyū: Yakuchū hen* 真誥研究: 譯注篇 (Kyoto: Kyōto daigaku jinbun kagaku kenkyūjō, 2000). A solid study of some aspects of the *Zhen'gao* and its history, strongest on the subject of Yang Xi's relations with his clients, may be found in Zhong Laiyin 鍾來因, *Changsheng busi de tanqiu: Daojing Zhen'gao zhi mi* 長生不死的探求—道經真誥之謎 (Shanghai: Wenhui, 1992).

Yang Xi 楊羲

Declarations of the Perfected (Zhen'gao 真誥)

From Yang Xi's Transcriptions

On the night of the twenty-sixth of the sixth month, eight Perfected beings descended. There were: (1) the Lady of the Left of Purple Tenuity,[3] (2) the Perfected Consort of Nine Flowers of the Upper Palaces of Purple Purity, (3) the Lady of the Southern Marchmount,[4] the Director of Destinies of the Higher Perfected, (4) the Perfected of Purple Solarity, (5) the Perfected of Pure Numinosity, (6) the Central Lord of Mount Mao, and (7) the Younger Lord of Mount Mao. There was also a person who was very young but of formal demeanor. He wore a lotus crown, a scarlet robe, and a sword belted to his side. I had never seen him before. I imagined that this was the Perfected of Mount Tongbo, Wang Ziqiao. He spoke quite a bit about the affairs in Golden Court Mountain, but most of what he said I could not understand. He was respectful toward the Lady of Purple Tenuity and the True Consort of Nine Flowers, in all cases saluting with folded hands before his breast as he spoke and referring to himself as their subordinate.[5]

The Lady of Purple Tenuity said: "Yesterday I visited the Palace of Pure Vacuity with [Senior Lord Mao] Shushen. They were collating the merits and demerits of the Perfected and Transcendents. Recently, they summarily dropped from the roles forty-seven people while only elevating three. But I saw your name-slips and all is well for you just now. Xu —— has gotten his name on the list of earls.

[Tao's note: Xu —— is Senior Officer Xu (Mi). Yang presented this to him and thus did not record his given name.][6]

"I was not aware that [Xu's] excellence was this great. He cleanses his heart and diligently advances to the extent he is capable given his endowments. His heart is pure and he exhausts his mental powers, all as carefully as if walking on ice[7] or through fire. If he can persist in this manner, the Perfected will not flee from him, nor will the Way of Transcendence be hidden from him. He must block only lascivious thoughts, and we [Perfected] will be able to appear to him. You may show him this [communication] in broad outline."

The Middle Lord [Mao] said: "The rank of earl is only a lower official position. The elder [Xu] will have further prospects. East of the River[8] I have never met anyone so earnest in pursuit of the Dao. But he must not, through reliance on this promise of an earl's [position], forget the Dao."

The Lady of the Southern Marchmount said: "Reckless action is an illness of virtue; vainglorious display brings disaster to the body. Stagnation is the beginning of loss; shame is the key [for evil to enter] the human frame. If [Xu] can banish these four flaws, then he may begin to learn of the Dao, and after this, numinous carriages with singing axles will follow in a matter of days. One whose mind is given over to carnal excess should not practice the Dao of the Higher Perfected. Those people dropped from the roles in the Palace of Pure Vacuity have [for this very reason] just now begun to be interrogated and punished. They were transported to the Three Offices for investigation.[9] You must be cautious about this!"

The Younger Lord [Mao] said: "Senior Officer Xu [Mi] should avoid proximity to corpses or attending mourning rites; [otherwise] within the year we will have a display of Transcendent Marquis Xu in a similar [coffin]!" With that, he laughed loudly.

The Perfected of Pure Numinosity said: "Since [Xu] gave up his stinginess, has his income differed? If he does not eradicate his self-abasement and shame, registers of life will not be written for him. What Senior Officer Xu has already eliminated should be again eliminated and again . . ."

The Lady of the Southern Marchmount said: "The Eastern Chamberlain, Director of Destinies [Greater Lord Mao], is well aware of the kindness and seriousness of Senior Officer Xu. When the King of the Xiaoyou Heaven yesterday inquired, 'And where is this person? What Dao does he practice?' the Eastern Chamberlain responded that he was a person from his own neighborhood.[10] He added, 'He is bright within and of true uprightness, though he mixes outside in worldly affairs. He is of good quality.' Since these words express [the Eastern Chamberlain's] true opinions, it seems that [Xu Mi] does have the makings of an earl."[11]

On the twenty-seventh of the sixth month, Lady Wang of Purple Tenuity then composed verses to be shown to Xu [Mi]:

Calm, distant, the Perfected talent,	蕭邈眞才
Reflects what is within; harmonizes with what lies without.	內鏡外和
Consider what emanates from his [cinnabar] field:[12]	曾參出田
As red as his red heart!	丹心同丹
White threads thrice reduced,	素絲三遷
Protected by a square head.	來庇方頭

[Tao's note: When broken apart and reassembled, the characters of the last four lines form the words *xuan si* 思玄 (contemplating the mystery), which is the Senior Officer's byname.][13]

His name enregistered in the Grand Ultimate,	録名太極
With golden writings in the Eastern Continents,	金書東州
He lets hang his garment for the sevenfold crossing;[14]	褰裳七度
And rests in concentration in the cavernous towers.[15]	耽凝洞樓
Since his inner entanglements have dissolved,[16]	內累既消
His *hun* and *po* are compliant.[17]	魂魄亦柔

He keeps them within tirelessly,	守之不倦
Concentrating them with ease.	積之勿休
Since the five difficulties have been transcended,	五難既遣
He will be enfeoffed earl and later made marquis. . . .[18]	封伯作侯

On the twenty-ninth of the sixth month, the Perfected Consort of Nine Flowers bestowed the following writing:

"The sun is the concretion of rosy mist, and rosy mist is the essence of the sun. You have heard only of methods for ingesting the concretion of the sun but never of dining on the essences of rosy mist. The scripture for dining on mist is extremely secret, but the way of bringing down rosy mist is very simple. It is called the 'Shangqing Method for Bodily Emanating Jade Beams and the Reflections of Mist.'

"The eyes are the mirrors of the body; the ears are the doors of the physical frame. If one belabors sight, the mirrors dim. If one listens excessively, the doors are closed. I have a stone for polishing the mirrors and methods for reopening the doors. If you were able to penetrate to the myriad numinous beings and subtly investigate their cutoff resonances, would this do for you?

"The face is the courtyard of the spirits; the hair is the efflorescence of the brain. If one's heart is vexed, then the face becomes scorched; if the brain shrinks, then the hair turns white. This is because the essential unity is depleted within and the cinnabar ford [begins to] dry up. I have a scripture for [restoring] a youthful face and a method for returning white [hair to black]. Would this do for you?

"Essence is the spiritual [substance] of the human form, and understanding is a treasure of the body. If one belabors it, essence disperses. When one's enterprises come to an end, understanding dissolves. This is because age is followed by the depletion of *qi*, and decrepitude soon follows. I have a way for increasing essence and a scripture for extending understanding. Would this do for you?

"These four ways are inner writings of Shangqing, true stanzas that bring immediate results. I wish to show them to you to increase your luminous emanations. Once I have bestowed them on you, you may give them to [Xu Mi]."

I [Yang Xi] responded, "Yes, yes" and requested them [from her].

[*Zhen'gao, DZ* 1016, 2.2b7–6b5]

FROM XU MI'S COPIES OF YANG XI'S MANUSCRIPTS

THE PERFECTED OF PURE NUMINOSITY EXPLAINS THE *SCRIPTURE FOR TREASURING THE [BODILY] SPIRITS*

[Tao's note: The Senior Officer's copybooks were often given titles like this. This one refers to the matters concerning the eyes and ears, raised before. The following are miscellaneous explanations by various of the Perfected, as in the rest of the *Declarations of the Perfected*. People today call this the *Scripture for Treasuring the [Bodily] Spirits*, but that work was never released into the world! This is just a sheet of notes.]

When one sets his heart on the Perfection of the Dao and mysteriously contemplates the numinous, those in the hidden realms also thoroughly examine his intentions. If he has not yet cast aside outer difficulties, so that the false and the praiseworthy exist in equal measures, although in fact we are not able to return him to the age of the western elm,[19] we can still stimulate a mystical youthfulness. Even if one has been recalcitrant in the face of mystic encouragements, so long as the will is unshaken, even those with fallen teeth, wrinkled visages, and snowy caps of hair can be made into infants in a trice by my way. We inquire only into the quality of the will. The study does not reside in age or youth. We draw near only when we meet the proper person.

Those who wish to seek the Dao must first cause their eyes to be clear and their ears sensitive. This is the crux of the matter, since the ears and eyes are ladders in the search for the Perfected and the doors to the collection of numinous powers. One must establish unfettered [hearing and sight] and proceed [from an understanding] of their necessity. Now I have copied out this path [of practice] to show to you. You may put it into practice.

[Tao's note: This refers to an essential "path" (or "way") found in the *Scripture for Treasuring the [Bodily] Spirits*. This is why it says "copied out."]

The Dao said: You should often use your hands to press, for three times nine repetitions, on the small indentations behind your two ears. Then, with the fingers and palms of your hands, massage from the tops of the cheeks, circling the ears, for thirty repetitions. For this massage, only the number of repetitions is mandated, not the time of day. Once you have finished this, do not fail to rub the hands up and across the forehead, beginning between the brows and ending in the hairline, for three times nine repetitions. As you do this, swallow saliva from the corner of your mouth. There is no set number of times for this. The eyes of [one] who practices this unfailingly will clarify themselves, and, in a year, one will be able to write at night. You can also practice this secretly when others are around; just do not say what you are doing.

Within the small indentation behind the eyebrows is the Bureau of the Six Reaches of Upper Prime. It is responsible for transformations in the radiance of the eyes. It harmonizes the glow and keeps the essential beams, grows the orbs and communicates with the Pupil,[20] and is responsible for the protection and refinement of the gods of the eyes. This is an Upper Way practiced by the Perfected when in activity or at rest. One name for it is the *Inner Scripture of the Perfected for Activity and Repose*.[21] A saying among the Perfected states: "If you wish to write at night, you should practice Activity and Repose." The reason that the Perfected are able to see in all directions and cause the eight dawn mists to gleam and glow is because they have repeatedly clarified [their sight] with the Activity and Repose.

Below the eyes and just above the cheeks are the Treasured Chambers for Issuing Luminosity. The ultimate way for returning to infancy is the technique of collecting brightness by using the hands to circle the ears. The circling opens the conduits and distributes the blood so that wrinkles do not arise, the efflorescence of the eyes reflect with a mysterious brightness, the essences are mixed, and the spirits [are] replete. Few aging humans do not begin [the practice] with the ears and eyes. Also, the signs of aging first issue from beside the eyes.

When one massages up the forehead with the hands, one visualizes the fetus within, the sun and moon both aglow, and the Upper Prime joyous.[22] Repeat three times nine, beginning with the eyebrows, and stop when the repetitions are complete. This is called "Paying Court with the Hands to the Three Voids." It is a way to solidify the brain and strengthen the hair.

You should rub upward on the four sides of your head with your two hands, following the hair and reaching to the topknot.[23] You should do this repeatedly. This will cause the blood in your head to circulate and will not allow winds and damps to settle. Once you are finished, press on the four corners of your eyes with your hands for two times nine repetitions. You will feel a perception of brightness. This is a way to inspect the spirits of the eyes. If you practice it for a long time, you will be able to see the hundred numinous beings.

[Tao's note: Whenever one practices this way together with all the various matters in this chapter, there is a definite precedence and order. I have written all of this in my other volume, Secret Instructions for the Ascent to Perfection (Dengzhen yinjue 登真隱訣), and will not repeat it here.][24]

When one diligently pursues this practice, it is best that the hands do not leave the face while it is being done. This is the means by which I became Perfected, and I still have not abandoned the practice. If you wish to practice this way, gold should be given when you take your oath. The amount of gold depends on the sincerity of the person receiving the practice. Do not act in vain by undertaking the practice [without the oath and faith offering].[25]

A Perfected Official said: "If you wish to hear of the Activity and Repose, gold should be written [as faith offering] into your oath document. The method should not be transmitted to the wrong persons. The way came from the Most High Scripture for Treasuring the [Bodily] Spirits. Originally, this scripture was not transmitted in the world, but those destined to become Perfected do on occasion have access to it. The method for reverting white [hair to black] is entirely found within."

[Yang Xi's note: Although there is no set amount for the faith offering, to receive this, one should offer two golden rings.][26]

The Lady of Purple Tenuity's written instructions follow:[27]

When you awaken from a night's sleep, you should always knock your teeth together nine times and swallow saliva nine times. When finished, use your hands to press the sides of your nose, massaging, left and right, up and down, several tens of times while silently incanting:

The Most High, luminous in the four directions:	太上四明
The nine gates issue essences,	九門發精
The ears and eyes mysteriously penetrate,	耳目玄徹
Reaching the Perfected and the Numinous.	通眞達靈
The mysterious tower in the midst of the heavens	天中玄臺
Lets flow qi with even modulations.	流炁調平
Exalted women in ranks like clouds;	驕女雲儀
The Eye Pupils gleam and glow.	眼童英明
Aural efflorescence resonates clearly.	華聰晃朗
The hundred affairs are faint but clear.	百度眇清
Protect and harmonize the Upper Prime[28]	保和上元
Who roams the Nine Ramparts.[29]	徘徊九城
Roots are planted in the five viscera,	五藏植根
While the ears and eyes give birth to themselves.	耳目自生
The tower of heaven is shadowed and pure,	天臺鬱素
Its pillars and beams are not bent.	柱梁不傾
The seven po are bathed and refined;	七魄澡鍊
The three hun rest at peace.	三魂安寧
The fetus walks hand in hand with the Phosphors—[30]	赤子攜景
All are joined with ME.	輒與我并
Any who dare block my ears and eyes	有敢掩我耳目
Will be destroyed by the Most High with his flowing bell.[31]	太上當摧以流鈴
The myriad evils are destroyed;	萬凶消滅
All I wish will be accomplished.	所願必成
Sun and moon guard the gates[32]	日月守門
My heart stores the five planets.	心藏五星
That which this Perfected Luminary incants—[33]	眞皇所祝
Listen reverently to its multifarious reverberations!	羣響敬聽

You should always incant like this upon awakening, not missing a single time. Your way of Perfection will thus be complete. We [Perfected Ones] still perform this [incantation], though we no longer recline to sleep. Instead we perform it while seated.

This is a superior method from the *Most High Scripture for Treasuring the [Bodily] Spirits*. This incantation will render your hearing and vision acute, strengthen and broaden your understanding, [and] stabilize your breathing so that your nose does not run and your eyes do not water. You will hear even distant echoes from all directions, and your visage will be that of a young lad. It will control your *hun* and restrain your *po* and drive off the myriad demons. Your seven orifices will be unobstructed, and your coloration will be healthy. This is the wondrous Way of the Perfected for Activity and Repose. The reason it is called "for Activity and Repose" is because we constantly practice it.

Once you have completed the incantation, swallow saliva nine times while rubbing your face and across your eyes until your skin is slightly hot. You should make this a constant practice and keep count each time.

[Yang's note: These instructions were dictated on the night of the twenty-third day of the sixth month in the third year of the Surging Peace reign period (= 365). On that very evening, you (Xu Mi) told me that there were many humans who lack good hearing and sight and asked that I request these methods. That night those who descended to me brought me these instructions.]

[Tao's note: This was recorded by Yang Xi himself. Senior Officer (Xu Mi) was more than sixty years of age, and his eyesight was failing. This is why he made the request of Yang. Since Yang did not wish to refer specifically (to Xu Mi's age), he wrote, "Many humans lack good hearing and sight."]

The Perfected of Pure Numinosity, Lord Pei, also announced: "A Daoist whose hearing is bad will easily lose control when practicing the Way of the Yellow and Red Breaths."[34]

[Tao's note: This admonition was meant to warn the Senior Officer.]

The Lady of Purple Tenuity said: "When you comb your hair, you should use many strokes so that the blood and *qi* are stimulated to flow freely and vapors and damp are dispersed. Change your combs frequently. Be careful in their use. You also should not let your hair down."

Lady An of the Nine Blossoms announced the following for [Xu Mi's] use:

The *Scripture of Registries of the Grand Ultimate* says: "When combing your hair, face the regnant direction.[35] As you begin to comb, quietly intone the following:

Dark flowerings of the muddy pellet,	泥丸玄華
Preserve essence and endure.	保精長存
To the left is the hidden moon;	左為隱月
To the right is the root of the sun.	右為日根
In the six directions[36] they are clarified and refined;	六合清鍊
The hundred spirits [of the body] receive blessings.	百神受恩

"Once you have finished this incantation, swallow saliva three times. If you are able to constantly practice this method, your hair will not fall out but will become more luxurious. While it is true that you should constantly change combs and should use many strokes in combing, do not comb to the point of pain. Nor should you allow your servant to comb your hair too vigorously. If you maintain these procedures, your blood and fluids will flow freely and the roots of your hair will remain strong and firm."

The Lady of Purple Tenuity gave instructions as follows:

Through opening the sides of the Floriate Canopy, the Celestial Perfected are pacified. Through entering the valley of the mountain stream, the fountain of the celestial mountains becomes full. In this way, the void spirits will appear, and the myriad demons will be physically destroyed. This is what is called "raising the head to harmonize with the Celestial Perfected; lowering the head to stabilize the mountain spring."

[Tao's note: The "floriated canopy" is also called the "flowery court."]

Now, the "Celestial Perfected" are the two points between the brows right next to the bridge of the nose. The "mountain spring" is the spot right below the nose, the origin point of the body. The two points to the side of this are "the valleys of the mountain stream." The "flowery court" is just below the eyebrows. These are all the bridge to good vision.

For instance, the "Celestial Perfected" reside in the upper chambers for summoning spirits. If at sunrise, noon, and sunset you swallow saliva thrice times nine while at the same time pressing these spots thrice times nine, you will summon spirits to your body, perfect your vision, and block perversities from entering. You must practice this three times a day.

The Lady of Purple Tenuity told me, "Though someone is mortally ill and on the brink of death, the common physicians of this world only know how to acupuncture the body; they know nothing of 'acupuncturing' the valleys of the mountain springs. This is their big mistake!"

[Tao's note: This paragraph was added after Yang Xi received a query in a letter from Xu Mi.]

As you press on the spot, incant as follows:

Open up the Celestial courts;	開通天庭
Grant me long life.	使我長生
With penetrating vision over great distances,	徹視萬里
And my *hun* and *po* returned to youthfulness,	魂魄返嬰
I will destroy ghosts, drive off demons,	滅鬼却魔
And bring in the myriad spirits.	來致千靈
I will ascend to the Most High	上升太上
And join the sun in longevity.	與日合并
Joining the Perfected Ones,	得補眞人
My image and name will be ranked with theirs.	列象玄名

During the time of Duke Zhuang of Chu 楚莊公 [trad. r. 613–591 B.C.E.], Market Chief Song Laizi 宋來子 would sweep out the market every day.[37] After this had been going on for a long time, a beggar suddenly appeared in the market. Throughout the day, he begged for food and sang this song:

The flowers of the Celestial Courts bloom in tandem;	天庭發雙華
The mountain spring clears out dark perversities.	山源彰陰邪
In the clear dawn, they saddle their celestial steeds,	清晨按天馬
And come to visit the home of the Grand Perfected.	來詣太眞家
The Perfected has no need to hide,	眞人無那隱
Since he has destroyed the myriad demons.	又以滅百魔

No one in the market could make any sense of this song. But Song Laizi was suddenly enlightened: This must be a Transcendent being! So, while he still could not understand the verses, he immediately made this beggar his master. Abandoning his official post, he followed the beggar for thirteen years. As a result, the Master bestowed on Song Laizi the arts of midlevel transcendence. Today, Song Laizi is within the Central Marchmount.[38] The "beggar" was Feng Yanshou 馮延壽, the Perfected of the Western Marchmount.[39] He was a scribe in the court of King Xuan of the Zhou [trad. r. 827–782 B.C.E.]. [As to the song:] the hands are the "celestial steeds," and the "mountain springs" are the spots below the nose.

[*Zhen'gao, DZ* 1016, 9.6a1–10b4]

NOTES

1. These events transpired some years after the Jin dynasty lost Northern China to invaders between 311 and 317. After this, the capital of the Jin was moved to present-day Nanjing. Yang Xi and his patrons, the Xu family, lived near the Southern capital. This region was also known as Jiangnan (south of the [Yangzi] River).

2. Yang Xi was a libationer of the Celestial Master lineages of Daoism, but he seems to have developed certain innovations on traditional beliefs. Thus, the Shangqing scriptures he produced eventually led to a reform of Celestial Master practices.

3. Purple Tenuity is the name of a Chinese constellation near the Pole Star. I have numbered the participants in this meeting for clarity.

4. The Southern Marchmount was one of five holy mountains spread throughout the realm. These mountains were held to have particular associations with one of the five phases and to house deities responsible for the safety of that quarter of the realm.

5. This passage previously appears, in a slightly different form, in *Zhen'gao* 1.15a10–15b4. Tao Hongjing's note to the passage explains that the reason for this repetition is that this particular retelling was meant for Xu Mi's eyes and thus relates only the elements of conversation related to Xu. Presumably, the earlier relation of the scene was for Yang Xi himself.

6. That is, he politely does not use his patron's given name.

7. The text has "water" 水 instead of "ice" 冰. The two characters are very similar and this must be a copyist's error. I have restored the idiom.

8. This geographical term refers to the eastern stretches south of the Yangzi River.

9.   The Three Offices of heaven, earth, and water were regarded as the underworld bureaus where human infractions of the living were adjudicated.

10. As Tao Hongjing notes, this means that Xu Mi dwelt in Jurong County, under the jurisdiction of Mount Mao, and not that they hailed from the same native place.

11. Tao notes that the copy he had of the text to this point was in Yang Xi's hand.

12. The three cinnabar fields—in the head and breast, and just below the navel—were held in Daoist practice to be central assembly points of the gods inhabiting the adept's body.

13. The byname was not normally used while a person was alive. While the way Xu Mi's name is constructed here is difficult to explain, it is necessary to give some account, since the resulting verse is so odd: "field" and "square head" refer to the top element of the character *si* 思. "Consider" alludes to the four strokes underneath this element, and "heart" is in fact the character itself. The word "thread" 糸 with the bottom three strokes removed and two strokes added to the top is "mystery" 玄.

14. According to Tao Hongjing, the term "sevenfold crossing" refers to the ritual "flying paces" conducted in vision along the stars of the Dipper.

15. Tao notes that the "cavernous towers" refers to the "cavern chamber" or bedroom. If he is correct, this line implies that Xu Mi is able to concentrate his spiritual powers and no longer practices the sexual rite of "merging *qi*."

16. This may refer to the death of Xu Mi's wife. Certainly the injunctions that he not mourn or "attend coffins" seems designed to take his mind off this recent loss.

17. The *hun* and *po* are important spiritual constituents of the human body. The former number three, and the latter number seven. The *hun*, yang in nature, are volatile and tend to fly out of the body, as during dreaming. The *po*, yin and watery in nature, tend to leak from the body. Since they share their nature with the earth, they are the most dangerous and often work for the body's return to earth in death. See Stephen R. Bokenkamp, *Early Daoist Scriptures* (Berkeley: University of California Press, 1997), 286–88.

18. I have elided, as did Tao Hongjing, a poem that appears again later in the text, several fragments of revelation, and the opening passages of the True Consort's revelation that describes the prospects of her merging her vital forces with Yang Xi in a sexless union.

19. I have not yet found the source of this image, but it clearly means "ageless youth."

20. The "Pupil" is visualized as a young boy, who activates vision.

21. The text here and directly below has *changju* 常居 (continual residence), but the title is given further on in the text as *qiju* 起居 (activity and repose), a phrase derived from a genre of court record of daily imperial activities. Since the Perfected explain the meaning of this latter title, I suspect that the first references to the title are copyists' errors.

22. The "fetus" is the transcendent embryo—a sort of "mini-me"—that adepts were taught to cultivate through meditation and *qi* ingestion. The sun and moon are part of the inner landscape, associated with the eyes. The Upper Prime is a deity found in the head. Although the objects of these visualizations are not described clearly here, they are in other of Yang Xi's texts. See Bokenkamp, *Early Daoist Scriptures*, 283–89, 326–30.

23. "Following the hair" in an upward direction makes sense once we realize that Chinese males wore their long hair tied up with a single topknot.

24. Three chapters of this work survive in the Daoist canon, *DZ* 421. Tao may be referring here to the material now found in the central chapter of the work.

25. Given examples found elsewhere in the *Declarations of the Perfected*, we can assume that this oath primarily involved the promise not to transmit the text.

26. This is not marked as Yang Xi's footnote. In Tao Hongjing's original text, Yang's own words would have been in ink of a different color. Our editions are uniformly printed in black, so this distinction is erased. I base my supposition on the content of this note. For Yang's request of golden jewelry as faith offerings on other occasions, see Stephen R. Bokenkamp, *Ancestors and Anxiety: Daoism and the Birth of Rebirth in China* (Berkeley: University of California Press, 2007), 138–42.

27. Tao Hongjing concludes from the arrangement of these fragments that Lord Pei and the Lady of Purple Tenuity appeared on the same evening. The date is given later.

28. The Upper Prime is the chief god of the head, the upper of the three primes of the human body.

29. The Nine Ramparts likely refers to the capitals of the Nine Heavens.

30. The Phosphors are glowing bodily spirits that have been rendered numinous by Shangqing practices. The usual number given is eight in each of the three registers of the human body: head, chest, and lower abdomen.

31. In Celestial Master Daoism, the Most High would be the deified Laozi. Yang Xi at times seems to accept the same explanation. At other times, the term is said to refer to another celestial god.

32. In Shangqing meditation practice, the sun and moon of the body are the eyes.

33. The term "Perfected Luminary" here likely refers to the practitioner himself or herself. It is a way of signaling to any maleficent forces that one is marked for Perfection and high station by virtue of the mere possession of this incantation.

34. The Way of the Yellow and Red Breaths is another name for the "merging of breaths," the Celestial Master sexual practice involving the exchange of *qi* rather than physical substances during intercourse. See Bokenkamp, *Early Daoist Scriptures*, 44–46.

35. The "regnant direction" is that direction of the compass determined by the one of the five phases that is dominant on any particular day.

36. The "six directions" are the north, south, east, west, up, and down. The incantation here seems to make a connection between brushing the hair and visual and aural acuity.

37. The point here is that this is a lowly occupation for the Market Chief. Sweeping was usually done by menials.

38. The five Marchmounts are prominent mountains associated with the five phases. The central mountain is Mount Song, in modern Henan Province.

39. The Western Marchmount is Mount Hua, in modern Shaanxi Province.

34. Tales of Strange Events

ROBERT FORD CAMPANY

Beginning by at least the third century B.C.E., and in much greater numbers from the late second to the early seventh centuries C.E., official-class literati wrote a huge number of accounts of phenomena whose one common trait was that they were deemed marvelous, strange, and incongruous. The vast majority of these accounts describe ordinary people's encounters with normally unseen denizens of the spirit world (from celestial deities to local gods, ghosts, demons, and ancestors), with humanlike animals and animal spirits or with religious adepts displaying extraordinary abilities. Perhaps as much as 80 percent of the original contents of these so-called accounts of anomalies (zhiguai 志怪) from the pre-Tang period has been lost, yet several thousand of the relatively short textual items survive, facts that give some idea of the enormity of zhiguai textual output and the depth of early medieval authors' and readers' interest in what these texts contain.

Modern scholars of Chinese literature have tended to approach these texts formalistically, seeing their narratological devices as the origins of fiction in China. The texts may, of course, be studied in that fashion, but their early medieval authors did not see themselves as makers of "fiction" in any modern sense. The zhiguai genre was, instead, a literature of record, an amassing of accounts of events deemed or argued to have actually occurred, in short, a type of case-based history. Each of the many texts of this genre (fragments of more than sixty such texts remain, with untold numbers having been lost) is a compilation of particular instances of human contact with the extraordinary. Authors compiled these cases from written works of other genres (ranging from histories, including regional or theme-specific histories now otherwise lost, to stele inscriptions) and, in at least a few instances, from oral sources and even personal experience. They did so, furthermore, in light of an old complex of ideas and institutions that saw the gathering and reportage of information to the throne—particularly information about local customs and sayings, and about anomalies of all kinds—as essential to the proper ordering of the world and the maintenance of sound government. The resulting literature was deemed lacking in formal sophistication, and some of its compilers felt the need to defend it from charges of frivolity and even of impropriety, the latter since it delved precisely into matters of "prodigies, feats of abnormal strength, natural disorders, and spirits" of which, famously, Confucius had not deigned to speak (*Analects* 7/20).[1]

If *zhiguai* texts are short on complex wordplay, however, they are rich in socially constructed and transmitted views of the cosmos and humanity's place in it relative to other classes of beings both up and down the hierarchy of kinds. They give a vivid sense of what it *felt like* to ordinary people to live in the imagined cosmos of the time, an animistic world thick with unseen beings dwelling not only in the wilds and margins but also, potentially, beneath the head of one's bed. They portray for us the religious world to which the organized religious movements of Daoism and Buddhism were responding in their texts and ritual protocols, and they make clear how widely distributed in society that religious world was. They come much closer than many of the works produced by those religions to illuminating the religious views, concerns, and activities of nonclerical members of the population, from rulers and high officials down at least to the level of local functionaries and, arguably, to that of many illiterate commoners as well.

None of this is to say that *zhiguai* compilations were neutral in their own embedded attitudes toward these topics. They were compiled from varying ideological vantage points and with varying persuasive agendas in mind.[2] The particular texts sampled here, which are among the most representative of the genre, constitute arguments for a particular view of the world and of humanity's place and obligations in it. That worldview, associated to some extent with the early medieval designation "the teaching of names" (*mingjiao* 名教), as opposed to its rival, the tendency toward "naturalness" (*ziran* 自然), is best seen in action in the patterns of narration and deed recorded in the narratives but can be summarized as the affirmation of a profound moral and taxonomic order that pervades the universe and regularizes (or should regularize) relations between the human and the nonhuman.[3] In these works, the amassing of empirical cases would go to show this lawlike regularity at work beneath the surfaces of things. First, then, these works imply, spirits really exist, and they severely punish any flouting of the rules of propriety; and second, spirits, although apparently mysterious and appearing at random, actually behave according to discernible principles. Even the obscure ways of demons, transformed animals, ghosts, and local gods would be revealed through these assembled cases to follow patterns, their apparent inscrutability a function of readers' lack of sufficient familiarity with the facts rather than anything intrinsic to the denizens of the unseen world.[4] Knowing the patterns allows humans to deal with spirits effectively and appropriately.

The particular *zhiguai* text drawn on most heavily in the selections presented here is *Records of the Hidden and Visible Worlds* (*Youming lu* 幽明錄)—records, that is, of instances in which these two worlds visibly and vividly intersected—attributed to Liu Yiqing 劉義慶 (403–444).[5] I have chosen it for three main reasons: (1) it was one of the three or four largest and most important such compilations of its time; (2) it deals, unlike some collections, with a very wide range of anomalous phenomena;[6] and (3) it has not received as much scholarly attention as some of its peer works have. The putative compiler, Liu Yiqing, was a nephew of the military founder of the Song 宋 (420–479), the inheritor of the princedom of Linchuan, and the holder of a succession of regional administrative offices. He is reported to have displayed conspicuous Buddhist piety late in his life. He is best known for having his name attached to a collection of sparkling, character-revealing anecdotes and reports of conversations known as, in Jack Chen's translation, *Recent Anecdotes from the Talk of the Ages* (*Shishuo xinyu* 世說新語), although that work exemplifies a naturalist ideology quite foreign to the one implied in *Records of the Hidden and Visible Worlds*. Several modern scholars have plausibly questioned Liu's authorship of *Recent Anecdotes*, attributing it instead to a circle of sophisticated intellectuals and writers summoned by Liu, disaffected under the militarist Song regime.[7] For our purposes, who compiled *Records of the Hidden and Visible Worlds* is less important than what the work reveals about religious thought, experience, and practice in the early fifth century. Rather than point this out myself in each case, I leave it to the reader to see what may be inferred on these matters from the following entries in the *Records* casebook.

Two independent attempts to rethink the significance of the pre-Tang *zhiguai* genre as a whole are Liu Yuan-ju 劉苑如, *Liuchao zhiguai di wenlei yanjiu: Daoyi wei chang di xiangxiang licheng* 六朝志怪的文類研究: 導異為常的想像歷程 (Taibei: Guoli zhengzhi daxue zhongwen yanjiusuo boshi lunwen, 1996); and Robert Ford Campany, *Strange Writing: Anomaly Accounts in Early Medieval China* (Albany: State University of New York Press, 1996). Sizable English translations of early *zhiguai* texts include Karl S. Y. Kao, ed., *Classical Chinese*

Tales of the Supernatural and the Fantastic: Selections from the Third to the Tenth Century (Bloomington: Indiana University Press, 1985); Gan Bao, *In Search of the Supernatural: The Written Record*, trans. Kenneth DeWoskin and J. I. Crump Jr. (Stanford, Calif.: Stanford University Press, 1996); Alvin P. Cohen, *Tales of Vengeful Souls: A Sixth Century Collection of Chinese Avenging Ghost Stories* (Taibei: Institut Ricci, 1982); and Robert Ford Campany, *Signs from the Unseen Realm: Buddhist Miracle Tales from Early Medieval China* (Honolulu: University of Hawai'i Press, 2012). Recent thematic and interpretive studies include Liu Yuan-ju 劉苑如, *Shenti, xingbie, jieji: Liuchao zhiguai di changyi lunshu yu xiaoshuo meixue* 身體, 性別, 階級: 六朝志怪的常異論述與小說美學 (Taibei: Zhongyang yanjiuyuan Zhongguo wenzhe yanjiusuo, 2002); Rémi Mathieu, *Démons et merveilles dans la littérature chinoise des Six Dynasties: Le fantastique et l'anecdotique dans le Soushen ji de Gan Bao* (Paris: Éditions You-Feng, 2000); Robert Ford Campany, "Ghosts Matter: The Culture of Ghosts in Six Dynasties *Zhiguai*," *Chinese Literature: Essays, Articles, Reviews* 13 (1991): 15–34, "Return-from-Death Narratives in Early Medieval China," *Journal of Chinese Religions* 18 (1990): 91–125, and "Two Religious Thinkers of the Early Eastern Jin: Gan Bao and Ge Hong in Multiple Contexts," *Asia Major*, 3rd ser., 18 (2005): 175–224; and Mu-chou Poo, "Ghost Literature: Exorcistic Ritual Texts or Daily Entertainment?" *Asia Major*, 3rd ser., 13, no. 1 (2000): 43–64. For introductions to the religious background that informs these tales, see Donald Harper, "Warring States, Qin, and Han Manuscripts Related to Natural Philosophy and the Occult," in *New Sources of Early Chinese History: An Introduction to the Reading of Inscriptions and Manuscripts*, ed. Edward L. Shaughnessy (Berkeley: Society for the Study of Early China and Institute of East Asian Studies, University of California, 1997), 223–52; and Mu-chou Poo, *In Search of Personal Welfare: A View of Ancient Chinese Religion* (Albany: State University of New York Press, 1998). Only after I had completed work on this chapter did I learn of a doctoral dissertation on *Youming lu*: Zhenjun Zhang, "Buddhism and the Supernatural Tale in Early Medieval China: A Study of Liu Yiqing's (403–444) *You ming lu*" (Ph.D. diss., University of Wisconsin–Madison, 2007). Zhang translates selected tales from the work and offers an interpretation that, unlike mine, heavily stresses its pro-Buddhist themes.

Records of the Hidden and Visible Worlds (*Youming lu* 幽明錄)

I

Around the first year of the Shengping period of the Jin [357], the family of Chen Su 陳素 of Yan District[8] was quite wealthy. The wife he had taken ten years earlier had not yet borne a son, so he wanted to take a concubine. His wife made sacrificial offerings and entreated the gods and afterward suddenly became pregnant. A woman of a neighboring commoner family also became pregnant at the same time. So Chen's wife bribed the neighboring woman, saying, "If I give birth to a male child, it will be Heaven's wish. If it's a female, and your child is a male, we will exchange the infants." They agreed on this.

The neighboring woman gave birth to a boy, and, three days later, Chen's wife was delivered of a girl, and so the infants were exchanged. Chen Su was delighted. He raised the boy until he was thirteen, when it was time to perform the offerings.[9] Now in Chen's household, there was an old woman who habitually[10] saw spirits. She said that she saw "the Commandery Governor" [Fujun 府君][11] enter first, come as far as the door,[12] and then stop; then she saw a mass of lesser spirits swarm around the altar and gobble up all the offering items. At this the father grew very suspicious, so he called in a person who could see ghosts and had him[13] watch as the offering was made again. His verbal description [of what he saw] completely matched the old woman's. Chen Su thereupon went within[14] and questioned his wife, who, out of fear, broke down and told him of the whole affair. With that, the boy was returned to his original family, and the girl was summoned back to Chen's.

[Youming lu 93 (LX 223); TPGJ 319.9]

II

Behind the home of Chen Qingsun 陳慶孫 of Yinchuan was a divine tree. Many people went there seeking blessings, so a temple was built, called "Temple to the Celestial Spirit" [tianshen miao 天神廟].[15] Now Qingsun had a black bull. The god said to him from midair:[16] "I am a celestial spirit [tianshen 天神], and I fancy this bull of yours. Unless you give it to me, I will kill your son on the twentieth day of the coming month." Qingsun said, "Human life is determined by allotted life span [ming 命], and allotted life span does not depend on you." On the appointed day, the boy indeed died. The god again announced, "If you do not give the bull to me, I will kill your wife in the fifth month." Still Qingsun did not sacrifice the bull. At the appointed time, his wife indeed died. Once more the god came and said: "If you do not give me the bull, I will kill you in the autumn." Still Qingsun did not give him the animal.

When autumn arrived, however, Qingsun did not die. The spirit [gui 鬼][17] then came and apologized, saying: "Sir, as a person your heart is upright. You will soon receive much good fortune. Pray do not mention this affair, for if Heaven and Earth should hear of it, my offense will not be taken lightly. In fact, you see, I had managed to get appointed as tree trunk in charge of [soul] ferryings under the Director of Life Destinies [Siming dushigan 司命度事幹],[18] and since it was your wife's and son's time to die anyhow, I did that only to try to cheat you out of some food. I hope in your deep forbearance you will overlook this. According to the [life] registers [luji 祿籍], you will live to the age of eighty-three, your family will be complete, and all will be as you wish. Spirits will bless and assist you, and I myself will act as your obedient servant." Then could be heard the sound of someone knocking his head on the ground.[19]

[*Youming lu* 162 (*LX* 243); *TPGJ* 318.21]

III

There was a spirit that lived under the pavilion at [the headquarters of] Houguan District. At the end of every year, the functionaries of the district would slaughter an ox as an offering to it. But when Wu Zeng 武曾 of Pei Commandery became the magistrate of the district, he ended this practice. After a year passed, Zeng was promoted to a military adjutant post. The spirit then came to him one night and asked, "Why do you not reinstate my meal?" His voice and appearance were quite hostile, and he reproached Zeng severely.

The functionaries therefore bought a bull on the roadside and joined in making an apology.[20] The spirit then departed.[21]

[*Youming lu* 208 (*LX* 255); *TPGJ* 294.19]

IV

An adjutant in Xunyang dreamed that a woman knelt before him and said: "The place where I was buried is close to water and is now flooded. If you grant me the favor of saving me from this condition, although I cannot make you rich or powerful, I can enable you, sir, to avoid misfortune." The adjutant replied, "What should I look for as a marker?"[22] The woman answered, "Beside the stream you will see a hairpin in the shape of a fish. That's where I am."

The adjutant looked around the next morning and did indeed find a ruined tomb. On top of it was a hairpin. He relocated the remains to a high, dry spot.

A couple of weeks later, the adjutant was riding [by carriage] across the east bridge. The bull [drawing his carriage] suddenly ran directly toward the water. Just as it was about to fall over the side of the bridge, it turned around, and so he avoided mishap.

[*Youming lu* 185 (*LX* 249); *Taiping yulan* 太平御覽, comp. Li Fang 李昉 (925–996) (facsimile reprint of Shangwu yinshuguan 1935 printing from a Song copy), 4 vols. (Beijing: Zhonghua shuju, 1992), 718.3a]

V

The son of Wang Ming 王明, a native of Donglai, resided in Jiangxi. Wang Ming had been dead a year when his form suddenly appeared and returned to his home. He ordered all his relatives and friends to be summoned for a talk about the affairs of life; then, for the rest of the day, he spoke with them, saying that the celestial court had granted him a temporary leave to return. When he had spoken to the point that it was time to leave, he tearfully asked for news of the village and was deeply affected by what he heard.

Then he said to his son: "It is a full year now since I left the human realm. I have missed gazing upon the mulberry and catalpa trees. I command you to come with me to look over the hamlet." As they walked, they passed by the temple to Deng Ai 鄧艾.[23] Wang Ming told his son to burn it down. The son was astonished, exclaiming, "When Ai was alive, he served as the East-Quelling General, and after his death he displayed some efficacy.[24] The commoners make offerings there to pray for blessings. Why should it be burned down?" The father angrily replied, "All Ai does now is polish armor in the armory,[25] his ten fingers practically worn away from the work. How could he be said to possess divinity?" Then he continued, "Even General-in-Chief Wang[26] is harnessed like cattle, driven and spurred to the point of exhaustion and death. Even Huan Wen 桓溫 [27] is used like a lackey. Both of them are in the earth prisons.[28] If they are this hard-pressed, how can they bring blessings to people? If you wish to seek abundant blessings, then here is all you need do: be deferential, agreeable, and completely loyal and filial, and do not be angry. Then goodness will flow to you without limit." He also instructed him to save up his fingernails, as these could be used after death to redeem him from [punishment for] sins.[29] And he had him erect a taller threshold, for if spirits entering people's homes to record their sins and errors trip over the threshold as they cross it, they will forget why they came.[30]

[*Youming lu* 216 (*LX* 258–59); *TPGJ* 320.9]

VI

The Temple to Deng Ai 鄧艾廟[31] was located in Jingkou 京口.[32] Above it was a thatch hut.[33] Now the Jin era North-Quelling General, Sima Tian 司馬恬,[34] while ill,[35] dreamed of an old man who told him: "I am Master Deng. My hut is rather dilapidated. Why not repair it for me, sir?" Afterward the general made inquiries and, realizing it was Deng's temple that had been indicated, had a tile hut built for him.[36]

During the Prosperous Peace period [397–402], there was an episode in which a man met a woman for a tryst on top of this god's altar. A serpent came and coiled itself around them numerous times.[37] When the members of the woman's family who had gone out searching for her finally found her, they made offerings of wine and meats. Only then was she released.

[*Youming lu* 61 (*LX* 213); *TPGJ* 318.19; *Yiyuan* 異苑 7.16. I note variants in the *Yiyuan* version]

VII

There was a certain ghost of a newly deceased man whose form was fatigued and emaciated. Suddenly he ran across another who had been a friend during life and had died almost twenty years earlier. The friend was plump and healthy. Upon inquiring after each other's welfare, when the friend asked, "How are you?" the newly deceased ghost replied, "I am unbearably hungry. If you know of any means [to get food], you should teach me your method." The friend ghost said, "This is very easy. All you need to do is create anomalous disturbances among people, and they will be terrified and will give you food."

The new ghost entered the eastern part of a large market town, where there was a family of pious Buddhists.[38] In an outbuilding in the western part of their living compound there was a grindstone. The ghost began pushing this grindstone, just as a person would. The master of the house told his children, "The Buddha has taken pity on account of the modest means of our household and has ordered a ghost to push the grindstone." So they carted in more grain and placed it there. Having worked until nightfall and ground several *hu* of grain, the ghost, exhausted, left. He cursed his friend ghost, saying, "Why did you trick me?" The friend said, "Go back and try again, and you will surely get something."

The ghost then headed out again, this time to the western part of the town, and entered a residence. This was a Daoist household.[39] Beside the gate of the compound was a pestle. The ghost lifted the pestle as would a person who was using it to pound. The householders here said, "Yesterday a ghost helped some-one [across town], and today it has come back to help us. We should cart in some grain for it." They had servants carry in baskets full of grain. By nightfall, the ghost was exhausted, and the family had given him nothing to eat. At dusk the ghost returned and furiously scolded his friend: "I am as close to you as if we were kin—closer than anyone else. How can you treat me like this? For two whole days I have helped people, and I have not received even one small serving of food or drink." The friend ghost replied, "Don't worry! One of those families worships the Buddha, the other serves the Dao. Their feelings are naturally hard to affect. This time when you go, you should look for a family of ordinary people and cause an anomalous disturbance there; you will then get something without fail."

The ghost went out again. Coming to a household with a bamboo pole across the gate, he entered by the gate. Through a window he saw a group of girls in-side the house, eating together. Entering the courtyard, he saw a white dog, which he picked up so that it would appear to be walking in midair. When the family members saw this they were frightened, saying that they had never ex-perienced such a strange thing before. A diviner said: "There is a guest seek-ing food. You should slaughter the dog and offer it in the courtyard along with sweet fruits, wine, and rice. In this way, you can ensure that there will be no further disturbances." The family did as this master instructed, and so the ghost obtained an abundant meal. From this time on, he continually caused anomalous disturbances, as the friend ghost had taught him to do.

[*Youming lu* 256 (*LX* 274–75); *TPGJ* 321.4]

VIII

An Kai 安開 was a vulgar shaman[40] from Ancheng. He was skilled in arts of illusion.[41] Whenever he was about to perform offerings to the gods, he would strike his drum, slaughter the three [kinds of] sacrificial animals, pile up firewood, light it, and then, when it was in full blaze, he would tighten his sash and enter the flames. The paper on which the petitions were written[42] would be entirely consumed in the flames, but Kai's body and clothing would remain just they had been before.[43]

Once when Wang Ningzhi 王凝之[44] was Governor of Jiangzhou,[45] An Kai, serving him[46] as he was about to go on a journey,[47] pretended[48] to arrange his hair for him, clasping onto it a lotus leaf instead of a cap. Wang was not aware of anything unusual about his "cap" until after he had taken his seat [at the altar],[49] when the lotus leaf suddenly appeared as such. Everyone seated there was astonished, but Wang was not aware of it.[50]

[*Youming lu* 102 (*LX* 268); *Fayuan zhulin* 61 [749b–c];
TPYL 687.6b–7a, 737.7b–8a]

IX

Huan Gong 桓恭 was an adjutant under Huan Anmin 桓安民. In front of the bed in his residence at Dantu 丹徒[51] was a small hole. When he examined it closely, he found it led to an ancient tomb, inside of which the coffin had rotted away. Whenever Huan took his meals, he would always put a bit of fish[52] and rice through the hole. He kept this up for an entire year.

Later on, he awoke from sleep one night to see a man standing before his bed. The man said, "It has been seven hundred years since I passed away. After I died, my line of descendants was cut off, so there was no one to continue making food offerings. But now that you, sir, have extended meals to me, I am moved beyond measure by your virtue. According to the register entry on you,[53] you are to be made Regional Inspector of Ningzhou." This did indeed later turn out to be the case.

[*Youming lu* 165 (*LX* 244); *TPGJ* 320.12]

X

In the Jin, during the reign of the Duke of Haixi,[54] there was a man whose mother died. His family was poor and lacked the means to bury her, so he transported her coffin deep into the mountains and resolved beside it to demonstrate his filial piety by constructing a burial mound,[55] not resting day or night. As the sun was about to set, a woman cradling a baby came there seeking a place to spend the night. For the next several nights, the filial son was not yet finished with his work, and the woman returned each time seeking [a place] to sleep. [Once] she slept beside the fire so that [the man noticed that] she was, in fact, a fox, and what she held was a black chicken. So the filial son beat them to death and threw them in the hole behind [the mound].

Next day, a man came and asked detailed questions about the whereabouts of any travelers who might have come that way the previous day and might have happened to spend the night there. The filial son answered, "There was only a fox. I killed it." The man said, "You have wantonly killed my wife! How can you speak of a 'fox'? Where is this 'fox' now?" So they went together to the hole and looked. The fox had become a woman, lying dead in the hole.

The man tied up the filial son and turned him over to a government office for punishment by death. The filial son told the magistrate, "This [man] is really a rogue demon. If you will only bring forth a hunting dog, you will know that he is a demon."[56] So the magistrate asked the man about matters of hunting, and whether he was a good judge of dogs. The man replied, "By nature I'm afraid of dogs and am not a good judge of them." So a dog was released. The man transformed into an old fox, which was shot to death. When they went to look at the woman, she had by then become a fox again.

[*Youming lu* 105 (LX 227); *Fayuan zhulin* (T 2122) 53:526b–c]

XI

Pang Qi 龐企 of Taiyuan, Governor of Luling, whose byname was Ziji 子及, personally told [the following story] of one of his own distant ancestors[57] an unknown number of generations ago. He was accused of a crime and imprisoned, but he was not the guilty party. Unable to bear the whipping,[58] he falsely confessed and submitted. When he was taken back to prison and [his confession] submitted [for penal action], he noticed mole crickets crawling about him. He said to them, "If only you had divine power and could deliver me from death, wouldn't that be fine?"[59] He then threw some rice down for them. When the crickets had eaten the rice, they departed. But soon they returned, and their bodies were now slightly larger. He thought this very peculiar, so he fed them again. This went on for several weeks[60] until the crickets were as large as pigs.

When the sentence was finally pronounced, it was for execution. That night, the crickets came and dug a large hole at the base of the wall, then severed his shackles, allowing him to go free. Much later he was pardoned, and so he survived.

This is why members of the Pang clan for generations have made sacrificial offerings [to crickets] in each of the four seasons along the city streets.[61] Later generations have been somewhat negligent; they no longer bother with offering foods specially prepared but simply cast down the leftovers from other sacrificial offerings as offerings to the [crickets]. They still do so today.

[*Youming lu* 159 (*LX* 242); *Chuxue ji* 初學記 (Beijing: Zhonghua shuju, 1962), 20 [493]; *TPYL* 643.9b; *Soushen ji* 20.11; *TPGJ* 473.18]

XII

In Jianghuai there was a woman who was very amorous by nature. Day and night, she never gave up thinking about sex. Once, after having been drunk, she got up in the morning and saw two young men in the rear of her room. They were quite attractive and well groomed, like young functionaries from the palace. The woman was about to embrace and take hold of them when they suddenly turned into broomsticks.

She took them and burned them.

[*Youming lu* 231 (*LX* 244); *TPGJ* 368.4]

NOTES

My thanks to Professors Liu Yuan-ju and Wendy Swartz for comments on early drafts of this chapter.

1. For broad studies of the genre in early medieval times, see Robert Ford Campany, *Strange Writing: Anomaly Accounts in Early Medieval China* (Albany: State University of New York Press, 1996); and Liu Yuan-ju 劉苑如, *Liuchao zhiguai di wenlei yanjiu: Daoyi wei chang di xiangxiang licheng* 六朝志怪的文類研究：導異為常的想像歷程 (Taibei: Guoli zhengzhi daxue zhongwen yanjiusuo boshi lunwen, 1996).

2. For a preliminary map of the persuasive interests at stake and how various *zhiguai* texts advanced those, see Campany, *Strange Writing*, chap. 7. This is not to say that they were not also entertaining, which they clearly were and still are; but we modern readers must do our best to recover other purposes and meanings of this literature besides its obvious entertainment value. For a concurring view of slightly later tales of the same genre, see Glen Dudbridge, *Religious Experience and Lay Society in T'ang China: A Reading of Tai Fu's Kuang-i chi* (Cambridge: Cambridge University Press, 1995). For a contrary view, see Mu-chou Poo, "Ghost Literature: Exorcistic Ritual Texts or Daily Entertainment?" *Asia Major*, 3rd ser., 13, no. 1 (2000): 43–64. No one would be likely to disagree with

Poo's argument that ghost stories were entertaining; the question is whether the many huge compilations of tales of ghosts and other anomalous matters had any purpose other than entertainment. Some modern readers, especially scholars of literature, continue to find it hard to answer in the affirmative.

3. Or, in the useful typology offered by Jonathan Z. Smith, a locative worldview, rather than (and in opposition to) a utopian one. See Smith, *Relating Religion: Essays in the Study of Religion* (Chicago: University of Chicago Press, 2004), 465–79; and Robert Ford Campany, "Two Religious Thinkers of the Early Eastern Jin: Gan Bao and Ge Hong in Multiple Contexts," *Asia Major*, 3rd ser., 18 (2005): 175–224. This locative view somewhat resembles the Buddhist notion of karma in its positing of a pervasive and cross-species moral order and an inexorable cosmic moral reciprocity, but it is indigenous to China and predates the introduction of Buddhist texts and values. Buddhist karma is also exemplified in some *zhiguai* collections, but not in the selections I present here. For an overview of the Buddhist texts, see Donald E. Gjertson, "The Early Chinese Buddhist Miracle Tale: A Preliminary Survey," *Journal of the American Oriental Society* 101 (1981): 287–301; and, for translated examples, see Robert Ford Campany, *Signs from the Unseen Realm: Buddhist Miracle Tales from Early Medieval China* (Honolulu: University of Hawai'i Press, 2012).

4. For further analysis of the cosmological claims and persuasive goals of these works, see Campany, *Strange Writing*, 343–62, and "Two Religious Thinkers of the Early Eastern Jin."

5. Depending on attribution, approximately 259 tales from this text survive in various collections. Lu Xun 魯迅 assembled 265 textual items in his monumental *Gu xiaoshuo gouchen* 古小說鈎沈 (Beijing: Renmin wenxue chubanshe, 1954), 197–280. See also Wang Guoliang 王國良, *Liuchao zhiguai xiaoshuo kaolun* 六朝志怪小說考論 (Taibei: Wenshizhe chubanshe, 1988), 158–60, who has suggested revisions to the attributions that would result in a total of 259 items. I cite tales in the Lu Xun collection by sequential tale number (which I supply; unfortunately, items in Lu Xun's text are not numbered) and page number in the volume, abbreviated as *LX*. I also provide information on the major sources in collections on which Lu's transcription is based and point out any discrepancies between various versions, incorrect punctuation by Lu, and the like. In a few cases (and where noted) my translations are from different versions of the same story found in other *zhiguai* texts.

6. Some collections focus much more narrowly on particular classes of phenomena—for example, vengeful ghosts, single regions, miracles illustrating the truth and power of Buddhism, or even particular bodhisattvas or sutras.

7. For further discussion and bibliography, see Campany, *Strange Writing*, 76.

8. In what is now Zhejiang Province. I have no further information on Chen Su. I indicate in the notes the cases in which (to my knowledge) we have information about a protagonist or other personage other than that contained in the story at hand.

9. These are presumably offerings to accompany his coming-of-age, or capping, ceremony. In classical ritual texts, no offerings to spirits are mentioned as part of this ceremony (though divination is mentioned), but those texts were Confucian in ideology and the fact that offerings to spirits during the capping are not mentioned does not mean that

people in early medieval times did not sacrifice to spirits as part of the capping rite. What was classically prescribed is that a son should make an offering of food *to his mother*. See Patricia Buckley Ebrey, *Confucianism and Family Rituals in Imperial China: A Social History of Writing About Rites* (Princeton, N.J.: Princeton University Press, 1991), 19–22; and Ann Waltner, "The Moral Status of the Child in Late Imperial China: Childhood in Ritual and in Law," *Social Research* 53 (1986): 667–87.

10. *LX* (perhaps due to a printer's error) takes this *su* 素 as Chen's given name, but here it is an adverb.

11. In the context of a story about the afterlife, one might expect this term to refer to the divine Commandery Governor of Mount Tai (Taishan fujun 太山府君), who, as related in many other *zhiguai* tales, was the divine overseer of the human life span and who would thus have been an appropriate divine invitee to a coming-of-age rite for a youth—and would also have had access to the spirit-world records on the two children that would have alerted his office to the fact that they had been exchanged. But *fujun* was also a term of respectful address used by family members toward their elders. The chief guest, then, appears to be a recently deceased ancestor in the Chen family lineage who somehow detects that the boy for whom the rite is being performed is not the child of Chen's wife.

12. The door to the room in which the offerings were laid out.

13. Or "her"; the specialist's gender is not specified.

14. He went into the inner, private quarters of the household, where the women often stayed.

15. Ordinarily, a mere tree spirit would not rank as "celestial"; this is an example of the sort of flattery through using grandiose titles that can still be observed in local temples.

16. Or perhaps the sense is "from nowhere"; that is, the god remained invisible while speaking. The phrase is *shen yu kongzhong yan* 神於空中言.

17. The change in nomenclature, from *shen* to *gui*, reinforces the sense that this spirit being has crossed the fine line dividing the "normal" relationship of reciprocal exchange on which local cults are based from the making of excessive demands backed by threats—the sort of divine protection racket to which the early Celestial Master Daoist religion, in particular, vehemently objected (and which is also seen in the following two stories).

18. The final two characters, *shigan* 事幹, seem to be a pun on *ganshi* 幹事, a generic term for subofficial clerks in local administrative bureaus, often abbreviated to *gan*, which also means "trunk of a tree" or "torso of a body."

19. This is a gesture of all-out supplication, which has been adopted into English as the word "kowtow."

20. The implication is that they sacrificed the animal to the god.

21. This seems to mean not that it no longer resided at the headquarters but simply that it stopped its demands.

22. The marker of the location of the woman's grave.

23. See the next story, which also concerns this god and his temple.

24. *You ling* 有靈, meaning that offerings and requests at his shrine achieved notable results.

25. The armory, we are to understand, of the otherworld bureaucracy.

26. This refers to Wang Dun 王敦 (266–324), an important official under both the Western and Eastern Jin. For a biographical sketch, see Liu I-ch'ing [Liu Yiqing], comp., *Shih-shuo Hsin-yü: A New Account of the Tales of the World*, trans. Richard B. Mather (Minneapolis: University of Minnesota Press, 1976), 596.

27. Huan Wen was an ambitious general who deposed an Eastern Jin emperor and usurped the throne; he is mentioned again in a later note. The point is that even a figure as powerful and important in this world as Huan Wen may fare poorly in the other world.

28. *Diyu* 地獄, underworld sites of punishment of the recently dead, recently had been introduced into the Chinese *imaginaire* along with the newly imported Buddhist religion.

29. The notion that such trimmings from one's body, as well as hair and beard trimmings, could be used as surrogates to receive punishment for one's sins in the afterlife is documented elsewhere as well. See Jiang Shaoyuan 江紹原, *Fa xu zhao: Guanyu tamen di mixin* 髮鬚爪：關於它們的迷信 (Shanghai: Kaiming shudian, 1928).

30. Such thresholds are common in traditional Chinese architecture, including homes and temples.

31. Deng Ai 鄧艾 (197–264) was a talented general who served the Wei regime. For a biographical summary, see Liu I-ch'ing, comp., *Shih-shuo hsin-yü*, 575–76. After a brilliant military campaign against the Shu-Han kingdom centered in what is now Sichuan Province, Deng was unjustly executed along with all his sons, and his wife and grandchildren were banished to Central Asia, which explains the existence of a temple to the dangerous, vengeful spirit of this dead general.

32. The town of Jingkou lay on or near the bank of the Jiang River, near its mouth, in what is now Jiangsu Province, east and downriver from the southern capital (what is now Nanjing).

33. The *Yiyuan* version adds: "that had long been in ruins."

34. Sima Tian 司馬恬 (338–390) was a general who served the Eastern Jin and is mentioned in several historical sources.

35. Given contemporary understandings of the relationship between illness and spirit incursions, there is at least a hint here that the god is causing both the illness and the dream in order to secure his desired residential upgrade. On this, see Mu-chou Poo, *In Search of Personal Welfare: A View of Ancient Chinese Religion* (Albany: State University of New York Press, 1998), 137–41; and Donald Harper, "Spellbinding," in *Religions of China in Practice*, ed. Donald S. Lopez Jr. (Princeton, N.J.: Princeton University Press, 1996), 241–50.

36. The *Yiyuan* version ends here. One would normally expect this temple repair to be followed by the general's recovery and, perhaps, another dream in which the god thanks his benefactor. It is likely that both versions of the tale have suffered textual loss at this point (perhaps due to selective, partial quotation in the collections, a common phenomenon).

37. Or, possibly, around *her*.

38. *You yijia feng Fo jingjin* 有一家奉佛精進, literally means "there was a family that worshiped Buddha with utmost devotion."

39. *Jia feng dao* 家奉道, literally means "This household worshiped the Dao."

40. *Fayuan zhulin* and *TPYL* 737 have *suwu* 俗巫; *TPYL* 687 has *sushi* 俗師 (a vulgar master). "Vulgar" (*su*) here probably has the sense of "employed by the common people." *Wu* 巫 is a term long debated by scholars. Suffice it to say that *wu* is the designation applied, in early medieval hagiographies and anomaly accounts, to personnel of both genders who served as intermediaries between humans and spirits of many kinds, whether by acting as spirit-mediums or in other ways. Often they were attached to temples, in which case they were the oracles of the resident gods and also apparently managed the temple's affairs. The question of whether these *wu* served as passive mouthpieces for the god (i.e., as spirit-mediums) or whether their own personalities remained intact while communicating with the god (in the manner of shamans), while it is a question that has preoccupied modern scholars, is not one that may be resolved by reference to the early medieval nomenclature, nor is the distinction between male and female practitioners always clear from the terminology used. For a provocative argument concerning the origins of the terminology, see Victor H. Mair, "Old Sinitic *Myag, Old Persian *Maguš*, and English 'Magician,'" *Early China* 15 (1990): 27–47.

41. It is possible, though unlikely given the details mentioned in this story as well as the way in which the name is given, that An Kai was female, as were many *wu* in earlier times.

42. This clearly refers to written documents bearing messages to the gods that were burned along with the animal victims. The burning of such documents (but *not* to accompany animal sacrifices) is normally associated with Daoist (specifically Celestial Master) liturgical practice, and in Daoist contexts the clients' written requests were also referred to as *zhang* 章 (petitions). This mention of written petition documents used by a shaman or medium is therefore especially noteworthy. On the Daoist practices, see, for example, Kristofer Schipper, "The Written Memorial in Taoist Ceremonies," in *Religion and Ritual in Chinese Society*, ed. Arthur P. Wolf (Stanford, Calif.: Stanford University Press, 1974), 309–24; and Peter S. Nickerson, "The Great Petition for Sepulchral Plaints," in Stephen R. Bokenkamp, *Early Daoist Scriptures* (Berkeley: University of California Press, 1997), 230–74, and "The Southern Celestial Masters," in *Daoism Handbook*, ed. Livia Kohn (Leiden: Brill, 2000), 256–82, esp. 269–71.

43. *TPYL* 687 lacks this subnarrative.

44. Mentioned several times in the standard *Jin shu*, Wang Ningzhi (d. 399) served as governor of two regions and also at court in the office of history. Mather notes that since he was devoted to the Daoist religion of the Way of the Celestial Masters, he relied on its exorcistic procedures when threatened by Sun En's rebellion in 399 and consequently died. See Liu I-ch'ing, comp., *Shih-shuo Hsin-yü*, 592.

45. *TPYL* 737 has "Once when Wang Ningzhi was performing the river offering, he was about to proceed with the wine libation when . . ."

46. Apparently because of a copyist's error, *TPYL* 687 has *xiang* 向, which makes no sense in the context, whereas the *Fayuan zhulin* version has *ci* 伺.

47. *TPYL* 737 sets up the context of this event not as a journey but as a sacrifice to a river god. This sacrificial context better fits both An Kai's own involvement and the later mention of seated guests and participants. But because a sacrifice to a river god would

be appropriate when one was setting off on a journey by water, both versions might preserve the original sense of the story.

48. Reading *yang* 佯 for the *yang* 陽 given in both *LX* and *Fayuan zhulin*.

49. *TPYL* 687 has "After he had come to the [spirit] seat" (i.e., the altar).

50. *TPYL* 737 lacks this last clause. The point of this odd subnarrative seems to be to demonstrate the shaman's skill at "illusion," causing this powerful figure—whose anger at having been mocked could be fatal to the offending party—to remain unaware of the leaf on his head. The translation follows the *LX/Fayuan zhulin* version, but variations in both *Taiping yulan* versions, which differ from each other, are noted. (*LX*'s version does not incorporate any of these variations but simply quotes *Fayuan zhulin*.) An alternative, partial translation may be found in Fu-shih Lin, "Chinese Shamans and Shamanism in the Chiang-nan Area During the Six Dynasties Period (3rd–6th Century A.D.)" (Ph.D. diss., Princeton University, 1994), 33.

51. Dantu is located on the south bank of the Jiang River, northeast of Jurong.

52. Both *TPGJ* and *LX* give *gui* 鲑, a term denoting some variety of fish in the salmon family. Is there a pun here on "ghost" (*gui* 鬼)?

53. Compare *Youming lu* 162, translated here as story 2. The same term, *ji* 籍, is used in both cases to indicate a spirit-world ledger book containing vital information about individuals, their allotted life spans, and, for example, the official ranks they will achieve.

54. Haixi gong 海西公 was a title with which Sima Yi 司馬奕 (342–386), who reigned as the Jin emperor from 365 to 371, was invested. He was deposed by the would-be usurper Huan Wen 桓溫 (312–373).

55. That is, apparently, to do so with his own hands instead of hiring out the work, as was customary. This figure overlaps with the ones featured in Keith Knapp, chapter 37 of this volume.

56. *Fayuan zhulin* here notes that some texts insert an additional phrase not given in *LX*: "[The 'husband'] returned to press for the execution of the filial son."

57. *LX* writes 祖, but *TPYL* and *Chuxue ji*, quoting *Youming lu*, and *TPGJ*, quoting *Soushen ji*, all have 祖.

58. In this period, prisoners accused of crimes were often presumed guilty until proven innocent, and confessions were sometimes extracted by torture, matters well documented in *zhiguai* texts among others.

59. The *Chuxue ji* citation of the *Youming lu* version has "Shouldn't I be allowed to live?"

60. The *Youming lu* version (in its various sources) has "several days."

61. The streets, presumably, of the ancestral hometown of the Pang clan. The *Soushen ji* version is more detailed, and only it contains the concluding remarks about the offerings made by the protagonist's descendants. My translation is based on a comparison of both versions. *Taiping guangji* cites *Soushen ji* as its source but is actually much closer to the *Youming lu* version; the late Ming compilers of the *Soushen ji* version must have derived their text from some other source.

35. Texts for Stabilizing Tombs

TIMOTHY M. DAVIS

Over the past half century, archaeologists have unearthed hundreds of texts buried in ancient Chinese tombs. The variety of interred writing is remarkable. From about the fifth century B.C.E. on, works of philosophy, literature, and history appear with some frequency among the grave goods buried with the dead, as do documents concerned with legal, administrative, ritual, and military issues; treatises on medicine, macrobiotics, divination, and portent reading; and almanacs and examples of sacred cartography.[1] These manuscripts, written on silk and bamboo or wooden slips, were the treasured personal property of the deceased, and their placement in the tomb made them available for the deceased's use in the afterlife. A closer look at the particular texts interred reveals that they were not chosen as casual reading material. Some scholars have argued that certain texts may have guided the dead on their perilous journey to transcendent realms or provided esoteric knowledge that would aid in the pursuit of posthumous immortality.[2] Donald Harper has suggested that these buried libraries may also have served a "talismanic" function designed to protect the corporal remains and spiritual essences housed in the tomb.[3]

The most pervasive type of burial text is the "tomb inventory" (*yiwushu* 衣物疏 or *qiance* 遣策), which lists the personal items interred with the deceased individual. Occasionally these inventories are accompanied by letters to underworld authorities presenting the deceased to the subterranean bureaucracy and informing them how to appropriately handle the transfer of the burial goods.[4]

Shifting sociopolitical realities and changing views of the divine during the Eastern Zhou (770–221 B.C.E.) profoundly influenced the various ways in which early Chinese imagined the afterlife and their relationships with their dead.[5] Over several centuries, the Zhou feudal order, founded on lineage ties and noble birth, gradually gave way to centrally administered bureaucratic states in which government appointments were based on merit and one's social status could be elevated through service to the state. In turn, these new ways of organizing society altered the perceptions of the underworld, giving rise to an elaborate bureaucratic conception of the afterlife.[6] By the Eastern Han dynasty (25–220), we find a panoply of celestial and subterranean spirits mentioned in tomb-interred documents. These divine functionaries carried out numerous responsibilities inspired by the political and judicial institutions prevalent among the living.

In the mid-Eastern Han, two new types of text begin to appear in many tombs of low-level elites: "land-purchase contracts" (*maidiquan* 買地卷) and "tomb-stabilizing writs" (*zhenmuwen* 鎮墓文).[7] These documents, like the tomb inventories, differed from the other kinds of interred texts (e.g., philosophical, legal, or divinatory writings) in that their messages were directed to underworld divinities with the primary aims of securing the tomb and peacefully assimilating the newly deceased individual into the world of the dead. In other words, these texts are meaningful only in the immediate burial context and were not consulted by the deceased during his or her lifetime.[8]

Land-purchase contracts were written or inscribed on durable material such as lead, stone, brick, or jade and were buried inside the tomb to prove the lawful occupation of a plot of sacred space in which a grave could be constructed. The earliest authentic specimen excavated so far dates to 82 C.E., and similar contracts continue to be produced even today. Terry Kleeman highlighted two regionally distinctive types of entombed land-purchase contracts: those from the North, which are modeled on real-world documents and involve actual sellers, witnesses, and reasonable amounts of money,[9] and those produced in the South, which record transactions involving exorbitant amounts of cash paid to terrestrial divinities.[10] In most Southern contracts, deified natural entities such as the sun, the moon, the four seasons, Heaven, Earth, and the five phases, as well as supernatural entities like the Sovereign Sire of the East, the Queen Mother of the West, and the Lad of the Eastern Sea, serve as witnesses. Money is paid not only to cover the cost of the burial ground but also to make amends for intruding into the realm of the earth spirits.[11]

Proper documentation, in the form of a land-purchase contract, ensured that the deceased could not be evicted from his property by the contentious spirits of those previously buried in the same soil, or a later tenant whose own interment might encroach on the contract holder's authorized burial space.[12]

Without such a deed, an abandoned corpse residing within the same plot of land could threaten the deceased by laying claim to the tomb or unlawfully pilfering sacrifices that had been offered to him.[13] Land-purchase contracts address these potential problems by often including what Kleeman calls a "corpse clause." These are provisions stating that all deceased individuals previously buried in the land acquired by the contract will become the permanent slaves of the deceased purchaser; even plants and animals living on the land will become the property of the deceased.[14] Land-purchase contracts thus reveal the logical application of legal and administrative authority in securing a place for the dead that kept them close enough to be properly propitiated yet safely separated from their living descendants.

A second mortuary document prevalent during the late Han and early medieval period is the tomb-stabilizing writ. Unlike land-purchase contracts, which are still used in burials, tomb-stabilizing writs were in use for only about 250 years during the late Eastern Han and Jin (265–420) dynasties before their functions were apparently subsumed by land contracts.[15] The physical form of these burial objects differs markedly from that of land contracts. Instead of inscribing text on a flat slab of durable material, tomb-stabilizing writs were written with a brush, often in vermilion ink, on the outside of small, unglazed pottery jars. Some of the jars seem to have contained a kind of divine medicine (shenyao 神藥), which is occasionally mentioned in their texts.[16]

Besides providing sustaining nutrients, tomb-stabilizing jars and their accompanying texts served three main purposes: (1) to absolve the deceased from responsibility for violating the boundary between land appointed for human use and the realm of the soil divinities, (2) to present the newly deceased individual to the underworld authorities, and (3) to protect living descendants from the adverse effects of death pollution, including illness, misfortune, and additional family deaths, by stressing the segregation of the living and the dead.[17]

The content of the typical tomb-stabilizing writ consists of an appeal to the authority of heavenly deities—such as the Envoy of the Celestial Thearch (Tiandi shizhe 天帝使者) or the Yellow God (Huangshen 黄神), Lord of the Northern Dipper (Beidouzhu 北斗主)—who announce the arrival of the deceased to the underworld bureaucrats, which include such figures as the Elder of Haoli (Haoli fulao 蒿里父老),[18] the Tumulus Vanguard (Zhongqian 冢前), the Tomb-mound Assistant (Qiucheng 丘丞), and the Tomb Earl (Mubo 墓伯).[19] Commands or orders (ling 令) are sometimes issued stipulating how the dead and their living descendants should be treated. Three tomb-stabilizing writs are translated in this chapter (documents 11–13).

A subgenre of the tomb-stabilizing writ is the "infestation-quelling writ" (jiezhuwen 解注文). As with regular zhenmuwen, infestation-quelling writs were written on the surface of small pottery jars that were then buried in the tomb. It was hoped that the presence of such jars would help stave off the undesirable effects of death pollution (primarily disease) that might otherwise be inadvertently or deliberately passed to living descendants by their recently deceased ancestor.[20] Document 14 is an example of this type of text.

The final genre of entombed text that I discuss here is the tomb inventory. As mentioned earlier, this type of text is among the most common found in the tombs of early and medieval China. The geographical area across which tomb inventories have been discovered is vast. While most have come from tombs located in Hubei and Hunan, others have been discovered in Henan, Guangxi, Jiangxi, and Jiangsu Provinces. Perhaps the most outstanding specimen was found in tomb 3 (sealed 168 B.C.E.), constructed for the Marquis of Dai 軑 at Mawangdui 馬王堆 near modern Changsha 長沙, Hunan. This particular inventory, written on bamboo slips and continuing on seven wooden boards, lists more than four hundred items assembled to provide for the marquis's posthumous comfort. [21] Even more interesting for our purposes is the attached letter addressed to underworld authorities. This document, written on one of the wooden boards by the household assistant (jiacheng 家丞) of the Li family (the Marquis of Dai is surnamed Li), is addressed to the Gentleman of the Interior Responsible for Burial Goods (Zhuzang langzhong 主藏郎中). The document instructs this underworld official to transmit the list of funerary goods to his supervisor, the Chief Administrator of Burial Goods (Zhuzang jun 主藏君).[22]

Although only a fraction of the total number of tomb inventories are paired with letters addressed to members of the underworld administration, the fact that such lists were buried in tombs supports the assumption that they were meant to be read by officials serving in the subterranean bureaucracy. Document 15 is an example of a tomb inventory with an attached letter dating from the early medieval period.

The recovery of land-purchase contracts, tomb-stabilizing writs, and tomb inventories provides a rare window into the common religious beliefs and practices of early China, practices that continued to be widely implemented during the early medieval period. The famous adage, attributed to Confucius, that the dead should be treated with reverence but kept at a distance,[23] appropriately describes the ambivalent attitudes that the men and women of these eras held toward their dead. On the one hand, interred documents were deployed to protect departed loved ones from potentially malevolent or intrusive spirits, but on the other hand, they served to limit contact between living descendants and deceased ancestors. Overall, these texts aimed at directing the deceased's numinous power toward securing long-term family stability and prosperity.

FURTHER READING

The seminal study in English of excavated land contracts and tomb-stabilizing writs is Terry F. Kleeman, "Land Contracts and Related Documents," in *Makio Ryōkai Hakase shōju kinen ronshū, Chūgoku no shūkyō: Shisō to kagaku* 牧尾良海

博士壽計記念論集, 中國の宗教: 思想と科學 (Tokyo: Kokusho kankōkai, 1984), 1–34. But see also the excellent articles by Anna Seidel, "Traces of Han Religion," in *Dōkyō to shūkyō bunka* 道教と宗教文化, ed. Akizuki Kan'ei 秋月觀暎 (Tokyo: Hirakawa shuppansha, 1987), 221–57, and "Post-mortem Immortality, or: The Taoist Resurrection of the Body," in *GILGUL: Essays on Transformation, Revolution and Permanence in the History of Religions*, ed. Shaul Shaked, David Shulman, and Gedaliahu G. Stroumsa (Leiden: Brill, 1987), 223–37. For an informative article on land-purchase contracts from the Song dynasty (960–1279), see Ina Asim, "Status Symbol and Insurance Policy: Song Land Deeds for the Afterlife," in *Burial in Song China*, ed. Dieter Kuhn (Heidelberg: Edition Forum, 1994), 307–70. The most comprehensive study of medieval and early modern contracts, including those buried in tombs to secure land from underworld divinities, is Valerie Hansen, *Negotiating Daily Life in Traditional China: How Ordinary People Used Contracts, 600–1400* (New Haven, Conn.: Yale University Press, 1995). For a convenient list of excavated land contracts and tomb-quelling writs discovered up through 1980, including transcriptions, see Ikeda On 池田溫, "Chūgoku rekidai boken ryakkō" 中國歷代墓券略考, *Tōyō-bunka kenkyūjo kiyō* 東洋文化研究所紀要 86 (1981): 193–278; now superseded by Zhang Xunliao 張勛燎 and Bai Bin 白彬, *Zhongguo daojiao kaogu* 中國道教考古, 6 vols. (Beijing: Xianzhuang shuju, 2006). For informative overviews of the variety of religious practice in early and early medieval China, see Mu-chou Poo, *In Search of Personal Welfare: A View of Ancient Chinese Religion* (Albany: State University of New York Press, 1998); and Richard von Glahn, *The Sinister Way: The Divine and the Demonic in Chinese Religious Culture* (Berkeley: University of California Press, 2004). A number of valuable studies have been published that view land contracts and tomb-quelling writs as sources for understanding the development of early religious Daoism. See Angelika Cedzich, "Ghosts and Demons, Law and Order: Grave Quelling Texts in Early Daoist Literature," *Taoist Resources* 4, no. 2 (1993): 23–35; Peter S. Nickerson, "Taoism, Death, and Bureaucracy, in Early Medieval China" (Ph.D. diss., University of California, 1996); and Michel Strickmann, *Chinese Magical Medicine*, ed. Bernard Faure (Stanford, Calif.: Stanford University Press, 2002).

1. LAND-PURCHASE CONTRACT FOR THE NEIGHBORHOOD MARQUIS OF KUAIJI 會稽亭侯 (252 C.E.)

[recto] The Neighborhood Marquis [*Tinghou* 亭侯] of Kuaiji 會稽,[24] concurrent director of the Qiantang 錢唐 navy,[25] and General Who Subdues the Distant [*Suiyuan jiangjun* 綏遠將軍], has purchased from the Earth Sire [*Tugong* 土公] a tomb fortification—one mound. Its eastern and southern limits are the ridges of Phoenix Mountain 鳳山, its western limit is the lake, and its northern limit is

the end of the mountain [range]. Cash paid in total was 8 million. This day the transaction is complete. The Sun and the Moon are witnesses, and the Four Seasons are guarantors. For those who possess private contracts, it is fitting [to proceed according to] statutes and ordinances. In the third month of the first year, which was *renshen* 壬申, in the era of Shenfeng of the Great [State of] Wu 吳, we "split the contract" [*pobie* 破莂], [resulting in] "great auspiciousness" [*daji* 大吉].

[side] On the sixth day of the third month in the first year, which was *renshen*, in the era of Shenfeng [April 2, 252], Sun Ding 孫鼎 made this contract [*zuobie* 作莂].[26]

> [For transcriptions and images, see Ikeda On 池田溫, "Chūgoku rekidai boken ryakkō" 中國歷代墓券略考, *Tōyō-bunka kenkyūjo kiyō* 東洋文化研究所紀要 86 (1981): 225, no. 25 and fig. 2; and Zhang Xunliao 張勛燎 and Bai Bin 白彬, *Zhongguo daojiao kaogu* 中國道教考古 (Beijing: Xianzhuang shuju, 2006), 820, no. 4, and 821, fig. 3. See also Tian Hengming 田恒銘, "Yi fang hanjian de Wu zhuan—Shenfeng yuan nian diquan ji qi shufa" 一方罕見的吳磚—神鳳元年地券及其書法, *Wenwu tiandi* 文物天地 4 (1991): 40]

2. LAND-PURCHASE CONTRACT FOR HUANG FU 黃甫 (254 C.E.)

Today, the eighteenth day of the tenth month in the first year of the era of Wufeng [November 15, 254],[27] we raised a tumulus dwelling [*zhongzhai* 冢宅] behind Mount Mofu 莫府山 near its southern edge for the adult male Huang Fu 黃甫 of Jiujiang 九江, age eighty. From Heaven we purchased land, from Earth we purchased a dwelling. The cost was three hundred. The eastern [limits] extend to *jiageng* 甲庚, the western [limits] extend to *yixin* 乙辛,[28] the northern [limits] extend to *rengui* 壬癸, and the southern [limits] extend to *bingding* 丙丁.[29] If there are those who contest the land, they should direct inquiries to the Celestial Emperor [Tiandi 天帝]; if there are those who contest the dwelling, they should direct inquiries to the Soil Earl [*Tubo* 土伯].[30] [Observe this] in accordance with the statutes and ordinances of the Celestial Emperor.[31]

> [For transcriptions, see *Wenwu ziliao congkan* 8 (1983): 5; and Zhang and Bai, *Zhongguo daojiao kaogu*, 822, no. 5]

3. LAND-PURCHASE CONTRACT AND INVENTORY LIST FOR CAO YI 曹翌 (285 C.E.)

[recto] On the twenty-fourth day of the sixth month in the sixth year of the Taikang era [August 11, 285], the late Left Gentleman of the Interior [*Zuolangzhong* 左郎中] for the [State of] Wu 吳 and Commandant of Established Credentials [*Lijie xiaowei* 立節校尉] Cao Yi 曹翌, courtesy name Yongxiang 永翔, of Jiangning 江寧 [District] in Danyang 丹楊 [Commandery], died in his thirty-seventh year.

We purchased ten square *li* 里 of cultivated land at Luya Fields 虜牙田 near Shizi Ridge 石子崗. The cost was a million cash. [The land is to be] used for burial. May no one encroach on or seize it. The text of the contract is distinct and clear.

[verso] As for the slave Zhu 奴主, the slave Jiao 奴教, and the maidservant Xi 婢西, these three people [listed] at the right are [Cao] Yi's slaves and maidservant.[32] One garment of fine-twined linen,[33] one cloak of lustrous silk.[34]

[For transcriptions, see *Kaogu xuebao* 1 (1957): 189; Ikeda, "Chūgoku rekidai boken ryakkō," 226–27, no. 28; and Zhang and Bai, *Zhongguo daojiao kaogu*, 832, no. 16]

4. LAND-PURCHASE CONTRACT FOR LI DA 李達 (300 C.E.)

Completed on *yiyou* 乙酉, the twenty-seventh day of the eleventh month, the new moon of which was an *wuwu* 戊午 day, in the first year of the Yongkang era [December 4, 300]. Li Da 李達 of Geyang 葛陽 [District], Poyang 鄱陽 [Commandery],[35] age sixty-seven, today purchased land from Heaven and a dwelling from Earth. In the east it culminates at *jiayi* 甲乙, in the south it culminates at *bingding* 丙丁, in the west it culminates at *gengxin* 庚辛, in the north it culminates at *rengui* 壬癸, [and] its center is *wuji* 戊己. The money used to purchase the land and the dwelling was three hundred, [together with] a three-foot embroidered kerchief [*huajin* 華巾]. Guarantors acknowledging [the transaction] are the Sovereign Sire of the East and the Queen Mother of the West.[36] If later [there are those who have] ambitions [to occupy] this dwelling, they should consult the Sovereign Sire of the East and the Queen Mother of the West. [Observe this] in accordance with laws and ordinances.[37]

[For transcriptions and an image, see *Kaogu* 6 (1984): 540–41; and Zhang and Bai, *Zhongguo daojiao kaogu*, 834–35, no. 20, and 836, fig. 8]

5. LAND-PURCHASE CONTRACT FOR
MR. HOU 侯氏 (D. 302 C.E.)

[recto] On *gengwu* 庚午,[38] the twentieth day from the new moon, which was a *xinhai* 辛亥 day, in the second month of the second year of the Yongning era [April 4, 302], the Grand Palace Grandee [*Dazhong daifu* 大中大夫], and . . . of Ruyin 汝陰 [. . . Mr. Hou] of Congyang District 樅陽縣, Lujiang Commandery 廬江郡, Yang Province 揚州, [purchased] land at Caihu Village 漦湖里, Lai Township 賴鄉, Jiangning District 江寧縣, Danyang Commandery 丹陽郡.[39] Its dimensions are five *qing* and eighty *mu*,[40] cash paid was 2 million. This day the transaction is complete. The eastern quadrant [extends to] *jiayi* 甲乙, the southern quadrant [extends to] *bingding* 丙丁, the western quadrant [extends to] *gengxin* 庚辛, the northern quadrant [extends to] *rengui* 壬癸, and the center to *wuji* 戊己.[41] The Tumulus Vanguard [*Zhongqian* 冢前] witnesses and acknowledges [the transaction]. [Observe this] in accordance with statutes and ordinances.

If someone asks by whom this [contract] was written—it was a fish.	若有問誰 所書—是魚
Where is the fish?	魚所在
In deep waters swimming.	深水游
Those who desire to find him,	欲得者
Should seek out the River Earl.[42]	河伯求

[verso] The Grand Year Star [Jupiter] is in *renxu* 壬戌 [302 C.E.].[43]

> [For transcriptions, see *Wenwu* 6 (1965): 44; Ikeda,
> "Chūgoku rekidai boken ryakkō," 227, no. 30;
> and Zhang and Bai, *Zhongguo daojiao kaogu*, 835–37, no. 21]

6. TOMB-STABILIZING STONE BY ZHANG ZHENGZI 張正子 FOR HIS PARENTS (433 C.E.)

It was a *gengshen* 庚申 day, the twenty-sixth of the tenth month, with the new moon falling on *guihai* 癸亥, in the second year of the Great [State of] Dai's era of Yanhe,[44] with the Year Star in *guiyou* 癸酉 [November 23, 433 C.E.], that the orphaned and sorrowful son Zhang Zhengzi 張正子 ventured [to offer] a shining announcement to the God of the Tomb Ridge [Mugang zhi shen 墓崗 之神]. [The announcement] says: "I, Zhengzi, inherited this plot of ground. Today, having attained auspicious divination [results], I present the numinous encoffined body [*lingjiu* 靈柩] of my deceased father, the 'filial and immaculate gentleman' [*xiaosushi* 孝素士], for joint burial at the gravesite of his 'gentle spouse' [*ruren* 孺人], my deceased mother of the Zou 鄒 clan. It is situated at *qian* 乾 [northwest] facing *si* 巳 [south]. To the left is the mountain, to the right is the river; truly it is an auspicious burial place. Divine One [*shen* 神], may you watch over them. If imps and goblins infiltrate the tumulus or 'dark palace' [*yougong* 幽宮], or if dholes, wolves, foxes, or rabbits tread across the tomb path, Divine One, may you punish them and pacify the souls of my forbearers. At the spring and autumn sacrifices, Divine One, may you feast with them. [If anyone] oversteps [the conditions] of this covenant [*meng* 盟], proceed according to [the dictates of] this stone. I venture to make this announcement."[45]

> [For a transcription and images, see *Zhongguo shufa* 中國書法 10
> (2005): 27–29]

7. LAND-PURCHASE CONTRACT FOR NAI NÜ 嬭女 (443 C.E.)

The twenty-fourth day, *bingyou* 丙酉, of the eleventh month, the new moon of which was *guimao* 癸卯, in the nineteenth year of the Yuanjia era, the Grand Year Star is in *renwu* 壬午 [January 10, 443].

Nai Nü 嬭女 of Xincheng Village 新城里 in the East Township 西鄉 of Shi-xing District 始興縣 in Shixing Commandery 始興郡, age . . .-five, passed away during the hour of the dog 戌 [7:00–9:00 P.M.] on the twenty-seventh day of the fourth month of the *jiaxu* 甲戌 year [June 19, 434]. The *Demon Statutes of the Dark Metropolis* [*Xuandu guilü* 玄都鬼律] and the *Statutes and Ordinances of the Subter-ranean Nüqing Edicts* [*Dixia nüqing zhaoshu lüling* 地下女青詔書律令] [state]: "Since the coming of military disorder, all the dead under heaven must heed and obey the living at the district and commandery where they are buried." A sepulcher has been excavated and a mounded tomb [*qiumu* 丘墓] constructed for Nai Nü across from Xikou Settlement 夕口村 at Xincheng Village in the East Township of Shixing District in Shixing Commandery.

[From the guardian spirits] of the settlement, neighborhood, village, and fief, as well as the Subterranean Ancestors [*Dixia xianren* 地下先人], the Elder of Haoli [Haoli *fulao* 蒿里父老], the Tomb Ministers arrayed in order to the right [*Muqing yuozhi* 墓卿右秩], the Sepulchral Lords of the Left and the Right [*Zuoyou zhonghou* 左右冢侯], the Tomb Mound Assistant [*Qiucheng* 丘丞], the Tomb Earl [*Mubo* 墓伯], the Subterranean Two-Thousand-Bushel Officials [*Dixia erqiandan* 地下二千石], the Assistant of Andu 安都丞,[46] and the King of Wuyi 武夷王,[47] we purchase this sepulchral land. Its dimensions are five *mu* 畝.[48] We excavate it to bury Nai Nü's remains within. Cash provided was a myriad-myri-ads nine-thousand nine-hundred and ninety-nine. This day [the transaction] is complete.

May the Subterranean Ancestors, the Elder of Haoli, the Tomb Ministers ar-rayed orderly at the right, the Sepulchral Lords of the Left and the Right, the Tomb Mound Assistant, the Tomb Earl, the Subterranean Two-Thousand-Bushel Officials, the Assistant of Andu, the King of Wuyi, and others all rise and heed Nai Nü who is buried in the sepulcher that has been excavated out of this ground. May they not allow those [deceased individuals] dwelling to the right and left, [who may harbor] rash ambitions, to delimit [again] the boundar-ies of this sepulchral land.

Those acknowledging [this transaction] are Zhang Jiangu 張堅固 and Li Dingdu 李定度; each has been supplied a liter of purchased wine [*gujiu geban* 沽酒各半], and jointly [they] make [i.e., validate] the contract.[49]

[See Zhang and Bai, *Zhongguo daojiao kaogu*, 851–54, no. 27]

8. LAND-PURCHASE CONTRACT FOR OUYANG JINGXI 歐陽景熙 (470 C.E.)

The ninth day of the eleventh month in the sixth year of the Song 宋 era Taishi [December 17, 470]. The deceased "man of the Way" [*daomin* 道民], Ouyang Jingxi 歐陽景熙, from Dutang Village 都唐里 in the Metropolitan Township 都鄉 of Shian District 始安縣 in Shian Commandery 始安郡 passed away. To-day he returns to Haoli. The deceased purchased this burial ground with myriad 9,999 coins. The eastern [boundary] extends to the Azure Dragon [Qing-long 青龍], the southern [boundary] extends to the Vermilion Bird [Zhuniao 朱鳥], the western [boundary] extends to the White Tiger [Baihu 白虎], and the northern [boundary] extends to the Dark Warrior [Xuanwu 玄武]. The [boundary] above extends to the Azure Heavens [Qingtian 青天]; the boundary [below] extends to the Yellow Springs [Huangquan 黃泉]. Within these four regions, everything belongs to the deceased. This day [the transaction] is complete. Those present at the time are Wangzi Qiao 王僑, Chisongzi 赤松子, Li Ding[du], and Zhang [Jian]gu. We split the contract and make [its conditions] clear. [Observe this] in accordance with statutes and ordinances.[50]

[For a transcription, see Zhang and Bai, *Zhongguo daojiao kaogu*, 861, no. 31]

9. ENTOMBED EPITAPH AND LAND-PURCHASE CONTRACT FOR SHEN HONGZHI 申洪之 (472 C.E.)

His Excellency, surname Shen 申, taboo name Hongzhi 洪之, is a native of Wei District 魏縣 in Wei Commandery 魏郡.[51] His great-grandfather [Shen] Zhong 申鍾 was Minister of Education for the earlier [state of] Zhao 趙 and Duke of Dongyang 東陽公.[52] His grandfather [Shen] Daosheng 申道生 was Bulwark General of the State, Governor of Yan Province 兗州, and Marquis of Jinxiang District 金鄉縣侯.[53] His [i.e., Shen Daosheng's] sons and grandsons established their families there.

As a youth [Shen Hongzhi] met with tribulation and setbacks and, together with his elder brother, the "straightforward and diligent" director [Shen] Qian-zhi 申乾之, entrusted his life to the [state of] Wei 魏. His Excellency's memory was clear and his physique strong, his conduct was earnest, and his character upright. He was filial, friendly, compassionate, and humane; congenial, respectful, kind, and harmonious. Elder and younger brother dwelt together, and grew white haired together in joyful interaction. The inner quarters [of their households] were appropriately managed, and the [interactions among the] nine-clan relations set a pattern and model [for others]. Owing to his extensive abilities [in managing] the responsibilities placed in his charge, his eminence was appointed adviser to the Eastern Palace.[54] He was about to set forth flourishing achievements and accomplish exalted deeds for the ages, but the years granted him were not extensive; and in his fifty-seventh year, on the fifth day of the tenth month, in the second year of the Wei era of Yanxing [November 21, 472 C.E.], he passed away at the capital.

Since he was separated from the old burial grounds by great distance, returning [his remains] to the crypt for burial proved too difficult.[55] Moreover, spare and lavish burials indeed follow the [prevailing custom] of the times. Testing our plans with turtle shell and milfoil stalk, all proposals were declared auspicious. Subsequently, we constructed a hall at Pingcheng 平城 south of the Sangqian River 桑乾河.[56] His physical form, following transformation, has moved on. However, his virtue stands out among [those of this] era. We venture to cut this stone in order to illuminate that which does not decay [*buxiu* 不朽].[57]

From the former landlords Wenniuyu Wuti 文忸于吳提, Helai Tufuyan 賀賴吐伏延, Helai Tugen 賀賴吐根, and Gaoli Gaoyutu 高梨高郁突, four men, [we] purchased twenty *qing* [228 acres] of land with one hundred bolts of official [grade] silk taffeta.[58] From that point until now, twenty years have passed. To-day, Hongzhi's corpse and spirit [*sangling* 喪靈] find eternal rest here. Hence we make a record of this [transaction].[59]

[For a transcription with commentary and a rubbing of the epitaph, see Hibino Takeo 日比野丈夫, "Boshi no kigen ni tsuite" 墓誌の起源について, in *Egami Namio kyōju koki kinen ronshū, minzoku, bunka hen* 江上波夫教授古稀記念論集, 民族, 文化篇 (Tokyo: Yamakawa shuppansha, 1977), 189–91. See also Ikeda, "Chūgoku rekidai boken ryakkō," 229–30, no. 35]

10. LAND-PURCHASE CONTRACT FOR ZHANG SHENLUO 張神洛 (507 C.E.)

On the sixteenth day of the ninth month during the fourth year of the era Zhengshi [October 7, 507], Zhang Shenluo 張神洛, an inhabitant of the North Ward 北坊, purchased from Lu A'dou 路阿兜, an inhabitant of the district, three *mu* of cultivated land for a tomb.[60] To the south [it extends] to the tomb of Qi Wang 齊王, to the north it extends fifty-three paces, to the east it extends to the tomb of Qi Tu 齊塗, and to the west it extends twelve paces. Payment was nine bolts of satin. This land is guaranteed not to have been stolen. If another person claims [it as his], then [Lu A']Dou will need to give forth fine land of equivalent *mu*. . . . When people privately employ contracts, they cannot thereafter recant on a whim. The one who first reneges must put forth [an additional] five bolts of satin. Drafting [the contract] indicates an act of trust.

The one who wrote the contract was Pan Miao 潘藐.

Lu Shanwang 路善王 was present at the time.

Lu Rongsun 路榮孫 was present at the time.[61]

[For a transcription, see Ikeda, "Chūgoku rekidai boken ryakkō," 232, no. 39. See also Jacques Gernet, "Le vente en Chine d'après les contrats de Touen-Houang (IXe–Xe siècles)," *T'oung Pao* 45 (1957): 387–89]

11. TOMB-STABILIZING WRIT FOR SUI FANG 睢方 (LATE SECOND CENTURY C.E.)

May the Yellow God [Huangshen 黃神], Lord of the Northern Dipper [Beidou-zhu 北斗主], on behalf of the buried individual Sui Fang 睢方, stabilize [the tomb] and gain [his] release from culpability and calamity. If the burial has transgressed against the God of the Tomb [*Mushen* 墓神] and the Tomb Earl [*Mubo* 墓伯], may that which is harmful to the living be deflected and removed today. May the tomb house [*mujia* 墓家] be without calamity.[62] May Sui Fang, and the rest [of the subterranean spirits], lay no charge to [his] sons, grandsons, wife, nephews, or brothers. For these reasons we trouble [you], great god [*dashen* 大神], to benefit the living and descendants yet unborn. [Observe this] in accordance with statutes and ordinances.[63]

[For a transcription, see Ikeda, "Chūgoku rekidai boken ryakkō," 275, no. 10]

12. TOMB-STABILIZING WRIT FOR THE YANG 楊 FAMILY (LATE SECOND CENTURY C.E.)

The Envoy of the Celestial Emperor respectfully on behalf of the Yang clan 楊氏 stabilizes and renders peaceful the shadowy barrow and tomb. [Furthermore,] he respectfully, by means of the lead man [*qianren* 鉛人],[64] gold, and jade, absolves culpability on behalf of the dead and, for the living, removes crimes and transgressions. After receiving this jar, command the mother to be pacified, and the lineage gentleman to sustain himself from annual underworld rents of 20 million [cash]. Command that sons upon sons and grandsons upon grandsons of later generations become gentlemen officials and ascend to the ranks of duke and marquis and that their wealth and nobility as generals and ministers never be cut off. Dispatch [these ordinances] by means of the Tomb Mound Assistant and the Tomb Earl below to those who should implement them. [Observe this] in accordance with statutes and ordinances.[65]

[For transcriptions, see *Wenwu* 11 (1975): 79; Ikeda, "Chūgoku rekidai boken ryakkō," 275, no. 12a. See also Mu-chou Poo, *In Search of Personal Welfare: A View of Ancient Chinese Religion* (Albany: State University of New York Press, 1998), 173]

13. TOMB-STABILIZING WRIT FOR CUI ZONGYING 崔宗盈 (FOURTH CENTURY C.E.)

Cui Zongying 崔宗盈, your own meager life mandate at an early age has ended, your longevity exhausted, the accounts depleted [*shouqiong suanjin* 壽窮算盡].[66] The dead appear before the Eight Ghosts [*bagui* 八鬼],[67] the Nine Canals [*jiukan* 九坎],[68] and the Senior Inspector of Mount Tai [*Taishan zhangyue* 泰山長閱].[69] May you go forth and accept this. [The living and the dead] in suffering do not recall one another, and in joy do not think of one another. After the separation has been carried out, do not allow the deceased to walk among the living. As for the sacrifices of the *ci* 祠, *la* 臘, *she* 社, and *fa* 伏, [may he] seek them beyond the suburbs.[70] In a thousand years, myriad Jupiter cycles, perhaps we may again have occasion to meet. [Observe this] in accordance with statutes and ordinances.[71]

[For a transcription, see Ikeda, "Chūgoku rekidai boken ryakkō," 276, no. 13]

14. INFESTATION-QUELLING WRIT CONCERNING
CHEN XIAOQING 陳小晴 (297 C.E.)

On the twenty-eighth day of the eighth month in the seventh year of the Yuan-kang era [October 1, 297], [Chen Xiaoqing] died. Sir, you had a meager life mandate and came to an early end. May you be unable to infest your repugnant [pathogens on the living].[72] May you be unable to infest your mother, and may you also be unable to infest your elder and younger brothers, or your wife and children. As for all those yet to come [i.e., descendants yet unborn] may you be unable to infest them. Regarding affairs [in the world] below, all punishments are Chen Xiaoqing's 陳小晴. [Observe this] in accordance with statutes and ordinances.[73]

[For a transcription, see Zhang and Bai,
Zhongguo daojiao kaogu, 395–96, no. 10]

15. TOMB INVENTORY FOR LADY PAN 潘氏 (D. 357 C.E.),
WITH ATTACHED LETTER TO UNDERWORLD AUTHORITIES

One square-cut garment of damask; one garment of rep-woven lustrous silk;[74] one garment of rep-woven taffeta; two blouses of lustrous silk; one [upper garment] [front and back] of open-work leno-weave; one [upper garment] [front and back] of crepe openwork; [one] pair of scarlet double-layered trousers; one purple and cyan double-layered skirt; one purple and cyan lined skirt; one scarlet and cyan lined skirt; one lined skirt of purple gauze; one set of knee coverings [made of] fine purple and yellow silk; one scarlet jacket; one jacket of yellow crepe; one . . . of purple mesh; one [garment of] gauze, crepe, and openwork [fabric]; a pair of pearl earrings; a pair of silver and hematite [earrings]; one armband with round gems; a pair of silver bracelets; two silver hairpins; . . . tortoise shell hairpins; two . . . raw silk handkerchiefs; two . . . of miscellaneous silk fabrics; a pair of damask "flying garments"; a silk sash; seven strings of cash; one box of cosmetics and fragrances; a pair of male and female [i.e., fine-tooth and wide-tooth] combs; a bronze mirror; one clothing chest; one brush; one black[?] needle-and-thread bag; one yellow needle-and-thread bag; one set of scissors and ruler; five needles for silk cloth; one skein of hemp thread; one skein of silk thread; four hand towels of lustrous silk; two hand towels of silk pongee; a pair of lustrous silk socks; a pair of socks with striped uppers; one large towel of white linen; five bags containing the five grains; one yellow damask pillow; one cloak; one rain hat[?]; one fine bamboo mat; a pair of jade swine;[75] one coffin; five sturdy nails; one garment of rib-woven linen; [and] one violet skirt.

On *jiawu*, the twenty-ninth day of the sixth month, the new moon of which a was *binyin* day, in the fifth year of the Shengping era [357 C.E.], Lady Pan 潘氏, the wife of the Commandant of the Guard for the Dukedom, Zhou Fangming

周芳命 of Jiyang Village 吉陽里 in the Metropolitan Township 都鄉 of Linxiang District 臨湘縣, Changsha Commandery 長沙郡, Jing Province 荊州, "became unsalaried" [*bulu* 不祿]. She was fifty-eight when on the said day, she "became drunk on wine and unsalaried" [*zuijiu bulu* 醉酒不祿].[76] The articles of clothing and objects [listed] are all those that Lady Pan wore and adorned herself with when alive. Another person cannot falsely claim them to remit [their own] debts.[77] The Lad of the Eastern Sea 東海童子 wrote [this]. When the document arrives, [he will] return to the sea. [Observe this] in accordance with laws and ordinances.[78]

[For a transcription and a hand-copied reproduction, see Li Zhenguang 李正光, "Changsha Beimen Guihuayuan faxian Jin mu" 長沙北門桂花園發現晉墓, *Wenwu cankao ziliao* 文物參考資料 11 (1955): 134–36. For a revised transcription with commentary and a rubbing of the stone, see Shi Shuqing 史樹青, "Jin Zhou Fang mingqi Pan shi yiwushu kaozheng" 晉周芳命妻潘氏衣物疏考正, *Kaogu tongxun* 考古通訊 2 (1955): 95–99. See also Zhang and Bai, *Zhongguo daojiao kaogu*, 956–57, no. 5]

NOTES

1. For an extensive list of manuscripts excavated from tombs, see Enno Giele, "Early Chinese Manuscripts: Including Addenda and Corrigenda to *New Sources of Early Chinese History: An Introduction to the Reading of Inscriptions and Manuscripts*," *Early China* 23–24 (1998/1999): 247–337. Also available online at http://lucian.uchicago.edu/blogs/earlychina/research-and-resources/databases (accessed May 9, 2012). Although manuscripts and inscribed texts recovered from tombs constitute a valuable body of unaltered source material, tombs containing texts make up only a tiny fraction of the total number of excavated burials.

2. A. F. P. Hulsewé, "Texts in Tombs," *Asiatische Studien* 18–19 (1965): 78–89. Compare Enno Giele, "Excavated Manuscripts: Contexts and Methodology," in *China's Early Empires: A Re-appraisal*, ed. Michael Nylan and Michael Loewe (Cambridge: Cambridge University Press, 2010), 114–34.

3. Donald Harper, "Warring States, Qin, and Han Manuscripts Related to Natural Philosophy and the Occult," in *New Sources of Early Chinese History: An Introduction to the Reading of Inscriptions and Manuscripts*, ed. Edward L. Shaughnessy (Berkeley: Society for the Study of Early China and Institute of East Asian Studies, University of California, 1997), 227.

4. So far, only a half dozen tombs have been found to contain such letters: Fenghuangshan tomb 168, Gaotaishan tomb 18, and Maojiayuan tomb 1, all from Hubei; Mawangdui tomb 3, located near Changsha in Hunan; Huchang tomb 5, located in Jiangsu; and the tomb of Lady Pan (d. 357 C.E.), wife of Zhou Fangming, located at Guihuayuan, also near Changsha, Hunan. The document found in Lady Pan's tomb is translated here (document 15).

5. For two influential interpretations of religious change in early China based on archaeo-logical evidence, see Wu Hung, "From Temple to Tomb: Ancient Chinese Art and Reli-gion in Transition," *Early China* 13 (1988): 78–115; and Lothar von Falkenhausen, "Sources of Taoism: Reflections on Archaeological Indicators of Religious Change in Eastern Zhou China," *Taoist Resources* 5, no. 2 (1994): 1–12.

6. On the bureaucratic view of the underworld in the Warring States period, see Donald Harper, "Resurrection in Warring States Popular Religion," *Taoist Resources* 5, no. 2 (1994): 13–28; and Jeffrey Riegel, "Kou-mang and Ju-shou," *Cahiers d'Extrême-Asie* 5 (1989/1990): 53–83.

7. On the smaller size and less lavish furnishings of tombs containing land-purchase con-tracts and tomb-stabilizing writs, see Zhuo Zhenxi 禚振西, "Shaanxi Huxian de liang zuo Han mu" 陝西戶縣的兩座漢墓, *Kaogu yu wenwu* 考古與文物 1 (1980): 48; and Anna Seidel, "Traces of Han Religion," in *Dōkyō to shūkyō bunka* 道教と宗教文化, ed. Akizuki Kan'ei 秋月觀暎 (Tokyo: Hirakawa shuppansha, 1987), 227–28.

8. "Entombed epitaph inscriptions" (*muzhiming* 墓誌銘) constitute another important type of burial text that also began to appear in late Eastern Han and more widely in early medieval tombs. These objects differed from the more pragmatic genres of land-pur-chase contracts and tomb-stabilizing writs because as commemorative texts, their lau-datory function was designed to long outlast the initial funerary context. Although the "original" *muzhiming* text was inscribed on stone and buried in the tomb, manuscript copies circulated above ground and more admired examples were collected in antholo-gies or were preserved in the author's collected works.

9. Documents 9 and 10, translated in this chapter, are examples of northern contracts in-volving human sellers and witnesses.

10. Terry F. Kleeman, "Land Contracts and Related Documents," in *Makio Ryōkai Hakase shōju kinen ronshū, Chūgoku no shūkyō: Shisō to kagaku* 牧尾良海博士壽計記念論集, 中國の宗教: 思想と科學 (Tokyo: Kokusho kankōkai, 1984), 3–4. For studies of litigation in the courts of the underworld, see Valerie Hansen, "Why Bury Contracts in Tombs?" *Cahiers d'Extrême-Asie* 8 (1995): 59–66; Peter S. Nickerson, "The Great Petition for Sepulchral Plaints," in Stephen R. Bokenkamp, *Early Daoist Scriptures* (Berkeley: University of California Press, 1997), 230–74; and Michel Strickmann, *Chinese Magical Medicine*, ed. Bernard Faure (Stanford, Calif.: Stanford University Press, 2002), 1–57.

11. On the rites required to absolve the deceased from culpability caused by digging into the soil, see Wang Chong 王充, "Jiechu" 解除, in *Lun heng jiaoshi* 論衡校釋, comp. Huang Hui 黃暉 (Beijing: Zhonghua shuju, 1990), 25.1044; and Alfred Forke, trans., *Lun-Hēng* (Berlin: Kommissionsverlag von Georg Reimer, 1909), 1:535–36.

12. Kleeman, "Land Contracts and Related Documents," 20. The large monetary sums in-volved were chosen for their auspicious associations (e.g., the number nine, linked with yang and life, appears often) and do not represent real amounts exchanged.

13. For an early account of one spirit stealing the offerings meant for another, see Yang Bojun 楊伯峻, *Chunqiu Zuozhuan zhu* 春秋左傳注 (Beijing: Zhonghua shuju, 1990), 487 (Xi 31).

14. Kleeman, "Land Contracts and Related Documents," 3.

15. Some documents join features from two different genres of entombed text. For example, document 3 combines a land-purchase contract with a short tomb inventory.

16. For an example of such a jar, see Ikeda On 池田温, "Chūgoku rekidai boken ryakkō" 中國歷代墓券略考, *Tōyō-bunka kenkyūjo kiyō* 東洋文化研究所紀要 86 (1981): 274, no. 9. For a translation, see Seidel, "Traces of Han Religion," 25.

17. Kleeman, "Land Contracts and Related Documents," 4–9. Seidel explains that in addition to an apotropaic function, these texts served as "letters of introduction or passports to the underworld" ("Traces of Han Religion," 25). The jars are between 5.5 and 9.5 inches high.

18. Haoli is the name of a district in the subterranean geography of the dead located beneath Mount Tai. See documents 7 and 8.

19. Kleeman, "Land Contracts and Related Documents" 4–5. For more on the envoy of the Celestial Emperor, see Seidel, "Traces of Han Religion," 34–37.

20. For an informative introduction to "ghost infestations" (*guizhu* 鬼注), deadly contagions sometimes transferred from the resentful dead to their living posterity, see Strickmann, *Magical Chinese Medicine*, 23–39.

21. He Jiejun 何介鈞, *Mawangdui Han mu* 馬王堆漢墓 (Bejing: Wenwu chubanshe, 1982). Tomb 1, constructed for the wife of the marquis, also contained an extensive tomb inventory extending over 312 bamboo slips.

22. *Wenwu* 7 (1974): 43; Seidel, "Traces of Han Religion," 25.

23. *Analects* 6/22. Falkenhausen points out that this idea, rather than originating with Confucius, reflects the general attitude toward the dead that prevailed from around the Middle Eastern Zhou, in "Sources of Taoism," 8.

24. Present-day Zhejiang.

25. Present-day Hangzhou.

26. The provenance of this contract is not firmly established. It appears to have been discovered in the 1950s near Hangzhou, Zhejiang. It was carved into a brick slab measuring $5 \times 4 \times 1$ inches.

27. The second era of Sun Liang's 孫亮 (r. 252–258) reign in the state of Wu 吳.

28. The scribe who wrote the contract mixed up the usual combination of "Heavenly Stems" (*tiangan* 天干): *geng* 庚 and *yi* 乙 have been interchanged. The correct pairing should be *jiayi* for the east and *gengxin* for the west.

29. These four pairs of Heavenly Stems correlate with the cardinal directions as given in the contract. Kleeman suggested that this was a way of designating the vast dimensions of sacred space within which the spirit of the dead would be allowed to roam, in "Land Contracts and Related Documents," 14.

30. The Soil Earl (*Tubo* 土伯) appears in the "Zhao hun" 招魂 piece from the *Lyrics of Chu* (*Chuci* 楚辭) as the menacing guardian of the underworld dead. He is described as a monstrous creature with the head of a tiger and the body of a bull. Wang Yi 王逸 (second century C.E.) states that the Soil Earl's authority was granted by the Earth Sovereign (*Houtu* 后土). See *Chuci buzhu* 楚辭補注, *SBCK* 9.107.

31. This contract was recovered in 1979 from a tomb located near Nanjing, Jiangsu. It was written on a brick slab measuring 15 × 3 × 1 inches. See Zhang and Bai, *Zhongguo dao-jiao kaogu*, 822 and 823, fig. 4.1.

32. The authors of the excavation report suggest that Zhu, Jiao, and Xi are the given names of the three servants. They further note that no corresponding manikins were found in the tomb. See Jiangsu sheng wenwu guanli weiyuanhui 江蘇省文物管理委員會, "Nan-jing jinjiao liuchao mu de qingli" 南京近郊六朝墓的清理, *Kaogu xuebao* 考古學報 1 (1957): 189.

33. My translation of *gou* 溝 as "fine-twined" is based on Bernhard Karlgren, *Gramatica Serica Recensa* (Stockholm: Museum of Far Eastern Antiquities, 1957), 49, no. 109.

34. This portion of the text, inscribed on the back of the contract, constitutes a brief tomb inventory list. This contract was unearthed from tomb 1 located at Nanjing, Jiangsu, in 1955. It was inscribed on a thin lead slab measuring 11 × 2 × 0.04 inches.

35. Modern Jiangxi.

36. The Queen Mother of the West (Xiwangmu 西王母), often associated with the para-dise realm of Mount Kunlun in the far west and with the bestowal of deathlessness, is the embodiment of yin forces. Here she is paired with her cosmic counterpart, the Sovereign Sire of the East (Dongwanggong 東王公), the manifestation of yang energy. The male divinity of this pair is sometimes called Lord of the Eastern Regions (Dong-fangjun 東方君).

37. This contract was recovered in 1980 from a tomb located in Jiangsu. It was carved into a brick slab measuring 13 × 6 × 2 inches.

38. The scholars transcribing the tomb inventory have incorrectly identified the twentieth day of the second month as *gengzi*. The twentieth was actually a *gengwu* day. While mis-takes in cyclical dating are one of the criteria for identifying forgeries, I think this is merely a case of mistakenly reading *zi* 子 for *wu* 午. The two characters are very similar in appearance and could be easily confused, especially considering the poor state of preservation in which the lead contract was found.

39. Both Ruyin and Lujiang Commandery are located in modern Anhui. Lai District of Danyang Commandery is located south of present-day Nanjing, Jiangsu. The sur-name of the tomb occupant, which is obscured in the original document, is derived from additional inscriptions on several of the bricks used in the actual construction of his tomb.

40. About one hundred acres. (A *mu* is roughly equal to one-sixth of an acre, and a *qing* is the equivalent of one hundred *mu*.) The extensive area claimed here is perhaps best understood as referring to the size of the deceased's landholdings in the world of the spirits.

41. We should remember that these immense concepts of space and the exorbitant price were meaningful only in the world of the spirits, as Kleeman has suggested in "Land Contracts and Related Documents," 13–15.

42. The significance of this curious concluding section is unclear. A similar passage is found in the text of a contract dating to 226 C.E. that was excavated near Nanchang, Jiangxi. However, in that case the fish is paired with a crane: "The fish enters the abyss"

while the crane "flies up to heaven." For a transcription and translation, see Ikeda, "Chūgoku rekidai boken ryakkō," 224, no. 23; and Kleeman, "Land Contracts and Related Documents," 23–24. Perhaps the crane and fish serve as messengers to transport the content of the contract to divine authorities in the spirit bureaucracies of the celestial and watery worlds. This may reflect Daoist ideas regarding the Three Offices (*Sanguan* 三官) that were believed to direct the administration of the tripartite spiritual bureaucracies known as the Office of Heaven, Office of Earth, and Office of Water (with the copy buried in the tomb effectively delivering the contract to the Office of Earth). In a similar manner, the fish identified as the scribe of Mr. Hou's land contract is also the agent charged with transmitting the terms of the contract to his superior the River Earl (He Bo). The River Earl, or divinity of the Yellow River, is mentioned in several early texts, including the "Autumn Floods" chapter of the *Zhuangzi* and the "Nine Songs" (*Jiu ge* 九歌) section of the *Lyrics of Chu*. Another possible interpretation is that these sentences demonstrate the utter inaccessibility of the contract's divine scribe, thereby implying that the party with whom changes to the contract must be negotiated is so remote as to prohibit rewriting any of its terms.

43. This contract was recovered in 1964 from a tomb located near Nanjing, Jiangsu. It was carved into a thin lead slab measuring 7 × 2 × 0.06 inches.

44. Dai 代 was the name of an independent Tuoba state that controlled parts of northern China, including the region around Hohhot, Inner Mongolia, from 338 until 376 when it was defeated by Fu Jian 苻堅 (338–385) of the Former Qin 前秦 (351–394). Although this document was written during the Northern Wei 北魏 period (386–534), the author maintains the older designation for this territory.

45. This inscribed stone was discovered near Hohhot, Inner Mongolia, in the early 1990s.

46. The name Andu probably refers to the underworld habitations of the dead and might be rendered "Metropolis of Repose."

47. An announcement or prayer to Wuyi on behalf of soldiers fallen in battle was excavated from tomb 56 at Jiudian 九店, Hubei (slips 43 and 44). This tomb dates to the Warring States period. See Hubei Sheng Wenwu Kaogu Yanjiusuo 湖北省文物考古研究所, *Jiangling Jiudian Dong Zhou mu* 江陵九店東周墓 (Beijing: Kexue Chubanshe, 1995), 508 and pl. 103; and Rao Zongyi 饒宗頤, "Shuo Jiudian Chu jian zhi Wuyi jun yu fu shan" 說九店楚簡之武夷君與復山, *Wenwu* 6 (1997): 36–38.

48. Less than one acre.

49. The divinity Zhang Jiangu, whose name means something like "affirmer of what is certain," and his counterpart Li Dingdu, whose name perhaps means "fixer of measurements," appear as witnesses in a number of Southern land contracts. See, for example, document 8 in which they are listed together with the famous transcendents Wangzi Qiao and Master Red Pine (Chisongzi). This contract was excavated from a tomb located in Shixing County, Guangdong, during the 1980s. It was inscribed on a stone slab measuring 9.5 × 4 × 0.8 inches. A second contract bearing the same inscription was found in the same tomb. The translation is based on the composite transcription supplied in Zhang and Bai, *Zhongguo daojiao kaogu*, which combines the legible portions of both contracts.

50. This contract was recovered in 1938 from a tomb located near Guilin. It was carved into a thin piece of soapstone or steatite (*huashi* 滑石) measuring 7.2 × 4.5 × 0.2 inches.

51. Located in southern Hebei.

52. Shen Zhong served as Minister of Education under the Later Zhao 後趙 (319–351) ruler Shi Jian 石鑒 (r. 349–350). When Ran Min 冉閔 killed Shi Jian and assumed supreme authority in 350 C.E., Shen Zhong transferred his loyalties to Ran. See *JS* 107.2793.

53. Both the Dongyang fiefdom and the Jinxiang District are located in present-day Shandong.

54. The Eastern Palace is the residence of the crown prince.

55. A proper burial was one in which the deceased, having lived out his or her allotted life span, was peacefully laid to rest in the family cemetery, reverently remembered, and offered regular sacrifices. The inability to carry out this ideal internment was a source of concern among the deceased's posterity, not only because filial obligations to the ancestors continued after their demise, but also because the "unquiet dead" could inflict real harm on the health and prosperity of living family members. For a fascinating study of early medieval apprehensions concerning the dead, see Stephen R. Bokenkamp, *Ancestors and Anxiety: Daoism and the Birth of Rebirth in China* (Berkeley: University of California Press, 2007).

56. Located in present-day Shanxi Province.

57. In other words, his virtue.

58. The unusual names of landlords given at the end of this document are transliterations from a non-Chinese language. They are the names of real individuals and not deities. Helai is a Xiongnu surname originally the designation of one of nineteen Xiongnu tribes. See *JS* 97.2549; and Yao Weiyuan 姚薇元, *Beichao hu xing kao* 北朝胡姓考 (Taibei: Huashi chubanshe, 1977), 32–38. Surnames similar to Wenniuyu and Gaoli are also found in Yao's study, though not the exact names given in this document.

59. This epitaph and contract was unearthed about 1940 near Datong 大同, Shanxi 山西, the early capital of the Northern Wei regime. They were inscribed on a stone measuring 21 × 17 inches.

60. About a half acre.

61. The scribe and witnesses of this Northern contract are actual members of the local community and not divinities. The exact provenance of this contract is unclear. In "Chūgoku rekidai boken ryakkō," Ikeda states that it was excavated in Zhuozhou 涿州, Hebei.

62. The exact meaning of the term *mujia* is unclear. It could refer to the physical structure of the tomb or more figuratively to the living lineage (*jia* 家) members related to Sui Fang.

63. This tomb-stabilizing writ was recovered in 1979 from a tomb located near Baoji, Shaanxi. It was written in vermilion ink on the outside of a small earthenware jar measuring 9.1 inches high.

64. Representations of humans made from lead were placed in a number of tombs to toil on behalf of the deceased. One such specimen was recovered from tomb M1 constructed for Wang Xingzhi. See Nanjing shi wenwu guanli weiyuanhui 南京市文物管理委員會,

"Nanjing Rentaishan Dong Jin Xingzhi fufu mu fajue baogao" 南京人臺山東晉興之夫婦墓發掘報告, *Wenwu* 文物 6 (1965): 29.

65. This document was one of five nearly identical texts recovered from a tomb in Lingbao County, Henan, in 1972. Like the other four texts, it was written with a brush in vermilion ink on the surface of a jar. Perhaps the duplication of the document was meant to enhance the potency of its message.

66. One's life mandate (*ming* 命) was allotted at conception and, owing to moral choices, could be extended or reduced. On the mutability of *ming* through various bureaucratic, alchemical, and meditative practices, see Robert Ford Campany, *To Live as Long as Heaven and Earth: A Translation and Study of Ge Hong's Traditions of Divine Transcendents* (Berkeley: University of California Press, 2002), 47–60; and Stephen R. Bokenkamp, "Simple Twists of Fate: The Daoist Body and Its *Ming*," in *The Magnitude of Ming: Command, Allotment, and Fate in Chinese Culture*, ed. Christopher Lupke (Honolulu: University of Hawai'i Press, 2005), 151–68.

67. The Eight Ghosts (*bagui* 八鬼) may be what Sima Qian refers to as the "eight spirits" (*bashen* 八神) in "Fengshan shu" 封單書. The group consists of (1) the Lord of Heaven, (2) the Lord of the Earth, (3) the Lord of Weapons, (4) the Lord of Yin, (5) the Lord of Yang, (6) the Lord of the Sun, (7) the Lord of the Moon, and (8) the Lord of the Four Seasons. See *SJ* 28.1367.

68. The Nine Canals (*jiukan* 九坎) may be an alternative name for *jiuquan* 九泉, which are the Nine Springs of the underworld. In some contexts, the term *jiukan* refers to a cluster of nine stars located south of the Ox Herd star. These stars are among those that "govern matters pertaining to irrigation." If this reference is applicable at all, it is probably due to the association of these stars with water: the element linked with darkness, the north, and death. Another possibility is that the Nine Springs are the subterranean correlative to the astral configuration. See *JS* 11.305; and Ho Peng Yoke, *The Astronomical Chapters of the Chin Shu* (Paris: Mouton, 1966), 107.

69. Several grave-quelling jars refer to the bowels of the Eastern Marchmount, Mount Tai, as the location where the dead are assembled and evaluated for posthumous service in the underworld. Compare the tomb-stabilizing writ for Xu Wentai dating to 175 C.E., which states, "The living are under the jurisdiction of Chang'an in the West, the dead are under the jurisdiction of Mount Tai in the East." See Ikeda, "Chūgoku rekidai boken ryakkō," 273, no. 7; and Seidel, "Traces of Han Religion," 31.

70. These four sacrifices were performed during each of the four seasons: spring, winter, autumn, and summer, respectively.

71. This tomb-stabilizing writ was discovered with another jar bearing the same text in a tomb located near Dunhuang, Gansu, in 1944.

72. The phrase is *zhuwu* 注誤 (忤/忤; infest your repugnant [pathogens]). The graphic variations are discussed in Zhang and Bai, *Zhongguo daojiao kaogu*, 521–22.

73. This infestation-quelling writ was found in a tomb located near Dunhuang, Gansu, in 1987. It was written with a brush in black ink on the outside of a small pottery jar.

74. Lustrous silk refers to silk that has been treated or degummed to remove the gelatinous protein sericin.

75. Pairs of small stone pigs have been found in dozens of southern tombs. They were grasped in the hands of the deceased and may have served an apotropaic function.

76. The phrase *zuijiu bulu* and the connotations of joyfully passing from life to death after having imbibed the intoxicating wine of the immortals is discussed in Peter S. Nickerson, "Taoism, Death, and Bureaucracy in Early Medieval China" (Ph.D. diss., University of California, 1996), 187n.15.

77. That is, another ambitious spirit cannot appropriate Lady Pan's rightful possessions to pay debts they might owe the underworld authorities.

78. This inventory and letter was unearthed in 1954 near Changsha, Hunan. The text was inscribed on a stone slab measuring 9 × 5 inches.

36. Reciting Scriptures to Move the Spirits

CLARKE HUDSON

The text translated in this chapter is an early Lingbao 靈寶 (Numinous Treasure) scripture.[1] The first Lingbao scriptures were anonymously composed by Ge Chaofu 葛巢甫, a grand-nephew of Ge Hong 葛洪 (283–343), around 400 C.E. Ge Chaofu and his imitators drew on several sources: Shangqing 上清 scriptures, the older religious traditions of the region (as found in Ge Hong's writings), and certain Buddhist sutras.[2] The text seems to present itself as a series of extracts from an earlier text, *Most High Concealed Commentary on the Jade Scripture* (*Shangqing taiji yinzhu yujing baojue* 上清太極隱注玉經寶訣), with further comments by the Perfected of the Great Ultimate (Ge Xuan 葛玄) and an appended hymn. However, the text was probably an original composition made to look like a commentary and, when first composed, probably looked much as it does today.

Daoist texts are an important source of information about religion in early medieval China,[3] and the Lingbao scriptures are an important textual corpus from this period. Roughly one-quarter of all extant Six Dynasty Daoist texts are Lingbao texts. Surveys of the Daoism of this period sometimes frame it as a story of three successive traditions—the Celestial Master, the Shangqing, and the Lingbao traditions—each of which incorporated the ideas and practices of its predecessor(s) while transforming them and adding new elements.[4] One advantage of this view is that it highlights the ways in which the composers of texts in these three traditions simultaneously competed with and drew on the other traditions.[5] The text translated here, for example, shows great reverence for scriptures from earlier forms of Daoism (especially the *Classic of the Way and Virtue* [*Daodejing* 道德經] and Shangqing scriptures) yet uses them for recitation, a practice characteristic of (though not unique to) Lingbao Daoism, thereby thoroughly altering the significance of the earlier scriptures.[6]

There is, however, a flaw in this view of early medieval Daoism as a succession of three traditions: we do not yet have a good understanding of the institutional reality or social contexts of these early textual traditions. From a text-based perspective, we say that "Shangqing Daoism" and "Lingbao Daoism" differ from "Celestial Master Daoism," but in fact, probably all the composers of these texts were Celestial Masters.[7] There were also other textual corpora or isolated revelations from this period (such as the Sanhuang 三皇, Shenzhou 神咒, and Shengxuan 昇玄 scriptures), as well as Daoist institutions (such as the Louguan 樓觀 Daoist lineage) that do not fit this narrative. So it would be best to think of Lingbao Daoism as just a textual tradition rather than a "school of Daoism" and hope that future research will clarify its place in the social history of Daoism during this period.

This scripture tells us much about the relations between humans and spirit beings in the Lingbao teachings (and in the earlier forms of Daoism that they drew on). Yet the main theme of this scripture is "scripture" as such: the majority of this text is concerned with the transmission, care, and recitation of scriptures. Scriptures are not just religious records; they are sacred objects. According to Lingbao teachings, at the time of cosmogenesis, the Dao collected to form scriptures. They first existed as sacred writing in the dim void and have since been transmitted through a hierarchy of spirits to us, finally to be inscribed in language legible (or at least visible) to mortals of China. Receiving a scripture is the closest we can come, in this life, to the Dao; and with the aid of human and transcendent teachers, scripture recitation is our best path back to union with the Dao. If an adept purifies himself (or herself) in body and mind and recites the four categories of scripture (the Shangqing, Lingbao, and Sanhuang corpora, and the *Classic of the Way and Virtue*),[8] with deep and intense sincerity, then the celestial deities will recite the same scriptures in heaven, echoing his voice. The Most High will be moved to send dragon-drawn chariots of cloud to collect him and deliver him to heaven. This blessing will reach his deceased ancestors to the seventh generation, who may be suffering in the purgatories.

The text mentions dozens of individual spirits or categories of spirit being, from (1) abstract or individualized high gods (e.g., the Celestial Kings of Primal Commencement, the Most High of the ten directions, the Five Thearchs, the Three Officers, the Three Purities, the Three Ones, three Lord Laos, Mystic Father and Primal Mother, Queen Mother of the West, Lord of the Primal One, the Great One or Taiyi, Most High Jade August One, and Thearch One), to (2) the transcendent rank and file (e.g., transcendent chamberlains, earls, dukes, and princes, or perfected beings of low, middle, and high ranks), to (3) tutelary spirits (e.g., the demon kings, beasts of the four directions, or the dozens of jade maidens and lads who stand in attendance on each scripture), to (4) the spirits of one's own body (e.g., the spirits of the three elixir fields or the Lords of the Three Primes or Three Purities within the brain), (5) heroes (e.g., Lord Lao, his disciple Yin Xi 尹喜, the *Classic of the Way and Virtue* commentator Heshang Gong 河上公, and Ge Hong's great-uncle Ge Xuan), (6) ancestors, and (7) demons. This text discusses the recitation of the four categories of scripture and the different spirit beings who respond to each of them yet does not attempt to organize them into a synthetic pantheon. The various spirits coexist for the adept according to a functional, ritual logic. All that matters are the places of these spirits within specific recitation rituals, and the relationship between the spirits and the adept; the relationships between different sets of deities are left unexplored.

In this text, the dividing line between mortal humans and transcendent beings is not absolute. Some humans are predestined for transcendence, and the text sometimes speaks of them as if they already were transcendent or perfected beings. These humans predestined for transcendence may already outrank some celestial transcendents.[9] This should not cause adepts to doubt their own predestination and thus despair of achieving salvation: anyone who is accepted by a master must, ipso facto, have the destiny of transcendent-hood, based on past lives of spiritual merit.[10]

Relations between spirits and the adept are mediated by scriptures, and the same holds for relations between the adept and other mortals. The emphasis here on scriptures gives us the impression that masters exist mainly to bestow scriptures on worthy disciples and that the adept's religious engagement with the world (e.g., maintaining his ritual purity and virtuous power [de 德], succoring others in need, disseminating teachings, or enduring praise and abuse with humility and sincerity) has value mainly as part of a regimen of self-cultivation leading to scriptural transmission and recitation, rather than as simple moral duty.

The Lingbao teachings represent the first extended attempt by Daoists to appropriate language, ideas, and practices from Mahayana Buddhism. One significant Lingbao appropriation from Mahayana is the idea that the adept's own salvation is linked to the universal salvation of all suffering beings in *samsāra*. Some argue that the Lingbao-Mahayanist concern for other beings marks a break from Shangqing or earlier forms of Daoism, in which the adept seeks only to save himself.[11] Yet in this text we see concern for others, even the idea of remaining in *samsāra* until all beings have been saved, mentioned almost in the same breath with exhortations to overleap the realm of common humanity and leave them all behind. On the whole, we find more self-concern in this Lingbao text than concern for suffering beings, without much attempt to rationally harmonize the two concerns.

FURTHER READING

The best introduction to the early Lingbao scriptures is Stephen R. Boken-kamp, "Sources of the Ling-pao Scriptures," in *Tantric and Taoist Studies in Honour of R. A. Stein*, ed. Michel Strickmann (Brussels: Institut belge des hautes études chinoises, 1983), 2.434–86. Erik Zürcher discusses the links be-tween Buddhism and early Daoism (including Lingbao) in "Buddhist Influence on Early Taoism: A Survey of Scriptural Evidence," *T'oung Pao* 66, nos. 1–3 (1980): 84–147. For a discussion of the Shangqing scriptures (an important source for the Lingbao scriptures), see Isabelle Robinet, *Taoist Meditation: The Mao-Shan Tradition of Great Purity*, trans. Norman J. Girardot and Julian F. Pas (Albany: State University of New York Press, 1993). The most widely read Ling-bao scripture, *Duren jing* 度人經, is translated in Stephen R. Bokenkamp, "The Wondrous Scripture of the Upper Chapters of Limitless Salvation," in *Early Daoist Scriptures* (Berkeley: University of California Press, 1997), 373–438. For studies of medieval Lingbao ritual, see Catherine Bell, "Ritualization of Texts and Textualization of Ritual in the Codification of Taoist Liturgy," *History of Religions* 27, no. 4 (1988): 366–92; and Charles D. Benn, *The Cavern-Mystery Transmission: A Taoist Ordination Rite of A.D. 711* (Honolulu: University of Hawai'i Press, 1991). Isabelle Robinet discusses the links between early Ling-bao scriptures and modern Daoist ritual in "The Lingbao School," in *Taoism: Growth of a Religion*, trans. Phyllis Brooks (Stanford, Calif.: Stanford University Press, 1997), 149–83.

Precious Secret Instructions on the Jade Scriptures, a Concealed Commentary by the [Perfected of the] Great Ultimate of Highest Clarity

INTRODUCTION: A SYNOPSIS OF THE PATH[12]

The Most High[13] of mystic tenuity comes from the time of the origin of the Three Caverns.[14] His words are of ultimate profundity, recessed and distant in the darkness, difficult to hear of. As a stygian crown, towering and alone, they encompass and enfold the massed multitudes of things. Lofty in their ultimate virtuous power [*de* 德][15] and massively imposing in their grand eminence, they are a perch for beings of ultimate perfection and the gate of many wonders.[16] [These words are] the progenitors of the spirits and transcendents, who col-lected them together and gave them written form. Chanting sonorously,[17] the spirits ascend in the void, driving dragons or mounted on clouds. With utmost integrity, they regulate and focus their dispositions. Now, a gentleman [or lady] intent [on transcendent-hood] may seek these scriptures afar. Reverently serving a ritual master,[18] he [or she] should genuflect in a hall of virtue, asking and consulting again and again, beseeching the master to bestow the precious scriptures. If he has true trust in the correct *dao*,[19] with nary a doubt, then he may count on achieving divine transcendent-hood. Exhaling stale air and inhaling fresh,[20] scooping up and eating rare exudations,[21] he will receive a summons from void nonbeing and, in time, will fly up as a transcendent. The wheel of Dharma [helps him] concentrate his awareness; his penetrating gaze reaches to the nine extremities of space.[22] How peculiar and small in the distance are the secret instructions! How could [even] transcendents of middle rank know them? You are a fellow who is studying perfection! If you can contemplate in solitude the radiance that confronts you,[23] quickly draw together the sincerity of your feelings, refine and test your lustful thoughts [to rid yourself of them],[24] undergo hunger and cold, suffer without growing weary, take a meal [only?] at midday,[25] endure public ridicule without dejection and praise without gladness, [maintaining] solitary virtue [*de*] within and eliminating all your physical expressions of emotion without, and bathing with [flowers of] *Angelica dehurica*, [then you will have] no loss of fetal *qi*[26] [and may] climb to the [room for] ritual purification[27] and enter the [oratory] chamber,[28] censing with sandalwood smoke. Thereupon you don kerchief and short cape, straighten your ritual vestments, make obeisances to the ten directions of space, take refuge in and [entrust] your life mandate to the great perfected ones, and bow thrice before the scriptures.[29] Now, opening the eight-colored wrapper and laying out the most high and precious repository [of scripture], take up and recite the revered scriptures of the Great Cavern, the Cavern Mystery, and the *Classic of the Way and Virtue*.[30] The *Hidden Chapters of the Eight Purities*[31] and the *Jade Radiance of the Golden Perfected Ones*[32] exterminate demons and scatter the numinous beings and summon the transcendents to pace the void. The clear tones of the *Winged Scripture of Flight*[33] roll through the empyrean, and the myriad perfected beings descend to the [celestial] court. The Most High[34] orders them to hitch up, and [the gods] ride together in canopied carriages of cloud. Luxuriant mists, darkly flushed with vitality, unite with the distant stygian darkness. The Three Simplicities[35] attune their phosphors and bear round and radiant [halos] behind their necks. They wear short capes of gauze, with jade bangles and fire bells at their waists. Reverent and serious are the eminent perfected ones as they glide on a distant journey. With Jade Efflorescence[36] lending protection, all mount together to the [heaven of] Highest Clarity. There is no separation between the noble and the base; rather, the deciding factor [regarding who attains transcendent-hood] is a person's utmost sincerity. [Beings from] the Three Realms will pay their respects,[37] and the demon kings[38] will come respectfully to meet you. Your years will be long, without limit. How could you count how many *kalpas* long your life span will be?[39] You will wander freely at leisure; your "furtherance" and "perseverance"[40] will be eternal.

THE TRANSMISSION OF THE SCRIPTURES

The *Concealed Commentary* says, "When bestowing the *Classic of the Way and Virtue*, the ritual master faces north,[41] the scripture is placed on the low table, and the disciple crouches respectfully on the left. The master grasps the scripture, and the disciple proffers the ritual surety.[42] The master clacks his [or her] teeth thirty-six times and makes the Three Palaces present in his heart-mind. The Three Ones of the Muddy Pellet, Elixir Field, and Crimson Palace[43] come out, with thousands of carriages and myriad cavalry, to assume their positions protecting the scripture and master. Thereupon, [the master] incants the following:

> Floating [among] the mountain ranges of the great void are flowing phosphors in the upper mystic regions. The scriptures originally have no kalpic limit to their existence, and eternally protect heaven, earth, and humanity. Lords of the [secular] world study how to bring back Yao,[44] while the gentlemen [or ladies] of the Dao chant sonorously to attain transcendent-hood. The worthy one [the disciple] now respectfully receives it and [will] transmit it according to the code. If there are no fellows of utmost virtuous power [*de*] during these times, keep it secret and do not wantonly publicize it. If you follow its principles, you will ascend to Grand Clarity, but if you discard it, you will plunge to the Nine Springs.[45] I teach the *dao* of nonaction and the spontaneity of the pure and tranquil *de* [virtuous power].

This done, the disciple bows thrice and receives the scripture. If the disciple is female, she crouches respectfully to the right.[46] The same applies to all scripture [transmissions]."

The *Concealed Commentary* says, "When bestowing the *Perfected Scripture of the Great Cavern*,[47] the ritual master faces north, and the scripture is placed on the low table. The master grasps the scripture, and the disciple proffers the ritual surety. The master clacks his [or her] teeth thirty-six times, and makes the Most High Jade August One present in his heart-mind, causing the reflected radiance of sun and moon to shine on the scripture and on the bodies of master and disciple. [The master] then incants the following:

> Grand Tenuity[48]—how tiny it is in the distance! The perfected ones are generated [therefrom], taking form in the void. The spontaneous Dao [crosses over], taking emptiness as its bridge, and collects to form the *Great Cavern Scripture*. The perfected worthies respectfully take up the ritual surety; responding to this rare fortune, they pass in sequence through the Yellow Court.[49] The Most High expunges [your record from] the register of death, and the Director of Destinies[50] copies down [your] transcendent name. If you protect and keep it secret, your life span will be counted in *kalpas*. If you leak it out disrespectfully, you will suffer in the earth prisons. Calamities and investigative tortures [will be visited on your

family] down to ancestors of the seventh generation, and knives of wind[51] will carve up your form.

This done, the disciple bows thrice, and receives the scripture."

The *Concealed Commentary* says, "When bestowing [one of the] Most High Numinous-Treasure scriptures of Cavern Mystery,[52] the ritual master faces north, and the scripture is placed on the low table. The master grasps the scripture, and the disciple proffers the ritual surety. The master clacks his [or her] teeth thirty-six times and makes the colors of the five viscera[53] present in his heart-mind. When he has caused them all to be present, he unites them to make clouds [in the form of] a precious canopy, covering the scripture, master, and disciple like a veil. [The master] then incants the following:

> The writings of heaven are simple and not complex; their *dao* and their *de* [virtuous power] are spontaneously complete. If you cultivate them, you will certainly [become a] divine transcendent. What further desire could you have? The writing flashes within Great Nonbeing, fiery yet darkly luxuriant. In transmitting them, in all cases follow the code. If you leak them out disrespectfully, you will fall down to the earth prisons.

This done, the disciple bows thrice, and receives the scripture. Finally, bow once in each of the ten directions of space, beginning with the north and turning east until you have made a full circle. Visualize seeing or meeting the Most High of the ten directions in their perfected forms. They [look] like the images currently [in use]."

The *Concealed Commentary* says, "When bestowing the *Most High Celestial Writs of the Three August Ones*,[54] the ritual master faces north, and the scripture is placed on the low table. The master grasps the scripture, and the disciple proffers the ritual surety. The master clacks his [or her] teeth twenty-four times and, in his heart-mind makes present the Three Palaces, each with a perfected being. These beings are shaped like infants, unclothed, [and] exhaling purple *qi* from their mouths, which censes the scripture, master, and disciple. [The master] then incants the following:

> The most high celestial writs have been passed down orally from the time of the beginning of heaven and earth. The August Ones promulgate their mysterious instructions, which are written out by the beings of ultimate perfection. The worthy one now respectfully receives it; his [or her] intention is set on ascending into the great void.

This done, the disciple bows twice[55] and receives the scripture."

The *Concealed Commentary* says, "In transmitting the chapters, scriptures, and talismans of Highest Clarity, always face north. For writings of middle rank, or outer writings [from the category of] conscious action [*youwei*],[56] the master faces east. As for the registers of the latter-day followers of the transcendents and holy beings, the person who transmits them faces south.[57] Male disciples crouch respectfully on the left, and female disciples crouch on the right. The ritual sureties, incantations, and vows follow the code of the ritual master." . . . [58]

RECITING THE SCRIPTURES

The *Concealed Commentary* says, "When reciting the *Classic of the Way and Virtue*, clack your teeth and swallow saliva, each thirty-six times, then first make present in your heart-mind the blue-green dragon on the left, the white tiger on the right, the cardinal-red bird before you, and the murky warrior behind you.[59] The divine turtle with the eight trigrams [on its shell] is below your feet, and thirty-six lions crouch before you. Your head is kerchiefed with seven stars, your five viscera generate five *qi*, and veil patterns cover your body. Above you, the Three Ones[60] attend upon the scripture, each with a retinue of a thousand carriages and myriad cavalry. There are eighteen thousand jade maidens and jade lads protecting the scripture in heaven, and the same number on earth."

The *Concealed Commentary* says, "When reciting the *Perfected Scripture of the [Great] Cavern*,[61] clack your teeth and swallow saliva, each thirty-six times, then first make present [in visualization] a whirlwind mingling together Thearch One,[62] the hundred spirits, and the myriad perfected ones. Then chant the *Cavern Scripture* with extended tones."

The *Concealed Commentary* says, "When reciting a Cavern Mystery scripture, clack your teeth and swallow saliva, each thirty-six times, then make present [in visualization] the five *qi* of the five viscera, each a different color, rising to infuse [you with] the essences of the five naked-eye planets. Then recite the scripture."

The *Concealed Commentary* says, "When sonorously chanting the *Most High Cavern Mystery Scripture of Pacing the Void*,[63] first clack your teeth and swallow saliva thrice. Make present in your heart-mind the sun and moon on your own face, entering through your nostrils and traveling to the Palace of Golden Efflorescence in the Cavern Chamber.[64] [A halo] of radiance is emitted from behind your neck, making a flaming, round shape of nine colors. It approaches and enters the Jade Pillow [the occiput], where it shines penetratingly in the ten directions. [This radiance] moves in a circuit, following your movements as you circumambulate the scripture. The sun enters the nose from the left, and the moon from the right. This done, clack your teeth according to the first method."

The *Concealed Commentary* says, "When reciting a scripture [devoted to] the ascent to transcendent-hood, first clack your teeth and swallow saliva, each twelve times. With each chapter you chant, clack your teeth thrice. There are individual methods for each scripture or scroll. When the method is not recorded, you may use the secret instruction above."

The *Concealed Commentary* says, "Now, if a scripture of the Dao is not received from a master, then its spirits will not be activated. If there are no ritual masters during your generation and none to transmit the registers, then [as an alternative method] you should throw your ritual surety into your oratory.[65] Or you may make an announcement to Lord Lao, the Mysterious Teacher, in a secret chamber. Facing north, bow thrice. Next make donations to people suffering from hunger or want while maintaining equanimity in your heart-mind. Then you may use the scripture. If there are masters [active] during your generation, you need not use this method."

The *Concealed Commentary* says, "When chanting scriptures, sit on a small dais five *chi* in height, and equal in length and breadth. Wear only kerchief and short cape; these need not be hempen.[66] The Perfected of the Great Ultimate's ritual vestments for reciting scriptures are a cape of sparse-gauze nine-radiance brocade, and a precious sun-dazzling kerchief of cinnabar gauze, with lion-striped sandals on the feet. Nowadays, when gentlemen [or ladies] of the Dao recite scriptures, they labor hard at the affairs of ritual, and their capes and vestments are coarser. Later, when you have attained the Dao, the celestial thearchs will bestow on you a sparse-gauze nine-radiance cape and the ritual vestments of a flying transcendent [decorated] with celestial-treasure beadstrings, to repay your past merit [*de*]. Do not admire the crowns of this world; give them up for the base clothes of a gentleman of the Dao. Although worldly clothes may appear glorious to the eye now, [their wearers] cannot escape death. A gentleman of the Dao clothes himself coarsely in his ritual vestments but ascends to transcendent-hood, where he is to be clothed in celestial raiment. The celestial robes clothing his body will allow him to soar up to transcendent-hood and ride [through] the void."

The *Concealed Commentary* says, "The method for reciting scriptures is to take the tones of the Middle Kingdom [China] as your model. These are the correct tones of the Nine Heavens.[67] When [in] the sixty-fourth Great Brahma[68] [heaven, the gods] extol a scripture, controlling their voices as they chant: these are also the correct tones. The tones for reciting a scripture should take these correct tones as their model."

The Transcendent Squire[69] [Ge Xuan] says, "Laozi went west to convert the barbarians;[70] when he was teaching [the inhabitants of] the foreign lands to recite scriptures, he mostly used the tones of the Great Brahma Heaven, to suit the preference of the gentlemen of the Dao [in those lands]."

The *Concealed Commentary* says, "For every five hundred words that you recite from a scripture, clack your teeth thrice. Lick your upper and lower lips with your tongue, and swallow thrice. This way you will not exhaust your limits: even after a long time, your voice will be clear. If you do not know this method, then you will diminish your *qi* and belabor your spirit[s]."

The Perfected says, "Make a beverage from bamboo leaves which have been boiled to a thick [broth]. If you use this while reciting scriptures and visualizing [spirits], it will increase your essence and cause your spirit[s] to pervade, harmonize your *qi* and make it flow."[71]

The *Concealed Commentary* says, "At midday, quickly swallow the 'Most High Great Concealed Talismans [in nine stanzas]' with water.[72] If you do this for a thousand days, then you will be a transcendent being, able to come and go instantly, disappearing or appearing at will. If you wear the 'Five Numinous-

Treasure Talismans'[73] on your person, then you will be able to ride on dragons or vapors, passing through water or fire. With the Five Thearchs[74] lending protection, you can wander far and soar on high, [in this way] also becoming a transcendent. If you wear the 'True Forms of the Five Marchmounts'[75] or the great talismans of the Three Caverns, you may not come near the affairs of the bedchamber or come into contact with yin or defiling things. If you do so, it is certain that you will die and never have a hope of transcendent-hood. How can you not be cautious?"

The *Concealed Commentary* says, "If a gentleman [or lady] of the Dao enters the chamber, undergoes ritual purification, and recites the *Most High Jade Stanzas on Pacing the Void* and the *Winged Book of Flight*,[76] then he can drive the nine dragons at a gallop, and carriages of cloud will come to meet him. These two affairs ought to be kept secret."

The *Concealed Commentary* says, "If you are constantly able to recite the *Five-Thousand [Character] Writ*,[77] [to the extent of] ten-thousand repetitions, then the cloud dragons of the Most High will descend to meet you. If the ten thousand repetitions are complete and you have not yet departed, recite it thrice[78] for a month. It is certain that the cloud carriage will arrive, and then you can ascend as a transcendent."

The *Concealed Commentary* says, "If you constantly recite the *Yellow Canon Scripture of Inner Phosphors*[79] aloud, then you will be deathless. If you constantly ingest primal *qi*, this is also a *dao* of deathlessness."

The *Concealed Commentary* says, "If you constantly maintain [a vision in which] your head is perfectly blue-green like jasper, your two hands are like cinnabar, and your two feet are like snow, and while maintaining this concentrated imagination recite the scriptures, you will be able to carry out various marvels, and you will be close to transcendent-hood. If you constantly clack your teeth twelve times [a day,] [clacking them once every double hour throughout the day and night], then you will also be deathless, since your corporeal spirits will be constantly present and on guard."

COMMUNICATING WITH SPIRITS

The *Concealed Commentary* says, "One term for clacking the teeth is 'Celestial Drums.' It musters the spirits of the body, summons the perfected ones of the heavens, and brings the flocks of transcendents together. The term for clacking the teeth on the left is 'Ringing Celestial Bells,' and the term for clacking those on the right is 'Knocking Celestial Chimes.' When a gentleman [or lady] of the Dao has a fearful thought and, out of dread, wishes to avoid demonic thieves, if he rings his 'bells' and 'chimes' twenty-four times each, then the sprites will not dare to approach, the celestial demon[-kings] will protect his person, and many blessings will come to him at once."

The *Concealed Commentary* says, "In the *Laozi*, it is said, 'That which one looks at without seeing is evanescent; that which one listens to without hearing is rarefied; that which one brushes against without grasping is minute.'[80] These are none other than the Three Primes[81] and Lord Lao's reign title. It also says, 'These three things cannot be closely examined, so they are blended into one.'[82] The Three Simplicities unite to become Lord of the Primal One.[83] These are the Mystic Father and Primal Mother[84] of the Fetal Worthy. If you recite this scripture, the three Lord Laos will meet you. If you see them, then you have attained the *dao* of transcendent-hood. In this, the *dao* is complete. Writing does not exhaust speech, and speech does not exhaust thoughts. As for profound insight, there are none higher than in this writing. It is generally agreed that one can see it without being able to understand it."

The *Concealed Commentary* says, "Kunlun, Penglai, Bell Mountain, Mount Song, and Mount Wangwu[85] all are cited in the scriptures of Highest Clarity."

The *Concealed Commentary* says, "Kunlun, the mountain of the Man-Bird[86] in the country of Yuannaluowei,[87] is an outside region under the control of the Celestial Kings of Primal Commencement. Their halls and rooms are of the seven treasures, and their lofty platforms encroach on the skies. When the Queen Mother of the West was first learning the Dao, she also climbed this mountain. All the scriptures of the Three Caverns are there on the mountaintop. These writings were made in the void. The characters of the scriptures are each one *zhang* 丈 [eight feet] square. The chart of the true form of this mountain[88] is of utmost importance. If you wear it on your person, then you will attain [the status] of a mystic perfected being of the Three Caverns. All the many beasts of this mountain can fly and are deathless. [If the beasts can do this,] how much the more [powerful] must its people be! All the many rare things appear together here. When the assemblies of holy beings of this mountain sonorously chant the scriptures, they always use the controlled tones of the Great Brahma Heaven, without grief, lagging, or haste [in their voices]. [Their chanting] is of high elegance and profound beauty, giving a happy and harmonious feeling to those who hear it. The various transcendents atop Mount Kunlun mostly chant sonorously [in the tones of] the Nine Heavens of the Middle Kingdom, their refined and pleasing [voices ringing] far and unimpeded, their clear tones crisp and loud. Those who hear them lose their emotion and [have a feeling of] fainting away in the misty heights. The masses of transcendents assemble periodically to sing the Cavern Mystery [scriptures], with long-drawn-out tones. As they recite, singing in unison, the new sounds dash and echo. Profound and secret, audible through the distance, they flourish their coloratura singing in the empty vastness. They ringingly pluck strings of void, and [the entire heaven] of Jade Clarity is moved to joy. Thus, the perfected beings on high place importance on reciting the scriptures. The inscription on the high platform reads, 'If you want to ride emptiness and overleap the void, sonorously chant my

[Scripture of] Pacing the Mystic, and Winged Writ.'[89] The various transcendents do not understand this declaration. These two books, the [Scripture of] Pacing the Mystic and the Winged Writ, are mystic scriptures of the Most High and are not transmitted to middle-ranking transcendents."

The Perfected of the Great Ultimate said, "For the Scripture of Pacing the Void, make a Numinous Treasure ritual purification, and sonorously chant the [stanzas] on pacing the mystic.[90] The Winged Scripture is a Cavern Perfection scripture meant to be chanted in long tones."

ADDITIONAL WORDS OF INSTRUCTION, HOPE, AND WARNING

The Concealed Commentary says, "When learning the dao while living the life of a householder, you ought to receive the Five-Thousand [Character] Writ. In loud tones, chant it on the first and fifteenth days of the month, on your own birth-destiny [benming 本命] day and on the days of the eight seasonal nodes, chanting it through once at midday and once at midnight. If you are unable to recite it, ask your master to recite it for you. You must personally stand in attendance with burning incense, receiving the scripture's instructions with a unified heart-mind, and with your intention set on respectfully rendering most wonderful services related to this scripture. On the day when you entrust your physical form to the Great Yin,[91] the cloud carriages of the celestial thearchs will come to meet you, and your body and its spirits will not be required to pass through investigative tortures and punishment in the earth prisons of the Three Officers of Mount Tai 太山.[92] You will be born above in the halls of heaven, before the celestial thearchs, or [you] will be born below among humans, in the household of a marquis or prince. Your major and minor marks[93] complete, your numinous countenance will shine with rich radiance. Those who gaze upon you will have glad hearts and will ever desire to see and listen to you. Also, a woman will be transformed into a man,[94] you will form the karmic conditions for [reaching] Highest Clarity, and the dao of transcendent-hood will be possible. When this scripture is transmitted among the multitudes of beings, whether they be large or small, they will have no obstruction in whatever they wish to obtain. In every case it is appropriate for seeing off the dead or nurturing the living. Furthermore, the scripture can bring calm to the country and its people. [When it is used to] bring about the control and submission of the foreign border tribes, there are none [among them] who are not [made to] follow the Dao. This scripture is truly a marvel, and there is none higher!"

The Concealed Commentary says, "Although students may cultivate their virtuous behavior, some may suffer from a matching [burden] from a previous lifetime. As for those who suffer from disease or disaster, or frequent bouts of fatigue, the gentlemen of the Dao or masters of ritual methods ought to hold purification rites for them and recite the Five-Thousand [Character] Writ, and the middle chapters of the *Wisdom That Extinguishes Demons*[95] and the *Cavern Scripture of the Golden Perfected Ones of the [Heaven of] Jade Clarity*.[96] Mighty spirits assume positions to protect the sick person. This is what is called 'receiving succor when on the brink of woe.' For rescuing [people] from all crises, there are no 'dharma wheels' equal to these." ...

The *Concealed Commentary* says, "When you receive a scripture, always collate the characters [of the newly copied scripture with its parent copy] three times. If one character is in error, then one year of your life span will be deducted. If more than this, add up [the errors]. One character too many or too few will lead to the loss of one year. If you wantonly destroy scriptural writings, then in a later lifetime you will suffer the investigative torture of having your physical form carved up by knives of wind. If you receive the scripture without venerating a master, then in cultivating it, you will also not gain any blessing, and later you will be cast into a lifetime of disease or a lifetime as a domestic animal." ...[97]

DIVINE COMMENTS: THE *CLASSIC OF THE WAY AND VIRTUE* [*DAODEJING* 道德經]

The Perfected of the Great Ultimate says, "From the beginning of the *kalpa*, Master Red Pine, Wang Qiao, Xianmen, Xuanyuan [the Yellow Emperor], and Master Yin [Xi][98] have all received the *Five-Thousand [Character] Writ* and the secret instructions of the *Concealed Commentary*. They have worked hard at practicing the great *dao* and have become elders among the perfected beings above. Such is the wonder of this essential commentary. Going in the contrary direction, we come to the case of Emperor Xiaowen of the Han,[99] who took great delight in the *Classic of the Way and Virtue* and who had attained a pure sincerity of complete void. A most high perfected being descended to the riverside in order to [spiritually] transform the emperor.[100] The Perfected One was sonorously chanting the scripture by himself. The emperor had never promoted the *dao* or discussed[101] its dark, distant, and profound principles. Yet since this was what he thirsted for in his heart, as soon as he heard that there was a peculiar person [there], he enthusiastically leaped into his carriage and drove it over personally to genuflect [before the Perfected One], respectfully pay a call to him, and consult him about the Dao and its perfected beings. The Perfected One made a chapter-and-sentence [commentary] for the emperor, to sketch one corner [of the text] for him and help him penetrate where he was obstructed. Now, the profundity of this scripture [*Classic of the Way and Virtue*] is difficult to fathom. Thus it is said that you cannot discuss it [based merely on your own] contemplation.[102] Now, this [encounter] alone was sufficient to allow the emperor to print [the Heshang Gong commentary] by relying on the empyrean darkness [for this project] and allow him to preserve his phosphorescent [corporeal spirits] and ride the clouds, to bridle flying dragons and soar at random, to climb directly to the halls of heaven, and, with the various inhabitants of the heavens, to join in the activity of discussion and sonorous chanting[103] in the Palace of Golden Efflorescence. So, he too held a rank within the *dao* of transcendent-hood. How joyous that Emperor Wen could practice the *Classic of the Way and Virtue* and achieve this great and lofty state! Emperor Wu [of the Han][104] valiantly but vainly labored [to become] a spirit or transcendent, though he was by nature an unbending man. He also received the prediction of being [among] the ranks of the inhabitants of the heavens. Pliancy and sincerity are the basis for learning the *dao*. Now, if you recite a single section of [the *Classic of the Way and Virtue* commentary by] the Perfected on the River, then you will penetrate the Most High Jade Capitoline, and the transcendents of all the heavens will clasp their hands together and praise this as a wonderful thing. When the sound [of your voice] is transmitted throughout the Three Realms, the demon kings will make obeisance to you in the hall; [the officers of] Fengdu 酆都 will maintain strict reverence, genuflecting before you, the ritual master. The Perfected on the River is thus a ritual master of the *Classic of the Way and Virtue*; therefore we venerate his chapter-and-sentence [commentary]. The secret *dao* for regulating one's person[105] must not be revealed to a common, vulgar person. Vulgar people often mock the scripture as being vacuous and absurd and say that it cannot [cause adepts to] ascend to transcendent-hood and pass over the generations. In this matter, each person has karmic conditions from past lives. One may not force [on others] the lessons [of the *Classic of the Way and Virtue*]. If you teach another person and he (or she) does not practice, then both of you will receive guilt from this. Therefore it is best to hide it deeply away."

The Perfected of the Great Ultimate says, "When venerating this scripture, let your heart-mind be infused with [or, focused on] the Most High Lord Lao, and bow thrice. Next, think about Master Yin [Xi] and the Perfected on the River as each being a 'Ritual Master within the Mystic.' Again bow thrice, and face the scripture. Thirty-six thousand transcendent lads and jade maidens constantly attend upon the scripture, burning incense and scattering flowers, and sending [a message] through to the many transcendents requesting that deathlessness be ordered for you, and seeking for you the *dao* of ascending to the heavens in broad daylight."

The Perfected Person of the Great Ultimate says, "When a gentleman [or lady] of the Dao is making the golden elixir,[106] [first] sonorously chant [the *Classic of the Way and Virtue*] for a whole day and night. The Great One [Taiyi] will be delighted and will descend to your chamber. You can avoid the inauspicious [alchemical] transformations [caused by] demonic trials, and your labors will certainly be successful."

DIVINE COMMENTS ON PURIFICATION RITUALS

The Perfected of the Great Ultimate says, "Now, rites of purification and restraint are the root of learning the *dao*. You must perform a purification rite when sonorously chanting scriptures, when collating scriptures, when copying scriptures, when copying talismans, when combining ingredients to make a prescription, when making the golden elixir, when doing concentrated contemplation, when calling on a master to ask for learning, when bowing in veneration, when receiving a scripture, when rescuing the sick and quelling disasters, and when summoning perfected beings. Purification rites are revered and taken seriously by the Most High. Lord Lao protects them, and the various holy beings rely on them. There are a great many varieties of purification rite; [the one you should use] depends on what you are cultivating and what you have received."

The Perfected of the Great Ultimate says, "When I was learning the *dao* long ago, I heard this bit of guidance from a most high perfected being. I respectfully upheld and practiced it, and now I transmit it to you. Cultivate this in secret. You may teach it in secret to people of latter generations who are destined from past lives to ascend to transcendent-hood." . . .

HYMN OF THE *MOST HIGH WISDOM SCRIPTURE*[107]

The most high progenitors of the mystic void promote the Dao and venerate its scriptures. They attained transcendent-hood in [the brief duration of] a nod; through the *kalpa*s [they have enjoyed] innumerable years [of life]. The virtuous power [*de*] of the great perfected ones is massive and lofty. They came into existence in still and quiet, caused by nonbeing. The phosphors of the empyrean form a framework of emptiness. They travel spontaneously [on this], riding the void. Sun and moon make all bright, and there is peaceful and harmonious music without cease.

In studying transcendent-hood, cut off flowery thoughts, because one thought causes the next, and the thoughts pile up. Coming and going, [the thoughts] disturb one's spirits. The spirits become agitated and roam everywhere. Extinguish your thoughts, and linger in void and leisure; in utter silence, enter empty stillness. Beg for the scriptures as if starving and thirsty. Maintain your will like metal or stone. [This will] safeguard your flight along the mystic road. The five numinosities[108] will move your tally and registration across [from the book of mortality to the book of long life].

Ferried over by the six crossings,[109] you can thereby unlace the Three Veils.[110] Perform a purification rite to clarify the mind, venerating Great Purity; exhaling and inhaling, nurture the cloud sprouts [of the five directions].[111] You wander freely and at ease in the Golden Porte:[112] the Jade Capitoline is your home. There, the seven treasures are produced spontaneously, and all the people are seated on lotus flowers. You may raise your head to chew on the crab apples[113] of the Mystic Capital or lower your head to savor melons from the empty vastness. Your countenance will dazzle like ten suns: who can count how many *kalpa*s of years long [you will live thus]? The ritual drums [or dharma drums] unite the transcendents of heaven, and ringing the bells summons the great demon [kings].

Numinous winds fan the fragrant blossoms, which open their gorgeous, burgeoning bosoms. The great perfected ones stroke chime racks [ao 璈] made of cloud, and the crowds of transcendents pluck numinous zithers. Singing elegantly above in the Three Heavens,[114] they scatter wisdom in the grove of Jade Efflorescence. Your seven generations of ancestors ascend to the hall of blessings, and there they pace [in step with the] mystic tones. If your merit [de] from previous lifetimes is insufficient, this scripture will seem small and far away, difficult to find. If your feelings of trust in the Dao are not total, then although you hope to fly up, instead you will sink. Expand the most high Dao of nonaction in your heart-mind.

One studies the dao by means of sincere trust. Respect your teacher as a member of your immediate family. Restrain your phosphorescent [corporeal spirits], and match them with the clear void. Industriously make them new day after day. If the many people have not yet crossed over to salvation, then I will not cross my own person over, even until the end.[115] My great vow will bring a weighty response: the mystic virtue [de] is certainly trustworthy. My hidden evil transgressions are most deep, and my corresponding [retributions] will arrive like a revolving wheel [of death and rebirth].

Studying the dao is weighty and painful; from dawn to dusk, you must establish a field of blessing. Planting virtue [de] is like planting trees: if the roots are deep, then the fruits will be abundant. You will be able to linger in a high, mystic [state], floating up to the clear heavens. To cultivate this dao of nonaction, you ought to form attachments with good [people]. The Most High spreads the ultimate Dao, [in] a writing entitled "Chapters of Wisdom." Pluck [yourself] out of suffering through your great talent; overleap the common in order to attain perfected-hood. [Your] numinous bearing is seen by the world as a curious thing; radiant it is, like a lotus in a deep pool.

Each person's way of acting has its root, and all come from past-life merit. In establishing merit [de], you must be timely. Make the vow that all will follow [you, to salvation?].[116] Good and evil each depend on the other. The principles of the interdependence [of good and bad fortune] are difficult to examine fully. Worthy gentlemen [or ladies] uphold the words of the dharma, forgetting both dao and de. If you understand this great wisdom, you will become a duke of the Great Ultimate on high. You will be ordered to ride in a carriage of linked jade and with a precious canopy, drawn by nine dragons. [In the Hall of] Golden Efflorescence, [they] will offer Cavern scriptures [to you]; all those who bear incense in joined hands [in attendance on you] will be transcendent lads. Whistling and singing will pierce the Mystic Capital; ringing jade will strike the rose-gem bells.

You throw yourself upward, vaulting up to the [heaven of] Great Clarity; your phosphorescent [corporeal spirits], transcending, roam idly in the purple empyrean. Maintaining nonbeing, you grasp the mainstay of the Dharma. Roving in the mystic, you plumb *xiaoyao* 逍遙 [free and easy wandering] to its limit. Myriad *kalpas* [pass as quickly] as last night; a thousand springs are like a single dawn. Lofty and massive [peaks] overshadow the cloudy efflorescence, [like] hands [casting] mottled shadows[117] on the branches of the precious grove. Fragrant smoke appears spontaneously, and whirlwinds arise on the mystic stair. Numinous banners spread out, following the wind; in response to the moment, your superfluous thoughts disappear. Extinguish wisdom and broaden the great muddle; through nonaction, sing a clear song.

[*Shangqing taiji yinzhu yujing baojue, DZ* 425]

NOTES

1. *DZ* 425 is text 21 of the original Lingbao scriptures, according to Ōfuchi Ninji, "On *Ku Ling-pao ching*," *Acta Asiatica* 27 (1974): 34–56; and Stephen R. Bokenkamp, "Sources of the Ling-pao Scriptures," in *Tantric and Taoist Studies in Honour of R. A. Stein*, ed. Michel Strickmann (Brussels: Institut belge des hautes études chinoises, 1983), 2:434–86.

2. The early Lingbao scriptures draw especially on Pure Land Buddhist sutras. See Bokenkamp, "Sources of the Ling-pao Scriptures," 436. They also draw on other Buddhist genres, such as *jātaka* tales, the *Nirvana Sutra*, and the *Lotus Sutra*. Buddhist Perfection of Wisdom discourse is largely absent from early Daoist texts, which Erik Zürcher finds surprising in "Buddhist Influence on Early Taoism: A Survey of Scriptural Evidence," *T'oung Pao* 66, nos. 1–3 (1980): 119–20. However, Perfection of Wisdom discourse is found in later Lingbao scriptures from around the Tang dynasty.

3. Daoist texts are usually the best source of information about the history of Daoism, but whenever possible, they should be studied in conjunction with other sources. For the early medieval period, other sources include non-Daoist historical records (official histories and Buddhist histories) and archaeological evidence; for the latter, see Zhang Xun-liao 張勛燎 and Bai Bin 白彬, *Zhongguo daojiao kaogu* 中國道教考古, 6 vols. (Beijing: Xianzhuang shuju, 2006).

4. For example, Isabelle Robinet, *Taoism: Growth of a Religion*, trans. Phyllis Brooks (Stanford, Calif.: Stanford University Press, 1997), 149–83; and Stephen R. Bokenkamp, *Early Daoist Scriptures* (Berkeley: University of California Press, 1997).

5. Bokenkamp, *Early Daoist Scriptures*, 186–94, 377.

6. Recitation here means reading a sacred scripture aloud, in a private room, with a sonorous voice, and with the gods as one's audience. The reciter's voice was said to reach to the deities in the heavens, who reward him or her with blessings. This is unlike the Mahayana Buddhist practice of reciting sutras to generate karmic merit in that Buddhist merit is an impersonal effect that does not depend on the actions of deities. Lingbao recitation also differs from the more familiar Chinese practice of reading a text (or reciting it from memory) for the sake of moral learning or aesthetic appreciation.

7. Angelika Cedzich, review of *Early Daoist Scriptures*, by Stephen R. Bokenkamp, *Journal of Chinese Religions* 28 (2000): 161–76.

8. Five categories of scripture are mentioned in this text—the *Classic of the Way and Virtue* (*Daodejing* 道德經), the *Great Cavern Scripture* (*Dadong zhenjing* 大洞真經), and the Lingbao, Sanhuang, and Shangqing corpora—according to Bokenkamp, "Sources of the Ling-pao Scriptures," 484. But based on Robinet's point that the *Great Cavern Scripture* is the core of the original Shangqing revelation, we should take it as a metonymic reference to the Shangqing category as a whole, rather than counting it as a separate scriptural category here. See Isabelle Robinet, *Taoist Meditation: The Mao-Shan Tradition of Great Purity*, trans. Norman J. Girardot and Julian F. Pas (Albany: State University of New York Press, 1993), 97–98.

9. For example, "How peculiar and small in the distance are the secret instructions! How could [even] transcendents of middle rank know them? You are a fellow who is studying perfection!" This passage implies that the reader of this text, because he (or she) is receiving this and other texts, must be a (future) transcendent of high rank, more privileged than even a transcendent of middle rank currently dwelling in the heavens.

10. This sort of circular argument is also found in Mahayana scriptures such as the *Lotus Sutra*.

11. Yamada Toshiaki, "The Lingbao School," in *Daoism Handbook*, ed. Livia Kohn (Boston: Brill, 2000), chap. 9, 230.

12. I added all the headings in this translation, except for the final one, "Hymn of the *Most High Wisdom Scripture*." The paragraph divisions are in the original text.

13. The Most High Lord of the Great Dao (Taishang Dadao Jun 太上大道君) is a high god and the source of many Lingbao scriptures.

14. The "Three Caverns" (Sandong 三洞) are three high heavens, first appearing in the fourth-century Shangqing scriptures. These heavens are Jade Clarity (Yuqing 玉清), Highest Clarity (Shangqing 上清), and Great Clarity (Taiqing 太清). The Three Caverns are also the three categories of scripture. In Lu Xiujing's 陸修靜 (406–477) catalog (*Sandong jingshu mulu* 三洞經書目錄, presented 471, no longer extant), these three categories are (1) Cavern Perfected (Dongzhen 洞真), that is, Shangqing (Highest Clarity) scriptures; (2) Cavern Mystery (Dongxuan 洞玄), that is, Lingbao (Numinous Treasure) scriptures; and (3) Cavern Divine (Dongshen 洞神), that is, Sanhuang (Three August Ones) scriptures. The three categories of scripture are correlated with the three heavens: the Cavern Perfected scriptures are correlated with the Jade Clarity heaven, the Cavern Mystery scriptures with the Great Clarity heaven, and the Cavern Divine scriptures with the Great Clarity heaven. See Ōfuchi Ninji, "The Formation of the Taoist Canon," in *Facets of Taoism: Essays in Chinese Religion*, ed. Holmes Welch and Anna Seidel (New Haven, Conn.: Yale University Press), 253–67; and Ozaki Masuharu, "The History of the Evolution of Taoist Scriptures," *Acta Asiatica* 68 (1995): 37–53. In this text, the three categories of scripture are sometimes listed differently: (1) the Great Cavern (Dadong 大洞), representing the Shangqing scriptures; (2) the Cavern Mystery (Dongxuan), that is, Lingbao, scriptures; and (3) the *Classic of the Way and Virtue*.

15. *De* can simply mean "moral virtue," but it often is a sort of virtue with the power to awe or move the hearts of others. Here I translated *de* as "virtuous power," "virtue," or "merit" (i.e., spiritual merit, or good karma). When *de* is paired with Dao/*dao* 道 (as "*dao* and *de*"), it is left untranslated.

16. This is an echo of the *Classic of the Way and Virtue* (chap. 1 in the received edition).

17. *Song* 誦 means "to chant loudly."

18. The term *fashi* 法師, translated as "ritual master," was adopted from Buddhism, in which it means "dharma master"—that is, a master of Buddhist teachings. In Chinese Buddhism, a *fashi* is an adept who has mastered the sutras or *vinaya*, or any follower of the Buddha may be a *fashi*. Here a *fashi* is someone who has received Daoist scriptures, along with instruction in the practices associated with them.

19. In this translation, I distinguish between *dao* (a way or tradition) and Dao (the Way). In theory, this distinction would have been recognized by early medieval Daoists. Because they also speak of "perverse *daos*" (*xiedao* 邪道), we know that for them not every *dao* corresponds to *the* Dao. While they would recognize this distinction in theory, they might not always have it in mind when reading a scripture like this one, so the translation's distinction between *dao* and Dao may sometimes distort the text's original ambiguity.

20. These are breathing exercises for ingesting cosmic *qi*. The factor shared by both inhaling cosmic *qi* and eating rare exudations is the intake of sacred substances into the body.

21. *Zhi* 芝 are sacred growths—often growths of stone in caves or fungiform growths on the earth—but may also be trees, animals, or other things. When an adept ingests *zhi*, he or she may see this as the ingestion of a substance bestowed by deities, or a substance formed spontaneously from the primal *qi* of the earth.

22. The "nine extremities of space" are the limits of space in the eight cardinal directions plus the center.

23. *Duijing* 對景, here translated as "the radiance that confronts you," could mean instead "the phosphorescent [spirits] with whom you are paired." In this text, the word *dui* often connotes a metaphysical connection, match, or pairing between the adept and something else, such as quasi-karmic burdens or celestial deities.

24. Or "[rid yourself of] thoughts about things with form [*se*]."

25. "Taking a meal at midday" may echo a Buddhist monastic precept against eating a meal after noon.

26. "Fetal *qi*" here refers to the primal *qi* remaining in the adult, left from the state of perfect health that he or she enjoyed in the womb. At other times, it may refer to primal *qi* cultivated by the adult adept through "fetal breathing" (*taixi* 胎息). "Fetal breathing" came to mean two different things. Whereas in the early medieval period, the adept practicing fetal breathing slowed and softened the breath until it was imperceptible, at which point the adept would be respiring through the umbilicus like a fetus in the womb, in the mid-medieval period fetal breathing came to mean forming a spiritual fetus within the subtle body through internal respiration. See Henri Maspero, *Taoism and Chinese Religion* (Amherst: University of Massachusetts Press, 1981), 481.

27. Purification rites (*zhai* 齋) are not Daoist in origin (e.g., they were performed before state sacrifices throughout the imperial period), but Daoists developed them into uniquely Daoist rituals: complex public ceremonies, performed for the benefit of the dead, the living, or the empire, which lasted for days and involved an entire community. However, here the *zhai* are preliminary rites of individual purification rather than public ceremonies.

28. Each of the Daoist priests had a private chamber dedicated to ritual and meditative use. A Celestial Master priest(ess) would dispatch petitions to the celestial or netherworldly officers from his or her oratory. Priests who practiced the teachings of the Shangqing or Lingbao scriptures would commune with deities from the oratory.

29. This sort of formal, ritual veneration of scriptures may have been adapted from Mahayana Buddhism. Mahayana texts such as the *Perfection of Wisdom Sutras* and the *Lotus Sutra* reflected an Indian Buddhist cult of the book, in which veneration of a book itself is promoted as a superior alternative to veneration of the Buddha.

30. Note that in this list of three categories of scripture, categories 1 (Great Cavern) and 2 (Cavern Mystery) accord roughly with Lu Xiujing's catalog, and category 3 (*Classic of the Way and Virtue*) does not.

31. This may refer to the Shangqing text *Perfected Scripture of the Eight Purities* (*Basu zhenjing* 八素真經), extant in two parts as *DZ* 426, *Shangqing taishang basu zhenjing*, and *DZ* 1323, *Dongzhen taishang basu zhenjing fushi riyue huang huajue*.

32. This is the Shangqing text *DZ* 1378, *Shangqing jinzhen yuguang bajing feijing*.

33. This is the Shangqing text *DZ* 1351, *Dongzhen taishang feixing yujing jiuzhen shengxuan shangji*.

34. In Daoism, the title Most High (Taishang) often indicates the deified Laozi, Taishang Laojun 太上老君. In Lingbao texts such as this one, it may refer to the Most High Lord of the Dao, Taishang Dadao Jun. Yet here it probably does not refer to an individual high deity (or scripture) but, rather, to any or all of them.

35. According to the *Scripture of the Three Feminine Ones* (*DZ* 1313, *Dongzhen Gaoshang Yudi dadong ciyi yujian wulao baojing*), the Three Ladies of Primal Simplicity dwell in the Palace of Golden Efflorescence in the brain as three hypostases of the Feminine One (*Ciyi* 雌一). See Robinet, *Taoist Meditation*, 132.

36. This may be the name of a deity, as in *DZ* 330, *Taishang dongxuan lingbao zhenwen yaojie shangjing*, 11b1, 12b2.

37. The Three Realms are the desire realm, the form realm, and the formless realm. The term and concept come from Buddhism. Hell beings, hungry ghosts, animals, human beings, titans, and lower types of gods live on the various levels of existence in the desire realm. The dozens of layers of heavens in the form and formless realms are populated by higher types of gods called brahmas.

38. The Demon Kings of the Three Realms (*Sanjie mowang* 三界魔王) are demons converted to the Dao who test the adepts who are following the path to transcent-hood. See Bokenkamp, *Early Daoist Scriptures*, 383.

39. In Indian or Buddhist thought, a *kalpa* is an eon, 320 million years long—an unimaginably long period of time.

40. These two terms come from the archaic *Zhouyi* and were reinterpreted later in the *Classic of Changes* (*Yijing* 易經). Many hexagram statements in the *Zhouyi* contain a combination of four words, *yuan* 元, *heng* 亨, *li* 利, and *zhen* 貞. These words originally referred to sacrifice and divination, but later Confucians interpreted them as four virtues: sublimity (*yuan*), accomplishment (*heng*), furtherance (*li*), and perseverance (*zhen*). See Richard Rutt, *The Book of Changes (Zhouyi): A Bronze Age Document* (New York: Routledge Curzon, 1996), 126.

41. The master and disciple take the position of ministers (facing north), placing the scripture in the position of the ruler (facing south).

42. The ritual surety, or "liturgical pledge" (*faxin* 法信), is an offering to suppress or appease the gods, received and used by the officiating priest. See Charles D. Benn, *The Cavern-Mystery Transmission: A Taoist Ordination Rite of A.D. 711* (Honolulu: University of Hawai'i Press, 1991), 32.

43. These are the three "elixir fields" (*dantian* 丹田), inner-body sites roughly associated with the brain, kidneys, and heart, respectively. They are occupied by corporeal spirits, which correspond to celestial spirits, rather than being aspects of an individual's "self."

44. That is, the emperors study the moral teachings of the Confucian tradition in order to embody in themselves the enlightened rule of Yao 堯, the legendary sage-king.

45. The Nine Springs are in the netherworld.

46. According to Chinese cosmology, the right-hand side is yin and female, whereas the left-hand side is yang and male.

47. The *Perfected Scripture of the Great Cavern* (*Dadong zhenjing* 大洞真經; DZ 7, *Dadong yujing* 大洞玉經) is the central scripture of the Highest Clarity (Shangqing) scriptural tradition. See Robinet, *Taoist Meditation*, 97–117.

48. Grand Tenuity (Taiwei 太微) is a constellation, part of the Southern Palace (Nangong 南宮). It is "a curved wall manned by high stellar officials, protectors of the royal person, composed of stars mostly in our constellation of Virgo" (Edward H. Schafer, *Pacing the Void: T'ang Approaches to the Stars* [Berkeley: University of California Press, 1977], 208).

49. The Yellow Court is a corporeal site, usually associated with the spleen but sometimes glossed as the middle *dantian*. Since it is said here that the spirits receiving the offering transport it through the Yellow Court, they may in fact be corporeal spirits.

50. The Director of Destinies (*Siming* 司命) is at once a corporeal spirit dwelling in one's heart and reporting one's deeds to the celestial bureaucracy, and an officer dwelling in the heavens receiving such reports and modifying one's fated life span based on one's good or bad deeds.

51. This concept comes from Chinese Buddhism, where it is thought that at the moment of death, a person who has been a slanderer in life will be carved up by knives of wind. See *Foguang da cidian* (Gaoxiong, Dashu: Foguang, 1988), s.v. "Fengdao" 風刀. Note that here the knives of wind are a punishment meted out in the purgatories, rather than coming (as in Buddhism) at the moment of death.

52. That is, when bestowing one of the Lingbao scriptures.

53. These are the kidneys, liver, heart, lungs, and spleen. The five viscera are the governors of the body and the sites of connection between microcosm and macrocosm. See Robinet, *Taoist Meditation*, 61–63.

54. According to Lu Xiujing's early catalog of the Daoist canon (*Sandong jingshu mulu*, presented 471), the Sanhuang (Three August Ones) scriptures are the third of the three categories of Daoist scripture. Lu Xiujing's schema is based on the sort of schema we see here. Only a handful of the Sanhuang scriptures are extant; most of them were destroyed in the Tang dynasty. The fundamental Sanhuang text was the *Writ of the Three August Ones* (*Sanhuang wen* 三皇文), which contained talismanic writing.

55. Note that the Sanhuang scriptures receive only two bows: they are to be venerated somewhat less than the Shangqing or Lingbao scriptures.

56. In accordance with a dominant reading of the *Classic of the Way and Virtue*, Daoism usually gives nonaction (*wuwei* 無為) given a higher value than purposive action (*youwei* 有為).

57. The transmitting priest faces south because he outranks these beings, who may be spirit soldiers or the Daoist dead of low rank.

58. A section follows listing the incantations to be recited when opening the wrappers of the scriptures (with a different incantation for each category of scripture), but this has been omitted from the translation.

59. These are the protector beasts of the four cardinal directions: east, west, south, and north, respectively.

60. During the period when this scripture was composed, the Three Ones could be, at the same time, cosmogonic forms of *qi*, celestial deities, and corporeal deities. Here, they are celestial deities, though the other meanings are still present. For the Three Ones as cosmogonic entities (e.g., the three forms of primal *qi*, Mystic [Xuan 玄], Inaugural [Yuan 元], and Primal [Shi 始]), see Bokenkamp, *Early Daoist Scriptures*, 159. For the Three Ones as celestial deities (e.g., the Three Feminine Ones) and corporeal deities (visualized as infants), see Robinet, *Taoist Meditation*, 131–32; and Poul Andersen, *The Method of Holding the Three Ones: A Taoist Manual of Meditation of the Fourth Century A.D.* (London: Curzon Press, 1980).

61. Because Thearch One is mentioned, "Cavern Perfected scripture" here refers specifically to the *Perfected Scripture of the Great Cavern* rather than to the category of Cavern Perfected (Shangqing) scriptures as a whole.

62. In the *Great Cavern Scripture*, the whirlwind is a breath of primal *qi*, exhaled by Thearch One (*Diyi* 帝一), that unites the adept with the hundred spirits and with Thearch One himself. Although the *Great Cavern Scripture* is "consecrated" to this deity, Thearch One in fact did not become important in later Daoist tradition. See Robinet, *Taoist Meditation*, 109–17, 119.

63. This may be *DZ* 1439, *Dongxuan lingbao yujing shan buxu jing*.

64. The Palace of Golden Efflorescence is in the brain.

65. Throwing a talismanic object was a way of communicating with celestial officers; one example of this is the rite of throwing small dragon figurines of gold together with talismanic writing strips (*fujian* 符簡) from mountaintops into water or into the earth. See

Edouard Chavannes, "Le jet des dragons," in *Mémoires concernant l'Asie orientale*, ed. Émile Senart and Henri Cordier (Paris: Éditions Ernest Leroux, 1919), 3:53–225.

66. Wearing hempen clothing would signify thrift and humility.

67. The Nine Heavens could be the eight directions of celestial space plus the center, nine vertical layers of heaven, or a set of nine heavens.

68. In Buddhist cosmology, a brahma is a god residing in one of the many heavens of the form or formless realms. In Lingbao cosmology, the primal *qi* from the origin of the cosmos is called Brahma Qi, the heavens formed from this *qi* are Brahma heavens, and the language of these heavens is Brahma language. See Bokenkamp, *Early Daoist Scriptures*, 386. This sentence probably refers to a high Brahma heaven (envisioned by the composer of DZ 425), although it is also possible that the sentence refers to a Brahma deity.

69. Ge Xuan 葛玄 (fl. ca. 200 C.E.) was the great-uncle of Ge Hong 葛洪 (Baopuzi 抱朴子). In the fourth century, Ge Xuan was remembered as a "typical 'master of esoterica.'" See Robert Ford Campany, *To Live as Long as Heaven and Earth: A Translation and Study of Ge Hong's Traditions of Divine Transcendents* (Berkeley: University of California Press, 2002). In the Lingbao scriptures, he is a high-ranking deified human and an important middleman for transmitting teachings from the Lingbao deities to the human realm. Bokenkamp argues that Ge Xuan's exalted place in the Lingbao scriptures is a reaction by Ge Chaofu 葛巢甫, another member of the Ge clan and the author of the early Lingbao scriptures, to the recent Shangqing revelations that demoted Ge Xuan to the rank of a lowly earth-bound spirit, in "Sources of the Ling-pao Scriptures," 442–43.

70. The *Huahu jing* 化胡經, and its story of Laozi's journey west to convert the barbarians of India and other lands to "proper" religion and civilization, was at the center of most of the public disputes between Buddhists and Daoists throughout the imperial period. The original Daoist authors of this story in the second and third centuries harbored no malicious intent against Indian Buddhism. The story was simply a way for Daoists to make sense of the coincidental similarities between Buddhism and Daoism by positing Buddhism as a form of Daoism suited to the different environment in India. By the fourth century, Daoists had made the story polemical, yet in the text here, the story serves a cognitive rather than a polemical purpose. See Erik Zürcher, *The Buddhist Conquest of China: The Spread and Adaptation of Buddhism in Early Medieval China* (Leiden: Brill, 1959), 289–320; and Kristofer Schipper, "Purity and Strangers: Shifting Boundaries in Medieval Taoism," *T'oung Pao* 80 (1994): 61–81.

71. Essence (*jing* 精), *qi*, and spirit (*shen* 神) are the "Three Treasures" of later Daoist meditation traditions such as inner alchemy. The conception of essence and spirit here may differ from the conception of these terms in inner alchemy (here they probably refer to corporeal deities rather than to forces or aspects of a person). Yet there may also be significant overlap between early and later conceptions ("*shen*" here may mean, at the same time, personified corporeal *spirits* and impersonal corporeal *spirit*).

72. Ingesting talismans as medicine wrappers or ashes in water was practiced by the early Celestial Masters and has remained a common practice in traditional Chinese medicine.

73. The "Five Lingbao Talismans" predate the Lingbao revelations and serve as one of the sources or seeds of the later tradition. See *DZ* 388, *Taishang lingbao wufu xu*, an important text with the "Five Lingbao Talismans" as its core; and Gil Raz, "Creation of Tradition: The Five Talismans of the Numinous Treasure and the Formation of Early Daoism" (Ph.D. diss., Indiana University, 2004).

74. In Lingbao texts, the Five Thearchs are deities of the four cardinal directions plus the center. See Bokenkamp, *Early Daoist Scriptures*, 413.

75. The Five Marchmounts are five sacred mountains in the central area of China. As usually understood, they are Mount Tai (Taishan 泰山) in the east (Shandong), Mount Heng (Hengshan 衡山) in the south (Hunan), Mount Song (Songshan 嵩山) in the center (Henan), Mount Hua (Huashan 華山) in the west (Shaanxi), and Mount Heng (Hengshan 恆山) in the north (Shanxi). The "True Forms of the Five Marchmounts" were recorded as both maplike charts and talismans. While a number of extant texts are related to these sets of charts and talismans, the charts do not exist in their simple, original form. These charts and talismans had the power to reveal the "true forms" of spirits, demons, the mountains, and numinous entities in the mountains, for communication and protection.

76. *DZ* 1439 and 1351, respectively.

77. The *Five-Thousand Character Writ* was an edition of the *Classic of the Way and Virtue* used by religious Daoists. See Bokenkamp, *Early Daoist Scriptures*, 59.

78. This must mean three times a day for one month.

79. This is an early and much-cited scripture on the cultivation of the inner landscape and gods of the body; it is extant as *DZ* 331, *Taishang huangting neijing yujing*, and *DZ* 332, *Taishang huangting waijing yujing*. See Robinet, *Taoist Meditation*, 55–96, and Paul W. Kroll, "Body Gods and Inner Vision: The Scripture of the Yellow Court," in *Religions of China in Practice*, ed. Donald S. Lopez Jr. (Princeton, N.J.: Princeton University Press, 1996), 149–55.

80. This is from the *Classic of the Way and Virtue* (chap. 14 in the received edition). The translation follows Lao Tzu, *Tao Te Ching*, trans. D. C. Lau (New York: Penguin, 1963).

81. The term "Three Primes" (Sanyuan 三元) has been used throughout Daoist tradition to refer to many different sacred triads. Here it refers to both the Three Ones and the Three Simplicities.

82. This is from the *Classic of the Way and Virtue* (chap. 14 in the received edition).

83. The Three Simplicities (or Three Ladies of Primal Simplicity) are incarnations of the Feminine One (Ciyi). See Robinet, *Taoist Meditation*, 132.

84. Practices in which the adept venerates and invokes these two impersonal "parents" are found in the Shangqing scripture *DZ* 1382, *Shangqing jiudan shanghua taijing zhongji jing*. The Fetal Worthy has a complex identity. In *DZ* 7, *Jade Scripture of the Great Cavern* (*Dadong yujing* 1.22b10, 2.10b9), the Fetal Worthy is correlated with Taiyi 太一. Robinet cites a confusing account of a practice in which the adept visualizes himself fusing together with a young boy/embryo and Taiyi, in *Taoist Meditation*, 137. So the "Fetal Worthy" is the adept's new, ideal self as an object of cultivation.

85. Kunlun 崑崙 is a legendary mountain beyond the western border of China; Penglai 蓬萊 is a legendary mountainous isle in the eastern sea; Bell Mountain (鍾山) is a legendary mountain in the far north (or perhaps northwest of Kunlun); Mount Song 嵩山 is the Central Marchmount; and Mount Wangwu 王屋山 is a mountain range on the border of Shanxi and Henan.

86. Mount Man Bird is usually thought to be a sacred central mountain found in every heaven and the object of Daoist visualizations. It is also the "true name" of the Buddhist sacred central mountain Mount Meru. See *DZ 434, Xuanlan renniao shan jingtu.*

87. Zürcher cites the name "Yuannaluowei" 緣那羅衛 as an example of pseudo-Sanskrit in "Buddhist Influence on Early Taoism," 111. When the composer of this Daoist text invented the name "Yuannaluowei," he probably took the name "Jiaweiluowei" 迦維羅衛 as his model. "Jiaweiluowei" is a Chinese Buddhist transliteration of "Kapilavastu," the capital of Śākyamuni Buddha's Śākya clan. Perhaps the Daoist composer intended a correlation between the Lingbao site Yuannaluowei and the Buddhist site Jiaweiluowei, or perhaps he merely wished to add a Buddhist flavor to this passage.

88. This is in *DZ 434, Xuanlan renniao shan jingtu.*

89. *DZ* 1439 and 1351.

90. The gods are chanting while pacing the spaces between the stars. The related term *buxu ci* 步虛詞 (*ci* poems on pacing the void) became a common genre of Daoist verse.

91. In Lingbao teachings, the Palace of Great Yin is where the physical body of the adept is refined after death. The adept's spirits are refined in the Southern Palace. After this refining process, body and spirits are rejoined for a celestial existence or a human rebirth. See Bokenkamp, *Early Daoist Scriptures,* 382.

92. The Three Officers, of Heaven, Earth, and Water, are in charge of the fates of the living and the dead. The practice of sending petitions to these spirits was especially important in early Celestial Master Daoism.

93. In Mahayana Buddhism, a being on the path to buddhahood slowly accumulates the thirty-two major and eighty minor marks of a buddha over the course of millions of lifetimes. When all these marks are complete, a buddha is born.

94. This is a reward promised in Mahayana Pure Land sutras—for example, *T* 362, *Fo shuo Amituo sanye sanfo salou fotan guodu rendao jing.* See Bokenkamp, "Sources of the Lingpao Scriptures," 173.

95. *DZ* 1344, *Dongzhen taishang shuo zhihui xiaomo zhenjing,* is an extant text of similar title, but it may not correspond exactly to the text cited here. *DZ* 1344 may be a Tang dynasty compilation; the original Lingbao *Xiaomo zhihui* 消魔智慧 (or *Zhihui xiaomo*) scripture(s) may have existed in name only and never actually been written down. See Kristofer M. Schipper and Franciscus Verellen, eds., *The Taoist Canon: A Historical Companion to the Daozang* (Chicago: University of Chicago Press, 2004), 590–91.

96. While this title does not correspond to a known text, it may refer to the Shangqing text *DZ* 1378, *Shangqing jinzhen yuguang bajing feijing,* also mentioned earlier.

97. In a section omitted from the translation, the text warns against "yin thieves" and then describes different categories of scripture and gives similar instructions for transmission.

A title line then follows dividing the *Concealed Commentary on the Scriptures of the Dao* (which forms the majority of our text) from appended divine comments. (These comments were probably always an integral part of our text, however, not later additions.) The first section of these appended divine comments, on the *Daoji jing* 道迹經 (a Shangqing scripture probably lost before the Tang dynasty), has also been omitted from the translation.

98. These all are holy persons said to have lived in the Zhou dynasty or the distant past. Master Red Pine (Chisongzi 赤松子), Wang Qiao 王喬 (Wangzi Qiao 王子喬), and Xianmen 羨門 were transcendents from Southern Daoist lore. All three of them are mentioned in *Inner Chapters of the Master Who Embraces Simplicity* (*Baopuzi neipian* 抱朴子内篇), by Ge Hong 葛洪 (283–343), which is (or represents) one source that the composers of the Lingbao scriptures drew on. Xuanyuan 軒轅 (Yellow Emperor, Huangdi 黄帝) and Yin Xi 尹喜 (Laozi's disciple) were more widely known figures.

99. Han Emperor Xiaowen 孝文 (Wen, r. 180–157 B.C.E.).

100. This is Heshang Gong 河上公, the Sire by the Riverside. For this story about Heshang Gong's encounter with Wen of the Han, see Campany, *To Live as Long as Heaven and Earth*, 305–7.

101. *Yi* 義 is a loanword for *yi* 議.

102. The phrase *buke siyi* 不可思議 originates in Buddhist translations, usually in descriptions of the plane of attainment, wisdom, or powers of a buddha or cosmic bodhisattva, unimaginable to ordinary beings.

103. Note that the gods are chanting the Heshang Gong edition of the *Classic of the Way and Virtue* in the heavens.

104. Han Emperor Wu (r. 141–87 B.C.E.).

105. This may refer to a distinctive concept in the Heshang Gong commentary on the *Classic of the Way and Virtue*: bringing order to the state through regulating the self or body (*zhishen zhiguo* 治身治國).

106. The golden elixir (*jindan* 金丹) probably refers to potable gold (*jinye, jinyi* 金液), a solution of mercury and gold. Ge Hong's book *Inner Chapters of the Master Who Embraces Simplicity* provides an important early account of the preparation of *jinye*. See Joseph Needham, with Ho Ping-Yu and Lu Gwei-djen, *Science and Civilisation in China*, vol. 5, *Chemistry and Chemical Technology*, part 3, *Spagyrical Discovery and Invention: Historical Survey, from Cinnabar Elixirs to Synthetic Insulin* (New York: Cambridge University Press, 1976), 81–106.

107. This is probably a quotation from a scripture that "existed" only in the heavens and had not yet been written by mortal hands. This same eight-stanza hymn is also found in the early Lingbao text *DZ* 1439, *Dongxuan lingbao yujing shan buxu zhang* 5b3–7a7, and the later texts *DZ* 613, *Zhongxian zansong lingzhang* 8a2–9a8, and *DZ* 609, *Taishang dongxuan lingbao zhihui lizan* 1a6–3a4 (*DZ* 609 omits stanzas 7 and 8). Comparing *DZ* 425 and 1439, I have found fourteen variants in the wording of the hymn, but I mention only one of them in the translation. The other thirteen variants are of uncertain relevance.

108. Later Daoists would use the term "five numinosities" to refer to corporeal spirits (of the five viscera), but in this text, these may be spirits of the four cardinal directions plus the center.

109. In Chinese Mahayana Buddhism, the six crossings (*liudu* 六度) are the six *pāramitās* (perfections), six practices (charity, morality, forbearance, effort, meditation, and wisdom) that help one "cross" to nirvana. Just what the "six crossings" mean in this scripture is unclear. In later Daoism, the "six crossings" were a set of six virtues or precepts. See *Daojiao da cidian*, 310.

110. The Lingbao text *DZ* 345, *Taishang dongxuan lingbao jieye benxing shangpin miaojing* 23a, 4–6, describes the Three Veils (perhaps figuratively) as iron nets found in the heavens where the souls of the guilty dead are tortured before rebirth.

111. Ingest five-colored *qi* from the five directions.

112. The Golden Porte (double gate towers) is the entryway to higher heavens. See Bokenkamp, *Early Daoist Scriptures*, 304n.12.

113. *Nai* 柰, or the Chinese pear-leaved crab apple (*Malus asiatica*).

114. Here, the Three Heavens are Jade Clarity, Highest Clarity, and Great Clarity. See note 14.

115. This is a Mahayana Buddhist sentiment.

116. In Mahayana Buddhism, vowing to become a buddha (rather than being satisfied with a lower attainment, such as arhat-hood) is an important early moment on the path to buddhahood for any bodhisattva.

117. *DZ* 1439, 7a5 has *pan* 攀 instead of *yu* 鬱. This would change the translation from "[like] hands [casting] mottled shadows on the branches . . ." to "[like] hands climbing the branches . . ."

37. Confucian Views of the Supernatural

KEITH N. KNAPP

Common wisdom says that Confucianism, if not atheistic, was at most disinterested in the supernatural. After all, it was Confucius who said, "We are still not able to [properly] serve men. How is it possible, then, that we can talk about serving the spirits?" and "We still do not understand life. How is it possible that we can understand death?"[1] Nevertheless, in the early medieval period, Confucians assumed that the spiritual world affected our lives in many ways. Sacrifices not merely were exercises in reinvigorating communal solidarity, but were truly meant to provide for, or at least placate, the deities and the dead. To show this, I have translated three types of documents in this chapter: four narratives about filial sons, two anecdotes about assumptions that people made about ancestral sacrifices, and a death testament about its Confucian author's notions about death and the afterlife.

In early medieval China, narratives about exemplary filial behavior were very popular among the educated elite. A number of scholars and even royalty assembled collections of these tales known as *Accounts of Filial Children* (*Xiaozi zhuan* 孝子傳), many of which have miraculous content. Perhaps influenced by Mohism,[2] the filial miracles reveal that early medieval Confucians believed that heavenly and earthly spirits existed and took a great interest in human ethical life. The logic on which these assumptions rested is what I call "correlative

Confucianism," a system of thought articulated by Lu Jia 陸賈 (fl. 200–175 B.C.E.) and Dong Zhongshu 董仲舒 (ca. 195–ca.115 B.C.E.) that superimposed Confucian ethics on *yinyang* 陰陽 and five-phase (*wuxing* 五行) cosmology.[3] According to this system, people play a central role in the cosmos because they embody attributes of both Heaven and Earth. Since it is assumed that things of the same kind affect one another, by perfecting those attributes, such as benevolence and righteousness, that humans share with Heaven and Earth, they can elicit sympathetic responses from both heavenly and earthly spirits. This notion is called the "resonance between Heaven and People" (*tianren ganying* 天人感應). In other words, because both extremely good and extremely bad conduct affect the spiritual cosmos, supernatural responses automatically result in the form of either omens or rewards.

In these narratives, supernatural responses either are rewards for those people who realize the virtue of filial piety or are punishments for those who violate its dictates. In the first tale, Liu Yin 劉殷 (ca. 300–318) is distraught that he cannot obtain what his grandmother wants, and his anguish and sincerity move a deity to provide him with enough of the desired food until it comes into season. The second anecdote, which features Miao Fei 繆斐 (second century C.E.), indicates that the power of filiality is so great that it can protect a loved one from supernatural disease. It can even cause the offending deities to suffer otherworldly justice. In the third tale, the filial love of Ding Lan 丁蘭 is so intense that it causes the statue of his mother to come alive: it reveals the wrong his wife has committed; it somehow expresses its disapproval of Ding's lending an ax to his neighbor; and it bleeds when a neighbor cuts off its arm. The last narrative, which concerns Xiao Ruiming 蕭叡明 (fl. late fifth century), not only illustrates how the spirits reward earnest prayer and devotion but also discloses that Heaven will severely punish those who flout filial conventions. Obviously, for the Confucian (Ru 儒) authors who propagated these tales, people's behavior was closely monitored by a spirit world that hungered for virtuous acts.

Because ancestor worship was the most common religious activity practiced by all social classes in the early medieval period, the next translations are of two anecdotes from the dynastic histories that illustrate what people believed was happening during the ancestral sacrifices. The first text, derived from both the third-century *Treatise on the Three States* (*Sanguo zhi* 三國志) and its fifth-century commentary, indicates that participants in the ancestral sacrifices often believed that the dead ancestor was present at the ceremony. Consequently, it was imperative that all measures be taken to ensure his or her comfort and happiness. This text also reveals that to facilitate communication between the celebrant and the dead, shamans frequently took part in these ceremonies. At the end of the passage appears a Confucian complaint that the emperor is devoting too much time and energy to serving the dead. It is important to note, however, that the remonstrating official neither criticizes the presence of shamans nor casts doubt on the actual presence of spirits. The second account, from the sixth-century *History of the Southern Qi* (*Nan Qi shu* 南齊書), emphasizes that recently dead ancestors were served their favorite dishes because it was believed that they actually did eat these foods in the afterlife. Moreover, ancestors who no longer received food sacrifices had no choice but to become otherworldly panhandlers.

Many early medieval literati highly esteemed the virtue of frugality. As a result, the death testaments of a number of prominent men requested an "austere burial" (*bozang* 薄葬). These were simple funerals and burials more befitting poor commoners than well-to-do nobles and literati. Although early medieval burials were in fact much less extravagant than those of their Han dynasty predecessors, it is not clear whether this was because people were attempting to realize this ideal of an austere burial or because straitened economic circumstances demanded more frugal burials. Not mere formulas but statements of personal preferences, these death testaments explore their upper-class authors' beliefs about the afterlife. Here I have translated the death instructions of Huangfu Mi 皇甫謐 (215–282), a famous recluse and self-identified Confucian. I have chosen his testament "The Ultimate End" because it is the richest and longest example of such documents. At first glance, he seems to request an austere burial because it fulfills a classical Daoist view that one should allow one's body to disintegrate quickly, so that one's spirits and *qi* 氣 can transform into different things.[4] Nevertheless, on closer inspection, it becomes apparent that he was terrified by the possibility that grave robbers might disturb his grave and ruin his remains' postmortem welfare. Obviously, for Huangfu Mi, something conscious remained in the tomb, so he wanted to make sure that it was left undisturbed. The testament also indicates that the only grave good he needed was a venerated book that would call attention to his virtue.

From these texts, we can see that early medieval Confucians truly upheld their master's dictum that one "should respect ghosts and gods while keeping them at a distance."[5] Although Confucians probably had less direct relations with the spirits than did either Buddhists or Daoists, they still thought that deities, ancestors, and ghosts were important and that their needs and desires could not be neglected.

FURTHER READING

The most extensive treatment of the filial piety narratives is Keith N. Knapp, *Selfless Offspring: Filial Children and Social Order in Medieval China* (Honolulu: University of Hawai'i Press, 2005). In *The Wu Liang Shrine: The Ideology of Early Chinese Pictorial Art* (Stanford, Calif.: Stanford University Press, 1989), Wu Hung discusses the filial piety stories illustrated at a second-century C.E.

sacrificial hall. In *Auspicious Omens and Miracles in Ancient China: Han, Three Kingdoms and Six Dynasties* (Sankt Augustin: Steyler Verlag, 2001), Tiziana Lippiello analyzes many of the omens and miracles that appear in the filial piety narratives. Zongli Lu does the same in *Power of the Words: Chen Prophecy in Chinese Politics, AD 265–618* (Oxford: Peter Lang, 2003). Early medieval beliefs about ancestor worship are explored in Keith N. Knapp, "Borrowing Legitimacy from the Dead: The Confucianization of Ancestral Worship," in *Early Chinese Religion, Part Two: The Period of Division (220–589)*, ed. John Lagerwey and Lü Pengzhi (Leiden: Brill, 2010), 1:143–92. Keith N. Knapp, "Heaven and Death According to Huangfu Mi, a Third-Century Confucian," *Early Medieval China* 6 (2000): 1–31, analyzes the beliefs found in Huangfu Mi's death testament, while Albert E. Dien, "Instructions for the Grave: The Case of Yan Zhitui," *Cahiers d'Extrême-Asie* 8 (1995): 41–58, does the same for the death testament chapter found in Yan Zhitui's sixth-century *Family Instructions for the Yan Clan*.

❖

STORIES OF FILIAL PIETY

LIU YIN 劉殷

In the depth of winter, [Liu Yin's] great-grandmother, Lady Wang 王氏, desired *jin* 堇,[6] but she did not say anything. As a result, for ten days she did not eat her fill. Yin thought her mood was strange and asked her why. Lady Wang told him. At that time, Yin was [merely] nine years old. He thereupon grieved and cried in the marshes [after vainly searching there for *jin*]. He said, "My sins are extremely grave. While young I have already received the punishment of my parents' death. Now Lady Wang is in the hall of my home, but this month she has lacked a week's nourishment. Yin is a son, but he cannot obtain what his parent wants. Emperor of Heaven [Huangtian 皇天] and Lord of the Earth [Houtu 后土], I hope that you will show me pity." The sound of his crying voice did not stop for half a day. Thereupon, he suddenly heard something like the voice of a person say, "Stop, stop crying." Yin stopped and looked at the ground. *Jin* was growing there. He took more than a bushel and returned home. Even after eating the plants, their number did not diminish. Only when *jin* came into season did they decrease.

[*JS* 88.2288]

MIAO FEI 繆斐

Miao Fei was from Lanling 蘭陵 in Donghai 東海. His father suddenly became ill. Doctors and medicine were lacking. Day and night Fei kowtowed and would neither sleep nor eat. His own life was almost at an end. Around midnight, two gods pulling chains suddenly appeared. They sought pity by saying: "In the past, your honorable father passed by our home and offended us. For that reason, he received our angry retribution. Nevertheless, [Heaven] has been moved by your perfect filiality. Yesterday, heavenly officials arrested us, recorded our crime, and locked us up in these chains." Fei awoke with surprise and saw that his father was already cured.

[*Taiping yulan* 太平御覽, comp. Li Fang 李昉 (925–996)
(facsimile reprint of Shangwu yinshuguan 1935
printing from a Song copy), 4 vols.
(Beijing: Zhonghua shuju, 1992), 411.7b, 644.6a]

DING LAN 丁蘭

Ding Lan was from Henei 河内. While he was still young, his mother died. Upon reaching fifteen years of age, he stubbornly yearned for her and was unable to forget her. [As a result,] he carved wood to make an image of her. Day and night, he reverently cared for it as if it were his living mother. As a matter of course, before departing for a journey, he would report the affair to his mother and only then leave. On his return, he would also tell her all the details [of his travel]. He diligently served her without ever being remiss. Lan's wife had an evil nature and often took this [caring for her wooden mother-in-law] as repugnant. [One day] when [Lan] was not home, she used fire to burn his mother's wooden face. Lan returned home late in the evening, so he did not see his mother's face. That night, he dreamed that his wooden mother told him, "Your wife burned my face." At dawn the next day, Lan saw [his injured mother]. The situation was truly as the dream had stated. He immediately punished his wife; he forever detested her and never again showed her any favor.

Once there was a neighbor who wanted to borrow an ax. Lan reported this to his wooden mother. He perceived that her countenance was unhappy; consequently, he did not lend the ax. His neighbor was indignant. He watched and waited for an opportunity when Lan would not be home. He then used a large knife to cut off the arm of the wooden mother. Blood flowed out [of the wound] and covered the ground. When Lan returned and saw this, he cried grievously and immediately went and cut off the neighbor's head, which he offered as a sacrifice at his mother's grave. When the officials heard of this matter, they did not prosecute him for committing a crime; instead, they gave him an official position with a salary. Even though [his mother] was made out of hard wood, Lan still fulfilled his filial duties to the utmost. Thus the intelligent spirits responded, and blood came out of [wood]. Because his perfect filiality, he was exempted from capital punishment. The beauty of [his] filial respect will be talked about forever.

[Funahashi *Accounts of Filial Children* (Funahashi *kōkoden* 船橋孝子伝)
manuscript now held by Kyoto University. Also see Yōgaku no Kai 幼學の會,
Kōshiden chūkai 孝子伝注解 (Tokyo: Kyuko shoin, 2003), 81–82 and 354–56]

XIAO RUIMING 蕭叡明

Xiao Ruiming's byname was Jingji 景濟. He was a native of South Lanling 南蘭
陵. His mother suffered from convulsions. For many years she was bedridden.
Day and night, Ruiming would pray for her. When the weather turned cold, the
tears that he shed would become frozen like veins; the blood on his forehead
from kowtowing would also freeze and would not drip. Suddenly, there was a
person who gave him a small stone box; he said, "This will cure your mother's
illness." Ruiming knelt and received the box. The person abruptly vanished.
Ruiming took the box to give it to his mother. Inside the box was only a three-
inch piece of raw silk. On it were the characters for sun and moon written in
cinnabar. As soon as his mother consumed the silk, her illness was cured.

At that time, there was a man named Zhu Xu 朱緒 from Moling 秣陵 who
was immoral. His mother had been ill for many years. One day she wanted to
eat a stew made from sea grass [*jiaobai* 茭白]. Xu's wife went to the market to
buy the sea grass to make the stew, which she wanted to offer to her mother-in-
law. Xu said to her, "She is ill once again, how can she eat it?" He first tasted it.
He then hurriedly gobbled it up. His mother angrily retorted, "Because of my
illness, I wanted this stew. How could you have the heart to eat it all up? If
Heaven has awareness, it should cause you to choke to death." When Xu heard
this, his heart became heavy. Immediately, he began to lose blood. By the next
day, he was dead. When Ruiming heard of this incident, he was overcome with
tremendous grief. He refused to eat for many days. He made inquiries about
the location of Xu's corpse; he wanted to personally destroy it. Not long afterward, though, he said, "[To desecrate that corpse] would pollute my knife," so
he stopped. In 487, he mourned his mother, but he could not overcome his
grief and died. The emperor decreed that he should be given the title of Gentleman of the Secretariat.

[*NS* 73.1815]

STORIES OF ANCESTOR WORSHIP

SUN HAO 孫皓

There was an official who memorialized that [Sun Hao, r. 264–280, the last
emperor of the Wu] should establish a temple [for his father, Sun He 孫和] in
the capital. In the seventh month of 267, he ordered that the renowned carpenter Xue Xu 薛珝 build a hall of repose [*qintang* 寢堂], which Hao called the
Temple of Purity [Qingtang 清廟]. In the twelfth month, he dispatched the

Probationary Counselor in Chief, Meng Ren 孟仁, the Chamberlain for Ceremonials, Yao Xin 姚信, and others to assemble officials, foot soldiers, and cavalrymen of the Middle Army, adding up to two thousand men. They were to use a spirit carriage and procession to go east to welcome [his father's] spirit at the Bright Mausoleum [Mingling 明陵]. Hao summoned Ren for an audience and personally escorted him out to the courtyard. When the spirit carriage was supposed to arrive, he sent [another] Counselor in Chief, Lu Kai 陸凱, to sacrifice the three sacrificial beasts in a nearby suburb. Hao slept out in the open outside the capital's walls. The next day, outside the eastern gate, he looked toward the horizon and performed a sacrifice. The day after that, he visited the ancestral temple and presented sacrificial offerings. While doing so, he sighed pitifully and felt acute sorrow. For the next seven days, he sacrificed three times a day, and musicians and acrobats provided music and merriment [for the spirit of his deceased father]. An official memorialized the throne, saying, "In making sacrifices, one does not want them to be numerous. If they are numerous, they lack respect.[7] One should use the rites to control emotions." Only then did Hao stop.

[The commentary by Pei Songzhi 裴松之 (372?–451) adds:] The *Documents of the Kingdom of Wu* [*Wu shu* 吳書] says, "When [Meng] Ren was returning, private imperial envoys brought him edicts written by the emperor himself. Day and night they continually arrived. Hao respectfully inquired about the spirit's actions and moods. The shamans and shamanesses said that when they saw [Sun] He, his clothing and appearance looked just as they had when he was alive. [Sun] Hao shed tears of both sadness and delight. He [then] called on all the highest officials and imperial secretaries to go to the gate under the tall tower to receive gifts."

[*SGZ* 59.1371]

XIAO ZE 蕭賾

In 491, in regard to the four seasonal sacrifices performed at the imperial temple, the emperor [Emperor Wu of the Southern Qi 齊武帝], Xiao Ze [r. 483–493], decreed that Emperor Xuan 宣帝 be presented with wheat cakes and duck fat; that Empress Xiao 孝皇后 receive bamboo shoots, duck eggs, meat sauce, and broiled thigh meat; that Emperor Gaohuang 高皇帝 be given minced fish and meat broth; and that Empress Zhao 昭皇后 receive tea, three-cornered dumplings [*zongzi* 粽子], and braised fish. These all were things that they loved to eat [while alive]. Before this, Shizu 世祖 [Emperor Wu] dreamed that Taizu 太祖 [Emperor Gao 高帝 (Xiao Daocheng 蕭道成, r. 479–482)] said to him, "All the Song family emperors are often at the imperial temple, where they are always begging for food. Can you offer sacrifices to me somewhere else?" The emperor then ordered that Lady Yu 庾氏, the consort of the Prince of Yuzhang 豫章王, perform the Four Seasonal Sacrifices in the old residence named the Qingxi

Palace [Qingxigong 青溪宮]. She should place [the spirit tablets] in the same hall and respectfully sacrifice to the two emperors and two empresses. In regard to the domestic animals and clothing that should be offered, they should be selected according to the rituals of family members.

[NQS 9.133]

HUANGFU MI 皇甫謐

The Ultimate End (Duzhong 篤終)

Master Sagely Teachings [Xuanyan xiansheng 玄晏先生, Huangfu Mi's name for himself] believes that life and death follow the fixed rules of Heaven and Earth, which human reason can surely understand. Therefore, according to the *Record of Rites* [*Liji* 禮記], at the age of sixty, one prepares his coffin.[8] All the time until one is ninety, each decade has its own requirements and differences. This is to use simplicity to prepare for death. How is it possible to be like the vulgar, filled with doubts [about the certainty of death]? Although not yet having reached the age at which making a coffin is necessary, my childhood afflictions have grown more serious over the years. As a result, when I suffer hardships, my spirit and energy [*shenqi* 神氣] are diminished and grow weak; my fate becomes distressed. I always fear that I will suffer an untimely, premature death; I am anxious that my death might not come at the normal [time]. Therefore, I will roughly describe what I hold to be most dear [concerning the disposal of my remains].

What man hankers after is life; what he despises is death. Although hankering after it, he cannot surpass his allotted time; although he despises it, he cannot escape [from death]. When a man dies, his spiritual essence ends and his bodily frame scatters. His *hun* soul 魂 can go anywhere; his *qi* belongs to heaven. When the life span he has been entrusted with is spent, his exhausted body returns to its true state. Consequently, the corpse is hidden in the earth. Therefore his spirit does not reside with the body; together with his *qi*, it ascends or descends. The corpse does not remain there for long but combines its form with the earth. That the bodily form and spirit are not blocked is the nature of Heaven and Earth. That the corpse merges with the earth is the principle of returning to its true state. While alive I have not been able to protect my seven-foot body; when dead, why would I want to separate it from the earth with a coffin?[9] Moreover, clothes and robes defile the corpse; coffins and vaults keep it apart from its true state. Consequently, the stone sarcophagus of Huan Sima 桓司馬 is not as good as decaying quickly.[10] Ji Sun's 季孫 precious *yufan* 璵璠 jade can be equated with exposed bones.[11] When Hua Yuan 華元 gave an extravagant burial to Duke Wen 文公, the *Spring and Autumn Annals* [*Chunqiu* 春秋] regarded it as disloyal.[12] When the body of Yang Wangsun 楊王孫 became intimate with the dirt, Ban Gu 班固 (32–92), the author of the *History of the Han* [*Han shu* 漢書], stated that he was more virtuous than the First Emperor of the Qin.[13] If we assume the *hun* soul definitely has awareness, then men and ghosts will have different regulations. As for one's relatives in the Yellow Springs, the dead [there] outnumber the living [here], so they will certainly prepare vessels and goods for the use of the [recent] dead.[14] Now, if you treat the dead on a par with the living, this is not what the spirits intended. [But] if the [*hun*] lacks awareness, then [to bury it with precious goods] is to rob the living of what is useful; it harms them while benefiting no one. Furthermore, it will stir up evil thoughts. This is to invite the disaster of exposing the [corpse's] frame and making the deceased's catastrophes more likely.[15]

To bury [*zang* 葬] means to hide away [*zang* 藏]. You hide [the corpse] in hopes that others will not be able to see it. However, many provide coffins and vaults, prepare funerary presents, and store goods. This is no different from burying gold on the side of the road and writing the fact on a sign next to it. Even an extremely foolish man will certainly ridicule those who do so.[16] Abundant wealth and extravagant burials give rise to evil intentions. Some [grave robbers] break open the vault and the coffin. Some drag out and expose the body itself. Some cut off the deceased's arm to obtain its gold rings. Some grab hold of the corpse's intestines in search of jade and pearls. The punishment of being burned to death is no more painful than this. From the past until the present, it has never been the case that people have not died; likewise, it has never been the case that tombs have not been robbed. Therefore, Zhang Shizhi 張釋之 said, "If you put something desirable [in the tomb], even if you secure the tomb in a south-facing mountain, there will still be cracks [through which grave robbers can enter]. If you arrange it so that nothing desirable is in the tomb, even though the grave does not have a stone vault, what anxieties could you have [about the tomb's being opened]?"[17] This statement is insightful! This man is my teacher. No matter how generous one is in giving funerary presents, this is not treating the dead lavishly. A living person does so only for his or her own benefit. These thoughts of the living are without benefit [to the deceased]; instead, it leads to abandoning everything that belongs to the dead. One who realizes this will not do it. Consequently, the *Classic of Changes* [*Yijing* 易經] says, "When burying the dead in ancient times, the dead were covered with firewood and buried in the fields. No mound was erected and no trees were planted [to mark the tomb]."[18] Thus the dead were able to return to their true state without harming the living.

Hence, if I die in the morning, I want to be buried that evening; if I die in the evening, then I would like to be buried the next morning. I want neither coffin nor vault. Dress my corpse with neither robes nor grave clothes. Do not wash my body or hair. About the things to put in my mouth or funerary garments, you should include nothing. I originally wanted to enter the pit naked, so that my body would become intimate with the earth. Perhaps, though, since our human feelings have long been contaminated by the vulgar, it will be difficult for [people] to understand this improvement.

So now I will roughly set forth my rules. [My funerary wishes] are not so lavish as to require a stone vault, but they are not so frugal that they call for burying my body naked. After my breath has stopped, then immediately dress [my corpse] in old, seasonal clothing and a head scarf made from a single piece of material.[19] Wrap my corpse in a rough reed mat and hemp, about two yards' worth. Then place my corpse on the [funerary] couch. Select fallow ground and dig a pit that is ten feet deep, twelve feet long, and six feet wide. Once the pit is completed, lift up the couch and approach the pit. Then take away the couch and let the corpse drop into the pit. As for the ordinary goods I used while alive, not one should accompany me. Put in only the *Classic of Filial Piety* [*Xiaojing* 孝經] to show that I did not forget the way of filial piety [*xiaodao* 孝道]. Except for the places where the reed mat [covers my body], [my extremities] should become intimate with the soil. The soil and ground over my tomb should be flattened. Return the grass that was originally there and allow it to grow on [the tomb]. Do not plant trees there. If there are any, get rid of them. Make it so that there are no traces of the living there and that even if you wanted to find it, you would be unable to do so. If one does not see what one desires, then evil intentions will not arise. From start to finish, [the dead] will be neither startled nor alarmed; for a thousand years, they will have no worries. [Allowing] the bodily frame and bones to become one body with Sovereign Earth [Houtu 后土] and the *hun* souls [*hunshuang* 魂爽] to join its spirits [*heling* 合靈] with the primordial *qi* is the epitome of solicitude.

If [my wife] dies before or after me, you should not move us [in order] to be buried together. Joint burials began with the Duke of Zhou. [However,] they are not in accord with the ancient rites. When Shun 舜 was buried in Cangwu 蒼梧, his two wives did not follow him.[20] We can take this as a rule; there is no need to even consider the Zhou rites. Do not ask about musicians; do not believe prognosticators. Do not pay attention to what the vulgar say. Do not set out places for the spirit tablets. On the fifteenth day, do not present morning and evening offerings. According to the rites, one does not sacrifice at the tomb. On the first day of each month, you should merely set out mats [for a feast] to make a sacrifice. After one hundred days, you should stop. When you approach the tomb, it should be either in daylight or at dusk; you should not come at night. Wear your mourning robes at your usual residence: do not live at the tomb. In ancient times, no one revered the tomb. That was wise. Nowadays, people build tumuli and plant trees. This is foolish. If you do not follow my instructions, [it would mean] giving the corpse a death sentence [*lushi* 戮尸] under the ground. This is to die and again be harmed. If the *hun* soul has awareness, then its grief at being wronged will flood the world, and it will be a vengeful demon [*hengui* 恨鬼] for a long time. You should take [the actions of] Wangsun's sons as an admonition.[21] It is extremely difficult to disobey the wishes of the dead. I hope you will not change them!

[*JS* 51.1416–18]

NOTES

1. *Analects* 11/12.

2. The foundational works of Confucianism, the *Analects*, *Mencius*, and *Xunzi*, have little to say about spiritual beings. The *Mozi*, in contrast, argues that gods and ghosts do exist and that their primary duty is to keep track of human behavior, rewarding good acts and punishing bad ones. During the Western Han dynasty (206 B.C.E.–8 C.E.), Confucian thinkers undoubtedly incorporated these ideas into their reformulation of the Confucian worldview.

3. Keith N. Knapp, *Selfless Offspring: Filial Children and Social Order in Medieval China* (Honolulu: University of Hawai'i Press, 2005), 82–112. See also Robert Ford Campany, *Strange Writing: Anomaly Accounts in Early Medieval China* (Albany: State University of New York Press, 1996), 343–63.

4. A. C. Graham, *Chuang Tzu: The Inner Chapters* (London: Allen & Unwin, 1981), 86–89, 123–25; Keith N. Knapp, "Heaven and Death According to Huangfu Mi, a Third-Century Confucian," *Early Medieval China* 6 (2000): 15–18.

5. *Analects* 6/22.

6. *Jin* was a vegetable used in meat stew.

7. This statement appears in the "Jiyi" 祭義 chapter of the *Record of Rites* (*Liji* 禮記). See D. C. Lau and Chen Fong Ching, *Liji zhuzi suoyin* 禮記逐字索引 (Taibei: Commercial Press, 1995), 25.1.

8. According to the *Record of Rites*, at sixty, a person prepares his coffin each year. At seventy, he makes adjustments to his funerary preparations each season. At eighty, he does so each month, and at ninety, he does so daily. See Lau and Chen, *Liji zhuzi suoyin* 5.48 and 12.33.

9. This phrase somewhat resembles the following one found in the *Huainanzi* 淮南子:

    Waiting on the times of Heaven (or Nature) the True Man does not rush to prolong life. In life I have a seven-foot body; in death I have a coffin-length of soil. As a living being, I add one to the kind of those who have form; just as, in death, I sink into the formless kind. Thus the sum of matter is not increased by my living: even the thickness of the soil is not swelled by my death. How then should I feel the joy of life or sorrow of death, the gain of one or loss of the other?

    See D. C. Lau, *Huainanzi zhuzi suoyin* 淮南子逐字索引 (Taibei: Commercial Press, 1992), 7.56; and Evan Morgan, *Tao the Great Luminant: Essays from Huai Nan Tzu* (1933; repr., Taibei: Ch'eng Wen, 1974), 63.

10. According to the "Tangong" 檀弓 chapter of the *Record of Rites*, when Kongzi 孔子 saw that Huan Sima could not complete construction of his stone sarcophagus within three years, he said, "What extravagance! It would be better that when dead, he should quickly decay away" (Lau and Chen, *Liji zhuzi suoyin* 3.70; James Legge, trans., *Li Chi: Book of Rites*, 2 vols. [1885; repr., New Hyde Park, N.Y.: University Books, 1967], 1.149).

11. This is an allusion to a story found in the "Ansi" 安死 chapter of the *Annals of Master Lü* (*Lüshi chunqiu* 呂氏春秋). By warning that it would lead to the tomb's desecration,

Kongzi stopped the chief mourner from putting the precious Yufan jade in the coffin of the Jisun family's patriarch. See D. C. Lau, *Lüshi chunqiu zhuzi suoyin* 呂氏春秋逐字索引 (Taibei: Commercial Press, 1997) 10.3, 50.

12. D. C. Lau et al., *Zuozhuan zhuzi suoyin* 左傳逐字索引, 2 vols. (Hong Kong: Commercial Press, 1995), B8.2.4.

13. Yang Wangsun requested that he be buried naked, whereas the First Emperor was famously buried in an elaborate tomb. See *HS* 67.2907–8.

14. That is, since the dead are so much more numerous than the living, they will take care of the physical needs of the recently departed. Here Huangfu Mi assumes that dead relatives will help out their kin, just as living relatives would. For this reason, it is not necessary to bury goods to satisfy the deceased's daily needs.

15. In the early medieval period, tomb robbery was rampant. Many of the early medieval writers of death testaments worry that if anything of value were buried with the dead, the tomb would be robbed and the corpse would be desecrated.

16. For the passage on which this is based, see Lau, *Lüshi chunqiu zhuzi suoyin* 10.3, 49.

17. This line appears in the *Records of the Historian* (*Shiji* 史記) 120.2753.

18. D. C. Lau et al., *Zhouyi zhuzi suoyin* 周易逐字索引 (Hong Kong: Commercial Press, 1995), 66.82. Interestingly, in the *Classic of Changes* (*Yijing* 易經), this passage describes how the uncivilized people of past eras buried bodies before the sages introduced coffins and vaults.

19. In early medieval China, a head scarf made from a single piece of cloth was a sign of simplicity and the badge of recluses, which is what Huangfu Mi was.

20. In the *Record of Rites*, both these assertions are credited to Ji Wuzi 季武子. See Lau and Chen, *Liji zhuzi suoyin* 3.3 and 3.28.

21. At first, Yang Wangsun's sons did not want to go along with their father's strange request to be buried naked. Hence, they convinced his friend Qi Hou 祁候 to write a letter to dissuade him from this notion. See *HS* 66.2907–8.

38. Encounters in Mountains

GIL RAZ

I n traditional China, as in many other cultures, mountains were sacred sites, mysterious and dangerous. The best-known mountains in China were the Five Marchmounts (*wuyue* 五嶽).[1] As the terrestrial correlates of the five phases (earth, water, metal, wood, and fire) in the cosmo-political theory that supported the imperial edifice since the Han, these peaks were thought to secure the realm with their very presence.[2] Among imperial rites, few were more sacred and awesome than the *feng* and *shan* 封禪 rites at Mount Tai, the Eastern Peak.[3] But these five peaks were not the only sacred sites. In fact, any mountain could become a sacred site at the local level. As the texts translated here show, Daoist scriptures of the medieval era merged imperial conceptions of sacrality with local traditions to create narratives that transformed local sites into cosmic loci of efficacy and revelation.

In Daoist lore, however, the most important aspect of mountains were realms hidden within. These cavern heavens (*dongtian* 洞天), hidden inside sacred mountains, were conceived of as microcosms with their own sun and moon, in which mundane spatial and temporal limits were abrogated. Such caverns were accessible only to the select few who possessed knowledge of the Dao and could employ esoteric devices and techniques to enter them. These hidden precincts were sites for revelation, instruction, and transcendence.

There was not a singular, unitary Daoist discourse on mountains, however. Daoist lineages of medieval times developed their traditions from an array of earlier practices, including local cults, healing and exorcistic practices, and imperial rites and discourse. These complex interactions are evident in the two texts translated in this chapter, which present two types of Daoist geographical narratives.

The first selection, "Terrestrial Perfection" (Dizhen 地真), chapter 18 of the *Inner Chapters of the Master Who Embraces Simplicity* (Baopuzi neipian 抱朴子內篇) by Ge Hong 葛洪 (284–363),[4] recounts the Yellow Emperor's quest for the teaching of the Way of the Perfected One 真一. The quest takes the emperor to mythical mountains at the four quarters of the earth, where he encounters reclusive sages from whom he receives texts and instructions for various practices. The journey culminates in an encounter in a cavern within Mount E'mei 峨嵋山 (in modern Sichuan Province) where the Luminary Person 皇人 finally instructs him in the ultimate method. While we may see the journey through the mythical landscape as a metaphorical trek to attain true knowledge of the cosmos, we should also note that the narrative places Mount E'mei at the center of the realm and thus makes it superior to all other locations. We may thus speculate that this text was composed by a lineage based on or near Mount E'mei.

The second text consists of selections from chapter 11 of the *Declarations of the Perfected* (Zhen'gao 真誥).[5] Entitled "Investigating Sacred Regions" (*Jishenqu* 稽神樞), part 1, this chapter describes the esoteric topography of Mount Juqu 句曲, also known as Mount Mao 茅山 (in modern Jiangsu Province), site of revelation of the Shangqing 上清 scriptures. The chapter provides detailed descriptions of the mountain and its history.

My presentation of these two texts has several interrelated goals. First, the two texts are among the best examples of Daoist discourse on mountains, and they demonstrate two different modes of encountering the extrahuman on mountains. The chapter "Terrestrial Perfection," while assuming the sacrality of mountains as sites of encounter and instruction, does not in fact describe Mount E'mei in any detail. Instead, the focus of the chapter is an extended exposition of meditation practice, with its philosophical and cosmological entailments. The chapter "Investigating Sacred Regions," in contrast, is an exhaustively detailed description of Mount Juqu.

Second, the geographic discourse in these texts encodes many debates, both among Daoist lineages and between Daoists and other traditions, about communal identity, the efficacy of practice, and competition between traditions and lineages. The two texts translated here need to be seen as participating in a complex intertextual network, in which the respective authors claimed the superiority of their knowledge and practice. We therefore observe how both texts manipulate, appropriate, recast, and otherwise respond to earlier textual material. Several ancient narratives—imperial, local, and Daoist—are recast in "Investigating Sacred Regions" to demonstrate the sacrality of Mount Juqu. Similar manipulation of early material is also apparent in Ge Hong's "Terrestrial Perfection." For example, the narrative of the Yellow Thearch's journey in this chapter is a reformulation of a narrative from the Daoist classic *Zhuangzi*. But the most important text to which both chapters are responding to is a narrative in the late-third-century *Array of the Five Talismans* (*Taishang lingbao wufuxu* 太上靈寶五符序) describing the discovery of the five numinous-treasure (*lingbao* 靈寶) talismans.[6]

The narrative core of the *Array of the Five Talismans* relates the subterranean journey of the Elder of Draconic Awe (Longwei zhangren 龍威丈人) into the cavern inside Mount Bao in Lake Dongting (Lake Tai in modern Jiangsu), where he finds the talismans that had been secreted there by the great Yu 禹, the ancient sage-ruler who quelled the floodwaters.[7] This mythical explanation for the appearance of the *lingbao* talismans in the human realm provides ancient authority and precedent for the ritual described later in the text. Originally a transmission rite of the *lingbao* talismans, this is the earliest known description of a *jiao* 醮 rite. This complex ritual combines the practice of the five talismans with two other practices, incantation of esoteric names of the five celestial emperors and a method of breath cultivation named "ingesting the five sprouts," which refer to the nascent *qi* of the five directions. This ritual was the core of the *lingbao* ritual program of the early fifth century, the basis for the ritual codifications of the fifth centuries, and remains among the basic modules in contemporary Daoist ritual.[8]

The relationship between the *Array of the Five Talismans* and Ge Hong's chapter is very complex. Ge Hong, known by his sobriquet Baopuzi 抱朴子 (Master Who Embraces Simplicity, which is also the title of one of his famous works), is arguably the best-known author and compiler of esoteric techniques in medieval China. The *Inner Chapters* (*Neipian* 內篇) is dedicated to the quest for transcendence and attaining the Dao.[9] Whether or not we should consider Ge Hong a Daoist depends on our definition of Daoism,[10] but because the various practices he mentions were incorporated into the Daoist syntheses of medieval China, the *Inner Chapters* is critical to our understanding of Daoism. The quest for transcendence was a fundamental aspect of Chinese religion for centuries and encompassed a vast array of techniques and methods, including alchemy, sexual practices, gymnastics, and dietary regimens. Ge Hong presents dozens of these techniques and methods for attaining the Dao, among them the five *lingbao* talismans and the texts associated with them. Clearly, the sources for Ge Hong's compilation included various distinct lineages and traditions. It is thus intriguing that a different version of Ge Hong's chapter "Terrestrial Perfection" is included in the *Array of the Five Talismans*, but as a distinct text entitled *Scripture of the Perfected One from the Most High Great One* (*Taishang taiyi zhenyi zhijing* 太上太一真一之經). Both texts seem to be based on the same original source and to have been incorporated into the two texts, which manipulated it in different ways.[11]

Ge Hong's chapter and the *Scripture of the Perfected One* differ in several respects. Whereas Ge Hong presents the chapter as oral instruction from his teacher Zheng Yin, the *Scripture of the Perfected One* is presented as an independent teaching. While a major portion of the two texts is the same, the actual order of passages is different. The most important differences between the texts lie in the distinct teachings they present. The instruction by the Luminary Person in the *Scripture of the Perfected One* is far longer and is focused on the Method of the Five Sprouts, including detailed instructions for practice.[12] Significantly, these instructions do not refer to the celestial Five Celestial Thearchs or to the *lingbao* talismans, which are at the core of the *jiao* ritual of the *Array of the Five Talismans*. This scripture emphasizes that the source for transcendence is within the body and not external to it and aims at attaining, through the ingestion of the five sprouts, Perfect Unity (*zhenyi* 真一), the integrated human body, and the Three Ones (*sanyi* 三一) that are within the body.

Although Ge Hong's chapter includes several passages also found in the *Scripture of the Perfected One*, it does not refer to the five sprouts but does include several other methods not mentioned in the *Scripture of the Perfected One*. Also absent from the *Scripture of the Perfected One* is a paragraph describing the precise location of the One within the body and the instructions for transmitting this teaching, which entail blood oaths. These two notions were criticized by some Daoists, such as the Celestial Masters. The elision of this passage in the *Scripture of the Perfected One* thus hints at the debates among Daoist lineages. We must remember that each lineage claimed to possess the most efficacious methods for attaining the ultimate goal of integrating with the Dao, becoming a transcendent, and living beyond the limits of time and space. The authority of one's preferred method depended to a large extent on asserting the primacy of its source, that is, the location of the original revelation and the genealogy of transmission of the practice. We can find similar rhetorical strategies in many contemporary texts, but few provide such clear links as the texts under discussion here. The narrative in the *Array of the Five Talismans* was also a direct inspiration for the description of the cavern heaven under Mount Mao in the chapter "Investigating Sacred Regions" in the *Declarations of the Perfected*. In the sacred geography presented here, however, Mount Bao, also called Linwu 林屋, the site of revelation of the five talismans, is referred to as the eastern portal to the cavern under Mount Mao. In fact, Mount Mao is said to be connected by subterranean caverns to four other important sites (7a7): Mount Tai, the eastern Marchmount and abode of the netherworld bureaucracy; Mount Luofu, the final residence of Ge Hong; and E'mei, the site of revelation described in the *Scripture of the Perfected One*. These are not merely geographic details but a reflection of the strategies of co-optation, adaptation, and reformulation of earlier material in the Shangqing scriptures, which were revealed on Mount Mao.

Declarations of the Perfected is a critically important work for understanding Highest Clarity Daoism (Shangqing 上清), a new Daoist tradition that emerged among a closely related group of local elite families. At the core of Shangqing Daoism are revelations received by Yang Xi 楊羲 (330–386?), in a process described by Stephen Bokenkamp in chapter 33 of this book. Yang Xi was not only a conduit for scriptural revelation. In séances, Yang Xi also transmitted questions to the Perfected on behalf of his patrons and some of their relatives and friends, regarding illnesses, locations of deceased kin, and the fortunes of specific family members. Partial records of these sessions, along with fragments of Yang Xi's journal in which he recorded information regarding the Shangqing revelations, form the main body of the *Declarations of the Perfected*. The text was collated and annotated by Tao Hongjing 陶弘景 (456–536), also known as the Recluse (*Yinju* 隱居), after he retired to Mount Mao 茅 in 492. Supported by Emperor Wu of the Liang dynasty, Tao pursued Shangqing meditative practices and alchemy. His main goal, however, was to collate and edit the Shangqing scriptures, distinguishing the authentic texts from later forgeries and imitations. In *Declarations*, Tao interjects his comments after Yang Xi's words in order to explain and elaborate passages he finds problematic. These comments are invaluable, not just for helping clarify Yang Xi's sometimes gnomic words, but also as an expression of devoted exegesis. As a true believer, Tao gives precedence to Yang Xi's words even when these words are inconsistent with other passages, historical sources, or Tao's own experience.

At the heart of the Shangqing revelations is Mount Mao itself. Indeed, the tradition is also known as Maoshan Daoism. Mount Mao included three distinct peaks, named Elder, Middle, and Young, after the three Mao brothers who resided on the mountain during the Han dynasty: the eldest brother, Ying 盈 (byname Shushen 叔申); the middle brother, Gu 固 (byname Jiwei 季偉); and the youngest brother, Zhong 衷 (byname Sihe 思和).[13] In the text, they are usually referred to by their posthumous titles: Ying is known as Director of Destinies and Divine Lord, Perfected Person of the Supreme Primordial, Great Minister of the Eastern Marchmount (Taiyuan zhenren Dongyue shangqing siming shenjun 太元真人東嶽上卿司命神君); Gu is named Divine Lord Who Determines the Registers (Dinglu 定錄); and Zhong is named Protector of Destinies (Baoming 保命).

Owing to its topography, Mount Mao was also known as Hooked Bend (Juqu 句曲). Yang Xi describes Mount Juqu as a sacred site where spiritual realization (*xinwu* 心悟) is possible. Moreover, the soil and water here are said to be so efficacious that anyone who lives on the mountain, even if not a seeker of the Dao, will "cross over generations" (*dushi* 度世) and dwell in a world of "great peace" (*taiping* 太平). Both these two core ideas of salvation in the Daoist tradition are traceable to earlier notions. The term "cross over generations" shows up as early as the *Lunheng* 論衡 by Wang Chong 王充 (27–97), where it refers to living beyond one's expected lifetime, or extreme longevity. Wang Chong doubts the possibility of such attainment, but his many references to contemporary tales reveal the popularity and pervasiveness of the belief in longevity. The notion of "great peace" appears in ancient texts as a political and social ideal, which all rulers aspired to attain. The importance and popularity of this ideal are evident in that it was adopted by one of the early Daoist movements, also known as Yellow Turbans. This movement led a rebellion in 184 C.E. Even though the rebellion was soon suppressed, it hastened the collapse of the Han dynasty. In the succeeding Daoist lineages, "great peace" became an eschatological idea, the idealized state that would appear in the new epoch.

Among the more intriguing aspects alluded to in this chapter of the *Declarations* is the complex interaction between local cults and the emerging Daoist tradition. Yang Xi's words, augmented by Tao Hongjing's notes, reveal that the Mao brothers, perhaps in the physical form of cranes, were first worshipped at local shrines at various villages near the mountain, with drumming, dancing, and blood offerings. Daoists despised these practices of the common religion, and they were careful to distinguish their own "pure" practices from these "vulgar" ones.

The co-optation of the Mao brothers and the sacred sites associated with them is another excellent example of the Shangqing reformulation of earlier practices. We thus find that Yang Xi provides instructions for an alternative, and superior, method for encountering the Perfected, such as Elder Mao. After preparatory ritual fasts and abstentions (*zhaijie* 齋戒), one is to "direct one's heart" (*xiangxin* 向心) to the deity. While meditating, the adept is to pray for the arrival of the deity. If all is done correctly, the deity will spontaneously appear before one's eyes. This type of guided meditation is to be contrasted with the frenzied practice of the local cult.

The text also provides a rare glimpse of the annual religious cycle on the mountain. Yang Xi provides specific dates for revering Elder Mao. These apparently were popular days of celebration, for Tao writes that thousands of celebrants visited the mountain on the eighteenth day of the third month. Tao mentions that the participants, including Daoists and commoners, celebrated with a *lingbao* ritual, indicating a confluence of Daoist and common practice (13a). Although he disapproved of the *lingbao* ritual and was clearly upset by the noise of the crowds, his description of the event is intriguing, and we wish for more details about the actual social and religious activities at the site. Elsewhere, Tao hints at a lineage of female Daoists, as well as more examples of the variety of Daoist and non-Daoist practitioners on the mountain (15a–b). Again, we wish for more details on the rich variety of competing religious traditions.

The texts translated here reveal different aspects of Daoist notions of sacred geography. Ge Hong's "Terrestrial Perfection" and Yang Xi's words in the

Declarations of the Perfected show various narratological strategies by which Daoist lineages attempted to distinguish themselves as they competed for support and potential converts. Tao Hongjing's notes to Yang Xi's arcane revelations hint at the sociohistorical reality on Mount Mao, further revealing the contention between various religious practitioners, Daoist and non-Daoist, which is usually hidden in scriptures. Perhaps most important, the texts show the importance of understanding the local traditions and contexts from which Daoist lineages emerged.

FURTHER READING

For a detailed study of Ge Hong and his work, see Robert Ford Campany, *To Live as Long as Heaven and Earth: A Translation and Study of Ge Hong's Traditions of Divine Transcendents* (Berkeley: University of California Press, 2002). There is no full translation in a Western language of the *Declarations of the Perfected*. Yoshikawa Tadao 吉川忠夫 and Mugitani Kunio 麥谷邦夫, eds., *Shinkō kenkyū* 真誥研究 (Kyoto: Kyōto daigaku jinbun kagaku kenkyūjo, 2000), is a complete Japanese translation, with extensive notes and a punctuated and annotated Chinese text. On the Shangqing revelations, see Isabelle Robinet, "Shangqing—Highest Clarity," in *Daoism Handbook*, ed. Livia Kohn (Leiden: Brill, 2000), 196–224, and *La révélation du Shangqing dans l'histoire du taoïsme* (Paris: École française d'Extrême-Orient, 1984). On Tao Hongjing and his place in Daoist history, see Michel Strickmann, "On the Alchemy of T'ao Hung-ching," in *Facets of Taoism: Essays in Chinese Religion*, ed. Holmes Welch and Anna Seidel (New Haven, Conn.: Yale University Press, 1979), 123–92. For more on Mount Mao, based on the *Declarations* and later material, see Edward H. Schafer, *Mao Shan in T'ang Times* (Boulder, Colo.: Society for the Study of Chinese Religions, 1989). On Daoist geography, see Gil Raz, "Daoist Sacred Geography," in *Early Chinese Religion, Part Two: The Period of Division (220–589)*, ed. John Lagerwey and Lü Pengzhi (Leiden: Brill, 2010), 2:1399–1442; Franciscus Verellen, "The Twenty-Four Dioceses and Zhang Daoling: The Spatio-liturgical Organization of Early Heavenly Master Taoism," in *Pilgrims, Patrons, and Place: Localizing Sanctity in Asian Religions*, ed. Phyllis Granoff and Koichi Shinohara (Vancouver: University of British Columbia Press, 2003), 15–67, and "The Beyond Within: Grotto-Heavens (*dongtian* 洞天) in Taoist Ritual and Cosmology," *Cahiers d'Extrême-Asie* 8 (1995): 265–90; and James Robson, *Power of Place: The Religious Landscape of the Southern Sacred Peak (Nanyue* 南嶽*) in Medieval China* (Cambridge, Mass.: Harvard East Asian Monographs, 2009).

❖

GE HONG 葛洪

Inner Chapters of the Master Who Embraces Simplicity
(Baopuzi neipian 抱朴子內篇)

CHAPTER 18. TERRESTRIAL PERFECTION
(*DIZHEN* 地真)[14]

The Master Who Embraces Simplicity says:[15] I heard my teacher say: If one can comprehend the One, then all matters will be complete.[16] If you know the One, then nothing will be unknown. If you do not know the One, then nothing may be known. The Dao arises in the One; its value is unique. *All things harbor the One, and by it emulate heaven, earth, and man; hence it is called Three Ones.* By attaining the One, heaven gains clarity. By attaining the One, the spirits gain efficacy. By attaining the One, earth gains tranquillity. By attaining the One, humanity gains life.[17] [By it,] metal sinks and feathers hover; mountains jut and rivers flow. Look for it, and it is unseen. Listen for it, and it is unheard.[18] Maintain it and you will live, neglect it and you will perish. Facing it, you will have good fortune; turning your back on it, you will have misfortune. Protect it and you will have long lasting blessings without limit; lose it and your allotment will decline and the pneuma will be exhausted. Lord Lao says: Obscure! Dim! Within it are images. Obscure! Dim! Within it are creatures.[19] This is called the One. Therefore, the *Scripture of the Transcendents* [*Xianjing* 仙經] says: If you wish to have long life, you must clearly understand [the method to] Preserve the One.[20] Think of the One when extremely hungry, and the One will provide your victuals; think of the One when extremely thirsty, and the One will provide your beverage.[21] *The One has a surname and name, clothes of specific color. It is nine* cun *in height in men, six in women.*[22] *It is located either in the Lower Cinnabar Field* 丹田, *two* cun *and four fen below the navel, or in the Golden Porte of the Crimson Palace* 絳宮金闕 *below the heart, the Middle Cinnabar Field. Sometimes it is between a person's eyebrows. As you progress within, at one* cun *is the Bright Hall* 明堂; *two* cun *within is the Cavern Chamber* 洞房; *and three* cun *within is the Upper Cinnabar Field. This then has been cherished by generations of Daoists* 道家 *who transmitted the names as oral instruction requiring a blood oath.*[23]

The One can complete yin and produce yang, withdraw and advance cold and heat. Spring attains the One for sprouting; summer attains the One for growing; autumn attains the One for harvesting; and winter uses it for storing. Its largeness cannot be topped within the six directions; its smallness cannot be compared with a tip of a hair.

In the past,[24] the Yellow Thearch reached east to Azure Hill 青丘. As he passed Feng Mountain 風山, he met Master Purple Mansion 紫府先生 and received the *Inner Writ of the Three Luminaries* [*Sanhuang neiwen* 三皇內文][25] with which to investigate and summon the myriad spirits. To the south, he climbed the Round Tumulus and rested in the shade of the Establishing Tree [Jianmu 建木].[26] He observed *the place where the hundred numinous beings ascended*, gathered *ruo qian* 若乾 blossoms, *and drank the waters of the Cinnabar Hill* 丹巒.[27] Traveling west, he saw the Central Yellow Master 中黃子 and received the *Nine Additions Recipes* [*Jiujia zhi fang* 九加之方].[28] Passing by Lake Dongting 洞庭, he received the *Scripture of Self-Completion* [*Zicheng zhi jing* 自成之經] from Master Guangcheng 廣成子.[29] He went north to the Great Dike 洪隄 to Juci 具茨, where he met Great Lofty Lord 大隗君 and the Youth of the Yellow Canopy 華蓋童子 and received the *Divine Herbs Charts* [*Shenzhi tu* 神芝圖].[30]

He returned to climb Mount Wangshi 王室 and received the *Record of Instructions for Spirit Cinnabar and Gold* [*Shendan jin jue ji* 神丹金訣記].[31] He reached Mount E'mei and encountered the Celestial Perfected Luminary 天真皇人 at the Jade Hall and inquired about the Way of the Perfected One.[32] The Luminary Person said, "Since you are lord of the four seas, is it not greedy indeed that you also wish for longevity?"[33]

As I cannot repeat all the details of their meeting, I will in passing mention only one aspect. As for methods of longevity and transcendence, there are only the [methods of] gold and cinnabar; as for preserving the form and expelling miasma, then there [are] only the [methods of] Perfected One; therefore the ancients valued them greatly. A scripture of the Transcendents says:[34] The *Scriptures of Nine Refinements Cinnabar and Golden Liquid* [*Jiuzhuan dan jinye jing* 九轉丹金液經] and the *Instructions for Preserving the One* [*shouyi jue* 守一訣] are within the Five Citadels of Kunlun, encased in a jade casket, inscribed on golden slips, sealed with purple resin and stamped with a Central Seal.[35]

I heard the following from my teacher:[36]	吾聞之於先師曰
The One is in the Great Abyss of the Northern Culmen.[37]	一在北極大淵之中
Before it is the Bright Hall, behind is the Scarlet Palace,	前有明堂, 後有絳宮
Towering, is the Floreate Canopy, and the Myriad-Story Golden Tower stretches tall.	巍巍華蓋, 金樓穹隆
To the left is Mainstay 罡, to the right is Leader 魁, billowing waves rise in the void.	左罡右魁, 激波揚空
Dark mystical herbs blanket the cliffs, ruby grasses flowering in the thickets.	玄芝被崖, 朱草蒙瓏
Bright jade craggy and jagged, the sun and moon send down their glow.[38]	白玉嵯峨, 日月垂光
Traversing fire and crossing water, passing the dark and fording yellow.[39]	歷火過水, 經玄過黃

The guard towers of the citadel interlock, canopies and side curtains ring melodiously.	城闕交錯, 帷帳琳琅
Dragons and tigers line up as guardians, spirit people at their side.[40]	龍虎列紉, 神人在傍
Without spreading, without giving, the One secures its place.[41]	不施不與, 一安其所
Without delay, without haste, the One secures its dwelling.	不遲不疾, 一安其室
[If you are] able to rest and able to roam, the One will never depart [from you].	能暇能豫, 一乃不去
Preserve the One and contemplate perfection; you will be able to communicate with spirits.	守一存真, 乃能通神
Lessen desire and restrict your eating;[42] the One will prolong your breathing.	少欲約食, 一乃留息
As a sharp blade nears your neck, by contemplating the One you will gain life.[43]	白刃臨頸, 思一得生
Knowing the One is not difficult; the difficulty is in completion.	知一不難, 難在於終
Preserving it without loss, you may [continue] without end.[44]	守之不失, 可以無窮
On land you will avoid evil beasts, in water evade the kraken dragons.	陸辟惡獸, 水劍蛟
You will not fear the *wangliang* or be threatened by poisonous vermin.	不畏魍魎, 挾毒之蟲
Ghosts will dare not approach; blades will dare not strike.[45]	鬼不敢近, 刃不敢

This is a general outline of [the method of] Perfected One. The Master Who Embraces Simplicity says: I heard the following from my master:

In numerous writings, Daoist methods that allow us by contemplation, visualization, meditation, and practice to evade evil and protect the body number in the several thousand. There are innumerable methods, such as Hiding the Shadow and Secreting the Form [hanjing zangxing 含影藏形], Preserving the Form as though dead [shouxing wusheng 守形無生], Nine Changes, Twelve Transformations, and Twenty-Four Births, for contemplating and viewing one's corporeal spirits, for internal vision, and for causing the appearance [of the spirits].[46] Each is efficacious. But manifesting in mind thousands of creatures in order to protect oneself is troublesome and suffices to overtax one's mind. If you know the Way of Preserving the One, then you may dispense with all of these [methods]. Therefore he said: "If one can comprehend the One, then all matters will be complete."

There are clear written instructions for the receiving the Oral Instructions for the Perfected One. *One will receive them [after selecting a day] in accord with the ruler-minister hemerological system and smearing the lips with blood of a white sacrificial victim. Use white silk and silver as [pledge] for a contract, break a golden tally, and divide it [as sign of covenant]. If you discuss them lightly or improperly transmit them, their spiritual power will not be efficacious.*

If you can preserve the One, the One will preserve you. Due to it, the hundred knives will have no place in which to place their sharpness,[47] and the hundred injuries will have no place to intrude with their misfortune. Though dwelling in defeat, you will be able to succeed; when in danger, you alone will be safe.

If you are in a shrine of demons, in a mountain grove, in a plague-ridden land, among tombs and graves, in a lair of tigers and wolves, or in a nest of vipers, Preserve the One diligently and the various baneful creatures will scatter afar. If you inadvertently forget to Preserve the One and are harmed by diverse ghosts or by nightmares in your sleep, then you should walk out to the central court of your home and gaze at the star Fu 輔 while concentrating on Preserving the One. The demons will depart. If it is raining or cloudy, you may stay indoors, face north, and visualize the star Fu; this would be sufficient. If you are surrounded by armed bandits and you cannot return to your native place, you should immediately enter the shade of the Six-jia [liu-jia yinzhong 六甲陰中], then the five types of weapons will not harm you. One who is able to Preserve the One can travel myriad li, join the military ranks, and cross mountains and rivers without the necessity of divining a day and selecting an auspicious time. When beginning construction or moving, assuming residence in a new home, one will no longer need to depend on divining the geomantic astrological positions; one will no longer need avoid the generals of Taisui 太歲 and Taiyin 太陰 and will never again encounter the calamitous odium of the Monthly Establishing killing and decimating spirits and the annual taboos. This method was effectively tried and proven by worthies of the past.

The Master Who Embraces Simplicity says: *The way of Mystic-One [玄一] is also an essential method. There is nothing it cannot avert; it is as effective as the Perfected-One [method]. What I referred to in "Reaching the Mystic" [Changxuan 暢玄], the first chapter of my* Inner Chapters, *is precisely this method. "Preserving the Mystic-One" is [an] easier [method] than "Preserving the Perfected-One." The Perfected-One has a name and surname, size, and colored clothing; the Mystic-One is suddenly manifested. At first, seek it within the sun, as is said: "Know the white, embrace the black" or "One who seeks death should not attain this."[48] First, however, you should hold a purification rite for a hundred days, and only afterward can you inquire about a master and seek it. You would then attain it within three or four days. If you once attain and preserve It, then It will not depart again. As you [practice] "Preserving the Mystic One," you should simultaneously envision your body dividing into three persons. Once three have appeared, you can continue and increase the number, reaching up to dozens of people all looking exactly like you, which you can hide or manifest. This is all based on oral instructions, the so-called Way of Multiplying Oneself.*

By this method, Master Zuo 左君,[49] Ji Zixun 薊子訓,[50] and Transcendent Ge 葛仙[51] were able to be in dozens of places simultaneously. So while one master could be sitting in one room talking to guests, another master may be at the gate welcoming a guest, and yet a third may be fishing at the riverbank. The guests could never distinguish which was the real master.

My master also said: Simultaneously [practice] Preserving the One and the Bright Mirror [method]. When this method is completed, you will be able to divide your form into dozens of figures, all dressed and looking alike.

The Master Who Embraces Simplicity says: My master said if you wish longevity, you should diligently ingest the great herbal preparations. If you wish to communicate with the spirits, you should [ingest] liquid gold and [practice] multiplying the form. After multiplying the form, then you will spontaneously see your body's three cloud souls and seven white souls [sanhun qipo 三魂七魄]; you will also be able to see the celestial divinities and terrestrial deities and be able to command the spirits of the mountains and rivers.

The Master Who Embraces Simplicity says: Life may be regretted and death may be feared. However, extending life, nourishing one's nature, and avoiding death all begin with diligence and end with long-lasting vision. After the Way is completed, little needs to be done. Before it is accomplished, nothing can be done. Collecting and picking herbal medicines, laboring in the mountains and marshes, and frying, ingesting, regulating and preparing [elixirs] all expend your muscles and strength. Ascending dangerous [heights] and crossing perilous [waters], day and night you cannot relax, and unless your intent is absolute, you cannot last long. You may wish to concoct the gold elixir and ascend to heaven, but the ingredients are too expensive and you cannot complete it. Then you need to once again depend on farming, husbanding, trading, and selling to accumulate resources. After years of diligent work, you may be able to complete it.[52] On the day you compound the elixir, you must perform ritual purification and cut off all social contact. Although not easy, yet you must add to this contemplation of the spirits, preserving the one, expelling evil spirits, and guarding your body. You must constantly conduct yourself as a ruler protecting his state or a general awaiting the enemy; then you may attain longevity. Using acuity and wisdom as the vessel for managing the state and delivering the people, and cultivating these practices, you would be sure to attain it. Shallow common people, even with deliberate intention, will be unable to carry this out to the end.

Therefore it is said the human body is the image of the state.[53] The status of the chest and belly is like the palace halls, and the arrangement of arms and legs is like the suburbs. The divisions of the joints and bones are like those of the hundred officials. The spirit is like the lord, the blood like ministers, and the pneuma like people. Therefore, knowing how to administer the body, you will know how to administer a kingdom. [Just as] one cherishes the people so as to bring peace to the kingdom, one [must] nourish one's pneuma so as to keep one's body whole. If the people are scattered, the country will collapse; if pneuma is exhausted, the body will die. What has collapsed cannot be preserved, and what has died cannot live. Therefore, the person of ultimate attainment resolves disaster before it occurs and heals disease before infection. He cures it before it becomes a problem and does not chase it after it has gone. People are hard to nurture but easy to endanger; pneuma is difficult to clarify but easy to contaminate. Therefore, you should inspect the power of virtue in order to protect its principles; cut off desires in order to consolidate blood and pneuma. Then the Perfected One will thereby be preserved; the Three and Seven will thereby be maintained; the hundred harmers will be expelled; and your life allotment extended.[54]

The Master Who Embraces Simplicity says: My master says, by ingesting the great drugs of gold and cinnabar, even if you have yet to depart the realm [of mortals,] the hundred depravities will not approach you. But ingesting herbal drugs and a little of the eight minerals, while adequate for expelling disease and fulfilling your allotment, is insufficient for warding off external calamities, such as threatening incursions by ghosts, slights and offenses by mountain spirits, or attacks by goblins. Only the method of Preserving the Perfected One will be safe from all these. Next, you should wear spiritual talismans. If you do not understand these two matters and yet seek longevity, you will be in great danger. Even if you shut three of four doors, bandits may still enter; how then dare you keep them open?

[*Baopuzi neipian*, DZ 1185; Wang Ming, ed.,
Baopuzi neipian jiaoshi (Beijing: Zhonghua shuju, 1985)]

SACRED MOUNT MAO

Declarations of the Perfected (Zhen'gao 真誥)

CHAPTER 11. INVESTIGATING SACRED REGIONS (*JISHENQU* 稽神樞) (EXCERPTS)

1a. Golden Peak [Jinling 金陵] is the fat and lard of the Cavern Void, the Earth's Lungs of Hooked Bend [Juqu 句曲] Mountains.[55] A hundred million people may tread there, but not even one knows this.

Note: Lord Baoming dictated these words.[56] This dictation must have occurred earlier than the sixth month of 365 [*yichou* 乙丑 year], that is, in 364 [*jiazi* 甲子]. In the beginning, he discusses the mountain's receipt of such auspiciousness. The mountain's soil is good; hence it is called fertile earth. Water reaches it and comes to the surface; hence it is called Earth's Lungs. For generations, people have roamed and trampled here, yet none knew of this place.

The water sources on Mount Juqu are sinuous and embracing: hence the name Hooked Embrace [Jurong 句容] Town. One may get there by crossing the river and continuing for 150 *li*. If you ask and seek it, you will surely find it.

Note: Beyond this point, the text is in big characters written in purple, and it is the same as that recorded in the *Biography of the Three Mao Lords*

[*Mao sanjun zhuan* 茅三君傳]. The *Biography* is indeed kept in secret, and those who have seen it are few. Now, having reverently transcribed the discourse on the matters of the mountain, all is evident and clear. In accord with the twisting and sinuous form of the mountain that rises and fall from east to west, it has been named Hooked Bend. The administrative boundary follows the mountain range: the west and north is part of Jurong, the east and south is part of Yanling. Since the establishment of Jurong as a district, the village is no longer extant. In the past it must have been near Shuxu 述墟. It was probably where the current mountain village of Shitou is located, about 150 to 60 *li* from the river.

East of the River, to the right and left of Jinling, is a small swamp. To the east of the swamp, there is Mount Juqu. This is it.

Note: This must refer to the Jinling that is Moling, and not the Jinling that is Earth's Lungs. The small swamp must refer to the current Lake Chishan. From the river until one is directly in front of the mountains, the surroundings are precisely as described here.

1b4. This mountain is a cavernous void. Through inner vision, [one may see] inside a numinous hall. The cavern court has four openings where mountain grottoes intersect. The ancients named this the Void Tower of Golden Altar 金壇之虛臺, the Detached Palace of the Celestial Consort 天后之便闕,[57] the Eastern Window of Pure Void 清虛之東窻,[58] and Font Adjacent to Linwu 林屋隔沓. This is the meeting point for all the caves, where the hidden paths all lead; the seven roads and nine fonts from the four directions all reach here. This is a Cavern of the Perfected and a Transcendent Hostel.

Note: This passage explains that within the cavern heaven, all places are interconnected. The Celestial Consort is the Perfected Lady in the Linwu Cave. This location is below Mount Bao in Lake Tai 太湖苞山, which the Elder of Draconic Awe entered and where he obtained the five *lingbao* talismans.[59] Clear Void is the name of the cavern heaven in Mount Wangwu. This means that Floreate Yang [Huayang 華陽] and these other caves are interconnected.

. . . 2a1. As for Golden Peak, weapons and water cannot assail it; calamity and disease cannot encroach on it. The "Central Essential Primordial" chapter of the *River Chart*,[60] scroll 44, says: "Within the altar of hooked gold is a peak; war and pestilence do not reach here, [and] flood and waves cannot ascend it." Truly, this is an auspicious place. That your heart was awakened here proves that you are certainly fortunate. Again, consider by whom this realization was prompted.

Note: The *River Chart* was received by Shun and Yu; it is of a type with the *Luo Writ* 洛書. Today there are still more than forty scrolls extant. The [final] lines refer to the senior scribe [Xu Mi]. In discussing the cause of his realization, he means that he was inspired by following Yang Xi's explanations.

Within Hooked Bend Mountain is the site of Golden Peak. The area of the site is thirty-seven or thirty-eight *qing*.[61] This is the Earth's Lungs of Golden Peak. The soil is fertile, and the well water is sweet. It is wonderful to dwell at this place; one will surely attain "crossing over generations" and see great peace.[62] The *Inner Primordial Scripture of the River Chart* [*Hetu neiyuan jing* 河圖內元經] says: "The soil of Earth's Lungs is fertile and its water is pure; on the Peak on the Golden Altar at Hooked Bend Mountain, one may obtain longevity and ascend to the Qucheng 曲城 [Bent Citadel]." Also, the *Middle Chapter of the River Book* [*Heshu zhongpian* 河書中篇] says: "The mountain of hooked gold, within it there is a peak; war and pestilence do not reach, flood and waves cannot ascend."[63] This is the place it refers to.

. . .

2b3. In ancient times, Golden Peak was named the Place of the Crouching Dragon [Fulong 伏龍]. We can examine the *River Chart* for records of past epochal turning points as well as future events that determined the name changes of this place. The name Golden Peak has already been in use for more than two hundred years.

Note: In seeking the label Golden Peak, we begin at the time of Chu.[64] When the Qin Emperor crossed the river in order to suppress its *qi*, he consequently changed the name to Moling 秣陵. The ancient administrative name given during the Han establishment of counties was Minor Danyang 小丹陽. Today it is called by this ancient name. In the third year of the Taikang reign period of the Jin dynasty [282], its territory was limited to the southern banks of the Huai River. In the ninth year of the Yixi reign period [414], the district seat was moved to Douchang 鬥場,[65] and in the first year of the Yuanxi reign period [419], it was returned to its present location. This is the Golden Peak of the region east of the river. According to legend, more than two hundred years ago, Sun Quan 孫權 of Wu dispatched people to seek gold.[66] They encamped on Crouching Tiger Mountain. Hence its name was changed to Golden Peak. This spontaneously resonated with the *River Chart*, so we should praise its prophetic signs.

2b9. Juqu Mountain was named Hooked Gold Altar during the Qin because inside the cavern heaven there is a gold altar a thousand feet tall. Hence, it received this name. Outside, there was Accumulated Gold Mountain, which was also named for the accumulated gold. During the Zhou, the fonts and pools here were named Twisting Water Hollows. Because of the twisting and bending form of the mountain, later people renamed it Juqu.

During the Han, the three Mao brothers took up their administration on the mountain.[67] In time, the local elders changed the name to Mountain of Lords Mao 茅君之山. The three lords arrived, each riding a white crane that perched on three different locations on the mountain. Contemporaries who saw them were inspired to compose songs and lyrics. Then, in accord with the locations on which the cranes landed, Mount Hooked Bend was divided into three peaks, Elder Lord Mao, Middle Lord Mao, and Young Lord Mao. In speaking of them together, they are simply the one mountain, Juqu, without any distinct names. The three Mao Mountains are secretly linked and connected together; they all are simply Mount Juqu. Contemporaries had told stories based on these matters so that now there are dozens of branches and twigs that led to the formation of different names. In ancient times, it was not so.

Note: Today, the southernmost tallest peak is called Mount Elder Mao; in the center there are two peaks with linked ridges and a common base, the taller of them is Mount Middle Mao; nearby to the north stands a solitary peak with heaps of rocks on it, this is Mount Young Mao. The ridge between Elder Mao and Middle Mao is called Long Slope [Chang'e 長阿]; to the east it reaches Yanling and Hooked Bend slope, [and] to the west it reaches Jurong lake. [. . .] To the south of Elder Mao are the mountains Jiu, Zhuwu, and Fang. Following these layered barriers, one crosses the mountains of Wuxing, reaching Mount Luofu and finally reaching the Southern Ocean.

3b4. The mountain produces gold. The Han Emperor Ling [r. 168–189] ordered the people of the commandery and district to collect the gold of Juqu so as to fill the military coffers. Sun Quan dispatched his palace guards to collect gold, which they regularly shipped to the palace. A hundred families of the troops and commanders eventually took up residence at the land of Crouching Dragon. Consequently, they changed its name to the Barrens of Golden Peak. As this name, too, had already been mentioned in ancient times in the River Chart, this may be said to be exceptionally marvelous.

Note: Currently, there are several deep caverns and pits on the southern face of Elder Mao, which traditionally have been called gold wells. These must have been bored and drilled at the time of Sun Quan. Currently, to the east of this mountain are several piles of smashed rocks that contain gold dust. The passage refers to military families residing on Fulong; today they are no longer there. . . . The home of the Elder Officer [Xu Mi] was to the northwest, near the little ridge of Changyin, where now there are many old shards of pottery pieces and kiln-red bricks. This was probably a residence, as the land appears to have been tilled. But the foundations and borders are no longer extant, and there is no well. It seems that unfortunately the Elder Officer's well has collapsed. . . .

4a3. The soil of Gold Peak is substantial and fertile like that of Beimang 北邙 and the North Valley pass and suitable for wheat and grains. If you drill a well, the water will be just as sweet as that of the wells outside the Feng gate of Chang'an. The fonts are pure and the depths are overflowing; the springs extend far and deep. The water's color is clear. Even those who do not study the Dao but simply live here and drink the water will also attain longevity. Because this place is irrigated by flowing gold liquid, you must keep it secret.

I have already transmitted a record of this and written fully of this matter. I have shown it to you.

Note: Received and composed by Lord Dinglu[68] and secretly presented to Xu Hui. Mount Beimang is a few *li* to the north of Luoyang; the North Valley pass is the Mengjin pass. The soil is yellow-black and rich and fertile. The Feng gate is the northern gate of Chang'an. Currently, the place I determined was Gold Peak has no cultivated fields, homes, or dug wells. Furthermore, I do not know how to explain this, but I think that the perfected powers cherish and protect and do not lightly let anyone dwell here. "I have already transmitted a record" refers to the *Biography of the Three Mao Brothers* [*Sanmao zhuan* 三茅傳].[69] According to a note by Xu Mi, he had not yet seen the *Biography* by the year *jiazi* [364]. This means that this text was probably orally transmitted during the *guihai* year [363]. The *Biography* also praises the fertile soil and sweet water and claims that whoever lives there will attain transcendence. These matters are therefore clearly spoken of.

. . .

5b3. The Golden Court of Mount Tongbo 桐柏 at Yue and Gold Peak of Juqu at Wu are auspicious sites for cultivating one's perfection; they are numinous precincts for completing one's spirits. During Yao's reign, the Eastern Ocean flooded five times, overcoming the people who all became ill and died. The army of Wu An was even worse than that! At such times you should draw near to me and rely on the dark gateway of the cavern tower.

Note: Dictated by the Perfected Lord Wang, right royal assistant, and secretly transmitted to Xu Hui, these must be the words of the [Perfected of] Tongbo, minister to the Dawn Thearch.[70] This passage says that the two most auspicious sites in the Wu and Yue regions are the two "Gold" sites. Wu An was the Qin general Bai Qi 白起 who attacked Zhao at Changping. In one day he killed 400,000 men.[71] Since ancient times there were none greater in military violence. That is why he is specifically cited as an example to illustrate the verse: "War and pestilence cannot approach; floods and waves cannot ascend." Guarding the cavern heaven are divine transcendent guards, hence the three calamities do not dare approach. The previous five passages [*tiao* 條] were all inscribed by Yang Xi.

5b9. There are thirty-six terrestrial cavern heavens in the cosmos. The eighth of these is Mount Juqu. The circumference of the cave is 150 *li* in area, and it is named Gold Altar, Heaven of Floreate Yang 華陽之天.

Note: After listing the ten heavens, the *Biography* continues, listing Fengdu 酆都, the Five Marchmounts, eight seas, the remote places of the divine transcendents, and the caves in the regions of the Di and Rong. . . .

The four walls of the cavern are of stone; the level roof is underground. It is 13 or 14 *li* in height, where it rises above the surface. . . . From east to west the cave stretches 45 *li*, and it extends 35 *li* from north to south. It is perfectly level. Its interior open area is 1,700 feet high. Descending, the walls are 1,000 feet high. The surface of the ground is as though crisscrossed with springs and hills. The roof above is perfectly smooth.

. . .

6a8. Inside are the occluded glow that is the night's radiance and the root of the solar essence, which illuminate the interior of the void, just like the sun and moon. The occluded glow rules the night, and the solar essence rules the day.[72] They are as round as the sun and moon, and they hover in the dark void.

Note: All cavern heavens have such suns and moons, although their names may differ slightly. They are like the sun and moon of the macrocosm that illuminate by disseminating their essence. Referring to night and day means that they rise and set and, just like the mundane sun and moon, have their times of brightness and darkness. While the limits of the mundane world cannot be fathomed, the limits of this heaven may be touched and seen. Just as the sun and moon rise and set, there must be regularity. Were they to randomly rise and set, then one would not know their size, as they are inside hollows and caves.

6b4. The cavern palace of Juqu has five gates, two to the south, one each to the east and west, and a main gate at the north. In total, there are five gates.

Note: Now, the great cave on the south face of the mountain is the western gate of the southern face; the eastern gate is in Bozhi 栢枝 hill. The cave at Liangchang 良常 to the north is the great gate at the north. But the locations of the gates to the east and west are unclear. The Middle Lord says: The east gate is at the opening in the slope between east Middle Mao and Young Mao. This entrance is the nearest to the cavern court, but the outer opening is very small and it may be blocked by rocks. This all is detailed later. The west gate is also like this; it must be at a place that is today blocked by rocks. At Bozhi there are two or three cave openings, but it seems that the true opening is not open. If you meditate and fast at the three gates when you seek them, they will appear by themselves. Now, although the opening of south gate is wide, it is blocked inside; this is probably because of too much polluting vapor. The great north gate is that from which demons and spirits come and go. The Perfected and Transcendents do not use the five gates, as they silently cross into that which has no space. The [discussion of the] arrangement of these gates is in order to present the structure of the mountain cave or perhaps to show where people must enter.

6b10. Within the void are stone staircases winding down from the opening, by which those who enter ascend and descend. People who happen to travel here may enter and leave without realizing that they were inside a cavern heaven and say to themselves that it is an open-air path. The radiance of the sun and moon is not distinct [from the mundane sun and moon]; the grass, trees, streams, and ponds are no different from those on the outside. With birds flying to and fro and abundant clouds floating in the wind, why would anyone have any doubts [that they are still in the mundane world]? That which is called the divine palace of the cavern heaven is numinous and marvelous without limit; it cannot be comprehended, it cannot be apprehended.

. . .

7a7. The cavern heaven of Juqu connects to the east with Linwu 林屋; to the north it connects with Mount Tai [Daizong 岱宗]; to the west it connects with Mount E'mei; and to the south it connects with Mount Luofu 羅浮.[73] These all are great roads and, between them, are many intersecting paths and trails that crisscross and intersect at several points.[74] During the Jian'an era of the Han [196–220], Zuo Yuanfang heard a tradition that spoke of a divine mountain in the region east of the river. He therefore crossed the river in search of it. After conducting fasts and abstentions for three months, he finally ascended the mountain and located the gateway and entered the cavern void, where he encountered the Occluded Palace 陰宮. The three lords presented him with three types of divine herbs. Yuanfang wandered throughout the cavern palaces for several years. The structures of the palaces and halls were so perfectly square and round that it was terrifying. Nowhere in the world was there anything as special as this. Spirits and deities came and went, calculating the life and death [of the people],[75] just as in the bureaus and homes of the mundane world.

Note: According to actual topography, Linwu is to the southeast and Luofu is in the southwest. Only Mount Tai and E'mei are precisely in the direction indicated. The direct roads must extend some five thousand or six thousand li. These routes must reach Yingchuan 潁川, and they must pass by and connect with Pure Void Heaven of Mount Wangwu 王屋. Yuanfang must have come after he was summoned by the Wei Emperor Wu.[76] The revelations by Later Perfected state: "Only after fasting in purity for five years can one finally closely approach the inner and outer palaces." As for the three types of herb, I think they are of a lower grade.

. . .

8a7. There is a peak named Liangchang by the cave opening in the north face of Mount Mao. Because it is connected to Juqu, they originally had a single name. In his thirty-seventh year, the First Emperor of the Qin [on a *guichou* day in the tenth month] set out on an expedition. In the eleventh month, he reached Yunmeng 雲夢 and sacrificed to Sage-Emperor Shun at Mount Jiuyi. He sailed down the river, viewed Jike 籍柯, and forded at Meizhu 梅渚. He passed Danyang 丹陽 and reached Qiantang 錢塘. As he approached the river Zhe 浙江 the waves were so torrential that he continued 120 li to the west and crossed at the narrowest straits. He ascended Mount Kuaiji, where he sacrificed to Yu of Xia. He performed the *wang* sacrifice to the Southern Sea and erected a stone praising Qin's virtue at Mount Kuaiji.[77] Li Si asked to compose an inscription, so he returned and passed through all the mountains and rivers and finally ascended

Mount Juqu, where he buried a pair of white jade discs.[78] The emperor, therefore, assembled all his officials and followers and gave a feast for them. Sighing, he said: "Of the pleasures of the imperial inspection, none surpass the mountains and seas. Henceforth this goodness [*liang* 良] shall be constant [*chang* 常]." The assembled officers then together wished for longevity and cried: "Goodness shall be constant." They also beat great drums and rang great bells. The myriad sounds harmonized and echoed, penetrating and terrifying, through the mountains and waters. They praised and gloried in the auspicious signs; young and old were all blessed. Hence, the name of the north slope of Juqu was changed to Mount Liangchang. This is the source and meaning of the name Liangchang.

. . .

9a6. On the *wushen* day in the seventh month of the third year of the Dihuang reign period [22], Wang Mang 王莽 [r. 9–23] dispatched his envoy Zhang Yi to make an offering of one hundred *yi* of gold and five copper bells to the three Transcendent Lords at Juqu.

. . .

9a9. On the *dingsi* day in the third month of the seventh year of the Jianwu reign period [32], the Han Emperor Guangwu [r. 25–58] dispatched his envoy Wu Lun to present an offering of fifty pounds [*jin*] of gold to the three lords. This gold is now buried at the highest point on Mount Young Mao.

. . .

9b3. In the second year of the Yongping reign period [59], the Han Emperor Ming ordered the commandery and district officials to renovate and restore the shrines of the Perfected at Juqu in Danyang commandery.

Note: When they first attained the Dao, the Mao brothers rode white cranes to the top of the mountain.[79] They were seen by the residents of the villages and hamlets, who all prayed and revered this numinous proof [of their attainment]. Therefore, they erected a shrine, named White Crane Shrine, on the east face of the mountain. Whenever anyone made food offerings, they would hear someone speaking, see a white crane in the curtains, or hear delightful music. As a result, all finally came to make offerings. These shrines still stand today. At Ping'A village, on the east side of the mountain, a woman surnamed Yin 尹 is the invocator. On the west of the mountain, each of the various villages has erected a shrine. To the west of Elder Mao, there is a shrine called Wuxu 吳墟廟, and on the mountain behind Middle Mao there is a shrine Shuxu 述墟廟. During the annual festivals, these shrines celebrate by drumming, dancing, and making blood offerings. These practices must be in reverence for Lord Ximing, for they cannot be for the Perfected Transcendents.[80]

9b8. Mystic Peak is the tallest point on Middle Mao. Here the Director of Destinies [Elder Mao] had buried six thousand pounds of cinnabar from Yumen in the region of the western barbarians. The cinnabar is buried twenty feet underground. On the four sides of the pit he placed small rocks that secure the place. To the left and right of the mountain are springs that flow with water. The water is a little red in color. If you drink it, you will be nourished. Below this mountain, to the left and right, are some small flat areas that are suitable for building a meditation chamber [*jingshe* 靜舍]. When Zuo Yuanfang arrived here, he requested cinnabar from the Director of Destinies and received twelve pounds.

. . .

11a3. Precious gold and white jade are buried by the four sides of the Altar of the Celestial Market [Tianshi tan 天市壇] on Mount Mao. Weighing more than eight thousand or nine thousand pounds, these treasures extend some twenty feet to the left and right of the altar and penetrate nine feet into the earth. In ancient times, the Lord Azure Lad of the Eastern Sea 東海青童君,[81] riding alone in his typhoon-wheeled chariot, traveled to all the mountains with cavern heavens. Finally he arrived at this mountain. To the left and right of this mountain are springs, which all flow with the liquid *qi* of gold and jade. It would be good if you could locate here a small level place suitable for a meditation chamber. If you drink this water, it will replenish your essence. It can be used to compound elixirs. The stones of the Altar of the Celestial Market are precisely at the center of the cavern heaven, above the mystic window. These stones are from the Celestial Market Mountain in Persia [Anxi guo 安息國]; hence they are called Rocks of Celestial Market. During his reign, the Mystic Thearch ordered the spirit envoys of the four seas to transport these rocks to the cavern heavens, not only to Juqu. Below the Celestial Market of the Transcendents is the window at the center of the cavern palace. The void emptiness in the innards of Juqu mountain is called Transcendent Office in the Cavern Tower 洞臺仙府. . . . The traces of the typhoon carriage are still clearly visible today.

Note: All the records and explanation regarding Mount Juqu are quite clear. Only the location of rocks of the Celestial Market is still unknown. As for the discussion of the traces, I suppose they must be at the vicinity of Elder Mao, but walking through the area, I have not seen any strange sites. I think the traces may have been covered by bushes; therefore I cannot discuss this further. According to Baoming, whenever Zhao Cheng 趙承 ascended to the altar, he made a long whistle, and the wind and clouds immediately collected.

. . .

12b9. There is another small cave on the south face of Mount Elder Mao. . . . It is called South Doorway, and its opening, too, is blocked by rocks. But you should meditate and fast and direct your heart toward the Director of Destinies. Then, on the morning of the second day, you should ascend the mountain and appeal for my arrival by requesting and incanting. You will, then, spontaneously get to see me.[82] If one is absolutely sincere in this, would it not suffice to view the Occluded Palace? What kind of man indeed was Zuo Ci?

Note: This refers to the main doorway on the south face, which must be within the cavern of ground stones at Bozhi. Because there are several caves here and it very difficult to distinguish among them, you must have a response to your meditation in order for the cave to open. Then you may enter as you wish. The term "second day" refers to the second day of the twelfth month. According to the *Biography*, there are two [special] days each year. I think the eighteenth day of the third month is too riotous and rowdy, so it cannot be suitable for meditation and prayer.[83] In order to become a transcendent, Zuo Ci had to change his physical essence from that of a common person. He therefore purified and fasted for three months and then could enter the cave. Xu Mi, although he has received a lofty and remote allotment and his intelligence and form were especially fine, why could he not rival Zuo? These words were meant to encourage Xu. In his later response, Xu expressed this intention reverentially.

13a6. On the eighteenth day of the third month or the second day of the twelfth month, the Lord Director of Destinies of the Eastern Peak, along with the Fully Perfected Lord Wang 總真王君, the Perfected of the Great Void 太虛真人, and the Azure Lad of the Eastern Sea meet on Mount Juqu. They travel and look at the cavern chambers. Those who cherish the Dao and who seek transcendence are to prepare by fasting and abstaining. On these days they should ascend the mountain and request and plead with focused intention and a sincere heart. The three lords will then by themselves appear to them. The lords will draw them in, leading and guiding them, in order to transmit to them the essential ways by which one can enter the cavern heaven, avoid the calamities of war and floods, and see the Sage-Lord of Great Peace.

Note: The Middle Lord wrote: "Regularly ascend the mountain on the second day and appeal for my arrival by requesting and incanting." This, then, refers to the second day of the twelfth month and does not speak of the eighteenth day of the third month. The second day of the twelfth month is soon followed by the middle of the first month. It is freezing and snowy during these two days of the La 臘 festival, so there are very few who come from near and far. But on the eighteenth day of the third month, when the lords personally meet in the clouds, hundreds of carriages and four thousand or five thousand people gather, men and women, Daoists and commoners, like crowds at a city market. The onlookers ascend the mountain together and perform *lingbao* chants and psalms. Their reverence and requests are scattered; how can any of them have deep sincerity or possess the secret tally [of Shanqing]? One who wishes to encounter the divine transcendents should, at an appropriate time, come with full sincerity, either alone or with a companion. Again, I regret the noise and dust, as one can never concentrate and be at ease. If one tries to attract the attention of the spirits and request their grace, one will have no result. I, the Recluse, dwell among the cliffs, cutting myself off in purity and solemnity, not traveling among the masses. I depart to another cave in an adjacent peak, and nobody knows my whereabouts."[84]

. . .

15a6. Below Mount Elder Mao there is a spring. You can erect a meditation chamber here, the closer to the source, the better. But it is a little dangerous and unstable.

Note: Now, nearby to the south there is a large cave opening. There is a fine stream but too many rocks. A little farther out, it is more level. In recent years, some practitioners have come to reside here. During the early Liu Song, Xu Piaonu 徐漂女, a female Daoist, who received offerings from Lu Hui 陸徽, Inspector of Guangzhou,[85] came to live by the mouth of the cave until she died several years later. She was followed by a female disciple, surnamed Song 宋, whose nature was pure and who could not hurt any creature. She lived to a very old age and was buried at the south face of the mountain. She was followed by a female disciple surnamed Pan 潘, who is still there at present. During the Yuanwei era [473–477], some male adepts came to live there. At the beginning of the Qi, the emperor commanded Wang Wenqing 王文清 of Jurong town to establish a shrine here. Named Revering the Primordial [Chongyuan 崇元], its hall, roof, side rooms, and corridors all are extraordinary. Regularly there are seven or eight Daoists here, who all receive state emolument. For the last twenty years, male and female Daoists from near and far come in accord with their vows. They travel about for several *li* to a dozen or so government-sponsored hostels. But among them, very few study the superior Dao; their practices do not go beyond the *lingbao zhai* 靈寶齋 and petitions and talismans [*zhangfu* 章符].[86] Recently, another female Daoist came to dwell at the cavern mouth. Diligently sprinkling water and sweeping, she styled herself Cavern Officiate [*Dongli* 洞吏] and performed shamanic acts and divinations [*wushi zhanbu* 巫師占卜]. There are many and various fake and empty practices, examples of which can be found everywhere. There is a stream in the southeast of Elder Mao. Ren Dun 任敦, who attained the Dao, lived there and compounded medicines during the late eastern Jin. Remnants of his furnace are still visible. Currently, Xue Bao 薛彪 and several others reside here, including Zhu Fayong 朱法永.

[*Zhen'gao, DZ* 1016, *juan* 11]

NOTES

1.   James Robson, *Power of Place: The Religious Landscape of the Southern Sacred Peak* (*Nanyue* 南嶽) *in Medieval China* (Cambridge, Mass.: Harvard East Asian Monographs, 2009).

2. For an introduction, see A. C. Graham, *Disputers of the Tao: Philosophical Argument in Ancient China* (La Salle, Ill.: Open Court, 1989), 315–82; and for an extensive study, see Wang Aihe, *Cosmology and Political Culture in Early China* (Cambridge: Cambridge University Press, 2000).

3. On the *feng* and *shan* rites, see Mark Edward Lewis, "The Feng and Shan Sacrifices of Emperor Wu of the Han," in *State and Court Ritual in China*, ed. Joseph P. McDermott (Cambridge: Cambridge University Press, 1999), 50–80. For a translation of a report on one such ritual, see Stephen R. Bokenkamp, "Record of the Feng and Shan Sacrifices," in *Religions of China in Practice*, ed. Donald S. Lopez Jr. (Princeton, N.J.: Princeton University Press, 1996), 251–60.

4. *DZ* 1185. The most accessible edition is Wang Ming 王明 ed., *Baopuzi neipian jiaoshi* 抱朴子內篇校釋 (Beijing: Zhonghua shuju, 1985). James R. Ware, *Alchemy, Medicine, Religion in the China of* A.D. *320: The Nei p'ien of Ko Hung (Pao-p'u tzu)* (Cambridge, Mass.: MIT Press, 1967), is an outdated translation.

5. *DZ* 1016.

6. The *Array of the Five Talismans* (*DZ* 388) (hereafter *Array*) was compiled in the late third century and includes material dating back to the Han. For the complex history of the text, see Gil Raz, "The Creation of Tradition: The Five Talismans of the Numinous Treasure and the Formation of Early Daoism" (Ph.D. diss., Indiana University, 2004).

7. For a translation and study of the impact of this passage on Chinese literature, see Stephen R. Bokenkamp, "The Peach Flower Font and the Grotto Passage," *Japan Association of Overseas Studies* 106, no. 1 (1986): 65–77.

8. Gil Raz, "Imperial Efficacy: Debates on Imperial Ritual in Early Medieval China and the Emergence of Daoist Ritual Schemata," in *Convictions and Means in Daoism, a Berlin Symposium*, ed. Florian Reiter (Wiesbaden: Harrassowitz, 2007), 83–109.

9. Here "transcendence" is a translation of the term *xian* 仙, more conventionally translated as "immortality." However, as this term does not refer to eternal life, and because the same term and others allude to a variety of attainments beyond the limits of mundane life and death, "transcendence" seems more suitable.

10. Nathan Sivin, "On the Word 'Taoist' as a Source of Perplexity; with Special Reference to the Relations of Science and Religion in Traditional China," *History of Religions*, 17 (1978): 303–30; Robert Ford Campany, *To Live as Long as Heaven and Earth: A Translation and Study of Ge Hong's Traditions of Divine Transcendents* (Berkeley: University of California Press, 2002), 6–8.

11. *Array* 3.16b9–23b4.

12. The instructions are given on *Array* 3.21a–b. Another version is found earlier in the text (3.16a1–10), in a section that is also said to be part of the *Scripture of the Perfected One* (*Zhenyi jing* 真一經).

13. *Declarations of the Perfected* does not describe the brothers' mundane careers and the practices they followed to attain transcendence. These details may be gleaned from the various citations and versions of the hagiography of Elder Mao (preserved in two versions, entitled *Taiyuan zhenren dongyue shangqing siming zhenjun zhuan* 太元真人東嶽上卿司命真君傳, in *Yunji qiqian*), *DZ* 1032, 104.10b–20a, and, without title, in *Maoshan*

zhi 茅山志 (*DZ* 304), chap. 5. For details, see Isabelle Robinet, *La révélation du Shangqing dans l'histoire du taoïsme* (Paris: École française d'Extrême-Orient, 1984), 2.389–98.

14. In the notes to the translation, I refer selectively to parallels and divergences between this chapter and the *Scripture of the Perfected One from the Most High Great One* (*Taishang taiyi zhenyi zhijing* 太上太一真一之經), which is preserved in *Array* 3.16b9–23b4, focusing on those that carry substantive or ideological significance. Italicized passages are absent from this *Scripture of the Perfected One.*

15. This section parallels *Array* 3.22a10–22b9.

16. *Array* 3.22a10 says: "If you know the cinnabar [method] of the Perfected One, then the myriad affairs will be extended."

17. *Classic of the Way and Virtue* (*Daodejing* 道德經) 39: "Those who attained the One in ancient times: Heaven attained the One and thereby became clear, Earth attained the One and thereby became tranquil, the spirits attained the One and thereby became numinous, the valley attained the One and thereby became abundant, the myriad creatures [*wanwu*] attained the One and thereby gained life." The sequence here switches the positions of Earth and Spirits, ignores the valley, and replaces *wanwu* with humanity.

18. *Classic of the Way and Virtue*, chap. 14.

19. *Classic of the Way and Virtue* 21. The *Scripture of the Perfected One* does not mention Lord Lao at this point.

20. *Array* 3.22b8 has "Three Ones" 三一 instead of "Preserve the One" 守一.

21. It is not clear where Ge Hong ends the citation of the scripture. The context and rhyme imply that the citation includes the following lines, which are not in the scripture. This is a major difference between the two texts.

22. During the Han, a *cun* 寸, of ten *fen* 分, was approximately 0.9 inch.

23. This entire paragraph is absent from the *Scripture of the Perfected One.*

24. This section parallels *Array* 3.17b3. In the *Scripture of the Perfected One*, this section is preceded by a passage describing the Yellow Emperor's reason for this journey as having acquired but not understood the *Scripture of the Perfected One of the Celestial Luminary* 天皇真一之經 and the *Essentials of the Perfect Pneumas of the Three Ones* 三一真氣之要.

25. *Array* 3.17b4 adds "Celestial Script in Large Graphs" 天文大字.

26. *Array* 3.17b5 adds "he climbed the Dark Mountain Stream of Five Numinous Herbs" 五芝玄澗. *Jianmu* is the world tree at the southern extremity of the universe, which, as explained by John Major, "marks the midpoint of the sun's path." It is described in the *Huainanzi*: "The *Jian* [Establishing Tree] on Mount Duguang 都廣, by which the ancestors ascend and descend, casts no shadow at midday, if one calls [from there] there is no echo. It forms a canopy over the center of the world." For discussion, see *Huainanzi* 4/5; John S. Major, *Heaven and Earth in Early Han Thought: Chapters Three, Four and Five of the Huainanzi* (Albany: State University of New York Press, 1993), 158–59. I read 壟 for 隴, as the *Huainanzi* mentions that "the grave mound of Lord Millet *Houji* is to the west of Establishing Tree" 后稷壟在建木西 (*Huainanzi* 4/14; Major, *Heaven and Earth*, 196, 204). See also *Shanhai jing* 13: "In the southwest, where the Black River flows, is Du-

guang Wilderness and the tomb of Houji." The Ruo tree is west of the Establishing Tree, and "within its branches are ten suns, its blossoms illuminate the earth" (*Huainanzi* 4/5; Major, *Heaven and Earth*, 158). These blossoms may be the *qian*, ultimate yang, flowers being collected by the Yellow Emperor. The phrasing in *Array* differs, implying that the numinous beings collect the flowers.

27.   This sentence is absent from the *Scripture of the Perfected One*. Beyond its obvious alchemical connotations, it is unclear what the referent of this phrase is.

28.   *Array* 3.17b6 names it the "Nine *Acanthopanax* Methods" (*jia* 九茄之方). It may well be related to the recipe for *Acanthopanax* liquor listed in *Array* 2.29b3–9.

29.   According to *Array* 3.17b6, Master Guangcheng dwells atop Mount Kongtong 崆峒, and the text is named *Scripture of Spontaneity* 自然之經. Elsewhere in *Master Who Embraces Simplicity* (13.241), Ge Hong also locates Master Guangcheng on Mount Kongtong. The locus classicus for this encounter between Master Guangcheng and the Yellow Emperor is in *Zhuangzi* 11, "Zaiyou."

30.   In *Array* 3.17b8, the text is named *Divine Herbs Chart of the Spirit Transcendents* 神仙芝圖 in twelve scrolls.

31.   The location given here is a mistake for Mount Wangwu 王屋山, as in the *Scripture of the Perfected One* and in *Master Who Embraces Simplicity* 13.241. In *Array* 3.17b9, the text is named *Spiritual Cinnabar Scripture of Golden Liquid Nine Times Refined* (*Jinye jiuzhuan shendan jing* 金液九轉神丹經) and is bestowed by the Mystic Maiden 玄女. This text is related to one or more of the alchemical works received by Ge Hong himself and described in *Master Who Embraces Simplicity* 4. Note in particular the *Yellow Emperor's Nine Tripods Spiritual Cinnabar Scripture* 黃帝九鼎神丹經, transmitted to the Yellow Emperor by the Mystic Maiden and transmitted by him to the Mystic Lad 玄子. For a detailed study of the alchemical tradition, see Fabrizio Pregadio, *Great Clarity: Daoism and Alchemy in Early Medieval China* (Stanford, Calif.: Stanford University Press, 2006).

32.   Ge Hong omits the encounter with Master Ning described in *Array* 3.17b10–18a3 and also the description of the Luminary and the initial encounter with the Yellow Emperor in *Array* 3.18a3–18b2. In *Array*, the Luminary 皇人 is never called Celestial Perfected, a title that may be based on *Array* 3.18a1, in which Master Ning mentions having received instructions from the Celestial Perfected officials of the Three Luminaries 三皇天真之官.

33.   *Array* 3.18b2 has "not dying" 不死 instead of "longevity" 長生.

34.   Which scripture is referred to here is unclear, but the following line seems to be a summary and adaptation of *Array* 3.18a10–19a4.

35.   *Array* 3.19a6–7 has "The Queen Mother of the West has placed this text [*Scripture of the Perfected One*] in the Five Citadels. Guarding it outside are twelve transcendent towers. It is hidden in a chest of purple jade, carved on a golden tablet, sealed with herbs of cinnabar radiance, and imprinted with the Central Emblem of the Most High."

36.   This section corresponds to the opening lines of the *Scripture of the Perfected One* in *Array* 3.16b9.

37.   This line is preceded in the *Scripture of the Perfected One* by "The Three Ones rely on one another, yet their dwellings are not the same. Sometimes they are in . . ." This line

is one example of the different foci of the two texts: Ge Hong's focus is on the One, while the *Scripture of the Perfected One* stresses the Three-One.

38. *Array* 3.17a2–3 differs considerably. This line is preceded by "Deep ravines plunge straight down, vermilion bamboo lush and teeming," followed by "Bright jade craggy and jagged, the sweet springs never run dry / the sun and moon hang down their glow, the golden furnace [stands] lofty and exalted."

39. These are alchemical technical terms: "dark" 玄 refers to cinnabar, and "yellow" is gold. The parallel line in *Array* 3.17a4 is "traverse the square [earth] and enter the round [heaven]."

40. *Array* 3.17a5 has "spirit people throng." The cosmological imagery and descriptions in this section refer to the human body, particularly the interior of the head.

41. This section parallels *Array* 3.23a3–8, whereas 3.23a3 has "leaking" 瀉 for "giving" 與.

42. *Array* 3:23a5 has "lessen drink" instead of "lessen desire."

43. This line corresponds to and compresses *Array* 3:23a5–6: "When approaching danger, have no doubts, the One will eliminate all calamities. When faced with heavenly disasters, contemplate the One and you will gain life."

44. *Array* 3:23a4 has "Knowing of Perfection but not practicing it is the same as not knowing. Seek for it incessantly and you will ascend to the nine radiances."

45. *Array* 3:23a8–9 has "All anomalies will be avoided and all infernal beings will be sequestered."

46. These names of methods may refer to texts listed in *Master Who Embraces Simplicity*, chap. 19: *Scripture of Twenty-Four Births* 二十四生經, *Scripture of Nine Changes* 九變經, *Scripture of Twelve Transformations* 十二化經, *Scripture of Internal Vision* 內視經, and *Scripture of Hiding One's Radiance (Shadow)* 含景 (影) 經.

47. *Array* 3.23a10 has "measure" 揣 for "place" 措. The line is based on *Classic of the Way and Virtue* 9: "Hammer 揣 and sharpen 錯 it; it cannot be preserved forever" and *Classic of the Way and Virtue* 50: "A rhinoceros will not have a place to goad its horn; the tiger will have no place to cling to with its talons; weapons will not have a place to intrude with their blade. Why? Because he has no place of death."

48. *Classic of the Way and Virtue* 28.

49. Master Zuo is Zuo Ci 左慈, styled Yuanfang 元放, a central figure in Ge Hong's own lineage. Originally from northern China, Zuo Ci established his reputation as an adept at the court of Cao Cao in Sichuan before arriving in the southern coastal region. He is the source for the alchemical teachings most esteemed by Ge Hong, which he transmitted to Ge Xuan 葛玄, Ge Hong's grand-uncle. Zuo Yuanfang is mentioned several times in the *Declarations* chapter translated here (7a7, 9b8, 12b). For a detailed study of his hagiography, see Campany, *To Live as Long as Heaven and Earth*, 279–86, 470–78.

50. Ji Zixun, named Ji Liao 薊遼, was a well-known adept during the late Han and was a recipient and transmitter of several key practices adapted by the Shangqing lineage. See Robinet, *La révélation du Shangqing*, 12–19. For a detailed study of his hagiography, see Campany, *To Live as Long as Heaven and Earth*, 169–72, 412–16.

51. Transcendent Ge is Ge Xuan, Ge Hong's grand-uncle. Ge Hong inherited his teachings by way of Zheng Yin. For details of his hagiography, see Campany, *To Live as Long as Heaven and Earth*, 152–58, 401–6.

52. Note Ge Hong's descriptions of his apprenticeship in *Master Who Embraces Simplicity*, chap. 4.

53. This sentence parallels *Array* 3.20a10–b10.

54. *Array* 3.20b9 has "The Three-Ones will thereby be maintained; the body will thereby be strengthened; and the life span will thereby be extended."

55. In the following, Yang Xi's words are the regular text, and Tao Hongjing's comments are indented and marked "Note." Sections of this chapter have been eloquently translated by Edward H. Schafer in his seminal *Mao Shan in T'ang Times* (Boulder, Colo.: Society for the Study of Chinese Religions, 1989). I borrow several of his felicitous expressions.

56. Lord Baoming is the title of the youngest Mao brother.

57. Citing lines from the *Array of the Five Talismans* 1.6a2.

58. Pure Void is the name of the cavern heaven within Mount Wangwu 王屋, about thirty-one miles north of Luoyang, the site of the apotheosis of Wei Huacun 魏華存 (251–334), the main transmitter of the Shangqing revelations, in which it came to be known as the Microcosmic Heaven of Clear Void (Xiaoyou qingxu zhitian 小有清虛之天) and was listed as the first of all cavern heavens.

59. This is a brief allusion to the narrative in the *Array of the Five Talismans* of the discovery of the five talismans.

60. The translation of this title, *Hetu zhongyaoyuan* 河圖中要元篇, is tentative. The title seems to refer to a weft text associated with the famously obscure *River Chart*, but this particular title is not mentioned elsewhere.

61. A *qing* 頃 is approximately 110,000 square feet.

62. "Crossing over generations" (*dushi* 度世) and "great peace" (*taiping* 太平) are core ideas of salvation in the Daoist tradition, as mentioned in the introduction.

63. This line is almost precisely the same as that cited earlier from the *Hetu zhongyaoyuan*. The title, too, is similar enough to suggest that it may in fact be the same line, yet there is a slight difference in the first clause.

64. A brief history of Jinling and its name changes is preserved in a citation from *Biographies from South of the River* (*Jiangbiao zhuan* 江表傳), in *SGZ* 53.1246.

65. I have emended the missing characters in accordance with the chapter on administrative geography in *SS* 35.1029.

66. Sun Quan 孫權 (182–252) was among the leading warlords during the final years of the Han dynasty. He established himself as King of Wu (r. 200–222), still nominally under the Han. When the Han finally collapsed, he declared himself emperor (r. 222–252), thus ushering in the era of the Three States.

67. The three Mao brothers are the elder brother, Ying 盈, whose title is Director of Destinies and Divine Lord, Perfected Person of the Supreme Primordial, Great Minister of the Eastern Marchmount (Taiyuan zhenren Dongyue shangqing siming shenjun 太元

真人東嶽上卿司命神君; the middle brother, Gu 固, whose title is Divine Lord Who Determines the Registers (Dinglu 定錄); and the youngest brother, Zhong 衷, whose title is Protector of Destinies (Baoming 保命).

68. Lord Dinglu is the title of the middle Mao brother.

69. According to *Declarations* 8.2a, this text was written by Li Zhonghou 李中侯. The text is partially preserved as the hagiography of Lord Mao.

70. All these labels refer to Wangzi Qiao 王子喬, who is introduced in chapter 1 as the Perfected of Tongbo, Right Royal Assistant, Commander of the Officers of the Five Marchmounts, and Minister of the Dawn Thearch 桐柏真人右弼王領五嶽司侍帝晨. See *Declarations* 1.2b. Among the most famous of ancient transcendents, Wangzi Qiao was reputedly the son of King Ling of the Zhou (r. 571–545 B.C.E.). He attained transcendence on Mount Song, the central Marchmount. Later he appeared riding a crane on Mount Goushi (in Henan). After that, he was revered at shrines on these mountains. According to Yang Xi, his administrative domain was on Mount Tongbo in the Tiantai range (in Zhejiang). The mountain is further described in *Declarations* 14.19a8.

71. A succinct statement of this event is in the *Records of the Historian* (*Shiji* 史記) 5.213. The longer account in Bai Qi's biography stresses that the Zhao troops were killed after surrendering to Bai Qi. Later, having fallen out with the future inaugural emperor of Qin and forced to commit suicide, Bai Qi regarded this massacre as a grave offense. See *SJ* 73.2331–38.

72. *Array* 1.7b.

73. Mount Linwu refers to Mount Bao, the site where the Elder of Draconic Awe discovered the Five Talismans. See *Array* 1b7. Here it is referred to as the eastern extremity of the subterranean paths. Mount Tai is the easternmost of the Five Peaks, the site of the imperial Feng rite. In the common religion, since at least Han times, the center of the netherworld bureaucracy was below Mount Tai. Mount Luofu was the final destination of Ge Hong, the great alchemist and uncle of the Xu family, recipients of the Shangqing revelations. The inclusion of Mount E'mei in Sichuan here is probably due to its importance in the narrative in the *Scripture of the Perfected One* that describes the Yellow Emperor's journey. Mount E'mei was to have a glorious history in Buddhist geographic lore. See "Terrestrial Perfection."

74. *Array* 1.7b6–7.

75. Among the core beliefs regarding the netherworld, in both Daoism and the common religion, was its bureaucratic aspect. The narrative introduces the cavern heaven at Juqu as one of the administrative centers.

76. Emperor Wu is the posthumous title of Cao Cao 曹操 (d. 220). Although it was his martial ability that led to the establishment of the Wei by his son Cao Pi 曹丕 (187–226), Cao Cao himself never ruled as emperor.

77. This passage is a citation and elaboration of the journey of the inaugural emperor described in *SJ* 6.260–61. Yang Xi inserts the lines concerning the ascent of Juqu and the burial of the jade rings.

78. The words of the inscription are cited in the previous passage: "The Inaugural Emperor of Sagely Virtue emblazoned and pacified the mountains and seas, inspected and hunted in the azure river, and engraved and incised the white jades."

79. On the significance of cranes, see Edward H. Schafer, "The Cranes of Mao Shan," in *Tantric and Taoist Studies, in Honour of R. A. Stein*, ed. Michel Strickmann (Brussels: Institut belge des hautes études chinoises, 1983), 2.372–93.

80. The Mao brothers were originally the center of a local cult. Even after they were absorbed by the Shangqing lineage, local reverence continued. "Invocator" is the translation of the word *zhu* 祝, which may also indicate a medium or shaman. This brief discussion illustrates the Daoists' distinctions between local and shamanic practices and their own visualization practices and scriptural revelations.

81. The Azure Lad of the Eastern Sea, also known as the Azure Prince of Fangzhu 方諸青童君 or, more regally, Lord of the Golden Porte of the Eastern Sea 金闕東海君, is a major deity in the Shangqing revelations. His origins remain obscure, perhaps traceable to the King Father of the East, a deity that appeared during the Han and served as consort to the ancient deity Queen Mother of the West. Ge Hong mentions the "Talismans of the Little Lad of the Eastern Sea" as one of the devices necessary for expelling the hundred dangers when crossing seas and waterways. See *Master Who Embraces Simplicity* 17.7a7–9; Wang Ming, *Baopuzi neipian jiaoshi*, 307; and Ware, *Alchemy, Medicine, Religion*, 294.

82. These instructions for meditatively encountering Elder Mao are important to indicating how one was to meditate on the tutelary deity of the mountain. "Directing one's heart" and praying for the appearance of the deity led to a spontaneous vision of the deity. This type of guided meditation should be contrasted with the frenzied practice of the local cult.

83. The *Biography* records that before his death, the Director of Destinies told his two brothers that henceforth if anybody wished to see him, they could do so only by visiting the mountain on the eighteenth day of the third month or the second day of the twelfth month. See *Yunqi qiqian* 雲笈七籤 (*DZ* 1032) 104.19b. It is unclear whether these dates were celebrations of the local cult or for Shangqing practice, but this passage may be evidence of a distinct religious calendar in the area.

84. Referring to himself as "the recluse," Tao Hongjing expresses his personal preference for personal cultivation practice rather than communal ritual, as well as suggesting competition among Daoist lineages or styles of practice.

85. For a biography of Lu Hui, see *SS* 92.2267–68.

86. Two different traditions of Daoist practice are mentioned here. First, the Lingbao *zhai* was a public ritual performed for the safety and health of the community and the state. First appearing in the Lingbao scriptures of the late fifth century, the rituals were systematized by Liu Xiujing 陸修靜 (406–477). "Petitions and talismans" probably refers to the earlier tradition of Celestial Master Daoism that used bureaucratic methods, such as petitions, to communicate with the officials of the Three Bureaus (heaven, earth, and water), along with talismans in healing and exorcistic practices. Once again, Tao expresses his disdain for the ritual practices of other Daoist traditions, implying rivalry and competition among different traditions or styles of practice.

CONTRIBUTORS

Robert Ashmore is an associate professor of Chinese literature at the University of California, Berkeley. He is the author of *The Transport of Reading: Text and Understanding in the World of Tao Qian (365—427)* (Cambridge, Mass.: Harvard University Asia Center, 2010) and articles on medieval Chinese poetry.

James A. Benn is an associate professor of Buddhism and East Asian religions in the Department of Religious Studies, McMaster University. He is the author of *Burning for the Buddha: Self-Immolation in Chinese Buddhism* (Honolulu: University of Hawai'i Press, 2007) and a number of articles on religion in medieval China.

Alan Berkowitz is the Susan W. Lippincott Professor of Modern and Classical Languages and a professor of Chinese at Swarthmore College. His primary research interests are Chinese literature and culture, Han through Tang, especially the intersections of ideas, values, and literary expression. Besides *Patterns of Disengagement: The Practice and Portrayal of Reclusion in Early Medieval China* (Stanford, Calif.: Stanford University Press, 2000), he has written works on biography and hagiography, Daoism and Buddhism, traditional medical texts, medieval poetry, literary and ritual eulogies, and the cultural role of the *qin* zither and tea. He served as president of the Early Medieval China Group and is a board member of the T'ang Studies Society.

Stephen R. Bokenkamp, a professor in the School of International Letters and Cultures of Arizona State University, is the author of *Early Daoist Scriptures* (Berkeley: University of California Press, 1997), *Ancestors and Anxiety: Daoism and the Birth of Rebirth in China* (Berkeley: University of California Press, 2007), and other works on early medieval Daoism.

Robert Ford Campany is a professor of Asian studies and religion at Vanderbilt University. He is the author of *Making Transcendents: Ascetics and Social Memory in Early Medieval China* (Honolulu: University of Hawai'i Press, 2009), three other books, and numerous articles on the history of Chinese religions and the comparative study of religion.

Ian Chapman is a lecturer at the University of Washington. His research interests include popular ritual and religion, local social organization, and identity construction in medieval China.

Huaiyu Chen is an assistant professor at Arizona State University. He has published two books and many articles on Buddhism and Nestorian Christianity along the Silk Road, Chinese religious history, manuscripts from Dunhuang and Central Asia, medieval monasticism, and medieval Chinese social and cultural history.

Jack W. Chen is an associate professor of Chinese poetry and thought at the University of California–Los Angeles. He is the author of *The Poetics of Sovereignty: On Emperor Taizong of the Tang Dynasty* (Cambridge, Mass.: Harvard University Asia Center, 2010) and has written articles on imperial poetry, gossip and historiography, the meaning of the donkey's bray, and the practice of reading in medieval China. He is currently at work on his second book, which examines *Recent Anecdotes from the Talk of the Ages* from the perspective of both narrative theory and social network analysis.

Jessey J. C. Choo specializes in the cultural history of medieval China. Her current research examines Buddhist-influenced transformation of mortuary and commemorative rituals. She received her doctorate from Princeton University (2009) and is currently an assistant professor at Rutgers University.

Timothy M. Davis is an assistant professor of Chinese history at Brigham Young University. He specializes in the social, cultural, and literary history of early medieval China.

Albert E. Dien has taught at the University of Hawai'i, Columbia University, and Stanford University, from which he retired in 1993. His primary interests are the social and political institutions of the early medieval period in Chinese history (220–589).

J. Michael Farmer, an associate professor of Chinese history at the University of Texas–Dallas, specializes in the history, literature, thought, and culture of early medieval China. He has published extensively on the history of early medieval Sichuan and is currently the editor of the journal *Early Medieval China*.

Charles Holcombe is a professor of history at the University of Northern Iowa. His research interests are China's great age of division, from the third century through the seventh century. His most recent book is *A History of East Asia: From the Origins of Civilization to the Twenty-First Century* (Cambridge: Cambridge University Press, 2011).

Clarke Hudson teaches Chinese religions at the University of Virginia. He is completing a book on Chinese inner alchemy, which argues that alchemical writing is a spiritual practice.

Keith N. Knapp is a professor and the chair of the history department at The Citadel, the Military College of South Carolina. He is the author of *Selfless Offspring: Filial Children and Social Order in Medieval China* (Honolulu: University of Hawai'i Press, 2005) and the president of the Early Medieval China Group.

David R. Knechtges is a professor of Chinese literature at the University of Washington. He is the author of more than one hundred articles and ten books, including *Two Studies on the Han Fu* (Seattle: Far Eastern and Russian Institute, University of Washington, 1968), *The Han Rhapsody: A Study of the Fu of Yang Hsiung, 53 B.C.– A.D. 18* (Cambridge: Cambridge University Press, 1976), *Wen xuan, or Selections of Refined Literature*, 3 vols. (Princeton, N.J.: Princeton University Press, 1982–1996), and, with Taiping Chang, *Ancient and Early Medieval Chinese Literature: A Reference Guide* (Leiden: Brill, 2010).

Paul W. Kroll is a professor of Chinese and comparative literature at the University of Colorado–Boulder. He has published extensively on early and late medieval Chinese literature, religion, and cultural history.

Jen-der Lee is a research fellow at the Institute of History and Philology, Academia Sinica, Taiwan. She is studying legal and medical history from a gender perspective and is teaching at several universities, including National Taiwan University and National Tsinghua University. Most of her work focuses on early imperial China, but she recently extended her interest to women's encounters with law and medicine in modern Taiwan. Her publications include two books, three edited volumes, and many articles.

Yang Lu is a historian of medieval China and a Buddhologist. His research interests include the cultural and political history of Tang dynasty, Buddhist scholasticism in

China, and the history of the Silk Road. He received his doctorate from Princeton University (1999) and is currently teaching at Peking University.

Stephen Owen is the James Bryant Conant University Professor and a member of the Department of East Asian Languages and Civilizations and the Department of Comparative Literature at Harvard University. He is the author of twelve books on Chinese literature and on comparative literature, and he has edited others, most recently, with Kang-i Sun Chang, *The Cambridge History of Chinese Literature*, 2 vols. (Cambridge: Cambridge University Press, 2010). He has received various awards, including the Mellon Distinguished Achievement Award (2007–2010).

Gil Raz is an associate professor of religion at Dartmouth College. He is the author of *The Emergence of Daoism: Creation of Tradition* (New York: Routledge, 2012) and other articles on medieval Daoism.

Wendy Swartz is an associate professor of Chinese literature at Rutgers University. She is the author of *Reading Tao Yuanming: Shifting Paradigms of Historical Reception (427–1900)* (Cambridge, Mass.: Harvard University Asia Center, 2008) and articles on early medieval Chinese poetry and classical literary thought and criticism.

Xiaofei Tian is a professor of Chinese literature at Harvard University. She is the author of *Tao Yuanming and Manuscript Culture: The Record of a Dusty Table* (Seattle: University of Washington Press, 2005); *Beacon Fire and Shooting Star: The Literary Culture of the Liang (502–557)* (Cambridge, Mass.: Harvard University Asia Center, 2007); *Visionary Journeys: Travel Writings from Early Medieval and Nineteenth-Century China* (Cambridge, Mass.: Harvard University Asia Center, 2011); and several books in Chinese.

Eugene Wang is the Abby Aldrich Rockefeller Professor of Asian Art at Harvard University. A 2005 Guggenheim Fellow, he also received an academic achievement award from Japan for his book *Shaping the Lotus Sutra: Buddhist Visual Culture in Medieval China* (Seattle: University of Washington Press, 2004). He is the associate editor of the *Encyclopedia of Buddhism* (2003).

Ping Wang is an assistant professor of Chinese literature at Princeton University. She received her doctorate in Chinese literature from the University of Washington–Seattle in 2006. Her research focuses on classical poetry, and she is currently writing a book on landscape poetry.

PERMISSIONS

The editors and publisher acknowledge with thanks permission granted to reproduce in this volume the following material.

"The Epitaph of a Third-Century Wet Nurse, Xu Yi," from Jen-der Lee, "Wet Nurses in Early Imperial China," *Nan Nü: Men, Women and Gender in Early and Imperial China* 2, no. 1 (2000): 1–39. Reprinted by permission of Koninklijke Brill NV.

Huangfu Mi, *Accounts of High-Minded Men*, from Alan Berkowitz, "Preface to and Biographies from *Accounts of High-Minded Men*," in *Hawai'i Reader in Traditional Chinese Culture*, ed. Victor H. Mair, Nancy S. Steinhardt, and Paul R. Goldin. Copyright © 2005 by the University of Hawai'i Press. Reprinted with permission.

Pei Ziye, "Discourse on Insect Carving," from Jack W. Chen, *The Poetics of Sovereignty: On Emperor Taizong of the Tang Dynasty* (Cambridge, Mass.: Harvard University Asia Center, 2010). Reprinted by permission of the publisher.

Stories of Filial Piety: Liu Yin and Miao Fei, from Keith N. Knapp, *Selfless Offspring: Filial Children and Social Order in Medieval China*. Copyright © 2005 by the University of Hawai'i Press. Reprinted with permission.

Stories of Ancestor Worship: Xiao Ze, from Keith N. Knapp, "Borrowing Legitimacy from the Dead: The Confucianization of Ancestral Worship," in *Early Chinese*

INDEX

Account of the Travels of Emperor Mu of Zhou (*Mu Tianzi zhuan*), 448

accounts of anomalous events (*zhiguai*), 10, 308, 486n.34, 489n.57, 540, 576–91; and Buddhism, 445, 577, 578, 583, 587n.3, 589n.28

Accounts of Filial Children (*Xiaozi zhuan*), 640

Accounts of High-Minded Men (*Gaoshi zhuan*; Huangfu Mi), 9, 326, 333–49

Accounts of Sages, Transcendents, and High-Minded Men, with Encomiums (*Shengxiangaoshi zhuan zan*; Ji Kang), 336

adoption, 10, 118–19, 431, 432, 440, 443, 460, 511–29

Ai (emperor, Eastern Jin), 13, 17

Ai (emperor, Han), 521, 527nn.43–44

Ai Jiang, 163, 164n.10

"Airs of Zheng" (*Shijing*), 214, 222, 224, 225, 229n.44

Allen, Joseph R., III, 276

Amitābha Sutra, 179

An, Lady (spirit), 562, 565

An Kai, 584, 590n.41, 590n.47

Analects (*Lun yu*; Confucius), 205, 285n.57, 400n.7, 558n.36; and accounts of anomalies, 577; and biographies, 384; on music, 226nn.11–13, 228n.31, 272n.10; on parents, 525n.17, 526n.31; and poetry, 266n.22, 273n.19; and recluses, 348; on spirits, 650nn.1–2; and Sun Chuo, 242n.11, 242n.26, 242n.29, 243n.44; on women, 299n.11; and Zhong Rong, 302n.40, 303n.44

ancestor worship, 348, 524n.8, 641–43, 645–47; imperial, 14, 527n.42, 528n.46, 529n.53; and spirits, 298n.2, 541, 561, 576, 594–95, 610n.55, 614, 615, 619, 628

Annals of the Jin (*Jin ji*), 267

Annals of the Southern Qi (*Qi chunqiu*), 166

Anqisheng, 343

anthologies, 8, 256, 307; and cultural capital, 195, 197–98; and genres, 275–76; of poetry, 259, 289, 305n.69; for women, 259

Anthology of Literary Compositions Divided by Genre (*Wenzhang liubie ji*; Zhi Yu), 197–98, 274–76, 289–90, 304n.53, 305n.68

Aoki Masaru, 452

Apocryphon to the Classic of Filiality (*Xiao jing yuanshen qi*; Song Jun), 480, 492n.85

archaeology, 182, 606n.5, 629n.3; of everyday life, 429, 436, 449, 459, 466n.5, 510n.42; and texts, 92, 95–99, 102–5, 456n.29, 592, 595. *See also* tomb documents

architecture, 436–37

Array of the Five Talismans (*Taishang lingbao wufu xu*), 654–55, 675n.6

Arrayed Accounts of Transcendents. See Biographies of Immortals

Arrayed Accounts of Women (*Lie nü zhuan*; Liu Xiang), 333

art theory, 406–7

Asim, Ina, 596

astrology, 109, 122n.7, 489n.61, 662

"Attending Banquet" (*Shiyan*; Liu Xiaochuo), 250, 253

Auerbach, Erich, 37

"Autobiography as De-Facement" (De Man), 384

autocremation, 543–60

"Autumn Day, An" (*Qiu ri*; Sun Chuo), 233, 236–37

Baba Eiko, 472

Bai Bin, 596

Bai Qi, 356, 367n.20, 668, 680n.71

Balazs, Étienne, 112, 498

Bamboo Annals (*Zhushu jinian*), 448

Ban Biao, 282n.18, 323n.45

Ban Gu, 282n.18, 283n.28, 284n.32, 356, 367n.17; on burials, 648; categorization by, 303n.46, 314, 331n.2; on Dong Zhongshu, 526n.30; work by, 278, 281, 293, 299n.13. *See also History of the Han*

Ban Si, 316, 323n.45

Ban Zhao, 282n.18

Bao Jing, 62

Bao Quan, 312, 320n.12

Bao Zhao, 272n.16, 291, 294–95, 302nn.41–42

Beasley, W. G., 39

Bei Si, 45, 57n.33

Bell, Catherine, 616

Benjamin, Walter, 309

Benn, Charles D., 616

Benn, James A., 539, 540, 548

Berkowitz, Alan, 81, 311, 326, 337

Bi Chen, 285n.57

Bian He, 214, 228n.26

Bian Rang, 361, 368n.30

Bianzhu (encyclopedia), 483n.4

Bielenstein, Hans, 39, 134

Bing Ji, 162, 164n.9

Bing Yuan, 189, 192n.42, 348

biographies, 9, 10, 450, 479; autobiographies, 328–30, 382–86, 390; categorized, 333–34; in dynastic histories, 326, 333; fictionalized, 382–85; of recluses, 333–49

Biographies of Divine Immortals (*Shenxian zhuan*; Ge Hong), 383, 547

Biographies of Eminent Monks (*Gaoseng zhuan*; Huijiao), 313, 322n.27, 540, 546–47

Biographies of Immortals (*Liexian zhuan*; Liu Xiang), 333, 383

Biographies of Men of Letters (*Wenshi zhuan*), 305n.70

Biographies That Broadly Extol the Lotus (*Hongzan fahua zhuan*; Huixiang), 546

"Biography of Master Great Man" (*Daren xiansheng zhuan*; Ruan Ji), 383

"Biography of the Master of Five Willows" (*Wuliu xiansheng zhuan*; Tao Yuanming), 328–30, 382–86

"Biography of the Master of Wonderful Virtue" (*Miaode xiansheng zhuan*; Yuan Can), 385, 386–87

Blader, Susan, 112

Bo, Lady, 463, 467n.15

Bo Changqian, 217, 229n.34

Bo Ya, 210, 227n.19

Bo Yi, 121, 227n.26, 250, 335, 338

Bodde, Derk, 473, 483n.11

Bokenkamp, Stephen, 539, 540, 564, 616, 656

book collecting, 199, 307–23; and cataloging, 309–10, 313–19

Book of Dong Zhongshu (*Dong Zhongshu shu*), 478

Book of Lord Shang (*Shang jun shu*), 150

Book of the Yellow Emperor (*Huangdi shu*), 475

Boqi, 214, 228n.26

Bourdieu, Pierre, 5

Boxiu (Han Kang), 83, 87n.22, 346–47

"Brass Hooves from Xiangyang" (*Xiangyang ta tongti*; Emperor Wu), 260

Brown, Miranda, 514

Buddha, 9, 445; clothing of, 435; former lives of, 559n.44, 559n.52, 629n.2; shadow image of, 330, 405–27

Buddhabadra, 180, 330, 422n.4; and shadow image, 405–6, 409, 412–15

Buddhism: and art theory, 406–8; and autocremation, 543–60; and class, 440; and *Family Instructions*, 494, 497, 498, 507, 510n.45; and festivals, 469–70, 480–81, 484n.15, 488nn.46–48; in Gaochang, 8, 93, 177–93; and Jiang Yan, 395, 403nn.47–48; and Lingbao Daoism, 613, 615, 629–39; and literary groups, 373–75, 381n.28; and local customs, 444–45; monasteries of, 434, 439; on mourning, 523n.1; and poetry, 259,

381n.28; Pure Land, 179, 629n.2, 637n.94; scriptures of, 178–79, 312, 315–18, 381n.25, 406, 410–15, 542, 552, 558n.33; and Sun Chuo, 232, 244n.49, 244n.54; and supernatural, 10, 445, 540, 577, 578, 583, 587n.3, 589n.28, 642. *See also* sutras

bureaucracy: centralized vs. feudal, 147, 148; and character appraisal, 135, 136, 327, 350–51, 443; and class, 90, 439–41; and examination system, 62–63, 67, 72n.5, 126, 127, 129, 495; in *Family Instructions*, 495, 498, 502–5; in Han dynasty, 125, 138, 141, 350–51; local, 8, 95–107; in Northern Wei, 158–60; vs. reclusion, 334–35; recruitment for, 90, 91, 125–46, 350–51, 498; sale of offices in, 126–27; streamlining of, 137–40; in underworld, 540, 541, 593, 595, 609n.42, 655, 680nn.73–75, 681n.86; in Wei dynasty, 128–34; Xiahou Xuan on, 135–40

Buzhan, 214, 228n.26

Cai Yong, 270, 271n.8, 280, 285n.50, 478, 489n.62

calendars, 10, 271n.2, 318, 681n.83; and festivals, 469–93

calligraphy, 143n.23, 284n.42, 363, 495, 562; and book collecting, 309, 312–13, 322n.31; in Dongpailou documents, 96; Ge Hong on, 69, 74nn.29–34

Campany, Robert Ford, 578, 579, 658

"Canon of Yao" (*Yao dian*; Shujing), 328

Canonical Studies (*Dianshu*), 475, 488n.51

Cao Cao (Wei Emperor Wu), 78, 128, 143n.19, 144n.37, 192n.42, 272n.12, 368n.30; and festivals, 489n.63; Jiang Yan on, 394, 402n.32; and literary patronage, 371, 381n.27; in *Recent Anecdotes*, 357, 358, 363, 364; and sacred mountains, 680n.76; Zhong Rong on, 289, 293, 299nn.14–17, 306n.79

Cao Chong, 192n.42

Cao Daheng, 401n.18

Cao Daoheng, 269, 391, 392, 531

Cao E, 479, 491n.79

Cao Fang (Wei Emperor Fei), 130, 143n.28

Cao Hong, 311

Cao Kai, 144n.28

Cao Mao, 368n.26

Cao Pi (Wei Emperor Wen), 1, 131, 144n.37,
264n.7, 272n.12; and festivals, 489n.63;
and literary genres, 275, 280; and
literary groups, 328, 371–75; Nine Ranks
System of, 128–29, 303n.46; in *Recent
Anecdotes*, 357, 358; and sacred
mountains, 680n.76; Zhong Rong on,
293, 299nn.14–17, 300n.19, 306n.79

Cao Qiusheng, 356, 367n.19

Cao Rui (Wei Emperor Ming), 130, 144n.28,
144n.37, 146n.66, 351, 451; and Xiahou
Xuan, 131–33; Zhong Rong on, 306n.79

Cao Shuang, 130–32

Cao Wu'an, 184

Cao Xu, 292, 298n.9, 301n.28, 479, 491n.79

Cao Yi, 597

Cao Yu, 130, 144n.29

Cao Zhen, 131, 144n.37

Cao Zhi, 255n.31, 264n.7, 265n.18, 266n.21,
280, 490n.67; on literary groups, 372;
Pei Ziye on, 270, 272n.12; and Shu Xi,
447; Zhong Rong on, 293, 294,
299nn.14–15, 303n.52, 304n.57, 305n.72,
305n.74, 306n.78

Caspani, E., 411

categorization: of books, 309–10, 313–19; of
human types, 9, 198, 326–27, 333–34,
350–69, 368n.28; of literature, 274–86;
of poetry, 287–306

caverns, sacred, 652, 654–55, 659, 664–66,
668–74. See also *Great Cavern Scripture*

Cedzich, Angelika, 596

Celestial Master (Tianshi) Daoism, 551,
557n.23, 588n.17, 590nn.42–44, 635n.72,
681n.86; and *Declarations of the
Perfected*, 562, 563, 573n.2, 575n.31,

575n.34; and Lingbao Daoism, 613, 614,
632n.28; and mountains, 655

Cen Boran, 69, 74n.31

Central Collection of the Classics (Zheng Mo),
315

Certeau, Michel de, 5, 429–30

Chang, Kang-i Sun, 251, 385

Chang Jianhua, 473

Chang Qu, 124n35

Chang'an, 18, 20, 77, 176, 179, 263, 265n.14,
266n.20, 346, 381n.23, 403n.34, 404n.50,
405, 406, 442, 471, 482, 496, 532, 534,
611n.69, 667, 668

Changsha, 92; documents from, 8, 95–107

Chaofu (Nest Father), 239, 243n.40, 338–39

Chapman, Ian, 431, 444

character appraisal, 9, 198; and bureaucracy,
135, 136, 327, 350–51, 443; in *Recent
Anecdotes*, 246, 326–28, 350, 357, 360,
361, 363, 364

Chen (dynasty), 2, 14, 65, 72

Chen, Duke of, 165n.11

Chen, Jack W., 198, 327, 578

Chen, Jo-shui, 160, 525n.15

Chen (kingdom), 165n.11

Chen Baoyin, 321n.24

Chen Baxian, 245

Chen Chen, 359, 368n.22

Chen Fan, 347

Chen Huang, 463

Chen Ji, 368n.22

Chen Jinhua, 411, 558n.40

Chen Lin, 371

Chen Mo, 523, 529n.55

Chen Nong, 314

Chen Ping, 356, 367n.16

Chen Qingsun, 580

Chen Qun, 128

Chen Shi, 368n.22

Chen Shou, 91, 275, 281n.11, 519

Chen Su, 579–80

Chen Xian, 52, 53, 58n.51

Chen Xiaoqing, 604

Chen Xu, 522, 528n.50

Chen Yanjie, 302n.41

Chen Yanzhi, 466n.9

Chen Yinke, 20, 22, 30, 66, 161

Chen You, 22, 23, 30n.19

Chen Yuanfang, 359

Chen Yurong, 483n.8

Chen Zhi, 110, 114–17, 123n.10

Cheng (emperor, Han), 282n.21, 527n.43

Cheng (King of Zhou), 111, 117–18, 123n.16

Cheng Gongbao, 464

Cheng Han (kingdom; Bashu; Di), 19, 23, 30n.23

Cheng Ju, 464

Cheng Tang (king; Shang [Yin]), 117, 123n11, 367n12

Cheng Tianfu, 49

Cheng Tianzuo, 48, 49, 58n.40

Cheng Ya-ju, 514

Cheng Ying, 522, 528n.49

Cheng Zhangcan, 168–69

Cheng Zheng, 505

Chengdu, 19, 108, 109, 110, 557n.24

Chenggong Zian (Chenggong Sui), 475, 488n.50

Chennault, Cynthia L., 251, 374

Chi Jian, 363, 369n.36

Chittick, Andrew, 473, 484n.17

Choo, Jessey, 431–32, 440

Chu (kingdom), 11, 292, 370, 482n.1; music of, 215–19, 221, 222, 265n.17, 266n.19

Ch'ü T'ung-tsu, 160

Chuci. See Lyrics of Chu

Chung Hung, 292

Chunqiu. See Spring and Autumn Annals

Chunyu Yi, 514

class, 5, 439–42; and bureaucracy, 90, 439–41; changes in, 92, 148, 245, 247; and cultural capital, 195, 196–97; and family, 439–40, 494–95, 498; and festivals, 472; and food, 450; in household registers, 167–68; and Liu Hui case, 159–60; and marriage,

166–75, 442; in North vs. South, 61, 71, 439; and poetry, 245–47, 439; and wet nursing, 458–61. See also commoners; elites; gentry class; literati class; slaves

Classic of Black and Yellow (Xuanhuang jing), 474, 486n.35

Classic of Changes (Yijing; Zhouyi), 109, 282n.14, 303n.49, 448; and book collecting, 312, 314, 319n.2; on burials, 648, 651n.18; and conversation, 202, 205; and cultural capital, 196; on festivals, 473; Huangfu Mi on, 337; and Lingbao Daoism, 633n.40; on music, 227n.18, 229n.37; and recluses, 348; and Sun Chuo, 26, 233, 240, 243n.37, 243n.41, 243n.45, 244n.55

Classic of Divine Marvels (Shenyi jing), 474, 486n.34

Classic of Documents (Shujing; Shangshu), 61, 123n.13, 205, 242n.29, 298n.4, 508n.10; and book collecting, 312–14, 319n.2; "Canon of Yao" in, 328; and genres, 279; on Jing-Chu, 482n.1; on music, 228n.29; Qiao Zhou on, 111, 117, 118; and recluses, 346; and self-representation, 328

Classic of Filial Piety (Xiaojing), 70, 348, 443, 480, 492n.85, 649

Classic of Music (Yuejing), 313

Classic of Poetry (Shijing), 73n.20, 74n.25, 86n.8, 198, 367n.18; on adoption, 518, 520, 524n.10, 525n.18; "Airs" in, 214, 222, 224, 225, 229n.44, 299n.12; and Analects, 273n.19; and book collecting, 312–14, 319n.2; and classical poetry, 287; and genres, 276–79, 282n.20, 283n.24, 284nn.33–37; and Jiang Yan, 403n.44; on Jing-Chu, 482n.1; line lengths in, 290; Mao commentary on, 205, 207; on music, 226n.10, 226n.14, 291; and North vs. South, 79; and Pei Ziye, 268–69, 271n.7, 272n.17; and Recent Anecdotes, 368n.32; and recluses, 346; and self-representation, 328; and shadow

Classic of Poetry (continued)
  image, 424n.38, 426n.47, 427n.53; and
  Sun Chuo, 242n.10, 242n.15, 243nn.
  32–34, 244n.50; and Zhong Rong, 292,
  300n.23, 301nn.28–29, 304n.55. *See also*
  "Great Preface"
Classic of the Way and Virtue. See Laozi
Classification of Rhymes (Qieyun; Yang
  Xiuzhi), 71, 76n.56
Classified Assemblages of the Arts and Letters
  (Yiwen leiju), 235, 264n.8, 471–72
clerical households, 98, 102–3, 106n.15
clothing, 68–69, 140–41, 429, 435–36, 504
Cohen, Alvin P., 579
Commentary on the Classic of Waters
  (Shuijing zhu; Li Daoyuan), 257
commoners, 92, 135, 440–42; and
  bureaucracy, 439, 494, 498; clothing of,
  435; and law, 148, 153, 159, 161; and
  marriage, 167–68, 170; and North vs.
  South, 71; and poetry, 246; and rituals,
  642, 657, 673; and supernatural, 577,
  582; wealthy, 34, 148; and wet nurses,
  459, 461
Comprehensive Customs (Fengsu tong; Fengsu
  tongyi; Ying Shao), 475, 487n.43
Comprehensive History of Institutions
  (Tongdian; Du You), 111, 268, 350,
  466n.7, 512, 526n.32
Concise Account of the Song (Song lüe; Pei
  Ziye), 268
"Concise Exegetical Principles for the
  Subtle Points of the *Laozi*" (*Laozi weizhi*
  lilüe; Wang Bi), 202, 225n.2
Confucianism: and accounts of anomalies,
  577, 587n.9; correlative, 640–41; in
  Family Instructions, 494, 495, 497, 498,
  500, 507, 510n.44; and Ge Hong, 62, 67;
  and genres, 275–76; and Huangfu Mi,
  336; and legal systems, 156–65; and
  Lingbao Daoism, 633n.40, 633n.44; and
  local customs, 445; and motherhood,
  513–14, 516; and North vs. South, 12,
  15–16, 60, 61; and other traditions, 8,
  196, 202–3, 234; patriarchal family in,
  158–60; and politics, 89, 91; Qiao Zhou
  on, 109, 111; and *Recent Anecdotes,* 358;
  in Shu, 109; and Sun Chuo, 232; and
  supernatural, 541, 640–51; and women,
  92, 432, 460, 461–62
Confucius, 305n.74, 337, 341, 495; on the
  dead, 595; and genres, 280, 284n.43,
  285n.57; and *Laozi,* 340; on music, 208,
  210–12, 222. *See also Analects*
Continuation of Literary Compositions
  Divided by Genre (Xu wenzhang liubie;
  Kong Ning), 276
conversation, 195, 201–29, 249. *See also*
  pure conversation
Courtyard Announcement (Tinggao; Yan
  Yanzhi), 496
Crespigny, Rafe de, 134, 514
Criticism of Poetry. See Grades of the Poets
Cui Shi (Cui Zhiti), 466n.9, 470, 475,
  488n.49
Cui Xieli (Cui Yeli), 35, 51–53, 56n.4
Cui Yin, 279–81, 284n.40, 285n.48, 286n.64
Cui Yuan, 280, 285n.48, 285n.52
Cui Zhan, 71, 76n.53, 76n.55
Cui Ziyue, 71, 76n.53
Cui Zongying, 603
Cui Zuan, 158–61, 164
cultural capital, 5, 6, 8–9, 195–200; and
  book collecting, 310; and class, 195,
  196–97; and Confucian classics, 196;
  and conversation, 203, 204; poetry as, 8,
  195, 196–97, 245–47
culture: elite, 10, 196–97, 432; estate, 530–37;
  of everyday life, 430; manuscript, 199,
  258, 309; material, 6, 9–10; North vs.
  South, 6–7, 11–16, 60–87; and regional
  festivals, 470, 471; of Turfan, 176–77
currency, 97, 149

Dai, Marquis of (Mawangdui tomb 3), 595
Dai Dalu, 112, 113

Dai De, 479, 490n.72

Dai Liang, 241, 244n.59

Dai Mingyang, 226n.14

Dai Sheng, 490n.72

Dai Shi, 22

Dai the Elder's Record of Rites (*Da Dai Liji*; Dai De), 479, 484n.18, 490nn.72–73, 491n.84

dairy products, 434, 435

Daoan, 559n.46

Daodejing. See *Laozi*

Daoism, 7, 8, 10, 264n.6, 300n.23; and accounts of anomalies, 577, 583, 588n.17, 590nn.42–44; in autobiographies, 383; and Buddhist autocremators, 547; and fall of Jin, 300n.20; and *Family Instructions*, 497, 508n.19, 510n.42; and festivals, 470, 484n.15, 485n.28, 487n.45; and Ge Hong, 61; and Huangfu Mi, 336, 337; Jiang Yan on, 395; Maoshan, 656; in *Recent Anecdotes*, 358, 362; and recluses, 341, 343; and sacred mountains, 573n.4, 575n.38, 611n.69, 622, 636n.75, 637n.85, 652–81; scriptures of, 316–18, 542, 613–39; and Shi Chong, 533, 535; in Shu, 109; and simple burial, 642; and Sun Chuo, 232, 235, 244n.54; and supernatural, 561–75, 609n.42, 642; and tomb documents, 596. *See also* Celestial Master (Tianshi) Daoism; *Laozi*; Lingbao (Numinous Treasure) Daoism; Shangqing (Upper Clarity) Daoism; *Zhuangzi*

Daowang, 557nn.24–25

Davis, Timothy M., 91, 540, 541

De Man, Paul, 384

Declarations of the Perfected (*Zhen'gao*), 539, 540, 542, 561–75; and Celestial Master Daoism, 562, 563, 573n.2, 575n.31, 575n.34; "Investigating Sacred Regions" in, 653, 655–58, 664–74

Declercq, Dominik, 337, 452

Deng (empress, Han), 278, 282n.19

Deng Ai, 582, 589n.31

Deng Guoguang, 276

Deng Xia, 23

Deng Zhi, 282n.19

DeWoskin, Kenneth J., 113, 207

Dharmarakṣa, 492n.93, 557n.13

Dharmaṣena, 179

Di people, 2, 19, 20, 30n.23

Dien, Albert E., 14, 66, 134, 432, 499, 643

Diény, Jean-Pierre, 235

Ding Fulin, 392

Ding Lan, 641, 644

Ding Lingguang, Lady, 257

discourse (*lun*), 195, 201–29, 249; arcane (*xuanyan*), 232, 300nn.20–23, 301n.24. *See also* pure conversation

"Discourse on Insect Carving" (*Diaochong lun*; Pei Ziye), 8, 198, 267–73

"Discourse on Literary Compositions Divided by Genre" (*Wenzhang liubie lun*; Zhi Yu), 8, 274–86

"Discourse on Literature" (*Lun wen*; Cao Pi), 275

"Discourse on Music" (*Ruan Ji*), 207

"Discourse on Music" (*Yue lun*; Xunzi), 273n.20

Discourse on Truths and Falsehoods in the Five Canonical Texts (*Wujing ranfou lun*; Qiao Zhou), 111, 123n.18, 123n.25

"Ditties of Yongzhou" (*Yongzhou qu*; Xiao Gang), 260

divination, 62, 122n.7, 587n.9; in Shu, 109–10, 113; in tomb documents, 592, 599, 601. *See also* necromancy

Dong Xun, 474, 475–76, 486n.39

Dong Zhongshu, 478, 490n.71, 526nn.30–35, 641; on adoption, 519–20

Dong Zhuo, 77

Dongfang Shuo, 202, 225n.1, 284n.41, 486n.34, 495

Dongguan Han ji, 321n.23

Dongpailou documents, 92, 96–99

Dongyuan Gong, 343

Dou Rong, 282n.18

Drège, Jean-Pierre, 311

Du Gongzhan, 469–71, 481, 483n.4, 489n.53, 493n.98

Du Guangting, 489n.57

Du Qiong, 109–10

Du Taiqing, 469, 471, 482n.2, 483n.6

Du You, 254n.18, 268, 466n.7, 512, 513

Du Yuan, 521, 528n.48

Duan Fang, 180

Duanmu Ci, 342

Dubs, Homer H., 39

Dudbridge, Glen, 310

Dull, Jack, 161

Eastern Wei (dynasty), 15

Eberhard, Wolfram, 113, 473

Ebrey, Patricia Buckley, 135

economy: commercialization in, 147–51; currency in, 97, 149; documents on, 96, 97–98; in North vs. South, 3, 7; privatization in, 147–55

Eight Companions of Jingling, 258, 303n.50, 328, 372–74

Eight Imperial Princes, Rebellion of the (bawang zhi luan), 17–18

elegies (jiwen), 329, 382

"Elegy for Myself" (Zi jiwen; Tao Yuanming), 329

elites, 89–90, 92; and book collecting, 310; and bureaucracy, 128–29; culture of, 432; and estate culture, 530–37; and frugality, 642; individualism of, 325; local Southern, 19, 78; and marriage, 442; new cultural, 196–97; Northern émigré, 13, 15, 18–19, 21, 24, 26–27, 65–66, 78, 91, 439; transregional, 15, 61, 64. See also gentry class; literati class

Elvin, Mark, 151

"Encountering Sorrow" (Li sao; Qu Yuan), 79, 293, 298n.6, 300n.19, 312, 325, 403n.42; and genres, 278, 283n.26, 283n.28

entombed epitaph inscriptions (muzhiming), 601, 606n.8

Erhuang, 465, 467n.17

Essential Digest in Four Categories (Sibu yaolue), 373

Essential Techniques for the Common People (Qimin yaoshu; Jia Sixie), 149, 433–34, 451

ethnic groups: Han, 2–3, 79; and Liu Hui case, 159–60; non-Han, 2–3, 17–18, 28, 32, 71, 97, 98, 432. See also Di people; Qiang people; Xianbei people; Xiongnu people

Etiquette and Rituals (Yili), 123n.15, 123n.26, 124n.30, 158, 466n.7; Commentary to (Yili zhushu), 516, 517, 524n.11, 525nn.13–23

eunuchs, 128, 442

Europe, 147–48, 150, 153n.2, 156

Evaluations of the Poets. See Grades of the Poets

everyday life, 5, 6, 9–10, 429–46; vs. daily life, 430

examination system, 126, 127, 129, 495; exemptions from, 62–63, 67, 72n.5

Explaining Simple and Analyzing Compound Characters (Shuowen jiezi), 449

"Exposition on Literature" (Wen fu; Lu Ji), 275

Extensive Records of the Taiping Era (Taiping guangji), 14, 60, 65

Fachi, 312

Facun, 552

Faguang, 547, 552

Fairbank, Anthony B., 134

Fairbank, John K., 38

Fajin, 180, 554

Fajing, 557n.21

Fakai, 180

family: vs. clan, 440; and class, 439–40, 494–95, 498; vs. cultural capital, 196–97; and poetry lineages, 290; and social change, 245, 494–98

Family Instructions of Mr. Yan, The (*Yanshi jiaxun*; Yan Zhitui), 15, 60, 167, 432–33, 440, 494–510; on bureaucracy, 495, 498, 502–5; on filial piety, 496, 499, 500, 506, 507; on marriage, 442–43, 501–2, 504; on mourning ritual, 64, 70–71, 505–7, 643. *See also* Yan Zhitui

Fan Guang, 313, 322n.27

Fan Li, 355, 367n.11

Fan Pu, 313

Fan Qiao, 142n.4

Fan Qin, 492n.87

Fan Xiaocai, 249

Fan Xu, 313, 321n.27

Fan Ye, 272n.15, 285n.48, 297, 306n.82, 560n.58

Fan Yun, 246, 249

Fang, Achilles, 134

Fang Zhuan, 313, 322n.33

fangshi (mantic artists), 109, 113

Fangyan (Yang Xiong), 449

Farmer, J. Michael, 91, 113

fashions, 67, 73n.17, 74n.28; Ge Hong on, 62–63, 68–69. *See also* clothing

Faxian, 330; and shadow image, 405, 408, 411–12, 419

Fayu, 547, 549, 554

Fei (emperor, Wei). *See* Cao Fang

Fei Changfang, 481, 493n.100

Fei Hui, 450

Feng Yanshou, 573

festivals, 431, 444–45, 468–93; and Buddhism, 469–70, 480–81, 484n.15, 488nn.46–48, 510n.45; and Daoism, 470, 484n.15, 485n.28, 487n.45; and food, 451, 472, 475; La, 444, 469–70, 475, 483n.11, 487n.44, 488n.49, 673; in North vs. South, 469, 471; Qingming, 469, 470, 477, 478, 484n.12. *See also* New Year festival

feudalism, 4, 147–48, 153n.2

filial piety: in accounts of anomalies, 539, 540, 585; and autocremation, 555; in

biographies, 386; and bureaucracy, 135, 136, 351, 443; of Duke of Zhou, 527n.44; in *Family Instructions*, 496, 499, 500, 506, 507; and festivals, 491n.79; and Luoyang, 17, 20, 21, 27; and motherhood, 443, 513; in *Recent Anecdotes*, 360, 365; and spirits, 640–41, 643–45; and Sun Chuo, 232. *See also Classic of Filial Piety*

Filliozat, Jean, 548

Fine Blossoms from the Garden of Letters (*Wenyuan yinghua*), 268

Five Barbarians (*wu hu*), 2–3

Five Classics, 203, 311, 319n.2, 373, 502. *See also* Confucianism; *specific classics*

Five Phases (*wuxing*), 208, 492n.86; in Celestial Master Daoism, 575n.38; and correlative Confucianism, 641; Liu Shao on, 352, 354; and sacred mountains, 652; in tomb documents, 593

Five-Thousand Character Writ. See Laozi

food, 433–35; fermentation of, 448; and festivals, 472, 475; in North vs. South, 72; pasta, 434

Forest of Tales from the Tang (*Tang yulin*), 256

Former Qin (state; Di), 20, 23, 30n.15, 31n.29

Former Yan (state; Xianbei), 20, 22, 23, 31n.29

Four Hoaryheads (Si hao), 343–44, 346

Franke, Otto, 180, 182

Fu Chai (King of Wu), 401n.21, 491n.80, 491n.83

Fu Jian (Former Qin Emperor Xuanzhao), 30n.15, 363, 609n.44

Fu Junlian, 353

"*Fu* on the Eastern Metropolis" (*Dongjing fu*; Zhang Heng), 257

Fu Qian, 319, 486n.31

Fu Xi, 23, 302n.41

Fu Xuan, 281n.11

Fu Yi, 278, 282n.22, 314

Gan Bao, 579

Gao (emperor, Han), 344

Gao (emperor, Qi). *See* Xiao Daocheng

Gao Botong, 346

Gao Min, 151

Gao Shiqi, 483n.4

Gao Wei, 443

Gao You, 322n.27, 493n.101

Gaochang (Turfan), 8, 93, 176–93

Gaohuang (empress, Qi), 646

Gaoyang (Zhuanxu), 403n.39,
    493n.101

Gaozong (emperor, Tang), 514

Gaozu (emperor, Han). *See* Liu Bang

Gardner, Daniel K., 113

Ge Chaofu, 613, 635n.69

Ge Hong, 7, 12–13, 15, 60–65, 476, 487n.46,
    635n.69; on fashions, 62–63, 68–69; on
    sacred mountains, 653–55, 658; and
    spirits, 613, 615. See also *Biographies of
    Divine Immortals; Master Who Embraces
    Simplicity*

Ge Lu, 215, 216

Ge Xuan, 61, 613, 615, 621, 635n.69, 663,
    678n.49, 679n.51

Genghis Khan, 177

gentry class (*shi*), 5, 6, 9, 10, 258; and book
    collecting, 310; and cultural capital,
    195–96; and marriage, 167–68

Gernet, Jacques, 548

Gong She, 338

Gong Sheng, 335, 336, 338,
    345

Gonggong, 482, 493n.101

Gongsun Du, 348

Gongsun Shu, 121

Gongsun Yuan, 348

Goodman, Howard, 134

Gou Jian (King of Yue), 115, 367n.11, 401n.21,
    479, 491n.83

Grades of the Poets (*Shipin*; Zhong Rong),
    8–9, 198–99, 246, 247–48, 272n.16,
    287–306, 390

Graff, David, 22, 38

Grafflin, Dennis, 128, 134

Granet, Marcel, 473

Great Cavern Scripture (*Dadong zhenjing*),
    617–18, 620, 623–25, 628, 630n.8,
    632n.30, 633n.47, 634nn.61–62

"Great Preface" (*Da xu*; Mao commentary to
    Classic of Poetry), 205, 207, 226n.8,
    226n.16, 228n.28, 229n.42; and genres,
    283n.24; and Pei Ziye, 268, 271n.7,
    272n.17; and Zhong Rong, 298n.3,
    301n.29, 304n.55

"Great Tradition of the *Shang shu*"
    (*Shangshu da zhuan*), 298n.4

Grünwedel, Albert, 179, 182

Gu Kaizhi, 80, 357

Gu Rong, 522, 528nn.51–52, 529n.53

Gu Xiangming, 66, 169

Gu Zhi, 303n.47

Gu Zhu, 121

Guan, Master (Guan gong), 367n.18

Guan Gao, 265n.12

Guan Ning, 347–48, 359, 368n.23

Guan Zhong, 355, 356, 366n.10, 368n.23,
    490n.68

Guangwu (emperor, Han), 87n.13, 87n.15,
    490n.69, 671

Guanyin Sutra, 56n.3

Guanzi, 478, 484n.18, 490n.68

Guo Huai, Lady, 459–60, 463

Guo Jingchun (Guo Pu), 293, 301n.24, 390

Guo Shaoyu, 276

Guoyuan, 178

Hachiya Kunio, 235

Han (dynasty), 4, 7, 177, 325; bureaucracy in,
    125, 138, 141, 350–51; continuities with, 2,
    3, 8, 91; documents from, 95–97,
    99–102; economy in, 148; fall of, 1, 12;
    and Northern Wei, 157–59; poetry of,
    292; and Shu, 108; and sumptuary
    regulations, 140; and Yellow Turbans,
    657. See also *History of the Han; specific
    rulers*

Han Anguo, 356, 367n.16

Han Kang (Boxiu), 83, 87n.22, 346–47

Han Xin, 356, 367n.20

Han Zhao (state), 18, 26, 29n.4

Handan Chun, 479

Hanfeizi, 74n.26, 227n.21

Hansen, Valerie, 182, 596

Harper, Donald, 579, 592

Hayashida Shinnosuke, 269, 270

He (emperor, Han), 142n.11

He Chengtian, 268, 271n.2

He Jin, 348

He Mian, 312

He Pan, 531

He Qiao, 360, 368n.28, 511–13, 515–16, 518, 522, 529n.53

He Qimin, 208

He Qun, 512, 513, 515–16, 518, 522, 529n.53

He Shuai, 512–13, 515–18, 522–23

He Xiu, 284n.32

He Xun, 40, 57n.21, 522, 528n.51, 529n.53

He Yan, 132, 202, 225n.2, 233, 300n.23, 361, 451

He Zeng, 162, 365, 369n.39

Henderson, John, 113

Henricks, Robert, 207, 227n.17

Heshang Gong, 615, 625, 638n.100, 638n.103, 638n.105

Heshang Zhangren, 343

Hightower, James, 251

histories, dynastic, 326, 333, 641

historiography, 9, 36–39

History of the Han (*Han shu*; Ban Gu), 303n.46, 338, 367n.17, 384; and Ruan Xiaoxu, 314, 317; and Xiao Yi, 311, 312, 321n.19

History of the Jin (*Jin shu*; Fang Xuanling), 274, 275, 311, 459, 460

History of the Latter Han (*Hou Han shu*; Fan Ye), 272n.15, 312, 314, 317, 321n.19, 489n.61

History of the Liang (*Liang shu*), 267–68, 389

History of the Song (*Song shu*; Shen Yue), 14, 38, 267–68, 326

History of the South (*Nan shi*; Liu Xiaochuo), 248, 288, 389

History of the Southern Qi (*Nan Qi shu*), 372, 642

History of the Sui (*Sui shu*), 198, 275, 288, 351

History of the Wei (*Wei shu*), 14, 38, 156–65

Holcombe, Charles, 92, 134, 196

Holzman, Donald, 134, 207

Hongya, Master, 337

Hou Gansui, 184

Hou Jing, 258, 307–8, 503, 509n.24, 509n.34

Hou Zhaobo, 490n.66

household registers, 98, 102–3, 167–68; for clerical households, 98, 102–3, 106n.15; for service households, 441–42

Hsiung Ping-chen, 462, 465n.4

Hu Baoguo, 22, 66

Hu Dalei, 236, 375

Hu Guang, 280, 285n.48

Hu Kongming, 69, 74n.33

Hu Sanxing, 56n.11, 57n.25, 485n.28

Hu Shengzhi, 52, 53, 58n.52

Hu Zhiji, 391

Hua Tuo, 488n.46

Hua Xin, 348, 358–60

Hua Yuan, 647

Huai (emperor, Jin), 18, 26, 29n.5, 529n.53

Huai (King of Chu), 491n.78

Huainanzi, 243n.32, 258, 424n.40, 650n.9, 676n.26; and festivals, 484n.18, 492n.84, 493n.101

Huan, Duke of Qi, 164n.10

Huan Anmin, 584

Huan Gong, 584

Huan Jing, 481

Huan Sima, 647, 650n.10

Huan Tan, 83, 87n.16, 323n.45, 422n.6

Huan Wen, 235, 508n.17, 582, 589n.27, 591n.54; memorial of, 22–25; military career of, 19–20; poetry of; 293, 300n.23; on return to Luoyang, 7, 13, 17–31, 231; Sun Chuo on, 26–29

Huan Xuan, 114

Huan Yi, 364, 369n.38

Huang, H. T., 451, 452

Huang Fu, 597

Huang Hao, 123n.10

Huang Qiong, 347

Huang Wenbi, 181

Huang Xian, 241, 244n.59

Huang Xiang, 69, 74n.29, 316, 323n.46

Huangdi. *See* Yellow Emperor

Huangfu Mi, 9, 326, 333–49, 539, 642,
    647–49

Hudson, Clarke, 540, 542

Hui (emperor, Jin), 464, 529n.53, 531,
    532

Huijiao, 313, 322n.27, 322n.34, 540, 546–48,
    554–56

Huishao, 549–50, 559n.48

Huishen, 552

Huishi, 549

Huixiang, 546

Huiyan, 320n.15

Huiyi, 547, 550–51

Huiyuan, 330; and shadow image, 406–10,
    415–19

Huizi, 74n.26

humaneness (*ren*), 136, 342, 352

Huo Guang, 169, 172n.14

Ikeda On, 181, 182, 596

Illustrations of Far-Flung Lands (*Kuoditu*),
    475, 487n.42

"Impeaching Wang Yuan" (*Zou tan Wang
    Yuan*; Shen Yue), 5, 166–75

"In Answer to Xu Xun" (*Da Xu Xun*; Sun
    Chuo), 234, 237–39

individualism, 9, 325, 334–35, 365

"Inscription for Mount Taiping" (*Taiping
    shan ming*; Sun Chuo), 233, 236

inscriptions, 10, 320n.16, 374, 497, 553;
    bronze, 108; entombed epitaph, 601,
    606n.8; as genre, 280–81, 371; by Lu
    Chui, 374; on shadow image, 415–21;

425n.41; on stele, 179–82, 280, 281,
    285nn.50–54, 309, 577; tomb, 608n.39,
    609n.49; from Turfan, 176–93

Instructions for the Youth (*Youxun*; Wang
    Bao), 496–97

Investigations of Ancient History (*Gushi kao*;
    Qiao Zhou), 111–12, 120–22

Islam, 177

Jan Yün-hua, 548

Jansen, Thomas, 269

jātaka tales, 559n.44, 559n.52, 629n.2

Ji Dan, 142n.4

Ji Han, 62, 72n.4

Ji jiu pian (Shi You), 449

Ji Kang. *See* Xi Kang

Ji Pingzi, 490n.66

Ji Sun, 647

"Ji Tumulus Texts" (*Ji zhong shu*), 448

Ji Wuzi, 651n.20

Ji Xuanjing, 52, 53, 58n.53

Ji Zha, 79, 355, 366n.9; listening skills of,
    208, 211–12, 226n.10, 228n.27, 271,
    273n.18

Ji Zixun (Ji Liao), 663, 678n.50

Jia Chong, 459, 463

Jia Kui, 285n.55

Jia Mi, 258, 328, 532

Jia Nanfeng (empress, Western Jin), 431,
    459–65, 532

Jia Shunxian, 112

Jia Sixie, 433–34, 456n.29

Jia Yi, 79, 141, 146n.70, 241, 244n.58,
    367n.18, 507n.3; and genres, 278,
    283n.29

Jiang Ge, 312, 320n.18

Jiang Hong, 373

Jiang Lu, 312, 320n.18, 502, 508n.18

Jiang Wenguang, 182

Jiang Xu (Yuanqing), 83, 87n.21, 386

Jiang Yan, 9, 87n.18, 321n.21, 329–30,
    388–404; autobiography of, 390; poetry
    of, 390–91, 395–400

Jiangling, 444, 509n.37; as Liang capital, 307–8, 471

Jiankang, 18, 36, 254n.25, 260, 509n.38; culture of, 63; and economic growth, 149; food in, 434; as Jin capital, 5, 11, 17, 27, 33, 73n.16; layout of, 438

Jianwen (emperor, Liang). *See* Xiao Gang

Jie people, 2

Jie Tui, 478

Jie Zisui, 478

Jie Zitui, 477

Jin (dynasty): bureaucracy in, 126; capital of, 5, 11, 17, 27, 33, 73n.16; Eastern, 5, 6, 230, 300n.22; in *Family Instructions*, 503, 504; vs. Han dynasty, 9, 325; histories of, 267, 274–75, 311, 459–60; and Luoyang, 7, 17–31; pure conversation in, 196; retreat of, 6, 11, 13, 32; and Shu, 12, 108; and Sima Yi, 145n.51; Western, 1, 6, 160, 290, 300n.20; and Wu, 12, 61, 73n.16, 74n.27, 531. *See also specific rulers*

Jing, Duke of Jin, 75n.37, 173n.24, 217, 528n.49

Jing Cuo, 283n.31, 370

Jingling, Prince of, 258, 303n.50

Jingzhou, eight categories of, 202, 203

Jinlouzi. See *Master of the Golden Tower*

Jizi of Yanling (Duke of Wu), 340, 346

Johnson, David, 135, 167, 168

Juan, Music Master, 212, 227n.21

Juan Buyi, 169, 172n.14

Juqu Anzhou, 178–81

Juqu Mengxun, 178

Juqu Mujian, 180

Juqu Wuhui, 180

"Justification for Living in Reclusion" (*Xuan ju shi*; Shu Xi), 448

Juyan documents, 95

Kamitsuka Yoshiko, 564

Kang Le, 160

Kao, Karl S. Y., 578

Kao Yu-Kung, 251

karma, 541, 547, 555, 587n.3; in Lingbao Daoism, 624, 629n.6

Kawai Kōzō, 385

Kawakatsu Yoshio, 151

Khotan, 177

Kierman, Frank A., Jr., 38

kinship groups, 4, 72n.5, 92, 148, 248; and elite power, 89–91. *See also* family

Kishiro Mayako, 168

Kleeman, Terry F., 593–95

Knapp, Keith N., 499, 539–41, 642, 643

Knechtges, David R., 79, 81, 92, 392, 430, 431, 434, 441

Kong Ang, 312

Kong Anguo, 123n.13, 301n.30

Kong Ning, 276

Kong Rong, 371

Kong Yinda, 73n.15

Koreans, 2

Kōzen Hiroshi, 533

Kroll, Paul W., 22, 81, 197, 329, 330

Kuai Ying, 40, 41, 56n.8

Kuang, Music Master, 211, 214–17, 227n.21, 228n.27

Kumārajīva, 179, 180, 330, 422n.2, 557n.13; and shadow image, 405–6

Lan Qin, 312, 321n.25

land: documents on, 96–102; and *juntian* (equal land) system, 441; privatization of, 147–55

land-purchase contracts (*maidiquan*), 593–94, 596–602

landed estates (*shu; zhuangyuan*), 147, 148

language, 69, 204, 232, 233; Yan Zhitui on, 64–65, 71

Langye Wang family, 78, 200n.6, 203, 204

Lanling (princess), 92, 157–64

Lanting gathering, 80, 233, 328

Laolaizi, 341

Laozi (*Classic of the Way and Virtue*; *Daodejing*), 109, 196, 300n.21, 312; and conversation, 202, 205, 225n.2; Heshang Gong edition of, 638n.103, 638n.105; and Lingbao Daoism, 614, 615, 617, 618, 620, 622–26, 630n.8, 630n.14, 631n.16, 632n.30, 634n.56, 636nn.77–82; and recluses, 340, 342; and sacred mountains, 676nn.17–19, 678nn.47–48; and Sun Chuo, 233, 235, 240, 242n.28, 243nn.48–49, 244n.54

Laozi (Lao Dan), 68, 293, 340, 343, 395, 557n.23; and Celestial Master Daoism, 575n.31; journey to the West of, 635n.70; and Lingbao Daoism, 621, 632n.34

Later Qin (dynasty), 556n.7

Later Zhao (state), 30n.11, 610n.52

Lau, D. C., 499

"Laud for Zhao Chongguo" (Yang Xiong), 198, 282n.21

lauds (*song*), 276, 277–78, 280, 282n.20

Laufer, Berthold, 449

Le Blanc, Charles, 112

Lee, Brigitta A., 392

Lee, Jen-der, 92, 160, 169, 431–32, 443, 462

Lee, Tim, 235

legal systems, 92; and Confucianism, 156–65; documents on, 98–99, 104–5; and women, 440, 511–29

Legalism, 92, 150

Leslie, Donald D., 39

"Letter to Yang Dezu" (*Yu Yang Dezu shu*; Cao Zhi), 303n.52, 305n.72

Leung, Angela Ki Che, 462, 465n.4

Lewis, Mark Edward, 90, 134

Li Chong, 296, 304n.65, 315

Li Da, 598

Li Daoyuan, 257

Li Feng, 132–33

Li Jianguo, 486nn.34–35, 489n.57

Li Jijie (Li Gai), 71, 76n.55

Li Jinhe, 169

Li Kang, 305n.74

Li Ling, 270, 272n.11, 292, 298n.7

Li Lou, 213, 228n.30

Li Qiang, 344

Li sao. See "Encountering Sorrow"

Li Shan, 166

Li Shi, 19, 30n.23

Li Shibiao, 277

Li Si, 670

Li Tao, 133

Li Wai-yee, 359

Li Wei, 71, 76n.54

Li Wenchu, 235

Li Xian, 489n.61

Li Xianzhang, 488n.46, 489nn.55–56

Li Xiaobo, 7, 14, 32, 35, 39–55

Li Xie, 76n.54

Li Yan, 299n.13

Li You, 280, 285n.55

Li Zhi, 277

Li Zhonghou, 680n.69

Li Zhu, 215

Li Zuren, 71, 76n.54

Liang (dynasty): capital of, 307–8, 471; and cultural capital, 197; elites in, 92; and Gaochang, 178–80; histories of, 267–68, 389; and Jiang Yan, 390; literary groups in, 372; poetry of, 256–63, 264n.5, 264nn.9–10, 267, 269; Southern, 15, 64; and Western Wei, 308, 309. *See also* Wu (emperor, Liang)

Liang Fanian, 41, 57n.29

Liang Hong (Liang Boluan), 336, 338, 345–46, 392, 400n.9

Liang Ji, 173n.23

Liang Mancang, 66

Liebenthal, Walter, 411

Liji. See Record of Rites

Lin Jiali, 168

Lin Xiangru, 228n.26

Ling (emperor, Han), 114, 271n.8, 667

Ling (empress dowager, Northern Wei), 157–64

Ling, Duke of Wei, 227n.21

Lingbao (Numinous Treasure) Daoism, 540, 542, 613–39, 681n.86; and mountains, 654–55

Link, Arthur E., 235

Lippiello, Tiziana, 643

literary criticism, 8, 307; and cultural capital, 195, 198–99; and genres, 275–76; and literary groups, 374; and poetry, 247–48; of Zhong Rong, 287–306

literary groups (*wenren jituan*), 257–58, 328, 370–81

Literary Mind and the Carving of Dragons, The (*Wenxin diaolong*; Liu Xie), 247, 276, 298n.10; on genres, 281n.5, 284n.40; and Zhong Rong, 287, 302n.31

literati class, 4, 439–40; and accounts of anomalies, 576; and bureaucracy, 128; and cultural capital, 8–9, 195, 197; and frugality, 642; and pure conversation, 196

literature: and accounts of anomalies, 576; as cultural capital, 8–9, 195; genres in, 197–98, 274–86; of Liang dynasty, 267; North vs. South in, 7, 77–87; oral discourse on, 288; patronage of, 370–81; schools of, 288–89. *See also* poetry

Liu An (Prince of Huainan), 370, 401n.21

Liu Bang (Han Emperor Gaozu), 37–38, 115, 197, 350, 367n.11, 367n.16; Jiang Yan on, 394, 402n.32; in Liang poetry, 256–63, 264n.5, 264nn.9–10

Liu Bao, 248, 440

Liu Bei, 97, 108, 114, 131

Liu Biao, 77, 79, 203, 349

Liu Chi, 66

Liu Ciqing (Liu Juanzi), 476, 489n.56

Liu Cong, 1, 18, 29n.6

Liu De, 323n.40

Liu Fang, 130

Liu Hong, 488n.51

Liu Huan, 312, 321n.21

Liu Hui, 92, 156–65, 199, 248–49, 288, 291, 295, 303n.45

Liu I-ch'ing. *See* Liu Yiqing

Liu Jinggong, 321n.22

Liu Jingsu, 329, 389, 390, 393, 401nn.15–20, 402nn.22–27, 488n.51

Liu Jixu (Liu Xiu), 305n.72

Liu Jun (commentator), 357

Liu Jun (Liu Song Emperor Shizu/Xiaowu), 155n.35, 167, 247, 401n.12, 550; and disputation at Pengcheng, 39–55, 56n.6, 56nn.10–12, 57n.25

Liu Kaihua, 358

Liu Kangzu, 51, 52, 58n.49

Liu Kun (Liu Yueshi), 293, 301n.24

Liu Lan, 248

Liu Ling, 327, 365, 369n.40

Liu Mian, 248

Liu Qinghua, 533

Liu Quan, 248

Liu Ru, 248, 319n.5

Liu Shan, 114

Liu Shao, 9, 206, 327, 351–57

Liu Shi (Han Emperor Yuan), 447

Liu Shizhen, 358

Liu Shufen, 151

Liu Song (dynasty), 7, 14, 157, 167, 179; elites in, 91–92; histories of, 267–68; and Jiang Yan, 389, 393; and Pei Ziye, 269, 271; and Pengcheng, 32–36; and Yangzi River, 34, 36, 54. *See also specific rulers*

Liu Taotu, 285n.48

Liu Wu (Prince of Liang), 370

Liu Xi, 449

Liu Xiang, 199, 303n.46, 490n.68; advice to family from, 495; biographies by, 333, 383; and book collecting, 314–17

Liu Xiaobiao, 315

Liu Xiaochuo, 8, 196, 197, 245–55, 375, 378–79

Liu Xiaosun, 373

Liu Xiaoyi, 259, 261–62, 375, 379–80

Liu Xie, 234, 247, 276, 290, 291, 298n.10. *See also Literary Mind and the Carving of Dragons, The*

Liu Xin, 303n.46, 314, 316–18, 490n.64

Liu Xiu (Liu Jixu), 305n.72

Liu Xiufan, 248, 389, 401n.17

Liu Xiuruo, 401n.18

Liu Xuan, 464

Liu Xuanming, 161

Liu Yao, 1, 319

Liu Yi, 90–91, 360, 368n.29

Liu Yigong, 39–55, 56n.9, 57n.23, 550, 551, 557n.18

Liu Yilong (Liu Song Emperor Taizu/Wen), 14, 34, 39–55, 56n.5, 57n.26, 389, 401n.15

Liu Yin, 641, 643

Liu Yiqing, 358, 578

Liu Yu (Liu Song Emperor Ming), 33, 245, 248, 357, 389, 401n.12

Liu Yuan, 3, 18, 29n.4

Liu Yuan-ju, 578, 579

Liu Yuejin, 310

Liu Yueshi (Liu Kun), 293, 301n.24

Liu Zhen, 270, 272n.12, 281, 285n.61, 371; Zhong Rong on, 293, 294, 299n.15, 305n.74

Liu Zhiheng, 312, 320n.14

Liu Zhiji, 268, 383

Liu Zhilin, 312, 313, 320n.14, 322n.36

Liu Zhiyuan, 313

Liu Ziluan, 401n.13

Liu Zishang, 92, 152, 155n.35

Liu Ziye (Liu Song Emperor Qian Fei), 401n.13

Liu Zizhen, 393, 401n.12

Liu Zuan, 69, 74n.30

Liu Zun, 248, 259, 262

Liuxia Hui (Zhan Huo), 68, 73n.23

Liye documents, 105n.4

Long Xianzhao, 113

longevity, 191n.15, 480, 481, 487n.45, 492n.91; and mountains, 657, 660, 663–64, 666, 667, 671

Lotus Sutra (Miaofa lianhua jing), 179, 558n.41; and autocremators, 543–48, 553; and Daoism, 629n.2, 630n.10, 632n.29

Louguan Daoist lineage, 614

Lü (empress, Han), 367n.16

Lu, Zongli, 113, 643

Lu Chui, 374, 375, 377

Lu Hui, 477, 478, 674, 681n.85

Lu Ji, 79, 231, 270, 272n.13, 275, 434, 532; in Recent Anecdotes, 357; and Zhong Rong, 293, 296, 300n.19, 304n.64, 305n.74

Lu Jia, 37–38, 641

Lu Jue, 299n.13

Lu Kanru, 130, 536n.7

Lu Lingxuan, 443

Lu Shanjing, 175n.40

Lu Sidao, 14, 60, 65, 72, 73n.9

Lü Wang (Tai Wang Gong), 356, 367n.12, 193nn.49–50

Lu Xiujing, 630n.14, 632n.30, 634n.54

Lu Xun, 587n.5

Lu Yaodong, 113

Lu Yun, 300n.19

Luli Xiansheng, 343

Lun yu. See Analects

Luo Chong, 344

Luo Guowei, 168, 235

Luo Zhenyu, 181

Luoyang: Buddhism in, 445; classes in, 442; descriptions of, 438, 439; fall of, 1, 11, 18, 77, 78; festivals in, 444; food in, 434; Ge Hong on, 62, 63; return to, 5, 7, 13–14, 17–31, 231

Lü's Spring and Autumn Annals (Lüshi chunqiu), 193n.49, 484n.18, 492n.84, 650n.11

Lyrics of Chu (Chuci), 87n.20, 265n.11, 265n.13, 266n.19, 287, 328; on festivals, 479, 491n.75; and genres, 278, 283n.26; and Jiang Yan, 403n.42; and Pei Ziye, 269, 270; and shadow image, 427n.54; and Zhong Rong, 301n.28

Ma Baoji, 248

Ma Guohan, 122n.3

Ma Lianghuai, 533

Ma Liao, 74n.28

Ma Rong, 202, 225n.2, 278, 280, 283n.23

Ma Wengong, 39–41, 51–53, 56n.7

Ma Yuan, 74n.28, 495

Mackerras, Colin, 39

Makeham, John, 207

"Making Offerings in the Temple of the
    Han Exalted Emperor" (*Han Gao miao
    saishen*), 256–66

Man Chong, 173n.30

Man Fen, 173n.30, 174n.33

Man Zhangzhi, 167–68, 170

Manichaeism, 177

Mao, Master (Mao Heng), 356, 367n.18

Mao brothers, 562, 565, 656–57, 664–74,
    679n.67, 681n.80

Mao Chang, 367n.18

Mao Qu, 114

Mao Zeng, 131

Marney, John, 260, 269, 392, 499

marriage, 7, 89, 91, 442–43; and class,
    166–75, 442; and divorce, 157, 447,
    511–13, 515, 521, 524n.5, 527n.40; in
    Family Instructions, 501–2, 504; and legal
    systems, 156–75; and motherhood, 513;
    Qiao Zhou on, 111, 118, 120; and role of
    women, 92

Marsh of Discourse (*Tansou*), 72n.1

Master of the Golden Tower (*Jinlouzi*; Xiao
    Yi), 9, 199, 246, 308–9, 311–13

Master Who Embraces Simplicity, The
    (*Baopuzi*; Ge Hong), 480, 484n.15,
    492n.88; *Inner Chapters* of, 638n.98,
    638n.106, 653–55, 659–64; *Outer
    Chapters* of, 5, 12, 61, 62, 67–70

Masters Literature (*zishu*), 308, 310, 312, 317,
    323n.43

Mather, Richard B., 66, 167, 168, 331n.5, 358,
    366n.1

Mathieu, Rémi, 579

Matsuura Takashi, 452

Mawangdui texts, 456n.29, 595, 605n.4,
    607n.21

Medicine King (Yaowang), 544–49, 551,
    553

Mei Sheng, 279, 283n.31, 292, 298n.10

Mei Tsu-Lin, 251

Mencius, 242n.22, 243n.43, 305n.74

Mencius (*Mengzi*), 305n.68, 558n.37,
    558n.40, 559n.43, 650n.2

Mi Heng, 77–78

Miao Fei, 641, 643

Miao Yuan, 174n.33

military, 98, 102, 110–11; and elite power,
    89–90, 92; in Europe vs. China, 147

*Mimesis: The Representation of Reality in
    Western Literature* (Auerbach), 37

Min (emperor, Jin), 18, 26, 29n.8, 31n.31

Ming (dynasty), 177

Ming (emperor, Han), 142n.11, 282n.22,
    671

Ming (emperor, Jin), 19

Ming (emperor, Liu Song). *See* Liu Yu

Ming (emperor, Wei). *See* Cao Rui

Miyazaki Ichisada, 134

Mohism, 449, 558n.40, 640, 650n.2

"Monthly Ordinances" (*Yueling*), 470,
    471

Monthly Ordinances for the Four Walks of Life
    (*Simin yueling*; Cui Shi), 470, 475

Monthly Ordinances of the Hall of Clarity, 338

Morino Shigeo, 261, 375

Moriya Mitsuo, 469, 472, 483n.9, 485n.25

*Most High Concealed Commentary on the
    Jade Scripture* (*Shangqing taiji yinzhu
    yujing baojue*), 613

motherhood, 431–33, 443, 511–29

Mou Shijin, 277

mountains, sacred, 59n.61, 264n.6,
    608n.36, 623, 637n.86; and Daoism,
    573n.4, 575n.38, 611n.69, 622, 636n.75,
    637n.85, 652–81; spirits of, 562, 565,
    566, 572, 588n.11, 603, 624

mourning ritual, 75n.45, 76nn.46–49; and
    adoption, 517, 521; in *Analects*, 525n.17;
    for children, 527n.45; and Daoist spirits,

mourning ritual (*continued*)
566; in *Family Instructions*, 64, 70–71,
505–7, 643; Ge Hong on, 69–70; and
Liu Hui case, 158, 160; and North vs.
South, 61; Qiao Zhou on, 111, 118–20; for
wet nurses, 460, 461, 464, 466n.7; for
women, 118–19, 513, 514, 523n.1, 527n.41
Mozi, 449, 558n.40, 640, 650n.2
*Mr. Zuo's Commentary on the Spring and
Autumn Annals (Zuo shi Chunqiu)*. See
*Zuo Tradition on the Spring and Autumn
Annals*
Mu (King of Zhou), 448, 504
Mu, Duke of Jin, 113
Mugitani Kuniō, 564, 658
Mulian, 480–81, 492n.94
Muramatsu Kazuya, 472
music, 273n.20, 313, 362; and calendars,
484n.20; of Chu, 215–19, 221, 222,
265n.17, 266n.19; *Classic of Poetry* on,
226n.10, 226n.14, 291; Confucius on,
208, 210–12, 222, 226nn.11–13, 228n.31,
272n.10; and dance, 206; and genres,
277–78; and poetry, 291, 297, 306n.78;
and recluses, 335, 341, 342, 346; *Record of
Rites* on, 205–7, 226n.8, 226n.17,
298n.4; and Shi Chong, 534, 535; *yuefu*
song series, 260; of Zheng, 214, 222,
224, 225, 229n.44, 270, 272n.10,
303n.44; *Zhuangzi* on, 227n.22, 228n.31
mysterious, conversation about (*xuan tan;
xuanyan*), 202, 225n.1, 232, 300nn.20–23,
301n.24. See also pure conversation
mysterious, poetry on (*xuanyan shi*),
230–44
mysterious learning (*xuanxue*), 8, 91,
225n.2, 233, 272n.15, 327, 361; in Shu,
109–10, 112

Nagarahāra shadow cave, 330, 405–27
Nāgārjuna, 422n.2, 555
Nakamura Hiroichi, 472, 473
Nakamura Takashi, 473

names, 206, 208; school of (*mingjia*), 327,
351; teaching of (*mingjiao*), 577
Naito Konan, 181
necromancy, 312, 315, 316, 318
Needham, Joseph, 449
Nestorianism, 177
*New Songs from the Jade Terrace (Yutai
xinyong)*, 259, 298n.10, 527n.36
New Year festival, 473–77; and La festival,
444, 469–70, 475, 483n.11, 487n.44,
488n.49
Nickerson, Peter S., 596
Nieque, 339
Nine Marks (*jiuzheng*), 352, 353–54
Nine Ranks system (*jiupin zhi*), 7, 90,
128–29, 134, 143n.19, 247, 303n.46
Nobuyoshi Yamabe, 411
North vs. South, 1, 11–87, 433; architecture
in, 436–39; class in, 61, 71, 439; clothing
in, 435; Confucianism in, 12, 15–16, 60,
61; culture in, 6–7, 11–16, 60–87;
economy in, 3, 7; festivals in, 469, 471;
food in, 434–35; and identity, 6–7, 60,
61; literature in, 7, 62, 65, 77–87; in
tomb documents, 593, 606n.9; women
in, 440, 442–43, 461–62; and Yangzi
River, 11, 19, 26, 78–79
Northern Qi (dynasty), 14, 15, 64, 65, 72,
471; Buddhism in, 445; and *Family
Instructions*, 505, 509n.31. See also Qi
(dynasty)
Northern Wei (dynasty), 7, 14, 441, 442; and
Gaochang, 178, 180; law in, 89, 156–65;
and Pengcheng, 32–36
Northern Zhou (dynasty), 64, 65, 471, 509n.31
Nüying, 465, 467n.17
Nylan, Michael, 112

Offices of Zhou (Zhou guan), 312, 348
"On Explicating the Way" (*Yudao lun*; Sun
Chuo), 232, 235
"On Nourishing Life" (*Yang sheng lun*;
Xi Kang), 204

"On the Worthies of the Way" (*Dao xian lun*; Sun Chuo), 232

Ouyang Jingxi, 600

Ouyang Xun, 472, 485n.26

Owen, Stephen, 198, 251, 385

painting, 179, 408–10

Palace Style poetry (*gongti shi*), 258–60

Pan Ni, 189, 192n.43, 300n.19

Pan Puti, 313

Pan Shouzhi, 184

Pan Yue, 79, 174n.35, 231, 293, 300n.19, 301n.26, 532; and Pei Ziye, 270, 272n.13

Pang, Venerable (Pang Gong), 337, 349

Pang Meng (Beihai), 82, 87n.12

Pang Qi, 585

paper, 198, 310, 312

pasta (*bing*), 447–57; history of, 448–49

Pearce, Scott, 499

Pei, Lord (spirit), 562, 565

Pei Fangming, 552, 557n.26

Pei Songzhi, 267, 646

Pei Yin, 267

Pei Zhaoming, 267

Pei Ziye, 8, 198, 246, 267–73

Pengcheng: attack on, 35–36; disputation at, 7, 14, 32–59; and historiography, 36–38

Pengcheng Laofu, 345

Pengcheng Liu clan, 248

Perfection of Wisdom Sutras, 381n.25, 629n.2, 632n.29

Persians, 176

"Petition on Closing Off Mountains and Lakes" (*Shangyan shanhu zhi jin*; Liu Zishang), 92

"Petition Submitted by Lady Yu in the Fifth Year of the Xianhe Reign of the Eastern Jin Emperor Cheng" (*Dong-Jin Chengdi xianhe wunian sanqi cilang He Qiao qi Yushi shangbiao*), 511–29

Pillow Book (*Zhenzhongpian*; Wei Shou), 496

Ping Wang, 12, 13, 15, 196, 328

Pingcheng (Northern Wei capital), 36, 438

Piqiu Gong, 340

poetry: allusions in, 247, 249–51, 291, 296, 304n.55; ancient-style (*gushi*), 272n.11; categorization of, 287–306; and class, 245–47, 439; competition in, 65, 196, 245, 246, 370; as cultural capital, 8, 195, 196–97, 245–47; euphony in, 288, 290, 291, 305n.75, 306nn.76–84; *fu*, 370, 371, 388, 390, 448; on Han Gaozu, 256–66; landscape imagery in, 231, 232–33, 235; lauds, 276, 277–78, 280, 282n.20; and Liang Emperor Wu, 246–48, 260; and literary groups, 372–74; of Liu Xiaochuo, 245–55; on mountains, 233, 235, 236–37, 241n.8; on the mysterious, 230–44; and North vs. South, 7, 62, 65; Palace Style, 258–60; restoring antiquity (*fugu*), 269; and Ruan Xiaoxu, 317, 318; self-representation in, 328; and Shi Chong, 532–33, 535; in Shu, 108; Tang, 260, 269; for women, 259; of Xiao Tong, 9, 375–77. See also *Classic of Poetry*; *specific poems and poets*

Poo, Mu-chou, 579, 596

Pratyutpanna Sutra (*Banzhou sanmei jing*), 409

Precious Canon of the Jade Candle (*Yuzhu baodian*; Du Taiqing), 469, 471, 477, 478, 482n.2, 483n.6, 485n.28, 492nn.90–91

Prescriptions of the Celestial Physician (*Tianyi fang*), 476, 489n.55

"Presented to Xie An" (*Zeng Xie An*; Sun Chuo), 234–35, 239–41

Pulleyblank, E. G., 39

pure conversation (*qingtan*), 8, 132, 202, 204, 205, 225n.1, 327; and cultural capital, 195–96; in *Recent Anecdotes*, 357, 361, 362

pure criticism (*qingyi*), 128, 361

Qi (dynasty), 79, 248, 269, 389–90; elites in, 92; literary groups in, 372; music of, 218, 219, 221, 222 *qi* (ethers; vital forces), 242n.22, 297n.1, 301n.24; and autocremation, 555; and death, 647, 649; and Laozi, 340; in Lingbao Daoism, 617, 622, 631nn.20–26, 634nn.60–62, 635n.68, 635n.71, 639n.111; and sacred mountains, 654, 666, 672; in Shangqing Daoism, 563, 564, 570, 571, 574n.15, 574n.22, 575n.34, 642

Qi Hou, 651n.21

Qian Fei (emperor, Liu Song). *See* Liu Ziye

Qian Lou, wife of, 384, 386, 387n.5, 387n.7

Qian Nanxiu, 359

Qian Qin. *See* Former Qin (state)

Qian Yan. *See* Former Yan (state)

Qiang people, 2, 30n.15, 282n.19

Qianlong (emperor, Qing), 177

Qiao Xuan, 363, 364, 369n.37

Qiao Zhou, 89, 91, 109–22

Qiao Zong, 114, 122n.9

Qili Ji, 343

Qin (dynasty), 108, 116, 140; bureaucracy in, 125, 138, 141; documents of, 95, 105n.4; music of, 218

Qin Jia, 299n.13, 520, 526n.36

Qin Mi, 109–10

Qin Shihuang, 35, 314, 343, 485n.29, 504; and sacred mountains, 666, 670; tomb of, 648, 651n.13

Qing (dynasty), 177

Qiu Chi, 400n.3

Qiu Guobin, 373

Qiu Lingkai, 373

Qiu Pangtong, 452

Qu (dynasty; Gaochang), 178

Qu Baomao, 181, 186

Qu Binzhi (Qu Bin), 183, 187, 179, 181–82, 188, 190, 192n.41

Qu Jian, 181

Qu Liang, 181, 182, 189

Qu Ming, 476

Qu Qiangu, 186

Qu Ren, 188

Qu Shaohui, 186

Qu Xuan, 187, 189, 192n.41

Qu Yuan, 12, 79, 302n.36, 370; and festivals, 479, 491n.75, 491n.78; and genres, 278, 283n.26, 283n.31; individualism of, 325; and Jiang Yan, 403n.39, 403n.42

Qu Zhen, 187

Queen Mother of the West, 540, 562, 598, 608n.36; in Lingbao Daoism, 614, 623; and sacred mountains, 677n.35, 681n.81; in tomb documents, 593

Questions on Rites and Customs (*Wen lisu*; Dong Xun), 487n.39

Ran Min, 610n.52

Ran You, 305n.74

Raz, Gil, 539, 540, 542, 658

Recent Anecdotes from the Talk of the Ages (*Shishuo xinyu*; Liu Yiqing), 78, 196, 357–66, 508n.17, 578; and character appraisal, 9, 198, 246, 326–28, 350, 357, 360, 361, 363, 364; conversation in, 205, 225n.4; on Sun Chuo, 31n.36, 230, 231; title of, 366n.1; on women, 365–66, 459

Record of Buddhist Monasteries in Luoyang (*Luoyang qielanji*; Yang Xuanzhi), 434, 439

Record of Local Folkways (*Fengtu ji*; Zhou Chu), 470–71, 476, 480, 488n.52

Record of Marvels (*Luyi ji*; *Luyi zhuan*), 476, 489n.57

"Record of Music" (*Yueji*; *Liji*), 205, 207, 226n.8, 298n.4

Record of Rites (*Liji*), 61, 75n.39; on adoption, 516, 520, 521, 523, 524n.12, 526n.33; on ancestor worship, 650nn.7–8, 650n.10; and biographies, 384; and book collecting, 312, 313, 319n.2; on burials, 647, 651n.20; calendars in, 492n.84; and *Family Instructions*, 70, 498, 504; and festivals, 473, 484n.18, 486n.36, 490n.72; on food, 450, 452, 456n.27;

and Ge Hong, 67, 72n.5; and genres, 282n.15; Huangfu Mi on, 338; and Liu Hui case, 162; on motherhood, 513, 514; on mourning, 75n.45; on music, 205–7, 226n.8, 226n.17, 298n.4; and Qiao Zhou, 118, 119, 123n.21; and recluses, 348; and Sun Chuo, 242n.16, 243n.30; and Zhong Rong, 304n.54

Record of the Buddha (Fo ji), 319n.6

Record of the Three Kingdoms (Sanguo zhi; Chen Shou), 74n.30, 91, 267, 351, 363, 641; and book collecting, 311, 312; and Xiahou Xuan, 130, 131

Record of the Year and Seasons of Jing-Chu (Jing-Chu suishiji; Zong Lin), 431, 432, 444, 468–93

Records of the Hidden and Visible Worlds (Youming lu; Liu Yiqing), 540, 578, 579–91

Records of the Historian (Shi ji; Sima Qian), 38, 111, 124n.33, 267, 367n.17, 680n.71; and biography, 329, 383, 384; and book collecting, 311, 312, 323n.42; on burials, 651n.17; on festivals, 473, 478, 485n.29; Huangfu Mi on, 338; and individualism, 325; and Laozi, 340

Records of the States South of Mount Hua (Huayang guo zhi; Chang Qu), 124n.35

Records of the Ye Court (Yezhong ji; Lu Hui), 477, 478

Rectifiers, Office of (zhongzheng), 90–91, 128–29, 135–37, 145n.53

Red Eyebrows, 47, 57n.35

Reflections of the Court Dietitian (Shiyi xinjing; Shiyi xinjian; Zan Yin), 476, 488n.53

religion, 5, 6, 8, 577; and festivals, 469–70; and politics, 92–93; texts on, 10, 539–42. See also Buddhism; Confucianism; Daoism; supernatural

Ren Dun, 674

Ren Fang, 197, 246, 249–52, 296, 304n.62, 315

Ren Yong, 121

renwu (personality), 351–52

Resolving Doubts About Sounds and Rhymes (Yinyun jueyi; Li Jijie), 71

Retreat of the Elephants (Elvin), 151

"Rhapsody on Climbing the Tower" (Denglou fu; Wang Can), 77

"Rhapsody on Fulfilling My Original Resolve" (Suichu fu; Sun Chuo), 29

"Rhapsody on Pasta" (Bing fu; Shu Xi), 431, 447–57

"Rhapsody on Regret" (Hen fu; Jiang Yan), 388, 389

"Rhapsody on Roaming the Tiantai Mountains" (You Tiantai shan fu; Sun Chuo), 232–33

"Rhapsody on Separation" (Bie fu; Jiang Yan), 388, 389

Rhie, Marylin Martin, 411

righteousness (yi), 342, 352, 496

Rites of Zhou (Zhouli), 118, 173n.26, 277, 456n.28, 478

ritual, 525n.15, 681n.86; Ge Hong on, 63, 68; jiao, 654, 655; lingbao, 657; and motherhood, 514; and North vs. South, 61, 79; purification, 626–27, 632n.27; Qiao Zhou on, 111, 117–20; and sacred mountains, 652, 654; and sumptuary regulations, 140

Robinet, Isabelle, 564, 616, 658

Robson, James, 658

Rong tribes, 49

Rong Xinjiang, 182

Ruan Ji, 207, 290, 299n.18, 357, 360, 365, 383

Ruan Xiaoxu, 9, 199, 281n.4, 310, 313–19

Ruan Yu, 371

Sabban, Françoise, 450, 452, 457n.30

Sailey, Jay, 66

salt monopoly, 99, 104

Sanhuang scriptures, 614, 630n.8, 630n.14, 634nn.54–55

Sargent, Clyde B., 39

Satake Yasuko, 452

Satō Ichirō, 498

Schafer, Edward H., 658

Secret Instructions for the Ascent to Perfection (*Dengzhen yinjue*; Tao Hongjing), 569

Seidel, Anna, 596

Selections of Refined Literature (*Wen xuan*; Xiao Tong), 166, 197, 232, 257, 276, 373, 388

self-narration (*zixu*), 383

self-representation, 5, 7, 9, 325–31; and group identity, 327–28

Sengfu, 554

Sengming, 548, 553

Sengqing, 547, 551–52, 557n.24

Sengqun, 554

Sengyao, 549, 550

Sengyu, 559n.48

Separate Biography of Zhuge Liang (*Zhuge Ke biezhuan*), 450

Separate Version of Literary Compositions Divided by Genre (*Wenzhang liubie bie ben*; Xie Hun), 276

Sequel to the Treatise on Literature (*Xu Wenzhang zhi*), 531

Serventi, Silvano, 452, 457n.30

service households, 441–42

Seven Accounts (Wang Jian), 317

Seven Catalogs (*Qi lue*; Liu Xin), 303n.46, 314, 316–18

Seven Masters of the Jian'an period (*Jian'an qizi*), 285n.54, 285nn.60–61, 328; and literary patronage, 371, 372, 374

Seven Records (*Qi lu*; Ruan Xiaoxu), 9, 199, 310, 313–19

"Seven Reliances" (Cui Yin), 280, 284n.40

Seven Sages of the Bamboo Grove, 232, 327, 328, 331n.5, 431; in *Recent Anecdotes*, 360, 364, 368n.27, 369n.40

"Seven Stimuli" (*Qi fa*; Mei Sheng), 279, 284n.39

sexuality: Ge Hong on, 63, 68; and *qi*, 563, 574n.15, 574n.18, 575n.34

shamans/spirit-mediums (*wu*), 502, 561–75, 584, 590nn.40–41; and ancestor worship, 641–42, 646; and sacred mountains, 681n.80; women as, 674

Shan Tao, 364, 365

Shang (Yin; dynasty), 117, 123n.11, 138, 367n.12

Shang Yang (Lord Shang), 150, 355, 366n.10

Shangguan Si, 173n.30, 174n.33

Shangqing (Upper Clarity) Daoism, 561–75, 613–16, 634n.55; and Lingbao Daoism, 630n.8, 630n.14, 632n.28, 632nn.31–33, 633n.47, 635n.69, 636n.84, 637nn.96–97; and mountains, 653, 655–58

Shangshu. See *Classic of Documents*

Shanjuan, 337

Shao Weng, 410

Shen Daosheng, 601

Shen Hongzhi, 601

Shen Jiaben, 159

Shen Jin, 30n.19

Shen Qianzhi, 601

Shen Qingzhi, 40, 57n.17, 57n.22

Shen Youzhi, 394, 402n.30

Shen Yucheng, 531

Shen Yue, 143n.19, 387n.1, 390; on marriage, 5, 89, 92, 166–75; and poetry, 246, 247, 249, 250, 288, 297, 303n.50, 306n.76, 306n.85. See also *History of the Song*

Shen Zhong, 601, 610n.52

Shengxuan scriptures, 614

Shenzhou scriptures, 614

Shi Bao, 530

Shi Bing, 62

Shi Cen, 278, 282n.19

Shi Chong, 430–32, 441, 442, 530–37

Shi ji. See *Records of the Historian*

Shi Jian, 447–48, 610n.52

Shi Kuang, 491n.77

Shi Kuang's Divination (*Shi Kuang zhan*), 479, 491n.77

Shi Tong, 530–31

Shi You, 449

shihan zong (school of stored consciousness), 361–62

Shishu, 285n.57

shishuo ti ("talk of the age" genre), 326

Shizu (emperor, Liu Song). *See* Liu Jun; Tuoba Dao

Shryock, John K., 353

Shu (region; Sichuan), 108–24; mysterious learning in, 109–10, 112

Shu Guang, 447

Shu-Han (kingdom), 12, 108, 110, 113–17, 130, 132

Shu Mengda, 447

Shu Qi, 121, 227n.26, 250, 335, 338

Shu Qiu, 447–48

Shu Xi, 432, 447–57

Shujing. See Classic of Documents

Shun (emperor, Han), 127

Shun (sage-king), 121, 193n.49, 386, 467n.17, 649; and sacred mountains, 665, 670; Xi Kang on, 208, 210, 214

Śibi (king), 554, 559n.45

Silk Road, 176–77

Sima Huang, 448

Sima Jun, 531

Sima Lun, 173n.30, 532

Sima Qian, 73n.13, 79, 227n.26, 250, 316, 338, 356; autobiography of, 329, 383; and genres, 278, 283n.30; individualism of, 325, 329; Qiao Zhou on, 111, 112, 122, 124n.36; in *Recent Anecdotes,* 367n.17; on spirits, 611n.67. *See also Records of the Historian*

Sima Rui (Jin Emperor Yuan/Zhongzong), 1, 18, 19, 26, 29n.9, 31n.31, 62, 78

Sima Shi, 132–33

Sima Tan, 174n.30

Sima Tian, 582, 589n.34

Sima Xiangru (Sima Zhangqing), 172n.19, 270, 392, 400n.9; and genres, 278, 283n.30, 285n.55; and literary patronage, 370–71; and poetry, 108, 252, 255n.29, 292, 298n.10, 300n.18; and shadow image, 427n.55

Sima Yan (Jin Emperor Wu), 145n.51, 360, 463, 531

Sima Yi, 129–33, 135, 141, 144n.37, 145n.51, 368n.26, 591n.54

Sima Yue, 18, 29n.3

Sima Zhao (King Wen of Jin), 110, 114, 122n.7, 360, 362, 368n.26, 531

Sima Zhen, 485n.29

Sivin, Nathan, 112

Sixteen States (*shiliuguo*), 32

slaves, 98, 438, 441, 442, 501, 505; criminals as, 158, 161, 162, 443, 458; and Shi Chong, 532; in tomb documents, 594, 598; as wet nurses, 460, 462

Sogdians, 2, 176

Song (dynasty). *See History of the Song*

Song Duanlin, 464

Song Jun, 492n.85

Song Laizi, 572–73

Song Yu, 278, 283n.27, 283n.31, 370

Soper, Alexander, 410, 422n.1

"Sound Is Without Sadness or Joy" (Xi Kang), 8, 196, 201–29

Southern Qi (dynasty), 15, 167; histories of, 166, 372, 642. *See also* Qi (dynasty)

spirit (*shen*), 407, 635n.71

spirits, 561–75; and accounts of anomalies, 576; and ancestor worship, 641–42; and Confucianism, 640–51; in Lingbao Daoism, 614–15, 622–24; of sacred mountains, 562, 565, 566, 572, 588n.11, 603, 624. *See also* shamans/ spirit-mediums

Spring and Autumn Annals (*Chunqiu*), 91, 304n.54, 338, 526n.31, 527n.36; on adoption, 519, 520; and book collecting, 312, 314, 317, 319, 323n.42; on burials,

Spring and Autumn Annals (continued)
647; commentaries on, 348, 473;
Gongyang Commentary to, 348, 367n.14,
519; *Guliang Commentary* to, 123n.18,
367n.14; and Liu Hui case, 159, 163; and
recluses, 348; Sima Qian on, 329
Śrīmitra (Gaozuo daoren), 364
Stele for Establishing a Temple (Qu Binzhi),
181–82
Stele for the Virtue of Establishing a
Buddhist Temple (Juqu Anzhou), 179–81
stele inscriptions, 179–82, 280, 281,
285nn.50–54, 309, 577
stimulus–response, law of (*ganying*), 541,
545–46, 641
Strategies of the Warring States (Zhanguo ce),
313, 322n.27
Strickmann, Michel, 564, 596, 658
Su Jun, 30n.12
Su Shao, 534, 537n.17
Su Shun, 280, 285n.59, 336, 338
Su Wu, 270, 272n.11
Su Yu, 537n.17
Su Ze, 537n.17
Sui (dynasty), 1–2, 14, 64, 65, 129, 149,
269, 471. See also *History of the Sui*
Sui Fang, 602
Sun Chu, 477, 489n.60
Sun Chuo, 5, 7, 8, 13–14, 17–31, 197, 293;
and Luoyang, 21–22; memorial of,
25–29; and the mysterious, 230–44,
300n.23
Sun En, 590n.44
Sun Hao, 645–46
Sun He, 645–46
Sun Qing, 278
Sun Quan, 79, 97, 173n.30, 450, 666,
667, 679n.66
Sun Sheng, 143n.28
Sun Simiao, 466n.9, 488n.53
Sun Zi, 130
Suo Jing, 69, 75n.35

Suo Ning, 180
supernatural, 5, 539–681; and Buddhism,
10, 445, 540, 577, 578, 583, 587n.3,
589n.28, 642; and Confucianism, 541,
640–51; and Daoism, 561–75, 609n.42,
642. *See also* accounts of anomalous
events; divination; necromancy;
shamans/spirit-mediums; spirits
Supreme Mystery (Taixuan; Yang Xiong), 109
*Sutra of Immeasurable Life (Wuliangshou
jing)*, 552, 558n.33
*Sutra of the Oceanic Samādhi of Visualizing
the Buddha (Guanfo sanmei hai jing)*,
406, 410–15
*Sutra on the Contemplation of the Buddha of
Immeasurable Life (Guan wuliangshou
jing)*, 552, 558n.33
sutras, 56n.3, 179, 409;. *Perfection of
Wisdom*, 381n.25, 629n.2, 632n.29.
See also *Lotus Sutra*
Suzuki Torao, 168
Swartz, Wendy, 385

Taizu (emperor, Liu Song). *See* Liu Yilong
Takahashi Kazumi, 392
"Tale of Lu Sidao" (*Lu Sidao*), 60. See also
Extensive Records of the Taiping Era
tan he rong yi (talk is cheap), 201–2
Tancheng, 554
Tang (dynasty), 129, 149, 177; poetry of, 260,
269
Tang Code, 165n.12
Tang Le, 283n.31, 370
Tang Yongtong, 208, 353
Tang Zhangru, 22, 90, 151
Tanhong, 552–54
Tanzhi, 312
Tao Hongjing, 540, 561–72, 574n.11,
574nn.14–15, 657, 658, 679n.55; as
recluse, 656, 681n.84
Tao Qian. *See* Tao Yuanming
Tao Shiheng, 497

Tao Shixiang (Tao Kan), 29n.11, 507n.2

Tao Shunzhi, 236

Tao Xisheng, 151

Tao Yuanming, 9, 80, 496; autobiography
    of, 328–30, 382–86

taxation, 3, 148, 498; documents on, 96,
    97–98, 101–3

tea, 434–35

Teng Ssu-Yü, 66, 499

Terms Explained (*Shi ming*; Liu Xi), 449

Thích Quang Du'c, 544

Three Mysterious Works (*san xuan*), 196,
    197, 202–4. See also *Classic of Changes*;
    Laozi; *Zhuangzi*

Three Standards Calendrical System (*San
    zheng li*), 348

Thucydides, 37

Tian, Xiaofei, 81, 196, 197, 199, 251, 260,
    270, 310

Tian Yuqing, 20, 22

Tibet, 177

Tiyang, petition from, 514

tomb documents, 10, 540, 541, 592–612

tomb inventories (*yiwushu*), 592–93, 595,
    604–5

tomb-stabilizing writs (*zhenmuwen*), 593,
    594–95, 599, 602–4

toutuo (*dhūta*; ascetic practices), 547, 549,
    552, 553

*Treatise on Literary Compositions Divided by
    Genre* (*Wenzhang liubie zhi*; Zhi Yu),
    274–75

Treatise on Personality (*Renwu zhi*; Liu Shao),
    9, 227n.23, 327, 350–58

Tsukamoto Zenryū, 235

Tuoba Dao (Northern Wei Emperor Shizu),
    14, 32–36, 39–55, 56n.10, 57n.28

Tuoba people, 32

Tuoba Ren (Prince of Yongchang), 51–53,
    58n.48

Tuobo Khan, 181

Turban, Helga, 472

Turfan (Gaochang), 8, 93, 176–93

Turks, 2, 181, 182, 188

Twenty-Four Companions of Jia Mi, 328,
    532

Uygurs, 176, 177

van Gulik, Robert Hans, 207

Verellen, Franciscus, 658

Vervoorn, Aat, 112, 337

von Glahn, Richard, 596

Wada Hisanori, 472

Wagner, Rudolph G., 112

Wallacker, Benjamin E., 38

Waltner, Ann, 514

Wang, Eugene, 330, 411

Wang, Ping, 197, 269

Wang Bao, 108, 292, 298n.10, 496–98

Wang Bi, 112–13, 132, 202, 225n.2, 233, 361

Wang Can, 77, 78, 266n.20, 280, 285n.54,
    293, 299n.15, 371

Wang Chang, 495–96

Wang Changxuan, 249

Wang Che, 320n.16

Wang Chong (Zhongren), 67, 73n.14,
    265n.12, 422n.6, 490n.71, 657

Wang Ci, 174n.31

Wang Dajian, 66

Wang Dan, 537n.18

Wang Dang, 256

Wang Dao, 13, 78, 204, 231, 363, 369n.36

Wang Dun, 30n.12, 582, 589n.26

Wang Feng, 344

Wang Fu, 142n.12, 503, 509n.33

Wang Gungwu, 39

Wang Guoliang, 587n.5

Wang Guowei, 181

Wang Hun, 508n.17

Wang Huzhi, 150

Wang Ji, 531

Wang Jia, 536n.9

Wang Jiakui, 564

Wang Jian, 15, 79–86, 199, 288, 315, 317, 318

Wang Jun, 249

Wang Kai, 531, 536n.7

Wang Kuo-ying, 385

Wang Lang, 359, 360, 368n.24

Wang Liang, 315

Wang Liqi, 71

Wang Mang, 280, 285n.51, 336, 495; and pasta, 450; and recluses, 338, 345, 386

Wang Ming, 581–82

Wang Mo, 122n.3

Wang Ningzhi, 584, 590n.44

Wang Qing'e, 562, 565

Wang Rong (Wang Yuanzhang), 249, 296–97, 304n.62, 306n.80, 360, 364–66

Wang Sengbian, 312, 321n.22, 323n.39

Wang Sengqian, 202–5

Wang Sengru, 373

Wang Shaoqing, 170, 173n.27

Wang Sheng, 450

Wang Shumin, 292, 302n.41, 304n.58

Wang Su, 166, 435

Wang Taiqing, 259, 262–63

Wang Tao, 466n.9

Wang Wei, 296, 304n.66

Wang Wenjin, 260

Wang Wenqing, 674

Wang Xianzhi, 322n.31

Wang Xingzhi, 610n.64

Wang Xizhi, 80, 143n.23, 231, 233, 322n.31, 357, 363, 533

Wang Xu, 534, 537n.16

Wang Xuan, 170

Wang Xuanmo, 35, 51–53, 56n.3

Wang Ya, 166, 173n.26

Wang Yi, 607n.30

Wang Yifu, 537n.16

Wang Ying, 249, 491n.74

Wang Yongping, 81

Wang Yuan, 173n.29; impeachment of, 92, 166–75

Wang Yuanzhang (Wang Rong), 249, 296–97, 304n.62, 306n.80, 360, 364–66

Wang Yun, 200n.6

Wang Yurong, 472

Wang Zhan, 249

Wang Zhaojun, 302n.37

Wang Zhenzhi, 313, 322n.27

Wang Zhongluo, 20, 22

Wang Ziqiao (spirit), 562, 565

Wangsun Man, 402n.33

Wangzi Qiao, 601, 625, 680n.70

Watson, Burton, 283n.30

Wei (dynasty), 1, 9, 12, 299n.18; bureaucracy in, 128–34, 138; conversation in, 203; vs. Han dynasty, 325; Qiao Zhou on, 110, 114–17. See also *History of the Wei*; Northern Wei (dynasty); Western Wei (dynasty)

Wei (King of Chu), 342

Wei Guan, 448

Wei Heng, 448

Wei Huacun (spirit), 562, 565, 679n.58

Wei Rui, 313, 322n.29

Wei Shou, 38, 496

Wei Xiangdong, 66

Wells, Matthew, 66

Wen (emperor, Han), 28, 141, 241, 266n.20, 514

Wen (emperor, Liu Song). *See* Liu Yilong

Wen (emperor, Wei). *See* Cao Pi

Wen (King of Jin). *See* Sima Zhao

Wen (King of Zhou), 115, 116, 193n.49, 211, 212, 336, 527n.44

Wen (Prince of Jin), 365

wen (refined literature), 8, 195, 196

Wen, Duke of Jin, 478, 647

Wen Li, 114, 122n.6

Wen Qiao, 364

Wenguan cilin, 234, 235

Wenhuan (emperor, Later Qin). *See* Yao Xing

Wenxuan (emperor, Northern Qi), 64, 65

Western Wei (dynasty), 15, 308, 309, 471

Wilhelm, Hellmut, 533

Williams, Nicholas Morrow, 392

Wixted, John Timothy, 247, 292

women: and adoption, 511–29; biographies of, 333; Daoist lineage of, 657, 674; education of, 511, 513; elite, 440; in *Family Instructions*, 500–501; and Liu Hui case, 159–60; medical texts on, 466nn.8–9; as mothers, 431–33, 443, 511–29; mourning for, 118–19; in North vs. South, 442–43, 461–62; in *Recent Anecdotes*, 365–66, 459; as wet nurses, 458–67

Wu (emperor, Han), 126, 370, 410, 504, 626, 638n.104; and bureaucratic recruitment, 350–51

Wu (emperor, Jin). *See* Sima Yan

Wu (emperor, Liang). *See* Xiao Yan

Wu (emperor, Qi). *See* Xiao Yi

Wu (emperor, Wei). *See* Cao Cao

Wu (King of Zhou), 117, 123n.11, 193nn.49–50, 250, 335, 337, 367n.12

Wu, Duke of (Jizi of Yanling), 340, 346

Wu Bei, 401n.21

Wu Feng, 66

Wu Fusheng, 269

Wu Guangxing, 311

Wu Hui (fire god), 453, 457n.33

Wu Hung, 642

Wu Jiaju, 353

Wu (kingdom), 8, 11, 12, 67, 71, 72, 89; documents of, 96–99, 102–5; and Jin, 61, 73n.16, 74n.27, 531

Wu Xianqing, 151

Wu Zeng, 581

Wu Zetian (Empress Wu, Tang), 513, 514

Wu Zixu, 401n.21, 479, 491n.80

Wuling tribes, 97, 98

Xi Kang (Ji Kang), 8, 196, 204, 206–25, 336; and *Recent Anecdotes*, 357, 360, 362, 365, 368n.27, 368n.34

Xi Zhong, 121

Xia Huanggong, 343

Xia Ji, 163, 165n.11

Xia Zhengshu, 165n.11

Xiahou Can, 180

Xiahou Shang, 131

Xiahou Tan, 311, 319n.6

Xiahou Xuan, 91, 129–33, 135–42

Xiahou Yuan, 131

Xiahou Zhan, 524n.4

Xianbei people, 2, 18, 42, 56n.13, 91, 157, 501; clothing of, 429; kingdoms of, 20, 22, 23, 31n.29, 32; legal systems of, 158; and women, 443

Xiang (King of Chu), 370

Xiang, Music Master, 211, 212

Xiang Xiu, 232

Xiang Yu, 115, 367n.16, 394, 402n.32

Xiangyang, 256, 260, 266

Xianling tribe, 282n.21

Xianyang (Qin capital), 264n.5

Xiao (Prince of Liang, Han), 258

Xiao Ben, 312, 321n.21

Xiao Cha, 322n.37

Xiao Daocheng (Qi Emperor Gao), 179, 389–90, 394, 402nn.28–32, 403nn.34–38, 646

Xiao Daqi (Prince of Xuancheng), 503, 508n.23

Xiao Fang, 472

Xiao Gang (Prince of Jin'an; Liang Emperor Jianwen), 8, 197, 256–66, 307, 320n.10

Xiao Gong, 321n.24

Xiao Hezi, 392

Xiao Ji (brother of Xiao Yi), 320n.11

Xiao Ji (Prince Yang of Ancheng), 320n.13

Xiao Ke, 322n.37

Xiao Lun, 322n.28

Xiao Mai, 321n.23

Xiao Mian, 552, 558n.30

Xiao Ni, 403n.37

Xiao Ruiming, 641, 645

Xiao Sihua, 57n.20

Xiao Tong (Crown Prince of Liang), 9, 198, 248, 250, 307, 320n.7; literary patronage of, 328, 373–74, 381n.27; poetry of, 375–77. See also *Selections of Refined Literature*

Xiao Wenyan, 373

Xiao Xiu, 320n.13

Xiao Xu, 321n.24

Xiao Yan (Liang Emperor Wu), 196, 199, 303n.50, 319n.6, 553, 656; in *Family Instructions*, 503, 508nn.22–23, 509n.34; and festivals, 488n.48; and poetry, 246–50, 256, 257, 260, 291, 303n.48

Xiao Ye, 320n.8

Xiao Yi (Liang Emperor Yuan), 319–23, 471, 508n.22. See also *Master of the Golden Tower*

Xiao Yi (Qi Emperor Wu), 167, 248, 403n.37, 646

Xiao Ying, 320n.8

Xiao Yu, 322n.37

Xiao Yuanyou, 322n.35

Xiao Yue, 312, 321n.22

Xiao Zao, 322n.37

Xiao Ze. *See* Xiao Yi

Xiao Ziliang, 249, 328, 372–73

Xiao Zixian, 374–75, 378

Xiaojing. See Classic of Filial Piety

Xiaopinfang (Chen Yanzhi), 466n.9

xiaoshuo ("small talk" genre), 326, 357–58

Xiaowen (emperor, Han), 625, 626, 638n.99

Xiaowen (emperor, Northern Wei), 157, 429

Xiaowu (emperor, Eastern Jin), 166

Xiaowu (emperor, Liu Song). *See* Liu Jun

Xiaozi, 178

Xie An, 80, 231, 234, 235, 239–41; in *Recent Anecdotes*, 357, 363, 364

Xie Fei, 315

Xie Hun (Xie Yishou), 276, 282n.13, 293, 301n.25

Xie Lingyun, 245, 315; on images, 408–9; and Pei Ziye, 270, 272n.14, 272n.16; and shadow image, 419–21; and Zhong Rong, 290, 293, 296, 301nn.26–27, 304n.59, 305n.69, 305n.74

Xie Shi, 363

Xie Tiao, 245, 288–89, 291, 295, 297, 302nn.41–42, 303n.50

Xie Xuan, 363, 364

Xie Yanyuan, 311

Xie Yishou (Xie Hun), 276, 282n.13, 293, 301n.25

Xie Zhuang, 272n.16, 296, 297, 304n.60, 306n.82

Ximen Bao, 356, 367n.13

Xin Jia, 284n.46

Xin Zhongyou, 185, 191n.18

Xinjiang Uygur Autonomous Region, 176

Xinting (New Stop), 13, 78

Xiongnu people, 1–3, 11, 18, 78, 177, 302n.37, 367n.16, 610n.58

Xu Chi, 258, 259

Xu Deping, 310

Xu Di, 99, 104

Xu Gan, 206, 207, 281, 285n.60, 304n.56, 371

Xu Jingzong, 234

Xu Ling, 259, 263

Xu Mi, 563–73, 574n.13, 665, 667, 668, 673

Xu Mian, 249, 311, 320n.9

Xu Piaonu, 674

Xu Shu, 299n.13, 520, 526n.36

Xu Xun, 232, 234, 237–39, 293, 300n.23

Xu Yi (wet nurse), 431–32, 443, 458–67

Xu You, 121, 242n.19, 337–40, 361, 368n.31, 381n.22

Xu Yuan, 41, 57n.27

Xu Zhen'e, 358

Xu Zhi, 347

Xuan (emperor, Han), 367n.15, 450

Xuan (emperor, Qi), 646

Xuan (King of Zhou), 25, 30n.26, 467n.18

Xuanzang, 177, 427n.52

Xuanzhao (emperor, Former Qin). *See* Fu Jian

Xue Bao, 674

Xun Xu, 315, 317

Xunzi (Xun Qing), 206–7, 271, 273n.20, 283n.25, 305n.74; on music, 229nn.36–40; on spirits, 650n.2

Yamabe Nobuyoshi, 422n.4

Yan Buke, 72n.5

Yan Han, 508n.17

Yan Hui (Ziyuan), 341, 384, 387n.4, 505, 509n.33

Yan Kejun, 285n.59

Yan Shigu, 449

Yan Yan (Ziyou), 67, 73n.13

Yan Yanzhi, 270, 272nn.14–16, 496; and Zhong Rong, 293, 296, 297, 301n.27, 304n.60, 304n.67

Yan Ying, 355, 366n.9

Yan Yuan, 210, 227n.19, 305n.74

Yan Zhitui, 60, 63–65, 167, 319n.4, 427n.52, 432–33, 437, 494–510; and class, 15, 441; on concubines, 440; on language, 64–65, 71; on marriage, 442–43, 501–2, 504; on mourning ritual, 64, 70–71, 445, 505–7, 643; on North vs. South, 15, 16

Yan Zhiyi, 73n.7

Yan Zun (Yan Junping; Zhuang Zun), 109, 344–45, 386

Yang (empress, Western Jin), 460, 464

Yang family lineage, 109–10

Yang Jian, 1

Yang Jun, 464, 531

Yang Lin, 473

Yang Mingzhao, 67

Yang Puwei, 113

Yang Songjie, 72n.1

Yang Wangsun, 647–49, 651n.13, 651n.21

Yang Xi (medium), 152–53, 155n.34, 540, 561–75, 656–58, 665, 668, 679n.55

Yang Xiong, 109, 124n.36, 172n.19, 344, 384, 386, 449; and genres, 198, 278, 280, 281, 282n.21, 283nn.28–31, 284nn.42–45, 285n.55, 285n.62; and literary patronage,

371; and Pei Ziye, 268, 270, 272n.9, 272n.14; and Zhong Rong, 292, 298n.10

Yang Xiu, 266n.21, 531

Yang Xiuzhi, 71, 76n.56

Yang Xuanzhi, 434, 439

Yang Xuanzhu, 440

Yang Zhao, 174n.35

Yangshe, 215, 216

Yangzi (philosopher), 558n.37, 558n.40

Yangzi River, 6, 11, 19, 26, 34, 36, 54, 78–79

Yanzi, 173n.24, 228n.30

Yanzi chunqiu, 173n.24, 229n.34

Yao (sage-king), 338–40, 361, 368n.31, 467n.17, 668; in Lingbao Daoism, 618, 633n.44

Yao Chongxin, 182

Yao Dazhong, 81

Yao Kai, 312

Yao Xiang, 19, 20, 30n.15

Yao Xing (Later Qin Emperor Wenhuan), 556n.7

Yao Xu, 549, 556n.7

Yasui Kōzan, 112

Yellow Emperor (Huangdi), 293, 475, 625, 638n.98; and mountains, 653, 654, 659, 676n.24, 677n.26, 677nn.29–32, 680n.73

Yellow Turbans, 47, 57n.35, 657

Yewang, Two Elders from (Henan), 82, 87n.13

Yi Ya, 214

Yi Yi, 284n.46

Yi Yin, 142, 356, 367n.12

Yi Zhongxuan, 184

Yi Zhou shu, 484n.18

Yijing. See *Classic of Changes*

Yili. See *Etiquette and Rituals*

Yin (Shang; dynasty), 117, 123n.11, 138, 367n.12

yin and yang, 216, 243n.46, 318, 453, 497, 659; and correlative Confucianism, 641; Liu Shao on, 352–54

Yin Chun, 315

Yin Hao, 19, 30n.14

Yin Jun, 313, 322n.30

Yin Xi, 340

Ying Shao, 475, 487n.43

Ying Yang, 371

Yinwan documents, 95

Yongjia disorder (*yongjia zhi luan*), 11, 12, 18, 20, 24, 31n.31

Yongzhou region, 256, 266

Yoshikawa Tadao, 112, 168, 564, 658

You Zhao, 158, 159, 163

Yu (sage-king), 121, 654, 665, 670

Yu, Lady, 431–33, 440, 511–29

Yu Bing, 231

Yu Chan, 311, 319n.6

Yu Fakai, 361–62

Yu Ge, 312

Yu Jianwu, 258–60, 263

Yu Jiao, 313

Yu Liang, 29n.11, 231, 293, 300n.23

Yu Qiao, 312, 320n.14

Yu Rang, 265n.12

Yu Shaochu, 391

Yu Xi, 373

Yu Xin, 259

Yu Yan, 302n.42

Yu Yingshi, 112

Yuan (dynasty), 177

Yuan (emperor, Han). *See* Liu Shi

Yuan (emperor, Jin). *See* Sima Rui

Yuan (emperor, Liang). *See* Xiao Yi

Yuan Can, 385, 386–87

Yuan Jun, 362

Yuan Lang, 361, 368n.30

Yuan Qiao, 232

Yuan Shansong, 314

Yuan Shao, 131, 173n.30, 394

Yuan Shuming (Yuan Bing), 391, 393, 400n.10

Yuan Xian (Yuan Zisi), 342, 505, 509n.33

Yuan Xiuyi, 159, 163

Yuan Zhen, 22

Yuan Zhun, 369n.35

Yuanqing (Jiang Xu), 83, 87n.21, 386

Yue Facai, 312, 320n.14

Yue (kingdom), 11, 71, 75n.38

Yue Region Biographies (*Yuedi zhuan*), 479

Yue Yanchun, 313

Yue Yi, 143n.23, 356, 367n.19

Zach, Erwin von, 392

Zan Yin, 488n.53

Zati sanshishou (Jiang Yan), 388, 392

Zengzi, 75n.39

Zhan Huo (Liuxia Hui), 68, 73n.23

Zhang (emperor, Han), 127, 142n.11, 346

Zhang Aibo, 533

Zhang Bowei, 292

Zhang Chang, 7, 14, 32, 35, 39–55, 356, 367n.15

Zhang Chengzong, 66

Zhang Chong, 15, 79–86

Zhang Daoling, 557n.23

Zhang Gang, 173n.23

Zhang Guangda, 182

Zhang Heng, 257, 281, 286n.65, 478, 490n.69

Zhang Hong, 178

Zhang Hongsheng, 311

Zhang Hua, 300n.19, 304n.58, 359, 368n.25, 448, 486n.34

Zhang Huaiguan, 74n.34

Zhang Jinyao, 533

Zhang Kai, 522, 528n.51, 529n.53

Zhang Kang, 300n.19

Zhang Liang, 115, 355, 367n.11

Zhang Ling, 109

Zhang Lu, 131, 144n.29

Zhang Pu, 391

Zhang Qi, 133, 144n.37

Zhang Rong, 249

Zhang Shenluo, 602

Zhang Shizhi, 648

Zhang Shoujie, 485n.29

Zhang Wan, 313, 321n.27

Zhang Weizhi, 358

Zhang Xie, 293, 300n.19, 400n.3

Zhang Xunliao, 596

Zhang Yaxin, 391

Zhang Yi, 671

Zhang Yongzhou (Zhang Zuan), 313, 321n.27, 322n.37

Zhang Yue, 552, 557n.25

Zhang Yun'ao, 168

Zhang Zai, 300n.19

Zhang Zhengzi, 599

Zhang Zhenjun, 579

Zhang Zhi, 69, 74n.34, 75n.35, 296

Zhang Zongyuan, 120–22

Zhang Zuan (Zhang Yongzhou), 313, 321n.27, 322n.37

Zhangjiashan documents, 95, 98

Zhao, Duke of Zheng, 172n.13

Zhao Chongguo, 282n.21

Zhao Guanghan, 356, 367n.15

Zhao Lixin, 321n.20

Zhao Qi, 450

Zhao Wu, 522, 528n.49

Zhao Xiangzi, 265n.12

Zhao Xuan, 464

Zhao Yi, 299n.13

Zhaoming (Crown Prince of Liang), 248

Zheng, music of, 214, 222, 224, 225, 229n.44, 270, 272n.10, 303n.44

Zheng Jiaofu, 256–57, 265n.11

Zheng Mo, 315

Zheng Xuan, 202, 225n.2, 298n.4, 301n.30, 319, 348, 486n.32, 486n.36; advice to family from, 495; on mourning, 111, 119, 282n.15

Zheng Yin, 61–62, 655, 679n.51

Zhengshi reign, tone of (Zhengshi zhi yin), 204, 207

Zhi (emperor, Han), 450

Zhi Dun, 231, 232, 361–62

Zhi Yu, 8, 197–98, 274–86, 290, 296, 304n.53, 305n.68

Zhibiao, 313, 322n.28

Zhizang, 374

Zhong Hui, 204, 524n.4

Zhong Laiyin, 564

Zhong Rong, 8, 198–99, 246, 247–48, 272n.16, 390. See also Grades of the Poets

Zhong Shilun, 311

Zhong Yi, 69, 75n.37

Zhong Yuanchang (Zhong Yao), 69, 74n.32

Zhong Ziqi, 210–14, 227n.19

Zhongren (Wang Chong), 67, 73n.14, 265n.12, 422n.6, 490n.71, 657

Zhongzong (emperor, Jin). See Sima Rui

Zhou (dynasty), 12, 79, 108, 125, 138, 292, 335–36

Zhou, Duke of, 48, 58n.38, 63, 121, 123n.16, 142; on adoption, 521; and Family Instructions, 507, 510n.44; and filial piety, 527n.44; Qiao Zhou on, 117–18

Zhou Chu, 470–71, 476, 484n.20, 488n.52, 492n.90

Zhou Fangming, 604

Zhou Hongzheng, 503, 508n.23

Zhou Hongzhi, 312, 321n.21

Zhou Ju, 477, 478, 489n.61

Zhou She, 321n.21

Zhou Weiquan, 533

Zhou Yaozhen, 184

Zhou Yi, 78, 364, 369n.38, 520

Zhou Yiliang, 66, 359

Zhou Yishan (spirit), 562, 565

Zhou Yong, 249

Zhou Zhengsong, 269

Zhouli. See Rites of Zhou

Zhouyi. See Classic of Changes

Zhu Bo (Shuyang), 83, 87n.17

Zhu Daiwei, 66

Zhu Danyuan, 312

Zhu Fayong, 674

Zhu Gongshu, 280, 285n.53

Zhu Jiping, 69, 74n.31

Zhu Lingshi, 114, 122n.8

Zhu Maichen, 243n.42

Zhu Zhuyu, 358

Zhuang (King of Chu), 165n.11

Zhuang, Duke of Lu, 164n.10

Zhuang Jiang, 519

Zhuang Xi, 69, 75n.38

Zhuang Zun (Yan Junping; Yan Zun), 109, 344–45, 386

Zhuangzi, 109, 196, 255n.33, 264n.5, 312, 654; and conversation, 202, 206, 207; and Huiyuan, 424n.32, 425n.42; on music, 227n.22, 228n.31; in *Recent Anecdotes*, 362; and sacred mountains, 677n.29; and shadow image, 425n.44; on spirits, 562; and Sun Chuo, 232, 233, 241n.9, 242n.13, 242n.21, 243n.31, 244n.53

Zhuangzi (Zhuang Zhou), 342–43; on festivals, 474, 476, 486n.37

Zhuanxu (Gaoyang), 403n.39, 493n.101

Zhuge Liang, 111, 122n.2, 275, 450, 519, 526n.25

Zhuge shi ji mulu (catalog of *Collected Works of Zhuge Liang*; Chen Shou), 275

Zhuo Shi, 505

Zhuo Wenjun, 255n.29

Zichan, 285n.57, 356, 367n.13

Zigong, 342

Zilu, 75n.40

Zither Tunes (*Qin cao*; Cai Yong), 478, 489n.62

Zixia, 356, 367n.14

Ziyou (Yan Yan), 67, 73n.13

Zizang, 338

Zizhang, 243n.44

Zong Lin, 431, 444, 468–72, 491n.76

Zong Mengjian, 312

Zong Ze (Zong Ce), 479, 491n.76

Zong Zhonghui, 312

Zou Shi, 386

Zou Yan, 386

Zoumalou documents, 92, 95–99, 102–5

Zu Di, 29n.11

Zu Xuan, 315

Zuo Ci (Zuo Yuanfang), 663, 670, 672–73, 678n.49

Zuo Si, 293, 300n.19, 301n.26, 532

Zuo Tradition on the Spring and Autumn Annals (*Zuozhuan*), 243n.43, 348, 498; on adoption, 519; on festivals, 478, 485n.30, 486n.31, 490n.66; and genres, 280; on music, 228n.30, 273n.18; and Qiao Zhou, 111, 113

Zuo Xiong, 127

Zuo Yuanfang (Zuo Ci), 663, 670, 672–73, 678n.49

Zürcher, Erik, 235, 411, 422n.1, 423n.12, 616